CH01506503

LIST OF TEXT FIGURES AND MAPS   ix

PHOTOGRAPHIC ACKNOWLEDGEMENTS   xiv

MAP REFERENCES   xv

EDITOR'S FOREWORD   xvi

ACKNOWLEDGEMENTS   xvii

INTRODUCTION   1

GEOLOGY AND TOPOGRAPHY, BY ANDREW A. MCMILLAN   3

BUILDING MATERIALS, BY ALEC CLIFTON-TAYLOR   8

ARCHAEOLOGY, BY HUMPHREY WELFARE   12

PRE-NORMAN SCULPTURE, BY RICHARD N. BAILEY   18

THE EARLY MIDDLE AGES   21

BORDER CONFLICT, C14–C16   25

FROM THE UNION OF THE CROWNS TO *c.* 1750   33

INDUSTRIAL ARCHAEOLOGY, BY GAVIN WATSON   45

THE LATER GEORGIANS, *c.* 1750–*c.* 1840   52

VICTORIAN AND EDWARDIAN   59

FROM THE FIRST WORLD WAR TO THE PRESENT   70

FURTHER READING   78

GAZETTEER   87

GLOSSARY   713

INDEX OF ARCHITECTS, ARTISTS, PATRONS AND RESIDENTS   739

INDEX OF PLACES   761

LIST OF TEXT FIGURES AND MAPS

Every effort has been made to contact or trace all copyright holders. The publishers will be glad to make good any errors or omissions brought to our attention in future editions.

Crossing Lancaster Sands, etching and engraving by
Robert Brandard after J. M. W. Turner, 1828 (S. Wilcox,
ed., *Sun, Wind and Rain: The Art of David Cox*, 2009)   1

Geological map   4

Eskdale, Hardknott Roman Fort, plan (P. Bidwell,
M. Snape, and A. Croom, *Cumberland and Westmorland
Antiquarian and Archaeological Society Research Series 9,
Kendal,* 1999)   15

Westoe farmhouse, Skelton, elevation and ground-floor
plan after R. W. Brunskill (*Transactions of the Cumberland
and Westmorland Antiquarian and Archaeological Society*
vol. LIII, 1953)   39

Whitehaven, Queen Street, drawing (J. B. Crossland,
Looking at Whitehaven, 1971)   44

Barrow-in-Furness, steelworks, engraving, 1872   49

Rydal, The Rash, proposed design, drawings by George
Webster, 1826 (A. Taylor and J. Martin, *The Websters of
Kendal,* 2004)   56

Ambleside, The Knoll, engraving by William Banks
(H. Martineau, *A Complete Guide to the English
Lakes,* 1855)   103

Appleby Castle, plan (RCHME, *An Inventory of the
Historical Monuments in Westmorland,* 1936)   107

Barrow-in-Furness, port, plan by James Ramsden, 1856,
courtesy of the Cumbria Record Office and Local Studies
Library   130

Barrow-in-Furness, prefabricated church (St Luke),
engraving (J. Richardson, *Barrow-in-Furness, its
History, Development, Commerce, Industries, and
Instititutions,* 1881)   133

Barrow-in-Furness, Town Hall, plans of original design
(*The Builder,* vol. 37, 1879)   136

Bewcastle Cross, drawings, c20   154

THE BUILDINGS OF ENGLAND

FOUNDING EDITOR: NIKOLAUS PEVSNER

CUMBRIA
CUMBERLAND, WESTMORLAND AND FURNESS

MATTHEW HYDE AND NIKOLAUS PEVSNER

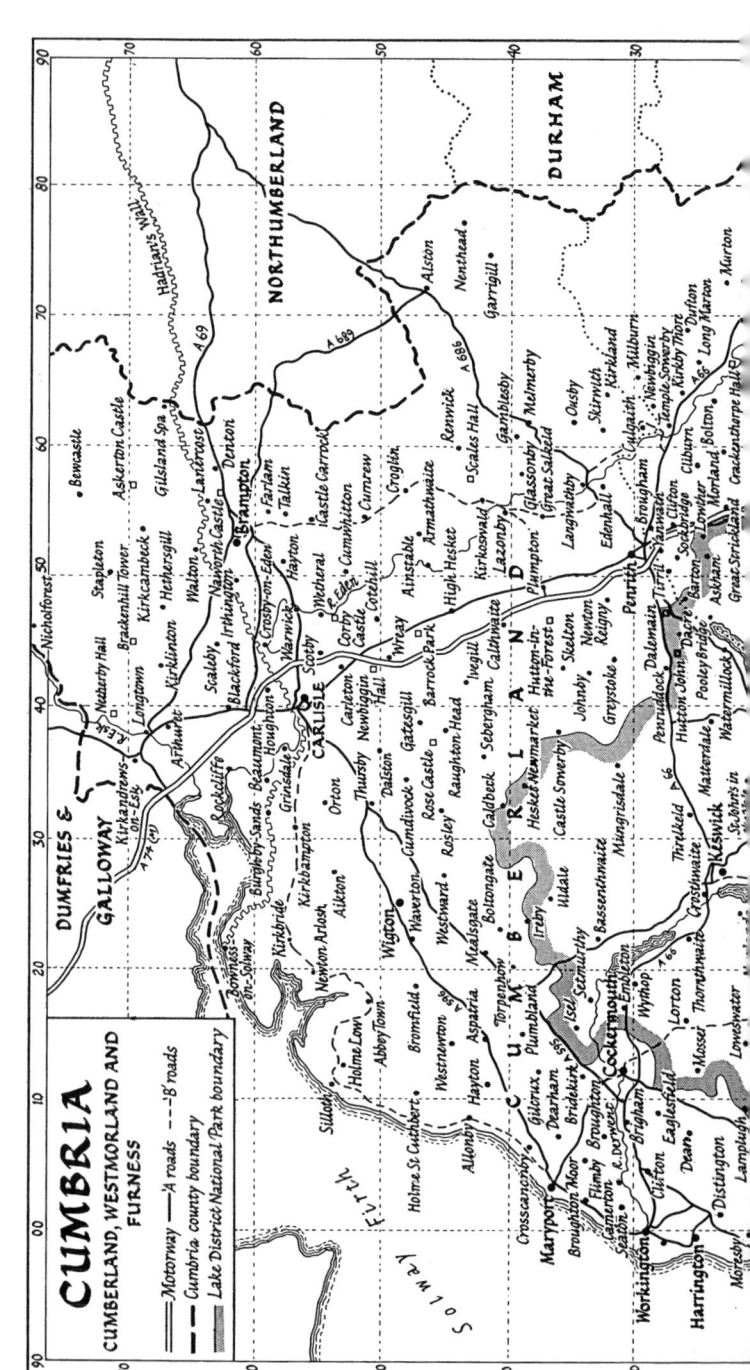

CUMBRIA

CUMBERLAND, WESTMORLAND AND FURNESS

— Motorway   — 'A' roads   ---'B' roads

--- Cumbria county boundary

Lake District National Park boundary

DUMFRIES & GALLOWAY

NORTHUMBERLAND

DURHAM

CUMBERLAND

Solway Firth

Hadrian's Wall

Bewcastle
Nicholforest
Stapleton
Askerton Castle
Gilsland Spa
Nether Denton
Lanercost
Brackenhill Tower
Kirkcambeck
Kirklinton
Hethersgill
Walton
Nabworth Castle
Longtown
Brampton
Farlam
Talkin
Castle Carrock
Cumwhitton
Croglin
Renwick
Scales Hall
Melmerby
Gamblesby
Ousby
Skirwith
Kirkland
Milburn
Newbiggin
Kirkby Thore
Long Marton
Dufton
Crackenthorpe Hall
Murton
Morland
Bolton
Cliburn
Temple Sowerby
Clifton
Brougham
Cliburn
Sockbridge
King's Meaburn
Great Strickland
Askham
Barton
Dacre
Tirril
Penrudock
Dalemain
Pooley Bridge
Watermillock
Hutton John
Newton Reigny
Greystoke
Johnby
Skelton
Plumpton
Iggassonby
Great Salkeld
Langwathby
Edenhall
Penrith
Lazonby
Kirkoswald
High Hesket
Armathwaite
Ainstable
Cotehill
Corby Castle
Wetheral
Cumwhinton
Wreay
Scotby
Warwick
Crosby-on-Eden
Houghton
Beaumont
Grinsdale
Rockcliffe
Kirkandrews-on-Esk
Arthuret
Scaleby
Blackford Irthington
CARLISLE
Thursby
Dalston
Cummersdale
Orton
Cumdivock
Rosley
Raughton Head
Caldbeck
Sebergham
Catlowdie
Hutton-in-the-Forest
Ireby
Castle Sowerby
Mungrisdale
Threlkeld
KESWICK
St. John's-in-the-Vale
Crosthwaite
Matterdale
Thornthwaite
Applethwaite
Wythop
Embleton
Lorton
Loweswater
Mosser
Cockermouth
Brigham
Dean
Clifton
Eaglesfield
Distington
Lamplugh
Harrington
Workington
Moresby
Camerton
Seaton
Flimby
Dearham
Broughton Moor
Maryport
Crosscanonby
Allonby
Hayton
Aspatria
Westnewton
Bromfield
Holme St. Cuthbert
Silloth
Gilcrux
Plumbland
Bridekirk
Isel
Sunderland
Blennerhasset
Torpenhow
Bassenthwaite
Bothel
Boltongate
Mealsgate
Westward
Waverton
Wigton
Aikton
Newton Arlosh
Kirkbride
Kirkbampton
Burgh-by-Sands
Bowness-on-Solway
Holme Low
Abbeytown
Oughterside

A69
A689
A686
A66
A7 (M)
M6

S c o t l a n d

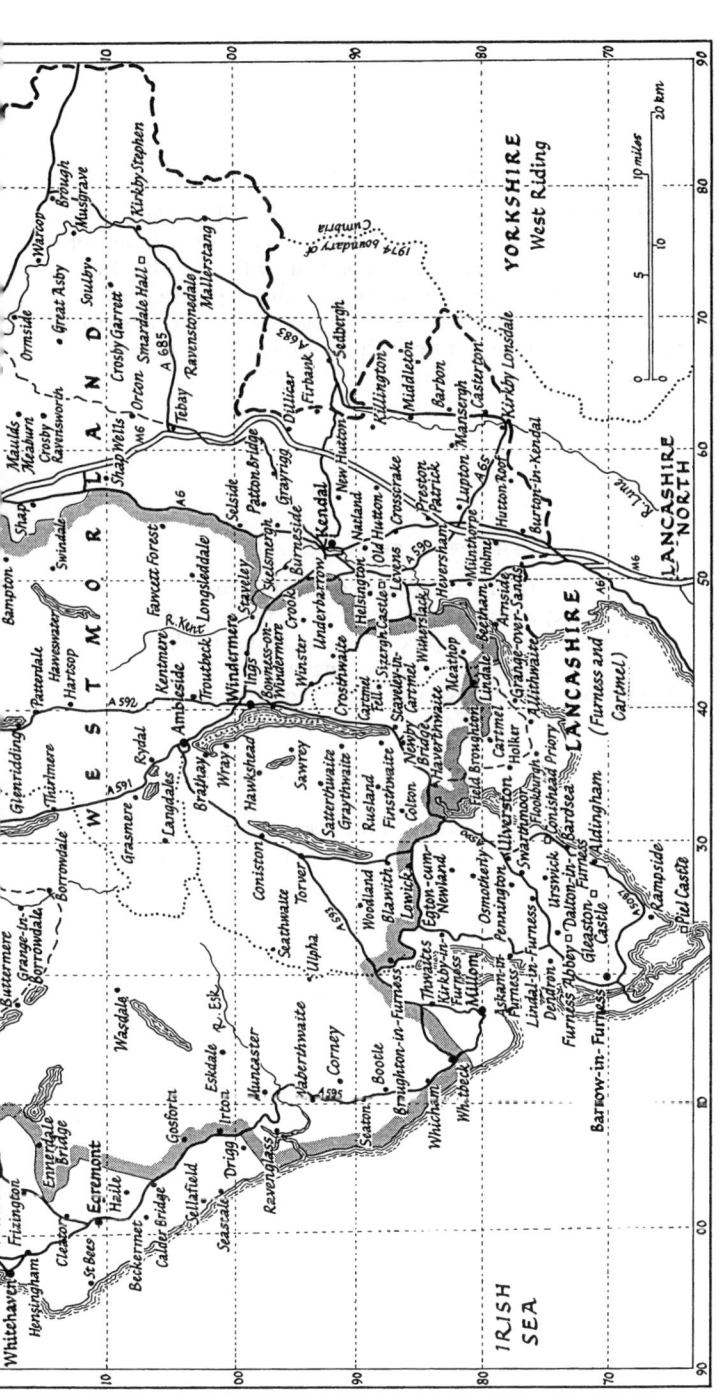

PEVSNER ARCHITECTURAL GUIDES

The Buildings of England series was created and largely
written by Sir Nikolaus Pevsner (1902–83). First editions of
the county volumes were published by Penguin Books
between 1951 and 1974. The continuing programme
of revisions and new volumes has since 1994 been supported
by research financed through the Buildings Books Trust
(now the Pevsner Books Trust)

THE PEVSNER BOOKS TRUST

formerly the Buildings Books Trust,
is an independent registered charity, number 1042101.
It promotes the appreciation and understanding of
architecture by supporting and financing
the research needed to sustain new and revised volumes of
The Buildings of England, Ireland, Scotland and *Wales*

The Trust gratefully acknowledges
a major grant from

THE LEVERHULME TRUST
towards the cost of research and writing

assistance with photography from
ENGLISH HERITAGE

and an additional grant towards the costs of maps
and other illustrations from
THE C.J. ROBERTSON TRUST

Cumbria

CUMBERLAND, WESTMORLAND AND FURNESS

BY

MATTHEW HYDE

AND

NIKOLAUS PEVSNER

THE BUILDINGS OF ENGLAND

YALE UNIVERSITY PRESS
NEW HAVEN AND LONDON

YALE UNIVERSITY PRESS
NEW HAVEN AND LONDON
302 Temple Street, New Haven CT 06511
47 Bedford Square, London WC1B 3DP
www.pevsner.co.uk
www.lookingatbuildings.org.uk
www.yalebooks.co.uk
www.yalebooks.com
for
THE PEVSNER BOOKS TRUST

Published by Yale University Press 2010
2 4 6 8 10 9 7 5 3 1

ISBN 978 0 300 12663 1

Printed in China
through World Print
Set in Monotype Plantin

Bowness-on-Windermere, Blackwell, ground-floor plan
(H. Muthesius, *The English House*, translated by
J. Seligman and S. Spencer, vol. I, 2007), courtesy of
Frances Lincoln Ltd   172

Brampton, Lord Carlisle memorial shelter, drawings
by Christopher Nicholson, 1928, courtesy of the RIBA   181

Bridekirk, cross-slab grave cover, drawing (P. Ryder,
The Medieval Cross Slab Grave Covers in Cumbria,
2005), courtesy of Peter Ryder and The Cumberland
and Westmorland Antiquarian and Archaeological
Society   184

Brougham Castle, plan (RCHME, *An Inventory of the
Historical Monuments in Westmorland*, 1936)   193

Brougham Castle, oratory, engraving (*The Beauties of
England and Wales, Westmorland*, 1807)   194

Burneside Hall, plan (D. Perriam and J. Robinson,
Medieval Fortified Buildings of Cumbria, 1998), courtesy
of Dennis Perriam and The Cumberland and
Westmorland Antiquarian and Archaeological Society   206

Burneside, Tolson Hall, stained glass, drawing
(R. Bingham, *Kendal, a Social History*, 1995),
courtesy of the author   207

Calder Abbey, plan   214

Carlisle, bird's-eye view of the walled city, engraving
after a drawing of 1590 (D. and S. Lysons, *Magna
Britannia* vol. IV, 1816)   221

Carlisle Cathedral, plan (R. W. Billings, *Carlisle
Cathedral*, 1840)   227

Carlisle Cathedral, choir north aisle, engraving
(R. W. Billings, *Carlisle Cathedral*, 1840)   230

Carlisle Cathedral, cathedral and precinct, plan
by J.H. Martindale (*Transactions of the Cumberland
and Westmorland Antiquarian and Archaeological Society*
vol. XXIV, 1924)   237

Carlisle Castle, Great Tower, cutaway drawing
(J. Goodall, *British Archaeological Association Transactions*
vol. XXVII, 2004), courtesy of John Goodall   243

Carlisle, the Cumberland pub, elevation by Henry
Redfern, 1920s (O. Seabury, *The Carlisle State
Management Scheme*, 2007)   258

Cartmel Priory, plan (*Victoria County History of
Lancaster* vol. VIII, 1914)   267

Coniston Hall, ground- and first-floor plans (*Victoria
County History of Lancaster* vol. VIII, 1914)   296

Crosscanonby, St John Evangelist, cross-shaft, engraving
(W. S. Calverley, *Early Sculpted Crosses, Shrines and
Monuments of the Diocese of Carlisle*, 1899)   312

Dacre Castle, ground- and first floor-plans
(E. H. A. Stretton, *Dacre Castle*, 1994), courtesy of
the author   321

Furness Abbey, plan   353

Furness Abbey, sedilia and piscina, engraving
(T. A. Beck, *Annales Furnesienses*, 1844)   355

Gosforth Cross, drawings (*Transactions of the Cumberland
and Westmorland Antiquarian and Archaeological Society* vol.
XVII, 1917)   368

Grasmere, Jerwood Centre, plan, courtesy of Benson &
Forsyth/Napper Architects   376

Grayrigg, St John, elevation by George Webster, 1837
(A. Taylor and J. Martin, *The Websters of Kendal*, 2004)   378

Great Asby, Gaythorne Hall, plan (RCHME, *An Inventory
of the Historical Monuments in Westmorland*, 1936)   381

Greystoke, Greenthwaite Hall, drawing (*Transactions of
the Cumberland and Westmorland Antiquarian and
Archaeological Society* vol. VII, 1907)   391

Hayton Castle, ground-floor plan (D. Perriam and
J. Robinson, *Medieval Fortified Buildings of Cumbria*,
1998), courtesy of Dennis Perriam and The
Cumberland and Westmorland Antiquarian and
Archaeological Society   402

Hutton-in-the-Forest, ground- and first-floor plans
(*Archaeological Journal* vol. CXV, 1958)   416

Keswick, High Moss, ground- and first-floor plans
(L. Weaver, *Small Country Houses of Today*, 1922)   451

Kirkby Lonsdale, St Mary, plan (RCHME, *An Inventory
of the Historical Monuments in Westmorland*, 1936)   459

Kirkby Lonsdale, Devil's Bridge, engraving (T. Pennant,
A Tour from Downing to Alston-Moor, 1801)   462

Kirkby Stephen, the 'Loki Stone', engraving
(W. S. Calverley, *Early Sculpted Crosses, Shrines and
Monuments of the Diocese of Carlisle*, 1899)   468

Lanercost Priory, plan   481

Lanercost Priory, section of nave, drawing by David
McNay (S. Harrison and H. Summerson, *Lanercost
Priory*, 2000), courtesy of the artist   483

Langwathby, station, platform elevation, drawing
(D. Jenkinson, *Rails in the Fells*, 1973), courtesy of
Railway Modeller magazine   490

Levens Hall, gardens, plan (RCHME, *An Inventory of the
Historical Monuments in Westmorland*, 1936) 494

Lowther Castle, garden front, engraving (J. P. Neale,
Views of the Seats of Noblemen and Gentlemen vol.
V, 1825) 504

Lowther village plan (R. W. Brunskill, *Transactions of
the Ancient Monuments Society* vol. XIV, 1967), courtesy
of Ronald Brunskill and the Ancient Monuments Society 509

Naworth Castle, plan (D. R. Perriam and J. Robinson, *The
Medieval Fortified Buildings of Cumbria*, 1998), courtesy of
Dennis Perriam and The Cumberland and Westmorland
Antiquarian and Archaeological Society 544

Ormside, St James, plan (RCHME, *An Inventory of the
Historical Monuments in Westmorland*, 1936) 558

Rose Castle, plan (T. Tatton-Brown, *British Archaeological
Association Transactions* vol. XXVII, 2004) 590

St Bees Priory, engraving by Samuel and Nathaniel
Buck, 1739, courtesy of Ian McAndrew and
www.stbees.org 597

Scaleby Castle, plan (*Transactions of the Cumberland
and Westmorland Antiquarian and Archaeological Society*
vol. XXVI, 1926) 605

Sizergh Castle, first-floor plan (I. Goodall and
C. Gapper, *Sizergh Castle*, 2005), courtesy of English
Heritage 621

Whitehaven, map, 1774 671

Windermere, St Mary, drawing, 1848 (G. G.
Cunninghame, *The Church and Parish of St Mary
Applethwaite*, 1900) 688

Yanwath Hall, plan (RCHME, *An Inventory of the
Historical Monuments in Westmorland*, 1936) 709

MAPS

Ambleside 100
Appleby 110
Barrow-in-Furness 139
Carlisle 249
Cockermouth 286
Kendal 436
Kirkby Lonsdale 464
Penrith 571
Ulverston 648
Whitehaven 678

PHOTOGRAPHIC ACKNOWLEDGEMENTS

We are grateful to English Heritage and its photographer Alun Bull for taking most of the photographs in this volume (© English Heritage Photo Library) and also to the sources of the remaining photographs as shown below. We are grateful for permission to reproduce them as appropriate.

English Heritage (NMR): 8, 68
Matthew Hyde: 2, 41, 56, 59, 67, 84, 86, 98, 103, 110, 114
National Trust Photo Library/Andreas von Einsiedel: 45

MAP REFERENCES

The numbers printed in italic type in the margin against the place names in the gazetteer of the book indicate the position of the place in question on the index map (pp. ii–iii), which is divided into sections by the 10-kilometre reference lines of the National Grid. The reference given here omits the two initial letters which in a full grid reference refer to the 100-kilometre squares into which the county is divided. The first two numbers indicate the *western* boundary, and the last two the *southern* boundary, of the 10-kilometre square in which the place in question is situated. For example, Abbey Town (reference *1050*) will be found in the 10-kilometre square bounded by grid lines 10 (on the *west*) and 20, and 50 (on the *south*) and 60; Yanwath (reference *5020*) in the square bounded by the grid lines 50 (on the *west*) and 60, and 20 (on the *south*) and 30.

The map contains all those places, whether towns, villages, or isolated buildings, which are the subject of separate entries in the text.

EDITOR'S FOREWORD

Nikolaus Pevsner's foreword to his *Cumberland and Westmorland* (1967) began with apologies: 'One ought not to publish a volume on Cumberland and Westmorland without the Furness part of Lancashire. I had to do it, simply because preparation of Lancashire had not proceeded far enough for me to travel when the Cumberland and Westmorland travels took place.' This revised volume makes good the omission, under the name of the new administrative county created in 1974. The gazetteer is thus ordered in a single alphabetical sequence, with the letter (C), (W) or (L) against each entry to indicate its historic county. The Introduction also uses these letters where the original county is not clear from the context. The exception is the Sedbergh district, part of Cumbria since 1974 but historically within the former West Riding of Yorkshire, and therefore described as such in Peter Leach and Nikolaus Pevsner, *Yorkshire West Riding: Leeds, Bradford and the North* (2009).

ACKNOWLEDGEMENTS

The foundations of this text are Nikolaus Pevsner's *Cumberland and Westmorland* (1967) and the Furness part of *North Lancashire* (1969). These were written with support from the Leverhulme Trust, who pleasingly have also supported this new book. Alec Clifton-Taylor contributed the first of his many essays on building materials to *Cumberland and Westmorland*, and that is reprised here, along with an introduction to the Geology and Topography by Andrew A. McMillan. Humphrey Welfare has written the archaeological entries and the relevant section of the introduction. Richard N. Bailey has written the introductory section on Pre-Norman sculpture as well as giving me a concentrated day visiting some of them on site. Gavin Watson contributed the industrial introduction and entries on many of the industrial sites, and on Carlisle schools. Andrew Martindale has written the entry for Appleby Castle, Adam Menuge that for Acorn Bank at Temple Sowerby.

I am grateful to the Department of History at Lancaster University where a Visiting Research Fellowship was created for the duration of the project, and where Angus Winchester and Mike Winstanley have been unfailingly helpful.

Other thanks must go first to those many Cumbrians who opened doors for me. The private houses, often off the beaten track and seldom open to the public, were a cumulative revelation, as I hope these pages reveal. Thanks too to those who opened churches, and also to all those who keep their churches open every day – one of the pleasures of working in Cumbria.

Whilst many allowed access to buildings in their care, too many indeed to list here, some have gone further. David Altham at Yanwath not only allowed a thorough inspection of that fascinating house on two occasions, but also sent me with an introduction to other houses in the area. Thanks to Hugh, Baron Cavendish of Furness, for his tour of Holker Hall and estate, and for taking my wife and me racing at Cartmel. Lord Chorley gave advice and contacts at an early stage. Thanks to Bethan and the late Nicholas Howard of Johnby, for their hospitality, introductions, and site visits. Robert Wells kindly lent his cottage at Cockermouth, providing a regular base in the NW of the territory. Bill Shaw and Sylvia at Swarthmoor Hall provided my favourite place to write.

The Venerable David Thomson, then Archdeacon of Carlisle, entertained me at No. 1 The Abbey and provided some gentle chivvying of churchwardens in his archdeaconry. David Weston,

Canon Librarian, was my guide to Carlisle Cathedral and Rose Castle. Diana and David Matthews are owed a special debt of gratitude, offering generous hospitality at Rayrigg and almost too many introductions to Westmorland society. Vicky and Oliver Barratt of Cowmire took me round the industrial sites at Back-barrow and Low Wood as well as supplying introductions in w Cumbria. Bed-and-breakfast hosts with their local knowledge helped in the same way, e.g. Jean Jackson at the Hermitage, Shap; Frazer Allison of Wallfoot; and Anne Sandell at the Croglin Castle, Kirkby Stephen.

Merrilyn and Henry Sawrey-Cookson of Newbiggin were very generous with their hospitality, introductions, and site visits. Christopher Terry was a genial host at High Head and Brougham Hall. Thanks to Janet Martin of Finsthwaite for tea, contacts and the fruits of her researches. Charles Blackett-Ord and Elaine Rigby opened their office records at Appleby and took me on various sites where work was in progress. Mark Blackett-Ord was an entertaining guide at Warcop, as were the senior Blackett-Ords at Helbeck. Thanks also to Charles Ecroyd at Armathwaite; to Margaret Edwards of the CWAAS; to Phyllida Entwisle, an invaluable contact in Cumbria's water industry; to Peter de Figueiredo for information on Dawstone, Windermere; and to the late Anthony Gaddum for family reminiscences and pho-tographs of Brockhole. Susan Thornely assisted with the Curwen archives of Belle Isle and Workington, as did Anthony Hothfield for Appleby Castle. Thanks to Myles and Camilla Sandys of Graythwaite, Tim and Jean Sturgis of Longhouses, Charles Woodhouse of Quarry Hill, Boltongate, Arthur Sanderson of The Croft, Cummersdale, and Harvey Wilkinson at Blackwell. Thanks to Roger Bingham for his hospitality, books, introductions, driving, and door-to-door visits in and around Milnthorpe, Hev-ersham and Burton-in-Kendal; to Mary Burkett at Isel; to Jocelyn Holland and James Carr for introductions and hospital-ity; to Alan Chapman (Sutton Cheshire) for loan of his mines survey; to John Borron; to the Revs Robert and Wendy Brace-girdle at Millom; to Mollie Clough at Stanegarth; to Gill Colling-wood for information on G. F. Armitage; to James Cropper for taking me round his farms and cottages in Burneside.

Stephen Gorton gave a guided walk around Hartsop, as did Bryan Sparrow around Ambleside, and both Steve Matthews and John Higham at different times around Wigton. Special thanks are due to Michael Bottomley of Kendal, who did a full peram-bulation of the town with me, read my text, and also took me round some of the villas old and new in the area.

John Lee of Lanercost was a strong supporter in the Northern regions, contributing hospitality and introductions and accom-panying me several times on fieldwork. Nina Jennings was a tren-chant guide to the clay dabbins of the Solway Plain, visiting some with me. Alastair Robertson and Peter Ryder gave much practi-cal help with fieldwork with the Alston area. Clare Hartwell managed to find time while working on North Lancashire to look at some Cumbrian buildings with me. Her Lancaster landlady

Gwenda Meredith also provided occasional accommodation. Wardens of Youth Hostels have been helpful too.

Denis Perriam is a well-known and prolific researcher and author on matters Cumbrian, which he was generous to share, as were John Martin Robinson, Henry Bowring at Whelprigg, and Heather and Alan Rhodes at Moor Crag. Thanks to the late Christa Grössinger for her lively interpretation of misericords, and to Penny Hebgin-Barnes for pre-Reformation glass in Lancashire. John Prag of Manchester Museum gave much useful information and literature on the Bewcastle Cross. David Cross gave much encouragement and help on public sculpture of the later varieties. Peter Ryder's researches on defensible buildings and on medieval cross-slabs have been invaluable. Ian Jones is a fellow enthusiast for the villas of Windermere. Julian Lambton provided much insider help with Rydal. Frederick O'Dwyer provided information on c18 buildings in Whitehaven. Peter Lockhart-Smith sent details of Stonegarthside hall, and Terry Friedman explained Penrith church. Details of bank architects were supplied by the Barclays archivists Nicholas Webb and Maria Sienkiewicz, and by Rachel Spree at HSBC. Geoffrey Fisher, Patrick Garman and Philip Ward-Jackson assisted with church monuments and John Kenworthy-Browne with the Howard Chapel at Wetheral. Graeme Moore supplied information on Dan Gibson, and Ian Wells on the Jerwood Centre. Andrew Lowe, lately Conservation Officer with the LDNP, was always willing to share his knowledge and enthusiasms.

Libraries, Record Offices and museums are of course an essential resource. Thanks to the staff of Kendal Library Local Studies, of the four Record Offices at Carlisle, Whitehaven, Barrow and Kendal, of the branch libraries such as Ulverston and Cockermouth, of Tullie House Museum in Carlisle and the idiosyncratic museums at Keswick, Coniston and Millom, and to the unique Armitt Library at Ambleside and the Rylands Library in Manchester. The collections of the Wordsworth Trust at Grasmere are especially valuable. Robert Woof, before his untimely death, was an inspiring help especially on the c18 and c19 discovery of the Lake District.

I am grateful to Stephen Matthews of Bookcase, Carlisle, who augmented my personal library for the duration by hiring out a century's worth of CWAAS *Transactions*. Tim Walton has helped out on several occasions with IT problems.

Staff of the National Trust and English Heritage, both on the spot and in the regional offices in Manchester and York, have given valuable help at different times and in different places. Thanks go especially to Adam Menuge, Sarah Woodcock, the late Ian Goodall, and Wayne Cocroft. Ian's top-to-bottom tour of Muncaster with my wife and myself was a high spot of the project, as in an entirely different way was Wayne's introduction to Spadeadam.

Thanks to all those who wrote in with corrections and new information. Geoff Brandwood has given much help on Paley & Austin (as also has James Price), and his snippets from archival delvings have been invaluable. Geoff Brandwood, Ron Brunskill, John Goodall, John Lee, Adam Menuge, Julian Munby, John Todd, and Angus Winchester are among those who have read through and commented upon parts of the text. Alun Bull of English Heritage took most of the photographs.

Finally I am indebted to the team at Yale, to Sally Salvesen, Sophie Kullmann, Louisa Lee, Gavin Watson and especially to my perspicacious editor Simon Bradley. A certain pitting of wits and wills has been fruitful in the end.

MH, 2010

INTRODUCTION

Bounded as it is by sea or by bleak hills or sparsely inhabited forest, the Cumbrian peninsula, comprising the historic counties of Cumberland and Westmorland and a detached part of Lancashire, has never been particularly easy of access. The sea however, being shallow at the edges, is fordable, as the name Lancashire-across-the-Sands makes clear. The race against the galloping tide across the endless mazy sands of Morecambe Bay toward the distant Cumbrian mountains could hardly have been a more exhilarating, or hazardous, way to arrive. John Wesley (1703–91) grumbled about it many a time, but wrote when he got there, 'God is nowhere more present than in the mountains of Cumberland' – a very modern sentiment. The Solway can be forded too at low tide from Scotland, and there are over-sand shortcuts all round the coast. Grange-over-Sands, Cartmel, and Flookburgh (all Lancashire-across-the-Sands), Waberthwaite, Ravenglass and Bowness-on-Solway (Cumberland) all preserve a memory in their geography of the Sands routes. You can still – with a guide – make the over-sands crossing, but a good

Crossing Lancaster Sands
Etching and engraving after J.M.W. Turner, 1828

substitute today is to take the train along the S coast to Ulverston. On a high Spring tide, when the waves lap right up to Grange-over-Sands station, the train seems to ride over the sea itself. The motorway, arriving from N or S, offers just tantalizing glimpses of mountains over gleaming sand and ruffled water. Otherwise it is up and over the whale-backed barrier of the high Pennines, or round the forbidding border forests N of the Roman Wall.

'The main structure of the landscape has remained little changed since the last Ice Age, but the detail is almost wholly man-made,' observed the *Observer's Book of the Lake District* in 1978. We are concerned with the man-made detail here, but the setting is always the grandeur of the landscape. It is all rewarding, from the great radially fissured dome of the Lake District, one of the most celebrated landscapes in the world, to other parts known hardly at all: the spacious muddy coasts and estuaries, the well-named Eden valley, the bare Pennine shoulders, the rough borderlands. The native architecture rarely attempts to compete, or embellish. No need. Summits and skylines are seldom accentuated by more than a simple cairn. Only the limestone ridges of Cartmel and Ulverston (L) are pimpled with towers and follies. The instinct seems to have been to keep low and horizontal, making a visual impact if at all with gleaming whitewash. Towers are broad rather than high, defensive in aspect and often in fact, though the alien spires introduced by the Victorians at Ambleside (W), Cockermouth (C), Silloth (C) and Field Broughton (L) can look good. Even the C20 era of tower blocks has left the region unmarked, save for the solitary Civic Centre (*Charles B. Pearson, Son & Partners*, 1960–3) at Carlisle (C).

Cumbria, among the largest of the post-1974 English administrative counties but with a population of less than half a million, is almost all hinterland. The towns are relatively insignificant, though sharply differentiated visually by their colours. Kendal (W) is silver-grey, and so is Ulverston (L). Penrith (C) is deep red, Ambleside (W) green, Coniston (L) black. Dalston (C) is piebald, and Keswick (C) flaunts every colour in joyful juxtaposition. Then there are the painted towns of W Cumberland: Whitehaven especially, Cockermouth, and the Georgian parts of Maryport and Workington. And finally the red brick towns, Carlisle and Barrow (L), both with red stone highlights. Towns very often bear witness to a degree of formal planning, from Norman Appleby, through C17 Whitehaven, right up to mid-Victorian Barrow and Silloth.

Villages (locally also called towns, hence Town End, Town Foot etc.) are often laid out in an orderly fashion round a communal green, which may ante-date any surviving building. Sometimes this is still perfect, as at Milburn and Dufton (both W) on the Pennine fringe, with houses on all four sides of a rectangular green with strip fields radiating behind to a back road. The planting of such villages may be linked to the resettlement after the Norman Conquest, i.e. late C11. Strip widths are generous, allowing for a house and its attached barn to stretch across each one – a very different effect from the urban row of gable-ends. In neither Milburn nor Dufton is the church part of the plan. At Hesket Newmarket (C) the rectangle is not quite complete, and it has no church. Nor does Blennerhasset (C). Ormside (W) developed no further than its stepped cross and hall below the church on its mound. Newby (Morland, W), Crosby (Cross-canonby, C) and Hayton near Aspatria (C) are little bigger. Askham (W) has three sections of green, like a string of beads, the uppermost of which is hardly built up. In other villages the green can be discerned only with difficulty because it has been encroached upon. The village school at Milburn, built upon the green, shows how this can start. Dean (C) is another example. Maulds Meaburn (W), Great Asby (W), Temple Sowerby (W), Gamblesby (C) and Caldbeck (C) have plenty of communal green but the dwellings are scattered haphazardly upon it. It is hard to say whether this was planned or not. Penrith (C) and Hawkshead (L) may be urban versions of the same thing – islands of buildings with irregular linked open spaces in between.

As for the isolated settlements, they are more likely to be little clumps than single dwellings, e.g. Watendlath (Grange-in-Bor-rowdale, C), and Colthouse near Hawkshead (L), although sometimes the clumps have been simplified down to a single dwelling, e.g. at the heads of the Lake District dales; evidence of rural population shrinkage.

GEOLOGY AND TOPOGRAPHY

BY ANDREW A. MCMILLAN

Formed between 500 and 400 million years ago, the Lower Palaeozoic (Ordovician to Silurian) rocks of the Lake District mountains, the Highlands of England, occupy the core of the modern county of Cumbria. This major geological inlier is surrounded by younger rocks of Upper Palaeozoic to Mesozoic age which crop out over the lower ground of the w coast, the N Cumberland plain, the Vale of Eden in the former county of Westmorland, and to the s.

The LANDSCAPE of Cumbria is intimately related to the geology and its complex structural history. The variable but comparatively hard and resistant Lakeland rocks developed in a variety of environments ranging from oceanic to volcanic, with granite masses that crystallized deep in the earth's crust. The earliest rocks were laid down on the floor of an ancient ocean. As the surrounding continents converged the ocean was destroyed, and the rocks of today's Lake District were deformed and uplifted by tectonic forces during a mountain-building episode. The mountains may have been of a Himalayan scale until rapid erosion began 400 million years ago (Ma). Thereafter, the later Palaeozoic to Mesozoic sedimentary rocks (Devonian to Jurassic) were deposited in shallow seas, rivers and low-lying deserts. These rocks are generally less resistant to the processes

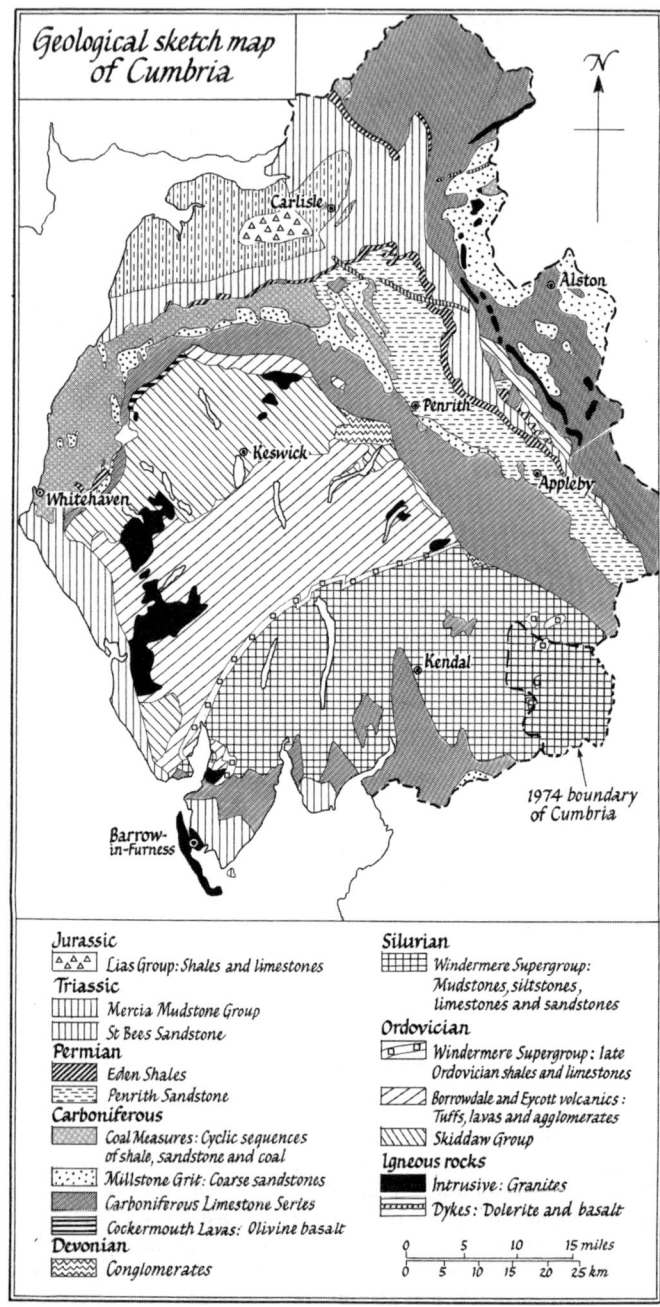

Geological map of Cumbria

Legend:

Geological sketch map of Cumbria

N

Carlisle

Alston

Penrith

Keswick

Whitehaven

Appleby

Kendal

Barrow-in-Furness

1974 boundary of Cumbria

Jurassic
Lias Group: Shales and limestones

Triassic
Mercia Mudstone Group
St Bees Sandstone

Permian
Eden Shales
Penrith Sandstone

Carboniferous
Coal Measures: Cyclic sequences of shale, sandstone and coal
Millstone Grit: Coarse sandstones
Carboniferous Limestone Series
Cockermouth Lavas: Olivine basalt

Devonian
Conglomerates

Silurian
Windermere Supergroup: Mudstones, siltstones, limestones and sandstones

Ordovician
Windermere Supergroup: late Ordovician shales and limestones
Borrowdale and Eycott volcanics: Tuffs, lavas and agglomerates
Skiddaw Group

Igneous rocks
Intrusive: Granites
Dykes: Dolerite and basalt

0   5   10   15 miles
0 5 10 15 20 25 km

of denudation and weathering. The effects of glaciation during the most recent geological period (the Quaternary – the last 2.6 million years) include over-deepened valley floors, some now occupied by lakes; erosional cirques (coves or corries) and depositional moraines (moundy deposits of till, boulders, sand and gravel) of the Lake District glaciers; and other glacial features, including drumlins (elongate ice-moulded drift mounds) and extensive deposits of till, sand and gravel, on surrounding lower ground which has been periodically inundated by ice from the Irish Sea basin. Locally, dry valleys are seen, the product of erosion by meltwater channels as the ice sheets dispersed. In post-glacial times (from *c.* 12,000 years ago) peat has developed on hillsides and valley floors, alluvial sands and gravels accumulated on the river flood plains, and raised beach and tidal flat deposits built up in the coastal zone. From N to S, the Cumbrian coastline now changes from the generally low land fringing the Solway Firth, occupied by raised tidal flat deposits and peat, via the spectacular red sandstone cliff scenery of St Bees Head, to the varied morphology consisting of coastal dunes, beach and glacial landforms which flank the E coast of the Irish Sea from St Bees to Morecambe Bay.

The Lake District MOUNTAINS of the Lower Palaeozoic core include the highest in England: Scafell Pike (3205 ft, 977 metres), Sca Fell (3163 ft, 964 metres), Helvellyn (3114 ft, 949 metres), Skiddaw (3054 ft, 931 metres) and Great Gable (2949 ft, 899 metres). To the W, the lower rounded granitic hills of Eskdale and Ennerdale overlook the W Cumbrian coast. E of the high Lake District lie the granite and Palaeozoic rocks of the Shap Fells, and further E, flanking the eastern margin of the broad Vale of Eden, is the Palaeozoic inlier of Cross Fell (2930 ft, 893 metres).

The oldest ROCKS of Cumbria were formed from sediments deposited on the floor of the long-vanished Lapetus Ocean. They belong to the Early Palaeozoic sub-era, divided into the Ordovician (488–443 Ma) and the Silurian (443–416 Ma). The earliest rocks belong to the SKIDDAW GROUP, which occupies the Northern and Western fells, Black Combe (1969 ft, 600 metres), and small inliers around Ullswater and Haweswater. Skiddaw Group rocks also occur at the foot of the Pennine escarpment below Cross Fell. The principal types are wacke (a compact, hard, dark grey sandstone composed of mineral and rock fragments), siltstone and mudstone (some now metamorphosed into slate). The Skiddaw Group was uplifted from its deep marine origins, and deformed in the process, to form the terrestrial foundation to the succeeding volcanic rocks. The latter were the product of an intense igneous episode which lasted some 15 million years. A chain of volcanoes then extended at least from eastern Ireland, through the Lake District and English Midlands, and into Belgium.

In the Lake District, two volcanic successions were built up, each originally *c.* 25–30 m. wide. Preserved in the northern one is the EYCOTT VOLCANIC GROUP, more than *c.* 10,500 ft (3200 metres) thick primarily of lavas and sills (intrusive sheets).

To the S, the BORROWDALE VOLCANIC GROUP comprises at least c. 19,680 ft (6000 metres) thick of lavas and sills, along with voluminous pyroclastic rocks (accumulations of rock and lava ejected from a volcano) and sedimentary rocks derived from volcanic material. The last are particularly important as a source of green slate, which continues to be used as a roofing material. Components of the Lake District composite granitic basement were emplaced at this time, and exposed by subsequent erosion. A range of more unusual rocks including gabbros, picrite and microgranite was also intruded.

Sedimentary rocks of the WINDERMERE SUPERGROUP (Late Ordovician to Silurian) stratigraphically overlie the volcanic pile. They comprise a c. 16,400-ft (5000-metre) succession of marine mudstones, siltstones and sandstones. These rocks crop out eastwards from the Duddon estuary, across the southern Lake District to the Howgill Fells. Within the succession are formations such as the Brathay Formation (Brathay Flags), laminated blue-black mudstone and siltstone much quarried until the mid C20 for building and flooring stone.

The continents surrounding the ocean started to collide around 440 Ma and the rocks were compressed, tightly folded, faulted and stacked against each other. Out of this collision a new landmass, the present Lake District, was formed. Granitic masses were emplaced in Early Devonian times at Shap and Skiddaw. Swarms of microgranite dykes emanate from these granite centres and widespread basis igneous dykes cut the Lower Palaeozoic strata. The Skiddaw Granite (399 ± 8 Ma) is a partly porphyritic medium-grained biotite granite. The Shap Granite (397 ± 7 Ma) in the eastern Lake District, with its distinctive feldspar crystals up to 2 in. (5 cm.) long, set in a coarse-grained groundmass composed of feldspar, quartz and biotite, is much prized for building and ornamental purposes.

The Devonian (416–359 Ma) was a significant period of land uplift and erosion. This resulted in the deposition of coarse-grained river gravel deposits, remnants of which are now seen in the form of CONGLOMERATES such as the Mell Fell Conglomerate. The conglomerates rest on rocks of the Skiddaw and Borrowdale Volcanic groups, and crop out over a large area N of Ullswater. Equivalent conglomerates may be covered by younger sedimentary rocks in the Vale of Eden. The 'Polygenetic Conglomerate' outcrops in the Cross Fell Inlier, and once near Greystoke, W of Penrith.

Carboniferous (359–299 Ma) rocks form an extensive outcrop around the margins of the Lake District: along the W Cumbrian coast, around the N of the massif to Caldbeck, and along the western and eastern margins of the Vale of Eden, the Yorkshire Dales and S Cumbria. In the North and under the Vale of Eden they are concealed by younger strata, mainly of Permo-Triassic age. A period of crustal extension, which began in the Late Devonian, continued through Early Carboniferous times, gradually produced a rifted topography of fault-bounded blocks (highs) and intervening fault-controlled grabens and half-grabens (basins).

Comparatively thin shallow-water, cyclical sequences of marine limestones, mudstones, siltstones and sandstones formed on the block areas while much thicker successions accumulated in the intervening basins. By mid-Carboniferous times distinctive block-and-basin topography was gradually submerged beneath predominantly river-borne sediments.

From oldest to youngest, divisions of the Carboniferous in Northern England include the RAVENSTONEDALE GROUP (Tournaisian Stage), the BORDER GROUP and GREAT SCAR LIMESTONE GROUP ('Mountain Limestone' of the early literature; Viséan Stage), YOREDALE GROUP (including the Mill-stone Grit; Viséan to Namurian stages) and PENNINE COAL MEASURES (Westphalian Stage).

The earliest rocks of the Ravenstonedale Group include variable thicknesses of unfossiliferous conglomerates and sandstones derived from erosion of the Late Devonian landscape. Basaltic lavas at Cockermouth in N Cumbria record Early Carboniferous volcanicity. In much of S and W Cumbria limestones form a major part of the succession of both the Ravenstonedale and Great Scar Limestone groups. Flanking the Vale of Eden is a well-marked succession of limestones, mudstones, sandstones and thin coals, belonging to the Yoredale Group. Namurian deposition was increasingly dominated by sand, silt and mud, carried into the region by large river deltas draining a land area to the N or NE. Rocks of Westphalian age represent predominantly deltaic and freshwater swamp conditions, with the coal-forming phase generally much more pronounced than in the Namurian. It was in this environment that the coal-bearing strata of the Pennine Coal Measures Group of the coastal tract between Whitehaven and Maryport accumulated.

Bright red sandstones and conglomerates that formed in the generally desert conditions of the Permian period (299–251 Ma) follow the Carboniferous succession. These are represented in the Vale of Eden by the APPLEBY GROUP, comprising the Brock-ram (conglomerate with locally derived pebbles) and the Penrith Sandstone Formation, which has yielded notable building sandstone. The succeeding Eden Shales Formation of the Cumbrian Coast Group includes gypsum and anhydrite, minerals formed after evaporation and indicative of coastal mudflat and alluvial environments.

Red cross-bedded sandstones and interbedded siltstones and mudstones of the Triassic (251–200 Ma) St Bees Sandstone (SHERWOOD SANDSTONE GROUP) occupy parts of northern Cumbria and the W Cumbrian coastal plain, culminating at its northern end in St Bees Head. St Bees Sandstone has been long used as a building stone in Cumbria, eastern Dumfries and Galloway, and far beyond.

The youngest sedimentary rocks of Cumbria include the interbedded red (and less commonly green-grey) mudstones, silt-stones and sandstones of the MERCIA MUDSTONE GROUP, which occupy the Carlisle Basin under Carlisle, Silloth and district. These rocks are succeeded by Early Jurassic (200–176 Ma) strata of the LIAS GROUP in the small outlier at Great Orton.

The most recent igneous rocks of the county are Palaeocene (66–56 Ma) DYKES. These thin upright sheets of igneous rock include the Armathwaite-Cleveland Dyke, well exposed in the River Eden. The dykes are representatives of the major volcanic episode which was responsible for the formation of the igneous centres of western Scotland.

BUILDING MATERIALS

BY ALEC CLIFTON-TAYLOR*

Until recent times stone was the natural and obvious building material in almost the whole of the North-western Counties, a fact to which visually Cumbria owes a great deal. Nevertheless, the stone is not always visible, for a very large number of buildings have been given a coat of roughcast or have been cement-rendered, to make them drier. At Grasmere (W) the entire church wears an overcoat of drab-looking roughcast. In 1891 this was removed from the tower, and its unhewn 'beck cobbles' were duly pointed. The pointing proved incapable of resisting the rain, and after only twenty years the roughcast had to be reapplied. In some towns, Cockermouth for example, or Whitehaven (both C), there is hardly a house in which the stone walls are exposed. The facing materials are not attractive in themselves, but the use of applied colour is a help; and if white is the favourite, and often the most telling, many other colours can also be seen, almost always muted, as befits the visual character of the region. Only in a few places, mainly on or near the Solway Firth, in Carlisle and at Barrow-in-Furness, was red brick employed for some buildings from the Georgian period onwards. The Solway Plain is also a stronghold of mud-walled or 'dabbin' construction, while historic timber-framed building, formerly widespread, is now rare (for more on these *see* p. 41).

Where the building stones are left exposed to view, they display several marked characteristics. The texture is usually rough, sometimes very rough indeed, for with the exception of the friable Permian and Triassic sandstones these are very hard stones, intractable to handle. An ashlared face in this region of England is rare, and even the rubble stone is usually uncoursed. In the Lake District, where much of the stone is of volcanic origin, the lumps are so difficult to break that the majority were used unbroken and laid random. Many were retrieved from the beds of the becks or from adjoining fields or moors. These 'cobbles', with their surfaces smoothed by the mountain streams or by waters from melting glaciers – for up here the Ice Age came to an end only about 10,000 years ago – are still available in abundant quantity. Unbroken cobbles were a great standby for

---

*Revised 2010, incorporating material by Alec Clifton-Taylor from *The Buildings of England: North Lancashire* (1969).

the wallers. These rugged building materials suit the country perfectly, of course, being in fact part and parcel of it.

Nowhere in England, perhaps, can dry-walling – walls, that is, in which the stones are laid without mortar – be seen to better advantage. This method of construction is normal for boundary walls, but was also widely used for barns, as also for some of the humbler cottages; it was, and indeed still is, a traditional skill. Every wall is a complicated jigsaw of stones of the most diverse shapes, sizes, and maybe colours too. On the older walls it is not unusual to see large stones projecting at intervals from the plane surface; these are what the builders call 'throughs' – stones large enough to extend through the thickness of the wall, helping to give it strength and to add still further textural interest. Sometimes the topmost stones of a field wall were selected to be laid not horizontally but diagonally or vertically, yielding a vigorously serrated edge. This not only looks well but has the practical advantage of deterring jumping sheep. So effective is the dry-walling in this part of England that modern architects, especially in the Lake District National Park, often like to keep their mortar as far back as possible from the wall face in order to give the impression of dry-walling.

As for colours, the building stones are unrivalled in England for diversity: red, pink, brown, yellow, buff, fawn, grey, blue, green, lilac, white, black – all these are to be found in abundance. Outside the Lake District, the former county of Cumberland is predominantly 'red'. From Carlisle to Longtown near the Scots border, to Brampton and Lanercost by the Roman Wall, to Kirkoswald, Lazonby and Penrith, to Wigton, Aspatria and Maryport, nearly all the stone buildings are red or pink or brown; and so they are along the coastal strip stretching SE from St Bees. Some of the pinks are delightful, and the deep cocoa-powder-brown of the Bunter sandstone formerly quarried just to the N of Aspatria has a dark glow, but at Penrith it must be admitted that the similarly coloured Permian sandstone seems a little sombre despite its 'warmth'. These New Red sandstones are attractive to lichen, and some of the best colour effects, beyond the power of man to imitate, derive from the spottings and splashings of grey and grey-green on shell-pink stones.

In Cumberland even the Carboniferous rocks, which on the E side are the usual light greys and buffs, change colour farther W. The presence of haematite ore has stained the narrow strip S of Cockermouth quite a deep red, while in the district N and E of the lower end of Ullswater ferric oxide from the formations which once covered the Carboniferous limestone and Calciferous sandstone has changed the stone colour to a delicious grey-pink, paler than anything to be seen in the New Red sandstone country. At Dalemain near Dacre can be enjoyed some of the most beautiful building stone in the North of England. It was quarried only a mile away.

Red and pink are also the principal colours of the Cumberland granites. Most of the granite buildings are to be found in the area centring on Eskdale and running southwards to near

Bootle. Although the field walls are grey with lichen, the buildings hereabouts are mostly pale pink. This stone is unhappily no longer worked, but visually it is perhaps the most attractive granite in England. A similar stone may be seen in the walls of the farmhouses around Ennerdale Water. Threlkeld granite, occurring to the E of Keswick, is mostly bluish-grey with some pink patches. The tower of the R.C. church at Keswick, completed in 1964, is a late example of its use for building.

The principal areas of Cumberland in which the building stone is not red, pink or brown comprise the W slopes of the Pennines, from Alston to Gilsland and Bewcastle (Carboniferous limestone: light grey and some buff); the coast from Whitehaven to Maryport and for a few miles inland (Millstone grit: pale brownish-grey); and the NW half of the Lake District. Here the hard rocks from the Early Ordovician series provide an uncompromising-looking building stone, often very dark and sombre in tone, as can be seen at Keswick; on the other hand the Borrowdale volcanic rocks yield one of the most delectable of all roofing materials, the green slates from the Honister Pass. Mention must also be made of the excellent barn and field walls of 'cobbleducks' (water-washed cobbles), gathered from the adjacent beaches, that are to be seen at certain places along the W coast between Millom and St Bees, notably near Bootle. In the best of these walls the cobbles are of nearly uniform size, so could be coursed, sometimes with bands of roofing slates introduced at intervals as 'levellers'. Splashes of brilliant yellow lichen add the final touch.

The former county of Westmorland, in contrast to Cumberland, is decidedly 'grey'. Red brick and tiles are still, fortunately, rare, and red stone occurs in a few places only: Permian and Triassic sandstones in the upper Eden valley, a few miles above and below Appleby, and the far older Ordovician stone at the centre of the Lake District. Although low in tone, the colours of this volcanic stone can be rather rich. They range from grey through every shade of brown to dark red and deep purple, the two latter due to staining from oxides of iron or manganese. The stone formerly quarried on Helm Crag, above Grasmere, is all dark red. Shap, the granite of Westmorland, only began to be quarried about a century and a half ago, and in the county itself it would be difficult to find even one building constructed of it, outside the confines of the company's works. But in the Late Victorian period there was a considerable vogue for it outside the county, especially in its polished form, e.g. for gravestones. The colour of this grey stone enlivened with high crystals of pink feldspar might from a little way off be described, in its natural state, as 'dusty pink'.

For the rest, apart from a small area of buff-grey Millstone grit near Appleby (a useful sandstone for dressings and where ashlar was required), three kinds of stone, and three only, cover the whole area, while for roofing there was until comparatively recently but one: slate. The Westmorland roofs are beyond doubt among the most beautiful in England. Old slates are very heavy; the roof of even a modest house may weigh as much as ten tons.

But fortunately a great many survive, equally satisfying alike for colour, for texture and for scale.

In much of SW Westmorland, including Staveley, Bowness, Windermere and Ambleside, the sombre greys and blacks and browns of the local Silurian flagstone dominate the architectural scene. This stone was relatively cheap and accessible, for, occurring largely with shale, it could be dug from the floors of the valleys, and, although hard, it could be broken up fairly easily into rough blocks. For expensive buildings these could be carefully shaped, but most buildings in this material are very rough-textured. This dour Silurian stone can also be seen in strength in the Furness district (see below).

Much more enjoyable is the so-called greenstone from the slate quarries, which belongs to the Ordovician period. This is really the wastage (not by any means always green; from the Kirkstone quarry it is grey with a bluish tinge) which is inevitable in the production of roofing slates and of panels or slabs for cladding. These pieces, lopped off in the trimming, are often rather small, but have been much used for walling stone in and around the Lake District.

Finally, there is the light grey Carboniferous limestone, which is the most extensive of the three. This covers the whole of the NE portion of Westmorland apart from the Eden valley, as well as an area to the SE which includes Kendal and Kirkby Lonsdale. Ravenstonedale, a grey village in a leafy hollow, is typical. This stone could be used where some degree of dressing was required, as for quoins and lintels; but most walls are rubble stone and constructed of rather small pieces – sturdy walls, with a good deal of mortar. Both in towns such as Kendal and Kirkby Stephen and dotted about the countryside, limewash often serves to give it a still whiter appearance. The limewash is usually applied over roughcast or, one is sorry to have to add, pebbledash. Needless to say there are also many excellent dry-stone walls of Carboniferous limestone; yet for some the surprise will not be the quantity of Westmorland's walls but the profusion, even here, of excellent hedges.

Sandstone and limestone both show well in the former Furness division of Lancashire, alias Lancashire North of the Sands. The Triassic (New Red) sandstone encountered in W Cumberland appears also at the extremities of the Cartmel and Furness peninsulas. The light grey limestone, usually in rather small, rough pieces, carries on from Westmorland; as e.g. at Ulverston and Dalton-in-Furness. One of these limestones, from near Ulverston, will take a polish and so qualifies as a semi-marble, a handsome stone employed in the 1870s at Holker Hall. But it is the older, Silurian flagstone which characterizes that part of Lancashire which fell within the Lake District, and which spreads down to the coast at Grange-over-Sands and at Ireleth. This extremely hard, splintery, flaggy material was only normally used as rubble, and its dour colouring – dark greys, blacks and browns for the most part – does not make much aesthetic appeal; but it was a common practice, as can be well seen at Hawkshead, to render with roughcast, and so long as the roughcast is frequently limewashed, this is probably the best method of making use of this intractable stone. The only trouble is that for most people it requires a real effort to remember that this was ever Lancashire.

ARCHAEOLOGY

BY HUMPHREY WELFARE

The settlement of Cumbria began slowly. After about 11,000 B.C., towards the end of the last glaciation, PALAEOLITHIC man seems to have utilized some of the limestone caves in the area around Grange-over-Sands (L). In the succeeding MESOLITHIC period, from about 8000 B.C., scatters of small worked flints and chert were widely distributed, especially along the coast. These mark the passage of groups of hunter-gatherers who probably erected little more than light impermanent shelters. By the late fifth millennium B.C., however, these people seem to have started to supplement their food with small-scale agriculture within the heavily wooded landscape; this shift in subsistence would have encouraged a less nomadic existence and the beginnings of settlement.

The mountains could be exploited as well as the lowlands. Between about 3800 and 2300 B.C., in the NEOLITHIC period, the distinctive green volcanic tuffs around Langdale (W) – from Stickle Tarn to Scafell, NE to Glaramara, and beyond – were extracted and quarried on an industrial scale to produce polished stone axes that were distributed throughout England and southern Scotland. In contrast, archaeology still provides few glimpses of the settlements of the Neolithic: just some concentrations of pottery, or a scatter of post-holes or pits, found in excavations. Rather more evident are the charnel houses of the dead: the LONG CAIRNS. Often trapezoidal in shape, they vary greatly in size, the one at Lowther (W) being 110 yds (101 metres) in length, whereas the dumpy example on Skelmore Heads (Urswick, L) is only 56 ft (17 metres) long. Little is known of their internal structures, which often prove to be more complex than the cairn may at first appear: thus, at Rayseat Pike (Crosby Garrett, W) excavation has shown that two adjacent round cairns (one of which covered a timber mortuary structure) were incorporated into the long mound of stone.

Neolithic society had the capacity and the will to build extraordinary monuments that were designed to impress. Even more startling in their scale than the long cairns were the enclosures known as HENGES, each of which usually consisted of a bank with an internal quarry-ditch: a design that can be seen in the earthworks known as King Arthur's Round Table, at Eamont Bridge (Yanwath, C). Closely adjacent, however, is Mayburgh – another henge – the massive bank of which was laboriously constructed of rounded stones taken from the river; a quarry-ditch was evidently not essential to the rituals played out there. This form has more similarities with some henges in Ireland than with those in Britain. In the C18 four upright stones still stood within Mayburgh, and two more at the entrance, indicating a relationship (not clearly understood) between the henges and the other type of monumental enclosure that survives from the Late Neolithic and the BRONZE AGE: the STONE CIRCLE.

The 'circles' vary greatly in size, shape, composition, and (apparently) in function also. The largest in Cumbria is Long Meg and her Daughters (Glassonby, C), a slightly flattened ring of boulders up to 120 yds (109 metres) across. At Swinside (Millom, C), 31 yds (28 metres) in diameter, the stones are closely set, perhaps suggesting a timber precursor; sites of this kind (cf. also Orton), and those that have evident pairs of 'portal' stones (e.g. Swinside, Castlerigg (St John's in the Vale, C), and Long Meg and her Daughters) may have been erected solely for the active rituals of the living. Elsewhere, the smaller circles – such as Sunbrick (Urswick) – were so commonly used for the deposit of cremations that burial may have been a principal function; the remains were often covered by a low central mound, as at Seascale (C), at Gunnerwell (Shap, W), and probably at Little Meg (Glassonby) and Castlehowe Scar (Crosby Ravensworth, W) also. Indeed the latter two sites may have been formed as the massive kerbs that retained the rubble of large cairns. At Gunnerwell an inner ring may have been (or become) the kerb of a later cairn. There are many variations on these themes. The Cockpit, on Askham Fell (W), is a circle of boulders on the inner side of a rubble bank; nearby, the 'Cop Stone' stands on the arc of another low stony bank; both of these may have been small cemeteries for cremations. The relationships between all of these sites are complex; archaeologists assign labels to many prehistoric structures but the functional distinctions between them – especially where ritual met daily life – may have been less clear-cut.

A cairn at Glassonby has a kerbstone that is decorated with ROCK ART; so too has a boulder at Little Meg, and another at Castlerigg, and Long Meg herself has a spiral and concentric rings pecked out on one of its faces. The messages in these designs are obscure to us but when they are found on natural rock surfaces – as at Copt Howe, in Langdale (W) – they may have had some reference to the landscape, indicating routes, ownership, or affiliation.

The structure of the Neolithic long cairn at Rayseat Pike suggests that some of the ROUND CAIRNS may have had an early origin, but they are more usually dated to the Bronze Age. Many have been found to be structurally complex and to have been utilized over a long timespan. They may also have been more than simply places of burial; often set on conspicuous high places – as on Great Mell Fell, overlooking Mungrisdale (C) – they seem to have marked territory and to have proclaimed rights inherited from the ancestors. The power of this is evident in later periods also: the cairn on Dunmail Raise, on the watershed between Thirlmere (C) and Grasmere (W), marked the southern limit of Strathclyde in the C10 and C11.

Burials dating from the IRON AGE (from *c.* 600 B.C.) are rarely identified; many bodies may have been disposed of in lakes and marshes. In the valleys of the Lake District and of the Howgill Fells (W) the contemporary settlements are also little known: the best locations then may still be occupied today. In the Solway Plain, however, aerial photography has revealed a scatter of small, enclosed farms, some with adjacent field systems, many of which may have been occupied into the Roman period. Castle Folds, on Great Asby Scar (W), may date to this period; it is an extraordinary site, surrounded (and possibly defended) by acres of limestone pavement. The classic development in the Iron Age was, however, the HILL-FORT. In Cumbria most of these are small enclosures that made best use of the natural defences of rocky bosses or isolated knolls – e.g. Castle How (Wythop, C), Castlesteads (Natland, W) or Croglam Castle (Kirkby Stephen, W). Some may have had a timber palisade in their primary phase – as at Skelmore Heads (Urswick) – which was likely to be replaced by a rampart and ditch or, later, by a stone wall. However, as so often in prehistory, the picture is far from uniform. On the summit of Carrock Fell (Caldbeck, C), 2174 ft (661 metres) above sea level, an extensive area is enclosed by a rubble wall; was this place intended for anything more than occasional or symbolic occupation? (It is undated and, as at Great Asby, it may be earlier than at first appears; a case has been made for a Neolithic origin.)

By the time that the ROMANS came to Cumbria, in the late CI, the settlements were small FARMSTEADS: a clutch of round-houses, with low stone walls and thatched roofs, enclosed (along with stockyards and ancillary buildings) within a rubble wall or bank. Examples include Ewe Close (Crosby Ravensworth, W), beside the main Roman road from the S; the three farmsteads on Aughertree Fell (Uldale, C) in the Caldbeck Fells; and Wicker-slack Moor near Crosby Ravensworth, tucked into the lee of a crest, with wide views across the Eden valley. At Ewe Close and at Aughertree Fell the remains of the contemporary FIELD SYSTEMS can still be seen.

One of the key weapons of the invading power was the system of Roman ROADS. The great western route struck N from the valley of the Lune, through the Tebay gorge (W; guarded by a fort at Low Borrowbridge), across the limestone fells to Brougham, and on to Carlisle, and so into Scotland. Another major road led through the Eden valley from Brougham to Brough (W), over the Stainmore Pass and thence to the fortress at York. Lesser routes enabled the garrisons to control the mountains: roads were pushed SW from Old Penrith (Plumpton, C) towards Derwent-water (C), and from Low Borrowbridge (Grayrigg, W) towards Watercrook (Kendal, W). One of the great upland roads, 'High Street', linking Brougham with Ambleside (W), was laid out across the tops between Ullswater and Haweswater. From Ambleside, another took the Wrynose Pass to Hardknott and down Eskdale to Ravenglass (C). Thus was imperial order introduced to *barbaricum.* Two MILESTONES, significant parts of this

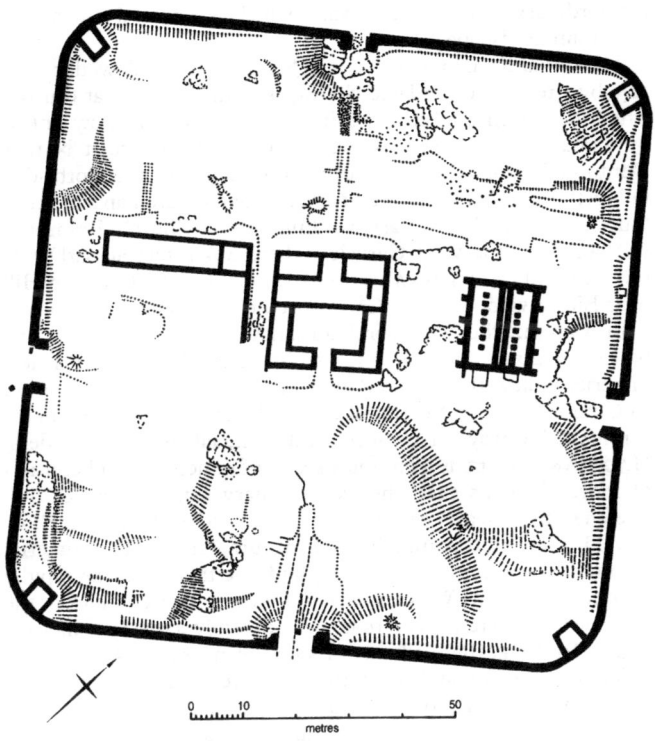

Eskdale, Hardknott Roman Fort.
Plan, 1999

infrastructure, still stand: one at Middleton (W), and another (in its original position) close to Temple Sowerby (W).

The ROMAN FORTS were almost invariably rectangular, with rounded corners; a notable exception is the fort at Bewcastle (C) where the plan was adapted to the knoll and was thus an irregular hexagon. At Ambleside (W) and at Hardknott (Eskdale, C) some of the internal buildings of the fort have been excavated and displayed. At the centre was the headquarters, set around a courtyard, and flanked on one side by granaries. At Ambleside the latter are particularly large, suggesting that this may have been a supply base. On the other side of the headquarters was the house for the commanding officer. The remainder of the interior of each fort was occupied by barracks, by workshops, and by stores. At Hardknott the simple external bath house has been exposed, but an even more remarkable set of baths stands next to the fort at Ravenglass; this survives to eaves height, its walls still bearing traces of the distinctive pink waterproof cement internal render, *opus signinum*. A more rigorous aspect of military life is illustrated by the parade ground at Hardknott, an extraordinary feat of engineering, which is terraced out of the mountain landscape.

The initial Roman advance into Scotland was followed, *c*. A.D. 103, by a retreat to the Tyne–Solway isthmus. The fort at Carlisle which had been established thirty years earlier was now linked by a road (later known as the Stanegate) to a fort at Nether Denton (Denton, C), and to those at Vindolanda and Corbridge in Northumberland. All of these were a day's march apart (about fourteen miles). A new base was built at Old Church, Brampton (C), and – to the W of Carlisle – there was a fort at Kirkbride (C). A number of SIGNAL TOWERS, including that at Pike Hill near Birdoswald (Walton, C), ensured quick communications.

In A.D. 122 the Emperor Hadrian visited *Britannia*. Disturbances in the N had coincided with the introduction of a new imperial policy: the consolidation of the bounds of the empire. In Cumbria, and in Northumberland, Hadrian undertook this in a remarkable way. Like most great artificial military frontiers, HADRIAN'S WALL is a complex series of structures, and consists of more elements than the extraordinary running barrier that stretched from sea to sea. To the W of the River Irthing at Birdoswald, the Wall was initially built of turf – the normal material for military ramparts at the time, and one that could be rapidly utilized. This TURF WALL was about 20 ft (6 metres) thick at the base, with battered faces that were possibly 12 ft (3.7 metres) high. (To the E, the Wall was of stone from the outset, perhaps reflecting the availability of the more resilient Carboniferous sandstones, and the poverty of the turf in the central sector along the Whin Sill, but turning all of this to advantage to the greater glory of the Emperor.) The Turf Wall can be seen W of Birdoswald, but elsewhere it was replaced in stone, on the same line, later in the C2. Between faces of squared rubble, with a rubble core bonded in clay, the 'Narrow Wall' that replaced the Turf Wall was just over 7 ft (2.2 metres) thick. This was much slighter than the STONE WALL to the E of the River Irthing, where, as the stubs on either side of the Turrets at Willowford (Denton, C) show, a 'Broad Wall' nearly 10 ft (2.9 metres) thick had been planned. Only the foundations and the wing-walls of the Turrets (the building of which preceded that of the curtain) were of this gauge. Above the foundations it was completed as the Narrow Wall: a substantial economy. The steps up to the wall-head at Milecastle 48 near Upper Denton suggest a height to the wall-walk there of about 12 ft (3.7 metres).

At an interval of one Roman mile there was a small fortlet (a MILECASTLE) providing access through the Wall; there was a gate tower in its N and S walls, and a small barrack block (for about eight soldiers) within the interior. The stone roofing slates and window glass found at Milecastle 48 give some insight into their construction and appearance.* Between each pair of Milecastles, equally spaced along the Wall, were two simple towers (TURRETS) which provided additional height for observation.

---

*For ease of reference, the Milecastles and Turrets have been assigned numbers from E to W: e.g. between Milecastles 49 and 50 stood Turrets 49A and 49B.

It is not known whether there was a wall-walk throughout the length of the Wall; such a provision is likely to have been part of the original plan but it may have been dispensed with in places later. All of this demanded an immense amount of stone: QUARRIES for the Wall and for its ancillary structures are known in several places and included those on the banks of the Gelt, s of Brampton (Permo-Triassic red sandstone), and at Combe Crag, near Nether Denton (fine-grained buff Carboniferous sandstone). The facing stones were probably rough-dressed at the quarries; ashlar is only seen in the fort at Birdoswald, and there it is likely to have been reused.

In front of the Wall was a narrow berm and then a broad DITCH, the upcast from which was thrown forward to accentuate the outer scarp. The ditch varies in form; a fine stretch survives at Willowford (Denton). The s side of the military zone was marked by yet another spectacular piece of civil engineering: the VALLUM. This was a broad, flat-bottomed ditch flanked on either side by a steep-sided upcast mound, revetted in turf. At first, access to this zone was tightly controlled: a causeway across the Vallum was only provided at each fort. However, the earthwork seems to have been slighted in the later c2.

In the first design for the Wall the intention seems to have been for the garrison to remain to the rear, on the Stanegate. This was rapidly revised to bring the troops up onto the line of the Wall itself. FORTS were established at Birdoswald, Castlesteads (Walton), Stanwix (Carlisle), Burgh-by-Sands, Drumburgh (Bowness), and Bowness-on-Solway. Forward posts were built at Bewcastle and at Netherby (also at Birrens, near Ecclefechan; *see The Buildings of Scotland: Dumfries and Galloway*). Only at Birdoswald are any significant remains displayed. Outside each fort a busy CIVIL SETTLEMENT soon established itself; at Castlesteads and at Maryport these were quite as large as most medieval villages. The settlements reached their peak in the c3, but by A.D. 300 many had been abandoned.

The fortress at Stanwix, just across the Eden from Carlisle, was the centre of Wall command. This may seem eccentric until the extent of the frontier to the w is taken into account. Beyond Bowness-on-Solway the Roman defences continued down the coast, probably as far as Risehow, between Maryport and Flimby (C). There was no linear barrier – the sea that offered a possible route for incursions also provided some protection – but there were MILEFORTLETS rather like the Milecastles of the Turf Wall, with, equally spaced between them on the coastal road, two small stone TOWERS, analogous to the Turrets of the Wall. (Possible merlon-caps found at two Towers suggest that they may have had flat roofs.) Of the thirty-one sites known – another fifteen are inferred – only the excavated Milefortlet on Swarthy Hill, between Allonby and Maryport, is now visible. The forts known at Beckfoot near Silloth and at Maryport were clearly parts of this system, and those further s at Burrow Walls (Workington, C) and at Moresby (C) may have been also, but the chronological and functional relationships are unclear.

In the early 140s – within a generation of its inception – Hadrian's Wall was largely abandoned as the Roman army moved N to build another frontier – the Antonine Wall – between the firths of Forth and Clyde. Retrenchment, however, came about twenty years later, and the southern Wall was reoccupied. Some Turrets were abandoned at this time but others, along with the forts and Milecastles, were used into the C4. At Maryport there are indications that the defences of the fort were strengthened, possibly in the early C4, with the addition of external bastions, as at Lancaster. At Birdoswald excavation has revealed something of the transition to the post-Roman world. Around 400, a granary seems to have been converted into a 'hall' for a defended community. A larger hall, its uprights supported on post-pads, was built about a century later, but the site seems to have been abandoned in the early C6. In Carlisle, archaeological and literary evidence suggests that some Roman structures survived intact for some centuries after formal support from Rome ceased *c.* 410.

Elsewhere, the settlements of the POST-ROMAN PERIOD are difficult to identify, although there are indications that small fortified sites such as those on Castle Crag, Shoulthwaite (W of the N end of Thirlmere, C), and on Castle Crag, Mardale (W), high above Haweswater, may have been constructed and occupied at about this time.

Roman architecture was certainly appreciated by later generations if only because it offered them ready supplies of building stone; this is particularly evident at the forts of Old Carlisle (Westward, C) and Birdoswald, at the medieval castles of Bewcastle, Brough (W), Brougham (W) and Carlisle, and at several medieval churches, such as those at Lanercost, Burgh-by-Sands, and Crosscanonby (all C).

PRE-NORMAN SCULPTURE

BY RICHARD N. BAILEY

In the crosses at Bewcastle, Irton and Gosforth (all C), Cumbria possesses three of the most important STONE SCULPTURES to survive from pre-Norman England; all still stand in their original positions to the S of the church. Like most such carvings in Northern England they were produced in the immediate locality, and thus provide an index of local tastes which is denied us by the more mobile contemporary arts of metalwork or manuscript illumination.

Stone sculpture in the PRE-VIKING PERIOD was largely a monastic art form, one of the technologies reintroduced from the Mediterranean heartland of Christianity in the later C7. Its figural styles and many of its motifs, like the ubiquitous vine scroll, ultimately derive from eastern Mediterranean prototypes, but were probably mediated through Byzantine Italy to Northern Europe on textiles, paintings and metalwork carried home by pilgrims. The earliest of the Cumbrian carvings is the C8

p. 154

cross-shaft at Bewcastle, its lengthy and battered runic inscription claiming that it was a *sigbecn* (victory symbol) set up by three people in memory of a fourth. Like the more elaborate contemporary cross at Ruthwell in Dumfriesshire, it has stylistic links to work from the monastery at Wearmouth/Jarrow in Co. Durham. To a monastic audience, accustomed to reflective rumination and aware of the commentaries of the Church Fathers, the monumental figural panels on its w face would have expressed awareness of Christ's divinity, particularly within the Eucharist – a theme echoed in the vine scroll of the E side, which provides sustenance for animals and birds. Scrolls and interlace knotwork fill the other panels, along with a sundial whose marking of the liturgical hours reminds us that this monument was designed for a monastic enclosure.

11, 12

Most of the other pre-Viking carvings in Cumbria belong to the late C8 and C9. Many (like those at Beckermet St Bridget (C), Carlisle Cathedral, Irton, Urswick (L) and Workington (C)) carry inscriptions which reflect the literacy which came through monastic training. The most complete of these is the cross at Irton, whose delicate carving and surface richness would have been immeasurably enhanced by its original painted form. Here again are scrolls, but they are now combined with smaller panels of interlace and metallic-looking spirals which conceal and reveal a series of cruciform shapes. Other C9 carvings, in their stylistic variety, betray the far-flung contacts of the Northumbrian monastic network: thus the shafts at Heversham (L) and Kendal (W) have scroll forms which relate to work at Lancaster, while the bolder and more deeply cut carving at Dacre (C), with its moustachioed lion, can be compared with work at Rothbury in Northumberland and Hoddom in Dumfriesshire.

9

The VIKING settlement of Cumbria from the early C10 involved Hiberno-Norse groups from western Scotland and Ireland as well as Danes from the slightly earlier settlement of Yorkshire. Whatever their origins and however disruptive their initial impact, these settlers rapidly integrated with the pre-existing community and adopted many of its religious and social practices. One of the most significant of these was the patronage of stone sculpture, a medium which had not been exploited in their Scandinavian homeland. Stone carving, hitherto an exclusively ecclesiastical art, was now enthusiastically taken up by the new aristocracy who recognized its potential for lordly display. So popular was stone carving in the Viking age that surviving pieces outnumber earlier monuments by a factor of five.

p. 468

Among the forms characteristic of this C10–C11 period are CROSS-HEADS connected by rings or circles, a motif adopted from western Scotland. These occur in a variety of types – as a simple connecting ring at Addingham (Glassonby), Penrith and Gosforth, or as a continuous circle at Aspatria, Bromfield, Dearham, Muncaster and Rockcliffe (all C); this latter form also occurs at Chester and on the Wirral, reflecting sea-borne links between Viking colonies around the Irish Sea. The most striking innovation in sculptural forms, however, is the HOGBACK. These are solid building-shaped monuments which represent an adaptation of an earlier Christian shrine (like Hedda's tomb at Peterborough) to the shape of a Viking-age house. Characteristic of Hiberno-Norse Cumbria and Yorkshire, examples survive at Addingham, Aspatria, Brigham (C), Crosscanonby (C), Gosforth, Lowther (W), Penrith and Plumbland (C).

In many ways Viking-age carving continued in an earlier tradition. CHRISTIAN SCENES still formed part of the ornamental repertoire: a shaft at Burton-in-Kendal (W) carries a panel showing Christ Triumphant treading down the beasts, whilst at Dacre (C) a Fall scene is depicted below the Sacrifice of Isaac. Similar continuity can be seen in ZOOMORPHIC ORNAMENT: the winged beasts at Waberthwaite (C), whose lower parts dissolve into interlace, derive from the same C9 menagerie as the Trewhiddle-style beasts on a shaft at Crosscanonby and a socket at Brigham. Equally drawing upon a pre-Viking past is a populous, if somewhat crude, group of C10 carvings stretching down the coastal strip from Aspatria to Beckermet which used scroll and knotwork segments to form incoherent and all-covering patterns; examples of this 'spiral scroll' school can be found at Aspatria, Bridekirk, Haile, Isel and St Bees (all C).

p. 312

Alongside such traditional themes, however, are other motifs which originated in the SCANDINAVIAN homeland. Among them are the ring-chains of Dearham, Muncaster, Gosforth and Rockcliffe (all C); these also occur on the Isle of Man and derive from a popular element in the Borre style. Examples of later phases of Scandinavian art are admittedly rare, though the Jellinge style of the late C9–early C10 is well represented by a powerful carving at Clifton (C) on which men ride the swelling outlined bodies of serpentine beasts in a depiction of the terrors of Hell.

The most interesting Viking-age carvings, however, portray scenes from Scandinavian HISTORY AND MYTHOLOGY. Some of these narratives are no longer recoverable. Such is the case with the large hogback from Lowther whose lightly incised depiction of an encounter between warriors on a boat and a land-based army is exactly matched by a carving from Lärbro St Hammars in Gotland. The so-called Warrior's Tomb at Gosforth provides a similar statement of warrior traditions. Other carvings at Gosforth, however, carry scenes which *can* be identified from later Icelandic sources, and they reveal a wholly unexpected, and very radical theology in which traditional Scandinavian mythology is harnessed to Christian purposes. The most striking example is the tall slender cross, whose shaft is covered with figural and animal ornament, arranged without panels in the Scandinavian fashion of the shield paintings, wooden panels and wall coverings which inspired its iconography. One scene shows Christ crucified, but the rest depict encounters and figures from the story of Ragnarök which tells of the Doom of the Old Norse gods. In a riddling manner, with unexpected juxtapositions and visual echoes, the decoration explores the identities and the contrasts between the ends of three worlds: of the Old Covenant which came with Christ's sacrifice; of the present age which will come with Doomsday; and of the world of the Old Norse gods. Within

10

p. 368

the church is a panel by the same artist which pursues similar themes. It shows a stag battling with a snake – a familiar Christian symbol of the struggle between Good and Evil – and sets this against a picture of Thor's fishing expedition in which he hooked his traditional enemy, the World Serpent. No other source but stone sculpture could have suggested that such sophisticated and subtle thinking existed so far from known centres of political and ecclesiastical power.

THE EARLY MIDDLE AGES, TO *c.* 1300

Important pre-Norman sculpture survives at Bewcastle, Dearham, Gosforth, Irton (all C), Lowther (W) and Urswick (L). So where is the PRE-NORMAN ARCHITECTURE? It is bewildering to find so little, especially when compared with Northumberland or Durham. The only candidate is the w tower of Morland church (W), with its deep-set baluster mullions in the belfry, and even that may be Saxo-Norman and as late as 1120. There are tall narrow doorways of early type at Long Marton and Ormside (W), and at Kirkbride (C). Crosby Garrett's chancel arch (W), rudely intercepted by a later and wider one, could be pre-Conquest, and so could the narrow tower base at Beetham (W). Reused Roman stones on the other hand are often seen in churches, e.g. Lanercost, Crosscanonby. What may be Roman arches reassembled are at Crosscanonby and Denton (all C).

The NORMANS came late, and slowly. By 1086 William had given the barony of Kentdale (i.e. Kendal), and also Kirkby Stephen, in what was to be the barony of Appleby, to his Steward, Ivo de Tallebois. Roger le Poitevin seems to have held Furness and Cartmel (L) under Rufus (William II). In 1092 Rufus took Carlisle from the local lord, Dolfin. By 1106 Ranulph de Meschines was lord of Carlisle and Appleby, while to the w William de Meschines held the barony of Copeland. Henry I had established the baronies sw of Carlisle by 1120, although in 1136 Stephen ceded territory back to David I of Scotland; so it was in 1157, when Henry II reclaimed it, that the barony of Gilsland (C) completed the delayed conquest.

In their earliest form, the CASTLES are little removed in style from the putative early medieval defended sites at Mardale (Haweswater, W) and Shoulthwaite (near Thirlmere, C). Some EARTHWORK CASTLES may have been straightforward adaptations of prehistoric defences. The builders of simple ringworks, such as those at Pennington (L), Pendragon (Mallerstang, W) and Tebay (W), made economical use of the natural defences, supplementing these with short lengths of earthwork. Similarly, MOTTES such as those at Egremont and Brampton (both C) were carved out of natural ridges. On the s coast, at Aldingham, the relationship between the principal types of early castle was startlingly demonstrated by excavation. The C12 ringwork there was heightened to form a motte, and was provided with a timber revetment in the late C12 or early C13. Documentary references to castles before they were rebuilt in stone are scarce, but there are records of buildings within the interior of the massive castle of Liddel Strength (Kirkandrews-on-Esk, C) in 1282. It is likely that mottes continued to be thrown up into the C14.

Juxtapositions at Aldingham appear to illustrate the transition from occupied mottes to the construction of defensive MOATS which enclosed a timber hall or other buildings. Moats are not common in the region, and are difficult to date without excavation; they seem to have flourished in the C12 and C13, and elsewhere many evidently remained in occupation for centuries. The medieval parish churches at Crosby Ravensworth and at Warcop (both W) each have a rectilinear moat immediately adjacent.

Among the STONE-BUILT CASTLES, Carlisle, the Border city and royal stronghold, was always the strategic kingpin. In 1092 Rufus ordered the town to be fortified and a castle built, but there
²⁷ is nothing identifiable left. The stone keep was probably started c. 1133 by Henry I and, highlighting its front-line position, completed by David I of Scotland before his death there in 1153.
²⁸ Brough (W), also started by Rufus, appears unusually to have
^{p. 107} been of stone from the start, but the stone keeps at Appleby (W) and Brougham (W) were not built until the later C12 and c. 1200 respectively. Pendragon, a keep with no stone castle, dates from c. 1180. Bewcastle (C; late C12 and probably after 1292), Egremont (c. 1120), the second castle at Kendal (W; late C12 onwards) and Cockermouth (C; c. 1220) were without keeps. Castle works of later phases, and lesser fortified houses, are described below, p. 26.

Of medieval PLANNED TOWNS AND VILLAGES, New Appleby of the C12 (W; there was an older settlement) is the best and most obvious, with its wide street named Boroughgate running down from the castle to the church. Egremont and Cockermouth (C) have wide market streets, lined with burgage plots running back to lanes behind, and overlooked by their respective castles. Kendal (W) is similar, very stretched out in fact, but the early motte on the town side was superseded by a stone castle across the river (*see* above). At Brough (W) the castle, green and church form a textbook group, but the main part of the town developed along the Stainmore road across the river. Flookburgh (L) and Ravenglass (C), landfalls after potentially hazardous sand crossings, are both clearly planned with broad market places, but undefended, and in the case of Ravenglass without a church either. Ireby (C) seems to be another tiny planned town. Newton Arlosh (C) is a dated example, laid out by Holm Cultram Abbey in 1304 after Skinburness was swept away; it never took off, and the broad market green, discernable on a map, can only with difficulty be made out on the ground.

Castles established the Norman presence in no uncertain terms, but more effective in the long term was the parallel foundation of monasteries, of the parish system, and of the Diocese of Carlisle. For MONASTIC FOUNDATIONS, Henry I and his court favoured the regular canons of the Augustinian order, and the Augustinians are well represented. Carlisle was founded in or around 1122, followed by Lanercost (C; 1169), Cartmel (L; *c.* 1189) and Conishead (L). In 1133 Carlisle was elevated to a cathedral, while remaining at the same time a priory, and the southernmost portion of the bishopric of Glasgow was hived off as its diocese.* Wetheral (C; founded *c.* 1100 by Ranulph de Meschines) and St Bees (C; *c.* 1120, William de Meschines) were Benedictine foundations from the great abbey of St Mary's, York, the most powerful monastery in the North of England. Kirkby Lonsdale (W) may have been intended for a third. Furness (L) was founded in 1127 as a Savigniac abbey, becoming Cistercian with the rest of that order in 1148, and in time growing to be much the greatest of the region's monastic houses and one of the richest of the order. Calder (C) was a daughter house, also Savigniac then Cistercian; but Calder was never rich. Holm Cultram (Abbey Town, C) on the bleak N coast, founded in 1150 from Melrose in Scotland, was Cistercian from the start. Surprisingly it flourished, though it was always a tempting target for the Scots. Armathwaite (C) and Seaton (Bootle; C) were small Benedictine nunneries, both founded *c.* 1190–1200. The Gilbertines had an outpost of one of their curious double houses at Ravenstonedale (W). Lastly the Premonstratensians, having first stopped at Preston Patrick (W), settled a house in a remote valley at Shap (W) by 1201, and the friars as usual proselytized in the towns: Dominicans and Franciscans at Carlisle both from 1233, Carmelites at Appleby *c.* 1281, Austin Friars at Penrith, 1291.

What survives is the following: nothing of the friars, or of Conishead; at Cartmel the church complete, but little else save the gatehouse; at Carlisle and Lanercost the greater part of the churches, and more besides; of the rest in alphabetical order, Armathwaite, traces within a later house; Calder, ruined church of the late C12–C13, with later buildings; Furness, ruined church, cloister and more; Holm Cultram, nave only, with a few monastic fragments; Ravenstonedale, excavated foundations only; St Bees, church only; Seaton, chancel E wall only; Shap, base courses of the church and of the monastic quarters, with the early C16 W tower nearly complete; Wetheral, gatehouse only. On the major remaining architecture more is said below, as also on the granges and vaccaries that fed the monasteries.

17, 21
20
23
18, 19

p. 597

22

The mighty fragment of N arcade of *c.* 1115 at Kirkby Lonsdale (W; *see also* below) is the outstanding monument among the NORMAN PARISH CHURCHES. Something grand was intended here, though it did not get very far. Lowther (W) and Crosby Garrett (W) have arcades of *c.* 1165–75 with fleshy leaves to the abaci. The most complete Norman churches, which are numerous especially on the Solway Plain, are small, two-cell jobs. Torpenhow (C) and Crosscanonby (C) are perhaps the best.

14

---

*The ancient cairn of Dunmail Raise, above Grasmere (W), marks its southern edge: just two-thirds of Cumberland and half of Westmorland. Except for the Alston area, which was Durham until the creation of the Newcastle diocese (where it still remains) the rest of the present area of Cumbria remained in the vast diocese of York until passing to Chester at the Reformation, and finally to Carlisle in 1856.

¹³ Warwick (C) is remarkable for its pilastered or arcaded apse (C). Many have decorative doorways, a few decorative chancel arches. Few had towers: Workington (C), Barton (W; a crossing tower), probably Bolton (W), possibly Warwick. Very often only the fancy bits are preserved – a doorway, a chancel arch. This may be because aisles have been added or widened (Bromfield (C), Cliburn (W), Cumwhitton (C), Gilcrux (C)), or chancels extended (Brampton old church; C). Basic construction may have been quite poor: rubble set in clay or not much more, relying on mass and a good covering of limewash for their integrity. Orton (C) is like this, as are part of Aikton (C) and the remains of the nave at Mealsgate old church (C). Reports of rebuildings, e.g. at Aikton, describe the same thing. The original windows were often very few (Bewcastle (C), Bolton (W), Barton (W)), small (Kirkbampton (C), Mealsgate (C)), and high (Melmerby (C)). When structural alterations were made, such as new or widened openings, it generally meant that the whole wall had to be rebuilt.

Of SCULPTURAL DETAILS, the doorways at St Bees (C; ¹⁵ c. 1160) and Great Salkeld (C; particularly impressive because of the narrowness of the opening) have multiple chevron with protruding, staring faces, which must have been alarming when new. Both have interlace on the capitals. At Isel (C) the zigzag voussoirs alternate, more or less, red and yellow. Cartmel (L) gives a salutary lesson to architectural historians because the choir arcades are either round or pointed according to circumstance, and zigzag decoration is applied or not apparently at random. ¹⁴ One of the great NW piers at Kirkby Lonsdale (W) is incised with a net pattern, irresistibly calling to mind Durham, although the missing link may be St Mary's, York. As at Durham the pattern is cut into identical pieces of stone, probably before assembly, but it is much rougher and smaller in scale. Little figures and faces abound at Torpenhow (C), and can also be seen in the chancel-arch capitals at Gosforth (C). Sculpted TYMPANA are at Pennington (L), which is signed in runes by Gamul the founder and *Hubert* the mason, and at Bridekirk (C), Kirkbampton (C) and Long Marton (two; W). A very fine sculpted lintel, with a roiling Viking dragon, is loose at St Bees. The best FONT is at ¹⁶ Bridekirk, densely carved with monsters and biblical scenes and signed in runes by *Rikard*. Dearham (C) and Bowness-on-Solway (C) run it close. The tiny carved scene of knightly combat over the N door at Bolton (W) has a similar liveliness.

Where VAULTING is found, of any date, it is usually of the tunnel variety, i.e. the simplest. The Norman church towers at Workington and Barton are tunnel-vaulted. In higher-status buildings the tunnel-vault may be reinforced by square cross-ribs, as in the Prior's Tower at Carlisle and in Greystoke and Naworth castles. Proper rib-vaults are confined to major churches and castles, such as Carlisle Cathedral (choir aisles) and Cockermouth Castle's 'Mirk Kirk'. The only tierceron-vault is over the crossing tower at Carlisle. But we are getting ahead of ourselves.

EARLY ENGLISH follows seamlessly from Norman *c.* 1200. The E terminations at St Bees and Kirkby Lonsdale, of about that date, have their walls hollowed out with walks behind detached shafts, a sure sign of a turning away from sheer mass towards a new airiness, as at Coldingham Priory in the Borders and in more extreme form in Burgundy. Seaton Nunnery (C) may have had something similar, and perhaps Beaumont, Caldbeck and Ireby old church (all C). The second chapter house at Furness, of c. 1230–40, is or was exceptionally fine, with decorative incised roundels above paired windows, i.e. on the principle of plate tracery. Hugh of Beaulieu's new choir at Carlisle was started c. 1220, though its piers and upper parts had to be rebuilt after a fire in 1292. The dormitories at Furness and Calder are elegant examples of the lancet style, and so is most of Lanercost, especially its clerestory, culminating in the beautiful W front, finished perhaps as late as c. 1280, with its statue of the Magdalen. A cruciform E.E. town church survives in fragmentary form at Kirkby Stephen. Morland (W) has kept its E.E. transepts (c. 1225). Arcades and/or crossing piers survive at Appleby, Crosby Ravensworth, Orton and Warcop (all W): trefoiled or quatrefoiled and keeled or filleted, with waterholding bases, steep chamfered arches, and occasional nailhead. The beautifully sharp E.E. SEDILIA and PISCINA at Cartmel were later ruthlessly cut up to insert a monument. Kirkby Stephen has another good E.E. set. A second set, with Decorated nodding ogees, is in the Town Choir at Cartmel. There are C13 FONTS at Aspatria (C) and Crosscanonby (C), very boldly modelled with droopy volutes.

The flowering of the later DECORATED style should follow on here, from about 1300, but this is when the architectural history was rudely interrupted by the Border Wars (*see* below). Building work was not immediately subverted everywhere. Calder Abbey built a new chapter house in the late C13 with an E window boldly wide, with Geometrical tracery. In the early C14 Furness built a new infirmary and chapel with windows, also Geometrical, having their arches straightened out into almost pure triangles, as in the N transept at Hereford. Slightly earlier, of c. 1300, is the chancel at Aldingham (L). Flowing tracery is best seen in the parts of Carlisle Cathedral's choir rebuilt after the fire of 1292, especially the gorgeous E window of c. 1340. Flowing tracery appears again in the SE chapel or Town Choir at Cartmel, and in the S aisles at Millom (C) and Brigham (C; 1323), both with vesica windows. The rebuilt piers at the Carlisle choir have deliciously bossy capitals with intricately realistic foliage from which peep little animals and people, and a notable series of the Labours of the Months. The barrel ceiling is later still, c. 1355.

Early medieval CHURCH MONUMENTS, and also STAINED GLASS, are described below, p. 31.

BORDER CONFLICT, C14–C16

By and large the border established by Rufus in 1092, ratified again in the early C13, was peaceful to begin with, allowing monasteries to flourish and manor houses to be built. All this changed with the coming of Edward I (1239–1307), *Scotorum Malleus*. Attempts to set John Balliol as king over Scotland were undermined by Edward's interference, whereupon (1295) the leading Scots rose up. The campaign that followed up and down the border until Edward's death in 1307 on Burgh Marsh so embittered cross-border relations that it entrained three centuries of intermittent conflict, as rapine and retaliation flared up at times into open warfare. Parts of the Western March, ruled by the infamous Graham and Armstrong warlords or reivers, were so ungovernable as to be officially written off as the Debatable Land.

DEFENSIVE BUILDINGS or places of strength were now the norm. The following account treats them as classifiable, but in reality they grade one into another.

Existing CASTLES developed and were strengthened, with the addition for instance of mighty round towers at Appleby (W) and Brough (W). At Carlisle the outer gatehouse was reconstructed 1378–83 (*John Lewyn*, mason) and the Tile Tower (1483–5) was added; the earliest documented brick in the region. Brougham (W) gained two successive gatehouses in 1296–1306, and an extra storey to the keep, with a gorgeous little oratory. In 1327 the monks of Furness were licensed to crenellate their curious castle of Piel (L), at the extreme sw of the peninsula, to defend the channel.

A different sort of castle arose when a previously undefended manor house was rebuilt inside massive curtain walls. Licences to crenellate date them: Scaleby 1307, Millom 1335, Naworth also 1335, to the Bishop of Carlisle at Rose 1336, Highhead 1342, Greystoke 1353 (all C). Penrith (C), where licence was granted to Bishop Strickland in 1397 and 1399, is of the four-square type of Bodiam (Sussex) and Bolton (Yorkshire), but with just two asymmetrically placed towers.

HOUSES WITH TOWERS are lower down the social scale than castles, and much more numerous; about fifty survive in Cumbria. A private refuge and defence in time of trouble, they take the form of a thick-walled rectangular tower with vaulted basement, attached to an existing house. Usually but not always the tower was carried up to a fighting top with parapet walks and battlements. Solar towers, i.e. those attached at the high end of the hall, are much the commonest, Yanwath (W) being the most famous example, but a few are at the service end, like the Jerusalem Tower at Newbiggin Hall (W) and the lost tower at Sockbridge (W), and there is a group in w Cumberland (Isel, Muncaster) where the relationship between tower and the rest seems quite casual. A free-standing tower like that at Dalton-in-Furness (L), which was Furness Abbey's court house, is a rarity. Kirkandrews and Brackenhill (both C) are clearly related to Scottish towers, and Arnside (L), more complex than usual, was a hunting lodge. An early tower is Linstock at Houghton (C), built by the Bishops of Carlisle probably early in the C14. It is impressively businesslike, with great strength in the 8-ft (2.5-metre)-thick walls. The floors communicate by straight mural stairs in

27

p. 194

2

p. 544

29

31

the thickness of the wall. Isel is similar, but soon they became standardized with a spiral stair in one corner. The biggest towers are Askham (W), Sizergh (W) and Broughton-in-Furness (L), the smallest, Catterlen (Newton Reigny, C). A textbook example, sectioned in half by partial collapse for our perfect understanding, is Hardrigg near Skelton (C).

An element of bluff crept in as the danger receded. Wraysholme at Allithwaite (L) for instance has no vault, and walls not particularly thick. Blencow (Greystoke, C), remodelled in 1590 with a tower at each end, looks fearsome, but their walls are no stronger than those of the house part, and again there are no vaults. In the centuries after 1603 many lost their fighting tops, as the nuisance of maintaining flat roofs and parapets in a wet climate became more important than defiance. However, it is clear from their pitched and decorative roofs that some towers never did have a fighting top, even though thick-walled and vaulted, e.g. Kirkby Thore (W), the priest's houses at Great Asby (W) and Croglin (C), and the tower at Preston Patrick (W). The latter introduces a variant in which the base storey is bisected by a vaulted passage between vaulted chambers. The other example is Burneside (W), identical in plan. These are both service-end towers above a three-door screens passage (rare in the region), which may go a long way to explaining their unusual plan. Curiously however the two are completely different in elevation. Where the upper floor at Preston Patrick is a fine open room with contemporary roof – i.e. it never was a true tower – Burneside is built up into a formidable little castle. A third example with this plan is the enigmatic ruin of Lammerside at Mallerstang (W). All three are C14.

At true TOWER HOUSES the whole is raised up high over vaults, giving a great sense of strength and superiority. Howgill, at Milburn (W), is a wonderful C14 example, unguessed-at from outside, hugely strong and refined in design. Johnby (Greystoke, C) is later (1583), more compact and evolved, with Scottish affinities. Interestingly, the family at Johnby decamp in winter to a lower, warmer wing (*see* Bastles, below), which may be a clue to interpreting other complicated houses. Scaleby (C) is another tower house, if the great room over the hall vault represents the principal living space. The priors of Carlisle had a tower-house retreat at Newbiggin (Carleton, C) while the bishops had Bewley (Bolton, W). Dacre (C) fits no neat category; tower house or free-standing keep? Askerton (C) works as a tower house, with all the living space upstairs, although lacking vaults it could be called a bastle. Upstairs living, vaults or no vaults, is always worth looking for when interpreting houses in the region. 30

Another strategy was to make the principal defence of a house an encircling CURTAIN WALL or BARMKIN. Middleton (W; C15) is the most striking example, otherwise defenceless behind its high wall. Beetham (W) retains most of its curtain, partly immured in later buildings, and so does Wharton (Kirkby Stephen, W), with an impressive gatehouse. Brougham Hall (W) has a fine curtain though the house has gone. Burneside (W) has a gatehouse and a section of curtain, as well as the strong service-end tower mentioned already. Scales Hall (C) retains its gatehouse of *c.* 1580, possibly not terribly serious. The gatehouse at Preston Patrick (W) has gone but is documented. Houses such as Rose Castle (C) and Askerton (C) have multiple defences including a curtain. Scaleby (C) has everything – a solar tower, a high hall over a vault (i.e. tower house), a high curtain wall and gatehouse, a polyangular forebuilding, and a wet moat.

BASTLES housed animals below, family above, in a single defensible building – if you like, a poor man's tower house. They are generally fairly late in date – C16 and even C17 – and are unique in England to the border regions of Cumberland and Northumberland. The term took on its specific meaning with the RCHME publication *Shielings and Bastles* in 1970, although the word is old (*bastile*), and like most such terms is a somewhat loose fit. The thick-walled ground storey, its floor grooved and drained for animals, will be almost windowless, with a single, barred door. The living accommodation above, with one or two fireplaces, is reached only by external steps to an upper door. No vault, but the mid-floor may be reinforced with flags over massive joists (Clarghyll at Alston, C). The best-known Cumbrian examples are at White House Farm, Glassonby, and Naworth Park, Stonehouse; also Townhead near Croglin, the vicar's bastle and The Temon at Denton, and Randalholme at Alston. They are often found in small groups (Clarghyll, Denton), or in company with a tower (Randalholme). They are mostly confined to N and E, but an excellent, and previously unnoticed, example is attached to the more glamorous tower house at Johnby (Greystoke). Other possible bastles outside the area they are looked for are at Forest Hall (Selside, W), and at Dalegarth Hall (Eskdale).

In Alston Moor (C), in the high Pennines, the bastle principle persisted well into the C18 and even C19. Upper front doors and outer steps of ALSTON BASTLES are still common on the streets of that town, and there is a good example on the green at Garrigill (C). Another sub-category is what is called a SOLWAY BASTLE, represented especially by Drumburgh (C), remodelled in 1518 by Thomas, Lord Dacre, into a large, formidable block-like house of three or four storeys. The smaller Barrocks House nearby names its purpose: more of a garrison than a single dwelling.

A scattering of CHURCHES (why only some?) are explicitly adapted for defence. In the most obvious cases the tower is vaulted and thick-walled, with tiny windows, and is only entered through a barred door from the church, as at Brigham, Burgh-by-Sands (*c.* 1360), Dearham, Great Salkeld, and Newton Arlosh (all C). An additional upper-level entry from the tower into the church is a common but mysterious feature. The towers at Ormside (W) and Scaleby (C) have very tall and narrow slit windows, but are unvaulted. At Newton Arlosh (*c.* 1303) the body of the church is defensive too, with a single narrow doorway and small high windows. The curious C15 tower at Edenhall (C), unusually pretty for Cumbria with a short spire, seems also on examination to have been defensive. Boltongate (C) is a unique

case. Here there is no tower, but the nave itself is covered
with a splendid pointed tunnel-vault which is buttressed by   36
subsidiary half-vaults. It has a full parapet walk, including round
the bellcote, reached by a chancel-arch turret. But the windows
are large, and the chancel unvaulted, so it was perhaps a case
of fireproofing and a defended vantage point. Like Kirknewton
in Northumberland, it reflects the Late Gothic fashion in Scotland (Bothwell 1397; Roslin c. 1450; Ladykirk c. 1500–7; the
inserted kirk at Melrose 1620s), which came from France (e.g.
churches of the Grandmontine order). Tunnel-vaulted porches
are an occasional curiosity: Caldbeck (C), Kirkby Thore (W),
Warcop (W).

The clergy sometimes provided themselves with defensible
buildings. Besides those already mentioned for the Bishop and
the Prior of Carlisle, the Prior had a very fine solar tower by the
cathedral, distinguished by a cross-ribbed vault, oriel windows
and a painted ceiling. There are 'VICAR'S PELES' – houses with   40
solar towers – at Boltongate (C), Croglin (C), Great Asby (W),
Great Salkeld (C), Lanercost (C), and perhaps Old Brampton
(Brampton, C). At Kirkoswald (C) the rectory tower was incorporated into a larger, lay house. Attached to the E end of the
church at Burgh-by-Sands (C) was what may have been the
vicar's pele. The vicar had a bastle at Denton and Nether Denton,
and at Cumrew (all C). Workington rectory (C), which seems
undefended, may have had a curtain wall.

Most buildings in the Border Country had heavily barred
windows. The bars survive here and there, but can always be
looked for in cut-off stumps and scars in the stone. The narrow
doorways to defensive towers were furnished with massively iron-
bound gates called YATTS, reinforced by a heavy drawbar slotted
into the masonry. Three remain at Naworth Castle, one at
Dalston Hall (both C); one at Broughton Tower (C) survived into
the C19. Great Salkeld and Burgh-by-Sands churches (both C)
retain their yatts.

As for TOWN DEFENCES, the only walled city is Carlisle. The
walls, under construction in 1130, enclosed a rough lozenge   p. 221
shape with three gates – English, Scottish and Irish. The Citadel
(1541–3, *Stefan von Haschenperg*) replaced the Bochard Gate as a   94
modification for artillery. Walls and gates were 'in very good
repaire' when Celia Fiennes visited in 1698, but the N and W
walls, and gates, came down largely in 1811 15. C14 documentation for walls round Penrith is so far unmatched by any evidence
on the ground. Towns like Penrith and Appleby may arguably
have been defendable on account of their few and narrow entries.

Things became somewhat more peaceful in the C16, i.e. the
later years of the PERPENDICULAR style. In the more secure
parts churches widened their aisles and windows (e.g. Crosthwaite (C), Appleby (W)), and added clerestories and towers,
though there is nothing like the flatland glories of the East
Riding. Kendal (W) is the prime example, grown by the addition
of outer aisles into a huge rectangle. Kirkby Lonsdale (W) added
one outer aisle (1574). Towers are broad and sturdy, often with

paired bell-openings not architecturally coordinated: Appleby, Brough (W), Crosthwaite (*c.* 1554), Kendal, Penrith (C). The only tower that can be called elegant is at Kirkby Stephen (W; probably 1540s). Furness and Shap abbeys were also building mighty W towers in the decades before the Dissolution, and the integrated Perp set of sedilia and piscina at Furness with its run of little vaulted canopies is outstanding. In 1507 Abbot Chambers added his W porch at Holm Cultram, and probably much else besides, and in 1528 Prior Slee built his gatehouse at Carlisle. The canons of Cartmel (L) finally finished their nave in the C15, with windows very similar to those at Kendal; it was part of a major campaign involving the rebuilding of the monastic quarters on the N side and the unique diagonally set belfry.

Cartmel's spectacularly enormous E window of *c.* 1420 is of imported Tadcaster stone, its pattern related to York Minster's E window and the W windows at Southwell (Notts.) and Bridlington (Yorks. East Riding). Because of the intractability of the local stone, tracery is relatively uncommon, and when it does occur it is often uncusped: Bowness-on-Windermere (W), Grasmere (W), Greystoke (C), Hawkshead (L). Late Perp is characterized by arched uncusped windows in long ranges: the rebuilt chancels of Morland (W) and Kirkoswald (C), at Cartmel Fell (L), and in the tall courtyard windows at Naworth Castle (C) and Wharton Hall (Kirkby Stephen, W). With Greystoke we see the Perp style continuing beyond the Reformation, as with the inserted early C17 E window at Holm Cultram.

At the DISSOLUTION OF THE MONASTERIES in 1536–40 the cathedral church at Carlisle was for the time being preserved entire, as were the conventual quarters. The monastic churches at Cartmel, Holm Cultram, Lanercost and St Bees also survived in parish worship, as already noted. The vicissitudes of the next couple of centuries meant that Carlisle, Holm Cultram, Lanercost and St Bees were unable to keep up the whole church, but even in their reduced state it is a remarkable rate of survival. Of other monastic structures, a few of the GRANGES still have something to show from the C14 to the C16. Grange Hall near Great Asby (W) is one of the best; it belonged to Byland in Yorkshire, which had been colonized from Calder. Furness Abbey's grange at Hawkshead (L) preserves its C15 gatehouse. Raby Cote at Abbey Town (C) belonged to Holm Cultram, and seems to have passed at the Dissolution to relatives of the last abbot; many carved stones from the abbey fetched up here. Characteristic of the Lake District are the monastery VACCARIES or high cattle pastures in the dale heads, such as Brotherilkeld in Eskdale (C; belonging to Furness), and Watendlath near Grange-in-Borrowdale (C; for Fountains, Yorks.).

Of MEDIEVAL CHURCH FURNISHINGS there are three sets of STALLS: forty-six at Carlisle, twenty-six at Cartmel and twenty at Greystoke (C). The Greystoke ones are of *c.* 1400, slightly anticipating Carlisle; four misericords survive. The Carlisle ones are of *c.* 1400–19, with splendid canopies (said to be later). The misericords are sinuous, deeply undercut, full of life. The Cartmel stalls of 1430–40 are distinctive, not least because of their C17 screen backs. The misericords exhibit a curious crystalline style, especially stylized trees, e.g. unicorn and the Tree of Life.* (Like misericords in impulse are the lively CARVINGS in Carlisle Castle, done in the 1480s possibly by a single prisoner, *Richie Graham*.) The two late C15 Flamboyant SCREENS now in the cathedral shop (St Catherine's Chapel) are thought to be the remnant of a set round the choir, part of the general glorification by Prior Gondibour. The Salkeld Screen of 1541 at Carlisle is a different kettle of fish, entirely in the Renaissance manner. The screens of the Cowmire Pew at Cartmel Fell, probably of *c.* 1521, still have traces of colour. Of screens elsewhere there are only bits here and there, e.g. at Greystoke, Kendal, Morland (W). Of other WOOD CARVING, the sculpted figure of Christ from Cartmel Fell is now in Kendal Museum. Continental woodwork imported in the 1840s confuses the issue at St Wilfrid, Brougham (W). The work is C16 and C17, both Gothic and Renaissance. The finest, a triptych of *c.* 1520 made by the *Antwerp Guild of Carvers*, was taken to Carlisle Cathedral in 1979. The cathedral pulpit, dated 1559, was bought from Cockayne Hatley (Beds.) in 1963, having come there from Antwerp in 1825.

No significant medieval WALL PAINTING survives in the churches, but Carlisle Cathedral has extensive PAINTING ON WOOD on the backs of the stalls. There are four cycles: St Anthony, St Cuthbert, St Augustine, and the Apostles; sixty-eight scenes in all. They are associated with Prior Gondibour (*c.* 1455–1500). Inscribed octagonal Perp FONTS are at Crosthwaite of *c.* 1396, with beasts at the base, and at Bootle, *c.* 1535. Kendal has a big black concave-sided font of North Riding C15 type.

It is surprising that any medieval STAINED GLASS has survived in this troublous region. The earliest, fragmentary and very austere, is a cross over green grisaille of *c.* 1200 at Kirkby-in-Furness (L). The great E window of Carlisle Cathedral retains original glass of *c.* 1340 in its tracery. The best place for the strong ruby, green and ochre glass of the mid C14 is the Town Choir at Cartmel, including parts of a Jesse Tree. The bestiary window at Greystoke, *c.* 1400, is all silver stain and black. There are some silver-stain angels too in the porch at Cartmel. The huge E window at Cartmel retains some of its glass of *c.* 1418. The late C15 glass at Bowness-on-Windermere is related to it in a not-fully agreed way, especially the Cartmel prior and named canons in the lower lights. The E window of Cartmel Fell has very interesting glass of *c.* 1520 showing the Seven Sacraments, each miraculously issuing from the body of Christ by a stream of blood. Of a slightly earlier time is the entertaining E window at Greystoke.

MONUMENTS include grave-slabs decorated with foliated crosses, a type distinctive to the Northern Counties. Peter Ryder has recorded 452 of them in Cumbria, dating from the C11 to C16 but predominantly of the C12 and C13. Because they are usually anonymous they have attracted little attention, and have

*There are incidentally C20 stalls with misericords at St Mary (R.C.), Workington, by *Robert Thompson*, 1926, including a dog with a real bone.

been variously reused, e.g. as lintels, steps or foundations. Victorian restorers mounted them in porches (Gosforth, C) or parked them against the outer walls (Bridekirk, Kirkoswald, both C). A fine collection at Egremont (C) is thought to have been removed in the 1960s. Cross-legged mid-C13 knights in bucket helmets are in the Abbey museum at Furness, as are a fine C14 lady and knight. Two Purbeck marble bishops are at Carlisle, one 1250s, one early C14. Also of the C14 are the wooden effigy of a knight at Ousby (C), the effigy identified as Thomas de Caldebec, priest, at Great Salkeld (C), and an alabaster knight at Greystoke (C). The outstanding monument of this time is the Harrington Monument at Cartmel (†1347); somehow more poignant for the damage sustained in its relocation. The little frieze of singing canons at the base bears witness to the vanished life of the priory, as does the unnamed Augustinian prior who was displaced and now lies in front. At Workington St Michael (C) the tomb-chest and effigies of Sir Christopher Curwen †1450 and his wife have been painstakingly reassembled after the 1994 fire. A relation was Black Tom (Curwen) o' the North †c. 1510, whose effigy is at Camerton (C). The roofless chancel at Lanercost (C) houses a remarkable collection of heraldic Dacre tombs. Those of Sir Humphrey and Lady Mabel, and of Lord Thomas and Lady Elizabeth, both probably made in the 1520s during Lord Thomas's lifetime, must have been barbarically splendid when painted. Of much the same time is the elaborate tomb of Abbot Chamber or Chambers at Holm Cultram, with its prevalent name and rebus. Like the Harrington Monument, though of lesser quality, it is moving in its damaged state. Bishop Bell †1496 is commemorated by a splendid brass in the midst of the choir at Carlisle. Other BRASSES are at e.g. Crosthwaite, Edenhall and Greystoke (all C), Kendal (W), and Ulverston (L).

A hint of the coming Renaissance appears in the naïvely CLASSICAL MONUMENTS of Lord Wharton (†1568) and his two wives at Kirkby Stephen (W), and of William Sandys and his wife (dated 1578) at Hawkshead (L). For church monuments of the early C17 see p. 36.

The ELIZABETHAN HOUSES show that mansions in the region were not devoid of decoration and comfort, especially in the more secure s and e. Levens and Sizergh (both W) revel in virtuoso panelling and carved chimneypieces, ornate ceilings and leaded glass. The earlier ceilings at Sizergh are quite restrained, with wooden ribs. The hall screen and many of the superb chimneypieces are dated: 1558, 1563, 1564, 1569. One carver or team seems to have been at work over the full span. At the end of the series comes the fantastic Inlaid Chamber of shortly after 1575, very different from the earlier work with a pendant plasterwork ceiling, armorial glass and Renaissance inlaid panelling. Work at Levens started after 1578, just as Sizergh was complete, and ran on until at least 1640. Levens's ceilings are geometrical with pendants, as in the latest work at Sizergh. The chimneypieces are bigger, richer and coarser than at Sizergh, the allegories more explicit. Both houses are very atmospheric.

Muncaster has a couple of good Elizabethan or Jacobean chimneypieces, though it is not certain they are *in situ*. Percy House in Cockermouth (C) has an ambitious, if naïve, figurative plaster ceiling and overmantel dated 1598. More PLASTERWORK is in the Fretwork Room at Dalemain (w), the Two Lions Inn at Penrith (C), Low Hall at Little Strickland (W), Burneside Hall (W), Hornby Hall at Brougham (W; dated 1584), and Calgarth Hall (Troutbeck; W: the best, of the 1630s, but damaged). Naïve domestic WALL PAINTING is best seen at Kirkby-in-Furness Hall (L; mid C16), and in the C16 clock face (no hands) in Yanwath Hall (W). Grotesque work of the later C16 – a cultivated taste – remains fragmentarily at Lanercost (C) and Yanwath. Calgarth also had sophisticated Renaissance panelling akin to that at Sizergh, some of which is now in Troutbeck church. At Isel (C) the hall was subdivided with a mid-floor, its timbers heavily moulded but not stopped, and linenfold panelling divides off a corridor and a parlour. Several houses gained intermediate floors or ceilings which were enriched with elaborate mouldings and a distinctive arch motif, in the manner of Prior Senhouse's tower at Carlisle (1510–20): Barwise Hall (W; 1579), Dacre Castle (C), Hartsop Hall (W), Scales Hall (C), Sizergh tower, Yanwath tower. Smardale Hall (W) of *c.* 1580 is a long narrow house – evidently once a wing – with a pair of conical-roofed turrets flanking each end.

46

FROM THE UNION OF THE CROWNS
TO *c.* 1750

On the death of Elizabeth in 1603 James VI of Scotland became also James I of England. In theory cross-border enmity was now at an end. In practice there was a slow healing, interrupted in the mid C17 by Civil War and in the early C18 by Jacobite irruptions. But there was a major surge of building, particularly of houses. This is when the characteristic and still very numerous vernacular buildings took their shape. Over much of Cumbria C17 datestones predominate.

One immediate effect among JACOBEAN CHURCH WORK was the rebuilding of the church at Arthuret (C) from 1609, perhaps indirectly due to James himself. The style is still pure Perp, except for the E window (replaced) and perhaps the mid-piers. Equally remarkable was the rescue and refurnishing of the priory church at Cartmel (L) by George Preston, between 1618 and his death in 1640. The style of his choir enclosure is a fascinating mix, naïvely classical for the columns with their Corinthian capitals, Flamboyant Gothic for the fretted backs. Carved in relief on the columns are vines, twining both ways, and symbols of the Passion. The old church at Martindale (W) has just longitudinal benches and low pulpit (1634). Churches of the mid C17 onwards are described below.

42

LADY ANNE CLIFFORD (1590–1676) richly earns a section to herself. Daughter of the Queen's champion George Clifford, Earl of Cumberland, she was a countess twice over (Dorset and Pembroke), mistress in turn of the great houses of Knole and Wilton, but always hankered after her Northern inheritance. Not until 1649 was she able to claim it. A 'repairer of breaches and the restorer of paths to dwell in', she spent the rest of her life making her Northern castles habitable again, at Appleby, Brougham, Brough, Pendragon (all W), and Skipton in Yorkshire (West Riding), making stately progresses from castle to castle. The antique names she gave to her medieval keeps are revealing: Roman Tower at Brough, Pagan Tower at Brougham, Caesar's Tower at Appleby. She restored the two churches in Appleby, and rebuilt the churches at Brougham and Mallerstang (L). Her almshouses at Appleby were carefully endowed to ensure their long-term maintenance, as was her Countess Pillar, in memory of her mother, on the present A66 at Brougham. Her church monuments are described below, p. 36.

Lady Anne tended to exaggerate the ruination that preceded her restorations, but nevertheless hers was a remarkable achievement. Her architectural taste was not just conservative but positively medievalizing, but she should not be seen as a completely lone and eccentric figure; Sir Thomas Dacre, Earl of Sussex, took care to preserve the battlements and turrets when he modernized his Northern castle at Dacre (C) from 1675. Gabriel Vincent is named 'Chief Director' of all Lady Anne's building in the North on his tomb at Brough church, but she was directly in control. It was her curious habit to give away elaborate locks and keys, made by *George Dent* of Appleby. George Sedgwick, her secretary, received one at Collinfield near Kendal (W). The one at Rose Castle (C) is still in daily use. Others are at Dalemain (C) and Dacre church, and there was another at Great Asby rectory (C).

Later C17 CHURCHES include Lady Anne's two at Brougham. These are Perp, but their shape is C17 – short and wide, well lit, with an unlinked pair of windows to E and W. Of the two, Ninekirks is furnished with robust simplicity, but St Wilfrid has a highly wrought screen to the hall pew, a palisade of jazzily carved posts linked by little stilted arches decorated with lively figures like tiny misericords – if this is indeed C17. In the 1660s Soulby (1662–3), Witherslack (1668–9, modified 1768), and the little chapel at Armathwaite (shortly after 1660) were also built or rebuilt. Sir John Lowther carried out a very interesting rebuild of Lowther church in 1686, again with paired unlinked windows E and W, but with rectangular side windows (cf. Dacre Castle, c. 1675), and a dome over the crossing tower – now alas replaced by something considered more respectable.

Churches, like farmhouses, were given a regular coat of white limewash, inside and out. Bowness on Windermere (W), Crosthwaite (C), Buttermere (C), Grasmere (W), Troutbeck (W), Hawkshead (L), all shone out white against the fells. A very few still do, e.g. Uldale and Castle Sowerby (both C). Kendal church was de-whitewashed in 1844, Windermere in 1869–70,

Hawkshead 1875–6. White limewash was reapplied to the W tower at Orton (W) in 2005–6. In some areas the absence of freestone for carving encouraged a naïve tradition of PAINTED DECORA-TION. Hawkshead church has the best remaining, with colourful curlicues and texts done in 1680 by *James Addison*, with later additions in appropriate style. Addison painted what sounds like a wondrous scheme inside and out at Kendal in 1684 (alas it is all gone), and another at Grasmere in 1687.

Church building in the C18 was set in motion by William Nicholson (1655–1727), the most gifted, energetic and colourful of Carlisle's bishops. His visitations of his 105 churches in 1703–4 found that thirty-one were good, e.g. Torpenhow (C) with its new ceiling; forty-three tolerably good; twenty-one neglected or ill-cared-for; and ten in a really bad state, e.g. Stapleton which was without glass, surplice or bell, with the roof caving in. The new URBAN CHURCH TYPE, a two-storey preaching box with galleries and an embraced tower, starts in the late C17 with St Nicholas at Whitehaven (C) in 1693 (rebuilt 1883), followed by Holy Trinity in the same town (1714–15; dem.). St Andrew Penrith (C), 1721–2 by *William Etty*, is more ambitious in its architec-ture, making the most of the red sandstone. Later C18 churches of the two-storey urban type are St James Whitehaven (1752–3)   77 and St Mary at Maryport (C; 1760, much altered), St Michael Workington (C; 1770–2, destroyed by fire), St Cuthbert in Carlisle (1778–9) and Wigton (1788). Country cousins, with but a single storey, are at Bampton (W; 1726–8), Ravenstonedale (W; 1738 and 1744), Ings (W; 1743), Allonby (C; 1743–4), Temple Sowerby (W; 1754, rebuilt), Culgaith (C; 1756) and Raughton Head (C; 1761).

Threlkeld church of 1776–7 (C) is interesting because it is designed with a symmetrical S face around a central porch, like a meeting house. MEETING HOUSES begin in the region in the later C17, with the QUAKERS. Lancashire-across-the-Sands is what they call 1652 country, where the Society of Friends first took root (cf. Swarthmoor Hall). Early examples are at Colthouse (Hawkshead; 1688–9), Swarthmoor (an adapted cottage, given by George Fox in 1688), Rookhow (Rusland; 1725); also White-haven (C; 1724–5), and Pardshaw (Dean, C; 1728–9), both   76 perhaps by the same mason. All are white, vernacular, simple but thoughtful, with characteristic furnishings such as movable screens. The Congregationalists' Redwing Chapel at Garrigill   /5 (C), 1756, is well preserved.

The larger C18 churches have not on the whole retained their FURNISHINGS. The best ensemble is at Ravenstonedale (W), seated college-chapel-wise with raked rows of pews on each side, and the three-decker pulpit dominating from the middle of the N side. Typical of the tenor of religious life in the region in the C17 and C18 are the plain box pews and three-decker pulpit at Brougham Ninekirks (W) already mentioned, and at Cartmel Fell (L; dated 1698). More ornate PULPITS are at Bampton (W; probably *c*. 1726) and Urswick (L). Ravenstonedale also houses some good C18 paintings, including a ROYAL ARMS. These are picked out in the Gazetteer because they can be the most lively

and colourful item in a plain church, and because fourteen are
attributed to the painter *Mathias Read* of Whitehaven, the best
being at St Nicholas Whitehaven (1693). The jolly Baroque
organ of 1661–2 at Appleby was given in 1683 from Carlisle
Cathedral.

Lady Anne Clifford put up at least seven FUNERARY MONU-
MENTS in different places, including two in Westminster Abbey.
The great veneration she held for her mother, who died in 1616,
is expressed in the black marble tomb and alabaster effigy erected
at Appleby by *Maximilian Colt*, the royal sculptor, in 1617. Lady
Anne's own memorial at Appleby, ordered in 1654 from, it is
thought, *Thomas Stanton*, although she lived until 1676, belongs
to a different age. No effigy; instead a heraldic display on a kind
of reredos with Doric pilasters and a broken segmental pediment.
Of equally high quality to Colt's monument and also of alabaster
is Sir Richard Lowther †1608 at Lowther. The effigy type is also
at Penrith (†1637), and at Kendal (†1656; under a table top
carried on Tuscan columns). Classical again at Lowther is the
later C17 monument to the two Sir Johns †1637 and †1675 attributed to *Jasper Latham*, and that to John, Viscount Lowther, †1700
by *William Stanton*, with a typically relaxed figure. More
Lowthers (†1700 and 1705, †1745) are at Cartmel. Incongruous
are the refugee monuments at Hawkshead in sophisticated
Baroque style, brought from St Dionis Backchurch in London
when it was demolished in 1878, to Daniel Rawlinson †1629 and
Sir Thomas †1708, of Graythwaite.

Few houses had survived the long years of border strife unless
they were strongly defensive – which meant inconvenient. As the
threat of warfare and violent thievery receded, the MAJOR
HOUSES began to open out. However, being both conservative
and relatively impoverished, Cumbria is not the place to look for
grand sweepings-away; on the contrary the old tower was almost
always retained, though it might be disguised. Hutton-in-the-
Forest (C) is a typical case. Here *Alexander Pogmire*, between 1641
and 1645, added a reaching-forward gallery wing with an open
loggia below. Its windows are still mullioned-and-transomed, but
it is symmetrical, with both Tuscan and imitation C13 quatrefoil
columns. An intended matching fellow was engraved by Kip; that
its absence was tolerated says as much about the region as the
retention of the medieval tower. In about 1680 the mason *Edward
Addison* (1656–1705) added a new Baroque front. When we take
into account the C19 counterpart to the medieval tower, and
remember that each component at Hutton is a different colour,
it will be appreciated how informal the great houses of the region
are. Sizergh (W) tells a very similar story. 1663 is the date of the
C17 addition at Lorton Hall (C), with upright three-light
windows under triangular pediments: firmly on the road to
classicism.

At Lowther (W) there was a pair of wings of 1640–56 by
Pogmire, similar at least in plan to the one at Hutton. *Talman* supplied a design for the central block, though Sir John, having dis-
cussed it with *Sir Samuel Morland*, and 'consulted strength as well

as ornament, suitable to the coldness of our climate', claimed the house built in 1692–4 as 'principallie my own thought'. *Edward Addison* was again the builder. But it burnt out in 1718, and it took nearly a century of chronic indecision and unrealized designs by *Gibbs* (*c*. 1728), *Colen Campbell*, *Matthew Brettingham* (1759–63), '*Capability*'*Brown* (1763), both *Robert* and *James Adam* (*c*. 1767–73), *Francis Webster* (1802–4), *Thomas Harrison* and *George Dance Jun.* (1803–5) before the castle was rebuilt in the early C19 (*see* p. 54).

Of other NEW HOUSES, a flurry of the tall, compact, progressive type was built from *c*. 1600 to a double-pile plan, often with a display of chimneys along the central spine: Gaythorne near p. 381 Great Asby (W), Marsh Grange at Askam (L; altered), the former Angel Hotel in Kendal (W). Hesket Hall, Hesket Newmarket (C) is symmetrical in all four directions, with a central stack. Other new houses of this time commonly conformed to a T-plan – a line of rooms in a single pile, with the stair behind in a short rear wing. Tullie House (1689) and the prebend houses at Carlisle are like this, as is Hutton Hall at Penrith (C). The double pile in other words seems to have fallen from favour, perhaps in order to avoid roof complications, although these houses have often since become double piles by filling in the angles.

The new work of *c*. 1670 at Moresby Hall (C), attributed to 51 the mason-architect *William Thackeray*, has weird, insistent rustication, as did the similar Ribton Hall (C; dem.), which can be related to Bishop Cosin's rebuilding at Bishop Auckland. The link may be *James Swingler*, carpenter, who often worked with Thackeray. The doorcase at Moresby, which Nicholas Cooper derives from a 1631 design by Henryk de Keyser, relates to the doorcase of the banqueting house of 1657 at Catterlen (C), and that at Marsh Grange at Askam (L). *Thackeray* may have refronted Branthwaite near Dean (C) in the 1670s and added to Acorn Bank at Temple Sowerby (W). He patched up and remodelled Rose Castle (C) in 1668–74 for Bishop Rainbow, and refronted 29 Drawdykes Castle at Houghton (C) in 1676. He seems therefore to have been the pioneer classical architect in the region.

Thomas Machell (1647–98), rector of Kirkby Thore and amateur architect, is our other hero of this period. We are indebted to him for his voluminous observations on Westmorland, and his tiny but seemingly trustworthy sketches and plans. He recast Howgill Castle (Milburn, W, with *Edward Addison*) for Sir Edward Sandford, and designed the charming Crackenthorpe Hall (W) in 1685 for his brother, and probably the Mansion House of 1686 at Eamont Bridge (W).

Both Machell's and Thackeray's houses were fronted with cross-mullioned windows. The earliest mention of SASHES is Celia Fiennes at Carlisle in 1698: 'ye Chancellors built of stone very lofty, 5 good sarshe windows in the front'; probably Tullie House. The ample front of the College at Kirkoswald (C), built at just this time, 1696, is sashed, but its wings were cross-mullioned. William Bird's great house of 1690 in Cockermouth (C), now Wordsworth House, was probably not sashed until 1745.

The early C18 was the age of the gentleman architect, and it is reasonable to see cultivated owners having a considerable say in the design of their new houses, and giving and receiving advice or designs from others. Henry Richmond Brougham's Highhead Castle (*c.* 1740–5), heartbreakingly ruined today, may have been designed for him by his uncle *John Brougham*, possibly assisted by *Susanna Richmond*. In a similarly crisp Gibbsian style is part of Warcop Hall (W), 1744. The pre-Webster Dallam Tower (Milnthorpe, W), built 1720–5 for Daniel Wilson, is at present unattributed. Dalemain's new front of *c.* 1747 (C) was very likely designed by the owner *Edward Hasell* himself.

There is not always a heavy line in Cumbria between the polite and the VERNACULAR. There are also several distinct vernaculars, notably those of the Lake District and the Solway Plain; but they all have to cope with a wet, windy climate and the general awkwardness of the building materials, and share a long, low look, with the components joined in line – very noticeable in the wetter parts such as Borrowdale (C) and Martindale (W), and in the clay houses of the plain. Simplicity is the key to resisting the climate, especially of the roof. Hips and valleys are avoided, outshuts limited to perhaps a porch in front and a stair-turret behind. Where valleys are necessary the slates may be swept around, avoiding leadwork, as at Kitty Hall in Great Langdale (Langdales, W), Thwaite at Troutbeck (W), and – a polite example – Gaythorne Hall (Great Asby, W). Thwaite has a roof ridge of the aptly named wrestler slates, interlocked to obviate ridge stones. Windows are deep-set under simple horizontal dripmoulds, and often mullioned in wood; stone mullions in many areas are a sign of higher status, as are transoms. Whitewash distinguishes the dwelling from the outbuildings; the whitewashed farmhouse standing out against a brackeny fellside is an essential Lake District sight. Without a protective layer of whitewash driving damp will penetrate even the thickest of walls, making necessary the ugly pointing that often disfigures de-whitewashed buildings.

Most significantly, these houses share a common longhouse-derivative PLAN. The firehouse (which may be called the big house, or simply 'house') is the nucleus, centred on the vital fire. The fireplace is appropriately huge, a walk-in job lit by its own little fire-window, either under a timber bressumer or a broad segmental arch, and fitted with dry recesses for salt and spices. Entry is at the end, in the corner beside the fire, but draught-proofed from it by a heck or stub screen, which is sometimes prolonged into a rear corridor. This doorway may come in from outside but commonly opens from a cross-passage behind the stack, in an attached outbuilding – i.e. not structurally part of the dwelling house. This, the everyday entry, is often initialled and dated and may even be fitted with a porch (a porch opening into a barn looks quite odd). Where there is a central front door it is invariably later, and seldom used. The rest is more variable. Opposite the fire end may be a small parlour or snug, its wooden floor raised a step above the flags of the firehouse, and sometimes

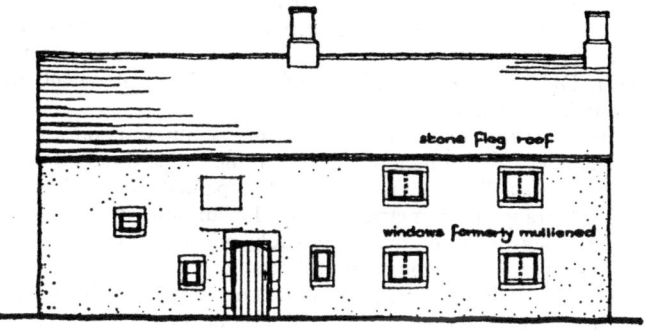

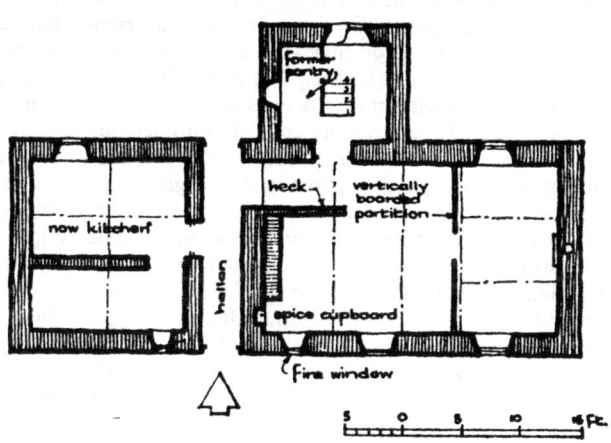

Westoe farmhouse, Skelton.
Elevation and ground-floor plan

also containing a bed. Next to that, or beyond, is the downhouse or kitchen, and the stair. Examples are manifold, widespread and socially inclusive. A few included for collateral reasons are White House Farm at Glassonby (C), opposite the well-known bastle; Ona Ash at High Windhill, Kirkoswald (C), picked out for the combination of red sandstone with thatch; Longhouses at Kentmere (W); Ratten Row, a clay house near Dalston (C); and Widewath near Askham (W). Even high-status houses such as Isel Hall (C) and Cowmire Hall (Crosthwaite, W), or No. 1 The Abbey in Carlisle, demonstrate the plan, and are used accordingly.

The true SCREENS-PASSAGE arrangement, where the cross-passage is inside the dwelling house at the service end, is confined to a few early and high-status houses: Castle Dairy in

Kendal (W), Preston Patrick and Burneside halls (all W). The
BAFFLE-ENTRY PLAN, where entry is into a lobby at the side of
the stack, is also uncommon: Bowness-on-Windermere rectory
(W), Dalehead Hall at Thirlmere (C) and Hornby Hall near
Brougham (W), all late medieval.

DATESTONES on houses appear, most commonly on a lintel,
in the later C16, proliferate mightily in the C17 and tail off in the
C18 and C19. The date is usually accompanied by initials, commonly arranged symmetrically with the surname in the middle.
There may be decorative or possibly magical devices as well.
Datestones are obviously useful, but are to be treated with
caution; strictly speaking a datestone only dates itself. The building they referred to may be altered or gone, or the stone moved,
e.g. at Newbiggin (W) and Hutton John (C). C17 court cupboards and spice cupboard doors are also frequently initialled
and dated, as is decorative plasterwork (*see* below).

The huge round CHIMNEYS of the southern Lake District are
highly characteristic, much imitated, but not common. The five
great stacks of *c.* 1580 at Coniston Hall (L) are rightly famous,
but travellers on the A590 may spot the equally dramatic bank
of four at Low Levens (Levens, W), probably of 1594. Sizergh
(W) has four outsized but square ones of much the same date on
its kitchen wing. Squatter, more conical examples can be seen on
Levens Hall and a couple of houses in Kendal. They are quite
widespread, always signifying status. Although sometimes called
Westmorland chimneys, they appear on the hall at Kirkby-in-
Furness (L), and also at Dalegarth Hall in Eskdale (C). Less
demonstrative ones, sometimes conjoined, are common: Rayrigg
at Windermere, High House Farm at Natland (1666), Glencoyne
Farm at Glenridding (1629). Another distinctive type is the cantilevered chimney, balanced on the firehouse gable originally –
though seldom now – over a timber-framed smoke-hood.

SPINNING GALLERIES – picturesque, first-floor wooden galleries under an extension of the roof – are again not very
common, but highly characteristic. Sometimes they are on the
house, more often on a barn. The gallery opposite Town End at
Troutbeck (W) and the very pretty one at Yew Tree Farm near
Coniston are the most photographed. There are others in the
Coniston area, one at Hodge Hill, near Cartmel Fell (L), and
smaller ones at Hartsop, Ravenstonedale and Rydal (all W). It is
not certain they were for spinning, though the image is attractive. Similar galleries can be seen in other wet mountain areas,
such as Galicia in northern Spain.

The stone carcase may be a simple thing – see How End at
Hartsop, or Mullender in Swindale, just a matter of recesses and
door pins – but when fully fitted out with INTERNAL WOOD-
WORK the Cumbrian farmhouse is a dwelling of considerable
vernacular sophistication. By the fire is the decorative spice cupboard, often initialled and dated. Opposite is a plank-and-muntin
partition with two doors, between which may be recessed an
ornate, dated and initialled court cupboard. Burneside Hall (W)

and Coniston Old Hall (L) have elaborated first-floor hall screens. Swarthmoor Hall (L) has an unusual chimneypiece, relating to George Preston's early C17 work at Cartmel Priory (*see* p. 33). Upstairs is often intricate, with plank-and-muntin partitions not necessarily following the downstairs arrangement, and built-in storage. Examples in the Gazetteer (all W) include Town End and Thwaite at Troutbeck, High House Farm at Natland (1666 on spice cupboard), Millerground at Windermere, Longhouses at Kentmere (dates 1703, 1704, 1711) and Collinfield at Kendal (1663, 1674, 1675).

The STAIR is often a simple stone half-spiral, without a proper newel, shut off top and bottom by thin doors. Otherwise a short wooden out-and-back with turned balusters. The stair at Swarthmoor Hall (said to be of 1586) shows an interesting halfway stage, winding round an open timber cage. Superior staircases with newels, balls and bottle balusters are quite plentiful: Barwise Hall (W; 1676), Beetham Hall Farmhouse (W), Weary Hall near Boltongate (C), Cowmire Hall (Crosthwaite, W), Lower Graythwaite (Graythwaite, L), Maulds Meaburn (W; also 1676), Moresby (C), Nether Levens (Levens, W). The very handsome stairs at Appleby Castle (1686–8) were made by *Mark Gardner*; the similar stairs at Askham Hall (W) are attributable to him.

49

DECORATIVE PLASTERWORK is quite common, if naïve: occasionally a whole ceiling, as at Blease Hall at Old Hutton (W); more often confined to an overmantel, e.g. at Waterside at Finsthwaite (L; 1675), and Hollins farm and Tolson Hall at Burneside (W; 1687; 1638 and 1639).

CLAY DABBINS are distinctive to the Solway Plain (C), where there is no stone and little wood. Wigton and Carlisle were once full of them, and they are still quite plentiful in country districts, though well-preserved examples are few. They are built of clay with dung added as what would today be called a plasticizer. Wobbly crucks of minimal quality, often reused, carry the roof, and the roof in turn stabilizes the top of the walls. The cruck feet are embedded in the wall, sometimes on padstones, so it is not true timber framing, as there is no sill or wallplate. The walls were built quickly, not as usual in staged 'lifts'. Between the wet clay of each course was a bed of straw which acted as a wick, allowing the water to be squeezed out as the wall rose. When dry it is thickly rendered inside and out, but where the naked surface appears, e.g. inside a barn, it looks not unlike irregular brickwork. These houses were originally thatched, as a few still are. Burgh-by-Sands and its dependent villages of Moorhouse and Longburgh are now the best places to look. Other good dabbins are noted at Ratten Row near Dalston (1689 datestone; timbers dendro-dated 1505 and 1586), Meadow Bank at West Curthwaite, near Thursby, and Howard Cottage at Warwick (all C).

The scarcity of true TIMBER FRAMING is highlighted by the survival of a single excellent example, in Carlisle of all places: the Guildhall, built by Richard de Redness between 1396 and 1407.

There is nothing hesitant here; fully accomplished timber framing on three storeys with jetties on two sides, dragon beams, continuous windowing. Also in Carlisle is the Priory Tithe Barn (*c.* 1470s; see St Cuthbert), resting upon part of the precinct wall at the back but otherwise fully timber-framed, with massive posts, braces and wall-plates.

If we except crucks within masonry or mud walls the rest of the list is this. Kirkby-in-Furness Hall chapel wing (L) retains posts and wall-plate within the present masonry structure. Coniston Old Hall (L) shows some evidence of former timber framing, and so perhaps does the non-defensive wing at Kentmere Hall (W). There are a few jettied town houses in Kendal (W), Burton-in-Kendal (W) and Hawkshead (L), probably of timber slung between masonry cross-walls, like at Totnes (Devon), though roughcast makes analysis difficult. Cote How at Rydal (W) is the only other building to display timbering, red herringbone sheltered by a spinning gallery. Bits of internal timbering suggest that it was once fully timber-framed.

Beryl Lott* put forward the theory that lost or rebuilt hall ranges, e.g. Clifton (W) and Crake Trees near Crosby Ravensworth (C), were timber-framed. Surely, however, sound timbers would be reused; where are they? An alternative theory put forward here is that these ranges were built of intractable stone – cobbles, slate – set in poor mortar or even clay, and have had to be rebuilt, sometimes repeatedly, as alteration, gravity and weather loosened their integrity.

AGRICULTURAL BUILDINGS include a characteristically simple but neat labour-saving invention, adapted to climate and terrain: the BANK BARN. The name was bestowed by R.W. Brunskill, who borrowed it from New England. The lower floor is for beasts, with entrances along the front often under a pentice roof; the upper floor for threshing grain, and for storage, with its own access at the back by a ramp, or simply by the slope of the land. Sizergh (W) has what may be the earliest, recorded in 1569; a double one, ten bays long, with two ramps. Park Barn at Rydal (w) was built in 1659 by Sir Daniel Fleming, another at Coniston Hall (L) in 1688. These early barns are commonly ramped, and not so different from big early barns not of the bank type, e.g. at Dalemain (C; 1685), and Sockbridge (W; 1699). Bank barns of a more modest size, built along a slope so the ramp was hardly necessary, soon became standard, from the one at Barwise Hall (W) dated 1681 right through to the many mid- or late C19 examples. Magnificent double bank barns were still built from time to time, as at Selside Hall (W) and at Farleton House near Holme (W). Sometimes an older building has been converted into one: a wing at Kentmere Hall (W), the tower at Wraysholme (Allithwaite, L), the upper hall at Coniston, the banqueting house at Thornthwaite Hall near Bampton (W).

*PhD, University of Nottingham, 1995.

PLANNED SETTLEMENTS are again prominent in the C17 and C18. Whitehaven, on Cumberland's remote w coast, is of great interest as England's first post-medieval planned town. The plan is a grid of streets and rectangular building plots running up from the harbour, with a plot in the middle set aside for the church, and a degree of enforced uniformity in the street frontages. The harbour and the germ of the plan originated with Sir Christopher Lowther from 1634, but credit for it goes chiefly to Sir John (1642–1706), M.P. and F.R.S. He must have known Wren's unrealized plan to rebuild London after the Great Fire of 1666, although Whitehaven is much less sophisticated. Trade was with Ireland and with Virginia, and Whitehaven's plan may have been a pattern in turn for many another planned town. The grid eventually came up against the natural limits of the site, so that the streets often end in wooded steeps, and the C18 saw a number of view-stoppers constructed, as in the formal gardens of the time, creating a highly enjoyable urban ensemble with a satisfying sense of completion. p. 671

Maryport (C) was laid out in the same manner by Humphrey Senhouse II in 1748–9, and named after his wife. Workington (C) followed with a planned district round a square, laid out by John Christian Curwen *c.* 1790. Both are a welcome surprise to those unfamiliar with w Cumberland, but unlike Whitehaven they fade out at the edges. Another square was laid out at Broughton-in-Furness (L) by Gilpin Sawrey in 1764, lined with handsome three-storeyed and colourwashed houses. In the far North, Dr Robert Graham of Netherby laid out Longtown in the later C18 with wide streets and two- and sometimes single-storey colourwashed houses. Allonby (C) has its own tiny square where two grandiose early C19 buildings, admittedly on a doll's-house scale, face each other. Lowther village (W) was removed *c.* 1682 and rebuilt in regular form on the NW boundary of the park, round a manufactory. By the 1760s this was again thought too close, and a second village was laid out by the *Adam Brothers* with a circus and linked squares. It was only half-realized, and built up with the humblest cottages, but remains the most ambitious planned settlement in Cumbria. p. 509

CUMBRIAN GEORGIAN 'is a genuine sub-species, more than merely a local variant. It has a distinctly Northern sturdiness, characterized by heavy window-surrounds, squat upper windows high under broad eaves, low-pitched roofs – also rendered or what in Scotland would be called harled, and colour-washed' (from the *Times Literary Supplement* review of the 1967 edition of *Cumberland and Westmorland*). p. 44

Of the GARDENS AND LANDSCAPING of the period, the first and most intriguing object is Sir Daniel Fleming's little grot of 1669 at Rydal (W), which frames a painterly view of an untamed waterfall. It seems a century ahead of its time, but Fleming's accounts and Machell's description prove the date. The Hasells did something similar at Dalemain (C), with their huge terrace wall and walk of 1688 rising up to a delightful little viewing house

Whitehaven, Queen Street.
Drawing, 1971

overhanging the river. It shows us perhaps that Cumbrians did
not need to discover the Lake District. At Lowther (W), the estate
papers record that Sir John had by 1697 spent £1,500 on his great
terrace and elaborate formal gardens. The great wall is still there
but the garden, densely planted out with forestry conifers, awaits
rediscovery. A formal geometric garden of 1692–7, famous for its
topiary, survives at Levens (L). James Grahme, a military man
and a Jacobite, compelled at times to take refuge abroad,
employed a Frenchman, *Guillaume Beaumont*, to extend his house
and create the garden. On one side it is bounded by the usual
high wall of the times, but on the other by a bastion and ha-ha,
opening it up 'that it might assort with the wilder country
without', as Horace Walpole said. If this was indeed made in 1692
it may be the first in the country.

Thomas Howard's elaborate garden at Corby Castle (C),
1708–*c*. 1739, is without formality. Nature dictates the form – the
drama of the Eden gorge gave little choice – but Howard added
plenty of extra incident: a cascade issuing from the jaws of a
monster, a giant Polyphemus, survivor of what was probably
quite a population of statuary, walks and steps, caves and grottoes, and a tempietto overlooking the salmon traps. Nunnery
Walks at Armathwaite (C), probably of much the same date (the
house is 1715), does without the imposed incident; steps, slippery
paths and viewing points are exciting enough. The Aira Force
walks near Charles Howard's Lyulph's Tower (Matterdale, C; *see*
below) are in the same mode, though overlaid by C19 exotic
planting and C20 improvements. Steep paths, vertiginous steps,
bridges and viewpoints make accessible a natural drama that
needs no embellishing.

p. 493,
47

INDUSTRIAL ARCHAEOLOGY

BY GAVIN WATSON

It is hard to generalize about industrial history in this region. Apart from a shared interest in slate quarrying and metal mining, the three historic constituents of the area have faced in different directions, and based their economies on different activities. Cumberland has looked N and W to Scotland and Ireland, turning its back firmly on Furness and Cartmel which gazes S across the sands of Morecambe Bay to Lancaster and beyond. Westmorland, true to its name, has always had strong connections to the E over the Pennines to Yorkshire and Co. Durham, whose western moorland fringe it was. The isolation of the area itself and of the settlements within it has meant that, for much of its history, the towns have been largely self-sufficient in trades like milling, brewing and tanning, so that local centres have always been underdeveloped, and centres answering wider regional or national needs have scarcely developed at all. Except for the special cases of the settlements on the rich coal and iron deposits of the western seaboard, the only towns to sustain a varied industrial base serving more than local needs have been Carlisle (C) and Kendal (W).

Sometimes, however, commodities won and worked within the Cumbrian Mountains have commanded national – even European – attention. Earliest must be the prehistoric cutting tools from the 'stone axe factories' of Langdale (W; *see* p. 487). Much later, the Borrowdale volcanics (C) yielded the 'Wadd' or graphite, which Thomas Fuller reported in 1662 as 'being so much transported beyond the seas'. The deposits were worked from at least the mid C16 until the 1870s, and were the foundation of the Keswick pencil industry. Similarly, the richness and purity of the haematite ores along the coast between Egremont (C) and Ulverston (L) fed an extraordinary C19 explosion of iron- and steel-making at Workington, Millom and Barrow-in-Furness. Rails rolled in Workington carried trains in every continent of the world, and nuclear submarines patrolling the world's oceans are still built in the shipyards of Barrow, created to exploit the products of those now abandoned mines and works. The isolation of the district and its lack of a populated hinterland have been prime reasons for the development of the nuclear complex at Sellafield (C), the site of the world's first nuclear power station, opened in 1953, and now the proving ground for techniques for decommissioning nuclear installations and the management of the wastes they produce.

The varied geology of the district provided useful minerals for local consumption. SLATE was used to roof buildings in the Roman fort at Hardknott, above Eskdale (C), and there is later evidence of it in the ruins of C13 Calder Abbey (C). Beautiful green slate from the Ordovician series is still extracted from underground workings at Honister (Borrowdale, C; opened 1648) and a greyish-green variant from quarries at Coniston (L), and there are plentiful remains in both places of disused C19 and

C20 workings. Hodge Close Quarry, in the Tilberthwaite Valley N of Coniston, is probably the most dramatic and at the same time the most instructive site for close (but careful) inspection. The Burlington Quarry at Kirkby-in-Furness (L) is the biggest working producer, winning blue-grey slates from formations of the Silurian period. There are C16 records of slate being shipped away, but full exploitation of wider markets had to await the coming of the railway in the mid C19. Burlington had its own private branch line, and the prospect of its traffic was in the minds of the first projectors of the Furness Railway.

LIMESTONE does not show itself much in the mountainous centre but outcrops frequently around the fringes of the region, most obviously in the S around the shores of Morecambe Bay. It was everywhere burnt as a soil sweetener, and for mortar and limewash. Small farm kilns are common and there is a particularly charming example, dated 1848, behind the pub at Bampton (W), suggesting that an enterprising citizen combined the roles of publican, farmer and lime-burner in his attempt to wrest a living from the unpromising soil of this remote corner. A fine example of a larger commercial kiln is at Ousby, on the Cumberland Pennines.

Miners invited over from Augsburg at the instance of Queen Elizabeth opened COPPER MINES in the Skiddaw slates of the Newlands valley (C) in 1556, and The Company of Mines Royal soon built a smelter near Keswick (C), taking power for its bellows from still-flowing water courses alongside the River Glenderamackin. The Germans brought the latest technologies and in 2008 wooden rails, dated by dendrochronology to the mid C16, were discovered in one of their LEAD MINES in Silver Gill, in the Caldbeck Fells (C). These are the earliest *in situ* evidences of rail transport to be found in Europe so far (on later railways *see* p. 50). Towards the end of the C16, copper deposits in the hard rhyolite around Coniston were opened up, though the ores still had to be transported by pack animals to the smelter at Keswick. Metal mining in the central Lake District seems to have fallen victim to the disturbances of the Civil War, and the industry did not revive until the mid C18. Thereafter, operations expanded rapidly and continued vigorously throughout the C19, finally petering out in 1962 with the closure of the Greenside Mine at Glenridding (W). BARYTES is generally associated with galena, the common lead ore, but was of little interest until its usefulness in glass and paint manufacture was discovered in the 1870s. Its presence in waste tips and old workings encouraged resuscitation of a number of closed mines in the late C19 and throughout the C20, and prolonged the life of others. Force Crag Mine, on the slopes of Grisedale Pike W of Keswick, opened for lead in 1775, yielded zinc in the C19 and survived on barytes until 1990. It was the last working mine within the Lake District National Park and has been conserved almost complete by the National Trust. Meanwhile, in the late C18 on the flanks of the northern Pennines, the London Lead Company did much work on Alston Moor (C) and developed a clutch of villages at the foot

of the western scarp as model settlements for their miners. There
is much to be seen in and around the charming village of Murton
(W), and the processing works in the company's remote town-
ship at Nenthead (C) near the Durham border are being conserved and turned into a splendid museum of the industry.

Coal was also mined on Alston Moor, won from drift mines
on the Pennine slopes as far s as Stainmore above Brough (W).
The mines were tiny, and have left little evidence except for the
remains of a network of tramways and early railway lines laid
down on the Earl of Carlisle's estates s of Brampton (C). The
main story of COAL MINING was played out elsewhere, where
Cumberland met the Irish Sea. The principal coalfield ran for
14 m. parallel to the coast between Whitehaven and Maryport,
with a tapering tail stretching inland to Wigton, and towards the
s stretching out for some miles beyond the coast. Drainage was
difficult, and dangerous firedamp (methane) added to the problems. Records survive from the 1560s, but for obvious reasons
the first workings were largely confined to surface outcrops.
Major capital to exploit the deeper seams arrived in the C17,
when the northern part of the estate of the former St Bees Priory
came into the hands of the Lowther family. Sir Christopher
Lowther in 1634 began to develop a HARBOUR and to lay out a
regularly planned town beside the tiny village of Whitehaven N
of the headland. His son, Sir John, carried on the work energetically, importing experts from the Newcastle area to develop the
coalfields. His ambition was to capture the lucrative export trade
to Ireland. His success encouraged his neighbours, particularly
the Curwens at Workington and the Senhouse family at Maryport, to exploit the coal beneath their estates and develop
harbours to ship it.

By the mid C18 there was a string of newly improved harbours
at Parton (N of Whitehaven), Harrington, Workington and Maryport, some already linked by tramways to inland coalpits and all
provoking rapid urban growth along the coast. Whitehaven is still
the best place to appreciate the beginning and the end of this
story. It was the site of many early advances in deep mining technology, and the 1729 Saltom Pit, disgracefully neglected at the
foot of the cliffs s of the harbour, was not only the first under-
sea mine in the world, but also the first to be designed from the
start with a systematic ventilation system. On the cliff above it
stands the last deep COLLIERY, Haig Pit, omega to Saltom's
alpha, closed in 1986 and now under restoration as a museum,
where one of the steam winding engines installed for its opening
in 1914 can still be seen running.

Where the coal measures gave out s of Whitehaven, IRON
MINING country began. Astonishingly pure haematite, almost
completely free of phosphorus, occurred in unpredictable large
'flats' of solid ore. Egremont has records of mining leases going
back to 1179 and the Cistercians of Furness Abbey were certainly
mining deposits near Dalton-in-Furness in the early C13, but
the operations were scattered and small-scale until successful
blast furnaces arrived in the district in 1711 at Backbarrow

(Haverthwaite, L) and Cunsey (Ulpha, L). This technology – new to this area, though already nearly two centuries old in Sussex – increased demand for ore, and thereafter the deposits were exploited on an increasing scale between Ulverston and Barrow-in-Furness, and around Egremont, Cleator and Eskdale in Cumberland. After Henry Bessemer patented his steel-making process in 1855, demand rose rapidly to new heights, since the area's non-phosphoric ore was ideal for the purpose. The Florence Mine at Egremont remained in operation in 2008, the last working deep metal mine in Europe. Further s at Millom (C), the remains of the Hodbarrow Mine, closed in 1968, still bring drama with their scale and boldness. The curving mile-long sea wall of 1900–4 contains the breached wreck of its predecessor of 1888–9, remains of lighthouses and pumping-engine houses, and a calm lagoon where there were once mine buildings, steelworks and a dense network of railway lines.

IRON-MAKING in the area remained small-scale and technically backward for surprisingly long. Furness Abbey seems to have claimed a monopoly in its area in 1273, but there is no convincing evidence that it used this privilege to develop an iron trade, or to produce anything more than was needed on its own estates. Place-name elements suggest iron-making, especially in the s and w of the region, but for the medieval period there are very few documentary references and physical evidences are slight. Production expanded in the C17, and there are records of 'stringhearths' and 'bloomforges' (the nomenclature is inconsistent and confusing) shipping iron as far as Preston. A stroll along the w shore of Coniston Water (L) can show the cinder heaps that remain of this palaeotechnic stage, together with the coppice woods and in them the flat pitsteads of the charcoal burners who provided their fuel.

A BLAST FURNACE was built at Cleator in 1694, but it was the furnaces of 1711 at Cunsey and Backbarrow (both in Furness) which set the pace for the region in the next half-century. The new furnace their owners constructed at Duddon Bridge in 1736 (Ulpha, C) is England's finest surviving example of an C18 charcoal-fired blast furnace. Nevertheless, with so much coal around, it was inevitable that Cumbrian ironmasters should experiment with it as a fuel. Unfortunately, the local mineral had more serious impurities than the Coalbrookdale 'clod' coal that enabled Abraham Darby to smelt successfully in 1709. Even as late as 1765, Gabriel Jars, a French industrial spy, reported that a furnace built expressly for coke fuel near Maryport was proving incapable of producing useable iron. Carrying small amounts of ore was much easier than moving and storing vast quantities of charcoal and keeping it in dry storage, so the centre of gravity of the industry continued to lie not near the orefield but in the coppice woods of Furness, close to assured sources of charcoal and water power. Steam, railways and Bessemer's discoveries had changed the balance decisively by the mid C19, but the old furnaces survived surprisingly long. Duddon Bridge worked until 1867, faithful to the end to charcoal. Since charcoal-made iron

Barrow-in-Furness, steelworks.
Engraving, 1872

had particular qualities needed for a number of special uses, Backbarrow carried on using charcoal exclusively until 1926, the last furnace in the country to do so, and did not close finally until 1967. But, for iron-working, the next century belonged to the coastal strip. Of the vast buildings and structures of these C19 and C20 iron and steel works at Barrow and elsewhere virtually nothing remains, though Workington's last Bessemer converter was taken to Sheffield in 1975 as an exhibit in the Kelham Island Museum.

The GUNPOWDER industry also depended on the southern coppice woods for the charcoal which was a vital ingredient of their product. Gunpowder manufacture grew in tandem with the development of mining and, particularly, slate quarrying, where the use of explosives could speed up the work dramatically. In addition to charcoal, the main materials needed were saltpetre and sulphur, which could be imported through Milnthorpe (W) and Greenodd (North Lancs.) on Morecambe Bay. The grinding, mixing and pressing processes needed plenty of power, and the rivers and becks of South Lakeland could provide this reliably and safely. The first gunpowder works opened in 1764 at Old Sedgwick, on the River Kent s of Kendal (Natland, W), and eventually there were seven, Blackbeck in High Furness opening last in 1860. The market was wider than local; there was considerable trade with Africa, and Westmorland supplied most of the blasting powder for the North Wales slate industry. Gatebeck was the last mill to close in 1937. Under Board of Trade regulations controlling this potentially dangerous industry, most of the works were comprehensively dismantled as soon as they finished. New Sedgwick (1858), however, has a comprehensive set of remains, sympathetically incorporated into a private caravan site, and Low Wood near Haverthwaite (L) has an impressive set of offices, complete with an ostentatious clock tower.

BOBBIN-MAKING was another trade which consumed huge quantities of coppice wood, and whose products met national needs. As the textile industry mechanized and expanded from the end of the C18, demand for bobbins soared. A typical large Lancashire spinning mill might have 10,000,000 bobbins in use at any one time, and they needed constant replacement as the bobbins travelled with the yarn to the weaving mills. At the peak, around 1850, there were nearly fifty bobbin mills at work in the Cartmel and S Westmorland districts, meeting about half of the national requirement. Most relied on water power for the whole of their working lives, Gilkes of Kendal fighting an effective battle against the advance of the steam engine with successive developments of their turbines and Pelton wheels. Stott Park Bobbin
68   Mill at Finsthwaite (L) at the foot of Windermere was the last survivor, closing in 1971, but happily preserved in working order by English Heritage. Although bobbin-making was concentrated in the S of the area, there were occasional mills elsewhere. There is a fine example, roofless but substantially complete, in Caldbeck (C), convenient for the textile mills of Carlisle. A well-
69   preserved WATER MILL survives at Eskdale (C). Dixon's Mill at
70   Carlisle, 1835–7 by Richard Tattersall, is a giant TEXTILE MILL of the type more common in S Lancs.

CANALS came late to the area, and there has never been any connection with the national system. The first was the Ulverston Canal, a 1½-m. ship canal opened in 1796 to bring coastal vessels into the town. It was reasonably successful until the Ulverstone [sic] & Lancaster Railway arrived in 1857. Kendal waited a long time for its canal connection; the Lancaster Canal Co. secured powers in 1792 to build a line N from Lancaster to the town but, reaching the Westmorland boundary at Tewitfield by 1813, work stopped and it took a further six years to finish the job. The Company's original engineer was *John Rennie*, but the northern extension was handed over to *Thomas Fletcher*, his assistant. Fletcher varied Rennie's line but the simple robust style of the major structures, Hincaster Tunnel (Heversham, W) and a substantial aqueduct at Natland (W), bear a close resemblance to Rennie's designs further S. It is not clear whether Rennie left drawings which Fletcher adapted, or whether Fletcher, as an attentive pupil, absorbed his master's precepts into his own designs. The last loaded boats reached Kendal in 1944, the final two miles were filled in, and the building of the M6 motorway severed the line in six places. There are bold plans to reopen the whole length.

The Carlisle Canal was part of a grand plan for a ship canal from the Solway Firth to the Tyne. Only the first 11 m. from the Solway to Carlisle were built, 1821–3. A planned settlement was developed at the seaward end and glorified with the name of Port Carlisle (Bowness-on-Solway, C). It has hardly grown since. Initially very successful, the canal was overtaken by railway development, and a branch line was laid along the filled-in bed.

Cumberland has a particular importance in the history of RAILWAYS. Early C18 tramways were laid down in Whitehaven to carry coal from pit to harbour. Contemporary illustrations and maps are possibly the first recorded use of the switching rails now

known as points. The courses of some of those lines are still traceable. In the N of the county, the Earl of Carlisle's railways
between Brampton and Tindale Fell were laid down as early as
1775 with some surprisingly heavy engineering.

The earliest recognizably modern railway in the county was the
Newcastle & Carlisle, opened in 1836 and blessed with some
exceedingly handsome bridges, of which the Gelt Viaduct
(Hayton, C) and Wetheral Viaduct (C) are the finest. The tiny
Maryport & Carlisle Railway followed in 1840–3 and stoutly
maintained its independence until the compulsory 'grouping' in
1923. Financed by local capital, it resisted all temptations to
expand, paying handsome dividends from the profits of moving
coal from the West Cumberland field to its harbour at Maryport.
Its water tank at Curthwaite (Thursby, C), proudly dated 1843,
is probably the oldest piece of railway operating equipment in the
world still in its original position.

The main line from London reached Carlisle in 1846 in the
shape of the Lancaster & Carlisle Railway, engineered by *Joseph
Locke*, over the steep gradients of Shap Fell (W). A year later,
northbound traffic could be handed over to the Caledonian
Railway to carry to Glasgow and Edinburgh. Carlisle has been a
great railway centre ever since. The western seaboard had to wait
until 1854 before a necklace of separate lines was joined up to
connect Maryport and the other coalfield towns to Furness
– whence the name, Furness Railway – and around to the main
line again at Carnforth (North Lancs.). Ferocious competition
to share in the glamorous traffic between London and Scotland
brought two more Scottish companies to Carlisle, the Glasgow
& South Western via Dumfries in 1848 and the North British
from Edinburgh via Hawick in 1861. Similar politics of competition between English companies impelled the Midland Railway
to incur massive expenditure in constructing the magnificent
Settle and Carlisle line over some of the most inhospitable and
unprofitable territory in the land, to bring the number of companies serving Carlisle Citadel station up to seven in 1869. It is
remarkable that, of the seven, only the North British presence
has disappeared completely. The Midland route has left us with
a splendid suite of stations and a series of superb viaducts. The p. 490
stretch of line through the Eden gorge S of Carlisle must be 106
among the most picturesque in the country.

In 1862 another line forced its way across the Pennines over
Stainmore, England's highest railway summit, to connect the
Durham coalfield with the West Cumberland iron-ore deposits.
A spindly iron viaduct nearly 200 ft (62 metres) high, designed
by *Sir Thomas Bouch* (of Tay Bridge fame), used to carry trains
over the Belah Beck. Sadly it was demolished in 1962, but the
same engineer's masonry bridges on the line, hardly less impressive (e.g. Smardale Gill Viaduct, Ravenstonedale (W)), are still
with us in the safe hands of the Northern Viaducts Trust.

The final pieces of the complex net of the area's railways
include the beautiful route laid in 1864 W from Penrith, through
Keswick and along the shore of Bassenthwaite Lake to Cockermouth and Workington (more surviving *Bouch* bridges); the dense

tangle of competing lines twisting and climbing through the hills behind Whitehaven and Egremont; and the bold Solway Junction Railway striking across the sea from Bowness to Annan on a mile-long iron viaduct in 1869. All were heavily dependent on the West Cumbrian iron trade, and all have gone. Of the branches from these through routes, only the 1864 line through Kendal to Windermere survives.

THE LATER GEORGIANS, c. 1750–c. 1840

In the mid C18 a great change occurred in English taste. Arcadia, the paradise for which it was the human condition to yearn, had been given visual substance in the paintings of Claude and Poussin, so desirable to the English milord, and given language in the Beautiful and Sublime of Edmund Burke's *Essay* of 1757. The sublimity of distant mountains, the pastoral beauty of foreground trees and water, the innocence of shepherds and their simple dwellings, a few melancholy evocations of past glory: these were the ingredients. Gardeners and landscapers in the gentler parts of England set to to create Arcadia with sham ruins, hermitages, sinuous rills and so on, all open to the wider landscape. The DISCOVERY OF THE LAKE DISTRICT began some time in the 1750s, when classically educated travellers, deterred from the Continent by war, found our own real, primitive, northern Arcadia. Paintings by William Bellers and Thomas Smith of the natural amphitheatre of Ullswater, or of Thirlmere with its three little bridges to point up the scale, showed that the essential ingredients were there for the taking. Painting pure landscape on the spot was something new, celebrated in Thomas Hearne's delightful study of 1777 of Sir George Beaumont and Joseph Farington sketching *en plein air*. Lady Mary Lowther herself toured the southern Lakes and made large-scale panoramas of Windermere.

Thomas West's *Guide to the Lakes* (1778) took tourists, unsure of the drill, to a series of 'stations' where they could be sure of perfectly composed tableaux; a Western counterpart to the Japanese tradition of ritualized viewing. Claife Station at Sawrey above the Windermere ferry, Brantwood on Coniston, Armathwaite Hall on Bassenthwaite all occupy West's selected spots. The Rev. William Gilpin, born at Scaleby Castle in 1724, supplied the word 'Picturesque' to fit West's composed views: the application of the rules of painting to a real scene. 'Shall we suppose it a greater pleasure to the sportsman to pursue a trivial animal, than it is to the man of taste to pursue the beauties of nature?' he asked. Aquatints after Gilpin's sketches in his *Observations Relative to Picturesque Beauty* (1782) and his 'Scottish tour' (published 1789, including a trip round Derwentwater), are as though seen in a Claude glass, a tinted mirror in which the tourist, turning his or her back, framed an idealized view.

William Cockin of Kendal, in his second edition of West's *Guide* (1780), encouraged the building of Arcadian VILLAS in the Lakes. According to Wordsworth, Thomas English of Nottinghamshire was the first to do so; his Belle Isle of 1774, an island   56
Pantheon by *John Plaw*, was also the most distinguished. On Derwentwater Joseph Pocklington built his own island villa in 1778, and in 1780 Charles Howard of Greystoke built a mock castle called Lyulph's Tower overlooking Ullswater (Matterdale, C). All three are Picturesque objects in themselves, consciously contributing to the grand view of their respective lakes. Moreover, much as a gentleman's park was best embellished not by a single temple but by a series of Picturesque incidents interlocked by vistas and viewpoints, so Belle Isle was answered by the castellated viewpoint of Claife Station and the jettied temple of Storrs. At Derwentwater *Pocklington* put up a series of island follies, a mock church, a stonehenge, and built two more houses at each end of the lake. Both lakes began to take on the air of designed playgrounds – as indeed they were, figuring in mock battles and races, with much noise and animation.

More followed, especially around Windermere: Fellfoot *c.* 1780 (Newby Bridge, L), Brathay Hall 1794–6 (L), Calgarth Park before 1796 (Troutbeck, W), Storrs *c.* 1795–7 and *c.* 1808–9 (Bowness-on-Windermere, W). Overlooking Ullswater is Thomas Clarkson's Eusemere of *c.* 1794, by *Thomas Wilkinson* (Pooley Bridge, W). Greta Hall of 1799–1800 (Keswick, C) gave views over Derwentwater and Bassenthwaite, while Tent Lodge (1806–7) and Monk Coniston (*c.* 1820) embellished Coniston (L). Many of these houses sit straight on the ground, without visible services to obscure the views. Services were hidden in buried basements, accessed by a tunnel at Storrs and Derwent Island, or in the case of Tent Lodge placed in a subsidiary house across the road.

Gilpin with his posturing came in for some satire, and with the publication in 1794 of Uvedale Price's *Essays on the Picturesque* with its non-interventionist aesthetic, so did the early villas. In deference to critcism they were planted out, gradually disappearing as the trees grew. Lord William Gordon at Derwent Bay   55
(Keswick (C); *c.* 1790), William Gell at Silverhowe (Grasmere (W), 1797/8) and John Wilson at Elleray (Windermere (W); from *c.* 1807) took a different approach, deliberately building low and unobtrusive. Both moreover were extensions of existing vernacular houses, which in the long run were to prove the enduring model (*see* below).

The CASTLE STYLE or GOTHIC REVIVAL was also popular, especially for greater houses outside the Lake District. *John Hird* of Lancaster sometimes essayed a tentative Gothic, as in his new front to Sizergh (W) of 1773–4, and perhaps at Broughton Tower (Broughton-in-Furness, L) in 1777.* Artisan Gothick can be seen

---

* His internal modifications to Witherslack chapel (W) in 1768 are classical, though the external changes match the C17 work.

at the White House, Appleby (W), and its relation Helbeck Hall at Brough (W; 1775), both attributed to *Henry Bellas* or *Bellhouse*, and at Tolson Hall, Burneside (W).

Charles Howard (1746–1815) of Greystoke (C), 11th Duke of Norfolk, seems to have designed for himself. Coarse, generous, clumsy, clever, Protestant, patriotic, an opponent of the slave trade and pro-American independence, Howard spent his youth among the rugged northern landscapes and the Dacre–Howard castles and traditions. He liked architectural tricks and jokes, such as the seven-sided towers of his s wing *c*. 1789 (mostly dem.) at Greystoke, and Stafford House there, apparently of one storey at the end, two storeys at the sides, but in fact of three full storeys within. His three folly farms at Greystoke – Spire House, Bunkers Hill and Fort Putnam – are typically provocative. His Lyulph's Tower on Ullswater (Matterdale, C), has already been high-lighted above.

Designs for Lowther (W) in both castle and 'abbey' mode had been made since the mid C18, and from 1806 *Robert Smirke* finally

58
p. 504

gave them reality with a splendidly scaled, mansion displaying a façade to the park and an abbey front to the garden. Augill Castle at Brough (W), 1841, is not much more authentic than Lyulph's Tower. In 1830–47 *L.N. Cottingham* refashioned Brougham Hall (W) for Lord Brougham and his brother in the coarse, skin-deep Baronial style that also characterized his work at Snelston and Elvaston in Derbyshire. Similar were *William Burn*'s contemporary recasting of Netherby (C) for Sir James Graham, and *Philip Wyatt*'s reinvention of Conishead Priory (L), 1823–9. In 1833–7 *John Dobson* built Holme Eden, Warwick (C), in a bristling Tudor style, for Peter Dixon, cotton manufacturer.

Thomas Rickman owed his influence in the North to Bishop Percy of Carlisle, who was raised to the see in 1827. For the

29
59

Bishop Rickman Gothicized Rose Castle (C) in 1828–30. On a smaller scale he designed the charming Brunstock, Houghton (C), also 1828–30, for the chapter clerk. His designs may have been used at Scaleby Castle (C), 1838. Reminiscent of Brunstock, though by an unknown hand, is Calthwaite Hall (C) of *c*. 1837, with its free-standing wooden spiral stair.

From the Early Victorian period are Aldingham Hall (L), 1846–50, attributed to *Sir Matthew Digby Wyatt*, which imitates

62, 63

Conishead in a more controlled manner, and Wray Castle (L), 1840–7 by *J.J. Lightfoot*, a much more serious affair. It is the only real attempt at such a castle in the Lake District, and mighty incongruous it is too.

Of other Northern architects of the C18 and early C19, *John Carr* of York is linked, with more or less certainty, to a number of fairly minor jobs in the region. He remained a Palladian, except perhaps for the original Claife Station of 1799, and at in

107

his work at Holker Hall (1783–93) which was mildly Chinesey-Gothick. For the Curwens he designed the rich interiors of Workington Hall (C; 1783–95, destroyed), and simpler ones at Belle Isle (Bowness-on-Windermere, W). He may also have had a hand in Christian Curwen's model farm at Schoose, Workington.

The Howards of Corby Castle (C) turned to *Peter Nicholson* (1765–1844), mathematician and geometrician as well as architect, who favoured a severe Greek style in his new work there of 1812–17. For Robert Mounsey, a Carlisle lawyer, Nicholson built Castletown House at Rockcliffe (C; with *William Reid*) in 1809–11, one of a group of gentleman's houses collectively nicknamed by Angus Taylor The Dukery of Carlisle. Others by Nicholson – all Grecian – are Houghton House, *c.* 1810, and the delightful Eden Grove at Crosby-on-Eden, 1837–9, for Richard Carruthers, a portrait painter – just a single storey over a basement, and only three bays, but given great presence by its Doric portico. Nicholson's granddaughter Jane married Alexander 'Greek' Thompson of Glasgow in 1847. The Neoclassical Tynefield House, Penrith (C), 1804, remains unattributed.   57

Finally the WEBSTERS of Kendal: *Francis* (1767–1827) and *George Webster* (1797–1864), whose practice was continued by *Miles Thompson*. The Webster style is ubiquitous in the limestoney south of Cumbria, and widespread in N Lancs. and Yorkshire. The family started as masons and marble-polishers in Cartmel, as remembered by the Webster memorial on the S transept of Cartmel Priory (L). *Francis* worked as a contractor, at Lowther for example, while himself designing in dignified Georgian mode or occasional Gothic. *George* was more the professional architect. At Underley Hall near Kirkby Lonsdale (W; 1825–8) and Whelprigg at Barbon (C; 1834) he showed himself a very early exponent of Jacobean Revival. At Hutton-in-the-Forest (C) he   61
designed the rebuilt, over-scale tower in 1826, and even proposed re-cladding the Baroque front. The spectacular Gothic mansion of Conishead Priory (L) is more George Webster than Philip Wyatt, whom he followed in 1838. Rigmaden at Mansergh (W, 1825–8) and Helme Lodge near Kendal (W; 1824–7), both jointly by *Francis & George*, are Greek. Their Esthwaite Lodge near Hawkshead (L; 1819–21) is a sweet Greek doll's house with charming if slightly overpowering plasterwork. In Kendal, *Francis*'s Aynam Lodge of 1823 and Beezon Lodge of 1825, and *George*'s Sand Aire House of 1827–8, are notable for the quality of their limestone work. In the Italianate, Osborne style is Belsfield at Bowness-on-Windermere (W), of 1840 and 1853.

The Websters' yard and showroom was Bridge House in Kendal, 1819. No. 4 Thorny Hills in Kendal was *George Webster*'s own, one of a row of pretty Webster houses. They also had a country house called Eller How at Lindale (L), in *cottage orné* style with a fanciful garden, and *George* built an Italianate sea-bathing house dated 1841, Black Rock Villa, at Grange-over-Sands (L).

A VERNACULAR REVIVAL can be seen beginning with William Wordsworth. He was critical of much new building in the Lakes, especially of Allan Bank at Grasmere, which he could see from Dove Cottage – and which he eventually took himself. In 1825–7 a perceived threat to the tenure of Rydal Mount (Rydal, W), which the Wordsworths had taken in 1813, stimulated him to think about building a new house, embodying his ideas, on a

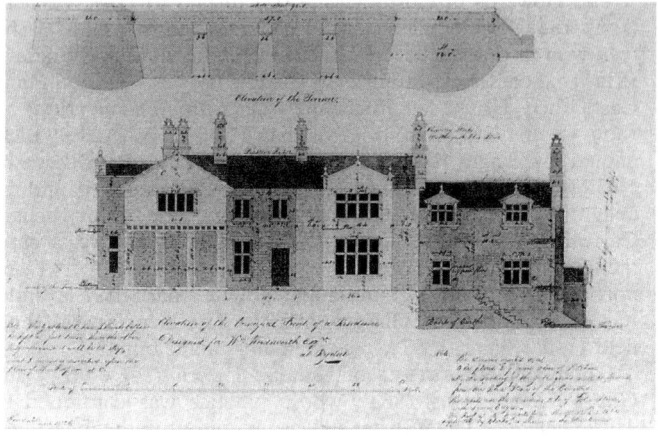

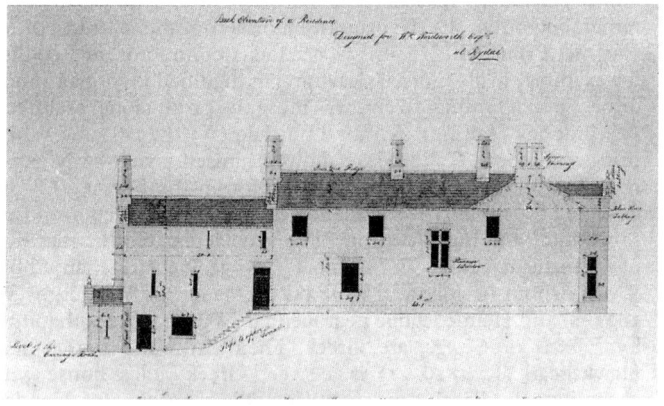

Rydal, The Rash.
Proposed design, drawings by George Webster, 1826

patch of land called The Rash, now Dora's Field. It was to be irregular, with round chimneys and mullioned windows under slate dripmoulds, and emphatically not white. Wordsworth's daughter *Dora* may have sketched it out, *George Webster* was taken on as professional architect. Both Wordsworth and Webster approved of modern planning, so the designs ignore the characteristic low horizontals and in-line plan of the region. Dormers and valleys abounded, and the low-pitched Regency roof dates it immediately.

The Rash was never built. However, Wordsworth's fame and longevity and the Webster firm's voluminous practice ensured that the views crystallized in its design were widely influential. Wordsworth advised directly on Thomas Arnold's Fox Howe at Under Loughrigg, Rydal (1832), and Harriet Martineau's

The Knoll at Ambleside (1845–6). Indeed the Rash design and p. 103 its immediate progeny, reinforced by Ruskinian ideas on truth to materials, and inevitably influenced by fads like steep roofs and twiddly bargeboards, set the style of building in the Lakes right up to 1900. All those dark stone, mullioned, round-chimneyed, multi-gabled villas and hotels (The Prince of Wales of 1855 and 1863, by *Miles Thompson* opposite Dove Cottage at Grasmere is typical), not to mention whole streetscapes in Coniston, Ambleside and Windermere, can be traced back to Wordsworth's inexact idea of the vernacular.

PUBLIC BUILDINGS of the period begin with a might-have-been. *Robert Adam* designed a Town Hall, County Court and Gaol in 1766–7 for Appleby (W), then the county town of Westmorland. As always Sir James Lowther prevaricated, and the job – quite modest by now – was given to his agent, *Daniel Benn*, 1776–8. Appleby and Kirkby Stephen both have little covered arcades or cloisters between church and town. Kirkby Stephen's is classical, by *George Gibson* 1810, and the better of the two. Appleby's (replacing a C17 one by *Thomas Machell*) is toytown Gothic by *Smirke*, 1811. Hawkshead's dignified Palladian Town Hall of 1790–1 – disapproved of by Wordsworth – could be by *Carr*, though *Francis Webster* was also involved. The Moot Hall at Keswick, pretty and memorable rather than distinguished, dates in its present incarnation from 1813. Its pagoda-roofed tower was a minor fashion at the time, the scooped shape a commonplace of Regency verandas and porches. Brampton's Moot Hall of 1817 is octagonal, and also originally open below, as was usual. Carlisle's endearingly demure C17 Town Hall was given its present shape *c.* 1825 with the addition of a l. extension to balance the present r. wing and ogee-roofed clock turret of 1717. (Carlisle incidentally built a municipal Fish House in the C18 at King Garth, where the salmon catch was monitored and sampled.)

The City of Carlisle carried out a major programme of improvement from 1807, with the removal of the city wall on the E and the construction of Lowther Street leading to a new bridge. The old gates were taken down and a new southern entry made between *Smirke*'s mighty twin towers of the Citadel (1810 *et seq.*, 94 superseding designs by *Thomas Telford* and others), which housed the new courts. The Infirmary at Carlisle was built by *Richard* 95 *Tattersall* in 1830–2 in Greek style with a giant portico, similar to what Richard Lane was doing in Manchester, made successful by its grandeur of scale. Carlisle Athenaeum of 1839–40, by *Arthur Y. & George Williams* of Liverpool, is in a more inventive Grecian style with giant pilasters turning into square columns at the ends. A giant order appears again in the unlikely surroundings of Allonby (C) on the N coast, on the Baths and Assembly Room of 1835, perhaps by *William Alderson*, and also on the Westmorland Bank in Kendal, of 1834–5 by *George Webster*, not the best of the several designs he made for that building. Of other COMMERCIAL ARCHITECTURE of the first half of the C19, Ulverston's Trustee Savings Bank of 1836–8, also by *Webster*, is Italianate, with a clock tower added in 1844, while

Miles Thompson's Savings Bank of 1847 at Kirkby Lonsdale (W) juggles the same architectural elements. As for SCHOOLS, the Tudor range at St Bees (C) was heightened in 1820, and in 1842–4 expanded into an open court with thinly turreted gate-house motifs, designed (or merely built) by *Thomas Nelson*.

Romantic Gothick is represented in CHURCH ARCHITECTURE by the attenuated, ghostly Howard Chapel of 1791 at Wetheral parish church. At Carlisle Cathedral, *Thomas Pitt* (1737–93), later Lord Camelford, carried out an economical restoration for his uncle Bishop Lyttelton from 1765 – which is early for the Gothic taste – including an inserted plaster vault and spiky furnishings. It was largely undone in the mid C19, but bits can be seen here and there. Similarly obliterated by later work was the jolly rebuild of Crosby Ravensworth church (C) from 1811 by *George Gibson*, including an openwork crown to the tower. Just a pair of vigor-ous porches remain.

New ANGLICAN CHURCHES untouched by Gothic are Kirkandrews-on-Esk (C; 1775), *Thomas Hardwick*'s splendid St John, Workington (C; 1821–3), built under the Commission-ers' first grant, and *Smirke*'s church of 1832–3 at Askham (W). Thin Gothic of the sort we call Commissioners' included *Rickman*'s two of 1828–30 in Carlisle, Commissioners' in fact, and relatively expensive for their second grant; both have been swept away. Even thinner are a series of small churches by *George Webster* at Haverthwaite (L; 1824–5), Natland (W; 1825, since rebuilt), Lindale (L; 1828–9), and New Hutton (W; 1828–9). Casterton church (1833), along with a parsonage and notorious schools, was built for the Rev. W. Carus Wilson, Perpetual Curate, whose views are explained in his *Helps to the Building of Churches and Parsonage Houses* (1835 and 1842). *Webster* perpetuated the type at Grayrigg (W; 1837–8) and Holme (W; 1839).

Bigger lancet-Gothic churches by *Webster*, with aisles, are St Thomas, Milnthorpe (W) and St Thomas, Kendal (W), both 1835–7. His St George in Kendal (1838–41) is more ambitious still, with twin turrets. The best of the bunch is Webster's R.C. church at Kendal (1835–7). This is a rare early example, for CATHOLICISM had not retained the hold it had in central Lan-cashire; a Catholic house like Sizergh (W) is very much the exception.* The (former) R.C. church of 1821 at Ulverston (L) with its iron tracery and plaster vault, but squeezed in on almost no land, has nothing like the same confidence – although after the Emancipation Act of 1829 a tower was added. Of other non-Anglican places of worship from the early C19, *Francis Webster*'s elegant Friends' Meeting House at Kendal (1815–16) is straight-forwardly Georgian.

Of CHURCH MONUMENTS, *Joseph Nollekens*'s memorial to Lady Maria Howard and infant †1789, for which the Howard Chapel at Wetheral (C) was built, is a touchingly poetic group.

*It is interesting however that Fr Thomas West (*c.* 1720–79), a Jesuit priest, was able to minister openly to his minuscule flock around Dalton-in-Furness (L), and maintain friendly correspondence on antiquarian matters with the likes of Richard Burn, Chancellor of the diocese, and Lord George Cavendish of Holker.

In the plain conventicle of Allonby (C) is an unexpectedly fine memorial to Joseph Huddart signed *Petrus Fontana*, 1821. *Musgrave Lewthwaite Watson* (1804–47), a native of Cumberland, created a sensational Neoclassical monument to his father (†1823) at Sebergham (C), a big white marble plaque in the lowest possible relief of the three Fates. A portrait bust of Watson by *George Nelson* is in the s transept of Carlisle Cathedral.

74

A collective pleasure are the common graveyard HEADSTONES of Cumbria. Handsomely scaled in the stone of the neighbourhood, elegantly lettered and flourished, they stand free in the usual way or may equally be fixed against the church wall. Good examples are at Aspatria, Beckermet, Caldbeck, Dean, Gosforth and Uldale (all C). Outstanding are the early C19 slate headstones by the *Bromley* dynasty, especially *William Bromley*, at Crosthwaite (C) and Threlkeld (C). Other early C19 monuments are described below, p. 64.

VICTORIAN AND EDWARDIAN

Victorian architecture was as vigorous here as anywhere. The new RAILWAYS were the key to development, as outlined on p. 50. The town of Barrow-in-Furness (L) was created and nurtured by the Furness Railway under its dynamic manager James Ramsden (1822–96). The company gave virtually all its building design work to the first-rate firm of *Paley & Austin* (*see also* p. 62), so the STATIONS and even quite humble structures are excellent. The Lancaster & Carlisle opened in 1846, with a great covered station at Carlisle. Its architect, here and at Penrith (C) and Oxenholme (Natland, W), was *Sir William Tite*. The Midland Railway's Settle and Carlisle line, opened in 1876 and celebrated today for the way it challenged the Pennines, used a standard range of station buildings. Their present state of preservation and smartness is outstanding in national terms. Of stations on other lines, Keswick, which has not seen a train since 1972, is in good shape.

104
105

p. 490

PLANNED SETTLEMENTS are again a feature. The Warwick Road area of Carlisle was laid out in the 1830s with broad, straight streets and squares, and built up over the following decades with handsome two-storey, Flemish-bond brick terraces with pillared porches of stone. The style is conservative, retaining Georgian proportion and restraint until the 1860s when, particularly in the two squares, florid Victorian began to appear. Distinctive railway districts were laid out in Maryport (C), with stone-fronted terraces with incised names, and in Workington (C). Barrow's plan was made by *James Ramsden*; first the Hindpool estate in 1856 as a grid of streets, leaving space for a market, then Abbey Road and the Strand with their two *ronds-points* in 1860, and a further grid up to St James's church in 1863. Not far behind was Millom (C), set out by *Wadham & Turner* of Barrow c. 1865–6, though the position of the market square was not

96

p. 130

settled until *c.* 1876. Askam-in-Furness (L) started at much the same time, with equal ambition, but didn't get as far. Cleator Moor (C) in the early 1860s was intended to be an ideal town, but again the town square did not materialize until the 1880s. None of these towns reached its full potential. Straight streets peter out in industrial wasteland, town squares remain unfinished. The grandest piece of townscape, given unity and completion by its geographical constraints, is Barrow Island with its great blocks of tenements (1872–4, 1879, 1880–1 etc.), designed by *Paley & Austin* and built by *David Caird* of Dundee.

Several new RESORTS came into being. Windermere (W), dating its birth to the arrival of the railway in 1847, developed rapidly with no overall plan, although several individuals stamped their mark upon it. The Rev. J. A. Addison conceived an ideal Gothic community round his new church. His architects were *Miles Thompson* and *J. S. Crowther*, his builder *Abraham Pattinson*. Later C19 Windermere and Bowness-on-Windermere (W), built by the *Pattinsons* and *William Harrison*, was in an elaborated vernacular, like Pattinson's own community of Elim Grove around his yard. Of coastal resorts, Grange-over-Sands (L) is successful because of its favourable position, but Seascale (C), planned by *Edward Kemp* in 1879 – with curvy roads, not a grid, for once – barely got started. Both depended on James Ramsden and the Furness Railway, as did the development of Furness Abbey (L). Silloth (C) on the other hand – another railway creation – has Scottish affiliations. The North British Railway, having rescued the original company in 1862, carried forward the projected dormitory town and seaside resort to a plan of *c.* 1857 by *W. & J. Hay* of Liverpool. It is a grid with a block left for the church, exactly as Whitehaven two centuries earlier.

VICTORIAN CHURCHES commonly replace not the medieval church, which if it had survived was now likely to be restored, but an C18 or even early C19 building considered to be unecclesiastical, e.g. at Chapel Stile (Langdales, W), Irthington (C), Patterdale (W), Underbarrow (W).

But first we must consider *Sara Losh* (1785–1853) of Wreay (C), a true original whom Pevsner puzzled over at some length. Coming from a wealthy and cultivated family, and well-travelled, she had a particular interest in archaeology and in the natural sciences. She reshaped the family home, Woodside, after the death of her father in 1814, but most of her building, always at her own expense, was done after the death of her sister in 1835. Her work harks back beyond the Gothic to the Early Christian or rather Italian Romanesque style, the style then called Lombardic. That in itself was remarkable, for the principal English examples of the style had yet to be built. She may perhaps have known of Klenze's and Schinkel's designs in Munich and Berlin, but the most likely source is Thomas Hope and his *Historical Essay on Architecture* (1831). 'Early Saxon or modified Lombard' was the phrase she used to describe her church at Wreay (1842) and her church addition at Newton Arlosh (C), but for her mortuary chapel at Wreay she copied the newly rediscovered church at Perranzabuloe, thought then to be the most ancient in England. The fat naturalism of the carving seems strangely anticipatory of Arts and Crafts Byzantinism of about 1900. Its iconography, drawn almost wholly from the natural world and including fossil forms, reflects contemporary science through the *Natural Theology* (1802) of William Paley, a family friend: from Creation we infer the existence of an intelligent creator. So her church was pantheistic, rational, even taxonomic, but not yet evolutionary. Comparisons can be made with James Bateman's contemporary Geological Gallery at Biddulph Grange in Staffordshire, and with the Oxford Museum. The furnishings too are replete with symbolism, including pulpit and lectern made from semi-fossilized bog oak and left in tree form. The forward position of the altar at Wreay too seems startlingly prophetic, this time of mid-C20 liturgical theory; more realistically it shows her knowledge of Early Christian custom. 82

Another independent thinker was *R. W. Billings* (1813–74), best known as an antiquary (his *Carlisle Cathedral* came out in 1840) and architectural theorist. His church at Crosby-on-Eden (C; 1854) is crazily inventive, and his cemetery memorial to Peter Nicholson at Carlisle (1856) is like an unbalanced geometric theorem. A comparably licentious Gothic design is *Benjamin Band*'s Lowther mausoleum (W), 1857. 83

Losh and Billings stand out because the course of Victorian architecture, especially the vigorous field of ecclesiastical architecture, was hijacked into True Gothic in those very years by *A. W. N. Pugin*. His little Catholic church at Warwick Bridge (C; 1840–1) is a perfect document of the new attitude, the revival of an ideal English Gothic with religious fervour. In much the same mode and scale are St Catherine (R.C.) at Penrith (C), of 1849–50 by *Atkinson* of Carlisle, and the extensions of 1857 to *Ignatius Bonomi*'s R.C. church at Wigton (C; 1836–7). 80

In the next generation, the influx of Irish Catholics to the West Coast towns led to a grand series of churches by *E. W. Pugin*: Whitehaven (1865–8), Cleator Moor (1869–72) and Workington (1873–6). Wide, airy, level-roofed, with good sightlines and acoustics, they are very different from his father's Warwick Bridge. Maximum and immediate impact was the aim, not mystery. Whitehaven is the best of the three, with its daringly huge windows, though it has lost its bellcote and spire. E. W. Pugin's fourth church, at Barrow, is smaller and more hysterical, though still very effective with its great width and strong light accentuating the immediacy and power of the altar. 88

Where Pugin led, the Anglican church followed. *George Gilbert Scott*'s church at Ambleside (W; 1850–4) is a fine sample of his work, owing nothing to local style but standing proud in its own convictions. *Joseph Clarke*'s church at Cockermouth (C; 1852–4) is equally ambitious but lacks Scott's sure proportions. *J. S. Crowther* (1820–93) of Manchester was another medievalist of Puginian persuasion. Notable is his sweeping restoration of

Kendal parish church (W), and the incremental restoration of
1848–87, amounting almost to a rebuild, at Crosby Ravensworth
(W). *Butterfield* showed more individuality in his reconstructions
of the small churches at Lamplugh and Brigham (both C), and
in his fine restoration of St Bees (C), with a new crossing tower
87   and a characteristic polychrome internal E wall and screen.

This is the moment to introduce a local man, *Joseph Bintley* of
Kendal, who had an astonishing ability to copy other men's
styles. His St John, Beckermet (C; 1878–9), fearlessly polychrome, with a starkly prismatic font, could easily pass for Butterfield. At Underbarrow (1869 and later) his work is so like that
of Crowther that one wonders whether the records are wrong.
He was even prepared to do a convincing Georgian, in extensions to the churches at Ings (W; 1877) and Moresby (C; 1885–8).

Two major practices came to the fore in the mid- and Late
Victorian years. Dominating Westmorland and Lancashire were
Paley & Austin (the name varied as the practice evolved) of
Lancaster, a firm of national importance. The founder, *Edmund
Sharpe*, built in the region only one church, St Bridget (1840–2)
at Calder Bridge (C), but *E. G. Paley* was very active. A typical
Paley church might be St Anne at Thwaites (W; 1852–4), and a
better than typical one St James (1867–9) at Barrow (L). At
Barrow, as well as almost everything for the Furness Railway, the
firm designed shipyards, jute works, and housing including
Scottish-style tenements (*see* above). *Hubert Austin* had joined
Paley in 1867, but the industrial rocket of Barrow was beginning
to fizzle out, and they failed to get the town hall contract which
would have crowned their work there. Where the partnership did
shine was in a series of tip-top village churches: Finsthwaite
86   (L; 1873–4), Barbon (W; 1892–3), Field Broughton (L; 1892–4),
Flookburgh (L; 1897–1900), Natland (W; 1909–10). They are all
inventive and satisfying; it is hard to choose the best. More towny
is Dalton-in-Furness (L; 1883–5), with a superb tower. A neat,
p. 133   dateless simplicity is shown by their four temporary churches of
1878 in Barrow, one of which survives. *Huddart*'s little church
at Eskdale Green (C; 1891–2) is similar, as is the mission church
at Kirkland, Lamplugh (C) by *T. L. Banks & C. H. Townsend*
(1886).

Occupying an equivalent position in Cumberland to Paley &
Austin was *Charles John Ferguson* (1840–1904) of Carlisle, sometime in partnership with *J. A. Cory*. Ferguson's repertoire, like
theirs, included numerous churches new and restored, country
houses, public buildings. His work has a similarly high standard
of execution, marked perhaps by a certain opacity of texture. His
mountain church at Tebay (W; 1878–80) can be compared with
Finsthwaite, as could his major church of St Nicholas (1883) at
Whitehaven – though burnt and mostly demolished – with Paley
& Austin's at Dalton-in-Furness. Neither firm went in much for
reproduction Gothic, particularly in their furnishings, nor for
revived vernacular. A particular strength was the unfashionable
Norman style, coupled with an interest in vaulting. Cleator Moor
84   (1870–2) indeed is fully vaulted, and Bridekirk (1868–70) which

is happier in its proportions, partly so. Like Bintley, Ferguson seems to have enjoyed the occasional stylistic challenge, as in his church hall at Brampton (C) of 1895, where he followed *Philip Webb*'s only church (1877–8). 89

Charles Eaglesfield was another who could make a good shot at Norman, as at Ennerdale Bridge (C; 1858) and Maryport cemetery (C; *c.* 1855). Worth an individual mention is *James Murchie*'s church at Lindal-in-Furness (L; 1885–6), a design of some originality and quality of execution. Characteristic of a rapidly growing settlement is a church such as *Salvin*'s St John at Keswick (C), begun 1836, which has compressed a lot of evolution into a short time. The Anglican and Methodist churches at Arnside (L) have had to do likewise, as has St Mary Applethwaite at Windermere (W). *Lorimer*'s little church at Plumpton (C; 1907–8) is stylish, as are *W. D. Caröe*'s at Broughton Moor (C; 1905), and *J. H. Martindale* at Calthwaite (C; 1913), and his revamp of Threlkeld church (C) in 1911.

Few would undertake a pilgrimage to Cumbria for its Victorian churches, but they are often unusually complete and well-preserved. Skirwith (C; 1856 by *Frederick & Horace Francis*), Longsleddale (W; *Miles Thompson* 1863), Great Asby (W; *W. & J. Hay* 1865–6), Ivegill (C; *R. J. Withers* 1868), Hethersgill (C; *Habershon & Brock* 1875–7), Distington (C; *Hay & Henderson* 1884–6), Haverigg (Millom, C; *Settle & Farmer* 1889–91), Martindale new church (W; *J. A. Cory* 1880–2), and Chapel Stile (Langdales, W; ditto, 1857–8), are all valuable as consistent and complete samples of Victoriana; the last three also worth seeing also for their modern stained glass (*see* below, p. 75).

VICTORIAN CHAPELS include a memorable one for the Congregationalists at Carlisle, built in 1842–3, by *John Nichol* from 85
Edinburgh. It follows the common Nonconformist formula of a showy street front, often with twin entrances, and not much else, like the Congregational chapels in Cockermouth (C; *C. W. Eaglesfield* 1850), Kendal (W; *Stephen Shaw* 1896), and Bowness-on-Windermere (W; *Robert Walker* 1879–80). The Methodists are at their grandest at Penrith (C; 1873) and at Alston (C; 1868), and boldest at Workington (C), by *Charles W. Bell* (1890) in Renaissance style, with a tower and dome. Exceedingly spiky and churchy is *T. L. Banks*'s Methodist church in Whitehaven (1877). Small country chapels, mostly Methodist and minimally Gothic, are only occasionally picked out in the Gazetteer, though the former Presbyterian chapel at Bewcastle (1891) is remarked for its exceeding remoteness. Of a classical chapel type is the Temperance Hall of 1856 at Kirkby Stephen (W). 99

Particularly good among the CEMETERIES is that at Dalston Road in Carlisle, by *J. M. & J. Hay* of Liverpool, 1855–6, a pleasing mix of formal layout and informal planting. Cockermouth cemetery (C), of 1856 by *Charles Eaglesfield*, is well preserved, as are those at Egremont (C), Penrith (C), and Wigton (C). Barrow cemetery (L), set out by *Edward Kemp* in 1872–4, was provided with a fine set of *Paley & Austin* buildings, but some have gone.

Cumbria is not outstandingly rich in VICTORIAN STAINED GLASS, nor perhaps is it desirable in some surroundings. Much is by Northern and local firms. *William Wailes* of Newcastle (fl. 1840–81, latterly as *Wailes & Strang*) often supplied the E window, the first to be fitted; e.g. Caldbeck (C). Blue is the usual overall tint. Wailes got the job in 1856 of restoring the medieval glass in the tracery of the great E window at Carlisle, but the main lights (1859–61) are by *John Hardman Powell*, as are several others in the Cathedral. Skirwith (C) has a full set of *Wailes* glass, and so (to *Butterfield*'s specifications) does St Bees. *John Scott & Son* of Carlisle (fl. *c.* 1845–70) failed to get any significant glass in the Cathedral, though they did carry out *Owen Jones*'s stunning decorative scheme for the choir ceiling. Their glass at Irton (C) of the late 1860s and 1870s is especially good. *Abbott & Co.* of Lancaster was a prolific and long-lived firm, established in 1860 and active, with strong full-blooded work, into the late C20, e.g. Allithwaite (L), Arnside (W), Whitehaven (C). *Shrigley & Hunt* of Lancaster (fl. 1870–late C20) are the best-known of the local firms, particularly associated, over many years, with Paley & Austin, e.g. at Flookburgh (L). Their W windows at Cartmel (L) are a personal favourite. The work of *A.* and *F. Burrow* of Sandside near Milnthorpe (fl. 1850s–60s) is quite bad; e.g. Beetham (W).

Of the national firms *Morris & Co.* is pre-eminent. Thanks to the friendship between George Howard, 9th Earl of Carlisle, and *Philip Webb*, Brampton (C) has a unique set of Morris glass, installed over a long period and illustrating the firm's changing styles. The E windows at Staveley (W; 1881) and Troutbeck (W; 1872) are exceptionally beautiful in their different ways, as is the one at Kirkbampton (C; 1871), though tragically deteriorated. More animated than Morris is the glass of *Henry Holiday* (1839–1927; he built a house for himself at Hawkshead, L). His best is at Casterton (W; 1893–9), where it is combined with wall painting, and also at Keswick (C) and Muncaster (C). But now we are getting near the Arts and Crafts, for which *see* p. 68.

MONUMENTS and SCULPTURE of note include the installation by the self-taught *Thomas Bland* (1798–1865), who opened his Image Garden at Reagill (Crosby Ravensworth, W) in 1837. It was overcrowded with statues of worthies from every age, nymphs, urns, lions and greyhounds. Niches displayed his paintings and geological collections. His figures may be dumpy, their stances awkward, but sometimes, like his lion and globe at Shap Wells (W), they have life. The sculptor *David Dunbar* (1793–1866), baptized at Dumfries, was a wanderer. In 1809 he was working at Lowther (W) for Paul Nixson, and in 1821 he was in Carlisle, where he carved the touching likeness of his infant daughter Elizabeth (†1821), but in between he had been in London with Chantrey. At Wreay (C) he modelled the statue of Katherine Losh †1835 on a sketch by her sister *Sara Losh*, with portrait medallions to their parents; and at Crosby Ravensworth he made the entertaining memorial to George Gibson †1835. Prominent in the middle of Wigton (C) is the fountain of 1872–3 commissioned by George Moore (on whom *see also* p. 67) in memory of his first wife, by *J. T. Knowles Sen.*, with reliefs by *Thomas Woolner*. Moore (1806–76) is himself commemorated by a bust by *John Adams-Acton* in the old church at Mealsgate (C), with memorials to both his wives – a memorable ensemble in a tiny, almost lost building. Another bust of Moore by the same artist is in the Cathedral. Here also are Adams-Acton's effigy of Bishop Waldegrave †1869, effigies of Dean Close by *H. H. Arm-stead*, 1885, and Bishop Goodwin by *Hamo Thornycroft*, 1894, and the strange leathery tablet to Bishop Bardsley by *Andrea Carlo Lucchesi*, 1906. Lucchesi also made the bronze portrait medallions on the Cropper memorial at Kendal (W) and the Ruskin memorial at Keswick (C). Lowther church (W) is full of funerary sculpture, including the huge white marble double sarcophagus (unsigned) of William and Augusta, Earl and Countess Lonsdale, †1844 and 1838, the builders of Lowther Castle, and a magnificent brass by *Matthews & Sons* of London to Henry, 3rd Earl of Lonsdale †1876. Lord Frederick Cavendish, assassinated in 1882, is commemorated in Cartmel Priory by an effigy by *Thomas Woolner* and by a statue in Barrow by *Albert Bruce Joy*. Public sculpture articulates Barrow's Victorian townscape: James Ramsden's statue by *M. Noble*, 1872, with evocative reliefs showing the transformation of the town between 1848 and 1871, and Henry Schneider's by *Percy Wood*, 1891. 103

DECORATED CROSSES in Anglo-Saxon or Viking style are a Cumbrian speciality, paralleling revivals in Ireland and Scotland. *Sara Losh* led the way *c.* 1840 with her version of the Bewcastle cross at Wreay (C). Scholarly replicas of ancient Crosses, acting like Wreay as both archaeological experiments and practical memorials, followed in the 1880s and 1890s at Aspatria, Bassenthwaite and Bowness-on-Solway (all C), the moving force being the antiquarian vicar W. S. Calverley. When Ruskin died in 1900 a cross designed by *W. G. Collingwood* and made by *H. T. Miles* was considered appropriate for his grave in Coniston churchyard (L). It was made in hard smooth green slate from Tilberthwaite, which seems to stay crisp forever. The model was the Irton Cross, not copied exactly, but now to reappear simultaneously as a Boer War memorial at Millom (C), in Kendal churchyard (W), and at Irton itself (C). A variant, with inset portrait heads, is the Boer War memorial at Eamont Bridge (W). The great proliferation of 102 Celtic crosses as memorials is probably due to Canon Rawnsley and his wife (*see* p. 70). Crosthwaite churchyard (C) presents a forest of them amongst the funereal cypresses, including their own.

The tradition continued after the First World War, whose memorials in Cumbria seldom take figurative form (the bronze reliefs by *Alex Carrick* on *Sir Robert Lorimer*'s abstract column of 1928 at Workington (C) are an honourable exception). Good examples are at Bowness-on-Windermere (W), Brougham Ninekirks (W), Grasmere (W), Hawkshead (L), Heversham (W), Kendal (K Shoes company memorial), Penrith (C) and Ulverston (L). Collingwood was the guiding force, though they are rarely signed. The memorials by *Beattie* of Carlisle seem in contrast almost light-hearted in their rough whiteness and the asymmetry of their inscriptions. The one at Croglin (C) is known to have been designed by *J. H. Martindale*.

Of MUNICIPAL BUILDINGS, only Barrow (L) has a really grand Victorian town hall, of 1877–87 by *W. H. Lynn*, and even that went off at half-cock. Alston (C) has a proud town hall, 1857 by *A. B. Higham*, but scaled to a small town. Kendal's is on a street corner, i.e. is not free-standing, and was arrived at in stages by adapting Francis & George Webster's Assembly Rooms of 1824–5, first by *George Webster*, 1858–9, and then by *Stephen Shaw*, 1891–3. Penrith Town Hall (C) is surprisingly good, considering that it was made out of two houses by *J. J. Knewstubb*, the council's Surveyor and Engineer, in 1905–6. The only significant COVERED MARKET is Carlisle's, by *Arthur Cawston* and *Joseph Graham*, 1887–9 etc. The triple-arched iron and glass roof is by *A. T. Walmisley*.

MUSEUMS, as so often, had their origins in private collections. John Senhouse's collection of Roman inscribed stones, described by Camden and Cotton in 1599, is now in Maryport's Roman Museum (C), housed in a naval battery of 1885. More unusual was Peter Crosthwaite's museum of 1780 at Keswick (C), gathered as an unashamed trap for tourists; now in an appropriately eclectic Arts-and-Crafts building by *Thomas Hodgson*, 1897–8 and 1906. Tullie House Museum at Carlisle, by *C. J. Ferguson* with the City Surveyor *W. Howard-Smith*, was opened in 1893. The exteriors are strappy Jacobean, more old-fashioned than the C17 Tullie House itself, and the interiors are cheerful with curly ironwork and *Craven Dunnill* tiles. Carnegie LIBRARIES of the first years of the C20, an easily recognizable type, are at Cockermouth, Kendal, Whitehaven and Workington.

Perhaps the most interesting EDUCATIONAL BUILDING, though a minor work, is *Butterfield*'s New College Hall of 1863 at St Bees (C), for the theological college founded in 1816 by Bishop Law of Chester. It is now used by St Bees School, which expanded further from its Tudor and early C19 buildings into a fine complex of 1886, 1899 and 1906–7 by *Austin & Paley*. Appleby Grammar School (W) is another that developed from C17 beginnings into a big Victorian complex, of 1886–7 by *George Watson* of Penrith. Two sets of over-designed ALMSHOUSES are at Milnthorpe (W): by *J. Bintley*, 1884 and (probably) *Eli Cox c.* 1881. By Cox also is the row so prominent by the Kendal riverside (W) of Organ Works, residence, and Sleddall Jubilee Almshouses and chapel, 1884 and 1887.

There is not a lot to say on PARKS. Such is the availability of open land that not many places have felt the need to provide them. Barrow Park (*Thomas Mawson*, 1904–7 and 1920), Penrith's Castle Park (1923), Kendal's Abbot Hall Park (1897), and Carlisle's Bitts Park can be contrasted with the rough open hillside round the monument to Sir John Barrow which serves – very popularly – as Ulverston's park, or the Serpentine Walks above Kendal.

COMMERCIAL ARCHITECTURE includes a strong representation by HOTELS. Each of the prime locations in the Lake District has one, often showing scant sensitivity to the *genius loci*. Low Wood on Windermere (W) of *c.* 1824, 1843, *c.* 1859 etc. was the first big one. Windermere Hotel (*Abraham Pattinson* builder, *Miles Thompson* architect) was opened by John Riggs, coach proprietor, in time for the arrival of the railway in 1847. Particularly gross is the station hotel at Keswick (by *John Ross*, 1869), and amusingly self-important the one (1894, probably by *Arthur Huddart*) by Beckfoot Halt on the little Ravenglass & Eskdale Railway (Eskdale, C). There are big *Pattinson* hotels on Windermere at Lakeside (Newby Bridge, L), Bowness (W; the Old England of 1869 and 1879), and Waterhead (Ambleside, W; 1895), as well as the Ferry House Hotel of 1880–1 on the w side (Sawrey, L). The Prince of Wales at Grasmere (W; *Miles Thompson*, between 1855 and 1863), the Inn on the Lake at Glenridding (W), the Borrowdale Hotel (1866) by Lodore Falls (Grange-in-Borrowdale, C) all share a certain joyless lumpishness, too big in too-dark stone, with meretricious detail, and are frequently disfigured by tacked-on sun lounges and air conditioning. The Crown and Mitre in Carlisle (*George Dale Oliver*, 1903–5), although hardly pretty, is better, with some rich fitting-out. Gilsland Spa Hotel (C; *James Stewart*, 1859–60) is on its own, an oasis of popular culture in the northern wilderness, though quite a grim piece of architecture. Shap Wells Hotel (1830–3, altered 1914–16) is another unexpected watering place, also grim but worth visiting for the obelisk of 1842 with naïve sculpture by *Thomas Bland*.

The best place to enjoy exuberant Victorian STREET ARCHITECTURE is Keswick (W). Here among the mountains, with a wide palette of coloured stone at hand for structural polychromy, not to mention coloured bricks and patent materials like *Harkewitz* tiles, our Victorian forebears could let themselves go. Windermere (W) and Ambleside (W) are more sombre in colour, Arnside (W) and Grange-over-Sands (L) lighter in tone. The BUILDERS include *Thomas & Isaac Hodgson*, and *F. & W. Green*, of Keswick, the *Pattinsons* and *William Harrison* of Windermere, and *Grisenthwaite* of Penrith.

Among VICTORIAN COUNTRY HOUSES – surprisingly, perhaps – there is nothing as preposterously self-confident as the early C19 Conishead or Holme Eden, though the monstrous Stone Cross at Ulverston (L; 1874, by *J. W. Grundy*) runs them close. Irton Hall (C), a sprawling house by *G. E. Grayson*, also 1874, is rather gloomy. *Anthony Salvin* (1799–1881) was kept busy restoring castles for the landed gentry: Greystoke (C; 1837–45 and 1875–8), Newbiggin (W; 1844), Muncaster (C; 1862–6 and 1872–4), Naworth (C; 1844–51), Hutton-in-the-Forest (C; 1862–7, following *George Webster*). He was favoured too by the different branches of the Marshall family at Patterdale (W) and Derwent Island (Keswick, C), as well as for churches at Keswick and Patterdale. Much of this work is pre-Victorian in spirit. George Moore (1806–76) of Wigton transformed Whitehall

(Mealsgate, C) into a *Salvin* mansion with *Nesfield* gardens, but their works there have largely gone. Barbon Manor (W; 1863 by *E. M. Barry*), a sophisticated French-style building in the forest, is a hunting lodge not intended for permanent occupation, and often informal. Witherslack Hall for Lord Derby (1874 by *Paley & Austin*) is another hunting lodge, deliberately quite rough and ready inside, and so is the Earl of Lonsdale's tin Bungalow in Martindale (W), 1910.

'Offcomers' from Liverpool and Manchester often brought in an architect for their Lakeland homes. *Waterhouse*'s two on Derwentwater (Fawe Park, 1856–8, and Lingholm of 1871–5, both Keswick (C)) are, to use Grevel Lindop's words, somewhat funereal. His Rothay Holme at Ambleside (W), of 1854 and 1890, manages a heavy cheeriness. Underscar near Crosthwaite (C), *c.* 1856–63 by *Charles Reed* (later *Verelst*), is an Italianate set piece, with Osborne towers, a splendid conservatory, and *Edward Kemp* gardens. *G. Faulkner Armitage* of Altrincham built Pullwoods (1890–1 etc.), one of the plum Windermere villas at Wray (L), and in 1906 carried out an unattractive enlargement of the mansion attached to Calder Abbey (C). Netherwood at Grange-over-Sands (L) was done by *Willink & Thicknesse* of Liverpool, 1893, and in *c.* 1886 *R. Knill Freeman* of Bolton built Bryerswood (dem.) at Sawrey (L), all decorative timber framing and tile-hanging. At Graythwaite (L) Freeman was assisted by *Dan Gibson* and, in the garden, by *Thomas Mawson*, his first major job. Gibson and Mawson went briefly into partnership in 1897. At Langdale Chase at Troutbeck (W), of 1889–94, *J. L. Ball* and *J. T. Lee* of Manchester worked with *Joseph Pattinson* of Windermere, and again there is a *Mawson* garden. Meanwhile in 1871 Ruskin, the sage of the age, had taken up residence at Brantwood, Coniston (L), to which he added until his death in 1900.

Of the local firms, *Paley & Austin*'s country houses are less pleasing than their churches; their eternal quality seems inappropriate. Holker (L; 1871–3) is much the grandest. Like their work at Underley (Kirkby Lonsdale, W; 1872), it is only part of the house, replacing *Webster* work. *Ferguson*'s country house work is similarly excellent but unyielding, and has not fared particularly well. Armathwaite Hall (1881) at Bassenthwaite (C) serves well as a grand hotel but is hard to imagine as a home. The later work at Muncaster (C; 1880s) again seems more public than private, as does the drawing-room wing at Newbiggin (W; 1890). Kirklinton (C; 1875, with *Cory*) has been partly demolished, as have some of his additions to Dalston Hall (C; 1899–1900).

Philip Webb's two houses near Brampton (C), Green Lane of 1877 and Four Gables of 1875–7, fairly minor in themselves, broke new ground. Both are remarkably wilful, taking the local style and rethinking it from first principles.

The end of Victoria's long reign and the turn of the century heralded a golden moment in English house design. Emblematic are three famous ARTS AND CRAFTS HOUSES just S of Bowness-on-Windermere (W): Blackwell by *Baillie Scott*, and Broadleys and Moor Crag by *Voysey*. All three were started in 1898–9. They were widely publicized at the time, and have grown in stature since. Their language was revolutionary: white simplicity, with long ranges of plainly mullioned windows under sweeping roofs with big chimneys. Inside all is cheerful lightness, low ceilings, plank doors and latches (beautifully designed of course), window seats and inglenooks. Their stylistic derivation is upwards from the farmhouse, not downwards from the stately home. Of the three *Baillie Scott*'s is the most complex, with its occasional historicism and clever blurring of conventional room divisions, but Moor Crag achieves a perfection that is given to few to realize.

112

The Lake District, and the E shore of Windermere in particular, was fertile ground for the style because the local vernacular was already celebrated, and because holiday villas could be informal, not needing the full paraphernalia of a country house. *Pattinsons* of Windermere built the Voysey houses, and they were quick to learn. Gossel Ridding (also Bowness), built in 1907–11 for G. H. Pattinson by his brother *Joseph Pattinson*, is an obvious derivative, although too much the builder's showpiece, losing the sweet simplicity essential to the style.* *Thomas Mawson* was another who learned on the job. The Corbels in Windermere was his own house, of 1900, followed there by Burrowfield and Shrublands. *Dan Gibson* and Mawson took up the style at Brockhole (Troutbeck, W; 1897–1902), which like Blackwell still has a few historicisms, and Gibson went on to build Dawstone (Windermere, 1904), White Craggs (Ambleside, *c*. 1900), and finally Birket Houses at Winster (W), 1907–8, before his early death. *Francis Whitwell* and *W. L. Dolman* extrapolated Gibson's style but, like Pattinson at Gossel Ridding, neither could resist making them too rich. The perfect holiday house was *Henry Holiday*'s own Betty Fold, of 1907–8 at Hawkshead (L), which takes an appropriately eccentric slant on the white ideal, as does *J. F. Curwen*'s Horncop at Heversham (W), 1899–1900. High Moss at Portinscale (Keswick, C) by *W. H. Ward*, 1901, springs from an overlapping artistic circle, independently reaching the same conclusions. Ward (1865–1924) and Herbert Luck North had quit Lutyens's office in 1898, setting up an association called the Bedford Square Group. Before joining Lutyens in 1894 Ward had worked with Dan Gibson under Ernest George & Peto. *North*'s one Lake District house is Keldwith at Windermere (1910–11), more imaginative and lavish than his Welsh houses, and better publicized. *Dolman*'s Waterbeck at Windermere (1913), like High Moss and Keldwith, spreads angled wings to make the so-called sunshine V, though in the region this could be traced back to 1798 and Derwent Bay.

p. 451

110

Out on a limb in Eskdale (C) is Gatehouse, 1896–1901, by *Arthur Huddart* for J. H. Rea (whose nephew built Keldwith), with a *Mawson* garden. *Robert Lorimer*'s Brackenburgh of 1902–3 (Plumpton, C) still belongs to the Victorian age in scale and function, even if leaning towards Arts and Crafts in its detail.

---

* Pattinsons built dozens of white sub-Voysey houses to let in and around Windermere, right through until the 1970s.

Grizedale Hall (Satterthwaite, L), by *Walker, Carter & Walker* of Windermere, 1905, for Harold Brocklebank of Cunard, was again Baronial in concept. It lasted a mere half-century. *Lutyens*'s weird Abbey House of 1913–14, by Furness Abbey (L), is unclassifiable; neither country house nor hotel, austerely designed and sparingly detailed.

This section must close with a celebration of the CRAFTS that make these houses such a pleasure. Gatehouse, unusually, displays the work of Manchester firms, but there were plenty of local ones. The *Keswick School of Industrial Arts (KSIA)* was started by the Rev. Hardwicke Rawnsley and his wife Edith in 1883–4 as a social as well as artistic enterprise. Housed initially in Crosthwaite Parish Hall (C; 1875 by *C. J. Ferguson*), the school moved to purpose-built premises by *Paley, Austin & Paley* of 1893–4. Neither seems perfect for the School's ideals. *Arthur Simpson* (1857–1922), who worked with Faulkner Armitage in Altrincham for a while, founded his hand-crafted furniture firm in 1885, as well as teaching at the KSIA. Simpson built himself Little Holme in Sedbergh Road, Kendal (W), 1909–10, designed by his friend *C. F. A. Voysey*. Simpson's domestic work can be enjoyed at Blackwell and Broadleys. Staveley church (W) has Simpson woodwork, and the work of his classes is at St Martin's, Bowness-on-Windermere, at Burneside (W) and at Crosby Ravensworth (W). Amongst woodcarvers may be named *Joseph Kilbride* of Windermere (Barbon church (W), Gossel Ridding in Bowness), and *George Fendley* of Carlisle at the churches of Threlkeld (C) and Calthwaite (C; by *J. H. Martindale*). *Harry Hems*'s carving can be seen at Distington church (C), *Alec Miller*'s at Urswick (L). *Robert Fell* did the carving at Ings church (W), including his own portrait. Other designers at the School included *Harold Stabler*. Langdale Linen, started in 1883 by Albert Fleming and Marion Twelves in Elterwater, moved to Crosthwaite in 1889 under the aegis of the KSIA. Influenced by the Langdale Linen Industry was The Spinnery at Bowness-on-Windermere (W), set up by Annie Garnett in 1889, with a purpose-built shop of 1912.

A summary of the ideals of the Arts and Crafts movement is provided by the loving rehabilitation of Swarthmoor Hall (L) by *Emma Clarke Abraham* in 1912–14. All the alterations, including her own handiwork, are conscientiously and prominently recorded on the spot.

FROM THE FIRST WORLD WAR TO THE PRESENT

Evidence for the continuance of the Arts and Crafts ideal after *c.* 1920 is provided by Gatesbield (1926) at Windermere. It was designed and built by *Stanley* and *Emily Davies* themselves, using natural and local materials. Much of the carving was done by

Emily. Pubs in and around Carlisle provide a bigger and more official example. 1916 saw the building of a vast munitions factory on the Scottish border near Gretna, employing at its height in 1917 nearly 20,000 people. An unanticipated side effect was the descent of hordes of weekend drinkers into Carlisle, causing alarm to the citizenry and hazardous working on Monday mornings. The STATE MANAGEMENT SCHEME (1916) of pubs and breweries was the Government's response. In *Harry Redfern* (1861–1950) they got the right architect, able to address the problem creatively with an eclectic series of Arts and Crafts-inspired pubs. Standing was discouraged by shorter bars surrounded by tables. Open rooms replaced small partitioned areas. Women were welcomed, often with a separate entrance to an upstairs room, and wholesome entertainment was on offer, such as a bowling green. The Apple Tree in Lowther Street (1925) was the first new Carlisle pub, followed by the Horse and Farrier (1927–8) on Orton Road, the Cumberland (1928) on Botchergate, and the Rose and Crown (1930) at Upperby. Styles were generally English and comfortably historical, but The Crescent of 1931 was white and gold and Moorish, the Earl Grey of 1934–5 is Deco, with chrome doors and patches of diagonal brick. The Redfern, Etterby (1939), was designed not by Redfern but by his former assistant *Joseph Seddon* as a tribute. The scheme was wound up in 1972.

p. 258

The slick rebuilding of Warwick Hall (C) in 1930–4 by *Guy Elwes* is a landmark. Although Neo-Georgian in its elements, it is unmistakably Deco in the way they are put together. The MODERN MOVEMENT arrived with Brackenfell (1936–7) at Brampton, and Cockley Moor at Matterdale, both houses by *Sir Leslie Martin* and *Sadie Speight*.

Of inter-war PUBLIC BUILDINGS, Barrow-in-Furness library (L) by *J. A. Charles*, 1915–22, is ponderous Beaux-Arts. Westmorland County Hall at Kendal, 1937–9 by *Verner O. Rees*, is a prominent if dullish specimen of official architecture of the period. Ulverston's Coronation Hall, 1914–20, is more festive. WAR MEMORIALS are described above, p. 65. CHURCHES of the period include the ambitious rebuild of St John on Barrow Island (L) by *Seely & Paget*, 1934–5. They also did St Barnabas on the Raffles estate in Carlisle, 1935–6. Both are Mediterranean white and overcomplicated without, calm and ordered within.

There is much good STAINED GLASS, further evidence if any is needed for a continuance of Arts and Crafts principles. For rich streakiness go to Great Asby (W) for *Leonard Walker*'s window (1929), Bardsea (L) for *Wilhelmina Geddes*'s apse windows (1924), or Arnside Methodist Church (L) for *Norris Roscoe*'s work of 1920–1, made by *Barrowclough & Sanders* of Lancaster. *Edward Payne*'s windows in Arnside parish church, 1948 etc., are plated, like the window at Great Asby, to create subtle colour combinations. Gentler in colour are *Joan Howson* and *Caroline Townshend*'s windows variously at Carlisle Cathedral, Seascale (C) and Skelsmergh (W), which resemble the work of *Christopher Whall* at Killington (W), and that of Whall's

daughter *Veronica* at Aldingham (L) and Keswick (C). *Abbott &
Co.* had a good C20 phase, with strong colouring e.g. at Whitehaven St Nicholas (C) and St Mary, Allithwaite (L). Richest of
all in colouring are the hieratic *Earley & Co.* windows at Cleator
Moor (R.C.; C) in the style of Harry Clarke. For quirky composition see *Alice Gordon*'s window in the generally dull collection at Kendal (1924), and again at Holme (W), or climb up to
Colton (L) for the little windows by *H. Warren Wilson* and *Gamon
& Humphry*. *Shrigley & Hunt*'s latest, almost abstract style can
be seen at St Thomas Kendal and Aldingham, and there is a fine
set by *A. K. Nicholson* at St Aidan, Carlisle.

Taking a view of LONG-TERM CHANGES, what is surprising is
that a land that was celebrated for the sturdy independence of its
statesman or yeomen, a region noted for its relative freedom from
major landowners, is now to a great extent under the control of
national bodies with property portfolios. This is the result of two
strongly opposed but complementary forces: that of exploitation,
and that of preservation. The Northern industrial cities, especially Manchester, eyed up the Lake District for WATER. The first
battle, in the 1880s, was over Thirlmere. Manchester's proposed
scheme called into existence a fierce opposition led by the
Rev. Hardwicke Rawnsley and the Lake District Defence Society
he had founded in 1883. Curious to note, the society's strongest
support was in Manchester, Liverpool and London, not the
Lakes – indeed Rawnsley himself was an offcomer; this is a recurring pattern. The scheme was unstoppable, the lake was dammed
into a reservoir, the landscape – all now owned by United
Utilities in succession to Manchester – depopulated and forested,
with new roads. Thirlmere was followed in 1919 *et seq.* by the
Haweswater scheme, and now many of the lakes are tapped.

Large-scale afforestation with conifers was also the prerogative
of the FORESTRY COMMISSION, set up in 1919 with powers of
compulsory purchase. The head of Ennerdale was planted from
1925–6, and the landscape effect of similar planting is obvious
when driving over Whinlatter from Keswick to Cockermouth.
For many years anti-conservation, indeed anti-people, the
Commission now actively woos the public, e.g. at Grizedale
Forest.

The NATIONAL TRUST represents the opposing force. It was
founded in 1895 by Octavia Hill, Sir Robert Hunter and Canon
Rawnsley. Brandlehow on Derwentwater was its first Lake District property (1902); it now owns a high proportion of the Lake
District. Beatrix Potter, a close friend of Rawnsley, became a
major landowner, bequeathing fourteen farms and 4,000 acres
to the Trust. Her concern for farming and farmers is still
influential, but the Trust in the Lake District is driven first by the
desire to preserve landscape, and there have been significant losses
of buildings in its care (eg. Claife Station, Sawrey (L)).

A new generation of visitors was catered for by the YOUTH
HOSTELS ASSOCIATION, which came to Britain in the 1930s.
Their Cumbrian portfolio of twenty-six hostels and fourteen
camping barns includes the *Websters*' delightful Esthwaite Lodge
at Hawkshead and *Joseph Pocklington*'s best house at Grange-in-

Borrowdale. It is interesting to see the early YHA feeling its way towards the conservationist policies which would become the norm after the War. Pattinson's barn conversion at Elterwater in 1939, while it did keep the original building, would be considered heavy-handed today, but in his Eskdale hostel of 1937–8 *John Dower* pioneered fitting-in but modern architecture.

Dower was one of the principal protagonists of NATIONAL PARKS, drafting the Council for the Preservation of Rural England's proposal in 1938 and continuing the campaign after the Second World War (just before his early death). The Act came into force in 1949, and the LAKE DISTRICT NATIONAL PARK (LDNP), all 880 square miles of it, was designated in 1951. The Park Board has tight planning control within its borders, ensuring that buildings are preserved and that new buildings fit in: local stone, pitched slate roofs, vernacular language. At the Park's boundaries, as the teashop quotient drops, so barn conversions are suddenly ubiquitous.

If the Second World War affected the region relatively lightly, the same cannot be said of the COLD WAR that followed it. For a few years at the end of the 1950s indeed Cumberland was in the front line. The former TNT factory at Sellafield, on the W coast, was already the site of a nuclear reactor and now was chosen to produce weapons-grade plutonium. This is Britain's major nuclear landscape. Meanwhile a 9,000-acre swathe of the northernmost waste at Spadeadam, between Gilsland and the Scottish border, was chosen for the development of the Blue Streak missile. The indestructible, mysterious remains of the test structures in the cold Northern forest are an extraordinary memorial to that era of bluff and double-bluff. In the far NW at Bowness-on-Solway (C) the Anthorn Array of tall stayed radio masts, erected *c.* 1965, communicates with nuclear submarines. At Barrow the enormous Devonshire Dock Hall was erected in 1985 by *J. T. James & Partners* for building Trident nuclear submarines. An ongoing consequence, as every lover of the Lakes will know, is the use of mountain valleys by the RAF for low-flying practice.

The MOTORWAY AGE, inaugurated by the Preston Bypass in 1958, changed the face of Britain. The M6 through Cumberland and Westmorland was constructed in the late 1960s, narrowly skirting both the Yorkshire Dales and the Lake District National Parks and threading its way on two levels through the Lune gorge s of Tebay. Killington Lake Services (W; 1972), a clever building in itself, is beautifully situated to be invisible from the motorway but to command a fine view; a very different concept from the landmark Modernism of Forton (Lancaster) Services in Lancashire. Westmorland Services at Tebay (W; 1972 by *Gordon Stables*, and 1993 by *Unwin Jones Partnership*) likewise keeps low, under big pitched roofs.

CUMBRIA was created in 1974 from the union of Cumberland and Westmorland with Lancashire-across-the-Sands. Also included was a small area of the Yorkshire Dales including Sedbergh and Dent (for which *see The Buildings of England, Yorkshire West Riding: Leeds, Bradford and the North*). The Furness and

Cartmel part of Lancashire had not made much sense since the old route across the Sands fell out of use, and the union was anticipated as long ago as 1804 by the Quakers, and in modified form by the Carlisle Diocese in 1856. The late C20 increase in prosperity evident over much of the country is not so noticeable here. Cumbria in 2005 had, along with Cornwall, one of the lowest average incomes *per capita* in the UK, though there is an island of serious money at Windermere. From an architectural point of view this is no bad thing.

If we consider now the first couple of decades of POST-WAR ARCHITECTURE, a welcome sign of optimism is the playful Rose-hill Theatre at Moresby (C) near Whitehaven of 1959, for Sir Nicholas Sekers by *Gavin Paterson & Son* and *Oliver Messel*. The 1960s era of steel, flat roofs, pilotis and glass had little impact. Carlisle's Civic Centre by *Charles B. Pearson, Son & Partners* (1960–3) is the chief exponent, wholeheartedly of its time. Others are relatively small beer, including schools at Alston (1957), Cockermouth (1958) and Egremont (1962–5) by the *Cumberland County Architect's Department* under first *J. H. Haughan* then *D. W. Dickenson*. The 1960s Provincial Insurance building in Kendal by *Basil Ward* of *Murray, Ward & Partners*, has been toned down in a conversion to flats, but Peter Scott's own house, Long Dales near Bowness-on-Windermere (W) also by *Basil Ward* (1961), is as confrontational now as it was then, as is *Brian Dockray*'s own house, Skewbarrow Top in Kendal, 1964, which hangs over a cliff face. Both are notably successful inside.

Clough Williams-Ellis took a completely different direction with his rebuild of Dalton Hall (1968–71), near Burton-in-Kendal (W). This is a proper classical country house with pediments, giant pilasters and sash windows. Perfect in photographs, it is a stagy illusion: the scale is small, the diagonal views unsatisfactory. Blackberry Hill at Beetham (W), five houses in a shallow crescent by *N. Keith Scott* of the *Building Design Partnership*, *c.* 1976, shows that the Modernist ideal was by no means dead. In contrast, *Frederick Gibberd & Partners'* housing at Low Fell-side (Kendal, W) of *c.* 1974 is notable for the reintroduction of pitched roofs and roughcast.

Taking a middle road were the local firm of *Gill, Dockray, Rhodes & Moore*: 'Few counties have firms of architects who specialize in producing modern buildings for their own area which at the same time carry on the local vernacular tradition' (John Martin Robinson). The Pearson Freshwater Laboratories by Ferry House, Sawrey (L), 1967 by *Gill & Rhodes*, the little Bank in Ambleside (W) by *Dockray & Moore*, 1967, Shepherds' boat-yard and pleasure dome (1975) at Bowness-on-Windermere (W), by *John Moore* – all are worthwhile buildings.

CHURCHES after 1945 include several minimally Romanesque R.C. examples by *Wilfrid C. Mangan*, e.g. the attractive model-like Grasmere (W), 1964–5. The former seminary chapel at Underley Hall, Kirkby Lonsdale (W), 1964–5 by *William White* and *John Sheridon* of the *Building Design Partnership*, was praised by Pevsner for its impressive, severe and exacting design. Similarly cryptic is *Weightman & Bullen*'s R.C. church at Milnthorpe (w), 1970, although once penetrated it houses some interesting artworks. SCULPTURE by the long-lived and prolific *Josefina de Vasconcellos* (1904–2005), sometime resident of Ambleside and of Isel, frequently of fibreglass, is in several Cumbrian churches: Ambleside, Cartmel, Greystoke, St Bees.

Several communities marked the Millennium with new STAINED GLASS in their church. Millennium windows tend to celebrate niceness and not much else: local scenery and wildlife, maybe a shepherd and sheepdog – e.g. those by *Alex Haynes* at Boltongate (C) and Rosley (C). Stronger stuff is the set of 1975–81 by *Jane Gray* at Martindale (W). *Christine Boyce*'s window of 2002 at St George, Millom (C), commemorating the poet Norman Nicholson, all deepest blues, is splendid, and the *Peter Strong* window, also 2002, nearby at Haverigg even better.   117
The rebuilt St Michael, Workington, has an unusually coherent narrative and figurative scheme of *c.* 2000 by *Roy Comber* of *Pendle Stained Glass* (E) and *John Lawson* for *Goddard & Gibbs* of London.

The only postscript needed is the reconstruction of St Nicholas, Whitehaven, after a fire of 1971, and the rebuilding inside the burnt-out shell of St Michael at Workington (C), 1994–2000 by *John Bailey*. Holm Cultram Abbey (C), burnt out in 2006, is set to follow.

LOSSES since the 1967 edition include *Rickman*'s one remaining church in Carlisle, and the closure of several other parish churches. The Mechanics' Institute at Wigton whose pediment sculpture Pevsner enjoyed has gone, and so has most of Netherhall at Maryport. Planning control means that a case like Cliburn Hall (W), comprehensively trashed in architectural terms in 1966, is a rarity, although the threatened demolition of Brockhole at Troutbeck – by the LDNP no less – shows that it can still happen.

PUBLIC ART was an essential element in the regeneration of Whitehaven, set in motion in 1992, with the sculpture programme centred on the docks. Most is figurative but anonymous, representing types not individuals. This and the way the sculptures are sited and displayed provides a telling contrast with the Victorian statues of Barrow. *Colin Telfer*, an ex-miner, has made figure sculptures of resin representing past industry, at Whitehaven, Maryport, Egremont, Millom and St Bees (all C). Naïve, small-scale, they are coloured either red with haematite dust or black with coal.

Other artworks have rural settings. A Millennium programme, generally abstract, is presented in the ten 'Eden Benchmarks' by different artists that mark the course of that river (which requires no embellishment) from source to sea. Most are forgettable, perhaps inhibited by the beauty and drama of the river itself, the exception being *Mary Bourne*'s dramatically simple Water Cut near the headwaters at Mallerstang (W). Stenkrith Park at Kirkby Stephen (W) provides another Millennium project. A dramatic spot made accessible by *Charles Blackett-Ord*'s footbridge, it plays host to an exquisite small-scale sculpture trail by *Meg Peacocke* and *Pip Hall*, 2004; perhaps a little dainty for the robust setting. The most thought-provoking public sculpture is found – with some effort on the finder's part – scattered in Grizedale Forest (Satterthwaite, L). The sculptures are unlabelled, unsigned, sometimes hard to spot. A virtue is made of using the natural materials to hand, with all that that implies for change and decay. *Andy Goldsworthy*, who started his working life as gardener at Helbeck, Brough in the 1960s, celebrates this. He likes his creations to be unlabelled, unmarked, found by accident. His sheepfold at Tilberthwaite (Coniston) is typical.

In the search for notable ARCHITECTURE SINCE THE 1980s Cumbria may seem at first to be quite barren. The Lanternhouse at Ulverston with its blue spire is a clever and witty adaptation by *Francis Roberts* (1987) of an existing building. The Buddhist Temple (1995–7) at Conishead, so much more relaxed than the Priory, stands in the walled garden and flashes gold. Curiously echoing it in its compressed pagoda shape, and size, is Low Furness Primary School at Urswick (L; 1992–6 by *Cumbria County Council*). The Beacon of 1994–6 at Whitehaven fits in by being shaped like a lighthouse. The boldly white, cubic swimming pool by *Hodder Associates*, 2001 at Grange-over-Sands (L; future uncertain) is an unusually brave statement. The towns on the whole have opted for fitting in rather than bold interventions, e.g for their SHOPPING PRECINCTS. The major one is Carlisle's The Lanes of 1982–4 by the *Building Design Partnership*, project architect *David Cash*, where a sugar-coated envelope of pastiche façades encloses standard late C20 arcades. Penrith's Angel Square shopping centre of *c.* 1986 by *Nichol Armstrong Lowe* and the *Hives Partnership* does the same sort of thing on a small scale. Carlisle's Tullie House Millennium project by *BDP*, *Stanton Williams* and *Johnston & Wright*, largely underground, was meant to be signalled from above by glass pyramids; in the event only the underground and internal parts were realized.

Even well away from the National Park it is a fact that many of the most recent developments hide themselves away. Outside Penrith is Rheged (by *Jak Jones* of *Unwin Jones Partnership*, 2000), a combination of shopping trap, visitor centre and road services, which makes a virtue of its hidden location in a disused quarry. Bolder and more convincing is Oasis Whinfell Forest (Brougham, W), a spectacular development by *Holder Mathias Alcock*, 1997, which despite its great size is completely hidden in forest and isolated behind barriers in a way curiously reminiscent of the Spadeadam missile site.

Within the National Park the tendency to hide new architecture under a bushel, or to disguise it, is even more marked. As *Building Design* reported (29 August 2008), 'in recent decades the planning climate has been implacably conservative'. The magazine picked the Jerwood Centre at Grasmere, next to Dove Cottage, by *Benson & Forsyth* then *Napper Architects* 1992–2004, as the only Modern building of note. A more sensitive location is hard to imagine. Considerably delayed by amenity societies and watchdogs, the building resorts to subterfuge, being partly underground and heavily camouflaged above; nevertheless it manages to make a contemporary statement. The extension to the Ruskin Museum at Coniston (1999, by *Ian Gibson* of *Gill Dockray*) is so restrained as to be almost invisible. Also by *Benson & Forsyth* are the tiny, exquisite interventions of 1986 at Boarbank Convent, Allithwaite (L). Invisible from above despite its size is the Lakeland Limited store at Windermere, an excellent multi-functional building by *Don Hanson* of *Hanson Walford Marston* of Kendal, 2003–5.

119

However, as Andrew Lowe asks at the end of his long career as LDNP Conservation Officer, what is there of our time for his successors to conserve? A change of heart can be seen in *Paul Grout*'s Parish Hall of 2005–6 at Ambleside (W), standing out boldly on its rock beside George Gilbert Scott's church, which has managed the trick of being unashamedly Modern and yet fitting in. More startling, although out of general view in the garden of Duddon Hall (Ulpha, C), is the bravely Modernist Temple House by *Alan Jackson* of *Ashworth Jackson & Walker*, 2007. More surprising is Grizedale Forest's striking education centre (*Sutherland Hussey Architects* 2004–6), which was initially designed to turn a shy face to the forest, but was brought into full view at the planners' own instigation.

In any case planning constraints may be overturned by eco-demands. Standing proud over the M6/A66 roundabout at Penrith (C) is the Environment Agency Building (*Ross Erwin* of *Hills Erwin Partnership*, 1998), which although exceedingly prominent ticks all the eco-friendly boxes. Deliberately eyecatching in colour and shape is the Eco Centre at Cockermouth School (C), by *Rod Hughes* of *ad.hoc associates*, 2006. The National Trust's own Footprint building, outside Windermere, was built in 2006–7, after a design by *Paul Crosby*. Using locally sourced materials, including old car tyres, the building fits its woodland setting beautifully while being entirely contemporary.

The current hot potato is the conflict that arises when two environmental imperatives collide, notably green power – i.e. renewable energy – versus natural beauty and wildlife. Cumbria has plenty of both. Both incidentally can generate plenty of money; it is not just an aesthetic and moral equation. WIND FARMS are not enumerated in the Gazetteer because they are all so similar, simply scaled up in number and size as required. The first was commissioned at Haverigg (Millom) in 1992, and in 2009 Cumbria has a hundred or so turbines on a dozen wind farms. More are planned. The National Parks are no-go, so they are concentrated on the coast, e.g. round Workington and Askam in the W, and Ulverston in the S, and in the M6 corridor, e.g. the five at Lambrigg near Junction 27 of the M6. Their great size – they can be 400 ft (123 metres) tall – means that they make their mark even in the longest prospects. HYDRO-ELECTRICITY is more tricky still. A number of waterfalls are already generating electricity, sometimes unobtrusively as at Backbarrow (Haverthwaite, L), sometimes with obvious sad effect as at Barrow House Youth Hostel, Grange-in-Borrowdale. Harnessing the falls at Rydal is particularly contentious – one has only to think of Tivoli whose famous falls are no more. All this fades into insignificance compared with the potential, for good and ill, of a tidal barrage across Morecambe Bay or the Solway Firth. As long ago as 1840 a railway embankment was proposed across Morecambe Bay. A motorway crossing would have obvious benefits for Barrow, which frets at being on the end of a twenty-five-mile cul-de-sac, and standing on the beach at Roa Island the thing looks entirely feasible. The apparent potential for tidal power and for fresh-water storage is seductive, but at the cost of enormous damage to one of the finest tidal mudflat habitats in Europe – and the joy of that coastal train ride with which this Introduction started.

FURTHER READING

Cumbria has a voluminous but partial literature. This is exemplified in the most valuable resource of all, the *Transactions of the Cumberland and Westmorland Antiquarian and Archaeological Society* (CWAAS), founded in 1866; Lancashire-across-the-Sands was included in honorary fashion from the start. 1913, poignantly, is a bumper volume, worth a place on anyone's Cumbrian bookshelf. With the 1930s and the demise of antiquarian-architect practitioners like W. G. Collingwood, J. F. Curwen and J. H. Martindale, the architectural content has faded in favour of archive-delving and archaeology. Publications of the Centre of North-West Regional Studies at Lancaster University are another useful resource.

The LISTINGS of the Department of National Heritage are again voluminous but partial. The forty-four 'greenback' volumes of *c.* 1967–9 are less informative than the revised blue-covered ones, post-1990, for Carlisle, Barrow, Ulverston and Grange-over-Sands. All the list descriptions are now available online at *www.heritagegateway.org.uk.*

COUNTY AND REGIONAL SURVEYS include early histories such as Sir Daniel Fleming, *Description of the County of Westmoreland* and ditto *Cumberland*, compiled in 1671 (published 1882 and 1889); J. Nicholson and R. Burn, *History and Antiquities of the Counties of Westmoreland and Cumberland*, 1777 (2 vols; part reissued 1976), and W. Whellan, *History and Topography of the Counties of Cumberland and Westmoreland*, 1860. Lancashire histories such as that by E. Baines (1831–6) will of course include Lancashire-across-the-Sands. A more concentrated account is provided by Thomas West, *Antiquities of Furness*, 1777. For the Cartmel peninsula the best source is J. C. Dickinson, *The Land of Cartmel, a History*, 1980. The *Victoria County History* covers Lancashire-across-the-Sands in the second half of vol. VIII (the Lonsdale Hundred), 1914. Cumberland has got as far as vol. I (1901) with an essay by W. G. Collingwood on the pre-Norman remains, and vol. II (1905) on ecclesiastical history, the religious houses, industries, and sport. Nothing for Westmorland, but that county does have the inestimable benefit of the Royal Commission on Historical Monuments' *Westmorland* volume (RCHME), 1936, which covers buildings and monuments up to 1714. County directories such as those by Mannix and Whelan, Bulmer, and Kelly are full of mostly second-hand information. C. A. Parker, *The Gosforth District*, 1904, is valuable for that corner of Cumberland – Egremont, Calder, Muncaster and Eskdale. The best of the more modern histories is perhaps W. G. Collingwood, *The Lake Counties*, 1902 onwards (various edns). Angus Winchester's landscape study *The North West* (English Heritage, *England's Landscape* series), 2006, with its many aerial photographs, gives a beautiful overview.

The LAKE DISTRICT has its own place in English literature. Essential works are Thomas West, *A Guide to the Lakes in Cumberland, Westmorland and Lancashire*, 1778 etc. (like most Lake District guides, it went through later editions and revisions), followed by William Gilpin, *Observations Relative Chiefly to Picturesque Beauty, Cumberland and Westmoreland*, 1786, and William Wordsworth, *A Guide through the District of the Lakes*, 1835. The writings of William and Dorothy Wordsworth, Coleridge and their circle are full of direct observation, as is an early and highly enjoyable secondary source, Thomas de Quincey's *Recollections of the Lakes and the Lake Poets*, 1834–40. Harriet Martineau's *Complete Guide to the English Lakes*, 1855, is unusual for her clear-eyed and unsentimental interest in what was new. An inspirational book is *The Discovery of the Lake District*, an exhibition catalogue published by the Victoria and Albert Museum in 1984, owing a good deal to the late Robert Woof and the Wordsworth Trust. Joseph Pocklington, one of the first 'offcomers', and Peter Crosthwaite, one of the first natives to make a living by exploiting them, are amusingly written up in A. Hankinson, *The Regatta Men*, 1988. Norman Nicholson is always worth reading, e.g. his *Portrait of the Lakes*, 1963, as is the trenchant Alfred Wainwright with his seven *Pictorial Guides to the Lakeland Fells*, 1955–66. He was a mountain man, but not immune to '. . . the curling smoke from the chimneys of the farm down below . . . oil lamps in flagged kitchens, huge fires in huge fireplaces . . .' Wainwright's *A Coast to Coast Walk*, 1973, has actually changed the cultural geography of Cumbria and North Yorkshire. John Parker's little *Observer's Book of the Lake District*, 1978, is a personal favourite. Grevel Lindop's *Literary Guide to the Lake District*, 1993, is an excellent guide to the guides as well as an enjoyable itinerary in its own right.

For GEOLOGY there is the British Geological Survey volume by P. Stone *et al.*, *British Regional Geology: Northern England* (5th edn), 2009. WATER, the Lake District's hidden industry, is highlighted in J. J. Harwood, *The Thirlmere Water Scheme*, 1895, and Bampton Local History Society, *A Cast Iron Community*, 2006, on Haweswater and the temporary village of Burnbanks.

Most TOWNS and some VILLAGES have their history and guide, such as 'Ewanian', *Penrith*, 1894, and J. F. Curwen, *Kirkbie-Kendall*, 1900. There are plenty of recent ones, some amazingly fact-free. The following selection runs through the spectrum. G. Bott, *Keswick*, 1994; D. Birkbeck, *A History of Kirkby Stephen*, 2000; T. Duffy, *Cleator Moor Revealed*, 2003; J. M. Carnie, *At Lakeland's Heart* (on Ambleside), 2002; and J. Bernard Bradbury's books on Cockermouth. *The Parish of Lamplugh*, 1993, is a laudable joint effort by the Parish Council. M. W. Holdgate, *The Story of Appleby in Westmorland*, 2006 is useful as history. Best of the bunch is Mary Scott-Parker, *Silloth*, 1999. *Whitehaven 1660–1800* is well served by the RCHME book (1991) of that title. Thinner but more inclusive is J. B. Crossland, *Looking at Whitehaven*, 1971. J. Richardson, *Barrow-in-Furness, its History, Development, Commerce, Industries and Institutions*, 1881, is one of the few books to glory in its own age. The town is also given valuable coverage in Michael Andrews, *The Furness Railway in and around Barrow*, 2003, as is Grange in Leslie R. Gilpin, *Grange-over-Sands, a Resort and its Railway*, 1997.

ARCHAEOLOGY is covered for many aspects by the CWAAS *Transactions*. For PREHISTORY there is, surprisingly, no authoritative modern account, but good summaries are included in Angus Winchester's book of 2006 and in M. Brennand (ed.), *The Archaeology of North West England* vol. I (Resource Assessment), 2006. The ROMANS, and especially Hadrian's Wall, have received more focused attention, even since John Horsley's magisterial *Britannia Romana* (1732). The standard guide is *J. Collingwood Bruce's Handbook to the Roman Wall* (14th edn by David J. Breeze), 2006, complemented by the *Archaeological Map of Hadrian's Wall* (English Heritage, 2010). Accounts of other sites are in P. Bidwell and N. Hodgson, *The Roman Army in Northern England*, 2009. The attitude of later generations to archaeological sites and topographical features can be glimpsed in D. Whaley, *Dictionary of Lake District Place-names*, 2006.

On the PRE-NORMAN period, W. S. Calverley, *Notes on the Early Sculptured Crosses, Shrines and Monuments of the Diocese of Carlisle*, published by the CWAAS in 1899, is still useful for its wide coverage and its drawings. Richard N. Bailey and Rosemary Cramp, *Corpus of Anglo-Saxon Stone Sculpture in England*, vol. II, 1988, illustrated with photographs, is more focused in date range. Individual monuments have their own voluminous and often polemical literature, especially the Bewcastle Cross.

MEDIEVAL BUILDINGS can start with CARLISLE CATHEDRAL, until recently the least studied of English cathedrals. R. W. Billings, *Carlisle Cathedral*, 1840 is the best early source, with fine plates and an explanatory text. David W. V. Weston, *Carlisle Cathedral History*, 2000, is a model of conciseness and easy reference. More exhaustive enquiries are in the British Archaeological Association's Conference Transactions of 2004, *Carlisle and Cumbria, Roman and Medieval Architecture, Art and Archaeology*.

Coverage of MONASTERIES is uneven. For Furness, T. A. Beck, *Annales Furnesienses*, 1844, is a surprisingly good read. There is also extensive coverage in the VCH, and the current English Heritage guide is good. Christine Dade-Robertson,

Furness Abbey, Romance, Scholarship and Culture, 2000, is in effect an extended bibliography – a study of studies of the Abbey. For Holm Cultram, Stuart Harrison's paper in the B.A.A. Transactions referred to above attempts a detailed analysis and reconstruction; see also the CWAAS *Transactions*, and likewise for St Bees. Calder lacks any sort of guide; the best source is Parker, 1904 (see above) and the CWAAS. There is a paper on Seaton Nunnery (1980) by John Todd. The situation at Lanercost is much better, with Stuart Harrison and Henry Summerson's monograph *Lanercost Priory* (CWAAS), 2000, and the English Heritage guide. Shap is best served by the RCHME Westmorland volume. For Cartmel see J. C. Dickinson, *The Priory of Cartmel*, 1991, plus Eric Rothwell, *The Misericords and Screen in Cartmel Priory*, 1997, and *The Stained Glass in Cartmel Priory*, 1995. Penny Hebgin-Barnes has kindly provided her notes on the glass for the forthcoming *Corpus Vitrearum* volume. Details of the founding of Cartmel are in D. Crouch, *William Marshal*, 1990.

For PARISH CHURCHES, Bishop Nicholson's pithy comments in the early C18 (Carlisle Record Office) are often enlightening. The most recent overall survey, indeed the only one to date of the present Diocese, is by Pevsner himself in the first *Buildings of England* series, *Cumberland and Westmorland* in 1967 and *North Lancashire* in 1969. Mike Salter, *The Old Parish Churches of Cumbria*, 1998, is derivative and goes not beyond 1790, but does have handy plans. Churches with defensive capabilities are dealt with in Christopher J. Brooke, *Safe Sanctuaries, Security and Defence in Anglo-Scottish Border Churches 1290–1690*, 2000. Peter Ryder's *Medieval Cross Slab Grave Covers in Cumbria* (CWAAS), 2005, includes a brief account of each church. Individual histories include Euston J. Nurse for Windermere, 1908, F. C. Eeles for Crosthwaite, 1953, and Gervase W. Markham, *Past Alive*, 2003 (on Morland). There are two valuable books on St Mary, Windermere: G. G. Cunninghame, *The Church and Parish of St Mary, Applethwaite*, 1900, and Ian Jones, *St Mary's Church in Applethwaite, by Windermere*, 2000, both with a good deal of social history. Other monographs include R. Bingham, *The Church at Heversham*, 1983, A. Penn, *Brampton Church and its Windows*, 1993, and M. Armstrong, *Linen and Liturgy*, 2002 (on St John Keswick and the Marshall family). S. Matthews, *Sarah Losh and Wreay Church*, 2007, also reprints Henry Lonsdale's biographical account of Miss Losh (1867), and a description of the church by A. R. Hall (1929). Leslie N. S. Smith, *Stained Glass in the Churches of the Anglican Diocese of Carlisle* (CWAAS), 1994, lists C19 and C20 GLASS without evaluation. There is also W. Walters, *The Stained Glass of Shrigley & Hunt of Lancaster and London*, 2003.

Information on Roman CATHOLIC CHURCHES is harder to come by, with a few exceptions such as Pugin's Warwick Bridge (for which see the national literature on Pugin). A selection of CHAPELS is in the RCHME volume *Nonconformist Chapels and Meeting-houses in the North of England*, by Christopher Stell, 1994.

Quakers are great record-keepers, as David M. Butler, *Quaker Meeting Houses of Britain*, 1999, bears witness. It was preceded by his *Quaker Meeting Houses of the Lake Counties*, 1978.

Among the GREATER HOUSES, the defensive buildings are particularly well served. J. F. Curwen, *Castles and Fortified Towers of Cumberland, Westmorland and Lancashire North-of-the-Sands* (CWAAS), 1913, formed the basis of subsequent studies. On proper castles, the *Carlisle Castle Conservation Plan* of 2001 for English Heritage is good, as is the current guide and the out-of-print English Heritage monograph. Brougham Castle is the subject of a monograph by Henry Summerson, Michael Trueman and Stuart Harrison (CWAAS), 1998, as well as sharing an English Heritage guide with Brough.

On defensive houses see Anthony Emery, *Greater Medieval Houses of England and Wales* vol. I, 1993; this can only be selective for Cumbria, and later authors don't always agree with him. Denis Perriam and John Robinson, *Medieval Fortified Buildings of Cumbria* (CWAAS), 1998, is invaluable for its plans and references, and for its considerably broader scope than the title would imply. Peter Ryder's unpublished report, *Medieval Defensible Buildings in Cumbria*, 2000–2, for English Heritage sticks more closely to the brief, with much fresh material. A useful handbook is Mike Salter, *Castles and Tower Houses of Cumbria*, 1998. Finally the RCHME volume *Shielings and Bastles*, 1970, opens up that knotty subject.

For later periods, Nicholas Cooper, *Houses of the Gentry 1480–1680* covers the C17, including the brief flurry of double-piles *c.* 1600 and the Machell/Thackeray era around 1680 – for which see also articles by Blake Tyson in *Transactions of the Ancient Monuments Society*, 1983 and 1984 (all Blake Tyson's papers are in Kendal Library). After that the only really useful book is John Martin Robinson's anecdotal *Guide to the Country Houses of the North West*, 1991. Geoffrey Beard, *The Greater House in Cumbria*, 1978, is of limited use today. Angus Taylor and Janet Martin, *The Websters of Kendal* (CWAAS), 2004 – the sole biography to date of a Cumbrian architectural firm – covers their whole output, which is dominated by houses. For another locally prominent firm see *Sharpe, Paley and Austin, a Lancashire Architectural Practice 1836–1942*, 1998, by James Price. A further study of the Austin & Paley practice is in preparation, edited by Geoff Brandwood. George Pattinson's privately printed *Pattinson's, Builders of Windermere*, 1973, has a good deal of interesting material on C19 and C20 developments round the lake and beyond.

Individual houses such as Netherby Hall, Rose Castle and Dalemain have been written up in *Country Life*. E. H. A. Stretton, *Dacre Castle*, 1994, is a good read. Ian Goodall and Adam Menuge of English Heritage have made studies of the astoundingly complicated Sizergh (2000), the frankly rather dull Belmount at Hawkshead (also 2000), Wordsworth House at Cockermouth (2002), Storrs at Windermere (*Georgian Group Journal* 15, 2006) and the extraordinary Wray Castle (2006). Sir

Clement Jones's biography *John Bolton of Storrs*, 1959, is revealing, as is A. G. Banks' *H. W. Schneider of Barrow and Bowness*,
1984. An unusual study of a Victorian mansion is Ian Jones, *The
House of Hird*, 2002, on Holehird at Troutbeck.

GARDENS are highlighted in the *Occasional Papers* of the
Cumbria Gardens Trust, e.g. on Corby Castle in 2003, and
Thomas Bland's Image Garden at Reagill in 2004. T. H.
Mawson's autobiography, *Life and Work of an English Landscape
Architect* (1927) is also relevant.

For VERNACULAR ARCHITECTURE, R. W. Brunskill, *Traditional Buildings of Cumbria* (new edn 2002) is the first port of call,
though it includes a good many polite, architect-designed buildings. J. H. Palmer, *Historic Farmhouses in and around Westmorland*,
1952, is a book that is locally valued. Susan Denyer, *Traditional
Buildings and Life in the Lake District*, 1991, concentrates on
National Trust properties, drawing on surveys such as Martin
Higgins, *Farmhouses owned by the National Trust in the Langdales*,
1985, and upon Janet Martin's researches. An unpublished thesis
on Martindale by Neil Birdsall (n.d.) is in Kendal Record Office.
Nina Jennings with her *Clay Dabbins* (CWAAS), 2003, has cor-
nered the market on the clay buildings of the Solway Plain.

For INDUSTRIAL ARCHAEOLOGY the essential survey is J. D.
Marshall and M. Davies-Shiel, *Industrial Archaeology of the Lake
Counties*, 1969 (revised 1977), usefully arranged both thematically
and by gazetteer. It tends to favour the southern part of the area,
so needs to be supplemented with the brief *Guide to the Industrial Archaeology of Cumbria* (J. and J. Bennett, eds), for the Association of Industrial Archaeology's 1993 conference. The
southern and western bias in printed sources is being corrected
by Graham Brooks in *The Cumbrian Industrialist*, a series of occasional papers published by the Cumbria Industrial History
Society, and in his contributions to the Society's excellent
website. Under Roger Baker, this is building up a series of introductory essays on all aspects of the area's industrial history. The
CWAAS *Transactions* and those of the History Society of Lancashire and Cheshire have also published usefully on industrial
matters. Other general sources include R.W. Rennison, *Northern
England*, 1981, in the Institution of Civil Engineers' *Civil Engi-
neering Heritage* series, W. Rollinson, *Life and Tradition in the Lake
District*, also 1981, and Marshall and Davies-Shiel, *The Lake Dis-
trict at Work*, 1971. The Newcomen Society *Transactions* (now
International Journal for the History of Engineering and Technology),
Industrial Archaeology Review (Journal of the Association for
Industrial Archaeology) and the Railway and Canal Historical
Society's *Journal* should not be overlooked.

For particular industries, M. Bowden, *Furness Iron*, 2000, is
excellent. D. Kelly, *The Red Earth*, 1998 is useful on exploitation
of the Furness and W Cumberland orefields. A. Raistrick, *The
History of Lead Mining in the Pennines*, 1965, is still the best introduction to its subject. The other extractive industries – including, surprisingly, coal – await something of the same quality.
A. Cameron (ed.), *Lakeland Mining Heritage* (Cumbria Amenity

Trust Mining History Society), 2000, is worth a look. E.G. Holland, *Coniston Copper Mines*, 1981, and Geoff Brambles's chapter on Tilberthwaite slate in the Cumbrian Geological Society, *Exploring Lakeland Rocks and Lansdcapes* (2008, ed. S. Beale) are both informative, well-written guides to exploration on the ground. For gunpowder, Alice Palmer, *The Lowwood Gunpowder Company*, 1998, has to stand as examplar for all the works that operated in the region. M. Davies-Sheil's characteristically dogmatic *Watermills of Cumbria*, 1978, has not been improved upon.

On RAILWAYS, David Joy's *Lake Counties* volume (1983) in the *Regional History of the Railways of Great Britain* series offers a thorough survey, and in the Booklaw *Rail Centres series*, P. Robinson, *Carlisle*, 1986, is essential. As everywhere, G. Biddle, *Britain's Historic Railway Buildings* (2003, revised edn forthcoming) is invaluable. V. R. Anderson and G. K. Fox, *Stations and Structures of the Settle and Carlisle Railway*, 1986, records in drawings and photographs a project without parallel in Victorian railway engineering. The Cumbrian Railways Association has an active publication programme, of which H. Quayle, *Whitehaven: Railways and Waggonways of a Unique Cumberland Port*, 2006, sheds fresh light on early railway development. It should be read with B. Scott-Hudson, *Whitehaven Harbour*, 1994. C. Hadfield and G. Biddle, *The Canals of North-West* England (2 vols, 1970) remains reliable on the area's WATERWAYS, but only J. Satchell, *Kendal's Canal*, 2000, gives a satisfactory account of an individual undertaking. For ROADS, B. P. Hindle, *Roads and Trackways of the Lake District*, 1984, is useful. R. Bray, *Walking on Bridges*, 2009, celebrates the district's minor BRIDGES, with circular walks designed to show off interesting examples.

The ARTS AND CRAFTS MOVEMENT around 1900 is the most recent to attract much attention, with extra impetus given by the opening of Blackwell at Bowness. Jennie Brunton, *The Arts and Crafts Movement in the Lake District*, 2001, concentrates on four Cumbrian episodes. Barrie and Wendy Armstrong's excellent *The Arts and Crafts Movement in the North West of England*, 2005, gives a broad coverage.

The scarcity of material on the C20 AND C21 is symptomatic of conservative, conservationist Cumbria. Loosely in the Arts and Crafts category is Olive Seabury, *The Carlisle State Management Scheme*, 2007, with a good deal on Harry Redfern and his 1920s pubs. For R.A.F. Spadeadam see Wayne Cocroft and Roger J. C. Thomas, *Cold War* (English Heritage), 2003. On public sculpture see Bill Grant and Paul Harris (eds), *The Grizedale Experience*, 1991, and *Natural Order*, 1996, plus the numerous publications on and by Andy Goldsworthy. The ten Eden Benchmarks are pictured on the moderately useful website *visitcumbria.com*, along with much material on churches and historic houses. For war memorials the UK National Inventory of War Memorials has a website, *www.ukniwm.org.uk*.

Of MANUSCRIPT MATERIALS the most valuable are Thomas Machell's unpublished notebooks and sketches of 1675 etc. in

Carlisle Record Office, though they are hard going. Bishop Nicholson's early C18 diaries and visitations are full of interest also at Carlisle, and the sketchbooks of Thomas Bland (*c.* 1843–50), in various collections, are informative. The Record Office situation in Cumbria incidentally is extremely odd and anomalous. For Cumberland, and some of the more important county-wide records, go to Carlisle. Records for the W coast however will probably be at Whitehaven. Westmorland records are at Kendal, though a good deal of Appleby material went missing when that ceased to be the county town. Here again there are two ports of call, for Kendal Library is almost as useful as the Record Office. Finally Lancashire-across-the-Sands records will be at Barrow, or maybe in Preston.

Information on INDIVIDUAL ARCHITECTS can be found in H. M. Colvin, *Biographical Dictionary of English Architects 1600–1840*, 2008 (4th edn), the *Directory of British Architects 1834–1900* (British Architectural Library), 1993 (expanded edn 2001, up to 1914), and A. S. Gray, *Edwardian Architecture, a Biographical Dictionary*, 1985. For SCULPTURE see I. Roscoe, *A Biographical Dictionary of British Sculptors 1660–1851*, 2009; also B. Read, *Victorian Sculpture*, 1982. An extensive bibliography of English architecture is available on the Pevsner Books Trust's educational website, *www.lookingatbuildings.org.*

GAZETTEER

ABBEY TOWN (C)

HOLM CULTRAM ABBEY. One of only four British Cistercian churches still used for worship. Just part of the late C12 nave is left, minus aisles and clerestory, but what a superb church it makes.

The abbey was founded in 1150 by King David of Scotland and his son Earl Henry, and was seeded from David's foundation of Melrose. The stone was brought from N of the Solway too. When Henry II of England retook Cumberland he confirmed possession, in 1157. The church was *c.* 265 ft (81.5 metres) long, of standard Cistercian plan: a short rectangular presbytery, transepts with rectangular E chapels, and an aisled nave of nine bays with arcades eleven paces apart (Melrose also eleven, Carlisle ten, Cartmel twelve). Later it may have acquired choir aisles, and certainly a crossing tower. Engravings show that a vast W window had replaced what Stuart Harrison suggests was originally a rose above three lancets.* In 1507 Abbot Robert Chamber or Chambers added the deep W porch, replacing what may have been a galilee of Fountains type. Despite border troubles it was at the Dissolution in 1538 one of the wealthier Cistercian houses (£477), still with twenty-four monks.

Holm Cultram was unusual among Cistercian houses in accommodating a parish congregation in the nave, which was the saving of the church. The parishioners pleaded, and were granted, its preservation as 'a greate ayde, socor and defence for us against our neighbors the Scots'. In 1561 stone from the conventual parts was being sold off, but the church and infirmary were suffered to remain as parish church and vicarage. However, the tower fell on New Year's Day 1600, carrying down the choir and N transept. Repairs undertaken by the University of Oxford, to whom the endowment had passed, were partly nullified by fire in 1604. Bishop Nicholson, shocked by its state, ordered further repairs in 1703. Between 1727 and 1739 (Buck's engraving) the nave was reduced to its six westernmost bays, and shorn of its aisles by building screen walls

---

*In *Carlisle and Cumbria: British Archaeological Association Conference Transactions*, 27 (2004).

in line with the arcades. The clerestory was removed, and a flat ceiling and galleries added. The galleries came out again in 1883, and in 1913 *J. H. Martindale* removed the ceiling, discovering the C18 (reused medieval) roof timbers. This roof fell on 9 June 2006, when the abbey was burnt by a thief. The stonework and stained glass survived, though damaged.

For a Cistercian foundation the setting is unusual: no rolling pasture and forest here, but a quiet village street and windswept saltmarsh. The present church looks like a capsized hulk in the flat landscape, the sides featureless except for two tiers of small round-arched Georgian windows, the ends of sloping silhouette with tumbling-down buttresses, the roof low and hipped behind a plain parapet. The W front is fascinating. The gable, sticking up higher than the roof, has two C18 piercings to hold bells. Flat buttresses r. and l. are all that can be seen of the Norman front. In the N one a niche for a statue inserted probably in the C14, richly appointed with ogee canopy and supporting pinnacles. Also arcading and decoration probably of the C16. Abbot Chambers's PORCH of 1507 displays his name and punning emblem of a chained bear on its round arch. It has angle buttresses below but classical quoins, cornice and round-arched windows above, where it was heightened (dated 1730). The bits of carving between the three shields over the door, including anachronistic dogtooth, were parts of a large and elaborate C16 niche, which was topped by the eagle now on the gable bellcote. The Norman W doorway inside the porch is a sumptuous piece, with four orders of columns and enriched waterleaf capitals. The arch is round with manifold mouldings, one of them keeled. The outermost has the Late Norman bobbin motif. A Norman W doorway to the lost S aisle now opens to the link corridor of 1973 (*see* below). The E window is an oddity of latest Perp, dating presumably from the 1600s but relocated in the C18 to the shortened nave. It has a jumping castellated transom and uncusped tracery, all lights and panels ending in uncusped arches, under a segmental head. Only here at the E end, where a pair of great clustered piers emerge out of the partition wall, do we gain an inkling of what is inside. Excavation to the E shows a portion of an E.E. doorway, with dogtooth, presumably from the crossing to the N transept. Also a portion of the NE crossing pier which appears to have required strengthening.

The interior is still astonishingly impressive, thanks to its great width and splendid piers and arches. In the thickness of the wall above the W door is a singer's gallery, as at Rievaulx, Fountains and Kirkstall, reached by a turning stair behind the SW buttress. The great piers had eight strong round shafts, as at Furness, but the slightly pointed arches are twice chamfered with a step between, rather than moulded as at Furness or Melrose. The easternmost pair lacking a shaft on the inner face must have marked the limit of the parochial nave. The next W pier on the N has a peculiar capital formed of curling leaves –

a motif also on the fonts at Aspatria and Crosscanonby; was there perhaps a pulpit here? The organ extension of 1884–5 allows these columns to be seen in the round. Other capitals plain or of waterleaf type, and one with decorated scallops of the trumpet variety. The roof was a tie-beam affair with extremely short kingposts and short curved wall struts. In 2008 *Purcell Miller Tritton* made a new roof in oak.

FURNISHINGS. A couple of ancient CHESTS survived the fire. – SCULPTURE. Many fragments in the porch, from coffin-lids with foliated crosses to Flamboyant tracery. – Large fragment of a Virgin, C15. – Virgin and Child, seated, quite casual, by *Josefina de Vasconcellos*. – STAINED GLASS. E window by *Wailes*, 1890. Others by *Wailes & Strang*, *Powells* (nave S, second from E), and *E. & C. O'Neill* (two, nave N). – MONUMENTS. Joseph Saul †1842 with profile medallion, in the porch. – Rev. Arthur Sheppard †1905, a copper scroll. By *KSIA*? – In the link corridor what remains of the tomb of Abbot Chambers, †1518 or 1519. In the centre the abbot enthroned, with crook and mitre, flanked by kneeling monks each with a book and a raised banner. At one end a censing angel, at the other the chained bear rebus. Also two fine early C14 grave-slabs.

ABBEY SHOP, SW of the W front. Supposed to incorporate part of the abbot's lodging or guest house (cf. the Vicarage at Lanercost in the same position). The only visible relics are the plinth and a fireplace upstairs with Abbot Chambers's name and rebus, again.

MILLGROVE, 200 yds S of the church. A partial rebuilding of the abbey infirmary, probably of 1472 and earlier (DCMS). Later the vicarage, now a farmhouse. A long narrow house of odd plan, with an oppressive number of massive cross-partitions. Three doors, three stairs and more than three stacks suggest division into three dwellings. The northernmost is distinguished by an unusual two-storey bow with mullioned windows, jammed between a buttress and a rectangular protrusion for the inglenook. The doorway is inscribed RF FF (Robert and Frances Fayrish) 1664. It opens into a wide through passage like a slype between dwellings 1 and 2. Stair-turret at the back. Inside dwelling 1 are two wide cross-arches, one across a huge fireplace with its own internal fire-window; the other spanning the room instead of a joist. At the S end a cottage with a tiny stair tucked in by the stack. At the N end a long BARN.

The town had an interesting form of self-government by 'The Sixteen Men', probably originating as a muster against the Scots, then responsible for the sea defences. The ordinary HOUSES were of clay or cobbles, with cruck frames. Nina Jennings notes the Smithy (rebuilt?), Brownrigg Cottage, Kingside Hill Farm, Swinsty Villa, Stankend Farm. Abbey stone was recirculated at the Dissolution, and from the C18 brick came into use.

WHEATSHEAF INN. By *Harry Redfern*, 1935. A good example of his country-house style. White-painted brick, sweeping tiled hipped roof, dormers, weatherboarding, shutters. It had a tearoom as well as the public bar and off-sales, and a bowling green laid with Millom turf.

RABY COTE, 1 m. NNE. One of the five abbey granges. Rebuilt by Thomas Chambers after 1600, when the abbey's tower and choir fell. The E front plinth is made up of sections of cornice used upside-down, with jumbled-up blackletter including the date 1513. Above, arms of Abbot Chambers held by an angel. At the back a seated and crowned relief figure of the Virgin in a niche, with miniature vaulting. She is flanked by kneeling figures, including the abbot himself, and sits over the abbey's and Chambers's arms. Also bits of tracery, one piece with a mullion reaching up into the apex of an ogee arch (cf. the late C14 staircase tower of Carlisle Castle, and Dean and Brigham churches).

1 m. W of the village, at Abbey Cowper, an early C19 STEAM CORN MILL. Brick, two storeys, six bays, gabled central projections.

ADDINGHAM (C) *see* GLASSONBY

2050

AIKTON (C)

ST ANDREW. Solid C12 W front with a double bellcote topped with St Andrew's cross. Fine stone catslide roof on the S. The side walls were rebuilt in 1869, with paired lancets. The old walls were then found to be built of cobbles set in clay which, if general, explains why so many Solway Plain churches have needed rebuilding. The N wall of the chancel is still like this; the rest was rebuilt in 1732, the date over its S door. Nave S doorway with three continuous hollows between ridges, probably late C13, as is the S arcade on dumpy octagonal piers, and the trefoiled PISCINA. Narrow Norman chancel arch with scallop capitals, the arch single-stepped. The top of an E.E. lancet window is visible in the vestry. Rustic tie-beam roof with king- and raking queenposts; apparently C15. – FONT. Square, chamfered at the corners and decorated with plain rounded and pointed trefoils; Pevsner thought C14, Bond C12. – MONUMENT. In the porch, upside-down C13 grave-slab with cross and sword. Associated since the C16 with Hugh de Morville, one of the assassins of Thomas Becket. – WAR MEMORIAL, 1919. White granite. Cross and wreath on a heavy base with tin hat and sword. Motifs, material and asymmetrical composition typical of *Beattie & Co.*

At the entrance to the FARM E of Bragg's House, C17 cannons reused as bollards to protect wall corners.

AINSTABLE (C)

St Michael. Rebuilt by *George Watson*, 1870–1. The tower was demolished in 1983, leaving a funny NW porch with a bellcote. Two tight lancet triplets of even height on the s side of the nave, but none at all on the N. Also plate tracery. – PILLAR PISCINA, loose. Norman, with decorated shaft. – Fancy wooden SCREEN with brass gates, 1885. – STAINED GLASS. E window by *Wailes*; also one chancel s (†1876). Another chancel s, *Clayton & Bell*. – MONUMENTS. John Aglionby, and his wife Katherine Denton of Ainstable, †1428. Removed from St Cuthbert, Carlisle, in 1778 when that church was rebuilt. Fine recumbent effigies. He wears a beard. – Aglionby tablets in the chancel. – Francis Aglionby by *M. L. Watson*, 1843. Very bare and intense; with a tall, slim urn in a recess. – Tablet to J. Y. Beall, Captain in the Confederate Army of America.

Wesleyan Chapel. 1861. Two bays, porch in the long side. Basic Gothic, with Y-tracery and diagonal iron glazing. A pair of flyers at the back to retain the hillside.

Townhead, Newbiggin. *See* Croglin.

ALDINGHAM (L)

St Cuthbert. On the brink of the vast sands of Morecambe Bay. Partly roughcast, with a big roof over nave and aisles and low Dec tower. The long chancel must date from *c.* 1300, see the trefoil-headed s doorway, E window with three stepped cusped lancets, and low-side window of two such lights with a transom. There is also a C15 window, and one probably of the C17 with (renewed) mullions fashioned like columns. Nave re-windowed 1845–6, and the N aisle added, by *Edmund Sharpe*. Low interior with a flat ceiling to the nave. The s arcade is latest Norman, with two short round columns and one octagonal. One capital has waterleaf. The arches have one step and one chamfer. The N arcade, taller and all octagonal, looks reconstructed, i.e. in 1845–6 (further restoration by *Hicks & Charlewood*, 1931). The tower pushes into the nave with its diagonal buttresses. Low and broad chancel arch, *c.* 1300, with headstops. The chancel has a rustic tie-beam roof with thin wind-braces making untidy circles. SQUINT on s side. PISCINAS in chancel and SE chapel. – COMMUNION RAIL. C17, with fattish turned balusters. – BOX PEWS. – FONT. Possibly C12 (DCMS). A peculiar fluted bowl with four legs and a centre stalk. – STAINED GLASS. E window by *Harcourt M. Doyle*, 1964. SE, Annunciation to the Shepherds, by *Veronica Whall*, 1934. Delightful, if not as intensely coloured as her father's work. Also Christ in Glory, N, bold 1970s *Shrigley & Hunt*. – MONUMENTS. Two worn C12 or C13 slabs in the chancel, one bearing part of an inscription; bits of three more. –

Alabaster, marble and bronze plaque to four grandsons of the Rev. John Macauley, all killed in wars 1874, 1901 and 1916. Signed *J. Underwood*, London. – Other tablets signed *Knowles*, Manchester, and *S. Gibson*, Liverpool.

ALDINGHAM HALL. By the church. Of 1846–50, for the wealthy Rev. John Stonard, who left it to his butler. Attributed to *Sir Matthew Digby Wyatt*. Very Gothic, of squared and coursed limestone with buff sandstone dressings. It has a big square stair-tower at the back, with a higher turret and battlements, but its seaward elevation is symmetrical. The ends project, framing the three large windows of the hall. They have canted bays between pinnacled octagonal turrets. These are set in from the corners, giving a blinkered look. All the main windows straight-topped. The entrance porch is on one short side, and a corridor runs across between hall and staircase.

MOTTE, ¾ m. SW. Surrounded by a broad ditch and partly eroded by the sea. At first a C12 ringwork, subsequently filled in and heightened; the height was increased further and a timber revetment provided in the late C12 or early C13. A broad causewayed ditch to the NE may be contemporary. At Moat Farm, N of the motte, and probably succeeding it, a square MOAT.

1 m. N on the road between Baycliff and Scales, an impressive LIMEKILN. C19, coursed rubble, rounded front corners. Segmental-arched draw-hole to the road.

ALLITHWAITE (L)

ST MARY. Routine Dec by *E. G. Paley*, 1864–5. SCHOOL and VICARAGE were part of the same job. Nave and S aisle separately roofed. Polygonal W spirelet carried on an arch or giant niche. Plate tracery. Five-bay arcade, collar-beam roof of two alternating designs. The chancel roof is single-framed. – Good STAINED GLASS. E window, late *Morris & Co.*, 1921. S aisle E by *Abbott & Co.*, 1950. Also by them two little musical windows, chancel S (designer *Paul O. Chapman*).

BOARBANK HALL, ½ m. SW. First built for Mary Lambert *c.* 1837 by *George Webster* in white symmetry, with a pedimented centre, links and taller wings behind a decorative veranda. Following a fire in 1870 it was rebuilt with an Italianate front in red rock-faced stone with buff dressings, with the same massing minus the veranda, but gaining an Italianate tower at the back r. Overdecorated interiors of the 1870s, but with some delicate floral wall paintings and brasswork in the drawing room that look more like *c.* 1900. LODGE of 1837 by *Webster*. STABLES by *J. W. Grundy* of Ulverston, 1876–8.

Augustinian Canonesses have run a nursing home here since 1921, gradually adding a series of linked buildings in a long line behind the hall. CHAPEL. 1958–61 by *Jacksons* of

Fleetwood, in a simple Romanesque style with windows in threes. Congregational nave and nuns' choir, originally invisible one from the other, focus in an L on the altar. In 1994–5 *Jonathan Pritchard* added a SACRAMENT CHAPEL behind the altar, with wrap-around walls and a faceted altar, and a tiny LADY CHAPEL. – Also by *Jacksons* MARYMOUNT, a nursing home of 1955, neo-1700 style, and BETHANY, 1967, bolder but cruder. Contrived inside the junction is the serene ORATORY by *Benson & Forsyth*, 1986, a white translucent drum with the single door and single window boxed out to create a sense of detachment. Also a PHYSIOTHERAPY ROOM (body and soul!) at the back, floating free over an earth bank. Ribbed metal outside. Diagonal floorboards and metal ceiling. Walls mirrored, of glass, or ribbed metal.

WRAYSHOLME TOWER, ½ m. SW. C15 tower of the Harringtons, passing to the Dicconsons in the late C15. The tower is impressive (40 by 28 ft, 12 by 8.5 metres), with three remaining corner turrets; the SW one mounted on a garderobe projection has lost its top. The walls however are not particularly thick, and there is no vault. It has been converted into a bank barn by making a bridge ramp and a wide E entrance, and removing the midfloor. A rough spiral stair climbs the SW turret. Wall-walks cross the N and S gables, but the present roof comes down over the side ones. Paired trefoil-headed windows light the upper floors N and S. Otherwise small square windows with the marks of bars. Small fireplace, upper W. Under a pent roof W, by the front of the hall range, is a surplus C14 doorway, steeply pointed – which makes one want to search for the other doors of a screens passage. The hall range carries a worn date R & AB 1674, carved on what looks like a bit of tracery upsidedown. Also 1848 over the front door.

KIRKHEAD TOWER, 1⅓ m. SE. Prominent C19 castellated summerhouse.

ALLONBY (C)

0040

Windswept coastal resort favoured by the Quakers. Already in 1748 it was said to have 'considerable concourse for bathing'.

CHRIST CHURCH. On the main B5300 road ¼ m. S of the village. Simple classical box with keyed-in windows, erected in 1743–4 by Dr Robert Thomlinson (*see also* Wigton). In 1845 spacious transepts and the shallowest of chancels were added, a plan like a Scottish kirk. Italianate triple windows at the E end and the ends of the transepts. A tripartite arch, the side openings exceedingly narrow, divides the addition (which is evidently the main worship space) from the nave. The SUNDAY SCHOOL blocks all the C18 nave windows on the N. – STAINED GLASS. E window, *Wailes & Strang*, 1898. – MONUMENT. Joseph Huddart †1816, signed *Petrus Fontana*, Carrara, 1821.

Oval portrait medallion and instruments of navigation. The captain 'pointed out a more secure path in the trackless deep'.

CONGREGATIONAL CHAPEL (former), Moss Lane. Typical that a genteel resort should have had a Congregational not a less 'respectable' Methodist chapel. 1844, quite sizeable, with a justificatory inscription in a quatrefoil.

QUAKER MEETING HOUSE, close by. The Friends in 1703 bought a low cottage, windowless to the coast road, and added a doorway and pediment. When the somewhat larger Main Meeting was added in 1732 this became the Womens' Meeting. (Separate burial ground a little N.)

LEISURE CENTRE, Moss Lane. The fruit of local enterprise, not Local Authority. By *Green Design Group* of Cockermouth, 1992, to serve Spring Lea caravan site. Roughly octagonal, on a laminated wood frame. Allonby is a good place to study chalets and mobile homes.

Only with the building of the present B5300 road through the dunes did Allonby turn to face the sea. The old coast road, now a long, intermittent, cobbled backwater, is built up on both sides, i.e. half the houses had their backs to the sea. Generally they are small and colourwashed, sometimes single-storeyed, though sometimes handsome, as Moss House of 1760 with a shell canopy. Facing each other across The Square two surprisingly grandiose buildings: ALLONBY GRANGE, single-storeyed on a basement, with a grand Doric porch and cottage wings, and the saltwater BATHS and assembly room of 1835, of five bays with a giant portico of Ionic columns *in antis*. On the seaward side this has a delicate iron balcony and four tall windows with tapering surrounds, like the Meeting House at Wigton, so perhaps also by *William Alderson*. The gaunt red brick building marooned on the sea turf near the Ship Inn was the READING ROOM by none other than *Alfred Waterhouse* for Joseph Pease, 1861. Both belonged to Quaker dynasties, and this modest building was the prelude to a string of Pease commissions around Darlington and Middlesborough. NORTH LODGE is a row of houses in a formal composition of seventeen bays, with two-storey centre, pavilions, and six-bay single-storey links; modest enough, but almost the only such thing in Cumbria. It was built in the early C19 for another Quaker, Thomas Richardson, as his occasional residence flanked by six cottages 'in which Mr Richardson generously allows as many poor to live rent free'. A simple Doric porch faces the sea, but the doors are on the landward side.

ALSTON (C)

High up and pent in by inhospitable, repeatedly dug-over Pennine moors. Geographically it is peculiar in that the E-flowing river South Tyne links it with Northumberland rather than

Cumbria. It is an ecclesiastical Peculiar in the Diocese of
Newcastle, not Carlisle. Mining was its business, especially lead,
with useful quantities of silver, iron and coal. Its vernacular architecture is unique in the North of England. As late as the C18 and
C19 houses were built on the bastle principle; not defensive   64
in terms of thick walls or tiny windows, but with the living
accommodation upstairs and the front door up external steps.
The population of Alston Moor in 1841 was 6,063; today only
2,000 or so.

ST AUGUSTINE. A plain building of 1770 by *Smeaton* was rebuilt
in 1869–70 in C13 style, by *J. W. Walton*. The S porch-steeple,
completed in 1886 by *G. D. Oliver*, looks inappropriately suburban, but the plate traceries of the N side and the punchy
wheel window in the W gable hit the right note. S aisle, but no
N aisle, so the nave has a two-storey elevation on that side.
Tympanum over the tower entrance, finely carved: Christ in
Majesty. Augustine was to fill the niche above, but the bishop
objected. Tall, well-lit interior. Thin arcade columns of polished
granite with fat foliage capitals. – STAINED GLASS. E window
of 1872 by *Powells*, designed by *Wooldridge*. N, probably by
O'Connor. – MONUMENTS. Several quite good tablets including Thomas Lancaster, vicar, †1789 by *C. Regnart*, a pair for
the Salvin twins †1850 and 1852 by *Davies* of Newcastle, and
Faithful and Faith Bridgwood †1833 and 1835, by *Green*. Loose
STONES: two bits of a fine foliated cross-slab, with flower and
nailhead on the chamfered edge. Two small grave-lids from
Garrigill.
    The sub-circular CHURCHYARD was open to the market-
place until the 1680s, then blocked by houses and only acces-
sible through a tunnel. Now there is a narrow gap for the gate.
ST PAUL'S METHODIST CHURCH, Front Street. 1868, by *F. R. N.
Haswell* (Kelly). Grand, polychromatic, two-storeyed; but
closed. Front of brown and yellow stone, with twin entrances.
ST WULSTAN (R.C.), King's Arms Lane. It was the C18 gaol,
then a Toc H centre, then a stable, before in 1953 becoming a
Catholic church. Now also used by the Methodists. Very plain,
with oblong windows.
QUAKER MEETING HOUSE, Front Street. A single-storey building of 1732, with mullioned windows, was heightened in 1764.
Partly re-fitted with sash windows. Porch added *c.* 1850,
though with the 1732 lintel. Disused between 1902 and 1981,
refurbished 1996. Fairly complete inside apparently, though
the loft has been removed.
TOWN HALL, LIBRARY, and SAVINGS BANK, Front Street.
1857, by *A. B. Higham* of Newcastle. A Town Hall of the sort
that would be recognizable in industrial Yorkshire or
Lancashire. Gothic, of balanced asymmetry, with a clock tower
in the middle. Savings Bank originally l., library r., hall above.
MARKET CROSS. A reproduction of 1765 of the previous cross
(Kelly), with stubby Tuscan columns. In fact it has been repeatedly demolished by runaway vehicles and reconstructed.

SAMUEL KING'S SCHOOL, Church Road. Reputedly the smallest state secondary school in England. 1957 by *Cumberland
County Architects* under *J. H. Haughan*. Flat roof and glassy
screen walls of the period, but an unusually deep plan to offer
minimum external surface to the Pennine weather.

STATION, Station Road. By *Benjamin Green*, 1852, as the terminus to the Newcastle & Carlisle Railway's branch. The line
closed in 1976, but part now operates on a narrow gauge as
the South Tynedale Railway. In a cottagey Tudor style, similar
to the architect's stations for the 1847 Newcastle & Berwick
Railway. Symmetrical, with gabled cross-wings. A stationmaster's bay window on the platform side. An overall roof here was
lost in the 1960s. Across the road, a handsome contemporary
GOODS SHED, with generous arched entrances for railway
wagons and in the E wall for road vehicles.

BASTLES. Although thinned out by demolition, the town is intricate, with flying freeholds, alleys and tunnels. Upstairs living
is signalled by outside steps to an upper front door. Where the
steps have gone the upper door can still be seen, blocked or
converted to a window. The ground floors were for animals,
shops or workshops. In times of growth these were let as
further dwellings, and then as the population shrank again the
downstairs became part of the main dwelling, and the upstairs
door was closed off.

  The following have dates into the C18 or even C19. On Front
Street is CROSS VIEW COTTAGE, 1690s, white-painted, with
two storeys above the first-floor entry. Another is at Town Foot,
opposite the Town Hall, with WHITEFIELD COTTAGE and its
pair on Station Road, below. On Kings Arms Lane, below the
W end of the church, is HAMILTON HOUSE, which was two
or even four dwellings: pair of upper-level doors, two doors
below. The incongruously elegant overdoor hood, also seen
next door at LINDEN HOUSE, is concrete of the 1920s.
Further round in the Butts are ARBOREAL SUNSET VIEW
(1752 WB) and CHURCH VIEW COTTAGE, both heavily
restored with the rest of this quarter. MOUNTHOOLY (MEW
1739), still with steps up to a first-floor entry, has again been
two or even four dwellings. On Back o' th' Burn is JAYCOTT
FOREST, the best-known Alston bastle. An alley called Katie's
Lane down from Front Street leads to OLD HOUSE and OLDE
COTTAGE (dated 1621), both still with living accommodation
upstairs.

Other buildings of note include the POLICE STATION, Townhead, 1850, oddly mixing Tudor and Greek detail. ALBERT
HOUSE opposite is a purpose-built guest house of the same
date. In Front Street the VICTORIA INN, originally a Temperance hotel. A plaque gives the date 1901, the architect *William
Young*, the patron, and the builders, 'all of West Hartlepool'.
Under the render it is brick. Also BARCLAYS BANK, 1898
by *Johnstone Bros* of Carlisle. Red sandstone, semicircular
porch with Corinthian pilasters and stained glass. Inside,
mahogany doors and panelling, black-and-white tiles, glazed

brick fireplace, moulded ceiling: a great statement of prosperity, though by then the mines were failing fast.

N of Market Square, HIGH MILL, equipped in 1767 with machinery by *John Smeaton*. Backshot wheel, a replacement of 1817, restored to working order 1992. The steep site reveals unexpected chasm-like alleys below the entrance at street level and the foot of the building.

NENTHEAD LEVEL was one of the sights of Alston: an adit 8 ft (2.5 metres) square in section, driven towards Nenthead (q.v.), 5 m. SE, to drain the lead mines there. Planned by *John Smeaton* in 1776 for the London Lead Co., it was hoped that boats would also use it to carry ore. Work proceeded until 1842, at first under the supervision of *John Gilbert*, who had designed the celebrated underground canal system in the Duke of Bridgewater's coal mines at Worsley (Lancs.), and was resumed 1870–1904. Though it was never completed, it did drain much ground, but only pleasure boats ever navigated it, carrying sensation seekers into the darkness. The tunnel mouth in Alston is now blocked and invisible in a builder's yard.

RANDALHOLME, 1¼ m. NNW. At the S end of the narrow farmyard is a square tower of uncertain date, of four storeys. A tunnel-vault at the base. In one corner a tiny mural stair, not spiral, rises through the vault – a very unusual feature – continuing in the S then W sides to the top. The tower was dressed up in 1746 with sash windows, cornice, and the Richardson arms in a cartouche. A stair extension of perhaps the same date is attached. In the farmyard is a second defensive dwelling, a bastle house of superior type, perhaps early C17. Round-arched door to the lower storey. Upper entry and small square windows upstairs, formerly barred.

CLARGHYLL HALL, 1⅞ m. NNE. Odd-looking group with a curious history. It is built around two C17 bastle houses. That they are exactly in line, as Peter Ryder points out, suggests a missing building between, perhaps a longhouse. The bastles were separately owned until 1674, when both passed to Nicholas Whitfield. He heightened the S one, leaving his initials on window heads dated 1678 and 1679 and a spice cupboard 1688. Both bastles were given a N extension, so that the end entries to the byres underneath were protected by crosspassages. Some time in the C18 the two buildings joined up again. In 1841 the whole was bought by the *Rev. Octavius James*, later the designer of the eccentric church at Kirkhaugh, just in Northumberland. In 1889 he perished in a fire in the study he had created in the N bastle. This remains ruinous. James added the top floor to the S bastle, with its crazily steep crowstepped roof, and the bowed seven-light oriel, its level row of tracery heads cut progressively by a segmental arch, an unconventional but effective device. The main room still gives a good idea of the reassuring security of a bastle. Reached by external steps and an upper porch, thick-walled, paved with flags over heavy joists. James added the large dining room projecting at the S end, with Dec windows in raised gables.

Fishtailed slits light the undercroft. Derelict at the furthest s, behind the dining room, is what looks like a third bastle, connected by a flying bridge. A neatly kinked slype creeps underneath. In front, a rectangular pool and a duck house, with room for doves above.

AMBLESIDE (W)

At a focal point of the Lakes, hence Wordsworth's Stamp Office on Church Street, whence he distributed legal stamps. A market charter was granted in 1651. The town is built of dark green and black stone, but it is a cheerful little place.

St Mary, Vicarage Road. By *George Gilbert Scott*, 1850–4. Second Pointed, with Geometrical tracery. A strongly pyramidal tower and Lincolnshire broach spire rise on the s side of the chancel. The sophisticated design and towny scale seem unsuited to the Lakes. Nevertheless it has the right degree of irregularity, complication and sturdiness to guard the little town and take on the beetling fells. The interior too is both Ecclesiologically fashionable and perfectly judged: broad nave, elegant arcades, chancel arch as tall and wide as it will go, spacious chancel stepping up to the altar, ne chapel. Heavy hammerbeams for the nave, wagon ceiling over the chancel. The clerestory is relatively low, with small trefoil windows. No carved work, but plenty of fine moulding. Alabaster REREDOS designed in 1895 by *Paley & Austin*, made by *Shrigley & Hunt* (mosaics) and *Bridgeman* of Lichfield (woodwork). – CHOIR STALLS also by *Bridgeman*. – CHAPEL REREDOS incorporating a sculpture of the Nativity by *Josefina de Vasconcellos*, who lived here, in memory of Charles Hales †1986. – WALL PAINTING under the w window by *Gordon Ransom*, 1944, done while the Royal College of Art was evacuated to Ambleside during the war. The figures of the annual rush-bearing procession are dabbed in powdery paint, with plenty of white showing through. Many are singing; not a pretty sight. – STAINED GLASS. The great e window is by *John Scott & Son*, 1854. w window by *Warrington*, 1857. Two aisle windows by *Holiday* (makers *Powells*), 1889 and 1891, face each other at the w end. Centre n, †1862, in ghastly browns, yellows and purples: supposedly by *Wailes*, one of several here. Opposite, St Anne and St Mary, with their respective Ambleside churches above; by Mr and Mrs *Dean Walmsley* of Langdale, 1952. *Wailes* windows in the ne chapel, deprived of their backgrounds; the e window figures designed by the sculptor *Thomas Woolner*. – MONUMENTS. nw corner, a group brought from St Anne (*see* p. 101), including Isaac Knife, rector, †1829, and Jane Harden of Brathay Hall †1829; she looks up from a book, an angel beckons. – Tomb-chest, niche and canopy, like an Easter sepulchre, to Henry Thomas Lutwidge R.N. †1861. By *Chapman &*

Son of Frome. – Brass to James Christopher Wilson †1884 by *Singer & Sons*, Frome, with St Christopher.

PARISH CENTRE, N of the church. 2005–6 by *Paul Grout Associates*. As ambitious and sophisticated as the church; perhaps a little precious. Skirts of rough stone anchor it to the rock. Entrance by a round turret topped by a ring of stylized carving by *Danny Clahane*. Another balances it on the N. Both are top-lit. Curved W apse, big E oriel. The interior, articulated by laminated crucks, is divided into a parish room (with carvings of Earth, Air, Fire, Water by *Trevor Singleton*), offices, and the Wesley Room in the E end, a glass-ringed semi-rotunda. – VICARAGE (former), dated 1832.

MATER AMABILIS (R.C.), Wansfell Road, off Lake Road. 1933, by *George J. Hughes*. Within the square he has contrived a tower-like lantern over the altar, and four corner spaces variously arched internally to form chapels, baptistery and porch. PRESBYTERY attached. On the corner with Lake Road is TOWER LODGE, dated 1891, intended as the nucleus of a priory, school and college. The tall Gothic stair window and an inserted wide entrance of orange terracotta look ill at ease in stone country.

METHODIST CHURCH (former), Millans Park. 1898. Attached HALL 1903–7, architect *W. Mason*. Eye-catchingly large gable window with flowing Art Nouveau tracery and coloured glass. The Tudorish hall has a streamlined gable-end with sloping verticals and hipped skirts. Converted to flats 2006.

The TOWN is divided into two parts, called Below Stock and Above Stock, by the rushing Stock Ghyll, once intensively used for water power.* The best-known building, also one of the oldest, is the comical BRIDGE HOUSE of 1723, a tiny house one bay wide and one bay deep on a minute bridge. The bridge led from Ambleside Hall to its orchard, now a car park, and the little upper room was the apple store.

BELOW STOCK, on flattish ground, is the town familiar to visitors and since the late C19 unabashedly geared up for tourists. By the stream in BRIDGE STREET is Stock Cottage, with little decorative lunettes, and No. 4 with a front crowned by six chimneys and a blank diamond-shaped clock face. The MARKET PLACE to the S looks as though a broad space between the Salutation and the Royal Oak and bounded by Cheapside has been encroached upon by island buildings: the White Lion, Market Hall, Courthouse, and the monstrously jutting-out Queen's Hotel opposite. Early views show timber-

---

* From the crossing of North Road and Stock Ghyll, a footpath on the l. bank leads down past a former industrial complex, now retail or holiday accommodation. On the r. bank OLD MILL STUDIO, essentially C18, and once the manorial corn mill. A wooden launder and overshot wheel survive. The mill opposite on the l. bank was served by a branch launder, only opened when the manorial mill could spare the water. The footway emerges on Rydal Road opposite another former mill, now GLASSHOUSE RESTAURANT. Mill race and wheel remain outside, and some machinery within. The building dates mainly from the C19, when it was used as a sawmill.

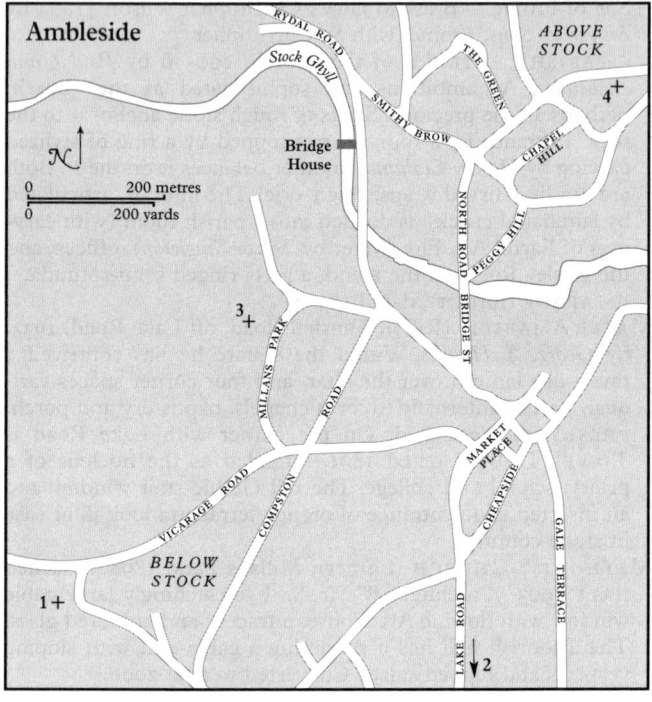

Ambleside

ABOVE STOCK

RYDAL ROAD
Stock Ghyll
Bridge House
SMITHY BROW
THE GREEN
CHAPEL HILL
NORTH ROAD
PEGGY HILL
BRIDGE ST
3
MILLANS PARK
ROAD
MARKET PLACE
VICARAGE ROAD
COMPSTON ROAD
CHEAPSIDE
GALE TERRACE
BELOW STOCK
1
LAKE ROAD
2

0 — 200 metres
0 — 200 yards

1   St Mary   3   Methodist church (former)
2   Mater Amabilis (R. C.)   4   St Anne (former)

framed houses here. The MARKET HALL is an entertaining Alpine-style building dated 1863 with a clock tower. The clock faces are in the tower roof. Insistent trefoil heads to every opening. COURTHOUSE, adjacent. 1858, Italianate. Both were paid for by the Benson Harrisons.[*] On Cheapside is the WESTMINSTER BANK, now NatWest, by *Dockray & Moore*, 1967. A clever little building designed around a series of fins and glass slots, like a row of books. Some of the glass is clear, some opaque. The fins are clad in local stone, and white marble is introduced for the entrance and sills.

At the bottom of North Road THE ROCK SHOP, by *Nigel Hutchinson, c.* 1990. Like a small barn with wood and glass excrescences. Spiral staircase with a handrail spirally bound in stainless steel. Close to the church, SPORTS PAVILION by *Robert Tarbuck, c.* 1986. Roughcast, with sloping buttresses and a half-hipped roof with a little cupola.

[*]No. 2 Gale Crescent, a drab terrace above the Market Hall, was home from 1945 to the refugee Dada artist Kurt Schwitters.

ABOVE STOCK is steeper, more intricate, without defined streets or pavements. On Chapel Hill, the church of ST ANNE, in its final incarnation a plain box of 1812 with a W tower. Low entrance bays l. and r. The body of the church with lancets filled with Victorian tracery. Converted to flats by *Gill Dockray & Partners c.* 1984. By it is HOW HEAD, a picturesque H-shaped house of unimproved texture with cylindrical chimneys, evidently long in multiple occupation. The Old Washhouse on Peggy Hill, SW, was the sculptor Josefina de Vasconcellos's workshop. The former BLACKSMITH'S, at right angles to the Golden Rule pub (*c.* 1683) uphill on Smithy Brow, is cruck-framed. On The Green, N, THE HAVEN has a demure three-bay Georgian front, but the firehouse at the rear keeps its plain spice cupboard inscribed TDM (Thomas and Dorothy Mackereth) 1652, and a large court cupboard with the same initials and the date 1658. A narrow two-storey porch dated 1674 juts out into the road.

OUTER AMBLESIDE

South of the town

ROTHAY MANOR HOTEL, Rothay Bridge. A former private house of *c.* 1825 called Rothay Bank, attributed to *Francis Webster*. White, of three bays with one-bay wings, a nice doorway, and a nice balcony railing.

LOG HOUSE, Lake Road. Imported from Norway by the artist *Alfred Heaton Cooper* (1864–1929) for his homesick wife. It was erected first at Coniston, then nearby at Wansfell, ending up here in 1922. Of interlocking pine logs, with ornamental door and window frames applied.

WATERHEAD, S, was developed by Pattinsons of Windermere; G. H. Pattinson bought the land in 1895. The GARAGE complex is late C20 work by *Nigel Hutchinson*.

WANLASS HOWE, now called Ambleside Park. 1841–2 for James Brooks; John Borron suggests it is by *Matthew Habershon*.* Later owned by David MacIver, founder of Cunard and M.P. for Birkenhead. Spectacularly sited on a blasted-out rock outcrop overlooking the head of Windermere, with a large circular bastion like The Knoll (*see* below). Business owners have spoiled it, removing veranda, bargeboards and many of its mullions. Warm air for heating was conducted through a tunnel from furnaces at the back of the STABLES below.

WANSFELL, Waterhead. Angus Taylor attributes it to *George Webster*, 1840–1, for Thomas Wrigley, papermaker, of Bury, Lancs.** Large many-gabled house with ornamental bargeboards bracketed out, and many octagonal chimneys.

*But attributed to *George Webster* by Angus Taylor.
**But George Pattinson says it was started in 1849 by *Abraham Pattinson* for the Rev. J. T. Hornby.

STAGSHAW GARDEN (National Trust) was created by the Trust's agent, *Cuthbert Acland*, from 1957.

LOW WOOD HOTEL, further s, where the A591 touches the lake shore. An essential port of call from the earliest days of Lakes tourism. An C18 hotel done up *c.* 1824 and again (by *G. Webster*) in 1843, with many later additions. The most striking feature is the side entry in the front yard: a tripartite veranda of *c.* 1859 fronts the two wide arches of a loggia, at the back of which is another triplet of door–niche–door. Inside, amid the accumulative mishmash, an oval cantilever stair of wood, some Gothic doorways, an iron column with lotus capital.

ROMAN FORT. On the N shore of Windermere about ½ m. s, beside the mouth of the River Brathay, the platform of a Roman fort, early C2, with a single defensive ditch (unnecessary elsewhere) surviving on the NE. Visible remains are those of the second fort on the site (the first, of turf and timber, constructed in the late C1). Excavated footings of the central range of buildings are displayed: headquarters, of the standard plan, with three rear rooms and a sunken strongroom; commanding officer's house – a dozen small rooms round a courtyard; double granary with characteristic multiple buttresses and rows of axial dwarf walls to carry a raised floor. Other internal buildings were of timber. The main E gate was a double portal, the other three were single portals.

(Adam Menuge notes a number of small and medium-sized early villas on OLD LAKE ROAD, by-passed by Lake Road in the C19, e.g. Iveing Cottage (1790s), mentioned in West's *Guide*, 1796 edn.)

North and west of the town

THE KNOLL, W of Rydal Road, was built in 1845–6 by *Harriet Martineau*, writer and economist. Unadorned and unpretentious, just fitting the knoll. Local stone. She claimed the design as her own, with the advice of Wordsworth, and certainly the great bastion derives from Rydal Mount. Her *Complete Guide to the English Lakes* was first published in 1855.

SCALE HOW (alias Green Bank), home of the Benson Harrisons. Georgian three-bay box of *c.* 1790, remodelled in Tudor Gothic and enlarged in 1824–5 (*Webster* again). The nucleus of Charlotte Mason College, now part of the UNIVERSITY OF CUMBRIA.

ROTHAY HOLME, now called Ambleside Lodge. A substantial villa for Elizabeth Head, 1854, by *Alfred Waterhouse*, extended 1890; his first new build. Almost pretty, with its varied bargeboards and timber veranda. Three principal gables. The big end room has panelling and a chimneypiece dated 1710.

CROFT LODGE, Clappersgate. Spectacularly vulgar; anything but a croft. Originally a white villa of before 1796, of three bays and three storeys plus two-storey wings with canted bays, with a very tall stair window at the back. All this is still visible. In 1828–30 James Brancker of Liverpool made it monstrously

Ambleside, The Knoll.
Engraving by William Banks, 1855

Gothick, probably abetted by *George Webster*. After Brancker came the Fletchers of Lever Bridge, Bolton, colliery owners and pioneers of terracotta. The chimneys are unreasonably tall, overbalanced by the hollows at the corners of their high bases, the eaves exaggeratedly deep with gloriously elaborate cast-iron brackets, each sporting a grimacing mask. An iron veranda links the two bays, between octagonal stops. An end entrance faces Ambleside, with a three-bay Tudor Perp porch. (The entrance hall is Gothick but most of the interior, now flats, is heavily Greek.)

LOUGHRIGG BROW, under Loughrigg. 1863 by *Ewan Christian*. Dour Gothic, roughcast, with dormers and wooden mullioned and mullioned-and-transomed windows. Over the door: God's Providence is my Inheritance.

(Barrie and Wendy Armstrong, *The Arts and Crafts Movement in the North West of England* (2005) add WHITE CRAGGS, Clappersgate, by *Dan Gibson c.* 1900, and ASHLEY GREEN by *Percy Worthington*, 1906, 1 m. w. NANNY BROW HOUSE, Clappersgate, was built in 1902 by the architect *Francis Whitwell*.)

APPLEBY (W)

Appleby, as Camden wrote, is almost encompassed with the River Eden. Its beauty consists in one broad planned street which ascends easily N–S from the church of St Lawrence at the foot to the castle at its head. This is New Appleby, founded *c.* 1110 by Ranulph de Meschines and given borough status by charter in 1200. E of the loop of the Eden, linked by the bridge and ford, is the older Danish settlement of Bongate, strung out along the winding course of the old A66 road. In 1281 a Carmelite friary (Whitefriars) was established in Battlebarrow, though there is nothing left. Scots raids came in 1314, 1322 and 1388. Lady Anne Clifford arrived in Appleby in 1651 and the town is strongly associated with her, as indeed is the county of Westmorland. The Eden valley railway opened in 1862 (closed 1962), the Settle and Carlisle line of 1876 is still with us. The A66 by-pass opened in 1981. The June Horse Fair attracts gypsies and travellers from all over the country to the town.

Appleby was England's smallest county town, with a population of under 3,000. When the County of Westmorland was abolished in 1974 the suffix IN WESTMORLAND was added to its name.

ST LAWRENCE, Boroughgate. Externally an unimproved Perp town church (though the aisle windows are renewals of 1863), low-roofed, battlemented and pinnacled, aisled from end to end, with a solid W tower of Westmorland type (Brough, Kendal) with two unlinked belfry lights each side. The clerestory over the nave with its gargoyles and arched three-light windows, round-topped but cusped, must be C16 or C17. In fact the bottom part of the tower is Norman (see the deeply splayed window in its N wall), the S porch entrance with its dogtooth and hollow chamfers is reused C13, and the S aisle wall is Dec. Inside, the five-bay arcades are early C14 Dec. They have quatrefoil piers, the foils more than semicircular and with fillets, and double-chamfered arches. The tower arch, off-centre, is of the same type; so is the W bay of the S aisle half embracing the tower, and the chancel arch and the two-bay S chancel chapel. The N chapel arcade with its flat square capital on its octagonal pier must go with Lady Anne Clifford's family chapel, built in 1655–6. *C. B. Martindale*, carrying out repairs in 1959, found an inscription on a beam: ANN CONNTESSE OF PEMBROKE IN ANO 1655 REPAIRED ALL THIS BUILDING. The nave ceiling, with rather parsimonious Gothick panelling and roses and what looks like an iron truss at the W end, was done by *Christopher Hodgson* in 1830–1. His chancel ceiling was removed presumably in 1959. Bracing arches either side of the chancel arch.

FURNISHINGS. SCREENS of *c.* 1500 with one-light divisions to both chapels. Plenty of graffiti. – FONT. C19, of black fossily marble, octagonal, on an octagonal base of the same stuff. – ORGAN. Free-standing in front of the tower arch. Made for

Carlisle Cathedral in 1661–2 by *Roger Preston* of Skipton, and given in 1683. The composition is of three turrets. Three fine achievements of arms on top of these, three cherubs' heads below the cornice. It has been moved within the church at least twice and bears the marks of modification. Some of the carved decoration has found its way to the CORPORATION PEW with its red baize in front of the pulpit. – STAINED GLASS. Three in the S aisle by *Heaton, Butler & Bayne*, the rest by *Wailes* (E and S chapel E) or *Wailes & Strang*. – MONUMENTS. NE chapel. Margaret, Countess of Cumberland, beloved mother of Lady Anne Clifford, †1616. Free-standing altar tomb of black marble with an alabaster effigy, attributed to *Maximilian Colt*, the royal sculptor. The tomb, of excellent workmanship, took a year to make, i.e. 1617. She wears a gilt-metal coronet. Her mantle is draped in the same way as that of Colt's Queen Elizabeth in Westminster Abbey. On the ends arms and supporters in red, on the sides symbols of mortality. The epitaph must have been composed by Lady Anne herself: 'Who fayth, love, mercy, noble constancie/To God, to virtue, to distress, to right/Observ'd, exprest, shew'd, held religiously/Hath here this monument thou seest in sight/The cover of her earthly part. But passenger/Know heaven and fame contaynes the best of her.' – Lady Anne, who died at Brougham Castle in 1676, caused her own monument to be built in her lifetime. It was begun *c.* 1655, and completed in 1657. It is very different. Austere, in black-and-white marble, with a reredos background with no effigy but a proud family tree of twenty-four shields. Again the epitaph is very typical, referring unflinchingly to 'ye dead body of ye Lady Anne Clifford'. Attributed to *Thomas Stanton* (GF). – Big Heelis family slab just W of N chapel arch. – In the former window opening between chancel and S chapel, designed indeed very like a sill, C14 effigy of a lady praying, with a floriated cross where the mullion would be. – N chapel, unsigned C18 tablets, all rather artisanish.

ST MICHAEL, Bongate. The church of the Old Town. Said to have been 'raised from its ruins' by Lady Anne Clifford, but that is a gross exaggeration. The N doorway is of pre-Norman proportions. The S doorway with dogtooth and rolls with fillets is E.E. Lady Anne may have been responsible for the ogee arch of the porch. S aisle and transept are Early Dec, with an E.E. arcade quatrefoiled with fillets but, like St Lawrence, with polygonal capitals. The low N tower was added in 1885–6. Cartouche AP 1659 (Anne, Countess of Pembroke) on the chancel N wall. The church closed in 1975 and is now an artist's studio (the nave), and house (the tower). Furnishings and some stained glass removed. – MONUMENTS. C10 hogback reused as a lintel over the S doorway. Carved with a single row of tiles above, then a broad three-strand plait over an unworked side panel. – Very crude C14 effigy, reassembled from fragments found in 1886, in a recess in the S wall. It has the arms of Roos and Vipont carved on mantle and pillow. – In the wall of the former vicarage opposite, now Courtfield Hotel, many fragments, C14 and after, including parts of a tomb canopy with the arms of Roos and Vipont.

OUR LADY OF APPLEBY (R.C.), Garth Heads Road. 1958. Dark brick and concrete, with a copper roof to the tower. Windows in threes with canted heads, but parabolic arches inside to Lady Chapel, sacristy, and behind the altar.

METHODIST CHURCH (Wesleyan), The Sands. 1888, extended 1904. Gothic, with a show front and utilitarian sides.

ROCK CHAPEL (KINGDOM HALL), The Sands. 1872. Slotted into the red sandstone cliff, and built upon a plinth of solid rock. Side-entry chapel, mildly Gothic.

APPLEBY CASTLE.* The earliest documentary evidence appears to be in a Pipe Roll of 1130. The castle belonged to the Viponts before it went to the Cliffords in the late C13. It remained Clifford property to the death of the Lady Anne, who had carried out a major restoration following the Civil War, beginning in 1651. It then went to her daughter the Countess of Thanet, whose son Thomas, 6th Earl of Thanet, was subsequently responsible for reconstructing the domestic ranges. Later works, largely aimed at improving the silhouette of the castle, were minor in nature, so allowing a rare impression of an ancient fortress repaired and remodelled in the C17 but never heavily restored or remodelled during the Romantic era. Today the castle looks surprisingly similar to Buck's engraving of 1739, although its landscape setting has matured and softened. The estate passed by descent in the Tufton family, earls of Thanet (up to 1849) and subsequently barons Hothfield, until 1962.

The splendid castle stands at the top of the town up on the steep bank of the Eden, surrounded by moats marking an inner and at least two outer baileys. The castle dominates the neck of the peninsula formed by the river. The oldest building is the later C12 KEEP, of squarish silver-grey stones, kept happily isolated from all else and finished off with four turrets with pretty lanterns. Decorative weathervanes, dated 1784. The ground floor has a round-headed entrance. Another doorway on the first floor, approached by an external staircase. The partition walls on all floors are Lady Anne Clifford's, neatly dividing the plan in half to provide lodgings. As the castle roofs are known to have been stripped after the Clifford involvement in the Rising of the North of 1569, it is likely that Lady Anne's alterations were based on structural, as well as practical, considerations. The new transverse wall contains flues and provides support for the new floors, making easier the installation of beams into existing sockets in the outer walls. Large windows, their details altered, on the first as well as more customarily on the second floor. It is difficult to determine how much may be original fabric and how much an intervention of the conservatively minded Lady Anne. The keep was originally lower, as the former roof-lines indicate. The merlons of the battlements have slits.

---

* This entry was revised by Andrew Martindale.

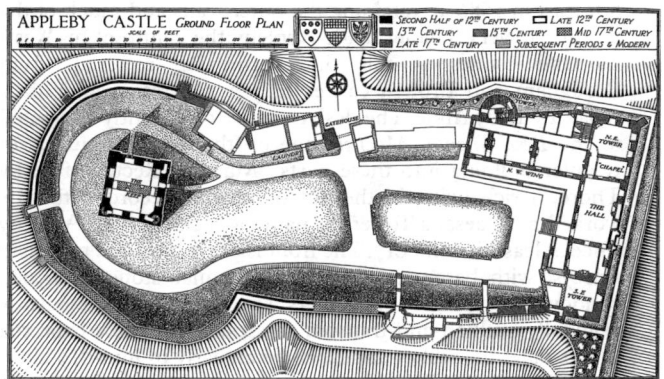

Appleby Castle.
Plan, 1936

The form of the CURTAIN WALLING is largely late C12, but with much C17 rebuilding after Civil War damage. It is note-worthy that the Lady Anne did not risk any restoration of the wall-walk or crenellations. There is evidence of at least one semicircular wall tower, probably of *c.* 1310, on the S side, and a well-preserved tower of similar date is attached to the later N range, with a garderobe projection high up on corbels. In the NE tower wall is another garderobe, complete with stone seat. The principal entrance to the courtyard, from the N, dates from the C17, although parts of the western pier are survivals of a large gatehouse, built 1418 and destroyed in the Civil War.

E RANGE. The outer walls of the principal domestic range, with N and S towers, are attributed to the C15, though not many features remain to demonstrate it. The POSTERN in the middle was ascribed by the RCHME to the late C12, but is more likely to belong to Robert Clifford's adaptations in the C14 (cf. Brough). It has a round, single-chamfered arch and in front of it a giant blank arch. The portcullis groove is preserved. Most of the SE tower is of 1883, when it was extended, raised a storey and battlemented. Of the C15 the NE tower, with a tunnel-vaulted sub-basement, a two-light window to the N, and a doorway in the basement in the S wall. Another leads from the N to the E wing. On the first floor (now the principal floor of the E range) a former CHAPEL or oratory has its C15 piscina. It is tempting to associate this work, and other evidence in the E range, with the recorded rebuilding in 1454 of the decayed hall, chapel and great chamber by Thomas Clifford. The S wing close to the SE tower has a one-light window with a shouldered lintel inside. This must have belonged to a room not otherwise preserved and is probably earlier than the C15.

But the E range is really remembered not as medieval, but as a stately piece of late C17 architecture. The COURTYARD FRONT was rebuilt, and the rest largely reconstructed, by the

6th Earl in 1686–8, retaining the outer walls and much of the
N and S towers. Thanet made Appleby the centre of his Westmorland estates at this time, removing materials from
Brougham and Brough castles only a generation after their
repair by Lady Anne. The design can be confidently attributed
to the *Rev. Thomas Machell*, one of 'the first introducers of
Regular building into these parts'. Machell, Rector of Kirby
Thore, a rich living in the gift of Thanet, recorded that he
worked at 'Caesar's Tower', a name associated with Appleby
since at least the mid C17. The front is of six bays and two main
storeys, with basement and attics. Regular stone-mullioned
windows, flat pilasters in two tiers. The windows were evidently
originally mullion-and-transom crosses, as would be expected
at this date; the sashes appear to be an early to mid-C19 alteration. The RCHME speculated, on the evidence of assembly
numbering, that the basement windows are the work of Lady
Anne, reused by Thanet. Doorway in the fourth bay, with an
open curly pediment on brackets. The window above it has
brackets too, and in the parapet of this bay, a length of
balustrading. The N range was added in 1695. This is more
utilitarian, although the floor heights and windows are the
same.

The HALL rises through a storey and a half, and is entered
at its S end: surely a reflection of the layout of the medieval
hall that Thanet rebuilt, keeping its proportions but dispensing with a screens passage. Coved ceiling, its Gothic detail
clearly C19 (cf. the parish church). The panelling however is
certainly of *c.* 1690. The STAIRCASE, adjoining the N tower, has
strong twisted balusters and a ramped handrail, and is apparently of 1695. The quality of joinery in the staircase and adjacent rooms is high, with boldly sized mouldings. The N WING
has a middle corridor all along its length on each floor, evidently inserted. The suites of rooms facing the courtyard, originally *enfilade*, have some good original bolection-moulded
doors and panelling. Some fireplaces enriched with brought-
in antiquarian carvings, evidently in the C19. In the NE tower
adjoining the main staircase, two major rooms: on the principal floor the dining room, and above the best bedroom. Both
have C17 woodwork, the latter with fitted tapestries.

In the courtyard w of the main gate, a detached SERVICE
RANGE incorporating a brewhouse of 1651 and a later C18
laundry. NW of the castle the STABLES, of 1653. A large building with an inner quadrangle, but modest in its details. To its
NE Lady Anne's BEE HOUSE, square, with a pyramid roof. The
structure of the GARDENS, with a yew-lined walk from the E
terrace overlooking the Eden to the walled gardens to the S, is
evidently C17 or early C18. Plain later C19 LODGE at the
entrance to the park from the head of Boroughgate.

BATHS, Chapel Street. By *Eden District Council* under *Paul Bruns-
don*, 1994. White, with bowed front and arched roof, vaguely
Deco. Lynn Pearson notes a large pictorial tile panel (1995) by
Maggie Angus Berkowitz.

GRAMMAR SCHOOL, Battlebarrow. 1886–7 by *George Watson* of Penrith, in grey and red stone with red tile cresting. It incorporates in a corner porch a doorway from the original grammar school building, dated 1671: square pilasters with strapwork and a plaque with a pediment. The Victorian front has mullioned-and-transomed windows. Former master's house l., chapel r., with a four-light Perp window. Further buildings 1927, 1936, 1960–3 and 1971–2. The school is now co-educational and comprehensive.

STATION, Station Road. 1876. Very smart. The largest of the Midland Railway's three standard Settle and Carlisle designs (cf. Kirkby Stephen), but carried out, unusually, in brick. Frilly bargeboards, glazed centre section. Stationmaster's house and railway terraces nearby.

PERAMBULATIONS

1. Old Appleby, east of the river

The single long S–N street comprising Bongate–The Sands––Battlebarrow is cut into the red rock in places, in the middle coming down at The Sands to the Eden BRIDGE. This is of 1889 in the style of the late C18. Two segmental arches with quatrefoiled Gothic circles in the spandrels. Near it are the Police Station and former Shire Hall. Both white-rendered with red sandstone dressings. The POLICE STATION was converted in 1971 from the county gaol, of 1770–1 by *Robert Fothergill*. Three bays and a hipped roof with two low projecting one-bay wings (restored), one arched through. The SHIRE HALL to the l., originally a court house, is of 1776–8 by *Daniel Benn* of Whitehaven, Agent of Sir James Lowther, with additions of 1813–14 (r.), 1879 (behind) and the late C20. A long plain building of eight bays with several entrances at the l. end. High walls of the former gaol behind.* *Francis Webster* carried out extensive work to the gaol in 1818, 1824 etc.

In Bongate, S, OLD HALL FARMHOUSE was a longhouse, without solid cross-partitions, gentrified and sashed in the C18. Chimney at each end, door roughly in the middle. Dining room with panelled wainscot, shutters. Sitting room with good panelling and built-in cupboards either side of the fireplace, with fluted pilasters. Good doors throughout, very thin; many five-panelled, i.e. with a single centre panel. Behind St Michael's church, Mill Hill leads down to the former BONGATE MILL. Three rubble stone storeys under a pyramidal roof. Large sandstone arch for the now-lost wheel. Fine diagonal stone WEIR.

---

* *Robert Adam* prepared Palladian plans for Town Hall, County Court and Gaol in 1766–7 which would have transformed Appleby's architectural fortunes, but as usual Sir James left them on the drawing board.

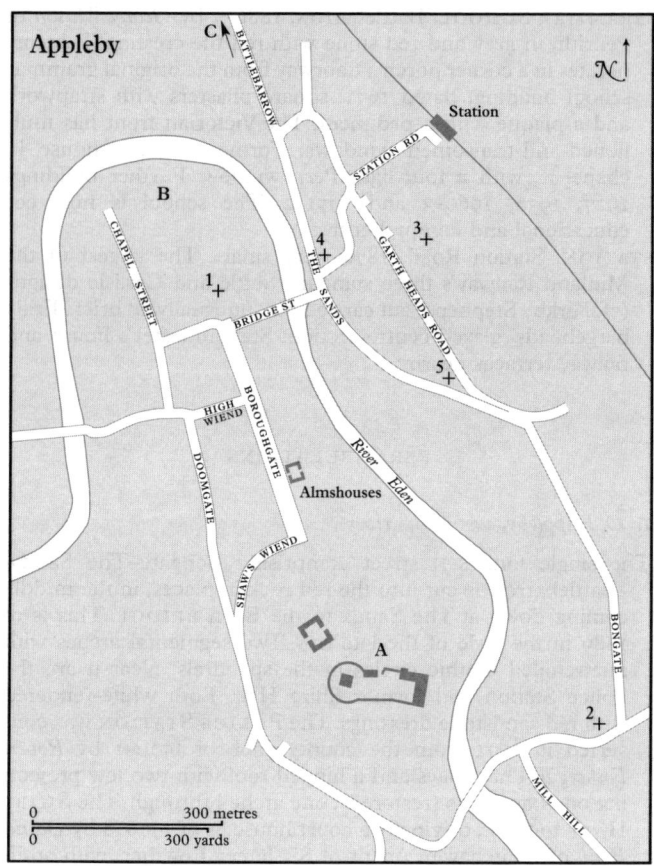

1   St Lawrence
2   St Michael
3   Our Lady of Appleby (R.C.)
4   Methodist Church
5   Rock Chapel

A   Castle
B   Baths
C   Grammar School

Going N, THE FRIARY at the N end of Battlebarrow commemorates the house of the Whitefriars. Early C19. Three bays, with
a porch of two pairs of thin Ionic columns.
By the river next to the footbridge, s, is *Joss Smith*'s Millennium
SCULPTURE, Primrose Stone. There are ten of these Eden
Benchmarks in all.

2. *New Appleby, west of the river*

Over the bridge is the plain, wide-spaced, ashlar front of the
former King's Head (C19). Then a rounded corner takes us
into BOROUGHGATE, Ranulph de Meschines's planned town.

Other such single wide streets are the new towns planted by
the Bishops of Winchester about 1200 (Alresford, Downton).
It is a pretty sight, wide, not quite straight, with the smartly
painted Doric columns of the High and Low crosses at the
ends and the C16 Moot Hall in the middle, closer to the W than
the E frontages, with grass and trees higher up. At the bottom
a CLOISTER or screen, by *Robert Smirke*, 1811, divides church
from town. Gothic, toy-like and unsophisticated; two two-
storey end pavilions with corbelled parapets, seven arches
without capitals between. It replaces a 'cloister' commissioned
by Bishop Smith of Carlisle from *Thomas Machell* in 1694–5.*
The MOOT HALL is dated 1596 RAW over the S door, but has
C18 windows. Bellcote on S gable.

Boroughgate is short, so it is best to take one side at a time. Starting at the Cloister, LOW CROSS is a Doric column with strong
entasis, on a square base and carrying a square top. Said to be
an C18 copy of the High Cross. The weathervane bears the date
1836. Going up the E SIDE, the first building of interest is
EDEN PHARMACY (No. 11), C17, with stepped three-light
windows in the dormer gables, like those of the church
clerestory but simpler; round-headed but uncusped. Each light
is given its own length of straight dripmould. The lower two
floors are probably earlier but still most likely mid C17. They
have the same big scrolls to the drip-ends as Tarn House at
Ravenstonedale (q.v.). More scrolls to the imposts of the side
entry. The earlier fenestration type can be seen. After the Hare
and Hounds (C18) and a couple of shops, comes BARCLAYS
BANK, originally the Carlisle and Cumberland Bank, of 1876
by *George Watson*. Confidently prosperous bank language in
Gothic, faced in pink snecked rubble with buff dressings. Three
storeys. Granite colonnettes with stiff-leaf capitals, white-
painted iron balconies. Openwork parapet, dormer windows
on the roof. Curved corner entry. HSBC is its companion, also
late C19. Buff ashlar. Segmental arch to rear yard, round-
arched ground-floor windows, segmental-headed first-floor
windows, top-floor sashes, castellated parapet on brackets.
After another shop and the Court 2 entry is the WHITE
HOUSE, Appleby's most individually memorable building. It
dates from 1764–5, and the design is attributed to a carpenter
called *Henry Bellas* or *Bellhouse*, for John (Jack) Robinson,
Agent for the Lowthers and Secretary to the Treasury under
Lord North. Oblong and tower-like, stuccoed, of three very tall
floors with string courses and quoins. Each floor has three
widely spaced Rococo Gothic windows front and side, and
there are little ovals on their sides in the N attic. The entrance
is on this side, with an ogee head under an odd and graceful
ogee pediment with two rising curves. Rear wing and coachhouse have polygonal bays with similar windows. After the
A'board Inn comes No. 30, as frivolous in its way as the
White House. A former Mechanics' Institute, prominently

*Kirkby Stephen built a classical screen in the equivalent position in 1810,
see p. 470.

dated 1851, of pink stone with frilly bargeboards, clustered chimneys on the diagonal, dripmoulds and Tudor windows. Three bays with a centre gable, but entry is via the arched carriageway, l. WHITE RAILS is an L-shaped C18 house of red ashlar with a garden in the angle. The MASONIC HALL is the former Bank House, early C19, of five bays, three storeys with a centre arch. A short run of low cottages precedes ST ANNE'S HOSPITAL, 1651–3: Lady Anne Clifford's almshouses for twelve poor women (cf. her Beamsley Hospital, Yorkshire West Riding). Red stone, low, seven well-spaced windows, roof-line sloping down the hill. Arms over the plain central archway, with further arms by every door round the trim cobbled yard. The centre house on the E has been removed. There is a little CHAPEL in the lower l. corner, lit only by a pair of round-arched E windows. Simple pulpit with C17 panelling in NE corner, benches with simply shaped ends at the sides, segmental plaster ceiling. – WALL PAINTINGS. Commandments W, texts N and S with cherubs' heads, and a Doom E, with angel trumpeters, cherubim, the heavenly host, skull and crossbones, and God at the top. All monochrome except for red for the text references. A few quieter houses near the top, and the Castle Lodge (*see* p. 108) facing down.

The HIGH CROSS is before the castle gates. Like the Low Cross, but this time inscribed 'Retain your Loyalty Preserve your Rights'. C17. Now proceeding down the W side, starting where Shaw's Wiend comes in around the castle perimeter. On this side the houses have railed front gardens – not the other side. The ROYAL BRITISH LEGION building is early C19, a symmetrical composition (Nos. 42 and 44) about a centre arch flanked by pedestrian arches and a tripartite window over. The door to No. 38 opens not into the house but into a hallan or cross-passage going through to the garden. C18 maps show that this was a common feature. The shambles were outside on the street here. The former Black Bull at No. 36 has been stripped of its render, revealing its architectural history, with two generations of windows, mid-C17 (blocked) and C19. The earlier windows are small and square, with fire-windows on both floors by the front door. C17 moulded doorway with decorated lintel. Next door is the WHITE HART, late C18 or early C19. Then the COURTYARD GALLERY, which was a C17 granary, then in about 1900 a dame school. RED HOUSE, distinguished and prominent, is dated 1717. Seven-bay house in red ashlar for Thomas Carleton, steward to Lord Thanet. The façade was achieved by uniting several burgage plots. Ground floor on a rusticated basement behind railings, so steps up to the front door with its segmental pediment. Doorway with bolection moulding. At the back a displaced doorway dated 1663. Blake Tyson notes the similarity of the staircase to that at Appleby Castle, both made by *Mark Gardner*. Next door is also C18 but in pink ashlar with contrasting white quoins and a thin semi-circular door hood. Then comes the narrow entry of High Wiend, followed by the POST OFFICE of 1912 and the hugely

confident CONSERVATIVE CLUB probably of same date, both
in red ashlar. In the narrow space behind the Moot Hall is a
house dated 1772 on a hopper. Red sandstone with quoins,
three storeys. The centre has been nastily built out in white
brick on iron columns, over a porch and shopfronts. TUFTON
ARMS, 1873. Cheerful, prettily polychrome in pink and buff,
with a rhythm of dormer–gable–dormer–dormer–half–hipped
gable, the last with a big oriel window (maximum variety!).
Veranda raised at one end to form an entrance canopy. Appropriately fussy stair within. Finally the SPAR shop, with a nice
twiddly Victorian iron shopfront extending forwards, and the
CROWN AND CUSHION INN, C17–C18 with a bolection-
moulded doorway.

RUTTER MILL, in a picturesque spot below the waterfalls on
Hoff Beck, 2¼ m. S. It started as a corn mill in the early C19,
and became the power station of the Great Asby Electric Light
Co. in the 1930s. The breast-shot wheel survives. Now holiday
cottages.

ARKLEBY (C) see PLUMBLAND

ARLECDON (C)   *0010*

Former mining village, composed chiefly of two long terraces in
the form of a V.

ST MICHAEL, ½ m. N. The chancel arch, twice chamfered,
remains of the C13 church. A rebuild of 1829 left it as a roughcast box with wide lancets and a W porch. In 1904–5 *J. H.
Martindale* built a rock-faced tower, Perp in style with a large
W window and paired bell-openings, outside the W end with a
short link to join it to the nave. Polygonal baptistery attached
to the tower on the S, stair-turret N. The rest was cased and
battlemented to match with the same red stone, and a new
open roof installed. – REREDOS and PULPIT of Caen stone,
painted white. One ought to disapprove, but the effect is
charming. – FONT. Dated 1578. – WALL PAINTING. Early C20,
floral. – STAINED GLASS. E, three medallions of C17 Continental glass set in a painterly background *c.* 1829. Side
windows of the 1870s–80s, pictorial, grungy; attributed by
Leslie Smith to *Gibbs*, or *Powell Bros* of Leeds.
   WAR MEMORIAL. By *Martindale*, 1923. Unusually good
Celtic cross made in several sections. He must have done the
elaborate LYCHGATE too.

At ROWRAH, SE of the village, a ravaged landscape with flooded
quarries and complicated former railway junctions: testimony
to the rivalry of Victorian entrepreneurs to exploit the convenient closeness of the limestone to the coal and ore needed for
steelmaking.

ROWRAH HALL, ¾ m. SE. In a pretty hollow surrounded by the remains of three railway lines. Built *c.* 1703 by the Skelton family. Five-bay front with cross-mullioned windows and an open segmental pediment over the door. The three-bay house attached l. was built in 1729 by Richard and Deborah Skelton. Walled garden with rusticated gatepiers dated R & DS 1739.

(SCALLOW, 1¼ m. E, nearer Kirkland. Dated 1687. Mullioned windows connected by a continuous dripmould. Above the door a blank vertically placed oval. 'Renovated out of all recognition', and in 1968 'virtually all features mentioned have been erased'.)

ARMATHWAITE (C)

CHAPEL OF CHRIST AND ST MARY. A simple cell with a bellcote, half-buried in the hillside. According to Bishop Nicholson in 1703, it was built and endowed by Richard Skelton of Armathwaite Castle soon after the Restoration, a chapel built in 1402 having fallen into disrepair. It has a few small round-headed windows with one hollow chamfer. Tie-beam roof with kingposts. – STAINED GLASS. E window by *William Morris & Co.*, 1926, the l. light designed by *J. H. Dearle*, the r. a *Burne-Jones* design. S, by *A. L. Moore & Son*, 1915, after Rubens. W by *A. K. Nicholson*, 1937.

SCHOOL HOUSE below. More church-like than the church, with a huge clock on the gable dated 1854.

ARMATHWAITE CASTLE. First mentioned in the early C16. Big cubic block standing almost in the river. Three storeys, double-span roof. The plan shows a massive thick-walled double pile with a spine wall. The only parallel in the region is the C16 tower at Millom Castle; but this has no vaults. The C18 front wall, away from the river, is thinner. The style is typically North Country, reminiscent of Duncombe or Gilling (Yorkshire North Riding) and a little of Vanbrugh. Broad rusticated door surround with straight entablature. The same entablature for the ground-floor windows. Flat raised window surrounds. A façade of few words and great dignity. *J. H. Martindale* in the early C20 Frenchified an C18 wing with large dormers in a mansard roof.

(ENGLETHWAITE HALL. By *G. H. Hunt*, 1880–2. Demolished.)

LOW HOUSE, 1½ m. NE. I + SG 1793 (Graham) on the stair protrusion at the back. Pretty five-bay house, colourwashed pink and standing on an enviable plat above the river. One-bay wings r. and l. The porch has battlements made like triglyphs and pillars with a curious seaweed-like encrustation and capitals of no known order. The rear wing, stables and lodge were added in the 1880s by *J. H. Martindale* for the Eckroyds. The entrance hall and stair have a delicate cornice with little conoids, like fan-vaulting. The hallway has been thrown into the dining room by means of a segmental arch. The stair is a cantilever, curved at the turn, with mahogany rail and turned balusters.

DRYBECK FARM is below Low House on the river bank. Dated JJS 1704 over a blocked doorway at the back. The house is unusually narrow and clearly had a steeper roof than now, presumably thatched.

NUNNERY, 2¾ m. SE. The earliest reference is 1200. The nuns were so harassed by the Scots that in 1480 they had to reinvent their own charter, spuriously dating their foundation to 1089 and William Rufus. At the Dissolution in 1537 there were three Benedictine nuns and the prioress. The buildings were granted (1552) to William Grayme, passing to the Aglionbys in 1694. The present house was rebuilt in 1715 by Henry Aglionby. 3-3-3 bays, two storeys, the centre advancing just a little – very like Hutton Hall in Penrith, and like it built of deep red stone. Channelled base, sill course, windows with flat raised frames, coved cornice and a balustrade. The doorcase has Doric pilasters, a metope frieze, and segmental pediment. The building, unusually for the time in the region, is a double pile, with a partial valley and regularly spaced chimneys. It is older than it seems, in fact the older remains may have determined the double-pile plan. At the ends four or five storeys of small mullioned windows. At the back several large mullioned-and-transomed windows, probably belonging to John Aglionby's alterations of 1694, and an odd shelf-like projection of the ground floor. This lower part is a remnant of the nunnery.

The interiors, badly cut about for hotel use, are mostly of 1715. Broad stair with three balusters per step and modestly carved tread-ends. The spine wall incorporates odd openings and niches. In the back wall is a beautiful mid-C13 segmental arch, hollow-moulded with dogtooth paterae; perhaps a tomb niche or a lavatorium.

STEADING, round a large attached courtyard. Many-arched, with a castellated wall to the garden.

NUNNERY WALKS. A landscaped promenade a little removed from the house, as at Stourhead, but very different in character. Dramatically engineered paths, vertiginous steps and viewing platforms capitalize on the antics of little River Croglin in its efforts to break through a band of harder rock. 'The rocks excite the struggling stream to tenfold fury, who with difficulty pushes his waters through an horrible fissure, and forms a cascade . . . The over-arching cliffs and solemn shades reverberate the roar in a manner truly tremendous.' (Richard Warner, *A Tour Through the Northern Counties of England*, 1802.) Having created a series of waterfalls and scooped-out hollows, the Croglin falls, exhausted, into the broad and beautiful Eden. Nature dictates: there is no attempt at imposing a design, no embellishments or artificial aids to contemplation, except a small SUMMERHOUSE.

RAILWAY VIADUCTS. Two splendid viaducts of 1875 by *J. S. Crossley* for the Midland Railway's Settle–Carlisle line. Both of red sandstone with brick soffits, and 80 ft (24.5 metres) high. s of the village, ARMATHWAITE VIADUCT: nine arches, 176 yds (162 metres) long. 1 m. N, DRYBECK VIADUCT: seven arches, 139 yds (128 metres) long.

ARNSIDE (W)

Railway resort facing NW towards Grange over the broad sands of the Kent estuary. The promenade is lined with tall board-ing houses of the 1860s–80s, well furnished with timber-framed bays, verandas and porches. In contrast, the little sugar-plum of UNDERHILL and UNDERWOOD, Nos. 16 and 17, *cottages ornés*. Peeping through from behind them is a folly tower with wonky battlements of bits of limestone pavement, silhouetted amongst great beeches. Higher up are large houses such as OAKFIELD LODGE (YHA) of 1911, until the late C20 typically occupied by a private school; and, well out of sight, the Leeds Poor Children's Holiday Camp (opened 1905, rebuilt 1919), and, until demolished in 2000, Grange View Convalescent Home of 1938–9.

Every now and then a train clanks over the KENT VIADUCT, carrying the former Furness Railway to Barrow across Milnthorpe Sands. Its construction barred navigation to the port of Milnthorpe, upstream, and assisted in much land recla-mation. The building of the 522-yd (482-metre) bridge in 1856–7 was difficult. The original iron structure, by *Sir James Brunlees*, was very similar to the same engineer's Solway Viaduct at Bowness (q.v.; also Leven Viaduct, Ulverston). The contractors, *W. & J. Galloway* of Manchester, developed a novel method of pile-driving using high-pressure water jets. The single line was doubled in 1863. Cast-iron girders replaced by wrought iron in 1887, original piers encased in masonry 1915–17. Major refurbishment in the 1990s has not signifi-cantly altered the viaduct's appearance.

ST JAMES. The nucleus is a small nave and chancel by *Miles Thompson* of 1864–6, founded with the establishment of the resort. Plate tracery. It was extended w in 1884 by *Stephen Shaw*, with further enlargements 1905 (*R. Morton Rigg*, N) and 1912–14 (*Austin & Paley*, s) as the town grew. N aisle a lean-to, with a low arcade of octagonal columns, enabling a minute clerestory to be squeezed in. s aisle with taller round columns and its own roof, necessitating a pair of dormers to light the nave. One of them rises picturesquely above the N clerestory. – STAINED GLASS. Vivid E window, †1880, by *F. Burrow* of Milnthorpe. No fewer than four war memorial windows in the s aisle, by *Shrigley & Hunt* and *Abbott & Co.* (one, far w). British Legion window signed CB (*Christine Boyce*), 1995. Good Shepherd, a three-lighter (†1936) by *Edward Payne*, with some plating to obtain subtle colours. A single N window also by Payne, 1948.

OUR LADY OF LOURDES (R.C.), Silverdale Road. It was the National School of 1880, converted in 1977. A simple but entertaining building with exaggeratedly shouldered windows cleverly grouped at the road end under a bipartite relieving arch.

METHODIST CHURCH, Chapel Lane. The same story of incremental growth as the Anglican church, but not so obvious. The chapel built in 1875 was end-on to the lane. A big social room was added at right angles in 1888, then in 1899–1900 *Stephen Shaw* of Kendal made a new nave at right angles to the chapel, in front of the wing, making it a T. The original doorway was turned into a plate-tracery window with a buttress in the middle. Inside, two-bay arcades divide the old chapel into three. Refurnished 2006. – STAINED GLASS. Ritual E window by a former minister, *Norris Roscoe*, made by *Barrowclough & Sanders* of Lancaster, 1921. W, a Te Deum, by the same makers and possibly the same designer, 1920. Both with plenty of streaky purple.

CEMETERY, Silverdale Road, S. With a pretty domestic-looking CHAPEL, 1904. – HEADSTONE of the cricketer John Popplewell †1936, with a lively representation of 'Owzat!', and the rhyme 'And when the one great scorer comes . . .'

ARNSIDE TOWER, in a beautiful position 1 m. S. Adam de Thweng(?) is said to have built Arnside, Dallam and Hazelslack towers *c.* 1375, though Anthony Emery and others see the existing structure as mid- or later C15. Damaged by 'a mighty wind and was burned which it pleased the Lord to per-mitte' in 1602, but repaired after that. A self-contained tower house, *c.* 48 by *c.* 33 ft (44 by 30 metres), with no sign of an attached hall range. Limestone rubble with red sandstone dressings. A projection on the NE corner houses a huge oven at ground level and four small rooms above. Smaller garderobe attachment at the opposite corner. The walls stand to the height of the corbelled parapet on three sides, but the W wall fell in 1884 in great chunks of masonry, revealing the interior with its carious walls: fireplaces on four floors, garderobes also on four levels, and spiral stairs in the remains of a cross wall. The entrance was at ground level in the E wall, next to the stair.

HAZELSLACK TOWER, 1¼ m. E across Arnside Moss. In a farm-yard with a pair of cottages and a bank barn in close atten-dance. Ruinous C14 solar tower, much smaller than Arnside Tower. Clear marks of a hall roof and fireplaces on the E side, so it was not free-standing. On the same side is a small origi-nal doorway, with a pointed head, and unchamfered. Lime-stone rubble with sandstone for a few of the small square windows and a single two-light cusped window on the W side of the upper floor. The ground floor is partly tunnel-vaulted. The plan is quite complex – a blunt L divided into two chambers, with a stair and garderobes (the dig-out hole can be seen) squeezed into the SW corner.

ARTHURET (C)

ST MICHAEL, ¾ m. S of Longtown. 'In 1607 James I passing this way took compassion on the church here which had been frequently laid waste by the Scotch, and ordered a brief for rebuilding of it. Much money was raised and a handsome church built.' So writes Chancellor Walter Fletcher in his summary of *c.* 1815. The new church, begun in 1609, is built to a spacious medieval plan (on the medieval footprint?), with a strong W tower (top stage *c.* 1700), long nave, and aisles to both nave and chancel. It is long and very even, with just a small step in the parapet to mark the junction of chancel and nave. The style is Perp, with flat roofs, battlements and blunt pinnacles throughout. The windows with four-centred heads; of three lights to the clerestory and S aisle, two lights to the N aisle. These aisle windows are transomed. Only the E window suggests the C17 date; a six-lighter with two sets of intersecting tracery and a circle in the head – originally an oval set vertically, and with a round and not a pointed arch. This original 1609 window, removed at the restoration of 1868, is at Whoof House, Scotby (q.v.).

The inside is more peculiar. There is still a chancel arch, which is unexpected in a through church, though the slight step noted outside might have suggested it. The capitals are more similar to the C13 than to later centuries. The two-bay chancel arcades and the two W bays of the nave have plain octagonal piers and capitals and twice-chamfered arches. The piers of the middle bays however are made up of half-octagons facing in all four directions. Those facing N and S, i.e. across the nave and aisles, continue above the capitals to the level of the chancel arch springing, then change to flat pilasters. Were cross-arches, or even vaulting, contemplated?

FURNISHINGS. Bishop Nicholson intriguingly recorded in 1704 the choir 'in cathedral modes', but the present CHOIR STALLS, PULPIT and SIDE SCREENS are early C20. – FONT, nine-sided, 1609. Baptistery furnishings 1908. – STAINED GLASS. E window, 1868–9, by *John Scott & Son* of Carlisle. S window, †1970, St Michael and the building of this church, by *Stanley M. Scott*. Baptistery, *Mayer & Co.*, 1908. – MONUMENTS. Brass, late medieval; tiny, on the chancel arcade N. Two slim hands holding a heart, a cross fleury behind. It represents a heart-burial. – Graham tablets to 1997, including Sir George Graham †1657, small, with a curly pediment, and Dr Robert Graham of Netherby †1782, with an urn.

CROSS, outside, W. Chamfered socket stone. Tapering shaft with a rude Maltese cross incised upon it. Broken and incomplete ring cross-head, mounted in an iron armature. It is post-Conquest.

ASBY (W) *see* GREAT ASBY

ASKAM-IN-FURNESS (L)   2070
with Ireleth

Ireleth is the old village on the hillside. Askam on the flat below
is a product of the C19 and the West Cumberland ore field. Ironworks were established in 1865 on the saltmarsh, rows of brick
houses laid out close by, and within a few years a large village
had come into being. There was to have been a church, square,
hotel, market hall, public park; not realized. Long dun-coloured
terraces end in slag banks or the sea. The works closed at the end
of the 1914–18 war and were cleared away in 1933–4.

ASKAM STATION. Opened 1877 (Furness Railway). It is excep-
    tionally pretty. Long platform range with external timber
    framing. The roof is brought forward on big fat brackets to
    make a shelter. Small stone signal box on the same platform,
    and a smaller passenger shelter opposite. All by *E. G. Paley*.
    Large CO-OP building opposite. The village has a cast-iron
    DRINKING FOUNTAIN (1897) like those at Dalton-in-Furness
    and Nenthead.
ASKAM PIER is essentially a long slag bank projecting into the
    sea. The outer end was levelled and piled to form a quay.
BRICKWORKS, 1 m. S (Furness Brick and Tile Co.). Impressive.
    Large continuous kiln, with a single tall chimney.
ST MARY, Ireleth. High up, overlooking the Askam terraces and
    across the Duddon estuary to Millom and Black Combe.
    1864–5 by *E. G. Paley* for the 5th Duke of Buccleuch. The cost
    was £2,044. Silver and red stone. Interestingly quirky build-
    ing with Dec tracery N and E but proto-tracery W and S.
    A square turret rises roguishly by the chancel arch N, carrying
    a tiny spire. (STAINED GLASS. E window by *Shrigley & Hunt*.)
    – Outside, by the tower door, stone tub PULPIT from the old
    chapel of 1612 (the pulpit itself is not so old).
    (SCHOOL. 1862.)
MARSH GRANGE, 1⅜ m. N. C17, with a walled front garden and
    massive GATEPIERS topped with outsize stone balls. They are
    heavily moulded and have up their middles thin pilasters with
    sunk panels – all very English Baroque. The front range makes
    quite a show. Five bays grouped 1–3–1, wooden cross-
    mullioned windows. Doorcase with bolection moulding, pulv-
    inated frieze and pilasters hollow-moulded like those of the
    gatepiers. Behind the ridge four diagonal stacks in a row (cf.
    Rampside Hall, q.v.), off-centre, indicating the earlier C17
    house behind. (At the back a long early C17 farmhouse range,
    making a bent T.)

ASKERTON CASTLE (C)

3 m. s of Bewcastle

30 Stern fortress house on the lonely road from Hadrian's Wall to Bewcastle. The front range, taken as E, i.e. facing the road running N, is twin-towered. It has three floors, and is built of very large stones roughly coursed – not Roman therefore – on a massive rough plinth. Surviving early windows are mere slits below, small, rectangular and heavily barred above. A high barmkin wall, similarly constructed, encloses a small courtyard behind.

Askerton was closely linked to Naworth (q.v.) from its first recording in 1295 until the 1920s. We have few dates, and the structure is open to different interpretations. There may have been, as Anthony Emery postulates, a c13 ground-floor hall, though the only possible c13 relic is a blocked doorway with two-centred head at the N end, an odd position (but cf. Newbiggin Hall, Carleton). In 1391 Ranulph Dacre was granted licence to crenellate, and it was probably he who moved the living accommodation upstairs for security. The end towers may have been added then, although it is difficult to see a break in the stonework. A century later Thomas, 2nd Lord Dacre (1467–1525), made it a bit more civilized, with mid-storey mullioned windows with three lights and hoodmoulds, and a new roof. Dendrochronology gives us a date c. 1494 for the trusses. Perhaps to compensate for the loss of defensive parapets, the towers were then heightened. They may be compared with the watch turret at Drumburgh (Bowness-on-Solway), also altered by Dacre at this time. Both towers at Askerton show an obvious discontinuity near the top, above which, on the s tower, are Thomas Dacre's initials. The subsidiary wings round the barmkin walls were added soon after.

The castle was dismantled in 1567 because of the involvement of Leonard Dacre in the Rising of the North. However, later c16 accounts recommend its repair and in 1598 it was again a house of strength, the only house in Gilsland fit for the Land Sergeant to dwell in. Nothing then was done until the mid c19, when *Salvin* put in large characterless windows and fireplaces on the ground floor and a stone stair to the first floor. In the 1920s Captain *Edmond L. Warre* carried out further modernization, including a full-height stair in the s tower.

FRONT WING. Entry today is by a c19 porch at the N end of the front block, next to the N tower; the c13 doorway is disused and hidden in a cupboard backing onto a c19 fireplace. A lump of masonry here could represent a turning stair. Otherwise there is no evidence for permanent pre-Salvin access to the first floor; in fact there is very little to see at ground level, but it gets more exciting as you get higher. Ascent is by the c19 straight stone stair in the centre, or by Captain Warre's Arts and Crafts stair in the s tower, a nice piece in c17 style (although its flat balusters are not Cumbrian). So the family lived upstairs, bastle-fashion. The two upper floors are linked by a steep half-turn stair in the thickness of the courtyard wall. The top floor gives a great feeling of comfortable security, as was no doubt intended. It is dominated by kingpost trusses, set low, closely spaced and of impressive scantling, with raking queenposts and with longitudinal braces up to the ridge, like the Dacre hall at Lanercost. The ties are cambered, without moulding or chamfer. Captain Warre noted that the N end truss has been cut in order to gain access to the tower top, and the s end truss removed altogether – proof that the tower tops are later than the roof. Stone stairs meander evocatively up into the tower tops, branching in the N tower to a dovecote. Both towers have flat leaded roofs with much graffiti, including a reference to 'when the rebels came'.

The REAR WINGS have kingpost trusses like the front wing but of lesser quality. They have been tree-ring dated to *c.* 1505. In the s wing is an upstairs hall; its fireplace is signed Thomas Carleton Junior 1576. Carleton was the opportunist Land Sergeant, responsible for the defence of the barony. These were presumably his quarters, while the family held the front wing. Adjoining at the SW corner is his solar, looking W through a tall three-light window with trefoil heads. It has been well barred. Aborted stone stairs rise in the outer corners to the presumed fighting top above. A section of parapet moulding and a gargoyle outside provide the evidence that it was indeed a third tower. The W wing has been greatly altered, but it seems clear that there were stables below, lodgings or barracks above, with five garderobes at the N end and evidence for several fireplaces.

ASKHAM (W)   *5020*

A planned village (Lowther Estate) around a long green, wide enough to incorporate clumps of big trees. The green runs W–E up the hill in three instalments, the uppermost of which has only one farm on it. Strip fields radiate behind, and most of the houses have a barn attached which gives the village its informal rhythm. On the s side of the green, a charming small SMITHY with a square cupola vent. There is much pleasure to be had in perambulating, but the houses, mostly dated C17, C18 and C19, do not need itemizing. The village can provide an object lesson in good and bad barn conversion.

ST PETER. Rebuilt in 1832–3 by *Robert Smirke*, after the plan of the medieval church, and incorporating features from it. *Joseph Mawson* was the superintending mason and builder. Smirke tried to be Norman here, and the result is rather depressing. NW tower, narrow N aisle with bald Gothic arcade with four-centred arches, long s transept. The windows (except for one) all round-headed. The arcade, whitewashed like everything else, consorts ill with these windows and the plain up-and-over plaster ceiling. The transept certainly existed before. Its S window, which looks like a triple lancet outside, is a C17 square-topped mullioned job inside. The initials ED and TS (Edmund Dudley and Thomas Sandford) and date 1593 found on a roof spar may relate to it. – FONT. 1664. – Leaded GLASS, cockled in order to catch the sun. – MONUMENTS. Elizabethan tomb-chest with simple geometrical pattern. Only partly preserved. – Mildred, wife of William Sandford of Askham Hall, †1684. Tablet attributed to *A. Quellin* (GF). – Two successive William Sandfords †1717 and 1730, both with economical Latin eulogies done with bracketed alternatives. – In the transept, Edward Bolton of Askham Hall †1803 'who said to corruption thou art my father, and to the Worm, thou art my mother'.

ASKHAM HALL, at the bottom end of the village. Built by the Sandfords, who held it from 1375. The senior Lonsdale house following the gutting of Lowther Castle in 1957. It is an H-plan house of the North-western variety, with a big C14 defensive tower across the S end, a relatively insignificant hall in the middle, a low service wing across the N end, recognizable internally by its three service doors, and a kitchen beyond that, via a kitchen corridor. This is not all, for there are two further wings, forming an oblong courtyard on the W side. However, the hall is so modified as to be hardly recognizable, and it is the great S tower, rising above a series of descending terraces with yew topiary, that dominates the picture, throwing the rest, low, grey and irregular, into relative insignificance. The tower was turned S to face the road in 1685–90, with an even fenestration of five bays and three storeys. The windows are cross-mullioned on the lower floors. The doorway is central, with a broken segmental pediment and some rustication. The four corner turrets seem to be in order, but the intermediate crenellation is a reconstruction. In the late C17 a grand stair was inserted in what had been the hall range, now emphatically at the back. Part of it was raised to accommodate the stair, and is roughcast. The long wing on the N side of the yard has five identical doors, suggesting a set of lodgings. The W wing, with its through arch, was the stable, though the finely moulded timber floor running right through seems to belong to something more important. The arch is semicircular with a nice cable moulding stopped by knots. It has been chopped away to take a higher vehicle. Over it the Sandford arms dated 1574, and an entertaining selection of windows – a square, a trefoiled ogee, one like a B on its side – all with the same moulding. Inside the yard the stable has four four-light windows with dripmoulds. One has a lion shield on a mullion. One of the five doors of the N wing opens into the stable, suggesting that the stable came later. Ahead the service cross-wing, with a worn Sandford arms set into it, and the hall range.

The solar tower retains part of its tunnel-vault at the W end, which is set quite high, like that at Scaleby, with a small ogee-headed window at each end just under the apex. A step in the external masonry indicates the upper floor. Also a double-chamfered doorway from the N. In the N wall a mural stair. Both N turrets accommodated garderobes. The great stair rises through an open well, with twisted balusters and ramped handrails. The striking similarity with the stair at Appleby Castle suggests the hand of *Mark Gardner*.

WINDER HALL, Celleron, 2 m. WNW. L-shaped, of two phases. Stripping for refurbishment by the Lowther Estate in 2005 revealed its construction. The downhill part, its openings all arched behind the lintels, is probably the older. The upper part, with lintels only, is dated 1617 (Machell says 1612) over the door, and 1619 on part of a frieze. In an outshut at the back is a stone turning stair, its treads covered with wood, with door reveals top and bottom.

Associated with the hall, and deserted in 2005, is a fine C19 MODEL FARM. A fifteen-bay barn and matching shippons with louvred roofs form a courtyard round a central midden under a pillared roof. The roofs are hipped (not a regional type), and the slender queenpost trusses are of Baltic softwood, ingeniously jointed. Red sandstone is used for the recurring half-moon windows, and in great blocks to support the midden roof.

WIDEWATH, Heltondale. Little has changed since it was painted in its setting by Mathias Read *c.* 1700. 1671 RM (Mounsey) on the end-entry door, RIM 1674 with hearts on the porch, so Mounsey presumably built the house, or part of it, and improved it on his marriage. Barn attached one end, byre the other and a neat hennery-piggery beyond that. Two packhorse bridges and a mill complete the picture.

FARM KILN, I m. NW, alongside the limestone quarry which served it. Late C19. The oval pot is typical of this part of Westmorland at this period.

PREHISTORIC REMAINS, 1¾ m. SW. On Moor Divock, a saddle between Askham Fell and Barton Fell, several prehistoric sites. A prominent STANDING STONE, the 'Cop Stone', 5 ft (1.5 metres) high, on the S arc of a low, stony ring-bank. A CAIRN, 450 yds (410 metres) NNW, with an almost continuous kerb of large upright stones. Excavation in 1866 revealed a cremation and two food vessels. Beside the later High Street (the Roman road), nearly I m. NW of the Cop Stone, is The Cockpit, a STONE CIRCLE of upright boulders forming the inner face of a rubble bank. Two low cairns to NNW and ESE.

ASPATRIA (C)

1040

The name is a corruption of St Patrick. The town is long, without a definite centre, and generally red, though for instance opposite the church are a pair of white stuccoed houses with Greek Doric doorcases with triglyphs. Mining coal from the extensive 'yard band' seam was the principal industry, dominated in the years of Victorian prosperity by the figure of Sir Wilfrid Lawson. Depression hit hard in the 1930s; the mines finally closed in 1942, putting 1,200 men out of work. Small-scale manufacture has taken their place.

ST KENTIGERN. Towny church of deep red stone by *Travis & Mangnall* of Manchester, 1846–8. Exceedingly tall and narrow. A Norman arch with zigzag now uncomfortably re-set on two big scalloped capitals over the NW vestry door inspired the architects to make the W doorway and tower arch Norman too. The reused arch was originally part of the chancel arch. In the tympanum a length of the former hoodmould with criss-cross decoration. The rest is in an attenuated E.E, earnestly Puginian, with an ungainly tower and higher stair-turret. Very steep and quick-stepping arcades, the piers alternating round and twelve-sided. Six bays. Tall bare clerestory with tiny quatrefoil lights, steep open roof lost in the gloom. The chancel and its arch again high and narrow, the windows set excessively high. Triple SEDILIA and PISCINA painted blue. The tiny SE chapel is a Musgrave mausoleum.

FITTINGS. ROYAL ARMS, 1711, by *Mathias Read*. – FONT. C13, like the one at Crosscanonby: square on an octagonal base, with gross hanging scrolls. – STAINED GLASS. Seven very good lancets on the N side illustrating the canticles – Te Deum, Benedicite etc. – with figures and scrolls. By *Powells*, 1911. By Powells too the E window, a vision of Heaven, 1908, in memory of Sir Wilfrid Lawson (*see* below). The lancets were given by the seven children of Lady Lawson. Four by *J. Scott & Son*, 1847 (N aisle E, SW, and S chapel) and 1859 (chancel S). – Musgrave MONUMENTS, naïve and brightly painted. Sir Richard †1710, with an open curly pediment, volutes and garlands. – Another Sir Richard †1739. – Nicholas †1500, Thomas †1532, William †1597: panels under the altar in the same style as the monument at Ireby old church (q.v.). – On the S wall a synopsis of Musgraves up to 1800, Anne relict of Sir Richard †1755 and Sir Thomas †1738. – Nave, William Lamb M.D. †1823 by *P. Nixson*, with a draped urn. – First World War memorial, beaten copper, by *William Morris & Co.*

Pre-Conquest SCULPTURE. C10 CROSS-SHAFT, remounted in front of the tower arch. It has been turned round, i.e. E was W. Enough survives to show it was circle-headed, like Dearham. – Part of an exceptionally ambitious HOGBACK, also C10, tall and thin in the Cumbrian fashion. Roof imitating tiles or shingles, with a crest, and a rope decoration as though for tying it down. Each tile has a triquetra carved upon it. The eaves are decorated with a kind of Greek key, the sides have pilasters with bordered interlace.

CHURCHYARD. E of the chancel, a replica of the Gosforth CROSS (q.v.), set up in 1887. A valuable piece in its own right, it was made as an experiment by the antiquarian vicar *W. S. Calverley* with his churchwarden and quarrymaster, *Henry Graves* and *Christopher Dickenson.* – Close by, Calverley's own memorial, †1898, a less convincing copy of the Dearham cross. Both pieces have carved surface detail that in the originals was probably painted. – Some very fine gravestones by the church-yard E wall. – Built in by the vicarage gate pieces of Norman zigzag and two cross-heads. – VICAR'S DOVECOTE, behind the former vicarage. Probably C17, white and square, with gablets and half-hips to the roof.

TOWN HALL, now Fitness Centre, off West Street. Late Victorian, small, of red stone, with a Frenchy top with cast-iron crown to the little tower.

MEMORIAL in the Market Place to Sir Wilfrid Lawson, 'strenuous advocate of Temperance and Peace', by *L. Fritz Roselieb*, 1907. On a stone plinth, bronze reliefs of Peace (a Roman and ancient Briton shake hands), Temperance, and a eulogy. On top a spirited St George spears the dragon (drink).

(BEACON HILL SCHOOL, at the W end of town. 1963–5 by *G. K. Seed*.)

STATION. 1841, for the Maryport & Carlisle Railway, probably by *J. Blackmore*. Single storey, cruciform plan. Tudoresque with plentiful gables and tall hexagonal chimneys. Red sandstone. Elegant late C19 lattice-girder FOOTBRIDGE, on cast-iron columns with acanthus capitals.

BRAYTON HALL, 1½ m. E. Sir Wilfrid Lawson's vast C18 and C19 house was largely demolished in 1940. A fragment remains, in relict parkland with an ornamental lake. – LODGES on the A596 and the B5299, both early C19 Gothick and mid-Victorian. – At Baggrow, ESTATE HOUSES. Lawson's son William developed in the 1860s a co-operative model farm called MECHI, 1 m. SE of the mansion, with long ranges of barns with polychrome arches, clock tower and bellcote.

BLENNERHASSET, 2 m. E of Aspatria. The houses are neatly grouped around a broad green, no doubt a medieval arrangement. Amongst them is the former SHOP (1867) for Mechi Farm, which was run on co-operative principles. Also the WAR MEMORIAL *c.* 1921 by *Beattie* of Carlisle, on a reused plinth with worn inscription dated 1881. Of pink granite, left rough except for the names and a sword and wreath. EVANGELICAL MISSION. Tin tabernacle, painted green.

PEARTREE HOUSE. IN (John Noble) 1686 on the lintel, with the words FEARE GOD inexpertly set out, and a quatrefoil over. The windows have lost their mullions. The hoodmoulds of the two ground-floor windows form a continuous band, rising over the middle doorway. WINDER COTTAGES are similar, with the same motto, initials W & MB and the date 1678. Continuous dripmould on both floors. Inglenook fireplaces back-to-back, as indicated by their small fire-windows.

BAMPTON (W)

St Patrick. Rebuilt 1726–8. W tower with slender doorway with open segmental pediment and still C17-looking bell-openings. Quick rhythm of seven rather thin round-topped side windows. Inside, a row of timber columns, Doric with egg-and-dart in the capitals. They carry arches, and also cross-arches to the outer walls. The C18 church was probably seated college-wise, like Ravenstonedale (q.v.). If there were galleries *C. J. Ferguson* did away with them in 1884–5, retaining a set of posts and bracing them with wooden arcading across the aisles as well as longitudinally to support an unconventional double-arcaded roof. He was a resourceful as well as a sensitive architect. The tower arch was reworked at the same time, and the chancel arch introduced or reworked.

FITTINGS. REREDOS. 1885, carved by the contractor, Mr *Grisenthwaite* of Penrith. – ALTAR RAIL and PULPIT both probably of *c.* 1726, the pulpit with slender blank arches and slender angle colonnettes still derived, though distantly, from the Jacobean type. – ORGAN and VESTRY occupy matching Jacobean-style pens, of 1885 again, at the E end of the nave. A full screen in the same style was intended. – FONT. A square tub, with circular cutaways at the base, dated 1662. – STAINED GLASS. Chancel made dark by *Ward & Hughes* windows of 1888 etc. N aisle, †1998, a St Christopher. Millennium window by the font, St Patrick. Both by *Ann Southeran* of York. – MONUMENTS. Tablets to John Noble †1816, and to William Noble †1823 by *Regnart*, Grecian, with lush leaves.

The village lies below the Haweswater dam (q.v.). Immediately behind St Patrick's Well Inn, a small LIMEKILN. Most unusually, it is dated: 1848. Well-preserved. The surrounding catchment was bought up by Manchester in the 1920s (now United Utilities). The FARMS have stood still, resulting in dereliction for some, e.g. High Drybarrows and High Roughill, but lending an unusual authenticity to others, and a great quietness to the landscape.

STANEGARTH, 1 m. W, can be taken as an example. Moss-grown and grey, it lies in a sheltered valley by a peaty beck that has been diverted into Haweswater by means of a tunnel. 1679 over the S door. Semicircular stair-turret with a couple of tiny windows. The stair is a rough spiral of stone, with no newel. On the N side a porch with one tiny vigilant window and a slate bench. At the W end a blocked arch, then a cottage and finally a barn. Above to the N, a fine BANK BARN.*

---

*The house has attracted notable tenants: in the late C19 and early C20 the Lucas sisters, potters and Suffragists, who invited to Stanegarth the likes of Alma-Tadema and Henry Holiday; in the 1940s–50s Alastair Morton of Sundour Fabrics and Edinburgh Weavers (*see* Brampton, p. 181; also Carlisle, p. 263), who designed a fabric called Steel to Stanegarth; and not least Mollie Clough, who has done much to champion the Haweswater farms.

THORNTHWAITE HALL, 1 m. S. Mute C16 and C17 Curwen house, long in decline. Hall and downhouse in the centre. Tower added NW after 1576, its battlements replaced by a pitched roof in the C19. In *c.* 1612 Lord William Howard added an upper-floor banqueting hall on the E end. It has been converted into a bank barn with the addition of a ramp. Mullioned windows and fireplace remain, and a garderobe turret.

BECKFOOT, 1 m. N. 1892, built onto on an older house. The home of the Noble family for whom Ferguson restored the church. Did *Ferguson* design this too?

BARBON (W)   6080

The main road from Scotland came this way and through Kirkby Lonsdale until the road we call the A6 was turnpiked in 1830.

ST BARTHOLOMEW. By *Paley, Austin & Paley*, 1892–3. An excellent work in a freely treated Perp style with a big crossing tower with stressed square stair-turret. The tower is a little wider than nave and transept, a subtlety which makes all the difference. Stone roofs. The composition of the S side, with gabled porch, gabled transept, and an aisle between which starts only some way E of the porch, is subtle too. This arrangement of the aisles is also effective inside. The arcades are of two bays, the piers an elongated octagon, with the arches dying against them. The crossing tower is open at the top of its lower stage, with pairs of windows to N and S. The whole interior is ashlar-faced. The cross-arches step up towards the E window.

CHOIR STALLS, PULPIT, SCREENS and PEWS all characteristic of the architects. *J. Mattison* of Burton is said to have made the chancel fittings. Barbon around 1900 nurtured some notable woodcarvers. *J. M. Kilbride* is credited with the eagle LECTERN. *John Carlisle* probably did the screen and font cover. – FONT. Octagonal, buttressed, with a two-stage balustered cover. – ROYAL ARMS. 1815. – STAINED GLASS. All made by *Shrigley & Hunt* except the W window, which is by *Powells*, 1893, to a design by *Harrington Mann*.

The chapel-of-ease recorded in 1610, rebuilt in 1815, was immediately N. Its PORCH remains, used as a shed.

VICARAGE (former). By *Brade & Smales* of Kendal, 1873.

BARBON MANOR, high above the village. A shooting lodge built for Sir James Kay-Shuttleworth in 1863 by *E. M. Barry*. Pevsner called it no more than an Italianate villa in a street; actually it is more like a small French town hall, with architectural dress far too grand for its mere three bays (four at the back). Basement floor of pecked rustication, emphatically battered. Florid cast-iron balconies at first-floor level encircling the semicircular E bay and the tripartite SW window. On the cornice the vaguely threatening motto KYND KYNN KNAWE KEPE ('keep your own kin-kind'). The mansard roof has big arched dormers all round. It was greatly extended in 1893, reduced again *c.* 1940 when a cone-capped tower was removed – the scar can be seen NW – and reduced further by *Claud Phillimore* in 1986. – KENNELS below in the woods, in the same style.

BECKSIDE, Beckgate. Sweet yellow-washed house of 1767 for George Turner. Attributed by John Martin Robinson to *John Hird*, and full of good carpentry.* Doorcase after Gibbs, incorporating a 'celtic' face. Paired side windows in vernacular mode. Lots of characteristic architectural detail, in particular a trellis pattern combined with trefoil shapes, often combined with leaves turning over at the tips. This appears on the chimneypieces, the hall arch, and on the mullions of the downstairs windows. The principal stair rises two floors, with two balusters to a tread and a nice plaster moulding under the soffit. The drawing room was upstairs, over the dining room. The wings were added in 1998 by John Martin Robinson and *Michael Bottomley*; a perfect foil.

61   WHELPRIGG HOUSE, ¾ m. SE. Exciting approach through a disused railway arch and up a long avenue. The house dates from 1834 and is by *George Webster* in his Jacobean style, contrasting with the Greek Rigmaden (Mansergh, q.v.), clearly visible across the valley. S and W faces are gabled, with ball finials and mullioned-and-transomed windows, those in the gables being stepped (a local motif). At the N end an addition of *c.* 1910 (with a re-set stone EMG 1700), and on the E an unexpected fragment of a house of *c.* 1815 with Gothick windows. The house is planned around a comfortable top-lit staircase hall, with its own fireplace. The upper landing manages to be bigger, by adding a corridor behind a tripartite screen at a slightly higher level.

2070

BARDSEA (L)

HOLY TRINITY. 1843–53, by *George Webster*. Of intractable limestone, hence the harsh detailing especially of the windows. The W tower pulls in to an octagon before the spire starts, silhouetted against the sweep of Morecambe Bay. Polygonal chancel (later?) on a battered base. Wide barn-like interior. Hammerbeam roof. Over-sized but low-set pulpit and reading desk. – STAINED GLASS. In the apse three lights by *Wilhelmina Geddes*, 1924, painted by *Michael Healy*; outstandingly rich, with deep colours. By *Shrigley & Hunt* the nave N window at the W end, †1903 (designed by *Carl Almquist*), the next one of 1883, just as good. Round the W several by the same of the late 1930s, with much more clear glass. Nave S, three by *J. Scott & Son*, 1850s.

---

* Colin Stansfield says it is by *John & Thomas Bennison*.

GALE MONUMENT, ⅔ m. NW. 1792 (DCMS). It crowns the long bare ridge at the top of the golf course, with a few doubled-over thorn trees for company. Shape and size vary disconcertingly from different angles, because it is triangular. Broad rather than tall, well-buttressed, with a big niche in each face. Dome surmounted by a tiny lantern, triangular pyramid obelisks on the angles. In the niches elegant urns like cinerary urns, inscribed to members of the Gale family. The legible *obit.* dates range from 1772 to 1814. Bardsea Hall, the seat of the Gales, was demolished in 1927.

BARROCK PARK (C) *see* HIGH HESKET

BARROW-IN-FURNESS (L)   2070

Churches	131
Public Buildings	135
Perambulation	138
Outer Districts	141
Barrow Island	141
Roose	142
Walney	143

A government report of 1588 reckoned Barrow's deep-water harbour the best between Milford Haven and Scotland. Sheltered by the long spit of Walney and guarded by the castle on Piel Island, it had afforded the monks of Furness Abbey safe passage to their daughter houses in Ireland and the Isle of Man. The monks had smelted iron with wood as early as the C13. In the early C18 charcoal was used, and the first blast-furnaces appeared. Jetties were built at Barrowhead to ship out Furness ores from 1790. In the C19 came the third ingredient, the railway, and Barrow took off.

A map of 1843 shows a cluster of just thirty or so houses by the Barrow Channel. We may picture something like Biggar, on Walney, built of beach-picked cobbles. Already however three or four ore jetties are reaching out into the deep water. Snooping around for more iron was Henry Schneider, a young speculator and dealer, who built a fourth jetty in 1844. The Furness Railway received assent in 1844; isolated to begin with, supplied by sea, only gaining Ulverston and then Carnforth in 1857. In 1850 Schneider was rewarded by the discovery of the phenomenal Park deposits of haematite, an exceptionally high-grade ore, and the stage was set. In 1849 the Furness orefield produced 182,000 tons, in 1850 465,000; and so in 1857 Schneider erected blast furnaces. Nor was the port neglected. Barrow Channel was enclosed by the railway company from 1863 to make the Devonshire Dock (open 1867) and Buccleuch Dock (open 1873), named after the chief landowners. Designed by *J. R. McLean & F. C. Stileman* and

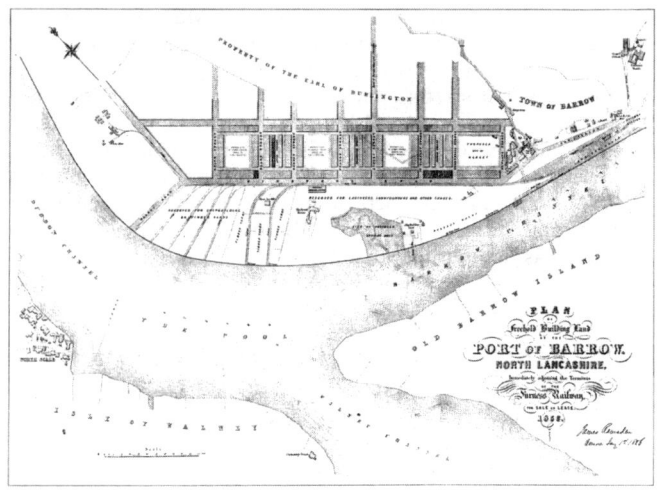

Barrow-in-Furness, port.
Plan by James Ramsden, 1856

built by *Brassey & Field*, each dock enclosed about 31 acres of water; with the later Ramsden and Cavendish docks, the total reached 450 acres. The population burgeoned from 8,000 in 1864 to 12,000 in 1867, when *Punch* reported that Barrow had swelled 'from the quiet coast-nest of some five-score fishermen, into the busy, bustling, blazing, money-making, money-spending, roaring, tearing, swearing, steaming, sweltering seat of twenty-thousand iron workers.'* By 1870 the Haematite Iron & Steel Co. was rolling 3,000 tons of rail a week. By 1876 Barrow was the largest steelworks in the world. W. G. Collingwood in 1902 gave a vivid picture of the enormous Babylonian towers of the retorts bulking in the darkness, from which 'flared out great banners of fire, lighting up the cloud into a brown glow against inter-spaces of deep violet'.

p. 49

With the railway came the twenty-three-year-old *James Ramsden*, then locomotive superintendent of the Furness Railway, a man with a vision of a thriving, and planned, city. He negotiated the purchase of the Hindpool estate in 1854, and in 1856 set out a grid of streets between Hindpool Road and Duke Street, leaving space for a market. Abbey Road (to the NE) and The Strand (to the SE) followed in 1860, and in 1863 a further grid of streets up to St James's church, N. The rigid layout, lined by long two-storey terraces and dignified by the generous widths of road and pavement and by street trees, is what makes Barrow. The first mayor of the belatedly formed Town Council in 1867 was of course Ramsden. He ruled from the railway offices until

---

*Compare Middlesbrough, Gladstone's 'Infant Hercules', growing from forty in 1829 to 7,500 in 1850 and 91,000 in 1901, likewise through railways, docks, iron and steel.

the town hall could be built. Ramsden also instigated the Barrow Shipbuilding Co., incorporated in 1871, on Barrow Island.

During the boom years of the 1860s–70s Barrow was dominated by a single architectural firm. Luckily it was of the best: the *Paley & Austin* practice of Lancaster. They designed all the churches, the cemetery and the market; almost everything for the Furness Railway from its headquarters and the mansion of its manager to the humblest signal box; banks, hotels and baths, tenements, terraces and shipyards. It is only unfortunate that the machinations of local architects deprived them of the town hall job, and that their years of greatness started just as Barrow's were ending: the boom was already faltering at the end of the 1870s, when the best ore had gone, and technological advances meant that such pure ore was no longer needed.

Vickers of Sheffield bought the shipyard in 1896, and the years leading up to the First World War saw warships built for Japan, Russia, Brazil and China as well as for the Royal Navy. To these years belongs the expansion of the town onto Walney Island. The population peaked in 1917 at 90,000, but peace brought slump: Vickers' workforce dropped from 23,000 in 1918 to 3,000 in 1923. To some extent Barrow has never recovered. In the 1960s much of the old centre was cleared away, and the ironworks closed in 1963. Miles of railway loops and branches, dock and steelworks lines, works, engine sheds and stations, all gone; it is hard to imagine it all. Meanwhile the first nuclear submarine was built in 1960, and Devonshire Dock Hall went up in 1985. On 1 June 2004, as fieldwork for this book was beginning, the amphibious assault ship HMS *Bulwark* slipped out of Barrow after fitting out. But in the early c21, with the population down to *c.* 61,000, Barrow is attempting to leave behind its origins in heavy industry for an uncertain future in light industry and tourism.

CHURCHES

St George, St George's Square. By *E. G. Paley*, 1859–61, N aisle 1867. Intended as the parish church of Ramsden's new Barrow, but left behind by the town's growth and the relocation of the station in 1882. Green Kirkby slate dry-jointed, red sandstone dressings. Geometrical tracery. Squat SW tower with a higher turret, many gables. The Ramsden Chapel (S) was added in 1883, when the chancel was rebuilt longer and higher. The interior was spoiled by the *K. C. White Partnership* in 1982, crudely partitioning off the N aisle and removing most of the furnishings. Timber rib-vault and wall arcading to the Ramsden Chapel. The arcade piers have moulded alternating with foliage capitals. On the N side of the chancel an arch to the organ, on the S side two to the chapel, a motif *Paley & Austin* made much of. Chapel arcades and chancel arch are quatrefoiled and keeled. – STAINED GLASS. E window by *A. F. Erridge* of *Wippell & Co.*, 1951, replacing the Schneider window blown out in the

Second World War; also s chapel E. W, *Hardman*, good in effect but crude faces. s aisle, two by *Shrigley & Hunt*, C20. – MEMORIAL. George K. Thompson Fisher †1917; mosaic and inscribed alabaster in a grey marble frame. – Former VICARAGE, E.

ST JAMES, Hartington Street. The steelworkers' church, 1867–9 by *E. G. Paley*. Well placed at the summit of Hartington Street to rise above the serried terrace roofs. Of red brick with blue accents, with yellow stone for the dressings and spire. The splendid steeple is unusually placed on the s side of the chancel, which terminates in a three-sided apse. The ringing-chamber windows are set in a continuous band of trefoil arches. *Hubert Austin* joined Paley in 1868; his influence may perhaps be seen in the bell-stage, which repeats the multifoiled circles of the W window, and the spire which, dispensing with broaches, rises directly from four gables, with a marked entasis. Broad and high interior. Slim red stone piers, C13 style, alternately round and foiled, on waterholding bases of yellow stone. The arches are of exposed brick; so were the walls, but these have been painted white. – REREDOS. A war memorial, 1919. – STAINED GLASS. War memorial window by *T. F. Curtis* of *Ward & Hughes*, 1922: the only survivor of bomb damage in 1941. It shows the Blomfield 'Cross of Sacrifice' surrounded by wooden crosses. The rest by *G. E. R. Smith*, 1952–5, except for the W panels from St John, Bowness (q.v.) by *James Clark* and *Henry Holiday*, 1905–8, set in plain glass. – MEMORIAL. John Sawyer †1901, beaten copper, by *KSIA*.

SCHOOLS and school houses also by *Paley*, for Henry Schneider, 1867.

SS MATTHEW, MARK, LUKE and JOHN. They were prefabricated churches of wood and brick by *Paley & Austin*. The initiative was James Ramsden's in the 1870s, when the population was booming and the Established Church was losing out to the Dissenters. £24,000 was collected from the dukes of Devonshire and Buccleuch, Lord Frederick Cavendish, Ramsden himself, and Schneider. All four churches were opened on 26 September 1878. Only one survives.

ST MATTHEW, Harrogate Street, N of the Centre. Rebuilt in 1965–8 by *Schomberg Scott* of Edinburgh. Massive s tower missing its s wall – a horrid motif, it looks ready-ruined – with a bell hanging from a beam. Glazed link to the church, which is of dull blue brick with metal-framed recessed slit windows. Canted E end. (Harled inside, with laminated trusses.)

ST MARK, Rawlinson Street. The only one of *Paley & Austin*'s original four of 1878 still standing (*see* above). It was doubled in size in 1882–3, so it has two naves and a single N aisle, and has lost its bellcote and narthex. Lightly framed in pitch pine, with red brick infilling and large domestic windows. No chancel. The interior is admirably light and simple. The doubling was carried out without disturbing the wall-posts, simply re-inserting the braces at a higher level and adding battens to hide the mortices. The 1880s work is slightly more churchy, the

Barrow-in-Furness, prefabricated church (St Luke).
Engraving, 1881

braces padded out to a Gothic curve and the walls articulated with bands of moulded brick. In a building like this pink wall-to-wall carpet and padded chairs jar not a bit.

ST LUKE, Roose Road, E of the Centre. Rebuilt by *Cruickshank & Seward* of Manchester in 1963–4. Bell-tower completely open, just four cross-braced concrete legs and a roof. The church concrete-framed, brick-clad, with a sawtooth roof. (STAINED GLASS. Some by *Dom Charles Norris* of Buckfastleigh, 1963.)

ST JOHN. *See* Barrow Island, below.

ST PAUL, Abbey Road. Of 1871 by *Habershon & Brock*, before the area was built up. Stone chancel and part of a nave, with double transepts. The W part was completed by *C. L. Mawson* of Kendal *c.* 1965 in a simplified, white-rendered style, with an oculus in the W gable and a Scandinavian-looking spirelet. Further W extension 2005–6 by *Paul Grout*, for coffee lounge and kitchen with offices above. The mix works surprisingly well, largely because Mawson, although working in a completely different idiom, continued the high and steep Victorian roof-line, with the same pendants and notched tie-beams inside, and because the newest section has a bold double-height segmental window to the W, letting in plenty of sunshine. – STAINED GLASS. In the big Dec windows of the Victorian part; nave NE, †1888 by *Heaton, Butler & Bayne*, the rest *Shrigley & Hunt*, 1905–*c.* 1926.

ST MARY OF FURNESS (R.C.), Duke Street. By *E. W. Pugin*, 1866–7. Large and ornate. Polygonal ritual E end flanked by rose windows in a pair of raised gables like embryo transepts. The thin and fussy SW steeple was added in 1888, the tall polygonal NW baptistery, like a fat turret, in 1894. In the middle a low lobby, with a big W rose above. This supplies most of the light to the high, cradle-roofed interior, which is made bright with stencilling and gilding. Steeply arched arcades, becoming ultra-steep where the easternmost bay does two overexcited steps in the space of one under the chancel gables. With this crowding of piers and arches corresponds a change in the clerestory, where equally suddenly a little rose appears above the lancets. The capitals alternate between thin and abstract and bulgy with foliage. The w responds have been left uncarved. It looks as though carved detail was intended in the spandrels at the springing of each arch too. – Towering ALTAR, TABERNACLE and REREDOS, by *O'Neill & Pearse* of Dublin. – PULPIT, carved by Mr *Lane* of Preston with the four Evangelists in bas-relief. – Iron SCREEN to the Lady Chapel by *Francis Roberts*, early C21.

PRESBYTERY by *J. Byrne* of Liverpool, *c.* 1874. 'The house merits no special commendation', said the *History of Barrow* in 1881.

TRINITY PRESBYTERIAN CHURCH, School Street. By *Paley & Austin*, 1873–5. An odd façade, where a short tower l. is balanced by a polygonal feature facing s. Red and silver stone. Burnt out; future uncertain.

(WESLEYAN CHURCH (former), Hartington Street and Nelson Street. 1907 by *H. T. Fowler* (Kelly). Red brick and yellow terracotta, with a corner cupola.)

(UNITED METHODIST CHURCH (former), Allison Street and Storey Square. 1894. Fiery red brick with a sw cupola. The features are a mixed C17 to Baroque assembly.)

TRINITY CENTRE (Methodist, now with United Reformed), Abbey Road, NE of the town centre. Of 1902 (Kelly). Grey sandstone with red dressings and spire. w window divided up the middle. Belfry lights push up into the spire, which is square, to suggest lucarnes. Blank panelling in gable and tower top.

BAPTIST CHURCH, diagonally opposite. 1953. Red brick, with a ribbed brick tower. Thin concrete surrounds to the windows. Tiers of small square windows at the end. Hall behind in yellow brick. All typical of date and denomination.

PSYCHOLOGICAL HALL and SPIRITUALIST CHURCH, Dalkieth and Buccleuch streets. 1893, in red and yellow brick.

SALVATION ARMY CITADEL, Abbey Road. 1910. Red brick and yellow terracotta.

CEMETERY, Devonshire Road, N of the centre. 1872–4. Laid out by *Edward Kemp* of Liverpool. The buildings are by *Paley & Austin*, of silver limestone with red dressings. – GATEHOUSE, triple-arched and carrying an upper storey. The carriageway is rib-vaulted in two bays. – N LODGE and service yard. – R.C. CHAPEL (former), at the far N end. Cruciform with an octagonal central lantern on sandstone broaches with a pyramidal cap, like an Armenian church. An excellent little building on its windswept hillside. The central chapels have been replaced by the 1950s CREMATORIUM, with banks of small square windows with concrete surrounds.

PUBLIC BUILDINGS

Town Hall, Duke Street. By *W. H. Lynn* of Belfast, completed   p. 136
1887. The grandest town hall in Cumbria, and the only one to
approach the municipal palaces of industrial Yorkshire and
Lancashire. However, it was not a happy job. Paley & Austin
had submitted a design earlier in the year, which Schneider
declared 'the very best . . . he had seen in his life'. It was
readily voted in by the council. After a protest by six Barrow
architects the decision was rescinded, but in the resulting open
competition, assessed by Alfred Waterhouse, no local men were
premiated. Lynn's design appeared in *The Builder* in 1879,
which reported building in progress, but by then Barrow's first
boom was already over, and in 1882 the design was pruned.
The subsidiary N tower and link to the market hall had to go;
fire station, police station and courts on the s side were all cut;
the façade was shortened by two bays at the ends. Lynn only
salvaged the rest by reshuffling the mayor's suite and council
apartments along the whole of the front. Even now the aprons
below the Council Chamber windows are uncarved, the
statue niches empty. To make things worse, in 1884 the tower
threatened collapse and had to be partly rebuilt.

The style is Gothic of the C13 Dec variety, like Manchester   97
and Rochdale town halls and Lynn's own Chester (1864–9).
The design owes a lot to Manchester, but the red sandstone
lends it a softer air. Front and central tower rise sheer from
the low-rise Duke Street, making a tremendous impact. It is
what might be termed symmetrical enough – so much more
satisfying in a Gothic building than slavish item-for-item symmetry. Symmetrical tower and entrance, and equal flanks with
corner tourelles, punctuated on each side by a three-storey bay
raised on corbels and pushing into the roof. Asymmetrical floor
levels and fenestration. The Council Chamber on the r., with
four extra-large windows, takes the place of two full storeys on
the l., and dormers and chimneys are allowed to vary. The
tower with a top one would not have expected: four steep
gables and an octagonal top stage. The rear, facing the empty
garden and car park (where *Paley*'s brick Gothic market hall
of 1866 is no more), reads as a U with a central porte cochère
and turrets in the angles, but the return wings are of different
lengths and end abruptly.

INTERIOR. There is no symmetry to the plan beyond the
central lobby and cross-entrances. The space under the tower
is the only bit of vaulting. Out of the FOYER with its fireplace
and dedication plaque rises the GRAND STAIR, of stone
carried on arches. The QUEEN'S HALL at its head is the one
apartment which richly fulfils expectations. A wall of stained
glass, canted in an oriel, faces w, a stone fireplace backs against
the tower opposite. Arcades with quatrefoil piers. Stained glass,
a composite including glass by *Shrigley & Hunt* and *Abbott &
Co*. Main upper lights glorifying the Cavendish family, 1893.

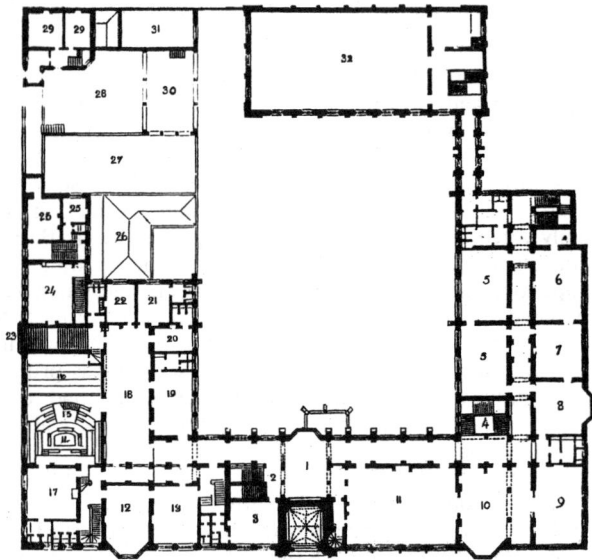

PRINCIPAL FLOOR PLAN

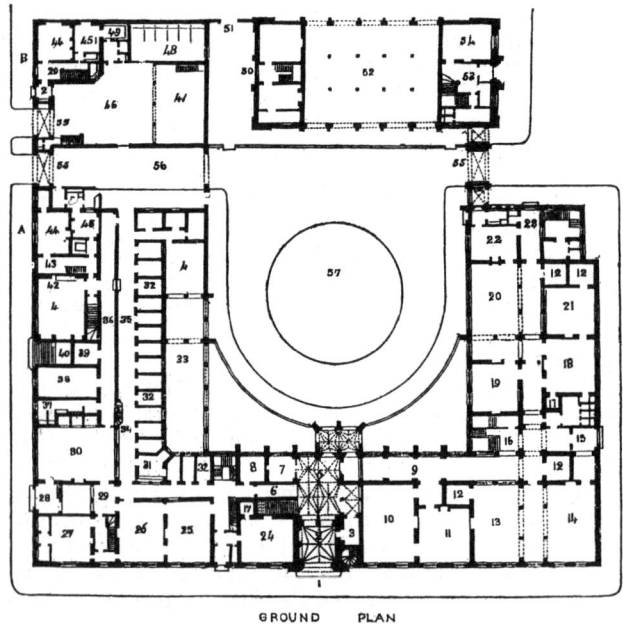

GROUND   PLAN

SCALE OF FEET

Barrow-in-Furness, Town Hall.
Plans of original design, 1879

Lower lights incorporating 1960s scenes of Barrow industry: the chemical and shipbuilding vignettes are good. To either side glass brought from Ramsden's house, Abbotswood, setting forth a history of Furness Abbey. They are a delight. BANQUETING HALL, RECEPTION ROOM and COUNCIL CHAMBER are grand apartments as one would expect, with stone fireplaces and coffered ceilings, but penny-pinched in the detail. A SECONDARY STAIR in the S wing ascends to the top of the building. It is cantilevered, with fancy iron railings, and rises in a stone cage. The upper floors are given to offices, with access by spiral stairs to the tower. Here it can be seen that the octagon is carried on eight arches behind the clock faces, an awkward arrangement. From the top platform with its eight rams (for Ramsden – they are by *H. T. Miles* of Ulverston) Barrow's geography can be appreciated as it cannot from the ground – the muddy channel guarded by Piel Castle (q.v.), the Irish Sea beyond the long spit of Walney island, the Cumbrian mountains away to the NE. At the N end of the building a two-storey flat for the superintendant. Back on the ground floor it remains to note the very tall clustered piers with iron filigree capitals in the PUBLIC OFFICES in the N wing. The CELLARS are brick-vaulted, with a great wodge of emergency concrete against the foot of the tower.

MAGISTRATES' COURT, Abbey Road. 1995. Red and yellow brick with bands of red concrete, and some mullions and transoms. The waiting area is a top-lit atrium. In the adjoining garden, SCULPTURE (*c.* 2000) of cushions and crowns.

POLICE HEADQUARTERS, next to the Town Hall, E. Utilitarian but decent building of 1958, characteristic of its date, of pale red brick and concrete with metal windows. It surrounds a small courtyard opening at the front through a five-bay colonnade – a happy invention. The windows above run together vertically, visibly lightening the load.

POST OFFICE, Abbey Road. Very good example of Wren-style officialese, 1931. Pantiled roof, hipped and sprocketed. Upper walls of small red bricks, lower walls panelled in ashlar, with reeded aprons under the round-arched windows.

FIRE STATION (former), Abbey Road, S of Ramsden Square. Of 1911–12 by the Borough Surveyors under *Arthur Race*. Red brick, yellow *Burmantofts* terracotta, with giant consoles over the garage doors.

TECHNICAL SCHOOL, now Nan Tait Centre, Abbey Road. A typical *Woodhouse & Willoughby* job of 1900–3. Red brick and yellow terracotta, with two reliefs. Asymmetrical, with a cupola on a turret. Varied C17 and C18 motifs.

LIBRARY, Ramsden Square. By *J. A. Charles*, 1915–22. Beaux-Arts classical, with bundled fasces dangling from the Ionic capitals. It fits the circus by having a centre and two diagonally projecting wings.

DOCK MUSEUM, North Road. By *Craig & Green*, 1994 and 1996. All roof, with a glazed semicircular section to the road. Much bigger inside, with two extra storeys inside the stone-stepped GRAVING DOCK, constructed for the Furness Railway in 1872, that blocks the N end of the channel. The glazed section fits the head of the dock.

FURNESS GENERAL HOSPITAL, Dalton Lane, NE of the centre. 1984 and later. Long red brick ranges on the brow of a hill.

BARROW PARK, Abbey Road. Laid out 1904–7 by *Thomas Mawson* and extended, again by Mawson, in 1920. – WAR MEMORIAL, *c.* 1920, given by the Barrow Haematite Steel Co. Prominent white obelisk on a railed platform. The names on bronze plaques. Representations of the three armed services and Liberty on the angles. The architect was *Major C. Oakley*, the sculptors *Fairbairn & Hull*, both of Barrow.

STATION, Abbey Road. Opened in 1882. The ungainly overall roof by *E. G. Paley* was destroyed by bombing in 1941. The Furness Railway WAR MEMORIAL (1921) survives; a bronze tablet on a red stone stele, both holed by shrapnel. The concourse of 1958 is quite a bold statement, Modernist, fresh and cubic with glass walls front and back; but pathetically small, eloquent of the reduced ambitions of both railway and town.

SIGNAL BOX, 1907. Wooden, fully glazed superstructure on a brick base with five recessed panels, each with a central blocked opening into the locking room.

PERAMBULATION

Grid layouts are never easy to explore, but in Barrow's case the triumvirate of founding fathers, Ramsden, Schneider and Lord Cavendish, continue in statue form to give structure to the town.

RAMSDEN SQUARE is where ABBEY ROAD, Barrow's gateway and principal thoroughfare, crosses DUKE STREET, the inner road of Ramsden's grid (*see* p. 130). It is a diamond, with the roads entering at the corners. Decent buildings on three sides: the Library (p. 137), others by *Paley & Austin*, but on the fourth side nothing at all. Ramsden's MONUMENT, by *M. Noble*, 1872, is marooned on the central roundabout behind municipal shrubs and railings. A pity, because here the meteoric rise of Barrow is summarized on a pair of bronze reliefs on the plinth.

103   One represents Barrow in 1848: thatched cottages, a cottager and her child, sleepy goats, the masts of a small ship. On the other side is Barrow in 1871, a tremendous image of industrial energy. This transformation is laid, literally, at the feet of Sir James Ramsden.

Exploring the streets in turn. On the stub of Abbey Road to the SW two Deco buildings: JOHN WINNERAH INSTITUTE, 1937–8 by *John Charles*, 'façaded' in the most literal way in 2004, and LAKELAND HOUSE, very similar. On the bottom corner, facing Hindpool Road, the former CUSTOM HOUSE, *c.* 1870. Large cubic house, stuccoed, with a wave frieze under the parapet. Labels and voussoirs rusticated like cracked and drying mud.

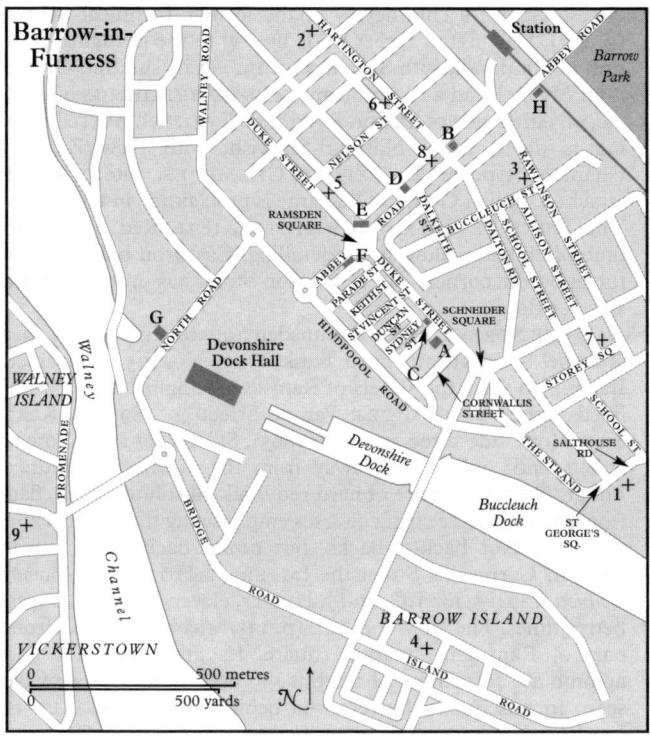

Barrow-in-Furness

1	St George	A	Town Hall
2	St James	B	Magistrates' Court
3	St Mark	C	Police Station
4	St John	D	Technical School
5	St Mary (R. C.)		(former)
6	Wesleyan church	E	Library
7	United Methodist Church	F	Fire Station
8	Salvation Army	G	Dock Museum
9	St Mary, Vickerstown	H	Post Office

On the NW continuation of Duke Street is St Mary's church
(p. 133), and a STATUE of the rugby player Willie Horne
(†2001). Bronze, 2004, by *Chris Kelly*. An action figure, with
lengthy eulogy, and apparently an excellent likeness.

Heading NE on Abbey Road, The CONSERVATIVE CLUB (E side)
by *J Y McIntosh*, 1897–9, of yellow ashlar, with chastely
handled mixed Georgian motifs, seems to look down on the
WORKING MEN'S CLUB opposite. This was the first building
of the new Abbey Road, 1870–1, the gift of the Furness Railway and Henry Schneider. A silly French château by *H. A.
Darbishire*, with a pediment and a cupola. On the l. RAMSDEN
HALL. Built 1872 as public baths but converted to a public
hall in 1886. Sweetly small. Red brick with a black-and-white

clerestory and a chimney. N of the former Technical School
(p. 137), Hartington Street leads up NW to the draughty gridiron of Hindpool, with St James (p. 132) at its summit. On the
r. on Abbey Road a run of former CO-OP BUILDINGS of 1889
etc. on either side of Dalton Road. The EVENING MAIL building is dated 1903; Norman-Shawish, with New Zealand
Chambers-type oriels. OXFORD CHAMBERS, dated 1875, is
attached. Italian Gothic. The name is proclaimed in terracotta.
The DUKE OF EDINBURGH HOTEL, 1871. Red brick with
blue brick and yellow stone detailing. Cast-iron balcony. The
turret on the corner with Rawlinson Street has probably lost a
spire or dome.

Now DUKE STREET, SE from Ramsden Square. First, the former
Wakefield, Crewdson & Co. bank, 1873 (No. 125), restrained
Italian. On the l. the streets of Ramsden's original grid are still
lined with low TERRACES: Parade Street (c. 1895–6), Keith
Street (one side three-storey, c. 1865), St Vincent and Duncan
streets and, only a step away from the Town Hall, Sidney
Street. The terraces are of hard red brick, absolutely even, flat-
fronted, with white string courses emphasizing their length and
evenness. Not back-to-backs, but tunnel-backs with a rear
alley. In Cornwallis Street the IMPERIAL HOTEL by *Thomas
Bennett*, 1874–5, for T.C. and J. Hunter, eleven bays; it has seen
better times. The TOWN HALL (p. 135) was built on the front
part of Ramsden's market square. Its great presence and
aplomb are something of a rebuke to everything else we have
seen. Inconsequentially removed behind it is the STATUE of
Lord Frederick Cavendish, by *Albert Bruce Joy*, 1885. Opposite
the town hall but, with the bloody-mindedness of the time, not
axial with it, is the desperate MARKET CENTRE of 1971,
redeemed only by its reverse-curve six-storey block fronting
Schneider Square. The rest is two low storeys only, of grey textured concrete with windows in horizontal bands, flat-roofed
with car parking on top. The market hall, without natural light,
has retro decoration of abstract splashes of colour on its upper
walls. The Civic Hall was revamped in 1990 as FORUM 28 with
a new entrance of white tubular steel and glass. The Dalton
Road front and the ghastly internal mall are unchanged.

SCHNEIDER SQUARE is the second node point. Henry Schneider's STATUE, in bronze by *Percy Wood*, 1891, stands on a traffic
roundabout leading to the high-level bridge to Barrow Island.
On the S side the MAJESTIC HOTEL, 1904 by *J. Y. McIntosh*,
with shaped gables.

Duke Street continues SE. ALFRED BARROW SCHOOL, 1888, by
McIntosh and symmetrical. On the S side the Albion pub,
c. 1865. The last traces of OLD BARROW can be sought behind
here, where the road comes down to the Barrow Island
channel. A knot of narrow streets, a concentration of pubs, and
a few fugitive and crumbling bits of wall built of beach-
scrounged stones, all different colours; that is all. Along THE
STRAND, SE, the Furness Railway occupied the land between
road and waterfront. Morrison's supermarket and car park

waste the prime dockside site now, preserving as a token the three-arched GATEWAY to the railway works. To the S, the former STRAND STATION and much of its associated engine shed survive. Of 1862–3, by *E. G. Paley*. Coloured brick and light stone, very grubby now. Four-bay centre with twin arched entrances, not a happy frontispiece for an essentially Palladian composition with its low wings and end pavilions. It forms the S side of the irregular ST GEORGE'S SQUARE. Immediately beyond were the railway's General Offices, a picturesque composition also by *Paley*, erected between 1850 and 1864 (dem. 1978). The complex occupied the site of Barrow's first station, opened in 1846. Traffic now rushes diagonally through the sloping space between the railway buildings and the church (N side; p. 131). Behind the church is ST GEORGE'S SCHOOL, low, of sandstone rubble, built for Furness Railway employees' children in 1849. In SCHOOL STREET, N, a block of eight three-storey houses with punctuations labelled BARROW HOSPITAL, 1875. They were for hospital staff. To the E, Nos. 1–20 SALTHOUSE ROAD are reckoned to be the first houses of the new Barrow. Built in 1846 of red sandstone rubble by the Furness Railway, and set back to make a widely splayed entrance to Rawlinson Street. For many years a whopping square iron-banded chimney stood within the embrace of the two terraces, connected by underground flues to the railway works across the road.

OUTER DISTRICTS

BARROW ISLAND

The fordable channel that made the island was transformed into floating docks, Devonshire, Buccleuch and Ramsden, from 1867 (*see* above, p. 129), crossed by Michaelson Road with its high-level bridge (rebuilt in 1965). The channel's NW end is blocked by Devonshire Dock Hall, Barrow's great landmark (*see* below). North Road runs straight across what was the channel's western exit, and the Dock Museum (p. 137) covers the graving dock to its E. Visually this geographical obfuscation is a pity. Barrow Island however remains distinct, an extraordinary townscape of large-scale items: giant shed, giant cranes, giant pubs, streets literally wide enough to accommodate ships, and great blocks of four- and five-storey TENEMENTS. A pair of brown stone ones (1872–4) with corner turrets face Michaelson Road, with long access balconies at the back; behind that an entire district of red brick ones, of 1879, 1880–1 etc. on Schooner Street, Brig Street, Steamer Street and so on. They are all by *Paley & Austin*, but the contractor for what is such a Scottish building type was *David Caird* of Dundee. The environment they create is strict but not threatening.

ST JOHN, Island Road. By *Seely & Paget*, 1934–5, replacing the fourth of *Paley & Austin*'s temporary churches of 1878 (*see* p. 132). Of concrete; its Mediterranean whiteness and complicated massing shine out amongst the regimented tenements. An open cloister links the street to the W door. A small campanile breaks the level roof-line, propped by an open arch, l. The miscellaneous blocks are not easy to interpret, and even inside it seems to be more a product of incomplete evolution – or curtailment – than a single concept. A square central space, lit by tiny windows in the corners, stands on four semicircular arches. Flat beamed ceiling, not the shallow dome it cries out for, but even so the great arches confer a sense of spacious calm. They are prolonged just enough to suggest the four equal arms of a Greek cross. However, added to that is a full chancel with a smooth semicircular apse and a full nave under a partly pitched roof. The block supporting the campanile turns out to be the organ chamber. The walls are noticeably thin.

FURNISHINGS. From the old church, the fruits of an indigenous designer and a carver in the 1920s, *Clifford Green* and *F. J. Lord*, including ALTAR RAILS with flat-carved symbolic plants such as wheat with a sickle, CHOIR STALLS with inset panels of Christ's ministry, and BAPTISMAL BOARD with a carving of 'Suffer Little Children'. Of pale limed oak, they look well in Modernist surroundings. – STAINED GLASS by *Heaton, Butler & Bayne* from the old church (†1893), in windows shaped specially for it. The nave was partitioned off in 2005 by a glass screen. A neat job, by *Craig & Green*.

ST PATRICK (R.C.), Michaelson Road. 1933. An unexpected oasis of green. Brick, lancets, very plain. Large PRESBYTERY adjoining in a more friendly style.

SHIPYARD BUILDING. 1871–2 by *Paley & Austin*, with extensions. Massive red stone screen wall along Michaelson Street punctuated by tall windows and a single arched doorway, whence a railway line crosses the street to the opposite building. A huge quadrangle is marked on the map, but parts are missing or replaced by crinkly tin: bomb damage?

DEVONSHIRE DOCK HALL was erected in 1985 by *J. T. James & Partners* for building Trident nuclear submarines. Unmissable tin shed with six vast cross-roofs. Enormous folding doors at the ends. Inside, a ship lift which can move 24,000 tons.

ROOSE

METHODIST CHURCH. 1877.

ROOSE COTTAGES. 196 cottages in two interminable terraces. Built by *David Caird* of Dundee, 1873–6 (cf. Barrow Island, above), for Cornish miners. Of Hawcoat sandstone, with a suggestion of Gothic in the door lintels and a long line of gables.

WALNEY

An eleven-mile spit of sand and cobble sheltering Barrow from the open sea. Connected to the town by JUBILEE BRIDGE, a rare example of the Scherzer rolling lift system. Tapered girders roll back as they lift, Tower Bridge-style, giving a clear opening of 120 ft (36.5 metres). By *Sir Benjamin Baker* and *C. A. Hurtzig*, 1897–1905. The old settlements are Biggar and North Scale (*see* below), with the chapel of St Mary in between, but this central part is now heavily built up. The houses start in garden suburb style by the bridge, but later developments are progressively bleaker, until we reach the featureless North Walney estate and the huddled caravans of West Shore Park.

ST MARY, Promenade. A chapel is marked on Saxton's map of 1577. The church of 1853 by *Sharpe & Paley* was replaced in 1907–8 by *Austin & Paley*, but the w end was not completed until 1928–31, and without the intended crossing tower. It is in their latest Perp style, blocky of silhouette. Tiled roof. Luminous interior with exposed stonework. The piers are of ungeometric section, with arches dying in. Taller, non-matching arcades for the chancel (one N, two S), and a pair of fat round piers for the chancel arch. – STAINED GLASS. E window by *R. R. Nichol* for *Abbott & Co.*, *c.* 1990.

VICKERSTOWN was planned in 1899 as a marine garden suburb on the lines of Port Sunlight, with playing fields and a park, although laid out on a Barrovian grid. Building started in 1900, with designs by *W. Moss Settle* of Ulverston. Powerful Street (the names are the best part – Niobe, Melampus, Latona) is the main avenue of North Vickerstown. By 1903 several hundred houses were occupied; inevitably corners were cut and specifications diluted. Windows are hung outside. Pebbledash, timber framing in the gables, wooden fencing. Houses for munitions workers were rushed up in 1914–16, some 'semi-permanent'.

BIGGAR. A tight knot of houses and barns on slightly higher ground to the S, mostly roughcast but built of multicoloured cobbles and beach pickings. NORTH SCALE is similar but entangled with modern housing. Nothing grows higher than the wind-blown hawthorns; when the cow parsley of the lanes flowers in May, quite a sight.

WALNEY LIGHTHOUSE, at the far S of the island. 1790, for the Lancaster Quay Commissioners. Tall stone octagon, tapering to a fully glazed lantern surrounded by a delicate iron balcony.

Close to the northern tip, WALNEY AIRFIELD. In 1937 the town acquired a site for a municipal airport, but construction started in 1940 under R.A.F. auspices, and military use continued until 1955. The present facilities date essentially from 2006.

BARTON (W)

No village. Pooley Bridge (q.v.) is a recent upstart.

St Michael. On a mound, in a round churchyard. Stubby
central Norman tower – the only one on a medieval parish
church in the county. No transepts however; lean-to aisles continue past the tower. The N doorway is Norman, with a continuous roll moulding; the S doorway a little later, still
round-arched but with a fillet on the roll. Two orders of shafts
with high, simply moulded capitals. Windows generally Late
Perp with ranges of slightly flattened uncusped lights under
square heads, but the chancel E window of three stepped
lancets. S porch among other parts repaired in 1699, with
Lancaster arms, 1703, designed by *Thomas Webster*. The church
is documented as being thatched in the C18.

The interior is made exciting by its mysteriously dark centre.
Under the tower is a forward altar, lit indirectly by the narrowest slit window in its S wall (proving that the tower originally stood free). On its E and W faces, a very strange sight, are
two superimposed arches; a narrow Norman one above, with
a big roll moulding, and a wide but extremely low one underneath, segmental, with a roll moulding and no capitals. The S
window is stepped inside. High up in the darkness is a barrel
vault, set transversely N–S: a highly exceptional, decidedly
Northern feature. Its thick render shows marks of basket formwork. A tiny door high up on the W wall gave access to the
space above.

Now for the rest. The nave arcades were broken through the
Norman N and S walls in the C13. Octagonal piers with plainly
moulded capitals on the S side, quatrefoiled with fillets on the
N, the foils more than semicircular, in both cases of three bays
with waterholding bases and twice-chamfered arches. The S
arcade may be earlier or later than the N. Nave roof of 1904
(Kelly). The chancel, lengthened in the C14, is windowless on
the N (the church is generally short of windows). On the S side
a succession of chapels overlapping the tower, see the two piscinas. Late Perp, with corbels with a figure and a shield. A broad
wide arch opens into the chancel. The vestry N of the tower
was until the C19 a stable open only to the outside.

FURNISHINGS. COMMUNION RAILS. C17. With strong
balusters. – LECTERN and STALLS, early C20 by *J. M.
Kirkbride*. – FONT. Medieval. Big octagonal bowl. – ROYAL
ARMS, 1730. – STAINED GLASS. E window by *Hardman*, W by
Kempe & Co., with the tower symbol of *W. E. Tower*; both 1913.
– MONUMENTS. Slab in the chancel with a fine foliated cross,
sword and shield. – Damaged wall monument, WD 1674, S
chapel. – Plenty of black-and-white marble tablets and
inscribed brasses. Brass at E end to Francisca Dawes †1673: 'In
her concenter'd did all grace's dwell/God pluckt my Rose yt he
might take a smell.' – Behind the S chapel altar a slab carved
with trees, flowers and birds.

NW is the unmistakable former VICARAGE of 1857, with a fine
garden. Then a confusingly juxtaposed but rewarding group.
Furthest, and tallest, is BARTON CHURCH FARM. L-shaped.
The W wing is C16, with a big stack-and-stair combined on the
W, and a porch added in 1693 by Thomas Dawes on the E.
(The great room over the hall has or had a geometric plaster
ceiling and a plaster overmantel dated 1628.) The S wing has
its own great stack on the front, entrance at the E end, and
newel stair at the back. One house, two dwellings in fact.
Between here and the church is the former PARSONAGE, now
called Glebe Farm, built by Lancelot Dawes 'non mihi sed suc-
cessoribus' 1637 – not for me (he lived in Barton Kirk) but for
my successors. This has mullioned windows, a two-storey
porch with Tudor-arched doorway, and the usual hallan entry
on the l. behind the stack and fire-window. 1701 and 1702 datestones on outbuildings.

KIRKBARROW is by the church drive on the main road. Late
C16–early C17 and later. L-shaped house with a two-storey
porch in the angle and a massive stack on the S end. Modern(?)
statue on porch. (Upper crucks.)

(BARTON HALL. 1710 and 1863. The early part is of five bays.
The doorway has an open curved pediment. The windows still
have cross-mullions. The Victorian part forms a cross-wing and
porch.)

BARWISE HALL (W)

2¼ m. SW of Appleby

In a spot perfectly chosen for shelter. Very long range of house
and byres facing the walled farmyard, sheltered top and bottom
by further outbuildings. Over the door the arms of Sir John
Sudwick, 1579. The doorway is moulded, its head like a B on its
side. Mullioned windows in fives, fours, and threes, the lower
ones linked by a continuous dripmould rising above the windows,
and a fire-window at the E. Unusual plan, a step above the norm.
Two apartments end to end. Both principal chambers have show
ceilings, moulded and stopped with the principals curving down
to what may have been bosses (cf. Prior Senhouse's ceiling at
Carlisle Deanery, c. 1510–20). The lower chamber has a big fireplace with moulded surround. The upper one, presumably a
withdrawing room, is panelled. The doorways have standard C16
lintels with obtusely pointed arches incised on them. The stair
outshut is dated 1676 R & E D (Reginald Dobson) over the back
door. The stair ascends in shallow stages round a well, with
dumb-bell balusters and squashed balls on the newels. This is
presumably the date of the cross-passage taken out of the E apartment – the moulded floor joists continue over – leading to the
stair.

BANK BARN dated E & E D 1681, an early example. BYRE in line with the house inscribed J. Barham Esqr M.P. 1835.

BASSENTHWAITE (C)

ST JOHN, on the A591 ½ m. S of the village. 1878 by *Daniel Brade* of Kendal. Expensive but ill-proportioned church of pinkish rock-faced stone with yellow dressings. E.E. Lancets in super-arches, shallow S transept sporting a prominent clock, and a thin tower and needle spire in the angle between transept and semicircular chancel. The interior is better, lined with silky-smooth buff ashlar. The transept has a mid-column. – PULPIT and ORGAN SCREEN carved with passionflower, grape, fig, pomegranate. – FONT, a monster block. – STAINED GLASS. Apse, *Clayton & Bell*, 1900. Three by *W. Wilson*, 1961. – WAR MEMORIAL. Celtic cross, 1921 by *W. H. Ward.*

OLD CHAPEL, at the crossroads. Now a church room. Rebuilt 1805. Prominent bellcote and stepped buttresses. Round-arched door and windows. Tiny SCHOOLROOM attached; its porch dated 1862 serves as the bus shelter.

ST BEGA, 1⅞ m. S. Probably a pre-Norman foundation, given to the Scottish abbey of Jedburgh in the C12. The situation on the lakeshore could hardly be more romantic, or the approach more beautiful. All the more disappointing therefore to find a church apparently Victorian, the exterior almost entirely of 1874, by *S. Watson* of Penrith, with po-faced triple E lancets, steep roofs and bellcote. Inside, however, a low unmoulded semicircular chancel arch on the simplest imposts, perhaps C12, a low spreading S chapel arch, also semicircular but with a slight chamfer, and a single slightly pointed and chamfered arch to a narrow S aisle. – FONT, low and octagonal. – ROYAL ARMS. George II, with spirited lion and unicorn. – HOUR-GLASS STAND by the chancel arch. – STAINED GLASS by *Powell Bros* (Leeds). – MONUMENTS. Walter Vane †1814 at Bayonne, with military trophy; by *Nixson* of Carlisle. – Outside, S, a copy of the Dearham CROSS (q.v.) for H.A. Spedding of Mirehouse †1887.

MIREHOUSE, ¼ m. SE of the last. The situation is poetic, with a view over parkland to St Bega, Bassenthwaite Lake and the fells. The house is low and spreading, neither grand or formal as major family seats go, but memorable for its literary and artistic associations. Neither front is entirely symmetrical, despite efforts to appear so. The centre of the N front with its seven crowded sashed bays is *c.* 1666, the taller ends with their canted windows 1790. The rear pile was added in the 1830s around the staircase projection. The music room at the W end was added in 1851 by *Robert Cantwell* of London. The four-column Doric porch in front is probably as late as this too. Interiors charming, without great architectural dress. The dining room shows a touch of Gothickry in the bundled shafts of the window and the fan hood and pinnacles of the sideboard recess, though its fireplace and doorcases are classical. The stair, a wooden cantilever, belongs probably to the 1790 phase, as does the charming longitudinal corridor with its succession of fanlights and little vaulted cross-lobby. A lot of work was done in the 1960s.

A curved open loggia links the back of the house to a square C17 or C18 DOVECOTE. Of brick, but switching to stone where it does not show.

ARMATHWAITE HALL (hotel). At the foot of the lake, 1¾ m. NW of St John. Over-inflated Cumberland baronial by *C. J. Ferguson*, 1881, for Thomas Hartley, M.P. and banker of Whitehaven. Asymmetrical hall range with a tower at each end. Vast mullioned-and-transomed windows in red rock-faced and yellow ashlar stone. The Jacobean interiors are over-sized too, and indigestibly rich. The NE service wing added by *J. H. Martindale* is nicely comfortable in comparison, its casement windows informally distributed. Was the Billiard Room, a charming top-lit apartment with red tiled fireplace, added then?

BASSENFELL MANOR (Christian centre), 1 m. NW. Italianate villa of 1847 for William Rathbone V or VI of Liverpool, with an Osborne tower and a high-level Alpine balcony. It appears to have grown from a three-storey holiday villa with a spectacular billiard room on top. Materials and detail are unattractive: fissile stone is laid crazy-paving-wise (over what?), string courses of sandstone or cement, applied timber framing. Rich Victorian fireplaces in over-ripe colours, figured pitchpine panelling, twirly balusters for the principal stair.

(SCARNESS DOWER HOUSE, 1 m. SW of St John's church. 1726, five bays. DCMS.)

ORTHWAITE HALL, 2 m. NE. Inscribed CR 1675 (Christopher Richmond of Highhead). House and barn in an L. The house is a single pile with stair projection at the back. Five bays plus one, of two-light windows, each with its own piece of entablature as a hood. Doorway with segmental, nearly semicircular pediment not as wide as the opening, and full bolection surround. Window frames with stepped surrounds. Close at hand the effect is a trifle overbearing, especially with the present bright pink wall paint, but from the other side of the tarn, against the mass of the mountain, it works well.

OVERWATER HALL (hotel), 2 m. N. Originally (*c.* 1810) named Whitefield, after the builder Mr Gaff's home town in SE Lancashire. Extended in 1840 by Joseph and Mary Gillbank, according to an inscription over the blocked back door. Castellated, with two ample bows flanking a three-bay centre. Projecting centre bay with giant angle pilasters and an inset porch with two pairs of Roman Doric columns. The windows are tripartite, and the upper middle window uses pilasters as dividers. A broad hallway runs right through. To one side a curved staircase with iron handrail. Mahogany doors, elaborate cornices. Marble fireplace with seated maidens and furled lily leaves in the drawing room.

BEAUMONT (C)

ST MARY. On top of the 'beau mont' by the River Eden. Re-set Late Norman s doorway; perhaps a chancel arch, with a thick roll moulding and waterleaf capitals. Semicircular responds. Trio of E lancets in double reveals, set oddly off-centre. Inside, arcading enframes these windows, but it is too thickly white-washed to be certain how much is late C12, how much C19. The shafts have steep bases, too steep really for a date to go with lancets, and very plain moulded capitals. The arcading returns by one bay on the N, but stops short of the s end of the E wall. Simple C16 roof with cambered ties and kingposts, made more impressive by cusping inserted by the deceptive architect, *David Walker*. The work was done in 1887–9 and included replacing all but the E windows. – STAINED GLASS. E window by *J. Scott & Son*, 1872.

Small triangular GREEN E of the church, with an attractive mix of houses in Carlisle brick (Beaumont House), buff stone (Orchard House), mixed cobbles (the remaining working farm), and a few of whitewashed clay (low wing to Orchard House). HILL TOP FARM, immediately s of the church, is the best clay house. Long and narrow, with bowed-out walls like a hogback, and a single central chimney set off the ridge to allow for the ridge beam between crucks. The door is to one side of the stack, indicating the cross-passage behind it. Because the stack sits in the middle of a bay, Nina Jennings interprets the stack and cross wall as inserted into a true longhouse, possibly C16.

BECKERMET (C)

The village shelters in a shallow, bendy valley among the low coastal hills.

ST JOHN, on a steep knoll in the village. Rebuilt by *Joseph Bintley*, 1878–9. Although subordinate to its antiquities, a worthwhile building. Nave, chancel, transepts, N aisle, and an octagonal sw turret with slated spire. Geometrical tracery. The s transept incorporates a fine C13 doorway, slightly pointed under a crocketed gablet. The interior might almost be by Butterfield, who was busy nearby at St Bees. N arcade banded in red and yellow stone. Walls lined with brick, laid in tricky patterns between the windows, with black bricks in simple patterns and a text under the wall-plate. Equally Butterfieldian the FONT.

Starkly geometrical: a cube, an inverted pyramid and an upright pyramid twisted by forty-five degrees. – STAINED GLASS. E window given 1870, by *Shrigley & Hunt.* W, 1888 by *Wailes & Strang.* Both with very large dedicatory brasses. – SCULPTURE. Many C10–C11 fragments found at the rebuilding. Part of a cross-socket with interlace. Parts of at least three cross-shafts, one distinguished by drillings at all the interstices of the tangled interlace design. The patterns, probably derived from Irton (q.v.), are distinctive enough for a Beckermet School to be postulated, seen also at Haile and Workington. – C12–C13 grave-slabs, small and large. Fragments of dogtooth.

ST BRIDGET. The 'Low Church', ½ m. SW, within sound but not sight of the sea. Date uncertain. Nave with bellcote and chancel, small and humble, roughcast and crooked, with plain domestic windows. Simplest interior, white with segmental plaster (?) vault. – ALTAR. A stone *mensa*, with George III's arms over. – PULPIT. Cut down from a two- or three-decker but retaining Doric colonnettes. – MONUMENTS. Row of fine headstones against the S wall, e.g. Nicholas Mossop †1820. – CROSS-SHAFTS. A pair, S of the church. Fat and round at the bottom, squared above, with a cable moulding between. The S one, dated by Bailey and Cramp to the C9, bears five lines of text on its W face. It looks legible at first, but has had five different translations in three different languages. The N one, a little taller, is C10–C11; its shape evidently copied from its neighbour, but the plait patterns like those at St John (*see* above).

For ST BRIDGET, the new church, and SELLA PARK, *see* Calder Bridge.

In the village N of St John is BARWICKSTEADS, a Victorian Tudor villa. TD 1858 on the rainwater hoppers. Steep gables with kneelers, crowned with finial chimneys. The WHITE MARE, immediately E of St John, has a date 1863 and pretty bargeboards, though part must be older. Opposite is CROFT LODGE, coolly Greek with a bust in a niche, but perhaps preserving a memory of an earlier building in the asymmetrical entry. INGLEBERG, on the Braystones Road, was built in 1900 by the Robley family, and is little changed. High-quality villa, roughcast with generous sandstone dressings and a little carving.

BECKSIDE (L) *see* KIRKBY-IN-FURNESS

BEETHAM (W)   *4070*

ST MICHAEL. The lower part of the W tower is early, perhaps even pre-Norman, only 15 ft (4 metres) square, and unbuttressed. The corbelled-out top stage, like that at Sedbergh, was added in the C16. Straight-headed three-light bell-openings.

The body of the church is C16 in character too; a spreading
rectangle with continuous clerestory and flat lead roofs, partly
embattled. The windows are varied, but all Perp, the earliest
being in the SE chapel. However the S arcade is Late Norman,
with tall cylindrical piers with square bases and abacuses and
shallow plain capitals.* Round arches with a slight chamfer,
like the tower arch, though this is slightly pointed. The imposts
are still many-scalloped. The close spacing of the piers and narrowness of the original church – proved by the position of the
tower arch as well as foundations discovered in 1872–4 – would
have been very powerful. However, in the C15 a new N arcade
was built further N. It is lower but more graceful, of standard
elements. Only three nave bays to the four on the S. Octagonal piers, finely moulded pointed arches. This arcade marches
straight through to the E end, five bays in all. The SE chapel
arcade has the same elements. Between it and the S arcade
a piece of the C12 wall remains. The clerestory is not coordinated with either arcade. The church was restored in 1873–5
by *Joseph Bintley*.

FURNISHINGS. Mostly C19 and C20, including quite an
elaborate coved SCREEN. – FONT COVER. 1636. Octagonal,
steeply spire-shaped. – STAINED GLASS. Medieval and C17
fragments in the SE chapel S window. They were re-set in
the 1870s by *Frederick Burrow* of Milnthorpe, who is also
responsible for the anaemic SE chapel E window. A more vivid
one by him, dated 1852, just W of the S chapel. More medieval
bits in the tower W window, also re-set by Burrow, include a
Crucifixion, Virgin and Child, a layman in a squashy hat, and
two bishops in the tracery. The lovely E window, †1881, is by
Heaton, Butler & Bayne: Christ in Majesty with heavenly host.
Nave windows by *Shrigley & Hunt*, later and looser on the N.
– MONUMENTS. Effigies of c. 1490 in the SE chapel, badly
damaged in 1647. Identified as Sir Robert Middleton of
Leighton Hall and Anne Beetham his wife. The tomb-chest has
shields and a large rude head in quatrefoils. – Huttons, S aisle.
Free-standing black urn, on a window sill; to William Hutton
†1811. – Wilsons of Dallam, chancel and S chapel, some quite
good: e.g. Edward †1707, with an urn and two sporting dolphins; another Edward †1764, a white urn by *Fishers* of York;
Daniel †1784, a cartouche; George Edward †1879, Gothic. –
More tablets in the NW corner including William Yeats †1770,
obelisk and urn by *Benjamin Bromfield*, and John Johnson
†1730, with broken pediment and arms.

(Immediately N of the churchyard PARSONAGE FARM. Probably
late C17, but the part appears to incorporate remains of a
medieval college demolished in 1756, including a blocked
doorway with two-centred head towards the churchyard.
DCMS.) Facing the churchyard, S, a pair of three-bay
Georgian houses with fine doorways. Both have segmental
pediments, and one also a frieze rising in the middle.

---

*A coin hoard of the late C11 was found in 1834 buried by a nave pillar.

ASHTON HOUSE, about 100 yds s of the church. T & SI 1678 on a side doorway, and below that JJ (James Johnson) 1744, which refers to the present five-bay, three-storey front range of gleaming whiteness. Pedimented doorcase and both windows above adorned with faces, including a profile with wreath on the top floor. The one-bay wings with their sparing tripartite windows are *c.* 1830. Well-preserved interiors with generous panelling, good chimneypieces and a handsome stair with enriched tread-ends. The little vaulted compartment in the cross-corridor is particularly charming. Extensive GARDENS with Victorian conservatory (and embattled GAZEBO dated 1791).

BEETHAM HOUSE, NE of the church, just across the River Beela. Of five bays, built by the Rev. William Hutton in 1771–2, and lower one-bay wings attributed by Angus Taylor to *Francis Webster,* 1792.

WAR MEMORIAL, by the bridge. 1919, by *Austin & Paley.* Variation on the usual Celtic cross. This is made of sandstone and has an angel and lily in the head of the cross.

HERON MILL. A fine three-storey C18 manorial corn mill on the River Bela. A wooden launder leads water to an internal 14-ft (4.5-metre) pitch-back wheel. Four pairs of stones, supported by a lowder frame, necessary to accommodate the great spur wheel running above the main floor. As is virtually universal in corn mills in these damp North-western Counties, there is an ample drying kiln, here housed in a narrow extension to the NW. Three pairs of upper crucks support the roof. Upstream, the former Waterhouse PAPER MILL.

BLACKBERRY HILL, Leighton Beck Road, SW. Five houses in a shallow crescent slung between massive party walls of limestone; *c.* 1976 by *N. Keith Scott* of the *Building Design Partnership.* The front is quite aggressive, with jabbing shapes clad in dark wood. The steeply rising hillside makes it possible to take the entries at the back via bridges to doors at mid-height. This side is limestone-clad with a big lead dormer at the top. The effect of the curve – the houses are slightly in echelon – and the five bridges crossing from the rocky hillside is pleasing. Interiors split-level, open-plan, upside-down: living/kitchen on top, bedrooms in the middle, bathroom on the ground.

BEETHAM HALL. A suitable introduction to Cumbria as one enters from the s on the A6, standing limestone grey on its defensive rock.

The HALL, at the SE end of this complicated site, has not been lived in since the C17. A full-blown C14 hall-and-cross-wing house. The windows, mostly square-headed, have flowing traceries of the chunky dimensions determined by the local stone, with hoodmoulds and shouldered reveals. The hall doors have wide two-centred arches finely moulded (cf. Wharton Rectory, Lancs.), again with hoodmoulds and shouldered reveals. The wings, still of three or even four storeys, may have been carried up into towers. The low end was nearest the road. If there was an external kitchen it has gone, and the service wing has been partly rebuilt, retaining however its traceried window to the courtyard and a turning stair at the outer hall corner. There may have been four rather than three service doors, the extra one, part of whose hoodmould can be seen, serving a stair. All wood has gone, so there is no indication of screens or roof. No fireplace either (a good deal of ash and wood was found in front of the dais position). At the high end a door goes through to the ground level of the family wing, and a second one in the corner to its upper floors via a spiral stair. The wing has garderobes and fireplaces on several floors, and an outer wing, s, with a clearly indicated chapel on the first floor (piscina and three-light straight-headed end window).

The defensive BARMKIN WALL stretched N of the hall in a rough rectangle, kinked at the present entrance. A good section is preserved and free-standing towards the road. It is about a yard thick and stands 10–12 ft (3–3.7 metres) high, with a wall-walk and corbelled-out parapet. Arrowslits, widely splayed, pierce the wall at regular intervals. Inside the long straight stretch N of the entrance are slots for cruck feet, indicating a building of at least six bays. Holes in the wall above each slot may have been for the cruck spurs. The building must have been planned with the wall. Much of the w curtain is inside the present farmhouse and its barns, including in the farmhouse a complete turret, with well-worn steps.

FARMHOUSE, N. IB or TB 1693 on a blocked doorway. TMB on the porch with its three ball-finials. Its plan is a double pile, with the barmkin wall forming the spine. The roofs indicate that it has grown in stages. Surviving windows of two lights, with hollow-moulded mullions. The inner porch doorway was clearly a window; its wooden jamb inscribed JW 1799. It is likely that this was the fire-window, and that the hallway was the ingle fireplace. The large windows in the l. room were probably put in at the same time. The earlier door is axial with the stair, a fine piece of woodwork ascending broadly in four flights, with nicely turned balusters.

The FARM BUILDINGS are not without interest. To the l. of the farmhouse three arches to implement or cart sheds, and a narrower one to a through passage. Above, reached by the external stair, a large bunkhouse for temporary labourers indicates the scale of operations here. In the bunkhouse, now a museum and display space, can be seen the top of the barmkin wall. The wall appears again in the barn at the other end of the farmhouse.

5070   BEWCASTLE (C)

Described in 1754 as 'a parish . . . in which there is neither town nor village, but a few wretched huts only, which are widely scattered in a desolate country' (*Gentleman's Magazine*). Bewcastle is at the end of a long lonely road N from the Roman Wall into the debatable land, through undulating, soggy, largely unfenced country. Cross, church and castle stand within a polygonal Roman fort. It was a religious sanctuary throughout its early history.

CROSS. 'Art in Cumberland started its course through history at p. 154 its climax' wrote Pevsner in the first words of his *Cumberland and Westmorland* (1967). 'The crosses of Bewcastle and of Ruthwell in Dumfriesshire, only 30 m. W, are the greatest achievement of their date in the whole of Europe . . . The technical mastery is as amazing as at Ruthwell. How can it have been possible, in stone, and at so early a date?'

The date is still open to question; *c*. 685 or *c*. 730 being the most likely. Deeply mysterious in spite of all that has been written, the cross stands 14 ft 6 in. (4.5 metres) high without its head, in its original socket. It is evenly tapered, with a roll moulding at the edges, and nearly square in section, giving four equal fields for decoration. On the W SIDE are three figures in deep niches, beautifully calm, majestically sized, classically posed and dressed. At the top John the Baptist holds the Lamb of God, reminding us of the *Agnus Dei* which was introduced into the Mass at the very end of the C7. In the centre is Christ, 12 haloed, with a pair of eager mole-like creatures worshipping at his feet, rather than trodden down like the young lion and dragon in Psalm 91 (inscription on the Ruthwell Cross). Next comes a long inscription in runes. It appears to be a commemoration of victory set up by three people for a fourth, the counterpart perhaps to the closed scroll held by Christ. The figure at the foot may be identified, with nice symmetry, as John the Evangelist with his eagle; or he may be a secular per- 11 sonage, perhaps the one commemorated, engaged in the noble pursuit of falconry. The style of these figures, which distinguish Bewcastle from all the other crosses in Cumberland or Westmorland, may be linked back to Romano-British tomb sculpture, such as the examples from Murrell Hill and Bowness-on-Solway now in Tullie House Museum, Carlisle. Their ultimate derivation is Eastern Mediterranean, perhaps via imported ivories. The link is Bede's Northumbria, a high spot of civilization. Details of expressions and dress are fugitive: fourteen centuries of the North's trying weather have done their worst, but it is more than possible that such details were rendered in gesso and paint.

On the N SIDE, now blackened in the church's shadow, are alternating panels of vine scroll and knotty interlace with, in the middle, a section of chequer which may have been inset with contrasting stones, in imitation of jewellery. The knots may strike us as barbaric, i.e. un-Antique, yet they are Mediterranean too, occurring in the *cancelli* or choir screens of S. Sabina and S. Clemente in Rome, both of the C6. Absent in the Ruthwell Cross, they were increasingly preferred to the more natural vine scrolls; they feature prominently in the Book

Bewcastle Cross.
Drawings, C20

of Durrow and the Lindisfarne Gospels, both before *c.* 700.
On the E SIDE a majestic vine scroll occupies the whole field,
inhabited by birds and animals. They diminish in size in an
almost musical way, turning this way and that as the vine rises.
The tendrils pass in front or behind in an organized fashion.
That this is more than decoration is suggested by the lines from

The Dream of the Rood inscribed on the Ruthwell Cross, in which the Cross is wound around with light, clothed in honour, and dressed in gold. Vine scrolls are Eastern Mediterranean too. A close parallel is provided by the ivory throne of Bishop Maximian at Ravenna, of *c.* 550 and made perhaps in Constantinople. More alternating interlace and vine scroll on the S SIDE, this time with a sundial near the top, scratched for the hours and with a hole for the gnomon. This has been taken to indicate the presence of a monastic community, needing to mark the hours. Was the cross used like a reredos, behind the celebrating priest? Collingwood records a mortice on top for the cross-head, and there exists a single tantalizing C18 image of a free-armed cross-head lying loose, decorated with chequer.

St CUTHBERT. A single cell, rather like an isolated chancel, with three stepped E lancets of *c.* 1200 and clasping buttresses. No windows on the N. The S side was rebuilt in 1792, and made Gothic by *J. F. Curwen* in 1901. Thin buttresses here. The funny W tower only just clears the roof and has a bellcote, not a proper bell-stage. It is really a stair-tower, set off-centre to the N, with a pair of staggered round-topped windows. W gallery on clumsy monoliths; there was a N gallery too.

UNITED REFORMED CHURCH, formerly Presbyterian, at The Knowe, a long way N. Unexpected urban-looking building by the lonely wayside. Gothic. Dated 1891 on the W porch, over which is a wheel window. – WAR MEMORIAL. White granite obelisk with a sheathed sword and sword-belt hung over the point – a motif also at Nicholforest (q.v.). By *Beattie & Co.*, 1922.

ROMAN REMAINS. The FORT was an outpost of Hadrian's Wall, hexagonal in plan to conform to the six-acre natural knoll. Rebuilt in stone in the mid C2, after a Hadrianic timber phase; reconstructed *c.* 300 but probably abandoned in the early C4. The single defensive ditch, utilized by the Castle at its NE angle (*see* below), is obscured by a later boundary on the SW. A double-portal gate is known from excavation on the WNW, just SW of the farm; the headquarters, commanding officer's house, and barracks have also been examined. The baths (exceptionally, inside the fort) stood outside the E wall of the churchyard. A road ran SSE to Birdoswald (p. 657); more rapid communication to Hadrian's Wall was via a SIGNAL STATION on Barron's Pike, 1¾ m. E – where a rock-cut sub-circular ditch probably surrounded a timber tower – and thence to a stone TOWER on Gillalees Beacon. When excavated, the latter was 20 ft (6 metres) square and still nearly 6 ft (1.7 metres) high; its original height is unknown.

CASTLE. At the end of the C11 Buerth, Lord of Gilsland, used the ditch at the NE corner of the Roman fort to defend his little castle, cutting two more ditches and building on the spoil. It was rebuilt in stone probably by Edward I after he seized it in 1296, in the form of a square shell with lean-to buildings inside. It was last garrisoned in 1639, then dismantled. Major repairs by English Heritage, 2004. The S wall stands to full height and retains most of its facing skin. Massive joist holes for the upper floor, with fireplaces and a window high up at the SE corner, with window seats. Another window at the SW corner is blocked, not surprisingly since the wall is rent below; it retains its mullion and transom. Entrance gateway in a forebuilding, with a mural stair to a garderobe. An additional bank, outside the ditch, strengthened the E side (and probably the N also).

(In the bleak neighbourhood are the remains of several bastle houses, all superseded in the C18 or C19 by more comfortable farmhouses. CREW CASTLE, 2⅛ m. N; HIGH GRAINS, 1½ m. E, where there may have been three bastles across the stream from the present house; LOW GRAINS, ¾ m. NE; and WOODHEAD, 1 m. SE. None survives as more than wall footings and doorway jambs. Peter Ryder identifies gunloops at Crew Castle and High Grains. To these may be added ROANS TREES, 3¾ m. NW, with its round-house in the middle, and SLEETBECK, 4⅛ m. WNW, a seven-bay, three-storey house of the late C17 and 1744, signed WAG for William and Anne Greenwell.)

BIRDOSWALD (C) *see* WALTON

BLACKFORD (C)

On the A7, N of Carlisle.

ST JOHN BAPTIST. Nave and chancel, with a square spirelet on a short tunnel-like bellcote carried over the roof ridge. By *Borough* of Carlisle, 1870 (Kelly), though very like one of Ferguson's simple Dec churches, e.g. Bigrigg (Egremont).

BLAWITH (L)

ST JOHN BAPTIST (Churches Conservation Trust). 1862–3, a humdrum, under-windowed effort by *E. G. Paley* of local rubble and red sandstone. Nave with short chancel, lancets, plate tracery.

Opposite and up the hill are the ruins of the preceding CHAPEL of *c.* 1560.

BOLTON (W)

ALL SAINTS. Long narrow church with a long chancel. A length of blank wall at the W end, thicker than the rest, may represent a lost or unfinished tower. Against it a MONUMENT, recumbent C14(?) effigy of a lady uncomfortably fixed upright. Big clasping buttresses at the w end, plus a central one, support a little enclosed belfry – neither bellcote nor tower – of the local type (cf. Warcop, Crosby Garrett); probably late C17. It has a saddleback roof. The heads of the two w windows are made from stones bearing dogtooth. Narrow Norman s doorway with one order of columns. Incised rosettes on the hoodmould. In one capital a figure holding two staves(?). Saltire crosses chip-carved in the abaci. On the N a matching but wider doorway, now blocked, with billet on the hood-mould. Above that a very interesting carved stone: two Norman knights on horseback (the stirrups are shown), tilting at one another. They have pointed helmets and shields. One, possibly both, has a banner on his lance. A similar relief at Fordington, Dorset, is dated *c.* 1100 by the RCHME, though Bolton church is unlikely to be before *c.* 1130. The church was restored in 1848.

Small-scale interior with blue walls and white ceiling. Chancel arch opened out. No N windows except at the extreme E, a tiny Norman lancet, and one inserted in the N doorway. A collection of painted BOARDS, TABLETS, and BANNERS combats *horror vacui*. Miscellaneous s windows including a matching Norman one, extreme E. The chancel windows lancets with round arches inside, i.e. late C12. – C19 or early C20 wooden SCREEN filling the chancel arch with delicate cusped Dec tracery. – Big ARMS of Queen Victoria over. – Medieval FONT. Round bowl on a square pedestal; COVER of plain spire shape inscribed TG 1687. – STAINED GLASS. E window and one chancel s by *Clayton & Bell*.

EDEN GROVE (now a school), immediately N of the church. Rebuilt by *George Webster*, 1844, for Richard Tinkler in what J. M. Robinson calls a jolly Tudor style. Further alterations *c.* 1900.

BEWLEY CASTLE, 1½ m. SSE. Granted to the Bishops of Carlisle *c.* 1170. Hidden away in an idyllic valley, a place of pleasure and occasional refuge rather than serious defence. Hugh of Beaulieu, Bishop 1219–23, was probably responsible for its name, but its present form is mid or late C14. Ordinations in the chapel are recorded in the C14. Repaired, re-roofed 1402 by Bishop Strickland. Tenanted from the C15 by the Machells, it passed to the Musgraves of Edenhall and was ruinous by 1774. The conserved ruins were taken off the at-risk list in 2006.

The ruin can be mentally reconstructed as a first-floor hall of good size, with attached chamber blocks probably once carried up into towers, well provided with garderobes and some decorative detail. A traceried window and seat at the s end of the hall hang over the little river, presumably behind the dais. Beside it a small door opens off SW to a garderobe turret. On the other (SE) is a substantial chamber with an E-facing traceried window and fireplace and another garderobe turret, almost complete. This is still vaulted underneath. The service (N) end of the hall stood over a basement which was evidently vaulted cross-ways. Just the springing is left. Parallel to that on the E was a second chamber, this time on a basement vaulted in line with the hall.

All this is on a good scale, with a continuous hollow-moulded plinth stepping up and down as necessary. Window mouldings are generally hollow. The remaining hall window was of two lights with tracery under a flat head and a transom. The basement window below, without tracery, shows holes for bars, a groove for leaded glass and hinges for shutters.

Adjacent C16 or C17 FARMHOUSE, so rebuilt in the 1990s as to be unrecognizable as such.

BOLTONGATE (C)

2040

ALL SAINTS. One of the architectural sensations of Cumbria, as well as offering fine views of the back of Skiddaw. Externally all one sees is a Perp church, with two-light side windows in the chancel, cusped with a little panel tracery (the E window with three lights), uncusped with panel tracery again in the nave, with only the upper w window cusped. Curiosity is aroused however by the way the nave roof and w bellcote sit well inside the walls, behind an embattled parapet walk, as in a pele tower, reached by a NE stair-turret with prominent pentagonal cap. The N and s porches, transepts and NE vestry are unusual too, because they are lean-tos, with stone roofs. There are carved gargoyles, a rarity in Cumbria (cf. Dean), a fine double plinth, and an irregularly polygonal little rood-stair turret (N) to finish the unusual picture.

36

The interior is the sensation. The nave is covered by a steeply pointed barrel-vault, in beautiful ashlar, on which the stone roofing originally lay direct. Its great outward thrust is resisted by the regularly spaced transverse walls of the porches and transepts, and reinforced by their half-tunnel-vaults, like continuous flying buttresses, with the stone roof still immediately on them. The arches into the transeptal chapels (two chamfers, dying into the imposts) cut into the nave vault. At the springing of the vaults are rows of corbels, presumably for centring rather than for any upper floor, though it is interesting to note that the w corbels carry the outer wall-walk. In Scotland pointed tunnel-vaults for churches occurred from the late C14 (Bothwell, Lanarks.), and became an accepted device after 1450 (e.g. Ladykirk 1500–7, the inserted kirk at Melrose as late as the 1620s, both Borders). Only the half-tunnels of the transept are not a Scottish custom.* The large Perp windows are integral with the vault, which is groined back for them. Their size seems incompatible with defence, but the nave

---

* Pevsner noted parallels for these, as for the tunnel-vault generally, in the South of France; also the C14 vaulted aisles at Elsdon, Northumberland.

would certainly be fireproof, as well as impressive. The long chancel, also Perp though probably on older foundations, is a little meaner in its windows and plinth, and not vaulted. – FONT. Plain, octagonal, but on four primitive heads. – STAINED GLASS. Chancel sides, two by *Wailes*, 1884. One *Kempe* window, S, also 1884. Lower W, by *Thomas Willement*, 1860. N transept, a nice but typically non-committal window by *Alex Haynes* of *Albion Glass*, 2000.

OLD RECTORY, S of the church. Probably early C15, with extensions of the early C17 and 1889 (DCMS). A solar tower is incorporated at its E end. Its ground floor, tunnel-vaulted and with a single minute slit window, stoutly barred, is only accessible from outside. Its upper room is reached off the hall range via a Victorian stair. The inside walls of the solar are stripped, and a fine old puzzle they exhibit. Probable small window to the N, possible one to the W. On the S a large sash has been inserted. Now it has a pitched roof, and there is evidence for a lower pitched roof, but also traces of another storey. On the W side of the Victorian hall is the corresponding C17 wing, not so thick-walled but with a huge fireplace in its W wall.

QUARRY HILL HOUSE, ¾ m. NW, was the factor's house for the vanished Killhow estate. Of *c.* 1830, still Georgian; five bays, two storeys. Cantilever stair with square iron balusters.

WEARY HALL, 1 m. NW. A fascinating house, of two tall ranges at right angles. A lintel (now not visible) was inscribed JCJC 1576. E range with Early Georgian sashes and a good cornice, but also showing small blocked windows and a blanked-off stair-turret. Inside, a big arched fireplace and a broad, black C17 stair rising right to the top, with bold bottle balusters. In the S wing a low, subdivided ground floor with another arched fireplace and a partly blocked C16 window, uncusped. Above, hardly accessible, is an extraordinary abandoned hall, its ruined walls, gable and even chimney wrapped up in later masonry. It belonged to the Porter family who owned Weary Hall Colliery, and who sold it to the Drury family *c.* 1710.

BOOT (C) *see* ESKDALE

BOOTLE (C)   1080

Described in 1811 as a small and mean market town (charter 1347). Not much more than a hundred-yard narrowing of the A595 road, with just three prominent buildings.

ST MICHAEL. Cruciform with lancets. 'Ancient', but only the chancel, low and roughcast, retains much medieval fabric. The transepts were added in 1837 by *H. J. Underwood*, who re-windowed the nave to match. A substantial W tower was started shortly after 1850, the belfry stage being completed in 1882.

It is a fine accent in the landscape, with pinnacles and a pyramid roof, blank arches to either side of the belfry lights, and, right at the bottom, massive buttresses. Dark interior. Two-bay screen to the transepts, octagonal columns with octagonal caps and bases, conventional. The chancel arch could be c14, twice chamfered, the outer ring rebuilt. Nave and transept ceilings of 1891 (Kelly), of a peculiar coved form raised in the centre over tie-beams, reminiscent of Paley & Austin. Chancel with a barrel-boarded ceiling, 1888. Good tower arch with four chamfers. – FONT. Octagonal, bearing two shields per face, inscribed R.B.: probably Richard Brown, rector *c.* 1535 – and an inscription in blackletter which appears to add up to an 'In Nomine'. The bugle may refer to John Huddleston of Millom. – STAINED GLASS. E window by *Hardman*. Chancel N, †1899, by *Henry Holiday*. N and S transepts ('terrible': Pevsner) by *Ward & Hughes*, mid-1880s. – MONUMENT. Small (*c.* 14 in., 36 cm.) brass to Sir Hugh Askew †1562 (*see below*), in full armour.

Austin & Paley did the CROSS by the churchyard in 1897.

CHAPEL. Built in 1780 by Joseph Whitridge for the Countess of Huntingdon's Connexion, and now Independent. Three by three bays, two-storeyed at the front, attached at the back to a house dated 1780 and another 1808. (Interior largely c19.)

CAPTAIN SHAW'S SCHOOL. 1830. Tall oblong two-storey box, Tudor, faced with scored stucco. Scriptural inscription over the paired doors.

HYCEMOOR, 1 m. NW, is a second settlement round Bootle STATION, a standard 1870s Furness Railway design in crazy-paving granite by *E. G. Paley*. An embryo resort with several three-storey villas, a bank (1902) and a hotel.

Former WORKHOUSE, between Bootle and the railway station. The main buildings of 1856–7 demolished. The substantial infirmary block, with a hipped roof, symmetrical chimneys and large sashes, is now a house called Meadow Croft. Also a casual-ward block of 1880, used by the council.

The lane leading SW from the workhouse goes through a series of coastal farms, the farm buildings e.g. SYKE BECK, HYTON, KISKIN of water-worn cobbles, the field boundaries of stones and earth.

SEATON HALL AND PRIORY, 1 m. N. In a sheltered hollow just out of sight of the sea, a small priory for Benedictine nuns was founded *c.* 1190–1200 probably by Henry Fitzarthur. Nearly every record of its life refers to its poverty; at the Dissolution there were just two nuns and a novice. Of the CHURCH the E wall of the chancel survives as a romantic garden feature: three tall E.E. lancets of equal height, shafted with a continuous hoodmould inside and with a little nailhead. In the spandrels a re-set blank trefoil and cinquefoil. Another shaft in the SE angle and remains in the S wall suggest a display of arcading like the E ends of St Bees or Kirkby Lonsdale (qq.v.). The buildings were granted to Sir Hugh Askew in 1542. His HALL stands in the likely position of the nuns' refectory, indicating the small scale of the cloister. After reconstructions in the c17

and C19, and further changes in the 1970s, it retains little of
antiquity. Peter Leach notes a blocked mullioned-and-transomed window on the E wall, bits of string course and a couple
of big segmental-arched fireplaces. On the S an octagonal
chimney with a stone cap.

BORROWDALE (C)

2010

'Dark rocks yawn at its entrance, terrific as the wildness of a
maniac', wrote Ann Radcliffe in 1794. Beyond, the valley opens
out to a lost world, pastoral, flat, scattered with four or five
hamlets, hemmed in by mountains on every side.

CHURCH, on the Stonethwaite side turn. C17 and 1825. White
dale church with bellcote, with dull inserted tracery and a sad
chancel added in 1873. – (PULPIT. Late Georgian, with pretty
panels. Brought from Mardale in 1937.)

ROSTHWAITE. The side lane leads to a cluster of farms all in
each other's back yards. NOOK FARM, cottage–three-bay
farmhouse–barn, C18, all in line. OAK COTTAGE, C17 house
and small barn in line; the house keeps its fire-window, the
barn has the common behind-the-fire entry. YEW TREE FARM
has kept its deep-set windows and door. KILN ORCHARD, in
contrast, is a new-build exemplifying the National Park's planning policy: five houses in a terrace artfully varied within strict
rules of scale and materials; by *ADK Architects* (*Andy Prickett*
and *Steve Harwood*) of Keswick, *c.* 1993.

STONETHWAITE. C17. A National Trust idyll, all olive paint and
unconverted barns.

SEATHWAITE. The wettest habitation in Britain; the buildings
are adapted accordingly, avoiding all complications of roofing.
The barns are all in a continuous row nearly 100 yds long, the
three C17 houses across a cobbled yard in a second row.

SEATOLLER. At the foot of the Honister Pass. The YEW TREE,
now a restaurant, is dated 1628. Comb Gill CORN and
SAWMILL, 1796. Single-storey, of rubble, with drying kiln
attached to the N. 10-ft (3-metre) undershot wheel.

PLUMBAGO MINE, ½ m. S of Seathwaite Bridge on the slopes of
Grey Knott. Shafts, adits and rudimentary foundations of the
famous 'Borrowdale Wadd' mine, Europe's only source of
natural plumbago, from which the Keswick pencil industry
developed in the C18.

HONISTER SLATE MINES. At the crest of Honister Hause, a collection of undistinguished sheds for splitting ('riving') and
dressing the beautiful pale green slate still being extracted from
mines under the fells to the W. To N and S of the road to Buttermere are substantial and sometimes dramatic remains of
350 years of quarrying and mining. The oldest workings, simple
surface operations started in 1648, show as terraces on the
flanks of Fleetwith Pike close to the 2,000-ft (615-metre)

contour. Ledges, tracks, and the walls of two tiny slate-dressing bothies are recognizable. These huts, squeezed into gullies 400 ft (123 metres) below, are built of rounded stones, clearly gathered from the surface. The raw slate 'metal', worked into finished material in the quarries themselves, was carried on sledges down still-traceable but alarmingly steep SLED ROADS to where wheeled vehicles could take over. By the 1830s attention was shifting to the N side of the Hause, and quarries were opened on Yew Crag. On the Fleetwith side extraction continued, increasingly from underground mines.

Railed INCLINES, already common in Welsh slate quarries half a century earlier, did not arrive until 1879/80. The first connected Yew Crag Quarry with a road to the Hause and is still substantially complete. The DRUM HOUSE at its head was consolidated in 1994. The DUBS INCLINE on the W flank of Fleetwith Pike, 1891, is now a footpath. Drum house at 1,750 ft (538 metres), also restored in 1994, along with the QUARRY OFFICE AND BOTHY, 1860. The most dramatic of the inclines, inaccessible but clearly visible, cuts across the precipitous N face of Fleetwith Pike from the C17 workings in Ash Gill at 1,900 ft (585 metres) to join the 1888 'Monkey Level' road to the Hause: lower stage built 1888; upper, with a tunnel section, 1894.

Closed in 1986, Honister reopened in 1994. Tourist tours of the underground workings and processing sheds supplement the income from slate.

BOWNESS-ON-SOLWAY (C)

At the northernmost point of the Cumbrian peninsula. Wonderful approach along the flat shore of the Solway. The village is densely packed, which is unusual for Cumberland. Its business was salmon fishing using haaf nets from the shore. At the W end of the village the road passes through the sites of the E and W gates of the ROMAN FORT at the W end of Hadrian's Wall. From the NW corner the Wall continued onto the shore. Beyond that, a system of forts, mile fortlets and towers, without a linear barrier, extended beyond Maryport (*see* p. 575).

ST MICHAEL. A characterful church, long, low, massively buttressed all round, built of stones from the Wall. Plain oblong double bellcote with an oblong stone pyramid roof and arched openings, on a broad buttress. Victorian windows in ones, twos and threes, but the N and S doorways are damaged Late Norman, both with one order of columns. The S one with a single-chamfered arch, the N with a continuous inner roll up the jambs and round the arch, and fine mouldings in the arch. One capital with nice leaves off a stem. One Norman N window in the chancel. The chancel arch and N transept are probably of the restoration of 1891–2. Before that there was a flat ceiling, square windows and box pews. – FONT. Late Norman and excellent. Square top, octagonal bottom, i.e. a bowl like a cushion capital. Boldly carved with leaves or vines on three sides, the stems beaded. Net or trellis on the s with individual nailheads and ballflowers in its meshes. – STAINED GLASS. E window by *Daniel Bell*, 1891. N transept: N by *Powells*, 1918, W by *Clayton & Bell*, 1900. Good C20 collection, often with a watery, fishy theme. Two W by *Millican, Baguley & Atkinson* of Newcastle, 1954. Nave s, Good Samaritan, *A. E. Buss*, 1957. Two-light s window by two designers: *R. R. Nichol* (Christ with young people, 1990), *Alex Haynes* (St Michael, 1999); Haynes also made the porch window. Nave N, St Mary, *R. R. Nicholl*, 1988. Chancel N, Ascension, by *G. Maile & Son*, 1972. A length of nailhead forms the sill.

Outside, E, copy of the Aspatria CROSS to the Rev. S. Medlicott †1899. Several good TABLE TOMBS, including Sally Sharp †1785 with urns and swags, knots and a dancing figure.

RECTORY of 1922, s of the church. Successor to a demolished defensive tower, to which was added in the C16 a bastile or bastle.

In the middle of the village is BOWNESS HOUSE FARM. Tall Late Georgian house, L-shaped, white, attached to an endearing, much lower C17 or early C18 house, of three bays with sixteen-pane sashes. The doorcase at one end is too big, pushing into the sill above. Bolection moulding with an extra roll (as Easton Hall, below), open pediment on brackets. Built in over a doorway, a Roman ALTAR to Jupiter. Extensive walled (defensive?) FARMYARD with a gin house. A formerly open shed has three stone piers, cylindrical monoliths, with proper capitals and bases. Where are they from, and how old?

SOLWAY VIADUCT. W of the village a broad embankment, lined with huge blocks of finely jointed sandstone, stretches N for ¼ m., its crest 20 ft (6 metres) above the sands. At the seaward end a transverse row of cast-iron columns, *c.* 5 ft (1.5 metres) high. This was the approach to a viaduct 1 m. 190 yds (1,800 metres) long, built in 1869 to carry Cumberland iron ore to the steelworks of Lanarkshire, avoiding the railway bottleneck at Carlisle. Piers of six cast-iron columns supported 181 single and twelve double spans of wrought-iron girders. Designed by *James Brunlees* (cf. the viaducts at Arnside and Leven). Closed 1921, dismantled 1934.

PORT CARLISLE, 1 m. E. The Late Georgian terrace of Port Carlisle faces up the estuary across the docks and basin of the CARLISLE CANAL, a ship canal built 1821–3 as part of an ambitious scheme to connect the Irish Sea with the North Sea. In 1853–4 the canal was converted to a railway laid along the filled-in bed. The Solway Viaduct (*see* above) effectively cut off the port from open sea after 1869.*

---

*The economic value of the railway can be judged from its persistence with a horse-drawn passenger service until 1914 – the last such in Britain.

The VILLAGE is just a long, straight, interrupted two-storey terrace, rather like a one-sided Carlisle street (but without the brick). Houses of two or three bays; near the middle the former SOLWAY HOTEL, a detached five-bay house with a Tuscan porch. It served passengers waiting for the tide, or for fly boats along the canal to Carlisle. At the N end of the main street, HESKET HOUSE (once the Packet Boat Inn) incorporates a small ROMAN ALTAR in its masonry immediately above the door. C20 houses now fill gaps along the original three streets. A pair of link-detached 1980s houses facing E down Scotch Street are surprisingly good: well proportioned, and acknowledging local traditions without resorting to pastiche.

HARBOUR AND CANAL STRUCTURES include a sea lock, two warehouses, a custom house, the remains of a wooden pier from which steamers ran to Liverpool (and occasionally across the Atlantic), all early 1820s. Also a substantial block of well-engineered masonry out in the estuary, the remains of a never-completed FLOATING HARBOUR, authorized by Act of 1836. In 1844 the company made an attempt to promote the place as a bathing resort, and a tiny single-storey BATH HOUSE survives on the N-facing shore. Symmetrical, with heavy architraves, in fine red sandstone ashlar. Very similar to the lodge cottage at the former canal basin in Carlisle (p. 261).

DRUMBURGH, 3¼ m. SE. An island in the saltmarsh, now mostly flat pasture. Site of the Roman fort of Congabata, on Hadrian's Wall.

33   DRUMBURGH CASTLE. Described in 1580 as 'Neyther castle nor tower, but a house of convenyent strength and defence', though it seems to have been more of a barracks than a house. Tall, perfectly rectangular, built of Roman stones of even size. The early house was perhaps C13 (Richard le Brun was granted licence to crenellate 1307). It had services W, solar E, and a broad round-arched door on the ground floor. In 1518 Thomas, 2nd Lord Dacre, remodelled it (cf. Askerton and Naworth castles) into what is now called a Solway bastle, i.e. upstairs living, with first-floor entrance by a splayed external stair immediately W of the earlier doorway. Over the upper door a damaged panel with the Dacre arms, and a section of parapet with two eagles (cf. Abbey Town). It appears to have had four floors, the middle two lit by narrow windows, and a watch turret on the W gable (rebuilt in 1977). Its purpose was to protect the inhabitants and their goods 'if the Scottes should happen to make any sudden rode or forroo as when the sea ebbeth they may easily do'. In 1680 Sir John Lowther made the upper three floors into two, inserting large cross-mullioned windows, now sashes. All the windows were formerly barred. The ground floor is low and dark, with inserted fireplaces and corridor. The narrow stair cuts through a joist, i.e. evidently secondary. The first floor is much taller, and well lit. The big room at the E end retains small-scale panelling with a reeded top section, but the equivalent upper-entrance room near the W end is bare. The lock to the upper front door says IL (John

Lowther) 1681. Good stair up to the second floor, with fat bottle balusters. This floor also has good head-room; a step-back about 3 ft (1 metre) above the present floor indicates the earlier floor configuration. A proper stair up to the watch turret was lost when that end was rebuilt. The roof trusses are kingposts (morticed for longitudinal braces) with raking queenposts.

By the front door two Roman ALTARS, one painted.

DRUMBURGH GRANGE, a grange of Holm Cultram Abbey (Abbey Town), stands between the road and the sea on the site of the Roman fort. Part of a rectangular MOAT remains. The Excisemen's watch tower which stood behind has been demolished. Most of the houses were of clay, thatched, opening straight onto the road; some slight remains on the inland-leading lane: HAZELDENE of 1720, with a cruck or two, and LOW FARM. Hugging the shoreline was the Carlisle Canal.

A smaller example of a Solway Bastle is BARROCKS HOUSE in Glasson, 1 m. NW. C16. The slit windows can be seen.

EASTON HALL, ¾ m. SE of Drumburgh. Eye-catchingly smart house of five bays, rendered and coloured, dated TBH 1724. Swan-necked open pediment over a round-arched doorway, with pilasters of the oddest section, like a half-hearted bolection with an extra roll.

ANTHORN ARRAY, on the peninsula 5 m. SW. Oddly festive circle of stayed radio masts dancing around a taller one. Erected for the Ministry of Defence c. 1965 on a former naval air base, for very low frequency (VLF) communication with nuclear submarines.

BOWNESS-ON-WINDERMERE (W)

4090

On a summer's day Bowness Bay is the liveliest of the Lake District's hot spots. Swans, crowds, steamers, piers with *Paley & Austin*'s wooden booking office and café, the (rebuilt) Cushion Huts for hire boats, Sir William Forwood's FOUNTAIN 'in sunny remembrance 1862–1912', all benignly overlooked by the Belsfield Hotel (*see* Villas, p. 171). As a backdrop, the unbroken woods on the far side, and beyond them the fells. So, although the lake can be very busy it is like a bubble of bustle and racket in a great silence.

CHURCHES

ST MARTIN (Windermere parish church), Lake Road. Mostly of c. 1483 when it was made parochial, but retaining the tower base from the earlier chapel-of-ease, as indicated by a W doorway with a two-centred arch hollow-chamfered, with a dripmould. The priest's door in what appears to be a Perp s aisle follows the same pattern, and pieces of the hollow moulding appear in the N and S main doors. The church is rectangular, of rubble, with full-length aisles. Clerestory and flat lead roofs probably C16. Only in the openings is there worked stone, and only the E window exhibits tracery. In 1870, as local magnates such as Henry Schneider competed to spend money on it, it was thoroughly restored by *Paley & Austin*. Theirs is the saddleback tower top and stair-turret and the extended chancel. The external whitewash came off. The NE vestry was added in 1911 by *W. L. Dolman*, then made into a chapel in 1922 by Dolman and Sir William Forwood.

The interior is a strange sight. Lacking freestone for respectable mouldings, columns or arches, it is entirely of rubble, thickly plastered and painted white. The piers, some markedly tapered, are chamfered squares in section. The painted TEXTS in the spandrels of the arcades were rediscovered in the C19. The texts can be dated quite closely. Some are Robert Openshawe's *Short Questions and Answeares*, penned in 1548 and published in 1590; the biblical texts seem to come from Coverdale's translation of 1535. Christopher Philipson's 'preyer' for deliverance from the Gunpowder Plot (1605) is dated 1629. The rest of the scheme is Victorian, in tempera and oil, by *Henry Hughes*, with verses and spiky linear decoration using a limited palette of browns with some black, red and yellow. The scenes in the chancel are meant to be read with the E window.

FURNISHINGS. REREDOS, 1870, marble, executed by *Bell & Almond* of London. – FONT. It could be C12, a small octagonal bowl with heads carved at four corners. – SCULPTURE. Well-carved wooden group of St Martin and the Beggar. The RCHME calls it probably C17 and foreign. It looks considerably re-carved *c.* 1850. – SCREEN to the SW chapel, brought here in 1995 from St John (*see* below); beautiful Arts and Crafts work by its vicar *E. S. Robertson* and parishioners under the direction of *Arthur Simpson* from 1896 onwards, with openwork panels of briar roses, grapes, pea pods. – DISPLAY CASE also by Simpson, in memory of the architect Dan Gibson, 1907. – The WAR MEMORIAL CHAPEL, NE, looks like an encapsulation of late Paley & Austin, but is by *W. L. Dolman*, 1922: reredos, altar, panelling, seating, organ, blackletter inscription in raised letters round the E window arch, memorial of alabaster and brass. Stained glass by *Shrigley & Hunt*.

Other STAINED GLASS. The E window retains much of its 1480s glass. The Crucifixion occupies the centre three lights. Streams of blood from Christ's wounds are being caught by angels into gold chalices. In the side lights St George, St Barbara and St Katherine, but the outer r. light lacks a large figure. Below are kneeling donor figures including a named Prior of Cartmel, and a group of named Augustinian canons in characteristic attire. It seems likely that these were brought from Cartmel. In the tracery centre fragments, e.g. an early

C14 Virgin. The window was conscientiously made good in 1870 by *Henry Hughes*; every new piece has a tiny HH. In an otherwise plain window on the N, emblems commemorating Bellman the C16 carrier who brought the lead for the roof. The rest is C19 and C20 by various makers, all of good quality. Individual war memorials in the NW corner. J. R. Lingard †1915, smooth and rich, by *Powells*, J. E. Bownass †1915, more scratchy, by *A. K. Nicholson* including Ypres in ruins. W window, gold-tinted, by *Ward & Hughes* to Elizabeth Schneider, 1881. – Etched glass SCREEN by *Sally Scott*, 2000, in the tower arch.

MONUMENTS. SE, Richard Watson of Calgarth Park, Bishop of Llandaff, †1816, by *Flaxman*, displaying the emblems of his neglected office. The crozier sticks out oddly, far below the tablet. – In front of the Simpson screen, 'Author's epitaph on himselfe, made in the tyme of his sickness' by Robert Philipson, 1631: 'A man I was, wormes meat I am/To earth returend from whence I came.' – Fletcher Raincock †1840. Tablet with bust in recess. By *R. W. Sievier*. – Rayrigg memorial, commemorating Flemings from †1835 to 1902; brass in alabaster frame. – Outside, South African WAR MEMORIAL, 1903. Cumbrian-type wheel-cross of green stone, with grapes and birds, signed *J. Swallow*, W-mere. Against the W wall of the S aisle, John Bolton of Storrs †1837. The monument encapsulates the man. A slab of white veined marble, without a trace of decoration or even finished edges, but so boldly lettered as to issue a silent challenge.

Former RECTORY, now Parsonage Wyke, Glebe Road. Logically of *c.* 1483, when the parish was formed. The Rector of Windermere was an important person, and the house has been updated several times in some style: E. A. Nurse quotes 1645, 1680, 1770 and 1857. Superior house of vernacular type, roughcast with round chimneys (cf. Town End, Troutbeck). Four-room plan, with hall and kitchen in the middle. Two-storey porch with an eye-catching chimney corbelled out over the door. It opens onto the side of the enormous stack, i.e. baffle-entry. Fireplaces back-to-back, each with a walk-in hood on a bressumer, fire-window and cupboards. The hall fireplace was big enough to be turned into a complete washroom and toilet. Tiny stair in a cupboard at the W end, turning round a mast. Tucked in by the hall stack upstairs is a powdering room. At the E end is a pretty Chinoiserie staircase, of perhaps 1770, and on the S a large Victorian wing with two bays.

ST JOHN, Lake Road. Closed, now flats. *Joseph Pattinson*, aged twenty-one, won a competition in 1881 with an advanced design with a long chancel and Geometrical E window to the road, completed 1886. Roughcast. Large, cruciform, aisleless. No tower.*

OUR LADY OF WINDERMERE AND ST HERBERT (R.C.), Lake Road. 1962–3, by *Hill, Sandy & Norris*.** Cut slate base, pinky-

---

*Some stained glass went to St James, Barrow, p. 132.
**But given to *Cuthbert Baines* on a plate in the narthex.

grey blocks above, concrete mullions. The sanctuary is a high pentagon, with two lower naves added to make a V, like an C18 parson's bands. The low entrance and higher baptistery are in the angle of the V, allowing the two naves at least a glimpse of each other. Slab glass in the baptistery, continuous high windowing of streaky glass round the pentagon.

CARVER MEMORIAL CHURCH (United Reformed), Lake Road. By *Robert Walker* of Kendal, 1879–80. William Carver of The Priory (Windermere) died in 1875 leaving no will. Sons and daughter built the chapel as a memorial, whereupon the will was discovered. Typical Congregational architecture, prosperous, churchy, even scholarly, with sw steeple and Geometrical tracery.

CHRISTIAN SCIENCE CHURCH, Birthwaite Road. By *David Matthews*, 1978. Ingenious roof of four petals making a square and held in tension, plus a little detached quarter-square, with a single petal, for the Sunday School. Auditorium on the diagonal and slightly raked. The roof floats a few inches above the walls, allowing light to enter. More light along the slits separating the petals, as well as at the corners.

THE TOWN

The TOWN, called a 'little, ill-placed, ill-built Cluster of Huts' by Richard Holden in 1808, is now solidly Victorian and Edwardian, with fussily detailed shops and terraces employing a wide range of materials and vernacular techniques, some local, some decidedly not, to create a mood of elephantine jollity. Around the irregular spaces called Queen's and St Martin's squares can be seen red, green and yellow stone, bargeboards and finials, pargetting, timber framing, jettying, even a couple of painted figurehead-like corbels. *Thomas Pattinson*, and from 1877 *G. H. Pattinson* (*see* below) were the great builders.

Jutting out into BOWNESS BAY is SHEPHERDS', a neat multi-function structure by *John Moore* of *Gill Dockray Rhodes & Moore*, 1975 – boatyard below, tourist trap above – taking the form of an abstract mountain of restless diagonals. Answering it on the r., the ROYAL WINDERMERE YACHT CLUB, 1964–5 by *John Gill* of *Gill & Rhodes*. Laminated timber frame with cedar cladding, but also two heavy stone screen or baffle walls. The building is quite small and has an odd sawtooth roof like the awning of a launch, one set of teeth pointing downward, another in a syncopated order upward. – BANDSTAND, 2005, by *Chris Brammell*. Wing-like roof, copper-covered, supported by rusty steel trees. It does not focus the sound as a traditional bandstand would.

Proceeding roughly from the bay uphill towards Windermere, N. The ponderous OLD ENGLAND HOTEL by *Thomas Pattinson*, the dark mass on the shore just s of the Royal Windermere Yacht Club, replaces a Georgian house pulled down

in 1869; extended W 1879, S extension 1926, etc. To the SE,
beyond St Martin's church, the SPINNERY (now a restaurant),
on the corner of Brantfell Road and Brayfield Road. Probably
early C18, but altered. It has a semicircular bay sheltering under
a three-sided upper storey, and an oriel overlooking the lake.*
Behind, on the wall of the former girls' school, is a MEDAL-
LION of John Bolton of Storrs (*see* p. 175), by *Webster*, from
Bolton's demolished School of 1836. High up on Biskey Howe,
NE, is the HYDRO HOTEL, opened in 1881. White, with an Italianate tower and semicircular bay. To the N in Rayrigg Road,
in front of the World of Beatrix Potter centre, SCULPTURE by
Anthony Bennett, 2005. Bronze, with three children and char-
acters from every book. Is it unbearably twee? On LAKE ROAD
the OLD BATH HOUSE of 1853 has Gothic windows of terracotta, washed over to look like stone. POLICE STATION and
former MAGISTRATES' COURT (closed in 2000), 1926. Of
green stone with red stone dressings. Long symmetrical composition, with the frowning police house at one end and offices
at the other. On the r. side, by Beresford Road, PATTINSONS.
In 1850 *Abraham Pattinson* bought some ground which he
named ELIM GROVE, for his builders' yard and office. He had
built six houses by 1854. ELIM BANK was built by *Thomas Pattinson* in 1886 for his son G. H. on his wedding; charmingly
over-egged with fretted bargeboards, coloured glass, fancy
porch and conservatory. GOODLY DALE COTTAGES, below
St John's church, are 1930s almshouses by *Joseph Pattinson*.
Symmetrical roughcast row strung out in a gentle curve. By
the road a larger house called Sunny Bank. Vernacular detail
gone self-conscious: dripmoulds of three courses of slates,
kneelers of stacked slates, slate covers to the roof overhangs.

  CLOCK TOWER. Small but prominent, marking the boundary with Windermere. By *Joseph Pattinson*, 1907, in memory of
'The Thorough Guide': Mountford John Byrde Baddeley.

VILLAS

An alphabetical selection of those on the blest E margins of the
lake (*see also* Newby Bridge, Windermere, Ambleside, and especially Troutbeck).

BELLE ISLE. Thomas English of Nottinghamshire bought the   56
  island, originally Longholme, in 1772 and started to build
  probably in 1774. Wordsworth said that this was the first house
  built in the Lake District for the sake of the beauty of the
  country. *John Plaw* designed a house like no other: a Pantheon,
  cylindrical, with a dome and lantern, and a tall portico of four

*This was Annie Garnett's shop of 1912, where she taught spinning, weaving and
embroidery. She established the Windermere Industries in 1889 in the converted
stable of her family house, Fairfield, up the hill, after a visit to Elterwater and the
Langdale Linen industry (q.v.).

slender unfluted Ionic columns facing Bowness, E.* It appears
in all the early views of the lake, providing the necessary Picturesque focus. English over-reached himself and had to sell.
It was bought in 1781 for the sixteen-year-old Isabella Curwen,
heiress of Workington Hall, and named in her honour. She
married her cousin John Christian and together they completed it. Isabella was a native of high standing, which helped
defuse early criticism of the house. They did away with
English's 'cabbage patch garden' and, with the advice of
Thomas White of Retford, planted trees *au naturel*. Today you
could be forgiven for not knowing the house is there at all, so
dense has the screen grown. White revetted the shoreline in
stone, and laid out a perimeter drive. His plan of 1783 shows
stables, kitchen garden, seats, 'a thatched building' and 'a
handsome building or temple', but it is not clear if these were
built.

The Curwens sold up in 1991. In 1994 the house burnt out.
The reconstruction was carried out under *David Walker*, then
of *Buttress Fuller* of Manchester. The fire revealed the house's
secrets. It is a true drum 54 ft (16.5 metres) in diameter, sitting
in a deep square area screened by a low wall. It is built of hard
Ecclerigg stone, laid watershot-fashion and not now (though
originally) disguised by limewash or render. The shafts of the
portico are of sandstone in fairly small pieces, but the capitals
are carved of wood. The frieze is pulvinated, and there is a pediment. A curved two-arm staircase rises inside the portico. The
body of the house has three Venetian windows in the other
three main directions. Their middle arch is set in a blank arch.
A pair of low square rooms added *c.* 1800 fill the NW and SW
corners of the area. Detached on the W side is a BILLIARD
ROOM built by J. R. Bridson of Bryerswood, Sawrey, when he
was renting the island in the later C19.

The INTERIOR is cleverly contrived to create sensible-
shaped rooms within the circle. The fitting-out can be credited
to the Curwens rather than to English, and to *John Carr* of
York. The ground floor has a vestibule, then in the centre the
full-height stair, of wood, with square balusters (though the fire
revealed that a stone cantilever had been intended). It has an
apse, but overhead an oblong with two semicircles. On either
side are the Eating Parlour, with a frieze of fox heads, and the
Withdrawing Room, simply panelled with a hunting-horn
frieze. Adamish fireplaces. Both are rectangular except for their
bowed outer walls. Fine curved mahogany doors. At the back
is the oval library, with a groin-vaulted centre, apses, and a
shallow curved projection for the Venetian window. The secondary stair fits in one of the left-over spaces. The offices were
in the basement, servants' bedrooms in an attic hidden in
the dome. All the flues are carried up invisibly through the
lantern.

---

*Ballyscullion in Co. Londonderry, begun in 1787 by the Earl of Bristol, Bishop of
Derry, to an oval plan, was inspired by Belle Isle; the Earl-Bishop's better-known
oval mansion at Ickworth in Suffolk followed in 1796.

Pevsner remarked that it is the house that makes the island *belle*. It still does; the temple villa and its island Arcadia are perfect. Only the sounds of the Bowness boatyards, so close in reality, and the commentaries of passing steamers, remind us of the outside world.

BELSFIELD (hotel), Kendal Road. White and stuccoed, very prominent by Bowness pier. Italianate villa with an 'Osborne' tower, of 1844 etc. by *George Webster* for Baroness de Sternberg, a Cumbrian lady who contracted an exotic marriage. In 1869 it was bought by H. W. Schneider of Barrow, ironmaster. His daily commute has become legendary: breakfast on his steam launch *Esperance*, then special train from Lakeside. From 1890 a hotel, gaining a large ballroom to the s, then a whole extra storey, by *Robert Walker*. Hotel interiors in Adam or Wyatt style, the Adam Suite to the l. of the entrance rather over the top for Adam.

Immediately below and N is a smaller version, ST ANDREWS, with its own little Osborne tower, the initials FEW and the date 1843; all typical of *Webster*.

BLACKWELL, on the upper road s to Newby Bridge. 1898–1900, by *M. H. Baillie Scott* for Sir Edward Holt of Manchester, brewer, philanthropist, and Lord Mayor. Not all the craftsmen are known, but *Arthur Simpson*'s woodwork, with its recurring Rowan motif, is a constant delight. Restored and converted from 1997 by *Allies & Morrison* for the Lakeland Arts Trust.

The original front drive, no longer used, climbs up the hill from the lakeside road, revealing more and more of the view, to the long comfortable whiteness of the roughcast house sitting end-on to the lake. Asymmetrical but balanced, the style Lake District vernacular (though no statesman's house was ever anything like as big), with odd disconcerting Tudor details. Large mullioned and sometimes transomed windows irregularly placed, flush and unmoulded on the outside, though with an ovolo moulding inside. Artistic leadwork, doorways with Tudor heads.

The INTERIOR does not reveal its pleasures all at once. Every built-in seat, and there are plenty, commands carefully composed views. The dark woody cross-corridor draws you inevitably to the white brilliance of the DRAWING ROOM, W, with its broad square bay window. As you approach the tantalizing view, the window opens up, being wider than its opening, and at the last minute discloses fabulous views N and s as well as W. This is a most delicate and feminine room, with slender iron shafts supporting cup-like capitals carved with foliage and birds. The GREAT HALL resembles Baillie Scott's competition fantasy of 1901, 'House for an Art Lover'. As Muthesius pointed out in 1905, it is a new concept of a room, effectively several rooms in one, with the space free-flowing. Partly double-height, with Cheshire-type timber framing, and partly of normal height and originally accommodating the billiard table – usually a male preserve shunted off to distant reaches. The painted peacock frieze is by *Shand Kydd*. The panelling is partly reclaimed, with a conscientious copper plate to tell us

112

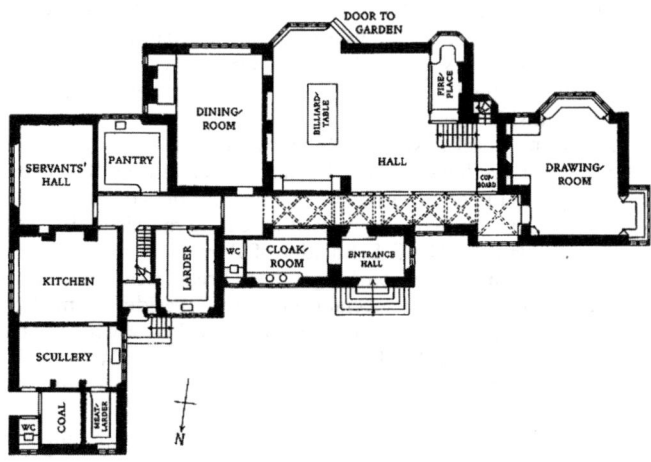

Bowness-on-Windermere, Blackwell.
Ground-floor plan

so. Both halves have their room-within-a-room seating. Beside
the inglenook rises the stair, sending off a branch to a little
minstrel room over the ingle. One can see Waterhouse in the
spatial interlocking, Burges in the fun and games, Pearson in
the beautiful little rib-vault – all Victorian architects; it is hard
to remember that Blackwell is also Victorian, so modern does
it seem. Lower and upper corridors look into the hall space.
The stained glass disconcerts in its eclectic mix: Art Nouveau
tulips and birds for the sliding partition and inglenook,
straightforward heraldry for the outer windows (is it all *Shrigley
& Hunt?*). The DINING ROOM beckons, with its huge joggled
voussoirs over the fireplace next to delicate Art Nouveau glass.
Rowan, bluebell and daisies on a hessian wall covering.
Charming naïve Backbarrow fireback of 1772. Upstairs are
further complexities, partly determined by what happens
below. The broad corridor rises and falls, some bedrooms push
up their coved ceilings into the roof space. Even here there are
two inglenook fireplaces, each with Art Nouveau glass. Fireplaces are flat and Voyseyish, each with a few *de Morgan* tiles
set into a hand-coloured and fired ground – except for a little
corner fireplace in a dressing room, which echoes the huge
joggled voussoirs of the reception rooms below.

In GREENSTILE PARK, near Blackwell, a telling late C20 group
by *Gill Dockray Rhodes & Moore*. GREENLANDS came first,
c. 1970: cubist, frankly Modern, with a flat roof, picture
windows and a cantilevered balcony. It is designed with living
accommodation upstairs, and has the characteristic open stair,
flush doors and decor of the period. HEATHWAITE immediately below (by *Gill*) consists of four connecting units each with
a monopitch roof, originally copper-covered. BELLMAN'S
KNOT is the latest, *c.* 1998. Bigger, richer, safer, more defer-
entially Voyseyish.

BROADLEYS, 2½ m. S, just past the former Lancashire boundary. By *C. F. A. Voysey*, 1898–9, in the years of his greatest
success and fertility (cf. Moor Crag nearby, p. 174), for Henry
Currer-Briggs of Yorkshire, colliery owner. Later owned by the
Milnes of Manchester, and since 1950 by the Windermere
Motor Boat Racing Club. Built by *Pattinsons* (with electric
lighting), and fitted out by *Simpson*. Towards the lake Broadleys
is, for Voysey, unusually formal in composition, and yet not in
any set symmetry. The front has three full-height curved bows,
the middle one with two transoms, the l. and r. ones representing two storeys and expressing them. Some bare wall to
the r., not matched to the l. On the landward side, E, it is an
L with a long low service wing under a big roof. The main block
has a porch and to its l. a square projection with continuous
windows to the staircase. On the seldom-seen N elevation five
tiers of windows are artfully disposed to suit the interior
requirements. White roughcast, green paint, unmoulded sandstone mullions and transoms set flush with the wall, battered
buttresses, iron brackets under the eaves, graded blue-green
slates and big plain chimneys. A continuous dripmould of
rough slate links the windows. What is so surprising about the
interior is its cosy scale. We enter into a low space which opens
into the double-height hall, lit by the full height of the centre
bay and warmed by a huge walk-in fireplace – but these words
imply a grandeur which is conspicuously missing; the scale is
always human, even slightly dwarfish. The upstairs corridor
bridges and looks down into it. Oak panelling without mouldings. At the N end is the DRAWING ROOM, now the bar, with
the shallowest tiled bow for the fireplace. At the other end the
DINING ROOM, with a green-tiled fireplace and more simplified panelling. That is all; it was, after all, a holiday home. The
STAIR winds round four posts and a decorative slatted cage of
balusters with inset hearts: Voysey's signature. The upstairs
rooms and corridor are very low for the date, but the roof
slopes intrude nonetheless. Only four bedrooms. Three have
fireplaces of narrow yellow-glazed bricks. The views from the
curved bows are sensational.

109

LODGE. Also by Voysey. The stone is exposed, except in the
gables. Dovecote in the N gable.

FALLBARROW, Rayrigg Road, just NE of the town. Large Gothic
villa built *c.* 1869 on the site of an earlier house, for John and
Elizabeth Rawson of Halifax, by *Pattinsons*. Attributed to *Joseph
Stretch Crowther* of Manchester on grounds of style, detail and
plan form, though he usually employed a steeper roof pitch.
Of dark local stone with golden sandstone dressings and carved
work. The charming oriel with its iron crown on the lake front
is pure Crowther (cf. Parkside, Kendal). The plan is a slightly
stretched version of his demolished Kendal Vicarage. The end
door leads into a square lobby, then a spine corridor offset to
allow end lighting. Halfway down is the main stair, admitting
more light through Gothic arches, and at the far end a cross-
passage to the lake-front door, and the back stair. Gothic
arches, two to a side, articulate the lobby, and lobby and

corridors are encaustically tiled. Gothic woodwork, all done by chamfering. The magnificent promontory site is nullified by dense specimen trees, now past their best. The grounds are packed full of mobile homes, but they do surprisingly little harm.

GOSSEL RIDDING, Craig Walk, in the E part of the town. Built for himself in 1907–11 by the Windermere builder *G. H. Pattinson*. The architect was his younger brother *Joseph Pattinson*. A hundred men were on site on occasions, and even though the expense was 'in-house' it cost £10,000. Pattinson had built Voysey's two nearby houses, and it shows. Roughcast, with curly gutter brackets. Flush windows with unmoulded mullions and plate glass. The Billiard Room wing with its curved end is set at an angle to command the view, creating a lot of complicated geometry – but is then only given three smallish windows per floor. HALL and BILLIARD ROOM are richly panelled with strapwork and bog oak inserts. The gigantic fireplace, atlantes, and an inset panel 'school in uproar' were carved by *J. M. Kilbride*. The MORNING ROOM in abrupt contrast is coolest Adam; decor and furnishings were supplied by *Kendal Milne*, whose designs are signed *R.A.T.*; other room designs by *Waring & Gillow*, the Adam drawing room by Mr *Durand*. Broad stair of oak, perfectly seasoned and assembled never to creak. Baillie Scott's influence shows in the timber framing of the upper corridor. Heating was by a warm-air system. Extensive service wing, with yard and back drive blasted from the rock. Balustraded terraces, tennis and croquet lawns, kitchen garden, two LODGES.

[114] LONG DALES, ¾ m. SW. Cheerful, stylish, outward-looking, uncompromising Modernist house by *Basil Ward*, 1961, for Peter Scott, chairman of Provincial Insurance, Kendal. Concrete and wood cladding, with strip windows, a chimneystack of slate, monopitch roofs, and a jabbing cantilevered balcony on pilotis. Free-flowing spaces within, and dynamic volumes. Fireplaces and main stair stand free. Many of the bedrooms have their own balconies. Owing nothing to the vernacular, it does nevertheless derive from Baillie Scott's open planning at Blackwell. Surprisingly, it still has a back stair, with service flat and garages attached at right angles. Complemented by the mature parkland of MATSON GROUND, a house of *c.* 1830 which is higher up the valley.

[111] MOOR CRAG, a little S of Broadleys (p. 173), and on the other side of the road. By *C. F. A. Voysey*, 1899–1900, for J. W. Buckley of Altrincham near Manchester, where he had a house called Westwood. The quintessence of the Lake District, in spite of the fact that Voysey had one style wherever he built, and of the vernacular, even though it copies no local precedent. Muthesius's admiration was echoed by Pevsner in 1969, who said of Moor Crag and Broadleys that 'there is nothing of the date on the Continent to come up to their standard. The future and the past blend effortlessly indeed. They are C20 pioneer work and yet free Tudor.' Yet the sweet simplicity of

the house, and its absolute rightness in the landscape, were not
arrived at without effort. Moor Crag was on the drawing board
in 1898 but it was more than a year before the design was final-
ized, and the catslide roof sweeping down at the lake end was
the result of changing its position (like Blackwell, p. 171, it is
end-on to the lake, with long N and S sides). The great hipped
roof is the thing, punctuated by gables and dormers on both
main sides, without formal correspondences, and set off by the
massive verticals of the chimneys and the long horizontals of
the eaves and dripmoulds. There is no service wing to disturb
the perfect 'house that Jack built'; servants were accommodated in an existing building down the garden path. The
window dressings and mullions, absolutely flush and
unmoulded, the steps and the floors are of Buttermere slate of
a most beautiful blue: a different palette to Broadleys and
Blackwell. The three upper cross-windows on the entrance side
represent the staircase landings. (Staircase again with close vertical slats.) Voysey took double care to ventilate the house when
empty, with tiny opening lights in each window, and an extra
chimney flue connecting to all the little air vents: typical of the
extreme thought lavished on what was, after all, only a holiday
home. *Thomas Mawson* did the site survey and blasted out the
romantic drive.

STORRS HALL, Newby Bridge Road, 1¾ m. SSW. A hotel since
1892. Low-slung Grecian mansion of somewhat sinister character occupying a prize promontory S of the Windermere ferry.
Sir John Legard in *c.* 1795–7 built a square, two-storey house,
with a four-column entrance portico on the N and a canted bay
looking S down the lake. It stood on a full service basement lit
by a moat-like area, communicating with the outside by a long
subterranean passage to the E. In *c.* 1808–9 the Liverpool slaver
John Bolton employed *Joseph Michael Gandy*, better known as
visionary artist than architect, to extend it. *Francis Webster* was
the clerk of works. Gandy faced Legard's house in ashlar (since
stuccoed), and book-ended it with taller and deeper wings,
linking them across the N front by a four-column loggia *in
antis*, and round the canted bay S by a decorative veranda. The
loggia columns are Doric of the Samian type, i.e. fluted at the
top of the shaft only, with a strong entasis. Fleshy lotus-bud
finials in a row on the entablature; more on the bracketed-out
heads of the pedimented three-light windows on the wing-
ends. At the angles of the wings are sunk-panelled pilasters or
antae. The basement having lost its natural light, a long, mostly
two-storey service wing was added on the E, over the tunnel.
This was raised to a domineering three storeys *c.* 1892 by
Joseph Pattinson as part of the hotel conversion.

The interior is arranged around a circular atrium formed by
Gandy, which has niches on the ground floor, a cantilevered
gallery around the upper floor, and a dome with coloured glass
in the lantern. Paired with it on the E is the staircase hall, also
remodelled by Gandy, under a smaller, oval dome. Cantilevered stair with a crisp two-column screen, Ionic below,

Corinthian above. Balustrade of brass. The W landing, in Gandy's wing and up two steps to allow for the taller rooms below, has rather different detailing. The former library occupies most of the W wing; fleshy plaster cornice and a marble chimneypiece with a tablet of Leda and the Swan. In the S room of the E wing a Thomas Hope-ish Greek Doric chimneypiece in black marble with gilt embellishment.* Also a magnificent bar of c. 1900, all bulging mahogany and floriferous stained glass, part of the hotel conversion. The labyrinthine basement is segmental-vaulted throughout, except for a hexagonal room formed in the C20 under the middle S bay room.

The grounds are laid out with romantic paths and an engineered lakeside walk, the shore regularized with a bund of rubble. The octagonal TEMPLE, with Belle Isle and Claife Station an essential Picturesque addition to the lake, was built for Legard in the 1790s (parapet altered by *Gandy*). It stands on a barely submerged rock, linked to the land by a causeway formerly with a castellated parapet. Four arched openings. Tablets on the four diagonal sides commemorate admirals Duncan, St Vincent, Howe and Nelson. Coloured glass gave an impression from within of different seasons and weathers. Legard's BOATHOUSE shelters in a bay N of the house. Its dock shows the remains of another castellated parapet; behind was a fish pond (for char). In 1804 Gandy exhibited a wonderful primitive Doric boathouse design *à la* Paestum for Legard, never built.

PARK. For Bolton *John Webb* made long drives N and S. These, linked by a sharp bend in front of Storrs, have become part of the A592, while still giving the impression of a parkland drive. *Pattinsons* divided and developed the estate, starting in the late 1890s with Blackwell, Broadleys and Moor Crag. LODGES and GATES are by (or after) *Gandy*. Middle Entrance Drive goes up to THE YEWS, which was the home farm, enlarged in 1896 by *Joseph Pattinson* for Sir James Scott of Bolton, and still further by *W. T. Dolman* in 1906 in contrasting Neo-Georgian style, with double pilasters copied from Gandy's lodge. The C17 firehouse remains more or less intact, with its stair and downhouse at right angles. The adjacent cow byre was made into an open hall, gaining a big fireplace and bay. The kink in the footprint, which makes the house so confusing but attractive, was there from the beginning where another barn adjoined. Dolman's section grows out of the join. All parts are rendered pink. Garden laid out in 1912 by *H. Avray Tipping*, with a sunken garden, ha-ha, and miniature bastions.

---

*The brass fittings to some of the mahogany doors may be products of the brief partnership between Gandy and the furniture-maker *Thomas Bullock*; *see* Ian Goodall, 'Storrs Hall, Windermere', *Georgian Group Journal* 15, 2006.

BRACKENHILL TOWER (C)

4060

4½ m. E of Longtown

Free-standing pele, dated 1586, built by Richard Graham, though Mike Salter suggests this is when he bought it from the Dacres. One of the best-preserved towers in Cumbria, though more Scottish than English (cf. e.g. Gilnockie, Dumfriesshire). Free-standing, with steep crowstepped gables inside a corbelled-out parapet walk. The windows are square-headed, with moulded surrounds, and often barred. (Vaulted basement and generously scaled newel stair. The first-floor chamber, now subdivided, retains a damaged fireplace with moulded surround, and window seat. Third floor apparently always subdivided, both chambers partly retaining their fireplaces, one chamber accessed by a narrow mural passage. A pair of garderobes in the N wall served the two chambers. HOUSE dated RG JG (Richard and Jane Graham) 1717, in brick with mullioned windows, and an L-shaped link dated CS 1860 in Scottish baronial style for the Standish family.)

BRAMPTON (C)

5060

ST MARTIN, Front Street. By *Philip Webb*, 1877–8. His only church. George Howard of Naworth, the future 9th Earl of Carlisle, and the Rev. Henry Whitehead were the prime movers. The tight site is that of the 1788 church, built on the site of Brampton Hospital (almshouses). Webb's church is designed from first principles, and is as wilful and unconventional as we would expect, though 'with the character, necessarily, to visibly express its office'. Webb fiercely mixes his styles, choosing sometimes old-fashioned motifs reminiscent of Barry's or Richard Lane's pasteboard Gothic, even harking back to Georgian ideas of comfort and open sight lines, sometimes conforming to the mainstream of the Gothic Revival, and sometimes seeming to look dynamically ahead.

w tower, nave and aisles, traceried windows. There is no chancel. Indeed the five-light E window, with flowing tracery partly blank to allow for the ceiling inside, is recessed between the bare projecting walls of organ chamber and vestry. The public side on the N has large two-light windows in cross-gables decorated with almost Gothick climbing battlements. Then a two-storey vestry with bare wall below, windows high up, and a consciously over-stressed chimney. The committee asked Webb to put the vestry at the back, but he wanted it here to balance the tower. The tower has a giant niche on its w side – another feature smacking of the Gothick – in which is a large window to the ringing chamber over two very small two-light

ones for the baptistery. The belfry stage was added in 1906 by
George Jack to one of Webb's designs. It has an E–W saddleback
roof out of which grows a lead spirelet, with low spurs with
pitched lead roofs going N and S. This makes the sides different; twin belfry lights N and S, deeply recessed, with the
mullion bending forward at the top like a corbel, single large
ones in the style of *c.* 1250 E and W. The S aisle W window is
round with tracery. The S side of the church, facing the small
steep graveyard, is mostly roof, sloping up from the aisle eaves
to the nave ridge, and punctuated by three small dormers.
Broad and bare gabled buttresses alternate with small rectangular windows, with just one larger Perp three-lighter to the E.

Entry is at the tower foot on the N. Webb intended a long
porch to the street, but instead a shallow open arch with a small
fragmentary gable shelters three doors and a TERRACOTTA of
St Martin by *Ellen Mary Rope*, 1906. We enter a low wide room
under the tower, then turn into the church through two arches.
A clear-glazed traceried window over shows the ringing room,
brightly lit from the W. Webb's interior is astonishingly informal, though rather overwhelmed by the superb glass. The space
is virtually square and the choir almost in the middle, but orientation is maintained by the crisply conventional four-bay
arcades with octagonal piers and chamfered arches. No
chancel arch. Open roofs had been *de rigueur* since Pugin, but
here we have comfortably boarded ceilings, white-painted, flat
in the centre with wooden vaulting covering the braces. Both
aisles are bridged by tie-beams, but are otherwise treated differently; on the N transverse tunnel-vaults, on the S a complicated false clerestory. Domestic quarry tiles for the floors,
except for the sanctuary which was paved in 1894 with the
'dullish red marble' recommended by Webb. No pulpit or
lectern, merely extensions of the stalls westward. The
REREDOS was added in the 1920s by *Hicks & Charlewood*
incorporating a *Morris* gesso panel of corn and grapes. – FONT
COVER by the *Keswick School of Industrial Arts*. – MONUMENT.
Rev. Thomas Ramshay †1840, with a free-standing bust on top.

STAINED GLASS. All by *Morris & Co.* to *Burne-Jones* designs.
'Believe me, the time will come when strangers will seek
Brampton, not for the sake of the town itself, but for the
windows in St Martin's church,' said the Rev. Henry Whitehead to a sceptical populace, the 'somewhat unliftable citizens
of a really mean north country town' as Webb called them. The
windows are wonderful. E, commemorating the Hon. Charles
Howard †1879, richly coloured and jewel-like. In the centre
light at the top is the Good Shepherd, and in the l. and r. lights
are angels. Then a tier of angels only, and below are saints (St
George in pink armour is particularly fetching), and in the
middle a magnificently drawn Pelican in her Piety, an intricate
composition, proving how near Morris and his circle could get
to the forms and rhythms of Art Nouveau. The cartoons for
these were all made for this church; *Webb* himself usually drew
the animals. SE, by the organ, is in contrast an oft-repeated

trio: Spes (blue on blue), Caritas (red on red), Fides (red on blue), of 1887. The rest on this side are small square scenes on the theme of children and teaching, set in lightly flowered quarries. The westernmost, of Samuel and Eli, is particularly nice. w-facing, large and solemn angels and prophets, with solid colour, in memory of Whitehead (†1896). The scheme of 1878–81 on the N is of large individual figures floating against a light quarry background, starting with Homo Primus (Eve is in the tracery), and finishing with St Paul. The war memorial chapel windows were the last: Sacrifice and Victory, 1920.

PARISH HALL, immediately W. 1895. By *C. J. Ferguson*, evidently enjoying working in Philip Webb's anti-style, with white-painted woodwork and plenty of light from the broad round-arched windows. The roof trusses of the main hall are of laminated wood. Smaller rooms are at a lower level, by the road, with Norman Shaw-ish windows but a doorway with pilasters and pediment. Steps down to the kitchen, now teashop, within a wide arch. The fireplace is flanked by cupboards to make a triple-arched composition in the local fashion.

OLD CHURCH, 1 m. W. Mostly demolished in 1788. The remaining chancel is small but complicated. The oldest part, pre-dating Lanercost Priory, is the W, with a narrow Norman lancet on the N. It was extended E in the late C12 or early C13, with a tomb-recess outside S and piscina and aumbry inside. The W porch was added in 1861, other details made good in 1891. Extensive CEMETERY, well planted. The early churchyard was round. – W of the church, an unusual ceramic MEMORIAL to the Rev. John Wesley Hetherington †1942: male and female angel, tree, bird. Signed by his daughter, *Rene Hetherington*. – OLD CHURCH FARM next door was the vicarage. Probably defensive, with medieval masonry in its W end.

The church was built in the NE corner of a short-lived early C2 ROMAN FORT, about 400 ft (120 metres) square. Excavations S of the churchyard revealed a headquarters building and granaries, founded on clay-bonded stone sleeper-walls, presumably having timber superstructures. Demolished when the garrisons moved from the Stanegate (*see* p. 16) to the Wall.

METHODIST CHURCH, Main Street. Opened 1900. Red and yellow stone, with a spire.

UNITED REFORMED CHURCH, opposite. Built 1854, on a very tight site, by Robert Barbour of Manchester and Bolesworth Castle, Cheshire. Well-preserved interior with typical dais and benches. – STAINED GLASS by *Reed Millican*, 1931, Hope and Light. – ROYAL ARMS hung diamond-wise; Hanoverian. – The chapel of 1722 survives as the HALL. Immediately behind, interlocking with the cruciform shape, is the ZION CHAPEL (former) of 1818.

THE TOWN is uncommonly attractive, with the main road running immediately N of Front Street and the Market Place but entirely separated from it. The A69 by-pass has in any case taken the pressure off.

MOOT HALL, in the cobbled market place. Octagonal, with a clock turret on top. 1817; the lower floor was open until 1896, when the N and S wings were added. Outer steps to the upper floor on the W side. Pointed windows and a square turret. The townish terrace behind on the E side was built for Thomas Ramshay, vicar, in 1819. The deep-plan part to the r. stands back-to-back with the MANSION HOUSE, now Masonic Hall, a very plain classical house also of 1819, brick, with a four-column porch. LIBRARY, shops and flats in the NE corner of the square are by the Cumberland County architect, *D. W. Dickenson*, 1964, with a then-fashionable raised pavement. In the opposite corner MAYFIELD and LEAFIELD peep through the evergreenery, a pair of very large red stone semis. Continuing clockwise, the NAG'S HEAD is probably C17, with a two-storey porch. HSBC, the former Cumberland Union BANK, and the chemist (built as such) are by *C. J. Ferguson*, 1883, pushing forward into the market place. Behind, where it widens out again, the early C19 HOWARD ARMS and former Eden Hotel side-by-side, with all windows tripartite. The sturdy tower and spike of St Martin work well as a viewstopper. Opposite HSBC is the CONSERVATIVE CLUB, another *Ferguson* building, this time Italianate in a brownish stone. Set back in a subsidiary open space, beyond the absurdly thin 'Bird Cage Corner' with brick castellation, is the WHITE LION, C18 and mid-C19, stucco. Further afield, the C18 SCOTCH ARMS on Main Street has retained its stone door hood, once a common Brampton feature.

INDUSTRIAL BUILDINGS. Traces of old mills and workshops survive along the Brampton Beck winding through the town. The best is the OLD BREWERY on Tarn Hall Road, partly reopened in 2005. Formal, two-storey brewery office; other sections of various C19 dates, around a triangular courtyard.

THE MOTE, E of the town. Substantial oval motte carved out of the end of a ridge. Ditch and counterscarp bank on the NW. On the summit a STATUE of George William Frederick Howard, 7th Earl of Carlisle, by *J. H. Foley*, 1869. Bronze, over-life-size.

WILSON MEMORIAL HOMES, The Sands (facing the green). 1930. Red brick, mock timber framing, red flat tiles. The group looks good from the Mote. On the green is an octagonal stone SHELTER commemorating George Howard, 9th Earl of Carlisle, †1911 and Rosalind his wife †1921. Of 1930, by *Christopher Nicholson* (1904–48; known as Kit), brother of Ben (cf. Banks, Lanercost). Central pillar with a ring of flying buttresses supporting the flagged roof. An old grindstone from Walton Mill is on top.*

FOUR GABLES, ¾ m. ENE. By *Philip Webb*, 1875–7, for the Naworth agent, John Grey. A free paraphrase of the Border tower and hall. The tower is square. Short lengths of parapet at the corners, rising to gables in the middle of each side. The

---

*Thanks to John Lee for this and much other information.

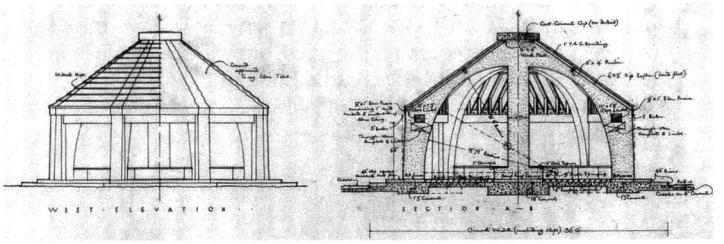

Brampton, Lord Carlisle memorial shelter.
Drawings by Christopher Nicholson, 1928

parapets sit on over-sized dentils, with boldly projecting water-spouts. Long service range attached, N, with catslide roof. Webb's ceaseless experimentation makes the house a joy to the architectural historian but awkward to live in. Every detail is freshly thought out, but not necessarily an improvement. Even the tooling of the stonework is unconventional. Ashlar dressings form an irregular apron under the windows. Windows are usually segment-headed, with an ashlar arch then a chisel-dressed one like the upper part of a segmental pediment. Windows are double-sashed with glazing bars deliberately thick, harking back to Wren. The porch doorway is round-headed under a gable. The bay window on the opposite side is canted, with splayed fins and a firm hat-like lid. The house is crowned by a splendid oblong chimney assembling the flues. Inside, rooms are low, circulation spaces markedly irregular, woodwork painted white. Balusters are plain Regency squares, but mounted diagonally. The general effect is both comfortable and restless.

GREEN LANE HOUSE, ¾ m. SW. Built as the vicarage by *Philip Webb*, 1877. The entrance side is markedly unceremonious, with the front door unobtrusive under a catslide outshut between unequal wings. Hall, stair and landing in the outshut are lit by a very large dormer. The garden front is more formal, though not quite symmetrical in any particular. Two-storey polygonal bay nearly in the middle, with Webb's characteristic fin buttresses and a square roof set low, so that the upper side windows have to be reduced. Windows flat or segment-headed, and one emphatic blank where a window should be.

(BRACKENFELL, Capon Hill, ¾ m. S. 1936–7, by *J. L. (Sir Leslie) Martin* and *Sadie Speight* for Alastair Morton of Sundour fabrics, Carlisle.* The only private house designed by Martin, later Chief Architect to London County Council. Mostly alien red brick, but with a concave porte cochère wall *à la* Corbusier of local stone. To the r. a N-facing studio with a large sloping window. Also a double garage and workshops.)

Close by is the CAPON TREE MONUMENT. Celtic cross of 1904 by *Laing & Beattie*, marking the tree from whose branches five followers of Bonnie Prince Charlie hung in 1746.

(BOOTHBY. Garden House by *Christopher Nicholson* for Charles Roberts, 1928.)

₃₀₀₀

BRATHAY (L)

HOLY TRINITY. 1836. Built by Giles Redmayne, who had made his money in the London ribbon trade. The architect was, it is thought, *John Latham*, though Redmayne undoubtedly had a hand in it. Romanesque, with a tall SW campanile for Redmayne's beloved bells. It perches dramatically on a low crag, but is itself drab in its dingy rendering. Round-arched windows, some with inserted tracery. – STAINED GLASS. E window by Powells, 1916. Nave S, three, *c.* 1910s, designed by the Rev. *E. Geldart* and made by *Taylor & Clifton*. – MEMORIALS. Metal plates inside, including one by the *Keswick School of Industrial Arts*. There is a Redmayne mausoleum underneath. – Outside, WAR MEMORIAL, *c.* 1920. Of green stone, based on Reginald Blomfield's war cross with a sword. Below the W end a Celtic cross to Robert Ellis Cunliffe †1902. At the bottom of the path a sweet SCHOOL of 1859 in Redmayne's memory; perhaps by Giles's son, the young *George T. Redmayne*. G. T. Redmayne married Waterhouse's sister Katherine, became his junior partner, and settled in Alderley Edge, Cheshire.

BRATHAY HALL. Plain Georgian house, built in 1794–6 for George Law, West India merchant, and early C19 home of the artist John Harden. The prospect down the lake is perfect, artfully framed by trees and parklanded to the water's edge. But conversely, it is a conspicuous presence. Coleridge hated it ('Mr Law's white palace – a bitch'). Faced in alien sandstone ashlar, tall and square (five bays, three storeys), with attached wings reaching back and a semicircular porch portico with Adamish columns. Restrained Neoclassical interior. Cantilever stair curving round in a semicircular projection at the back. For the Redmaynes, who came in 1834, *Alfred Waterhouse* made alterations in 1855, and in 1858 built the LODGE. Stone, asymmetrical, Italianate. From 1946 a Trust for outdoor activities and training founded by Francis C. Scott of Provincial Insurance in Kendal. DINING HALL ANNEXE, 1974 by *Stables & Gilchrist*.

---

* *Lorimer* supplied a design in 1914 for James Morton, which was abandoned.

BRIDEKIRK (C)

ST BRIDE. The OLD CHURCH survived long enough to be photographed. It was big, with a lumpy W tower. Part of its
chancel, with a Late Perp E window, still stands by the churchyard gate, and foundations of its nave.

The NEW CHURCH is by *Cory & Ferguson*, 1868–70. In the
Norman style, at which Ferguson excelled; cruciform, with an
apse, W front with a wheel window over three widely spaced
lancets, and a forceful crossing tower, flat-topped with pairs of
big two-light belfry windows. The E doorway in the S transept
is clearly genuine Norman, with one order of columns with
scallop capitals and zigzag at right angles to the wall in the
arch. Billet hoodmoulds too. A fragment of carved stone
depicting the Sacred Heart is built in next to it. In the S porch,
tunnel-vaulted in yellow brick, the inner doorway is another
real Norman piece, of two orders with zigzag and billet. One
of the colonnettes is delicately diapered all over. On the tympanum, cut away at the bottom (or unfinished?), is a majestic
Christ with forked beard, staring eyes, halo, and a robe draped
over one arm.

Pleasing interior lined with buff brick, with reddish stone
dressings. Crossing arches and cornice picked out with
restrained polychromy and notching. Chancel and crossing are
rib-vaulted, with brick webs, the rest boarded to a barrel shape.
Another Norman arch has been redeployed over the organ.
Malcolm Thurlby sees this as the old chancel arch, which
would give the old church a mid-C12 date. Built-in REREDOS
of intersecting arcading round the apse, with crisp leaf carving
at the top and a background of fleur-de-lys tiles. – ALTAR
RAIL. Stone, like miniature arcading. – Neo-Norman CHOIR
STALLS. – PULPIT and READING DESK, the pulpit just a bit
more solid and a trifle higher. – ORGAN, N transept. The organist sits right underneath.

FONT. A remarkable piece. Rectangular, not big, with tapering sides carved all over in crisp and lively fashion, probably
in the mid C12, i.e. of a piece with the other Norman survivals.
The style is like that of Yorkshire, the decoration has Italian
touches. On the E side the top band has two affronted monsters, half-bird half dog, eating plants. The bottom band, with
a scrolly plant with a dog and a little man in a skirt munching
grapes, is horizontally divided by a scroll with a runic inscription and signature, a rare thing (but cf. Pennington): Rikard
he [has] me iwrocht [wrought] and this merthr gernr me
brokte [to this glory – i.e. glorious place – carefully brought
me]. Below is foliage, and *Rikard* himself industriously chipping with an outsized hammer and long chisel – not an axe or
adze. To the S a cross growing into a vine, above a wheel with
monsters r. and l. in a very classical frame. To the N a bird with
two snaky-necked heads biting its own tail, which grows into
a big three-petalled flower. Below is the Baptism of Christ and

Bridekirk, cross-slab grave cover.
Drawing, 2005

a scrolly tree. W side, hard to see, a centaur (his head is missing) being attacked by a dog and a monstrous bird. The scene below can be interpreted as the Expulsion from the Garden of Eden. An angel in a long robe brandishes a sword. Adam stands craven, with a staff, Eve clasps the Tree. Both are clothed.

STAINED GLASS. E window by *Wailes*, 1869. W window and transept ends by *Clayton & Bell*, 1870s. Chancel sides by *Powells*: two N, 1907; one S to Lamplugh Frescherville Ballantine Dykes, 1893, designed by *Henry Holiday*. The other S is signed *Reed Millican & Co.*, 1962. – MONUMENTS. Brasses to John Lancaster, musician, †1666, and C19 ones to three members of the Ballantine Dykes family, by *John Hardman*, Birmingham. – Just inside the W door, free-standing marble urn on a pedestal to Sarah, wife of the Rev. H. A. Hervey, †1827. – Outside, against the apse, a number of C13 and C14 slabs including an exceptionally fine cross fleury in relief, upside-down.

(Former VICARAGE, by the church. Georgian with moulded window frames and a Tuscan porch.)

DOVENBY STATION (Maryport & Carlisle Railway), 2 m. SW. Now a private house. One of those rarities, a private station, built in 1867 for the exclusive use of the owners of Dovenby Hall. Two-storeyed, of sandstone.

DOVENBY MILL. A mid-C19 three-storey water-powered corn and sawmill. It makes a handsome group with its four-square miller's house with stone mullioned windows under chamfered hoodmoulds.

(DOVENBY HALL, 1½ m. WSW. Built *c.* 1680 by Richard Lamplugh, with a Georgian five-bay front added by the Ballantine, later Ballantine Dykes, family. Porch of four unfluted Ionic columns. Behind and not at all noticeable from outside is the medieval tower, variously dated from the late C13 to the C15. Its ground stage is tunnel-vaulted. An old loop window opening into the present stair hall, round-arched and single-chamfered, is in this context probably C16.)

(TALLENTIRE HALL, 1½ m. NE. Classical house of *c.* 1770 incorporating a C16 turret stair. Recessed centre with colonnade of unfluted Doric columns. Extended in 1863 by William Browne, who also built the SCHOOL opposite.)

BRIGHAM (C)   *0030*

ST BRIDGET. An important and early medieval church, carefully if not conservatively restored by *Butterfield* in 1863–76. Telescopic two-stage W TOWER, unbuttressed, wider N–S than E–W. Early C13 bell-openings, with two pointed openings under a round arch. The W window is later (C14), the saddleback roof

is of course Butterfield's. Nave N wall and chancel also without
buttresses, of rough stonework retaining traces of whitewash.
Blocked N doorway under a higher and narrower relieving arch
or niche. The N windows are Butterfield's, but he redeployed
a round-arched Perp window with ogee heads to the lights in
the vestry, and left another *in situ* on the S side of the chancel.
The S aisle, a rare example in Cumbria of full-blown Dec,
was rebuilt as a chantry chapel *c.* 1323 by the rector, Thomas
de Burgh. It resembles the Dec aisle at Millom (q.v.) specifi-
cally in its almond-shaped W window with flowing tracery.
This has a sunk-quadrant moulding and a slight ogee tip.
The (restored) E window has flowing tracery too, with a
heart shape like the great E window at Carlisle. S windows
also Butterfield's restorations, S doorway with a reused late
C13 arch. The arcade however is Late Norman, of three bays,
with square abaci on round piers with waterleaf capitals. High
bases probably indicate a lowering of the floor. Tower arch
probably only a little later than the S arcade. The arch
has responds with round abaci. The ground stage of the
tower has a barrel-vault set high. In its SW corner not a vice
but a mural stair climbing so steeply that the treads have
had to be made triangular, i.e. two steps in the space of one.
In the S chapel triple SEDILIA, PISCINA with tracery, and a
tomb-recess with openwork mouchette tracery and a gable
and buttress-shafts. The gable has rather summary foliage. In
the recess an exceptionally fine and well-preserved foliated
CROSS-SLAB – surely de Burgh himself. To l. and r. of the E
window are niches for images. The *Robinson* family were
responsible for painting and gilding Butterfield's roofs: red,
green, grey.

FURNISHINGS. SCREEN, PULPIT, LECTERN, BENCHES and
FLOOR TILES all by *Butterfield*. – FONT. Small, octagonal,
probably C17 (or C13: DCMS). – STAINED GLASS. E window
(1876) and S aisle (1864, 1865 etc.) by *Alexander Gibbs*, under
Butterfield's direction; dense and hot, with dominant reds and
yellows. – MONUMENTS. Ann Mary Harris †1860 in child-
birth. An angel takes her up to heaven, behind an elaborate
curtain. The babe lies on a rolled-up mat. – SCULPTURE. Fragments of at least three C10 crosses. One socket stone in two
pieces, with interlace, and a piece of a hogback.

The medieval PARSONAGE is N of the church, by the A66
road which severs both from the river. Single central stack. One
gable-end has two buttresses and in between them a blocked
two-light window with a circle over, i.e. the window of a later
C13 upper hall.

On the old main road S of the church is the COLLIERY RESCUE
STATION of 1914, Neo-Georgian with a red stone entry, and
the former POLICE STATION, small, but expressing its importance with the full language of International Modernism:
pilotis, four floors, strip windows and a flat roof. By the Cumberland County Architect, *D. W. Dickenson*.

BROMFIELD (C)   1040

ST MUNGO. Low and spreading. Nave and bellcote, porch, N
aisle, long chancel with transepts. Tall and narrow re-set
Norman S doorway, with zigzag voussoirs alternating red and
yellow. The tympanum, decorated with sunk chequer, is a
reused hogback: you can just see the edges of its roof tegulae
from the inside. (In the E wall of the nave, either side of the
chancel arch, are lengths of the Norman frieze of an aisleless
nave, decorated with saltire crosses.) N arcade of three bays. The
piers round, with four flat fillets (a motif not seen elsewhere).
Round arches with one step and one chamfer. Pevsner dated it
to the early C13. The aisle itself was rebuilt in 1861. The chancel
arch seems bits and pieces; the faces at its springing do not look
C13. It has three proper chamfers and is pointed. The responds
have the same broad fillet, grotesque faces on the capitals (cf.
Gosforth) and a pointed arch thrice chamfered. Opening
transept-wise off the chancel S is the chantry chapel of St
George, founded in 1395, suppressed in 1546, and restored in
1925. The S window has simple but curious bar tracery, a late
C13 motif. Dec window. The N transept was rebuilt in 1861 with
the aisle by the Ballantine Dykes family of Dovenby as a family
chapel, with posthumous brasses to their Crookdale ancestors.
The chancel was restored in 1893. – ROYAL ARMS by *Mathias
Read*, 1711. – STAINED GLASS. Much by *Wailes & Strang*. E
window by *R. B. Edmundson*; also S transept S and one nave S
(these 1862). Sanctuary S, *J. Scott & Son*. – MONUMENTS.
Many coffin-lids with foliated crosses. – Fine foliated grave-slab
under an arch in the N transept; the re-cut inscription refers to
Adam of Crookdale, 1514. – In a tomb-recess on the N side of
the chancel, the Rev. Richard Garth †1673, a tomb-chest with
a long rhyming inscription in typical Roman capitals. – Frederick and George Bouchier, twins †1838 in infancy, with tiny
images of them both. – Outside, the Taylor vault set up in 1890,
using the churchyard cross steps surmounted by a stack of
cyclopean stones.
    ST MUNGO'S WELL, in the field N of the church. Under a
little round building, half-sunk and with a doorway.
BLENCOGO SCHOOL, 2 m. NE. It looks like a small but florid
railway station. Gothic, steep-roofed, with a bold central gable
with plate-traceried window, diamond-paned, to the schoolroom. Flanking chimney-breasts display the initials GMD
(George Dixon) and date 1854, and a shield of arms. Gabled
porch, r., bellcote on the r. end gable.
(LANGRIGG HALL, 1 m. SW. Five-bay house of *c.* 1735 for
Thomas Barwis, who had bought the medieval house from
Cuthbert and Mary Osmotherley. Their initials appear with the
date 1703, reused from a dovecote, on a side wing.)
LANGRIGG MILL. A notable feature in a county where windmills were very rare: an early C19 three-storey tower windmill,
with a domed wooden cap. The sails were removed by 1860.

BROUGH (W)

Market Brough and Church Brough are separate places, definitively so now that the upgraded A66 cuts between them.

The by-pass has left MARKET BROUGH, the road settlement to the N, high and dry; a wide dusty street with a faintly military echo about it. CLOCK TOWER at the junction of the Kirkby Stephen road to the S. Square pedestal, smaller square clock stage, then a column tapered rather than with entasis, and a finial; all rather small. Dated 1910 but, as Pevsner remarked, it looks C17. Indeed Machell *c.* 1690 drew a 'well at Brough Spaw' with similar elements, though squatter and with a figure on top. At the same junction the CASTLE HOTEL. Five bays, three storeys, with a Tuscan porch. Late C18.

CHURCH BROUGH (with the Castle) is a planned settlement round a small triangular green.

35 ST MICHAEL. A big church hugging the ground: plain parapets, low blind-storey, flat roofs, flat-headed windows. Its extreme horizontality is set against a strong W tower, though even that is broad rather than high. The tower was built in 1513 under the direction of *Thomas Blenkinsop* of Helbeck to a characteristic design with two unrelated and widely separated belfry lights on each face (cf. Penrith, Appleby). The N aisle was widened at much the same time. The windows all straight-headed and of the Perp centuries, i.e. late C14 onwards. Those of the chancel come last. They are tall with depressed-rounded heads to the lights: C16, or C17? It is only on the S side, away from town and castle, that the Norman fabric appears. Splendidly barbaric S doorway with one order of columns, the abaci decorated with little lozenges, the inner arch with beakhead faces, cat-like and moustachioed. The outer arch has zigzag at right angles to the wall. This may date from the 1180s, after the destructive raid of 1174 (*see* below). All the windows have been opened out except the westernmost, which may be Norman. A Celtic face – which could be of any age – is carved on the jamb of the W window.

The interior, broad, whitewashed, well lit and homely, slopes up markedly towards the altar, narrowing as it goes. C14 seven-bay arcade of standard elements and uneven construction. One of the octagonal columns is markedly thinner than the rest, requiring adjustments as the arch comes down. The tie-beams of the nave roof are simply packed out to achieve the necessary fall for the leads. Tower arch of 1513 with three continuous chamfers. In the S wall is a tomb-recess.

FURNISHINGS. REREDOS. Incorporating C17 panels with stylized leaves and columns. – COMMUNION RAIL. 1704. – PULPIT. Of stone, plain except for its moulded base; dated 1624. – LECTERN, a powerful eagle in black wood. C19. – FONT, looking 1660s. – WAR MEMORIAL, 1921. Typical roadside or churchyard cross, but mounted indoors by the font. – STAINED GLASS. E window, *Wailes & Strang*, 1870. N, by the organ, Victorian setting of C15 bits. John the Baptist/Christ the Good Shepherd, female crowned head, group. More bits were set S, by the pulpit, in 1982: four C15 heads, and two heraldic pieces, one dated 1638. Another S by *J. Scott & Son.* – MONUMENTS. Plain slab in front of the pulpit: HERE LYE– MR GABRIELL VINCENT. STEWARD TO THE R– COUNTESS DOWAGER OF PEMBROOKE DORSETT AND MONTGOMERY AND CHIEF DIRECTOR OF ALL HER BVILDING IN THE NORTH WHO DYED IN THE ROMAN TOWER OF BROVGH CASTLE LIKE A GOOD CHRISTIAN THE 12 OF FEBRUARY 1665 1666 LOOKING FOR THE SECOND COMMINGE OF OVR SAVIOUR IESVS CHRIST. Who could have composed that but the Lady Anne herself? – Also a cast of a Roman tablet with a Greek, though Runic-looking, inscription, found in the restoration of 1879. It commemorates Hermes, a youth of Commagene, in Syria, who died aged sixteen.

BROUGH CASTLE. The site is superb, commanding the York–Carlisle road on its descent from Stainmore to the N, and the road from Westmorland as it joins from the S. The medieval castle uses the same N-facing scarp as the Roman fort whose platform and ditch can be seen on the S (*see* below). Its keep still stands to full height at the W, but is rent from top to bottom, with chunks of masonry lying where they fell. The other principal standing parts are on the S: the round Clifford Tower, hall range and the gatehouse.

This was one of William Rufus's castles, and appears to have been at least partly stone-built from the first. The base of the keep and parts of the curtain wall date from *c.* 1100, the latter marked by patches of coarse herringbone masonry near the NE corner. In 1174 the castle was captured and fired by the Scots under William the Lion, but was repaired by the end of the century. During the siege a knight is described as hurling timbers from the parapets of the keep at the Scots, proof that it was then of wooden construction. In 1203 King John granted the castle, together with Appleby, to Robert de Vieuxpont or Vipont. The gatehouse is his work, though it has been drastically quarried away. In 1268 it passed, with Brougham, to the Cliffords. Robert Clifford carried out much rebuilding and added the semicircular tower at the SE corner. Roger Clifford in the late C14 built the first-floor hall, over vaulted basement rooms, whose windows look out over the moat on the S. Domestic ranges were added along the N wall. In 1521 the place was accidentally burnt out after the Christmas feast, and lay empty until Lady Anne Clifford came to the rescue in 1659. She recorded her restoration in 1663 (the stone is lost) and occupied the top room of the SE corner tower, now called Clifford's Tower, which she rebuilt with characteristically fine masonry and square mullioned windows. Similar work is seen in the N face of the hall range, and the keep, which she called Caesar's Tower. However fire struck again in 1666, and by 1715 most of the roofs were stripped, and the castle was pillaged for stone until 1920, when it was taken into care. The appearance

28

of frozen warfare is therefore deceptive, the result of quarrying not cannon.

The GATEHOUSE has lost the whole of its outer face, though
the two triangular-ended buttresses are plain to see. A Buck
engraving of 1759, when it still stood to its full three storeys,
shows that they rose no higher than the entrance. This was
originally tunnel-vaulted with big, broad, single-chamfered
transverse arches. Ahead, against an early section of the N wall,
the remains of Lady Anne's kitchen range. In a C13 section
towards the keep a double latrine. The hall range, a maze of
wall bases and mostly collapsed tunnel-vaults, represents the
basement of Roger Clifford's upper hall against the S curtain.
Above are its Dec windows with reticulated tracery (the side
mouchettes left solid) originally of two lights indicating its lost
elegance, and an inner range added by Lady Anne. In the midst
of this the approach stairs to the hall inserted by Lady Anne
can be seen.* The vaults are hers too, but very probably they
replaced C14 ones (cf. e.g. Bolton Castle, Yorkshire North
Riding).

The KEEP has two offsets and flat clasping buttresses rising
to corner turrets. A mid-buttress appears in the top stage on
the N and S sides. Near the top some odd sections of stones
laid in an open zigzag, creating black, presumably decorative,
shadows. A Norman window survives on the W side, with a
shaft between two lights, the shaft having in section two
semicircles and a spur between. A low roof-line can be seen at
the level of the second set-off, suggesting a possible heightening – or more likely, as at Carlisle, the whole upper floor
was void. It seems that a later roof was inverted, to catch rainwater. The windows on the N side belong to Lady Anne's
restoration.

The ROMAN FORT (*Verteris*: 'the summit') underlies the
castle site, with its S half comprising the outer bailey. The E,
W, and possibly the N walls of the castle overlie the Roman
ones, but the S wall crosses the earlier fort obliquely. The
massive ditch (with a counterscarp bank) is an enlargement of
the earlier, playing-card-shaped defences, the scale of which
can be appreciated around the S perimeter. Occupied from
c. A.D. 79, and into the late C4; an inscription built into the
church porch records rebuilding in A.D. 197. The rampart and
ditch to the W – aligned with the fort – may be that of an
annexe, an outwork, or the first fort. A broader ditch across
the ridge, further W, and another partly covered by the farm,
provide additional protection but are undated. Outside the E
ditch of the castle a short ditch defines a triangular area – possibly part of a larger early defensive scheme, in timber – containing a square earthwork, possibly a garden from the time of
Lady Anne. The date and significance of a stump of wall
descending the E ditch, close to its N end, are unknown.

---

*Built against a wall from an earlier hall block against the E curtain; excavations
have shown that this in turn replaced an earlier, timber-framed hall.

HELBECK HALL, 1 m. N of the castle. On a big platform high
above the valley, which extends at the back over impressive
vaults.* The present house is Gothick, and of great charm;
probably by *Henry Bellas* or *Bellhouse*, like the White House in
Appleby (q.v.). IM 1775 on the hoppers for John Metcalfe
Carlton, then aged twenty-one; he also built a cotton mill at
Yoss Gill. Five bays, two storeys, with one-bay wings. Ogee-
headed windows, even for the dormers; Batty Langley doorway;
urns along the parapet. Simple plan: all the principal rooms
overlook the E view, linked by a longitudinal corridor on the E.
Plain stone stair in the middle with square wooden balusters.
Only the little sitting room at the NE end retains its Gothick
character. The Breeks family, who acquired the house in the
1850s, made a new entrance at the S end and added the billiard room at the back. From the Lowther sale came the fabulous silk wall hangings in the library and dining room.
    The present STABLE, also Gothick, is below the house plat-
form on the N. Agrippina, a statue from Lowther – probably
Roman, but heavily restored – stands nearby. WALLED
GARDEN, brick-lined, with ogee doors. – FOX TOWER, to the
E and higher up, stands on a semicircular bastion and is itself
round, with a much taller round tower attached, tapering like
a chimney. Large arched windows (not Gothick) and a fireplace show that it was a banqueting house – dining room
above, services below – and the tight spiral stair in the turret
suggests a viewing platform.
AUGILL CASTLE (hotel), ¾ m. E. 1841, for John Bagot Pearson.
Gatehouse centre with pencil-thin turrets, porch, wooden traceried window and swooping-up castellations. The stair-tower
at the back is not quite in line with it. Symmetrical side pieces
again with castellations swooping up to a point, ending in more
round turrets. Mannix (1851) reported that the main staircase
window was after one at Melrose Abbey and that the library
and its stained-glass window were based on those at Sir Walter
Scott's Abbotsford. Stables on the l. also castellated, with
wooden Dec tracery.
1¼ m. E, at Augill Bridge, the remains of Augill LEAD SMELTER,
erected 1843: reminders of the little-known Westmorland
mining industry. The external walls still stand, the main chambers and flues visible.
SOUTH STAINMORE CHAPEL, 3 m. ESE. High and remote. Simplest three-bay nave and chancel, with Y-tracery; probably of
1842–3. But the projecting square bellcote must be C17, and
the remaining sash window under it perhaps C18 (the chapel
was founded in 1608 and repaired in 1699: Kelly). Anomalous
E window, flat-headed with Dec tracery. Inside, a flat ceiling
with tiny bosses. At the back a three-bay school building with
a misplaced datestone 1673. – ALTAR RAIL, three-sided with
just twelve balusters. – FONT. Minute, C17. – STAINED GLASS.
E and S windows (1922), by *W. Pearce*. N, by *J. Holmes & Co.*

---

*A drawing exists for a classical Helbeck of about 1700; Mark Blackett-Ord sug-
gests that its stable stood over these vaults.

MAIDEN CASTLE, 2 m. W of the chapel. A Roman fortlet guarding the road over the pass, and crossed by a later packhorse track. Occupied from the mid C2 to late C4, and defended by a mortared wall (now reduced to rubble), a ditch and an outwork.

BROUGHAM (W)

No village, but plenty of what the RCHME calls monuments. Any settlement on the flat land round St Ninian's church has long gone. The village near Brougham Hall, mapped by Machell in about 1680 with its green and cross, was swept away c. 1686 to enlarge Brougham Park. The present village is at Eamont Bridge (*see* Yanwath).

BROUGHAM CASTLE. The ruins stand tall and compact by the River Eamont, where the Lowther falls into it, commanding both E–W and N–S routes. It was built on the NW corner of the Roman fort of Brocavum (*see* below), which served the same purpose.

King John (1199–1216) granted the site to his agent in the North, Robert de Vieuxpont or Vipont. This is the date of the keep. There are three main phases thereafter.* The first is 1296–1309, at the opening of the Anglo-Scottish wars, under Robert Clifford whose father Roger had married into the Vieuxponts. The gatehouse complex and curtain wall belong to this phase, and so does the Tower of League at the SW corner and the fourth storey to the keep. The castle's heyday was under Robert's grandson, another Roger, in the 1380s. Due to him ('thys made Roger', on a stone now set over the main gate) are the Hall and chapel. The last of the line was Lady Anne Clifford who, as an inscription re-set on the outer gatehouse tells us, restored the castle in 1651 and 1652 'after it had layne ruinous', although she added nothing of significance. It was her favourite castle, and the place of her death in 1676. Gutted in the early C18, the castle underwent repairs in 1848–9, and after further ruination was taken into the care of the state in 1928.

As Brougham Castle is very unusual in plan, it is best described as it is seen. The two GATEHOUSES are strangely butted up against the N side of the keep, separated by a murderous little courtyard. The OUTER GATEHOUSE is the later, of the early C14. It has three storeys, with transomed Dec windows with some reticulation units, and shouldered doorways. Diagonally set turrets to the N like overfed buttresses (cf. Dacre, Kirkoswald, both c. 1320). A portcullis groove, and a

---

* *See* Henry Summerson, Michael Trueman and Stuart Harrison, *Brougham Castle, Cumbria*, CWAAS, 1998.

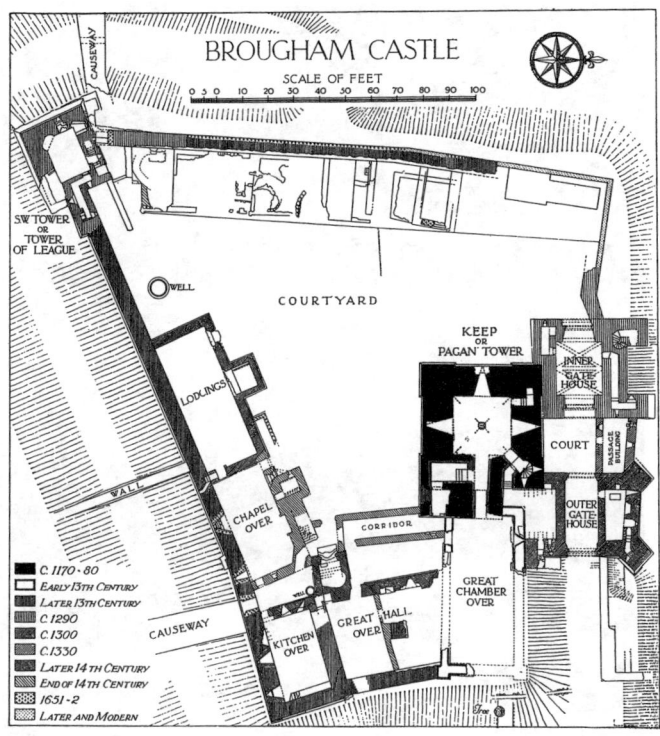

Brougham Castle.
Plan, 1936

pointed tunnel-vault. On the r. a porter's room with a garderobe in the big NE angle buttress. This feature repeats on the
second upper floor. The INNER GATEHOUSE is a little earlier.
A two-light window has pointed-trefoiled lights and a pointed
quatrefoil over, i.e. pre-ogee motifs. There is again a portcullis
groove. Two-bay rib-vault with single-chamfered transverse
arches and ribs. In the N wall is an L-shaped passage leading
to an arrowslit. More wall passages on the first and second
floors.

Through the Inner Gatehouse one enters the cobbled
INNER COURT. This is roughly L-shaped. Along the w side was
a range of buildings not now exposed. The TOWER OF
LEAGUE at the furthest sw corner is of c. 1300, with fireplaces
on all floors and garderobes on two.

The KEEP can be seen from the Inner Court on its w and s
sides and also, as it has lost the attached forebuilding, on its E
side. It stands almost to its full four-storey height, with characteristic flat buttresses and upper windows large and shafted.
On the s side the top storey is partly corbelled out on two faces,
and further to the r. there is more corbelling for a garderobe.

Brougham Castle, oratory.
Engraving, 1807

The main entry was originally on the second floor. This is badly preserved: one jamb shaft; arch with a keeled roll and hollows. The interior of the lower three floors is very ruinous; the vaults inserted in the C13 and the fireplaces have all collapsed. These vaults had single-chamfered ribs on a middle pier. The blank arcading on the second floor (see N wall, W part) is also C13. Looking at the top floor now from inside it is at once recognizable that this is also an addition. Chamfered corners and squinches. It is possible to imagine the Painted Chamber that occupied the centre, encircled by a mural passage which widened out at the corners, with shouldered doors again. The window to the E is of two lights with a circle over, i.e. a form of *c.* 1300. In the SE corner, the corbelled-out part contains an ORATORY, which although severely damaged is an exquisite place of high romance. In this minute space is a narthex or ante-chapel with two recesses each in the N and S walls, one on the S side trefoil-arched, and a polygonal nave whose windows are angled to see the chapel across the court-yard below. Doorway with an inner and an outer cusped arch. The mouldings are typical of the late C13–*c.* 1300. Large E window under which presumably was the altar. In its N jamb two small figures. Piscina in the SE wall, cupboard-like sacristy to the N. The oratory's ribbed dome is an irregular heptagon, with radial single-chamfered ribs and a two-faced boss.

Still stranger than the placing of the gatehouses, the earlier GREAT CHAMBER was built E of the Keep, so that it later flanked the gatehouse approach. There is very little preserved of this, but the clasping SE buttress shows the date. S of the Great Chamber was the GREAT HALL, of the late C14. It was on the first floor and was moderate in size. Small outer two-light windows with ogee-headed lights to the E. To the N one jamb of the doorway to the Great Chamber. The KITCHEN lay S of the hall, also on the first floor. Fireplace in the S wall. Next to it to the W, i.e. along the S wall, was the CHAPEL of the late C14 and the very ruinous LODGING (with a square projection). The chapel is easily identified, on the first floor, with its triple sedilia, piscina and the remains of two single-light Dec S windows.

The DITCH of the castle (radically scoured out in the 1930s) was supplemented on the W by a second one, possibly pre-dating the angular overall plan of *c.* 1300. The Norman keep may thus have stood within a larger defended area than the present one.

The ROMAN FORT, a convenient quarry for the castle, lay imme-diately to the SE, where the great western road from Man-chester to Carlisle met those from Ambleside (over High Street) and Stainmore. Occupied from the C2 to the C4. Inside a broad ditch a bank marks the line of the fort wall. Between the reduced N defences and the ditch of the castle lay Lady Anne Clifford's mid-C17 GARDEN; the ditch of the fort on the W and on part of the S may have been cleared out at that time. The garden stretched to the road where the visitor centre is, corresponding to the area now dotted with trees.

COUNTESS PILLAR. 2 m. ESE. At a rise of the road (A66) linking Brougham with the other Clifford strongholds of Appleby, Brough and Skipton (Yorks.), Lady Anne said her last farewell to her beloved mother. Forty years later she marked the spot with a permanent memorial (1656) and long inscription. Tall octagonal pillar with base and cap, carrying a block with a truncated pyramid roof and a finial. Sundials on three sides of the block, one with the commemorative inscription; a double achievement of arms on the fourth. Lady Anne provided for largesse to be dispensed annually from the low plinth immediately E, ensuring that her pillar would be kept in good order.

St Ninian (Ninekirks), 1⅝ m. ENE. The parish church; now Churches Conservation Trust. Two great bends of the River Eamont beyond the castle, and utterly alone. One of the good works of Lady Anne Clifford, who rebuilt it in 1659–60. It is both typical of its time and consciously old-fashioned. The windows are of single lights, round-headed and uncusped, with hoodmoulds. Buttresses between. Nave and chancel are in one, and it is only the evenness of the whole and the two windows E and two windows W which betray the century. The porch is of 1841. Inside, a wide, white room, well lit and furnished with robust simplicity. Roof with collar-beams on long arched braces.

FURNISHINGS almost completely as in the Lady Anne's time. REREDOS. Painted Commandment board. Above it in the plaster, AP (Anne Pembroke) in a wreath and the date 1660. – ALTAR. A plain table, standing on the medieval stone *mensa*. – ALTAR RAIL. Full width, which is to say wide, with chunky turned balusters on the way to the dumb-bell form of the later C17. – SCREEN with balusters still in the Jacobean tradition. – BOX PEWS, and some FAMILY PEWS with an upper screen, their balusters like those of the main screen. – BENCHES, one with the date 1661. – PULPIT. Against the S wall. A three-decker with tester, not tall. The sounding board has little pendants. – FONT. Dated 1662, plain octagonal bowl, stem and base. – One anomaly: a bit of fancy CARVED WOOD against the S wall in front of the altar rails, and an empty space. Charles Tracy says there was a row of imported Continental stalls here; presumably it was the Brougham Hall pew. – MONUMENTS. Three bogus Brougham brasses inside the altar enclosure. Commemorations run from 1570 to 1830, but the date is *c.* 1846, following the discovery of Odard de Burgham, a putative ancestor. They have delicate flowery crosses, names in scrolls rather like leaves, small figures like fruit, set in slate slabs. – WAR MEMORIAL outside, 1920s. Just two names. Gracefully foliated cross set in an ancient socket.

St Wilfrid, in a strong position SW of the Castle. The chapel of Brougham Hall (*see* below), linked to its boundary by a bridge of 1842 across the sunken road. Rebuilt by Lady Anne Clifford in 1658, like Ninekirks, though differing surprisingly in the details – the single-light windows, for instance, are pointed. One of the two large S doors was presumably for the hall pew. *Cottingham* Normanized some of the windows internally for Lord Brougham and Vaux *c.* 1843–6, and added the W rose window. The interior is dark and baffling. Seated college-wise around a sunken centre, it is cram-full of carved woodwork and crusty stained glass. Both Brougham and Cottingham were enthusiastic collectors of Continental *spolia*, but it is too easy to write this off as a purely C19 creation. Charles Tracy reckons the only complete importation was the triptych now in Carlisle Cathedral (q.v.), and even that had to be separated at Brougham into its three components to fit round the E windows. Otherwise carved panels and stall-ends are incorporated into C19 and older work like a mixed-up jigsaw. – REREDOS. Replacing the triptych now in the Cathedral. Made up with inserted traceries and sculpted panels. – STALLS. Designed by *Cottingham*. Eight, with canopies after those of *c.* 1308 at Winchester Cathedral, against the N wall; uncanopied stalls in front and across the way. Flamboyant tracery for the fronts. The stall backs have similar work to the screen at Cartmel, and to the Gondibour screenwork in Carlisle Cathedral. A couple of the stall-ends are late medieval Flemish work. – PULPIT, in the centre of the S wall. Cottingham, like Pugin, bought Renaissance pieces as well as medieval – see the dancing cherubs on the door. – What about the hall pew SCREEN at the W end? This is a mysterious piece. It has closely set uprights, each jazzily carved in three sections with chevrons, spirals, flutes, diamond-shaped flowers, scales and leaves, linked at the top by highly stilted little cusped arches. In the spandrels, on both sides, delightfully inventive faces, figures and animals, all having to tumble or recline in order to fit the space. – LECTERN. Of brass, on four animals as feet; made to look convincingly late medieval. Presumably by *Cottingham*. – FONT. A small octagonal bowl on a straight-sided stem, as at Ninekirks (and probably also of *c.* 1660), but the stem decorated with chevrons and with eight sides all coming out diagonally. – STAINED GLASS. Older than the building; badly preserved pieces of the C14 and later.

BROUGHAM HALL. It was a C14 manor defended by a curtain wall or barmkin, like Wharton at Kirkby Stephen, or the other Brougham seat at Scales. In 1830–47 Henry, 1st Lord Brougham, the reforming Whig Lord Chancellor, and William his brother turned it into a romantic castellated pile of the sort that looks best from a distance.* The architect was *L. N. Cottingham. Richard Charles Hussey* did the octagonal vaulted billiard room. The curtain wall is largely complete in its C14–C17 and C19 form, but the rest was demolished in 1935. However a fatal accident brought the work to a halt, leaving the lower parts of the walls standing and quantities of worked stone on site.

Brougham in its present *déshabille* gives little idea of either incarnation. Some idea of the overwhelming vulgarity and superhuman scale of the Cottingham house can be gained from architectural salvage scattered at the sale, which has often ended up in other Lakeland houses (e.g. the bar of the Pooley Bridge Inn), and from the chapel (*see* above). There were two courtyards. An archway between them copies the rib-vault of

---

*For the evolution of the design, as well as evidence for the old house, *see* Janet Myles, *L. N. Cottingham 1787–1847, Architect of the Gothic Revival*, 1996.

the inner gatehouse at Brougham Castle. Dec windows in the so-called pele tower (too thin-walled to have been defensive) may be salvage from Brougham or Brough castle. At the back is a terrace supposed to echo Windsor Castle. The remains are being restored by a charitable trust, founded in 1985.

HOSPITAL FARM, now Pembroke House. Intended by Anne, Countess of Pembroke, to provide income for her almhouses at Appleby. Big busy farm with extensive barns, one now used as a church. The house has mullioned windows in twos, threes and fours.

HORNBY HALL, ⅝ m. E, near Ninekirks. Arched lights to several windows. Three-storey porch, dated 1584 in the plaster of its first-floor chamber. Its cambered roof is still there under the pitched one, so presumably it was parapeted, and defensive. Arrowslits in the side cover the front of the house. It blocks a window of the long main range, which must therefore be older (its roof gave a tree-ring date of 1552–4). Edward Birkbeck was granted the manor by Henry Clifford in 1553. In the hall are restored arms in stained glass of Clifford and Birkbeck. Hall and kitchen fireplaces are back-to-back with the porch entrance coming into the connecting passage, i.e. in baffle position, where there is also the turning stair to the Great Chamber above. Hall and chamber have the remains of geometric plaster ceilings. In the late C19 a coloured frieze was recorded in the chamber, with full panelling and an overmantel – all gone now. A barbarously decorated doorcase stands in the SE corner of the hall, inscribed TIB (Thomas and Joan Birkbeck) 1602. Its hood is asymmetrical and sports dogtooth in three and four rows, with spiral motifs at the drip-ends. What is it doing here? It may have been removed from a blocked entrance further W, in baffle position to a second stack and possible spiral stair. Curwen saw it as *in situ*, an internal front door. Either way it suggests the presence of a second household; it is interesting that Thomas Dalston, whose obliterated arms are on the porch, let the hall but reserved for himself lodging, food and stabling. The Victorian porch near the W end opens into a wide cross-passage behind this second stack.

OASIS, Whinfell Forest, 2 m. SSW of St Ninian. Gated holiday compound, opened 1997 by Rank. Now part of the American-owned Center Parcs franchise. *Holder Mathias Alcock* were the architects, *AMEC* the builders. Hidden away in conifer forest, with just a single winding approach, it comes as a surprise to find 4,500 holidaymakers in residence, backed by 1,300 staff and a massive infrastructure. The site is centred on an artificial LAKE, which acts as a heat sink as well as reservoir for the many water features.

VILLAGE CENTRE. Enormous and dramatic building kept below the treetops, therefore invisible from afar. Butterfly plan with a central rotunda. Glass curtain wall S, towards the lake, but otherwise not much exterior. The roof swoops in a curved and twisted plane, and is covered with membraneous ridges of glazing. It is supported on laminated wood trusses braced with white tubular steel. The interior is kept at a constant 29.5 degrees, with semi-tropical plants and running water in abundance. One wing is dotted with refreshment booths, bridges and minor amusements, the other is for water sports. Gambling and entertainment spaces off, vast plant rooms underneath.

COUNTRY CLUB. Also enormous, enclosing six games courts and pitches as well as two storeys of shopping under a triple-wave roof. Again the exterior is unimportant, simply clad in wood, but the interior is sensational. The ground level drops in three terraces; columns support wooden branches to the mesh of wooden girders and Meccano-like fishplates and bolts that constitutes the curvaceous roof. A pedestrian bridge crosses from one side to the other.

LODGES. 853 of them, densely but picturesquely arranged beneath the pine trees. They are timber-framed with split-pitched roofs. – APARTMENTS opposite the Village Centre, again based on a butterfly plan with a distinct hinge, the wings not quite symmetrically placed. – CYCLE CENTRE. A perfect sea of bikes under another wave roof.

BROUGHTON (C)   *0030*

Populous former mining area with several scattered settlements. The narrow part of Main Street appears originally to have run through an open green between two distant rows of houses, i.e. a medieval plan, but this has been encroached out of existence.

CHRIST CHURCH, Great Broughton. N, between Main Street and Moor Road. 1856 by *Charles Eaglesfield*. Nave with bell-cote and chancel. Lancet windows. (PULPIT. Charming late C18 piece. – STAINED GLASS by *Powells*: †1907 (E), the rest Art Nouveau with leaf motifs.)

ST COLUMBA, Broughton Moor, 1½ m. NW. 1905, by *W. D. Caröe*. One of his most appealing churches. Small, of local rock-faced stone, simply detailed so that it could be built by unskilled labour under the local mining engineer, who was a relation. A virtue is made of simplicity and roughness. Dwarf tower on the S, designed on a big scale. Big wide round-arched entrance between E–W buttresses, so wide it has to cant inwards inside. Tall ringing-chamber lancet above, then a wide-open, segmentally arched bell-stage between diagonal buttresses which only start here, and a spike on top. The nave, sloping down to the W, has a broad segmentally arched open roof in the Caröe fashion. Round-arched windows. 'Caröe has left C19 historicism far behind. He may not have been as refined as, say, Temple Moore, but he had the virtue of originality.' (Pevsner). – FONT. Designed by *Caröe*, a big round tub, spirally fluted.

ROYAL NAVAL ARMAMENTS DEPOT. Military hutment with blast-proof banks occupying most of the 1,200-acre triangle between Broughton, Broughton Moor and Camerton. Established *c.* 1937, mothballed in the 1980s.

BROUGHTON EAST (L) *see* FIELD BROUGHTON

BROUGHTON-IN-FURNESS (L)

At the head of the Duddon estuary. The town was laid out by Gilpin Sawrey in 1764, with a handsome SQUARE and MARKET HALL. This is of seven bays, not detached, with arcading formerly open. Clock face dated 1766. Most of the houses, three-storeyed and colourwashed, also date from around then. In the middle of the Square an OBELISK, 1810. On the N side are the gates of Broughton Tower (below).

ST MARY MAGDALENE. It sits beautifully in a slight hollow among the drumlin-like hillocks S of the town. The S aisle is the nave of the old chapel of ease. Its E window is Perp; several of the other windows are of the earlier C16. The new, taller nave was built in 1873–4 by *Paley & Austin*, and the broad saddle-back tower by *Austin & Paley* replaced the old one in 1900–1, both largely at the expense of Richard Cross of Eccle Riggs (*see* below). The style was taken from the old Late Norman S doorway, which has waterleaf. The tower is just tall enough to look over the nave roof as you approach from town. – FONT. Octagonal, with a goblet bowl and shields. – STAINED GLASS. By *Kempe* the E window (1883), chancel N (three single lights, 1875), one nave N window (1902) and baptistery, W. In the old nave, S, Spes by *William Morris & Co.* (designer *Burne-Jones*), from Redcar, installed here 1948. Some others by *Shrigley & Hunt*.

WESLEYAN CHAPEL, Princes Street and Brades Street. 1875 by *William Culshaw & Sons* of Liverpool, builder *Nathaniel Caine* of Liverpool and Broughton. Chapel, hall and kitchen form an attractive group round a little courtyard. Gothic. Double bell-cote on chapel gable is balanced by a tall triple chimney on the kitchen. No fixed furnishings left.

BROUGHTON TOWER. The view up the drive from the market square is of Gothick symmetry, with corner towers, an uncommonly pretty porch with clustered shafts, the windows all ogee-headed, and a belvedere rising over the top. The belvedere is a real C14 tower, built probably after 1322 when the whole area was wasted by the Scots, heightened with a screen wall. It is larger than most (41 by 31 ft, 12.5 metres by 9.5 metres), three-storeyed (visible on the N side up to *c.* 60 ft, 18.5 metres), with two tunnel-vaulted chambers at the bottom and a turning stair. The Broughtons lost the estate after Sir Thomas, on the losing side at Bosworth, followed Lambert Simnel from his landing

at Piel Castle. It went to the 1st Earl of Derby, then by purchase to the Gilpin Sawreys. They rebuilt the house in 1744
(rainwater hopper), wrapping round three sides of the tower.
The house was Gothicked in 1777 (another hopper) possibly
by *John Hird*. At this stage it had pretty pavilion wings, the l.
of which is still there in principle. More work in 1838–41 by
George Webster, including perhaps the screen walls. The outer
towers were added in 1882–3 by *Settle & Farmer* with red stone
dressings; on the front they keep in harmony with the Gothick
work. The last private owner, Sir Robert Rankin of Liverpool,
made some alterations and importations in the 1920s. A special
school for years, now it is divided into flats.

Interiors. Porch and two-storey hallway have circular ceilings with pendentives, i.e. suggesting domes. In the hall the
first of Rankin's importations, a very fine Renaissance doorway
(early C16 French, thought Pevsner) with a pair of flying angels
at the top. Through to the former solar in the tower, a fine
spacious room with that sense of comfort and security given
by 6-ft (2-metre)-thick walls. Immensely deep and splayed
window reveals, a cross-framed ceiling, and a splendid Renaissance fireplace (Italian) with winged lions. This and the double
doors closing off the lobby must be thanks to Rankin again.

HA-HA, GATES and extensive rocky PARKLAND.

ECCLE RIGGS, ¾ m. s. Substantial Tudor Gothic house of 1865
by *E. G. Paley* for Richard Assheton Cross M.P. (1823–1914),
Disraeli's Home Secretary from 1874, later Secretary of State
for India and eventually Viscount Cross of Broughton. As
chairman of the Great Central he was able to commandeer
parts of the old hall at Ashton-under-Lyne (South-east
Lancashire) when it was demolished for the railway. Two stone
turrets flanking a building called the Dungeon were re-erected
here as gatepiers (one removed *c.* 1980), and panelling and fireplaces were used in the house. In 1880 a large dining-room
wing was added by *J. S. Crowther*, with a canted bay linking it
to the hall. Iron shutters wind up from below, on the sash principle. Cross was evidently concerned for his security.

FOXFIELD STATION. 1½ m. s. Neat set of buildings by *E. G.
Paley* in the middle of nowhere. Large signal box combined
with a small waiting room; exterior timber framing and hipped
roofs. Water tower adjacent, and the station house. The station
opened in 1858–9 as a junction for the Coniston branch.

BROUGHTON MOOR (C) *see* BROUGHTON

BURGH-BY-SANDS (C)   3050

Pronounced Bruff. Solway Plain village strung out in the space
between Hadrian's Wall and the Vallum. E of the crossroads, the
site of a ROMAN FORT on the Wall, guarding an ancient cross-

ing of the Solway; the road rises over the E and W ramparts. The church is in the SE quadrant.

ST MICHAEL. The church is built of Roman stones. The Norman W doorway is probably that now transferred to the N aisle, with stylized beakhead, and bits of the outer orders. Signs of a canopy porch. But apart from this doorway all that is medieval is E.E., see the one chancel N lancet and the N aisle windows (a pair of lancets in the E wall, which is unusual). This aisle was added *c.* 1200, when the church was given to Holm Cultram Abbey. In the C14 the church was lengthened E and W by a pair of defensive towers. An enquiry of 1360 refers to the digging of the W tower's foundations which caused the N arcade to collapse. The tower E of the chancel – a very unusual feature – was perhaps the vicar's residence. Reduced in height probably in 1713, it no longer looks like a tower, being roofed in line, but is two-storeyed (no vault) and communicates with the church only by a small door by the altar. Its present windows are C18. The top storey of the W tower with its round-arched bell-openings is of different masonry and probably Georgian. The S wall has required rebuilding more than once, and shows the outline of flat-topped windows above the late C19 Dec ones. The restoration was in 1880–1.

The arcade of three bays was rebuilt after 1360 with octagonal shafts, but retains the damaged, but interesting, E.E. capitals with primitive stiff-leaf. The small internal doorway to the broad W tower is protected by an iron GATE or yatt with huge hinges and bolts. The inner lintel seems to be made of a carved tympanum, possibly with birds. The thickness of the walls leaves little volume for the barrel-vaulted interior. Many steps up to the W window slit. A gunloop covers the (blocked) NW doorway, and a spiral stair rises in the SW corner. – STAINED GLASS. All by *Seward & Co.*, 1897, except the five lancets of the N chapel (†1898) which are by *Heaton, Butler & Bayne*; one depicts Edward I who lay in state in the church.

VICARAGE (former). A successor to the E pele of the church (*see* above), it occupies a corner of land taken out of the churchyard, NE. Very modest, yet a terrier of 1578 mentions accommodation for the vicar, a curate, and the vicar's stable. It is clay-built, with crucks. The ridge beam has curved wind-braces down to the cruck collars. Date 1652 on a raised cruck, upside-down. The roof has been altered to a flatter pitch to take stone flags, allowing an upper floor to be inserted. The W end is C18, as is the Gothick screen wall to the churchyard.

Burgh, with its satellite villages (listed below), is one of the best places to see the clay houses called DABBINS or daubins. They can be recognized by their wobbly walls on a stone plinth often incorporating large padstones, the long and narrow shape, and single-storey form, perhaps with attics in the roof. The chimneys emerge to one side or the other of the ridge. A few are still thatched. Inside will be crucks to hold the roof up, while the roof, often weighted at the eaves, holds the walls down.

Diagonally across from the w end of the church is the thatched gable-end of LAMONBY FARM, one of the best remaining clay houses. Reckoned to be of *c.* 1615 (dendrochronolgy), it is a longhouse of ten bays in all: cottage, house and barn in line, with the cross-passage between barn and house. The nine cruck-trusses march straight through with only the smallest variation in the standard width (17 ft, 5 metres) and spacing (11 ft, 3.5 metres) – a slight widening for the house, a stretching of the spacing for the cottage at the s end. The step down into the cottage marks the line of Hadrian's Wall. Splayed window openings, cut straight through the clay without stone surrounds. The construction can be seen inside the barn. The clay is laid in pillows separated by chopped straw, the cruck feet are buried in the wall. The walls taper as they rise, coming to a point at the apex. The crucks are very slight and wiggly, with no attempt at tidying up their appearance. The blades do not meet at the top, but are jointed by a short collar upon which the ridge rests. The roof, originally of the local type of thatch called stapple, with a few sandstone slabs to weigh it down, is now of reed for the house, corrugated iron for the barn. The flying buttress on the s side is an addition of the 1980s. ROSE MOUNT, next to Lamonby, is c18 brick. Slate roof with courses of stone at the bottom, perhaps a hangover from dabbin technique. Opposite is CROSS FARM, with chimneys off-centre and a good cruck barn behind, both c16 and of clay. A Roman inscribed stone ALTAR, found nearby in 1802, is incorporated in a wall. Next comes BUCK BOTTOM, also clay – it is characteristic that the village consisted largely of a string of farms. WHITE ROW. Six houses (the plan suggests converted from farm and barn) of clay, single-storeyed, with big stones sticking out at the base. Next an unnamed house of 2+1+2 bays with an Ionic porch. FULWOOD HOUSE and BURGH HOUSE. Long front with two pediments and two doorways, one with an Ionic porch. Dated 1769 W & EH over the side door.

n from the crossroads, YEW TREE COTTAGE has the distinctive walls and off-centre chimney of a dabbin. Likewise EDNA'S COTTAGE, still thatched, with two buttresses. LEIGH COTTAGE, three bays end-on to the road, has a tin roof and the clay construction partly exposed. The crucks are set high in the wall, emerging at shoulder height.

MONUMENT TO EDWARD I, 1¼ m. NNW. Square stone pillar about 20 ft (6 metres) high, with a cross on top. Erected 1685 (by *Thomas Langstaff?*), rebuilt 1803, restored and fenced 1876. It marks the desolate non-place where in 1307 the Hammer of the Scots met his death. In 2007 a STATUE of the king by *Chris Kelly* was given by Fred Story.

BRIDGES. The Carlisle Canal (*see* p. 163), s of the village, was crossed by a series of wooden lifting bridges. The railway conversion of 1853–4 replaced these with fixed cast-iron structures, on sandstone abutments built directly on the more elegantly curved bases for the 1821 crossings. The best example is at the w end of the village at West Green.

LONGBURGH, 1½ m. WSW of Burgh. LONGBURGH HOUSE is dated 1782 with initials W & AH over the carriage arch at the side. Two storeys of numerous bays, enclosing a courtyard. The low four-bay centre section, with a door at each end, may be older that the higher wings. WHITE COTTAGE is built of clay, with large projecting plinth stones and small windows cut straight through the clay. Originally two cottages. The door of the lower one is blocked; it retains the fire-window and, apparently, a clay hood over the inglenook. CROFT COTTAGE is another, recently dendro-dated to 1510, and a genuine long-house, though it looks unpromising having had a second storey added in brick. Four crucks.

BOUSTEAD HILL, 2½ m. W. Impressive and spacious parade of houses on a bluff overlooking the sea, exhibiting the Cumberland sureness of proportion. From l. to r. HILLSIDE FARM. Late Georgian, of red and yellow chequer brick. Three bays with one-bay wings. Greek Doric porch with triglyph frieze. Unnamed house of perhaps 1810 with a broad Grecian front, smoothcast, very plain. FRITH HOUSE. Victorian five-bay yellow brick front with stone trim; gabled centre with arms. CROFT HOUSE. Three bays of chequered brick with an arched fanlight. Early C19. BOUSTEAD HILL HOUSE, at the end. White, four bays with low wings, Doric porch with triglyph frieze. Also early C19.

MOORHOUSE, 1½ m. S on the B5307, a younger, less prosperous settlement than Burgh, is full of interest.

Former QUAKER MEETING HOUSE, set back behind trees at the E end of the village. Handsome building of 1733. No longer of the earliest and humblest cottage type, but the brickwork surprisingly amateurish, and lumps of stone project at intervals. Six bays, of which the fourth is the doorway, with a keyed-in round arch. Nothing left inside except the big roof trusses, set low, with kingposts and raking queenposts. They rest on the lumps of stone, their weight carried down to the ground by stone posts against the walls. What an odd way to build. Was the builder more familiar with clay and crucks? A piece of wood dated 1681 – the date of the first meeting house – was found during the conversion. Walled GRAVEYARD opposite, dated 1694.

MOORHOUSE HALL FARM is a dabbin, with outshuts also at least partly of clay. The crucks are said to have been put up as late as 1742. Barn at the W end of the farmyard of clay too. Slender roof trusses resting on top of the wall. However, a slot for a cruck shows that they are replacements. ROYAL OAK INN is dated TS 1742 (Thomas Stordy), who probably added the upper storey and the brick front. The attached COTTAGES, unpromisingly faced in brick with modern windows, are dabbins with reused crucks (felling range 1376–1401). THE STONEHOUSE. Slate and flags for the roofs, huge erratics for the base and padstones, cobbles for some of the walls, brick for others, clay for the barn walls, oak crucks for the barn structure, and buff ashlar, perhaps reused, applied to the front.

1703 over the door, with the initials SWT (William and Tirzah Stordy). The same initials occur on the parlour fireplace, with the motto HERE WE RESIDE. OUR NEXT REMOVE WILL BE. FROM TOILING TIME. TO VAST ETERNITY. The phrases can be read in any order. The plan suggests it was one long dabbin. The E end, a three-bay byre with crucks jointed at the elbows, remains as built. The house remained until 1703 when it was stone-faced, losing its crucks with the raising of the roof. The detached BARN to the W is also partly of clay and has evidence of removed crucks.

MOORHOUSE HALL. Large mid-Georgian house set back behind a sweep of lawn. Five bays with a tripartite doorway, Venetian window over, and a half-hearted pediment. Strange fan-shaped antefixae on the parapet.

MOORHOUSE FARM, at the W end. Converted to residential, including a ten-bay clay barn, i.e. nine crucks. Barn crucks have given a tree-ring date of c. 1462.

BURNESIDE (W)   5090

A company village with much company housing. Paper making started in the area in 1746. The various mills came under the control of the Cropper family during the C19. The trackbed of Croppers' tramway, connecting the works with the Windermere branch railway, can be traced up the valley as far as Cowan Head.

ST OSWALD. James Cropper added the present N aisle (to *George Webster*'s church of 1823–8) in memory of his wife, who died in 1868. The rest was taken down and rebuilt by *C. J. Ferguson* in 1880–1. It is Dec, rather stumpy in its forms, short and wide, with nave and chancel in one and a broad SW tower-porch. The W door is framed inside-out. Some nice foliage carving in the arch. Small-scale arcades, their piers alternating circular and octagonal. – REREDOS. Beautifully carved in 1890 with roses etc. in panels, by the sixteen members of an evening class and their tutor *A. W. Simpson*. – The ALTAR looks like an 1828 survival. – Tub FONT with yellow water-lilies carved round the rim and passionflowers on the capitals of the clustering columns. – STAINED GLASS. Good E window of 1936 by *Caroline Townshend* (a pupil of Christopher Whall) and *Joan Howson*; Nativity and swallows in the tracery, large figures in the five lights with more birds, smaller scenes below. S aisle E, two panels from the 1820s E window by *Gardner & Ellis*. W window and S aisle W by *Ward & Hughes*, 1880–1. N chapel E by *Lavers, Barraud & Westlake*, †1869. The others by *Shrigley & Hunt*. Also small bits of C18 or C17 glass brightly remounted in the S aisle.

BRYCE INSTITUTE, 1897–8. The adjacent building looks like *Curwen*.

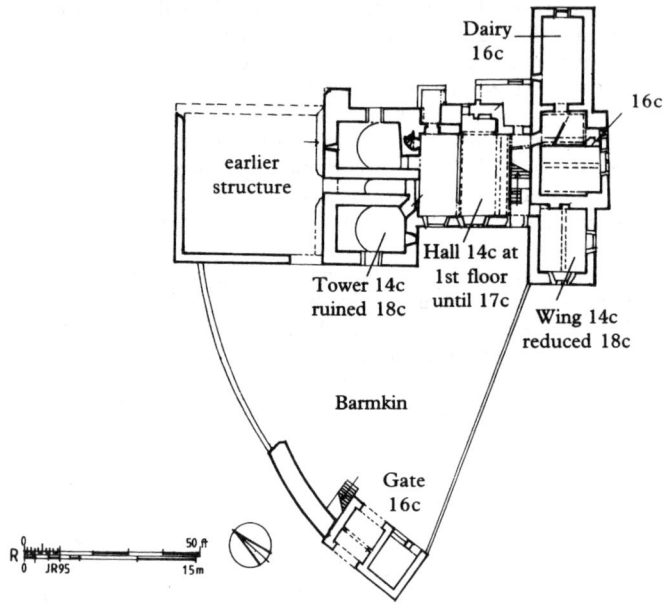

Burneside Hall.
Plan, 1998

STATION HOUSE. 1847. Angus Taylor attributes it to *Miles Thompson*. Window reveals and base mould of chunks of lime-stone pavement.

MILLS. To the E on the River Sprint is the picturesque SPRINT MILL, on a medieval site and successively a woollen, bobbin, and sawmill. ½ m. further upstream, OAK BANK BOBBIN MILL. Large, with a fine coppice barn with circular pillars, indicating an early C19 date.

BURNESIDE HALL. The formidable C14 N tower of the Belling-hams, long ruinous, dominates. Its base storey has two tunnel-vaulted chambers with a narrow tunnel-vaulted passage between, without direct doorways to the chambers, as at Preston Patrick (q.v.). The tower forms the N (solar) wing of a hall-and-cross-wings house. The hall, as so often, is unim-pressive, hiding behind an enormous early C17 chimneystack. On the W side to the N two three-light windows with transoms and cusped heads, to the S one small two-light window. Door-ways two-centred and chamfered with mason's marks. The outer doorway is at the N end. Originally four screens door-ways in a row – one for the through passage, two for the vaulted buttery and pantry, one to a turning stair to the tower solar. In the late C16 or early C17, when the stack was added, the hall was moved upstairs, level with the solar, reversing ends at the same time. The new entrance, as shown by Machell in the late C17, was up a ramp at the S end, where the stair is now. At the

s end was a single room attached to the sw corner of the hall
(as at Coniston Hall, q.v.). This was extended across the end
of the hall and further E, where it was vaulted below and probably carried up as another tower. The upper middle chamber
has a good plaster ceiling of *c.* 1600: quatrefoils with patterns
of tendrils in them and in the spaces between them. There is
a fine panelled screen, pre-C16 so probably moved.

An altered C16 GATEHOUSE and part of the barmkin wall
are on the w side. Below to the N, evidence for a pair of fish
ponds.

TOLSON HALL, ½ m. WSW. Heralded from the A591 road by
James Bateman's OBELISK in honour of the younger Pitt, 1814,
by *George Webster* (⅜ m. SSE of the hall) and on the by-road
down to the village by a castellated Gothick ARCHWAY of
1750. An older house was in 1638 made comfortable by
Thomas Townson or Tolson, tobacco grinder. In 1750 it went
Gothick, with sash windows with circles and ovals in the heads.
In *c.* 1840 the upper floor was heightened, with the substitu-
tion of bargeboards for battlements and the introduction of the
small centre gable and typical *Webster* porch. Inside are elements of the C17 house, including panelling and a wooden
overmantel on the ground floor. Stained-glass quarries bearing
the initials TT and the dates 1637 and 1638 with disarming
mottoes: 'God by this meanes hath sent/what I on this howse
hath spent', depicting pipes and tobacco; and 'All prayse unto
his name/that gave the meanes to build the same', picturing
piles of money. The same initials and the dates 1638 and 1639
in a couple of coarse plaster overmantels in the wing.

ELLERGREEN. Large many-gabled house lower in the park, built
for James Cropper in 1847. Angus Taylor suggests that it is by
Thompson & Webster.

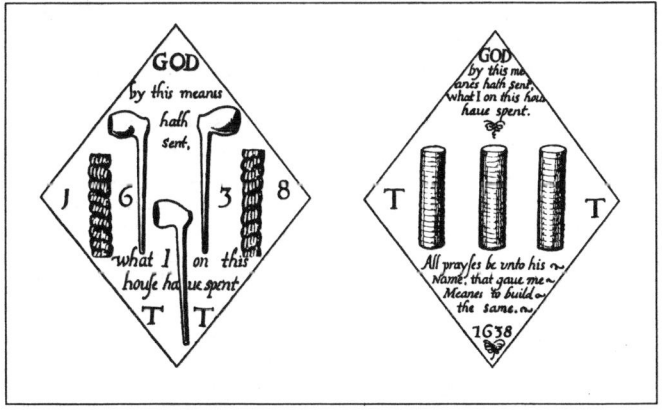

Burneside, Tolson Hall, stained glass.
Drawing, 1995

HOLLINS, Strickland Ketel, 500 yds SSW and close to Tolson Hall's gateway. A simple white farmhouse. In the C17 the two upper rooms got their plaster ceilings, friezes and overmantels, one with close and intricate leaves and the date 1687. Stair with stout balusters and an unusual cupboard or chest in the well. Cruck-truss in the W wing.

LOW BRUNDRIGG, 1½ m. WSW on the Crook Road. The house is a standard two-room, two-stack unit with a narrow centre passage. What makes it unusual is the end extension, which has a big square upper chamber, like a courtroom. Bench seating round two walls, an internal porch, a plaster frieze with stylized grapes, and an overmantel with the royal arms and the initials GD and AD (for Dodgson or Dixon) and the date 1667. What could be a retiring room is attached. Downstairs the same initials appear on a spice cupboard with the date 1664.

(GODMOND HALL, 1¾ m. N. Small C15 tower with no notable features, and late C17 five-bay house attached.)

PLUMGARTHS (Cumbria Wildlife Trust), Crook Road, 1 m. SW. A pretty picture. Small farm carefully gentrified and extended in 1934 for the Somervell (K Shoes) family by *Geoffrey Morland*. The wing with its four-pane sashes is proportioned to complement the farmhouse. Recessed balcony evoking a spinning gallery at the end, but with contemporary metal windows at the back. Beautifully simple woodwork and metalwork inside.

BURTON-IN-KENDAL (W)

ST JAMES. The massive low and broad W tower is Norman in its lower part, with an unmoulded arch to the nave and the reveals of the W window filled with Dec tracery. Norman also the NW corner of the nave. Where the roughcast is stripped on the N this shows construction of water-rounded stones. The nave goes through without a break, and so, under its own roof, does the C14 S aisle. The N aisle is a lean-to, but the E part was rebuilt as a vestry with a gable to balance the S side in the restoration of 1844. Of this date also the clerestory and the remodelling of the chancel. Re-set E window of the N aisle with intersecting tracery, i.e. *c.* 1300, that of the S aisle slightly later, with undeveloped cusps. Other windows Perp and straight-headed. The arcades, too far out of step to have ever allowed a chancel arch, are of standard Perp elements, the N slightly later and cruder than the S. In 1872 the E part of the S arcade was rebuilt. – PULPIT. Jacobean, with intricate patterns including low blank arches. – STAINED GLASS by *Clayton & Bell* (E window), *H. W. Bryans* (S aisle to W), *Shrigley & Hunt* (S aisle to E), and *Lavers, Barraud & Westlake* (W, and N aisle). – MONUMENTS. Brass to Sarah Hornby of Dalton Hall †1886. Several good C18 tablets in the S aisle. – SCULPTURE. Piece of a late C10 or C11 cross. The central scene of the front shows, within an inner arched frame, Christ in Majesty treading a serpent, and, above, the nimbed figures of John and Mary by the empty cross. Plenty of scrolls and interlace. Another fragment has irregular zigzag, and yet another a defaced figure and also a wheel head.

The VILLAGE is mostly one long street (Main Street), with a few side yards. It widens briefly into THE SQUARE, laid out *c*. 1810 with a row of modest three-storey houses on each side. The ROYAL HOTEL overlooks the NE side with a fine display of Venetian windows. Reportedly the cottage attached to the N has a full cruck within. Several houses on the W side are jettied out over the pavement on stone columns. Walking S, DEVENANT HOUSE of hammered limestone, three bays with a square fanlight and blank attic floor; early C19. Then HUTTON HOUSE, dated 1728 with a doorway with pulvinated frieze and pediment, and the chapel-like Manor House STABLES, of six bays with double entrance and double first-floor windows under an applied pediment. Opposite is FERNLEA with an apsed hood on excellent carved brackets. On the same side FERN BANK with a doorway with Tuscan columns, and then, again on the E, The MANOR HOUSE of 1701, but all the details late C18, i.e. flat window frames and flatly framed Venetian window.

Lastly BURTON HOUSE. Built by William Atkinson *c*. 1795, and quite splendid. Faced in fine sandstone ashlar, it lies back and has a centre of three generously spaced bays and two-and-a-half storeys with the main windows pedimented. Low two-bay links, recessed quite a distance, connect with one-bay pedimental pavilions. The links each have their own pedimented doorway, and have clearly been raised at some time. The main doorway, of the Venetian type, is at the side of the centre block. It leads straight into the staircase hall which occupies one of the three bays. Beyond in the other two bays is the apsed drawing room with an Adamish ceiling. Halfway up the stairs a small sitting room similarly embellished. Spacious cellars, fully lit from broad areas front and back. The back windows are tripartite with flat raised frames, the wall roughcast over rubble. On the N side of the garden a low SCHOOL HOUSE with big sashes and a sundial, then a sunhouse or ORANGERY with tall arched windows. The walls on the S reflect the same rhythm in blank recesses.

DALTON HALL, 1 m. SE. Stately doll's house of 1968–71 for the Mason-Hornbys by *Clough Williams-Ellis* – his last commission. Symmetrical front and rear, of seven bays and two storeys with giant pilasters and pediments to the centrepiece, colourwashed yellow and white under a hipped roof. Sash windows with stout glazing bars. Generous black-and-white paved hallway. The language is of the grandest but the scale is small, with an air of stage scenery. The house sits inside the ghost of its prede-cessor, a bigger house with an early C19 centre and major addi-tions by *E. G. Paley* in 1859. Its main entrance, preserved to waist height, faces a turning circle on a polygonal bastion.

Further rooms can be seen outside the present kitchen, and the stables are complete on the other side of Clough's paved and cobbled courtyard. A circular TEMPLE reuses the columns and entablature of the early C19 porch. 'It is very warming to have ended my long building career with so satisfactory a last fling,' said the architect.

BUTTERMERE (C)

Sequestered valley and lakes, but the hamlet is one of the Lake District's hot spots.

CHURCH. Celebrated for its very lowliness, contrasting with the superbly grand surroundings. Tiny, with a bellcote and lower chancel. The dates are 1840, extended E 1884, W porch 1933. Of an earlier chapel the stumpy half-column gatepiers to the enclosure, and the C18 FONT. Iron GATE in the porch, with shepherd and dog, made in 1968 by *Gilbert Hodgson* of Warcop. – STAINED GLASS. E window by *Holiday*, 1893. – MEMORIALS. Bronze portrait medallion, 1945, by *Cyril Catherall* to his son Alan, who died in Java. – View of Haystacks from a S window appropriated by inscription as a memorial to Alfred Wainwright †1991.

LOW HOLLINS, Brackenthwaite. *See* Loweswater.

CALDBECK (C)

Loosely knit village in magnificent open country, with important industrial remains.

ST KENTIGERN. A painted inscription dates the thin W tower to 1727; bells for it were made in 1724. At that time the church had an overall roof and round-topped windows like those of the tower, which has a small unmoulded arch towards the nave. The clerestory is by *C. J. Fawcett Martindale*, 1932–3, and so are the roofs and the aisle windows. So far so good. The rest poses some interesting problems. The outer doorway of the S porch is misplaced Norman, with beakhead. More beakhead, so highly stylized as to be abstract, on the inner side – which suggests it was originally the (very narrow) chancel arch; cf. Kirkbampton. The porch itself is tunnel-vaulted, an occasional regional phenomenon (also Warcop, Kirkby Thore). The inner doorway is C13, with continuous roll mouldings. The E end is E.E. in its lower parts, with flat clasping buttresses and two intermediate ones. The upper E wall is Late Perp, with a broad window of five uncusped lights under a segmental head. It carries an *orate* inscription of about 1512 to John Whelpdale,

rector also of Greystoke. He may have added the substantial
sacristy.

Both arcades are of six bays. The N arcade piers are round,
the S octagonal and slimmer, both with a clear hiatus midway;
in fact the mid-pier on the S was an E respond. The W columns
on both sides are monoliths. That the arches change from slight
to proper chamfers indicates W before E here. So a lengthening to the E seems indicated, and must have taken place as
building went on. The only trouble is that in the chancel S wall
a column has come to light, with a steep base and an elementary moulded capital, and this looks earlier than the arcades,
i.e. would imply a chancel in a place to the E of the whole six-
bay nave. A shafted window reveal on the S side suggests a composition like Ireby or Beaumont or Kirkby Lonsdale. The
interior of the tower apparently shows medieval masonry, and
Martindale built some Norman zigzag into its first-floor
opening. Chancel roof of 1880 (restoration by *C. J. Ferguson*).

FURNISHINGS. FONT. Big, octagonal, Perp, with a thickly
moulded stem. – ROYAL ARMS. George IV. – STAINED GLASS.
E window, chancel S, and baptistery, typically blue, by *Wailes*.
Chancel S, *Wailes & Strang*. Nave NE, St Kentigern and
St Cuthbert, 1938 by *Powells*. SE by *Peter Strong*, 2000, the
Good Shepherd, and Mary, in a densely imagined local setting.
– MONUMENTS. Outside, painted white, John Peel †1854, with
hunting horns and a hound, signed *J. Crosthwaite*. Nearby is
Mary Harrison, the 'Maid of Buttermere', †1837.

Specimen conifers in the churchyard proclaim a gentleman
parson.

RECTORY, to the W. Gentlemanly house of 1785. Front with
canted entrance bay in the middle, behind a screen of four
Doric columns. At the side, overlooking the churchyard, a pair
of delightful Gothick windows, tripartite, the sides with steep
lancet arches, an ogee head over the central light. The gateway
to the churchyard reuses an early C18 doorhead.

(LOW BROWNRIGG, 1⅛ m. NW. Dated 1695. Mullioned windows of two lights in moulded frames. Between ground floor
and first floor a moulded string course. Above the doorway a
round window. The inscription is worth reading:

> Grace brings salvation by an inward light
> Works reformation in a pious might,
> Then listen well unto Christ's voice within
> And tender that which keeps us out of sin.)

(At WHELPO, 1⅛ m. W, is a former FRIENDS' MEETING
HOUSE of 1698, sold 1932. A plain three-bay single-storey
house, now with new windows. No furnishings.)

INDUSTRIAL REMAINS. The beck that flows so picturesquely
through the village formerly powered a variety of industries.
¼ m. to the W, it plunges over a waterfall into the narrow gorge
of The Howk, where stands a former BOBBIN MILL. Built
c. 1847, it was powered by one of the largest water wheels in
England, 42 ft in diameter and 3 ft wide (33 and 1 metres),

brought from Carrock End Mine (*see* below). The main building is roofless, but the large open-sided coppice barn is complete, with on each side five columns of the later square form.
Downstream, at the W entry to the village, the OLD BREWERY
(now houses) incorporates an earlier mill and mill house, dated
1671. Originally probably a corn mill, by 1829 a cotton-
spinning mill, it became a brewery *c.* 1847. The square tapering brewery chimney rises through the roof of the original C17
house. To the l. the square cube of a two-storey MALTHOUSE,
under a pyramidal roof. Beyond is the original mill with a
splendid weir and headrace behind. The neighbouring HIGH
MILL, now also a house, is probably late C18. The miller's
house incorporates a one-time CORN MILL under its roof,
extending at right angles to the rear. A storage building,
looking earlier, projects awkwardly forward, r. Downstream
again, a splendid early C19 THRESHING MILL, later used for
wool and finally blanket-weaving and clog-making. T-plan, two
storeys; internal wheel and machinery complete. Finally,
beside the church is LOW MILL, now Priest's Mill Tea Rooms.
Datestone over the rear entrance: J WYBWERGH B OF LAWS
AND RECTR OF THIS CHURCH BUILT THIS MILL AD1702 ED
AD. Two storeys, U-plan. At first it ground corn, but finished
its working life as a SAWMILL in the early 1960s. Some
machinery inside; the unconvincingly 'restored' wheel turns by
a coin-in-the-slot electric motor.

The CALDBECK FELLS, SW, have been worked for minerals –
copper, lead, silver, zinc and more – for at least 800 years; the
last barytes mine closed in the 1980s. Recognizably modern
mining began in the C16 with *Daniel Hochstetter*, brought from
Augsburg for Queen Elizabeth's Company of Mines Royal.
Of the hundreds of sites, the best expedition, an easy 5-m.
walk, starts from Fellside on the southerly loop of the
Caldbeck–Uldale road. All the workings are dangerous, and
none should be entered.

From the end of the lane leading SE from the settlement, a
mine track leads r. into the valley of Dale Beck. The second
stream flowing under the road is Hay Gill, where below on the
r. are remains of a late C19 SMELT MILL. A collapsed flue
crosses under the road and extends E up the fell, while dry
watercourses run towards an empty wheelpit at the N end of
the foundations. Up the Gill, a ruined DRESSING FLOOR and,
100 yds further on, remains of a COPPER MINE, reputed to
have been worked in the C17 by the German experts of the
Mines Royal: wheel pit, bothy, drainage adit and dressing floor.
These mines last worked *c.* 1870. Looking W across the main
valley of Dale Beck, the great gashes of the Brae Fell HUSH cut
diagonally down the fellside. Near the horizon is the dam constructed to collect water, which was released to rip the covering of earth from the mineral veins. Further down, the adit
openings and waste tips show how productive this mine was
c. 1790–*c.* 1880.

Just before the track crosses the Dale Beck, a grass trod leads
l. across Birk Gill, to ROUGHTEN GILL MINE. The valley

opens out to the E, revealing adits, working levels and waste
tips all round a great amphitheatre. Ruined buildings by the
road, r.: the mine office, a bothy where ninety miners could
stay, a smithy, service buildings, stabling, etc. Ahead, working
down from the horizon, are the extensive remains of receiving
floors, the crushing floor, the jigging and secondary crushing
areas, and the final separation and settling tanks. The early
German workings are the highest, some 600 ft (185 metres)
above the modern waterworks valve house.

Returning to Fellside along the mine road on the l. bank of
Dale Beck, Silver Gill opens on the l., site of workings from
the C14. It displays some splendid German 'coffin' levels
(narrow hand-cut passages with a broadening at shoulder
height).*

CARROCK END MINE lies on the eastern slopes of CARROCK
FELL, ¼ m. W of Linethwaite Farm. The mine was attached
to the Company of Mines Royal in 1570, and the Francis Shaft
was sunk in 1836. A C16 cobbled dressing floor survives almost
complete. Remains of a powder store, a smithy, and a whim,
including the bearing stone in which the vertical axle of the
winding drum turned. A deep groove runs from the mine
arrow-straight across the moor for 300 yds (275 metres) to a
pit for a 40-ft (12-metre) wheel near the farm, indicating the
line of pump rods which drained a 27-fathom (50-metre) shaft.
At the back of the site, a leat comes down for 1 m. from a dam
at the ford on the Carrock Beck. Behind the leat, a deep diagonal trench down the fellside, with remains of a small dam at
its head: almost certainly from early hushing operations to
expose the mineral vein.

HILL-FORT, on the summit of Carrock Fell 4 m. SSE, overlooking Mosedale. A puzzling hill-fort of uncertain date, defined
by a broad wall, now a discontinuous bank of rubble. The surviving stretches of facing-stones suggest that the wall had a
stepped profile.

CALDER BRIDGE (C)   0000

CALDER ABBEY. In 1135 thirteen monks arrived from Furness,
then still a Savigniac house. Within four years they were driven
out by the Scots. Turned away from Furness, they settled eventually at Byland in Yorkshire. A second colony came from
Furness in 1143; this is often reckoned as the abbey's true
founding, and is associated with William FitzDuncan, the
leader of the marauding Scots but now, by marriage, Lord of
Egremont. All three abbeys became Cistercian in 1148, but
whereas Furness and Byland grew great, Calder remained poor
and obscure.

*Excavations in 2007 revealed wooden rails pegged to the floor of the Emmanuel
Stollen adit, carbon-dated to the Early Elizabethan period, and thus the earliest
known in Europe; a 1586 inventory records 'Rowle Wagons' at Caldbeck.

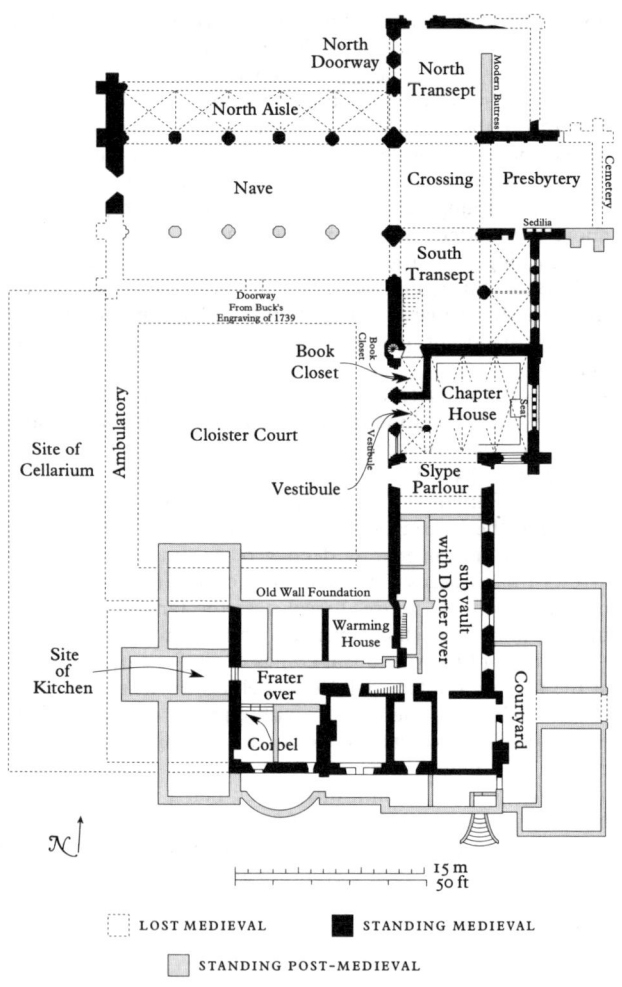

North
Doorway

North
Transept

Modern Buttress

North Aisle

Nave

Crossing

Presbytery

Cemetery

Sedilia

South
Transept

Doorway
From Buck's
Engraving of 1739

Book
Closet

Book Closet

Ambulatory

Chapter
House

Site of
Cellarium

Cloister Court

Vestibule

Slype
Parlour

Vestibule

Old Wall Foundation

sub vault
with Dorter over

Site
of
Kitchen

Warming
House

Frater
over

Courtyard

Corbel

𝒩

15 m
50 ft

☐ LOST MEDIEVAL   ■ STANDING MEDIEVAL

☐ STANDING POST-MEDIEVAL

Calder Abbey.
Plan

The church lies by the river, as was the rule among the Cistercians. A splendid Norman w doorway, the presbytery, and
parts of the transepts (with their E aisles) and monastic quarters were erected in stone. John Todd suggests that the slen-
derness of the abbey's endowments may not have allowed
much more. A plausible time-frame is provided by a raid in
1216 which may have destroyed temporary buildings, and the
death in 1240 of Thomas de Multon of Egremont. Further
raids especially in 1332 may account for signs of downsizing

e.g. in the succession of nave roof scars at the crossing. Its value in 1536 was assessed at £50, when there were nine monks. In 1538 Thomas Leigh, one of the two 'visitors' of religious houses in the North, acquired the suppressed abbey and its lands. While the church fell to ruin the buildings of the cloister were incorporated into a mansion. In the 1780s the Senhouse family built a new front block, diverted the road, planted woods. In the 1840s Mary Senhouse married Thomas Irwin, and together they rebuilt the N wing, added the W porch, and created the long riverside walk to their new church at Calder Bridge, ¾ m. WSW.

ABBEY CHURCH. An ideal ruin, romantically overgrown and precarious. The W front stands to the sill of the window. The N arcade is complete. Four tall crossing arches support the stump of a tower, unusual in a Cistercian church; it was perhaps defensive. The S transept, chapter house with one bay of its vaulting, and dormitory wing are all there, with the arch from the S aisle to the S transept. Excepting the Norman W doorway and possibly parts of the transepts it is very consistently C13 E.E., with the same twice-chamfered and steeply pointed arches everywhere and lobed and filleted piers. The Dec style only makes its appearance with the great E window of the chapter house, and perhaps in the lost E parts of the chancel. 23

The W DOORWAY, dated by Pevsner to c. 1175, is round-arched, much-moulded, with an outer ring of lobes and water-leaf capitals to the colonnettes. (Similar capitals also appear in the outer shafting of the S transept chapels.) The five bays of the NAVE N ARCADE, built between 1215 and 1240, are elegant but relatively low in comparison with the great height and width of the crossing. The piers are alternately octagonal and quatrefoiled with fillets, both on waterholding bases. The easternmost octagonal capital is decorated with a zigzag of leaves, which occurs at the same time at Egremont Castle. The start of a triforium can be seen on the N, and there are traces of what must have been quite a tall clerestory, with a wall-passage. Foundations of the PULPITUM appear one bay W of the crossing. The CROSSING ARCHES, twice chamfered, are splendidly tall and wide. N and S responds canted, E and W ones semicircular and resting on brackets, short in the E arch, somewhat longer in the W arch. The tower has needed a massive shore against its NE corner, cutting off the N TRANSEPT CHAPELS, of which there is little left. However the start of the N chapel arcade, and traces of its vault, can be seen. N transept doorway with two orders deeply moulded, similar to the W doorway but slightly pointed. Over on the S TRANSEPT is a pair of E chapels originally rib-vaulted. Each of the two bays has two lancet windows. The central pier is quatrefoiled with deep narrow hollows between the foils. The foils carry fillets. Double-chamfered arches. Above, a handsome blank arcade, single-chamfered with continuous mouldings, two lights for one arch below, and with big blank quatrefoils in the spandrels. The W wall has a tall clerestory of lancets (with later tracery), and a wall-passage to a narrow newel stair up the SW corner of the tower. In the s wall is the upper doorway which connected the dormitory with the transept by means of the night stair. This also has continuous mouldings. The EASTERN LIMB, normally the oldest part, is cut short at the w reveals of a pair of very tall transomed lancet windows. It appears therefore that the chancel was rebuilt but not lengthened, keeping its short Burgundian termination to the end (known from excavation). Three SEDILIA and the door to the s transept chapel are gathered into one composition under trefoiled arches, which also appear in the tall lancets in the w wall of the s transept. Above this the side walls, as far as they are preserved, had very tall blank arcading, the slender shafts with several shaft-rings.

MONUMENTS at the crossing. Damaged effigies of three knights in mail, with triangular shields. One can be identified by his heraldry as Robert de Leyburne, early C14. Also an abbot(?) under what could have been a nodding ogee canopy. Now for the MONASTIC PARTS. Unusually the CHAPTER HOUSE butts directly against the transept (as also at Furness, as reconstructed). It was a fine apartment rib-vaulted in three bays; the eastern vaulting bay stands. The ribs were single-chamfered. There is the usual entrance from the cloister: a doorway with two window-like openings l. and r. The northern one is walled off as a small treasury or book cupboard, also vaulted with single-chamfered ribs. The chapter house E window is as wide as it is tall, with stumps of Geometrical tracery, seemingly with cusps to the lights but not the circles (cf. the infirmary chapel at Furness). These details indicate a late C13 date. s of this was the slype, then an UNDERCROFT which runs on into the basement of the house. Above was the DORMITORY. This preserved many well-spaced lancets set within super-arches, to the w as well as the E. It was linked to the night-stair door by a passage across the chapter house vestibule. Above the chapter house vault was a small room (for the sacristan), reached by a narrow passage in the thickness of the s gable wall and a small plain doorway. (The day stair in the SE corner of the cloister is walled up in the house.) Of the cloister itself, and the w range, there is no visible trace.

The s range is subsumed into a MANSION of startling ugliness. The w-facing wing of the 1780s is gauntly fenestrated with patchy red and yellow render.* Venetian window upper centre, above a hideous porch of 1859. This has a Doric frontispiece with a flat entablature, and above that a semi-attic lit by an open oculus, and then a floating pediment. Three bays to the l., three to the r. The s elevation in dusty red stone is by *George Faulkner Armitage* of Altrincham, 1906, for Thomas Harrison Rymer. Rusticated basement with round-arched windows, lobed like the abbey's w doorway. The Georgian windows have been given hoodmoulds. The bowed section with its fiddly ornament represents the abbey's REFECTORY, built Cistercian-fashion at right angles to the cloister. The

---

* *John Carr* made a design, not used, in 1785.

echoing opulent interiors are Faulkner Armitage's. Central stairwell with decorative timber framing. In the SE oak room a huge inglenook with Art Nouveau glass and fine carving, and a frieze of roses and hips above the high panelling of the walls. All this is raised up over a labyrinthine basement in which evidence of the abbey's S range may be sought, but not readily found.

GATEHOUSE, now a garage. W of and somewhat above the church. C14, with double-chamfered arches; the outer one is continuously moulded, the inner has proper responds. No vault.

The abbey's water supply crosses the field to the E, emerging next to a domed structure with a low arched door which was apparently an OVEN. Next to it a C19 TURBINE HOUSE, magnificently constructed with a roof of interlocking stone slabs.

ST BRIDGET, Calder Bridge. By *Edmund Sharpe*, 1840–2, for Thomas and Mary Irwin. Lush site, plain red sandstone building in lancet style. W tower and transepts, short chancel, thin buttresses along the nave, clumsy pinnacles on the tower – i.e. not yet archaeologically accurate. Exceedingly plain interior lifted by fine Pre-Raphaelite STAINED GLASS of 1879 by *Powells*, artists *H. E. Wooldridge* and *H. J. Burrow* (E).

PONSONBY CHURCH, ¼ m. S. On a hilltop overlooking Sellafield, islanded by a ha-ha in the park of Ponsonby Hall (now Pelham House). A medieval church, belonging to Conishead Priory, but after the addition of the low W tower and broach spire in 1840 and a thorough restoration in 1874 it looks High Victorian. Red sandstone; lancet windows. Of the old church some rougher masonry, part of the chancel arch. – STAINED GLASS. Fragments of late C16 heraldic glass in the lowside window. – E window by *Morris & Co.*, 1877. Oblong sacred stories, clearly and simply told, in charming foliage squares. – W (†1893) designed and made by *Henry Holiday*. – MONUMENTS. Two coffin-lids with cross, sword, and shears. – Thomas Curwen †1653. Square tablet in a frame of dogtooth (cf. Corby Castle, Lanercost), with rustic supporters in C17 dress in relief l. and r., one drawing a sword, the other contemplating a skull on a curly stand.

PELHAM HOUSE. Built for George Edward Stanley of Ponsonby and Dalegarth (Eskdale) in 1780, possibly by *John Hird*, to a published design by *James Paine*. The five-bay ashlar front rises in the middle to light the semicircular staircase hall. The four-column Doric portico, of fluted monoliths without bases carrying a triglyph frieze, was added probably about 1810, as was the large rear wing and Tuscan rear portico. The stair is a slender cantilever, with iron balustrade. On the principal floor good doorcases, some curved for the rooms interlocking with the staircase hall, with broken pediments framing a tripod-and-snake motif. – LODGES on the A595. Early C19, both with stout Doric columns *in antis*. The S lodge has in addition a pediment and arms. The GATEWAYS and BRIDGE are of 1796–7.

SELLA PARK, W of the former. C17 house of the Curwens. Nearly square double pile of three storeys, symmetrical, with mullioned-and-transomed windows and a blocked central entrance. The stair is symmetrically placed at the back, with shallow treads, closed string and bottle-shaped balusters. Bolection-moulded hall fireplace (and two more upstairs). At the side a wide spiral stair without a proper newel, like that at Gosforth Hall.* *T. L. Banks*, who surveyed the building in 1883, probably made the new entrance tower and generally tidied it up. Further alterations in the late C20 for BNFL: ground floor opened up, extensions.

On the A595 as it winds through the village is CAUDER HOUSE, dated IM 1727. Above the door a quatrefoil, presumably from the abbey.

4040

CALTHWAITE (C)

Cut through by the West Coast main railway line and M6.

ALL SAINTS. By *J. H. Martindale*, 1913 (builders *T. Lowthian & Sons*). Red stone. Still Gothic, with lancets and very small voussoirs. Bright no-fuss interior, except the trio of arched doors on the N. By one of these the parson gains the PULPIT, a pretty conceit jutting out polygonally like a little opera box, with a back window. Angels of the easternmost hammerbeams, stalls, lectern all carved by *George Fendley* of Carlisle.

CALTHWAITE HALL. Light-hearted Gothic villa, in the Italian sense, i.e. with a farm. It was built *c.* 1837 by Thomas Dixon. The steading is dated TD 1840. The main façades symmetrical, with sashed windows in splayed reveals, one centring on a Gothic porch with reeded pillars, the other on an E.E. bay. The great feature of the interior is a free-standing spiral stair of wood, which rises through a circular opening, beyond which can be seen a higher and wider gallery, and then an octagonal glass dome: quite a trick in so modest a house.

0030

CAMERTON (C)

ST PETER. All by itself in a loop of the River Derwent, a spot long disfigured by mine spoil banks but now returning to beauty. Small and white. Gothick windows made correct with C19 Dec tracery, a little W tower and spire of 1855 leaning westwards, and a S transept. Over the inner door a whole list of dates: 1633, 1745, 1892, plus 1644 on the threshold. Peter Ryder identifies the last as a reused C12 grave-slab. Parts of the

---

* This has been taken as evidence for a defensive tower.

structure could be medieval, for instance the transept arch with its step and chamfer. – MONUMENT. 'Black Tom of the North.' Black-painted effigy of Thomas Curwen, *c.* 1510, with a fearsome sword. On the tomb-chest shields in circles.

CAMERTON HALL, ½ m. NW. Late Georgian, white, with two shallow bows and a Tuscan porch. IVY LODGE is delightfully Gothick, octagonal and castellated, with fancy glazing and coloured glass.

CARLETON (C)

4050

GARLANDS. This was the lunatic asylum for Cumberland and Westmorland; a large, closeted, multi-faceted community. *Thomas Worthington* of Manchester, who took a particular interest in hospitals, won the competition in 1851 with a full set of designs. Two years later the site was changed; Worthington was dismissed, and the complex was built, using Worthington's designs, by the County Surveyor *J. A. Cory* in 1858–62. Additions up to the mid C20. It closed in 1997 and was redeveloped for housing by Fred Story, 1999–2003. Worthington planned the big central block with long male and female wards and cells on either side. Buildings to his designs are round-arched and Italianate, with shallow-pitched and wide-eaved roofs; e.g. HOLLY HOUSE of 1862, the former main entrance, in red ashlar striped with buff stone and buff and blue brick. *Cory*'s later buildings are in plain red stone, often rock-faced, such as the former CHAPEL of 1875, large, Perp, with a SW tower with octagonal top and short spire. Further down the hill, pavilions like OVAL COURT (with shaped parapets to the bays) were built in the 1880s and in 1902–6, staff houses in the 1930s. The C21 environment is remorselessly nice.

NEWBIGGIN HALL, by Junction 42 of the M6. Handsome seven-bay E façade of Tullie House (Carlisle) character, with a good cornice and four evenly spaced chimneys. The clue to its real age lies in the stinginess of the ground-floor openings – only the door and two windows – and their 7-ft (2-metre)-deep reveals. It is in fact a large tower house (50 ft by 30 ft, 15 by 9 metres) of perhaps the C14, vaulted on the ground floor, which belonged to the Priors of Carlisle. Described still in 1650 as 'tower with a battlement above', it was made polite by William Graham *c.* 1698, possibly to *Thackeray*'s designs (Blake Tyson). Central doorcase with swan-necked pediment, upper-floor windows in an even row – both these in contrasting yellow stone – and a stair outshut at the back to make the standard Cumbrian T-plan of the period. It was further gentrified in 1820–6 by Henry Aglionby, who added the service accommodation at the SW end. Aglionby also opened up the ground-floor windows, made tripartite, with curly heads like the doorcase, but in red stone. The NE gable with its crowsteps and blunt pinnacles belongs to this phase, with a Venetian window replacing a large C17 basket-arched opening. The interiors are early C19, overlaid by a further facelift *c.* 1930 by *Harrods* of London for the Carrs, biscuit manufacturers. It seems likely that the living accommodation was originally upstairs, on top of the vault (cf. Askerton, Johnby (Greystoke), Scaleby). The upper floors are reconstructed, with thin walls. The lower chambers serve as entrance hall, dining room, and drawing room (the last without a vault, though one is assumed). The original tower entrance is in the W corner (cf. Askerton), with the possible remains higher up of a turning stair. The present stair, an elegantly curvaceous Regency piece, rises through a cross-arch broken through at the back, with Grecian plaster-work at the groin. It ascends three storeys, with a plaster rib-vault (cf. Kirklinton House) at the top. Thick walls at the back of the service wing are perhaps the remains of a barmkin. WALLED GARDENS, HA-HA, small towered STABLE.

CARLISLE (C)

Carlisle Cathedral	224
Exterior	225
Interior	227
Furnishings and Monuments	231
Monastic buildings	236
Churches	239
Public Buildings	240
Perambulations	249
1. *The walled city*	249
2. *The eastern edge of the walled city*	253
Inner Districts	256
1. *The south-eastern quadrant: Botchergate and Warwick Road to the Eden*	256
2. *West and south-west of the walled city: the early suburbs, with Caldewgate and Denton Holme*	260
Outer Districts	263
1. *South and south-east: Currock, Harraby and Upperby*	263
2. *West of the Caldew: Morton, Raffles and Newtown*	264
3. *North of the Eden: Stanwix, Kingmoor, Etterby and Belah*	265

As Arthur Mee put it, Carlisle was 'born under Mars on the highway of war'. *Luguvalium*, the civil settlement on the site, was the northernmost city of the Roman empire, watched over by the biggest fort on Hadrian's Wall across the River Eden at Stanwix. The position is strong, a leaf-shaped bluff of high ground protected by the Eden to the N and by its tributary rivers Caldew and Petteril to the W and E respectively. The castle occupies the

ANCIENT PLAN OF THE CITY OF CARLISLE,
from a Drawing in the British Museum.

Carlisle, bird's-eye view of the walled city.
Engraving after a drawing of 1590

northernmost and highest point, and from it the West Walls still
run almost complete above the banks of the Caldew to the
Citadel guarding the southern entry. Little survives of the rest of
the ring of walls.

The settlement began in A.D. 72 as a Roman timber fort which
occupied the S portion of the site of the later castle and that of
Tullie House. It had a turf and timber rampart, and an annexe
to the S containing the maintenance and service industries for
the garrison. A series of three subsequent forts (built in stone
from the C3) continued in occupation at least until the early C5.
The town grew up S and SE of the fort, between it and the
main road – now represented by Botchergate, Scotch Street and

Rickergate, leading N to the crossing of the Eden. By the early C3 Luguvalium, a town of over 75 acres, had probably been designated the *Civitas Carvetiorum*, the seat of government for the local people, the Carvetii.

Of the time between Romans and Normans we have only glimpses. The headquarters building of the fort continued in use in some form well into the early medieval period; Bede tells us that St Cuthbert came here *c.* 685 to speak to Ecgfrith's queen in her sister's monastery, and was taken to see the walls of the city and a marvellously constructed (*mire olim constructum*) Roman fountain. Here we have evidence of Roman survival, providing a context for the Bewcastle cross (q.v.) of much that date. John of Worcester tells us that Carlisle lay unoccupied after Viking raids in the C9, but we have late C9 references to the continued existence of the monastery, and know that one Dolfin was in charge when William Rufus came to annex the area to England in 1092.

In 1122 Henry I founded an Augustinian priory, probably at the site of an older church, whose congregation were allowed to occupy the nave. The other parish, equally ancient, was that of St Cuthbert. Eleven years later Henry elevated the priory to a cathedral, although inadequate endowment left the see vacant between 1157 and 1204, and probably also ordered the building of a great stone keep in Rufus's fortress. The Scots had turns in the C12 as well. Charters are recorded for *c.* 1158, 1251, 1316, 1352, 1358, empowering the corporation to maintain the walls which saw the city safe through later sieges. There were two friars' houses, Greyfriars and Blackfriars (both 1233), and several hospitals including St Nicholas, none of which have left remains above ground. 1292 saw a major fire, with another in 1352. Around 1300 Edward I used the castle as his northern base against the Scots – though there were no great works commensurate with those in Wales – and in 1307 he summoned a parliament to Carlisle. His unresolved territorial ambitions meant that Carlisle was in the front line of ceaseless strife between England and Scotland, right up to the Union of Crowns in 1603. Defences of castle and town were radically reconfigured for artillery under Henry VIII and Elizabeth.

The C17 was a depressed time, partly from the ending of border garrison status after 1603, but also following the siege of 1644–5 and destruction of cathedral nave and precinct. Celia Fiennes (1698) noted how few brick or stone houses there were, the rest presumably being of timber and clay. The capitulation to the Young Pretender in 1745 was the last significant episode of civil strife. The city was perceived as poor until the mid C18 at least. Turnpikes (the 'Military Road' towards Newcastle, 1751; after 1755 to London) and canal (1819–23) were the turning points. In the later C18 and early C19 Carlisle enjoyed a solid prosperity, supported by an ecclesiastical bureaucracy and the cotton industry. The county town and legal centre of Cumberland, it supported two banks in 1750, six by 1810. Until 1812 the Eden meandered by in at least two channels, each with a bridge.

Robert Smirke's new bridge was finished in 1816, the southern channel being filled in.* The eastern walls were mostly demolished in 1813 for the creation of Lowther Street. The rebuilding of the Tudor citadel as The Courts by *Smirke* and others in the early C19 asserted Carlisle's regional importance, as did *Tattersall*'s splendid Infirmary of 1830–2. *Rickman & Hutchinson*'s two churches of 1828–30, Christ Church in Botchergate and Holy Trinity in Caldewgate, have been demolished, but the architectural legacy of this period includes a whole suburb of dignified Georgian brick terraces in the Warwick Road area, and a string of fine villas in places such as Houghton and Crosby-on-Eden (qq.v.). Their dates extend well into the railway era.

The population, less than 10,000 in 1801, grew to 25,000 by 1851 and reached 45,000 by 1901. However, the Victorian age did not bring much of an architectural flowering. Nothing could be more telling than the absence of a Victorian or Edwardian town hall. The new railway age made the best show, with Citadel Station (1846–7) and the adjacent County Hotel, where Queen Victoria sometimes stopped on her journeys to and from Scotland. Of the other, increasingly sumptuous hotels, the Red Lion (now County) and Crown & Mitre are the best remaining.

In 1922 Carlisle was characterized as 'a great railway centre, long noted for its silesias [cotton], its biscuits [Carr's], its decorated tin boxes [Hudson Scott], and its giant cranes [Cowans & Sheldon]'. To this list ought to be added munitions, established in the First World War a few miles N between Longtown (q.v.) and Gretna. Lloyd George's concern about drinking by munitions workers led to the creation in 1916 of the STATE MANAGEMENT SCHEME, which took over the city's four breweries and 253 pubs. 'Fewer and better public houses' was the motto, as the Home Office sought, 'saner, cleaner, soberer but at the same time merrier inns', freed from competition and promoting food, family and non-intoxicating refreshments. *Harry Redfern* was appointed architect, with the interior designer *George Walton*. Initially *C. F. A. Voysey* (who designed the letterhead) and *Basil Oliver* were on the board, and eventually *Joseph Seddon*. Most of the pubs were built by *Robert & James Bell*. Redfern had a quiet sense of humour as well as an eclectic taste, and his pubs are a collective treat, lending Carlisle an unusual flavour. Denationalization in 1972 however has done them no favours.

The city council embraced its new housing powers enthusiastically, and for most of the C20 its efforts outstripped those of private house-builders. The first council flats appeared in 1900 in a small development at the Willow Holme. Large estates were built successively at the Raffles, St Ann's, Upperby, Botcherby, Currock, Belah, Harraby and Morton Park. The boldly modern civic cluster arose in the early 1960s, with the county's first and still only tower block. The cohesion of the city was ruptured in

* But still occasionally reasserting itself, as in the floods of 2005, when the medieval enceinte was once again almost an island.

the late 1960s by two grossly insensitive dual carriageways, thrust between the centre and the castle and the centre and its early suburb to the E. They failed to solve the traffic problem. In the 1980s in a telling change of tack the medieval Lanes were replaced by a pastiche shopping centre of the same name. Carlisle's civic hesitancy was again highlighted in 2000 by the incomplete Millennium expansion of Tullie House. The population of the urban area in 2001 stood at about 72,000, modest for such a significant regional centre.

CARLISLE CATHEDRAL

'Like a great wild country church' is how three army officers found it in 1646, 'neither beautify'd nor adorn'd one whit'. The greater part of the Norman nave was largely dismantled shortly after. This was the church's lowest point. Today, though plenteously beautified and adorned, it is still not much more than half a cathedral.

Henry I founded an Augustinian priory *c.* 1122, appointing as prior Athelwold, an Anglo-Saxon (prior also of Nostell, Yorks.). In 1133, needing to stabilize the newly established border with Scotland, and to ward off the Bishop of Glasgow, Henry elevated it to a cathedral, Athelwold to its bishop. It retained that peculiarly British duality of cathedral and priory until the Reformation.

The C12 church was narrow. In the absence of both its ends we can say it had an aisled nave of probably seven bays, unaisled transepts each sprouting a small semicircular eastern chapel, and an aisled chancel of two or more likely three bays, ending – according to foundations seen in the 1850s, and by analogy with other Augustinian churches – in a trio of apses. It has been suggested that the tall blank arcading round the apse of the dependent church at Warwick (q.v.) may reflect the exterior treatment.* The canons' choir extended a couple of bays into the nave, with a screen or pulpitum at that point. In 1218 Hugh, first abbot of the royal Cistercian house of Beaulieu, Hants, was appointed bishop, instructed to reclaim the canons who had sworn allegiance to the King of Scots. Bringing with him an augmentation of the revenues of the see, Hugh embarked on an ambitious new choir around 1220. It was 12 ft (3.7 metres) wider than the old, and much longer. The conventual buildings blocking enlargement to the S, the extra width was all on the N side, allowing the new N and E walls to be built round the old choir. It is noticeable that the W bays on the old C12 alignment on the S side, the last to be rebuilt, are more untidy than the rest.

Hugh's choir was complete by *c.* 1290, but fire swept the city in 1292, burning off the roofs. Their fall must have caused sec-

*By Neil Stratford, in the first edition of *Cumberland and Westmorland*, 1967.

ondary fires at ground level, damaging the piers. No doubt a temporary patch-up disguised this when Edward I held his parliament here in 1307, when excommunication was pronounced upon Robert the Bruce. Permanent repairs followed. The great E window, the cathedral's chief glory, was ready to be glazed in about 1340. The roof was on by about 1355. In 1380 however came a second disaster when the Norman crossing tower fell, destroying the N transept. Tower and transept were rebuilt by Bishop Strickland (1400–19) on the Norman piers, perpetuating the awkward junction with the wider choir. There was a resurgence of work under Prior Gondibour, *c.* 1465–1500. In 1540 the priory surrendered, with twenty-three canons and four chantry priests, and in 1541 the buildings were granted to a new dean and chapter. The monastic buildings survived until the 1644–5 siege, when all except for the Fratry, the Prior's Tower, and Prior Slee's gatehouse were cannibalized for the city's defences. The parochial part of the nave survived a little longer, but the congregation moved to St Cuthbert's in 1650, and in 1652 a new W wall was erected at the position of the pulpitum, allowing the rest to be demolished. A reduced parish congregation squeezed back into the remaining two bays between 1666 and 1669.

A major internal restoration took place in 1765 under Bishop Lyttelton, to Gothic designs by his nephew *Thomas Pitt*, later Lord Camelford. Pitt's work was condemned as 'barbarous' in 1852–6, when it was largely undone by Dean Tait and *Ewan Christian*. Christian restored nave and transept roofs to their original pitches, and generally replaced Perp and Perp-survival work with the more approved-of Dec. He made a grand doorway into the S transept entry, making good at last the loss of the presumed W door. The parish congregation moved out again to his new church of St Mary (*see* No. 3 The Abbey, p. 238), allowing *G. E. Street* in 1871–80 to clear the vacated nave of pews and galleries, and remove the partition between nave and crossing. Street provided new presbytery furnishings, although only the bishop's throne survives, and remodelled the Fratry. *Sir Charles Nicholson* followed, with an abortive scheme to rebuild the nave and part of the cloister, and then from 1947 *S. E. Dykes Bower,* who created the regimental chapel in the nave and St Wilfrid's Chapel in the N transept. Excavations for the TREASURY in 1988–90, under the demolished nave N aisle, showed that the Norman nave had been built upon Roman remains and a Viking cemetery, so it is not surprising it gave trouble. The Treasury is by *Ray Nichol.*

EXTERIOR

The mismatch between the truncated Norman nave – narrow, crooked, hoary – and the lantern-like E.E. and Dec choir, so much higher, wider, and ruddier, remains disconcerting. The unhappy junction at the crossing is not helped by Strickland's weak, off-centre tower.

The NAVE is built mainly of small square blackened stones, probably Roman, with buttresses at the chopped-off W end tumbling down to a pair of orphaned piers. Discontinuities in the masonry, as on the W side of the S transept where it switches to red stone above the second storey, tell of different building campaigns. The master of the clerestory level has set the work out more evenly than the rest, with more decoration, but in general the Norman work is pretty rough. Windows where they survive are shafted, with scallop capitals and enriched arches: on the N side to both aisle and clerestory, on the S side to the clerestory only. Beneath the parapet is a corbel table of masks carrying stones flat on face but moulded in their reveals. At the E end of the nave is the doorway into the missing cloister, blocked since the transept S entrance was made. The present W window in the partition wall is by *Ewan Christian*. Against the N side a vestry by *Dykes Bower*, 1957. The SOUTH TRANSEPT has its Norman E and W clerestory still, and a single triforium window on the W. A little survives of the S gable too, but otherwise the transept front is all of the 1850s. The NORTH TRANSEPT is largely a rebuilding by Bishop Strickland (1400–19), necessitated by the fall of the tower. It has neither a W nor an E clerestory. The large N window in Early Dec style is by *Christian*, and likewise the round window over, with its seven circles. Strickland's narrow TOWER, aligned on the Norman nave, has Perp bell-openings and battlements and a higher, square stair-turret. The odd length of wall extending N from its NE corner was needed to make the connection with the widened choir.

The CHOIR is a spectacular piece. It is confusing only at first that it patently belongs to two styles, E.E. and Dec. The N and S walls of the aisles are E.E., with a system of regular lancet pairs with blank arches l. and r. on the N side and on the E bays of the S side. Shafts with shaft-rings, and canted buttresses. The western bays on the S side, where the Norman choir was finally taken down, are more irregular, with chamfered lancets in stepped groups of three, without shafting; the two westernmost have proto-tracery in the form of circles in the spandrels. The short easternmost bay has two-light windows with cusped and enriched Y-tracery, i.e. Dec. The remains of a vaulted building on this side are those of a sacristy. The clerestory is entirely Dec, and completely flat with tripartite windows simply punched into it. Tracery patterns differ considerably, but reticulation occurs several times. The C14 E termination is the show front of the building. The great E window is a gorgeous display of flowing tracery, 51 ft (16 metres) high, of nine lights, divided 4–1–4, with the middle light expanding into a bulbous shape with internal tracery and the side parts developing tracery of the type with leaves off a stem. Big buttresses l. and r. with niches plus Victorian statues in two tiers on its upper parts. In the gable a big spherical-triangular window with tracery in the form of three spherical triangles. Pinnacles from the 1850s restoration climb the gable

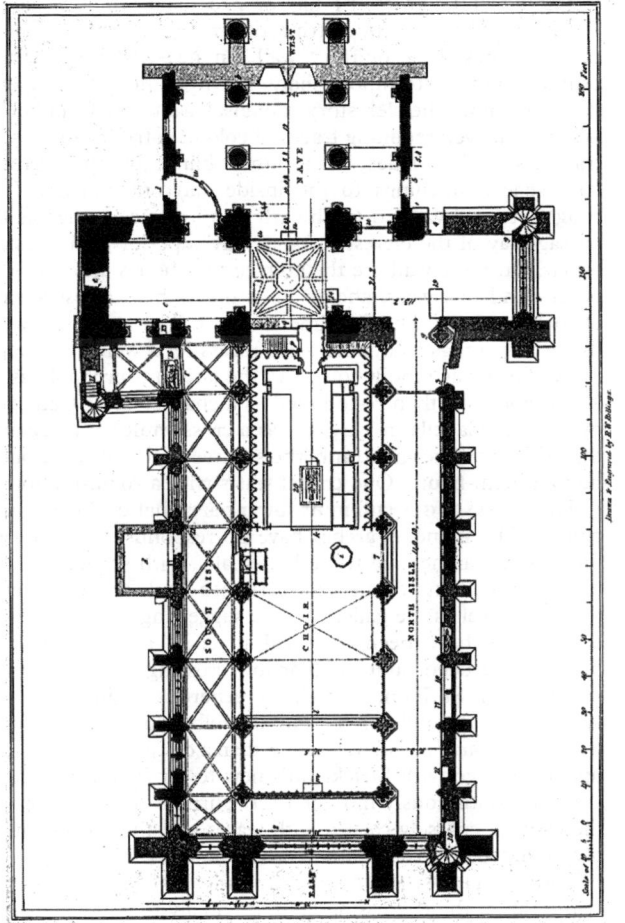

Carlisle Cathedral.
Plan, 1840

slopes. The aisle ends are unequal, with a stair-turret N and heavy pinnacles S, and windows like the easternmost of the S aisle.

INTERIOR

Entry to the cathedral is by *Christian*'s door into the S transept. [17] Transept, crossing and stumpy nave pack a massive punch, claustrophobic, austere, poorly lit, overhung by the enormous organ pipes on the screen, and thrown off-balance by the asymmetric entrance to the choir.

The SOUTH TRANSEPT has or had plain windows and a clerestory with the stepped tripartite arrangement so typical of the Norman style, as on the W wall. On the S wall only the easternmost and westernmost shafts survived the insertion of a larger window. The clerestory capitals, hard to see from below, are carved, even retaining traces of colour. A triforium passage traverses all three sides, but is almost blind: just three irregularly spaced openings to the inside and one outside. It is roughly tunnel-vaulted (with early C19 iron ties), whereas the passageway of the clerestory, generally superior to the rest, is ashlar. On the E wall are the arch to the choir S aisle, with an outer band of zigzag, and to its r. the arch to a lost apsidal chapel (as at e.g. Dunfermline Abbey, begun 1128). Between the two openings a cupboard-like recess for a well. The chapel (now shop) was rebuilt square in the late C13, probably as an E transept aisle, then re-founded as a chantry of St Catherine by John de Capella in 1342. It has a cross-vault with elegantly thin E.E. ribs standing on corbels, three with stiff-leaf, one a human demi-figure. One corbel starts with a roguish knot.

The CROSSING is still in its lower parts that of the Norman church. The E and W arches have no responds, but those on the N and S arches are triple half-shafts, with scalloped capitals of a broad and elementary early C12 kind. These are set at the same level as the gallery string, suggesting that diaphragm arches may have been intended to cross the transepts, or indeed have been built. Similar low crossings can be seen at e.g. Chester St John, though its generous width takes the arches up to a good height, and at Melbourne in Derbyshire, where they carry a walkway rather than a diaphragm wall.* The upper parts go with Strickland's new tower. The triple shafts are now continuously moulded (cf. Furness Abbey W tower), the capitals coarsely carved with leaves and the arches multiply moulded. Overhead a tierceron star-vault.

The NORTH TRANSEPT, mostly early C15, has Perp tracery at the top of the N crossing arch, originally to allow light into the crossing over its flat roof; nave and S transept were the same, but all three roofs were raised to a more 'correct' pitch by *Christian*. The arch to the Norman choir aisle, with zigzag like the S one, is ruthlessly interrupted by an E.E. arch to the present, wider aisle. Arch and wall above are horribly fractured. From the choir the blocked Norman gallery arch can be seen.

Of the NAVE there remain just two bays, walled off W of the second pair of piers. It feels as though there is almost as much stone as air, so little free space is there. The closely spaced piers, fat and round, but not tall, carry round arches with two slight chamfers, a late C12 characteristic. Round capitals, many-scalloped on the S side, plain on the N. Some of the bases have spurs, as at Melbourne and Warwick. There are triple responds against the aisle walls, and wall arches too on the N

*See Richard Plant in *Carlisle and Cumbria: British Archaeological Association Conference Transactions* 27, 2004.

side, but no aisle vaults. The gallery has raw single-step openings without subdivisions, the clerestory the same tripartite
arrangement as the transept. Half-shafts start up above the
arcade capitals but only get as far as the gallery string.

CHOIR. After the dim confines of the nave, its breadth and   26
height, light and colour are exhilarating, all the more so for the
unpromisingly offset entry under the organ. Looking back at
the crossing we have the reverse effect; the entry is now central,
but crossing arch and organ pipes are jammed to one side of
a blank expanse of battered stonework. Otherwise we are in a
sublime room. Six full bays, plus a shorter bay at each end,
giving an almost classical sense of completion and contain-
ment. Arcades, triforium and clerestory in balance, with
nothing extreme, neither a vertical rush to the heavens, nor a
horizontal one towards the altar. The brightly lit depth between
the two skins of the clerestory is the most notable spatial effect.

The puzzle is to determine the effect of the fire of 1292. Stylistically there is no problem: E.E. equals pre-fire, Dec equals
post-fire. Clearly E.E., i.e. *c.* 1220–50, are the outer walls,
cinquefoiled with small dogtooth on the N but not the S, and
the shafted lancets. Likewise the ribbed aisle vaults, and the
main arcade arches, of many mouldings with prominent dogtooth on the inner sides, and a hoodmould with small nailhead. Equally clearly Dec, i.e. early C14, are not only the
triforium and clerestory above, and the easternmost bay, but
the piers beneath. How was this done? Either the damaged
piers could have been replaced one by one under the propped-
up arches and aisle vaults, or the vaults and arches were taken
down and rebuilt. The piers have eight strong shafts with sharp
fillets on the diagonals. Deep continuous hollows between the
shafts. The beautiful bell-shaped capitals are made of several
pieces of stone. Peeping forth from the nobbly foliage are, on
the outer sides, fox and goose, harpies, musician and tumbler,
owl and mouse – similar subjects to the misericords (*see* p. 231).
On the inner sides the Labours of the Months. Starting SE: 24
January as Janus (three-faced, not two) is feasting. February
toasts his toes by the fire. March digs, April prunes. May offers
new growth, June goes hawking. On the N side July is mowing,
August weeding, September reaping, October harvesting
grapes. November sowing, while December is killing an ox and
feeding pigs. It is frustrating that the western carvings are
hidden by the choir canopies. Reaching down to the triforium
sill string are the long, finely carved Dec corbels of the wall-
shafts, showing that above here all is post-fire. The triforium
has three small two-light openings per bay with reticulation
units. The clerestory is still tripartite, but very bare, except for
the wall-passage parapet with its quatrefoil openings.

The arch into the N transept from the aisle, already noted
above, is of the same kind as those of the choir arcades. As it
happens a complete E.E. pier, presumably like those removed
from the choir after the fire, has been left to its N, visible from

Carlisle Cathedral, choir north aisle.
Engraving, 1840

the aisle. The outer wall swerves out to avoid it. The pier base is waterholding. All eight shafts have flat fillets. The capital would also hold water were it upside-down, i.e. it is deeply scooped, with a little dogtooth. The arch-and-a-bit that it carries are like those of the main arcades, with prominent dogtooth. What is it doing here? Jennifer Alexander suggests that the N transept had been given an eastern aisle which was not rebuilt after the fall of the tower. A bit more arcading heading N may be seen outside.

Now for the short half-bay at the E end. This probably represents an extension of the C13 aisles up to meet the line of the E wall of the central vessel, which would therefore have projected a little beyond the aisles. The wall arcade loses its dogtooth, and its capitals and corbels now have naturalistic Dec leaves. For the great E window, rivalling the W window of York Minster (1338), we have a date c. 1340.* The puzzle lies with the arcade arches and the aisle vaults, both still E.E., albeit rather distorted. A pair of abortive flying ribs sprout from the E respond. Is this the start of an intended rebuild of all the choir aisle vaults?

The brightly coloured barrel CEILING is, surprisingly, medieval. The collar-beam trusses that support it have been dated c. 1355 by dendrochronology. *Thomas Pitt* in 1764 hid it above a plaster vault, cutting the tie-beams. *Ewan Christian*, having revealed and restored it in the 1850s, left their stumps like three pairs of functionless hammerbeams. Its stunning colour scheme, bright blue with gilded stars and angels, was devised by *Owen Jones* and carried out by *Scott & Drape* of Carlisle in the 1850s. Repainted in 1970 under *Dykes Bower*, and superbly lit by a new system of 2005, it is especially exciting from outside at night.

UPPER PARTS. The NE corner stair, presumably of about 1340, is unusually broad, topped with a pretty umbrella-vault with a rib-ring. Behind the triforium openings, entirely unmoulded at the back, are the medieval aisle roofs. The clerestory passage runs between the two skins of the wall with flat paving overhead. A long mural passage links them up and over the E window, giving access to the space above the barrel ceiling of the choir, where a forest of criss-crossed stainless-steel braces supplements the single-framed medieval structure. The lower part of the tower stair belongs with the rebuilt choir, and seems to have survived the fall as it has a decorative umbrella-vault just like that at the NE. A passage crosses the spur wall to a mural passage round the tower proper at vault springing level.

FURNISHINGS AND MONUMENTS

Choir and choir aisles

ALTAR, REREDOS and BALDACCHINO are by *Charles Nicholson*, 1936. The trick was to make an impact in front of the powerful back-lighting of the E window while blocking as little of it as possible. Filigree detail on a simple rectangular form; the effect Gothic, taking its cue from the SE chapel screens, but the forms Free Renaissance. All-over gilding in 1970 by *S. E. Dykes Bower* enables it compete on more even terms. – BISHOP'S THRONE by *Street*, 1880; the only survivor of a whole set of Street furnishings. Boxy openwork above, and a spire. – STALLS. Forty-six. Attributed to Bishop Strickland

---

*On grounds of stylistic similarity John Harvey attributed the Carlisle E window to the mason *Ivo de Raghton*, his candidate for the designer of the W window at York.

(1400–19), so between the late C14 sets at Worcester and
Chester and the late C15/early C16 sets at Ripon and Manchester, and perhaps closest to the westermost stalls at
Norwich of *c*. 1420. They have unusually good poppyheads
composed of upside-down lions, grimacing monsters etc. Arms
with figure and leaf-work, ends with blank tracery. The
canopies are said to be Prior Haythwaite's, i.e. after 1430, originally with many statuettes. The stall-work retains traces of
colour, especially where it wraps around the w end of the choir
under the organ. The organist's pulpitum is a survivor of
Thomas Pitt's work, *c*. 1765, likewise the DOORS to the Bishop's
and the Dean's stalls. Much graffitti of the 1590s on the stall
fronts. The lower stalls are by *Nicholson*, extended 1976 by
Dykes Bower, with Renaissance detail. Full set of MISERI-
CORDS, deeply undercarved, with expressively drilled eyes,
sharply delineated feathers and scales, and flexible and curvaceous postures. Splendid laughing wyvern under stall S5.
Nearby s the Pelican in her Piety, lion and wyvern fighting,
wild man and dragon, mermaid and mirror. On the N side the
Coronation of the Virgin, angels making music. – PAINTINGS
on the stall backs, facing the choir aisles. On the N the Apostles, each accompanied by a phrase of the Creed, and cycles
of St Anthony and of St Cuthbert. On the s, appropriately for
an Augustinian priory, a cycle of St Augustine of Hippo. Each
scene has a blackletter caption in northern English ('unthek'
for un-thatch). Pevsner was dismissive ('all bad'), but they are
bold and lively, and this is one of the most complete survivals
in the country. They are later than the stalls themselves; the
monogram of Prior Gondibour (*c*. 1465–1500) appears in the
Augustine cycle. The Cuthbert scenes can be linked to a
Durham illuminated *Life* of *c*. 1200, which may have been
made available for copying through Bishop Bell (1478–95). –
SALKELD SCREEN, to the N aisle. Lancelot Salkeld was the
last Prior, surrendering in 1540 to Thomas Cromwell himself.
The screen is perhaps the first thing he did on being made
Dean in 1541.* The screen is an uncommonly complete
example of English Early Renaissance decoration, a world
away from the Gothic stalls. Profile heads in lozenges and
medallions, stylized dolphins, balusters instead of mullions. –
PULPIT. Inscribed 1559, it concords well with the Salkeld
screen, but has an entirely different provenance. It was bought
from Cockayne Hatley church (Beds.) in 1963, whence it had
been imported in 1825 from St Andrew in Antwerp. Hexagonal, on a foot with bulbous brackets ending in claws, with a
curved stair which has false-perspective architecture carved
upon its solid sides. Brackets of straining figures trapped in
strapwork support the pulpit proper. Fluted angle colonnettes
and little pedimented aedicules with statuettes of the Evangelists. – ARMOIRE in the N choir aisle. Also associated with Prior
Gondibour. It is painted with plants, like a herbal; graffiti

44

*Ejected in 1548, reappointed under Mary in 1553, he survived Elizabeth's acces-
sion (though the Bishop was ejected), and died in 1560.

include the name Sawrey Gilpin 1747. – SCREENS to St Catherine's Chapel (choir s aisle and transept). Late C15 and again associated with Prior Gondibour, with intricate Flamboyant but flat forms of Scottish or Flemish type. Thought to be *ex situ* remnants of screening round the whole of the choir.

STAINED GLASS. The great E window retains much glass of *c*. 1340–50 in its tracery. It was restored by *Wailes* of Newcastle in 1856. It is a Doom. Christ in Majesty appears in the topmost quatrefoil. Below that is a pair of yellowish quatrefoils depicting the Heavenly City, and under that a splendid Hell, with a huge eye, red flames, and the damned against blue and green. The lesser lights show the saved and the damned, often as single figures contorted to fit the opening, with fully modelled, characterful faces. The main part of the window is by *John Hardman Powell* of the *Hardman* firm, 1859–61. Bluer and less opaque than the tracery. The subject (originally probably a Tree of Jesse) is the New Testament narrative from the Annunciation to the Ascension. The many individual scenes are linked transversely by bands of tiny roundels. In the two outer lights some scenes run together vertically, and the three central lights can read as one, with figures clustered in mandorla shapes around the central representation. The faces are diagrammatic, often wearing a slightly pained expression. – Choir s aisle E by *Wailes*, easternmost s by *A. K. Nicholson*, 1920, the next two of 1922 and 1931 by *Powells*. – Choir N aisle E and second from W by *Clayton & Bell* (†1893, †1909).

MONUMENTS. Behind the High Altar, Bishop Waldegrave †1869, marble effigy on grey tomb-chest, by *John Adams-Acton*, 1872. White and asleep. – On the E wall, Archdeacon William Paley †1805; just the simplest plaque. – Sir James Robert George Graham of Netherby †1861; half-figure in relief. – Bishop John Wareing Bardsley †1904. By *Andrea Carlo Lucchesi*, 1906. Strange bronze tablet, as though cut out in leather. The style similar to Alfred Gilbert, but broader and balder. – In the middle of the choir the splendid BRASS of Bishop Bell †1496, a former Prior of Durham. He stands in full canonicals, reciting the credo, under a triple canopy, with four hexameters under his feet (*see also* Rose Castle).

Choir s aisle. Brass to Bishop Henry Robinson †1616. Behind his kneeling figure is the complete cathedral, but disappointingly generalized; it could represent any church. Many figures and inscriptions in the style of the time, e.g. 'Deadly feude extinct', and one in Greek. – Dean Hastings Rashdall †1924; portrait head in bronze relief. – Canon Hardwicke Rawnsley †1920; profile bronze set in green Lake District slate. – Dean Francis Close †1882. Marble effigy under a wooden canopy. By *H. H. Armstead*, 1885. – Bishop Harvey Goodwin †1891. Bronze effigy by *Hamo Thornycroft*, 1894. – Purbeck marble effigy of a bishop, identified by the VCH and others as Bishop Barrow †1429, but dated by Pevsner a century earlier. Very good. He lies on a plain Purbeck tomb-chest with thinly outlined large quatrefoils.

Choir N aisle. Double tomb-recess, with a segmental head starting on short vertical pieces. The arch aggressively decorated with short stumps running in two different directions. They appear to be broken off; perhaps originally an undercut zigzag. One recess is empty; under the other an excellent though battered Purbeck marble effigy of a bishop, perhaps Bishop Sylvester †1224; the same type as those at Ely of the 1250s. He has a pointed trefoiled canopy and originally shafts l. and r. One stiff-leaf capital survives. – Bishop Edmund Law †1787, tablet by *T. Banks*. Faith resting. Her hand on the mitre. Fluted obelisk behind.

Transepts, crossing and nave

INSCRIPTION. Scratched on a stone immediately inside the S door is a Runic inscription going back to Henry I's time, translated as 'Dolphin wrote these runes on this stone'. – FONT. Overcomplicated piece of 1891 by *Sir Arthur Blomfield*. Hexagonal, in an unpleasantly shiny stone with three bronze figures bracketed out (sculptor *F. W. Pomeroy*). The cover is missing. – BROUGHAM TRIPTYCH, St Wilfrid's Chapel (N transept). Made *c.* 1520, perhaps for a church in Cologne. Bought for St Wilfrid's Chapel at Brougham (q.v.) in the 1840s, and installed here in 1979. It is a typically animated, coloured and three-dimensional narrative of the Passion of Christ in framed compartments, with smaller scenes of his Life below and, at the base, the Tree of Jesse. The open hand of the *Antwerp Guild of Carvers* appears on nearly every group of figures. Other chapel fittings by *S. E. Dykes Bower*, 1979, include an iron SCREEN incorporating C19 altar rails etc. from Chelmsford Cathedral, and STALLS by *Bodley* from St Paul, Manchester. – The REGIMENTAL CHAPEL in the nave was created by *Dykes Bower* in 1949 for the Border Regiment, rearranged in 2000. The SCREEN is modelled on C16 Spanish work, with widely spaced bars like attenuated balusters, and candlestick-like finials and cresting on top. STALLS and ALTAR RAILS, Renaissance, with cherubs and wreaths.

STAINED GLASS, clockwise from the SE. In St Catherine's Chapel a beautiful and poignant window by *Veronica Whall c.* 1926, to a young man killed at Arras in 1916. By *Hardman* the attractive rose over the S door (1883) depicting the Seven Days of Creation. Nave S aisle, Border Regiment memorial of 1884 by *Hardman*, possibly to a design by *Matthews & Hodgson*. Standard-bearers in C19 uniform below. Also by Hardman the S aisle W window (1880), and main W window, like the E window, but later (1870) and more economical, with small scenes against a geometric background. – Nave N aisle W, Fisher Memorial window, 1987 by *Harry Harvey*. – Fragments of old glass in the nave N, with purplish grisaille background, re-set by *Caroline Townshend* and *Joan Howson* in 1925. – N transept W by *Wailes*, *c.* 1846. – Large N transept window by *Hardman*, 1858.

MONUMENTS. N transept. Simon Senhouse, Prior, †c.1520. Plain black slab on a tomb-chest with shields in quatrefoils. – Capt. J. R. Graham †1830; grieving lady, broken column. – Richard Assheton, Lord Privy Seal and 1st Viscount Cross, of Broughton-in-Furness, †1914. Brass set in a stone frame with a grand achievement of arms over. – Hugh James †1817 by *Regnart*, and exceptionally busy. Two small allegorical figures l. and r. of a short sarcophagus. Urn on the top. – Tablet to Elizabeth and John Johnson †1792 and 1800, by *Nollekens*. – Canon Fletcher †1846, brass designed by *Pugin*, made by *Hardman*.

S transept. Something of a literary and artistic *omnium gatherum*. Elizabeth Dunbar †1821, infant daughter of the sculptor, *David Dunbar*. Of 1860. Poignantly chubby figure asleep on a fat cushion. – Also by *Dunbar*, Robert Anderson †1833, with profile portrait. – Musgrave Lewthwaite Watson, sculptor †1847; good relief portrait by *George Nelson*, 1859. – Norman Nicholson †1987, bronze bust in a niche. – Thomas Sheffield. Roundel by *G. Nelson*, 1856; seated figure, reading: a Flaxman motif. – George Moore of Wigton †1876, suitably bold profile bust in Victorian dress by *John Adams-Acton*. – Susanna Blamire †1794, poetess; floor plaque 1994.

Nave. Mainly military, and concentrated in the short S aisle. Crimean memorial by *John Steell*, Edinburgh, 1859; sorrowing angel with trumpet and wreath. Also several individual brasses by *Hardman*. – South African War, 1908. Large plaque in alabaster, mosaic and *opus sectile*. – First World War, 1922. Green slate slab with lettering in relief picked out gold and red, a stone frame carved with the names of battles, and outside that the names of the dead. – Artillery memorial of beaten bronze. Roses r., vines l., Heavenly City on top. – N aisle, Melchior la Beaume of Bengal †1791. Adamish; urn and colonnettes elegantly swagged.

MONASTIC BUILDINGS

The Cloister

The CLOISTER was not large, and must have been a few steps down from the cathedral floor level. Not much is left, but a certain amount can be pieced together. S of the S transept is a path with a low wall on the E, a high wall on the W. This path represents the E range, i.e. the UNDERCROFT of the dormitory, as rebuilt in the C13. This was vaulted, as the heavy springers show. The ribs were single-chamfered. The double doorway from the cloister to the chapter house vestibule survives, as does the corresponding single inner doorway, half-sunk in the ground. Both are of the mid or later C13. The vestibule doorway has a trumeau, and the twin arches sit in a super-arch in the way Y-tracery is formed. The vestibule was rib-vaulted, the CHAPTER HOUSE itself octagonal, as the start of the wall N of the doorway and a single angle shaft prove, and almost certainly vaulted. It measured *c.* 12 ft (4 metres) to a side – about the same as Cockersand of *c.* 1250, which has a central pier, and Whalley (both North Lancs.). The upper storey of the E range contained the DORMITORY, 'utterly ruinated in the late times of troubles' and pulled down along with the chapter house after 1639. One small lancet opening remains in the E wall of the refectory (*see* below); also the outline of the roof upon the S transept. The Fratry or refectory (*see* below) was, as usual, in the S range. It also lay on the first floor. On the ground floor in the SE corner is the doorway to a passage or slype leading S out of the cloister. To its l., the doorway to the dormitory day stair, which survives enclosed within the refectory (the night-stair door into the church was lost when the present S transept entrance was created). The S view of the refectory range here is quite irregular and picturesque with a small turret.

The FRATRY or refectory stands to its full height. It was built *c.* 1300 and remodelled in the late C15 by Prior Gondibour, whose initials appear on a keystone of the undercroft vault. The corbels to the N show where the cloister roof was. The undercroft (now a café) is a beautiful room. It has a row of very low octagonal piers along its longitudinal axis and vaults with hollow-chamfered ribs. The difference in moulding marks the difference between *c.* 1300 and the late C15. The large upper room was re-created by *Street* in 1880–1. He was ticked off by the Society for the Protection of Ancient Buildings for destroying an interesting late C17 reconstruction, which had already been modified *c.* 1812 by *Smirke.* The room has to the W a large Perp window, to the S also large Perp windows, and to the N small two-light windows entirely Dec (one reticulation unit). Built into the S wall is the refectory pulpit for a reader at meal-times, set flush rather than jutting out oriel-wise as is more usual. It is a delightful piece with original Perp tracery to the S (a window, smaller than the others) and to the N as well. Its flat ceiling is also decorated with blank tracery. In the W wall are two hatches, no doubt to the former kitchen. Three niches were moved back to the E wall by *Street.* They contain over-large figures by *Josefina de Vasconcellos* (1989). Characteristic Street roof, door furniture, gratings, bookcases. The SW porch is a reconstruction by *Street* on the line of the cloister walk.

From the corner of the refectory the walls of the W range can just be seen for a few inches. The rest is missing.

The Abbey

The customary name given to the precinct of monastic and canonical buildings sheltered by the cathedral on the S. The description is from W to E.

GATEHOUSE to the precinct from the W. A rebuilding dated 1528 over the W arch. Also Prior Slee's inscribed *orate* in blackletter. Both E and W arches are round and triple-chamfered.

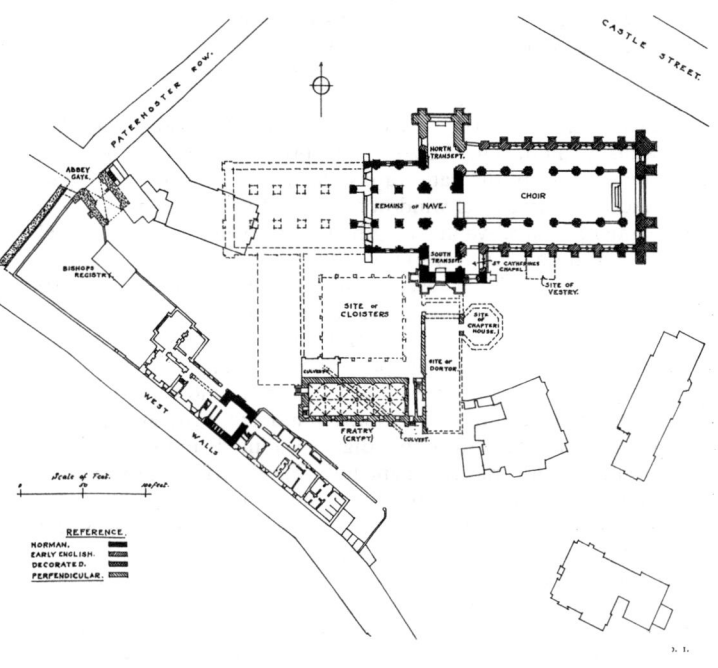

Carlisle, cathedral and precinct.
Plan by J.H. Martindale, 1924

Midway between the two a division between pedestrian and carriage entrance. Both parts of the gatehouse are tunnel-vaulted. Above the E arch a typical early C16 window with uncusped lights. Integral two-storey lodge to the NE.

No. 2 The Abbey adjoins the gatehouse on the N. It was rebuilt in 1669–70 of stone from Wetheral Priory; many masons' marks can be seen. Five bays. Broad rustication round the doorway. Originally a T-plan, with the stair in the downstroke. This has been filled in to make a double pile, with early brickwork. Windows, now sashed, were cross-mullioned (see the staircase window at the back). A couple of bolection-moulded fireplaces survive upstairs, one in a complete panelled room of the period. *C. J. Ferguson* was responsible for the inner porch and a nice two-bay screen to the stair. Canon Hardwicke Rawnsley and Edith left their mark on a pair of cupboard doors dated 1909.

BISHOP SMITH'S REGISTRY, to the s as one enters. Dated 1699 on the re-cut lintel. A fetching little building of brick, single-storeyed with just two bays plus one entrance bay, but fire-places at both ends. Restored by *S. E. Dykes Bower* in the 1950s, adding the moulded surrounds and the open curly pediment to the doorway.

DEANERY AND PRIOR'S TOWER, again on the s side, with West Walls behind. The TOWER was probably started by Prior Gondibour in the late 1490s; finished by Prior Senhouse (1500–20). Big oriel windows to N and S. Its basement has a segmental barrel-vault strengthened by seven single-chamfered ribs. A mural stair leads up from the vestibule to the splendid solar, its oriels (their reveals also rib-vaulted) looking over the town walls on one side, towards the cathedral on the other. Spectacular painted ceiling with Prior Senhouse's mottoes and badges – the Dacre scallop, Senhouse popinjay, and roses – repeated over and over again like a mantra, and carved bosses. The ceiling beams are moulded and stopped, and prettily arched in one direction. Big flat-jointed fireplace, finely moulded, with traceried panelling above, perhaps C16 French. The rest of the panelling, bolection-molded, probably dates from the time of Dean Smith (1671–84). Mural passages and chambers in all the corners. Another mural stair to the next floor, which may also have had a painted ceiling, and a turning stair to the roof. To the W and E of the tower are ranges for the DEANERY, as reconstructed by Dean Smith in 1671–4. The W range incorporates pre-C17 fabric interpreted as the hall range to the tower. To the outside here a blank, vertically placed oval with a coat of arms. The further W addition is of 1853. (In the hall range the C17 stair with dumb-bell balusters upside-down. In the further room an enormous fireplace.) The E range, of two-and-a-half storeys, keeps the lower walls of the late C15 structure. The segmental-pedimented doorway and the window surrounds are mid-C20 improvements by *Dykes Bower*. Late C15 STABLE range immediately E, now Nos. 9 and 10. Single-storey, mossily stone-roofed, with Prior Gondibour's initials on a doorway.

No. 1, E of the Fratry, is much altered but may contain C17 fabric. No. 3, S of the E end of the cathedral at an angle, is an amply proportioned house of *c.* 1683–5, of dark red brick. Seven bays, with segment-headed windows. String course with bricks sticking out triangularly. Originally one room deep, without corridors, with the broad staircase with its stout balusters in a projection at the back. From its garden can be seen the aisle wall, with blocked windows, of the lost St Mary's church by *Ewan Christian*, built in 1870 and demolished in 1954.

The GATES and SCREEN at the E end of the Abbey are by *Lorimer & Matthew* of Edinburgh, 1930. – LODGE, 1890.

BARN. *See* St Cuthbert, below.

CHURCHES

For churches outside the city centre *see* pp. 256–66.

ST CUTHBERT, St Cuthbert's Lane, off the Market Place. Solidly Georgian; rebuilt in 1778–9. Its orientation SW–NE suggests an origin when the Roman street pattern was still extant. The builders were Messrs *Hayton, Lowthian & Lowrey*. Of dark red stone. Stumpy W tower made to look more so because it is embraced by the gallery staircases. It has a lead cap of ogee outline. Nave of eight bays and two storeys, and a short, low chancel. The windows are square-headed with flat frames in two tiers, and there are gallery doors in bays one and eight. Venetian window at the E end. Inside, the gallery is carried on Tuscan columns, and on it is an upper tier of Doric columns, each carrying its own bit of triglyph entablature. Flat ceiling. Furnishings all C19 and C20. – PULPIT. A phenomenal contraption by *J. H. Martindale* and the crane-makers *Cowans, Sheldon & Co.*, which can be wound across on rails from the wings, as it were, to fill the space between the choir stalls. – STAINED GLASS. E window by *Ward & Hughes*, 1868. N, York School glass of high quality, C14 (a figure under a fine canopy) and C15. Reassembled by the *York Glaziers Trust*, 1961. Also N, St Mary, lilies, and the two Carlisle churches signed R.R.N., i.e. *Ray R. Nichol*, Surveyor to the Cathedral 1985–97, and a Latvian refugees' window of 1982 designed by *John Rees*, made by *Elders Walker Millican Ltd*. On the S side six oval scenes from the life of St Cuthbert, by *A. K. Nicholson*, 1948–54 except one by *G. E. R. Smith*. – MONUMENTS. William Giles †1797 and his wife †1814, by *Paul Nixson*. Urn in an aedicule with Roman Doric columns. – Elizabeth Connell †1825, by *Dunbar*. Big cherub with a torch, by an urn. – Rev. John Fawcett †1851, by *W. Jackson*. Marble bust in front of drapery. – Some late medieval monuments have fetched up in Ainstable church (q.v.).

PARISH ROOM NW of the church. One of the handful of Cumbrian buildings with a fully developed, if not complete, timber frame. It was built as a TITHE BARN by Prior Gondibour around the 1470s (his shield was found, but is no longer visible), in the SE corner of the abbey precinct. Low red sandstone building, 120 ft (37 metres) long, with a big roof. In the E gable a two-light window with cusped lights. Although the timbers are much renewed the structure is at it was, of seven bays, open on massive posts one side, resting on a section of the precinct wall on the other. The closed side, with splayed slit windows, has short wall-posts and cross-braces. There is no evidence for longitudinal bracing, and the wall-plate is discontinuous, not scarfed. The wall, in other words, is primary. The open side is properly jowled and scarfed, with big curved longitudinal braces up to the wall-plate. Heavy kingpost trusses with two or three pairs of raking queenposts. Restored and converted by *Norman Phillips* in 1969–71. The w end wall was rebuilt in blockwork in 1998.

VICARAGE, West Walls. *See* Perambulation, p. 253.

CHURCH OF SCOTLAND, Chapel Street. 1832–4. Straightforward boxy chapel of brown stone, very broad, three bays under a pedimented gable. The windows are tall and arched. It was floored at gallery level in 1979, bringing the church close to the pitch pine of the arch-braced roof.

85 CONGREGATIONAL CHURCH (now United Reformed), Lowther Street. 1842–3; designed *c.* 1838 by *John Nichol*, Edinburgh-born but then of Carlisle. Terrific Frenchy-Scottish Renaissance façade of three bays, set into the terrace – as Pevsner says, neither religiously nor stylistically in conformity. Curly gable and side-pieces with speared ball finials. The middle bay pushes out over the entrance, with quoins alternating like opening and closing brackets. Very tall square-topped windows, with mullions and four tiers of transoms in wood, the lights round-arched at the top. Over each window a strapwork flourish on consoles, and extra ears halfway down. The interior is quieter. Foyer with twin cantilevered stairs with curly iron balusters. Short auditorium with U-shaped gallery on slender quatrefoil-section columns, presumably of iron. Ceiling flat over the galleries, raised in a semicircular cove in the middle, with roundels. E. W. Hodge notes STAINED GLASS by *B. D. Walmsley* of Langdale, 1928 with *Lewis Davies*.

METHODIST CENTRAL HALL, Fisher Street. *See* p. 252.

QUAKER MEETING HOUSE, Fisher Street, at the castle end. On the remnant of their 1681 burial ground. By *Hodgson & Tritton*, 1963. Like a mobile classroom. For the earlier meeting houses at No. 23 Fisher Street *see* p. 252.

PUBLIC BUILDINGS

27 CARLISLE CASTLE. Triangular enceinte on the high promontory between the rivers Eden and Caldew, with marshy land, now Bitts Park, at its feet. The inner bailey forms another, smaller triangle at the eastern apex.

In 1092 William II (Rufus) gave orders to build a castle and fortify the town when he expelled the local ruler, Dolfin. There is no trace of Rufus's castle but he may well have established the shape of inner and outer baileys. Henry I came in 1122, founded the Augustinian priory and paid for the town's castle and walls. John A. A. Goodall makes a convincing case for Henry I as the builder of the Great Tower, starting then or in 1133 when he created the bishopric.* By 1136 however Carlisle was in the hands of the Scots, and it was King David who

---

* In *Carlisle and Cumbria: British Archaeological Association Conference Transactions* 27, 2004.

probably completed it. In 1157 they handed the castle back to Henry II, who was responsible for the stone inner and outer curtain walls. Edward I made it the centre of his Scottish campaign, ordering a hall to be built in 1301. A new outer gatehouse was built in 1378–83, the Tile Tower in 1483–5. The Pilgrimage of Grace of 1536–7, highlighting the poor state of the castle and the weakness of the king's hold on the North, led to modernization by *Stefan von Haschenperg* from 1539, matching the new citadel at the S end of the city. Battlements and turrets were cut down, giving the castle a streamlined look. The inner curtain walls were thickened with a huge earth bank to take guns, entailing massive buttressing on the NE, and outworks, and the Great Tower was reconfigured inside. However, Haschenperg was sacked in 1543, 'having spent great treasures to no purpose', and was succeeded by *William Garforth* then *John Rogers*. Mary Queen of Scots was here in 1568. Lord Scrope, appointed warden of the Western Marches in 1570, built a range (mostly gone) by the S curtain wall. By 1633 the castle was without portcullises or drawbridges, but in 1639 the king's impending war with Scotland brought emergency work to city and castle by *Heinrick van Peere*. NW and SW batteries (not extant?) were built of stone from the cathedral's chapter house and cloister, 1639–40. In 1645, when Charles I was defeated at Naseby, the city capitulated. With the Restoration in 1660 Carlisle's military significance once more decreased. The last time it saw action was in 1745. French prisoners of war were held here in 1758–63. A new role as a permanent garrison against civil unrest saw much unsentimental clearing away in the 1830s, when the raised and levelled outer bailey was ringed with barrack blocks. The depot closed in 1959.

The castle was separated from the town by two ditches, the inner placed some distance from the outer. The outer ditch, which had become built up, is now occupied by the A595 road (1972–4). In the W wall, strictly part of the town defences, is the Tile Tower, rebuilt in brick for artillery in 1483–5 by Richard of Gloucester (Richard III). The earliest documented brick in the city (it was thought resistant to cannonade), it has vaults of four-centre profile on two levels.

The Outer Gatehouse or De Ireby's Tower in the S wall was the Warden's house. Built in 1167–8, reconstructed 1378–83 for Lord Scrope's occupation. The rebuilding contract has survived, naming as mason *John Lewyn*, who was to be paid 500 marks for tower, barbican and gate. Lewyn built the cloister and the great cathedral kitchen at Durham, as well as rebuilding the keep there; he seems to have been primarily a fortifications man. The barbican has corbels for a wooden gallery. The outer arch is segmental, the inner pointed. Ground-floor rooms are tunnel-vaulted. Straight mural stair up to the living quarters, a complete little manor house. First a small hall with the portcullis mechanism beside the fire. A door beside the high table leads through to a family apartment; the kitchen is accessible from the low end, as is a chamber above via another mural stair.

The OUTER BAILEY is ringed with barrack blocks of brick named after campaigns. Surveying them clockwise from the sw corner, the stone-fronted officers' mess of 1876, occupying the site of the sw battery, is now regimental headquarters. There follows YPRES of 1836; GALLIPOLI of 1829, extended 1876, in front of the site of the NW battery; and on the N side ARROYO of 1804 by *Capt. Hartcup* for the Board of Ordnance. ARNHEM, Vanbrugh-like, was the master gunner's house of the 1660s, rebuilt 1804–5 again by *Hartcup*. ALMA, built 1932, from 1961 housed the county records.

Facing the parade ground on the E side is HALF MOON BATTERY, sunk into the inner moat in front of the inner gatehouse. It was made in 1542 by *Stefan von Haschenperg*. Partly demolished and infilled in the C19, excavated in the early C20.

The inner gatehouse behind the battery is called the CAPTAIN'S TOWER. A complicated building three storeys high. The front with its flat buttresses dates from the 1160s, the back from the late C14, but further modified in the C16 – see the window above the arch – when the curtain was widened for artillery. The passage has a pointed tunnel-vault, with murder holes in it. The C14 inner arch has a frill of cusped tracery, like an arched portcullis of stone: one of the few decorative features of the castle. A small doorway to the S leads into a vaulted chamber. The top doorway of the curving mural stair has a shouldered head.

The triangular Inner Bailey is crowded with buildings, with the keep in the sw corner. Along the NW side were the principal domestic apartments, long since replaced. The CURTAIN WALLS were thickened in the mid C16 for cannon, making a magnificent high-level promenade, with a wide ramp for access next to the N wall of the keep. On the N side at the W, MAGAZINE, 1827 and 1851. The outer skin is of red stone with minute windows; inside is a parabolic vault of brick reaching right up into the roof, lit by large end windows just under the crown. Next to the E a MILITIA STORE, 1881. The REGIMENTAL MUSEUM occupies the place of the HALL built probably 1301–7 for Edward I, but all that is left is the late C14 STAIR-TURRET of a lost gatehouse. It has polygonal buttress-shafts, two of them on head corbels, and blank tracery of an odd kind – two lights with a reticulation motif, cut by the upper continuation of a shaft which is the mullion of the two lights. A datestone of 1577 remains of Lord Scrope's connecting range.

27   KEEP. A mighty cube of red stone, 60 by 67 ft (18.5 by 20.5 metres), partly wrapped in the C16 ramparts. Its form and flat buttresses are typically Norman but its shot-off silhouette and thick incurved merlons – it originally had four corner turrets – are an adaptation in the time of Henry VIII for artillery. John Goodall derives the particular form of the keep from

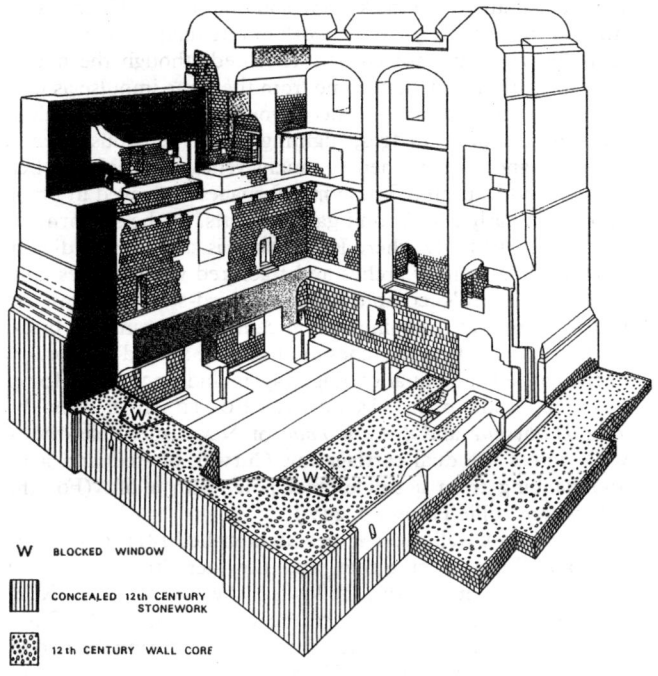

W   BLOCKED WINDOW

CONCEALED 12th CENTURY
         STONEWORK

12th CENTURY WALL CORE

Carlisle Castle, Great Tower.
Cutaway drawing, 2004

Bamburgh in Northumberland and thence from the White
Tower in London. Entrance is at ground level; the forebuilding whose foundation can be seen on the E side is clearly an
addition. The interiors are in a shattered state due to the explosion of a magazine some time before 1576, and to the installation of a central spine wall to take cannon on the roof; this
meant adding an inner skin to the walls as well, as can be seen
in the front mural stair. A wide spiral, also in a shattered state,
rises in the NW corner, missing out the third floor, which is
taken as evidence that the roof was countersunk within the
outer walls to this level – as in the White Tower in London,
and at Brough. The basement vaults are also insertions of the
C16, possibly replacing C12 vaults. The dividing wall makes the
apartments uncomfortably grim. None of the W rooms even
have fireplaces. The fireplace in the first-floor E room has signs
of nailhead, i.e. a C12 motif. There are small wall cabinets. The
mural passages and rooms on the E of the second floor are
embellished with PRISONERS' CARVINGS, the most humanly

interesting feature of the castle. Their heraldry points to the 1480s, at a time when the keep was in poor repair; Henry Summerson suggests they are the work of one man, perhaps *Richie Graham*. Vigorous, not crudely executed (though the figures are rather dwarfish), they come from the same impulse as misericords, and include some favourite subjects: fabulous animals, heraldic badges, fighting men, religious scenes, mermaid and mirror. There are many repeats, especially a helmeted head in profile. These mural spaces are paved in brick, and retain early iron-bound gates or yatts. In the SE corner is a possible ORATORY where King David is said to have died in 1153. Its fragmentary arches and fractured wall surfaces epitomize the keep's complexity. The third-storey rooms are vaulted across to the spine wall in cannon-resistant C16 brick.

CITY WALLS. The best stretches are from the SE and SW corners of the castle to the dual carriageway, including the Tile Tower – *see* the Castle, p. 241. IRISHGATE FOOTBRIDGE, 2000, by *Jane Darbyshire* and *Nick Kendall* of Newcastle, links the W walls across the dual carriageway. Curved, of steel and glass and hanging from a single steel pole, with a lift. (For the subway *see* Tullie House, p. 247.)

The N and E walls were largely demolished 1811–15 to make East and West Tower Street, and Lowther Street. The West Walls are still impressive, following the scarp of the River Caldew, and best seen close to the Tithe Barn (*see* St Cuthbert, p. 239). They were successively hidden during the C19 by warehouses and the slums of English Damside, and have only been revealed in the C20 with their clearing for car parks and landscaping. For dates and reclaimed datestones *see* Perambulation 1, p. 253.

CITADEL. The defensive counterpart at the S end of the city to the castle at the N. The medieval Bochard Gate was reconstructed for artillery under the German engineer *Stefan von Haschenperg* in 1541–3. It had two massive round towers, as now, and an enclosure embracing the square medieval tower in the wall between, where the road now is. In its early C19 recasting the Citadel forms a magnificent entry to the city. The E tower was kept, re-skinned and heightened, for use by the Nisi Prius court; the W one (nearer the railway station) rebuilt further W, forming the Crown Court. This was a protracted business. Road formed in 1804, Act for conversion to courts and offices in 1807, also reclamation of stone from the walls started, and a design prepared by *Thomas Telford*. *John Chisholme* acted as architect on site; he also designed a Judge's Lodging, not completed. Chisholme died in 1808 and was superseded by *Peter Nicholson*, and in 1810 Telford was displaced by *Robert Smirke*. Grand Jury room finished 1819, Crown Court finally completed 1822. Gothic two-light windows in the towers. Along the road, facing one another, two plain façades of six bays of Gothic windows. All embattled. The road is flanked at its SE end by a gate-like projection, pierced through in 1929 with pedestrian archways. There was an octagonal radial-plan gaol behind the w tower: built 1824–7 to a scheme by *John Orridge* (drawings by *Paul Nixson*, completion overseen by *Christopher Hodgson*.) Closed 1922, demolished 1930s. Part of its perimeter wall survives, and a good deal of its hospital, cookhouse and lodge.

INTERIORS, W tower. COURTROOM. A half-circle within the drum, in its arrangement owing something to Thomas Harrison's Shire Hall at Lancaster. Roof with a quatrefoil-holed girder over the judges seat. Is it iron? Figures of Justice and Mercy, bust of George III. GRAND JURY ROOM. Massively overscaled panelling with castellated top. Black marble fireplace, Tudor-arched. Half-cones of fan-vaulting form the cornice. GRAND STAIR. Wooden vaulting cove, skylight in the middle. Stone landing bracketed out on iron brackets.

OLD TOWN HALL, Market Place. At the focus of the town, where English Street broadens out into Greenmarket. Engagingly and surprisingly low and unbombastic, colourwashed orange, and not at all the sort of thing most Northern industrial towns lusted for (though *Ferguson* designed a Wrennish aggrandisement in 1887). Single storey on a basement only. The seven-bay centre is of 1668–9 on the site of the medieval town hall, with replacement paired and curved steps of *c.* 1825 up to the Council Chamber. Originally it had cross-mullioned windows and a single flight of steps. The medieval great chamber survived until 1717 when the present r. end was built, of stone and projecting a little, with the date on its sweet clock turret. This has five bays to the side. The l. extension was completed by 1825, with sash windows above and shopfronts below. The former council chamber at the top of the steps (now tourist information) has C19 panelling, and a dais. Some of the roof trusses have been cut through.

GUILDHALL, Greenmarket. Built by Richard de Redness shortly after a town fire in 1392; a date between 1396 and 1407 is suggested by documentation and confirmed by tree-ring analysis. This seems to be the only major timber-framed building remaining in the whole of Cumbria. Yet there is nothing half-hearted or hesitant about it. L-shaped, and jettied out on both fronts and both upper storeys, with dragon beams. Shops below and two storeys of tenements above. The ground floor of the Greenmarket front has been under-built, but the timber posts remain inside, and on the Fisher Street side the shop arches remain as well. The mid floor is infilled with early brick, the top floor faced with mathematical tile. Inside however are decorative curved braces, presumably intended to be seen. They run down to the floors, as in York but not in Lancashire or Cheshire. The face corbels are casts of 1844 (mostly renewed). On Fisher Street are a couple of little windows with C15 wooden tracery, and a charming wooden oriel like a ship's poop, probably C17. The main roof has raking queenpost trusses, perhaps a late C16 or C17 replacement, but the narrow trusses of the wing are original, crowded with crown-posts braced up from the tie and up again to the collar-plate. The timbers generally are massive but completely unmoulded, except for the simplest chamfer. Upper floors opened as a museum in 1978.

CIVIC CENTRE, Rickergate and Lowther Street. A building of which Carlisle should be proud, but is not. *Charles B. Pearson, Son & Partners* won the competition in 1957, and the building went up in 1960–3. It was intended to be part of a civic quarter but the money ran out. The three elements – offices, Rates Hall behind ceremonial rooms, Council Chamber – are clearly expressed. Offices are housed in a ten-storey point block on a recessed podium, with the frame extended at the top into a transparent air stage, which looks attenuated because the inter-mediate mullions are omitted: an effective silhouette. Civic Suite and Rates Hall form a two-storey link. The Council Chamber is octagonal, originally on stilts, with the peripheral posts sticking up on top. The interiors are a period piece. The RATES HALL is clerestory-lit, covered with a shallow concrete vault on mushroom columns. The COUNCIL CHAMBER occupies the upper part of the octagon. Double height, with steps up to a public gallery behind the podium. This features a three-dimensional collage including plans of the city, of the cathedral, and back-lit stained glass. The public stair has *Pilkington* tiles with spots arranged to make a silent explosion. CIVIC SUITE on the first floor above the main entrance. Doughnut tables, honeycomb ceilings, lighting in echelons, like ducks over a fireplace. The cross-lounge above the foyer features a spectacular white ceiling with inverted stepped pyramids, and Arabian fretted screens to the stairwell.

MAGISTRATES' COURT, POLICE (former) and FIRE STATION, Warwick Street and Rickergate, w of the Civic Centre. 1937–41. By *Percy Dalton*, City Engineer and Surveyor. Cotswold Tudor, stone-faced, with mullions and transoms. Even the fire tower has a four-centred top opening. The CLERKS' BUILDING adjoining to the N on Rickergate, *c.* 2000 by *John Robinson*, the last Cumbria County Architect, makes a very different statement. External frame and thin bracing partly exposed, continuous band of window under the roof behind it. White, blue and pink block facing.

CROWN AND COUNTY COURTS, Earl Street. *See* p. 257.

TULLIE HOUSE MUSEUM, Abbey Street and Castle Street. Set back from Abbey Street in a large garden, Tullie House is Carlisle's premier and most influential house, dated 1689 on the elaborate rainwater hoppers. As Pevsner remarks, it uses the classical apparatus with ease and yet a certain provincial licence. The architect may have been *William Thackeray*. Façade of seven bays and two storeys in red ashlar contrasted with yellow stone dressings. Odd to see constructional poly-chromy at this date; it appears occasionally elsewhere in the city. The doorway and all windows have broken pediments, alternating triangular and segmental. Celia Fiennes in her muddled way mentions '5 good sarshe windows' in 1698. The doorway has a bolection moulding. It was a single pile, with the stair in a stub wing at the back, like Nos. 1 and 3 in the Abbey (p. 239). The stair has twisted balusters. Fine panelled room and fireplace upstairs, mid-C18. Fluted pilasters with Corinthian capitals. *C. J. Ferguson* headed the scheme to convert and extend the house into a museum, executed 1892–3, with a façade to Castle Street, E. His exteriors are in red stone with yellow accents, like the old house, in a free C16 to C17 style, with pilasters in tiers and Henry VIII as well as Elizabethan windows. Many of the inset blocks remain uncarved. The former library is by the City Surveyor, *W. Howard-Smith*. The gate tower on Castle Street was the Librarian's house; it has a clock turret, and TVLLIE HOVSE on the parapet. Ferguson's interiors are cheerfully museumy, with shiny dados of *Craven Dunnill* tiles from Broseley, mosaic floors, and swirly iron balustrading to the stairs, complete with coloured and gilded municipal shields.

The present E entrance leads to revamped reception facilities by *City Architects*, 1989–90, opened 1991. Inward-looking. From the Victorian door is a tunnel-like corridor of unstructural section, its pointed ceiling not springing off the walls, lined with plastic honeycomb, like packaging. It leads to an atrium of complex shape, lined with dark brick. Beyond, towards the castle, ROTUNDA and MILLENNIUM GALLERY opened 2001, by *BDP*, *Stanton Williams* and *Johnston & Wright*. The rotunda has no obvious function except as a viewing deck. The underground Millennium Gallery is an impressively free-flowing space, leaf-shaped, but marred by the functionless triangle of concrete beams intended to support the unachieved glass pyramid which was to have lit it. Through a wall of glass bricks, incorporating found objects, can be glimpsed a public UNDERPASS intended to reconnect town and castle under the A595 road. On the other wall of the underpass is an artwork, Steel Wall by *Russell Coleman*, incorporating things made in Carlisle. The granite pavement is carved with reiving surnames; and a polished granite Cursing Stone by *Gordon Young* which immortalizes, rather inappropriately, the Archbishop of Glasgow's blood-curdling curse against the Border Reivers and their doings.

LIBRARY. *See* Scotch Street, p. 251.

SANDS CENTRE (leisure), next to the Eden bridge. 1983–5. Characterless. Brick, exposed inside.

COVERED MARKET. Entrances on Fisher Street, West Tower Street and Scotch Street, and a long blank wall to Market Street, W. By *Arthur Cawston* of London and *Joseph Graham* of Carlisle, 1887–9, extended NE in 1900–1. Red stone, Renaissance style, enlivened by some amusing sculpture: head of Mayor Creighton, carved *in situ* by *Beall* of Newcastle; Corinthian caps with ram, cock, and bull among the acanthus by *Richard Nelson* of Carlisle, from models supplied by *Jackson* of London. The interior space is spoilt by the insertion in 1990–1 of two cheap department stores, one above the other. The upper one is open to the roof, which is glazed and triple-arched with plenty of rivets and no frills. The engineer for the roof was *A. T. Walmisley*.

BITTS PARK, below the castle on the flat and formerly marshy land at the confluence of the Eden and Caldew. STATUE of Queen Victoria, by *T. Brock*, 1902. Powerful bronze, over-life-sized, imperial, majestic. She carries orb and sceptre and is richly costumed. Reliefs on the white granite pedestal: Commerce, Science and Art, Education and Empire. Much the best of Carlisle's meagre public sculpture. Also EDEN BENCHMARK No. 9, Towards the Sea, by *Hideo Furuta*, 2000. Four big stones in a row, like stages of a cannonball trying to break free but not succeeding.

EDEN BRIDGE.* By *Sir Robert Smirke*, 1812–16. Five shallow segmental arches lope across the fast-flowing river. Fine hard yellow sandstone ashlar, with restrained and stately detailing. At each end, broad stone seats with wrought-iron lanterns are built into the parapets. The bridge was doubled on the upstream side in 1932, largely respecting the original design. Upstream, on the N bank, the PIER of a 1743 predecessor, re-erected after it was uncovered during flood relief work in 1951–2.

105 CITADEL RAILWAY STATION, Court Square. By *Sir William Tite*, 1846–7. One of the grandest survivals of the railway mania years. Long row of Tudor Gothic buildings along the town side. The l. end, looking like a school of the period, included the first-class refreshment room behind the big bay window, and later a covered link to the hotel. In the centre is the booking hall behind a porte cochère, with a tall clock tower asymmetrically placed, and to the r. a long line of offices. The station was greatly enlarged in 1879–81, when the Midland Railway came in from Leeds. That is the date of the island platform with its grand refreshment room, and the ridge-and-furrow roof (made by *Blyth & Cunningham* of Edinburgh), which originally spanned right over to the great screen wall on the far side. The later parts are robustly Tudor. The roof was cut back in the 1950s, losing its Gothic end screens.

The glory days of Citadel Station have departed, when four English and three Scottish companies, each with its distinctive personality and livery, met under its seven-acre roof; but it is a place of romance still, especially on a winter's night when rain-streaked trains rumble in from the outer darkness, pause briefly in the great lighted room, and after a short space vanish out of sight.

---

*Locals still speak in the plural of 'Eden Bridges', in a folk memory of the multiple channels to cross.

PERAMBULATIONS

1. The walled city

The English entry to the city is as good as could be wished for.
Whether stepping off the train or driving in from the s, the fat
twin towers of the Citadel (p. 244) are a magnificent statement
of arrival. COURT SQUARE in front of the Citadel, though not
a set piece, is worthy of it. The station (p. 248) to the w is a

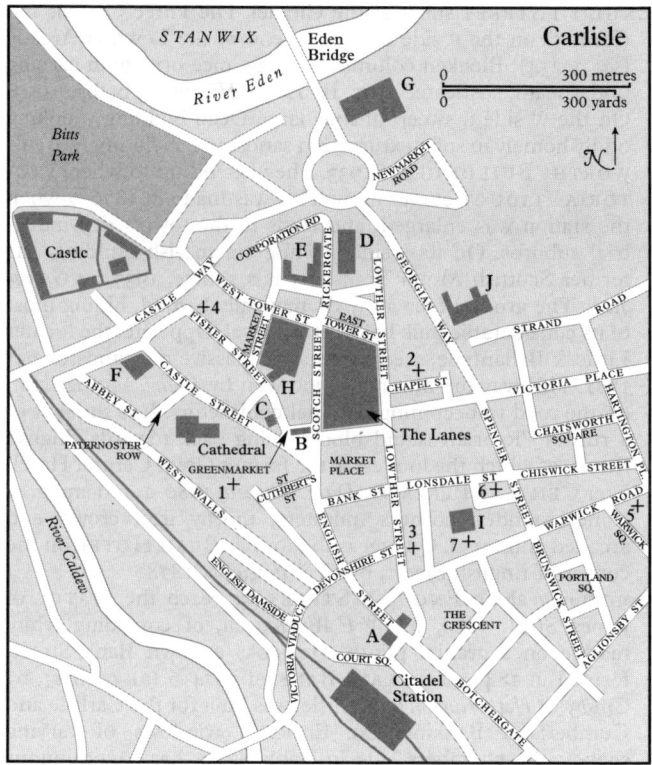

1	St Cuthbert	C	Guildhall
2	Church of Scotland	D	Civic Centre
3	Congregational church	E	Magistrates' Court
4	Quaker Meeting House		and Fire Station
5	St Aidan	F	Tullie House Museum
6	St Paul (former)	G	Sands Centre
7	St George	H	Covered Market
		I	Crown Courts
A	Citadel	J	Trinity School
B	Town Hall		

fine foil, making its own statement but, being lower, not competing. (For the buildings around Court Square, the Crescent, and Lowther Street *see* Perambulation 2, p. 254). The pattern of the city is simple. English Street leads N from the Citadel to the market place. There it fans out into three: Scotch Street (r.) going N to the bridge and the main road to Scotland, Fisher Street in the middle, and Castle Street NW past the cathedral and towards the castle gate. Beyond the cathedral precinct, which is called the Abbey, are Paternoster Row and Abbey Street.

ENGLISH STREET starts at the Citadel. The Three Crowns inn (former) on the E side marks the end of the Lowther Arcade (*see* p. 254). Blocked columns in pairs, nice oriel with carving underneath, rusticated attic. By *Henry Higginson*, before 1903. On the W side a sweep of four large Deco buildings, looking oddly homely in soft-textured red sandstone, including WOOL-WORTHS BUILDINGS of 1933. They extend up to where VICTORIA VIADUCT curves away. This was made in 1876–7 when the station was enlarged, and leads to the town's C19 industrial suburbs. On its S side a white cinema-ish building, the former Scottish Motor Transport bus garage, 1937 by *George Jack*. The ground falls away dramatically behind, hiding most of its considerable bulk below street level. Opposite, the former Little & Ballantyne, seed merchants, massive red sandstone of 1881. This was the first major job won by *Laing*, setting them on the road to becoming national contractors. It is the first of a run of Victorian island blocks going back towards English Street, of which the loudest is the former Great Central Hotel, later CENTRAL PLAZA. By *Daniel Birkett*, 1880–1; red and grey stone, rounded corners, pilasters, thorny iron crown and arcaded chimneys. Quieter is the former BUSH HOTEL on the corner of English Street, by *C. J. Ferguson*, 1878.

Continuing along ENGLISH STREET we reach the STATUE of James Steel, 1859, by *W. F. Woodington*, of corroding white marble on a granite plinth. He looks E down Bank Street, formed in 1849. BARCLAYS BANK of 1874–6 (SE corner), by *Crosby & Hetherington* of Carlisle, was built for the Carlisle and Cumberland Banking Co. Enriched windows of varying shapes; the chambers side in Bank Street has a continuous first-floor arcade. On the NE corner is HSBC, originally Carlisle City and District Banking Co., of Portland stone with granite pillars. The date is 1898 – an early use of Portland in the North – the architect *T. Taylor Scott*. Manager's house behind on Bank Street, with a big semicircular hood over the doorcase. It was the refronting of a bank building of 1849 by *T. J. Fox*, designed for the new street. In Bank Street itself is the former CLYDESDALE BANK of 1878 by *Hetherington & Oliver* (Nos. 10–14, S side). Rather Waterhouse-ish, in red sandstone. In English Street on the W side is a good MARKS & SPENCER store of 1931, in the usual Deco and Portland stone, with bronze windows and apron. The extension (1977–89) is not half so good. HOUSE OF FRASER (Nos. 30–40) was

Robinson Bros' store of 1902 by *Oliver & Dodgshun*, with additions by *Harry Foxall*; badly mauled.

English Street broadens out into the MARKET PLACE and GREENMARKET, round the astonishingly demure Old Town Hall (p. 245). The MARKET CROSS is dated 1682. Unfluted Ionic column on a square base. On top a sundial with balls at the four top and four bottom corners and on it a lion. The DCMS suggests that the initials ATM may be for *Thomas Machell*, architect, *Thomas Addison*, mason. The CROWN AND MITRE HOTEL on the W side makes up for the Town Hall's absence of civic pride. It is a monster. 1903–5 for Walter Scott, by *George Dale Oliver*. Symmetrical, of very red brick, with curly Flemish gables and strappy cartouches in red stone. Striped red and white marble lines the foyer and stair, an alabaster colonnade screens Reception, over-ornate iron balustrading runs up the stair. Along the first-floor front is a suite of large entertaining rooms, as in a Victorian town hall. The ballroom is almost detached at the back. Next door towards Castle Street is another blocked-column building like the Lowther Arcade buildings, and probably, like them, by *Henry Higginson*. Dated 1903 on the kneelers.

SCOTCH STREET offers plenty of simple late C18 and early C19 fronts, as well as the pastiche façades of Carlisle's main shopping precinct, THE LANES, between Market Place–Scotch Street and Lowther Street to the E. Site earmarked 1960, initial study 1977, built 1982–4, cost £10.5 million. This is by the *Building Design Partnership*, project architect *David Cash*. There are five major stores, fifty smaller shops, twenty-seven homes, the main library, and a covered car park. It is a relatively early example of mall-type shopping integrated in historic surroundings. The idea was to perpetuate the Lanes demolished for the scheme, but under cover. It has worked well enough, though only Globe Lane occupies its original site. The outer pasticherie, suggesting so many individual old properties, is not so good. Inside, by Debenhams, bronze STATUE by *Judith Bluck* (1986) of Jimmy Dyer, fiddler and ballad singer, sitting on a rock with his carpet bag. Upstairs in the middle is the LIBRARY, by *John Robinson*, not pastiche but boldly techno. It is marked by an overhanging then receding glass façade to the enclosed lane, over bright lime-green tubular steel. The interior is a machine for reading, its structure and services exposed as though in relief after the fake cladding elsewhere. Big cranked concrete supports carry fat pipes for the forced ventilation (making work uncomfortable), yellow one side, white the other. On the W side of Scotch Street, the former BLUE BELL INN at No. 60 retains part of its late C18 façade, with a segment-headed archway and Venetian window with pilasters over. Nos. 42–44, TOWER BUILDINGS of 1889, is by *G. D. Oliver*, in Jacobean style with a corner tower.

FISHER STREET starts narrow, behind the Town Hall, next to the Guildhall (p. 245). On the E side GUILDHALL OFFICES, Tudorish, 1874. Next door, No. 23 (now The Arches) is the former Quaker Meeting House, of 1776–7 with a new façade of 1867 by *James Stewart*; suitable for a small bank, fussy and important. The C18 front and back doors can be seen inside Kinmont Arcade, linking Fisher Street with Rosemary Lane. No. 19, good two-storey Georgian brick. Four bays, Doric half-column doorcase with flower roundels. The street widens where St Mary's Gate comes in, l. On the r. corner is a tall Grecian house. Doric porch with fluted columns and triglyph frieze. Giant Ionic pilasters to the upper floors. N of Market Street, No. 15 was the Town Clerk's Office, 1879. The YMCA, No. 22, occupies a good early C19 house of two tall storeys in brindled brick with Grecian Doric doorcase. Opposite is the former METHODIST CENTRAL HALL (for sale 2007). Of 1922–3 – so a late example of the type – by *A. Brocklehurst* and *A. W. Hornabrook* of Manchester with *H. E. Ayris* of Carlisle. Pedimented front of sandstone and red brick, over a steel frame. (Good and complete interior: octagonal hall with rostrum and organ; STAINED GLASS by *Humphries, Jackson & Ambler.*)* The WORKING MEN'S CLUB is next door, in a house built for Robert Ferguson *c.* 1790. An unusual wave front – the bays not treated as separate but merging in a Baroque fashion. Angle bays on the ground floor unimaginatively added, C19. At the castle end Nos. 4–8, a nine-bay early C19 terrace in chequered brick. Nice lacy overthrows. Then back to the Market Place.

CASTLE STREET, with Abbey Street, is Carlisle's best Georgian streetscape. At the corner with the Market Place an altered house of perhaps *c.* 1700, of five bays and three storeys with a bolection-moulded doorcase and segment-headed windows. Then open to the cathedral on the S side. Prominent on the other side is the CUMBERLAND BUILDING SOCIETY by *Johnson & Wright,* 1976, in brown brick. A large deep-plan office block, trying hard to disguise its mass. Beyond Bulloughs' store, No. 21 is a good brick Later Georgian house of five bays with Composite columns to the doorcase. Nos. 19 and 17 are BOOKCASE, a bookshop. No. 17, harmless enough, is dated 1798 on a decorative hopper. No. 19, larger and of much the same date, received a sophisticated stone façade in the early C19. Big windows, presumably once tripartite, and a broad doorway under wide semicircular arches divided by red stone pilasters on the ground floor. The pilasters have paterae on little blocks instead of proper capitals. Both houses have cantilevered staircases with wrought-iron scrolled rails. The larger house has good doors and plasterwork too, especially in the bay rooms at the back. This became the Head Office of the State Management Scheme (*see* p. 223).

Beyond Paternoster Row on the S side is *Paul Nixson*'s terrace of 1823, Nos. 26–30. Grecian, with a little incised decoration. Porches of unfluted Ionic columns, and an unusual oval of

---

*In the basement a ROMAN MASONRY FRAGMENT protected under an ingenious hardwood case with bronze-framed viewing panels. *By H. E. Watson.*

Greek key in the fanlights. Nixson made marble fireplaces, several of which are within. Then the *Ferguson* entry to Tullie House (p. 246). The low c18 houses opposite (Nos. 13–15) are occupied by Johnson & Wright, architects. No. 3 has a three-bay Grecian front with Ionic pilasters to the doorway.

PATERNOSTER ROW has smaller, simpler houses. Nos. 4 and 5, 1855, is a house and shop, with a central way through to a ware-house behind. Very finely jointed rosy brickwork with a little polychromy, fat granite columns and Corinthian capitals to the doorway. Tile inserts flank the entry. House and warehouse were joined by an airy stair hall in tubular steel and glass brick by *Alan Jones*, c. 2000. At the S end is the gatehouse to the cathedral precinct (p. 237). From here, ABBEY STREET runs NW. Nearest the gatehouse No. 48, late c17, retaining a bolection-moulded doorcase and a single early segment-headed sash. For Tullie House *see* p. 246. The plumber *John Cassidy*, who made Tullie House's elaborate rainwater goods, lived opposite at EAGLESFIELD HOUSE, No. 42 (late c17, with late c18 alterations). Utterly weird are Nos. 36 and 38, of ashlar, in a decidedly debased early c19 classical with eccentric variations on the tripartite window. No. 32 is a superior and very handsome town house of *c.* 1817 for Christopher Hutchinson. *Paul Nixson*, architect. Grey ashlar front of five widely spaced bays. Very sparing decoration. Doorway with Doric columns *in antis*, wreaths in the frieze, and a semi-elliptical fanlight above. Wavy iron railings, decorative overthrow for a lamp. (Hall with rib-vaulted plaster ceiling. Cantilever stair with cast-iron balusters.) No. 26, late c18 with Ionic columns and an open pediment for the doorway.

WEST WALLS is reached at the W end of Abbey Street. The cathedral built three adjacent vicarages near St Cuthbert's in 1832, designed by *Christopher Hodgson*, for St Mary (then still in the cathedral nave), and Holy Trinity and Christ Church (both now demolished). One vicarage now serves as Church House, the other two as St Cuthbert's vicarage. These face over the West Walls themselves, still c12 with rebuilding and refacing of 1746, 1876–7, 1985, 1988–9. They incorporate datestones from removed buildings – 1851, 1879, 1840 – towards the railway and the River Caldew.

2. The eastern edge of the walled city

In front of the Citadel and next to the station is LAKES COURT HOTEL, the former County and Station Hotel, 1852–3 by *Salvin* for George Head Head of Rickerby, costing £12,000. Five-bay front, now painted white, the centre with a segmental pediment, with a mansard roof and fancy dormers – i.e. very French; like P.C. Hardwick's Great Western Hotel at Paddington of 1851–4. Extended 1866–8, l., by *Cory & Ferguson*, with a much higher tower with a French pavilion roof. Coloured tiles in window reveals and cornice. The best interior is Cory & Ferguson's ballroom, in a detached block behind, with a high coved ceiling. Next door the former CUMBERLAND UNION BANK, 1865–7. Rich palazzo by *Daniel Birkett*; now a bar, with pastiche interior. Round the corner on Botchergate the Lakes Court Hotel comes out again with a frontage by *Cory & Ferguson*. Over the road is the COUNTY HOTEL, formerly the Red Lion, by *J. Murchie* for Samuel Bousfield, 1894–6. Notable for elaborate interior tilework. Inner foyer skylight lined with pale blue and cream swags. Bar at the back with remains of a sumptuous *Doulton* scheme. Coffered ceiling entirely of tilework (presumably over iron girders), coved cornice with brackets, frieze, two dark brown fireplaces, doorcase. The wall facing has been painted over, but a little shows by the door: it had horizontal stripes. Mosaic floor in fan patterns with a swirling foliage border. The former corner entrance, now BAR SOLO, is made through what must be an annexed older building: dated 1885, restored 1995. Ceiling of large rose and thistle tiles set in a mahogany frame, tiled walls with large inset pictures including the Four Seasons, and a greenish-brown tile dado with owls, parrots, storks. Next to the E THE CRESCENT, a quarter-circle of houses of *c.* 1821–4 in Carlisle brick. Opposite, a STATUE of William, 1st Earl of Lonsdale, 1846 by *Musgrave Lewthwaite Watson*, moved from between the towers of the Citadel. Of white marble, weathering ungracefully.

The Crescent straightens and becomes LOWTHER STREET, built over the East Walls in 1823. Plenty to see, especially at the Citadel end. First a sortie E for a few buildings at the start of Warwick Road, s side. White House was the CRESCENT INN, by *Harry Redfern*, 1931. Jokingly, in Moorish style. White blocks on a grey granite base, green pantiled roof. Decorative balconies to the first-floor windows. Three-bay recessed centre balcony, vaulted, with gold mosaic lunettes. Exotic interiors with floral tiles and arabesque ironwork. POST OFFICE next door, 1912–16, in Beaux Arts classical style. Then the LONSDALE CINEMA by *Percy Browne & Son*, 1931, much altered inside but retaining plasterwork and stained glass by *Reed Millican* of Newcastle. Back to Lowther Street, where the NE corner is announced by NORTH BRITISH AND MERCANTILE BUILDINGS of 1925 (or modified then), with a Scottish tourelle. On the w side the entrance to LOWTHER ARCADE by *Henry Higginson*, 1904, with lavish use of alternately blocked columns. Next on the E side the wild Renaissance front of the Congregational church (p. 240). Next a former Post Office, 1863 by *J. Williams* (*Office of Works*). In 1899 given its top storey; in 1916 converted to the first of the State Management pubs in Carlisle, as the Gretna Tavern (*see* p. 223). Then LLOYDS TSB, the former Athenaeum of 1839–40, facing down Devonshire Street. By *Arthur Y. & George Williams* of Liverpool. Broad five-bay late classical front with giant pilasters. The front is recessed in the end bays so the pilasters turn into square columns. Good carving including grimacing Fates in the parapet. In amusing contrast EXCHANGE BUILDINGS, formerly spirit vaults (r.) of 1868, shop and office of 1881. Both sections, rock-faced, are by *Daniel Birkett*. The differing storey heights are united by a common parapet with terracotta balusters. The 1868 section has a Gothic oriel with fairytale conical roof. The extension is itself enterprisingly asymmetrical; basket arches of different widths make a syncopated rhythm. BROAD-ACRE HOUSE, 1973, is given just sufficient modelling and mass to stand up to its neighbours. Faced in stone, pushed out into four shallow bows on all four storeys. With another jump in style and colour comes No. 22, dated 1892. Italian Gothic, polychrome stone, windows in pairs. Shaped gable, stone finial. Finishing the run, a pair of fine 1830s town houses, Nos. 24 and 26. Three storeys on a railed basement. Porches with Greek Doric columns and triglyph entablature. Balustrade and aprons of slabs of pierced stone, heavy cast-iron railings and stair balusters. The stairs are cantilevered. Nos. 35–39 (W side) are handsome 1830s houses set back from the street, built and probably designed by *Thomas Nelson*. Grecian, faced with buff ashlar. Doric columns set within the porch recesses. No. 35 (Liberal Club) has shallow curved two-storey bows.

A little further down Lowther Street on the E side, Nos. 30–40, a row of brick town houses, *c.* 1830. Three, including No. 34 in the middle, have kept their doorcases, with stone pilasters and wreaths. On the W side, No. 45 goes with the long run of three-storey shops and offices in Bank Street, built in 1851. PIPPINS was The Apple Tree, by *H. Redfern*, 1927, the first of his post-war model inns. Symmetrical front, gable at each end and three dormers between. Mullioned-and-transomed windows. Purply brick and buff stone, the ground storey partly faced with white faience but with a fruity carving in buff stone over the entrance. There was an upstairs bar as well, furnished with writing materials and periodicals, with a refectory table for farmers to conduct business after market. Murals by artists of the Carlisle School of Art on the theme of the Golden Apples of the Hesperides. Beyond the entrance to the Lanes (*see* p. 251), the HOWARD ARMS. Late C18 or early C19, the ground floor refaced with beautiful *Doulton & Co*. tilework in blue, green and yellow, with paired pilasters and fancy lettering. The interior retains its small-room intricacy, with Lincrusta friezes and a decent curved stair.

Off to the E is VICTORIA PLACE. No. 1 was built just after 1837 by *John Hodgson*, the rest followed mostly in the 1840s and early 1850s. Identical two-storey-on-a-basement pale ashlar terraces face each other, with unfluted Ionic columns to the porches. First a pair of five-bayers standing slightly forward, with a bit of fancy on the parapet and centre emphasized over the porch. Then addorsed pairs of three-bayers with double porches of four columns. The style is not quite pure Georgian, e.g. the bulky cast-iron railings. Next, CHAPEL STREET, laid out in 1824. Now a short cul-de-sac, its former outlet having been sacrificed to the barbarous GEORGIAN WAY, a four-lane dual carriageway named after the fine early C19 street and gardens cleared to make way for it in 1963. On the N side, DISPENSARY by *John Hodgson*, dated 1857, yet in the same classical tradition as Victoria Place. Ashlar, four bays, the doorway and ground-floor windows pedimented. Next to it the Scottish church of 1834, and opposite a good terrace in Flemish-bond brickwork.

Lowther Street fizzles out before its original destination at Hardwicke Circus, and ends with a whimper at EDEN BRIDGE HOUSE. A straightforward curtain-wall job by *E. H. Banks* of the *Ministry of Public Buildings and Works*, 1963–4. Behind the Civic Centre (to the W; *see* p. 246) is the Ristorante Adriano, on the corner of Corporation Road. This was the MALT SHOVEL, a *Redfern* pub of 1927–8 in sub-Lutyens Queen Anne style, with a giant order in brick and a very tall chimney right on the front corner.

From the roundabout at the end of Georgian Way, Newmarket Road leads E to the TURF INN. 1839–40, extended 1874 by *Daniel Birkett*. Its railed monopitch roof was a grandstand for the racecourse on the Swifts. It looks as though the first floor could have been open behind a colonnade.

INNER DISTRICTS

1. The south-eastern quadrant: Botchergate and Warwick Road to the Eden

Immediately E and SE of the centre, the area between Botchergate and Victoria Place was laid out in the 1830s with broad, straight streets and two squares. Over the following decades they came to be lined with handsome two-storey terraces, usually of Carlisle brindled brick with pillared porches of stone. The style is conservative, retaining Georgian proportion and restraint until the 1870s. Oddly enough it is in the two squares, Chatsworth and Portland (the names refer to the Duke of Devonshire's estates) that good manners were finally thrown to the winds.

ST AIDAN, Warwick Road. 1899–1902 by *C. J. Ferguson*, late in life. Large and dignified, though with a double bellcote not a tower. Dec, with two aisles and clerestory. An enormous BELL on an iron girder sticking out of the chancel was given to the Rev. Sidney Swann by the campanologist Edwin Banks of Highmoor, Wigton, who intended it for Carlisle market. Low W baptistery between the N and S porches, with a pointed tunnel-vault with closely set chamfered cross-arches. Interior with six-bay arcades, i.e. no chancel arch. Well-grouped parochial buildings to the NE. – STAINED GLASS. Almost all by *A. K. Nicholson*, over a long period, *c.* 1909–50.

ST JOHN THE EVANGELIST, London Road. By *R. Clarke* of Nottingham, 1867. Dark grey stone, rock-faced. No tower. Lancet style with shafts. Some stiff-leaf capitals. W porch, and a thin square turret next to the chancel arch. (STAINED GLASS all by *M. & A. O'Connor*.) Large parish centre attached to the E end, 1986.

St Paul, now Elim, Lonsdale Street. By *Habershon & Brock*, 1869–70. Stump of a tower/porch by the chancel, NE. Paired cinquefoil windows for the clerestory. Big W window all wheel shapes. Former VICARAGE, now Chatsworth House (No. 21 Chatsworth Square, E), by the same architects.

Our Lady and St Joseph (R.C.), Warwick Square. Assertive building of 1891–3 by *Dunn, Hansom & Dunn* of Newcastle, assisted by the local architect *Henry Higginson*. Square W tower with a higher turret, nave and chancel in one, with clerestory and aisles. Of red sandstone mechanically cut and coursed. Windows mainly square-headed, of Bath stone, which has either gone black or bleached white. Above the altar a circular window with flowing tracery like the Bishop's Eye window at Lincoln. The W porch cusped and sub-cusped. The aisle windows have two-centred arches set under straight heads. – FITTINGS mostly of 1952 (consecration), and by *Wilfrid C. Mangan*.

St George (United Reformed, formerly English Presbyterian), Warwick Road. 1862–3. Raised up on a basement. Brown stone, small NW tower. Manse next door in brick and buff stone.

Crown and County Courts, Earl Street, off Warwick Road. A setted enclave like a small square beside the United Reformed church. By *PSA Building Management*, 1990–2, at a cost of £9.5 million. It contains four courts, judges' chambers, library, robing and assembly rooms, custody area, refreshment rooms, offices. In the street a STATUE of Major Francis Aglionby, 1844, by *M. L. Watson*. He is suffering from the elements.

University of Cumbria, Fusehill Street. The central block (until 2007 St Martin's College, until 2000 the City General Hospital) was originally the UNION WORKHOUSE. 1863–4 by *Lockwood & Mawson* in Bradford Italianate. Long, even front with all the main windows arched. Pedimented centre flanked by towers with pavilion roofs. CHAPEL to the E, *c.* 1893. Extensive post-war additions, including the large LEARNING GATEWAY building, W, 2006 by *Architects Plus*.

Trinity School, Strand Road. At the W the former GRAMMAR SCHOOL of 1881–3, by *George Dale Oliver*, a local man. Rock-faced red sandstone, with stone-mullioned windows, hinting at Gothic. Near-symmetrical to Strand Road, with a pyramid-roofed entrance tower. To the E an attached two-bay house for the headmaster, squeezing three storeys into the height of the schoolrooms' two. The W façade gained a second storey in the 1980s. Abutting it, the churchy-looking assembly hall presents to the roaring traffic of Georgian Way a gable with a Perp-style window.

Streets. Those to the S are described first, then to the E, then to the NE.

Botchergate is the principal approach from the S, outside the Citadel. It has become rackety and gappy, part glitz and part tat. At the Citadel end is the CUMBERLAND, one of the best-preserved of *Harry Redfern*'s State Management pubs, of

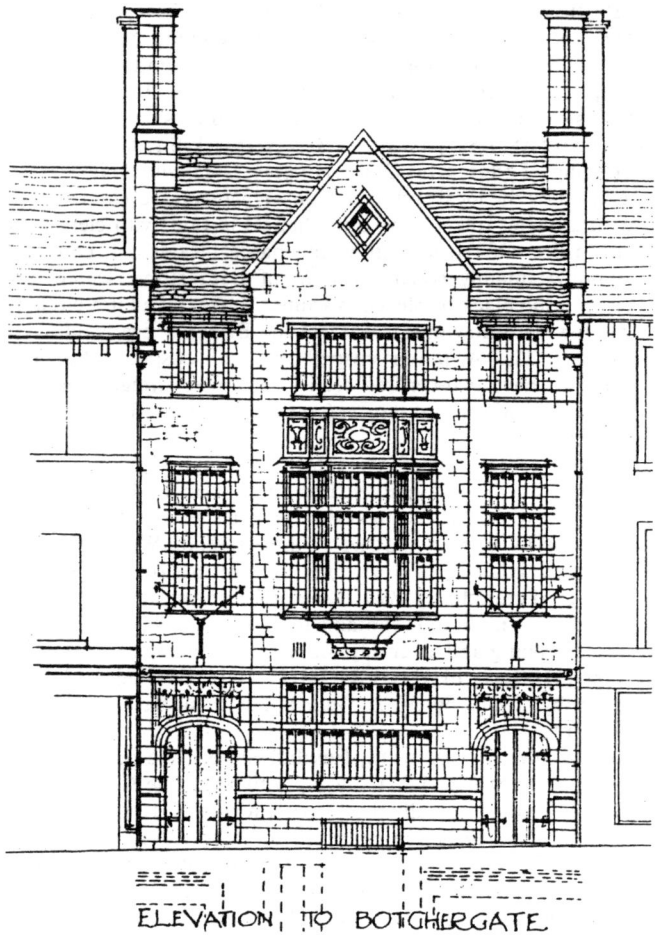

Carlisle, the Cumberland Pub.
Elevation by Harry Redfern, 1920s

1929–30. The front is of an unusual streaky brown stone, the style a metropolitan Gothic, symmetrical about the usual two entrances and a central oriel. The site is narrow but goes back a long way. Interior panelled in Japanese oak, with concrete beams stopped and grained like wood. Long bar behind a semi-screen of columns. Separate billiard room at the back. The upstairs bars were more clubby, with oak overmantels painted with appropriate verses and stained glass honouring the architects (Redfern and *Joseph Seddon*), clerk of works (*Ernest A. Streatfield*), builders (*Robert & James Bell*) and manager. On the r., in Crown Street, a handsome seven-bay hipped-roofed stone GOODS DEPOT of 1853 still proclaims the ownership of the Maryport & Carlisle Railway. Further out, on the corner of Rydal Street, is *Redfern*'s former Earl Grey Hotel of 1934–5 (later The Jester). Here the style is Deco, the materials blue brick for the base, buff brick in patterns above, blue glazed pantiles for the roof, chromium for the doors. Windows are metal, swooshing round curved corners. Recessed in the middle a robotic tower, of grooved brickwork, with a flagpole. On Lancaster Street, SW, the former OLIVETTI FACTORY, later C20, maltreated as Bee Gee Ltd (carpets). Green copper tent roof coming down to points originally shedding rain by chains.

Further out still, where Botchergate becomes LONDON ROAD, are a couple of handsome 1830s houses, now pubs. THE CRANEMAKER (No. 43, NE side), double-fronted, of Flemish bond brick, commemorates Cowans, Sheldon & Co.'s works across the road, cleared in 1989. The ST NICHOLAS ARMS is similar, with an Ionic porch. 200 yds further, on the NE side, the former TRAMWAY DEPOT, 1900 for the City of Carlisle Electric Tramways Co. A partly curved brick four-road shed with tall arched side windows and a stepped pedimented gable. Set at an angle to the main road to ease the curve for tramcars arriving and leaving. Now a hire shop and store, but little changed from the day the system closed in 1931. Next door, behind boundary walls, LONDON ROAD STATION, the abandoned and increasingly derelict remains of the city's first railway station, between 1838 and 1863 the terminus of the Newcastle & Carlisle Railway. Of the 1838 establishment the row of plain single-storey sandstone offices, l., probably by *John Dobson* of Newcastle. A large goods station occupies the site of the original train shed. By *J. Bell* for the N&CR's successor, the North Eastern Railway, 1863–4. A long straight shed behind a two-storey brick office. Lunette openings in the shed walls, crudely blocked up.

Across the road, the RAILWAY INN, built as a hotel in 1837. Red sandstone. It has lost a tetrastyle porch. Further along, on the SW side, the HILL TOP HOTEL has at its heart a plain three-storey flat-roofed brick hostel on a T-plan, built in 1947 by the London Midland & Scottish Railway for enginemen on 'lodging turns'.*

WARWICK ROAD, running E from near the Citadel, was laid out in 1829. Long, dignified, with wide pavements. Substantial terraces of brick houses, at first two-storey, with stone-pillared porches generally Doric. The brick is characteristic and attractive, Flemish bond, gently brindled. SPENCER STREET runs off to the N. Two-storey terraces of the late 1840s onwards. Doric porches in pairs. Few original railings. To the S, Brunswick Street leads to PORTLAND SQUARE. Laid out in 1853 but apparently not built up until the 1860s onward.

96

---

*A similar building for crews from Scotland survives at Etterby in the northern suburbs, now dignified as BALMORAL COURT.

Chunky cast-iron railings (1870) round the central garden. Stone terraces of decidedly Victorian over-eggedness on three sides. The square is marred by an intrusive C20 block imme- diately behind the W side, and a bit of vacant land just off the SE corner, showing how carefully a square has to be treated in order to work. Further E, WARWICK SQUARE opens to the S of Warwick Road, not a square because it has the R.C. church (p. 257) in the middle. Houses of the 1870s onwards, with some new door and entrance designs. Beyond the S side, AGLIONBY STREET crosses NE–SW. Rather more modest. One section dated 1873. A long run is brightly chequered in red and yellow brick.

CHATSWORTH SQUARE lies E of Spencer Street and N of Warwick Square. 1870s. Private garden in the middle, behind florid railings. It goes very Victorian at the outer end, with poly- chrome brickwork and bits of superfluous decoration, and the intrusion of individual detached houses, particularly the very assertive RED GABLES (No. 17, S side) by *G. D. Oliver*. 1884–5, of pressed brick, inset with *Burmantofts* flowers in the gables. The front steps turn to climb inside an arched colonnade. No. 21 was St Paul's vicarage (*see* p. 257). Nos. 22 and 23, floridly Gothic, of 1889, are by *T. Taylor Scott*. At the E end HARTINGTON PLACE runs S. Built up from the 1840s–50s. The two-storey terrace formula, but with some tricky Victo- rian porch designs. CHISWICK STREET returns W. Only six houses were shown here on Asquith's survey of 1853; generally 1860s–70s two-storey terraces in Flemish bond brick.

VICTORIA PLACE. *See* Perambulation 2, p. 255.

2. *West and south-west of the walled city: the early suburbs, with Caldewgate and Denton Holme*

The River Caldew runs close beside the West Walls. Its stream, more controllable than the Eden, more powerful than the Pet- teril, attracted the earliest extra-mural settlements. A contract of 1434 provides for a mill at Caldew Bridge End, but there were at least three earlier mills in the area. The C18 industrial development began here, and the arrival of the ship canal in 1823 stimulated rapid growth (cf. Port Carlisle, at Bowness- on-Solway, q.v.). By the 1850s 'superior' building-society housing was being developed at Denton Holme, and seven railway companies were pushing goods lines through the area – the Citadel Station was reserved purely for passenger trains – and building depots and sorting yards. The mill-owners moved away, upwind of the smoke, to villas along the rising Dalston Road.

ST JAMES, St James Road. 1865–7 by *Andrews & Pepper* of Brad- ford. The church of a well-off suburb. Rock-faced, quite large, with an apse and a SW steeple with a broach spire. Geometri- cal tracery. High scissor-truss roof. Low round columns, coarse leaf-crocket capitals of an entirely Victorian type.

(STAINED GLASS. Apse, by *J. Scott & Son*, 1867–8. Two by *A. K. Nicholson*, S (1906) and N (1932). Also one S by *G. E. R. Smith*.)

CONGREGATIONAL CHAPEL, now Carlisle Christian Fellowship, on a sliver of land between Charlotte Street and Junction Street. Octagonal, with two wings, by *Ralph Nicholson* of Halifax, 1860–1. Pyramidal roof with extra dormer gables. Little flying buttresses. Entrance stairs hooded in the thickness of the wall. The oval lecture room was added by the same architect in 1878.

BATHS, James Street. 1883–4. By *Joseph Hepworth*, a civil engineer (Kelly). The Turkish bath was added in 1909; tiling and flooring by *Minton, Hollins & Co*. The plunge room is a cross-in-square, with lunettes lighting the arms and a coloured skylight in the centre. The four columns bulge lasciviously with shiny faience. Striped keyhole doors, mahogany and coloured-glass cubicles. The whole room is richly tiled in shades of olive and pea. Also baths to the N, added 1975.

GAS WORKS, Rome Street. Carlisle was early into public gas provision, and a works opened in 1819. The elegant framework remains of a gasholder of 1878, a pioneer in the use of concrete in its construction.

ELECTRIC LIGHTING STATION, James Street. 1899. Two-storey offices in semi-glazed red brick with terracotta details, including a large panel under a fancy Flemish gable proudly declaring municipal ownership. Generator halls and boiler house behind. The electric tramway was to open in 1900 and guaranteed a continuing baseload for this costly municipal enterprise. Now part of Carlisle Enterprise Centre (small business units).

Also in James Street HUDSON SCOTT'S factory for printed tins, 1869 and 1887.

CANAL BASIN, at the foot of Caldewgate. Little survives of the installations. A pretty red sandstone pavilion built as a gate-keeper's cottage now guards an undistinguished industrial estate. A wheel pumped water up from the River Eden, 50 ft (15 metres) below. In 1839 a 60-in. (1.5-metre) Cornish engine was installed to supplement it. The sluices and pit for the water wheel and the foundations of the engine bed survive beside the footpath along the Eden's l. bank.*

CARR'S BISCUITS (now McVities), Caldewgate. Jonathan Dodgson Carr, a Quaker, came from Kendal in 1831. The prototype of his patent biscuit-cutting machine is preserved within the works. Demolition of the five-storey frontage building in the 1990s has left a visual muddle. TEMPERANCE HALL of 1861 opposite the works.

DIXON'S MILL (Shaddon Mill), Junction Street. By *Richard Tattersall* of Manchester, 1835–7 (i.e. before the railway arrived). 70

---

*After the canal closed in 1853 the North British Railway built a locomotive depot nearby, supplied by a steam pump to take water from the river. Remains of this installation survive beside the footpath, ¼ m. downstream.

Undeniably monumental. Red sandstone, seven-storey block 225 ft (69 metres) long, of twenty-two bays of unrelieved evenness, save for a slight stepping forward at the ends. The windows have flat raised frames and completely unmoulded horizontal architraves. Hexagonal chimney of strongly tapering outline, rising 270 ft (83 metres) straight from the ground. It unfortunately lost its top 35 ft (11 metres) and cap in 1931, but still plays an important role in the townscape. Attached engine house at the W end, its single window rising to the third storey. Interior of fireproof construction, designed by the great engineer (*Sir*) *William Fairbairn*, following the model of Charles Bage's pioneering Ditherington Flax Mill of 1795 in Shrewsbury. Iron beams and columns support shallow brick vaults and tile floors. The largest cotton mills of the moment in England; by 1847 they demanded the labour of 8,000 people. Later used as a woollen mill. Now workshops and flats, converted in 2004 by *Unwin Jones Architects*. A new lift and staircase tower in turquoise-tinged glass was added at the NE corner.

The mill forms a striking group with the octagonal church (p. 261) also on Junction Street. From the opposite side, Kendal Street is lined up exactly on the chimney – an awe-inspiring perspective.

FERGUSON BROS' WORKS, off North Street in Denton Holme, s. The most notable of a sequence of large C19 and C20 factories on North Street, Norfolk Street, Nelson Street, Junction Street and the Willow Holme, following the course of a mill race. In 1824 Joseph Ferguson established a bleach and dyeworks beside the Holme Head weir, adding by 1865 spinning and weaving sheds, an unusual early example of vertical integration. The 1850s OFFICES stand just upstream of the weir facing Denton Street, of sandstone with a pilastered porch in what was, until a three-bay r. extension, a central position in a nine-bay range. A third storey added 1899 (by *Henry Higginson*). Later extensions to the l. have further weakened the composition. The main works building rises behind (1865 and early C20). Immediately downstream, a three-storey thirteen-bay WEAVING SHED, expanded from a nine-bay two-storey block of the 1850s. Generous and regular fenestration, with flat brick arches and sandstone sills. The varying brickwork shades tell of enlargements, but the original proportions and details continue. Then the two-storey former MANAGER'S HOUSE of *c.* 1850, Georgian proportions under a shallow hipped roof with oversailing eaves. The canted bays either side of the square porch give the date away. Downstream again, BRIDGE TERRACE, workers' housing of 1852–4 by *John Hodgson*, with characteristic Carlisle use of pale header bricks between dark stretchers in Flemish bond. The earliest houses have a particularly shallow roof pitch. They look over open space, originally a bowling green, to the river. In 1881–2 the Ferguson brothers commissioned a TEMPERANCE COFFEE TAVERN from *G. D. Oliver*. Octagonal, with a high pyramid roof and timber-framed dormer gables, it neatly turns the angle between Bridge Terrace and North Street. The whole riverside prospect is a pleasing testimony to a self-confident and philanthropic management.

ST JAMES' ROAD. No. 10 is a house by *Sir Robert Lorimer* for Sir James Morton, 1923. Named TUETHUR at Lorimer's suggestion because Morton spent his weekends elsewhere. Voyseyish in style and quite modest in size. The house was intended to incorporate boardroom and textile museum. The Carlisle mill of Sir James's SUNDOUR FABRICS was nearby in Lorne Crescent. Fire destroyed a weaving shed in 1914 and *Lorimer* designed its replacement – a simple L-shaped brick affair with large windows, pleasant proportions and brick patterns.

CUMBERLAND WRESTLERS, Currock Street. A *Harry Redfern* pub, 1937, in Georgian mode. Plum brick, buff sandstone, small-pane sashes. The building is symmetrical about the two entrances, each brought forward under a small pediment.

OUTER DISTRICTS

1. South and south-east: Currock, Harraby and Upperby

ST ELISABETH, Arnside Road, Harraby. By *D. T. Johnson*, 1966–7. Bleakly situated amid cheap low-rise housing. Square block of yellow brick, with a concrete ring-beam, continuous clerestory and pyramid roof, linked by a flat-roofed narthex to a slightly battered tower, featureless apart from a row of slits (designed for bells).

(ST HERBERT, Currock. Built as a mission hall in 1932. Extended, 1967–9.)

ST JOHN THE BAPTIST, Upperby. 1843. Of the Commissioners' type, plain, with lancets and W tower. Bell-openings with Y-tracery. Chancel added in 1889–90 by *C. J. Ferguson*, with a Dec E window with STAINED GLASS by *Heaton, Butler & Bayne*, c. 1920. Parish centre on the N side, 1975. Surrounded by a municipal cemetery.

ST MARGARET MARY (R.C.), Scalegate Road, Currock. 1961–2. Early Christian basilica, brick, with an open five-arch narthex, a campanile, and three round apses. The detail is a little more adventurous than St Bede (p. 264), which is not to say better. Tear-drop-shaped windows at the sides, industrial-looking vents to the tower.

CEMETERY, Dalston Road. By *J. M. & J. Hay* of Liverpool, 1855–6. Elegiac landscape, just the right mix of formal layout and informal contouring. Broad roadways lined with shaped dark yews, nicely set off by the symmetrically placed chapels in warm brick. Lodge-cum-gateway. – MONUMENT to Peter Nicholson, architect (†1844), by *R. W. Billings*, 1856. In the form of an interpenetrating triangular plinth and obelisk. Just as weird as it sounds, but it composes well with the cypresses.

ROSE AND CROWN, Upperby Road. 1930, by *Harry Redfern*. One-and-a-half storeys, white, with shaped gables. Set back behind a cobbled forecourt, and originally a bowling green at the side overlooked by a loggia.

LOCOMOTIVE DEPOT (former), South Western Terrace, off Currock Road. Built in 1896 for the Glasgow & South Western Railway. The original plain six-road straight shed is now embedded in later accretions. Closed to locomotives in 1924; now the only surviving engine shed of the seven separate railway companies that served Carlisle. The charming contemporary red brick houses stepping in pairs down the street were built for GSWR workers, probably to designs by *James Miller*.

REPEATER STATION, London Road, at the corner of Hillcrest Road. Built for the G.P.O. in 1964. A mast 264 ft (81 metres) high, the highest object in the Carlisle sky. It is quite thrilling to look at, a steel skeleton in diminishing tiers, each with a perimeter platform, and now festooned with dishes; a touch of Blackpool, a touch of oil rig.

2. West of the Caldew: Morton, Raffles and Newtown

ST BARNABAS, Newtown. Built in 1935–6 by *Seely & Paget* to serve the Raffles housing estate. The long side elevation seems senselessly strung out. A pair of flyers at the E end, a section of aisle and clerestory, an oblong tower with a red stone doorway breaking the whiteness, a longer boxy nave with a mansard roof, broken by two transept-like but non-projecting gables, and a flat-roofed narthex with more red stone. Windows are round- or flat-topped, big or little, in groups or singles, with two domestic dormers for good measure, and oculi E and W. Once inside – high, white, light – it all falls surprisingly into place. Four great semicircular arches articulate the space, buttressed by the gables, the tower and the flyers. The worship space occupies the whole volume, but the tower, vestries and organ create a narrower chancel. This is articulated by a pair of opera-box-like projections for the organ pipes, matched by another pair over the E doors. Turning back, the W end presents another set piece of arches, with a groin-vaulted narthex. The FURNISHINGS are as original as the building. ALTAR, RAILS and CHOIR STALLS, streamlined Deco in flush woods. Stone PULPIT, matching READING DESK, and FONT, octagonal but on a streamlined base. Seating of bentwood folding chairs in fours. – RECTORY, adjacent. Also 1935, by *Fawcett Martindale*. Lucid, white, symmetrical, with an Italian loggia.

(ST LUKE, Morton. 1958–60. Big concrete crucks almost to the ground.)

ST BEDE (R.C.), Wigton Road. 1959 by *W. C. Mangan* of Preston. Italian Early Christian, of the type immediately recognizable in Britain as Roman Catholic. Red brick and pantiles, with an open-arched narthex and asymmetrically placed campanile. (STAINED GLASS. Baptistery window by *John Hardman Studios*, 1965.)

CUMBERLAND INFIRMARY, Newtown Road. The original building by *Richard Tattersall*, 1830–2, is extremely impressive. Grand and restrained ashlar front of eleven bays, with a giant tetrastyle portico of Greek Doric columns carrying a pediment. Wreaths in the frieze. One-storey corridor links of square piers and glass, each like an orangery, were added by *C. J. Ferguson* in 1870–4, but only one of his pavilions and rear wings is left. Their style matches Tattersall in front, turns domestic at the side, and is altogether utilitarian at the back. Further extensions 1908–13, by *Sir J. J. Burnet* – but what? Major additions include SCHEME ONE, behind and to to the w. Deepplan block, opened in 1975. Blue brick, striped with white matchboarding, under a flat concrete roof with upside-down brackets to hold the window-cleaning rail. Further w, the new MAIN BLOCK, 1997–2000 by *Llewelyn-Davies* under a Private Finance Initiative scheme. Four large courtyard blocks open off a glass-roofed mall, curving so as not to be too intimidating, with balconies and bridges. All white inside, with brightly colour-coded doors. In front, CROZIER LODGE, now a doctors' residence. Of the 1820s with an early c20 mansard roof.

(STRATHCLYDE HOUSE, Wigton Road. Built as the Home for Incurables, 1884–5 by *G. D. Oliver*, with additions. In a homely version of English Gothic.)

HORSE AND FARRIER, Orton Road. 1928–9, by *Harry Redfern*. Sussex vernacular after Lutyens, with hand-made flat tiles and bonnets over the numerous hips and dormers. White walls with weatherboarded gables and a hint of pargetting, bays with arched centre lights. Bowling green at the side, overlooked by a long wing for the tea and club room.

BUNKERSHILL, Orton Road, 2 m. SW. Large, white Late Georgian house. In the garden a re-erected two-light window in the Dec style, from the Abbey buildings (p. 237).

MORTON MANOR, Wigton Road, 1½ m. S. Early c19, of two storeys and five broad bays. Good staircase and metal railing.

At CUMMERSDALE, off Dalston Road, is THE CROFT, *c.* 1981 by *David Johnston* and *David Lamont* of *Johnson & Wright*. Extension 2002. Very large craft bungalow centred on the garden. On Cummersdale Road the SPINNERS ARMS, a State Management pub by *Harry Redfern*, 1930. White-painted brick, tile roof swept round the valleys. Rainwater channel stamped with a trumpeting elephant, gaping crocodile, tortoise, ostrich. Spaced out on the road are four little white COTTAGES of *c.* 1924 for the Land Settlement Agency (*see* Crofton Hall), each with its three-acre plot. One is scarcely changed, one derelict, one greatly extended, and one rebuilt by the Carlisle builder Fred Story, who was born here.

3. North of the Eden: Stanwix, Kingmoor, Etterby and Belah

ST MICHAEL, Church Street, Stanwix. It stands in the s corner of a Roman fort (*see* p. 266). A rebuilding of 1841–5 by *John Hodgson*. Commissioners' type; cruciform, with bald lancets. Straight-up w tower with octagonal buttresses (derived from Rickman's Holy Trinity, *see* p. 223) and blunt pinnacles.

The Early Christian apse was added in 1893. Broad open interior, flat ceiling with thin cross-ribs. – STAINED GLASS. Apse by *Powells*, 1890s-1914. S, 1966 by *Harry Stammers*. – MONUMENTS. Robert Ferguson †1816, by *Kirkbride* of Carlisle. With a figure of Faith. – Richard Ferguson †1860, almost a copy. – Capt. Hugh Patrickson †1821 by *Nixson*. Profile in relief, rather Neronic for an army captain. Military still life at the top. – Henry Hughes Dobinson, Archdeacon of the Niger, †1897, by *KSIA*, with a palm tree. – In the churchyard a table tomb to George Head Head †1876, with split-cusped piercings in the sides.

Of Uxelodunum, the largest ROMAN FORT on the Wall (10 acres), little is visible or known. It lies under the church and across the hilltop, bounded by Brampton Road and Well Lane. Part of the N wall, close to the fort's NW corner, is forlornly marked out in the car park of the Cumbria Park Hotel; this wall was built in the mid C2 when the Hadrianic fort was enlarged to project just N of the Wall itself.

ST MARK, Bracken Ridge, Belah. 1951–2. Plain, white-rendered walls under a copper roof. Perfunctory square E tower.

AUSTIN FRIARS SCHOOL, Etterby Scaur. 1891–2 for the Order of the Sacred Heart, and used successively as girls' school, boys' reformatory, orphanage and, since 1951, boys' school, always under the aegis of the Roman Catholic Church. Large, plain, three storeys and attic in red stone, with a big chapel making a T.

(BARN CLOSE, Well Lane. Arts and Crafts house of *c.* 1900 by *Norman Evill*, written up in *The Studio*.)

RICKERBY, 1¼ m. NE of the cathedral. The park is public, a fine playground for the city. WAR MEMORIAL by *Sir Robert Lorimer*, 1922. Inelegant granite stele, with wreaths and regimental badges ('. . . always difficult to design. This cenotaph business is a teaser,' he wrote). The park was laid out as part of the memorial. RICKERBY HOUSE and its environs, after some vicissitudes, have been developed by Fred Story for housing. The house was built round an C18 brick house *c.* 1835 for George Head Head, probably by *Christopher Hodgson*. Greek, faced with creamy ashlar. Tetrastyle Doric portico in front, hexastyle to the garden at the back. The entrance side is of five, the garden side of nine bays. (Staircase with heavy scrolly iron balustrade, immediately behind the entrance portico.) Extended 1879 for Miles McInnes, Head's nephew, in brick, with a tower. Doric LODGE, with a temple front of four columns at both ends and Head's motto, Study Quiet. The STABLES and various other eccentric outbuildings are by contrast Tudor, in deliberately rough and old-looking red brick, with much crowstepping. The exception is the former BOYS' SCHOOL, dated 1835, in ashlar with a little enclosed bellcote perched on the W gable.

REDFERN INN, Kingmoor Road. Of 1939, a tribute by *Joseph Seddon* to his boss Harry Redfern, architect of the State Management scheme. Designed round the bowling green at the back, to which it makes a shallow V with a balcony.

KING GARTH, ¾ m. NW of Cargo, off the road to Rockcliffe; on
the river bank. Carlisle Corporation's Fish House of 1733 and
1780, once occupied by the bailiff. Long building of whitewashed brick with lengthy inscriptions commemorating
mayoral visits for the annual salmon dinner.

CARTMEL (L)

3070

CARTMEL PRIORY. Founded for Augustinian Canons *c.* 1189 by
William Marshal, a landless second son who rose to be the parfait
knight, courtier and magnate. Marshal, granted the royal estate
of Cartmel by Henry II in 1186, was one of the four 'co-
justiciars' entrusted with the government by Richard I while he
was on crusade, and was Regent of England following the death
of King John in 1216. The Marshal's death in 1219 gives us an
end date for the eastern limb, crossing and transepts, and the
monastic quarters on the S; but apart from perhaps a section of
N wall only a stub of the nave had been built by then, and probably not the clerestories. In the mid C14 the S choir aisle was
rebuilt on a larger scale as the Harrington chantry, now called
the Town Choir. The following century saw the replacement of
most of the windows, and notably the insertion of an enormous
E window in about 1420. It is thought that in the mid C15 something drastic made it necessary for the canons to rebuild their
monastic precinct on the N side. Almost nothing remains either
side. The present nave was probably being built at the same time;
its outer walls post-date the changeover.

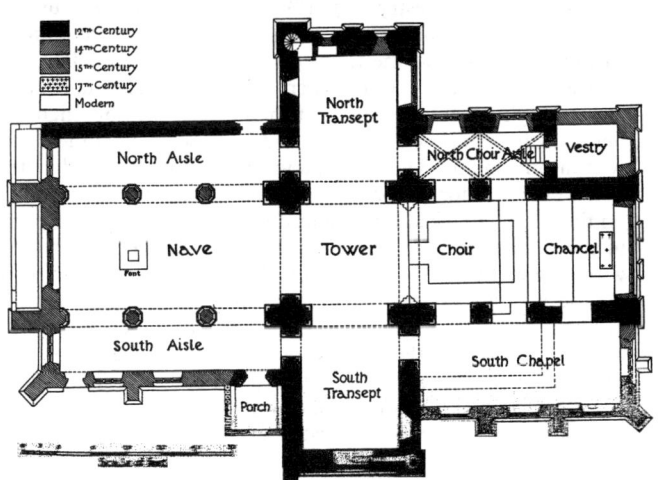

Cartmel Priory.
Plan, 1914

Cartmel Priory was suppressed in 1536, at which time there were ten canons.* The Chancellor of the Duchy of Lancaster ruled that the church, because used also by the parish, should 'stand still', but by the C17, like Lanercost and Holm Cultram (Abbey Town), it was in poor shape.

At this unlikely period in stepped George Preston of Holker (†1640), who from 1618, according to his monument, 'repaired this church being in great decay with a new roofe of tymber and beautified it within very decently with fretted plaister worke adorned the chancell with curious carved woodworke and placed therein a pair of organs of great valewe'. We have therefore the monastic church complete, giving an unparalleled impression of the relation of scale between it and the little town at its feet. Much C19 restoration, especially in 1857–c. 1870 by *E. G. Paley*.

EXTERIOR. The church is unusually broad and stubby: aisled chancel and nave each of three bays only, unaisled two-bay transepts, markedly broad crossing and tower. Broad buttresses with very slight set-offs. The low clerestory is Perp, with blocked tracery in the chancel. The unique feature is the diagonally set belfry stage: a three-dimensional demonstration of the medieval method of halving the square. It gives the church an extraordinary air of watchfulness. Nor should its defensive potential be overlooked. The church is battlemented throughout, with walkways in front of the s and w gables, square turrets on the transepts and raised corners elsewhere – i.e. not just for ornament. By building the belfry stage diagonally the fighting top of the low crossing tower was kept clear – it will be noted how its four sectors are linked.

The widened s chancel aisle makes a gorgeous display of flowing tracery of the 1340s in windows of four and five lights. There is virtually no E wall; the E window (nine lights) is of enormous size. NE vestry, 1677 (DCMS). None of the church's original lancets remain open, but their reveals can be seen at various points round the transepts and eastern arm. Two are in the N transept N wall, where the new night-stair door (round-arched) cuts into one of them. Perp window high up here. In the transept E wall a broad Perp window, and in the w wall one shafted lancet too, and in the least restored state. Some evidence for the original monastic buildings can be seen on the s – the blocked night-stair door (undoubtedly Norman) in the transept s wall, and in its w wall a square book recess with joggled head. Above this a blocked Norman window. Also on the s side a couple of corbels and a flashing-line for the cloister. The splendid s doorway of *c.* 1190 is hidden in the low C17 porch in the angle of the s transept: three orders of zigzag and three of colonnettes. The hoodmould ends in a snaky turn. The easternmost part of the nave wall is blank rubble, simply a back for the cloister. The rest is Perp. Its base-mould, but-

---

* The Priory held the right to appoint the guide over the treacherous sands, an official appointment that still exists – hence the sign at the s end of town: Lancaster over sands 15 m., Ulverston over sands 7 m. Both are much further now by road.

tresses and windows – which are hollow-moulded with three-centred heads, like Kendal – make it clear that this was built after the s cloister had gone. The N nave wall is thin featureless rubble – backing for the replacement cloister and nothing else. The crude corbels and flashing suggest that this was an unambitious affair, though there is a good N doorway with a snaky turn to the hoodmould, as on the s.

INTERIOR. The Norman s doorway opens into the E end of the nave. The scale of the crossing, a full twelve paces square (cf. Carlisle, only ten), determines the character of the whole building. Clustered shafting, with keels on the cardinal sides. The springing of the E arch is several feet higher. Round and pointed arches are employed where they fit best. The chancel arcades are round or even slightly more than round, whereas the entries to the aisles from the transepts are steeply pointed; their slight stilting suggesting an attempt to match the vaulting profile of the aisle. Rich decoration is bestowed upon some arches, both round and pointed, while others are finished with the simplest of chamfers. The decorative motifs of the s doorway reappear in the two-bay chancel arcade, though the arch mouldings are finer. But zigzag, also combined into lozenges, is present prominently, and on the (pointed) arch into the N chancel aisle. The arcade piers are of eight shafts, quite sturdy. As for capitals, the same basic type is applied everywhere, from the chancel arcade to the arches between transepts and nave aisles. In many cases it is left basic, but where it is carved the motifs are E.E., with crockets, a knotted snake motif, and even early stiff-leaf (small leaves, close to the bell). So the nave N doorway may mark the end of this one campaign, running *c*. 1190 to *c*. 1220. In favour of this interpretation, lancet windows occur, as we have seen, in the transepts. Tall pointed lancets (blocked) also at the E end of the choir, N and s. And the chancel triforium, admittedly of necessity later than the arcades below, consists entirely of a long row, originally unbroken, of small pointed arches on E.E. shafts. (More in the transepts, including the jambs of two in the N transept E wall that have been knocked together for the Perp E window, with the same arch moulding as the N nightstair doorway.) The choir clerestory is puzzlingly unsatisfactory. It has few and small openings, and they have flattened or segmental heads. Has the wall-plate been lowered, blocking the window heads, or was it never completed to its intended height? The square recesses between the windows, and the intermittent blocking of the triforium, seem to suggest worries about the loading. The choir was transformed by the vast E window, almost entirely doing away with the wall and flooding the church with light. It may have been the gift of Lord John Harrington (†1417). Its hard Perpendicular grid is softened and unified by the broad intersecting sub-arches of the tracery. The heads of the main lights are alternately pointed and ogee, creating a lively rhythm, and causing short lengths of transom to jump up and down too. Dr Murray Mitchell has shown that the tracery is of fine Tadcaster (Yorkshire) limestone, whereas the mullions are of local Quarry Flat stone. The inference is that tracery and glass were supplied together from York. The outermost lights of the tracery have been jigged about to make them fit. The even bigger E window of 1408 in York Minster, and the inserted W window of its dependency Southwell Minster, have the same fascinating rhythms. The beautiful SEDILIA and PISCINA, ruthlessly cut into for the Harrington monument (*see* below), are pure E.E.

Now for the choir aisles. The N aisle, called the PIPER CHOIR, is rib-vaulted, with the unexpectedly plain profile of just a single chamfer. The diagonal ribs spring from colonnettes and canted capitals. The S aisle is called the TOWN CHOIR, suggesting that no nave was available at the time for public worship. It was widened and extended E in the middle of the C14 to hold the Harrington tomb (*see* below). The springings for the removed rib-vault can be seen, and capitals at the W end. Two delightfully figured C14 corbels. The big windows mix Geometric and flowing motifs, and in the E window even Perp verticals alongside Dec mouchettes. Double SEDILIA with nodding ogee hoods, small PISCINA.

The C15 NAVE, although built of rubble rather than the fine ashlar of the rest, is a fine big-boned piece. The intended Norman nave is indicated by the toothing of the ashlar, by a set of responds, including diagonal ones for rib-vaulting in the aisles, and by blocked triforium entries under the aisle roof. The sturdy octagonal piers are well spaced, their arches rising considerably higher than the Normans – on the evidence of the triforium passage doorway – had intended. Three bays only, though wide; double-chamfered arches. A few capitals are carved with leaves, the rest left uncarved.

The high ROOFS are of C13 type throughout, massively single-framed with no longitudinal elements. George Preston's epitaph implies that these are C17 renewals; surely not, especially as his epitaph implies, and engravings show, that he hid the structure. The ceiling of the N transept is of 1850.

Finally we must assess the unique CROSSING TOWER, which means ascending via the SE transept turret and traversing the parapet. Pains have been taken to connect the accessible parts up here. Small bridges link the parapet walks around the angles of the tower. Higher up, the four triangular sectors of the intermediate roof are linked by doorways cutting through the corners of the belfry stage. The ringing chamber is spectacular. Its four corners are tunnel-vaulted out to the four great unmoulded diagonal arches, steeply pointed, which carry the bell-stage. The weight of the belfry is thus transferred onto the apexes of the crossing arches, balancing the extra thrust of the nave arcades. The haunches of the tunnel-vault also spread the load out evenly. The weight of the belfry is much less than that of a full-width structure of the same height, and is further reduced by the very wide four-light belfry windows. It is a brilliant exercise in medieval poise and counterpoise.

FURNISHINGS. The twenty-six STALLS were set up in 1430–40.   42
Their poppyhead finials are badly weathered, lending some
support to George Preston's assertion that the church needed
a new roof, but the MISERICORDS are mystifyingly perfect.
They include, on the S, a provocative double-tailed mermaid,
the Devil enthroned, ape and urine bottle (aping a doctor). On
the return, a Pelican in her Piety and a three-faced king. Under
the sub-prior's stall on the N is a unicorn and an oddly crystalline Tree of Life. Further along are a hart and hounds, and
the elephant and castle leaning against a tree. The style is
harder than that of the sinuous Carlisle misericords. The
CANOPIES and SCREEN, in fact everything above arm-rest
level, were installed by George Preston in the years following
1618. Their style is a fascinating mix. Naïve classical for the
columns with their Corinthian capitals, very elaborate Flamboyant Gothic tracery for the fretted backs. Carved in relief on
the columns are vines, twining both ways, and Instruments of
the Passion such as lamp, scourge, cross. Preston's motivation
for the re-creation of a functional enclosed choir is made clear
by the texts: 'Enter into his gates with prayse', and 'My soule
hath a desire and longing to enter into the courts of the Lord'.
In the screen the tracery panels are on hinges. – ROYAL ARMS
and COMMANDMENT BOARDS at the W end. 1681. These have
painted texts on the reverse; it is thought that they were
designed to stand upon the choir screen. – FONT COVER.
Simple, dated 1640. – FONT and stone PULPIT designed by
Paley, 1867. CHANDELIER. Of brass, 1734. Two tiers of arms.
– SCULPTURE. By *Josefina de Vasconcellos*: The True Vine, They
Fled by Night (1966), and Young Martyr, all fibreglass, and
Soul is Form and doth the Body Make, bronze (1991).

STAINED GLASS. The vast E window is filled mostly with
clear but not plain glass, tempering rather than hiding the view.
In the upper part of the three central lights and in the tracery
stained glass of about 1418 remains; York work in the soft style
associated with the workshop of John Thornton. In the centre
the Virgin flanked by an archbishop, perhaps William of York,
and John the Baptist. In the lights small figures of saints, some
labelled with scrolls. – In the Town Choir, portions of a mid-
C14 Jesse window of characteristic green and gold cast. More
medieval fragments in the N choir aisle and porch. – Of the
C19 glass the W (attributed to *Burlison & Grylls*) and N and S
transept windows (*Shrigley & Hunt*) imitate the E glass with
varying degrees of success. Aisle W windows also by *Shrigley
& Hunt*, 1886, stronger, with some particularly rich scenes in
the Te Deum window on the N.

MONUMENTS. In a C14 recess in the choir N wall Prior
William of Walton †1292. Slab with cross and inscription in
Lombard lettering. – Visible from here, but properly in the SE
chapel or Town Choir, is the Harrington tomb of *c.* 1345, one   25
of the best monuments of its date in England. It was originally,
it is thought, a small chantry standing in the midst of the
enlarged aisle, with a screened space at the head for priest and

altar. The overall form is not unlike like the shrines of St William in York and St Werbergh in Chester; the sculptural styles suggest a connection with contemporary monuments in Yorkshire.* Damaged in the Civil War, it was crammed by Thomas Preston into the N wall recess of the chapel, which was crudely opened through into the chancel for the purpose, as we have seen. The tomb-chest just fits but the altar was lost. Effigies of Lord John Harrington †1347 and Joan Dacre his wife, finely carved in white freestone. The diaper on her side includes the Dacre scallop shell. Both hold aloft presumably their hearts. A procession of little mourning Austin canons, minus their heads unfortunately, winds its way round the figures. They are carved direct out of the same stone as the effigies, and are not placed in niches: a unique feature. Below, a poignant frieze of crouching canons sing a requiem, some gathered round service books, one beating time. The architectural frame, although damaged and crudely repaired, is exquisite. The posts of the canopy are carved with shields, square fleurons, and also figures including the Virgin and Christ on a foliated cross. Both are of types internationally current in the early C14. In the corners the four Evangelists. The canopy has two bays, with slender ogee arches and a straight top with leaf motifs. On it Christ showing his wounds on the one side, the Coronation of the Virgin on the other. In the heads of the arches a representation of the soul being drawn up in a sheet by a pair of angels. The wooden tester is partly preserved, with a PAINTING of Christ in Majesty, medallions of the Signs of the Evangelists, and stars. – On the floor the recumbent effigy of an Augustinian prior, C13, presumably displaced by the Harrington monument. He is cowled, and holds up the chalice. – Disgracefully encroaching upon the SE window, Sir William Lowther †1705 and Dame Katherine Lowther †1700. Bust of Dame Katherine in an oval medallion with putti and an urn. – On the other side Sir Thomas Lowther of Holker †1745. A putto unveils a portrait medallion. An excellent piece. – Charles Goring †1843 aged nine, by *E. B. Stephens*. Mother, child, angel, broken wheels. – NE chapel, Edward Robinson, Clerk †1685, good wordy oval cartouche. Here and in the nave, plaques signed by *Webster* of Kendal, *Fawcett* of Lancaster (J. Newby †1834, with big draped urn), and *T. F. Tyson*, Ulverston. – Nave N, George Preston of Holker †1640. Painted board dated 1646, half given over to a splendid achievement of arms, the rest to his eulogy including the achievement of rescuing this church. – Lord Frederick Cavendish †1882, by *Thomas Woolner*, 1885. White marble effigy on an alabaster tomb-chest designed by *H. J. Austin*. – Outside against the S transept, Robert Webster of Quarry Flat †1799. The father of Francis and grandfather of George, architects. Urn of the said Quarry Flat stone in a pedimented niche.

* Mary Markus in *Church Monuments* II, 1996.

GATEHOUSE. Roughly contemporary with the Town Choir, i.e. early C14. Crudely built, with a high archway and two long windows of ogee lights high up, following the great scare created by the Scottish incursions of 1316 and 1322. This is the only identifiable part of the monastic precinct, though parts of the perimeter wall are under the houses of the market place or Square.

The SQUARE with its Cross, fish slabs and pump extends to the church, and is visually enjoyable everywhere. A bridge divides it in two. The best house is close to the church, early C18 of five bays, with arched, keyed-in windows and doorway with big segmental pediment. More attractive houses through the gate-house arch in CAVENDISH STREET, and E of the priory. (LOCK-UP, 30 yds N of the Post Office.)

(FRIENDS' MEETING HOUSES. The original meeting was at Height, a long way from Cartmel – 1 m. N of High Newton on the A590, 2½ m. SE of Newby Bridge. Built 1677, sold 1922 and now a dwelling called BARROW WIFE, with sashed windows. Burial ground across the road. Two cottages in Hagg Lane were converted into the present Meeting House in 1859; David Butler records the involvement of *Alfred Waterhouse*. It looks like a small school.)

RACECOURSE. Immediately W of the town. Beautifully situated on Cartmel Park, owned by the Cavendishes of Holker. The loop of the course weaves around outcrops of limestone with big trees. Organized racing started in 1856. New stand by *Rebecca Gibson* of *John Coward Partnership*, Cartmel, 2004.

CARTMEL FELL (L)

ST ANTHONY. Far away in the fells. Hard to find, and all the more rewarding for it. Built as a chapel of ease to Cartmel *c.* 1504 to fulfil the will of Anthony Knipe (†1500); carefully restored in 1911 by *John Curwen*. Long, low and grey, sloping down the hillside, half-hidden amongst rocks and verdure. Crouching saddleback tower, W, with low-pitched roof. Nave and chancel in one with curious lean-to extensions N and S added *c.* 1520 at the E end. Triplets of round-topped windows with minimal but nicely executed mouldings and hoods. An unmoulded pair over the priest's door on the S side is clearly later. The interior is perfect in its way, with its low-set slightly wonky windows, leaning-out walls and sloping floor. Low tie-beams with raking queen-struts. The NE outshut shows evidence of an intermediate floor, with tiny windows lighting both storeys, and a chimney; perhaps it offered occasional accommodation for the priest.

FURNISHINGS. ALTAR RAILS. A three-sided pen, with turned balusters. Later C17. – COWMIRE PEW. Probably *c.* 1521, with one-light divisions, and retaining traces of colour.

It is furnished as a rudimentary schoolroom, with aids to cal-
culation inscribed on benches and table. A sculpted figure of
Christ, probably from the rood, has been taken to Kendal
museum, but its small traceried Gothic canopy remains, not
in situ. – BURBLETHWAITE PEW. C17, but largely redone in
1810. – Another PEW made up of bench-ends, with the date
1696. – The rest made in the Kendal workshops of *Arthur
Simpson*, 1910–11. – Three-decker PULPIT, dated 1698. –
COMMANDMENTS BOARD with very charming Stuart angels.
– Some original STAINED GLASS, especially the radiant fragments of the five-light E window. Penny Hebgin-Barnes dates
it *c.* 1520. A careful restoration by *J. A. Knowles* of York in 1911
made it intelligible without adding anything new. On the far
l., a sly St Anthony with his T-shaped staff, bell and pig (with
its own bell). Outer r., St Leonard. Donor figures at their feet.
In the centre, the Crucifixion. In the intermediate lights, the
Seven Sacraments: Mass, Ordination, Matrimony (near-
complete), Unction and Penance (fragmentary), Baptism and
Confirmation (missing). A tiny figure of Christ stands upon
the altar of the Mass to signify the Real Presence. Matrimony
is especially charming for its faces and costumes. Each is linked
to the wounded Christ by an outflowing of ruby-red blood (cf.
Bowness, where the blood is collected into chalices; also
Llandyrnog in Denbighshire). More early C16 fragments in the
N side window.
(Close by is HODGE HILL, *c.* 1560, a beautiful old farm with a
charming spinning gallery.)
BROADLEYS and MOOR CRAG. *See* Bowness-on-Windermere.

CASTERTON (W)

The Rev. William Carus Wilson was an Evangelical clergyman at
whose Clergy Daughters' School the Brontë sisters suffered in
the 1820s. Appointed Perpetual Curate of Casterton in 1833, he
built a new church, parsonage, and schools both for his girl
boarders and for the village. He published *Helps to the Building
of Churches and Parsonage Houses* in 1835. Eastlake wrote, 'the
most jealous critic would have frankly pronounced them . . . free
from those artistic attractions in which one section at least of the
religious public saw at that time a pitfall and a snare'.

HOLY TRINITY. 1831–3. Clumsy lancet style, in almost
undressed limestone ('the rough appearance is preferred, as
giving more the appearance of antiquity'). Undersized W
tower, partly embraced. Originally a tiny chancel without side
windows, and a chimney over the chancel arch. The architect
was almost certainly *George Webster*, who built a number of similarly starved churches (the type was also recommended in
Carus Wilson's book). The pale sandstone chancel added

c. 1860 by *E. G. Paley* puts the rest to shame, with its scholarly
E.E. lancets, assured in their spacing and relation of window
to wall, and overtopping with its steep roof the low-pitched one
of the wide nave. Space for the new chancel was tight – its NE
corner stands on the retaining wall of the lane – so its scale is
perforce small. The nave interior is broad and unobstructed,
with a scissor-braced roof. The tower intrudes, forming a baptistery. Paley's chancel arch is as wide as it can be, without a
screen, so there is no sense of a separate room. – REREDOS,
CHOIR STALLS, PULPIT and PEWS look like *Paley*, but the
FONT, bulgy and polychromatic, does not. – MONUMENTS.
Rev. W. Carus Wilson †1859, and other Gothic tablets, mainly
1860s. What makes the interior exciting are the WALL PAINT-
INGS and STAINED GLASS. The chancel scheme of 1893–9 is
by *Henry Holiday*. Three E lancets represent the Ascension,
completed by the angels of Heaven in the painting above. N
and S lancets show scenes from the Life and Passion of Christ.
The painting over the S lancets, Christ preaching, is particularly engaging in the way Holiday has used the window surrounds for the figures to lean on. The two W lancets, also by
Holiday (1895) are delightful. The six days of Creation, in
roundels, alternate with verses from the Benedicite represented
with great vigour and movement. Especially good is 'O ye
Winds of God', with a wonderful vortex effect.* The baptis-   92
tery window (centre; †1884) is by *Shrigley & Hunt*. The rest of
the nave was painted in 1905–12 by *James Clark*. On the N wall
are three large scenes of Moses, prefigurations of Christ. On
either side of the chancel arch John the Baptist announces his
coming. Over the NW door the Annunciation, over the S door
the Magnificat; these two the most convincing of the cycle. The
Nativity is on the W wall, but the shepherds S of the tower have
been lost. Finally, one after the other along the S wall, Christ
as the True Vine, Light of the World, and Good Shepherd.
Clarke's paintings are more pastelly that Holiday's, and bear a
fatal resemblance to Sunday School prizes of the period. The
nave windows, inserted in 1919 with advice from Clarke, are
without colour, relying on texture and leading. – (WAR MEMO-
RIAL CROSS, churchyard. 1919–20 by *Comper*.)

CASTERTON SCHOOL. Carus Wilson also built a PARSONAGE,
now the headteacher's house; the SCHOOL, now OLD
SCHOOL, refurbished *c.* 1990 by *Gill Dockray & Partners*; and
a VILLAGE SCHOOL: all with diagonally set chimneys, decorative bargeboards and Tudor dripmoulds. The village school,
now extra classrooms, is the prettiest, with dormers and finials.
The school's ARTS CENTRE was built *c.* 1990 by *G. Dockray
& Partners*.

(CASTERTON HALL. 1811, and probably by *John Webb*, who also
designed Leck Hall in N Lancs. Five-bay ashlar front with
a semicircular Doric porch. Round the corner a big bow and
blank niches on either side. Entrance hall with shallow

---

*These windows were adapted from cartoons for Grace Church, Utica, USA.

segmental plaster vault. Staircase hall with oval skylight. John Martin Robinson notes a Tuscan CATTLE SHED in the park.)

CASTERTON OLD HALL, W of the church. C17, with mullioned-and-transomed windows. One overmantel is made up of early C16 woodwork – monsters and human heads.

(CASTERTON GRANGE, N of the school. By *Ewan Christian*, 1848.)

CASTLE CARROCK (C)

5050

No castle.

ST PETER. 1826–8 by *John Dixon*, incorporating bits of earlier fabric. Roughcast. Thin W tower, no separate chancel. It was violently, but incompletely, Normanized by *William Marshall* in 1888–9. He reorganized the windows in Early Romanesque style, French or Italian rather than English, with marble shafting. One approximates to Doric, with triglyphs, another to Corinthian, with foliage and volutes. Two of the windows however keep their plain early C19 character. – Norman ALTAR RAIL and PULPIT. – Queen Anne ROYAL ARMS, i.e. 1702–14. – STAINED GLASS. All commemorating members of the Watson family †1886–1904. E (1888), NW and S next from W are by *E. R. Suffling*. – MONUMENTS. John de Begho, rector †1346, slab with foliated cross, chalice and book.

WATSON INSTITUTE, on what looks like a grassed-over road in front of the church. 1897. Stage-set frontispiece of a backless tower with higher turret and battered base.

GELT LODGE. In the village. C19. 'Osborne' tower with a clock. Subdivided and extended.

TARN LODGE, 1 m. SW. 1807, for John Bell. Five-bay front with one-bay wings set slightly back, as at Low House, Armathwaite, but with hipped roofs. Doorway with broken pediment behind a convex porch with four Doric columns. (Polygonal FOLLY TOWER with an attached stair-turret on the hill.)

CASTLERIGG (C) *see* ST JOHN'S IN THE VALE

CASTLE SOWERBY (C)

3030

ST KENTIGERN. White, low, vernacular, but surprisingly spacious considering the absence of habitation. Powerful view W to the Northern Fells. Double bellcote, C16 or C17. Very wide porch arch with two chamfers, presumably C14 or C15. S doorway with a roll moulding, probably *c.* 1250. Of about the same time the extended chancel, necessitating a rise of six steps, with its lancets and traces of an eastern triplet – or was the nave floor lowered? The octagonal columns of the the five-bay S arcade stand on high bases. The W respond is round, perhaps C13. The chancel arch was removed in the C18. Restoration by *C. J. Ferguson*, 1888 (DCMS). – FONT, probably 1671. – ROYAL ARMS. 1752. – STAINED GLASS. E window by *Percy Bacon*, 1927.

CAUTLEY

See *The Buildings of England, Yorkshire West Riding: Leeds, Bradford and the North.*

CLEATOR AND CLEATOR MOOR (C)   *0010*

Not outwardly enticing, as Jollie remarked in his 1811 *Directory*, but abounding in coal, limestone and iron ore. It developed rapidly in the C19 with mines, furnaces and railways. The population progressed from 362 in 1801 to 1,779 in 1851, doubling to 3,995 in 1861, 7,061 in 1871, and in 1901 nearly 10,000. Cleator village, although mightily grown, was upstaged in the early 1860s by the planned town of Cleator Moor 1 m. N, with its municipal square of the 1880s. However the mines were all closed by 1925, and by 2001 the population had fallen to *c.* 7,500. The long rows of terraced cottages, roughcast and not quite even, are just beginning to blossom from drabness into colour. Green spaces, cycle tracks and light industrial sheds show where railways, works, mines and opencast pits once were.

St Leonard, Cleator. On the old village street off the A5086. The chancel is Norman – see the flat clasping buttresses and N window. The nave was rebuilt in 1841–2 by *George Webster* of Kendal in basic lancet style. In 1900–3 *J. H. Martindale* reshaped and re-clad it, adding the N porch and vestry linked by a two-bay cloister, with segmental arches and companionable seating. Double bellcote on the NW shoulder, heavily buttressed in preparation for an intended NW tower. One C15 window in the S wall. Martindale found a damaged PISCINA in the S wall and the Norman window and doorway on the N, as well as traces of wall painting. The broad undivided interior is a Webster relic, enlivened by Martindale with a pulpit in a

niche in the s wall and a baptistery at the w end, both with
ribbed arches. – FONT. Small, octagonal, with rolls up the
angles; perhaps 1660s. – CHOIR STALLS in a low curved pen.
– Early C20 STAINED GLASS of greenish cast, by *Heaton, Butler
& Bayne*, and *Abbott & Co.* (two, nave s).

ST JOHN EVANGELIST, Leconfield Street, Cleator Moor.
1870–2. In the Norman style by *C. J. Ferguson*, who was good
at it. Outwardly unenticing, but a structural *tour de force*. Few
and simple elements: w tower massively square, plain and
unbuttressed; nave, aisles and clerestory; chancel with a steeper
roof and longer lancets, as though a little later. The N doorway
takes up a whole bay, with three orders of arches and colonnettes under an extension of the roof. The interior is broad,
lighter than anticipated thanks to the wide window splays.
Astonishingly, it is vaulted throughout. Quadrant half-vaults
for the aisles, pointed barrel-vault to the high nave with groins
for the clerestory openings, both on transverse arches of brick
and stone. Domical rib-vault for the tower, and an intersecting rib-vault for the chancel. The vaults and internal walls
unfortunately painted white; they are of yellow brick with
bands of pinkish stone, as at Bridekirk. Arcade piers of quatrefoil section with acanthus capitals. Round chancel and tower
arches, with a fat roll of brown stone. – PULPIT and READING
DESK. Lovely Romanesque pieces in oak. – LECTERN. A spirited wooden eagle on a knot of conker-tree leaves and fruit. –
FONT. Big square tub under the tower. – STAINED GLASS by
Reed Millican, 1972 and 1985. E, Christ blessing, net and fishes,
corn and sickle. S, the Virgin.

ST JOHN'S MISSION, Wath Brow. 1881, using materials from a
Wesleyan chapel. Small but prominent stone tower and spire,
the rest roughcast.

OUR LADY OF THE SACRED HEART (R.C.), on the A5086
between Cleator and Cleator Moor. 1869–72 by *E. W. Pugin*,
the third and most spectacular of his w Cumbrian trio, built
to serve the many Irish immigrants. Large, rock-faced, with
lancets. w bellcote teeteringly tall, as Pugin liked it, and fanciful in its details. In the aisles two lancets per bay with a vesica
in between filled with a block of yellow stone. Were they meant
to be carved? Inside, this resolves itself to a jumpy rhythm of
cross-arch–window–niche–window–cross-arch. In the niches
brightly painted leaning-forward statues. The piers are of
toffee-coloured stone, each having an extra shaft emerging
glutinously from it, supported on a bracket off the high red
stone base. These shafts go straight through the lushly carved
capitals to their own capitals higher up. They carry nothing but
the wall-shafts notionally supporting the feet of the wooden
high roof, whereas the stone arches of the aisles emerge with
no preparation at all. It is all, as Pevsner said, exactly what what
one means by debased. Six steps climb up to the alabaster and
brass ALTAR RAIL. – Towering ALTAR and REREDOS by *Pugin
& Pugin*, 1885, with figure carving by *A. R. Wall*. In 1978 the
BAPTISTERY was pushed out of the N doorway, of flimsy glass

and wood with tall corner ears.* – STAINED GLASS. Many by
Earley Studios of Dublin, up to 1961, in the style of Harry
Clarke. Richly jewelled colours, sad green faces, attenuated
hands and feet. The best are the triplet in the N transept, and
in the narthex. Earlier windows by *Francis Barnett* of Edinburgh, and *Hardman*.

GROTTO constructed by unemployed men in 1926–7.

MARKET PLACE, Cleator Moor. The municipal buildings stand
in the middle, not round the edge. Local Government Offices
1879, former Library, 1894, and the present Library which is
dated 1906. All are essentially to the same design (architect
T. L. Banks?): a single storey on a basement, of red sandstone,
with grey granite columns for a portico. FOUNTAIN, 1903, in
two colours of granite, the pelican on top missing. SCULP-
TURE, 1988, by *Conrad Atkinson*. Three slabs of steel cut out
and stencilled: Miner, Phoenix and Hand. On the s side the
CO-OP has its factory with a tower, on the W side its shop with
a long iron veranda. In 1878 the *Northern Counties Gazette*
called the Cleator Co-op a 'monster Institution' with thirteen
branches, mill and farm.

THE FLOSH, now Ennerdale Hotel, on the main road SW of Our
Lady. Cream roughcast and red sandstone dressings. To a
house already enlarged in 1837 was added an Elizabethan S
wing with five gables dated 1866 TMA (Thomas Ainsworth),
with a phoenix emblem. A disused porch is castellated, with
gargoyles and much fussy carving. In the cross-hall a monstrously overdesigned Gothic fireplace, also dated 1866. The E
rooms overlooking the garden, with their elaborately moulded
and gilded ceilings, can all be thrown together by sliding
partitions.

INDUSTRIAL BUILDINGS. At the S entrance to Cleator village,
an early C19 former SPADE FORGE, of random red sandstone.
Two low storeys. In the gable-end, a semicircular arch indicates the position of the ring drive which took power from the
main water wheel to drive the forge hammer. Further N, on the
banks of the River Ellen, Thomas Ainsworth's monumental
FLAX MILL of 1859, on the site of a predecessor of *c.* 1800. It
tries to look like a country house in its setting in the meadows.
Two storeys with crenellations, large windows with hoodmoulds and central mullions. The main façade faces S, a block
of five of its thirty bays towards the W end set forward. At
the NE corner an engine house with a detached circular
chimney on a square panelled plinth. All in finely laid red
sandstone.

BREWERY. N of Cleator Moor, beyond the bridge over the former
Whitehaven, Cleator & Egremont Railway (1875), a handsome
former brewery, 1873. The hipped roof is broken by a lucam
in the SW corner. Mashing floor indicated by horizontal

---

*Remnant of a bold reordering, with a circular altar right in the middle, overhung
by a stainless steel CORONA by *Gilbert Ward*, and surrounded by seating arranged
diamond-wise. Removed 2006.

louvres, emphasized by heavy sandstone framing which makes strong rectangular patterns on the town- and road-facing sides.

CLIBURN (W)

St Cuthbert. A lovely spot overlooking a sweep of river with great oaks. Small Norman church with an unusually short chancel, turned into a near-square by a s aisle added in the thorough restoration and beautification of 1886–7. Norman s doorway and chancel N window. The doorway has a lintel at whose ends stand two small figures. Above that a blank tympanum and zigzag arch. The chancel arch may be Norman too, but is completely redone. – FONT. The shaft is round and Norman. Shallow zigzag pattern. – STAINED GLASS. By the font, the Baptism of Christ and Christ with children, by *Morris & Co.*, 1910.

Cliburn Hall. Towered house drastically modernized in 1966, erasing all appearance of antiquity. With its utilitarian windows and pebbledashing it looks like an unfashionable block of Modernist flats; an interesting contrast with the latest houses in the village with their 'period' detail. The C14 tower had an unusual mid-C15 well-tower linked to it by a bridge. Major improvements – a new entry, stair-tower, and domestic wing – were made by Richard de Cleburn in 1567, with a rhyming inscription. The tower was refenestrated then, though it kept its fighting top until *c.* 1872.

Crossrigg Hall, 1¼ m. ESE. Old house re-cased, plus new reception rooms, in 1864 by *Anthony Salvin*. Greatly enlarged with a notable staircase and tower in 1915–18 by *J. H. Martindale* of Carlisle. Tudor, with battlements and mullioned-and-transomed windows.

CLIFTON (C)

St Luke. On a spur of high ground at Bridgefoot, a fragment of village orphaned by the realigned A66 and A595 roads. Rebuilt in 1858, and in 1900 by *James Howes*, but retaining a Late Norman s doorway with a single-chamfered arch, hood-mould with billet and little flat triangles, and nailhead in the imposts. (CROSS-SHAFT, found in 1900. One of the most important pieces of C10 Jellinge-influenced sculpture in the country. Serpentine animals and little struggling men – an image of Hell. The arrangement of the carving in vertical strips is a local characteristic.)

At Bridgefoot, on the River Marron ¼ m. w of the bridge, a late C18 SPADE FORGE. The main building is now a house. Two in-line wheel pits survive on its w side, with the remains of a breast-shot wheel. To the NW the small building where the spades were made. Sizeable mill pond, and a good set of weirs and sluices.

CLIFTON (W)

5020

s of Penrith, on the A6.

ST CUTHBERT. Raised on a mound; the A6 goes round it. Small C12 nave, porch, long narrow C13 chancel, C14 aisle built of very large stones, windowless to the N. s doorway with undecorated tympanum and shouldered lintel. The blocked N doorway is like the screens doors at Clifton Hall tower (*see* below). Partly rebuilt in 1846, with original materials. A gas explosion in 1943 accounts for the partial rebuilding of the E end, and in particular the peculiar tripartite chancel arch. The N aisle has lost its arcade and opens to the church by a single shapeless arch. – PULPIT and CHOIR STALLS are made up with pieces from Brougham Hall, heavily carved in Continental style. – STAINED GLASS. A couple of medieval fragments were saved in the E lancets: St John, and the Virgin (supposed to be a portrait of Eleanor of Engayne, mistress of Clifton Hall in the C14). – MONUMENTS. Wybergh arms, 1738, in the N aisle. – In the churchyard, bronze urn on a square base to the Rev. William Hogarth †1816.

CLIFTON HALL (English Heritage). Preserved tower, reckoned to be a late example of the type (C15 or C16), quarantined in the middle of a busy farm. It looks impressive with its battlements and taller turret, but is not seriously defensive. Far too many doors for a start. Three and possibly once four on the s, one on the N and one at an angle on the NE corner. It has not moreover always been free-standing, as now. The s side shows the scar of a roof. If this was of a great hall, then the multiple doors declare the tower to have been a service wing with solar over. The N door is exactly opposite the widest s door, as if for a kitchen passage. However there is also a row of strong corbels unrelated to the roof scar. The canted NE door was the entrance from an earlier hall. In the SW corner a wide turning stair, with its own outer door, leads to the upper floors and parapet. To the E large C18 windows in three tiers. Hipped roof within the parapet walk, with complicated multiple struts. Walled pleasure garden opposite, with an arched alcove. The FARM, magnificently situated with huge views, has a semicircular open gin house, and big cobbled yard lined with stables. M6 motorway and West Coast main-line railway pass close by.

WETHERIGGS POTTERY, 1¼ m. ESE. A remarkable survivor of a working country pottery, started in 1855 as an estate brick-

works and tilery. The buildings appear to stand on a slight eminence, the result of the extraction of clay all around. The principal structures surviving from earlier days include the
RESERVOIR; the BLUNGER (a quaint outdoor mixing device
which washed stones out of the freshly dug clay); the 1860s
ENGINE HOUSE, built mainly of random rubble, with its 15-ft
(4.5-metre) square chimney; the SETTLING and SUN PANS
where clay slurry was dried out; and a 20-ft (6-metre) high circular beehive KILN embraced by a square hovel. The present
kiln dates from 1913 but occupies the foundations of the 1860s
structure. Among the tourist stuff it was in 2008 still producing earthenware to its old simple practical country patterns.

COCKERMOUTH (C)

1030

Castle and brewery occupy the peninsula where the River Cocker
joins the larger Derwent. The confluence renders the town peculiarly liable to flood, most seriously in November 2009. Across
the Cocker, the broad Main Street runs E–W, parallel to the
united rivers as they flow westward. When larger-scale industrial
processes began to develop in the late C18, this position provided
the town with the water and power needed. By the mid C19 there
were about fifty significant industrial sites.

ALL SAINTS, Kirkgate. 1852–4. 'Some very odd proceedings
have been taking place at Cockermouth,' reported *The Builder*
in 1851. *James Swingler's* church of 1709–11, which replaced
the medieval chapel of ease, had burnt down in 1850. A competition went to *Hay* of Liverpool. Then, in a *volte face*, a new
design was ordered from *Joseph Clarke* at a meeting at which
both architects were present. 'Some curious scenes then took
place.' Clarke's plan was rejected, but nevertheless his is the
church that was built. It is an academic exercise, owing nothing
to the genius of the place – too tall, too solemn, too Dec. Tall
crossing tower and recessed spire, nave and aisles, transepts
with E aisles, and a long chancel of course. The interior is dominated by the crossing. Effortful piers with arches dying into
them carry the tower, with a rib-vault. The nave piers are by
contrast tall, slender and cylindical, with rich foliage capitals.
Geometrical tracery. Anomalous plain corbels stick out of the
nave walls; a gallery may indeed have been contemplated, until
the pew problem was solved by the building of Christ Church.
– FITTINGS. REREDOS by *Caröe*, 1890. – FONT. A rich piece,
quatrefoil-shaped on four fat legs. – STAINED GLASS. E
window, a Wordsworth memorial, by *Hardman*, 1853; badly
faded. W by *Kempe & Co.*, *c.* 1891, with stock figures of martyrs.
S windows by *Cox, Sons & Buckley*, 1880s; Jesus walking on the
waves (baptistery) is particularly good. – MONUMENTS.
Embossed brass to Andrew Green Thompson †1889. –

Tablet to Henry Bell †1876 by *Walker & Emley*, Newcastle-upon-Tyne.

Atmospheric hilltop CHURCHYARD with big trees and fine gravestones. CHURCH ROOMS, S. 1896–7 in a somewhat severe Tudor style with mullions and transoms.

CHRIST CHURCH, Gallowbarrow. 1865, by *Bruce* of Whitehaven for the Rev. H.B.L. Puxley (a design by *Charles Buckeridge* of Oxford was rejected). An old-fashioned design, in rock-faced stone. Plain NW tower with blunt pinnacles, tall nave windows, but the plate tracery and drip terminations characteristic of the 1860s. Barn-like interior with galleries on three sides carried on iron piers with capitals like tyre-less car wheels. Lightly framed roof. – STAINED GLASS. Running across the five E lancets like a framed painting, Christ casting out spirits, *c.* 1882. Said to be by *Heaton, Butler & Bayne* but more like O'Connor. – PARISH ROOMS on South Street, added in 1880. – FAIRFIELD SCHOOL, immediately S; 1876, 1884 and 1887, with its own little tower.

ST JOSEPH (R.C.), Crown Street. By *T. G. Gibson* of Newcastle, 1856. Plain, with paired trefoiled lancets, bellcote, and a thin hammerbeam roof, the trusses closely spaced. The three-sided apse was added *c.* 1904.

CONGREGATIONAL CHAPEL (United Reformed). By *C. W. Eaglesfield*, 1850. Spiky Gothic three-gable façade in limestone ashlar set back from the Main Street. The outer gables are extremely steep. Interior divided horizontally in 1989. An older chapel of 1735, and a clumsily re-erected porch dated 1719, are behind.

METHODIST CHAPEL, Lorton Street. 1932. Red brick and white terracotta.

FRIENDS' MEETING HOUSE, Kirkgate. By *R. S. Marsh*, 1884, using the side and back walls of its C18 predecessor. Like a bank; Italianate, single-storey, with a Doric porch. (Interior divided by a movable partition of sashes.) Graveyard behind.

COCKERMOUTH CASTLE, Castlegate. No keep. The triangular inner bailey was built by William de Fortibus *c.* 1220 on the spur of high ground between the two rivers, with a D-shaped tower at the apex and a ditch across the land side. Within this a hall and family accommodation were built in the 1350s by Thomas de Lucy. This is all in ruins. In 1368–1408 the outer bailey took shape to the E, under Lucy's daughter Maud and her husband Gilbert de Umfraville, with an inner gatehouse and kitchen tower filling the original ditch, and a new ditch (since infilled) in front. Maud's second husband Henry Percy, 1st Earl of Northumberland, completed the outer gatehouse and Flag Tower, which are what you see from Castlegate. Georgian and Victorian buildings line the outer bailey's walls. The castle is the summer seat of Lady Egremont. Unsuspected from without, a lushly exotic garden flourishes within the ruined walls high above the town.

The OUTER GATEHOUSE is impressively large, with a three-stepped tunnel-vault. A forebuilding or barbican is partly preserved to the E. The inner doorway is round-arched with one chamfer. Five coats of arms under a hoodmould over it. (Spiral stair in the SW corner topped with a ribbed umbrella-vault, cf. Johnby Hall (Greystoke) and Carlisle Cathedral, with eight spokes, then a ring, then sixteen radial ribs.) The E curtain is lined with offices of 1847 (N) and 1904. At the SE corner the FLAG TOWER of *c*. 1400, ending in a stepped gable. Against the S wall are the pretty STABLES of 1805, Gothick, eight bays, two raised into a central clock tower. The WYNDHAM ROOMS on the N side are Lady Egremont's residence (1805, and 1847, E). Plain sashes inwards, Gothick ones out to the river valley and park.

The INNER GATEHOUSE lies about 6 ft (2 metres) higher than the outer ward, so the drawbridge must have had quite a slope. It has to the E an arch connecting the l. and r. parts high up and provided with machicolation. The archway is rib-vaulted, with doors into flanking tunnel-vaulted guardrooms. The N room has a hooded fireplace. Hatches down to rib-vaulted oubliettes in the former ditch below.

Access to the inner bailey is now through a window. The HALL here was at first-floor level. Its outer wall stands complete to the N, with Dec windows inserted in earlier embrasures. Part of the external stair remains, and a jamb of the doorway next to the Kitchen Tower, in the NE corner. By it is a trefoil-headed niche, and a turning stair up to a tiny room vaulted in trefoil section, lit by a small window to the W with a cusped rose window over.

The KITCHEN TOWER is massive and square, with 24-ft (7.5-metre) high lancets on the E side. Two huge fireplace embrasures fill the S wall; their hoods have fallen away. The C19 rescue arch towards the Hall may represent a third. In the outer wall, N, are two more embrasures, rib-vaulted, with a buttress between them pierced by a pair of later windows. There was probably a gallery here, supported on the stone shelf in the wall and reached by the mural stair in the E wall. A broad stone stair under a stepped tunnel-vault goes down to the MIRK KIRK below, a square room rib-vaulted like a chapter house from a single octagonal column. It is pitch dark, the only windows blocked by the Wyndham Rooms. The ribs are single-chamfered, springing from wall responds without capitals.

The hall and adjoining chamber and solar were on a curved plan. The chamber and solar windows with mullion-and-transom crosses are later. The ROUND TOWER at the W apex is really D-shaped, and open on the inside. Three deep embrasures with seats, above which the wall thins considerably, allowing a walkway. Diminutive BELL TOWER at the SE corner of the inner ward, leaning perilously.

In the outer garden is a SUMMERHOUSE, 1682–3, overlooking the bowling green. Octagonal, of brick with stone quoins, with a broken segmental pediment over the door.

WORDSWORTH HOUSE, facing Gallowbarrow on Main Street. Patrician house of nine bays and two storeys on a basement, limewashed apricot, behind good gatepiers with urns. Despite the inscription over the back door 'Joshua Lucock, Sherriff, built ye house 1745', the carcass is William Bird's great house of 1690; an up-to-date double pile with a hipped roof in front and three gables at the back. His quoins and cornice survive, and one rear window retains the moulding for a cross-mullion. Inside, the corner fireplaces of the smaller rooms are typical but not diagnostic of the late C17; one bolection-moulded fireplace remains upstairs, and the arched opening from the landing to the w passage. Otherwise it is Lucock's C18 house: Doric porch, façade with moulded window frames, and interiors. Between 1764 and 1783 it was occupied by John Wordsworth, agent to Sir James Lowther (later 1st Earl of Lonsdale), who treated him badly. William and Dorothy were both born here. The National Trust restored and reinterpreted it in 2003–4. The paucity of Wordsworth relics has freed the Trust to present, very successfully, a living house of the period, without ropes or signs. The grandest rooms, though not large, are the Dining Room, front r., and the Drawing Room above it. The latter is fully panelled with a chair rail, entablature, Corinthian pilasters, swan-necked overdoors, and a fireplace of Kilkenny marble. The stair has an open string with decorated tread-ends. Three sturdy balusters per tread, mahogany rail.

PERAMBULATIONS

1. The town

Wordsworth House in MAIN STREET is a convenient place to start. First a few steps w for the TROUT HOTEL, long and low, with a rustic Ionic porch and the moulded window surrounds that indicate the early C18. Opposite, N side, is the distinguished GRECIAN VILLA, now MANOR HOUSE HOTEL. Greek indeed, with giant pilasters and lesser pilasters marching past each other, tripartite windows with scroll brackets, and in the centre a recessed loggia on both floors, with a pair of Ionic columns below, square columns and scrolly brackets above. Band of fatly carved anthemion over the upper windows. A delicate cantilever stair with cast-iron balusters climbs up a semicircular recess under a little dome. Neoclassical going on Victorian in other words, which suits its date, *c.* 1844. It was built for Thomas Wilson, a hat manufacturer. Angus Taylor has shown that it is an enriched version of a *Francis Goodwin* design published in his *Domestic Architecture* of 1833/4.

E of Wordsworth House, Main Street broadens out, lined with rendered and colourwashed buildings of two and three storeys. In the middle the STATUE of the 6th Earl of Mayo, assassinated in the Andaman Islands in 1872. Marble, by *W. & T. Wills* of London, 1875. His viceregal stance looks a little awkward since

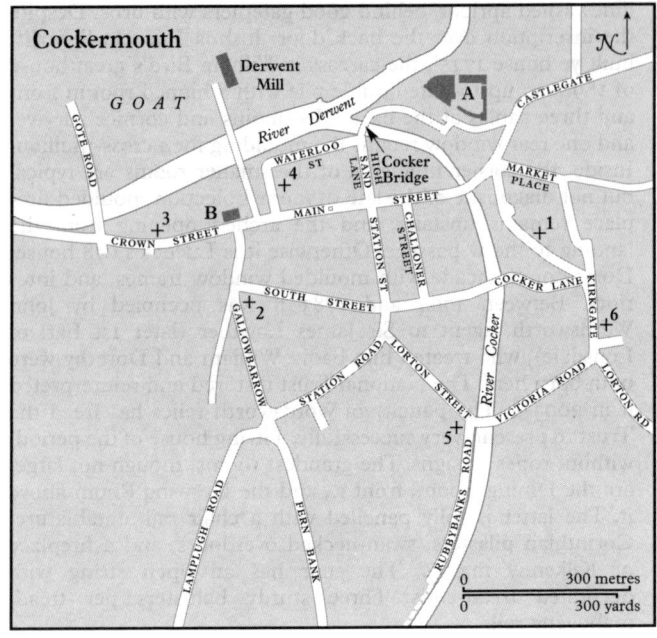

Cockermouth

GOAT

Derwent Mill

River Derwent

GOTE ROAD

CASTLEGATE

A

WATERLOO ST

Cocker Bridge

MARKET PLACE

HIGH SAND LANE

STREET

CROWN STREET

B

MAIN

CHALLONER STREET

STATION ST

4

3

COCKER LANE

KIRKGATE

1

6

SOUTH STREET

2

GALLOWBARROW

STATION ROAD

LORTON STREET

River Cocker

VICTORIA ROAD

LORTON RD

RUBBYBANKS ROAD

5

LAMPLUGH ROAD

FERN BANK

0   300 metres

0   300 yards

N

1   All Saints
2   Christ Church
3   St Joseph (R.C.)
4   Congregational chapel
5   Methodist chapel
6   Friends' Meeting House

A   Castle
B   Wordsworth House

he was discombobulated by a lorry in 1964. On the N side is
the CARNEGIE LIBRARY of 1903–4 by *A. E. Marsh*, of official
red sandstone, five bays, with a raised broken pediment over
the upper central windows. The ground floor breaks off into
asymmetry with an arched entry at one end and the entrance
next to that. The United Reformed church (*see* p. 283) is set
back in its yard. On the s side NORHAM HOUSE of 1725 has
five bays with quoins, moulded window surrounds, and a steep
roof. Strolling E it can be seen how the window surrounds go
flat in the later c18 and early c19, and then – this is a Cockermouth speciality – break out into ears, pediment shapes, and
continuous sills and lintels. The pubs seem particularly to
enjoy these fancies, e.g. THE BUSH, and HUNTERS, both
with a distinctive tri-lobed pediment over the door, and the
BLACK BULL.

E of Mayo's statue a crossroads, with on the NE corner BARCLAYS
BANK, originally the Carlisle & Cumberland Bank, 1897–9 by
Mr Oliver (probably *G. D. Oliver*). Baroque, in deep red sand-
stone ashlar. Five bays, with three prominent gable dormers.

Broken pediment framing a column and ball. Scrolly brackets
to the windows. The upper windows have alternately blocked
surrounds. Complicated door surround with two great brackets jutting out each side. Inside the front door a little barrel-
vaulted vestibule. High Sand Lane leads N from here to
WATERLOO STREET, running w and parallel with Main Street
and backing onto the Derwent. This was served by a culverted
mill race from the Cocker, and a few early small mills survive.
The best, Wharton's Mill, was working flax in the 1820s but is
obviously cobbled up from at least three building stages. Three
storeys and three cart entrances, two arched, one with a
straight lintel. Most of the original fenestration survived the
housing conversion, and the only jarring note is the plate glass
substituted for taking-in doors.

Continuing E on Main Street, on the s side the tall GLOBE
HOTEL shows Early Georgian characteristics – sash windows
closely set and with moulded surrounds. Where Main Street
narrows again on the N is the POLICE STATION of 1894. A
prime example of speaking architecture. Set back, of dark
stone. Under a crowstepped gable a pair of tall windows closely
set under an emphatic roll moulding and drip frowns suspi-
ciously over the gaping archway which leads to the cells.
Adjoining is the former SAVINGS BANK of 1846, attributed to
C. W. Eaglesfield of Maryport. Fine ashlar, channelled on the
ground floor, with an Ionic portico set in a semicircular recess,
and a clock turrret on the parapet. The OLD COURTHOUSE
of 1828 stands by the Cocker bridge, also of 1828. Tudor
Gothic with four-centre arches and square hoodmoulds.
Rickety interior, sloping and creaky, shaped to fit its irregular
site on the riverbank. The courtroom is upstairs, crammed now
with knick-knacks and old clothes. A wide wooden gallery
encircles the space, with a low flat ceiling with cornice and roof
vents. Opposite is HSBC, of red stone, Arts and Crafts asymmetry. Designed in 1886 by T. L. Banks & C. H. Townsend.

Across the bridge is the MARKET PLACE, lined with good three-
storey buildings with the same varied window surrounds we
have seen in Main Street. No. 35 is unusually grand, with a
Greek Doric doorcase and hammered limestone upper storeys.
PERCY HOUSE (gallery) on the N is earlier, lower, its ground
floor below street level. A tree-ring date of 1462–3 is recorded;
exceptionally early for a town house in the region. It was the
bailiff's residence for the Percy estates, with living accommodation above, reached by an external stair and upper door at
the back. In 1598 the upper room was given a fine plaster
ceiling and overmantel with the Percy arms and the initials
HN, for Henry, 9th Earl of Northumberland (the 'Wizard
Earl'). Evidently the arms were done first, for the top is hidden
by the ceiling. Traces of painting, perhaps grotesque work, on
the wooden partition.

Tucked away between street and river is the narrow BANKS
COURT, last survivor of an early form of factory development.
On the E side a terrace of two-storey workers' houses, on the
w side, less than 10 ft (3 metres) away, is the factory where

the inhabitants spent their day. No signs of a power source, so the factory was probably equipped with hand-operated spinning jennies. The generous fenestration on the first floor tends to support this supposition, and the small-paned metal-framed windows on the ground floor suggest storage downstairs.

Continuing for a moment NE up the narrow steep of CASTLEGATE, lined with good C18 houses but too narrow to linger, we reach the castle entrance and CASTLEGATE HOUSE (gallery), 1739. Widely spaced three-bay façade, the rendering rusticated on the ground floor. Pedimented doorway on pilasters. Delicate Rococo plasterwork in one ground-floor room.

Returning to the MARKET PLACE, we can dive S through any of several entries to the nondescript car park which represents the lost Elizabethan Hall, demolished in 1973. Overlooking it from the N slope of the churchyard is Cockermouth AREA OFFICE and TOURIST INFORMATION, a former Methodist chapel of 1841. Three bays, with Greek Doric columns to the doorway. A fine building in poor repair, partitioned horizontally at gallery level. The oval of the gallery can be seen, resting on slender iron pillars. A path crosses All Saints' churchyard to KIRKGATE, where it widens into an irregular square, French in feel, with pollarded trees and cobbles. Nos. 37/39 has the Cockermouth shaped window surrounds and three-lobed pediment over the door. No. 22 has the shaped window surrounds again, and No. 40 continuous sills and lintels. At the top of the square is the Quaker Meeting House (p. 283).

COCKER LANE returns steeply W down to the river, with a single-storey house at the bottom. Across the footbridge is CROFT TERRACE, well-preserved late C19, with each of the trades exhibiting its skill. Further on is the narrow CHALLONER STREET, with a good range of Cumberland Georgian houses. The lane comes out onto STATION STREET by the mid-Victorian TITHE HOUSE SALEROOM, of polychrome stone; diagonally opposite, FAIRFIELD HOUSE dated in frosted glass 1868. The Victorians were good at turning street corners. Turning S for a moment into Station Road, the former GRAND THEATRE of 1913–14, minus domes, and, a little further up on the site of the railway station, the COUNTY FIRE HEADQUARTERS of 1985–6 and the WAR MEMORIAL, by *F. W. Doyle Jones*, 1921. Bronze angel on a tall stone pedestal. Barebreasted, on tiptoe, with a wreath and palm: the same image as his Boer War memorial of 1906 in Penrith. Station Street returns N to Main Street.

2. The river banks and industrial buildings

On the S edge of the town, Gallowbarrow leads to FERN BANK, and thus S to DOUBLE MILLS. In 1470 there were two corn mills facing each other across the River Cocker. One survives, on the l. bank (now a youth hostel). Narrow, three storeys, apparently C18 – but on the W side, where substantial fragments of two wheels survive, the ground floor is ashlar, while

the upper storeys are of rubble. The tail race of the upstream wheel leads through the body of the mill and is probably the older. Of the r. bank mill only scattered stones and a wheel pit remain. An agreeable riverside walk leads downstream ¼ m. to the three-storey C19 RUBBYBANKS MILL, in use in 1900 as a woollen mill, but adapted at various times for other short-lived uses. Now housing. Then the charming OLD PUMP HOUSE, a tiny single-storey house like a lodge, in random coursed stone with fine ashlar surrounds. The pump itself, extracting water from the Cocker, lay behind and across the yard. RAILWAY TERRACE, four two-storey cottages dated 1882, completes the set. Immediately beyond the former railway bridge are remains on the opposite bank of the ATLAS WORKS. This used the Tom Rudd beck, once lined with mills and tan yards, joining the Cocker from the E. Built 1872–4 as a rug and blanket mill employing 400 people, but within a decade converted to confectionery manufacture. Under the Victoria Bridge on the opposite bank was an extensive tannery, where what appear to be full-height pilasters on the walls of the present-day house were once the supports of an open bark barn. The former HAT FACTORY, built by Thomas Wilson before 1857, follows shortly on the w bank. The housing conversion makes some acknowledgement of industrial origins with a grid of steel galleries on the river side, but is unpleasantly hard-edged in grey cement render. From the path, over the foot-bridge and on towards the Market Place, or l. towards South Street and thus back to Main Street (see Perambulation 1).
The final hundred yards of the Cocker's course to its confluence with the Derwent can be viewed from Cocker Bridge. The scene is dominated by Jennings Bros' CASTLE BREWERY. When John and Joseph Jennings bought the brewery in 1874 all its buildings backed directly onto the river. Elements of those early structures may survive in the present miscellaneous huddle, but the three-storey building of eight regular bays at the upstream end started in the early C19 as Stoddart's cotton mill. The fine four-storey MALTHOUSE beyond and behind, erected in 1889 at a cost of £10,000, now houses the company offices. Where the river makes its last bend to join the Derwent, dilapidated remains of a circular brick C18 WINDMILL tower, an odd thing to find on a site in the shadow of the castle hill, so close to flowing water, in a town of stone and in a county where windmills were always rare. It was set among tan yards, so it may have ground bark. Last on the r. bank, FOUNDRY HOUSE commemorates the iron foundry which succeeded one of the tanneries.

OUTLYING BUILDINGS

CEMETERY, Lorton Road (SE). 1856. Twin chapels by *C. W. Eaglesfield*, linked by an arch with belfry and spire on top. The

arch has a pointed tunnel-vault. Masonic Memorial 1902 in
the turning circle beyond: white marble column carrying full
entablature, abacus, and a ball.

Former INDUSTRIAL SCHOOL, Lorton Road, by the cemetery.
1881. Like a barracks: long even ranges in red and blue brick
with buff stone dressings, round a parade ground. Roofs all
hipped and shallow-pitched. A good and complete example of
the type. It became the Grammar School in 1929, closed 1990.
Now residential, and called Strawberry How.

COCKERMOUTH SCHOOL, Castlegate Drive (ENE). Opened as
Derwent Secondary Modern School in 1958. A typical, and
good, design by *James Haughan* of *Cumberland County Architect's Department*. Three storeys, mostly of glass, flat roof, with
one side on pilotis allowing access to an inner court. Extended
in 1987–90 under a Crystal-Palace-style arched roof. – MIKE
WILDE ECO CENTRE. Eye-catching and round, using recycled and renewable materials and power. By *Rod Hughes* of
ad.hoc associates, Penrith, 2006. Semicircular front, faced in
yellow and brown plywood in stripes and hung in a zigzag over
water, with Sedum roof. The rear, also semicircular, rises
steeply under a glass roof.

GOAT (INDUSTRIAL BUILDINGS). To avert the Derwent's sea-
sonal floods, its potential was harnessed by means of a ¾ m.
leat (the GOTE), running roughly parallel with its r. bank from
a point opposite the castle to the NE outskirts of the town. This
gave its name to the industrial suburb which grew up at its
lower end, N of the Derwent Bridge. At the foot of Goat Brow
the leat passes under HIGH GOTE MILL, mid-C18 in its
present three-storey form, which worked until 1969. The adjacent miller's house is dated 1802. The leat continues past the
chapel-like, Gothick-windowed HOSPICE, built in 1820 by
Jonathan and *William Harris* as a flax-drying house, to LOW
GOTE MILLS, another very early mill site. Of the two mills
only one remains, clumsily converted to housing with a
depressing display of half an undershot wheel sunk in concrete.
The Harris linen firm operated here from 1808 into the 1840s,
when they transferred their operations to their steam-powered
DERWENT MILL, begun in 1834 on the N bank of the Gote
at the end of the modern Wakefield Road. This was Cockermouth's most successful textile venture, extended in 1847 and
1855 to form the four-storey, twenty-bay mill of coursed rubble
with ashlar quoins which dominates the W side of the town. Its
Quaker founders also developed new methods of treating and
dyeing flax fibres for embroidery threads. Used as a shoe
factory 1940–90, now flats and offices.

The town of Maryport took its water from the Derwent, and
its PUMP HOUSE of 1810 still stands at Low Gote. Solid, rock-
faced limestone with red sandstone dressings over arched
windows. The tall stepped square chimney was felled in 1974,
when the complex was ignorantly converted to housing.

HAMES HALL, Gote Road, ⅝ m. NW. Tudor Gothic villa in a
small park across the Derwent, built for John Steel *c.* 1844.

Angus Taylor has shown that this, like Grecian Villa (*see* p. 285), is a *Francis Goodwin* design, called 'A Marine Residence in the Gothic Style'. Three bays. Oriel over the entrance, flanked by thin octagonal turrets. A more substantial octagonal tower at the back. A service wing provides the necessary Picturesque asymmetry.

THE FITZ, Lamplugh Road (SSW), in its own park. The home of the Senhouses from 1670 to 1990. Front of 1835, plainly Grecian, with an uncomfortable two-bay centrepiece and porch of fluted Doric columns.

COLBY (W)

6020

Quite a substantial village, though without a church or working chapel.

NETHER HOFF. G & IB 1683 on a triangular stone floating over the doorway, which has a pulvinated frieze but has presumably lost a pediment. It is not in the middle. Mullioned windows of three lights, and four for the hall. Windows of the two upper floors curiously linked vertically. Pevsner remarked how old-fashioned it was; cf. Crackenthorpe Hall nearby, of 1685, but wholly William-and-Mary.

COLTON (L)

3080

HOLY TRINITY. High up, where pasture gives way to moorland. No village. Roughcast, grey. W tower blunt and almost featureless. Nave and chancel in one. Assorted flat-topped, cusped and uncusped windows arranged partly in two storeys, indicating a former gallery. Bishop Gastrell in the early C18 mentions 'a mean, unconsecrated chapel . . . under ye abbey of Furness'. The priest's doorway probably belongs to this; two-centred arch, hollow-moulded, in red stone. This church was consecrated in 1578, made parochial in 1676, enlarged by a N transept in 1721, and restored in 1889–90 by *Settle & Farmer*. Rustic, with rough tie-beams for the roofs and sloping inner walls. DRAW NIGH UNTO GOD is painted on the W wall, the remnant probably of an overall scheme. – ALTAR RAIL. C18, with turned balusters. – Unusual STAINED GLASS. SW, very rich, to Harriet Dickson of Abbotts Reading †1918: Jacob's dream, Coniston water, local birds and flowers by *H. Warren Wilson*. Others by *Gamon & Humphry*: Daniel and St John, curlew and snipe, to Arthur Dickson †1901. War memorial window by the pulpit, *c.* 1920. On the N side Arthur Dickson †1934: cloudy glass, the words of Psalm 150, and tiny pine

branches. Rev. John Hull †1958, Good Samaritan in four spirited scenes. – MONUMENTS. Surprising number of good
tablets; the best John Machell †1771, by the altar.

TOTTLEBANK BAPTIST CHURCH, 1¼ m. S. Long low roughcast
building of c. 1750, extended in 1864 to accommodate a
schoolroom. The congregation dates from 1669.

COBBY HOUSE. *See* Finsthwaite.

3070

CONISHEAD PRIORY (L)
Ulverston

Now Manjushri Buddhist Centre. The Augustinians settled here,
like their brethren at Cartmel (q.v.), because of the perilous but
vital routes over sand and water which linked the Furness peninsula to Lancaster. Conishead was founded as a hospital in the
1150s and made a Priory in 1188. There is nothing to be seen of
it. The church is said to have been on the S lawn, in which case
the mansion is on a N cloister; the orientation is right. On Dissolution the site went to the Stanleys, and so eventually to Col.
Thomas Richmond Gale Braddyll. In 1823, newly rich from coal
and family alliances, Braddyll commissioned a new house from
Philip Wyatt, youngest son of James Wyatt. As feckless as any of
his family, he was sacked in 1829, having built a Z-shaped service
part.* Things stood still until *George Webster* took over in 1838.
The spectacular front parts of the house are his. Conishead
should perhaps be considered his *magnum opus*. Col. Braddyll,
ruined by his great house, was declared bankrupt in 1848.
However the date 1853 on the W wing shows that building carried
on. A palatial hydro called The Paradise of Furness took over in
1878. In 1928 the house was bought by the Durham Miners'
Welfare Committee as a convalescent home. It fell empty in 1972,
but was rescued in 1976 by English Buddhists. With a resident
community of a hundred or so and an attendance of 3,000 at the
annual festival it seems the best possible use for the place.

The house is sweepingly Gothic, of the late, i.e. Perp variety
handled with the freedom from antiquarian qualms handed
down from the C18. Webster's state rooms at the front strive
for height, with a bristling skyline of finials and patterned
chimneys. The removal of the stucco has revealed an embar-
rassing mix of hasty materials, including extensive use of *Coade*
stone, e.g. for the parapets and finials. The former grand
entrance on the N is wholly asymmetrical, with a large gate-
house-type centre flanked by turrets with spires. The great hall
is behind this and goes through two floors. The recessed wall
on the l. with its high three-light window, represents the staircase. The present entrance front on the E is symmetrical, with

---

* Philip Wyatt is notable for just one other work, the classical Wynyard Park in Co.
Durham of 1822–8. Here too he was sacked for his 'extreme inconsequence'.

a central gable and a bipartite porch projecting in the middle. The s (garden) side is symmetrical too, with a conservatory between projecting wings. Wyatt's work, appearing behind, is less bristly and more solid-looking, being faced in Bath stone and favouring square corner towers rather than spires or pinnacles. The five tall two-light windows (iron tracery) to the r. of the grand N entrance are Wyatt's work. A long wing comes forward from this, with a towered arch (dated 1853) through to the service yard, and behind that a long square-towered wing.

The lobby of the E PORCH is rib-vaulted (in plaster of course). It opens onto the Gothic CORRIDOR, white, rib-vaulted as well, and cross-lit. An incredible vista, much longer than seems possible. This is achieved by projecting the corridor right through the dramatic spaces of the house and out into the domestic wing: 170 ft (52 metres) in all. The main rooms have lost much of their finery to dry rot, but a number of ornate ceilings, Gothic to Jacobean, survive. At right angles N is the vast, echoing HALL, also plaster-vaulted, with stained glass by *Willement* in the great N window. At first-floor level it has a gallery, with a screen of genuine Perp tracery with one-light divisions, brought from Salmesbury Hall (North Lancashire). Next to the Hall is the flying staircase, rising in one and continuing in two, with glass by *Wailes* at the half-landing and badgers on the newel posts. More old woodwork in the OAK ROOM, although the importations have had to be eked out with reproductions in a substitute material. The chimney-piece has slender termini-caryatids and a date 1623.

GARDEN. Terraces N, E and s. Extensive pleasure gardens bounded by a ha-ha, and a path to the beach.

KADAMPA BUDDHIST TEMPLE, in the walled garden.   116
1995–7. The design by *Geshe Kelsang Gyatso*, carried out by *Mark Tole*, is based on a Buddhist mandala of the celestial mansion, with four doorways, a gilded deer and dharma wheel over each one, and three tiers. A cheerful, outgoing building, simple in concept and construction but lending itself to ongoing embellishment. The 78-ft (24-metre) square carries a low octagonal clerestory and lantern, both supported on ring beams. The glass walls can be opened out into the surrounding colonnaded loggias, which are extended into marquees during festivals. More lighting comes from the two octagonal clerestories, but there is also a sliver of top lighting round the outer walls, and round the lantern. Cast panels all round of Eight Auspicious Signs: flowers, fish, umbrella, banner, vase, conch, wheel, knot. Continuous floral frieze over the colonnade. Big calm space inside, embellished with athletic scarcely-clad dancers and symbolic panels picked out in happy secondary colours – mint green, pink, violet, and gold leaf. The community has developed considerable expertise in stone-casting from patterns carved by *Daniel Quall King* and others. Glass-fronted shrine along the w wall dominated by the 8-ft (2.5-metre) Buddha and two Bodhisattvas, modelled on site by

Alfredo Baracco and cast in bronze. Since 2006 the roofs shine forth with golden vajra finials at each level, golden edges to the parapets, and a pointed gold umbrella for the topmost roof, which looks green and translucent from below.

Three TOWERS can be seen. On Hermitage Hill, NW, a two-storey octagonal folly tower with higher turret. Across the road SW a smaller octagonal SUMMERHOUSE, early C19, with battlements and a pyramid roof. Further SW the Gales's triangular mausoleum in Bardsea Park (q.v.).

CHAPEL ISLAND. A rocky islet out in the bay, with a few trees and many nesting sea birds, commanding a magnificent prospect of the Lakeland fells at the head of the sands. A refuge on the dangerous crossing from Cartmel, provided with a CHAPEL by the Prior of Conishead. The E gable with three lancets was said to remain in 1969, but what now remains appears to owe more to Col. Braddyll, 1823.

CONISTON (L)

Originally a mining village, and looking like one, with its long lines of dark slate cottages huddled under the Old Man. Now a Lake District resort (though still somewhat removed from the lake) with a few old-established white hotels and a townish shopping street. Ruskin's long residence at Brantwood, across the lake, has left a strong mark.

ST ANDREW. Chapel of ease to Ulverston, known in 1586. The present nave and W tower were built in 1819 by *J. Matson*. The side windows have basket arches and wooden tracery (cf. St Joseph, Kirkby Lonsdale). Chancel added in 1891 with a Perp E window like that at Troutbeck. The low battlemented bays r. and l. of the tower were built in 1891. – STAINED GLASS. W window, 1894 by *Kempe*.

RUSKIN CROSS, in the churchyard. 1901, in hard green stone from Tilberthwaite. It was designed by *W. G. Collingwood*, who is buried close by, and made by *H. T. Miles* of Ulverston – so even here the artist was not the craftsman. The shape is that of the Irton Cross (q.v.). The scenes are biographical. E, starting from the bottom: Grecian youth with lyre, 'not very passionately inspired', says Collingwood. Then the inscription, followed by the youthful artist sketching *en plein air*, a winged lion for St Mark and Venice, and a menorah for the *Seven Lamps*. On the S an inhabited vine, as at Bewcastle, but the inhabitants are a recognizable robin, kingfisher and red squirrel. W, from the bottom again: the Parable of the Vineyard for *Unto This Last*, lilies for *Sesame and Lilies*, angel and key for *Fors Clavigera*, wreath and knot, and at the top St George for the Guild. The carving is distinctively flat but soft-edged. Collingwood quotes Ruskin: 'You have . . . your flat stone surface given you as a sheet of white paper, on which you are required to produce the utmost effect you can with the simplest means . . . leaving the block itself, when shaped, as solid as you can, that its surface may resist weather, and the carved parts be as much protected as possible by the masses left around them.' – WAR MEMORIAL, *c.* 1920. The distinctive style of the Ruskin Cross became the almost universal pattern in the region for memorials to the dead of the First World War.

SACRED HEART (R.C.), S of the village opposite the Old Hall turn. 1872, by *James O'Byrne*. SW tower/porch with saddleback roof. Sparse lancets. Gaunt presbytery at the back (N) with linked dripmoulds. – STAINED GLASS. The E window obviously by *Hardman*.

INSTITUTE and RUSKIN MUSEUM, Yewdale Road. The Institute and library was built in 1878, and a museum founded by Collingwood at the back, which was tiny, opened in 1901. Extension by *Ian Gibson* of *Gill Dockray*, 1999. Restrained to the point of invisibility.

MAJOR HOUSES

CONISTON HALL, ⅞ m. SSE. It stands by the shore S of the pier, its mighty display of chimneys, round and tapering on square bases, challenging the mountains. C16 hall and service cross-wing, and a ruined withdrawing room (possibly once towered) attached at the NE corner to the high end. William Fleming moved the principal apartments upstairs, probably between his second marriage in 1574 and his death in 1598, with two rooms in the space of the old hall, but Sir Daniel (1633–1701) having removed to Rydal, Coniston was by 1770 ruinous. William Green in 1819 lamented that the old hall, 'lately a splendid ruin', had been spoilt by the demolition of the NE wing and the erection of an inclined plane to convert the ancient hall into a depository for corn, i.e. a bank barn. The cart doorway was knocked through where old pictures show an oriel. The house was acquired by the National Trust in 1971 and extensively repaired.

The Hall trusses are arch-braced with angle pieces to continue the curve, and very generously pegged. Parlour trusses simpler, without the angle pieces. The partition truss is filled with close studding, and mortices indicate close studding below as well. The low-end truss looks as though it was designed to stand free, with a close-studded partition immediately behind to the cross-wing. The C16 screens passage is boxed out in front of it, with two doors and much-moulded square panelling, much renewed. Fireplaces are simply arched and chamfered, in red stone.

GREAT BARN. Built by Sir Daniel Fleming in 1688. Gutted by the National Trust in 1974–5.

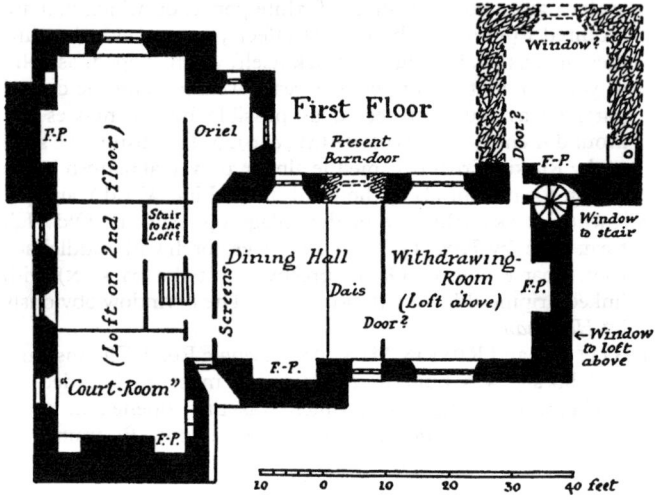

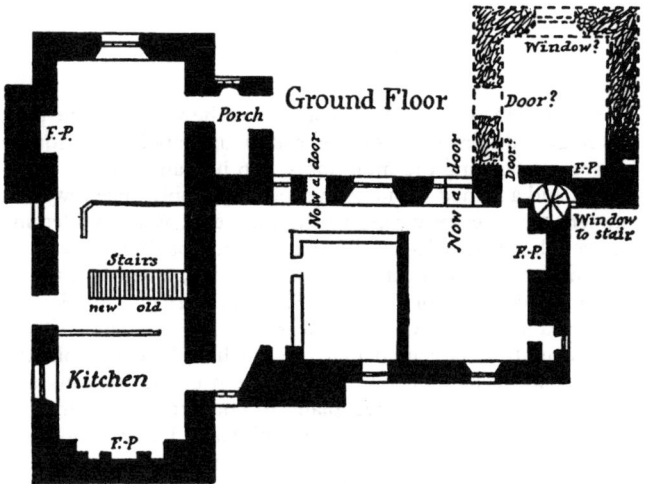

Coniston Hall.
Ground- and first-floor plans, 1914

MONK CONISTON HALL, 1¼ m. ENE, near the head of the lake.
Strawberry-Hill Gothic villa built *c.* 1820 by Michael Knott,
with additions with red stone dressings by *William Cecil Mar-*
shall of Leeds, 1881. There was an Early Victorian phase too,
e.g. the addition of the NW wing. A good deal of the early detail
has unfortunately been lost since it was pictured in the *Lons-*
dale Magazine in 1822; the castellations have gone, and the
turrets flanking the centre gable have been decapitated. Cross
arrowslits and quatrefoils have disappeared too. C20 iron-

hooped CONSERVATORY on the SW corner. Tall rear elevation
partly visible with a curved stair-tower and Gothic glazing bars.
The long corridors inside are Gothic-arched and the stair has
iron Gothic balustrading. The best room is at the W end. X-
framed ceiling with little bosses, fretting and scrolls. Regency
Gothic fireplace in white and pale brown marble.

The Marshall family created the famous beauty spot of TARN
HOWS in 1865 by damming a small mill pool.

TENT LODGE, I m. E, on the E shore of the lake at the N end.
Arcadian villa of c. 1815, built by George Smith on the spot
where his uniquely gifted but tragic daughter Elizabeth lived
out her last summer in a tent, where she could breathe more
easily. She was renowned as a linguist and scholar, as well as
an early fell-walker. The house and its wonderful setting was
painted by Turner in 1818. It is quite severe, a deep double pile
with widely spaced windows and a shallow wide-eaved
Regency roof. Just two storeys, with the principal rooms with
their tall windows on the ground. Oval entrance lobby. The
stair is in the NE corner.

BRANTWOOD, 1½ m. SE, on the E shore of the lake. Ruskin considered this the most beautiful spot on earth. It was a 'station',
one of the essential scenic viewpoints of the Lake District,
looking out across Coniston water to Coniston Hall below and
the Old Man above. Thomas Woodville built a villa in the late
C18. In 1852 it was bought by the poet, artist and republican
William James Linton and his wife Eliza, novelist and friend
of Harriet Martineau. In 1871 he offered it sight unseen to John
Ruskin, and here Ruskin was content to live until his death in
1900. Ruskin's circle included W.G. Collingwood, and Arthur
and Joan Severn who lived here with Ruskin, and stayed on
after his death. J.H. Whitehouse bought the house in 1932,
retrieved much dispersed material, and opened it as a Ruskin
shrine in 1934.

The cultural significance of the house outweighs its architectural merit. Each of the protagonists added their two penn'-
orth, governed always by the steepness of the hillside and the
desirability of the W view.* The house rambles up in steps and
back in echelon, with corner oriels peering round each other
towards the lake. Small sashes mark the first phase of c. 1797.
Linton put in the shallow semicircular bow that features in
Collingwood's famous portrait of Ruskin in his study. Linton's
studio was above the small outhouse immediately S, frescoed
in bold blackletter GOD AND THE PEOPLE. The 1830s 'estate'
windowed sections with diagonal ironwork come next. Ruskin
added his small turret room in c. 1871–2, the dining room with
its seven-light *Stones of Venice* window c. 1878–9. An upper level
with its Arts and Crafts wooden casements followed in the late
1880s. Behind, at the top level but back on solid ground, is
Severn's chapel-like studio.

*The sequence is illustrated by paintings in the collection.

FARMS

YEW TREE FARM. On the A593, 1¾ m. NW. The initials of
Richard Walker and the date 1665 are on the press cupboard
in the low house at the back. This is cruck-framed, with its
stack and fire-window at the SE end. The front house was built
in 1743 by George and Agnes Walker, whose initials are cut,
and the date scratched, on the latch of the front door. Good
panelling and chair rail, stair with stout balusters. The front
parlour was furnished as a tearoom in 1934 by Beatrix Potter,
to give the farmer's wife an income. Splendid BARN and
GALLERY. Ramp entrance at the end. The gallery is cantilevered out on the main joists, i.e. not an afterthought.

BOON CRAG FARM, 1 m. NW, on the Hawkshead road opposite
Monk Coniston Hall (see p. 296). Two C17 farms and their outbuildings round one yard; now a National Trust sawmill. End-
on to the road a barn with spinning gallery. Unlike the one at
Yew Tree it is clearly an addition, separately roofed and not
cantilevered but supported on lengths of wall. (Window sill of
one of the cottages, which are cruck-framed, inscribed
'William Sawrey built this house 1631'.) The top house has its
fire-window and firehouse window run together, with just a
wooden upright between, which is a local feature.

67   LOW YEWDALE, 1¼ m. NW. Attractive C17 and later group sheltered by a great outcrop of rock. Three houses. The main house
has lost its mullions but the fire-window is there, and the bressumer within. Stair in a lean-to outshut at the back. Cottage
attached beyond the main stack. Third house L-shaped and
small-scale. Mossy-roofed bank barn at right angles to the
cottage, and another barn behind the L-shaped house.

HIGH YEWDALE. Again more than one dwelling, though the l.
one, low and small, has been uninhabited since 1936. Behind
is a larger but probably older house, apparently cruck-framed,
and to the r. of that a barn with pentice roof, like an embryo
gallery.

The Tilberthwaite valley runs NW from High Yewdale. At its head
– a classic Lake District arbour – is LOW TILBERTHWAITE
FARM. A court cupboard is dated 1687. Small, with C18 barn
and spinning gallery attached in line. Nearby, and unmarked

118   as always, is one of *Andy Goldsworthy*'s reconstructed SHEEP-
FOLDS (2003), which has inset circles of slate-like stone laid
at different angles, as though rotating.

INDUSTRIAL REMAINS

Mining and quarrying have long histories in the mountains
around Coniston. The earliest known reference to slate working
concerns mining at Sladgill in 1283. Copper mining can be traced
back to the very end of the C16; the last ore came out in 1942.
For three centuries and more, water was the key to these opera-

tions, and the overwhelming impression is of the ingenuity and determination applied to harnessing water and controlling its power. A 5 m. walk around the Coppermines Valley, NE of the village, reveals much evidence of centuries of winning and working both minerals.

¼ m. from the Sun Hotel, the path bridges Mealy Gill and immediately on the l. are the remains of a COPPER HOUSE and WHARF where copper and slate were loaded onto an extension of the Coniston branch railway. A further ¼ m. and the track crosses Miners' Bridge to join the mine road leading to the COPPER MINES YOUTH HOSTEL, formerly the mine office and manager's house. The path rises to the r. after 200 yds, to pass above and behind a row of miners' COTTAGES. Above, remains of BLUE QUARRY (slate), worked from the end of the C18 until 1939. The path gives a panorama of the former ore-dressing floors, crushing mills and settling ponds grouped around the Hostel below. Ahead, a slate-built PILLAR, which once supported a wooden launder feeding a 20-ft (6-metre) water wheel, indicates the site of East Bonsor Upper Mill. Below, l., are early C17 copper workings of the German miners of the Company of Mines Royal, alongside the lagoon and leats feeding the EAST BONSOR LOWER MILL and an C18 pumping shaft. At the foot of the pillar an early C19 WHEEL PIT. Running back across the path into the hillside is the 'bob-plat level', which carried reciprocating rods taking the wheel's power to a pump in a 1,400-ft (430-metre) shaft. Over the footbridge across Red Dell Beck is a series of open stopes dropping deep into workings known in the early C18 as WHITE or NEW WORKS. At the W end of this complex is the C19 NEW ENGINE SHAFT. The square hole was a ladder way, the round hole beside it accommodated the pump chain. The water-wheel pit survives. Immediately beyond, the THRIDDLE INCLINE begins its steady 200-ft (62-metre) rise to workings high in the crag. Just upstream, remains of a cobbled DRESS-ING FLOOR.

From the incline foot, the reedy course of TONGUE BROW RACE can be followed round the fell to the dam at Levers Water. Constructed in the 1830s and over ⅓ m. long, the superbly engineered leat passes through a 30-yd (28-metre) tunnel, whose rock-cut entrance can still be seen. *John Barratt* built the stone-faced earth DAM to increase the capacity of Levers Water in the 1820s. Across the dam, under the slopes of Brim Fell are the dramatic gashes of early C17 COPPER WORKINGS at Simon's Nick and Back Strings. From here, a path leads s down Boulder Valley to Low Water Beck, giving a good view of the SLATE QUARRIES on the slopes of Coniston Old Man. From the beck crossing, still on the l. bank of the stream, the PUDDINGSTONE WATER RACE can be followed. A footbridge crosses the outflow from Levers Water below the waterfalls and joins the track leading down towards the Youth Hostel. On the way, remains of the C19 PADDY END COPPER

WORKS, including at the bottom of the slope the old GUN-POWDER HOUSE, with a portion of its protective blast wall.

BLOOMERIES are earlier metal-working sites, for smelting iron by means of coppice-wood charcoal. Very hard to date, they are recognizable today only by low overgrown mounds of slag. There are particularly significant sites on the W shore of Coniston Water ½ m. s of Coniston Hall at Water Park, and on the E shore at Beck Leven Foot. M. Davies-Shiel's plotting of their distribution estimates that each bloomery needed about 500 acres of coppice to maintain steady operation.

SLATE QUARRIES, along the delicious Tilberthwaite Valley NNE of Coniston. Worked as mines and pits from the C18 until the late C20. Black Hole Quarry, near Slater Bridge (W side), is the most dramatic, with a great arch, deep shafts and echoing caves. Hodge Close Quarry (E side) is the most instructive, affording spectacular views into the great flooded pits, the tunnels connecting them and the remains of anchorages for fixed cranes which teetered over the lip of the hole and for the overhead cableways which succeeded them.

CORBY CASTLE (C)

4050

The tower which is embedded in the NE corner of the house, to the r. of the entrance, is assigned to Richard de Salkeld and the C14. Invisible from outside, it is encased at a slight angle to the front, and makes its presence felt inside by the thickness of the wall and the spiral staircase. The property passed to the Howards in 1611 and 1624. Sir William Howard added to the W of the tower the long C17 three-storey range which is what you see from the Wetheral side, making the building L-shaped. We know from a drawing of 1793 that all its windows were pedimented, alternatingly triangular and segmental, which puts it in the last third of the C17 (cf. Hutton-in-the-Forest; Tullie House, Carlisle). It is irregular now, with plain sash windows of the early C18 and the early C19. In 1812–17 the space between the two parts was filled in to make a handsome Neoclassical rectangle by the mathematician and architect *Peter Nicholson* for Henry Howard.

The entrance (E) side is of five bays, with the middle bay pushed slightly forward, and so wide that it has a porch of four Greek Doric columns – quite an early use of this order – a tripartite window with pilasters above, and a tripartite lunette above that. Howard lion of *Coade* stone on a pedestal on top. Coming forward on either side an orangery with four round-headed windows. The other windows have finely moulded surrounds. To the s, with an even more spectacular view up the broad Eden, is a seven-bay front with a recessed centre under another lion, filled in on the ground floor by a loggia of two pairs of Greek Doric columns.

INTERIORS. The Howards sold up in 1994 to Edward and
Mary Haughey, now Lord and Lady Ballyedmond, who have
done it up to the nines with gold leaf and mirror-polished
marble. It keeps its irregular plan and levels. The broad
ENTRANCE HALL with its black and gold columns belongs
clearly to the Neoclassical phase. It has in one of its long sides
two niches. The rooms on the ground floor in Nicholson's part
have minor plaster ceilings, but the STAIRCASE, except for the
lantern, which is clearly Grecian, must date from *c.* 1730. At
the E end, hanging over the river, we are in the C17 house, subdivided with long narrow rooms. Stucco panelling and swirling
plaster low-relief ceilings here also of *c.* 1730–40. Above them,
on the first floor, are two quite spectacular ceilings of the same
date. Nicholson partitioned a passage off one of them and re-
set here two doorcases again of *c.* 1730–40. Of work in the
house at such a date nothing is recorded. S of the hallway we
are in the basement of the C14 tower, now wine cellars with
brick subdivisions under its tunnel-vault. Its turning stair goes
to the top and what may be its parapet appears in the uppermost cross-hall. The principal stair seems to be that shown in
a plan of 1803. A string of small bedrooms on the top floor.
Also a small S-facing room painted by *William Henry Nutter*
(1819–72): Italy on one side, Switzerland on the other. The
third side presents a real-life Arcadia: the spectacular view up
the River Eden.

MONUMENT. In the hallway the fragments of a slab to
Thomas Mowbray, 1st Duke of Norfolk. The Duke died in
Venice in 1400, and received his memorial at St Mark's. It was
saved from destruction in 1810 and brought here. It is an armorial plate entirely, with the White Hart of Richard II, and must
at least be re-tooled. It also received a frame of egg-and-dart.★

The GARDEN is the creation of Thomas Howard, who inherited in 1708. Largely complete by 1739 when it was depicted
by Buck, it is a very early example of allowing nature to dictate
the form, rather than imposing a design upon nature. The
house, as Howard remarked in 1733, is 'as it were suspended
over the River Eden', which, heading straight for the cliff on
which the house stands, turns aside obligingly at the last
minute and offers a multitude of picturesque possibilities. –
CASCADE, *c.* 1720. Water gushes from the jaws of a goggle-eyed
monster and a pair of three-headed dogs. The CASCADE
HOUSE, not roofed, has Venetian openings and horizontally
channelled masonry. Damaged figures with amphorae stand in
the niches. The cascade falls by many steps artificial and
natural into a semicircular basin in which stands an early C19
statue of Nelson, and then down into the river by more steps
under an arch. The effect is best seen from Wetheral Priory
gatehouse across the river, which was surely borrowed as part
of the design. Howard himself wrote a masque called *Sensuality*

★ Pevsner noted a CHAPEL and its fittings; not seen.

Subdued, 'adapted to the scene of the cascade at Corby from Milton's *Comus*', which concluded with the release of a mass of water into the basin below. – CAVES beneath the house, hollowed out of the red sandstone cliff. – GREEN WALK, along the river. Eventful with grottoes and alcoves. Originally much statuary too, of which a giant STATUE OF POLYPHEMUS with his reed pipes, *c.* 1720, is the lone survivor. Crude but forceful. The rest was removed by Philip Howard in the 1750s in the name of a more natural taste, to Gilpin's approbation. Lord Ballyedmond has re-populated it. – The TEMPIETTO of *c.* 1720 terminates the walk, with widely spaced Tuscan columns up a wide staircase. Pediment sculpture of Arcadian figures on an island, with supporting figures and seahorses. Paintings of classical maidens under the portico, *c.* 1720, recently uncovered. Inside, a gently curved ceiling, Doric pilasters and the remains of painted decoration of *c.* 1830s by *Nutter*. (At the S end, life-size STATUE of St Constantine, 1843.)

Towards the S end of the estate, SALMON COOPS. Although popularly ascribed to the monks of Wetheral Priory (q.v.), the earliest evidence of the present structures is the 1752 map of Corby Park. Three sandstone piers and two abutments stretch from the E bank of the Eden to the upstream end of the northerly island, and a sloping sandstone causeway connects to a southerly island further upstream. It is likely that these islands themselves are artificial. Easily visible from Corby Castle, the arrangement may be a deliberately managed element of a Picturesque landscape.

Above the house on Byre Hill is a four-column Ionic TEMPLE with gilded balls. It is a memorial to an Italian lady who died young, and has on the frieze the inscription 'A quella che merita'. On top, the Howard lion signed *W. Robinson Delt* 1865. Above a balcony. It fronts a C17 or C18 DOVECOTE, which is in good order complete with rotating potence. – KITCHEN GARDEN and STABLE, *c.* 1812–17. – FOUNTAIN. 2004. – The GATE LODGE, 1817–18, has a Tuscan temple front with four columns on high bases and deep eaves. In the pediment a spirited Apollo and chariot in relief.

EXEDRA in the village square, built in 1833 for the blacksmith with covered space for shoeing. It is a niche on short round piers with free capitals. At the back is a round-headed doorway with a continuous roll moulding, thought by Pevsner to be C12 and from a church.

The modest COTTAGE at the railway crossing seems to have been the prototype for the first wayside stations along the Newcastle & Carlisle Railway (e.g. Stocksfield, Northumberland). At the beginning of the railway age, *c.* 1840, stations were treated as estate lodges, and no specific provision was made for passengers and their comforts. Also a RAILWAY BRIDGE over Corby Beck on the same line, 1830–4. By *Francis Giles*. Five round arches.

LITTLE CORBY HALL. *See* Warwick.

CORNEY (C)

An out-of-the-way parish. The church stands on its own, high above the sea.

St John Baptist. Chancel, nave and bellcote. Medieval in origin, C17 in character, C19 in architectural dress after renewals of 1847 (the vestry) and 1882 (restoration and refurnishing by *Paley & Austin*, with Gothic mullioned windows replacing domestic ones). Removal of roughcast on the N side shows granite lump construction and a blocked nave door near the W end. Also original the chancel N doorway. The W doorway, sheltering in a suburban timber porch, is round-arched but the stones are C19. Rustic queenpost roof. – MONUMENT. Simple tablet by *D. Dunbar* to Joseph Benn †1860, agent to the Earl of Lonsdale.

COTEHILL (C)

St John Evangelist. By *Habershon & Brock*, 1868. Like a Congregational chapel, with its W frontispiece, except for a distinct chancel and the funny bell-turret, thin and battered, tacked on the chancel N. Geometrical tracery, big roof, paired W windows. – STAINED GLASS. Nave N by *Henry Holiday*, 1871.
(Holme House, Cumwhinton, 2 m. NW. 1778. The standard five-bay type with a pedimented doorway. But the graceful decoration of the frieze below the pediment reveals the date.)

COWGILL

See *The Buildings of England, Yorkshire West Riding: Leeds, Bradford and the North.*

CRACKENTHORPE HALL (W)

NW of Appleby, cut off between river and the A66.

The Machells lived here from the C13 to the C20, 'seldom or never ascending to the degree of knight, esquires or gentlemen constantly', as an C18 writer put it. The deliciously fusty-looking five-bay front is untouched since 1685, when it was, on the contrary, shockingly up to date. It was designed by *Thomas*

Machell, who was born here, for his brother Hugh. Machell described it as 'exactly uniforme & of such a surpriseing symetry, that it semeth greater by far than it is. The N haveing a pedament & 2 s[p]heres or Cupiloes either side on top of the house; the one being designed for pleasure only, the other for a stack of chimneys.' The three-bay centrepiece carries a triangular pediment and so does the doorway. The pediment has plenty of square modillions. The corners are regularly quoined, and the windows taller than wide, with stone cross-mullions and transoms. An attic floor shows above the main cornice. The 'cupiloes' have unfortunately gone. The colour scheme is brown stone and cream roughcast. (Staircase with twisted balusters. In the hall a chimneypiece made up of diverse C17 pieces.) The plan, characteristic of the North-western counties at the time, is a long single pile with a stair extension at the back. Major additions in the 1880s in the same style, SW, have taken away much of its charm.

CROGLIN (C)

ST JOHN BAPTIST. A funny little church, rebuilt in the Norman style in 1878 by *J. Howison* of Edinburgh. Nave and chancel. Shafted windows with zigzag arches. Double bellcote. – STAINED GLASS. E window by *Lavers, Barraud & Westlake*. – COLOURED PRINTS. Published in 1897 by the *Fitzroy Picture Society*, founded by A. H. Mackmurdo to provide cheap pictures for schools. Triptych of the Nativity by *Heywood Sumner*, costing 16s. 6d., and three by *Selwyn Image* at 4s. 6d. each. Late Pre-Raphaelite, on the way to the flat style of the C20 poster. – WAR MEMORIAL, 1921. Celtic cross, with the names of the dead pasted across the base at an incongrously cheery angle. By *J. H. Martindale*. – MONUMENTS, also in the churchyard. Completely defaced female effigy. – Bishop Robert de Chause †1278. Foliated cross on a stepped base, the slab inscribed upside down on one side only.

Former RECTORY, opposite, S. Usually interpreted as a hall and tower, but there is a good C14 or C15 roof over the solar, clearly meant to be seen. This seems to prove that it was never a true tower, even though its ground floor is vaulted (cf. Preston Patrick, Temple Sowerby, Great Salkeld and others). Secure but not actively defensive. The hall range has been heightened, blocking a small window in the wing. Its door positions suggest that it may have had a through passage at the low end, in the medieval way. As it is now, the house appears Georgian apart from the masonry.

TOWNHEAD BASTLE, Newbiggin, 1¼ m. NW. Superior bastle house, converted to a bank barn, in the yard of Townhead Farm. The farmhouse is dated 1702, with the initials GD JD and a rhyme. The upper door of the bastle is unconvincingly inscribed TD MDXX; a more likely date is mid-C17. Both doors are on the S; the byre door underneath towards the E end, the first-floor door a little W of centre, both with drawbar slots. Massive integral stack for the first-floor fireplace in the W wall. The fireplace has two rows of voussoirs in a segmental arch, which has slipped badly. There is what looks like an inserted second fireplace at the other end, with a massive lintel on corbels. The eaves of the roof have been raised, with a section of thinner wall, and the floor may have been raised too.

(CROGLIN LOW HALL, 1¾ m. SW of the village. C17 or possibly C16 house extended in the C19, and a long C16 barn wing making an L, much of it in poor condition. The barn is massively built, with two tiers of slit vents.)

In the yard of CROFT HOUSE FARM on the way to Townhead is a little WESLEYAN CHAPEL dated 1847. The porch is in the side not the end wall. Good set of unconverted farm buildings.

CROOK (W)

4090

Five footpaths converge at the humble TOWER of the old chapel of ease on its hilltop. It is said to date from 1620. The bell-openings and parapet indeed look Jacobean. No buttresses. The new ST CATHERINE is at the road junction below, ¼ m. N. By *Stephen Shaw*, 1887, it is roughcast but not white. Wide nave and aisles. The unbuttressed W tower is as blunt as the old one; the style is Late Perp.

HOLLIN HALL, 1 m. NE. Attached to the house at the E is a C14 or C15 tower with stepped gables, tunnel-vaulted at basement level. It may never have had a fighting top. The rest late C16 or early C17, with a W addition of the late C17 or early C18. Round chimneyshafts.

STONETHWAITE. By *Tom Mellor* for himself, 1968. Long and low with white roughcast walls and a single chimney. Single-storeyed, but it steps down as the ground falls. Semi-autonomous flat for carer or granny. Main rooms open to the matchboarded roof.

CROSBY-ON-EDEN (C)

4050

ST JOHN EVANGELIST. By *R. W. Billings*, antiquary and architect, 1854. Pevsner enjoyed it: 'A very inventive, rather naughty design . . . It is the tower which floors one. Short, with a spire with colossal crockets up the edges, and nightmarishly long, tight lucarnes.' The lucarnes are actually taller than the spire itself, dropping their sills below the spire base. Wheel-cross on top, cannon gargoyles at the corners. The canopy over the W

83

door repeats the over-sized crockets and the wheel-cross on a pedestal. An over-sized turret on the N continues the line of the nave wall. A continuous drip-course jumps excitedly up and down to get around the turret to the tower front, colliding in the process with a parapet moulding – but there are no parapets. Underneath all this, the form of the building is pre-archaeological: a single auditory space with little more than an alcove for a chancel. The windows however have fully developed flowing Dec tracery which is unexpected for the 1850s. Their inner reveals are segment-headed, each fitted with a frilly Gothic pelmet. An antecedent can be found in the inner gatehouse of Carlisle Castle, but there it is stone; here cast iron. The tracery is filled with cut or moulded glass with stars and crosses, a charming idea creating a glittering effect. They were made by *Williams & Watson* and date from 1957. Pew-ends and gallery front are of cast iron. The roof has arched braces forming big semicircular hoops. – PULPIT, LECTERN and VICAR'S SEAT are replacements of 1925 by *Arthur Simpson*'s firm, richly carved by *William Aumonier (Jun.)*. The FONT however is from the previous church – a square chamfered back to round, on a round stem and capital-like base. – STAINED GLASS. E window by *Heaton, Butler & Bayne*, 1885.

NATIONAL SCHOOL immediately W. 1844. Sweet, or would be were it not for the cage-like fence. Three bays, symmetrical, with iron lattice windows. Centre gable with bellcote, clock and inscription.

CROSBY HOUSE, High Crosby, ⅜ m. E. A five-bay early C19 brick house of standard type, with a four-columned Doric porch, hipped roof and one-bay lower wings. HIGH CROSBY FARM, opposite, has a three-bay façade of the late C18 with a prettily decorated frieze below the doorway pediment. CROSBY LODGE (HOTEL), round the corner, was a calm three-bay classical villa, hip-roofed with a central bow, of 1807–8. Attributed to *Peter Nicholson* and *William Reid*, for David Kennedy of Carlisle. It had single-storey wings reaching back, and another hip-roofed building enclosed a yard at the back. It has been swallowed up by a hysterical brick affair, castellated, ivy-clad, towered and turreted. The re-invention was complete by 1874, and can be attributed to George Saul of Brunstock, or to his son Silas, the sculptor. Present entrance in a side wing, raised to two storeys and given a porch. On the original front the bow can be recognized, but refenestrated with a series of narrow arched lights. An octagonal tower replaces the r. link. On the other side is a larger square tower, stone-faced, which partly obscures the wing. Their inequality, no doubt meant to be Picturesque, is merely annoying. Standing back in the field the original roof and chimneys can be seen, and it can be appreciated how the battlements swoop down and then up to a peak over the bow.

EDEN GROVE, ⅝ m. WSW. By or after *Peter Nicholson*, 1837–9, for Richard Carruthers, a portrait painter. Demure Greek villa of red ashlar, facing the river. Three by two bays only, and just a single storey over a channelled basement. Two pairs of fluted

Doric columns support a free-standing portico. The windows have tapered surrounds. The front door opens halfway up the stairs: two flights down, one up to an inner hall articulated by another pair of columns. The principal rooms are on the upper floor, with restrained Greek detail. A service wing on the r. leads on to an exceptionally high brick garden wall scooping round to catch the sun. The usual bothies and potting sheds are behind it, plus the stables, hidden by a parallel curving stone wall. The integration of house, garden, services and out-buildings is unusual.

CROSBY GARRETT (W)

7000

St Andrew. On a steep hilltop, with a bird's-eye view over the village and up to the viaduct. The chancel is already stepping down the hill. Miniature c13 w tower, really an enclosed belfry, corbelled out over a middle buttress. A local fashion (cf. Warcop), and rather fragile; this was last rebuilt in 1874. Flat floor right through to a clear E window. The chancel has c14 Dec features. E.E. chancel arch, very low. On the E side the top of a higher and narrower arch can be seen above. It is semi-circular, less than 6 ft (0.9 metres) wide, with proper voussoirs; perhaps pre-Conquest. Huge squint to the N aisle. Norman three-bay N arcade of c. 1175 on big square bases. Flat, square capitals and abaci with fleshy leaves, similar to Lowther (q.v.). Round arches, single-stepped. The aisle itself was rebuilt in 1866 by *E. Johnson* of Liverpool in fake-Norman style. – COMMUNION RAIL. C17. – MONUMENT. Matthew Thompson of Stobars Hall †1871, by *Gaffin & Co.*, 1882. Still Georgian, with a weeping lady, hourglass, and draped urn.

Old Rectory. The c18 STABLE is opposite the church gate. The house is dated 1637 and 1719, of two-and-a-half storeys, with upper crucks. (Some good c18 interiors, including a couple of panelled rooms and a fine stair with turned balusters, fluted newels, and inlaid handrail.)

Railway viaduct, 1871. Six skew arches of local limestone, 110 yds long, 55 ft high (102 and 17 metres). For the Midland Railway's Settle and Carlisle line.

Rayseat Pike long cairn, 3¼ m. wsw. Visible from the nw, across Sunbiggin Tarn. A Neolithic mound of rubble, 65 yds (60 metres) long, probably consisting of two separate round cairns later conjoined; higher and broader at the se end. Several disarticulated burials were found in c19 excavations.

CROSBY RAVENSWORTH (W)

6010

St Lawrence. An unexpectedly grand and fully developed church to find in so quiet a place. w tower with a corner spike, long nave with aisles and clerestory, transepts, and a long

81

chancel. The fruit of two successive remodellings. First in 1811–12 by *George Gibson*, who is thought to have taken advice from *Smirke*. Of this there remain the Gothick s w porch and chancel s doorway. They have a naïvety and vigour close to folk art, with large flat flowers, magical geometric devices, and slightly comical representations of the bread and the wine. The names of the five masons, including *R. Bland*, are recorded in the porch.* The second was in 1848–87, a long collaboration between an artistic, energetic incumbent, *George F. Weston*, and his architect friend *J. S. Crowther*. However the C13 s doorway, with two orders of colonnettes and much dogtooth, proves that the building is much older. The exceptionally dark interior indeed reveals a medieval church of considerable ambition. The oldest part is the crossing of *c.* 1190–1200. The piers are tripartite to each crossing arch, with the middle shaft sharply keeled, as at Orton. The capitals are crude, the arches triple-chamfered (the E arch is C19). The capital and arch springing of the NW pier of the crossing is much lower than the rest, indicating a raising of the floor levels. Next come the elegant early C13 nave arcades, slender, with quatrefoil piers with short diagonals between the foils, waterholding bases and twice-chamfered arches. The s side has a little nailhead and leaf paterae as label stops. The arch from s aisle to s transept is double-chamfered and steep. It is thought that Lancelot Threlkeld (†1492) dismantled the crossing tower, if there was one, took down the transepts, and built the w tower. Characteristic w window with grid-like tracery, plain tower arch. The Threlkeld chapel at the NE is Dec, with an E window now internal and another N. The wide segmental arch to the chancel must be C16, perhaps post-Reformation, with indeterminate mouldings.

The Weston–Crowther restoration took its cue from the E.E. arcades. The first new furnishings were introduced in 1850. The whitewash came off and the columns and arches were re-hewn, which makes one's heart sink somewhat. A surpliced choir was introduced in 1853, and in 1854 the chancel arch, which up until then had been a timber-framed partition with windows at the top, was inserted, plus a new vestry with medieval chimneys. The w tower was given a new belfry stage in 1866–8, an eminently characteristic Crowther job with gargoyles, an inhabited string, frilled louvres and an octagonal stair spirelet. In 1868 the clerestory was added, with quatrefoil lights too small to do the job, and a new steep-pitched, single-framed roof. The foundations of the lost s transept were discovered at this time, and in 1870–1 it was re-created at the expense of Mr Wilkinson Dent of Flass, Maulds Meaburn. St Lawrence at Morland (q.v.) was the model for its E.E. style, but a wheel window substitutes for Morland's upper lancets. Internally this is an elaborate piece with two tiers of arcading and encaustic

---

*Pictures show that the tower was then given a jolly Magdalen-College crown and the interior was whitewashed and decorated with scrollwork and texts chiefly done by *Gibson*. Chancellor Walter Fletcher, visiting in 1815, was delighted with it.

tiles. The simpler N transept followed in 1872–3. They made the crossing very dark, so big inauthentic dormers were introduced. Finally the chancel was rebuilt in Geometrical style, with the regulation piscina and sedilia. It was completed in 1886, just before Weston's death. *Robert Hogarth Parkin* of Orton was resident mason. Weston himself supplied working drawings and some of the ornamental designs. *J. R. & E. Williams* of Manchester were the sculptors; their portrait heads, chancel S, are characteristic of Crowther churches.

FURNISHINGS. REREDOS. 1897, by the ladies of the wood-turning class under *Mrs Webster*. Last Supper, blank tracery, canopy, foliage, cresting. – ALTAR, RAIL, CHOIR STALLS, *c.* 1850, all quite simple. – PULPIT, also 1850, highly wrought of stone from Hause quarry, with polished shafts, nailhead, ballflower and foliage: a demonstration-piece of what was to come. – FONT. Completely plain octagonal bowl dated 1662. Its cover comes from a second FONT of 1818, lurking in the NW corner like a monstrous chalice painted red and green, with acanthus leaves and a palindromic Greek inscription. – STAINED GLASS. Mostly by *Clayton & Bell*, following closely on each phase of the work. The N aisle W window was designed by *Weston* himself, with the tracery, in memory of his first wife †1855. W window by *Warrington*. *Shrigley & Hunt* made three on the S side in the 1880s, in one of which (chancel S) Weston appears, with angel orchestra and choir.

MONUMENTS. Big Threlkeld tomb-chest under the NE chapel arch. Polished black top, sides scalloped, rather like linenfold, with three blank shields. Possibly to Sir Lancelot of Crosby Hall †1512, but Pevsner thought it later. – Fine standing monument signed *Dunbar*, Newcastle, to George Gibson †1835, who superintended the first reconstruction, aiding 'with his own skilful hand so excellent a work'. White sarcophagus, figures of Faith, Hope and Charity, and a charming musical trophy with a chant by himself to Psalm 122. – In the tower, a plain slab records the rebuilding of 1811 and the influence of William Dent. – Wilkinson Dent †1886. White marble bust in recessed frame by *Thomas Smith* of London. – Brasses to the Rev. G. Weston †1887, perhaps by *Crowther*, and to Robert Hogarth Parkin †1903. – Arthur Evelyn Dent and his brother Reginald Teesdale, both killed in the First World War; white marble tablet with portrait medallion. – Other Dent plaques include Thomas Wilkinson John Dent †1902 in alabaster and porphyry.*

WESTON HOUSE, E, the former vicarage, was improved by Canon G. W. Weston with the addition of Gothic mullioned windows. Windows at the back with complex iron glazing may represent 1811 improvements. The house has been limewashed deep red.

Also E of the church, a little L-shaped former SCHOOL. Dated 1784 under the cornice. *Ingredere ut proficias* ('enter to make

---

*Recently destroyed is a PAINTING of the Blessing of the Children signed *I. N. Heineman*.

progress') inscribed in flowing copper-plate script in the pediment over the door. Windows round-headed with double keystones.

METHODIST CHAPEL. 1875. Mildly Gothic with a pinnacle on the end gable.

JENNYWELL HALL, in the village, s. It incorporates Victorian Gothic work such as the roofed front gate, porch, and two-storey bay. Details of style point to Crowther (or Weston).

(HOLESFOOT. Of *c*. 1845. Centre with a Greek Doric porch. Low flanking wings with niches.)

CRAKE (or CRAIK) TREES. On a wonderful high spot ½ m. NW. Romantic but deteriorating ruin of the high-quality late medieval house of the Lancasters. A cross-wing at the s end has a vaulted basement. Ogee-headed and cusped window head re-set on the s wall. Hall range in the middle, retaining a four-light front window and a fireplace lintel, but little more. The in-line solar at the N end had a spiral stair, but has suffered a recent collapse. Some of the stones have been reused in the adjacent farm and holiday let.

REAGILL GRANGE, 1½ m. NW. Fine old house, beautifully secluded. It was a grange of Shap Abbey, bought by the Wharton family after the Dissolution. L-plan house of probably the late C16 (1590 mention in the Parish Register), but with the date 1652 in an upstairs bedroom. Two-storey porch in front and a two-storey stair-tower behind. Roughcast, with two-light mullioned windows now largely converted to sideways sashes, and plenty of fat cylindrical chimneystacks. The porch door opens sideways. The wing was extended in 1700 by T. & E. D. (Thomas and Elizabeth Daws) as recorded on a displaced lintel, now over a first-floor window. In its end wall, overlooking Chapel Field, is a small window with pointed arch. Continuous hoodmoulds. The turning stair is stone to the first floor, wooden after that.

At Reagill is the IMAGE GARDEN made by *Thomas Bland* (1798–1865). He hosted a grand public opening in 1837, and thereafter it was the scene of regular fetes and entertainments with new sculptures added year by year. 'Bland seems to have attacked everything from science to sketching with furious but intermittent energy,' wrote Canon Weston. Bland's archaeological investigations reminded him of 'a terrier at a rabbit hole'. In a walled enclosure of only about fifty paces square he created a bewildering ensemble of sculpture in a strongly architectural setting. Lamps in niches illuminated his oil paintings. Bland made the flat garden theatrically three-dimensional, creating terraces and steps, raised walkways at the edges, two raised platforms or stages in the middle, and viewing steps and a balcony attached to the house. All the stonework is dry, so it is beginning to fall about. There are dozens of urns, often with figure decoration, and many animals. The human likenesses can sometimes be identified from contemporary accounts; Bland seems to have fought shy of lettering. They include Sir Walter Scott, Robbie Burns, a Norman king, a reclining nymph, Diana with a lyre, and many that are fragmentary. They stood on plinths inset with relief sculpture (as at Shap Wells, q.v., and at Black Dub, below), of which only a few survive.

The garden is such fun that it comes as a surprise to find that it is not at all Picturesque. Nowhere does it compose into a satisfactory picture. It is not formal either – no vistas or diagonals. Nor for that matter does there appear to be any narrative. The different elements are simply disposed where their creator fancied. As for style, the inspiration is hand-me-down classical, not Gothic.

BLACK DUB, on the limestone moor 2¾ m. SSW. Hard to spot, even in so featureless a landscape. MONUMENT made *c.* 1851 by *Thomas Bland* of Reagill at the spot where in 1651 Charles Stuart quenched his thirst on his way S from Scotland to the Battle of Worcester. Bas-reliefs on the square base show Charles II in profile, a crown, and a lion. Blunt obelisk on top.

STONE CIRCLE, 2 m. WNW, SE of Castlehowe Scar. Small. Ten boulders with an outlier to the NE.

EWE CLOSE, I m. SW. A Late Iron Age and Romano-British SETTLEMENT beside the Roman road from Low Borrowbridge to Brougham, the raised camber of which is clearly visible on the SW. A square enclosure, with three rounded angles, entered from the S. In the centre the footings of a large round building about 50 ft (15 metres) across internally. Excavation revealed Roman pottery, and stone walls with substantial basal courses. A circular enclosure lies across the SE quadrant of the square one and may have preceded it; the sequence is uncertain. A series of smaller walled yards and buildings extends E; some of these may represent medieval reuse of the site as a farm or sheepfolds (hence the name). A polygonal field to the S is bounded by a bank and ditch.

CROSSCANONBY (C)

0030

ST JOHN EVANGELIST. A small Norman church, given to the canons of Carlisle in 1130 or 1150, and built partly of square Roman stones probably from Maryport. Nave and chancel, and a narrow Dec aisle joining on to the S porch. Windows are few, small, and set high, especially in the aisle. The porch has a pointed arch with two continuous chamfers, and a trefoil niche above. The inner doorway is tall with blank tympanum.

The interior is full of good things. Chancel arch plausibly Roman, re-set: deep voussoirs of high quality but entirely unmoulded, tie-backs at springing level, imposts also unmoulded but incorporating on both sides a very classical niche. The aisle opens into the nave by a single wide twice-chamfered arch which has little faces at the springing. Above it appears the head of a Norman S window. A smaller arch opens into the chancel. Chancel S window also Norman.

Crosscanonby, St John Evangelist, cross-shaft.
Engraving, 1899

Restoration of 1880 by *C. J. Ferguson* (Kelly). – PULPIT. It
looks early C18. – Behind it on the wall a TEXT carved and
painted black and gold, with cherubs. – C18 too the carved
PANELS to the gallery front, dated 1730, with lush foliage, and
two more on benches, this time with mainly military emblems.
– FONT. Alabaster, square, with very boldly moulded curling
leaves mostly in scroll or volute contexts; C14, as Aspatria. –
PAINTING. The Last Supper, probably by *Mathias Read
c.* 1717. – Also by Read the ROYAL ARMS, 1733. – STAINED
GLASS. E window, 1849, signed *Carl Scott* (of *J. Scott & Son*).

MONUMENTS AND SCULPTURE. CROSS-SHAFT (part), C10,
in the porch. On the front four beasts, alternately reversed,
bend back to bite themselves; a wonderfully lively and
ingenious composition, the beasts not interconnected and set
separately against a worked flat background, not just chiselled-
away space. On one edge a more familiar dragon in the Jellinge
style. On the remaining two sides interlace. – LAWRENCE
STONE. CII(?) grave-cover crudely incised with a spiral-
stemmed cross, zigzags l. and r. of it, a small human figure on
the l. lower down, and what could be a gridiron. – Outside, a
C10 HOGBACK, worn almost smooth. Curved ridge with a

beast at each end, covered with the interlocking ring-chain design of Dearham. – Table TOMB of John Smith of Birkby, salt officer, †1730. Side panels with putti, skull and crossbones in relief, and a scribe – he might almost be an Evangelist – in a deep niche, Bewcastle-style. – Many C18 and C19 Musgrave tablets in the chancel.

The abbreviated CROSBY village is strung out on the A596 ½ m. SE, on either side of a broad open green.

(BIRKBY LODGE, ⅝ m. SW. A handsome late C18 or early C19 house of three bays with a porch of unfluted Ionic columns and the windows r. and l. set in blank arched recesses.)

MILEFORTLET, Swarthy Hill, ⅔ m. NNW. On a low sea cliff on Allonby Bay. Excavated and partly reconstructed remains, part of the Roman defences down the Cumbrian coast. Probably occupied only in the C2, during the reign of Hadrian. A rampart of dumped sand faced with turf enclosed a rectangular area, traversed by an axial gravel path. Outside the rampart a broad berm and a ditch, omitted on the seaward side. Over the W entrance a timber tower; on the E a narrow causeway across the ditch, and rampart ends revetted by timbers held in sleeper-beams. In the interior, S of the path, a three-roomed building, also founded on beams; to the N, a line of posts probably supported the roof ridge of a shed of four bays.

On the shore immediately below, remains of C16 SALT-WORKS. Brine was 'sleeched' from salt sand, and simmered in a pit or well (surviving in the shingle). W of the road, the foundations of saltworkers' cottages.

CROSSCRAKE (W)   5080

ST THOMAS. Rebuilt by *Paley & Austin*, 1874–5. Of square slate blocks. It had a bold saddleback central tower which was reduced in 1944 owing to structural failure and removed altogether in 1963–4. *T. Maldwin Jones* created a shallow S transept which effectively disguises the loss, and a weedy spirelet was placed over the crossing. A Dec window from a church in Barrow replaces the original lancets of the transept. Only on the N does a stump of the missing tower appear, flat-roofed, retained in order to clear the crossing arches. Internally the church is still good, though a modern narthex blocks half a bay w. The style is late C12 to early C13. N aisle with round piers and caps and two-step arches. High and wide crossing well lit from the dwarf S transept. The S arch is a 1960s creation. – FURNISHINGS by *Paley & Austin*, including a big square FONT in the N transept/aisle. – STAINED GLASS. E window, *c.* 1890 by *Clayton & Bell*.

Former VICARAGE, now Sellett Lodge. 1848 by *Miles Thompson* in rustic mode. Raw chunks of limestone pavement for the door and window surrounds. The split gable looks oddly C20.

SELLET HALL, 1 m. SE. No dates, but perhaps C16, with the stair wing and cross-corridor made in the C17. Mullioned-and-transomed windows on both floors, except the one l. of the entrance, which has mullions only. Plenty of rough timber framing within, including the lower reaches of the well staircase. Higher up it develops proper vertically symmetrical turned balusters.

At STAINTON, 1 m. S, is an Independent CHAPEL erected *c.* 1698, with W addition for schoolroom above, stable below in the banking. Completely plain exterior with rectangular windows. Interior re-fitted and turned *c.* 1870, but the C17 pulpit and communion table are, or were, still there. The chapel closed in 2007.

2020

CROSTHWAITE (C)

ST KENTIGERN. The ancient parish church of Keswick; indeed for centuries the only parish church in the central Lakes.* In 1180 Jocelin of Furness said the church was recently built, perhaps by Aelicia Pipard also called de Rumeli, who gave it in 1198 to Fountains Abbey. A NE chapel was added *c.* 1340. Donations for building work are recorded in 1523 (by Dame Alice Ratcliff; *see* below) and 1554. It was restored in 1844–6 by *G. G. Scott* with surplus funds collected for the Southey monument. Further work in 1889 (*C. J. Ferguson*) and 1915.

The present church is Perp and latest Perp. Thick roughcast without and plaster within, and the general ironing-out of telling discrepancies, make this a discouraging building to the architectural historian. Long, low, and grey, with a battlemented clerestory from end to end and a bluff W tower with square SW stair-turret. There does not seem to be much left of Aelicia's C12 church. Its footprint occupied the present nave and N aisle, and a few carved stones remain. The tower, probably *c.* 1554, was without a W doorway until 1921. The W window has uncusped panel tracery and an embattled transom. Side windows are mullioned in twos and threes under square heads. They are quite varied, especially on the N where they jump up and down alternately. The lower ones have ogee heads and shouldered rere-arches, probably C14, the higher ones are cinquefoil-headed, and later (S aisle except W, clerestory except two SE, N aisle easternmost). Both sorts display incised CONSECRATION CROSSES, of which there are twelve outside, nine in. The NE window is clearly Dec; the chapel was integrated with the aisle in the C16. The priest's doorway, S, has a re-set shouldered head of late C13–C14 type. The clerestory dates from the 1550s rebuild, although its easternmost windows may be reused. The main E window was until 1844 off-centre to the N, indicating a later widening to the S.

---

*Bowness, Grasmere and Hawkshead were chapelries until the mid C16.

Scott rebuilt it in the centre, and *Ferguson* refashioned it in 1889. S porch by *Scott*. The whole interior slopes up to the E. The tower arch is twice chamfered, dying into the jambs. Arcade arches also twice chamfered, on octagonal piers and capitals, running on for seven bays without a chancel arch. The easternmost arch on the S is much wider, where an intervening pier has been removed. Roofs all *Scott*.

The quality of the FURNISHINGS owes much to the Rev. Hardwicke Rawnsley and his wife Edith, who arrived in 1883, and the *Keswick School of Industrial Arts* (*KSIA*; *see* below). – REREDOS. By *Ferguson*, 1889, incorporating three gleaming repoussé panels by *Edith Rawnsley* and *John Birkett* of the KSIA. Likewise the hanging LIGHTS, MOSAICS, and PULPIT. – FONT. *Orate* inscription for Thomas de Eskhead (Hesket?) †*c.* 1396. The bowl is octagonal, with plant forms and shields alternating, and the sign of the Trinity. Square stem broached to an octagon, with blank Dec tracery. Square base with four damaged beasts, like those in Dacre churchyard (q.v.). – STAINED GLASS. N aisle, half-figure of C16 cleric with book, staff and bell – perhaps St Anthony. S aisle E, lady's head, and C16 coat of arms. By *Kempe & Co.* the E window of 1897 and two N, 1904. Several others by *Wailes*, and two by *Hardman* (S aisle, second and third from E). Four by *Mayer* of Munich in the chancel clerestory. Clerestory window over the Southey monument by *David Cross*, 2000.

MONUMENTS. BRASSES (SE chapel) to Sir John (†1527) and Dame Alice Ratcliff, on a large polished slab. The figures are 23½ in. (60 cm.) long. – Alabaster effigies of a civilian (with purse) and lady, retaining traces of colour; thought to be Thomas Radcliffe †1495 and wife. – Robert Southey (†1843) by *J. G. Lough*, 1846. Recumbent white marble figure, disturbingly awake, one hand on his heart, the other holding a book. Wordsworth wrote the epitaph: 'Ye Vales and Hills, whose beauty hither drew/The poet's steps, and fixed him here, on you/His eyes have closed.' – Many tablets. e.g. two by *Webster* (chancel N). – Several *KSIA* plaques including a South African War memorial. – First World War memorial in beaten copper by *E. Harrison*. – Canon Rawnsley, co-founder of the National Trust, †1920, and his wife Edith †1916. Slab with simple carved relief. – Outside, several outstandingly good slate GRAVESTONES by the *Bromley* dynasty of stonemasons. Joseph Dover †1810 by the porch (with Hope at the top; by *William Bromley*, erected 1840); George Wood †1812 by *John Bromley I*, free-standing close by; Joseph Cherry †1818 at the E end (with Father Time; by *W. Bromley*). On the N side Thomas Bowe †1838 with simple scythe and hay-rake, beautifully done. The churchyard presents quite a forest of Celtic cross headstones, including *Edith Rawnsley* †1916, who designed some, and certainly championed them.

(VICARAGE, Vicarage Hill. Late C18 front of five widely spaced bays, with a Venetian window rather than the door in the centre.)

CROSTHWAITE PARISH HALL. SE of the church, across the Greta bridge (so actually in Keswick). Green stone, white cove, timber-framed gable, Yorkshire lintel. By *C. J. Ferguson*, 1875.

SCHOOL OF INDUSTRIAL ARTS (KSIA), High Hill. The school was started in the parish hall by the Rev. Hardwicke Rawnsley and his wife Edith in the winter of 1883–4, with classes for woodcarving and metalworking. New building 1893–4, by *Paley, Austin & Paley*, with much illustrious advice, built by *T. & I. Hodgson* and *F. & W. Green*, a typical Keswick team. The style is supposed to be Old Lake Country Domestic, including a spinning gallery. The text on the front, 'The Loving Eye and Patient Hand . . .', is from Robert Browning. The school was wound up in 1984; now a restaurant.

CUMBERLAND PENCIL FACTORY, High Hill. Built in 1937 in what was hoped to be a forward-looking style. The main façade presents a three-storey white-painted concrete frame of twenty-six bays with metal-framed windows divided into eight horizontal strips. Projecting vertical ribs and the slight forward set of the four central bays fail to bring the composition to life, and the overall effect is mean – an impression reinforced by the cheap-looking single-storey former laboratory block, now the Pencil Museum, which sits in front at an unconsidered oblique angle. Pencil manufacture was transferred to Workington in 2008, ending over 300 years of the industry at Keswick.

Also on High Hill is PORCH COTTAGE, C17, the home of Marion Twelves (*see also* Langdales, p. 487), who in 1889 set up the spinning wheels and handlooms of the Keswick linen industry.

KESWICK SCHOOL. The Grammar School was housed near Crosthwaite Parish Hall in buildings of much the same period, now residential. The present Comprehensive school occupies the magnificent Lairthwaite site, SE of the church. A Secondary Modern school was built here in 1951–2, incorporating a Victorian house. New buildings by *Steve Harwood* (*ADK Architects*), *c.* 1995. Long and white with a slate roof, crank round to fit the contour, with a round turret as hinge, echoing Skiddaw.

ORMATHWAITE HALL, 1 m. NE. White house of seven bays, early C18 and later, for the Brownrigg family. Doorway with Doric pilasters and pediment. At right angles, like another house, was the chemical laboratory of Dr William Brownrigg (1711–1800). Five bays and lower two-bay wings, the doorway moulded and with a pediment. Pevsner thought the octagonal window must be later.

UNDERSCAR (hotel). N of Ormathwaite Hall, high up, with a wonderfully moody view over Derwentwater to the Borrowdale mountains. Villa of *c.* 1856–63 for William Oxley of Liverpool, by *Charles Reed*, who later changed his name to *Verelst*. Italianate, with two Osborne towers, one centrally placed. Shallow-pitched roofs, bracketed eaves. Opulent central atrium under a dome, like a Dresden villa, and a splendid conservatory added in the late C19. *Edward Kemp* designed the equally Italianate GARDEN.

MILLBECK TOWERS, Millbeck, 1¼ m. N. Made out of a carding mill, 1903. In many styles, with two pepperpot towers. Art Nouveau interiors.

CROSTHWAITE (W)

In the Lyth valley, famed for its damsons.

ST MARY. Chapel licensed 1537, chancel and tower 1626. Present church by the chameleon-like *Joseph Bintley*, 1877–8, here in Paley & Austin mode and Perp in style. The old tower was retained until 1885 when this one, a fine piece also by Bintley, was constructed. Rock-faced. Broad nave without aisles, transepts, polygonal apse. No architecturally defined chancel, but angel hammerbeams and steps mark the transition. – REREDOS. 1885. Gothic frames round the apse, painted in flat Early Italian style with plenty of gold. By *Shrigley & Hunt*? – STAINED GLASS. Apse, 1879 by *Heaton, Butler & Bayne*, in poor nick; also W window. One by *Harry Stammers*, 1953, nave s, another by *L. C. Evetts*, 1974. – MONUMENT. Portrait bust, William Pearson †1856. Signed *T. Doggett*.

HILL TOP, 1¼ m. NW. A very odd set-up. Reputedly built by Sir Daniel Fleming of Rydal in about 1808 for his mistress and illegitimate family. It is surrounded by an enclosing wall, fully 18 ft (5.5 metres) high and buttressed in places, built dry, but only about 18 in. (46 cm.) thick, and pierced by castellated arches. The wall has been dropped on the garden side to leave a ha-ha. Within stand a pair of houses, one with a Roman Doric porch, joined by a timber-framed link, and a pretty pavilion. Constructional details suggest one build: roughly shaped limestone quoins to the enceinte wall and both houses, shallow hipped roofs to both houses and pavilion.

COWMIRE HALL, 2 m. SW. Hard to find in the maze of tiny lanes. Plain roughcast front range of *c.* 1690, of three equal storeys divided by weatherings. Six bays. Cross-mullion windows of wood, and a semicircular wooden hood over the central door. The main hearth is at the r. end, with a blocked end entry beside it. Facing the front door, not necessarily *in situ*, is an ornate chimneypiece with arms. At the back is a defensive tower. This, judging by its three- and four-light windows, round-headed and well-barred under flat hoodmoulds, is mid-C16. Its ground floor is tunnel-vaulted in two chambers and it has garderobes on the upper floors in a slight projection. The C17 house stair has been accommodated within it. It is broad, with finely turned balusters of bold projection with ball finials and a drop pendant, and rises in double flights to the very top of the house. There are several fireplaces with bolection mouldings. The partition between the top-floor rooms of the tower is formed of heavy close studding. Court-yard of farm buildings. Bothy reached by outside stone steps with two end fireplaces, one of them a bottle-shaped recess for a hanging hood or lumb (cf. Forest Hall, Selside), now used as a damson gin factory.

POOL BANK FARM, ½ m. s of the above. Complex of houses and barns, heavily restored to conservation standards for residential use. IKH (John and Katherine Hartley) 1693 on a lintel with a castellated sink. Side range with stone cross-mullions. Small wooden gallery in the yard.

LIMEKILNS. A number of the C18 or C19 on the NE slopes of Whitbarrow, 1¼ m. SE. The best, a large rectangular farm kiln with a parabolic arch over the draw-hole, is 400 yds SW of Dawson Fold.

CULGAITH (C)

Long unplanned village of red stone.

ALL SAINTS. 1756 over the W door, but Dec windows inserted c. 1896 at the E and transept ends. The rest are slightly pointed. Two-storey W elevation. The church is cruciform with equal arms, like a Scottish kirk, and somewhat puritanical in character. Transept arms screened by roughly Doric colonnades of three bays; bases high enough to clear the pews, shafts and responds too tall and without entasis. The coved ceiling comes down to meet each column. Chancel re-fitted c. 1935. – PAN-ELLING of c. 1756.

(VICARAGE. 1856 by *Francis Bros.*)

METHODIST CHAPEL. 1830. Red stone. The door is in the long side, not the gable end as later became standard.

STATION (closed) and stationmaster's house. 1880. The only non-standard designs on the Settle and Carlisle railway.

(MILLRIGG. Built in 1597 by the Birkbecks. Their kinsfolk the Dalstons of Acorn Bank (Temple Sowerby, q.v.) purchased it in 1661. A 1669 datestone relates to a refurbishment including some splendidly chunky bolection-moulded stone fireplaces. The house has a two-storeyed porch with an adjoining spiral-stair projection.★)

CUMDIVOCK (C)
Dalston

ALL SAINTS. 1870–2 by *Cory & Ferguson.* Dec. Grey stone. Nave and chancel in one. The bellcote stands on two little hanging arches. – STAINED GLASS. E window by *Clayton & Bell,* 1872.

★Thanks to Adam Menuge for this and much other information.

CARDEW LODGE, ¼ m. NNW. It is a pity the church is so dull, for this is where *C. J. Ferguson* came to live. The house, a many-gabled affair, was built in the 1870s for Maj.-Gen. W. H. Lowther. Ferguson's additions are dated C & AF 1889. He added a round tower to the garden façade, and built a pair of fat battlemented round towers to flank the gateway, recalling Smirke's Citadel in Carlisle, and a LODGE on the road with a similar tower.

CARDEW HOUSE, ¼ m. NW, has an C18 show front with painted stone surrounds to the tripartite windows, the centre one raised. The doorway and middle bay have pediments. STONETHWAITE, a little further on, dated 1724 R & AN, is similar but quieter because the stone is unpainted. The frames of the windows have thin raised fillets along the outer and inner edges. Door surround bolection-moulded with ears.

CUMREW (C) 5050

ST MARY. 1890 by *George Dale Oliver*, replacing a church with a little W tower. Bad architecture, said Pevsner, with its busy rock-facing; 'neat and substantial', said a report of the time. NW tower. Geometrical C13 detail but round-headed chancel arch. – STAINED GLASS. E and chancel S windows by *Lavers, Barraud & Westlake*, 1890. – MONUMENTS. In the boiler room, C14 effigy of a lady in green stone. She is very tall, has a little sausage dog above her head but no face left. – Outside, on the S chancel wall, a fine Gill family monument signed *Bromley*, Keswick, 1829.

Bordering the path to the church a row of three C17 stone houses, no longer inhabited. The one next to the church gate was the rectory. It has a couple of bits of Norman carved stone built into it.

CUMWHITTON (C) 5050

Attractive red stone village clustered round bits of green.

ST MARY. Diminutive W tower with exterior steps at the side to the ringing room. Arched windows, with keystones on the S side, i.e. all C18. But the masonry is older, with marks of former openings. In the S wall a small length of Norman zigzag. Narrow N aisle. The chancel with its lancets may be Victorian; the arch has been opened up. The aisle E window, opening now into the vestry and probably *ex situ*, is narrow and double-splayed; Saxon or Early Norman? The N arcade of three bays is *c.* 1200: round piers and arches with one step and a slight

chamfer. – FONT. Plain octagonal bowl, dated 1662. – SCULP-
TURE. Part of a Maltese cross-head, regarded by Collingwood
as Norman. – STAINED GLASS. E window by *Percy Bacon*, 1924.
One N by *L. C. Evetts*, 1962.

4020

DACRE (C)

ST ANDREW. A monastery is recorded by Bede in the C8, and
again in the C10 (*see* sculpture, below). The church has W
tower, nave, aisles and clerestory, and long chancel; a common
enough complement elsewhere in England, but not in Cumberland. A link with Greystoke is likely. The tower was rebuilt
in 1810. Aisles and clerestory are Perp externally, the chancel
late C12. The chancel has round-headed windows and a shafted
S doorway (one crocket and one waterleaf capital); the triple E
lancets are C19 (repairs 1854, restoration 1874–5). Inside, the
unmoulded Norman tower arch remains. The quick-stepping
arcades date from the early C13; Pevsner put the N slightly
earlier on the grounds of its slighter chamfers. Piers mostly
octagonal, but two on the N are round and so are the responds.
    FURNISHINGS. ALTAR RAILS, late C17. Twisted and taper-
ing. S door with LOCK given by Lady Anne Clifford; cf. the initials and the date 1671. – STAINED GLASS. E window and
others by *Clayton & Bell*. Chancel S by *L. C. Evetts*, 1947.
Etched glass in an uncomfortably hybrid opening by *Lawrence
Whistler*, to Sylvia Mary McCosh of Dalemain †1991. S aisle E,
signed S, to William, Viscount Whitelaw †1999. Tree and dove
in pastel colours. – SCULPTURE. Two cross-shaft fragments.
One small-scale and intricate, like the font at Bridekirk; winged
beast with human face. Dated by Rosemary Cramp to the mid
C9. The other, C10 or C11, is more softly carved with beasts
and people; possibly a rare representation the Sacrifice of Isaac
from the Viking age. – Good MONUMENTS and plenty of them.
Tablets in the nave, including a war memorial of brass with lettering in black, set in green marble, by *Keswick School of Industrial Arts*(?). Many Hasells of Dalemain in the chancel,
including Edward †1707, Baroque cartouche with putto heads
in an architectural frame with segmental pediment; Edward
†1781, plain Neoclassical by *T. Taylor*, York; Edward †1825, by
Chantrey, 1830, weeping lady in relief, with draped urn and
sarcophagus labelled Hasell. – Worn effigy of a C14 knight,
cross-legged.
    The four corners of the original CHURCHYARD are guarded
by the four Dacre bears, sinister troll-like creatures with worn
features, that seem to be clinging to pillars or trunks of trees.
Their age is at present unknowable, as is their identity – one
looks more like a lion – and their meaning.
DACRE CASTLE. Keep-like C14 tower house with projecting
corner turrets, two square, the other two diagonal, like over-

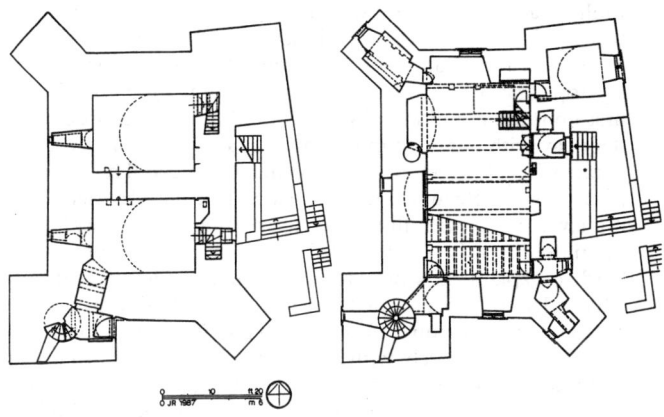

Dacre Castle.
Ground- and first-floor plans, 1994

fed buttresses (cf. Kirkoswald Castle, also built by the Dacres).
So, from any point of view, it looks unbalanced.* William
Dacre applied for a licence to crenellate in 1307, and in 1354
a licence for a chaplain was granted to Margaret widow of
Ranulph by the Bishop of Carlisle, which presumably marks a
completion. Modifications were made c. 1570, despite the dis-
array of Dacre affairs. It was thoroughly modernized from 1675
by Sir Thomas Dacre, created Earl of Sussex, on his coming
of age. He inserted large rectangular windows, cross-mullioned
in the tower, set flush with a shallow wave moulding. The Earl
set his arms over the new first-floor entry in the E wall. Perhaps
surprisingly, he preserved the fighting top with its turrets and
crenellations, and took care that the set-back which is the
tower's only articulation should go around his new windows.
However, the Earl had overspent, and after his death in 1716
Dacre was sold, passing to the Musgraves and then to the
Hasells of Dalemain. It is part of the Dalemain estate still,
restored from dereliction in the early 1960s by Bunty Kinsman
and her 'able and sensitive architect', Mr *Unwin*. The castle has
a double vaulted basement at the bottom, and then, despite its
bulk, just two principal rooms: the great hall, and above it the
great chamber or King's Room. But such is the wall thickness
that the window alcoves are almost rooms in themselves, big
enough for a table for four or a C21 work-station. In addition
little rooms are stacked up in the corner turrets, excepting the
SW one which houses the stair.
    INTERIORS. The broad studded door into the SW turret is
preserved. The ENTRY is tunnel-vaulted with strengthening
ribs, and so is the CELLAR PASSAGE – an immediate sign of
superiority. The two CELLARS are identical, with plain tunnel-

*There is much disagreement as to whether the square turrets are original or alter-
ations. The view taken here, following Anthony Emery, is that it is all one build.

vaults. Each has in the E wall a little stair up to the first floor (as at Howgill), both now blocked at the top. From the entrance a broad and well-built spiral STAIR goes right up to the top. The other three turrets are solid at the base. On the first floor the grand internal entry off the stair is guarded by a doorway with superior moulding and a wide landing with an aumbry. The GREAT HALL is splendid in size and height, with plenty to see. Beautiful trefoil-headed piscina (Pevsner called it a lavatorium) with fluted bowl, retaining traces of colour in the mouldings. It could indeed be of 1354, but its position is hard to explain: it is next to an E-facing window reveal, into which debouched one of the cellar stairs. This window was enlarged into the upper front door in the C17. The fireplace has a wide segmental arch, with an integral doorway next to it with pointed head. Its position near one end suggests that the room was divided. Splendid ceiling. Every member is hollow-moulded and stopped, with arch-shaped braces. Redundant corbels show that it is not the original ceiling; by analogy (Scales, Catterlen, Yanwath) it is probably Elizabethan, *c.* 1570. A 1960s stair, harmless enough, rises free to the next floor. As for the corner rooms, the diagonal SE turret was for garder-obes; a squeeze-in bathroom is now NW, a reasonably sized bedroom in the square NE turret, down a few steps. On the second floor, the great chamber or KING'S ROOM is as high as the hall, but much more bare. There are very tall tunnel-vaulted and pointed recesses in SW and NE corners. Two fire-places, neither very big. One has a Tudor arch but the same masons' marks as much older bits. Corner rooms as before, but this time fitting in two storeys. In the square NE turret a 1960s spiral stair goes up to a room called the CHAPEL. It does face E, and there is a blocked lancet in the E wall. All four turrets are tunnel-vaulted at the top. Splendid martial roofscape with battlements complete and steep steps up to the turret tops.

Square MOAT, in water but not complete – was it ever? Anthony Emery notes that it is cut by C14 work, so evidently older. – BARN. Like that at Dalemain, which is C17, but smaller. (ROSE BANK. 1689, with a symmetrical extension of 1773. DCMS.)

DALEMAIN (C)

Three principal phases: the medieval house at the back, an updating of 1685 by Sir Edward Hasell, steward to Lady Anne Clifford (a front-door lock was given to him by Lady Anne), and the mid-C18 E front and S side by his son Edward.

The exceedingly fine E front, of 1747 or a little earlier (1744 on a roof beam), may have been designed by *Edward Hasell* himself. It depends for its effect on proportion and on the beautiful pink Stainton ashlar, superbly cut and laid. *Ralph Smith* was the master mason. Nine bays, arranged 2–5–2. The 'wings' are marked out by rusticated quoins of even length, the centre by a balustrade. No pediment. Doorcase of whiter stone with fluted Ionic pilasters, ears, and a triangular pediment, windows with moulded surrounds, plinth and cornice, and an even parade of chimneys. There may be a link with Highhead (Ivegill). The s side, after a return of a couple of bays, was rebuilt in about 1756 to a simpler formula, with no cornice or window mouldings; seven bays altogether, overlooking the great terrace.

At the back (w), the visitor is presented with a different, older and irregular house, probably C15 or early C16, which is clearly going to take some working out. Although flat and continuously parapeted, it consists of a hall range in the middle, a possible tower at each end of it, and a narrow slip room at each extremity. Quoins mark some of the divisions. The mortar of the n tower is embedded with oyster shells, and the s one has a St Andrew's-cross window. The great kitchen stack on the n side is there, but it no longer sticks out because of the infill on the nw corner. What does stick out is a crude lavatory block of roughcast over red brick. In the centre of the house is an unsuspected internal courtyard. From here the rear range can be seen to have its own show e front, begun in 1685, with a big bolection-moulded doorcase and plain-surround windows.

INTERIORS. The visitor sees the C18 range first. The stair is in the ENTRANCE HALL. It is a wooden 'cantilever' of the Carr/Hird type, with three balusters of tassel motif per tread. The BACK STAIR in the long corridor behind is of the same type. The rooms *en enfilade* are sober, with raised and fielded panelling and good wooden chimneypieces, except for the CHINESE ROOM. That has painted wallpaper and a wild Rococo chimneypiece carved by *Nathaniel Hedges* after a Chippendale pattern. The bill for sixteen sheets of 'Indian paper' (at £10) is dated 27 December 1756. Little doodles can be spotted among the pheasants, including an artist signing himself *Thai*. In the DINING ROOM a quieter Nathaniel Hedges chimneypiece.

The transition into the rear wing is striking – darker, lower, crooked, with glimpses into the gloomy courtyard. The door to the little LIBRARY at the sw corner, added in 1756, breaks through a mullioned window. A broad turning stair rises to the FRETWORK ROOM, with an Elizabethan or Jacobean moulded plaster ceiling (patterns of thin ribs) and internal porch, and two bedrooms. The ATTIC above shows a splendid open roof, meant to be seen. Two trusses arch-braced with longitudinal braces to the ridge. The third truss at the s end has rudimentary hammerbeams, unless they have simply been cut short. At the nw corner successive alterations have produced a mystifying series of ups and downs and differences in floor level.

A broad straight STAIR cuts down to the kitchen door, lit by two superimposed mullioned windows. The SERVANTS' HALL, now tearoom, does not convince as a great hall – the ceiling is too low, and the moulded joists shallow and uneven in execution. The big central fireplace is made up of C17 bits. The plaster was stripped in the 1920s as part of a make-over by *Thomas Bonner* of Edinburgh. Was the principal accommodation above? Finally in the N range is the great KITCHEN, with a vast segmental-arched fireplace in the outer wall.

A new STAIR-TOWER designed by *Robert Hasell McCosh* was added on the N in 2006, tucked away behind the handsome early C19 hip-roofed BREWHOUSE, to enable the family regions of the house to connect up.

GARDENS. One of the most impressive features of Dalemain is the huge TERRACE WALL of 1688 on the S, which creates the level ground. This may have been done by *James Swingler*. At the top end is a delightful square BANQUETING HOUSE or grotto with a pyramid roof, now apple store, of much the same date, overhanging the river. The C18 garden wall has clearly been built up to it. The present plantsman's paradise is largely a C20 creation.

Across a fine expanse of cobbles to the N is the great BARN of 1685. It has a smaller brother at Dacre, and resembles the one at Sockbridge (1699); none are bank barns. Eleven bays, with an aisle on square stone piers open on the ground floor. The timberwork is silvery ash, retaining its bark in many places. Beyond that a long two-sided IMPLEMENT SHED. Central spine wall, open lean-tos front and back. Square stone columns, slender trusses of ash. The CART SHED N of the great garden wall is similar. – PIGEON HOUSE, probably C18, at the entrance corner, given importance by ashlar walls and a hipped roof. It retains pigeonholes but not its potence.

DALLAM TOWER *see* MILNTHORPE

3050

DALSTON (C)

ST MICHAEL. In a big and handsome churchyard by the River Caldew. The chancel is early C13, with slightly stepped triple E lancets, still with round rere-arches. The priest's doorway carries a little gable. The nave masonry is partly medieval too, with the jambs of a half-buried E.E. doorway of two orders on the S. A Norman capital with decorated scallops and leaves has been built into the N porch. The church was reconstructed in 1749, when the presumed medieval arcade(s) were taken out. A big C18 door is left in the N transept with egg-and-dart surround. The timber posts inside may have carried galleries, as perhaps at Bampton (q.v.). *C. J. Ferguson* undertook a second rebuild in Dec style in 1890. The wooden arcades were linked by a slender girder running E–W below the purlins. Chancel restored *c.* 1874. – REREDOS and ALTAR look early C20, carved and coloured: St George and St Michael in the reredos, Annunciation, Nativity, Baptism on the altar frontal. – N transept organ SCREEN by *Ferguson*. – PEWS with pretty baluster panels set in the ends. The C18 box pews were used to panel the walls. – FONT. C19, by *R. H. Billings*. The COVER is a charming piece of 1925 by *Lorimer*, similar to one for St John, Lattingtown, New York State. Rabbits, water birds, dove with sun and moon, and fire and clouds round the rim, for the Four Elements. – STAINED GLASS. Chancel by *William Wailes*, nave mostly *Clayton & Bell*. SW, 1996, by *Peter Strong*. Packed composition of figures, animals and Dalston itself in steep foreshortening. – MONUMENTS. The Rev. Walter Fletcher †1846, by *Musgrave Lewthwaite Watson*. Portrait head in profile, and a broad tapering Grecian block above with acroteria. – Isaac Sheffield †1881. Characterful portrait in low relief, by *G. Nelson*. – Outside, the genial Bishop Percy †1856, rebuilder of Rose Castle. Fine wheel-cross, of Irish rather than Cumbrian form.

THE SQUARE, not square, is in front of the church. Nice, predominantly C18 mixture, with entry arches to back yards. The houses, where they are not colourwashed, mix red, yellow and black stones, sometimes making a chequer pattern.*VICTORY HALL faces the Green. 1922, by *H. E. Ayris*. Brick and roughcast, with bands of tile. Sweeping slate roof. On the Green is the CORONATION SEAT, dated 1911 GR. Iron and red sandstone. Octagonal plinth with central octagonal back rest. At Buckabank, on the r. bank of the Caldew, a large two-storey COTTON-SPINNING MILL, 1902, on a late C18 site. Red sandstone, with a brick chimney. Extensive leats.

DALSTON HALL (hotel). Best seen from the garden. The solar tower is inscribed (backwards) 'Iohn Dalston Elisabet mi wyf mad ys byldyng', with emblems including cat and dog. With the arms on the higher turret this indicates a date *c.* 1498. Three storeys and a fighting deck, with an arched, uncusped, three-light window for the solar. The adjoining hall range was built either by Sir John Dalton *c.* 1612, or his son Sir George *c.* 1618. Its plan is intriguingly trapezoid, its elevation, of the local red and yellow stone randomly mixed, distinctly Scottish. Wide two-storey porch with a thrice-corbelled parapet curving around the corners in the Scottish way (cf. Highhead at Ivegill, 1550s), and gargoyles like cannon, bizarrely garlanded and decorated. Some have flat faces at the ends. Then the slightly recessed hall, and then balancing it at the NW end a slimmer and taller four-storey tower with higher semicircular stairturret starting on a corbel. The mullioned windows have curiously projecting frames, and are oddly moulded, with a double

---

*Nos. 25 and 26, single-storey, was taken by Nina Jennings to be a clay longhouse, but the walls are stone now.

roll and flat bit in between. In the 1680s *William Thackeray* carried out an interesting classicizing scheme, but this was obliterated by the new entrance front made in 1899–1900 by *C. J. Ferguson* (who had written a scholarly account of the house in 1875) and *John Wayland Benwell* (1859–1926). N porch, stair and dining room, with state rooms W and services E.

The hall range has been opened up through two storeys to form a magnificent space, with a gallery and a grand C17-style stair off. Huge ingle with EWS (E. W. Stead) 1900 on the hood. Through an original iron gate or yatt is the tunnel-vaulted ground floor of the tower, now the library. A spiral stair leads up to the solar, which has a C17 plaster ceiling. Dining and billiard room are richly panelled, with *de Morgan* fireplace tiles, but the circular ante-room made in the base of the C17 tower leads nowhere; a very large drawing room intended was never built – or has it been removed? The service yard at the pele tower end is certainly much reduced.

GARDEN. C17 terraces, mock wall-walks and bastions. The GATEPIERS may have been part of *Thackeray*'s work in the 1680s.

HAWKESDALE HALL, 1¾ m. SE. White, even, three-storey house, dated over the rear entrance 1704 J & MN (Nicholson). Five bays, in a 1–3–1 rhythm. Moulded window surrounds. Doorway with pulvinated frieze. Full-height stair with twisted balusters. The C17 house, now the r. wing, was the home of John Nicholson, brother of the Bishop of Carlisle and father of the antiquarian author.

HOLME HILL, now LIME HOUSE SCHOOL. Spreading mid-C18 U-shaped mansion, altered *c.* 1810 when acquired from the Holmes by Col. Thomas Salkeld. The staircase with faux-domed ceiling in the style of *Peter Nicholson* belongs to this phase. The house was transformed, but not improved, in 1887 (LCS 1887 over stable arch) when the centre was given an extra storey, a gargantuan tower built behind the l.-hand link, and a three-storey concave-gabled porch raised over the entrance. The wings retain their Venetian windows with lunettes over. Shunted to extreme l. is a mid-C18 Ionic porch with pulvinated frieze, broken pediment and shield. (Two fireplaces dated 1638.)

At RATTEN ROW, 1¾ m. E, a splendid clay dabbin, called LONG-HOUSE. The width is determined by the crucks, the single storey by the limitations of clay. The small fire-window and off-the-ridge stack indicate the living end, the door (with the date 1689, initials IM RM and an array of folk-art symbols) the cross-passage. The byre end is rebuilt in stone. Dating of the timbers gave 1505 and 1586. Benign gentrification has resulted in renewal of the thatch and a tasteful pale yellow and grey colour scheme. It is interesting that most of the houses and barns of the cluster, though rebuilt in stone or brick, retain the same long and narrow footprint.

DALTON-IN-FURNESS (L)

The principal town of Furness, though in the C18 eclipsed by Ulverston, and in the C19 by Barrow. 'A miserable and antiquated vill, once the pride, now the shame of Furness', is Father West's description (1774). It is a proper town, though, with a long market street rising to the market place at the church end (market grant 1239), and to Tudor Square at the other.

St Mary. The old church, itself largely a rebuild of 1825–6 and 1830 by *George Webster*, was replaced in free Dec style by *Paley & Austin* in 1883–5; their most prolific and fruitful period. The situation is dramatic: on the N and E it seems a pretty urban oasis off Market Square, but immediately W a lane plunges down to the valley to the N below. The architects made the most of it, keeping the nave relatively low, with three equal gables as in the old church, but making their W tower high and strong enough to command both the town and the long valley that runs down to Furness Abbey. Growing forcefully out of the rock, the tower is emphasized at the top by chequer- and flushwork, using the local silvery limestone to contrast with the red sandstone of the rest, and by a higher stair-turret. More chequers at the E end and over the porches. The old E window, of yellow stone, was incorporated on the N side, as were several of the side windows in the SE chapel. Polygonal porches, close to the W end; half-hexagonal on the N, a full hexagon on the S. Both have charming rib-vaults, and are entered from the E at an angle.

The interior suffers from lack of light at the centre, a fault the architects usually took pains to avoid. The porches lead into the W bay of the aisles. The tower is carried with little apparent effort on big piers – but not too big – on its E side. The arches die in. The nave is given a degree of N–S symmetry by the matching of the tower arch with the chancel arch, both propped by quadrant arches over the aisles. The NE one in front of the organ chamber is a flyer. The chancel too is given an overall symmetry by the two bays of blank arcading on either side, segmental-headed, with quatrefoil windows at the tops, but within that the openings are asymmetrical: two arches for the S chapel, one bigger one for the organ chamber, then E of it some blank wall. The arcades have octagonal piers. Chancel arch with five continuous mouldings. – FURNISH-INGS by the architects to their usual high standards; the wood-carving is by *Miles & Morgan* of Lancaster. – REREDOS canted at the sides, with alabaster panels let into the sandstone. – FONT. Medieval. Goblet-shaped, octagonal, with pairs of qua-trefoils and shields around the bowl and blank tracery round the stem. – STAINED GLASS. Early C16 fragments in N porch: Virgin with dove and ring, and an unidentified saint. – Schnei-der memorial window, N, from the old church, †1862, by *Heaton, Butler & Bayne*, designer *Alfred Hassam*; hot colours.

A number of the windows have faded badly, but not the two early C20 *Shrigley & Hunt* windows on the S. – MONUMENTS from the old church in the SE chapel, e.g. William Atkinson †1821 by *Webster*, and at the W end, including a couple of C18 ones. – In the churchyard, a simple slab to the artist George Romney, †1802, who was born in Dalton.

PARISH CENTRE, linked to the S porch. 1979–80, by *K. C. White* of London. Large, flat-roofed building of pinkish cement blocks, buttressed like the church, with the corners cut off to suggest an octagon and the roof edges sloped and slated to suggest a pitch. Not good in itself, but composing well with the church and the ravine below. Open-plan interior, with some late STAINED GLASS by *Shrigley & Hunt* from St Margaret (*see* below).

CHEQUERS HOTEL, in the quarry below, is the former SCHOOL, 1872. Red and silver stone, with many hooded gables.

ST MARGARET, Ulverston Road. Sold in the 1970s, and now OUR LADY OF THE ROSARY AND ST MARGARET OF SCOTLAND (R.C.). By *R. B. Preston*, 1902–4. Red and white stone. Long low roof-line, changing pitch over the aisles. Bellcote sideways-on over the N door. Grouped small lancets.

CASTLE, in the Market Place. Free-standing tower of *c.* 1350, perfectly rectangular, 44 by *c.* 30 ft (14 by 9 metres), with an eroded Armed Man standing atop each parapet corner. Thought to have been built as a courthouse and bailiff's residence by the Abbot of Furness, like a modest version of the Archbishop of York's Moot Hall at Hexham, Northumberland. Large ground-floor door on the S, close to the E corner. Smaller one broken through on the W giving straight onto the spiral stair. No vault. The courtroom occupied the first floor. This was raised, the upper floor done away with, and the large S window inserted in 1856 when the 5th Duke of Buccleuch converted it to a Masonic lodge. *E. G. Paley* was the architect. The other windows also 1856, except for one restored two-light window in the E wall.

TOWN HALL, Station Road. For Dalton Local Board, 1884, by *J. Y. McIntosh*. Of limestone and yellow sandstone. Plain C17 style, with a clock turret.

MARKET PLACE. Triangular, with friendly houses, the parish church, and formerly the shambles and encroaching houses round the Castle ('like another Gogmagog', said Pevsner), and fussily landscaped with shrubs and parking spaces. Small cast-iron DRINKING FOUNTAIN, 1897; 'Keep The Pavement Dry', it says (identical ones at Askam-in-Furness and Nenthead). TUDOR SQUARE, at the E end of town, is triangular as well. The POLICE STATION and COURT (former) of 1898 frowns over it from a great height. Silver limestone and red sandstone dressings, eagle and cherubs on the gables. The polychromy and sculpture fail to make it festive. This was the working-class end of town, with terraced housing and the working-class church, St Margaret (*see* above).

(TYTUP HALL, 1½ m. NNE. Five-bay house of *c.* 1713, with a pretty doorway. It has a segmental pediment and a frieze with the typical motif of two concave curves leading up to a truncated middle top. Father Thomas West, doyen of the Lake District guides, was chaplain here from the early 1760s.)

PARK SOUTH SIGNAL BOX, 1 m. NE. 1883. A particularly handsome example of the Furness Railway's practice, almost unique among Britain's railway companies, of building substantial signal boxes in local stone. Wooden operating floor. Hipped roof, as with all F.R. boxes.

INDUSTRIAL REMAINS. The town is surrounded by quarries and pits, many flooded, recalling the long history of haematite mining from the C17 until 1960. WOODBINE PIT CHIMNEY, 1½ m. S on the W side of Greystone Lane, is the last survivor of many on the Cumberland and Furness ore fields. The mines were served by a dense network of tramways and railways; much of the metre-gauge MOUZELL LINE is traceable, engineered in 1849 by *John Barraclough Fell*, later celebrated for his Mont Cenis Railway connecting Italy and Switzerland over the Alps. From the roughly parallel Butts Tramway, laid *c.* 1860, a BRIDGE ABUTMENT on Ireleth Road and TUNNEL at Crossgates, near Tytup.

DEAN (C)

ST OSWALD. Low nave, S aisle and chancel, with a double bellcote over the chancel arch. It looks C17. The chancel has carved gargoyles, unusual in Cumbria. On the S they are fully realized figures with legs and feet. Two-light chancel windows with ogee heads under a round arch, which Pevsner calls a Perp rather than a Dec motif; there was a rededication in 1447. Lumps of stonework at the E end suggest that it may have butted up to a lost building, perhaps the C16 Grammar School. Several original nave windows. The interior retains its ceilings and is cheerfully crooked. S arcade of four bays, late Norman with double-chamfered arches, round piers and elementary round caps. Chancel arch cut away to improve sight lines. Redundant corbels in the chancel, probably for a lower but steeper roof. Low, later TOMB-RECESS in the S aisle wall. A blocked doorway at the extreme NE, and a large archway at the W end, again suggest connected buildings. – CHANCEL FURNISHINGS, PULPIT and LECTERN by *Robert Thompson* (the mouse man) of Kilburn, 1967-8. – FONT. Small round Norman bowl decorated with thin continuous intersecting arches. – STAINED GLASS. E window 1884, W 1887, and chancel S (St Oswald and St Aidan; very rich), 1898, all by *Hardman*.

Outside, six-stepped octagonal base for a preaching CROSS. Dean village shows signs of a planned open GREEN which has been encroached upon: see the line of Manor Farm (1753 over door), Dean Farm and Dean Mains, all set back, but with Mains Barn (1844 on lintel) in front.

76 FRIENDS' MEETING HOUSE, 2½ m. E, at Pardshaw. To the road just a long low range, whitewashed with green-shuttered windows. This is the STABLE of 1731 and the SCHOOLROOM of 1745. A passage through, with Quaker hat-pegs, leads to the BURIAL GROUND and the MEETING HOUSE of 1728–9. L-shaped, of two rooms divided by wooden shutters.* Porch added 1740. The windows are sashes with simple moulded surrounds, except for a couple of mullioned windows from the old meeting house reused at the back, and one in the porch. The 1672 datestone over the stable door is also from there. Every detail is tried and tested for practical simplicity, making the ensemble extremely attractive.

BRANTHWAITE HALL, ⅜ m. W. Shadowed by alders, by a little river. Tower and hall range evidently built together, probably in the late C14. The tower is battlemented, and tunnel-vaulted at basement level in two compartments, with a SW spiral stair carried up into a turret with saddleback roof. Several small original windows. Lower and upper doors to the stair are chamfered and steeply pointed. Identical doorways at the other end; one, now internal, into the E wing, the other under the S stair into the hall range. The house was revamped in 1604 with mullioned windows with hoodmoulds, and a stone staircase in a projection on the S, with a window with arched heads to the lights. This is presumably the date of the hall floor, and the great stack dividing the hall range into two. Doorways and fireplaces of this phase have the characteristic obtusely pointed lintel of the period, with the addition of a little decorative twiddle in the spandrels (also at Haile, q.v.). The N front was redone in the 1670s, perhaps by *William Thackeray*: quite a swagger, if rustic job. Lower windows with lintels scored as though they were fanning-out voussoirs, and straight entablatures. Upper windows with pulvinated friezes and semicircular pediments continued with straight ends as if part of an entablature. The windows themselves have mostly been sashed, but one at least retains its cross-mullions. They have raised moulded frames. In 1984 the Coal Board, who were converting the house to regional offices, removed two emergency buttresses, whereupon this side fell down. The blocked openings of the 1604 phase have been faithfully reincorporated in the rebuilt façade.

BRANTHWAITE MILLS. C18 and C19 water mills side by side by the River Marron. The first worked as a paper mill in the 1800s, and a sawmill in the early C20. The later mill ground corn.

(FAR BRANTHWAITE EDGE, 1¼ m. SW. Dated 1683. Nearly symmetrical façade with two- and three-light transomed windows. Straight window entablatures.)

CRAKEPLACE HALL, Ullock, 1 m. S. Built by Christopher Crakeplace, 'servant to Baron Altham', in 1612. The inscription, re-

---

* David Butler suggests the mason also built the Whitehaven meeting house of 1724.

set in a lean-to porch, has a billet frame. Mullioned windows, some with headstops to the dripmoulds.

DEARHAM (C)   0030

ST MUNGO (C20 dedication). Norman church in a strong position, with a sturdy unbuttressed C14 W tower built for defence. Bell-openings of two ogee-headed lights, but the bells are in a double bellcote on its E parapet. The S doorway is Late Norman: a much-moulded round arch on capitals with rudimentary volutes and waterleaf, i.e. of c. 1170–90. Very strange jamb mouldings. Tiny Norman window with a wide splay in the chancel S, and possibly another N. Also one lowside window, S. The Norman W wall has gone, leaving the tunnel-vaulted tower base open to the nave by a wide segmental twice-chamfered arch dying into the walls, quite probably a C13 form. Much of the rest, including the N aisle (1882), is due to *C. J. Ferguson* and the Rev. W. S. Calverley, vicar 1877–84. – REREDOS. In Calverley's memory (†1898). – FONT. Norman, shaped like a cushion capital, with spirals instead of volutes at the corners, i.e. they go the wrong way. Dragon-like creatures on two sides, a symmetrical scroll or knot on the third, and a strange pattern on the fourth of a frieze of arched panels, a frieze of lozenges below, a frieze of rectangles below that. The style is connected with Yorkshire, e.g. Fishlake (West Riding), which is of c. 1170. – STAINED GLASS. E window by *Clayton & Bell*. N, St Mungo, by *Albion Glass* of Brampton, 2002.

Calverley uncovered much early SCULPTURE. Their names are his. 'ADAM' STONE, on a window sill by the font. Crisply carved slab with the word Adam upside down at the bottom and runes at the top. Episodic composition in relief including three figures holding hands under linked arches, palm-like trees in a quatrefoil, crossed arrows and another head the other way up. It may be as late as the font. – STANDING CROSS, brought inside in 1900. Complete C10 wheel-cross, its head and stout stem completely covered with snaky interlace and knots, with virtually no background sinking. One side grows from a bulbous root, interpreted by Calverley as the Viking world-ash Yggdrasil, though Bailey and Cramp remind us of the Christian cross as a tree of life. The cross-head is oddly subordinate to the wheel. – 'KENNETH' CROSS. C10–C11. A section of the shaft stands on the W window sill. Mixed up with untidy interlace are two figures, one on horseback, and a big bird. (A cross-head is built in by the vestry.) – Also many COFFIN-LIDS.

COTTAGES. The coal miners' rows have a flavour of Cumberland vernacular about them, with their heavy window architraves.

DENDRON (L)

A large farm sprawling both sides of the road (dates 1726 and 1662), an early C19 house with a walled garden across the road, a couple of cottages and converted barns, and the church.

ST MATTHEW. Trim classical building of some sophistication of 1795–6, attributed to *Francis Webster* (Angus Taylor). It replaced one of 1642. w tower 1833. Enlarged by *Charlewood & Hicks*, 1932–3. No chancel. Arched windows in super-arches, triumphal arch composition E.

    The SCHOOL was under the same roof until replaced in 1833 by the little building across the road, which functioned until the 1990s.

DENT

See *The Buildings of England, Yorkshire West Riding: Leeds, Bradford and the North.*

DENTON (C)

Immediately S of the Wall. Denton comes in several instalments strung out between river and railway, described from E to W.

DENTON MILL, at the edge of Naworth Park, is the studio of Albion Glass. Early C18 (dates 1724, 1726), with early C19 additions. DENTON FOOT, across the ford. Superficially C19, but it is a bastle, within sight and earshot of Naworth Park Stonehouse in case of trouble. Thick walls and a pair of tiny upper windows, well barred. Dated 1594. DENTON HALL. Fossilized in the middle of a farmhouse of 1829, and hidden by its overall roof, is a massive tower, probably the 'Turris de Denton' mentioned in 1415. It is square, with very thick walls. No vault, but a turning stair in the SE corner, with very narrow shouldered doorways. To the E and SE the shallow earthworks of a series of FISH PONDS.

LOW ROW has a fine signal box, and the original (but closed) Newcastle & Carlisle Railway station building, *c.* 1835–40.

At NETHER DENTON is ST CUTHBERT, of 1868–70 by *Cory & Ferguson*. Chancel, nave, porch, double bellcote on a central buttress – the same recipe as Gilsland church, also for the Mounseys, but by better architects. The inside is good, lined with plain ashlar. Very wide splays to the windows, wide chancel arch. The chancel has a barrel ceiling, its planking winding like a skew bridge. Fine CHOIR STALLS by the same hand as those at Lanercost. – Of the old church nothing is preserved except a SCULPTURE. A fine, smallish Norman figure of a king with sceptre(?), set against a cross with arms extending Maltese-fashion beyond a small central circle. It must have been a very good piece, and is reminiscent of the French mid C12. – STAINED GLASS. E window and chancel S by *C. A. Gibbs*. – Uninscribed ROMAN ALTAR beside the porch.

Church and vicarage stand within a late C1 ROMAN FORT, the rampart of which is evident at the SW angle of the churchyard. An earlier fort, or an annexe, extended S to the Gilsland road (the Stanegate; *see* p. 16). The OLD VICARAGE, immediately E, is or was a bastle.

UPPER DENTON (DENTON VILLAGE). A small dead-end settlement, hardly a village, across the railway tracks. It has its own CHURCH, probably early C12, disused but not forlorn. Small and low, with big quoins and a little bellcote. Tiny lancet on the N of four stones, splayed on the inside only. Plain S lancet. The rest of the windows are from *Ferguson*'s restoration of 1881 (another restoration in the 1930s). The S doorway is a rough attempt at a 'Caernarvon' arch. The chancel arch is plausibly Roman; it looks reassembled. Deep round arch, unmoulded. Flat imposts, hollow-moulded underneath. Plain jambs, plain plinth. – TOMB-SLAB with cross and sword set in the N wall. The former VICARAGE, immediately E, was another bastle. Now a roofless ruin, tied with a massive steel ring in 2004. Small, but of high quality; probably late C16. The upper living floor has a fireplace at both ends, chased out into the gable walls, each with an adjacent cupboard recess. In the SE corner what is interpreted as a lavatory with a drain.

THE TEMON. On the military road, now A69, at the Northumberland boundary. Front presumably added after 1757, when the road was completed. Four bays, Doric doorcase with bulgy columns. Back-to-back with it is a charming house dated 1730 on the keystone of its naïve-grand doorcase. Segmental pediment over. The windows were two-lighters, now minus their mullions, the upper ones heightened as well. Linked to it by the farmyard arch is a thick-walled late C16 or C17 bastle, retaining some of its small square barred windows on the upper floor.

MILECASTLE 48, on Hadrian's Wall. On a steeply sloping site S of the railway, above the W bank of the Poltross Burn (approached from the E side of the railway in Gilsland, q.v.). The S side of the milecastle was robbed when the railway was constructed (1835) but an accumulation of soil ensured better preservation on the N. One of the largest milecastles known. It is the original Broad Wall gauge (*see* p. 16), but as built subsequently the main curtain here was much narrower; a short wing-wall on the E shows the thickness originally intended. E and W walls meet the S face of Hadrian's Wall (the milecastle's N wall) at right angles in the usual way, but the surviving SE internal angle is rounded (cf. Harrow's Scar, p. 657). The massive N and S gates each carried a tower, the piers for their inner arches projecting from the face of the adjacent walls into the interior. An intractable local rock was used, and thus the masonry – uncharacteristically for gateways – is of squared rubble of uneven size, left rock-faced within chiselled margins. Each gate was later partly walled up and thus reduced in width. In the NW corner, a series of five successive ovens; in the NE, a broad flight of steps provided access to a parapet walk, and may offer evidence of the height of the Wall.

The larger size of this milecastle provided space for two free-standing BARRACKS (with possibly some stabling), flanking a cambered axial road. The buildings, occupied into the later C4, each contained four separate rooms, stepped down the slope; every room had a door on its r. side. Subsequently the internal partitions were moved to provide only three rooms in each barrack. The excavators (in 1909–10) found thin stone roofing slates and fragments of window glass. Outside, a kerbed and terraced veranda or path fronted each building.

At WILLOWFORD, ⅓ m. WSW of Gilsland, an instructive stretch of HADRIAN'S WALL. From the E: foundations of the Broad Wall are visible between the modern road and TURRET 48A with its substantial wing-walls; deeply recessed into the curtain, it was originally roofed with stone slates. Occupied into C4. To the W, a fine length of the ditch of the Wall, utilized by the farm road. Then TURRET 48B, similar to 48A but less well preserved on the S. Reused in the N wall of a barn, E of the steading entrance at Willowford, a 'centurial' stone inscribed by the century of Gellius Philippus, which had built an adjacent section of the Wall. Down the slope to the river, the Narrow Wall, with the Broad Wall foundations clear on the S side.

Then the ROMAN BRIDGE, carrying the Wall across the Irthing (which has shifted to the W). Three phases of the E abutment are visible. The first, for a footbridge only, was formed by a short length of Broad Wall into which a tower (containing steps, for access) was recessed; a baffle wall protected against erosion on the S. Subsequently a larger tower, with a central pier, was built to the E; two sluices were provided, the baffle wall was rebuilt, and a block of masonry retained the river bank on the N. In the late C2 or early C3 the tower made way for a ramp to carry the Military Way on a bridge with new rectangular piers. In the C3 some blocks from the bridge were reused to repair the E wall of the fort at Birdoswald.

For Harrow's Scar and the continuation of Hadrian's Wall to the W, *see* Walton (Birdoswald).

DILLICAR (W)

(CROOK OF LUNE BRIDGE. C17 or C18. Two unequal segmental arches.)

DISTINGTON (C)

HOLY SPIRIT. 1884–6 by *Hay & Henderson* of Edinburgh. E.E.
It stands very tall, even without the intended two-stage top of
its SE tower. Of Pica sandstone. Five steeply stepped lancets E,
excessively long thin trio W, plate tracery to the aisle ends.
Clerestory windows of plate tracery: three quatrefoils approx-
imating to a spherical triangle. The fall of the land allows for
a room under the chancel. Stone-lined interior, its noble tallness emphasized by the short length – only four bays. Arcades
with polished granite columns. The stiff-leaf capitals were not
carved until 1897. Sedilia, piscina, aumbry and an organ
gallery in the chancel. – ALTAR, arcaded, with angels in niches,
and PULPIT, wooden, with Gospel scenes. Both made by
Harry Hems. – FONTS. One octagonal, dated 1662. Another
round, of white, black and green marble, by *William Rhind*. –
STAINED GLASS. A fine collection. E quintuplet in always-
warm colours by *Powell Bros* of Leeds, 1886. The other original windows also by them. NW, by *Stanley Murray Scott*, 1975,
for *Reed Millican*. Pentecost: tongues of fire and speaking in
tongues. Next to that a simplistic Christ in a boat by *K. Ram*
for *Elders Walker & Millican*, 1981. Another Scott/Millican
window of 1963 by the font.
   The preceding church of St Cuthbert, a low white building
with a double bellcote, was not demolished until the new was
complete. Its chancel arch stands N; twice-chamfered arch
dying into the imposts, i.e. late C13–C14.
CREMATORIUM. 1974. On the site of the C19 Distington Hall,
and making the most of its sylvan surroundings. Brick, with
oval porthole windows, and swoopy screen walls.
At the SE of the settlement a small estate of 'Flat tops', perfectly
square semi-detached houses with flat concrete roofs, built by
the *Ministry of Supply* 1941–2 for workers in the mines and
munitions factories.
HAYES CASTLE, ½ m. S. A small quadrangular castle, on a motte
which presumably preceded Robert de Leyburn's licence to
crenellate in 1322. Wet ditch to N and W, reused on the S as
the leat for the adjacent mill; steep slopes to a stream on the
E. A single fragment of walling to the NNW.

DRIGG (C)

ST PETER. 1849–50, of tooled red sandstone. By *Miles Thompson*
with *G. T. Andrews* of York. Nave and chancel in one, with a
buttress to mark the division, plus a N aisle. Lancet style, the
single W lancet impressively tall. W bellcote. – STAINED GLASS.
Chancel, by *Wailes*, 1850. W window (†1897) by *Swaine Bourne
& Son*, Birmingham.

CARLETON HALL, 1 m. SSE, on the A595 where the old coast road joins it. Deliciously faded classical villa of *c.* 1785. It was built for Cuthbert Atkinson, steward to the 1st Lord Muncaster. Three bays, two storeys, with low two-bay wings and a porch with Doric columns. Atkinson's elegant MONUMENT (†1816) is set against the N end of the house.

DRIGG HALL. In the village, on the B5344. Three-bay pedimented centre, rendered with painted dressings. Fluted pilasters to the doorcase, with its own pediment. Slightly lower wings coming forward a little, dated 1795. One is a barn, of brick and stone, the other a cottage. Brick also the BANK BARN, r.

DRUMBURGH (C) *see* BOWNESS-ON-SOLWAY

DUDDON BRIDGE (C and L) *see* ULPHA

DUFTON (W)

5 A mining village right under the Pennine scarp, developed from the C18 by the (Quaker) London Lead Co. round the wide rectangular medieval green. The Company pulled down most of the old cottages and built new, with vegetable gardens. FOUNTAIN in the middle, a cylindrical pillar and ball standing in a basin, with Latin inscription (Ovid). Erected by the Company in the C19.

In the village one very grand house, DUFTON HALL. A massive double pile, it is C18 in external character though late C17 in origin, and interestingly asymmetrical. Five bays with a Doric doorcase at the far W end and a lower wing reaching forward from the E end. At the rear more asymmetry: two very large round-headed windows r. and a smaller one in the middle. EM (Edward Millward) 1779 over a side door. This doorway has what William Adam called a basket arch, and powerful rustication; the low outbuilding stretching E from here has the same features. The number of doors suggests long-term multiple occupation.

WESLEY HOUSE. 1820. The figure in the niche is not Wesley but Shakespeare, perhaps carved by *Thomas Bland* of Reagill, Crosby Ravensworth.

ST CUTHBERT. Completely separate from the village, on the road to Knock. Traces of window heads in the N wall show that the masonry is old. Now it is Toy Gothick of 1784, with Y- and intersecting tracery and fat obelisk pinnacles on the W tower: charming verging on the comical. Ceiling with pretty plaster tracery as a ceilure over the altar. Gothick PEWS, W GALLERY FRONT, and ALTAR TABLE. – Brass DONATION BOARD, 1778.

– GLASS. Brightly coloured glass quarries supplied by *Faucet* of Appleby in the windows also probably *c.* 1784. – SCULPTURE. Worn figure in a sunk field set into the chancel s wall. Cross grave-cover sw. – Kilner MONUMENTS, 1784 and 1785. INDUSTRIAL REMAINS. A mine road leads 2 m. NE to drifts in the narrow valley of Great Rundale Beck. Many ADITS on both sides between the 1,750 and 2,000 ft contours (540 and 615 metres), DRESSING FLOORS and WATER-WHEEL PITS at 1,500 ft (460 metres). At the mouth of the gill significant remains of BUDDLES and WASHING FLOORS (where the crushed ore was separated). What appears to be a large stone-lined adit to the l. of the beck is in fact a well-built LIMEKILN. All these are C19. High up on the fell, s of the gill, are dramatic HUSHES and DRESSING FLOORS, possibly earlier.

EAGLESFIELD (C)

0020

St PHILIP (John Dalton Memorial Church), ¾ m. E of the village. By *C. J. Ferguson*, 1890–1. Of roughly coursed limestone and chiselled sandstone. No structural chancel. Bellcote. Straight-headed windows, but Geometrical tracery in the w window. – (Arts and Crafts REREDOS. 1907. – PULPIT given, and perhaps carved, by Mrs *Sewell* of Brandling Hall. – STAINED GLASS. E window (†1906) by *Shrigley & Hunt.* Chancel s, *A. K. Nicholson*, 1931. Nave, two by *William Morris of Westminster*, †1915, †1924.)

Former FRIENDS' BURIAL HOUSE, immediately w of the village. A gate in the wall carries the date 1693, though the burial ground was mentioned in 1670. The meeting house was indeed used only for funerals. Over the back door JOHN BARN GAVE 40£ TO BUILD THIS HOUSE 1711. Humble, with two-light windows.

DALTON HOUSE, in the village. Over the fireplace JMD (Jonathan and Mary Dalton) 1741, though part is C17. The scientist and Quaker John Dalton was born here in 1766. Cottage with a barn attached, not in line but projecting forward, with a porch in the angle. The pattern is repeated several times in the same lane. The barns are almost all residential now.

EAMONT BRIDGE (W) *see* YANWATH

EDENHALL (C)

5030

St CUTHBERT. A curious building, prominent in the landscape, and commanding a fine prospect of the Pennines. It stands out of the village to the SE, surrounded by parkland.

The undersized tower with its unusual little stone spire was built in the mid C15, either by the last of the Stapletons, whose brass is within, or the first of the Musgraves who succeeded them. Good moulded base, buttresses and corbel table of the period. Two-light w window with shields in place of tracery lights. Towers are usually defensive in Cumberland, and despite appearances this seems to be no exception. The parapet is balanced upon points, forming a species of machicolation. The holes line up with slots in the base of the spire, providing defenders inside with cover. Long chancel, C12 with C13 lengthening, short C12 nave. Windows at odd heights and varied sizes, including a very narrow blocked Norman window and one Dec window on the N. The clumsy over-large s porch is balanced by a N vestry, both of 1834 and attributed to *George Webster* of Kendal. The desire for symmetry in plan is typical. The Norman chancel arch is of plaster – Webster again, possibly reflecting the genuine one. So is the Gothick ceiling of the chancel, which is grained like wood.

FURNISHINGS. Long C19 family STALLS in the chancel, which has the character of a family chapel. Their fronts are reeded linenfold. – FONT. Big square block on a round base. – STAINED GLASS. E window. Medieval fragments (two early C14 figures) and C17 Continental pieces (several Netherlandish roundels), made up in 1834 with bright and gruesome yellows, greens and purples. – Arms of Stapleton, Musgrave, Veteripont and Hilton in the side windows, plus more medieval fragments inventively rearranged, see e.g. the square halo of crowns on the N. – MONUMENTS. Brass of Sir William and Margaret Stapleton †1468. His good 35-in. figure, hers is only 27 in. (89 and 68 cm.). – A score of Musgrave tablets from 1659 to 1835 line the chancel. That to Sir Christopher Musgrave †1735 is attributed to *Sir Henry Cheere*. – Large *Webster* tablet to the Rev. Thomas Watson †1833 in the nave.

EDEN HALL, by *Smirke*, 1821, was demolished in 1934. It was Grecian, with a portico. Extensive and well-built outbuildings remain, converted to residential use by *Michael Bottomley* (of *E. Donald Haigh*, Kendal). STABLE YARD of 1842, attributed to *George Webster*, with tall octagonal clock tower with a lead dome over the arch. Landscaping by *Lanning Roper*, later C20. In the centre a 16-ton monolithic drinking trough of 1841. Former AGENT'S HOUSE, perhaps *Webster*. Stone-roofed BARN converted by Bottomley in 1974. LODGE, with columns; also the WEST LODGE and GATES. Attributed to *Webster* and the 1830s. Three sets of quadripartite gatepiers and a cruciform lodge with Greek Doric tetrastyle portico, all in white ashlar, not the local red stuff, and composed about a cross-roads. A second lodge would have made it more impressive still. On the gatepiers the strange emblem of the family, a pair of armoured arms bearing aloft a wreath.

The village, as its name implies, seems little more than an adjunct to the hall. Even now the estate ambience is strong.

EGREMONT (C)

The newly formed Barony of Copeland was given to William de
Meschines in the early C12. The town is a planned one, with a
broad main street widening out into a market place beneath the
castle, like Cockermouth. It is an iron-ore town, and suffered
severe depression in the 1930s with the working out of the ore,
though one deep mine was still working in 2009. Population
1,556 in 1811, 2,049 in 1851, 6,305 in 1911 (the peak of iron
mining), 7,205 in 1971.

St Mary. The old church was remembered by Parker in 1904
   as plain and uninteresting, but with four beautiful E.E. lancets
   (originally six) at the e end. Much else was discovered at the
   demolition, leading *Thomas Lewis Banks* of Whitehaven to
   design his new church of 1881–3 in E.E. style, though typically
   Late Victorian in ambition. The four genuine E.E. windows are
   now in the sides of the chancel. They are slightly pointed,
   moulded, and have inner shafting.* The sedilia are built into
   the vestry. Some voussoirs in the transept arches. The nave is
   big and broad, with a semicircular w baptistery given by the
   Freemasons. Narrow passage aisles, behind circular columns
   with stiff-leaf capitals. Two-bay transepts behind a pair of taller
   arches. The mid-pier is of quatrefoil section with dogtooth in
   the hollows – these details copied from the old church. The
   chancel and its arch are tall and narrow. The builder and carver
   was *John Smith* of Egremont. Undersized nw tower, placed
   outside the aisle. It was heightened in 1901–2 by *Oliver &
   Dodgshun*. – reredos of wood, 1927, by *Caröe*. – pulpit of
   alabaster, 1875. – font. An angel bearing a scallop shell, after
   Thorwaldsen, of white-painted cast metal. Given 1883. –
   royal arms, 1790, in the tower porch. – stained glass. By
   Wailes. e gable rose by *Christine Boyce* of Brampton, 1992.
St John, Bigrigg, 2 m. nw, on the A595. By *C. J. Ferguson*,
   1877–80, for Henry Jefferson. Nave, chancel, bellcote. Con-
   ventional Dec, modest in size. (stained glass. w and e
   windows by *Kempe*, †1886 and 1896.) Extension sw 1993 by
   Richard Lindsay.
(St Mary (R.C.), St Bridget's Lane. Early Christian brick basilica with an open narthex, of 1959–60. mosaic of Christ as
   Lord of Creation in the semi-dome above the altar.)
Methodist church, Main Street. 1875–6 by *T. L. Banks*. The
   former Free Methodist Church at Bookwell (s), by
   Moffat & Bentley, 1892–3, is now the Masonic Hall.
cemetery. 1864. Twin spiky chapels, short and cruciform. The
   s one is slightly more fancy. Both have enormously heavy
   canopy porches pressing down on thin colonnettes of white
   granite. Between them a teetering Gothic monument to Joseph

---

*The Norman church had been extended e and doubled to the n, making it two-
naved, as it were. An apse added in 1752 removed two of the e lancets.

Roberts, signed *W. & A. Gilbeck*, Egremont, and dated 1866. –
On the roadside immediately l. is a turnpike TOLL HOUSE
dated 1856.

CASTLE. Motte-and-bailey castle, much ruined, now maintained
in a municipal garden. Founded by William de Meschines
c. 1120, at much the same time as St Bees Priory. A round shell
keep built in the mid C12 by William FitzDuncan, still shown
by Buck in the C18, has left no visible trace, but the curtain
wall and adjoining W gatehouse with their herringbone
masonry remain. The early C13 saw the building of the great
hall on the S slope of the motte. Damage by Robert the Bruce
in 1315 was followed by repairs and improvements. By 1578 the
castle was in decay, except the court house on the E which continued in use until 1785.

The main GATEHOUSE faces SW, away from the town.
Round-headed arch with a segmental arch recessed behind it.
Inside are the corner columns and scar of a domical rib-vault
(cf. Castle Rising, Norfolk, *c.* 1138). The CURTAIN WALLING
is irregular. Of the HALL BLOCK only the S wall is left, higher
up to the N. It had the hall on the upper floor. Two big windows
remain, and the start of a third, plus on the l. the doorway with
its portcullis slot. The doorway, originally with a porch and
outer stair, is continuously chamfered. Linking the windows is
a dripmould with a delicate zigzag leaf motif, like flat half-dog-
tooth; the motif recurs in the nave at Calder Abbey. More
domestic buildings along the E side. The MOTTE belongs with
the impressive original earthworks, established on a natural
hillock and steeply scarped above the crossing of the River
Eden. Excavation revealed a substantial ditch separating the
motte from the bailey, extending well into the N portion of the
later bailey, and similar in scale to the external ditch on the SW
that formerly extended round the N and E sides also.

TOWN HALL (former), Main Street. 1889–90. Five-stage clock
tower with pyramid roof and gablets. The wings are not quite
equal, the r. being slightly stretched and set back. MARKET
HALL of 1883 behind.

WAR MEMORIAL, Market Place. 1922. Bronze soldier and rifle
by *C. W. Coombes*, on a granite plinth.

WYNDHAM SCHOOL, now WEST LAKES ACADEMY. 1962–5, by
the Cumberland County Architect, *D. W. Dickenson*. Progressive both architecturally and educationally: a complete community education centre on a town centre site, including a
comprehensive school for 1,600, public library and public
swimming pool. The stimulus came from the development of
the nuclear plant at Sellafield. The five Modernist storeys are
a statement not a necessity, as are the pilotis of the side block.
Complex window rhythm. Monopitch stair top. Its future is
uncertain. SCULPTURES by *Colin Telfer*, 1993, 'When I was a
lad' and 'Haematite worker'. Crude, self-explanatory.

MAIN STREET lost a good deal of texture in the 1960s, with
clearances of the medieval burgage alleys or wents. Small
houses dated 1662 and 1667 close to the war memorial have

retained little more than their datestones. LOWES COURT, opposite Wyndham School, has fared better, retaining its central stack and a big arch through to the former court. Late C17 or early C18. Several three-storey houses of some presence, e.g. Old Hall (Nos. 59–60), late C17 or C18, five bays, with mullioned-and-transomed windows. C19 Gothic porch, but the inner doorcase has a bolection surround. At Nos. 54–56, l., a five-bay Early Georgian house with a double Doric porch – three columns – and moulded window surrounds. Several substantial pubs, e.g. the King's Arms, Blue Bell (with a blue bell), Red Lion, Wheatsheaf and Horn of Egremont.

FLORENCE MINE, on the SE outskirts of the town. At the time of writing (2009), Western Europe's last working deep iron mine. The headgear rises from a boxy three-story brick building with chutes to direct ore into railway wagons below. It sits atop a shaft sunk in 1947. The working entry is by an adit.

MONKS' BRIDGE, 3 m. E, near Farthwaite Farm. One of the few packhorse bridges which have never acquired parapets, showing the original simplicity. It is exceedingly narrow, with a slightly pointed arch taking a single leap high over a rocky pool on the infant River Calder. Popularly claimed as medieval, it is probably C17 or early C18.

EGTON-CUM-NEWLAND (L)   2080

ST MARY, Penny Bridge. First built before 1786 as a white box with round-arched windows. Rebuilt by *William Smith*(?) in 1831 with a W tower and Y-tracery. A chancel was added by *Miles Thompson* in 1855–6, and the nave rebuilt at the expense of the Countess Blücher von Wahlstadt, 1864–5, by *E. G. Paley*. Plate and Geometrical tracery. The S transept is later still, *c.* 1890; *Grundy* of Ulverston is a likely candidate at this date. The little white saddleback NW tower and W gable that comes into view down the beech avenue is different again: a makeshift of 1969 by *Frearson*, substituting for Smith's W tower which was removed in 1893. The Victorian nave, S aisle and S transept, in slate rubble and red dressings, are quite rough in construction. Inside the surprise is the brick of the arcade arches. – Unexceptional STAINED GLASS all by *Wailes*. – PAINTING, formerly behind the altar. Descent from the Cross, given by T. R. G. Braddyll of Conishead. Now there is a carved wooden REREDOS of 1908.

(PLUMPTON HALL, 2½ m. S. Front of 1706 with sash windows, but a doorway with lintel and pediment in the C17 Yorkshire tradition. The l. wing is C16 or C17, with big chimneys.)

(SUMMER HILL, Spark Bridge. Minor Late Georgian villa with an interesting extension of *c.* 2006 by *Francis Roberts Architects* in modern-Regency manner, including a small tower and copper-clad first-floor living space.)

NEWLAND. *See* Ulverston.

1030

EMBLETON (C)

St Cuthbert, ¾ m. sw of the village, and s of the A66. Plain roughcast box of 1806, remodelled 1884. The thin w tower-porch with its funny bellcote is of the former, the s porch and plate tracery of the latter date.

0010

ENNERDALE BRIDGE (C)

St Mary. 1856–8 by *Charles Eaglesfield*. In the Norman style, and very good of its kind. Semicircular apse, its smooth half-cone of slates catching the light, with a little round se bell-turret alongside. Long nave, s doorway in a thickening of the wall. Clasping buttress at each corner. Pevsner thought there were genuine Norman bits in the chancel arch (one scalloped capital) and doorway, but it is hard to be convinced.

Ennerdale Water is the quietest of the major lakes. No farms at the dale head, so no perimeter road.

Stone circle on Blakeley Moss, 1¼ m. ssw, beside the road to Calder. Reconstructed in 1925 with eleven stones; low central cairn.

Sampson's Bratfull, 4½ m. sse, on Stockdale Moor. Remote Neolithic trapezoidal long cairn, 87 ft (26 metres) long, higher and broader at the se end. From here three smaller cairns occupy the e skyline.

1000

ESKDALE (C)

Two main settlements: Boot, and Eskdale Green, 2 m. wsw.

St Catherine, Boot. Idyllically placed by the swift clear River Esk. Single-cell church, with bellcote and porch, restored by *Paley & Austin*, 1881. Three-light Dec e window with heavy tracery; its head starts to narrow in for a point, but then finishes off flat. The rest have uncusped heads (one s window of two lights is c17). – Font. Octagonal, ornamented on alternate sides with a wheel and six-petalled flower, and what is presumably meant to be cusped tracery incorporating an ogee. c14, or 1660s? – Stained glass. All 1889–96. e and w windows by *Gibbs & Co.*, sides by *A. Savell & Co.*

Boot is a tight whitewashed cluster of cottages, farms and pub. Also Eskdale Mill, a typical small Cumberland bank mill, long and low, rubble-walled, beside a subsidiary stream. The first record is in 1547. Two 12-ft (4-metre) overshot wheels *en echelon*, the second added in 1750, each originally driving two pairs of stones. The still-working machinery is mainly wooden.

Grain could be unloaded directly into a kiln (essential in such a rainy area), where it was dried on a perforated metal floor over a gentle fire.

RAILWAYS AND INDUSTRIAL REMAINS. On the slopes behind Eskdale Mill are the old adits of NAB GILL IRON MINE, begun in 1871 under the auspices of the Whitehaven Mining Co. In 1873–5 the public, 3-ft (0.9-metre) gauge RAVENGLASS & ESKDALE RAILWAY was built to link the mine with the Furness Railway. The INCLINE to lower the haematite ore to its original terminus is clearly visible, NW. By 1877 both mines and railway were in the Receiver's hands, but from 1880 the South Cumberland Iron Mining Co. opened new workings at Gill Force, ⅔ m. SSE. The girders of its railway BRIDGE over the Esk are still in position (now a footbridge). The company also built the present DALEGARTH COTTAGES ¼ m. W of the original terminus site. The railway closed in 1913, but during the First World War *W. J. Bassett-Lowke*, a successful Northampton-based model maker (and patron of Charles Rennie Mackintosh) and *R. Proctor-Mitchell* bought the line and illegally converted it to 15-in. (38-cm.) gauge, initially as a test track for their miniature locomotives. In 1922 year-round goods traffic was secured when the MURTHWAITE GRANITE QUARRY opened, 1½ m. W.

DALEGARTH HALL, ½ m. W of St Catherine. The capital house of the dale, belonging to the Stanleys since 1345. L-shaped, seemingly growing from the bedrock, with five fat conical 'Westmorland' chimneys. It appears to have lost a section at the W end, possibly the hall, its fireplace back-to-back with that of the present sitting room. The entrance was probably between the two in baffle position; bent walls and dead space here suggest a turning stair. A bulge at the back suggests another. A plaster ceiling dated 1599 has gone. The roofs have massive raking queenpost trusses of C17 type; was the house once perhaps taller? The BARN in front, with former cottage attached, may have been residential; slit windows below but high-quality square windows of red sandstone above, suggesting a bastle arrangement. It has an upper-cruck roof.

YOUTH HOSTEL, 1 m. NE. By *John Dower*, 1937–8. His writings contributed to the 1947 report upon which the Minister took action to establish National Parks. The building is interesting as heading towards the planning standards the National Park would adopt. Of granite rubble with the mortar brought to a flat surface, with graded slate roof and metal windows. The entrance is in a formerly open loggia.

BROTHERILKELD, 2¼ m. E. The topmost farm, at the foot of Hardknott Pass. The whitewashed C17 house stands in the middle of a line of barns which have their entrances picked out in whitewash. Unusually, the downhouse with its chimney is detached, across the yard.

HARDKNOTT ROMAN FORT, 2½ m. E. High above the upper valley on a spur of Hardknott Fell, beside the Roman mountain road linking the forts at Ambleside and Ravenglass. Walls of roughly coursed local volcanic rubble, unpicked in the 1890s, and consolidated and partly reconstructed in the 1950s; the extent of reconstruction is approximately indicated by a narrow band of slate. Architectural details (nearly all robbed away) were of St Bees sandstone, and tiles came from kilns at Muncaster.

Occupied only during the reign of Hadrian (A.D. 117–38), the fort was square and had three simple dual-portal gates; on the NW, overlooking Eskdale, there was a narrower single archway. Four angle towers, within the thickness of the earthen rampart, were probably entered from the raised rampart-walk; there are no doorways in the basement levels that survive. In the interior of the fort, rocky knolls were cut back to accommodate the three buildings of the principal range: the largest, in the centre, was the headquarters, having the familiar narrow transverse hall with a dais at the E end, approached through an arcaded entrance courtyard. Along the rear wall, opening into the hall, offices flanked the central regimental shrine. To ENE, a heavily buttressed double granary (of more than one period), each half having a loading platform at its SE end and an axial row of piers to support a raised floor. To WSW, the remnants of the commanding officer's house, probably ranged round a courtyard. Knowledge of the other internal buildings is fragmentary.

The low walls of a BATH HOUSE stand outside, to the SE: a simple row of rooms, providing (from NE to SW) cold, tepid and hot water; the furnace was in the SW gable. A separate, circular, room for dry heat was probably a later addition. There may once have been a timber changing room also.

A PARADE GROUND, 205 yds (190 metres) NE of the fort, along a road from the NE gate, is an impressive and exceptionally rare survival. A massive engineering project, its SE side was built up to provide an almost level platform of 2.7 acres. A huge wedge-shaped mound of rubble on the NW side may have been the site of a small temple, or a tribunal from which the officers could review the troops.

STANLEY GHYLL, 1½ m. W of St Catherine, by Beckfoot Halt. Built as a hotel in 1894. The architect was probably *Huddart*. Brash and self-satisfied, its red tile-hanging, red-painted timber framing and bargeboards rendered preposterous by the minuscule station and sylvan setting.

ST BEGA, Eskdale Green. 1891–2 by *T. L. Banks & C. H. Townsend*, supervised by *Arthur Huddart*. Mission church/hall above, school beneath. Unchurchy, Home Counties, like their one at Kirkland (q.v.), but with a square E end, and now minus its flèche. – FONT. A strange affair of terracotta segments, by *Hope Rea*, 1904; trilobed, decorated with the interlocking Tree pattern from the Dearham cross, and the Midgard Worm of Norse myth.

ESKDALE GREEN is essentially a railway settlement. J. H. Rea of Gatehouse (*see* below) and the *Huddarts*, father and son, were responsible for its Home Counties style, e.g. POST OFFICE

Row (1897) opposite St Bega: mixed tile-hanging, timber framing, granite lump and roughcast. Several of the older houses display a distinctive stone porch with a neatly shaped and moulded hood. The BOWER HOUSE INN, ¾ m. w, has one with the date 1751 on the doorway. FORGE FARM and SWORD HOUSE, close to the George IV Inn ½ m. E, bear the dates 1750 and 1789 on a little flat on the porches themselves. IRTON ROAD STATION of 1875, ⅔ m. w, the only unaltered one on the Ravenglass & Eskdale line, has claims to be the oldest English narrow-gauge station. A basic stone open shelter with a small office. Overbridge built to accommodate 3-ft gauge trains.

GATEHOUSE, E of St Bega. Rubicund mansion of 1896–1901 by *Arthur Huddart* for James Henry Rea, later 1st Lord Rea, a local boy made good as a Liverpool ship-owner.* Huddart (1865–1951), whose father was the local builder, trained with T. L. Banks of Whitehaven at the time of his partnership with C. H. Townsend. Tudor, with mullioned-and-transomed windows, of the indigenous silvery granite with red sandstone dressings. The house was first a modest H with hall bay and porch, but it grew rapidly at both ends. The E addition is a massive pele tower with corner turrets. The external grouping is successful but indoor circulation was never worked out satisfactorily.

As the house expanded, simple panelling and C17-style fireplaces gave way to an ever-richer Arts and Crafts ambience. Linking the centre with the tower is an 80-ft (25-metre) long GALLERY, its ceiling deeply coved and moulded, with two non-matching fireplaces in deep alcoves. Above this is a top-lit DISPLAY GALLERY, now partitioned. Lord Rea collected pots. At the top of the tower was a large MUSEUM ROOM. On its first floor an elaborately interlocking suite of bedroom, dressing room, boudoir and bathroom. The DRESSING ROOM is supposed to reproduce Albrecht Dürer's room in Nuremberg. In the BOUDOIR a C17 German overmantel. Off the huge LIBRARY occupying the tower base opens a WINTER GARDEN, containing stained glass of 1921 by *Caroline Townshend* and *Joan Howson* brought from Platt Chapel, Manchester. Galleried BILLIARD ROOM at the NE end. The table winds up from below. Inglenook fireplace, timber framing above the panelling. The two large beaten copper pictures of galleons in full sail are by *J. Smithies* of Wilmslow (Cheshire), who may have done the copper fire-hoods elsewhere. The tiles are *Pilkington*.

GARDEN by *Thomas Mawson* with rhododendrons, specimen trees, rockeries and rills round an artificial tarn with boathouse. Also by him a JAPANESE GARDEN N of the house at Giggle Alley, c. 1912–14.

---

* Uncle of Alec Rea, the builder of Keldwith, Windermere (q.v.).

Facing the road to the s is the original c17 farmhouse, YATTUS ('gatehouse' in Cumbrian). Of lump granite, with a continuous dripmould over part of the ground floor. A blocked doorway to the r. of the porch, and blocked fire-window at the uphill end.

FARLAM (C)

5050

ST THOMAS À BECKET, Kirkhouse, 1 m. NE. Rebuilt by *Anthony Salvin*, 1859–60. It cost £1,570. Nave with double bellcote, N aisle, and chancel. Lancets, and simple plate tracery, e.g. under the cross-gables of the N side. Pretty entry to the pulpit out of the wall by a doorway with shouldered lintel. – STAINED GLASS. E window by *R. B. Edmundson*. Others mostly *Clayton & Bell*, 1897 etc.

PARSONAGE. By *Salvin*, 1856–7.

FARLAM HALL (hotel). Raised *c.* 1860 from a row of cottages (C18 and *c.* 1824), by James Thompson, mining engineer to the Earl of Carlisle.

INDUSTRIAL REMAINS. This was coal-mining country, with plenty of evidence of digging, spoil heaps, and tramways. The deep cutting rising to the E immediately N of the church was for the Earl of Carlisle's INCLINE, 1,500 yds (1,385 metres) long, made in 1836 to bring coal from mines established above Hallbankgate down to Brampton staithes on the new Newcastle & Carlisle Railway. Further W, a colliery GASWORKS dated 1883, including chimney.

At COALFELL, 1½ m. E, is a drinking fountain with bronze inscriptions commemorating miners killed in 1908.

TINDALE, 2¾ m. E, has an impressive CO-OPERATIVE STORE of 1888, by far the biggest building in this strange bleak settlement, and formerly served by its own railway siding. Double-fronted, half-hipped roof, with a central gable and, on the s side, clumsy parodies of Venetian and Diocletian windows. Also a great EMBANKMENT, another noteworthy survivor of early engineering, and large WASTE TIPS from zinc smelting (1794–1931), for which Tindale Tarn was dammed. Between the smelter site and the Tarn, on the s side of the valley, two splendid late C19 LIMEKILNS, finely built, with pointed arches to the draw-holes.

FAR SAWREY (L) *see* SAWREY

FAWCETT FOREST (W)

5000

BORROWDALE HEAD. Small C17 farmhouse and barn in line. The house is typically tucked into the fold of the hill, and whitewashed, unlike the barn. Porch to the house, but the barn shows the expected entry, now blocked, at the back of the fireplace. The house is said to have a stylized rose tree in plaster inside.

FIELD BROUGHTON (L)   3080

ST PETER. By *Paley, Austin & Paley*, 1892–4, replacing a church   86 of 1745. The tall crossing tower with its stair-turret and recessed shingled spire is entirely alien, but exactly what this broad vale required. The red tiled roof too is out of place, but just right. Unmistakable are the excellent proportions, perfectly judged to suit the rising ground, and the top quality of execution, in limestone with buff sandstone bands and dressings. The church is aisleless, unless you count the W extensions of the transepts as one-bay aisles. The long nave is stopped at the W by massive diagonal buttresses. Long porch, attached to the W bay, with an intermediate door as well as an inner one. The flat-headed Perp windows, especially the belfry lights with their unusual detailing, confer a purposeful look. The interior, stone-lined, follows the same concept as Flookburgh and Finsthwaite – a long vista punctuated by receding arches and artfully lit at the centre where you might expect it to be darkest. The sharp arrises of the arches die into the tower piers, which stand free, except for the SE one which is fatter to accommodate the stair. – FITTINGS. By the architects and integral to the design, including a sturdy FONT of fossily marble at the extreme W. – STAINED GLASS. War memorial N, and N transept aisle by *Abbott & Co.* of Lancaster. Faith, Hope and Charity, N, by *Morris & Co.*, 1920, to oft-used cartoons. Two *Kempe* windows, S, 1894 and 1898.
(HAMPSFIELD HALL, 1 m. SE. C17 (spice cupboard dated 1687), with mullioned windows.)
BROUGHTON LODGE. A holiday house (so early) built 1770–80 for Josiah Birch of Failsworth, Manchester. Five bays, three storeys, hipped roof, Palladian side wings and pavilions – and a park – all on a miniature scale. The porch has unfluted Ionic columns, the wings pediments and Venetian windows under super-arches. (Fine drawing room.)
LONGLANDS, ¾ m. S of Broughton Lodge, is similar but early C19, with more of a Regency look. Two equal storeys with the wings set far back.
HAMPSFELL. *See* Grange-over-Sands.

FINSTHWAITE (L)   3080

ST PETER. A brilliant essay of 1873–4 by *Paley & Austin*.★ Paid for by Thomas Newby Wilson of Newby Bridge, proprietor of

★Goodhart-Rendel named Finsthwaite, Flookburgh (q.v.), and St George, Stockport (Cheshire) as his favourite Paley & Austin churches.

the Bobbin Mill (*see* below), in replacement of Clement
Taylor's 'new chapel' of 1724–5. The design originated as one
of the architects' victorious entries to a competition for 'mountain chapels' held in 1873 by the Carlisle Church Extension
Society. Everything centres on the massive central steeple,
which bulges up like a wooden church in the Carpathians.
Instead of transepts, broadly set-off buttresses build up to a fat
pyramid roof. Simple wooden louvres N and S but – the only
false note – Norman belfry dormers of red stone E and W.

Inside it is the length that dominates, from the font at the
W end to the faint gleam of gold mosaic at the E, with only a
slight broadening between the arches of the crossing. This has
four equal arches and a rib-vault – hence the massive buttressing. On its N a belfry stair expressed by tiny internal
windows; on the S a tall clear-glazed lancet floods the crossing
space with light. Twinkling above the packed trusses of the
single-framed roof are gable windows to E and W, with stained
glass. – WALL PAINTINGS, angels and plant forms, above the
windows, at the E end and on the tower vault. – FURNISH-
INGS. By the architects, simple and excellent: altar rails,
chancel floor, low pulpit, lectern, and the tub font of fossiliferous marble. – REREDOS of alabaster and mosaic by *Salviati*,
1883. – STAINED GLASS E and W only, by *Shrigley & Hunt* who
worked so closely with the architects. In the two W windows
are musical quotes from Handel's *Messiah*. – MONUMENTS.
Several tablets of above-average quality by *Webster* of Kendal,
e.g. Margaret Taylor †1827 with urn and books, and an
unsigned one to Edward Taylor †1790, from the old church.

In the knot of houses and barns above the church is ROSE
COTTAGE, a good farmhouse of *c.* 1630, white-limewashed.
Largely original wood-mullioned windows set deep, including
a five-lighter. Entry was at the S end from a cross-passage
behind the fireplace in the former barn, now a separate house.
Internal partitions largely timber-framed, with slightly arched
doorheads. The small wooden-floored bower or parlour off the
firehouse can be identified.

FINSTHWAITE HOUSE. Five-bay front, perhaps by *John Hird*,
completed *c.* 1790. The centre advances a little; the porch has
paired Doric columns. Broad hallway and straight stair flanked
by handsome drawing and dining rooms. The rest is surprisingly complicated. Two phases show at the back, roughcast,
with a hopper dated 1763 at the join. The kitchen section is
correlated by Janet Martin to payments made in 1724/5. Two
men were paid in 1730 for making the back stair, with its bulgy
but quite slender turned balusters and square newels. In 1743
Isabel Taylor paid 'for pulling down & rebuilding the late
dwelling house at the south-end'. So there was a still earlier
part, which was replaced by the present library (without its
bay) and 'little room' with its coved niche. Walled pleasure
garden and kitchen garden, stables.

(TOWER on the hill, SE. Built in 1799 by James King of Finsthwaite House to honour the English naval victories over France,

Spain and Holland. He may also have built the short obelisk nearby called THE SPIRE.)

COBBY HOUSE, ¾ m. SW. Bought by Edward Taylor in 1684. White Lake District farm, in a small cluster of dwellings and outhouses. Centre stack with a baffle entry on its E side and a straight stone stair squeezed in on the W. In the kitchen the stubs of a cruck-truss embedded in the walls at knee height.

STOTT PARK BOBBIN MILL, ⅓ m. NW. The tall square brick chimney is a surprise in these Elysian surroundings, especially when it is filling the valley with smoke and escaping steam. Small manufactories like this turned millions of wooden bobbins from the local coppice for the Lancashire cotton industry. The water-powered Old Mill was built in 1835 by John Harrison. It was a speculation; the running of the business was always leased out. In the 1880s Elizabeth Coward and her son William took over the lease and decided to diversify, adding a new lathe shop, engine and boiler house, and the open-fronted coppice barn. In production until 1971, the last of many, and now preserved and open to the public.

COTTAGES built for the mill workforce.

WATERSIDE, 1 m. SW, by the Lakeside branch railway and River Leven. The lane in front was then the main Ulverston road, and this was a smithy, recorded in 1570. The earliest part probably the centre room with its great stack and wooden-mullioned fire-window, and the E end room back-to-back with it. In 1675 Agnes Taylor married Charles Robinson, and ornamented the chimneypiece of the rear wing with a celebratory wreath of plasterwork. The stair with its bulgy balusters is very similar to the 1730 stair at Finsthwaite House. In the 1760s the legendary 'Finsthwaite Princess', Clementina Sobiesky Douglas, lodged in two first-floor rooms, and their fine panelling belongs to this period. The third storey was probably added at this time, its upper crucks perhaps reused.

FIRBANK (W)   6090

ST JOHN EVANGELIST. 1841. In a lovely spot, a minuscule version of the Carus Wilson type (*see* Casterton), probably by *Webster*. Bell-turret like a weeny tower. Lancet windows, short chancel. Flat ceiling with a stucco roundel.

Two fine sandstone RAILWAY VIADUCTS, both of 1858–61 by *J. E. Errington* for the London & North Western Railway's Ingleton branch (closed 1967). LOW GILL VIADUCT, eleven segmental arches of 45-ft (14-metre) span in red Penrith sandstone, curves away from the London to Glasgow mainline across the Dillicar Beck at a height of 88 ft (27 metres). 2 m. S towards Ingleton, the LUNE VIADUCT crosses the River Lune at 100 ft (31 metres) with a 41-yd (38-metre)-long central cast-iron arch, set between three sandstone arches on each side. The

total length is 177 yds (163 metres) and the setting superb.
A fine C17 BRIDGE, repaired in 1780, carries the A684 over the
Lune on two segmental arches.

FLIMBY (C)

ST NICHOLAS. Built in 1794, but the features are all of the
restoration and enlargement by *Charles Eaglesfield*, 1860–1. W
porch, nave with Dec windows, small chancel. – STAINED
GLASS. E window, †1875, by *Wailes*.
FLIMBY HALL, Wedgwood Road. Five-bay three-storey hall
facing away from the road. Raised and moulded window surrounds, with straight entablatures above the first-floor
windows. Moulded top cornice. Hoppers dated 1766.
1½ m. E, in the bed of Furnace Gill deep in Flimby Great Wood,
the surprisingly complete remains of an early C18 BLAST
FURNACE. Is this the mysterious coke-fuelled furnace,
described by Gabriel Jars as under construction in the vicin-
ity of Maryport in 1765 and reported as incapable of producing useable iron, even when charcoal fuel was substituted for
mineral coal?

FLOOKBURGH (L)
with Cark

Flookburgh and Cark are more or less continuous with Holker
to the NW (q.v.), but they are all very different in character.
Cark is an C18 planned village around the Big Mill of 1785,
which has gone. Flookburgh is a tough medieval fishing town,
small but surprisingly urban. Main Street runs E–W, between
a nothingness of sand at both ends; the over-sands route was
the way from Lancaster to Ulverston. The square in the middle
of the village was the churchyard of the old chapel of ease. A
cross marks the spot. The MARKET PLACE – Flookborough
had a market, established in 1278 – is a smaller widening a few
yards E, with a market cross of 1882. A little further E is the
MANOR HOUSE, a showy little house dated 1686. Symmetrical
front, with the initials WS on the incised Yorkshire lintel. Mullioned windows and a triplet in the central dormer gable rising
a little in the centre.
ST JOHN BAPTIST. Lady Frederick Cavendish in 1872 wrote of
the old church, 'a mean conventicle is almost unbearable. It
insults the majesty of God.' On a new site, close to Cark
station, her daughter Lady Evelyn in 1897 laid the foundation
stone of its replacement. The new church by *Austin & Paley*,
given by Victor Cavendish M.P., was consecrated in 1900. The

church climbs the hill in four roughly equal steps: semicircular apse, chancel, nave, broad W tower. The apse, which stands
on an undercroft, has a lead roof; the rest sandstone flags. The
tower has a low saddleback roof, recessed on two sides. The
weathervane is a fluke, or flatfish, and the tower gables have a
fish-scale finish. The windows are lancets, single or occasionally paired. Exterior and interior of pale sandstone brought to
a near-ashlar finish, with dressings and string and sill courses
smoother still. The way the parts are articulated is very interesting. The aisles have been, as it were, slid eastwards, leaving
the W bay of the nave clear, but overlapping the chancel. The
S porch opens into the tower base, which is open to the nave
by a wide arch and functions as both narthex and baptistery.
The first bay of the nave is, as we have seen, aisleless,
allowing an extra-tall pair of lancets to give direct lighting.
The view E is punctuated by further arches for chancel and
apse. Advancing, it can be seen that the aisles do not quite
reach to the apse arch, allowing another pair of tall lancets to
be popped in here to provide another strongly lit accent. The
roofs are complex, especially that of the nave which combines
two types of trusses with unusually massive braced and tied
rafters.

FURNISHINGS. All by *Austin & Paley* and very good in a
quiet way. – STAINED GLASS. All by *Shrigley & Hunt* and
worthy of the church. The earliest are the brown-tinted E
window and the W pair, *c.* 1901. Latest in style is the N chapel
N of 1927, wholly naturalistic: St Cuthbert preaching.

RAVENSTOWN, SW of the town. Extraordinarily out-of-place
1930s estate. Semis with hipped roofs alternately of slate and
red tile, in a formal semicircular layout. Streets named after
First World War battles – Jutland, etc.

CARK AND CARTMEL STATION. 1857, one of the original set
built for the Ulverstone (*sic*) & Lancaster Railway. Random
limestone, cottagey under a steep roof. The two-storey gable
faces the platform. Later iron-lattice FOOTBRIDGE, an ornamental product of *W. Macfarlane & Co.* of Glasgow.

CARK HALL, ½ m. N. Late C16, with mullioned windows. L-
shaped, two components. The main part is three-gabled with
a grand late C17 doorway with attached Ionic columns and a
big segmental pediment.

CANON WINDER HALL, 1¼ m. SW, by the coast path. The property belonged to the Canons of Cartmel Priory. Probably C16,
with C17 additions. Handsome house with large mullioned
windows, transomed on the ground floor, and a two-storey
canted bay on the N end. Late C17 doorway with ears and a
roll on top, under the flat canopy. The older doorway, which
appears to be a baffle-entry, has a Tudor flat-arched head.
Huge stack at the back with a round top.

RAVEN WINDER, ½ m. SW of Canon Winder Hall, is plainer.
EJH 1746 over the central door, but as usual there is an older
doorway and cross-passage behind the main stack.

WRAYSHOLME TOWER. *See* Allithwaite.

FRIZINGTON (C)

The village consists practically of one long terrace of two-storey miners' cottages.

ST PAUL. 1864–7, by *W. Bruce*. Rock-faced, with a sw turret and needle spirelet like a cemetery chapel. Wide steep-roofed nave with lancets and a w porch, i.e. still derived from the Commissioners' type of the 1830s–40s. Another porch was added midway along the s side in 2000 to convert the w end to the LINGLA CENTRE, function rooms with community café over. The partition was crudely done with breeze blocks. The remaining worship space is too short for its height. Paired hammerbeams. Traceried opening for the organ l. of the chancel arch.

(RHEDA. The main house of 1881–3 by *Jonathan Shepherd* of Whitehaven has been demolished. The office court by *C. J. Ferguson*, altered by *Martindale* in 1900–6, survives.)

MARGARET MINE, 1½ m. E. Engine house, chimney, miners' 'dry' and offices of the mine, closed in 1923 but still remarkably intact.

FURNESS ABBEY (L)

In 1124 a colony of twelve monks and their abbot came from Savigny, near Avranches, where their order had originated in 1105. Tulket, near Preston, was granted them by Stephen of Blois, afterwards King of England, but in 1127 they settled on this secluded valley, flat-bottomed but steep-sided, which winds up to Dalton from the sea. The site was promising, with forest, red rock, mines 'exuberant in lead and iron', and a safe sea haven behind Walney Island. This was the senior Savigniac house in England. In 1148 Serlo, fourth Abbot of Savigny, merged his order with the Cistercians. Abbot Peter went from Furness to Rome to protest, but when he failed to return his place was taken by Richard of Bayeux, a Cistercian. By then the E end of the church was built, probably with five apses *en echelon* (the chancel, and two apses to each transept), together with the essential buildings around the cloister, including a chapter house also probably apsidal. The Cistercians remade Furness in their own standardized image later in the C12, but evidence for the Savigniac abbey can still be found – a fascinating subtext. The abbey grew to be one of the largest and richest Cistercian houses in Britain, challenging even Fountains, with lands reaching into High Furness as far as Coniston and Hawkshead. The ruins give a picture of progressive and vigorous growth, despite periodic Scots depredations, with a magnificently defiant tower rising at the Dissolution. Thirty-three monks, implicated in the Pilgrimage of Grace, surrendered in 1537.

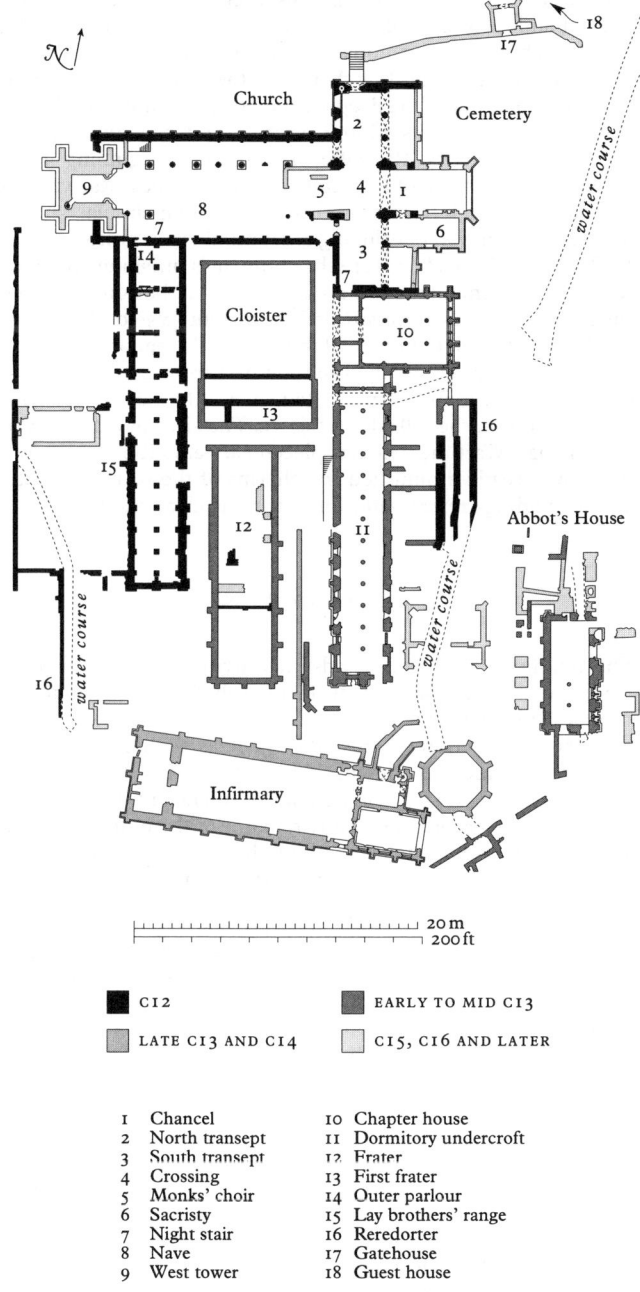

N

Church

Cemetery

water course

9

8   7

14

Cloister

13

10

15

16

12   11

Abbot's House

16

water course

water course

Infirmary

17   18

|⊢⊢⊢⊢⊢⊢⊢⊢⊢⊢⊢⊢⊢⊢⊢⊢⊢⊢⊢⊢⊢| 20 m
                         200 ft

▮ CI2   ▮ EARLY TO MID CI3

▮ LATE CI3 AND CI4   ▮ CI5, CI6 AND LATER

 I   Chancel   IO Chapter house
 2   North transept   II Dormitory undercroft
 3   South transept   I2 Frater
 4   Crossing   I3 First frater
 5   Monks' choir   I4 Outer parlour
 6   Sacristy   I5 Lay brothers' range
 7   Night stair   I6 Reredorter
 8   Nave   I7 Gatehouse
 9   West tower   I8 Guest house

Furness Abbey.
Plan

Church and conventual buildings, even the *capella extra muros*, were abandoned and pillaged. John Preston incorporated what was probably the guest house into his new manor house to the N, which passed to the Lowthers and then the Cavendishes. By Late Georgian times 'the deep retirement of its situation, the venerable grandeur of its Gothic arches, and the luxuriant, yet ancient trees' (Mrs Radcliffe, 1807) were beginning to be admired. A new lease of life came from the Furness Railway line, completed through to Lancaster in 1857.* Soon circular tours by train and steamer were bringing great numbers of visitors. *Sharpe & Paley* then *E. G. Paley* were the company's unfailing architects. Abbey Approach, marked by archways top and bottom and encircling the *capella extra muros*, led to the integrated station and hotel, the latter made out of John Preston's manor house. The abbey ruins were landscaped to look best from the hotel's lawn. For the chairman, James Ramsden, the company built Abbotswood on the hillside to the NE. The site passed into State care in 1923. Wartime damage, piecemeal demolition and railway cuts have greatly diminished the charms of the scene, but many minor buildings remain and the picture is clear enough.

THE ABBEY RUINS

The buildings are of red sandstone, artistically but alarmingly eroded, with occasional accents in a polished grey limestone. Not a lot is left of the nave, so what takes the eye is not so much the E–W axis of the church across the valley as the long N–S line of the transepts and the immensely long dormitory, and the E wall of the infirmary, all standing virtually to full height. The approach is from the N, through the scanty remains of the outer court. The following description takes the church first, the domestic quarters after. For the gatehouses and visitor centre *see* pp. 358–9.

CHURCH. The E end as rebuilt is of the standard Cistercian plan, with a straight-headed chancel and transepts with an E aisle divided originally into three chapels to each arm. Entry, unusually, is by the N TRANSEPT, standing tall with flat Norman buttresses leaning outwards somewhat. Good round-arched portal of three orders, the outer with bobbins, the others multiply moulded. Huge replacement window above, now tracery-less. The piers to the transept E aisle have eight shafts, with slightly pointed arches. They are part of the Cistercian rebuilding, and their waterleaf capitals determine the date, *c.* 1175. The triforium is complete, the opening of the middle bay retaining proto-tracery of trefoil sub-arches with a little sunk circle in the spandrel. Again waterleaf capitals. Furness and Roche (Yorkshire West Riding) are the first English Cistercian churches to exhibit a three-storey elevation. Late C15 Perp windows above, and inserted in the Norman openings else-

---

*The railway originally proposed a line slap through the abbey ruins, but the company's engineer recommended a short detour and tunnel to ease the bend.

Furness Abbey, sedilia and piscina.
Engraving, 1844

where. The three eastern chapels are reduced to plinth level, but their altar bases and steps can be seen. They were rib-vaulted on piers rather than divided by cross-walls. Pillar piscina nearest the chancel.

The CROSSING is essentially that of the Savigniac church, i.e. before 1148. Its piers have multiple shafts and waterleaf capitals. Only the E piers are intact, with the slightly pointed E arch with a chamfer and three thin rolls. It was probably heightened when the chancel was remodelled by the Cistercians. Against the NW pier some well-worn steps, perhaps to a pulpit or gallery. There are signs that the crossing tower gave cause for concern: the SW pier was strengthened in the C15, with Perp panelling to disguise its mass. The SW arch to the nave aisle was also filled in, as was part of the N transept triforium.

The CHANCEL, although rebuilt square from the Savigniac one, is still short and constricted. The first bay is sheer and blank, apart from a pair of filled-in arches interpreted as a Savigniac survival. Then two projecting bays, filled on the N with immensely tall Perp windows of the late C15, originally with transoms. The E window too is as tall and wide as it could be, and likewise had transoms. On the S side the windows come down less far, because the sacristy adjoins here. Below, four SEDILIA and a tripartite PISCINA with towel recesses, integrated into one splendid Perp set piece. Row of projecting canopies, straight top band with ogee cresting and complicated miniature vaults inside. It is one of the best ensembles of sedilia and piscina anywhere in England. C19 graffiti includes the name *W. B. Kendall*, supervisor of the restoration under Lord Frederick Cavendish. An ogee-gabled doorway with three continuous deep hollows and filleted rolls goes through to the sacristy.

The S TRANSEPT lacks a triforium. Its inner chapel has been extended E and closed by a wall on its S side to make the sacristy, with a beautiful piscina. Carved lozenges and sections of zigzag visible from outside above the chapel arcade are probably bits of the Savigniac chapel arches and apses. The rest has its eight-shaft piers, waterleaf capitals, and pointed arches. In the S wall the broad night stair to the dormitory, with a C13 arch at the landing. In the W wall two round-arched windows set sufficiently high to clear the cloister, and two upper Perp windows.

The NAVE was originally ten bays long. It is mostly reduced to a few base courses, but there is enough left at the crossing to show its system. The N aisle E arch to the transept remains in its original form, with waterleaf capitals. The corresponding S aisle E arch (also with waterleaf) is there too, but it has needed strengthening. A second arch was inserted, then it was blocked, as already noted, with just a small C15 doorway through. Also surviving is part of the first compartment of the S aisle vault. An arch, severely deformed before being blocked, went through at triforium level above. The nave piers, not particularly stout, were alternately round and eight-shafted. Stone bases for the choir stalls extend into the two easternmost bays. Then comes the pulpitum which occupies a whole bay, with steps and base for an altar against its W face in the N aisle. Behind the stalls in the N aisle is a plinth decorated with roundels of blank Flamboyant tracery. Steps at its W end suggest it was the base of a tiny chantry chapel. The lay brothers' night stair comes in near the SW end of the nave, through a round-headed upper doorway into the upper storey.

The building of the mighty W TOWER from about 1500 meant intruding into the last bay of the nave. The tower details are late: three-centred arch to the stair doorway, continuous mouldings to the tower arch, fleurons and faces in the hollow mouldings of the very large W window. The side walls are blank, as at Shap (q.v.). With walls 10 ft (3 metres) thick, and buttresses with niches for images spreading nearly as far again, it was clearly meant to go high; the stump still stands 60 ft (18.5 metres) to the head of the W window. It would have been an even stranger sight, poking out of the extreme edge of the valley, than Huby's tower at Fountains.

THE CLOISTER was oblong rather than the usual square, because when the Cistercians rebuilt the refectory the opportunity was taken to enlarge the cloister on the S side. The E RANGE first. The NE doorway to the church is round-headed with a continuous moulding. There is an additional doorway, completely

plain, into the s transept. If the Savigniac church had two-bay
rather than three-bay transepts, this was originally the door to
the slype. As it is, the rebuilt CHAPTER HOUSE abuts the
transept. This has the usual triple entrance, the central one to   18
the vestibule and the outer ones to tunnel-vaulted book rooms
(one vault is round, the other pointed). Slightly smaller
entrances follow to a warming house (formed within the dormitory undercroft) and to the displaced slype. The run of five
arches, still round, richly and multiply moulded, is Furness's
particular showpiece. All this must date from c. 1230–40. The
vestibule has blank pointed-trefoiled arcading along the N and
s walls, and is vaulted with diagonal and ridge ribs, all
moulded, and a small central boss. Wall seat and shafting
picked out in polished silver limestone. The chapter house,   19
though ruined, is still lovely. Of four by three bays, it was rib-
vaulted too, on slim piers of eight shafts, with fillets on the cardinal sides. Large blank arcading carried on all round, with
twin lancets with splendid sexfoil paterae – some with dogtooth – in the tympana. The windows in the E half are of the
same pattern. So is the doorway. To the outside the windows
have detached shafts, and the buttresses are chamfered. It had
a roomy upper floor, perhaps the scriptorium, lit by plain
lancets. Next in the cloister comes the walled-off N bay of the
dormitory undercroft, then the slype, then the DORMITORY
UNDERCROFT itself, with a row of octagonal mid-piers. Originally of fourteen bays (the longest known in England), it projected a full ten bays beyond even the rebuilt s walk of the
cloister. Against the walls corbels with stiff-leaf capitals in the
N bays, simpler capitals in the other bays. The dormitory above,
connecting to the night stair by a wide passage over the chapter
house vestibule, has lancets in a long, even row, as at Calder.
The scar of the day stair can be seen in the SE corner of the
cloister. E of the E range were more rooms. The stream which
any monastery needs runs roughly N–S here, and the late C12
lavatories or REREDORTER can be recognized. Pair of round
arches. For the original infirmary (later Abbot's House),
further E, *see* below.

Almost nothing remains on the s SIDE of the cloister. Here
was the warming house (at the E), and two or even three generations of refectory or frater – the Savigniac one aligned E–W
on the earlier, square cloister, and the Cistercian one at right
angles N–S, as was their custom, on the enlarged cloister. The
present N wall of the refectory was the s wall of the earlier
refectory.

The W RANGE, for lay brothers, is a little more eloquent. It
is long and again two-naved, sticking out to the s, though not
as far as does the monks' dormitory. The total length is fifteen-
and-a-bit bays, but is subdivided on the ground floor: cross-
walls create the outer parlour at the N end (two by two bays),
and the entrance passage further s. The N respond within the
range is semicircular with a scalloped capital and inverted
cones for two completely detached shafts, an early instance of
columns *en délit*.

To the SW of the W range is the LAY BROTHERS' RERE-
DORTER, again across a stream. This stream turns E and runs
under the INFIRMARY of the late C13, which is placed S of
refectory and dormitory. This was a splendid apartment,
130 ft by 50 ft and 40 ft high (40, 15 and 12 metres), with a W
chamber divided off and at the E end a vaulted chapel and a
smaller vaulted servery. Judging by the E wall, which is almost
complete, and by the single bays remaining of the N and S walls,
it had a stone seat all round and two tiers of continuous arcading. The lower tier incorporates the doorways to chapel (r.) and
servery; the upper tier, taller and thinner, presumably high-
level windows at the sides. It would be interesting to know how
this great room, much the widest single span on the site, was
roofed; there seem to have been no internal supports, and the
walls are powerfully buttressed. The chapel and servery are
both essentially complete. The CHAPEL is of three bays, with
a broad shallow rib-vault with a ridge rib and diagonal ribs, all
moulded, but no bosses. Seating all round, and a string at sill
level. Pillar piscina, SE. The window heads fit the vault, making
the side arches acute and almost straight, the E one very broad
and again almost straight. They have rere-arches and retain
some Geometrical tracery. The SERVERY is of two smaller bays,
with a plain rib-vault of diagonals only, and five doorways all
differently moulded. A twice-kinked passage linked it to an
octagonal KITCHEN spanning the stream. The relationship
between passage, kitchen, and servery and chapel is puzzlingly
awkward.

At the E edge of the site, against the cliff, is what is reckoned to be the ABBOT'S HOUSE, converted out of an earlier
infirmary. Successive alterations make it seem folly-like. Five-
bay undercroft with mid-piers of octagonal section. Small
lancets to N and E. To the E also a large fireplace preserving a
section of dogtooth on one corbel. Octagonal buttressing at the
back, like that of the chapter house, i.e. mid-C13. The upper
floor was extended back to the cliff, and required massive
flying buttresses at the front. A branch of the stream ran under
the building, and there is a sluice.

BUILDINGS TO THE N OF THE CHURCH

Moving northwards from the N transept.

E of the N transept is the C14 GATEHOUSE which led through
to the cemetery E of the church. Attached to the NE of that the
irregular remains of the C12 GUEST HOUSE, as rebuilt in the
C14. Two levels are evident, indicating the raising of the ground
against flooding.

The VISITOR CENTRE, at the N perimeter, is a self-effacing
red brick building of 1982 with monopitch roofs. MONU-
MENTS from the site are displayed here. Two knights of
c. 1250–60, fashioned in silver limestone; cross-legged but still

with cylindrical, slit-visored helmets. – C13 deacon in a pleated habit. – Early C14 lady with chinstrap and flowing dress, red sandstone. – Fine C14 cross-legged knight in mail and surcoat. – Several C13 and C14 inscribed grave-slabs.

Outside the English Heritage site to the N is the late C12 GREAT GATEHOUSE. It exists only as few base courses, one side displayed in the car park, the other, across the minor road that still goes through it, hidden in undergrowth. It was a powerful building with a long vault in two sections and a gate arch in the middle, like that extant at Whalley (North Lancashire).

ABBEY TAVERN, N of the car park. It is a pity no more is left of so tantalizing a building. It was the manor house of the Prestons, probably incorporating the abbey's guest house. The railway company rebuilt it as the Furness Abbey Hotel in 1847 and in 1866–9 (probably by *E. G. Paley*), linking it with the station and providing large windows and gardens overlooking the abbey ruins. What remains after demolition in the 1950s is the former second-class refreshment room, tap room and booking office. ABBEY COTTAGE (*c.* 1873) was the coachman's house, originally with stables adjoining.

N of the Abbey Tavern is the CAPELLA EXTRA MUROS, complete except for its roof. A single cell, with late C13 tracery, chamfered buttresses, and lovely triple sedilia expressed outside, with steep gables, plus piscina and aumbry. The plain N and W walls perhaps remain from the Norman building – no strings, no windows. W doorway and small S doorway also Norman. Statue niche, trefoil-headed, over the W doorway. The altar platform remains, and so does a possible base for a statue or relic in the NE corner. Rebuilt arches of an outer GATE attached W. It has a large and small arch.

PERIPHERAL BUILDINGS

PRECINCT WALL. Prominent on the southern skyline, and affording a wonderful view of the abbey in its natural amphitheatre. To the W it descends onto a gully and a small OUTER GATEHOUSE, arched front and back but not vaulted, with the remains of an upper chamber. Next to it, a pretty addition, WEST GATE COTTAGES, by *E. G. Paley*, 1873.

Adjacent to the Abbey Tavern are the former station platforms, and the private level crossing between them, with its LODGE, that led to Abbotswood (1857), Ramsden's house. It has gone, but some furniture and stained glass are in Barrow Town Hall. Three more lodges, a home farm and cottages, all by *Paley* or *Paley & Austin*, can be found.

ABBEY MILL, S of the Infirmary, across a lane. Once the custodian's cottage, now café. Small. The roof, partly destroyed in a recent fire, was dendro-dated to the late C15. The middle truss has short hammerbeams.

COTTAGES, SE of the Infirmary. *Cottages ornés* dated 1874, timbered black-and-white with coves, some pargetting, and red tiled roofs. If these are by *Paley & Austin* like the rest they are in an unusual idiom.

113 ABBEY HOUSE HOTEL, Abbey Road. In the NW corner of the abbey precinct, above but hidden from the car park. By *Lutyens*, 1913–14, i.e. a near-contemporary with the rigours of Castle Drogo (Devon), and the demure domesticity of Ednaston Manor (Derbys.). It was built for Vickers of Barrow, as a place to entertain ministers and heads of state for the purpose of selling them battleships. Vickers asked for a large hall, drawing room, billiard room and dining room on the ground floor, and 'a full little apartment for McKechnie [managing director] where he can receive a couple of friends, and his apartment should have a private entrance of its own . . . and be cut off entirely from the rest of the house'. Neither country house nor hotel, but with elements of each.

Of red sandstone and based on the Tudor E, with extra, lower wings at the ends, the building's startling austerity and rigid symmetry seem in tune with its purpose. The polygonal porch shows windows only at the very top. Windows are punched through, the mullions and transoms of the ground and top floors contrasting with intermittent bands of round-topped mezzanine windows between. Where mezzanine windows are missing, e.g. in the fronts of the wings, there is just blank wall. No sills, no drips, no strings or plinths, and only the slightest roll forward as a cornice. All we are left with is powerful massing and sharp edges reinforced by Lutyens's subtle battering, strong colour, a great run of roof behind its parapet, and massively grouped chimneys.

Entry is through the low domed porch to an equally low transverse hall with a pair of doors at each end; a claustrophobic and unsettling space. In order to reach the principal rooms you have to penetrate the spine wall. The great hall centres on the biggest bay at the back, despite which it is surprisingly dark. Through it climbs the main stair, wide and creaky, pausing on top of the screen. Over the whole is an unadorned coffered ceiling. The billiard room, now the bar, is double-height too, with a lower section originally containing the fireplace. Back-to-back with it is the former drawing room, with a saucer dome on pendentives. The dining room in the corresponding wing has a barrel-vault, a small gallery, and a suffocatingly large fireplace (many of the fireplaces are bolection-moulded). The main stair changes character when it cuts back through the spine wall to the mezzanine, abandoning the pale oak and symmetrically turned balusters of the lower part for black, chunky, cartoon-like slat balusters and newels.

A hotel EXTENSION to the N, 2001, kowtows to Lutyens in its red stone cladding, angled bays and strip windows; otherwise unremarkable. – LODGE. Also by *Lutyens*, and equally austere. A wide entrance on Abbey Road, designed for a cavalcade of cars to sweep in to the turning circle. A raised grass plinth to the house. A row of windswept pines to the S.

The neighbourhood of Furness Abbey is Barrow's West End. MILLWOOD was built *c.* 1860 for Edward Wadham, agent for the 5th Duke of Buccleuch, by *Edward Browning* of Stamford. Altered and extended *c.* 1876 by *Paley & Austin.* Very tall spooky chimneys. CROSSLANDS off Rating Lane, *c.* 1865, was the residence of J. T. Smith, manager of the Barrow Haematite Iron and Steel Co. Now Chetwynde School. Red and yellow voussoirs. Two LODGES. OAKLANDS is next to Abbey House: all silver limestone, mostly rock-faced.

GAMBLESBY (C)

Attractive open-plan village with an extensive irregular green ringed by good Cumbrian houses – the total greater than the sum of its parts.

ST JOHN, an excellent building of 1868 by *C. J. Ferguson,* is closed. Nave and chancel in one, with a smoothly rounded apse and continuous roof. The style is late C13. Wooden bell-turret and spire set in from the W end. Lancets.

METHODIST CHAPEL of 1864 with Y-tracery. Its 'chancel' is the school. Near-identical chapels in Ainstable and Glassonby.

GARRIGILL (C)

ST JOHN. Single-cell church of 1790, reconstructed within the shell in 1888–90 by *Hicks & Charlewood,* Newcastle Diocesan architects. They proposed the addition of a chancel, then a W extension, but in the end only a chancel arch with side arches was inserted, dividing the interior into nearly equal parts, both wider than long. The internal proportions were made still odder when a three-light Dec N window, too big for the church, was inserted in 1904. – STAINED GLASS of the Crucifixion.

REDWING CHAPEL (Congregational), ½ m. NW. 1756 on a lintel. Closed 1977; complete but slowly disintegrating in 2006. Four round-arched windows with moulded surrounds on the S side only. Stable at the far end. Grey-painted two-decker PULPIT in its pen, BENCHES. Good monuments in the churchyard, and a pair of splendid beeches.

CHAPEL (Wesleyan), Low Houses, N. 1859, not small. Now Thortergill tearoom.

CHAPEL (Primitive Methodist), Gatehead, S. 1885, on the site of two earlier chapels. Not small either, though without a gallery. Usual pattern of round-arched windows to the front, with a central porch.

The village surrounds a soft triangular green, a surprising find at this altitude. In the middle is a single Alston Moor bastle, now the POST OFFICE. Steps to the upper door at the back.

ROTHERHOPE TOWER, 2¼ m. NW. The house is dated JU 1717 on the front doorway. T & M H 187- on the gate arch dates its conversion to a shooting lodge, which it still is. A folly curtain wall with little castellated towers goes with the arch, as does a monstrously overscaled porch with a single slab of stone for the roof. There was a castellated tower too, with a Gothic window, but this has been cut down. Evidence for quite an elaborate garden.

GARSDALE

See *The Buildings of England, Yorkshire West Riding: Leeds, Bradford and the North*

GILCRUX (C)

Pronounced Gilcruse, with a hard G.

ST MARY. Little C12 church on an eminence above the green, commanding a grand view over the Solway into Scotland. Chancel, nave with bellcote, S aisle and porch. On the porch gable a fine stone SUNDIAL, 1836. The chancel is very narrow, with a Norman N window but Late Perp windows E and S, and has a yet narrower chancel arch of severest Early Norman type with just a single step on the W. The impost is cut away on the chancel side N, and on the S is a comical squint, like an oval porthole.* Two-bay Late Norman arcade, whitewashed. Its E end finishes dead in the wall. The mid-pier is round, with little incised scrolls on its big square abacus, like a memory of Ionic volutes. The W impost is a fully formed pier, indicating an intended third bay. Arches with one step and one slight chamfer. The aisle, only about 6 ft (1.8 metres) wide, has paired lancets of 1878. – FONT. Norman. Massive square tub on a short fat stem, all whitewashed. – ROYAL ARMS, 1759. – STAINED GLASS. The retable is a copy in glass of Leonardo's Last Supper by *Chance Bros*, 1865. Said to come from Holy Trinity, Whitehaven (dem.). – E window by *Abbott & Co.*, 1937.

---

*The Rev. Leslie Price writes that Bridekirk old church had something similar.

GILSLAND SPA (C)

A sulphur spring was known from the C17 but the spa only developed significantly in the C19, when chalybeate springs were discovered as well.

St Mary Magdalene. 1852–4 by *James Stewart* of Carlisle, for G. G. Mounsey. Nave and chancel. Lancets and pairs of lancets, steep bellcote. Dull. (– STAINED GLASS in E and W windows by *J. Scott & Son*, from Rockcliffe church.)

The former VICARAGE is a prominent, plain house of white brick, derelict but inhabited. Presumably also by *Stewart*. Chunk of HADRIAN'S WALL in the garden.

METHODIST CHAPEL and HALL. Gothic, with Y-tracery. 1869.

SPA HOTEL. The hotel, also by *James Stewart* for G. G. Mounsey, was built in 1859–60 after fire destroyed an earlier building. It is an ugly thing, nine bays wide by eight deep, blocky and quadrangular in yellow railway brick and token Italianate style – the occasional group of three windows with arched heads is unmistakable. The setting is what makes it. The River Irthing has cut a gorge here as it descends from Spadeadam Moor. Broad paths wind along the brink, or descend through delicious woods to the malodorous spring and the tea-coloured river. It was purchased by the Co-op in 1901 as a convalescent home, much favoured by miners from Northumberland and Durham. An aura of hospital still hangs over the place, with its long corridors and functional stairways. Only the principal stair has a bit of style; a broad cantilever running up to the top, with a fireplace at its foot. The ballroom occupies the central court; iron-framed and glass-roofed, but stripped of architectural interest. By the drive is SPA VILLA, 1815, of six widely spaced bays with a hipped roof.

ORCHARD HOUSE. Early C19 spa accommodation, originally several houses. Five bays and three storeys, with not-quite-matching four-bay wings. Matching C20 porches with Doric columns fashioned as wrought-iron cages.

Gilsland village is mostly across the River Irthing, in Northumberland.

FOOTBRIDGE at Willowford, to take the Hadrian's Wall path. 1999 by *Christopher Rainford* of the *Napper Partnership*. Engineer *Arup*. Single rainbow swoop of rusting steel, starting high at one end, ending low the other. Single support at the high end.

TRIERMAIN CASTLE, 2½ m. W. On a natural knoll, with a ditch and counterscarp bank on the E and SE. Form uncertain; possibly quadrangular, with a gatehouse; a single slender fragment of interior fabric survives. Robert de Vaux was given licence to crenellate in 1340; abandoned for Askerton, and in ruins by 1580.

R.A.F. SPADEADAM, 2½ m. N. The drearily undulating blanket bog of Spadeadam Waste, beyond the aptly named Moscow Farm, was taken over by the Forestry Commission in the mid 1950s, and then, with Cold War tension rising, selected as the testing ground for Britain's intermediate-range ballistic missile, Blue Streak. This was designed to deliver a nuclear warhead to Moscow in twenty minutes. Work started in 1956, testing in 1959, but in 1960 the Government, frightened by enormous and escalating costs, cancelled it. One missile is preserved on its cradle near the main gate. The five main areas are widely separated over more than 7,000 acres of conifer forest and bog, linked by roads floated on brushwood in time-honoured fashion, by high-tension electricity cables, clean and contaminated water economy (for cooling), kerosene and liquid nitrogen pipes, and instrumentation cables: a prime integrated Cold War landscape.

OFFICE AREA, at the southern edge of the site. Security, Fire Station (a 'Robin'-type hangar), accommodation blocks and a large metal-clad assembly shed. LIQUID OXYGEN (LOX) PLANT. Mysterious concrete platforms and anchorages tell little of the huge tanks and machinery they supported, nor the building that contained them. The circular platform on legs, like a walk-through hypocaust, held the liquid oxygen tank clear of the ground, which would otherwise warm it up. Close by is a high-capacity electricity substation.

COMPONENT TESTING, 550 yds N. Concrete stands for testing hazardous parts such as turbo pumps. The tests were powered by static jet engines and observed from an armoured bunker.

ENGINE TEST AREA, Priorlancy Rigg, 1 m. NW. The engines were taken to the top of each of the four stands, which were clean, while the rocket efflux and contaminated water were kept to the downhill side. Again there is a sunken bunker for instrumentation and indirect observation.

ROCKET TESTING AREA, Grey Mare Hill, nearly 2 m. N. The rockets were set upright, prepared and fuelled from movable eight-storey gantries, then test-fired at full power but tethered. All steelwork has gone, so what is left is a pair of giant concrete stands, each with its liquid oxygen and kerosene stores, cooling-water supply, emergency fuel dumps, efflux and waste water channel, and settling tank for separating out waste fuel. Great inclined legs support the rocket platform against the hillside, and a triangular frame underneath held the blast deflector bucket. At a safe distance is the observation bunker, buried in earth and linked to the stands by a long instrumentation tunnel.

These mute remains have a stark beauty of their own. Although their forms should be dictated only by function, a sinister aesthetic has been at work, highlighted by the gross incongruity that occurs when a contrasting aesthetic appears, such as the friendly and familiar presence of a couple of standard red K6 telephone boxes out on the range.

HADRIAN'S WALL. *See* Denton.

Coniston Hall (L), C16, from the NW, with Brantwood, late C18 and C19, behind, left (p. 295)

2. Piel Castle (L), C14, seen from Roa Island (Rampside, L), with watch tower, 1849, left (pp. 576 and 583)
3. Rydal Water (W) from the s side, with Nab Cottage, 1702 (p. 596)

4. Keswick (C), late C19 houses, with Skiddaw behind (p. 447)
5. Dufton (W), village green (p. 336)

6. St John's in the Vale (C), The Carles stone circle, Castlerigg, prehistoric (p. 601)
7. Ravenglass (C), Roman bath house (p. 585)
8. Walton (C), Birdoswald Roman fort, aerial view (p. 657)

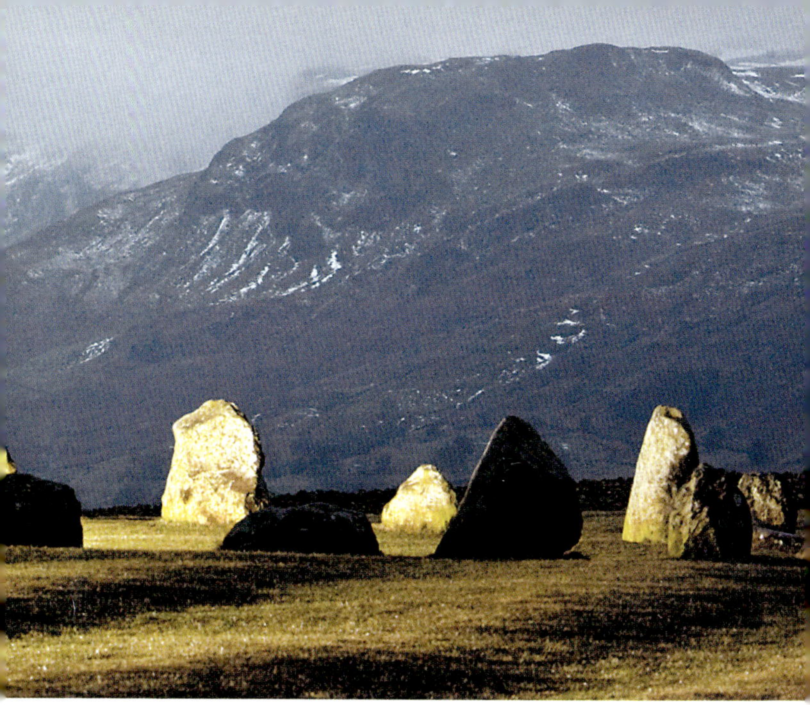

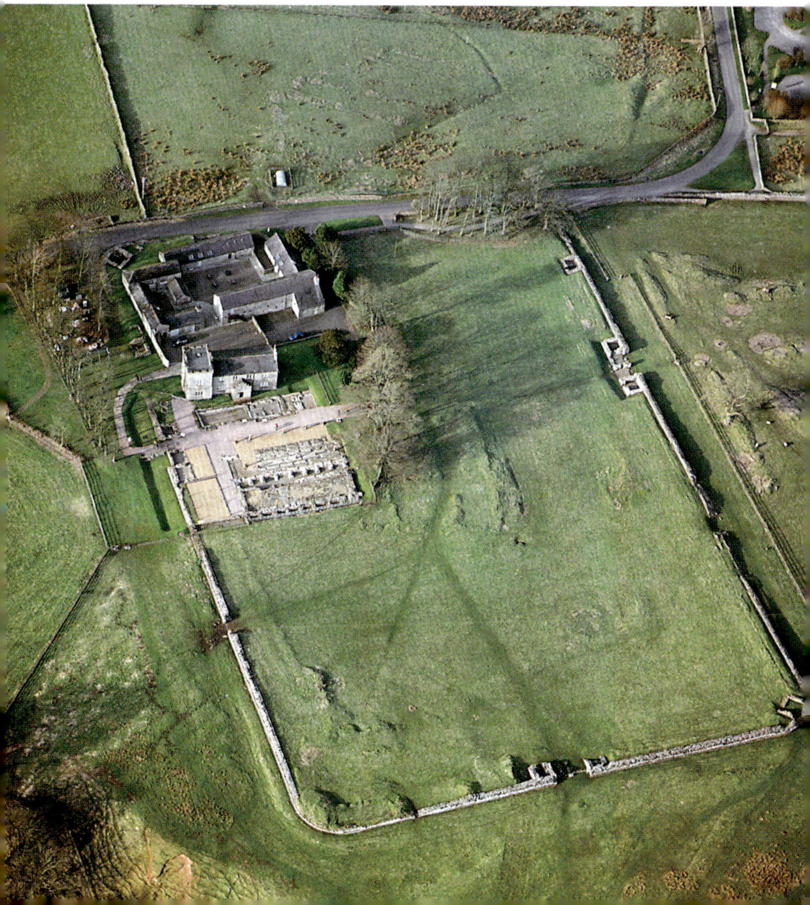

9. Irton (C), St Paul, cross, c9, w face (p. 423)
10. Gosforth (C), St Mary, cross, c10, w face (p. 367)
11. Bewcastle Cross (C), late c7 or c8, w face, St John the Evangelist(?) (p. 153)
12. Bewcastle Cross, late c7 or c8, w face, Christ (p. 153)
13. Warwick (C), St Leonard, apse, Norman (p. 661)

14　Kirkby Lonsdale
　　(W), St Mary, N
　　arcade, early C12
　　(p. 458)
15.　Great Salkeld
　　(C), St Cuthbert,
　　S doorway, C12,
　　detail (p. 384)
16.　Bridekirk (C),
　　St Bride, font, by
　　Rikard, mid-C12,
　　E side (p. 183)

17. Carlisle Cathedral (C), nave, C12, S side (p. 228)
18. Furness Abbey (L), S transept and S cloister range, with chapter house entrance, C12 and early C13 (p. 356)
19. Furness Abbey (L), chapter house, looking E, c. 1230–40 (p. 357)

20. Lanercost Priory (C), C12 and C13 (p. 481)
21. Carlisle Cathedral (C), C12–C15, exterior from the SW (p. 225)
22. Shap Abbey (W), tower, begun *c.* 1500 (p. 616)
23. Calder Bridge (C), Calder Abbey, C13, nave and crossing, from the W (p. 215)

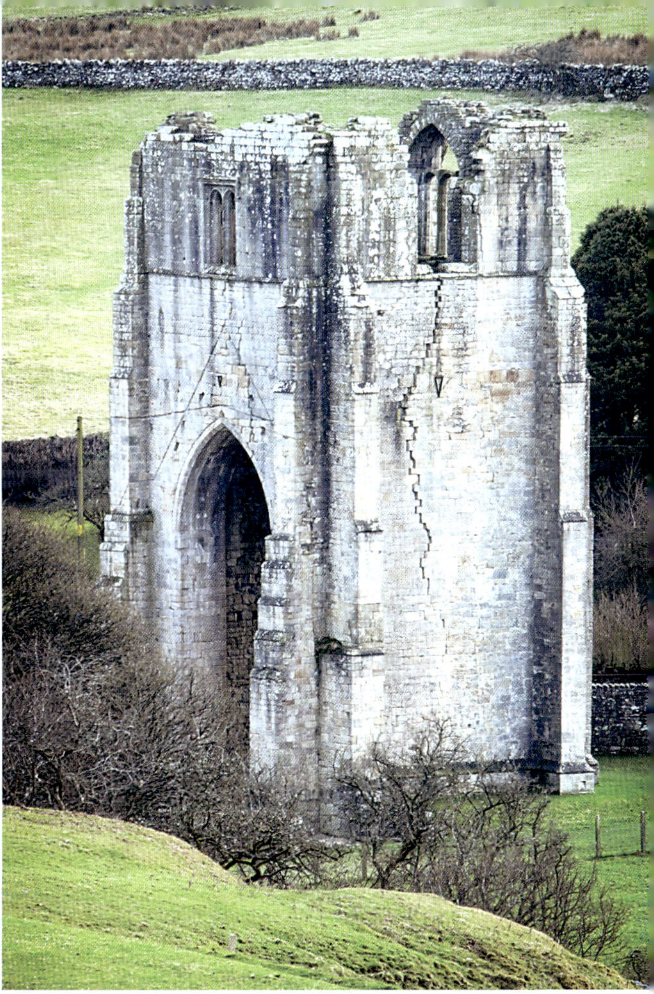

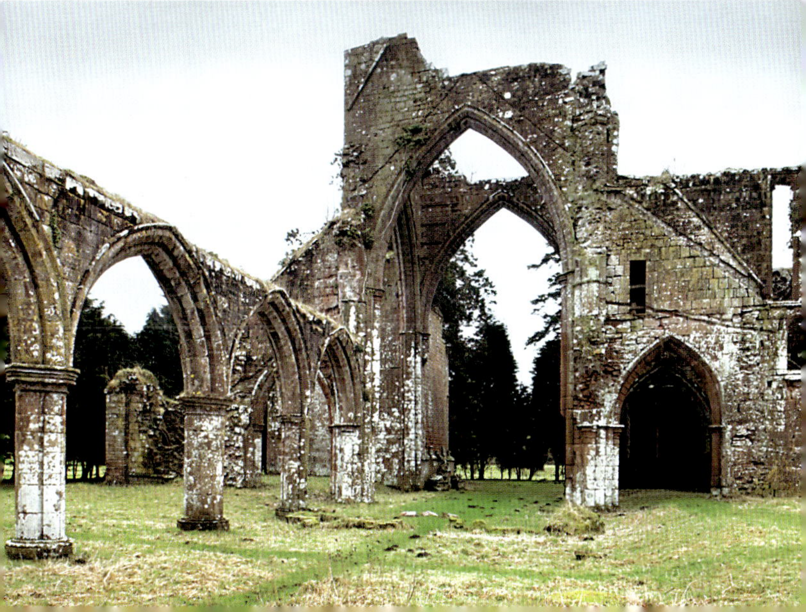

24. Carlisle Cathedral (C), choir, early C14, detail of capital (p. 230)
25. Cartmel Priory (L), Harrington monument, *c.* 1345 (p. 271)
26. Carlisle Cathedral (C), choir, *c.* 1220–*c.* 1355, from the W (p. 228)

27. Carlisle Castle (C), C12 and later, from the s (p. 240)
28. Brough Castle (W), *c.* 1100 and later, from the s (p. 189)
29. Rose Castle (C), mid-c14, restored 1828–30 by Thomas Rickman, from the NE, showing Bell's Tower, centre, and chapel, left (p. 591)

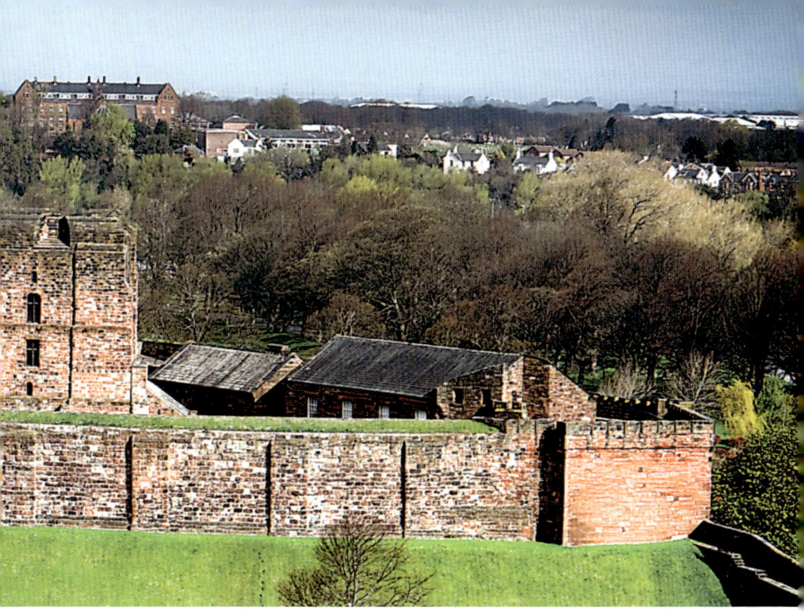

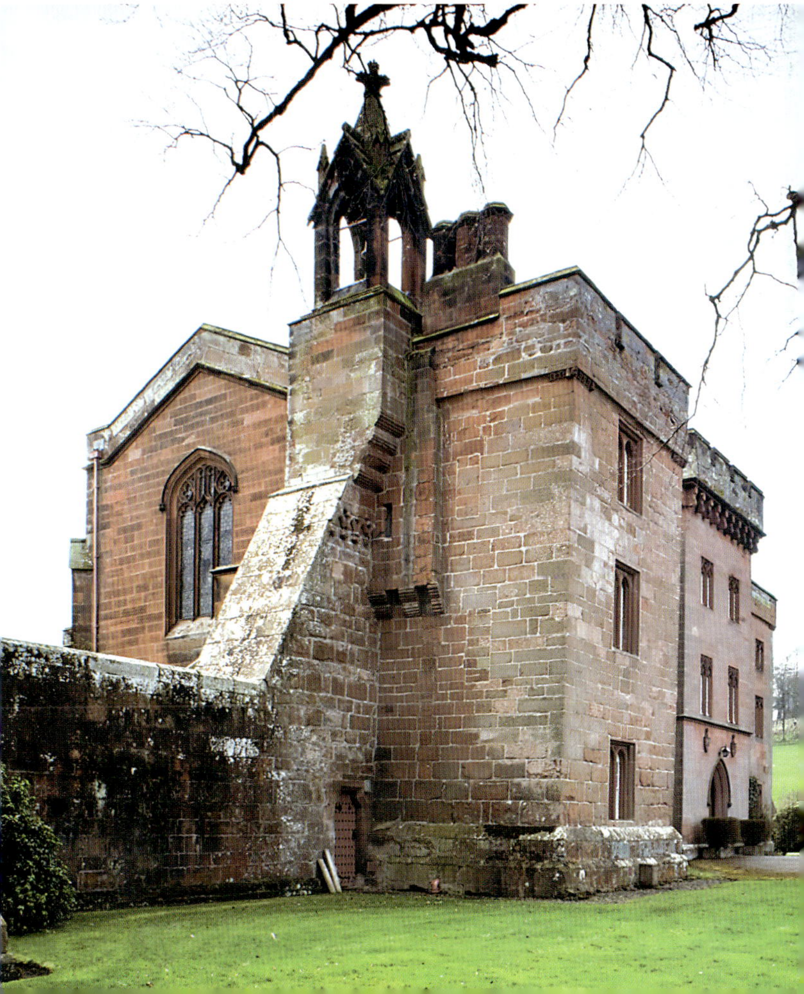

30. Askerton Castle (C), C13 or C14 and later (p. 120)
31. Yanwath Hall (W), late C14 and C15 (p. 708)

32. Newton Arlosh (C), St John, *c.* 1303, extended to the N by Sara Losh, 1843 (p. 554)
33. Bowness-on-Solway (C), Drumburgh Castle, C13 or C14, remodelled 1518 and 1680, N front (p. 164)

34. Grasmere (W), St Oswald, interior, N aisle and roof, 1490–1500 and *c.* 1562 (p. 374)
35. Brough (W), St Michael, N side, late C14 and later; tower, 1513, by Thomas Blenkinsop (p. 188)
36. Boltongate (C), All Saints, interior, probably C15 (p. 158)

37. Greystoke (W), St Andrew, E window, probably late C15, detail (p. 386)
38. Bowness-on-Windermere (L), St Martin, E window, 1480s, detail (p. 166)
39. Cartmel Fell (L), St Anthony, E window, c. 1520, detail (p. 274)
40. Carlisle (C), Deanery, painted ceiling, c. 1500–20, detail (p. 238)
41. Carlisle Castle (C), Keep, prisoners' carvings, probably 1480s, detail (p. 244)

42. Cartmel Priory (L), stalls, 1430–40 and after 1618, detail (p. 271)
43. Brougham (W), St Wilfrid, screen, probably C17, detail (p. 197)
44. Carlisle Cathedral (C), Salkeld Screen, *c.* 1541 (p. 232)

45. Sizergh Castle (W), Inlaid Chamber, after 1575 (p. 623)
46. Kirkby-in-Furness (L), Kirkby Hall, wall paintings, later c16 (p. 457)
47. Levens Hall (W), mostly late c16, E front, with garden, 1690s (p. 492)

.8. Hutton-in-the-Forest (C), Gallery Wing, 1640s (p. 415)

.9. Maulds Meaburn Hall (W), staircase, probably 1676 (p. 518)

0. Hutton-in-the-Forest (C), N front, centrepiece by Edward Addison,
   c. 1680 (p. 416)

1. Moresby Hall (C), S front by William Thackeray, c. 1670 (p. 531)

52. Ivegill (C), Highhead Castle, attributed to John Brougham, *c.* 1740–5, N front (p. 426)
53. Warcop Hall (W), dining room, 1744 (p. 661)
54. Appleby (W), White House, attributed to Henry Bellas or Bellhouse, 1764–5 (p. 111)
55. Keswick (C), Derwent Bay, *c.* 1790 (p. 452)

56. Bowness-on-Windermere (W), Belle Isle, by John Plaw, begun 1774 (p. 169)
57. Penrith (C), Tynefield House, 1804 (p. 574)
58. Lowther Castle (W), by Robert Smirke, begun 1806, N front (p. 505)
59. Houghton (C), Brunstock, by Thomas Rickman & Henry Hutchinson, 1828–30 (p. 413)

60. Greystoke Castle (C), w front by Anthony Salvin, 1837–45 and 1875–8; tower behind, C14 (p. 387)
61. Barbon (W), Whelprigg House, by George Webster, 1834 (p. 128)

62. Wray Castle (L), exterior, by J.J. Lightfoot, 1840–7 (p. 703)
63. Wray Castle (L), upper landing (p. 703)

64. Alston (C), Front Street, bastle-type house, C18 (p. 96)
65. Sizergh Castle (W), bank barn, probably C16 (p. 624)

56. Troutbeck (W), Town End Barn, dated 1666 (p. 641)
57. Coniston (L), Low Yewdale, C17 and later (p. 298)

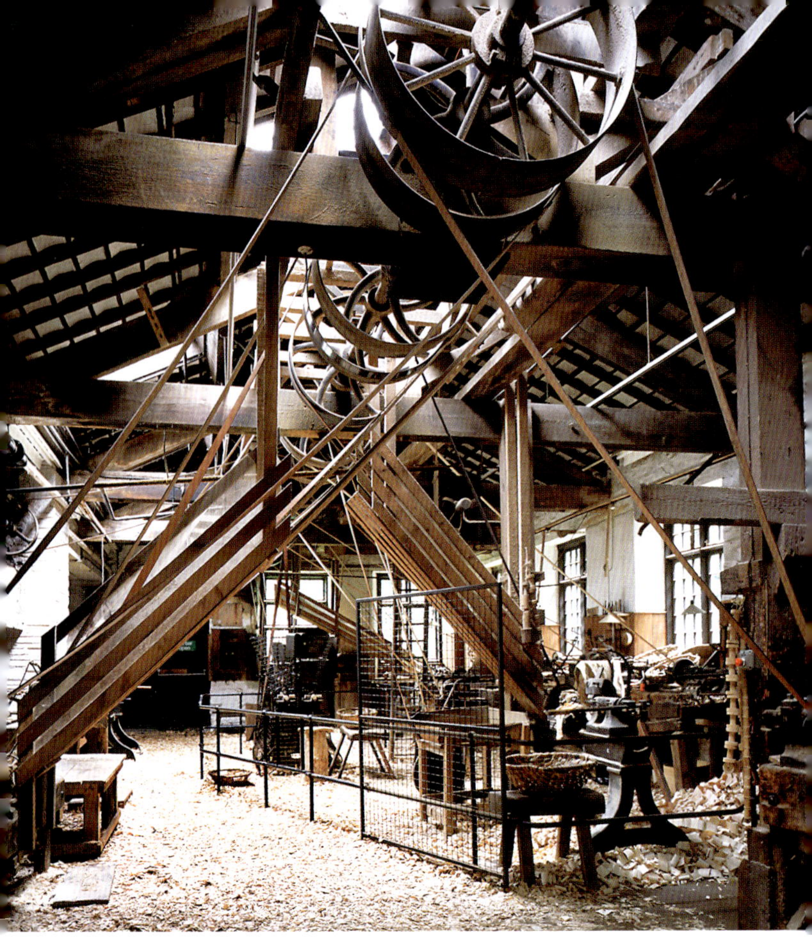

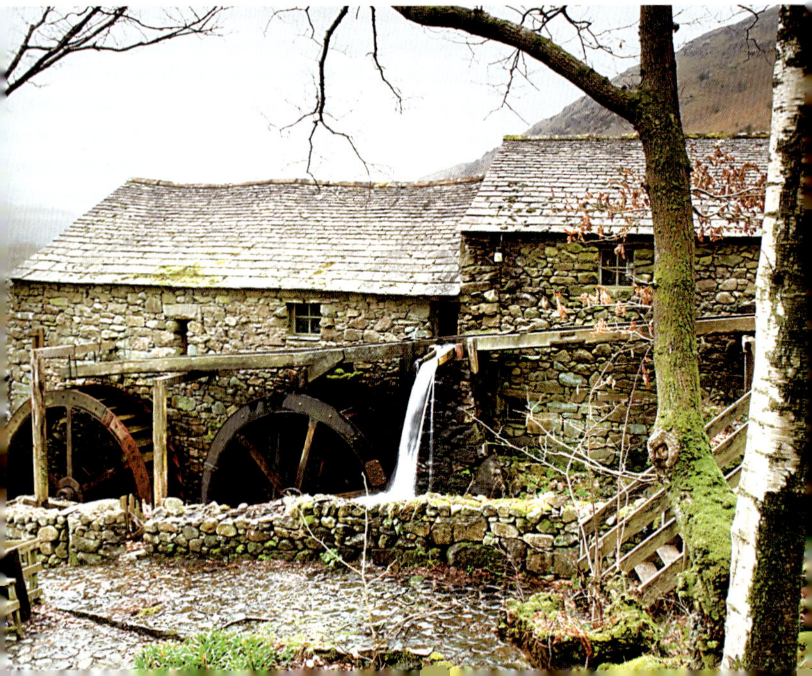

68. Finsthwaite (L), Stott Park Bobbin mill, 1835, interior (p. 349)
69. Boot (C), Eskdale Mill, before 1750 (p. 342)
70. Carlisle (C), Dixon's (Shaddon) Mill, by Richard Tattersall, 1835–7 (p. 261)

71. Lowther (W), St Michael, monument to Sir John Lowther †1637 and Sir John Lowther †1675, attributed to Jasper Latham (p. 507)

72. Appleby (W), St Lawrence, monument to Margaret, Countess of Cumberland, †1616, attributed to Maximilian Colt (p. 105)

73. Wetheral (C), Holy Trinity, monument to Lady Maria Howard †1789, by Joseph Nollekens (p. 668)

74. Sebergham (C), St Mary, monument to Thomas Watson †1823, by Musgrave Lewthwaite Watson, detail (p. 610)

"INTO THY HANDS I COMMEND MY SPIRIT; FOR THOU
"HAST REDEEMED ME, O LORD, THOU GOD OF TRUTH."

RESPECTED AND REGRETTED.

ERECTED BY HIS WIDOW MARY WATSON

ΑΓΡΥΠΝΕΙΤΕ ΟΤΚ ΟΙΔΑΤΕ ΓΑΡ ΠΟΤΕ Ο ΚΑΙΡΟΣ ΕΣΤΙΝ

75. Garrigill (C), Redwing Chapel, 1756 (p. 361)
76. Dean (C), Pardshaw, Friends' Meeting House, 1728–9 (p. 330)
77. Whitehaven (C), St James, attributed to Christopher Myers, 1752–3, interior (p. 673)
78. Kirkandrews-on-Esk (C), St Andrew, 1775 (p. 453)

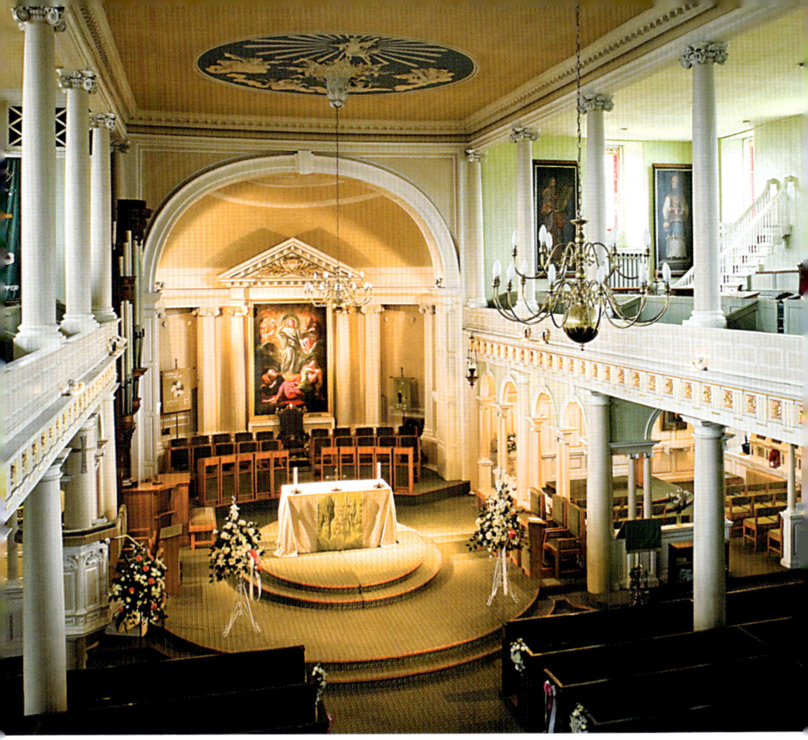

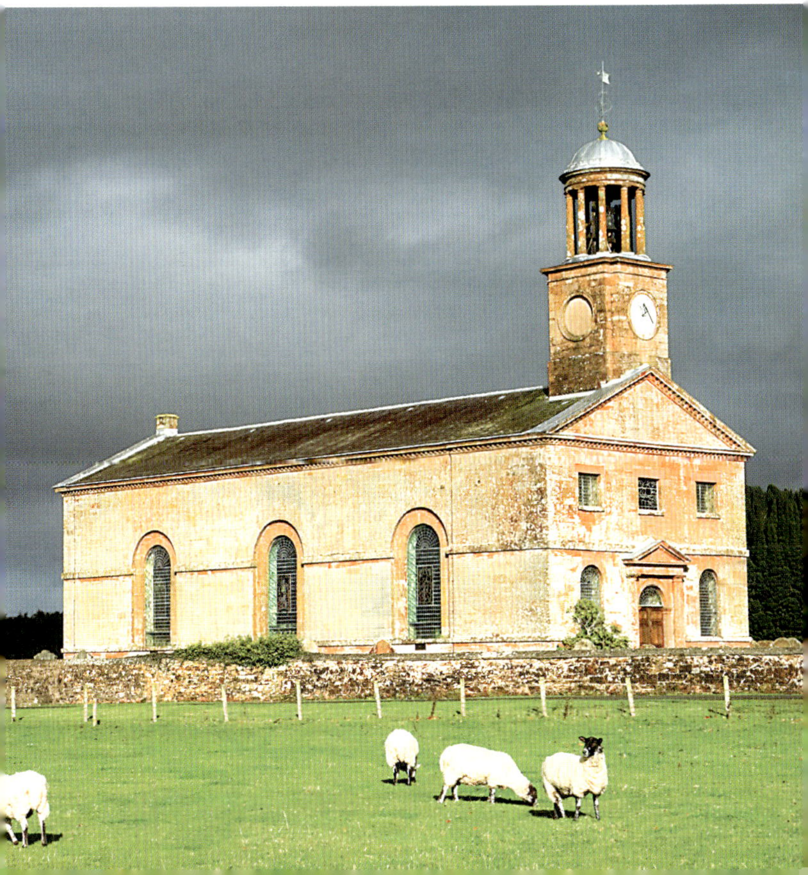

79. Workington (C), St John, by Thomas Hardwick, 1821–3, with lock-up, 1825, right (p. 699)
80. Lowther (W), mausoleum of the 2nd Earl of Lonsdale, by Benjamin Baud, 1857, with parish church, mostly of 1686 (tower altered 1856), right (pp. 508 and 506)
81. Crosby Ravensworth (W), St Lawrence, SW porch, by George Gibson, 1811–12 (p. 308)
82. Wreay (C), St Mary, by Sara Losh, completed 1842, apse interior (p. 704)

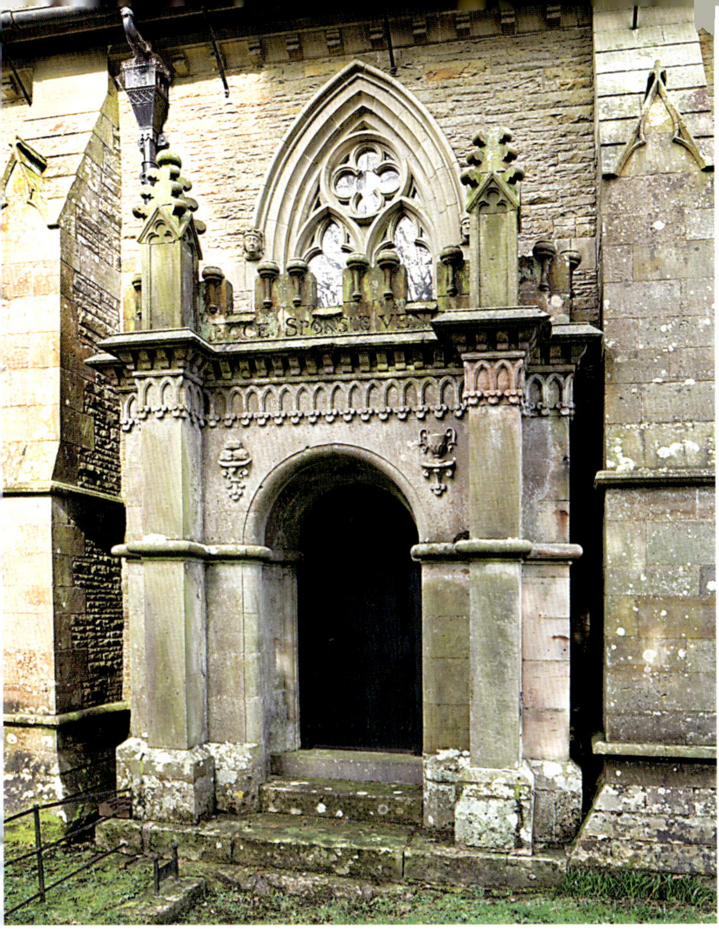

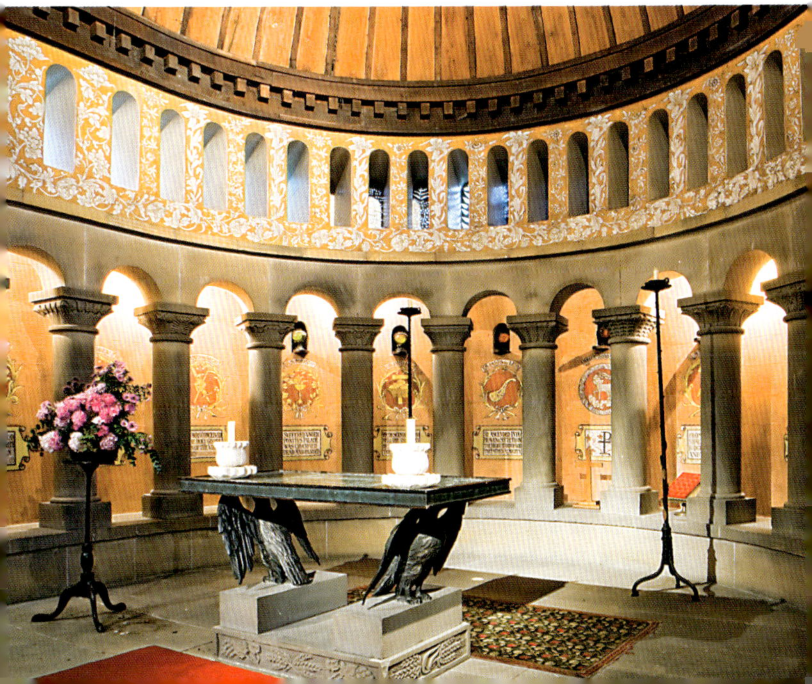

83. Crosby-on-Eden (C), St John Evangelist, by R.W. Billings, 1854 (p. 305)
84. Bridekirk (C), St Bride, by Cory & Ferguson, 1868–70 (p. 183)

85. Carlisle (C), Lowther Street Congregational Church, by John Nichol, 1842–3 (p. 240)
86. Field Broughton (L), St Peter, by Paley, Austin & Paley, 1892–4 (p. 347)

87. St Bees (C), St Mary and St Bega, chancel interior, remodelled by William Butterfield, after 1855 (p. 597)
88. Workington (C), Our Lady Star of the Sea (R.C), by E.W. Pugin, 1873–6, interior (p. 699)
89. Brampton (C), St Martin, by Philip Webb, 1877–8, interior (p. 178)

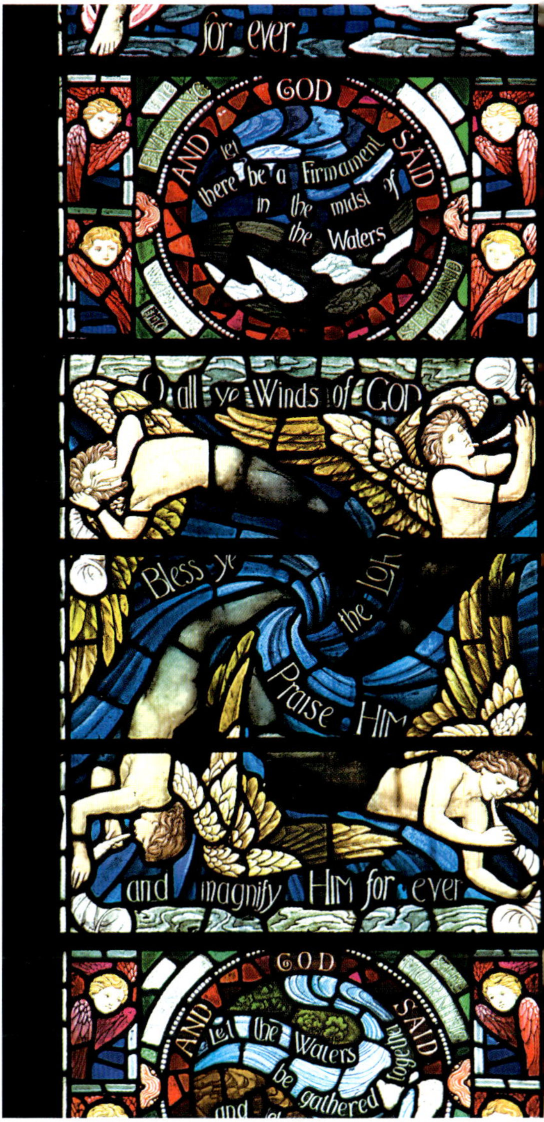

90. Brampton (C), St Martin, stained glass by Morris & Co., detail of E window, 1880 (p. 178)

91. Irton (C), St Paul, stained glass by John Scott & Son, *c.* 1870, detail (p. 422)

92. Staveley (W), St James, E window by Morris & Co., 1881, detail (p. 629)

93. Casterton (W), Holy Trinity, Benedicite window by Henry Holiday, 1895 (p. 275)

94. Carlisle (C), Citadel, by Robert Smirke, 1810s, incorporating a tower of 1541–3 by Stefan von Haschenperg, right (p. 244)
95. Carlisle (C), Infirmary, by Richard Tattersall, 1830–2 (p. 264)
96. Carlisle (C), Warwick Road, early C19 houses (p. 223)
97. Barrow-in-Furness (L), Town Hall, by W.H. Lynn, completed 1887, from the NE (p. 135)
98. Barrow-in-Furness (L), Michaelson Road tenements by Paley & Austin, 1872–4 (p. 141)

99. Kirkby Stephen (W),
    Temperance Hall, 1856 (p. 470)
100. Shap Wells (W), Queen Victoria
    monument, 1842, sculpture by
    Thomas Bland (p. 618)
101. Wigton (C), memorial fountain
    by J.T. Knowles Sen., 1872–3,
    sculpture by Thomas Woolner
    (p. 685)
102. Yanwath (W), Eamont
    Bridge, South African War
    memorial, 1901, sculpture by
    W. Grisenthwaite, detail (p. 711)
103. Barrow-in-Furness (L), Ramsden
    monument, by Matthew Noble,
    1872, detail (p. 138)

104. Grange-over-Sands (L), railway station, by E.G. Paley, 1872 (p. 373)
105. Carlisle (C), Citadel railway station, by Sir William Tite, 1846–7 (p. 248)
106. Ravenstonedale (W), Smardale railway viaduct, 1875 (p. 588)

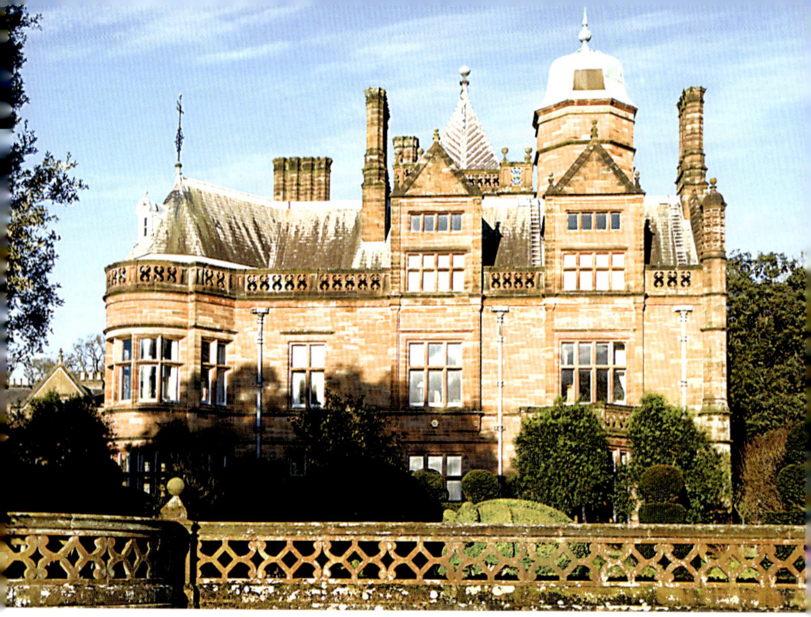

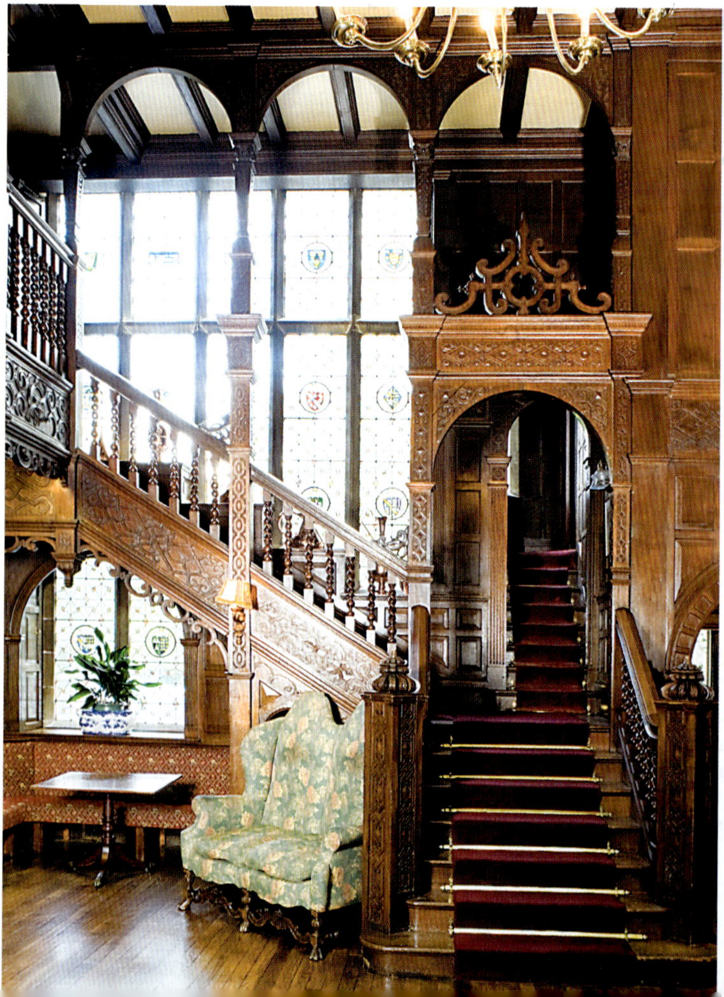

107. Holker Hall (L), garden front, by Paley & Austin, 1871–3 (p. 410)
108. Troutbeck (W), Langdale Chase, by J.L. Ball, J.T. Lee and Joseph
     Pattinson, 1898–94, hall interior (p. 644)
109. Bowness-on-Windermere (W), Broadleys, by C.F.A. Voysey, 1898–9
     (p. 173)

110. Windermere (W), Waterbeck, by W.L. Dolman, 1913, garden by Thomas Mawson (p. 694)
111. Bowness-on-Windermere (W), Moor Crag, by C.F.A. Voysey, 1899–1900 (p. 174)

12. Bowness-on-Windermere (W), Blackwell, by M.H. Baillie Scott, 1898–1900, Great Hall (p. 171)

13. Furness Abbey (L), Abbey House, by Sir Edwin Lutyens, 1913–14, entrance front (p. 360)

114. Bowness-on-Windermere (W), Long Dales, by Basil Ward, 1961 (p. 174)
115. Ulverston (L), Lanternhouse, converted by Francis Roberts, 1987 (p. 65)
116. Conishead Priory (L), Kadampa Buddhist Temple, by Geshe Kelsang Gyatso with Mark Tole, 1995–7 (p. 293)
117. Millom (C), St Luke, w window by Peter Strong, 2002, detail (p. 526)

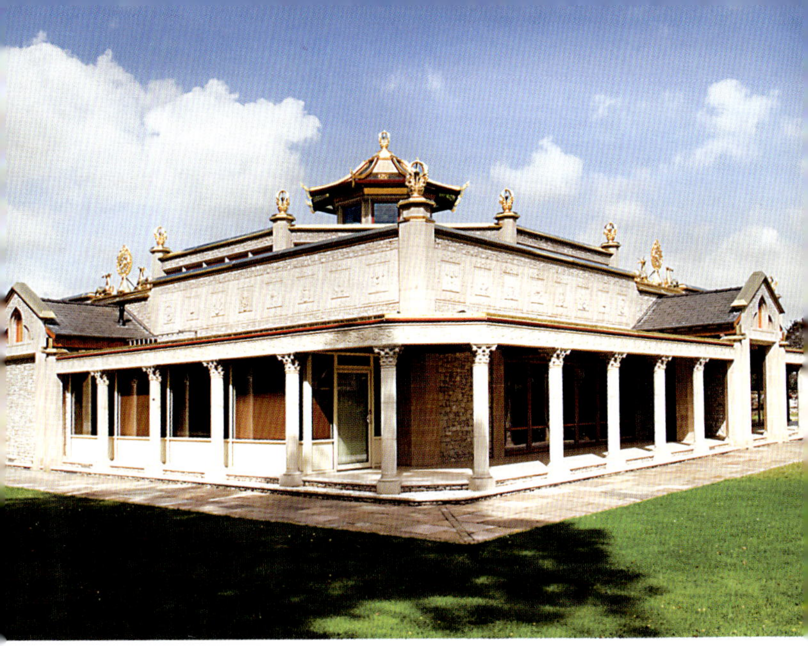

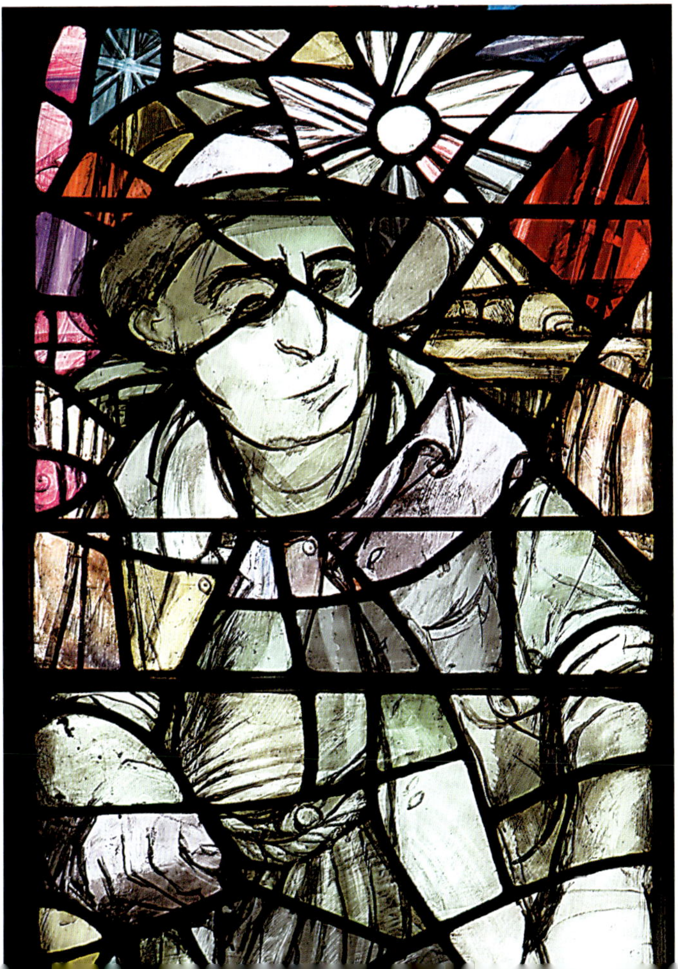

118. Coniston (L), near Low Tilberthwaite Farm, sheepfold reconstructed by Andy Goldsworthy, 2003 (p. 298)
119. Windermere (W), Lakeland Limited store, by Hanson Walford Marston, 2003–5 (p. 689)

GLASSONBY (C)

Served by the church of Addingham, ½ m. s, which was lost in
the River Eden some time in the C15 or C16 and rebuilt on higher
ground.

St Michael, Addingham. All by itself. Latest and simplest
Perp. Chancel 1512, re-roofed and given a new chancel arch,
wide and low, in 1786. A low-pitched roof can be traced in the
E wall. Further restoration in 1898, when 'an ornamental
chancel arch of plaster in imitation Norman style [presumably
early C19] was removed'. Porch rebuilt in 1840. Built into it is
a piece of zigzag. – STAINED GLASS. Chancel, by *Wailes*, 1862
etc. By *Heaton, Butler & Bayne*, s aisle (Faith and Fortitude,
1902), and N aisle (†1904; King David and St Cecilia). W
window, a spirited St Michael and the Dragon signed *S. M.
Scott*, 1973. – SCULPTURE, recovered from the river in 1913.
Two parts of a C9 cross, with interlace and vine scroll. C10
hogback with carved roof shingles. Cross socket with an incised
frame and drillings around the hole. – In the churchyard a
standing CROSS of the Viking age, C10–C11. Rather grotesque,
with hammerhead top and bottom arms; the cross seeming
subservient to the rectangle with holes. Incoherent scrollwork
over the whole.

BASTLE HOUSE in the yard of White House Farm. Stone steps
to the living accommodation on the upper floor. The upper
doorway has the Tudor-arched lintel of the late C16. Few and
small rectangular windows fitted with iron bars, and one in the
gable; so there was an attic. Entry to the ground-floor byre is
in the end wall, fitted with drawbar slots. The walls are easily
a yard thick. The farmhouse has an inscription WW 1723
appearing not over the front door, which is largely for show,
but over the door of the through passage in the lower wing,
behind the stack – the usual Cumbrian entry.

LONG MEG AND HER DAUGHTERS, Hunsonby. A huge stone
circle, 120 yds (109 metres) across – the third largest in
England, after Avebury (Wilts.) and Stanton Drew (Somerset) – of massive granite boulders weighing up to 30 tons,
on a sloping, dished site. Some stones in the W arc may be
set in a low bank. Two additional boulders, outside the circumference on the SW, mark an entrance. Further out here,
the tallest stone, Long Meg herself, is 12 ft (3.7 metres) high,
of red sandstone decorated with concentric rings, cup-and-
rings, and a spiral. The arc of the circle is flattened on the
N, probably respecting the ditch of a large earthwork (now
levelled) which enclosed the area around the modern farm
buildings.

LITTLE MEG, 700 yds NE. A small setting of rough boulders
(with others added from the field) which probably protected a
central burial. One stone carved with a spiral and concentric
rings.

GLEASTON CASTLE (L)

Scanty remains of a squareish curtain wall with corner towers of different shapes and sizes, perhaps never finished on the N. It was probably begun *c.* 1325 by John de Harrington. The details of construction and the form of the towers compare to Piel, nearby (q.v.). In 1540 Leland described it as a ruin, although part was inhabited until the late C17. The principal tower, 92 by 53 ft (28 by 16 metres), is in the NW corner. It stands in one corner up to *c.* 30 ft (9 metres). Immediately S of this is a narrow gateway. Midway down the W wall is a projection, once possibly a mid-tower. The SW tower is less than half the size of the NW tower. It stands up almost to the top and also has a straight staircase. The SE tower again has a straight staircase. On the first floor is a fireplace. Little of the NE tower is preserved.

GLENRIDDING (W)

Dark mining village on the SE shore of the long Z of Ullswater, now given over to Lake District pleasures.

GLENRIDDING HOUSE. At the water's edge. It was built for the Rev. Henry Askew of Greystoke, before 1819. Regency villa with shallow pyramidal roof, encircled by a pretty iron trellis veranda and balcony. Two canted bays towards the lake. Floor-length windows on both storeys. Its low-slung elegance makes a great contrast with the lumpish Victorian INN ON THE LAKE next door.

GLENCOYNE FARM. Flagship National Trust farm, donated by Sir S. H. Scott in 1948. The largest hill farm in the Lake District: 4,000 acres. The white farmhouse and its line of barns nestle into a fold in the fellside, while to the W an unbeatable panorama opens out of Ullswater at its widest turn. The house has untypical crowstepped gables, and two big round stacks of Westmorland type. It is larger than usual, the result of converting the low-end barn into a second dwelling unit, now the downhouse. The earlier dwelling is uphill, with entry as usual from the cross-passage behind the stack. Stone heck with a built-in bench and two spice cupboards. Stair with turned balusters in an oval projection at the back. Downhouse, with its own stack and fire-window, dated 1629 over the fireplace, with the initials TH and DH for Thomas and Dorothy Harrison. Specially designed SHEEP PEN, the first of many on National Trust farms, by *Bill Garlick*.

INDUSTRIAL REMAINS. 1½ m. up the Glenridding beck, the remains of GREENSIDE MINE, the area's last and largest lead mine. Between 1838 and 1961 it yielded 268,888 tons of lead and 1,222,288 oz. of silver. The former joiners' shop, stables, offices, miners' hostel and a smelter have all been adapted for reuse as hostels or climbers' bothies, but retain little of their original form. Above the l. bank of the main beck run the extensive remains of leats which brought water down from KEPPEL COVE RESERVOIR. An earth dam here burst in 1927. Rebuilt in mass concrete, it failed again in 1931, and was abandoned. N of the mine, up the valley of the Swart Beck, the remains of a masonry CHIMNEY which served the smelter stretch up the E flank of Raise for ¾ m., to the 2,250 ft (690-metre) contour.

GOSFORTH (C)

ST MARY. A decent, gently quirky rebuilding in the Dec style by *C. J. Ferguson*, 1896–9. Nave with two-stage bellcote and S porch, chancel, N aisle, vestry and organ chamber. Ferguson's red ashlar is easily distinguished from the rougher stone of an earlier reconstruction of 1789. Below that are the Norman footings; a blocked Norman doorway remains on the S, with a continous roll moulding. N arcade with nice capitals. A run of six lancets behind rere-arches of four and two openings looks into a little courtyard formed when the PARISH ROOM was built in 1995. Note too the little high-level balcony at the W end. The re-set C14 chancel arch rests on Norman imposts, with capitals wildly decorated. On the N three moustachioed and boggle-eyed heads, one with hands covering its mouth, another with what might be honeysuckle leaves issuing from it. On the S three more faces connected by a beaded twist. – Chinese BELL of 1839, captured from Anukry Fort on the Canton river, given 1844. – STAINED GLASS. Mostly late C19, mostly by *Ward & Hughes*, 1883–94. W lancets by *G. J. Baguley*. St Cecilia, chancel SE, by *F. Pickett & Co.*, c. 1954. – MONUMENTS. C13 grave-covers built into the porch. Outside, chancel N wall, John Hudlestone †1834, with an engaging lady and anchor in relief.

SCULPTURE. A unique Viking-age assemblage. All is of the first part of the C10, and much may be by the same artist. CROSS. About 15 ft (4.5 metres) high, amazingly slender, of red sandstone. A great contrast to the classically calm Bewcastle, by two centuries the elder. The shaft starts round, with interlocking decoration like crochet, and turns square. The junction is hanging semicircles. The flat parts are densely inhabited by plaited and knotted creatures, representing perhaps the forces of evil, and small but dynamic people, any way up. Calverley, Parker and Collingwood in the 1880s identified the scenes with the Viking Ragnorök, the Doom of the Gods. Only the cross-head, small and ringed, with triquetra on both sides, and the Crucifixion on the E, are Christian. The correspondences between the scenes and sides, and between the Viking

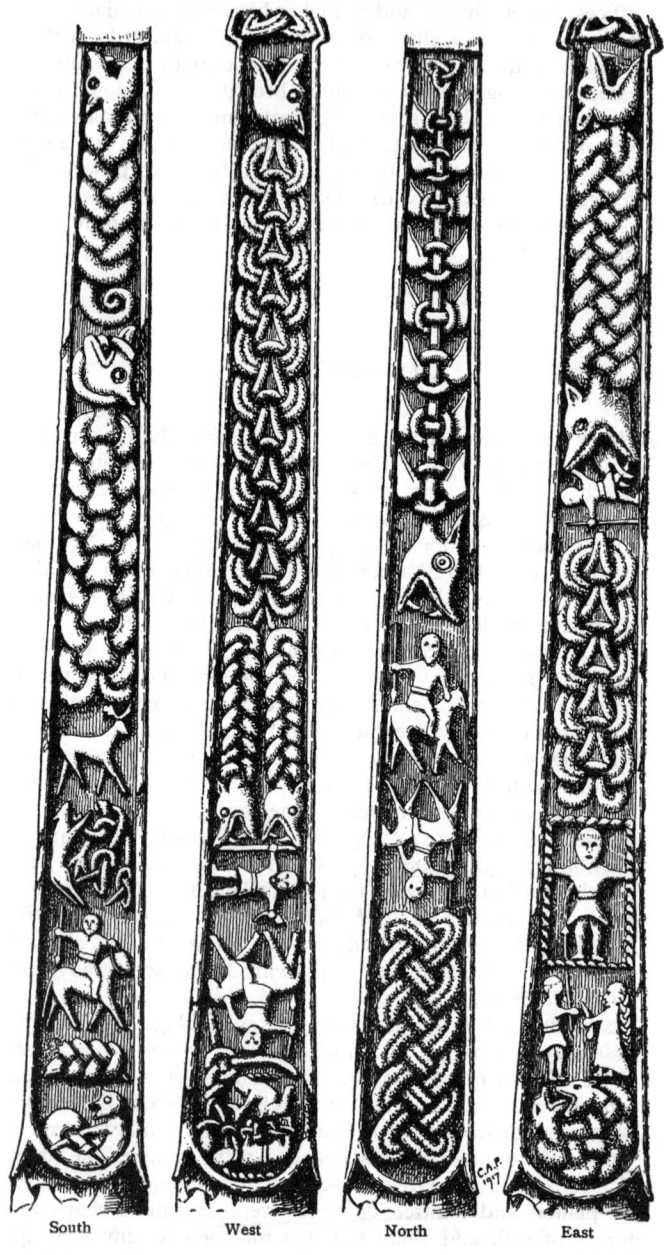

South   West   North   East

Gosforth Cross.
Drawings, 1917

and Christian stories, suggest that it was an aid to deep contemplation, which we may not yet have fully fathomed.

On the S SIDE, starting from the bottom, a reclining animal something like a seal. Then a horseman with downturned spear; a leaping wolf and stylized thicket; and a stag: Odin perhaps, with Mimir and the wolf Garm? At the top a plaited snake eating its own tail, and a knotted snake. – W SIDE. From the bottom again, the bound figure of Loki, with a long plait of hair, at the mercy of his enemy Sigyn in a gown, who holds a poison cup. A horseman upside-down, and a sideways figure with staff and horn corresponding to Heimdall, the watchman god. Above, wolves with knotted bodies, and a crocheted dragon. – N SIDE. Plaited knot, then two horsemen, one upside-down, and a splendid eight-winged dragon, its tail tied in a triquetra. – The E SIDE bears at its centre, in a rope frame, the Crucifixion, though there is no cross. Christ's blood flows from his side, and below are the Roman soldier with spear, and Mary Magdalene with a long plait and alabastron.* Above is a two-headed dragon; in the forked-tongued mouth of the lower one is the figure of Vidar, with spear, avenging his father's death.

A second cross, only 7 ft away (cf. Penrith) was cut down in 1789 to form a sundial. There may have been one or even two more. Two broken CROSS-HEADS are inside, built into the N aisle. Likewise the FISHING STONE. Thor goes fishing, with the giant Hymir with his axe, and an ox head as bait, for the World Serpent. The representation of a boat is rare (cf. also Lowther). Two HOGBACKS were found in 1896–7 in the foundations. The 'Saint's tomb' has the cross-less Crucifixion at both ends. The 'Warrior's tomb' is so called for the procession of men armed with spears and overlapping shields (cf. Lowther).

GRAVEDIGGERS' HUT, NE corner of the churchyard. Built of left-overs, including more C13 grave-covers, pieces of zigzag, and a corbel.

GOSFORTH HALL (hotel), NW. Two-and-a-half-storey house built by Robert Copley in 1658 (datestone now on a barn), probably consisting of a hall and kitchen in line W–E, with a spiral stair rising two storeys at the back. The kitchen retains its broad segmental-headed fireplace and integral doorway to the stair. The roof is framed with upper crucks. In 1679 Robert and Isabella (plaster overmantel) added a withdrawing room in front (S) of the kitchen, making an L, which was later extended back as well, making the house T-shaped. The additions retain two- and three-light mullioned-and-transomed windows. The ball finials on gables and gatepiers are the only up-to-date features.

The LIBRARY on the main street is a house dated 1628 and inscribed John et Margrat Shearwen. Mullioned windows

---

* Richard Bailey and Rosemary Cramp connect the particularities of this scene to a C10 coloured stone plaque originally from Penrith, derived from Irish metalwork.

under a continuous hood, inglenook fireplace. The rear wing, with its own inglenook, may be part of a house called Gosforth Gate, mentioned in 1598.

STEELFIELD HOUSE, at the W end of the village. For Sir Humphrey Senhouse, *c.* 1840. As Greek as can be; even its gatepiers are sturdy Greek Doric columns – a rare conceit. Two storeys. Doric four-column loggia *in antis.*

GRANGE-IN-BORROWDALE (C)

2010

The grange of Borrowdale was granted to Fountains Abbey in 1210–12 as a vaccary or summer pasture.

HOLY TRINITY. 1860–1, founded by Margaret Heathcote. With its graded roof, slab boundary wall and churchyard monuments it makes quite an exhibition of slate, and it is interestingly styleless. Nave and chancel in one, with a bellcote, and narthex/porch (1882). Sloping buttresses. Round-arched windows, the voussoirs cut to a point, like fangs. The beams of the tunnel-vaulted ceiling are treated the same way. – WAR MEMORIAL, 1922. Green wheel-cross with grapes and a dove.

BRIDGE over two arms of the Derwent. Early C19. A humpbacked slate arch carries the road over each channel, and a slate embankment connects them. Parapets are continuous throughout, giving the impression of a single oddly undulating bridge.

VILLAGE. Drawings for village houses of the 1850s and 1860s are marked TAT, for Thomas Threlkeld, and signed *C. L. Newby* of Keswick. The Threlkelds built the METHODIST CHAPEL too, in 1894.

BARROW HOUSE (Youth Hostel), 1¾ m. NNE. The last of *Joseph Pocklington*'s three houses (*see* Keswick, p. 450), and the best-preserved. Nearly square double pile with two wings, one containing the stair, originally under gauche lean-to roofs. Pocklington started building in 1787, but he tinkered with it, replacing the front Venetian windows with two full-height canted bay windows close together, and extending the E wing in 1798. Stepped tripartite windows in the wings. The house centres on a great upstairs dining room overlooking the lake, 'a noble room, made for the whole neighbourhood', wrote Coleridge. Pocklington's account book records 'Plaisterer Allin [*James Allen* of Whitehaven], £16 16s. od.' Coloured Adamish chimneypiece and marble relief of Belisarius by *Robert Shout* of High Holborn. Other rooms, despite being called 'mere pidgeon holes' by Coleridge, have enriched Venetian windows and fireplaces by *Nutter* of Carlisle and *Dawson* of Whitehaven. Even the cascade behind the house was partly Pocklington's creation. In 2006 it was tapped by a black plastic pipe to generate electricity: saving the environment in one sense, spoiling it in another.

Pocklington couldn't resist tinkering with the BOWDER STONE either, 2½ m. s. In 1789 he built a custodian's cottage, and 'improved' the stone itself, putting a ladder up it and excavating underneath to make it more dramatic.

BORROWDALE HOTEL is one of several on the B5289. Dated 1866, large and brash, with ingenious use in the porch and bay of built-up and turned slate to construct a fussy three-dimensional object out of a material that only cleaves in two dimensions. NEWTON PLACE, over the road, was built c. 1850 for Joseph Bell; another of Derwentwater's follies. Tower-like, with prominent angle buttresses. The porch is buttressed too. It looks as though intended to go higher, but is finished instead with a blunt pyramid roof. HIGH LODORE FARM, immediately N. C18 cottage, three-bay farmhouse, and two-storey barn all in line behind a yew tree. The house has a central porch made of four pieces of slate, but the white-edged doorway through the barn behind the house chimney is the commonly used entrance.

WATENDLATH, 1½ m. SW. Long dale-head arbour of fields, high above Derwentwater. Given to Fountains Abbey as a vaccary in the C12 by Aelicia Pipard or de Rumeli. A tarn, a car park, and three C17 farms. The road was only made in 1930; before that it was the focus of a network of tracks over the various passes. CAFFLE HOUSE has its firehouse in the middle, marked by the small fire-window under the single big stack. Bower and buttery are as usual facing the fire, and in this case the downhouse is at the other end, with its fire back-to-back with the main one. The stair is at the back in an outshut, and the usual entrance at the back also, in baffle position. STEPS END FARM has a very wide porch, with steps within it, and a good wide door. It has retained its wide deep-set windows. FOLD HEAD FARM, nearest the tarn, has a stone half-spiral stair opening straight out of the firehouse. All three farms were bought by the National Trust in 1960, with the whole valley.

PACKHORSE BRIDGES. A most attractive early C18 packhorse bridge crosses the beck at the outlet from the tarn. Single segmental span, very narrow, low parapets, hump-back. 2 m. N of the hamlet, ASHNESS BRIDGE, also single-span. Widened and strengthened for motor traffic in the C20, but still a striking feature in the famous view over Keswick and the northern reaches of Derwentwater to Skiddaw.

GRANGE-OVER-SANDS (L)

The name is a statement of fact: Cartmel Priory had a grange here, although nothing is left of it, at the point where travellers crossing the sands from Lancaster made dry land. A knot of little streets climbing off the shore by the Commodore Inn off Main Street represents the pre-C19 settlement. With the opening of the

Furness Railway in 1857 the town developed as a genteel resort, with hotels, boarding houses and bungalows rather than big villas.

St Paul, Crown Hill. Miss Sarah Anne Clarke, a holiday visitor from Liverpool, opened an appeal in 1851. Nave, short chancel, porch and baptistery were built in 1852–3, by *J. Murray*. N and S aisles were added in 1861 and 1867, by *T. D. Barry* of Liverpool, and in 1875 the chancel was lengthened, with a new organ chamber. The W porch is dated 1904. In 1912 a total rebuild was contemplated, but war intervened. Instead, and not until 1932–3, the E end was rebuilt with a new polygonal apsed chancel and SE chapel by *Austin & Paley*, i.e. *H. A. Paley*. Triple-gabled exterior with a bell-turret of 1853 between the gables of nave and S aisle. The interior is low and spreading, so the roofs dominate. Peculiar arcades with columns of dark polished stone set in pairs in depth, not much thicker than colonnettes. Each has its own capital, and the two then support a single block for the arcade arch. It looks flimsy, but does open up diagonal vistas. Fine oak furnishings of the 1950s including the CHURCHWARDENS' SEATS (W end) and the wood-covered FONT. – STAINED GLASS. S chapel E window by *S. Evans*, 1888. Otherwise C20, by *Shrigley & Hunt* or *Abbott & Co.*, mostly signed.

  CLOCK TOWER, by the church. 1912. Edgar Wood-ish, with battered diagonal buttresses. Small band of bell-openings, short octagonal spire.

METHODIST CHURCH, Kents Bank Road. Signed by *Ernest Bates* of Manchester, 1874, who may well have been proud of it. Gothic, with a very large Geometrical window over the narthex entrance. The side windows have powerful plate tracery, more stone than glass.

St Charles (R.C.), Kents Bank Road. 1883–4, by *E. Simpson* of Bradford. A plain little building, minimally Gothic, with lancets. Within, a surprise: an elaborate tripartite E end contrived by bringing out the corners on low arches and fat piers. The side spaces thus created are not chapels but ante-chapels: the chapels themselves are tucked away in outshuts behind another pair of piers. The piers are so compressed that their foliage caps are only at chest height. Pairs of flying angel corbels frame the altar space. The High Altar is by *A. R. Wall* of Cheltenham. – STAINED GLASS, unsigned but looking like *Abbott & Co.*, C20.

CONGREGATIONAL CHURCH (United Reformed), Kents Bank Road. 1894–5 by *E. H. Dawson*. Small but ambitious. The road façade is a transept front. Circular windows to the clerestory, chequered red and yellow gables. Porch angled towards the road, balanced by a little polygonal baptistery(?).

COUNCIL OFFICES and VICTORIA HALL, Main Street. 1898 by *John Hutton* of Kendal. Very broad mullioned-and-transomed windows, shaped gables with ball finials. Fine inside, with a balcony.

STATION by *E. G. Paley*, 1872. It is hard to think of a prettier [104] station, or one more beautifully placed. Of limestone with sandstone dressings. On the seaward platform a long shelter with a full-length seat and windows framing the sea view; a small waiting room at each end. Substantial entrance building on the land side, E-shaped, with originally a house at each end. Excellent detailing, e.g. Furness Railway lamp brackets and twirly downspouts.

GARDENS and ornamental pool, immediately outside the station. Created in 1865 from a piece of saltmarsh which had been cut off from the sea by the railway. Opposite, a row of late C19 SHOPS and tearooms called Yewbarrow Terrace, with an iron and glass loggia, some half-timbering, and fancy finials.

PROMENADE, 1902–4. The railway cut off the town from the foreshore. This is the compensation, parallelling the railway to seaward, and incidentally covering the town sewer. – TEAROOM, 1901. – LIDO, 1933, closed 1992, and now very forlorn.

SWIMMING POOL and sports centre, Berners Close. By *Hodder Associates*, 2001. A brave statement, stark, white and cubic. The pool roof is hung from grey steel gantries overhead. Swimmers looked straight out into Morecambe Bay. Sadly closed after three years owing to rumoured structural and financial problems, joining the long-dead lido below in unwelcome irony.

GRANGE HOTEL, facing the station. By *E. G. Paley*, 1866; much enlarged later. The same composition as the station, but taller. Mildly Frenchified, with a mansard roof and château tower. STABLES on the road, with a central arch.

BARCLAYS BANK, Main Street, a little way down from the Council Offices. Of 1910 by *J. F. Curwen*, for the Bank of Liverpool. Small but butch. Tudorish, with strapwork. Inside, stone cross-arches and a fireplace.

ROCKDENE, Morecambe Bank. Incorporating Black Rock Villa, built for himself by *George Webster* in 1837–41, with a seawater bath in the basement. It survives, just, as part of Rockdene holiday flats. BAY VILLA, close by on Main Street, is a little earlier: *c.* 1820, extended 1849 by *G. Webster*.

NETHERWOOD HOTEL, Lindale Road. Originally an Arts and Crafts house by *Willink & Thicknesse* of Liverpool, 1893, for George William Deakin of Bolton. It replaced an early C19 house called Blawith Cottage, of which there are traces here and there. Jacobean-style in silver and red stone. Hall composition, with porch, bay and family wing where you would expect them, but a three-storey tower interpolated at the low end. *Gill Dockray & Partners'* hotel extension of *c.* 1990 on the SW has improved the composition by cranking round to fit the valley head. Interiors supposedly by *Gillows* of Lancaster, rich with panelling and stained glass, with Sizergh-type ceilings. Terrific stair with Jacobean arched balustrade echoed in the stained glass. Rich Jacobean fireplace in the library initialled GWD. – Small castellated buildings a little higher up and to the r.

GRAND HOTEL, now Cumbria Grand. Opened as the Hazelwood Hydro in 1887. Very large rather than very grand. Of grey limestone, with several distinct sections.

NORTH EAST COUNTIES CONVALESCENT HOME, Risedale. 1914–16 by *W. Wadman*. Of grey limestone contrasted with red sandstone. Barrack-like, particularly at the back. Now holiday apartments called Hazelwood Lodge. This and the Grand are very prominent from Arnside.

CARTMEL GRANGE, Kents Bank Road. Convalescent home of the Working Men's Club and Institute Union, completed 1914. Very large block of red brick and white terracotta, turning at the back to silver limestone and red brick. Extra storey added in plain red brick. – WAR MEMORIAL, 1921, in a corner of the garden, given by Normanton Liberal Club. Rifleman in reinforced concrete.

HOLME ISLAND, ¾ m. E. An ornamental residence of just one storey attributed to *George Webster* was built *c.* 1832 for John Fitchett and enlarged, again by Webster, in the 1840s. In 1851 it was bought by John Brogden, engineer for the new railway. His son Alexander connected the rocky island to the mainland by a causeway in 1857. – Pretty LODGE. – (TEMPLE. 1840s, with statuary by *John Graham Lough.*)

HAMPSFELL HOSPICE, 1½ m. NW. Small look-out tower and shelter, one of two ornamental towers built by the Rev. Thomas Remington in 1834–46.

GRASMERE (W)

The pastoral, Samuel Palmerish setting under the beetling fells – but a little removed from the lake – is justly famous.

ST OSWALD. The whole exterior is roughcast grey, foxing any attempt at analytical dating. The tower is strongly battered with a distinct entasis, and corner ears. The tower arch is steeply pointed, unmoulded. It is a SE tower, because the church was doubled in size on the N in 1490–1500. This gives the roof an overall, gambrel profile, for reasons we shall see inside. Windows and doors were done over by *Webster* in 1840. At the E end two Perp windows and an upper one in C14 style. The inside is extraordinary. The Langdale or N aisle, really another nave, was made by knocking low arches through the N wall. Each half had its own roof. The S trusses have kingposts and raking queenposts, the N ones kingposts with curved four-way braces. Both N and S trusses are trenched for purlins on the inner sides for the former valley. Valleys however are troublesome in this wet climate, so in *c.* 1562 the roof was 'taken down and maide oop again'. A second tier of arches was built on the centre wall, and a third roof built to cover the valley from ridge to ridge. The spine wall, incomplete at the ends, looks like the ruin of a Roman aqueduct, with five wide and irregular arches below, four more regular ones superimposed above the span-drels. It does not touch the ridge of the roof, but reaches only to the upper tie-beams. The topmost trusses have raking queenposts only. They rest on the spine wall in the middle and on the apexes of the trusses on the s, but because the N trusses are out of synch an extra flying wall-plate had to be inserted. None of them is synchronized with the spine wall.

FURNISHINGS. ALTAR RAIL. 1725; closely balustered but with every fourth one removed. – POOR BOX. Dated 1648. – PULPIT. Nice Arts and Crafts piece carved with fruits and flowers. Behind it the FLEMING PEW, provided in 1633. – FONT. Medieval. Rough octagonal bowl on three stages of steps, like a village cross. – STAINED GLASS seems almost superfluous with such splendour around; in fact the E window was replaced in 1937 by plain glass. *Shrigley & Hunt* window of *c.* 1926, N; two by *Henry Holiday*, S, 1890s. Medieval fragments in the chancel S window heads. – MONUMENTS. Fleming tablets in the chancel, notably the great Sir Daniel †1701, Doric, in Latin. Also Jemima Quillinan †1822, Greek. – William Wordsworth, by *Woolner*, placed here 1851. Beaky portrait relief, daffodil and snowdrop. Epitaph by John Keble. – On the spine wall Elizabeth Fletcher †1858 with portrait medallion, by her son *Angus Fletcher.*

RECTORY. Plain house of 1690, enlarged in the C19, with thin hoodmoulds. The Wordsworths' home 1811–13. Tiny SCHOOL by the N gate, 1630; a gingerbread shop from 1854.

OUR LADY OF THE WAYSIDE (R.C.), on the A591. By *Wilfrid C. Mangan* of Preston, 1964–5. Cruciform, with a low central tower (34 ft; 10.5 metres) and W porch. Green cut slate without, whitewashed simplicity within. The interior is a T not a cross, with a flat E wall and the altar placed centrally under the lantern tower. Sacristy and confessional in the E arm. The transepts have nominal aisles, so there are eight, not four, round columns at the crossing. A late example of the minimal Romanesque style espoused by the Roman Catholics.

WAR MEMORIAL, *c.* 1920. In Broadgate Meadow. Celtic cross in blue stone signed *W. Bromley*, Keswick, but apparently designed by *W. G. Collingwood.* Good naturalistic carving of a dove and olive branch, and a stag trampling an intertwined serpent.

DOVE COTTAGE. White C17 and C18 cottage by the wayside. It is amazing to consider who has called at this obscure garden gate, for this was the home of William and Dorothy Wordsworth 1799–1808, with Mary Wordsworth from 1802. It was taken by Thomas de Quincey until 1835 although, driven out by his own books, he moved to Fox Ghyll (Ambleside) in 1820. The front windows have been enlarged, but otherwise the cottage is preserved, not too preciously, much as the Wordsworths left it. End entry by the stack under a little porch (of 1939), and straight into the little parlour, crudely panelled, with an iron range and black flag floor. A bedroom and kitchen complete the downstairs. The sitting room was upstairs, over the parlour.

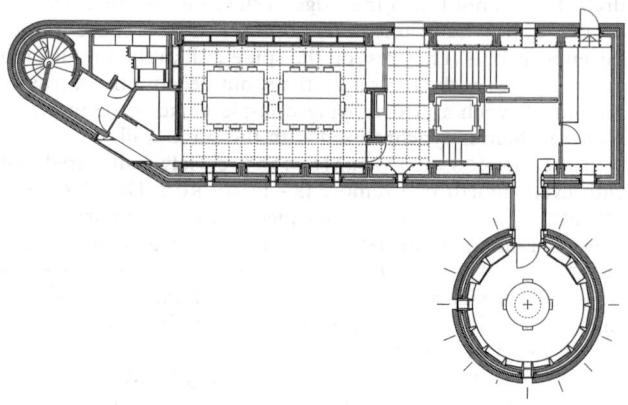

Grasmere, Jerwood Centre.
Plan

Dove Cottage was shown to the public from 1891, and the place remains a primary intellectual centre. A museum, with a pair of bulging round chimneys, opened in 1936. The present MUSEUM is a conversion 1981 of the carriage house and stable of the Prince of Wales Hotel (*see* below); architects *Newcastle upon Tyne University Projects Office*. The CAFÉ was a garage of 1928, built round trusses of 1820 from Langdale gunpowder works. The JERWOOD CENTRE is a notable addition. *Benson & Forsyth*'s design of 1992 was given the go-ahead after appeal in 1999, but *Napper Architects* of Newcastle took over as executants *c.* 2000. The building, finished in 2004, is a tightly planned building on a tight site, its construction constrained by the intense official conservatism of the Lake District in one of its most sensitive spots, by the exacting requirements of museum conservation, and by the pressure of rapidly expanding collections. These have been balanced triumphantly. Long building in line with the museum and exhibition building, and a circular tower or rotunda linked to it only by a glass bridge. The long roof floats on a deeply recessed clerestory, and there are a few, mostly small, windows. What we do not see is that the two are linked underground, with extensive plant rooms. The library interior is simple and satisfying. The few windows are deeply set and frame chosen bits of view. More light trickles in from the clerestory. A skew window looks towards the village, next to a spiral stair free at the edges in the building's prow.

PRINCE OF WALES HOTEL. Between Dove Cottage and the lake. 1855 and 1863, by *Miles Thompson* for Edward Brown. Great lump of a building, not improved by vernacular elements derived from Wordsworth's proposed house at Rydal (q.v.).

The VILLAGE consists mostly of hotels, of which we may single out the MOSS GROVE for its weird balcony over the porch, like an inside-out ziggurat. The LAMB INN has a similar feature at the side.

ALLAN BANK, on the other side of the valley. Wordsworth and his growing family moved here in 1808. He disliked it – 'a temple of abomination' whose chimneys smoked. It was built in 1805 for Mr Crump of Liverpool, and extended in 1834 perhaps by *George Webster*. Now mercifully hidden by trees, it is bleakly Italianate with bald sashes, hoodmoulds and peeling stucco.

SILVERHOWE, ½ m. SW. William Gell built a single-storey house here in 1797 or 1798, low and unobtrusive, like Derwent Bay (Keswick) and Elleray (Windermere). He was soon embroiled in Queen Caroline's affairs, and spent his later years in Naples, so much is due to the next occupant, Samuel Barber, principally in the 1820s. Gell's two sitting rooms and small kitchen, as described by William Plumptre in 1799, are still single-storeyed, commanding a magnificent prospect of the lake and island. The longer room is done up theatrically in Windsor Castle Gothick, with a coved and bluntly arched plaster vault, ogee overdoors and a grey marble fireplace. A taller section added at right angles behind acquired its own Gothick porch, and originally a porte cochère on octagonal piers, when the upper drive was blasted through the rock. The internal vista from the porte cochère, along the broad hallway to a distant stair, is reminiscent of Wray Castle (q.v.). Vertiginous GARDEN with steps, conversation places, and a little Gothick grot with patterned pebble floor and tent ceiling overlooking the croquet lawn.

THE HOLLENS (National Trust Regional Office). Three-bay cottage villa of the 1790s with lean-to wings, with a fabulous view. An Italianate hotel conversion of 1849 and later by *George Webster* or *Thompson & Webster* changed its character. Of green stone with irregular quoins. Three-storey tower, canted bay, glass and wood entrance porch. Quite a good staircase, Webster fireplaces.

(DALE END, ¾ m. S, across the lake. The core is a farmhouse of 1661. One fireplace and the roof structure remain. The bow window of the drawing room must be of *c.* 1800, but most of what makes the house prominent is of shortly after 1893.)

CAIRN, on the watershed at Dunmail Raise, 2¾ m. N. Partly rebuilt after roadworks in 1891 and now on the central reservation of the dual carriageway; up to 8 ft (2.5 metres) high and 60 ft (18 metres) across.

GRAYRIGG (W)

ST JOHN. Lean church of 'Carus Wilson' type, like Casterton (q.v.). It is by *George Webster*, 1837–8. Tower rebuilt 1869. Lofty well-lit interior. – STAINED GLASS. E window, †1892, by *Shrigley & Hunt.* – MONUMENTS. Several tablets of the earlier C19.   p. 378

Grayrigg, St John.
Elevation by George Webster, 1837

ROMAN FORT, Low Borrowbridge, 3¼ m. NE. A platform on a
small knoll in the Tebay gorge. Defences, a parallelogram,
much robbed in the early C19 and before; the rampart survives
best as a steep bank on the W. Two ditches and an additional
counterscarp bank on the SW, close to the W gate – probably
a single portal. Here the land rose (before it was cut away for
the railway and for the M6), and deeper defences were needed.
Footings mark the E gate: projecting guard-towers flanking two
portals, the N one blocked in antiquity. The fort faced S; its
interior much ploughed and featureless. Site first occupied in
the late C1, and as late as the late C4; excavations revealed substantial reconstructions.

3090

GRAYTHWAITE (L)
Far Sawrey

GRAYTHWAITE HALL. The GARDENS with their terraced walks
and rhododendrons were *Thomas Mawson*'s first major commission, begun in 1889 for Thomas Myles Sandys M.P. and
carried on for many years. The rocky ground made it difficult
and expensive (£120,000 in 1899).
The HOUSE has been through many stages under a string of
architects. Before Mawson was *George Webster* (*c.* 1840), mainly
on the W of the house, and some possibly unexecuted designs
by *James W. Grundy* (1875). Working at the same time as
Mawson were *R. Knill Freeman* and, inside, *Dan Gibson*.

Freeman's work is characterized by red St Bees sandstone, and is best seen on the S front, remodelled in a rich Jacobean style which is 'expressive of its history, and yet can keep rank with the present' (Mawson). An unexecuted perspective shows the whole house recast in Kirby Hall (Northants) style, with giant pilasters. But in the re-entry on the E, behind the C19 tower, an C18 house appears, with a modest Ionic doorcase and sash windows informally disposed. Earlier still was the house depicted in a painting resembling the C17 Rayrigg at Windermere: H-shaped with an extension at the rear, with deep-set windows.

The principal rooms owe their present form to *Dan Gibson* in the early C20. Behind the S loggia is the Oak Hall, made *c.* 1910 out of two rooms, with bolection panelling and a trellis-pattern ceiling. Rising out of it is the principal stair, quite modest and probably C18. Next to it on the SE corner is the dining room, the only really grand apartment, with an enormous inglenook fireplace, linenfold panelling and finely carved swags in Grinling Gibbons style by *Arthur Simpson*, who chose the wood off the estate. In the drawing room a crisp chimneypiece in red sandstone with the Lancashire arms, *c.* 1920.

Across the E yard is the ESTATE OFFICE, with a chapel above. The STABLES are by *R. Knill Freeman*, arranged round a railed courtyard, prettily but inappropriately timber-framed, with a clock turret. C20 works are recorded by *John Banks* of Kendal, *Francis A. Whitwell* and *E. Donald Haigh*, mainly on estate buildings.

LOWER GRAYTHWAITE, or Graythwaite Old Hall. The seat of the Rawlinsons, but now part of Graythwaite Estate. C16 or C17, with a six-bay front of *c.* 1710, three rooms wide and three storeys high. The pedimented doorcase is set to one side and paired with an ill-understood Venetian window like the one at the Heelis office in Hawkshead, which the National Trust attributes to *Ferdinando Taylor*. This is the hall, with a vestigial screens passage, and, at the high end, a great fireplace in which is inserted a typical C19 Graythwaite estate chimneypiece. The high-end parlour is fully panelled; behind the panelling is a spice cupboard. The low-end dining room has bolection panelling and the date 1646 over a window. Jacobean fireplace, perhaps *ex situ*. Good wide early C17 stair with balls. Above the family parlour is a fine bedroom with a door and fanlight, like a front door. It is fully panelled, with pilasters and chair rail. The rear parts of the house are older, supposedly of 1565. Plank and muntin panelling in the entrance hall, with its inglenook fireplace and fire-window and a narrow stair. In the kitchen adjoining a matching fireplace, this time with a door under the bressumer leading off to sculleries. In the bedrooms above are tiny closets and wig cupboards next to the stack. Topiary *à la* Levens. – BARN on the road with a clerestory dovecote, and behind it a BANK BARN with queenpost roof, restored in 2004, both with balls on the gables.

SILVERHOLME, or Graythwaite New Hall. A house with a view, built for J. J. Rawlinson in the 1830s. It has all the hallmarks of *George Webster*. Five-bay house, stripped of its roughcast and made rather bleak by its dropped window sills. The pinched tripartite entrance leads to an L-shaped hall, so the stair, a delicate cantilever curved in the middle, is at right angles. Eclectic plasterwork, some of it finely executed, and good Webster fireplaces.

On the lakeshore below is HULLETT HALL, inscribed WMR (William and M– Rawlinson) 1720. The simple long deep-windowed whitewashed pile of the vernacular.

FELLBOROUGH. Very prominent from the lake. Prim Victorian villa set on lawns with cypresses; stable, boathouse.

GREAT ASBY (W)

Open-plan village surrounded by immense limestone moors, brown, green and grey in sharply defined patches.

ST PETER. Rebuilt in 1865–6 for Ann Nevell Hill by *W. & J. Hay* of Liverpool, who have signed their work under the soffit of the porch entrance. Pink and unabashedly Victorian, it stands on a level and open green. Some Geometrical tracery and some single-light windows with pointed-trefoiled heads. Heavy bellcote carried on a buttressing super-arch around the w window. Ornate s porch. Interior a mid-Victorian set piece: pitch-pine furnishings; capacious chancel, encaustically tiled, with piscina, sedilia and aumbry, brass and iron altar rail; carved angel corbels. Wide-stepping s arcade of three bays with alternate pink and white voussoirs. Massive, overdesigned and overcrafted PULPIT and FONT. The organ, unusually, is at the w end. – STAINED GLASS. E window by *Burrow* of Milnthorpe, 1866, rich and full of colour, with clumsy faces. s aisle E by *Leonard Walker*, 1929: St Peter and St Bartholomew. It is partly plated, i.e. two sheets of glass back-to-back, giving great depth and subtlety to the streakiness. – Of the old church, which was low and whitewashed with a w turret, there survives a huge indent for a brass, now the porch floor, and a few MONUMENTS. William Fairer †1811 by *Francis Webster*. – James Park of Asby Grange †1830, draped urn on grey marble back. – The church has an 'A.P.' LOCK of 1670, presented by Lady Anne Clifford.

Former RECTORY, s of the church. The part nearest the road is a solar tower of the C14, thick-walled with a tunnel-vault to the ground floor, though it may never have been carried up to a fighting top. In the gable a two-light arched Geometrical window with a transom (cf. Kirkby Thore Hall). Flat-topped mullioned windows elsewhere. The doorway to the tower is single-chamfered and has a hoodmould. It is now inside the hall range, which is probably C17. s extension of 1866.

St Helen's Almshouses, e of the church. Founded and endowed by William Fairer, watchmaker, and his brother Joseph 1811, and built by 1814. Four houses in a square block, pyramid-roofed, with a four-way chimney.

Asby Hall, in the village. Tall three-storey house with big sashes, dated 1694 and enlarged in the mid C18. Stripping off the render has exposed the earlier fenestration. Lowther arms carved over the door. Immediately in front of the house fine C18 railings, then a broad forecourt flanked by low farm buildings and bounded by more iron railings and tall gatepiers with channelled rustication.

Gaythorne Hall, 2 m. w, off the Orton Road. In so wild and drear a district, so far from any other habitation, it is a surprise to find such a stylish house. It was built c. 1600 as a hunting lodge for the Bellinghams of Levens. Standing tall, it is an up-to-date double pile with a staircase tower at each end and a porch front and back. The plan therefore is a square with four projections, a condensed version of Robert Smythson's Chastleton House, Oxon, of c. 1602, and very close to a drawing of 1596 by John Thorpe labelled 'house at Potters Bar'. As in Thorpe's drawing the chimneys rise all in a row in the middle from a massive spine wall. The floor levels of front and rear piles are staggered. The front has two tall storeys plus cellar and attic, the service range at the rear three full storeys.

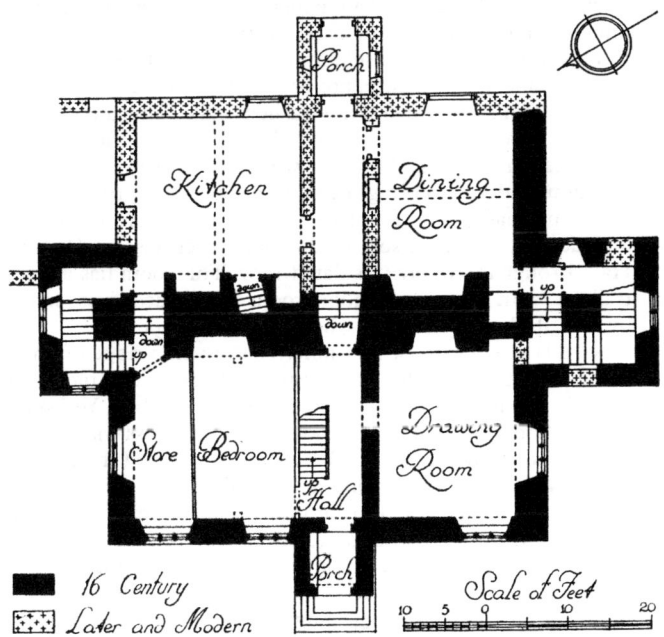

Great Asby, Gaythorne Hall.
Plan, 1936

The enigmatic Clegg Hall at Milnrow, SE Lancashire, is planned the same way, but without the paired stairs. Even more remarkably, Gainford Hall of 1600–3 in Co. Durham (over the Stainmore pass) is a virtual twin. Although the front entry is central, extra mullioned-and-transomed windows indicate the asymmetrical hall position. The two-storey porch has a round-arched entrance of complex moulding, with a square label surround decorated with diamond shapes and the Bellingham arms on the keystone. Over the inner door a provocative mermaid with two tails and a short leafy skirt. At the foot a grotesque lady in ruff and squashy hat, and a man with staring eyes and a tree out of his mouth. The rear is a come-down, with single-storey porch and workaday fenestration. The same goes for the present roofs, of practical vernacular form with continuous eaves and swept valleys. They were put on in 1702, as recorded on a hopper with the initials IG, and probably relate to its downgrading to a farm. Three ridges, not two, hide the central stacks, nullifying with heavy eaves the continuous upper dripmould. What was the intended top finish? Gainford has another storey, then roofs of similar form between coped gables with ball finials, but Chastleton and Clegg make a show of gables and cross-roofs. If this was a hunting lodge it is likely to have had at least some parapeted flats.

The INTERIOR is impressive for the height of the rooms – quite out of the ordinary for the region – and for the immense thickness of the spine wall penetrated by stepped tunnels linking the two sides. Little is left in the way of decoration or fittings. The tower stairs, seldom used because there is a third modern stair in the centre, are broad but completely plain, of wooden baulks between whitewashed walls. The unfinished-looking tower-top rooms suggest that they were once higher. Over the rear pile is an immense wool loft, with a simple crane and double doors to bring the stuff in. The sitting room in the SW corner has a good fireplace, flat-pointed in C16 local style and decorated with a sort of dogtooth, seen also at Hornby Hall, Brougham, where it is dated 1602. This room has a vine-trail frieze. In the corresponding room an identical frieze made by the BBC of polystyrene when filming in 1996.

GRANGE HALL, 1½ m. S. Very lonely, sitting on a ridge of limestone pavement in a dry valley. Built of large square blocks of pinkish sandstone. It belonged to Byland Abbey, Yorkshire (North Riding), which descended from Furness via Calder (qq.v.). Long tower house of three storeys, with lower and later wings N and S. Corbels on the N indicate an earlier wing. Although it has an overall roof now, the cove course running right round the top, with gargoyles mostly broken off but at least one complete and cannon-shaped, indicates that it once had a parapet-walk. However, the parapet base is interrupted by medieval windows, suggesting that it was itself secondary, and that the building was even taller than now.

The house retains a number of eye-catching features. The first-floor oriel on the E gable wall, although now unglazed and walled off from the interior, is a beauty of C15 design. It grows out of a corbel with a masked or blindfolded bearded face, through two sets of complex mouldings, to a solid dado and a five-sided window with cusped-headed lights and a lead-covered stone roof. On the entrance side (N) a mid-C14 pair of ogee-cusped windows, blocked, pushes into the former parapet. A shield or device of the Bellinghams, i.e. post-Reformation, is mercilessly cut into by a C17 mullioned window. At the back (s) is another ogee-headed window high up, a stack, and a garder-obe tower serving the middle floor; blocked windows suggest it was a double-seater. Tucked away behind the front wing on the NW corner is a round stair-turret, lit by one tiny window, and now with no top, the main roof simply coming down over it. It starts not at ground level, but boldly corbelled from the first floor. The way the corbelling grows out from the square corner, first in two arcs then in individual stepped corbels, looks specifi-cally Scottish of around 1600. We may surmise that the turret and defensive parapet-walk are due to the Bellinghams, after the Reformation but before the Union of Kingdoms, i.e between the 1540s and 1604. Also at this end, another massive stack, and what could be a dig-out hole for a garderobe.

The interiors are divided into two rooms per floor by studded partitions. (Peter Ryder reports a four-centred doorway to the NW turret and a flat-headed one at the top, both chamfered.)

PREHISTORIC SETTLEMENT. On Great Asby Scar, 3 m. SW, a sub-rectangular settlement of exceptional interest, CASTLE FOLDS, made almost impregnable by the surrounding lunar landscape of limestone pavement. A tumbled wall up to 9 ft (3 metres) thick, the external face up to 3 ft (1 metre) high. Slabs were set on edge to form the basal course of the inner face. Shelving interior, free of visible structures except for small enclosures attached to the wall, some of which may be original. Entrance through the s side, opposite a break in the pavement.

GREAT LANGDALE (W) *see* LANGDALES

GREAT MUSGRAVE (W) *see* MUSGRAVE

GREAT ORMSIDE (W) *see* ORMSIDE

GREAT ORTON (C) *see* ORTON (C)

GREAT SALKELD (C)   5030

ST CUTHBERT. Powerful W tower of *c.* 1380, unmistakably defensive. It has no external door, tiny one-light openings even for the bell-stage, and businesslike battlements. The church has defensive features too, but of an earlier period. The Norman S doorway is exceptionally narrow, though a splendid piece with three orders of zigzag and of colonnettes. Hideous masks are incorporated into the zigzag in the centre, as at St Bees (q.v.). Abacuses and capitals are carved. The absence of early windows suggests they were small and/or high. A small square window set right at the top of the N wall may be a survivor. Chancel and chancel arch were restored by J. S. Mulcaster, rector, in 1866. The door into the tower is a YATT, i.e. an iron grating with massive bolts and hinges, its interstices oak-planked. The tower room is tunnel-vaulted and gives a comforting feeling of strength, with its immensely deep-set window. C13 grave-slabs are used to cover the splays. The upper floor has a doorway into the nave as well; what for? – STAINED GLASS. Much of the C19 by *Cox & Sons*. Nave S, St Cuthbert, by *Powells*, 1929. C20 image of William Nicholson, rector 1682–1702 then bishop, in the high window in the N wall. – MONUMENT. Recumbent effigy of a priest, with tonsure and hood. Identified as Thomas de Caldebec †1319.

RECTORY. Due S, across a green. Medieval T-shape, with a solar over the services at the W end of a hall range. Modified in 1674 by Thomas Musgrave, rector (datestone) and again in the C19 with the addition of a two-storey bay.

SCHOOL. Founded 1515, rebuilt 1667 and 1856, enlarged 1906.

(NUNWICK HALL. 1892 by *C. J. Ferguson*. Red sandstone, Tudor style. Gables and mullioned windows with arched lights.) Fine GATEPIERS.

GREAT STRICKLAND (W)

5020

ST BARNABAS, at the E extremity of the cross-roads village. 1871–2 by *George Watson*. Three-sided E end. Bellcote and spirelet over junction of nave and chancel. Paired lancets without cusps, and a W triplet. Tricky open roof. No chancel arch, just a wooden cradle on dwarf colonnettes to carry the spirelet. The side windows sit in square holes with only the wall-plate bridging the top. STALLS and PULPIT skeletally open. An economical but original design, in fact. – STAINED GLASS. Apse, by *Shrigley & Hunt* for members of the Plumer family, 1880s.

VILLAGE HALL, at the cross-roads. Of corrugated iron with a veranda, painted dark green with a red phone box in front – rather pleasing. It came from Gretna in the 1920s, so presumably of First World War vintage.

GREAT URSWICK (L) *see* URSWICK

GREYSTOKE (C)

ST ANDREW. A major church, broad but markedly deficient in height. It was re-founded as a collegiate church (one of only two in the region) in 1382, following protracted negotiations initiated in 1358 by William, 14th Baron Greystoke, and had a master, seven chaplains and six chantry priests.* However, the building appears not to be C14 but essentially latest Perp, of the C16 or even C17. The inscription on the chancel records its repair in 1645 and restoration in 1848 (by *Salvin*; 1848–9), which does much to explain things, when another restoration of 1818 is taken into account.

Bulmer says the W tower was rebuilt in 1848, though its broad squat shape and few and small Dec openings suggest rather a re-cladding. The nave is narrow, the aisles wide and boxy, the chancel long, and wider than the nave. Windows are big for Cumbria, and set low. Traceries, except in the E window, are of round-headed lights and uncusped – a simple doubling of the lights and a halving of their size. Chancel and some S aisle window heads two-centred, of three lights, the rest straight-headed or segmental. Distinctively C17 is the S aisle E window with its three-centred head and emphatic interrupted transom, like that at Holm Cultram (Abbey Town) of *c.* 1605. Attached to the S aisle is a two-storey sacristy or chapter house, with a castellated chimney like those of Blencow (*see* p. 390) neatly incorporated in the aisle parapet, and an equally neat protruding stair-turret. Also two windows on its upper floor into the aisle. Above the S porch a straight-headed three-light window.

Despite the big windows the nave is dark: no clerestory or W window. Its narrowness is an early C13, pre-college legacy. Six-bay arcades, short-stepping with steep arches. At the E a widening for an intended crossing (though there is no western arch). It has keeled shafts, i.e. C13 again. The W responds are keeled as well. Bays one to five however have the oddest piers, of red stone, circular, with shapeless capitals moulded out of the same block. Perhaps of 1818, when Jefferson (1840–2) says they were heightened. They carry arches of two slight chamfers. The roofs of the contrastingly wide and light aisles are of the 1870s and 1880s by *C. J. Ferguson*.

FURNISHINGS. Stone MENSA set in the present altar steps. – Triple SEDILIA, PISCINA. Shields in the N wall, one dated 1557. – STALLS. Ten on each side. Four have medieval MIS-ERICORDS, perhaps slightly preceding the Carlisle set, i.e. *c.* 1400. Pelican, St Michael and the dragon, women groom-

---

*The college was on the site of Rectory Farm. In 1958 it was re-founded as a pre-theological college, which lasted until 1979.

ing a horse. The rest are C17. – SCREEN, partly medieval. One-light divisions, dainty tracery. Top rail with angels. – PULPIT. An odd openwork object of two storeys. – LECTERN. Wonderful contraption of iron and brass commemorating the Rev. Edmund Askew †1901. – SCULPTURE. Madonna and Child on the font carved by German prisoners of war at Greystoke Castle *c.* 1944. Crucified Christ by *Josefina de Vasconcellos.*

STAINED GLASS. E window probably of the late C15 and by a York workshop, and looking remarkably complete, though the order of the scenes is jumbled (it was reassembled in 1848). Tracery mostly heraldic, restored. In the main lights large figures and donors. Below, in two rows of five, each with black-letter commentary in Northern dialect, is the outrageous tale of St Andrew by Leucius Charinus, already discredited in the C5. After Pentecost Matthew went to Wronden, city of cannibals. Thence he is rescued by Andrew, who, after preventing the execution of a scapegoat, is himself tortured and sees a vision of trees bearing parts of his own flesh. The city is inundated, Andrew escapes, the dead are raised, but the executioner is swallowed up. – Chancel S, another medieval window, pretty complete: a bestiary of *c.* 1400. Ass, phoenix, antelope, eagle, mongoose, caladrius, each in a medallion and done in silver stain and black. – Also chancel S by *Wailes & Strang* (†1859), chancel N by *Hardman* (†1875). N aisle E, a very good *Kempe* window of 1901: Christ in the garden and Mary Magdalene. Angels guard the tomb, Jerusalem behind – or is it Greystoke? N aisle W end by *A. K. Nicholson*, 1920s: Suffer Little Children, St Cecilia, St Margaret of Scotland. S aisle E, *Heaton, Butler & Bayne*; S aisle S, *Clayton & Bell.*

MONUMENTS. The tomb-recess of 1848 on the N side of the chancel was for John Dacre, last provost of the college. Now it accommodates alabaster effigies of William, 14th Baron Greystoke, founder of the college, *c.* 1360, and John, 16th Baron, †1436 (will). Angels by William's pillow; a canopy over his head. One side of John's tomb-chest is preserved, with two saints still in the style of the C14, which remained so long in England, and otherwise standard angels holding shields. – Small BRASSES in the N aisle. John de Whelpdale †1526, dressed and tonsured as a priest of this college, with his shield of four whelps (bust 7 in., 18 cm., long). (Also Margaret Moresby †1528 (13 in., 33 cm.), Winifred Newport †1547 (11 in., 28 cm.), Richard Newport †1551 (11 in., 18 cm.), the latter two from the *'Fermer' workshop*, London.) N aisle W end, Henry Charles Howard of Greystoke †1914, red stone Arts and Crafts with bronze portrait medallion, by *Louis Reid Deuchars* and *Sir Robert Lorimer.*

GREYSTOKE CASTLE. The capital house of the barony. Licence to crenellate was granted to William, 14th Lord Greystoke in 1353. The two remaining towers, the N one ruined, are set at such a mad angle to one another as to suggest the curtain wall of a polygonal castle with courtyard rather than attachment to a hall range. The barony passed to the Dacres in 1505, and then in 1569 to the Howards. Much wasted in the Civil War, the house was rebuilt after *c.* 1675 for Henry Charles Howard in early classical style, like the large MODEL preserved in the hall. Bishop Nicholson notes further building work in 1702, and in 1705 'Charles Howard Junior . . . to wash with a white paint his pye-ball'd new building'. A s wing was added *c.* 1789 by *Charles Howard*, the convivial *11th Duke of Norfolk*, in a fanciful castellated style, including a pair of seven-sided towers – but this eminently interesting work was mostly taken down in the 1950s. The designs were probably his own, with *William Nixon* as mason, although the architect *Francis Hiorne* was here in 1787.* *Anthony Salvin* worked here twice: first in 1837–45 to rebuild the c17 part for Henry Howard, and again in 1875–8 for another Henry Charles Howard to reinstate it after a fire (1868), when he made some aggrandizing changes to the exterior as well.

Salvin is what we see first. His E-shaped Elizabethan w front   60
of pinkish Greystoke ashlar is made asymmetrical by the windows of the hall (Salvin phase two) to the l. of the entrance, but unified under a long level parapet. The two hall windows are tall, with four transoms, then the hall bay with five transoms, and then the chamber and solar. Rising above and to the r., and catching the eye in any plan, is the N tower with its inauthentic rounded corners, set at a different axis to the rest. The upper stage is Salvin's, but his battlements and turret were removed *c.* 1980 after stones fell through the roof onto the grand stair shortly after the last farewells of a party. Of the s tower there remains only the exposed inside of its N wall, with an upper mural passage running out into space. At the back is a splendidly long grassy terrace overlooking a pair of manmade lakes. This side consists of a suite of rooms added in the 1790s or earlier, but the architectural dress is Salvin. At the N end a spectacular canted bay of 1875–8 copied from another Howard house, Thornbury, Glos. The medieval masonry of the tower can now be seen, clearly differentiated from the Salvin top. A scar on its N side indicates the 1789 wing, now cut down to one storey and used as a garage. At its s end was one of the seven-sided towers. Its twin, the CLOCK TOWER, stands detached to full height, its quoins, roundels, and blank arches at the top very Vanbrugh-like. This section is aligned on the skewy s tower. Hall interior and stair belong to Salvin's post-fire restoration of 1875–8. (*Willement* glass.) The tower's genuine lower part has an unusually impressive tunnel-vault, reinforced with five broad square-section transverse ribs, and two slit windows.

Handsome STABLE range, N, early c19. (HOME FARM, N again. Signed and dated HH (Henry Howard) 1837, HH 1836, *John Barker* architect and *Joseph Turner* builder. Two-storeyed, with three-storey wings and a large courtyard.) Stable and

* *John Teasdale* (father and son), masons of Greystoke, and *James Teasdale*, surveyor and plan-drawer, worked for the Duke at Arundel, and surely here as well.

farm were highly innovative, collecting methane for instance to light the house.

STAFFORD HOUSE, just inside the gate. For the head gardener. One of the 11th Duke's follies, giving a flavour of what the castle looked like pre-Salvin. Gothick, with battlements, pointed windows upstairs, round-arched ones below. In the gable-end facing the gate a full-height churchy window of three lights, with intersecting tracery and a looped transom. The strange thing is that this house, apparently of one storey at the end, two storeys at the sides, has three full storeys within. The middle floor is lit from the front, the top floor from the back. Evidently the Duke enjoyed an architectural joke.

LODGE and gate, dated HH 1846.

PARK. 6,000-acre deerpark made in the 1780s when the Johnby and Greenthwaite estates were added to Greystoke. A 9-ft (2.8-metre)-high wall was built, and new roads made round the outside.

VILLAGE. The Howards are here still, and the village has an estate air. MARKET CROSS. By *Salvin*, 1844–7, on green lawns. A market was granted in 1350. Gothic SCHOOL, dated 1838 HH. POST OFFICE and cottages dated HCH (Henry Charles Howard) 1887 and 1893. Attached to them on Church Road, a fine five-bay house of the late C17. Segmental hood over bolection-moulded doorway. Strong quoins, coved cornice. The windows are still two-light mullions. The wooden building attached was built by Henry Charles Howard in the 1890s, when farming was in difficulties, as a co-op for produce.

The approach along the B5288 from Penrith is signalled first by the 11th Duke of Norfolk's GREYSTOKE PILLAR, a dumpy stone spire of *c.* 1780 on a pedestal bearing the Howard Arms. Then, as the village approaches, a crescendo of late C18 folly farms, Gothick, Picturesque, and provocative. First SPIRE HOUSE to the N, reputedly for a tenant with an abhorrence of steeple-house worship. The spire rises out of an octagonal castellated tower. Next BUNKERS HILL, commemorating the American victory of 1775 and making clear the Duke's sympathies. It has a three-sided 'barmkin' wall and a broad polygonal tower. FORT PUTNAM, named after the American General, has a high seven-sided wall enclosing the farm. Battlements, a five-sided tower, a large church window, and then a blank wall with arches, and round buttresses topped by coronets of stiff petals. The farmhouse itself is built into a corner, as at Lyulph's Tower (Matterdale, q.v.). The details have the Vanbrughian ring of the tower at the castle, and the *Duke of Norfolk* himself was probably the designer of all these, influenced perhaps by Francis Hiorne.

JOHNBY HALL, 1 m. N. Tower house of three sheer storeys, with a staircase projection and entrance to the S at the E end. First mentioned in 1200, Johnby was sold in 1300 and again in 1326, which is a likely time for the addition of a defensive tower wing which may form the W part of the present house. In 1583, according to a long inscription in an hourglass-shaped surround over the entrance, William Musgrave and Isabel Martindale made the present house. They added two more vaulted compartments in place of a presumed earlier hall, and made a new hall at first-floor level, with an entrance and double stair-tower at the SE corner, making an L. In 1747 the front was updated with sash windows and a central door, and the martial parapets and turrets were replaced by a hipped roof with eaves; in 1783 the house became part of the Greystoke estate. In 1897 *Maud Leyborne-Popham* made a new kitchen door, and replaced the sashes with large mullioned-and-transomed windows, finely moulded – as she tells us by a carved inscription.

The whole ground floor is vaulted: barrel-vaults in three compartments, and a vaulted corridor in front of the two E ones. A great arched fireplace, roll-moulded, in the N wall of the W chamber. A cunningly angled shooting window in the entrance angle commands both fronts. An unusually wide turning stair within the SE projection leads to the upper entry of the C16, which has a broad passage with an aumbry. The stair is capped at the top with an elegantly ribbed umbrella-vault, like those at Carlisle Cathedral (but so much later). The ribs and the top of the newel post have fillets. Immediately to the N and parallel is a smaller, service stair. (Torwood, near Stirling, was built to the same plan, including the duplicated stair, in 1566.) The fine great hall, nearly square, stands over the two eastern vaults. A tiny buttery and pantry are contrived partly in the thickness of the E wall, each with its own segmental vault carried on corbelled-out cross-walls. The fireplace surround was carved by *Maud Leyborne-Popham* herself, with an inhabited running vine *à la* Bewcastle. The toffee-coloured tiles were made in the tilery she set up in the 1890s (now Tilery Farm) to alleviate agricultural unemployment. Over the western vault is the C14 solar. Turning stairs in two corners continue up to the second floor, with another of Maud's fireplaces, this one carved 'from ancient oak piles from a lake dwelling at Neuchâtel, Switzerland, in 1883'. The NE turning stair continues up, presumably once to parapets and turrets, now to the roof space. The roof, an excellent hipped kingpost structure, was made in 1747.

Flanking the tower house on the W is the low and unobtrusive house called KELLY, where the family lives in winter. External steps lead to an upper doorway dated 1637 with the initials WM and GM, thought to be the widowed Winifred Musgrave and her daughter Grace. This wing has the characteristics of a bastle. No ready link between the two storeys. The ground-floor windows where they have survived are mere slits, the floor sloped and grooved for animals. The stout wooden intermediate floor supports stone flags over the boards. Toilet and bathroom are contrived in the big end stack; its fire-window remains. Access from the tower is through a linking passage made by Maud Leyborne-Popham, picturesquely stepped and kinked as it passes through the great thickness of wall.

Terraced former GARDEN E of the house, through one doorway with a Yorkshire lintel, or another dated 1689. W of the house an enclosed area called the Pleasaunce. STABLE. Curious stone in a gable with three heart-shaped holes, two upside-down. They have rope-moulded surrounds and scribed circles between. A DOVECOTE alongside, converted to a squash court, is dated WBB (William and Barbara(?) Williams) 1675.

BLENCOW HALL, 1¼ m. NE. An arresting sight with two ruinous towers, complete to their battlements, at either end of a long hall range. The N tower wraps round the hall in an odd way. The S tower is rent from top to bottom. Running back from it is a long wing, with an arch to the courtyard. The inscribed motto QUORSUM VIVERE MORI, MORI VITAE (Wherefore live to die; to die is life) over the hall door in the yard records Henry Blencow and the date 1590. The doorways with their flattened pointed heads under a square mould are consistent with this date. Mullioned windows, dripmoulds with variously sculpted terminations (cf. Scaleby, 1597–1604). The S tower proves to be less formidable than it looks, with walls no thicker than the domestic parts. Doorheads and dripmoulds are of the same type, so it seems that this too can be dated c. 1590, and was essentially for show. The N tower is a little more serious, with thicker walls. It also has some of its battlements. Its ground floor is unheated. A spiral stair in the SE corner, jutting out in front of the hall, goes straight up to the solar. Although the shell may be late C15 the detail is all late C16.

Blencow has been imaginatively restored, with inset glazing behind the gash in the S tower, by *Donald Insall Associates* with *Graham Norman* and *Charles Blackett-Ord* (2006–8).

Remains of a small CHAPEL, on the W side of the courtyard. Unconvincing as such, but shown by Mathias Read in a painting of c. 1700.

GREENTHWAITE HALL, ¾ m. SW. Pretty F-shaped house facing the park wall and with its back to the road. The three-storey porch bears the inscription PEREGRINOS HIC NOS REPUTA-MUS E 1650 with the initials MDH (Miles and Dorothy Halton). Above are Miles's arms, 1660, and a carved panel with flowers or suns, and plants (thistles?). Panels of strapwork (one C19?) over two of the mullioned windows. It is clear from the masonry that the F-shape is made up of two Ls: the earlier a hall and kitchen at right angles (W), the later (1650) the porch and two-room apartment to its l., characterized outside by continuous drips and strings. The interior is much altered, dividing the hall at the SW corner into two. It has a big arched fireplace with roll moulding, as at Johnby (Greystoke), of the 1580s. Its adjoining room has a flat-lintelled fireplace with a complex mould, and integral doorway by the side, through to the entry from a cross-passage behind, as usual. Some of the floors are laid with gypsum plaster. No old stairs remain, except a tiny stone stair giving access to the top porch room, which has a little aumbry.

HARDRIGG HALL, at the far end of the park. *See* Skelton.

Greystoke, Greenthwaite Hall.
Drawing, 1907

GRINSDALE (C)   3050

ST KENTIGERN. A short walk E of the village, immediately above
the wide Eden river. Rebuilt in 1738–40 on the old foundations. Very small, roughcast, with a little W tower. Nave of three
bays, chancel of two. FURNISHINGS mostly of 1895–6. – MON-
UMENTS. Mrs Clara Steel †1845. Tall, very unadorned urn in
an equally deliberately bare recess. Signed *Nelson* of Carlisle.
– Outside S, headstone of John Studholme †1847, draped with
carved willow fronds just as the little church is overshadowed
by a copper beech.

HADRIAN'S WALL

Selected portions of the Wall and of its associated structures are
described under the following gazetteer entries, listed from E to
W, with their place names where these are different: Denton
(Poltross Burn and Willowford), Lanercost (Hare Hill), Walton
(Birdoswald and Castlesteads), Carlisle (Stanwix), Burgh-by-
Sands, Bowness-on-Solway. For the Stanegate *see* Introduction
p. 16, for the outpost forts *see* Bewcastle and Netherby Hall.
For the defences down the coast *see* Crosscanonby, Maryport and
Ravenglass. For the history of the Wall, its Milecastles and

Turrets, and an explanation of the Vallum (ditch and linear earth-work) *see* Introduction, pp. 16–18.

HAILE (C)

CHURCH. In a dell. A Georgian rebuild with plain round-arched windows and prominent though flush voussoirs. The nave steps in, as though for a chancel, but there is no chancel arch (as also at Bampton and Penrith). W porch, roofs and SCREEN are by *C. J. Ferguson*, 1882–3. – SCULPTURE. Very large C10 or C11 grave-cover, in several pieces. Interlace decoration with zoomorphic termination of the sides is clear, but the top is worn almost away, except for the roll at the edges. – STAINED GLASS. E window by *Wailes & Strang*, S by *Heaton, Butler & Bayne*, 1898, N by *Powells* (†1952). – MONUMENT. John Ponsonby †1670, W wall outside, with rhyming epitaph in capital letters.

HAILE HALL. A short wooded drive drops down to a small C16 or C17 GATEHOUSE. In the courtyard beyond, a long barn l., rising ground r., and the HOUSE ahead. The five-bay, two-and-a-half-storey S front is early C18, with moulded window surrounds. The door surround has a bolection moulding, to which is fixed, for some reason, two wooden bedposts. The W front, overlooking the valley, is dominated by an outsized Venetian window in the southernmost of four unequal gables. On the N side SP 1591 AP (Simon and Anne Ponsonby) is carved over the doorhead, which has an obtuse point and a little spandrel moulding exactly as at Branthwaite Hall, Dean (1604). Upper crucks in the roof show that the C16 house was the same size as the present house, but H-shaped, i.e. with a recessed hall range in the middle between N and S ranges. A broad half-spiral stair ascends two storeys in the angle between hall range and N wing, and a wide arched fireplace occupies the S end of the hall. There may have been a second spiral next to the stack, but in 1625 (datestone) Sir John Ponsonby made a new staircase wing here, i.e. extending N from the E end of the S range. The stair itself is late C17 or early C18, part of a major reorganization that saw the W front filled in between the wings, and the creation of the magnificent LIBRARY. A ceremonious route leads from the S entrance hall, up the stairs, back through an arch to a panelled corridor, not over the hallway, but poaching space from the SE room, and allowing the library to be a good 30 ft (9 metres) long. The great Venetian window fills its W wall. A pair of overmantels in smaller panelled rooms, painted by *Mathias Read c.* 1710, provide an end date for this phase, though the splendid marble fireplace in the library with herms and reclining maiden must be later. The other datestone to notice is JP 1928, for another Sir John, who replaced many of the chunky sashes with mullions and transoms, installed numerous bathrooms, and imported architectural salvage. Sir John converted the barn into a gentleman's club, hence the fireplace and pilasters.

YEORTON HALL, ¾ m. s, along the river. An intriguing house. Large in-line block, smooth-rendered and scored, regularized in the late C17 or C18 to 1–5–1 bays with a central doorway with broken pediment. The upper storey is excessively tall, with very large windows, one a dummy. The ground floor and back are irregular. The windows themselves are plastic, replacing sashes. Did these in turn replace cross-mullions, perhaps double-transomed, like Thackeray's vanished Ribton Hall of 1680? An upper-level bridge at the back, removed in 1988, gave access to walled gardens and outbuildings. Their remains, with the front gatepiers and gappy avenue, speak of departed grandeur.

HARRINGTON (C)

9020

Church Road runs down from the parish church to the HARBOUR. Its two irregularly shaped basins grew from a quay built by Henry Curwen in 1760 for coal from his estate. In the C19 shipbuilding and steelmaking developed, but the main trade continued to be coal exports, which continued until 1929. During the Second World War a secret Magnesite factory was opened to extract magnesium from seawater for use in incendiary bombs, and the harbour was sealed off as a reservoir. It is once again open to the tides, and attempts are being made to develop it as a marina.

St MARY, Church Road. Medieval in origin, the church evolved from a simple box of 1634 which received a grossly over-sized E addition (it was called the 'snail church') in 1807–8. All except the tower was rebuilt into the present rock-faced form by Mr *Deighton* or *Daighton* of Workington in 1884–5; an unbelievably retardataire design. The tower with its oversailing w top was rebuilt in 1905–7 by *John F. Curwen*. Long plain building with Y-tracery, intersecting in the E window. Wide six-bay nave, four more for the chancel, which has added narrow aisles so it is wider than the nave. (The inner w doorway is considered to be of 1634, reusing C12 stones. – FONT. High octagonal bowl with intersecting arches on thin colonnettes. Dated 1634, but perhaps medieval. – ROYAL ARMS by *Joseph Faulder* of Cockermouth, 1812. – SCULPTURE. Norman capital with small figures, in the porch. – Part of an Anglo-Danish cross with disorderly entanglements. – STAINED GLASS. Harrington window, *c.* 2000 by *Alex Haynes*. Otherwise all by *Atkinson Bros*, Newcastle upon Tyne, *c.* 1912–16.)

St MARY (R.C.), Church Road. By *Charles Walker*, 1893. Nonconformist-looking façade, with a closed-in narthex and rose window above. Plain sides with paired lancets, and a three-sided apse. Hammerbeam roof. Contemporary PRESBYTERY alongside.

PRESBYTERIAN CHURCH (now UNITED REFORMED), Church Road. Opposite the R.C. church, raised up on a mound. Of 1881. Short octagonal turret, wooden bar tracery.

METHODIST CHAPEL (former; now Wesley Court), Church Road. 1881. Excited Gothic façade, excessively pointed.

SCHOOL, Church Road. 1875 by *Thomas Lewis Banks*. Large, Gothic, with plate tracery and polychromy. Closed.

No. 72 Church Road is worth noting. Seaside boarding house, Late Victorian and typically over-designed. French mansard-roofed bay in the middle, challenged by over-sized dormers on either side and a pair of pedimented doors (one to the back alley). Coloured glass, curved glazing bars, fancy rainwater goods. All this in the space of a door-and-two-windows cottage.

(BROOKLANDS, SSE of the church, below the playing fields. Late C17 house, of five bays probably originally with cross-mullioned windows. Pedimented doorcase.)

HARTLEY CASTLE (W) *see* KIRKBY STEPHEN

4010

HARTSOP (W)

Pretty hamlet in a side valley. In 2005 it was recorded that only sixteen of the fifty-five houses are permanent homes, which is a typical Lake District figure.

HARTSOP HALL. Lonely house at the head of Patterdale, commanding the Kirkstone and Scandale passes. It belonged to the Lancaster family, then the Lowthers, and now the National Trust. 'A little old black building', says Machell (*c.* 1675), 'wherein is nothing very remarkable but this coat of arms [Lancaster] and good beames and joysts over the parl(ou)r'. It is whitewashed now, a simple rectangle distinguished by uncusped Gothic arched windows of red Penrith stone of about 1500. A stair with vertically symmetrical turned balusters rises in the middle, clear of the external walls, into Machell's parlour, really an upper hall but now subdivided. This has indeed a high-quality framed ceiling of C16 type, deeply moulded and stopped. The Lancaster arms is on the stairs. A garderobe chute can be seen in the attached barn. Extending S is a longer wing, where Machell indicates the hall and kitchen, with a lean-to shelter in the angle supported on cylindrical piers.

THORN HOUSE, C17, has a spinning gallery.

HOW END. Probably mid-C17. Not inhabited for many years, and instructive for that reason. Extreme simplicity, but clever.

Small two-light windows, glazed in one half and shuttered over the other (a late modification). The two floors each now single spaces, their partitioning removed. The bressumer supports a stone fire-hood. Fire-window, aperture for spice cupboard. End entry by the fire heck is now blocked – it led from a cross-passage in the barn but the barn-side wall is secondary. Recess, perhaps for a bed, by the stair, which is a rough half-spiral with no newel. Roof trusses are simply triangulated, the tie-beams chamfered. – DRYING HOUSE by the farm gate. Diminutive crowstepped building with direct access to both floors, like a bank barn. Upper floor with a single cruck-truss, and a floor of slates on edge over joists to make a grille. Lower floor only at the downhill end, below the cruck.

HIGH BIELD. A little N, on a fellside ledge. Built for herself by *Ann Macbeth* (*see* Patterdale) in 1926. White, simple, with a studio in the roof. Three or four other holiday houses of similar date close by (the Ullswater road was only made in the 1920s), of which GREY RIGG, 1923, is the best.

The two functioning farms are modern: CROSS GATES FARM by *Ed Hill* for Alan Weir, 2000, and GREENGATES FARM, a barn converted in 1985.

LEAD MINE, ¼ m. SW of Hartsop Hall, and about 250 ft (77 metres) higher. Working 1696–1942. Ruins of the miners' bothy and crushing mill, and the leat. The early C18 open-hearth SMELTER, along the footpath to Hoggett Gill, is the district's oldest surviving example.

½ m. SE of the village, at the junction of Hayeswater Gill and Pasture Beck, are the remains of a small CORN MILL and the Myers Head and Dodd End LEAD MINES. The large water-wheel pit and the stone supports for the launders date from the 1860s. Further up the beck, two fine stone-arched levels indicate trial workings of *c.* 1800.

HAVERTHWAITE (L)

Cut in half by the A590.

ST ANNE, 1824–5. Plain church of *Webster* type: W tower, nave and chancel with pointed windows and Y-tracery. Outside, memorial to William Fell †1852, listing his many engagements in the Peninsular War.

STATION. 1869, by *Paley & Austin* in the polychrome style chosen for the Lakeside branch. Station building, goods shed and signal box in yellow, blue and red brick plus red stone. The WALL PAINTING centred on the tearoom fireplace, by *Mark Sharphouse*, 2006, is worth a look.

BIGLAND HALL. High above the village, in a bowl of parkland with a tarn. Important as a signed and dated work by *John Hird* of Lancaster, 1781. His designs and estimate were formerly at the house. A refronting probably by *Francis Webster* is recorded in 1809 (datestone). Five bays widely spaced, the middle brought forward a little, with quoins, and the centre window emphasized with brackets and a lion on the lintel. Four-column porch portico. Plain sashes, taller below.

At BACKBARROW, ¾ m. NE, is Ainsworth's Mill of 1823, now WHITEWATER HOTEL. For cotton, then the manufacture of Laundry Blue. – IRON WORKS. The blast furnace was built in 1711 on the site of a bloomery. All the other early furnaces had gone by the 1890s, but Backbarrow was casting iron until 1966. The natural fall of the river was a ready-made source of power, first for a wheel and then a turbine; the charcoal woods stretched far; Furness iron ore was close by. Water power was supplemented by a horizontal steam engine, then electric blowers. When the railway came in 1869 large ore and charcoal sheds were built across the road. A hydro-electric plant was installed in 1999 (replacing an earlier one) and a development plan for the whole site is in the offing. John Wilkinson's great FURNACE is still there, a massive stone cube with a later iron-bound brick stack on top. Cast lintel with date 1711 and initials. For the Wilkinsons' iron-making *see also* Lindale.

BARE SYKE was built for Isaac Wilkinson in the 1740s. A pretty house with square (double) ten-pane sashes. The house has an C18 back garden for which the rock had to be cut away.

LOW WOOD GUNPOWDER WORKS, ¼ m. S. Started in 1798 by Daye Barker and partners, to produce black powder for the Africa trade. The buildings are well scattered for safety between the main leat (which now powers another hydro-electric plant) and the river, with cross-lades powering individual wheels or turbines. The buildings were deliberately left open on one side, with flimsy roofs. The CLOCK TOWER building of 1849 housed the Saltpetre Refinery, a rare survival. Here is the little smoking house, the only place where the men could smoke; offices and stables, and works cottages. BIRK DAULT, over the road, was built for himself by Daye Barker in 1798–9, extended in the 1850s, modified to admit more light in the 1950s.

4010

HAWESWATER (W)

Time has not softened the shocking artificiality of the straight concrete dam, nor the lake's often bald shores. Manchester Corporation's Haweswater Scheme was authorized in 1919. The city acquired more than 22,500 acres of land, and 1921–35 saw the construction of the top end of the aqueduct. A temporary village for the workforce was built at Burnbanks in 1929. The dam was built in 1934–41; once the reservoir started to fill in 1942 the village was mostly dismantled, though some houses lasted until

2004.* The main aqueduct, and the Manchester terminal at Heaton Park, were not inaugurated until 1955. The pipeline is 82 m. long and can supply 72 million gallons per day.

MARDALE village, at the s extremity of the lake, had to go. The demolition of the little Holy Trinity church in 1935 is not yet forgiven locally. Nor is the loss of the Dun Bull in Mardale. The HAWESWATER HOTEL was built in 1936–7 as its contractual replacement.

DAM. Designed by *G. E. Taylor*. A pioneering example of a hollow-buttress structure, still rare in England. It consists of forty-four I-section units, each 35 ft (11 metres) long, stable in itself and structurally independent of its neighbours. A network of walkways runs throughout the interior of the dam. The reservoir is connected by tunnels to the catchments in the Swindale, Wet Sleddale and Haltondale valleys, all envisaged in the 1919 Act, and since 1971 it has also been able to receive water pumped from Ullswater. The DRAW-OFF TOWER incorporates stone from Mardale church.

PUMPING STATION below the dam, of 1978, civil engineers *Rofe & Raffety*. It is able to extract more water than the draw-off tower, which however remains in use. All we see is a large shed, windowless but with vehicle doors, clad in black stone and slate. Two-thirds is below ground, so the interior is highly impressive. Water comes in at the bottom by two huge pipes and shock absorbers. There are six vertical pumps. A giant cigar-shaped tank is another shock absorber. All the working parts are brightly colour-coded, green, blue, purple, yellow. No water is seen, but the sense of rushing power is palpable.** Only in such places, hidden from view, does the vast scale and extent of Lakeland water extraction and export become apparent.

SWINDALE, 3½ m. SW, suffered a similar fate. In 1937 Arthur Mee recorded the last service in the little C17 church, 'doomed by Manchester's water scheme', although in the event the reservoir is modest and little of the valley was flooded. SWINDALE FOOT farmhouse was rebuilt, on higher ground, in Manchester council-house style. The TREATMENT STATION is dated 1933. By a small dam/collection point is MULLENDER, C17, long uninhabited but instructive. The house can be identified by the fire-window and blocked end entry. Inside, holes for spice cupboard etc. and upstairs a bottle-shaped recess for a suspended smoke-hood.

CASTLE CRAG, Mardale. High above the w shore, 1 m. SW of the Haweswater Hotel. A very small FORT, possibly early medieval, only 65 ft by 30 ft (20 by 9 metres) internally, on the

---

* The dwellings were of prefabricated cast-iron panels supplied by *Newton, Chambers & Co.* of Sheffield. A pair of houses was re-erected at Shap Quarry, much of the recreation room became a library in Barrow, and the mission hall survives as the village hall in Legburthwaite, at the foot of Thirlmere.

** An eight-pump version of *c.* 1969 is sited at Ullswater completely underground.

tip of a precipitous spur. Two natural gullies, lightly enhanced, defended the only approach, from the s. A thick wall, now an arc of rubble, enclosed an uneven oval area.

HAWKSHEAD (L)

3090

A tiny town, complete with an important church, market place, police and court house, and a town hall. There are no true streets, but an intricate succession of interlocking spaces and islands of buildings. Flag Street, rough in old photographs but dainty now, has a good succession of jetties, and in the nearby Vicarage Lane a jetty goes clean over the street. The old town's integrity is preserved by drastic means: an avoiding road, a large car park, a ring of retail outlets; effectively New Hawkshead.

ST MICHAEL. The chapelry was constituted a parish in 1578, the building mostly of the C16–mid C17. It stands long, low and comfortingly sturdy on its little hill; one of the best Lake District churches, though no longer shining snow-white as Wordsworth described it. Stripping the whitewash and render in 1875–6 has made necessary the nasty pointing. Nave and chancel without division, full-length aisles, blunt w tower and s porch. 1578 is the date over the Sandys Chapel door, N, and the unusual rounded mouldings of the lights of the straight-headed windows indicate that Archbishop Sandys was responsible for the whole N aisle. 1633 is the date on the N side of the low clerestory, although this is thought to be a repair to the structure added in 1578.

The interior is thickly whitewashed over rubble. On the N side the piers are roughly cylindrical. Those on the s are nearer conical, going from squarish at the base to round at the top. There are no capitals, the unmoulded arches just come down onto the piers. Shapeless arches. Something was evidently felt to be lacking, for in 1680 *James Addison* was employed to effect a *trompe l'oeil* transition between pier and arch. He painted yellow and black zigzag and a corbel effect, but at the cardinal sides not under the squinches. More yellow and black outlines the arches. It works very well. Addison also painted twenty-six 'Sentances of Scripture decently florished' with swags and cherubs, such as 'But Godliness with contentment is great gain'. *William Mackreth* did further painting in 1711–12. They were restored in 1875–6 by *William Bolton*, under the direction of *J. A. Cory*. The style varies considerably – some are almost Neoclassical – and their distribution is somewhat random. – STAINED GLASS. E window by *Hardman*, 1894. Four good windows on the s by *H. W. Lonsdale*, 1884–1901. – MONUMENTS. In the Sandys Chapel, William Sandys and Margaret his wife, formerly dated 1578. They were the Archbishop's parents. A big sandstone chest with two rustically carved recumbent effigies, he a knight in early c16 armour. Traces of colour, e.g. in the mouth of the comical lion at his feet. – On the w wall, unexpectedly grand monuments brought from St Dionis Backchurch in the City of London in 1878, to Daniel Rawlinson †1629 and his son Sir Thomas †1708, both of Graythwaite. – Several good tablets over the arcades including the simple black-and-white memorial to Elizabeth Smith (*see* Tent Lodge, Coniston), †1806 aged twenty-nine. – Col. Thomas Myles Sandys M.P. †1911. Marble effigy by *Wade*, in military uniform and greatcoat.

FIRST WORLD WAR MEMORIAL. In the churchyard. Excellent design of 1919 by *W. G. Collingwood*, based on his antiquarian researches, executed by *Barbara Collingwood*, his daughter. Cross in red sandstone modelled on that at Gosforth, though not so attenuated. St George, looking very Viking, is entangled in the dragon's coils which have turned into interlace, but manages to spear its gaping mouth by his foot.

METHODIST CHAPEL. Behind an c18 or early c19 house converted in 1862. Squeezed in between pre-existing buildings and reached through the house door. – STAINED GLASS. Photographic portraits of Elizabeth Cooke †1866 who gave this chapel, and her daughter also Elizabeth †1916.

TOWN and MARKET HALL. The middle three bays were built in 1790–1 by *Francis Webster* for the Rev. Reginald Braithwaite of Belmount, perhaps to a *John Carr* design. The upper round-headed windows within wider blank arches are characteristic. The lower segmental arches have been filled in, as with market halls everywhere. It was extended at the ends in 1887.

GRAMMAR SCHOOL, s of and below the church. Now a museum. Founded in 1585 by Archbishop Sandys, and rebuilt in 1675 with its bold lintel moulding and curly pediment. The historicist windows were made in 1891 to replace sashes. Wordsworth attended the school from 1779 to 1787.

HAWKSHEAD HALL, N of the village. A grange of Furness Abbey. The GATEHOUSE was used as a courtroom. It is now a detached building, but was once part of a courtyard house. It dates from the c15 and has crowstepped gables. Alterations and restorations 1837, 1849 and 1932. Dec window gone wrong in the end gable, of red stone, as though assembled by workmen who had never seen such a thing. The entrance arch is also of red sandstone. Keystone like a reused boss, a replica of the original. Niche above it, again in Furness sandstone. Inside on the upper floor is a fireplace with a dogtooth moulding; c13? The hall and solar lay on the s side, sw of the gatehouse. Part of the c16 w range now forms a house.

ESTHWAITE LODGE (Youth Hostel), 1 m. s. Grecian doll's house attributed to *Francis & George Webster*, 1819–21, perhaps under the influence of Gandy (cf. Storrs Hall, p. 175). For Thomas Alcock Beck, valetudinarian author of *Annales Furnesienses*. Francis Brett Young, M.D. and novelist, lived here 1929–32. Doric porch, its columns fluted in their upper part, supporting a triglyph frieze. Pretty veranda towards the garden. Platform for a bow-fronted conservatory at the back. Charming interior with incorrect Greek detailing and a sweetly curved stair under a glass dome and vine ceiling.

ESTHWAITE OLD HALL, 1½ m. S. The original seat of the Sandys was rebuilt by Col. Sandys in 1925 after a C17 drawing by Thomas Machell. With its round chimneys and exaggerated stonework it looks like a model or caricature. CRUCK BARN largely rebuilt in 2004, with four new cruck-trusses, lovely to see, of Graythwaite oaks.

BELMOUNT. 1 m. N, between Hawkshead and Outgate. Plain five-bay, three-storey house, built 1774 for the Rev. Reginald Braithwaite, vicar of Hawkshead. Doorway with Tuscan columns and pediment. To l. and r. two-bay links to single-bay pavilions, for services (l.) and agriculture (r.). Similar to Brathay Hall, 1794–6, and Broughton Lodge, 1770–80. Bought by Dr J. W. Whittaker, vicar of Blackburn and architect, in 1840, then by Mrs Heelis (Beatrix Potter) in 1937 and given to the National Trust in 1944 by her husband.

BETTY FOLD, Hawkshead Hill. By *Henry Holiday*, 1907–8, for himself. The builders were *Ushers* of Coniston, and Holiday may have been advised by *Jonathan Bell* of Coniston (on grounds of style). The design of a free-thinking artist, but not a work of art in itself. It stands on a steep hill, shored by three immensely tall sloping buttresses. Holiday's studio is underneath, reached by a long descending stair external but roofed, lit by lunettes of bottle glass. The front door, under its own little canopy roof, opens onto another external but roofed corridor, going round an L to a cross-hall and stair. Altogether there are an excessive number of roofs and outside doors, but only one stack.

COLTHOUSE, ¾ m. NE. Three white farms. QUAKER BURIAL GROUND, 1658. Walled, with seating for open-air meetings. MEETING HOUSE, 1688–9. The tall sashes at the front were inserted in 1790, the kitchen extension 1978. On one short side two cross-windows, at the back one of three lights with a transom. Inside the double porch, one door leads to the schoolroom, the other to the full-height meeting room. The two can be thrown together by means of shutters; one leaf hinges up, the other slides. A low side door leads by a half-spiral wooden stair to the gallery.

CRAGG, ¼ m. N of Colthouse. Built in 1695 by William Satterthwaite, imprisoned for his Quaker obstinacy in 1665 and 1666. White four-bay house with cantilevered or balanced chimney at the uphill end; the former smoke-hood pushes the windows downhill, apart from a blocked fire-window. Internal porches and plank-and-muntin partitioning. Part of the barn fronting the road was converted to another house in the 1930s.

BROOMRIGGS. Very white and prominent across the water from Hawkshead. Built in 1900 for Thomas Thorneley but mostly of 1914, by *M. E. Whitwell* for Richard Rainshaw Rothwell. Long episodic composition in pebbledash, including a broad castellated tower. Hallway small-panelled in oak. Stair wide, plain, nicely moulded underneath, with fat square balusters and closed string. Divided into flats, 1973.

HAYTON (C)

1040

Near Aspatria

The village is a medieval planned one with a long wide street-green, big enough for a football pitch.

ST JAMES. 1865–7 by *Henry Travis* of Manchester. Nave with bell-cote, chancel. Closely single-framed roofs. – Slender iron SCREEN, 1875. – FONT. (C17?), with acanthus decoration, from the Castle chapel. – STAINED GLASS. E window predictably by *Wailes c.* 1872, W by *Gibbs & Howard*, 1882. Behind the organ two Marys, one with an enormous chin, and a self-satisfied Edwardian lady angel; 1910, by *Swaine Bourne*.

HAYTON CASTLE. Hard to understand, thanks to repeated ruination and rebuilding. Especially confusing are the changing floor levels. Its origin is probably a C14 tower house, or rather tall house, for the walls are not particularly thick. It was held by the Tirriols and then the Musgraves, who also held Scaleby, which it resembles in some respects. Mary Queen of Scots stayed in 1568 so it must have been reasonably complete then; probably an H-plan house, but the evidence for this will have to wait until we are in the roof. It was reconfigured in 1609 by Sir Edward Musgrave as a six-room double pile built around a thick spine wall, with staggered floor levels front and back, and large mullioned-and-transomed windows. The new centre and altered S wing had two floors of tall rooms, but the N wing has retained its three floors, giving the house an unbalanced look. In the 1660s, following Parliamentarian damage in 1648, a new front entrance was made on the W side, and some internal modification. Further updating in the C18 in two phases, when the windows of the two-storey part were sashed and then lengthened.

The plan is a rectangle, 90 by 50 ft (28 by 15 metres). The W front stands tall under a long level cornice and parapet. The doorway, not quite central, has a semicircular pediment not reaching to the ends, framing an urn; i.e. late C17. Bays two, six and nine from the l. are pushed out a little. A discontinuity after bay three may indicate where the hall was recessed. Bays one to three, i.e. the N wing, retain their Elizabethan mullioned-and-transomed windows on three floors. The rest is sashed on two taller floors, but the marks of wider openings can be seen. The back is a mess, marred by two enormous emergency buttresses close together in the middle and sloping right up to the top floor. A double discontinuity between the stair and the N wing shows where a recess has been walled in.

p. 402

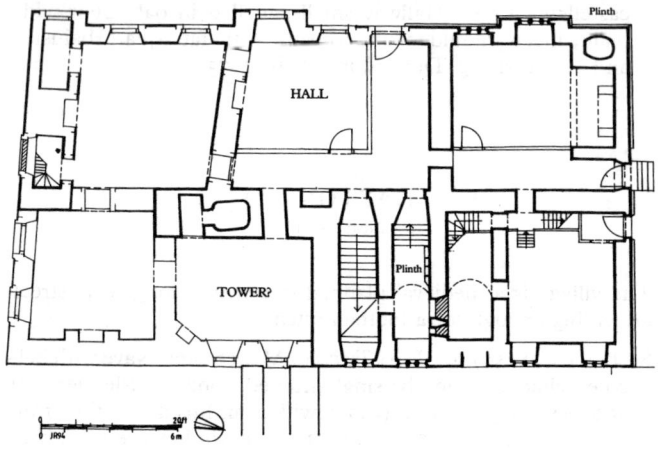

Hayton Castle.
Ground-floor plan, 1998

Windows are randomly placed to suit internal arrangements
until we get to the top, where eight square windows (one dated
1709 or 1719) march under the four equal gables and chimneys. It can be seen that the rear roofs have been raised to
create a vast attic.

Entrance is through the w door, but previously was probably from the E through what is now a tunnel-vaulted cellar. The
hall was subdivided in the late C18 to make a corridor and
smaller drawing room, with Neoclassical chimneypiece and
plasterwork, but its great chimneypiece of *c.* 1670 remains in
the spine wall. Earlier classical decoration in the sw dining
room, with much egg-and-dart. The room behind the hall fireplace is snug with late C17 panelling, and so is the one above
it. The stair opens between the hall fire and the original
entrance, climbing in two broad flights between solid walls. On
the turn are the arms of Sir Edward Musgrave, 1609; our first
firm date. At the top is a grand entrance to what was presumably an upper hall or great chamber, also now subdivided.
Flanking it are two smaller doors, one to a curious mezzanine,
the other to the labyrinthine N wing. There is at least one good
bolection-moulded mid-C17 fireplace, but another with its feet
cut off by a raised floor exemplifies Hayton's complications.
As one mounts higher the intramural spaces become more
evident. Both ends of the house have mural chambers on either
side of a huge stack, and there is an unplumbed space next to
the hall stack. A spiral in the spine wall continues up to a vast
uninhabited attic region. Up here, in a wall of excellent ashlar
between N wing and centre range, is a C14 ogee-headed
window. Below it is a roof-line, so it must have looked out from
a tall kitchen wing over a lower hall.

Traces of a formal GARDEN to the E relate to the 1660s front door, commanding a tremendous prospect over the Solway into Scotland and the Isle of Man. The large amount of stone needed for the emergency buttresses may have come from the chapel which stood w until the beginning of the C19.

HAYTON (C)
Near Brampton

5050

ST MARY MAGDALENE. Rebuild dated 1780 with Latin inscription over the door in the thin w tower. Nave of five bays with arched, keyed-in windows. Chancel added 1842 (by *Sydney Smirke?*), of two bays, with the Venetian E window re-set. Aisle and vault added 1793 on the N side for the Grahams of Edmond Castle (*see* below), with its own w doorway. It is eight steps higher than the nave, opening into it by three arches – a dynamic effect – and is full of family MEMORIALS, e.g. Thomas †1807, with a draped urn. Church restored by *T. Taylor Scott*, 1888 (Kelly). – STAINED GLASS by *C. Evans & Son*, 1888. Also nave sw, †1907–9, signed *W. H. A. Ward.*

SUNDAY HOUSE, on the site of the old thatched parsonage immediately N, for the Grahams so they would never miss a service. Charming stone villa of the 1860s in the Norman style, with a tower.

(FRIAR'S GARTH. By *Ryder & Yates*, 1956, for J. F. Tonner. NE of the church. Single-storey house with one curved wall, flat roof, oriel window with Gothick glazing bars of galvanized metal.)

SCHOOL. 1818, 1853 and 1871, with a Graham inscription and in the Graham style.

THE WOODLANDS is a footballers' close, built by Fred Story of Carlisle United, 2004–6, on the site of Stone House. Absurd row of five-bay Georgian manors each in slightly different stone or brick.

CASTLE HILL, on the N side of the village. A small RINGWORK CASTLE, scarped from the ridge, in the garden of Nook House.

EDMOND CASTLE, 1 m. NW. Now called Hayton Hall. Late C18, altered and extended by *Sir Robert Smirke*, 1824–9, for Thomas Henry Graham, plus a rear wing by *Sydney Smirke*, 1844–8 (library, conservatory, chapel and study). Rather dry Tudor, ashlar-faced. Three-bay entrance side of the 1820s with two shaped gables, and a Tudor porch of three narrow bays of the 1840s. Round the corner a larger 1820s front with two bay windows and also shaped gables. Divided into flats from 2005 by *Casson Conder* of London. The sw GATE has a tall two-centred arch and lodges l. and r. Straight, embattled top. 1820s, with later C19 and C20 extensions and alterations.

The Grahams were great builders; cf. Talkin.

GELT VIADUCT (Newcastle & Carlisle Railway), 1¼ m. ESE. Across the river of the same name at Middle Gelt, high above the old road bridge. A very handsome 64-ft (20-metre)-high three-arch viaduct on a skew approaching 45 degrees, it was famed on its completion in 1835 as the largest such structure in Britain. Stone panels in the rusticated red sandstone credit, in English and in Latin, *Francis Giles* as engineer and *John McKay* as contractor. (*Thomas Slack* of Langholm, the mason responsible, is not acknowledged.) Immediately to the w, the mile-long COWRAN CUTTING, 110 ft (34 metres) deep: another engineering marvel of the time. A million cubic yards of spoil were removed by human and equine muscle.

TOPPIN CASTLE, ¾ m. SW. Folly farm of 1861 for George Head Head of Rickerby, Carlisle. Four-storey tower house, ridiculously tall, with exaggerated corbelled parapets and a yet higher octagonal turret. Narrow windows and coat of arms disposed at random. In the farmyard a miniature Gothic TITHE BARN, fully buttressed, with transepts.

HAZELSLACK TOWER (W) *see* ARNSIDE

4080

HELSINGTON (W)

ST JOHN. High above the Lyth valley and commanding tremendous views over sea and fell. Simple and isolated building of 1726, restored 1857, 1898 and 1910. Roughcast box with bellcote and s porch. Y-tracery E and W, the side windows more correctly shouldered in pairs. The scissor-braced roof too must be an addition, and the rood beam which alone marks out the chancel. – ALTAR with coloured tooled leather panels, *c.* 1912. – E wall, PAINTING of 1920 by *Marion d'Aumaret*, kneeling angels and the Lyth valley. – STAINED GLASS. E window by *Kayll & Co.* of Leeds, 1898. – Tiny SCHOOL of 1854 next door, in use until the 1950s.

HELSINGTON LATHES. *See* Kendal.

9010

HENSINGHAM (C)

On the E edge of Whitehaven.

ST JOHN EVANGELIST. By *J. Slack*, 1911–13. Rock-faced red sandstone, with a NE tower. The W lancets are E.E., the E window Dec, the aisle and clerestory windows Perp. Only the tower top shows a hesitant break away from precedent. (STAINED GLASS by *Heaton, Butler & Bayne*. Also two s by *Wailes*, C19 and re-set, and N aisle w by *William Morris of Westminster*. – MONUMENT. Tablet to John Steward †1848 by *Kirkbride* of Carlisle.) Large PARISH ROOM NW, late C20. The old church, of 1790, 1843 and 1889, was close to the Square, on the N side, where there is still a graveyard.

METHODIST CHAPEL. Cleator Road. Early C20, with a spirelet over the porch. In West View, opposite is the former WES-LEYAN CHAPEL, dated 1856 but looking late C18; charmingly Gothick with a shaped gable and three obelisk finials.

Holly Terrace is typical Whitehaven Georgian, admittedly very late. Garden Villas, another terrace, is Tudor.

WEST CUMBERLAND HOSPITAL, ½ m. SE. By C. B. Pearson, Son & Partners, 1957–9 and 1961–4. One of the first new hospitals built under the National Health Service. Concrete-faced in buff with reddish stripes.

(WESTLAKES SCIENCE PARK, 1¼ m. SE. Established c. 1988 with a mixture of public and private funding. The masterplan is by the Green Design Group and others, with a loop road within 132 acres of landscaped grounds. Near the middle is INGWELL HALL, built by Joseph Gunson, reportedly in 1826. Five widely spaced bays, two storeys, one-storey wings, and a porch of two pairs of Greek Doric columns. Full-height staircase hall under a shallow dome, with a gallery landing all round. Plain iron balustrade with occasional acanthus motifs. Six office pavilions of 1992–6 (Green Design Group) are linked to it. Many other buildings, including the INNOVATION CENTRE facing the main road, 1998 by Eric Parry Architects and Day Cummins, and HERDUS HOUSE (Nuclear Decommissioning Authority), 2005, again by the Green Design Group.)

(NETHER END, 1¼ m. ESE. Dated 1624. Windows mullioned on the ground floor, mullioned-and-transomed above, not quite symmetrical. On the doorway fanciful head, lintel, and finial. C19 addition, r.)

HESKET NEWMARKET (C)

3030

Planted and planned medieval settlement round an oblong green, like Milburn and Askham. On the green is a big ash tree, tiny square MOOT HALL, early 1750s, roughcast with a hipped roof, and the MARKET CROSS – just a pyramidal roof with a ball finial on four round pillars. The plots round the green were never fully built up.

HESKET HALL. 'Sr Wilfrid Lawson's whim', Bishop Nicholson called it. That was probably the Sir Wilfrid who was baroneted in 1688, whose principal house was Isel. Probably a hunting lodge or villa, not a permanent residence. Cubic centre block and four gabled wings: twelve corners and four-way symmetry, like a rustic Villa Rotunda, enabling it to act as a sundial, as has been noted since at least c. 1809. An urn on each corner, a ball on each gable. All the flues are brought into the massive central stack. Some cross-windows. The W wing houses a fine

broad stair with twirly balusters behind a double-transomed
three-light window. Over the s door is an oval window placed
horizontally, under a square dripmould.

For such a transparent concept the house poses an uncon-
scionable number of puzzles. Why are the hoodmoulds of the
central cube chopped off by the wings? Yet the hoodmoulds of
the wings appear to be identical. Why, in addition to the main
stair, are there not one but two turning stairs, of opposite hand-
edness? Why does the impressive pyramidal roof, surely C17,
decapitate a whole series of C17 attic doorways? And who was
'A'? He signed every cut stone, with the significant exception
of the spiral stairs.

CARROCK END MINE. *See* Caldbeck.

HETHERSGILL (C)

Cross-roads hamlet of mainly single-storey houses in the Scottish manner.

ST MARY. 1875–7 by *Habershon & Brock* of London. Rock-faced.
Nave with bellcote and chancel. Will a Victorian set piece like
this, with its sparse lancets, pitch pine, polished tiles and
shaven grass eventually achieve interest?

WESLEYAN CHAPEL, 1901. A better building, though no longer
a chapel. Four-light arched windows fill the spaces between
sloping buttresses.

HEVERSHAM (W)

Spring-line village at the crook of the Kent estuary.

ST PETER. *Paley & Austin*'s strong Neo-E.E. tower (the drawings signed *E. G. Paley*) of 1869–70 is misleading, for this is
one of the oldest Christian sites in Westmorland. In the porch
is a chunk of a late C8 Anglian CROSS of the type of Bewcastle, though closer still to Lowther, with vine scroll and beasts,
amply proportioned. The body of the church is mostly Perp,
with flat lead roofs. The N side is latest Perp, perhaps even early
C17, with flat-headed windows; the church suffered a fire in
1601. In the NE chapel a re-set window of *c.* 1300 with intersecting tracery. The same flat-headed windows appear in the
SE chapel, but the nave s side has (renewed) windows of Early
Perp type, with two-centred arches and panel tracery. The big
five-light E window has loops and short sections of battlemented transom, and some of the mullions do not quite reach
the top. The lancet windows of the clerestory are of course Victorian. As for the interior, it is best to itemize first what Paley

& Austin did: the tower arch, N nave arcade, chancel arch, N and S chapel arches, and the E respond of the S arcade. The new work is striped, not too loudly, in red and yellow stone. The S arcade is chunky Norman work of the late C12, with baldly stepped pointed arches. One complete circular pier with a waterleaf capital, the shaft of a second pier, and the E respond with crockets and rather more fluted or streaked leaves. High square bases. The chancel N arcade is primitive Late Perp, steeply pointed on a slim pier. Roofs look to be mostly post-1601, with flat camber-beams. Small PISCINAS in the N and S chapels.

FURNISHINGS. Mostly *Paley & Austin*, of high quality. REREDOS of alabaster; ORGAN and CHOIR STALLS of 1888, i.e. later than the rest. – Rearranged SCREEN with balusters of 1605 in the N chapel, where there is also a massively iron-bound C14 CHEST. – Medieval S DOOR with bold ironwork, *c.* 1300. – STAINED GLASS. Damaged armorials in the N and S chapels, that in the S with a date 1601. E window by *Warrington*, 1844. S, mostly *Clayton & Bell* including the Wise and Foolish Virgins, suitably ditsy, by the organ. W window by *A. K. Nicholson*, 1924. NE chapel, *Shrigley & Hunt*, 1914. – Plenty of MONUMENTS. Dorothy Bellingham †1626, a tablet on the N side of the NE pier, alabaster. She lies underneath the inscription, a little figure with a swaddled child and a book. – Anne Preston †1767, signed *I. Stewart*, Dublin, N aisle. Classical urn in a shallow recess. – James Backhouse †1790. Richard Crompton †1797, black marble tablet. – Several more set high in the chancel. – Greville Howard †1850 and Mary Greville, huge pair of tablets inset in a Gothic frame, N chapel E wall.

Outside, WAR MEMORIAL CROSS, 1920 by *J. F. Curwen* of Kendal.

MILLENNIUM MONUMENT, on the hillside N. Designed by *Paul Grout*, with carvings by *Danny* and *Lara Clahane*. A topograph. Square pyramidal top with the sun and carved representation of the church and Arnside viaduct, then a circle of slate, a built-up octagonal shaft and a circular base.

HEVERSHAM HOUSE, W of the church across the road. This was *Hubert Austin*'s home, but he modified a Georgian house rather than building anew ('HJA JA 1900' in the stair window). The stair has three balusters per tread and decorated tread-ends. He must have added the top floor with its three gables, but how much is Georgian and how much Austin is not easy to determine. The semicircular bay over the front door for example looks like Austin outside but appears to have Georgian pilasters within.

HEVERSHAM HALL, ¼ m. W. C14 hall and in-line service wing, retaining many of its windows and doors, with a C16 upper storey and some other additions. The lower windows are of two lights, transomed, the heads pointed-trefoiled, and rebated for shutters inside; one each side of the doorway on the N front, two at the back and one to the l. The broad doorway is pointed, as is the solar stair doorway visible in the hall inside. Upper floor with paired mullions and massively framed C16 floor. Rear wing with circular chimney and fire-window. Ruin of a detached thin-walled tower, S.

PARK HOUSE BARN, ¼ m. S of the hall, may have been built for St Mary's Abbey, York. Seven C15 upper-cruck-trusses, very fine. Two tiers of purlins; curved braces come down from the lower ones, go up from the upper. Angle brackets to upper collars. The generous pegging suggests an early date. A flat wall-plate is set in under the cruck feet, and there may be another at the top. A C19 horsewalk is attached, largely complete. A three-bay C19 kingpost-roofed barn continues in line.

PLUMTREE HALL, 300 yds N of Heversham Hall. For Joseph Braithwaite of Kendal. Angus Taylor attributes it to *Francis Webster*, c. 1815. Substantial three-bay, three-storey centre of fine limestone ashlar, with lower links and wings. Porch with Adamish Ionic columns.

EVERSLEY HOUSE, ¾ m. N. Italianate mansion built c. 1855 for Thomas Atkinson Argles, and altered in the 1920s for the Drews. Of limestone in varying textures, with arch-headed windows in twos and threes and an Osborne tower.

HIGH LEASGILL, a little further N. The former vicarage. Substantial house dated RWE (Rev. Robert William Ellis) 1844 on the side-entry porch. Probably by *George Webster*. Tall fifteen-pane sashes with very slender glazing bars.

GIRLS' AND INFANTS' SCHOOL. 1839 for James Gandy of Heaves. Addition 1841 by *Webster*, further changes 1903 by *Joseph Bintley*.

HORNCOP, ½ m. S. 1899–1900, an especially interesting moment in English house architecture. It was designed by the Kendal architect and antiquarian *J. F. Curwen* for himself, which makes it doubly interesting. A touch of Tudor about the doors, of Queen Anne in the broad eaves, white-painted, but really almost style-less and in any case considerably altered. Two wings open at an obtuse angle like a book; in the angle a canted bay looks straight down the Kent estuary into the sunset. An Arts and Crafts stair climbs round the polygonal space thus created into a profligately empty landing. The top floor, even more profligately, is entirely open.

ELLER HOW, now TIDAL REACHES, close by Horncop. By *Stephen Shaw*, c. 1915. Modest but progressive white house with emphatically sprocketed roofs. Flush casements under slate eyebrows allow deep window reveals within. Arched doorway emphasized by bands of slate on edge. Hexagonal tile floors. Simple slatted stair. Bolection-moulded doorcases, two-panelled doors.

ROWELL, 1¼ m. W. Probably C16 though dated RP 1719 over the door. Small mullioned windows of three and four lights under hoodmoulds with end stops. Four-centred head to the doorway, its hoodmould linked to that of the window to the r.

HINCASTER HALL, 1 m. NE. Not big, but advertising its status with four round chimneys and ball finials on porch and gateposts. Front range and rear wing look to be all of one build;

the date 1660 on panelling inside may apply to the whole. Mullioned windows with hoodmoulds. The four-lighter for the hall or firehouse and the two-lighter for the fire-window have been run together to make seven. Good fireplaces inside, but the partitioning has been moved to make it open-plan. Stair with wooden treads in straight flights round a stone newel, which is unusual. It turns into a spiral round a mast to get to the attics. A BANK BARN behind has the stone balls too.

HINCASTER TUNNEL. Built in 1817–19 for the Lancaster Canal. Engineer *Thomas Fletcher*, builder *William Crosley*. 378 yds (349 metres) long. Portals of fine limestone ashlar. Tapering pilasters flanking a segmental arch, which rests on a rounded stone fender at towpath height. A bold string course connects the pilasters above, and the retaining wall continues up to a plain parapet. The composition is serious and impresses with its scale and solidity. Ashlar gives way to brick after ten yards into the bore of the tunnel. No towpath; anchors for a chain or cable allowed boatmen to haul their vessels through. Boat horses were led along a well-engineered path which passes under two arched BRIDGES, the first contemporary with the tunnel, the second – much heavier and clumsier – provided later by the Lancaster & Carlisle Railway.

HIGH HESKET (C)

4040

The A6 has passed it by, to wither.

ST MARY. The chancel arch is medieval, wide, with two chamfers dying into the imposts. Sturdy double bellcote, probably C17. C18 W porch. The roughcast nave and chancel with their keyed-in arched windows are of 1720 but the E window and the N aisle are Victorian. – (STAINED GLASS. E window by *Powells*, 1909. – MONUMENT. Bernard Kirkbride †1677; rustically classical, with a very curly wide-open pediment.) – Outside, Gothic early C19 MAUSOLEUM of the Parker family.
  (VICARAGE. Of *c.* 1927, by *Edward Unwin*, son of Raymond Unwin of Parker & Unwin.)

BARROCK PARK, 1¾ m. NW. From a small C18 LODGE by the A6, white and ogee Gothick, a long avenue descends straight to another, later LODGE, more seriously Gothic, then wanders along the river scarp to find the house. Slightly creepy five-by-five-bay block, built 1791 *et seq.* by James Graham around a C17 core. Plain sashed windows reaching low, quoins. The original roughcast has been removed. Good doorcases on both principal fronts: one (N) with fluted Corinthian columns and an open triangular pediment, the other (E) a full frontispiece with a broad Venetian doorway – enclosed in a glazed porch of 1862 – and free Venetian window over. This side has a bay added r. in 1820 by William James, who bought the estate in

1813. Older work behind is obscured by a large nursing-home extension. Stainless-steel chimney in the garden. – Derelict DOVECOTE near the stable yard. C18. Octagonal, minus its cupola and potence.

HOLKER (L)

HOLKER HALL. Pronounced Hooker. At the Dissolution the Prestons aquired massive land-holdings in Cartmel and Furness. George Preston, closet Catholic and restorer of Cartmel Priory, built Holker in the early C17. About 1700 it passed by marriage to the Lowthers, and in 1756 by marriage to Lord George Augustus Cavendish, whose descendants are here still. Through many incarnations and evolutions the mansion has kept its basic L-shape, and even the same rhythm of bays and gables. The Jacobean house was modified by *Carr* of York in 1783–93, and perhaps by *John Hird*. In 1815 the house was covered in Roman cement. There was a sweeping rebuild in 1838–41 for the future 7th Duke of Devonshire by *George Webster* in his Jacobean style. *Caldecotts* of London made alterations, largely internal, in 1858. *Paley* of Lancaster did more in 1859–61. Then a fire in 1871 destroyed Webster's front block. It was rebuilt immediately for the 7th Duke by *Paley & Austin* (1871–3) on the same footprint and in theoretically the same style; but the new wing is greater in every way, superbly confident, with red sandstone replacing the indigenous stuccoed limestone. It has gained two towers – one solid and square with a grey pyramid roof, the other slimmer, octagonal, with a Baroque hat of green copper.

The Paley & Austin STATE WING, shown in its entirety to the public, is their outstanding domestic work. The three sides – the fourth, NW, has the older leftovers – are calculatedly asymmetrical, the entrance side (NE) with a porch and four-storey staircase tower, the short side with the triangular library bay and a stately round angle bay, the garden side (SW) with that bay and then a flat front with asymmetrically placed dormers. It is a pleasure to follow the compositional finesse. Nor does it interfere with the unabashed display which was obviously expected. The motifs are all Elizabethan – mullioned-and-transomed windows, gables, etc. – yet the house is like no Elizabethan house and to that extent a pattern of Victorian originality. INTERIORS. 'Upholstered magnificence . . . an air of dull ecclesiasticism', thought John Buchan in 1926, though it is not at all Gothic. Much space is given to circulation: hall below, gallery above, each giving onto to the grand stair by a pair of shiny arches of fossily limestone. Nice quarries in the windows, probably *Shrigley & Hunt*. Otherwise four state rooms below, four bedroom suites above.

The OLD WING or family wing, extending at right angles behind, has externally the Tudor windows and hoodmoulds of *Webster*'s rebuilding of 1838–41. It is centred on what was no doubt the original firehouse. This is panelled from Canon Winder Hall, Flookburgh (q.v.), with a chimneypiece made up of bits from Conishead Priory; the Adam and Eve relief is probably Continental work. A pair of Baroque barley-sugar columns are part of the set imported to Chatsworth. Drawing room and small dining room continue in line. Behind is a long black-flagged corridor from the work of 1783–93, linking the twin end staircases in their semicircular projections with Chinese/Gothic ornamental glazing. Both are wooden, suspended in an open spiral, and go up two floors. The front staircase, by the entrance, is a little posher, with fancier balusters, but not wider. Behind the corridor are service rooms and courtyard.

STABLES, by *Miles Thompson*, 1863. Done up (well) as café and shop.

GARDENS. Laid out 1835–6.* Redesigned by *Thomas Mawson* in 1910, but owing a great deal to the present Lord and Lady Cavendish of Furness. *Kim Wilkie* did the cascade, the labyrinth and the new car park (2003–4), using plenty of Burlington slate. *Mark Lennox-Boyd* did the sundial. In the PARK W of the hall an ICE HOUSE, recorded 1732, on a knoll. Rectangular entrance room and domed storage room. (N of the hall, lead STATUE of Inigo Jones by *Rysbrack*, c. 1740s, brought from Chiswick House in the C19.)

VILLAGE, SSW. All in estate style with estate bargeboards and octagonal glazing, painted in Holker light blue. Much by *Miles Thompson*, 1861–2. ESTATE OFFICE by *Webster*, 1846. SCHOOL, 1864, by *Thompson*. U-shaped enclave of social housing, by the main gate, c. 2000.

HOLM CULTRAM (C) *see* ABBEY TOWN

HOLME (W)

HOLY TRINITY is a 'Carus Wilson' church, of 1839 by *George Webster*. Like Casterton (q.v.) but even rougher in execution, and its steeple wider and higher. – (STAINED GLASS designed by *Alice M. Gordon*, 1930. 'Original arrangement of familiar objects'.)

The LANCASTER CANAL opened here in 1819; the mile-long stretch through the village has no fewer than eight bridges and an aqueduct.

FACTORY COLONY, ½ m. S. Established to support linen manufacture in 1790. Two mills, reconstructed in the 1860s after a

---

* *Joseph Paxton* added an enormous ridge-and-furrow conservatory, which has gone.

fire, and now converted to housing. The mill ponds remain, as do the three-storey terraces for the workers.

CURWEN WOODS, ⅝ m. SE. Set in a small park with a pillared lodge. For Thomas Dicey Cotton, c. 1830. Angus Taylor attributes it to *George Webster*. Classical limestone ashlar with two pavilion wings, the recessed centre filled with a loggia of coupled square columns.

FARLETON HOUSE, 1½ m. NE, has a magnificent double BANK BARN, probably C18. Both doors are ramped. Projection on the N with pigeon holes in the gable done in brick, and another projection S, by the farmhouse. Balls and kneelers on all the gables.

HOLME LOW (C)

1050

ST PAUL, Causewayhead. Built as a chapel of ease to Holm Cultram in 1845, before Silloth developed. By *William Armstrong*, 1844–9, in conjunction with Holme St Cuthbert (q.v.). Nave with bellcote and chancel. Lancet style, the E triplet shafted inside.

SE of Skinburness, the road bounding the marsh follows the line of earthwork SEA DEFENCES, probably post-medieval but incorporating a medieval predecessor built after the inundation of Skinburness (*see* Newton Arlosh) in 1301.

HOLME ST CUTHBERT (C)

1040

ST CUTHBERT. By *Willam Armstrong*, 1845, in the same lancet style as its pair at Holme Low. The oblong W tower of 1924, hardly clearing the roof ridge, replaced a spired tower. It has a higher stair-turret. – MONUMENT. Broken C14 effigy of a knight, sans head, sans legs, and with but one arm.

(EDDERSIDE, 1 m. SSW. Two houses now called Neville House, dated JB MB 1739, and Manor House R & AB 1785. Manor House has a shell-hood. Also WEST END FARMHOUSE, early C18, with a semicircular overdoor and bolection-moulded door surround.)

HOUGHTON (C)
NW of Carlisle

4050

ST JOHN THE EVANGELIST. 1840–2. Similar to Stanwix church, Carlisle (p. 265). Cream-coloured sandstone from Dalston. W tower, nave with lancet windows, short chancel. The bell-open-

ings have Y-tracery. Interior renovated 1901 by *C. J. Ferguson*:
pine PEWS, carved oak PULPIT and LECTERN, pitch-pine panelled ceiling. Red cement floor with chancel floor of black-and-
white marble. – FONT of carved Caen stone, with red marble
pillars, of 1898. – GLASS. Windows of Moorish pattern, in plain
leaded glass by *Cleator & Sons*, London, 1897. – (TABLET. John
Dixon of Knells †1857. By *Nelsons*, Carlisle.) – Large attached
PARISH CENTRE.

DRAWDYKES CASTLE, 1⅛ m. SE, on the B6264 where it crosses
the M6 (the site of Milecastle 64 of Hadrian's Wall). C14 tower
with farmhouse of *c.* 1764 attached to its short side. The tower
was refronted for John Aglionby, Recorder of Carlisle, in 1676
(date and arms) by *William Thackeray*. Now three bays, with
alternating pediments over the windows of the ground floor
and first floor with Thackeray's characteristic flat bit at the
ends. Pulvinated friezes. The windows are sashed now, but
probably had his characteristic flush cross-mullions. The
doorway has a moulding like a bolection but flattened off. On
the parapet a comical bust after the Antique; two more are now
mounted in the yard. Roof flashing indicates that the original
hall range was taller than the present farmhouse.

LINSTOCK CASTLE, 1⅝ m. SE. Early tower of high status. The
estate came to the Priory of Carlisle with Walter the second
prior, *c.* 1250, and passed to the bishopric in the C13. Edward
I, and the court stayed here in 1307. The tower may be a little
later. Its walls are faced in ashlar, and extremely thick. Wide
doorway at ground level, pointed with a chamfer and hoodmould. A similar doorway on the first floor is blocked – was
there an external stair, or did it open off an attached building?
Sash windows were inserted in 1768, when the presumed
parapet and fighting top were lost. The basement has a pointed
tunnel-vault. A mural – not spiral – stair climbs up to the first
floor, but its presumed continuation to the second floor and
roof is lost. Attached to the NE corner of the tower is a C15 hall
range, much altered, with two mullioned windows. Parts of a
moat can be seen, and an avenue leading SE to the old Brampton road.

VILLAS. A rash of fine houses for the Carlisle *nouveaux riches* was
noted as early 1826 by James Losh; he called it the Dukery of
Carlisle (*see also* Crosby-on-Eden, Scotby).

HOUGHTON HALL, sandwiched between the M6 and A689.
Early C19 five-bay classical house with a porch of two pairs of
Greek Doric pillars and columns. In front opened in 2000 an
ambitious GARDEN CENTRE housed in a triple steel-and-glass
arched shed, slightly pointed. Lesser sheds to the side and
behind are segment-headed, of galvanized steel or laminated
wood. By *Chris Mackie* for the Klondyke Group of Polmont.

BRUNSTOCK, ½ m. ESE. Large three-bay villa of 1828–30 for   59
George Saul, chapter clerk to the Cathedral. By *Thomas
Rickman & Henry Hutchinson*, and Gothic. The style is oddly
undecided: Tudor domestic with bargeboards for the main
house, fairy-like E.E. for the portico, solid Perp for the ballroom. The perfectly even ashlar is just as Pugin would say not

to do. The interior decor is Gothic too, but the plan is that of a contemporary classical villa, round a central top-lit lobby with encircling landing. The stair is unexpectedly modest: a steeply curving cantilever with iron balusters of quatrefoil section. A much grander, Italianate stair has been added on the other side, together with a large billiard room with coffered ceiling. – GARDEN. Broad raised terrace overlooking parkland. – LODGE with bargeboards and Gothic oriel, no doubt by *Rickman & Hutchinson*, as are the castellated GATEPIERS. – LATCHEND COTTAGES. 1844. Brunstock estate Tudor with frilled bargeboards and faces above the windows.

HOUGHTON HOUSE, ½ m. N. Of *c.* 1810 by *Peter Nicholson* for William Hodgson. Plain five-bay, two-storey house with single-storey pedimented wings, covered in incised render. Small semicircular porch with two Ionic columns. What makes it delightful is the fanciful veranda, a filigree of Gothick cast iron, stretched between the porch and a pair of identical Ionic columns standing free at the ends, each carrying a bit of entablature and an elegant urn. The plain Neoclassical interior is enlivened by a beautiful little library in the r. wing. Nicholson called it an 'elyptical octagon' with a 'semi-ellipsoid' dome. The pendentives are fluted, the dome decorated with an incised fret. Unfortunately the pilasters and original bookcases are gone.

THE KNELLS. ¾ m. NE, on the Scaleby road. Classical three-bay villa of 1824 for John Dixon, remodelled for him in 1843–5 by *John Dobson*. Dobson may indeed have done it all. Fine buff ashlar on a base of pecked rustication, with a rope moulding under the parapet. The porch with two pairs of unfluted Ionic columns is set in front of a recessed centre bay, a favourite Dobson motif (Mitford, Northumberland, 1823). Tripartite windows, their entablature on console brackets. Coffered central light over the stair, with caryatids.

HARKER LODGE, 1 m. NW, on the A7. Three-bay C18 farmhouse facing N, to which Richard Ferguson added a wider garden front in 1816, probably designed by *Paul Nixson*. The new front, overlooking a one-field park, is of Carlisle brick. The ground floor has a tripartite Grecian doorway under a basket arch, and tripartite side windows, but above is an even parade of five windows. Shallow hipped roof with broad eaves. The flanking farm buildings (for this is a villa in the Palladio sense, with a farm) were given pediments to set it off. The hallway has a plaster rib-vault.

HOWGILL

See *The Buildings of England, Yorkshire West Riding: Leeds, Bradford and the North*

HOWGILL CASTLE (W) *see* MILBURN

HUGILL (W) *see* INGS

HUTTON-IN-THE-FOREST (C)   *4030*

Typical of a Cumbrian great house in presenting an informal, accretive front to the world: an asymmetrical group of clearly assorted parts. Before going round, it is as well to have in mind an outline of its evolution.

The N tower and a presumed N–S hall range were built by Thomas de Hoton (†1362), probably with outworks and a moat. Between 1641 and 1645 Sir Henry Fletcher added a long gallery 48 extending E from the N tower over an open cloister, attributed to *Alexander Pogmire* on the grounds of his very similar work formerly at Lowther. There is no evidence that a matching S wing was ever achieved, though one is shown on Kip's engraving of *c.* 1705. In *c.* 1680 the hall range was given a new swagger front 50 for Sir George Fletcher by the master mason *Edward Addison*: a white Baroque frontispiece whose design was probably influenced by William Talman. Like the gallery wing it relates to contemporary work at Lowther. Its cramped lateral proportions suggest that it had to fit a pre-existing space, i.e. there was a S tower as well as the N one. Henry Vane was responsible for adding a suite of Georgian rooms in and around the old tower, *c.* 1745, with plain sash windows overlooking the family entrance in the NW angle. In 1824 *William Nixon* of Carlisle remodelled the C18 family wing which stretches out behind the tower on the S front, with basket-arched windows, and in 1826 Francis Vane commissioned *George Webster* to rebuild the S tower into its present over-dramatic form. Webster even proposed a Gothic mask over the Baroque front. Finally in 1862–7 the inevitable *Salvin* built a new courtyard and offices on the N, and linked the series of parallel buildings beyond the N wing with a screen wall and gateways. He made a new porch and battlements for the medieval tower, and a new main stair behind the hall.

EXTERIOR. The absorbing interest lies in the two C17 parts, and in their links to the vanished C17 Lowther. They are an object lesson in how the century moved from Jacobean to Baroque without seriously going classical. The GALLERY WING of the 1640s first. The cloister below was open until the late C19. It has pairs of semicircular arches r. and l., reaching quite high, but in the canted centre four compressed flat-arched openings. Its columns are shaped to look clustered, in other words E.E., with unmistakable E.E. capitals, a most remarkable example of revivalism. But the rear wall is articulated by seats in niches framed by segmental arches on stout classical columns with over-swelling entasis. Capitals with egg-and-dart, but the mason, tiring of this, has carved one as a rope. The gallery above has a big canted bay projection in the centre, with mul-

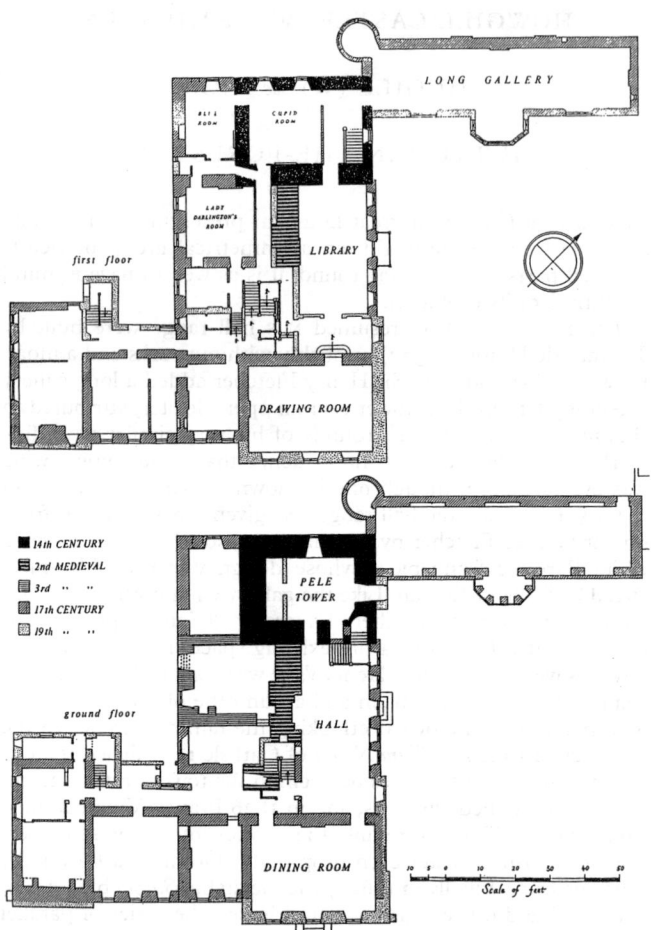

Hutton-in-the-Forest.
Ground- and first-floor plans, 1958

lioned-and-transomed windows, but only a single flanking
window each side, which sits over the spandrel of the lower
storey. At the back, where it joins the tower, is a circular
belvedere, the prettiest part of the whole design, overlooking
the N garden. The medieval TOWER in the corner makes little
impression, its impact diminished if anything by *Salvin*'s porch
and battlements. The CENTREPIECE of *c.* 1680 is a proud piece
of architecture, executed in white stone in contrast to the red
of the rest, but cramped by the flanking towers and missing
the support of a s wing to match the gallery. The doorway has
a broad rusticated surround, the window above it Corinthian
pilasters, a frieze with two garlands, and a bulgy entablature,
the windows l. and r. of this alternately broken triangular and

broken segmental pediments. The attic storey has in the middle, instead of a window, drapery and a shield. The Webster S tower is more bulky as well as taller than anything else, with a whole apparatus of romantic battlementing on top. Behind that, facing the south gardens, the family wing as remodelled in the 1820s by *Nixon*, modestly castellated.

Hutton's INTERIOR dispositions are unusually divorced from its exterior, and the public route doubles back in a confusing way. Entry is into the medieval N tower. Here is the expected tunnel vault, stripped of plaster, and evidence for a spiral stair in the NE corner. There is an inserted partition near its W end. The lower HALL is a space to pass through rather than a place to be in. It is a bay too long, extending by a bay beyond the frontispiece into the S tower, and the floor has been dropped. The C17 lock and key given by Lady Anne Clifford for the front door are now loose. Leading back up into the former solar in the N tower is the gorgeous CUPID STAIR, presumably contemporary with the C17 front, though there is nothing else remotely like it here. The balustrade is boldly modelled with pierced acanthus scrolls (cf. the Black Stair at Durham Castle, 1662), and chubby rustic cherubs. Its position may have been altered, but the one-sided nature of the design limits other possible configurations. The solar has lost its identity. Part is appropriated as a landing, leading to the long, cold GALLERY. This is fitted with a *Webster* ceiling and fireplace, but has Jacobean panelling apparently brought in by *Salvin* from Torpenhow church. The LIBRARY over the hall is at least partitioned in correspondence with the Baroque front, but is no more satisfactory as an apartment. A narrow cut-off corridor leads back to a suite of three Georgian rooms at the N end attributed to *Daniel Garrett*. A local man, *Peter Hardman*, carved the chimneypieces, while *Thomas Perritt* and *Joseph Rose (Sen.)* did the plasterwork. The ceiling of one of these rooms has Cupid in the middle. The top-lit main STAIR is by *Salvin*; its bottom flight has been moved. That leaves the two big rooms in the Webster tower. The DRAWING ROOM above is decorated with *Morris & Co.* papers and a fireplace to match. The gloomier DINING ROOM below has a characteristic *Webster* fireplace of grey marble.

GARDENS. The formal layout shown by Kip survives in outline to the N of the house, though he hardly indicates the steep drop on the W and S sides. It was given a romantic overlay c. 1874 by *Col. Markham*. Walled garden 1736. Park designed in the early C19 by *William Sawrey Gilpin*. – DOVECOTE. C17 or early C18, octagonal, apparently preserving its revolving potence. – HOME FARM by *John Ross* of Darlington, 1870.

ST JAMES, ½ m. N. Nave and chancel, with a bellcote. The medieval church was rebuilt in 1741, and modestly updated by *Salvin* in 1867–8 (£500). He rebuilt the W wall with its double bellcote, Gothicized the windows, took away the ceiling and made the open roof presentable. – ALTAR RAIL. C17. – GALLERY RAIL. Also C17, but from the chapel at Sizergh. –

MONUMENTS. Good collection of Fletcher (†1700, †1761) and Vane tablets in the chancel. – C14 tomb-slab in the entrance, and another, probably later, used outside as a table tomb.

Former RECTORY, opposite the church drive. Harmless three-bay Late Georgian house, retaining at one end a tough, thick-walled defensive wing. Slit windows, formerly barred, below; mullioned windows above. No vault, and with some evidence for an internal wooden stair or ladder. Good kingpost roof. Not a tower therefore, nor a bastle, but nevertheless a place of strength.

₄₀₂₀

HUTTON JOHN (C)

Unwelcoming huddle of buildings tucked away in trees below the A66. The seat of the Huddlestones into the C20, who described it in detail.

(The HOUSE, as complicated as any, is L-shaped and three-storeyed, with a pele tower in the SE angle. It has been repeatedly altered to fit changing ideas. Nothing is ever discarded, but it may well have been moved. This goes for datestones, windows, doorways. Any cogent story depends on family traditions and masons' reminiscences.

The C14 tower is tunnel-vaulted below, with solar above. Entry and spiral stair at the NW corner. In the ground stage a small fireplace with a smoke-hole in the wall. The tower has an unusual projection on the outer E side, said to have been carried up as a beacon turret. The upper windows are sashed. The N wing, adjoining the long side of the tower, is assigned by F. Huddlestone to *c.* 1460 but was thoroughly rebuilt by Andrew Huddleston and his wife Dorathie Fleming after 1660, with a first-floor entry (upstairs living) opening onto the side of the stack. On the other side of the stack (E) was a projection for a chapel and sacristy. In 1730 this was turned into a staircase tower, reached at ground-floor level through a tunnel forced between fireplaces back-to-back. The wing has mullioned-and-transomed windows, a staircase with three balusters to the tread and carved tread ends, and a plaster ceiling. Small heart-shaped windows on the ground floor, and one (carrying a cross; Andrew Huddleston was a Catholic) at the top of the N wall. The W wing was built by Cuthbert Hutton in the mid C16. It acquired a third storey in 1830, with C16 windows moved to the courtyard side to make it all look old. Each wing had its own hall, implying two households. In the work of 1730 the house was thoroughly Georgianized, only to be re-Tudorized in 1866 by *George Ledwell Taylor*, a relation, with a new entrance hall and library. The flat-roofed, double-height entrance and link in the courtyard angle is his. High Victorian Gothic chimneypieces.)

(The GARDENS were well-known. Terrace with large shaped yews along the E side. Andrew and Dorathie's 1660 front doorway is now in a garden wall, between S wing and dovecote.)

BURIAL MOUND, on the summit of Great Mell Fell. Of earth and stones, 26 ft (8 metres) across and 2 ft 4 in. (0.7 metres) high, surrounded at a distance of about 14 ft (4.3 metres) by a shallow ditch with a slight inner bank.

ROMAN REMAINS, WNW of Troutbeck, alongside the Roman road from Old Penrith (*see* p. 579) toward Keswick. Earthworks of a ROMAN FORT and three CAMPS, all probably late CI. The westernmost camp (which preceded the Roman road) and the fort are crossed by the old A66 road, by-passed in 1974. The camps differ markedly in size, from 1.6 acres to 24 acres; the gates through their simple bank-and-ditch perimeters were defended by short curving extensions of the rampart. The rampart of the small square fort was built of clay blocks, revetted with timber; it turned inwards on either side of the gate placed centrally in each of the four sides.

HUTTON ROOF (W)   *5070*

Approached from the W over high, roof-like limestone pavement – but there is good sandstone in the parish as well.

ST JOHN. Of 1880–1 (1881 on the weathervane) by *Paley & Austin*. A good, honest job. Perp, and not large, with a S tower acting as a porch, and a N aisle under a catslide roof. Excellent interior, without tricks but all of good quality, with a full set of FURNISHINGS: altar rail, choir stalls, screen, organ screen, pulpit. The chancel has a barrel ceiling with stars, the nave a tie-beam roof with tracery between the queenposts and the roof slope. – FONT dated 1870. – In the vestry a datestone 1610 with the 6 reversed, and a window head dated 1757, also from the previous church. – STAINED GLASS by *Heaton, Butler & Bayne*; also w window by *Shrigley & Hunt*, 1880.

The former VICARAGE, S, is by *Ewan Christian*, 1850. Tall, plain, handsomely scaled, a little gaunt. The floor-length sashes of the canted bay look straight E to Ingleborough. At the end of a garden walk S the Georgian BELLCOTE frames a more bucolic view.

INGS (W)   *4090*

ST ANNE, Hugill. Dated 1743 over the W door. Eight flame-like pinnacles to the unbuttressed tower with its quoins. The openings look CI7, i.e. old-fashioned, rather than CI8, and the reused lock of the w door says 1682. w doorway with broken pediment and Italianate shield painted with the arms of Robert Bateman, a child of the parish who, in Wordsworth's words, 'grew wondrous rich' as a merchant of Leghorn, and has his funerary monument there. E window of Venetian type under a broken pediment into which the arch reaches up. Six-bay nave and chancel, undifferentiated, with arched windows with blocky imposts and keystones. Urn on each corner. The N transept, very well done, was added by *Joseph Bintley* in 1877. The church was evidently meant to be whitewashed, as usual in the area. Good interior with coved ceiling, the chancel steps marked out by a pair of Ionic pilasters, perhaps of 1877. The tower arch is filled with what could be the remains of a chancel screen, now with swing doors like a Wild West saloon, classical pilasters with their capitals shorn off, and Greek key entablature. – Chancel PAVING in six-fold stars, of marble sent by Bateman from Leghorn. – ALTAR with a top with an inlay of marble too. – REREDOS, carved by *Robert Fell* of Common Farm, each panel of the wainscot carved differently. He made the PULPIT too, and the self-portrait with flowing beard and wideawake hat that hangs by it. – FONT. Square, bulgy bowl with four grown-up cherubs' heads. C18. – STAINED GLASS. E window by *Edward Frampton*, 1883. Very painterly. Others by *Shrigley & Hunt* (two S) and *Wailes* (one S and one N).

RESTON HALL, originally Leghorn Hall ¾ m. E. Dated 1743 on a rainwater head, and also for Robert Bateman. Plain seven-bay front with sashes, which is quite progressive for the Lake District proper. (Inside, a fine arch with pilasters connects entrance hall and staircase hall. The staircase has slim balusters. In an adjoining room an equally fine cupboard with pilasters.)

(THE ASHES, 1 m. S. Mid-C16 with additions. Mullioned windows. Pevsner noted interior features including a refined fireplace of *c.* 1730, reportedly from Rayrigg, Windermere (q.v.).)

IREBY (C)

ST JAMES, in the village. 1845–6. Bald lancet style, wide nave and short narrow chancel. Bellcote. W arch as though for a tower never built. – FONT. Norman, from the old church. Round bowl on an unusual pedestal with four 'clock faces', like the knop of a chalice, each ornamented with a cross or flower in relief. – Other FITTINGS were taken in 1961 from the demolished church of St John, Uldale (1869). – STAINED GLASS. E window by *Abbott & Co.*, *c.* 1950.

Ireby is a failed town, granted a market charter in 1236. The MARKET PLACE running E–W, the focus of four roads, is encroached upon by two groups of buildings. They include the former MOOT HALL: C17 centre and two later wings, doorway with segmental pediment, Salkeld arms above. The CROSS stands a little W in a leftover bit of open space. Octagonal shaft and plinth both C17. The C19 head copies the font now in St James.

(IREBY HALL. Two houses and two barns in a row, C17 and later.)

OLD CHURCH, 1 m. W of the village, in a rushy field. Just the chancel; nave and N aisle were taken down in 1845. Much repair and reconstruction then, and in 1880 by *Ewan Christian*. It was taken into care by the Redundant Churches Fund (now Churches Conservation Trust) in 1972.

So small, yet two distinct parts: the W of *c.* 1150, the E lengthening Transitional of the late C12, with clasping buttresses and a triplet of round-headed E windows of equal height, and one more above. The lower three are set in an inner arcade with colonnettes with waterleaf capitals. Pair of blocked pointed lancets, S. Two AUMBRIES and a small PISCINA. Old stones built into the walls include what could be part of the *mensa* – or is it the other half of George Crage's tomb-slab? (†1626, vernacular, with unskilful lettering.) – Also MONUMENT to Thomas Wilson †1769, Ionic with a broken pediment. – Outside, as though awaiting Simeon the Stylite, the octagonal monoliths of the N arcade with their caps and waterholding bases: i.e. C13. They were reinstated in 1977, having done duty elsewhere as gateposts.

SNITTLEGARTH, 1½ m. SW of the village. Behind a magnificent green cedar, a five-plus-two-bay, two-storey house with unusually small sashes. Early C18 and 1801 (date over the door). Doric pillared porch, with triglyph frieze. A large dining- and drawing-room wing was removed in 1935.

Higher up still, ½ m. SSW, is HIGH HOUSES, commanding a vast prospect over the Solway into Scotland. 1669 WW (William Williams) EW on the lintel. Mullioned-and-transomed windows blocked, replaced by Georgian sashes. The main hearth is on the l., with a wide-arched fireplace and end entry. Barns attached make a sprawling cross-shape, with a subterranean system for access to all parts under cover, including a brick-vaulted tunnel under the hay barn to take feed direct to animals below; probably C19.

IRELETH (L) *see* ASKAM-IN-FURNESS

IRTHINGTON (C)   4060

ST KENTIGERN. Bishop Nicholson in 1709 found 'both ye Chancel and Vicarage-House, as well ye Vicar himself, much out of repair'. A painting of 1842 shows a long whitewashed building without aisles or clerestory, fitted with domestic sash windows, with only a pair of lancets at the extreme E and a bellcote on the chancel arch to distinguish it as a church. The picture today is, not surprisingly, Victorian: 1849–53 and *M. H. Bloxam* of Rugby for the aisles with their lancets and the clerestory with its spherical-triangle windows, *T. Taylor Scott* of Carlisle, 1897, for the new NW tower outside the aisle. It comes as an agreeable surprise therefore to find inside the bones of a very fine Transitional and E.E. church. The chancel arch is early C13, of two orders of columns with spurs and crocket capitals. The innermost order is a continuous roll, and the arch has rolls as well as dogtooth. The stout arcades are yet older, *c.* 1170. They have round arches of one step and a slight chamfer carried on circular piers with square abacuses and capitals decorated with broad fleshy leaves, some crossed, and what looks like a corn-cob motif. The capitals are uncarved on the aisle side. (The C13 priest's doorway is now in the vestry.) Looking more carefully at the exterior it can be seen that the masonry of the long chancel is indeed medieval and that the lancets, though remade, are convincingly widely spaced. – STAINED GLASS, including E window by *Wailes, c.* 1858, and W window by *Percy Bacon Bros*, 1909.

MOTTE, SSE. Steep-sided; once landscaped as a garden.

CARLISLE AIRPORT, ¾ m. SW, was constructed in 1940–1, passing out of military ownership in 1946. Control tower with a bar in its ground floor, of three storeys with metal windows (some replaced by plastic). A few hangars.

IRTON (C)

0000

ST PAUL. In dull country, but offering stupendous views of Wasdale and the mountains at its head. 1856–7, by *Miles Thompson* of Kendal. Perp, roughcast with red stone dressings, with a big W tower with taller turret. The chancel was extended in 1872 by *William White*. White made the strange Gothic triumphal arch to accommodate the organ and vestry. In 1887 Sir Thomas Brocklebank installed a peal of bells (very unusual hereabouts); the coloured iron tower SCREEN was made, Thompson's ceiling was removed and the double-hammerbeam roof installed. *G. E. Grayson* was probably the architect. – STAINED GLASS. N aisle, two two-lighters by *Morris & Co.*, 1887 and 1888, unmistakable; large single figures on richly damascened backgrounds. St Catherine is by *William Morris*, the others by *Burne-Jones*. Contrasting, but equally good in their way, several by *John Scott & Son* in chancel and S aisle from the late 1860s and 1870s: small lively scenes in quiet colours, deliberately two-dimensional like early Clayton & Bell. The remainder, with their mauvish cast, are by *Wailes*, except the W window by *Gibbs*, 1856.

91

MONUMENTS.* George Irton and wife, †1744, 1749, coloured marbles. – Samuel Irton †1767, with draped urn. – Skeffington Lutwidge, commander in 1773 of HMS *Carcass* towards the North Pole, †1814, with trophy. – Several decorative brass plates to members of the Brocklebank family, supplied by *Morris & Co.* into the early C20. – Outside, against the E wall of the vestry, Daniel Brocklebank, shipbuilder, †1801, superbly lettered. – Due W of the tower, memorial to the Irton Hall servants; the earliest †1781. Square, with elegantly scooped cavetto sides and fluted top, like a tea caddy.

CROSS. S of the church. Of the first half of the C9, so between   9
Bewcastle and Gosforth in date, though closer to the Anglo-Roman discipline of Bewcastle than the Viking wildness of Gosforth. A beautiful piece, with just the right amount of entasis. The free cross-arms are well emphasized with scooped-out armpits. The decoration, to our eyes all abstract, is divided into panels with a wide rope or pellet border. On the W or 'public' face are two large panels of interlace separated by a space ruled for a three-line inscription, though none can be seen. Five pellets in a circle in the head. S and N are full-height vine scrolls. The E side, more worn, has five unequal panels including at the top an unusual chequer of sunk St Andrew's crosses. In the head is a boss and a circle of pellets in a wavy ring. Figures are said to be visible on the cross-arm.

CROSS. In the SW corner of the churchyard, at a respectful distance. Of 1911, commemorating the Brocklebanks, who had bought the hall. Like the C9 cross, but stouter, less aspiring, and fatally encumbered by a dwarf wall. The motifs are converted back from abstraction to naturalism, like the Ruskin cross at Coniston.

To the S, former VICARAGE of 1864 also by *White*, Gothic, very big, with several outbuildings, and a former SCHOOL.

IRTON HALL, 1 m. E. Dismal straggling pile of 1874 in granite and red sandstone, castellated, mullioned and transomed, by *G. E. Grayson* of Liverpool, for Jonas Burns-Lindow. It has had older incarnations, and incorporates at the back a C14 defensive tower; part of a C15 window with round-headed lights shows on the SW. It is four-storeyed, with a tunnel-vault; entry and newel stair are in the SE corner. Grayson's stable clock tower with its open top is frankly Victorian (1887), and rather more jolly. It holds the 'Pretender' bell of 1715 from the church.

ISEL (C)   *1030*

ST MICHAEL. A small early C12 church down by the River Derwent and bridge. Nave and chancel only. Mathias Read, usually trustworthy, painted it in the early C18 with a W tower

---

*The d'Yrton stone, which lay under the altar, is at St Bees (q.v.).

and spire – an unusual thing in Cumberland. Three tiny windows N, deeply splayed on the inside. One (chancel N) now gives on to the vestry. The S doorway with one order of columns with scalloped capitals and two orders of zigzag is Norman. So is the chancel arch, with a half-roll and two quarter-hollows, and one S window, externally of the C18. Restoration 1878 by *Ferguson*; CHOIR STALLS, PULPIT in his baluster style. – FONT. A heavy octagon, rounded below. Medieval – ROYAL ARMS, over the chancel arch. 1714, by *Mathias Read*. – SCULPTURE. Two parts of a C10 or C11 cross-shaft. – MONUMENT. Outside, a medieval tomb-chest with shields over ogee canopies, separated by buttresses.

ISEL HALL. Quite a spectacular building, especially since in 2003 its pele tower was limewashed ice-cream pink. The colour is traditional and, in the words of the limewasher, it lifts the whole valley.

Tower and hall range in a seemingly casual relationship: the tower presents a short side to the long side of the hall, the opposite to the usual set-up (but as Muncaster and Irton), and the two are separated by a narrow wedge-shaped space, now occupied by a staircase. The four-storey TOWER is late C14 or early C15, and more like a miniature castle than usual. Its basement is subdivided into a small and a large chamber, vaulted at right angles to each other, and a long vaulted passage to an inner doorway with a shouldered arch. Access between floors is by long mural stairs in the E wall, not the usual spirals. There are garderobes on each floor, and the caphouse and parapet-walk are well preserved. A few original windows. On the top floor a two-light window of early C16 type. On the first floor an original fireplace is preserved. The damaged NE doorway to the HALL RANGE, which is perhaps late C15, may also have had a shouldered arch. A mid-floor, its timbers heavily moulded but not stopped, was inserted *c.* 1520, perhaps by Sir John Leigh whose arms appear on the S wall. This probably dates the stack with its little fire-window at the W end. A timber-framed partition and linenfold panelling divide off a parlour at the E end, and a later passageway runs through to a C19 drawing room addition beyond. Although Isel is clearly a gentry house, the plan has evolved into that of a Cumbrian farmhouse: door and cross-passage at one end behind the stack, entry beside the fireplace, screened by a heck prolonged into a corridor, and a parlour or bower at the far end from the fire. In the hall also Elizabethan panelling with painting in imitation of tarsia. More such panelling in other rooms. In the room above the hall, reused, simpler early C16 panelling with plain muntins.

W of the hall range is a long and even three-storey range of mid-C16 date (WL IL 1531 on a fireplace), with three-light windows and obelisks on semicircular loops decorating the parapet. Mathias Read's painting shows a cross-wing at the far end, answering to the pele tower; now gone. To the N is a square sunken WALLED GARDEN, in essence probably C17. At the top of its steps, and on the S terrace, is displayed the punning device of the Lawsons – a sun supported by the long arms of the law. Mid-C16 STABLES, with obtusely pointed lintels.

WATER MILL, ¼ m. N of the Hall. Mid-C19, originally four-square of two storeys and two bays, now extended to the l. The attached single-storey wheel house still contains an overshot iron wheel.

HEWTHWAITE HALL, ¾ m. SW. A puzzling little house, which can be interpreted differently depending on whether one considers it vernacular or polite. Three bays only; a blocked N doorway suggests that there was more, perhaps farm out-buildings in line, with the usual cross-passage and end entry. Inscription over the central doorway with the date 1581, combined with royal arms of an earlier date, family arms upside-down, and four medieval-looking figures in niches, two above two; all brightly coloured. Ground-floor windows mullioned with round-arched heads and dripmoulds, probably c. 1581. Upstairs are bald-looking cross-mullions, i.e. more like 1680s. Above that a section of blank wall, as though the eaves have been heightened, or a third storey lost. This incorporates bits of sill and lintel as infill, like those of the ground floor. The stair window at the back has an embattled transom and cinque-foil-cusped heads, which looks medieval. The r. room is divided from the central cross-passage only by a stud partition, and has the larger fireplace; so it corresponds either to the gentry hall or to the farmer's firehouse. The l. room is smaller but has moulded and stopped joists of C15 type: the bower. Behind the hall is a small unheated chamber (downhouse?), and at the back a fine C17 stair with bottle-shaped balusters.

IVEGILL (C)

CHRIST CHURCH. Built at the sole expense of the Rev. Arthur Emilius Hulton of Southampton, 1868. The architect was *Robert Jewell Withers*. It has an octagonal bell-turret with spirelet on a W mid-buttress. Plate tracery. – (STAINED GLASS. Three windows by *M. & A. O'Connor*, 1868. Others by *Powells*.)

VICARAGE, E. Same date and architect. Bigger and more showy than the church, with some polychromy. – (STAINED GLASS by *Heaton, Butler & Bayne*. Peter Howell.)

PACKHORSE BRIDGE, downstream of the modern road bridge. Exceptionally elegant. A single span of over 20 ft rises to 12 ft above the water (6 and 4 metres). Large sandstone flags have been added to provide parapets, probably in the C19.

HIGHHEAD CASTLE, 1½ m. W. Henry Richmond Brougham's mansion burnt out in 1956 but has, if anything, gained beauty in tottering ruin. Demolition was sought in 1985–6, but Christopher Terry brought stasis if not rehabilitation in 1987.

A straight mile of neglected avenue descends gently to its grassed-over forecourt. Stables on one hand, garden wall the other, gorgeously elaborate GATEPIERS with Ionic columns ahead. Behind them what was the finest C18 house in the region. 1745 was scratched on a window, but if Brougham started to build as soon as he came of age in 1740 then the tradition that the architect was his uncle *John Brougham*, who died in 1741, may have truth. *Susanna Richmond* may also have assisted. In any case James Gibbs and his *Book of Architecture* (1728) was evidently the source. The masonry is still crisp, deep red with white dressings; both from the same Dalston quarry. Eleven-bay N front, with a three-bay centre and pediment but no expressed order. A W wing unbalances it on the r.; we shall see the reason for this. In the pediment a splendid achievement of arms borne by a merman with trident and mermaid. Shallow steps up to the *piano nobile* and the main doorway, with rustication of alternating sizes and its own pediment. Moving round to the l., we find that the terrace that hugs the house on three sides hangs vertiginously over the river far below, for this was a genuine castle site (licence to crenellate 1342), and much stronger than is at first apparent.* Part of the Georgian E façade fell in 1980, but the S side is mostly complete, with a sharply cut Venetian window to light the stair. The W wing, behind the Georgian front, turns out to be C16. It was built *c.* 1550 by John Richmond and Margaret, daughter of Hugh Lowther, and has typical details. Four-light windows, with hoodmoulds, round-arched but uncusped. There is a long parapet walk on a three-stepped cornice which curves in at the corners, Scottish-style.

The C18 plan was ambitious: a double pile built around a double spine wall. The broad hall intersected the cross-corridor with a double Doric colonnade, one of which still stands precariously amongst the saplings, leading to a central imperial stair at the back. Gibbs would have put a grand saloon here, with balanced stairs at either end; the drop at the back may have suggested this variant. Anthony Sharp, who made studies of the house in 1953, recorded Rococo plasterwork and a groined plaster vault for the cross-corridor. The plasterwork was apparently of variable standard, as is the external carving, lending credence to the tradition that both local and Italian craftsmen worked here. The basement floor is complete, segmentally vaulted in stone.

Brougham died in 1749, unmarried and childless, leaving the house, possibly still unfinished, to be squabbled over by relatives. By 1790 it was hastening to ruin. Repairs were undertaken in 1874, and in 1902 it was sold to Judge Herbert Augustus Hills of Alexandria and made habitable by *J. H. Martindale*. His new servants' wing N of the Elizabethan part is the only part now roofed. This was built across the filled-in ditch; the resultant subsidence may be noted, and the neat way it has been corrected. A cross-section of the ditch appears where the ground falls away to the E.

---

* A Buck print of 1739 shows a three-storey gatehouse, and a rock-cut ditch across the undefended N approach.

STABLES, now residential, dated 1747. A fine quadrangle, the front with windows and archway all heavily rusticated. Steep pedimental gable and cupola. – Walled pleasure GARDEN, steeply and expensively terraced. The wall is lined with heat-retaining brick. – LODGE and GATES by *Martindale*, early C20.

CHAPEL, in a field nearby. Long plain building, closed 1974, converted to a house in the 1990s. It was rebuilt in 1682 and bears a stone inscribed with the names of twelve trustees. Pointed-arched windows, and one mullioned window. Bell-turret and Y-tracery 1836.

HIGH HEAD SCULPTURE VALLEY, NE. An interesting example of farm diversification. *Jonathan Stamper* is both farmer and sculptor, and has brought in other artists. The artistic standard is not high. The effect of indifferent sculpture dotted about the valley – neither wild nor tame, but unkempt – is perilously close to a farmer's junkyard.

THISTLEWOOD, ASHES. *See* Raughton Head.

JOHNBY HALL (C) *see* GREYSTOKE

KENDAL (W)   5090

The historic plan is essentially just one very long street, climbing northwards from the Nether Bridge and the parish church to a summit at the market place, then dropping again before leaving by County Hall and St Thomas's church; a full mile. Off this spine open innumerable narrow Yards, like the Edinburgh wynds, each corresponding to a burgage plot. To the E they run down towards the river, although there was much clearance in the 1950s–60s. The better-preserved ones on the W are brought short by the steeps of Fellside and the motte of Castle Howe. Across the River Kent, to the E, is Kendal Castle. The town is built of the tough local limestone (hence 'the old grey town'), used as rubble and generally roughcast until in the early C19 the Webster dynasty (*see* below) perfected a hammered near-ashlar finish. 'Visiting' stones often look uncomfortable, especially when directly contrasted with the local stuff, as in the library or the chancel of St George.

Kendal was incorporated in 1575. Its business was wool, weaving and especially dyeing, which reached a peak in the C16 but thereafter declined gradually to nothing. In the C18 it was a centre of snuff manufacture; snuff is still made in Lowther Street and Canal Head North. The coming of the canal in 1819 ushered in an era of prosperity and growth, reinforced by the Windermere branch railway which arrived in 1846. The canal terminus was on the E side of the river, below the castle, and it created a new district, with a new bridge to serve it. K Shoes was a major employer in the C20, starting as Somervell Bros in the 1840s. The Provincial Insurance Co. was another; it moved to Kendal in 1919. The end of the C20 saw the demise of both. An unusual industrial presence is Gilbert Gilkes & Gordon, turbine manufacturers.

Kendal has nurtured quite a crop of ARCHITECTS. *Francis Webster* (1767–1827) was 'the first to introduce the public profession of architecture into Kendal'. Coming from a long line of masons and marble polishers, he arrived *c.* 1787, and was closely involved in the early C19 with the canal as promoter, builder and architect. His son *George* (1797–1864) dominated the architectural scene until mid-century, building in a variety of styles including the early use of revived Jacobean. *Miles Thompson* (1800–72), partner from 1845, seamlessly continued the practice. Then, but diminishingly, *Brade & Smales*. The term 'Webster' can be applied with variable exactitude to a great many Westmorland and Lancashire houses of limestone in the Greek, cottage, and Jacobean styles, with readily identifiable marble fireplaces; and to a batch of pre-archaeological churches. Other men to watch are *Joseph Bintley* (fl. 1860s–80s), and *Eli Cox*, who did the almshouses and the organ works along the river bank. *John Flavell Curwen* (1860–1932) was a progressive architect and observant antiquary, with numerous brisk papers in the CWAAS *Transactions* to his name. The practice of *Stephen Shaw* (1846–1931) and his son *Malcolm* was bought by *Brian Dockray*, taken over by *John Gill* of Ambleside, becoming *Gill, Dockray, Rhodes & Moore*, now *Gill Dockray*.

Traffic is the bane of Kendal. Despite The M6 to the E and the A591 by-pass W it is still difficult to dissociate the town from its terrifying one-way system, which speeds traffic along both river banks and across all three bridges, turning significant chunks of the town into traffic islands. The population was 24,000 in the mid 1960s. The 2001 figure shows little change, at 27,505: the largest town in the old county of Westmorland.

CHURCHES

HOLY TRINITY, Kirkland. Wide and spreading, like a hen covering her chicks, nicely symbolizing the mother church, its thriving town and vast parish. A dependency of St Mary's Abbey at York, Kendal was bestowed in 1553 upon Trinity College, Cambridge. It was the Master of Trinity, Dr Whewell, who initiated the great restoration that determines much of its present character. *J. S. Crowther* in 1848 found it 'about as melancholy a picture of neglect, ruin and irreverence as the imagination could conceive'. Nave and chancel were done in 1850–2, inner aisles 1863, outer aisles 1868.

Holy Trinity is one of the broadest parish churches in England, being fully five-aisled, and by far the biggest in Cumbria. The W tower is embraced by the aisles, and there is no projection even for the chancel, so only the SW porch stands outside the perfect rectangle. The elevation is almost as even, being in character entirely Perp of the mid C15 to early C16. The broad W tower is very plain, except for the large W window with its emphatic transom. The porch is by *Crowther*, and typical in all its details. The church is flat-roofed and battlemented throughout, with pinnacles, inhabited cornices and gargoyles characteristic of Crowther, not Cumbria (he derived the details from Manchester Cathedral, which he had measured and drawn and was in due course to restore). The windows, set in deeply scooped reveals, have repetitive Perp traceries and depressed heads, originally three-centred, i.e. without a point; the renewed ones are more pointed. Where the gables allow it at the ends they are more perky in shape, and for the main E window Crowther has managed the fully two-centred arch which he considered the ideal. The low C16 clerestory drops down by a timber-framed gable to a blind storey over the chancel. The Bellingham Chapel at the NE corner is taller than the rest, with its own upper storey.

The vast INTERIOR is gently dished down to the E, with little to interrupt the free-flowing space. The receding lines of columns never line up, reminding us that it was not planned as a single space. *Crowther* has left it cold and over-tidy. Until the C19 it was a maze of pews, stoves and galleries, with painted texts, cherubim and seraphim, and 'green hissing serpents and flying dragons'. The inner arcades make it clear that the church existed from at least the C13, and it was already aisled, but not outer-aisled, from end to end. The piers of the four-bay chancel are of C13 form (octagonal alternating with round) on waterholding bases. They have occasional bits of nailhead, and one incorporates a trefoil-headed aumbry. The piers were rebuilt by Crowther without disturbing the arches above, which are steep and twice-chamfered. No chancel arch, just a slightly extended pair of piers, without capitals. Crowther marked it with a pair of hammerbeams, having shortened the clerestory by a bay. Four bays for the nave, with taller arcades, and then the open base of the tower with its mighty piers. Its arches die in, like those marking the chancel, which is a C15 motif, but the mid-piers may be older (round piers, round or octagonal abaci, double-chamfered arches). The outer arcades run through from E to W without a break. The S arcade, probably early C16, has squat circular columns on conical bases, and elementary capitals. The outer N piers, also C16, are octagonal with no bases, just a ring moulding, and very matter-of-fact. The Bellingham Chapel at the E end of the aisle has a pendant ceiling with thin wooden ribs, like the Tudor ceilings at Sizergh (q.v.). It was renewed in the C19, with some original bosses, as were all the other roofs.

FURNISHINGS. The enormous width of the church is emphasized by long dark lines of benches. A conservative reordering in 2007 brought a forward ALTAR and CHOIR STALLS by *Nicholas Rank* in George Pace style. *Crowther*'s long CHOIR STALLS, some incorporating medieval bench-ends with poppyheads, had already been dispersed to the back and sides.

– SCREENS. There must have been many medieval screens; a doubtful survivor is in the Strickland Chapel (inner SE) with some genuine Flamboyant tracery. Crowther's re-created chancel screen has largely gone too. The Parr Chapel screens (outer SE) were designed by *J. F. Curwen* and made by *Arthur Simpson* in 1934. – A hanging CORONA of stainless steel, designed by *Michael Bottomley* and made in 1969 by *Keswick School of Industrial Arts* for the chancel is now in the Bellingham Chapel, where it has more headroom. – PULPIT, a nice example of *Crowther* design *c.* 1852, its stone base integral with the rebuilt pier. – FONT. Large octagonal bowl of black marble with concave sides and plain shields; a type which recurs in the North Riding of Yorkshire in the C15. The copper lining with Art Nouveau flower motif looks like the *Keswick School of Industrial Arts.* – PAINTING. Bell-ringers in Regency knee-breeches; the inn sign from the Ring o' Bells next door. – SCULPTURE. Fragment of a late C8/early C9 cross-shaft with vine scrolls, similar to the one at Heversham (q.v.).

STAINED GLASS. Thirty-two windows, few of them good. E window by *O'Connor*, 1855, good in effect but clumsy in detail. S aisle, in front of the Strickland Chapel screen, a gold-tinted window by *Ward & Hughes*, 1893. Fourth from W, 1928 by *J. C. N. Bewsey*, with old-fashioned canopy work. Next W, all blues, greens and yellows, made by *Shrigley & Hunt* in 1924 to a design by *Alice Gordon*. Below, a single figure kneels with her back to us in a dark overgrown garden. Above, the Heavenly Hosts. Simple, heartfelt. Several *Warrington* windows at the W end, dates 1852 to 1883, not good. (N aisle, some C19–early C20 glass from Fellside church (*see* p. 440), installed here 2008.) NE chapel N, single old coat of arms. Inner S chapel, C15 fragment with head of a king. In the clerestory, hard to see against the too-dark C19 grisaille ground, some old armorial glass.

MONUMENTS. Starting in the Bellingham Chapel, NE. Excellent but anonymous coffin-lid with foliated cross, sword and shield; late C13. – Tomb-chest with brasses of Sir Roger Bellingham †1533 and wife. The tomb is a restoration of 1863 and the brasses were made new at that time. – Brass of Alan Bellingham †1577 (20 in.; 51 cm.) with two coloured coats of arms. – Zachary Hubbersty †1787 by *T. Flaxman*, tablet with a relief in the tympanum: an angel hovers over the disconsolate family. – Strickland Chapel. Plain early C16 tomb-chest with just shields. – Walter Strickland †1656. Alabaster effigy, more dwarfish than child-like, under a canopy with Tuscan columns. The sides of the miniature tomb-chest decorated by chevron ornament. – On the N, S and W walls C18 and C19 tablets two and three deep, including more than twenty of *Webster*'s. – Against the W wall George Romney, the painter, a Dalton boy who died at Kendal in 1802. Niche with a black classical urn in relief. – John James of London †1823. Grecian tablet. – South African war memorial, also W, a fine brass.

CHURCHYARD. MEMORIAL to the Rev. John Cooper †1896, a good copy of the Irton Cross, signed *J. W. Bromley*, Keswick. – GATES, given by Trinity College in 1822; they look older. –

The PARISH HALL, immediately S but without its intended link, is by *J. Hutton*, 1912; the former PARISH INFANT SCHOOL by *Miles Thompson*, 1877.

ST GEORGE, Castle Street. By *George Webster*, 1838–41. 'Novel, chaste and beautiful', wrote the *Westmorland Gazette*. It had a pair of slender stair-towers 100 ft (31 metres) high flanking a narrowed W end, with 'neat side porches' giving access to the galleries. The E end was narrowed too, with a pair of vestries and thinner turrets to match, giving a degree of longitudinal as well as bilateral symmetry, a typical device of the time. Thin lancets and thin buttresses. The *Church Builder* in 1904 published a design signed HJA (*Hubert Austin*) and an appeal for a complete rebuild, but *Austin & Paley*'s new and longer chancel of 1907–11 takes a different form. Its brown sandstone and advanced Dec style disdain Webster's hammered limestone and basic E.E. The W towers proved troublesome, being shortened in 1927 and cut down to roof level in 1978. The tall E pinnacles have gone too. A narthex with twin pavilionettes was added by *Michael Bottomley* in 2004. All this makes the prominently seen S elevation seem excessively long and ill-assorted in its parts. The bare unobstructed nave, minus its galleries, seems enormous under its wide tie-beam roof with kingposts and lesser kingposts, even though two of its seven bays were partitioned off in 1963 to create a hall and meeting rooms. The tripartite nave E wall is essentially Webster's, though modified on the organ side by Austin & Paley. Their chancel is asymmetrical, with a large space for the organ (N) and a low passage aisle (S), each terminated on the E by a canted passageway. Green-tinted glass, exposed stone walls, canted ribbed ceiling. Chancel FURNISHINGS by *Austin & Paley*. – WAR MEMORIAL, *c.* 1920. A Gothic recess in the nave N wall.

ST THOMAS, Stricklandgate. By *George Webster*, 1835–7. Gaunt lancet-style box with embraced W tower. Lancets mostly in pairs, thin buttresses, short chancel. The tall pinnacles have been removed. It is somewhat upstaged by the buttressed form of the Parish Centre attached on the N, by *K. C. White*, 1980, of rain-streaked concrete blocks. The aisleless interior is drastically stripped, fully carpeted, and opened through into the Parish Centre. The galleries have gone, and so, alarmingly, have the tie-beams and kingposts of the roof. The commanding PULPIT of 1882 is cut down, the Gothic reredos gone. – STAINED GLASS. E, near-abstract, by *Shrigley & Hunt* (artist perhaps *R. Hayes*), *c.* 1970.

Handsome PARSONAGE, N (the church is not oriented), by *Thomas Hudson*, 1854.

ALL HALLOWS, Fellside. *See* Perambulation 2, p. 440.

HOLY TRINITY AND ST GEORGE (R.C.), New Road, facing the river. 1835–7. Much the best of *George Webster*'s three Kendal churches, and the best-preserved. No tower, but a frontispiece brought slightly forward, with *Thomas Duckett*'s sculpture of St George and the Dragon in the gable. Wide and brightly lit interior, appearing even wider since the floor was raised above flood level. W gallery on slender Gothic arcading. Enough rich-

ness at the E end to avoid bareness, with a very shallow
sanctuary, not much more than a giant niche, framed by receding arches, the outermost forming an ogee, and flanked by a
pair of excessively tall statue niches. – STAINED GLASS.
Four squares of C17 Flemish glass in the porch. E window
by *Hardman & Co.*: the Rev. Thomas Withington holds a
model of the church. Others signed *Mayer & Co.*, and *H. M.
Barnett*, Newcastle, 1874. E. W. Hodge (CWAAS *Transactions*,
vol. 76, 1976) mentions several in the style of *Earley Studios*,
Dublin.

ZION CHAPEL (United Reformed), set back from Highgate in a
Kendal yard. 1896, by *Stephen Shaw*. Flat plate-traceried front
with flanking stair-turrets. Interior completely preserved, with
steeply raked galleries slung from timber arcades, all focussing
on the massive dais. Posts, gallery fronts, pews and especially
the dais all worked and moulded in pitch pine.

METHODIST CHURCH. Close to St Thomas, on the corner of
Stricklandgate and Burneside Road. A large rectangle in the
Italianate style. By *W. Ranger* of London, 1881–2.

FRIENDS' MEETING HOUSE, set back from Stramongate. By
Francis Webster, 1815–16, in replacement of a late C17 building.
William Fisher, clerk of works, designed and perhaps made all
the internal fittings. Two-storey elevations front and rear, the
lower windows arched. Very large single windows in the gables.
A cross-lobby containing the stairways gave access to two
unequal rooms, divided by sash partitioning that could be
dropped into the cellar. The smaller (women's) section, further
subdivided in 1934, is the current meeting room. The larger,
stripped of its furnishings but retaining its gallery on two sides,
houses the QUAKER TAPESTRY of 1982–96.

MARKET PLACE CHAPEL (Unitarian). Built in 1720 (date on
hopper) by Dr Caleb Rotheram, who also founded in 1733 the
Dissenting Academy through whose archway the chapel is
reached. Plain white two-storey box with gravestones against
its walls. The stone porch dates from 1882, and so does the
Sunday School at the back. This is surprisingly jolly inside:
coloured glass top lighting, pink coved ceiling with plaster
foliage, Corinthian pilasters and a stage at one end. In the ante-
room some pew-ends dated 1691 and 1709. The chapel interior
is arranged round a dais opposite the entrances, i.e. probably
as built, but the fittings date from 1881–2. The ceiling and its
supports were altered in 1958.

EVANGELICAL CHURCH, Parr Street. *See* p. 443.

CEMETERY, both sides of Park Side Road. With matching Gothic
chapels of 1854 by *Miles Thompson*.

PUBLIC BUILDINGS

TOWN HALL, Highgate. Norman Nicholson called it 'municipal
comic', and it is true that there is something comical about the

attempt to meld together the parts of a multi-phase building, and about the exuberance of the latest part. First came the Whitehall Assembly Rooms by *Francis & George Webster*, 1824–5, Grecian, with just three bays to Highgate, fourteen wasted on Lowther Street, l. In 1858–9 *George Webster* converted it into a town hall, replacing the original cupola with a clock tower and revamping the interior. In 1891–3 it was extended another three bays along Highgate by *Stephen Shaw*. All, it will be noted, Kendal practices. Shaw replaced Webster's clock tower with a dormer and built a Frenchy domed clock tower (which houses a carillon) over his new entrance, big enough to unite the enlarged building. His efforts to create a unified façade are worth analysing. The rhythm is A–A–B–A–C–A, where C is Webster's upper Ionic portico *in antis*, B is Shaw's frontispiece and tower, and A is Webster's tall sashes over a rusticated basement, original or carried on unchanged. Shaw's entrance is florid Baroque with plentiful carving and superimposed pediments. Interiors, made irregular by the site, are gloomy with dark wainscoting and polished tiles. A pair of staircases, cantilevered and curved at the turn, rise in a crosslobby. Beyond is the Assembly Room with its high curved ceiling, wreathed frieze and gallery. At the back the former courtroom, and a fine wooden stair rising in a complete semicircle under a dome.

COUNTY HALL, Stricklandgate. For Westmorland County Council, 1937–9 by *Verner O. Rees*, in a Neo-Georgian style that Pevsner called anaemic. Nine bays. Good lead-clad clock turret on the roof. Brass roundels of G. H. Pattinson and James Cropper.

KENDAL CASTLE. It stands high above the town on an impressive drumlin, looking like ruined teeth. The castle began as a ringwork, with a ditch and a counterscarp bank. Now roughly circular, with a deep ditch, and crowned by a curtain wall. Entrance is over a causeway from the N. Only traces remain of the gatehouse sketched by Machell in the late C17. Part of the C14 hall to its immediate E stands over the remains of two parallel tunnel-vaulted basements, with a garderobe tower jutting out into the ditch. Its dig-out hole can be seen. Part-way round on the W is a C13 round tower. At the S end was a postern gate. Machell drew a small chapel on the bumpy greensward inside. There is a suspicion that the ruins were improved in the C18 by the Wilsons of Abbot Hall (*see* below) to make a more Picturesque silhouette. Castle and park were acquired by the Corporation in 1897.

CASTLE HOWE. Small much-landscaped motte-and-bailey, 2½ acres in size. Probably deserted in the late C12 when Kendal Castle was built on the E side of the river. The motte formed of upcast from a ditch across the ridge to N and SE; the bailey (Bowling Fell) to the E. On the motte a MONUMENT, an obelisk of 1788 celebrating the Glorious Revolution of 1688. Thought to be *Francis Webster*'s first work in Kendal; *William Holme* was the builder.

ABBOT HALL (ART GALLERY), N of the parish church. Rebuilt in 1759 for George Wilson, fourth son of Daniel Wilson of Dallam Tower, under the superintendance of *John Carr* of York. So said the *Lonsdale Magazine* in 1821, but J. M. Robinson attributes it rather to *John Hird*, and C. R. Hudlestone thought 1762 a more likely date, when the Colonel married.

The house is approached through an archway in the middle of the stables. They have blank arches towards the house. Construction is surprisingly unrefined, of the local limestone in small squared blocks and irregular courses. Entrance side of three widely spaced bays and slightly lower and bare projecting wings. Low pavilions attached at the ends. The doorway is pedimented and reached by an outer staircase. Towards the river the house has two canted bays. The tripartite middle doorway and the Venetian windows in the wings here are set in blank arches – a Carr motif. Steps up to the door. Plain parapets. The entrance hall, which goes right through, has a screen of two Roman Doric columns. To the r. a few Rococo swirls in the plasterwork, and a swan-necked broken pediment overmantel. The dining room on the other side is smaller. Doorways with pulvinated frieze and pediment. The far N room has a Gothick flavour, with a trefoil frieze and triple-colonnetted fireplace. The stair, typically of Carr, looks like a wooden cantilever; in fact probably suspended.

Abbot Hall was bought by the town in 1897, the garden turned into a public park. Almost derelict by the 1950s, the house was restored and converted to a gallery by *M. J. H. Bunney* and *Charlotte Gray* in 1957–62, with the loss of all the upper-floor detail. In the PARK, a DRINKING FOUNTAIN by *J. F. Curwen*, 1889; an obelisk with swirly Viking dragons. – CROPPER MEMORIAL with portrait medallion signed *A. Lucchesi*, 1901.

LIBRARY, Stricklandgate. 1908 by *T. F. Pennington*. In the free Baroque so typical of Carnegie libraries, with Gibbs motifs. Grey limestone and red sandstone in eye-watering contrast. Railings and outer doors verging on Art Nouveau.

MUSEUM, Station Road. *See* p. 442.

BREWERY ARTS CENTRE, Highgate. An undemonstrative but successful ensemble. Miscellaneous range of limestone rubble buildings, with a stubby octagonal chimney, reaching up the hill. Whitwell Marks' brewery was built in 1858, its last brew 1968. The Arts Centre opened in 1972. The original conversion was by *Gordon Stables*, more recent work such as the cinema by *Robert Tarbuck*.

RAILWAY STATION, Station Road. Built by the London & North Western Railway after 1859. The building now houses a medical centre (conversion and extension by *E. Donald Haigh*, c. 1990). Rough dark-grey rubble. Three storeys plus dormers, half-hipped gables. The impression from the main approach is threateningly Wagnerian. 'Quite picturesque' (Pevsner), but since shorn of its glass awnings and the platform side smoothed by unyielding cement render and dreary new glazing.

PERAMBULATIONS

1. Kirkland, Highgate and Stricklandgate

On the face of it nothing could be simpler, but in practice it is almost impossible to walk the straight mile directly from one end to the other, thanks to the enticing Yards which open off every few paces.

The start is at the s end in KIRKLAND at the NETHER BRIDGE, on a medieval site but showing in its soffits work of the C17 and of widening to the N in 1772 and again in 1908. Each successive build used larger and more regular stones. Facing the w end of Nether Bridge, KIRKBARROW MILL, *c.* 1798, the earliest spinning workshop in the town. Three storeys with a late C19 shop window inserted, and sadly neglected. 200 yds N along Kirkgate, in the car park of Abbot Hall (p. 434) is a little classical front, inscribed 1825 EX FUMO DARE LUCEM ('from smoke give light'). It is the re-erected meter-house façade of *Francis & George Webster*'s gasworks in Parkside Road, demolished in 1970. Two angle pillars, two Doric columns, and a pediment. Opposite, an amusing group. Nos. 34–36 is L-shaped, spuriously dated 1563, with the air of a *cottage orné*. It was built *c.* 1840 for John Yeates by *George Webster*. No. 32, small and tucked-in, with a plain shell hood, has the chimney and fire window in standard C17 juxtaposition. The POST OFFICE (No. 30), with big sash windows, is timber-framed over a Doric colonnade, while PEMBROKE HOUSE next door has three gable dormers (and upper crucks). Nos. 22–24 is by *Curwen*.
Blind Beck, which only flows in winter, marks the start of HIGH-GATE. On the w side BLIND BECK HOUSE, L-shaped, rebuilt in 1785 by Christopher Wilson, founder in 1788 of the Westmorland Bank (*see* below). Gillinggate leads off here; *see* Fellside perambulation, p. 439.[*] Nos. 134 and 136 are a tall pair of *Francis Webster* houses, six bays, ashlar-faced, *c.* 1798; Nos. 130–132 a pair of an earlier generation, perhaps 1760s, with much smaller sashes and the shopfront of G. Lightfoot, chemist, l. The HIGHGATE HOTEL, of 1769, incorporates a C17 doorway and inscription. Good staircase, splayed at the bottom, with three fluted balusters per tread. Beyond Captain French Lane is CONNEXIONS, an interpolation of *c.* 1970 by *John Gill*, frankly clad with squares of fossily limestone and green slate. It is surprising how little such a contrast grates. YARD 120 demonstrates the importance of these narrow entries. Two front doors face each other, one splendidly Doric with fluted pillars and a squashed fanlight, the other with concave octagon panels. No. 118, now the Youth Hostel, was built by the Wilsons of Dallam in 1757. Good open-well stair,

---

[*] On the E side, Dowker's Lane leads to HOUSING by *Frederick Gibberd & Partners*, 1971 etc., N of Abbot Hall Park, between Highgate and the river. 124 dwellings, partly arranged as four-storey maisonettes. Colourwashed walls with vertical strips of windows and slate-hanging, inadequate-looking pitched roofs. The entrances and continuous balconies all face inwards, overlooking the courtyards and access roads. Pedestrian ways follow the line of the old yards.

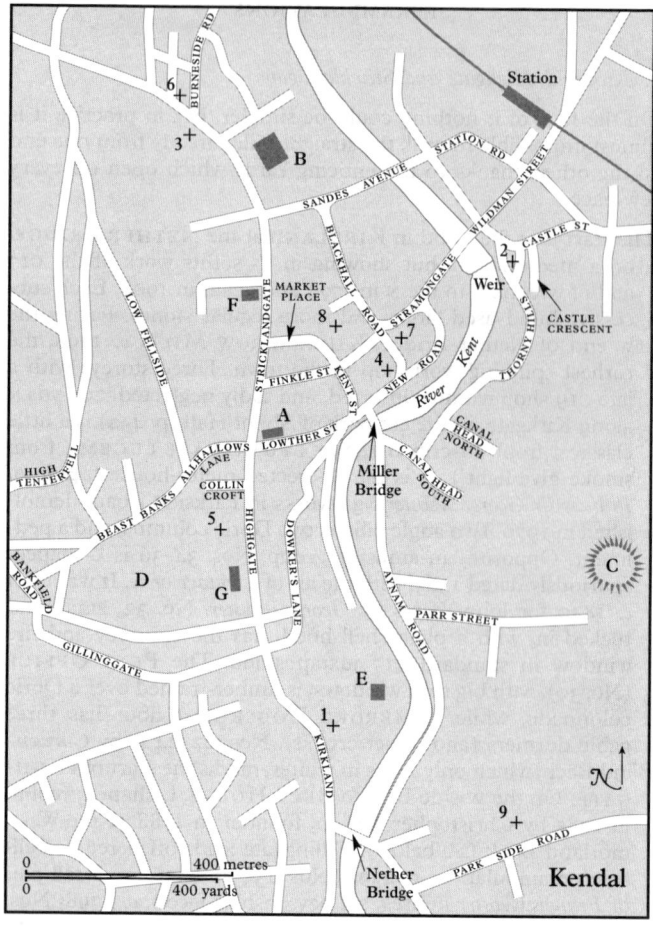

1   Holy Trinity
2   St George
3   St Thomas
4   Holy Trinity and St George
5   Zion Chapel
6   Methodist church
7   Quaker Meeting House
8   Market Place Chapel
9   Cemetery

A   Town Hall
B   County Hall
C   Castle
D   Castle Howe
E   Abbot Hall
F   Library
G   Brewery Arts Centre

splayed at the foot opposite the yard entrance, with two mahogany balusters per tread. A brewery was formerly attached to it. The long garden went right back to the steps and terracing behind the brewery car park. BANK HOUSE,

No. 112, was rebuilt by the Rev. John Wilson in 1787 to the plans of *Robert Furze Brettingham*. Front room with low-relief Adamish ceiling. Curvaceous wooden cantilever stair facing the side entrance, rising through two storeys under a little dome. No. 106, fronting the Zion Chapel (p. 432), bears the date 1868; for R. F. Thompson, one of *Miles Thompson*'s last designs. It is set back a little, allowing an extension of 1881, its openings framed in colossal pieces of limestone, to look down the street. No. 119 (1811) is opposite, and the adjoining ODD-FELLOWS HALL of 1833 by *George Webster*. Odd-fellows has a rusticated ground floor with a tripartite window, beneath a tall *piano nobile* with shallow pilasters and a segmental arcade. Heavy cornice and lettering sooted black, and an attic. Still on the E side, DR MANNING'S YARD (83) is a pleasant backwater with a terrace of houses and gardens. WEBSTER'S YARD has been redeveloped with housing by Russell Armer Ltd, architect *Mike Walford*, 1988.

SANDES HOSPITAL (w side) is a landmark. The gatehouse building is dated 1659, anticipating Thomas Sandes's formal foundation of 1670 (inside, in plaster, TS 1661.) Almshouses round a courtyard, like Lady Anne Clifford's at Appleby (q.v.), with a garden beyond, but rebuilt as a depressing row by *Miles Thompson* in 1852. Their backs in Shakespeare Yard look C17, so perhaps it was just a refronting. The SHAKESPEARE INN (No. 76), by *J. C. Richardson*, is dated TS 1830 on a hopper. It has a half-sunk shop underneath. Kendal once had many such two-tier buildings, like the Rows at Chester. At the end of YARD 76 is the former theatre, 1829–30, also by *Richardson*. Next the splendid WESTMORLAND BANK, now HSBC. Of 1834–5 by *George Webster*, demonstrating the different degrees to which the Websters could work the tough local limestone. Five concentrated bays, with giant pilasters in the centre, tapered window surrounds at the sides. Recumbent lion of 1840 on top of cast metal, painted. COLLIN CROFT at the side is a good example of a Kendal Yard, giving access to a variety of properties and cutting through, via arches and steps, to Beast Banks. *Miles Thompson* revamped several of the buildings. The whole was restored *c.* 1978 for the Civic Society by *E. Donald Haigh*, project architect *Michael Bottomley*.

There is a hiatus here, where the traffic is diverted w towards Beast Banks, or E down the gloomy canyon of LOWTHER STREET, beside the Town Hall (for which *see* p. 432) Lowther Street was made in 1782, and is lined by contemporary houses. An C18 wooden emblem of a Turk identifies Gawith's SNUFF WORKS.

Next to the Town Hall is the former Angel Hotel, with small sashes and a centre arch. Dramatic C17 roofscape of five-plus-five chimneys set diagonally on either side of a lantern, puzzlingly windowless but once lighting the stair. The KENDAL BANK of 1873 (now Barclays) is said to be by *Edward Salomons* of Manchester, though he is not usually so bland; the ground floor was altered in the 1920s. MILLETTS, Nos. 24–28 Highgate (W side), features two big dormers, three little oriels, and three dainty *Webster* shopfronts of 1828. No. 24 in a typically English contrast is twice as tall, with stucco pilasters and an iron crest on the roof. Then Nobles Amusements, a tiny one-bay house. The OLD SHAMBLES line the long yard behind the FLEECE INN, which is timber-framed and roughcast with a colonnade. Now we are in STRICKLANDGATE. Nos. 13–17 on the crest of the hill on the E side forms a continuous late C17 jettied range, presumably timber-framed, with a rack of four diagonally set chimneys. No. 13 (FARRER'S) retains its half-columned shopfront of 1822–3, installed by the *Websters* with their joiner *William Fisher*, and its interior, said to have been 'a sensation' at the time. Further N a replica of the Moot Hall of 1729, destroyed by fire in 1969. It has a corner tower or eminence with lantern and a Venetian window towards Highgate. Now an intermission for the MARKET PLACE. WAR MEMORIAL, 1921, with a Tommy in full kit signed *Chas W. Coombes*. Figure sculpture is rare for war memorials in the region. The timber-framed Globe Inn has been refronted in replica, next to another of *John Gill*'s unobtrusively modern buildings, the Royal Bank of Scotland (N side). At No. 16 the MARKET HALL. The job was secured by *Daniel Brade* in 1887, though *Eli Cox* had won the competition. Showy façade attempted in a small compass, but the stone has failed in places. The hall behind is a utilitarian affair of thin steel trusses and glass. Extended to create WESTMORLAND SHOPPING CENTRE, opened in 1989. The NEW SHAMBLES of 1803–4 curves down SE from the Market Place to Finkle Street, lined with single-storey shops. Perhaps by *Francis Webster* and *John Fisher*. Round the corner on Branthwaite Brow is an unexpected curiosity, IRON HOUSES, done when the street was widened in 1853 by the ironfounder *Joseph Winder*. Flat cast-iron façade trellised all over by strengthening flanges. Some ogee Gothick detail on the ground floor. The walls are very thin, the window frames hung in front. On the opposite side, the CHOCOLATE SHOP. Tiny multi-level house and shop, claiming the date 1657.

Back onto Stricklandgate. The former ABBEY NATIONAL (No. 35, E side) is by *John Gill*, c. 1960s, clad in squares of green slate with white granite for the recessed shopfront. Amongst a run of fake façades and another entrance to Westmorland Shopping Centre is the unconvincingly C16 BLACK HALL, though it retains one great round Westmorland chimney and a sign of a bristly boar, showing that it was, until 1953, a brush factory. On the W side at No. 92 STRICKLANDGATE HOUSE, c. 1776 for Joseph Maude, possibly by *John Hird*, set back a little to allow its flat seven-bay stucco front to impress. Doorway with Corinthian columns and pediment. No. 95 (CHARLIE'S café), just before Sandes Avenue, is one of the best of Kendal's town houses. It was built in 1690 and updated in 1724; griffins and date on the rainwater goods. Three storeys, five bays with small sashes and the door at one end. Wooden mullions at the back. The broad stair rises through two floors, with three balusters per tread. Treads are oak, balusters mahogany. The front room with plain fielded panelling fits the C18 date, but the small rear parlour has chunky C17 bolection panelling. Long rear extension, later C18. Opposite County Hall (p. 433), THE OLD HOUSE is a big town house at the front, with a labyrinthine interior, but a country house at the back with extensive gardens. Associated with Wakefield's Bank, established here in 1788, is the one grand room of 1797 by *Francis Webster*, behind a Venetian window; it has a curved end wall. On the garden side is a large room contrived in 1911 to house an early aeroplane called Water Hen. The parts of the plane were slung on the cross-beams, like oars and masts in a boathouse. Round the corner in SANDES AVENUE is the façade of *Thompson & Webster*'s Market Hall of 1854, re-erected in 1909 when it acquired a ridiculous fake French roof with scaly tiles and *œils de bœuf*. N of County Hall, at the junction of Stricklandgate and Burneside Road, a small MILL SETTLEMENT, three limestone storeys of the former Kent Carpet Mill, mid-1820s, dominating the rows of workers' cottages.

As a coda, STRAMONGATE descends NE to the river from the lower ends of Finkle Street and the Market Place, widening out like Highgate but disastrously bisected by through traffic on Blackhall Road. Nos. 7 and 23 are C16 or C17 town houses with large gable dormers. Nos. 48–52, opposite the Quaker Meeting House (p. 432), is a dignified thirteen-bay composition of *c.* 1800 probably by *Francis Webster*, of limestone ashlar with windows within super-arches. Twin rusticated entries, each with a tripartite window within a fan head above. The front doors are in the yard entries, e.g. in YARD 50 a grand Doric doorcase under a plaque of huntress and hound. Through Yard 52 is the former QUAKER SCHOOL of 1792. Overlooking Meeting House Yard is the tallest of Kendal's stair windows, of three full storeys.

SAND AIRE HOUSE, by the river, is the grandest of *George Webster*'s town houses, of 1827–8 for Daniel Harrison, with a Doric porch *in antis*. Expertly extended in 1926 by *Bradshaw Gass & Hope* of Bolton to make a symmetrical front along Stramongate. To this PROVINCIAL INSURANCE added in the mid 1960s Kendal's most prominent building (criticized as such by Pevsner), a five- and six-floor office block by *Basil Ward* of *Murray, Ward & Partners*. In 2000 the whole complex was converted to flats by *Stephenson Bell* of Manchester. The earlier parts look unchanged, but Basil Ward's building has come in for considerable modification, breaking up the modular windows with shutters and balconies, and sneaking in two storeys of penthouses on top, around the lift hoists. The new colour scheme is subtle, in shades of Lake District green and grey.

2. Fellside

A steep warren of narrow lanes and steps, much renewed in the LOW FELLSIDE housing development of *c.* 1974 by *Frederick*

Gibberd & Partners. This dominates the scene with its tall pitched-roofed ranges, though some of the intricacy remains. At the top and on Gillinggate are some grander houses taking advantage of the view.

GILLINGGATE starts at the junction of Highgate and Kirkland. First the DEAN GIBSON MEMORIAL SCHOOLS, by *John Stalker*, 1898, roughcast Neo-Tudor. Then a group of enterprising houses by *J. F. Curwen*, all growing organically out of the hillside. Nos. 56–62, dated 1889, is a relatively quiet white terrace, nicely asymmetrical. LYNNSIDE of 1891, for Gilbert Gilkes, is a big horizontal house on a massive revetted base, with a long ramp up to the front door, all slate-hanging and long ranges of pushed-forward windows. HILLCOTE, 1894, by contrast is a little tower, small and vertical. HILL HOUSE, 1970s by *Mike Walford*, takes the idiom and makes it modern; a little tower built over a carport. PLAYMATES, the former Cropper Memorial Hospital facing Bankfield Road, is by *J. Bintley*, 1869 and 1883. Gothic, with plate tracery and some bizarre detail, e.g. a thickening with a boss where mullion meets transom. On the common land at the top is the former INGHAMITE CHAPEL by *Miles Thompson*, 1844, oblong with thin round-arched windows and a pediment; clumsily converted to residential use in 1985. Up High Tenterfell, N, is SKEWBARROW TOP, *Brian Dockray*'s own house, 1964, recklessly cantilevered out over the abyss, like Frank Lloyd Wright's Falling Water. Spacious open-plan, the few internal walls being of local slate with dados of terrazzo or white brick. Matchboard ceilings, flush doors and cupboards. Originally square, now extended at either end. Further W in the allotment gardens behind Bankfield, traces of the terraces and fencing of the TENTERBANKS which gave Tenterfell its name, and to the E, remains of a large double LIMEKILN.

Descending Beast Banks, we meet MONUMENT HOUSE with an Early Victorian summerhouse, probably by *Miles Thompson*, who made the house Picturesque *c.* 1860. Behind it is Castle Howe and the Monument, *see* p. 433. AIREY CLIFFE, very prominent from below, is by *J. Hutton*, 1891. The silhouette is very well managed. Perched on the cliff edge is an octagonal SUMMERHOUSE of *c.* 1780 which went with the bowling green in the castle bailey. CLIFF TERRACE of 1851–3, opposite Monument House, is nicely varied along a gently curved walk, with some projecting bays. At the far end is a villa of 1866 with Italianate tower and bracketed eaves by *Miles Thompson* for Thomas Garnett. The SERPENTINE WALKS above the terrace were laid out in 1824.

Below, in the steepest and most intricate area of Fellside, is ALL HALLOWS, a former mission church of 1864–6 with an attached house, by *Miles Thompson*, attractively tucked into its tiny hillside site. The eye-catching E window copies the odd Perp design of the parish church's W window. Below that is JOB PENNINGTON'S MEMORIAL HALL, 1899. The raised lettering and the stone frame upon which it is carved are the memorable feature of this little building. Descending again there is much renewed housing and, cleverly slotted into the dense townscape, BOOTH'S SUPERMARKET of 2005 by *Tony Hills* of *Corstorphine & Wright Hills Erwin*, like a small Victorian railway terminus except that the steelwork is white and tubular. Arched roof with one end wall of glass, the other solid. In the basement storey is ARTISAN, for local foods, again taking its inspiration from railway engineering, with shallow jack arches on fat steel columns. Finishes are of slate and oak.

On Allhallows Lane is the former PUBLIC BATH HOUSE by *Miles Thompson*, 1863. It has a prominent chimney, like a brewery. The LAST ORDERS brings us out opposite the Town Hall. The pub, probably by *Curwen*, is a neat piece of Queen Anne revival, with chimneys set diagonally, big dormers, a strong cornice, wooden cross-windows and a shell-hood.

3. The Canal Town, east of the river

The enabling Act for the Lancaster Canal was gained in 1792. By 1797 it had reached the Westmorland boundary at Tewitfield. In 1813 work started under *Thomas Fletcher* on the locks of the long-anticipated link into Kendal, which was completed in 1819. Traffic finished in 1944, an Act of 1955 authorized closure, and the final 2 m. to the basin were filled in.

The perambulation runs from Stramongate Bridge southwards to Nether Bridge. STRAMONGATE BRIDGE was rebuilt in 1794–6. *Thomas Harrison*'s competition design in 1791 was for three semi-elliptical arches, but a pier of the old bridge proved to be indestructible – hence four segmental arches, with Harrison's characteristic flat deck and arched niches in the piers. The contractors were *Francis Webster* and *W. Holme*. JUBILEE BRIDGE (1887), iron, of three flat spans, by *D. Goddard*, is a little N. The RIVERSIDE HOTEL stands prominently between them; by *Haigh Architects c.* 1992, industrial-looking, though with a Websterish tower, and incorporating a genuine small industrial building at the bridge end.

CASTLE DAIRY, Wildman Street. The name may be a corruption of 'Dowry'. Small but complete C14 hall house of the pattern expected in most of England, but not in here, where they are usually defensive. The wings project to one side only (not H-wise). A two-centred hollow-moulded doorway indicates the low end. Three-light hall window with trefoiled heads, renewed 1983–4 with naïve headstops. The present high-end entrance is C17. Rounded chimneys. The hall is minute, but retains its dais canopy, now partly cut away for a staircase. Ceiling at purlin level, divided by thin moulded ribs. A very large fireplace was inserted *c.* 1560 to back onto the screens passage, with a wooden heck and framed smoke-hood. It has the usual fire-window, and a spice cupboard with tricky linenfold moulding. C19 chimneypiece and iron range. The wooden doorway through to the screens is dated 1560, with sloping shoulders and a flat head notched to make an ogee. In the screens passage the expected three service doors, hollow-moulded and very small, and similar entries front and back, the latter retaining its door. Screens and service wing are paved with stones set on edge. A small room is partitioned off to make a snug or bower of C17 Lake District type; is the framing partly retained from the medieval kitchen passage? At the other end, the upper chamber has a segmental ceiling divided, like the hall ceiling, by thin moulded ribs. Arms at the intersections, and a carved pair of griffins as a corbel or bracket. Stained glass with dates 1565 and 1567, initials of Anthony Garnett, and the Eagle and Child badge of the Stanleys. At the rear extends what appears to be a garderobe gallery.

BEEZON LODGE is behind on the l., hemmed in by later build-ings. Severe Grecian house of 1825 by *Francis Webster* for Richard Rawes. On Station Road, NW, ALBERT BUILDINGS, now Kendal Museum, was the wool warehouse of Whitwell, Hargreaves & Co., 1864, probably by *Miles Thompson*. Large plain building of limestone rubble with bay windows pushed out in place of Thompson's open arches, one of which accom-modated a railway siding. Backing onto it is the ALLEN TECHNICAL INSTITUTE by *Stephen Shaw*, 1912.

S of the bridge, Castle Street leads to St George's church (*see* p. 431) on a wide green, with Castle Crescent to its E. THORNY HILLS continues S in grander style, above the filled-in mill race for Castle Mills. Developed by *Francis Webster* from 1821, after the completion of Canal Head. It is not too regimented, and exceptionally attractive for that reason. The styles vary from Greek to mildly Italianate. No. 4 was *George Webster*'s own, with wreaths in the frieze, with cunning planning and lush interior Grecian decoration. No. 7 is the prettiest, with a first-floor balcony interrupted by a semicircular bay. OLRIG BANK, below the S end of the terrace, was built in 1879 for the mill-owner.

The CANAL has been filled in and its route is not obvious. It came in parallel to the river, then turned a dog-leg immediately S of Thorny Hills to a basin flanked by Canal Head North and South, with warehouses and cottages by *Francis Webster*. Arched entrances for boats and waggons can still be seen inside the premises of Gilbert Gilkes & Gordon, but the basin itself is covered by later buildings. In CANAL HEAD NORTH, two probable *Webster* buildings. A small two-storey stone building with an arched window in the E gable was the CANAL TICKET OFFICE. Further W, the neat symmetrical AGENT'S HOUSE of 1820. KENDAL BROWN HOUSE is still a snuff manufactory, built 1887 for Gawith Hoggarth. In Canal Head South was Day's CASTLE FOUNDRY of 1893, makers of kitchen ranges.

MILLER BRIDGE to the W was commissioned by the Canal Committee from *Francis Webster* in 1818, and completed within that year. Three shallow spans, with iron rail and stone posts to make an approach from the town. Facing the bridge is BRIDGE HOUSE, the Websters' marble showroom, by *Francis*

Webster, 1819. Modest though prominent façade with small iron balconies to the upper rooms. AYNAM LODGE is next to the bridge, an urbane three-bay Grecian house of 1823 by *F. Webster* for Thomas Harrison, surgeon, with a low wing for his surgery. Like Beezon Lodge it is of hammered near-ashlar, three well-spaced bays with corner pilasters and sunk window surrounds. CASTLE MILLS, originally the town corn mills, had converted to weaving by *c.* 1800. The main block, all in limestone, incorporates a central arched entrance of 1806 within an 1854 rebuilding for J. J. & W. Wilson. The tall engine house carries an 1854 datestone. Until 2007 the buildings housed Goodacres Carpets, the last survivors of Kendal's long weaving tradition. On the opposite bank can be seen woolwashers' STEPS, high and dry after the lowering of the river bed in the 1970s.

AYNAM ROAD runs s beside the river, from which PARR STREET leads up towards the castle, past the EVANGELICAL CHURCH by *Michael Bottomley*, 1970. This stands on a recessed base, with a double monopitch roof. Over a CANAL BRIDGE, widened in 1888 with curved iron girders, on the r. is the abortive FLETCHER SQUARE. Fine trees and a diagonal pathway, but it never developed beyond the single terrace of late C19 houses, N. Facing the river is the long line of the ORGAN WORKS and residence, 1884, and SLEDDALL JUBILEE ALMSHOUSES, 1887, all by *Eli Cox*. Very effective from the other side of the river, with the multiple dormers of the almshouses and the full stop of the chapel at the s end. Further s, by the roundabout, the GRAMMAR SCHOOL, now Kirkby Kendal School, is by *Stephen Shaw*, 1888. The K Shoes factory, tamed Deco by *Corby Hall & Sons* of Leeds, 1925, was totally demolished in 2007. Company WAR MEMORIAL by *W. G. Collingwood*, a green Celtic cross.

OUTLYING BUILDINGS

SEDBERGH ROAD, E. No. 103 is LITTLE HOLME, a small almost-square house by *C. F. A. Voysey* for his friend the craftsman Arthur Simpson, 1909–10. Voysey made no charge for the design. The external features are a huge pyramidal roof with a single chimney, its slates graded in the approved way but going small again for the sprockets, and an enormous wooden porch, flat-roofed and bracketed, sheltering the arched entrance. The mullions are flat and unmoulded, the walls are of roughly squared limestone without further dressings. The builder was *J. W. Howie*, the joiners *Hayes & Parkinson*, but *Simpson* himself designed the furniture, much of it made by his son *Hubert*, including a desk and sewing cupboard for the traditional inglenook which is indicated by the small fire-window next to the porch. Pevsner judged the house 'in its plainness and flushness on the way to the new style of the C20'.

Kendal Civic Society has recorded the architects of many of the neighbouring HOUSES. Nos. 98 and 105 are by *Geoffrey Morland*, 1929 and 1930, the latter altered in the late C20 by *Michael Bottomley*. No. 69 is by *H. Fowler*, 1909; No. 91 by *J. Hutton*, 1910; No. 97 by *P. W. Smith*, 1922.

PARKSIDE, Parkside Road and the new Sedbergh Road (A684), 1 m. E. 1865, by *J. S. Crowther* for Major Bousfield, M.P. Of cut slate and sandstone. Gothic, with a lot of charming detail. Fairytale oriel and bay to the garden, both with high conical roofs and sun-and-planets iron finials. The house is planned round a full-height hall, indicated by the tall traceried windows to the r. of the porch, which contains the stair. Plate glass in most of the windows from the start. STABLES, LODGE.

HELME LODGE, Burton Road, s. Excellent four-square Grecian house by *Francis & George Webster*, 1824–7, for William Dilworth Crewdson, whose father founded the Crewdson bank. Of finest limestone ashlar, finely jointed, with sparing dressings of Lancashire sandstone. Similar to Rigmaden at Mansergh (q.v.) but with eaves instead of parapets. The Ionic portico was carved by *William Coulthard* on Longridge Fell. Four-bay veranda, s, added *c.* 1914. w side remodelled 1916 after a fire by *W. A. Nelson*, with balustrading added to the bays and a curved veranda set between them. Pretty GIG HOUSE and STABLES, 1820s, by *William Airey*.

(WESTMORLAND GENERAL HOSPITAL, Burton Road, 1½ m. SSE.)

(KENDAL COLLEGE, Milnthorpe Road, ⅓ m. s. New three-storey range by *Taylor Young*, 2008.)

WATTS FIELD, tucked away E of Milnthorpe Road. C17. Round chimney to l., the window on this side pushed in for the hearth and maybe a blocked fire-window. Battered two-storey porch with an outsized doorcase with segmental pediment. In the pediment a comical cherub's head. Nice outer gatepiers and gates with a chained bear.

A little further s, along Collin Road to the w, is COLLINFIELD. Almost surrounded now by housing, but protected by its walled courtyard and very complete inside. Unusual plan, consisting of two units each with a stack at the s end and divided by a wide cross-passage. Porch with date 1663 and Latin inscription into the cross-passage. The inner door bears one of Lady Anne Clifford's locks, given to her secretary George Sedgwick, who bought the place in 1668 with the aid of £200 contributed by the Countess. Everyday access is through the C18 kitchen into the s unit. Ingle fireplace with fire-window and spice cupboard dated GS 1674. Panelled partition opposite the fire with the customary two doors (and two court cupboards), one leading to George Sedgwick's bower or prayer-room, with boarded floor and prayer-desk dated GS 1675, the other to the stone-floored pantry. In the corner by the fireplace a partitioned-off stair. A second stair in the cross-passage, and the date 1674 in plaster over the fire of the N unit. This section has an unusual second-floor dormer at the back.

Yet further s is HELSINGTON LATHES, a larger and not very pre-posessing house at least partly pre-Reformation. Essentially T-shaped but with many extraneous gables on the N. In the E cross-wing an otherwise apparently early C19 room has the date 1538 in plaster, with initials I and AB (probably Bellingham) in an incomplete geometrical pattern as though for a ceiling (and very like those at Levens). The hall part is confusingly divided up. At the W end the solar, in line but cross-roofed, with two huge stacks and a three-light ogee-headed window. Small two-light window below with depressed arched heads. Few solid partitions upstairs.

The substantial weir across the Kent here dates from *c.* 1800 for Webster's marble mill, converted to a SNUFF MILL in 1822. The mill worked until 1991, the last water-powered snuff works in Britain. The undershot water-wheel survives, but the machinery has gone and the modest buildings await other uses.

ROMAN FORT, Watercrook, 1 m. s. Within a meander of the Kent, the rectangular platform of a fort built in timber in the late C1, reconstructed in stone in the mid C2. Occupation continued, perhaps intermittently, until the late C4. Site of a civil settlement, beside the river; probably subject to flooding in the C4.

KENTMERE (W)   4000

A 4 m cul-de-sac, narrow and secluded, heading due N out of Staveley. The valley broadens at the end, only to be closed in by a wall of mountains. The mere was drained *c.* 1840 to make pasture land, although a small part has reappeared in peat diggings.

ST CUTHBERT. A simple building, roughcast but no longer white. The saddleback W tower was rebuilt in the restoration of 1866; its off-centre position suggests older foundations. Small side windows grouped in threes with arched tops, very widely splayed inside. E window with three mullions running straight into a segmental head. Boarded ceiling on stout C16 camber-beams. Thomas Machell in 1691–3 drew its triple-grouped windows, mentioning 'little windows placed very high', a high roof 'formerly designed for lead' (i.e. flat), and that it 'has had a steeple', so the basic structure dates at least from then. – MEMORIAL. Bernard Gilpin, the Apostle of the North, born at Kentmere Hall in 1517. Bronze tablet by the *Keswick School of Industrial Arts* with a frame of trees with intricate roots and branches, almost Art Nouveau. In 1901, in the course of a CWAAS visit, Canon Rawnsley 'was grieved to notice that there was no sort of memorial to the fame of Gilpin'. Subscriptions were gathered that very evening, and the plaque is the result.

KENTMERE HALL, ¾ m. W. 'An antique tower standing under a monstrous craggy mountain', wrote Machell. William Gilpin was here in 1375, but how much of the existing structure goes back so far is open to argument. A fine two-centred doorway arch of that sort of date leads into a wide cross-passage behind the hall stack. This feels like an exterior rather than an interior space, and it is noticeable that the passage widens because the E cross-wing is built at an angle to the rest. The wing is unusually steep-roofed. Now converted to a bank barn, it retains four elegant roof trusses with cambered collars and upper collars sitting on a timber wall-plate (cf. Coniston Hall). The hall range, entered originally from the cross-passage, was largely rebuilt in the 1660s when Kentmere was sold to the Philipsons, and is now uninformatively modern in appearance.

The eye-catching part is the W wing, which is raised into a defensive tower, long ruinous. Curwen thought this a late example of the genre, of c. 1545. It is smaller than most, but sophisticated, with a garderobe extension on the NW and a turning stair, ingeniously made from the uncuttable local slate, winding up in the NE corner to a taller turret. The parapet had machicolated projections on all four sides, surviving in part, and there are arrowslits on each floor at the front corners. The tunnel-vaulted basement, still with its dairy slabs, is accessible only from the house. The first-floor chamber has an external door at the back, up a few steps from the hillside, but there is also a blocked door through to the hall range. The two-light ogee-headed window on the S side makes it probable that this was a solar. The upper floors have gone.

BANK BARN in the front yard, lime kiln at the back.

FACTORY. 1940s. It processed diatomite, which was found mixed with the peat in the lake bed, for Max Factor powder puffs. The flooded diggings form the present lake.

LONGHOUSES, 1 m. S. Pair of white C17 farms, each with a C19 bank barn in line, and each, as usual, revealing little of the satisfying detail within. The S one is prominently dated WDF (William and Dorothy Fleming) 1703. Their initials appear again on the spice cupboard, with the date 1704, and the court cupboard (1711) which was built into the plank-and-muntin partition between firehouse and bower. Evidence for a built-in bed in the bower. The windows are either the original wooden mullions or C19 sideways-sliding sashes. At the back is the downhouse, with its own fireplace and fire-window, and the stair. The barn, accessible from the house, is equally well-preserved, with a stable, distinguished by its greater headroom, and shippon for twelve cows with a central fodder gang. Both parts are partitioned by slabs of slate slotted into timber framing. *Tim Sturgis* carried out the sensitive modernization.

OTHER INDUSTRIAL REMAINS. Upper Kentmere had eight SLATE QUARRIES, the last, Steel Rigg, working until the 1950s. 2 m. N of the village, the miners' barracks can still be seen, as can many of the levels and workings. Immediately beyond is KENTMERE RESERVOIR, behind a stone-lined earth dam built

1845–8 to maintain a reliable flow to the sixteen mills then in the lower valley. Cropper's paper mill at Burneside (q.v.) funded a major repair in 1996.

KESWICK (C)   2020

The setting amidst mountains and lakes is incomparable. In the C16 the town's business was mining: lead, silver, copper and especially wad or black-lead from Borrowdale, spearheaded by a community of German miners. 'There is no beauty in the primitive little town,' wrote Harriet Martineau in her *Complete Guide*, but that was before the railway arrived in 1865. Architecturally it is overwhelmingly mid and late C19, the richest place for Victoriana in Cumbria. The local stones produced the hot colours Victorians delighted in: green, red, yellow, black and pale grey; not delicate hues, but strong and dense. Add bricks in red, yellow and blue, a little red and cream terracotta, set one against another with Victorian relish, and you have a townscape of structural polychromy more vivid even than Bristol. *Thomas & Isaac Hodgson* were the great C19 builders, with *F. & W. Green*, joiners. Inside, look for coloured tiles made by *Herman Harkewitz* from Threlkeld granite dust from 1882.

ST JOHN EVANGELIST. By *Anthony Salvin*, 1836–8, for John Marshall. Even in the geological showcase of Keswick, its pink Lamonby ashlar is outstanding. Aisleless nave and chancel in one, W tower and spire, and a dainty octagonal S vestry with pyramid roof linked to it by a little corridor. The spire appears to rise inside a parapet, but in fact has almost flat broaches. A N aisle was added in 1862, a S aisle in 1882, reusing Salvin's windows. The chancel was lengthened in 1889 by *William Marshall*, grandson of the founder. The church is broad and low, without clerestory or chancel arch. Slender round piers looking too slight for their capitals and arches. Even so the wide aisles starve the centre of light. Windows uncusped, with plain circles, except for the extreme E windows of 1889 which have rere-arches. – STAINED GLASS. Much by *Powells*, mostly to designs by *Henry Holiday*. The best is the E window, 1879, though it is not in perfect condition. Also the chancel side windows, 1888–9, and the furthest W, S aisle. E of the last, *Veronica Whall* made the lovely window to John Marshall †1923, with tenderly drawn children. SW window by *Christine Boyce*, 1992. – MONUMENTS. Matching 'Easter sepulchres' in the E part of the chancel to the Leeds manufacturer John Marshall, founder, †1836, and the Rev. Frederic Myers †1851, with a brass to his son, also Frederic, †1901, one of several by the *Keswick School of Industrial Arts* (KSIA; *see* Crosthwaite).

PARSONAGE, S, now Holy Name House. Also by *Salvin*, 1838. Large, multi-gabled. Small modern vicarage in front. NE, the former SCHOOL, 1840 and LIBRARY, 1849, both mildly Tudor.

OUR LADY OF THE LAKES AND ST CHARLES (R.C.), High Hill. 1927–8 by *Oldfield, Simpson & Saul* of Workington, completed in 1962–4 by *Jonathan Saul* of the same firm with the w bay, Lady Chapel and tower. Early Christian style. Arched windows in threes, semicircular apse, semicircular baptistery, N. The interior is demonstratively stony. Fat columns of white granite frame the chancel arch. Massive tie-beam trusses. – STATIONS OF THE CROSS, bronze, signed *R. Gourdon.*

THE THEATRE BY THE LAKE, Lake Road. 1999, by the *MEB Partnership* with *Theatre Futures* as consultants. Unconfrontational building, using bank-barn vocabulary to be friendly, varied materials, broken outlines and mature trees to disguise its size. Octagonal auditorium, with traditional complement of proscenium, galleries and even boxes done in dark red welded steel and textured wood. CERAMICS by *Paul Scott* commemorating the itinerant 'Blue Box' that preceded the present building.

PERAMBULATION. A transect can be walked NE–SW from the former station, which was the C19 gateway, to the car park by Derwentwater which is the C21 equivalent.

The STATION (Station Road) was the headquarters of the Cockermouth, Keswick & Penrith Railway. 1865, by *John Ross* of Darlington. The last train ran in 1972, despite which it is well preserved. Green and yellow stone. The best feature is the extensive ridge-and-furrow glazed canopy over the spacious main platform. The station is linked directly to the great lump of the KESWICK HOTEL, also by *John Ross,* 1869. Pink and green stone this time, built by *Pattinsons* of Windermere. The MUSEUM is the descendant of Peter Crosthwaite's museum of 1780, a cabinet of curiosities. By *Thomas Hodgson,* 1897–8 and 1906; Arts and Crafts, of sawn Borrowdale stone with timber framing. FITZ PARK behind was opened in 1882, *in memoriam* H. I. Jenkinson, whose portrait medallion is over the gate. The BRIDGE over the Greta was made by the railway company, 1861, by (*Sir*) *Thomas Bouch* with ornamental castings by *Gilkes & Co.* of Middlesborough.* WAR MEMORIAL at the crossroads, *c.* 1920, incorporating a copper plaque made by *KSIA* for railwaymen. Here Station Road becomes STATION STREET, with a clutch of the tall Late Victorian boarding houses, in variegated materials, which are such a feature of Keswick. No. 27 of 1880, for instance, is of green stone with buff dressings and red frills, and a front garden displaying specimen rockwork. GRANDY NOOK of 1891 is a tall parade of shops, and the former ROYAL OAK HOTEL is partly C18 and partly of 1909, *à la mode* in the style of *J. H. Sellers* (cf. Kirklinton). Roughcast with shaped gables.

Bouch was also responsible for a series of bowstring GIRDER BRIDGES (five inverted, three upright) over the Greta as the railway squeezed its way E for 3½ m. through a narrow wooded gorge. The track is now a footpath, giving a splendid prospect of the boldness of the line's engineering.

Immediately NW is the MARKET PLACE, architecturally undistinguished except for the memorable little MOOT HALL in the
middle. Exceedingly pretty. In its present incarnation it dates
from 1813 and has a tower at one end, like a church, with a
pretty concave-sided pyramid roof. The body has three formerly open arches below, arched windows above. Beyond the
NW end of Market Place, the COUNCIL OFFICES, POLICE
STATION and MAGISTRATES' COURT (all 1902) form a
municipal group on Bank Street and Main Street. The Council
Offices are green and yellow, with a clock on a bracket, the
Constabulary red and green, with four attached houses, the
Court Italianate. Behind the offices a windowless building
exhibits green and white stone in morse-code patterns, with
yellow quoins. Immediately above, at the bend of Bank Street,
are four large boarding houses with typical names: Briarholme,
Thornleigh etc.; two vivid red-brown, the other two equally
vivid green. Stanger Street leads up r. to GRETA HAMLET, or
Derwentwater Tenants Estate, early co-operative housing of
1909–11. Twenty-seven cottages in Garden City style on 2
acres, with rustic porches and catslide roofs. The architect was
N. W. Hodges of Winchester.

GRETA HALL lies W of Greta Hamlet. Southey's 'palace of the
winds' was built in 1799–1800 by William Jackson, a Whitehaven carrier, to take advantage of the influx of Lakers.
Jackson, an educated man with a good library, let half to the
Coleridges from 1800 to 1803 – Coleridge wrote some marvellous descriptive work here – and then to Southey until his
death in 1843. Three bays and three storeys, with broad segmental bows at the sides and fluted Ionic columns and a pediment for the doorway.

Over the Greta is Crosthwaite (q.v.); an easy walk past the former
KSIA and the Catholic church to St Kentigern and then, if
desired, over a footbridge to Portinscale.

Back to Market Place. A few steps along ST JOHN'S STREET is
the ALHAMBRA CINEMA, *c.* 1920s Baroque in hard red brick
and terracotta, and then St John's church (p. 447) and its attendant buildings. Late C19 residential streets around St John's
may be savoured: Leonard, Southey, Blencathra, Helvellyn,
Eskin. Nos. 2–10 Eskin Street are especially enjoyable in their
vulgar notchiness, exhibiting stone, brick and terracotta in
every available colour.

From the cinema DERWENT STREET, lined with minor C18
colourwashed houses, drops down SW to Borrowdale Road.
GEORGE FISHER'S, with its blunt corner tower, is one of the
landmarks of Keswick. George Abraham, pioneer photographer of the early rock climbers, built it as his showroom in
1887. Green slate roof with hexagonal bands, green walls,
yellow sills, lintels and carved capitals, polished green shafts.
Continuing SW, LAKE ROAD passes a pair of otherwise identical houses of the 1880s in vividly contrasting green and brown
stone. Beyond the underpass is THE HEADS, overlooking the
immaculate Hope Park. A towering row of boarding houses of

the 1890s challenges the mountains themselves. And so to the Theatre (p. 448) and the lakeshore with its famous view of Derwent Island and the jaws of Borrowdale.

A short walk further s along the shore leads to FRIARS CRAG, given to the National Trust by subscribers in 1922 in memory of Hardwicke Rawnsley †1920. The RUSKIN MEMORIAL stands among the pines. Portrait medallion by *A. C. Lucchesi*, 1900, with the word TODAY, set in a slab of slate with incised quotations designed by *W. G. Collingwood*.

BRIGHAM FORGE, ½ m. E of the railway station. The WEIR in the river belonged with the historically important C16 forge operated by the Company of Mines Royal. Also the rock-cut LEAT forcing its way through the 15-yd (14-metre) tunnel known as the 'hammer hole' to feed the hammers and bellows. Later, the leat powered an exceptionally early attempt to generate electricity for public lighting (1890). A further ½ m. E reveals the BRIERY BOBBIN MILL, active from the 1830s until 1958, crudely incorporated with its associated cottages into a 'holiday village'.

BRIDGE over the Greta, 1 m. NNE. For the A66 by-pass, opened 1978. Concrete, elegantly brutal. Designed by *Scott Wilson Kirkpatrick*.

VILLAS round the lake.

DERWENT ISLAND. The Rev. William Gilpin, circumambulating the lake in 1776, advised 'not to . . . choose one of the little, flat and unvaried islands for my residence'. No such inhibitions had Joseph Pocklington, of Carlton-on-Trent, Notts. On its heightened summit he built a house (1778–80), white and cubic, looking all ways, pedimented over the full five bays on the E and W fronts, with pairs of full-height canted bays at the sides. It was raised on a hidden basement with a tunnel for access, roofed with great slabs of slate. The island's oval outline was regularized, a perimeter drive laid, trees planted. On the S tip Pocklington built a 'Druid Temple 56 feet (17 metres) in diameter', and a mock fort, which came into its own during the annual regattas he instigated with Peter Crosthwaite. Nothing much left of these, but behind the landing stage is still 'St Mary's Church' with its ivy-clad tower.

Pocklington's chestnuts have grown mightily, and so has his HOUSE. In 1850 *Anthony Salvin* extended it E and W for William Marshall. On the E an entrance tower, large dining room and stone stair running from cellar to attic. On the W a single-storey kitchen wing, flat-roofed; an Italianate loggia and roof terrace on top opens off Pocklington's upstairs drawing room. None of his internal decoration survives; in fact the roof terrace and loggia seem to represent a still later phase, c. 1900, with a drawing-room overmantel by *Ellen Mary Rope*. From here, Pocklington's houses at Portinscale (below) and Grange (q.v.) can be seen, giving the impression that the whole lake was his personal playground.

DERWENT BANK, Portinscale, ⅝ m. SSW. *Joseph Pocklington's* second house, 1784–5, probably to his own design. Again tall

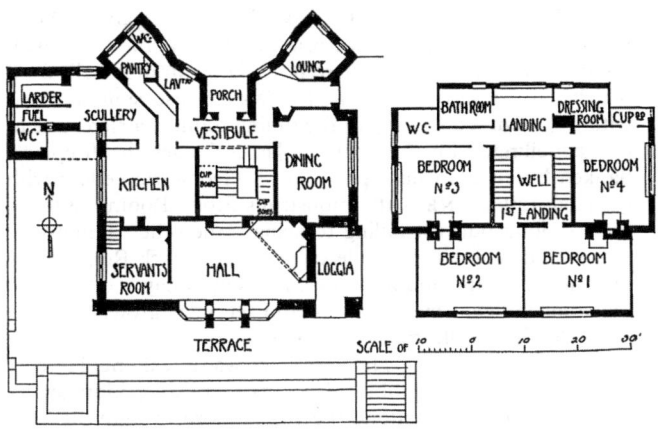

Keswick, High Moss.
Ground- and first-floor plans, 1922

and square with Venetian windows and lean-to wings, but now extended and institutional.

HIGH MOSS, Portinscale, on a back lane towards Uldale. For J. & L. Birket, 1901, and signed additionally *W. H. Ward* architect, *T. Hodgson* builder. High Moss is square in plan, designed around a central stair and a hall dominated by a huge corner ingle on the S, but the varied elevations deny any squareness. Front and back rooms are staggered to allow for the steep slope. The entrance, framed by low butterfly wings, is dominated by a tall slate-hung gable. At the back Siamese-twin gables, roughcast. Adam Voelcker notes its similarity to Wern Isaf at Llanfairfechan in North Wales by H.L. North. Ward (1865–1924) and North left Lutyens's practice together in 1898, setting up a loose association of architects called the Bedford Square Group. Before joining Lutyens in 1894 Ward had worked alongside Dan Gibson in the office of Ernest George & Peto.

(FAWE PARK, SE of Derwent Bank. By *Alfred Waterhouse*, 1856–8, a Picturesque holiday cottage for a fellow Quaker, James Bell, built tall with its sitting room on the top floor to enjoy the view. Enlarged in stages, partly to the design of *Spencer Bell* before his death in 1870, becoming more funereal as it grew.)

(Another small *Waterhouse* commission, nearby, was ROSE TREES, 1857–61, for Gilbert Henderson.)

LINGHOLM is a grander affair, an achingly gaunt house of 1871–5 by *Waterhouse* (£15,700) for Lt-Col. G. F. Greenall, brewer. Roughcast, steeply gabled and dormered, with tall cylindrical chimneys. The dining room at the S end was extended towards the lake to accommodate bought-in furnishings. After 1900 Col. George Kemp, later 1st Baron Rochdale, made further extensions to the N and E. As a result Waterhouse is scarcely visible on the lake front, which exhibits three phases in different styles and colour combinations. More recently it has been unsatisfactorily cut down at the s end, with a picture window like a square hole. The entrance hall, from which rises a surprisingly modest Waterhouse stair, is lined with C17 stamped leather. In the dining room is a rich suite of C17 panelling, with the arms of James I over the fireplace, flanked by cities in false perspective. Geometric ceiling with Greenall initials. NE is the monstrous Stone Room, 48 ft (15 metres) long but just failing to achieve the other dimensions that would make it a double cube. A vast black Renaissance fireplace faces the double-transomed central bay. – GARDENS. Once-magnificent views of lake and fell have grown out, the rhododendron collection gone to pot.

(ST HERBERT'S ISLAND. The hermitage was a real one; Herbert was a friend of St Cuthbert. By 1374 there were indulgences for those who would attend the vicar of Crosthwaite there on 13 April, St Herbert's day. About 1800 Sir Wilfrid Lawson built a new hermitage 'from a design by the Revd. Mr Wilkinson' of Ormathwaite – probably *Joseph Wilkinson*.)

55 DERWENT BAY, 1½ m. SW of Keswick. A lakeside pavilion built by Lord William Gordon, *c.* 1790. Only a single storey. In the middle is a 24-ft (7.5-metre) rotunda with three floor-length windows towards the lake. Blank arches round the other sides. Flanking are an unequal pair of rooms angled in to catch the cross-views up and down the lake, each with a canted bay. Each part has its own tent roof. Further rooms and links have been added from time to time. It is all extraordinarily informal, unassertive, and disarming.

MILLBECK, 2⅔ m. NNW at the foot of Skiddaw, was a small textile-working settlement. MILLBECK TOWERS, a confection of three storeys and three bays between circular flanking towers under conical roofs – Scottish baronial without the dignity – started as an C18 carding mill but was greatly altered in 1903 for John Banks. MILLBECK TOWERS COTTAGES have been created out of a water-powered FULLING MILL of 1805. Original mill windows survive on the first floor, the absence of the heavy architraves usual in houses in the region betraying the industrial origins.

KILLINGTON (W)

The village, in a fold of the hills and reached by high-hedged lanes, seems far from the M6. Hall and manorial chapel sit together, which is not common in Cumbria.

ALL SAINTS. Roughcast, nave and chancel in one, with a diminutive tower-porch. Domestic in character, with plain C17 mullioned windows, except for two on the N, one of which has three trefoil-headed lights: perhaps C14, and perhaps displaced from the E when the present window was introduced. It was re-roofed in 1868, and restored in 1895 with a new vestry. – STAINED GLASS. The E window is by *Christopher Whall*, 1907. Christ appears after the Resurrection, ringed in fire, to his gathered followers. Outside, a starry night and angels. – MONUMENTS. Several good C18 tablets, one (†1771) all of black marble.

KILLINGTON HALL. The ravine by the S wing makes a naturally defensive site. This is the ruined solar wing, formerly embattled, but not thick-walled. It seems C15 and has to the front a four-light, and above it a three-light window, the lights all cusped. The hall range is now partly three-storeyed, with dormer gables with stepped three-light windows, and a date 1640. Remodelled Gothick doorway, adjoining ogee-headed window made out of the low-end door, 1803. Round chimneys. Interior mainly C17.

(LOW HALL, Hallbeck, ½ m. SE. Dated 1684, yet still with irregularly placed mullioned windows. Pevsner noted characteristic Westmorland oddities about the doorway: 'It has pilasters, but they have the oddest sunk moulding. It has capitals, but they are almost Anglo-Saxon in their incorrectness. And it has a lintel with simple geometrical decoration and a pediment minus its base.')

KILLINGTON LAKE SERVICES, M6 southbound, immediately S of Junction 37. 1972. Excellently designed and cleverly sited, it turns away from the motorway, unlike earlier service stations, towards the canal reservoir with its piney island and the distant Pennines. A folded glass wall under a row of dormers provides maximum alcove seating along the view side. The big pyramidal roof, open and boarded on the inside, calms the space. The materials are natural without labouring the point – limestone cladding and slate roofing.

KIRKANDREWS-ON-ESK (C)   *3060*

A wonderful group. The church stands urbane and assured on the Scottish side of the Esk, a famous salmon river; the tower house, tall and tough-looking, overlooks it from the bluff above. A suspension FOOTBRIDGE of 1877 (Kelly) links the church to the aristocratic sweep of Netherby Hall and its Park (q.v.). By the A7 is the Grahams' private railway station.

ST ANDREW. The old church, ruined like all Arthuret's chapelries in 1606, was rebuilt in 1637, and again in 1775 by Dr Robert Graham of Netherby. Sophisticated simplicity. A box of perfect ashlar with just three widely spaced windows   78 in super-arches on each side. Pedimented W front with square gallery windows over the pedimented Tuscan doorway. Square W tower, topped by an open rotunda of columns at the bell-stage and a little dome. Slightly gauche E elevation, with a large window and two niches. The interior must have been austere, judging by the three arches of the Netherby gallery at the back, but in 1892–3 it was glorified by *Temple Moore* for Cynthia, second wife of Sir Richard Graham. A splendid set of classical FURNISHINGS (Temple Moore was usually a Gothicist) was introduced, all in dark green and gold, executed by *W. & H. Davidson* of Carlisle. The ensemble is arrranged like stage scenery to unfold as you advance up the nave: grand triumphal SCREEN to define a chancel, ALTARPIECE framing a copy of Raphael's Transfiguration, ALTAR RAILS brought forward in a half-circle to complete the other half of the internal apse, ORGAN PIPES in matching little opera boxes; the player has to sit in the vestry. – FONT COVER, a Corinthian temple, and iron crane, 1894. – STAINED GLASS, executed with Temple Moore's scheme by *Shrigley & Hunt*. In the gallery the Kirkandrews landscape (†1932) by *A. Ferdinand*.

KIRKANDREWS TOWER. A stronghold of the notorious Graham family (cf. Brackenhill), built by 1552; let after 1703 to the rector. Self-contained tower house in the Scots tradition, like e.g. Gilnockie Tower, N of Canonbie (Dumfriesshire), which was built for the Armstrongs at much the same time. Windows high up, small and irregularly disposed. Parapet-walk on corbels, with cannon gargoyles, surrounding a steep roof. First-floor entrance, above the vaulted undercroft. Retainers perhaps occupied this floor, with the hall on the second floor. Corner staircase. The barmkin wall was made into a garden feature in 1827.

THE SCOTS' DIKE. Remnants of a low bank, flanked by shallow ditches, running for over 3 m. from the Sark to the Esk, marking the Border agreed in 1552 through the lawless Debatable Lands.

LIDDEL STRENGTH, 1½ m. NNE. A fine earthwork CASTLE high above the Liddel Water (here, the Border); first mentioned 1174 when taken by William the Lion. A motte and an inner ward (unusually, not separated by a ditch) were defended by a semi-circular bank and ditch; outer ward on the SW. In 1282 the castle had a timber hall with two solars and cellars, and a chapel, kitchen, byre, grange, and granary. Within the inner ward, the footings of a later tower house, occupied by the Grahams until *c.* 1600.

KIRKBAMPTON (C)

ST PETER. Little Norman church of Solway type, restored in 1870–1 and 1882. Nave with porch and double belfry. Long narrow chancel with three E lancets and a tiny S lancet under a single stone with incised lines. A similar window re-set in the organ transept. N doorway with two orders of zigzag and a billet dripmould to the arch, and one order of colonnettes. The tympanum is damaged but a kneeling figure can be made out. On the s was another doorway with an order of columns half-buried in the ground. The blocked priest's doorway on the s side has a very odd tympanum: three horizontal bands each consisting of squares set lozenge-wise and connected with one another by pairs of stones one on top of the other. In the bottom row the squares are cream-coloured and the connecting stones red, in the next the colours are reversed, in the top row they are again as in the first. Red and yellow voussoirs too, but not strictly alternated. The doorway itself seems to have been extremely narrow. The chancel arch is Norman, probably not later than *c.* 1150. Zigzag and beakhead in the arch and scalloped capitals inventively varied with fish-scale, diaper and sunk chequer. The arch has one roll and one step. The back of the arch has beakhead so perfunctory as to be abstract. In the chancel a trefoil-headed PISCINA, SE, and what looks like another piscina further w, suggesting a lengthening, and explaining the odd position of the priest's door. Built in next to it what looks like a Roman stone. NE are two aumbries, one massively bolted and locked. Lamb-and-flag Victorian floor TILES. – STAINED GLASS. E triplet by *Morris & Co.*, 1871, sadly deteriorated: eight angel musicians by *William Morris*, and a beautiful figure of Christ with flag of St George by *Burne-Jones*. Pevsner contrasted it with the adjacent 'insufferable' window by *E. R. Suffling*, 1885. The nave windows by *John Scott & Son* and *Wailes* are not much better.

KIRKBRIDE (C)

ST BRIDE. Atop a hillock, once an island, overlooking the bridge. Small nave and bellcote and chancel, essentially Norman but revamped by *Oliver & Dodgshun* in 1895–9, when the chancel was virtually rebuilt. Plain s doorway, narrow and tall, and plainer blocked N one, straight-headed and even narrower. Norman also the unmoulded chancel arch on the plainest imposts, one nave N window, one chancel N window, and the chancel s doorway, round-arched with a continuous chamfer. Round arched niches for altars on either side of the chancel arch. – FONTS. One small, square with rounded corners, with Norman arches, a lamb and cross, and dogtooth and fleurons down the edges. The other square, larger and Perp, with trefoiled and quatrefoiled circles on the sides, knobbly leaf underneath. – STAINED GLASS. E window by *Kayll & Co.*, Leeds, 1904. s choir window designed by *J. F. Bentley*, 1896. – (SCULPTURE. Italian panel of the Entombment, small, approximately late C16.)

AIRFIELD, ½ m. s. Laid out in the Second World War as a receiving base for planes flown across the Atlantic. The brick control tower remains, and a scatter of hangars, some in industrial or storage use.

(FINGLAND FARM, 1¾ m. E. A good dabbin with a classic and very clear Cumbrian plan: the only door goes into the byre at the back of the stack. Fire-window in the house place by the stack. No middle front door, though it may have had one at one stage. Upper storey raised by piling a bit more clay on the wall tops and putting short posts on the cruck yokes to raise the ridge a little.)

KIRKBY-IN-FURNESS (L)

Also called KIRKBY IRELETH. It has several hamlets: Sandside, Wallend, Soutergate. The church is at Beckside, SE.

ST CUTHBERT. W tower, nave, long chancel, and a large N aisle. Quite an ambitious Norman S doorway, of c. 1170. Two orders of columns, one hexagonal, with decorated scallop, leaf and waterleaf capitals. The outer arch is continuously moulded, the inner with vertebra-like beakhead. It retains its red raddle colour. The westernmost chancel N window is Norman too. The outline of its opposite number can be seen. The chancel was extended E with Perp windows, the broad E window renewed in 1698. The N aisle originates as a chapel of 1523, later extended W. The tower was rebuilt in 1829. But it is all ruthlessly renewed: the chancel in 1881, the nave, aisle and arcade in 1884 by *Ewan Christian*, and the tower in 1904. The chancel arch and gable, interestingly, are timber-framed.

FONT. Later medieval. Octagonal, goblet-shaped, with panels, and a shield on the stem. – PAINTING. Moses and Aaron by *Mathias Read*, c. 1720. – STAINED GLASS. Chancel N window, grisaille with a small cross superimposed, c. 1200. Typically Cistercian in its austerity; Furness Abbey held the living until 1230. Chancel S, in the Y of the Y-tracery, Christ displaying his wounds, c. 1300; colourful by comparison. Chancel N easternmost, St Aidan and St Cuthbert, excellent, by *Hugh Arnold*. In the N aisle contrasting *Shrigley & Hunt* windows: of 1913, richly Kempe-like, with pearls, and 1953, floating multicultural figures in clear glass. – MONUMENT. Tomb-slab by the pulpit of Alexander de Kirby, mid-C13. Cross, sword, small shield, and the suggestion of a cushioned head and praying hands.

BECKSIDE GRANGE, S of the church, was the rectory. By *Paley & Austin*, 1881. A fine solid house of green cut stone with red ashlar dressings. The big roof indicates an L-shaped house, turning to make a big slate-hung gable at one end, but the front is flat, with an emphatic cornice.

CHRISTIAN MEETING HOUSE, Wallend. 1876. Plain and sensible building, minimally Gothic. The Christian Brethren were active in this westernmost corner of Lancashire.

KIRKBY HALL, 1⅜ m. N of the church. Home of the Kirkbys until mortgaged in 1689, passing with its slate quarries to the Cavendishes in the C18, when panelling and even floorboards were taken to Holker. A mountain of Burlington slate waste is getting ever closer behind.

Hall and cross-wings – but the front is flat – with the big round chimneys that so often signal status. Windows all plainly mullioned. The low end is identified by the big bluntly pointed and moulded doorway, the hall by its evident greater headroom and by a simple high-end bay. The service wing on the r. (SE) was considered by the VCH to be the oldest part, c. 1450. Belonging to this a wide wooden turning stair in an outshut at the back. The screens passage is not really a screens in the southern sense, not having the requisite number of doors, and leading to the stair not a rear door. The new hall was added, thought the VCH, c. 1530. It is big (24 ft, 7.5 metres, square) and plain, with a broad arched fireplace. A hollow-moulded doorway leads through to the family parlour at the NW end. In the NW corner, by the fireplace, a curiously long curvy passageway cuts through to the back dairy.

Upstairs, the SE bedroom has a plaster overmantel with cockle shell, arms (missing), grapes and flowers. From the back dairy a ladder and trap door give access to the CHAPEL, so called, above the W parlour. This was a comfortable chamber with a fireplace in the W wall and well lit by mullioned windows facing S and W; the latter, now blocked, retaining wooden mullions. In the N corners are sub-circular recesses, one over the long passage noted below. At a hazard one may have been a spiral stair, perhaps of wood like the main one, the other a garderobe. The roof is a crown-poster – an archaic form commoner in the South than the North – with just one longitudinal member under the collars, longitudinally braced from the crown-posts. Curved braces come down from the tie-beam to wall-posts, visible but buried in the stone walls, which are jowled for the wall-plates. So this is one of just a handful of surviving examples of timber framing in the region. It was also very likely free-standing, i.e. preceding the hall, the stones of which are simply built up to and piled on top of the wall-plate. All around, on walls and timbers, are PAINTINGS in black, white and red. On the walls exotic and mythical birds and beasts, like a bestiary. A bird, with ears no less, peers out with a horseshoe in its beak. Next to that a gormless-looking bird identified as a bustard, with a thin egret-like bird above. The feathery backgrounds are not feathers, however, despite the peacock 'eyes' in them, but palm trees, since they have trunks, with coconuts. Between each panel a twisted column with a bulgy red capital. More architecture shown small between the animals. Above, on a plaster cove, a blackletter frieze: the Lord's Prayer, Ten Commandments and Creed, well preserved except for the red initials, which have faded. The Os have smiley faces in them. On the timbers traces of chevron.

46

What is the date of all this? The paintings are not the Renaissance-influenced grotesque work of the later C16 (cf. Lanercost) but seem medieval in inspiration. The texts on the other hand – if contemporaneous, which they appear to be – must post-date 1549 and the Book of Common Prayer; so perhaps the 1550s is the best estimate.

BARN at the back r. with two upper-cruck-trusses. Ruined building to the l. of the front with remains of a full cruck of good size.

BURLINGTON SLATE QUARRY, NE. Small quarry sites were exploited by farmers from the C17 for the splendid slates which, laid in diminishing courses from eaves to ridge, make the local roofs such a pleasure. In the 1840s drainage difficulties and problems with overlapping workings gave *William Cavendish* the excuse to terminate his tenants' leases and take over all the mines and quarries. The scale of the current workings is Cyclopean.

KIRKBY LONSDALE (W)

6070

Compact grey stone market town (charter 1227) in what was Richmondshire, on the Yorkshire, Lancashire and Westmorland borders. The site is a significant one, at the head of possible Lune valley navigation and at an important bridging point on the Skipton–Kendal road. Much of its revenue came from the tolls. By-passed today, a great hush has fallen on on the town, although it is popular with day-trippers.

ST MARY. Hidden behind the houses of Market Street. The springy-turfed churchyard opens out beyond the church onto a marvellous view: a great sweep of the Lune, the turrets of Underley Hall, and the distant Yorkshire Dales. A little N is a low Norman MOTTE.

The church, a clean rectangle excepting only the S porch of 1866, exhibits an interesting and promising mix of styles and stonework. An extra N aisle makes it very wide, like Kendal. The church poses some knotty problems, so it is well to have an outline history in mind. There was a string of Saxon foundations up the Lune valley from Heysham, of which this may be one. In the 1090s Ivo de Taillebois, Baron of Kendal, gave Kirkby Lonsdale to the abbey of St Mary at York. The four western columns of the N arcade were then built. The tower and non-matching W columns of the S arcade are supposed to be *c.* 1180. The showy (inside) E termination is about 1200. In the C14, or perhaps *c.* 1400, the N and S walls were taken down and built further outwards, including the Norman S doorways. 1486 is the foundation date for the large Middleton chantry chapel (NE), later replaced. The C16 saw an updating, with a new clerestory, pinnacles, battlements and flat lead roofs. At

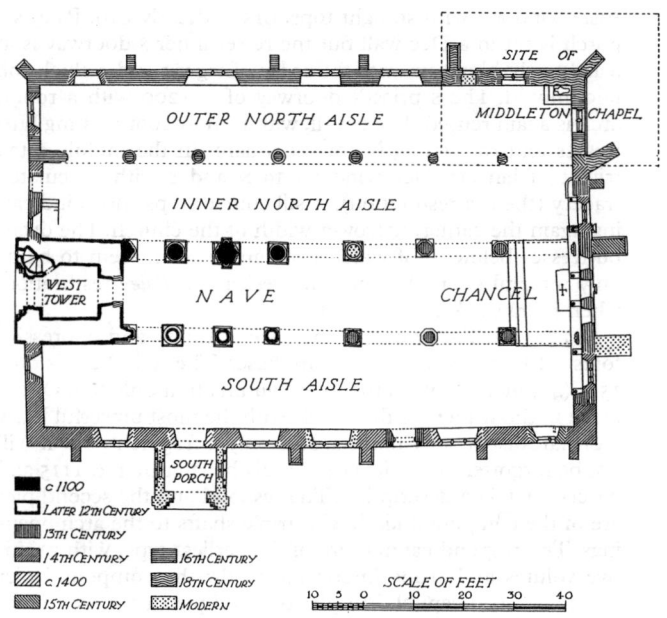

Kirkby Lonsdale, St Mary.
Plan, 1936

the Dissolution the benefice was given to Trinity College,
Cambridge, and in 1574 the outer N aisle was added. In 1705
the tower top was rebuilt. The Middleton Chapel was taken
down and brought into line with the outer aisle. In 1807 *Francis
Webster* did away with clerestory, battlements and pinnacles,
removing 36 tons of lead, and made an enormous sweeping
overall roof of slate.* 1866–8 saw a restoration by *E. G. Paley*
for Lord Kenlis, later 4th Earl of Bective, who replaced the
roofs – still a huge sweep, but raised a bit, and with the outer
N aisle roofed separately.

EXTERIOR. The W tower is embraced by embattled aisles.
Late Norman W doorway of two orders of shafts with reeded
capitals and additional inner mouldings. One arch order has
panels basically each a saltire cross, but with decoration
inserted. The outer order has a long, thin, much-weathered
archer(?), a dragon(?) etc. The lancets at the W end of the aisles
(one round-headed and one pointed) are set close in to the
tower, indicating the narrowness of the aisles at that time. The
small Norman doorway at its outer N edge (one continuous
chamfer) was presumably repositioned for the widened aisle.
The top stages of the existing tower, unbuttressed, are latest
Perp. Does the date 1704, below the lower W window, apply?

*Webster wrote that he would have given up architecture were it not for the fact
that it sold slate.

Aisle windows with straight tops, C15 and early C16. Paley's s porch is set in a Dec wall but the re-set inner s doorway is at least partly Norman, with an order of zigzag and a thick roll hoodmould. The s priest's doorway of c. 1200 with a round arch is again reused. The E wall, with its non-coordinating buttresses and roof scars, is not set square. In the middle a tall triplet of lancets. Dec windows to N and s with reticulated tracery (the N a restoration). A sill course stops short, indicating again the earlier, narrower width of the church. The dwarf buttresses below it, of which two can be seen, seem to be its only integral strengthening. The vesica is a *Paley* restoration, when he raised Webster's roof-line.

INTERIOR. The W end of the nave is a dark and oppressive forest of fat piers on high square bases. The nave here is only 15 ft (4.5 metres) wide, the intercolumniation only ten. One is faced in the W piers of the N aisle with the most powerful Early Norman display in Cumbria. It is only a fragment, but it will not be forgotten. The piers can hardly be later than c. 1115 and deserve detailed description. The respond and the second pier are of the compound kind, with triple shafts to the arch openings. The respond capitals are of the earliest type, with primitive volutes and crude interlaced bands; the compound pier has a scalloped capital. But pier one and pier three are round, and they have boldly incised or carved-in trellis like that of Durham Cathedral or the nave of Selby Abbey. The model is that of the Durham W end (c. 1105–20) rather than the spirals of its earlier parts, and it is executed in the same way, i.e. every stone has the same pattern cut into it in the same place. Malcolm Thurlby links the work also with Norman fragments at St Mary's Abbey, York.* The first pier has a trellis of three parallel lines of incisions, the third one of deep and quite broad grooves. The first pier has a square abacus and a capital of four big scallops. The capitals include some entertaining carving, which Durham lacks. The first arch has three parallel fat rolls, the second one step and one chamfer, the third a moulding of a half-roll framed by two half-hollows, again as at Durham. The fourth pier has an octagonal capital of later type.

The church thus begun must have been intended to have had a wider nave and altogether a different scale. It may have been started with a view to vaulting – cf. the shaft of the compound pier, clearly meant to be continued upward. The alternation of columns suggests that each vault bay would have spanned two arcade bays, as at Durham. Also, as one capital of this early work was left unfinished, we may assume a break in operations. Then came a reduction, and, later in the C12, the much simpler s arcade was started. Its first pier still has a square abacus. The capital is flat and has scallops, but the arches have two slight chamfers, and the next pier has the round capital of c. 1200. When the new church had reached

---

* In *Carlisle and Cumbria: British Archaeological Association Conference Transactions 27*, 2004.

that far, i.e. when not much upper wall and no roof were yet built, the work must have received a new impetus, and proceeded apace. The narrow nave now widens a little on the N, continuing with the chancel, but no intervening chancel arch, to a total of seven bays. The E bays on both sides have slender alternating round and octagonal piers and double-chamfered pointed arches. The beautiful E wall terminated the work. Its lancets are elegantly shafted inside, with boldly detached shafts with one shaft-ring. This treatment continues to the width of the original narrow aisles (the windows now, as we have seen, Dec), with a walkway behind the colonnettes at sill level. It breaks off abruptly at each end. Some of the capitals of the shafts at the E end have waterleaf, some crocket capitals. That also indicates that the end of the work was about 1200. The execution is curiously irregular, both in setting out and in applied decoration. Most puzzling is the way the aisle arcades crash into it, demanding the *ad hoc* buttressing we saw outside. It suggests that the E wall was built in advance of the arcades. The SE column has a PISCINA set in it. The late C12 piers were higher than the old, and so the W bays were rebuilt on high, square bases. The W tower was begun at the time of the S arcade, as the tower arch and the W portal show. *Paley* lowered the floor, with some new pier bases. The nasty stonework above the nave arcades must be *Webster*'s, when he abolished the clerestory.

The outer aisle arcade is Late Perp, but its two E bays relate to the Middleton Chapel which stood here. The piers are round – still, or again – and the capitals as plain and simply moulded as to make them quite similar to early C13 capitals. Only the chapel piers are octagonal. N windows also Late Perp.

It remains to notice the rubble E wall of the tower. Simple doorway – no shafts, just flat caps and a slight chamfer – and Neo-Norman ringers' window above.

FITTINGS. REREDOS of alabaster and mosaic. – Iron SCREENS around the chancel by *Paley*, 1866. – PULPIT dated 1619, but cut down. With closely ornamented panels in two tiers, the upper with the usual short, broad, blank arches. Other bits can be seen around the church, including one inscribed SEDES VICAR. – FONT. From the C14 chapel at Killington, set on a C19 base. – STAINED GLASS. Mostly by *Lavers, Barraud & Westlake*, with their typical down-in-the-mouth faces. The E triplet, also apparently theirs, is a surprise with its blue cast and small-scale scenes; it was designed by *Westlake* in 1863. E of the S door, Faith, Charity and Hope, by *Heaton, Butler & Bayne* to a *Henry Holiday* design. Two by *Shrigley & Hunt* NW, and an armorial window in the Middleton Chapel by *William Wailes*, c. 1856. – MONUMENTS. At the NE corner the pathetic remnant, half-buried in the wall, of the C15 tomb-chest and alabaster effigy of Edward Middleton, once in the middle of a much larger chapel. – Quite a number of Georgian tablets, including a symmetrical group on the tower N wall in dark fossiliferous marbles grouped round a big black urn on a pulpit-

Kirkby Lonsdale, Devil's Bridge.
Engraving, 1801

like excrescence (to Hugh Ashton †1749). – Urn in a niche to
the Rev. John Wilson †1792, N. – Janet Webster †1805, with the
urn in an unusual place. – Brass s of the altar to Amelia,
Countess of Bective, †1864, perhaps by *Hardman*.

In the CHURCHYARD, W, an obelisk to Alice Clark, Agnes
Walling, Hannah Armstrong and Agnes Nicholson, 'buried to
eternity, in the awful destruction by fire of the Rose and Crown
Hotel', 1820. – VICARAGE. 1783. The third storey and chalet
roof were added in the early 1830s. – By the churchyard w gate
a surprisingly weak WAR MEMORIAL with Norman niches and
zigzag spirals, by *Austin & Paley*, c. 1920. – Beyond the E end
of the church a pair of summerhouses. The octagonal GAZEBO,
late C18 or early C19, was in the vicarage garden but is now
part of the churchyard. It has lost its pretty roof. Four arched
openings in the main directions. CHURCH BROW COTTAGE
was built as a private summerhouse in 1820, and restored by
the Vivat Trust c. 1993. It is square with a bowed s side facing
the garden and a balcony over the river.*

METHODIST CHAPEL. Opposite the w gate of the churchyard.
1834. Simple Gothic, with lancets.

For other places of worship *see* Perambulation.

(PRIMARY SCHOOL, Kendal Road, to the w. By *Brian Dockray*
of *Gill Dockray & Partners*, c. 1986. Low, with big roofs.)

MOTTE. Low Norman motte on the w bank of the Lune, N of
the vicarage.

DEVIL'S BRIDGE. A very popular rendezvous. The earliest record
is a repair order of 1365. It was perhaps built by the masons
of St Mary's, York, at much the same time as the E end of the

---

*Church Brow Walk commands the view lauded by Ruskin and painted by Turner,
with a great sweep of the Lune valley and the turrets of Underley Hall (p. 466).

church, i.e. *c.* 1200. The three unequal arches of sandstone
ashlar stand high and slender on the water-sculpted limestone
bed of the river. They are ribbed underneath, and the arches
are round, with triple chamfers. The cutwaters are chamfered
back halfway up, so the refuges on top are polygonal.

The GATEPIERS by the river belonged to Lunefield, a pretty
white villa of 1815–16 by *Francis Webster* for Roger Carus,
demolished in 1868 for a Gothic pile by *Alfred Waterhouse* for
Alfred Harris, now demolished too.

The A65 STANLEY BRIDGE stands a respectful distance s. It has
a single arch, also ribbed underneath, and was built by the
Reinforced Concrete Construction Co. of Manchester in 1931–2.
Only the parapet is stone.

PERAMBULATION

The best place to start is MARKET SQUARE, though this was
created only in 1823. The important-looking building at its E
end is not a town hall but the SAVINGS BANK of 1847 by *Miles
Thompson* (*Thomas Garnett* of Kirkby Lonsdale was asked for
plans first). The ground floor is rusticated, the upper has paired
corner pilasters. Three bays, the middle one brought forward
with paired round-topped windows under an open pediment
and empty turret. Porch with two pairs of Doric pilasters and
a balcony. The MARKET CROSS is not a market cross either,
but a memorial built by the Rev. John Llewelyn Davies in 1905
to his wife. Octagonal vaulted shelter with a cross on top, originally carried on a flying crown, like the Chichester or Malmes-
bury crosses. It is by *J. F. Curwen* of Kendal. The ROYAL
HOTEL, C18 and C19, the principal hostelry of the town, completes the E side of the Square. Ashlar-faced, with a ground
floor in smooth rustication and a porch of unfluted Ionic
columns, pulvinated frieze and pediment. Here was the Rose
and Crown, burnt in 1820 (*see* St Mary, churchyard). On the
s side two handsome shopfronts, one bowed, the other with
Roman Doric columns.

First a brief walk s along TOWN END (Main Street). Carr &
Bleasdale's shop and the Tourist Information occupy a build-
ing signed AH 1897, with flowery bargeboards. TOWN END
HOUSE, with a Tuscan porch, dates from 1777, built by Robert
Gathorne whose initials are on the hoppers. Finally GREEN
CLOSE, of 1906 by *Austin & Paley*, enlarged *c.* 1985 by *Michael
Rowlinson*.

MAIN STREET going the other way, i.e. N of Market Square, is
narrow, with several decent doorways. It suffered fires in 1776
and 1780, so is mostly late C18 and early C19. An exception is
Lunesdale Homes and Gardens (Nos. 54–56), *c.* 1600 and
much lower than all the others. No. 9 juts forward, with its
gable treated as a pediment and pierced by an arched window.
The front is to the s, i.e. looking at it from the s, blocking part

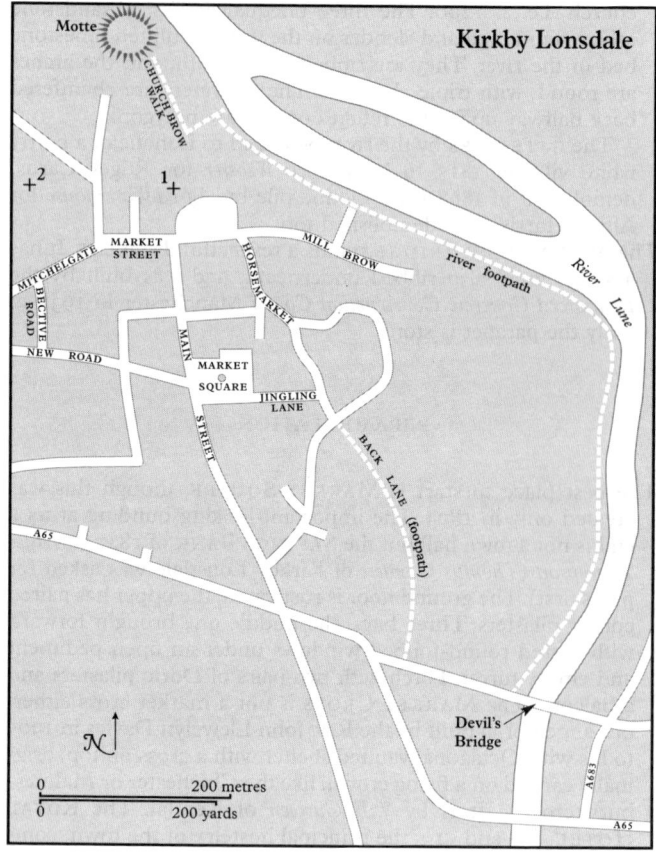

1   St Mary
2   Methodist chapel

NatWest Bank (No. 55) of 1855 has an ashlar
front of projection and recession, asymmetrical, with a pediment but with restrained detail.

Now up New Road (new in 1821), which heads W next to the
Royal Hotel. The Library was a Sandemanian chapel of
1820. Rowan Garth shows 2004 stone technique, as though
the stones are simply stuck on. The Institute, 1895, is at
the junction with Bective Road. Built and perhaps designed by
William Bayliff. Good Arts and Crafts architecture, of which
there are many other examples in town. Booth's Supermarket at the top, of *c.* 2000 by *Farrell & Clark*, is saved from
simple shed-dom by its echelon of four gables at the ends.

Bective Road has nice things too. The houses on the l. were
built for the Biggins estate. Nos. 2, 4 and 6, 1890s, are also by

Bayliff. Nos. 8–14 a nicely balanced row dated 1895 built by *Joe Dawson*. The houses on the other side, again nicely composed, were built for the Underley estate at much the same time. At the N end, on Mitchelgate, is ABBOT HALL. Dated 1632 on a court cupboard. Two-storey porch at the downhill end, so it must have been altered. Mullioned windows, in the l. half under one continuous string course, which is a later C17 motif. (Late C17 staircase, fireplaces, panelling.)

Now MARKET STREET, a continuation of Mitchelgate to the E. FOUNTAIN HOUSE, mid-C18, closes the W end of Market Street, where it bends round the churchyard. Five bays, the doorway with unfluted Ionic columns, pulvinated frieze, pediment and a nice lamp overthrow. (Very wide stone fireplace of C16 type.) To the l. of Fountain House, at right angles, No. 4 Beck Head, also of five bays, rebuilt in 1775. The SUN HOTEL (C17) is built over the pavement on three rough monolith piers. The KING'S ARMS has a grand C18 front with three Diocletian windows in the gables, and tripartite ones under them. This was the C16 manor house, and the interiors show elements of the C16 and C17. The MARKET HOUSE of 1854–5 by *Miles Thompson* successfully turns the corner into Main Street. Its ground-floor arches were originally open. Interior on iron columns, with concert hall and assembly room above. Mill Brow leads to the little SWINE MARKET. Medieval CROSS. Steps and column with octagonal cap. The ball finial was put on top in 1819 when it was moved here from Market Street. Also a little WEIGH-HOUSE with tallies scratched on its door and a half-height upper floor with louvred windows. OLD COURTHOUSE is dated 1880, with Merrie England timbering and pargetting. Mill Brow continues steeply down to the river. Part-way down is Kirkby Lonsdale's best house, the OLD MANOR HOUSE. Five-bay front of *c.* 1700 with cross-mullioned windows, doorway with shouldered architrave, triple keystone, broken segmental pediment. Back near the top, and stretching S, HORSE MARKET is a narrow way that has been encroached upon by Nos. 3–11, in Arts and Crafts style. Through an arch can be spied the houses of its earlier street frontage. ST JOSEPH (R.C.), on Back Lane, was built as a Congregational chapel in 1816, with basket arches. JINGLING END of 1829 was built for, and perhaps by, *Thomas Garnett*. Three bays. Ashlar at the front, watershot stone at the side, rendered rubble at the back. The door is set in a big blank arch, the roof is more complicated than it need be. From here Jingling Lane leads back to Market Square.

OUTLYING BUILDINGS

Kirkby Lonsdale's affairs, especially in the C19, were much influenced by the great houses that surrounded it: Underley Hall, The Biggins, Lunefield, and Rigmaden at Mansergh. The

Biggins, home of the Paget-Tomlisons, and Lunefield, rebuilt by
Alfred Harris, have both gone.

UNDERLEY HALL, 1 m. N. Now Underley Schools. By *George
Webster*, 1825–8, for Alexander Nowell. Purchased in 1840 by
Alderman William Thompson, ironmaster, under whose
daughter and son-in-law as 4th Earl and Countess of Bective
it eclipsed even Lowther. Its pepperpot turrets, reminiscent of
Stonyhurst (North Lancashire), are prominent in the famous
view from Church Brow, as is the uncompromising chapel.

 Webster's work is remarkable as an early revival of Jacobean.*
It has level, openwork parapets rather than the multiple gables
he used later at Whelprigg (Barbon, q.v.). Both main fronts are
strictly symmetrical. The entrance side has two angle turrets
with caps, two bay windows, and a frontispiece of pairs of
fluted columns in two tiers. A second portico on the garden
front, this time with four enriched Doric columns and with
pierced obelisks in place of the upper storey. Also two turrets
and two canted bays. Major additions were made by *Paley &
Austin* in 1872, continuing this façade. Their 100-ft (31-metre)
tower compensates for Webster's unexecuted belvedere over
the centre. All beyond the tower also belonged to this phase,
including a ballroom and a conservatory with a globular roof
and glass dome – would that it were still there. The road up to
the walled gardens affords an astonishing view over house and
offices with its multitudinous turrets and chimneys, like a city.

 CHAPEL, now sports hall. Dating from 1964–5 when
Underley was a junior Roman Catholic seminary. By *William
White* and *John Sheridon* of the *Building Design Partnership*.
Pevsner admired its 'impressive, severe and exacting' design.
Faced with thin concrete slabs with recessed horizontal
pointing, it appears at first to have no windows; apart from the
lantern over the altar position there are only slits between
projecting, completely sheer blocks of various shapes rising
above the roof. The roof hangs from these blocks, admitting
light from the top. Extensive sacristies on the N, and a whole
row of chapels for the individual daily masses made
unnecessary at exactly that moment by the Second Vatican
Council.

 Lune BRIDGE, in the park. 1872–5. Two wide ribbed arches
and a narrow one, castellated, costing £10,000.

 HOME FARM. C19. The yard gatehouse has the same
Jacobean features as the mansion. Three detached octagonal
buildings; one was the retort house for a private gasworks.

 Gigantic GATEPIERS, more Baroque than Jacobean.
Polychromatic Home Counties Tudor LODGE in preposterous
juxtaposition. Gothic village SCHOOL, 1902.

TEARNSIDE HALL, 1½ m. W, off the A65. Dated 1686 I and AB
on the door lintel, with carved branches. Two-storey house,
stable and barn in one long range. Mullioned windows of two

---

*In the same style as Webster's Netherside Hall of 1820–2, Yorkshire North Riding,
also for Nowell.

lights. Continuous dripmoulds over the windows. Pevsner noted the funny pilastered doorcase, with the same roll moulding and crude capitals as Low Hall, Killington (q.v.). Even odder the upper window of the two-storey porch, like a misunderstood Venetian window with the shoulders of the arched light glazed as well. The lower floor of the porch is ashlar, the upper rubble, implying two builds. A second doorway has an ogee head. A door in the barn leads to a passage behind the main stack, as expected.

SETTLEMENT, near Kilnerfoot, 1¾ m. W. Probably of late Iron Age date. Substantial irregular oval enclosure, much subdivided, with two circular buildings; suggestions of medieval reoccupation.

KIRKBY STEPHEN (W)

7000

Near the head of the Eden valley. A long town of Yorkshire character as much as Westmorland. Market charters 1361 and 1606. The town is built of an unusual stone called Brockram: limestone fragments in sandstone, which looks like coarse pink and grey concrete. Only a handful of public buildings exhibit ashlar. Plenty of chapels. The town has kept its iron railings – what a difference it makes. Front railings of dozens of different patterns even in so small a place, ranging from simple wrought spears to elaborately cast floral patterns. Population 1,141 in 1801; in 1991, 1,619.

CHURCH. Dedication not known (Stephen is a place-name corruption). Set back behind buildings and the market cloisters. The stately Perp W tower is quite out of the ordinary for Cumbria. Eight pinnacles, bell-openings of two pairs of tall lights under ogee hoodmoulds, stepped diagonal buttresses, three-light W window, W doorway with shields in the spandrels. Its heraldry suggests that it was built by the 1st Lord Wharton in the 1540s, rather than 1506 as usually quoted. Inside, a tall tower arch, the highest in Westmorland, and similar to that at Shap Abbey (q.v.). Otherwise little medieval fabric shows externally. The chancel and E chapels were rebuilt in 1847–51 by *R. C. Carpenter* in the local grey Brockram stone laid watershot-fashion, with steep roofs. The long and relatively low nave and aisles were rebuilt in 1871–4, with a new clerestory, in contrasting red ashlar. The architects were *Austin & Johnson* of Newcastle (Kelly).

On closer inspection it becomes clear that an E.E. church of long and narrow proportions, built or rebuilt by St Mary's Abbey, York, in the 1230s, is present in fragmentary form. Its chancel is represented by the very fine, steeply trefoil-pointed SEDILIA and PISCINA preserved inside Carpenter's rebuild. The capitals have awkward upright leaves. The S doorway of the S transept is there too, hollow-moulded with nice foliage

Kirkby Stephen, the 'Loki Stone'.
Engraving, 1899

tails to the dripmould, and the triple s responds (the middle member filleted) of the crossing. In the s chapel, re-set, is a C13 corbel, with a motif of zigzag consisting of lanceolate leaves. The N transept is more complete, retaining its clasping buttresses, w wall with sill string and a couple of lancets, and its E wall to string level, but the N crossing responds and arch are Victorian renewals. In the E wall of the N transept a Perp reredos niche. Also surviving is the w corner of a narrow N aisle, with its sill string, the line of a very steep roof, and an interesting small square w window, set high in a wide internal reveal. All these are executed in a yellowish sandstone. So there was an aisled cruciform church essentially as big as the present structure, and possibly defensive in character. The seven-bay arcades are complete but more problematic. Quick-stepping double-chamfered arches on circular piers with octagonal abaci. The waterholding bases, each on an octagonal plinth, stand on a larger circular bases. Are these the remains of a short-lived Norman church, or simply the result of dropping the floor level? We have not finished with the E.E. church, for the large SE chapel, although also rebuilt by Carpenter, retains a steep E.E. arch to the transept, hollow-moulded like the s doorway, on responds with short waterholding bases. The s aisle was rebuilt in the C15 to the full width of the transept, in Perp style. Its s doorway and sw corner are best preserved, and the wide arch into the transept. Also the roof bosses.

FURNISHINGS. Chancel SCREEN made by *A. W. Simpson* as a First World War memorial. – ORGAN CASE. Given in 1890, made by *J. M. Kilbride* of Windermere. – s chapel SCREEN partly medieval, with engraved post-war GLASS of St Stephen by *John Hutton*. – N transept, parts of a made-up SCREEN, with early C17 balusters, Flamboyant tracery, and Early Renaissance friezes. – Round PULPIT, given in 1871 by the Cumberland and Westmorland Archaeological Society and the Freemasons. An over-rich piece, of polished Shap granite, green Italian marble, alabaster and pink marble. Inset are white translucent stones carved with masonic symbols. – FONTS. A C17 one designed by *John Green Waller* with a COVER by *James Dent* of Ravenstonedale.

SCULPTURE. The 'Loki Stone'. Part of a C10 cross-shaft on which is a man chained at the wrist and ankle, with downward-turning horns or volutes. The top of his head is missing. Both head and torso are triangular. Other pieces behind glass in the tower, and hard to see. They include two pieces of a later C8 cross-shaft carved with a large-scale scroll. Two pieces of a C10 cross or possibly some other furnishing, half-columnar in section. A C10 hogback, undecorated. Also loose, in front of the tower arch, a beautiful Norman capital with leaves, an almost Grecian honeysuckle motif, and a square abacus. It must be *c.* 1170–80 at the latest.

STAINED GLASS. E window by *Powells*, before 1873. s transept, 1874, *Clayton & Bell*; also the s aisle window furthest E, 1903. s aisle further W, a striking window of *c.* 1951, by

Powells; the Empty Tomb, with much white glass. s aisle w, designed by *James Clarke* of Casterton, 1903. The cartoons, better than the executed glass, are displayed nearby.

MONUMENTS. In the s chapel, Richard Musgrave †1464, a plain black tomb-chest with his arms. It is set in a highly decorated gabled niche with crockets, beasts, a bit of blackletter, traces of colour. Musgrave arms on top, in a different stone, held by an angel, with supporters. – Free-standing tomb-chest with effigy of a knight, who could be Sir Thomas Musgrave †1376 or his grandson Sir Richard †1422. – Low tomb-recess in the n aisle. – In the n chapel, behind the organ, lies Thomas, 1st Lord Wharton †1568 with his two wives. Of stone, a huge triple tomb-chest, with kneeling sons and daughters in Renaissance niches and at the corners detached balusters. One of the sons, with forked beard, turns his head soulfully towards the beholder. Companion to one at Healaugh near Tadcaster (Yorkshire, North Riding) where he is actually buried. – Edward Hartley of Melbecks †1740. Tablet with swan-necked pediment, cut away for the inner s porch.

WESLEYAN CHAPEL, High Street. 1839. No longer really Georgian. Two arched doorways under one pediment, fancy corner tourelles. Sunday School 1879.

PRIMITIVE METHODIST CHAPEL, Market Street. With a pair of spirelets. 1902. Now the Youth Hostel.

CONGREGATIONAL CHAPEL (former), Market Street. With a tall turret and spirelet. 1864. Typical educated Congregational style, polychrome, with flowing tracery. Now a shop.

CEMETERY on the Brough Road. *c.* 1861. Neat double chapel with a central spirelet.

TEMPERANCE HALL, Nateby Road. 1856. An adorable building of lovely pink (Lamonby?) ashlar, with date and title. Tall doorway with a segmental pediment on big scroll brackets. Two equally tall windows, with the same brackets. Over the door in a niche the figure of Temperance in a relaxed pose. She appears to be smoking a cigar.

THE CLOISTERS form a 'piazza' to the market square and a screen to the church. Helpfully signed and dated *George Gibson*, architect, 1810, presumably he who has such a splendid tomb at Crosby Ravensworth and who supervised the reconstruction of that church in 1811–18 (q.v.). Doric colonnade in dark red stone with triglyph frieze, breaking forward in the middle as a temple front, with a little bellcote on top. Much more sophisticated than its Gothic equivalent at Appleby.

The best individual building in the town is BARCLAYS BANK in Market Street, formerly Martin's, given its present façade in 1903 by *John F. Curwen*. Slate-hung attic, roughcast first floor, buff stone ground floor. A stack divides the two unequal gables, corbelled out over the entrance and a sloping buttress. Blue railings and crested gate set it off nicely. HSBC in the same street, a rebuild of the 1920s by *Brierley & Rutherford* of York, has a three-bay temple front with the entrance in an extra bay to one side. Trophy of fruit in the pediment. Three-quarter Doric columns with rustication behind. A few Georgian five-bay houses, one E of the church, one in Market Place and one, with a pedimented doorway, down a narrow alley s of Barclay's Bank.

MILLENNIUM PAVILION, at the s end of town. 2004. By *Elaine Rigby* for the Town Council. A complicated little structure: star-shaped base with steps, square open pyramid roof, circular stone core with a tail, like a tadpole.

STOBARS HALL, ½ m. NW, on a hilltop overlooking the town. By *George H. Smith*, *c.* 1825. Front with Tuscan porch and sashed and tripartite windows, but the parapet castellated (probably in 1866: DCMS). Two unequal castellated towers asymmetrically placed behind. Derelict stables etc. at the back.

HARTLEY CASTLE, ½ m. SE. Almost nothing is left of the quadrangular castle of the Musgraves, drawn by Machell *c.* 1680; it was demolished not long after, the materials taken to repair Edenhall.

STENKRITH PARK, ⅔ m. S. Unsuspectedly dramatic spot below the road bridge. MILLENNIUM BRIDGE. Blue-painted steel footbridge by the engineer *Charles Blackett-Ord*. Of conventional design with arched girders, made superbly dramatic by the setting of sculpted rock, falling water, bridges upon bridges. – POETRY PATH, 2004. Twelve poems by *Meg Peacocke*, celebrating the hill-farmer's year, accompanied by a beautifully executed little square vignettes by *Pip Hall*. – SCULPTURE, Passage by *Laura White*, 2000. One of the Eden Benchmarks. Three lumps of sandstone, scooped less dramatically, indeed less sculpturally, than the natural limestone river bed is by the river.

RAILWAY STATIONS. East Station (South Durham & Lancashire Union Railway, later NER), 1 m. W. Opened 1862, closed 1962. Used as a bobbin factory until 1992 and from 2000 under hesitant restoration. Double train shed with an island platform still partly present. The Midland station, on the Settle–Carlisle line, was built in 1875–6. 1⅔ m. SW of the town, up the hill because the line is already climbing. It employs the Derby Gothic adopted as standard for the entire line, with the usual frilly bargeboards, decorative lamps and 'estate' glazing – the largest of the three station designs. Down on the road are two terraces of RAILWAY COTTAGES and the detached STATION-MASTER'S HOUSE.

WHARTON HALL, 2 m. SSW. An H-shaped house of probable C14 origin, greatly aggrandized by Thomas, 1st Lord Wharton, whose arms and the date 1559 appear on the gatehouse. Lost to the family in 1728 by the exiled Philip, 1st Duke of Wharton, since when it has fallen into semi-ruin as a tenanted farm and occasional hunting lodge.

The original C15 HOUSE is at the back of the irregular walled enclosure (E side), with solar and service wings, l. and r. It is battlemented in front to match the rest, but gabled behind. Its service wing is vaulted, with a through passage. So is the porch adjoining it. This led into the hall, which has its projecting chimney-breast. To its S Lord Wharton in the 1550s built a much larger BANQUETING HALL (68 by 27 ft, 21 by 8 metres), now reduced to its base courses, only the fireplace recognizable. Also in the SE corner a grand KITCHEN, preserved though roofless. It stands over a vault, so Wharton's hall was probably raised too, though not vaulted underneath. The kitchen has two enormous fireplaces and a pair of large three-light mullioned windows, with uncusped depressed-arch heads to the lights below and above the transom. Along the NW side Lord Wharton built a long, even range with four-light mullioned windows on both floors, also with arched (uncusped) heads to the lights. Parallels with Sizergh and Askham suggest a long gallery and chapel (one is known) above, possible lodgings below. Arms on the S end as on the tower of Kirby Stephen church. The GATEHOUSE and perimeter wall look powerful, but would not withstand serious attack; like at Blencow Hall (Greystoke) the walls are not thick, except for a short length around the postern at the SE. The gatehouse has segmental arches and was originally three storeys high. Outside the enceinte are ranges of contemporary barns and stables.

PARK. Its impressive WALL, well seen immediately E of the station, was erected probably in 1547, causing conflict with the Lowthers as well as with the locals who were evicted to Wharton Dykes. The park wall can be picked out by its irrelevance to the modern field pattern. It is taller than more modern walls, and topped with flat stones not upright ones. Lord Wharton made another park at Ravenstonedale (q.v.).

WINTON MANOR HOUSE, 1½ m. NE. DMC 1726 in the segmental pediment over the doorway, which has a bolection moulding. Plain three-storey ashlar house of six bays. The sashes are all the same – no *piano nobile* or attic, resulting in left-over walling at the top before you get to the cornice. Fancy hopper, l. It is only a single pile.

Winton has a little triangular green on which is built the village SCHOOLROOM of 1862, with a long list of trustees. Arched windows with intersecting glazing bars.

CROGLAM CASTLE, ¾ m. SSW. An oval bivallate HILL-FORT, covering 4 acres overall, its inner rampart and outer ditch levelled. Entrance on the NE.

KIRKBY THORE (W)

Now an industrial village based on the mining of gypsum for plaster.

ST MICHAEL. C12 tower like the early one at Long Marton, telescopic, with a narrow W door and no stair. Dec bell-openings. The calling bell rings from a two-light bellcote on its

E parapet, as at Dearham. Nave and chancel, with assorted windows mostly Dec, but at least one lancet. The imposts of the (widened) chancel arch are Norman. Long chancel, the windows Dec too, but the N window set in a Norman arch. E window of 1850 (DCMS). Low lean-to N aisle. The two-bay N arcade has quatrefoil piers with the foils more than circular in section, and capitals typical of the late C13. Broad rustic porch with pointed tunnel-vault (as Warcop and Caldbeck). Thomas Machell, rector in the mid C17 and amateur architect, may have put in the large square windows in the chancel; blocked now, having visibly weakened the structure. He was certainly responsible for the ALTAR RAIL inscribed Caroli II 35, i.e. 1684, taking the start of the reign as 1649 and ignoring the Commonwealth. Twisted balusters. – The FONT of 1688 carries Machell's arms, carved perhaps by *Addison* also of Kirkby Thore. Baluster stem, unusually generous octagonal bowl. – PULPIT dated 1631, with caryatids at the corners, arabesque panels above and blank arches below. – STAINED GLASS. E window and one nave S by *Powells*, 1891 and 1894.

KIRKBY THORE HALL. Hall and single wing, both retaining their medieval roofs. An arched brace has given a tree-ring date of 1438. The hall was divided horizontally in the late C16 and given a mullioned-and-transomed bay window. Another window fills its low-end doorway at the E end, and the lintel of the centre window can be seen over the present front door. The ash of a central fire was found when the hall was re-flagged. The wing, consisting probably of solar over kitchen, is little altered. A two-light Dec window in the gable lights the solar. The tracery is of two arched heads with a pointed quatrefoil over i.e. a form of *c.* 1300. High arch-braced solar roof. The high collars carry short kingposts and longitudinal braces. The hall trusses are without kingposts, having instead a shaped arch over the collar. C19 dairy wing at the back converted into a Gentleman's Residence in the 1980s, with surprisingly classy woodwork.

Hill in the C19 recorded 'a piece of old forestwork building' at the solar end, i.e. a rare example of timber framing in the region. Machell in about 1685 sketched a diagonally braced upper floor on a stone ground floor. An end of wall-plate exposed on the W, where the side wall is cut back, may be the remains.

KIRKCAMBECK (C)   5060

ST KENTIGERN. Rebuilt in 1885 by the Rev. Henry Whitehead, who commissioned Philip Webb at Brampton – so who designed it? Tiny single cell with a wooden bellcote on the roof. Closed, abandoned to the cows. E of it an arch built of materials from the old church.

6030

KIRKLAND (C)

3 m. NE of Culgaith.

(ST LAWRENCE. The church seems 'ancient', as Kelly would call it, i.e. the masonry is medieval, the pointed-trefoiled PISCINA E.E., and the triple-chamfered chancel arch partly dying into the imposts could be called late C13 or C14. The rest is of the rebuilding of 1880. Rebuilding also in 1768 (Kelly). – STAINED GLASS by *Talbot & Co.*, 1899, 1900. – MONUMENT. Effigy of a knight; C13. – CHURCHYARD CROSS, over 8 ft (2.5 metres) high, the head free-armed, but round holes between the arms. Collingwood.)

4060

KIRKLINTON (C)

ST CUTHBERT. Erected in 1845 on the site of the old church, of which the ancient arch at the W end, and those in its tower, are memorials. So states a plaque above the S door. The arch from the tower to the nave is indeed Norman, with two orders of zigzag and two sizes of colonnettes, but looks more an evocation than a relic. In the porch is an undoubted Norman capital with waterleaf. The new church is not Norman but Commissioners' Gothic, although unusually boldly sculpted, with an overhanging tower parapet, substantial diagonal buttresses, lancets, and a continuous drip-course running behind the side buttresses. – MONUMENTS. Edward and Dorothy Appleby both †1698, with armorials. – Joseph Dacre Appleby †1729. Standing monument with fluted pilasters and open segmental pediment, quite metropolitan. – Joseph Dacre Appleby †1738, a tablet with Ionic columns and an open curly pediment.

FRIENDS' MEETING HOUSE (former), at Sykeside, ½ m. SE. 1736. Small but with arched windows. Rebuilt 1997 as a dwelling.

KIRKLINTON HALL. Spectacular and deeply sinister ruin, with shaped gables, spindly chimneys and dormers outlined against the sky. The core is a late C17 (1661?) house of advanced design, for Edmund Appleby. More window than wall, on the lower two floors at any rate, where there are five closely spaced bays. The surrounds are moulded and have pulvinated heads and flat hoods. The top storey has only three spaced-out windows. The house was extended r. and l. in the C18, then greatly enlarged and made grander in 1875 by *Cory & Ferguson* for the Kirklinton-Saul family, with a big extra wing. The shaped gables, giving the C18 parts a Scottish look, date from then.

KIRKLINTON PARK, 1 m. ESE. 1822 for Hugh Patrickson, 'recently improved' in 1884. Plain five-bay two-storey house, originally rendered, with a wide tripartite doorway under a relieving arch. The dormers in the hipped roof were added *c.* 1900, as was the garden porch at the side with alternately blocked columns, and the incongruous prefabricated billiard room at the back. Spectacular oval cantilever stair with an elegant iron balustrade and ribbed plaster vault (cf. Newbiggin Hall, Carleton). In the principal bedroom a delightful Art Nouveau enclosure, *c.* 1900 again, for an *en suite.* The billiard room is fitted out in similar style, with an inglenook dated 1905. Axial at the back, through a tower entrance dated 1824, a cracking FARMYARD. Of a piece with the house, with plenty of elliptical arches.

LODGE. Of *c.* 1900 by *J. H. Sellers,* who worked in Carlisle with *G. Dale Oliver* before going to Manchester and Edgar Wood. Four-way symmetrical, with a polygonal bay at each corner and a dormer facing each way. ESTATE HOUSES further down the lane, roughcast with sloping corner buttresses, probably by *Sellers* again.

KIRKOSWALD (C)

ST OSWALD. Half-buried in the shoulder of the hill that hides it from college and village. Kirkoswald was collegiate; with Greystoke, one of only two such foundations in the present country of Cumbria. The college was founded by Thomas, Lord Dacre, and Isabel de Greystoke in 1523 for a provost and five secular priests.

The church is without a tower or even a bellcote, having instead a cute Gothic BELFRY topping the green hill immediately E (but invisible from it). Just a ringing room and bell-chamber with a higher stair-turret, standing on a grassy platform with corner balls. The lower parts are of rubble, the upper of ashlar. The weathervane bears the date 1743, but the present building is a restoration of 1893 (by *Ferguson?*).

CHURCH. Nave and aisles of three bays, all separately roofed. Blocked mid-C13 N doorway with thin roll moulding. Odd tracery of the late C15 in a N window. The chancel, rebuilt wider for the college in 1523, has large straight-headed windows filled with arched uncusped lights: five lights E, two each of three lights N and S. The church was restored by *Atkinson* in 1845, and again in 1878–9 by *John Cory.*

Cory proposed the following chronology. First a C12 nave and chancel, of which the footings of the chancel arch survive, and a chunk of plain wall in the arcades marking its W end. A N aisle was added *c.* 1160, and then a S aisle, and the chancel lengthened. The piers on the S have been rebuilt but their capitals and single-step arches remain from the late C12. The N arcade also has round arches, but one arch has two slight chamfers, the other two normal chamfers. Both aisles were rebuilt wider in the C13, leaving the C12 arcades in place. The whole church was extended by a bay westwards in the C14 or C15, according to the faces on the W responds. Also in the C14 chapels were extended to flank the chancel, hence the arches on either side of the chancel arch springing direct, without responds. The chapels were removed in 1523 when the chancel was rebuilt. The present chancel arch probably dates from then, and so do the clerestory and the N porch. The last is a rare example of Cumbrian timber framing, though it has needed propping. Stout posts, jowled at the top for the wall-plate, angle braces with very long tenons, tie-beam so steeply cambered as not to need packing out for the roof.

FURNISHINGS. The collegiate chancel was used by the Fetherstonhaughs as their private chapel; choir stalls, vestry and organ were all in the nave. Only after 1912 were the present conventional arrangements made. – COMMUNION RAIL. C18. – STAINED GLASS. All by *John Scott & Son*, 1847 etc., including the Fetherstonhaugh armorials in bright settings in the chancel sides. – MONUMENTS. Faceless stone effigy in the SW corner. – Small broken roundel of alabaster put up in 1609 (Browgham and Bertram). Kneeling figures and symbols of Death. – C18 and C19 Fetherstonhaughs line the chancel. – Good collection of grave-slabs outside against the N wall, including a fine foliated cross with sword, book and dragon of *c.* 1200.

COLLEGE. After the Dissolution it reverted to a rectory, but in 1590 was sold to Henry Fetherstonhaugh. The family, who are there still, have been conscientious about dating their many alterations. The beautifully assured entrance front (E) was built by Timothy and Bridget Fetherstonhaugh in 1696. Five-bay centre and two-bay wings advancing a little. Two storeys, hipped roof. The doorway has an open curly pediment on brackets and a pulvinated surround. The windows are sashes, but the sills of the wings were prepared for cross-mullions. The range forms a long single pile with the stair sticking out at the back, a common Cumbrian plan. In the gable here a small round-headed window. Beside the staircase wing to the S is the rectory tower, C16 but probably post-Dissolution, with a bay window added *c.* 1640. A slip of infill between the two indicates that stair wing and tower were independent. Adjoining the tower inside are parts of walls probably of the original college. The N corner was filled in in 1811 and 1910, the S end with domestic offices in 1840. So now the back is flat and the house is a double pile.

The HALL is entered traditionally at the low end, with a vestigial screens passage. The high-end overmantel incorporates the Dacre arms from Kirkoswald Castle (*see* below). The ceiling was given its plaster armorials in 1850. Beams decorated with egg-and-dart. The library in the high-end wing has floor-to-ceiling small-scale panelling, as at Hutton Hall, Penrith. The DINING ROOM decor is Victorian, with heavy gilded bosses in the ceiling and a horribly twiggy garlanded cornice. Its huge fireplace arch is in order for *c.* 1550 but has acquired a band of plaster foliage and an inserted chimneypiece with the Fetherstonhaugh motto, Valens et Volens. This work bears the initial TF and EW (Timothy Fetherstonhaugh and Eliza Were), dating it to the 1840s. The KITCHEN is in the low-end wing. In the kitchen corridor a pair of flattened ogee-headed doors, probably mid-C16, bearing the Dacre scallop. The 1696 STAIR rises broad and handsome in four flights (cf. Moresby Hall). Tapered spiral balusters, the stair-end hidden by a string. The drawing room was upstairs, over the hall. The tower, like that of Hutton Hall (Penrith), is square and not vaulted, with an unusually broad turning stair in one corner. Its ground-floor room has been made into a warm SITTING ROOM with cream-painted panelling and basket arches: 1740s? The SOLAR is richly panelled with the date 1639 on the internal porch and 1641 in the overmantel, with crude caryatids; the bay was pushed out at the same time.

Long TERRACE WALK at the back, and a HA-HA. WALLED GARDEN dated 1839, which may also refer to the castellated GATEWAY.

CASTLE. Licence to crenellate to Sir Hugh de Morville, 1201. In 1317 it passed by marriage to the Dacres. Rebuilt *c.* 1485 by Thomas Dacre, who died in 1525. Tall fragments only. Quadrangular, entered from the W; reduced to two S towers with vaulted basements and a N staircase tower, set diagonally at the corner of the site of the hall. In it is a spiral staircase, a full three storeys. At the base a stepped mural passage and a small room. The gatehouse was in the W side. The SE tower retains its tunnel-vaulted base storey. An island at the NW angle of the moat was probably a garden feature. Quarried for the restoration of Naworth *c.* 1620, and for the College.

EDEN BRIDGE crosses the river on four round arches of red sandstone ashlar. Two further dry arches on the curving approach from the village to the N. Dated 1762 on the parapet.

VILLAGE. Kirkoswald has a little cobbled market place, but the cross is the WAR MEMORIAL of *c.* 1920, and the 'town hall' is the CHURCH INSTITUTE, 1910. The MANSION HOUSE was built by the Musgraves of Edenhall. Handsome five-bay façade of the late C17 with cross-mullioned windows and, over the door, a curved pediment open a little at the top. The older side elevation is dated 1622. Also in the village a handsome early C19 former CORN MILL. A self-conscious composition in coursed rubble sandstone. Five bays under a hipped roof. The street elevation of two storeys with dormer windows in two transverse gables and an arched cart entrance to the r. An iron overshot wheel survives on the l. Now flats.

ONA ASH, on the B-road N at High Windhill, is a rare surviving thatched house. Over the door is the inscription WML 1693. It leads into a cross-passage entry through the former barn, also thatched. The cross-passage runs behind the hearth of the main house, where a small fire-window lights an inglenook. Entry to the firehouse from the passage behind a heck at the back. The house walls have been raised to take an upper storey. All this can be read from the road.

STAFFIELD HALL. Red Victorian mansion of the Denman family, now in untidy multiple occupation. Tudor. The castellated tower-porch carries the date 1848 and the Fetherstonhaugh motto.

NUNNERY. *See* Armathwaite.

LAMPLUGH (C)

ST MICHAEL. The old chancel and s chapel were unusually fully developed Perp, the rest largely C18, with a bellcote on the chancel arch. In 1870 the church was reconstructed by *Butterfield*. Characteristically wilful is the big double w bellcote, and the prominent chimney of the N side. He appears to have retained the chancel and chapel walls, and rebuilt the nave to match. New roofs were made to the approved high pitch, the E window rebuilt higher up, and the Perp openings restored as necessary. Perp chancel N doorway with continuous mouldings, Perp one-light window and doorway of the vestry. Three reclaimed gargoyles were mounted on the E gable; one is a flying pig. The interior is very interesting. The chancel arch, though re-tooled, appears to be the medieval one – otherwise why so low? Twice-chamfered, the imposts octagonal on square bases. The chapel arch is the same. Butterfield has inserted five-light Perp tracery in the wall above the chancel arch: is this the medieval E window? His FONT is octagonal, with an octagonal stem on a square base, like the chancel arch. – STAINED GLASS. Including four from the studios of *C. E. Kempe*: chancel N and s (1891 and 1901), w window (1910) and N aisle (1911). E window and nave easternmost N and s all *Clayton & Bell*. – Two big MONUMENTS in coloured marbles on the w wall. Margaret Brisco †1731, with a portrait medallion, and Thomas and Frances Lamplugh †1745.

GATEWAY, SE of the church. 1595, rebuilt 1961. Low-pitched two-centred arch, continuous mouldings, and stepped gable. It led to Lamplugh Hall, demolished in 1821, including a large detached pele tower.

(STREET GATE, 1⅛ m. NW, W of the A-road. Dated 1733 and still with cross-windows.)

KIRKLAND MISSION CHURCH (now C. of E. and Methodist), 2½ m. SSW. Not churchy except for the semicircular apse and the bellcote in the centre of the ridge. Of rough red stone with a continuous sill, also rough, and continuous windowing between strong buttresses. It is by *T. L. Banks & C. H. Townsend* (he of the Whitechapel Gallery), 1886.

LANERCOST (C)

LANERCOST PRIORY. Serene by the River Irthing, with a setting   20
of great trees. The church is exceptionally well preserved, the
monastic ranges have fared less well. The foundation charter is
traditionally dated 1169, for Augustinian canons; the founder
named as Robert de Vaux. His father Hubert had been set by
Henry II as overlord of Gilsland, newly wrested from the
Scots. Permanent building appears to have started *c.* 1175–80
with the cloister and the parts of the church adjoining it. Sleeper
walls found under the presbytery arcades could indicate that an
aisleless church was started, but if so it was soon replaced by the
present S side of the presbytery with its chapels, then the rest of
the presbytery, the crossing and the first bay of the nave. The
cross whose stump stands outside may mark this partial
completion in 1214. The beautiful W front with its statue of the
Magdalen suggests a final completion, with the three W bays of
the nave, about 1280. Edward I and his retinue made Lanercost
their base in 1306–7, living in temporary palaces probably before
the W front. The generations of border warfare and skirmish that
followed the king's death at Burgh-by-Sands in 1307 meant that
the priory was little altered thereafter. Raids are recorded in 1311,
1346, and 1366, when the prior was held to ransom. Dissolution
came in 1536–8, as late as 1542 for the Dacre Chantry, with
transfer of the buildings to the Dacres of Naworth. The nave was
retained as the parish church but fell into disrepair in the C17,
when the congregation retreated to the N aisle.

Things began to look up in the 1740s with the re-roofing of
the nave, and a new E partition wall. *Salvin* reported on the fabric
in 1846 and, after a roof fall had highlighted its plight, carried
out a conservative restoration in 1847–9. From 1869 into the
1870s George Howard, the future 9th Earl of Carlisle, and his
wife Rosalind, who had made their home at Naworth, undertook
with *C. J. Ferguson* a more searching restoration. In 1929 the
ruined parts passed to the Office of Works. The site is still in
multiple ownership: parish church, English Heritage, Dacre Hall
Committee, vicarage, Naworth estate.

EXTERIOR. The E end is square, flanked by two square chapels
in echelon on each side. The nave has just a N aisle, as
do the Augustinian houses at Hexham and Brinkburn (Northumberland), the S side being taken up by the cloister.
Construction is of rosy and grey sandstone in regular squarish
blocks assumed to come from Hadrian's Wall, but re-tooled.
Stylistically it is a harmonious Early English whole, except
for the Transitional characteristics of the earliest part. There
are signs of economy in the middle phases, lending an
almost Cistercian austerity to the presbytery elevations, but
increased richness towards completion in the clerestory and W
front.

The church can be seen as a whole from the N, standing virtually complete, missing only the roofs of the eastern limb, crossing and transepts. The E front has two tiers of three lancets between flat buttresses, even in height below and stepped above. Also traces of a stepped or crenellated gable associated with the lowering of the original steep-pitched roofs, perhaps as late as *c.* 1520. There is a change of masonry between the lower and upper half, visible also on the cloister side. To the N and S the chancel has first two lancets, and then the chapels attached to it, merging with the E aisles of the transepts. The N chapel has an E lancet and a Perp N window, followed by an identical one as the N window of the transept aisle. The S chapel windows have three lancet lights under one arch, a sign of the late C13. The lancets have hoodmoulds. The N transept N wall is flanked by polygonal turrets. Its fenestration is similar to that of the E wall, except that the large polygonal turrets leave room for only two lancets below. The clerestory is the unifying feature that really makes the building, inside and out. Above a continuous string its lancets keep their own even rhythm, ignoring what goes on below. Corbel table of three small hanging arches between every two corbels. It lacks only its parapet (save at the extreme W end). The crossing tower is blunt and almost windowless. A drawing of *c.* 1400 in the Lanercost Cartulary suggests that it had a spire by that time. Its crenellations are late medieval, perhaps again of *c.* 1520. The N and S sides show the marks of the original steep roofs. The S transept has the clerestory windows to the E connected by a string course from hoodmould to hoodmould – a change from the chancel. Its S front shows the roof-line of the E range round the cloisters. Above that three lancets of even height. The W side has windows only above the former cloister roof. They are lancets, in two tiers not vertically lined up. The hoodmoulds of the upper window are again connected by a string course.

There is evidence in this place of the earlier architectural history of the building. The S transept has to the W a broad, flat, i.e. typically C12, buttress. It also has a doorway into the cloister which has a round arch with two slight chamfers and columns with waterleaf capitals. That, in terms of Cumberland, might be as late as *c.* 1190, but in terms of an Augustinian priory may well be *c.* 1175–80. As one carries on along the S side of the nave the earliest phase clearly continues. The buttresses and the plinth type show that at once; the E nave doorway into the cloister, though pointed, again has waterleaf capitals; and the W nave doorway into the cloister is round-arched with two slight chamfers and has the same capitals. Tall lancets above that, and the eight clerestory lancets keeping their own rhythm. Except for the first they have big nailhead along the continuous string course, rising around the windows. The masonry is red throughout, i.e. the change in the upper parts does not continue. The nave N aisle, with narrow, irregularly spaced lancets, shows a clear break after the

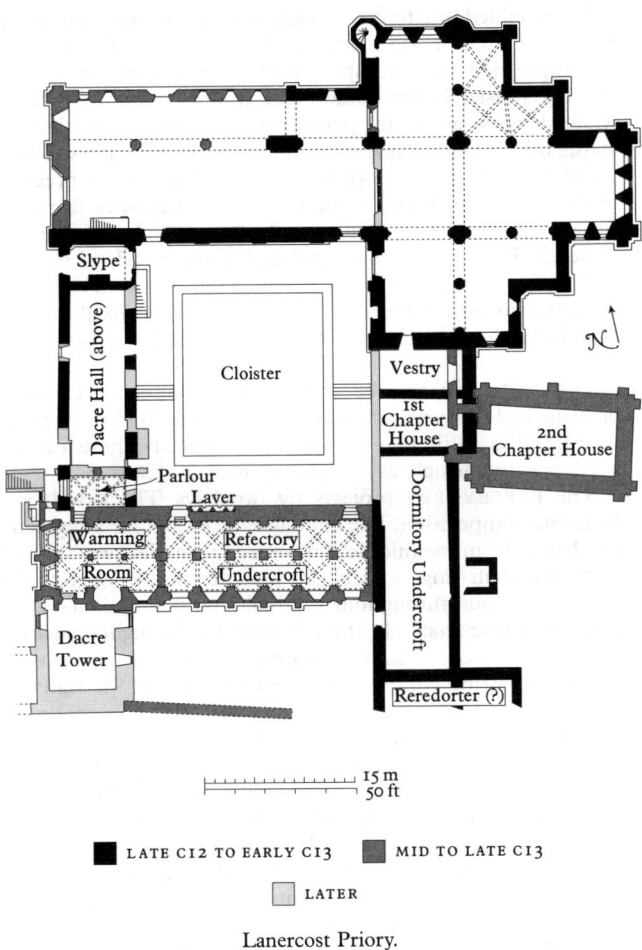

Lanercost Priory.
Plan

LATE C12 TO EARLY C13   MID TO LATE C13

LATER

easternmost bay. N doorway with two orders of columns, some
small nailhead enrichment, and a fillet along one of the arch
rolls. The aisle corbel table has two of the little hanging arches,
the clerestory – as from the beginning – three; but the last six
of the units in the aisle turn to three hanging arches.

The W FRONT is immensely satisfying, perfectly balancing
aspiration and repose. Framed by unequal flat buttresses   20
turning octagonal in their upper parts, the height is
emphasized by three tall lancets, the middle one taller and
wider, set in a continuous arcade defined by ringed shafts.
Below that, a thirteen-bay frieze of pointed-trefoil arcading.
The sumptuous portal has four orders of columns, their
moulded capitals with small nailhead. The arch is pointed and

richly moulded, the four rolls each with fillets. Dogtooth in the hoodmould. Door and frieze are slightly offset to the N, giving the impression that the upper parts lean slightly towards the missing S aisle. In the gable niche (more dogtooth) is Mary Magdalene, to whom the priory was dedicated: a genuine C13 statue miraculously preserved. Tall and willowy to allow for our foreshortened view, she presumably held the jar of precious ointment in one hand, while her mantle cascades from her raised arm. It is a favourite motif of *c.* 1250–80 (cf. e.g. the Wise and Foolish Virgins in the Angel Choir portal at Lincoln). At her feet, much smaller, the crouching donor figure of an Augustinian canon. Early C16 heraldic panels flank the niche, and there is a sunk quatrefoil on either side of the central lancet head.

The INTERIOR can only be seen in two instalments. Chancel, crossing and transepts are a controlled ruin in English Heritage guardianship. Although set out symmetrically these eastern parts are surprisingly asymmetrical in their elevations.

The PRESBYTERY projects by two bays. The E wall is a beautiful composition. The dado is bare, except for a segment-headed niche in the middle. Above are the tall lancets, shafted, and with shaft-rings and above that the wall-passage which was to continue throughout the building. It is articulated by clusters of four shafts. In the S TRANSEPT the night stair from the dormitory opens as usual halfway up the wall. Then there is a keeled string course in the S and W walls of the transept. The aisle windows have shouldered rere-arches (absent on the N side). The arcade responds and piers are slender, semi-octagonal and round. In the aisle a ceiling was put in – cf. the corbels – but that was an afterthought. In the N transept the keeled string course occurs where the E end of the aisle meets it. The N CHAPEL are rib-vaulted, the ribs single-chamfered. There is no evidence of any vaulting of the major spaces, i.e. chancel or transept. A straight joint in the N arcade wall immediately E of the NE crossing pier shows that the N side of the chancel was intended to be like the S side. Then, however, and no doubt very soon, the plan was altered and the N side was given a full-grown gallery. It has round arches subdivided into two pointed openings by two colonnettes set in depth and with a blank quatrefoil in the spandrel. The arcade below has details like those of the S side, but of necessity the responds and piers are much less tall. The arches are triple-chamfered. The clerestory continues its way, the wall-passage with quadruple shafts. Each bay has a small pointed transverse tunnel-vault. The wall-passage in the E wall is made to harmonize precisely, by shaft-rings corresponding to the capitals. The S clerestory is of the same design as the N clerestory.

In the N transept E wall the gallery continues (without the quatrefoils in the spandrels), and the rest continues too. In the S transept E wall also nothing changes. Of the crossing piers only the SW one is part of the earliest work. It is triple, with the main shaft keeled. The E arch is on short keeled corbels.

Lanercost Priory, section of nave, N side.
Drawing by David McNay, 2000

The N arch and SE respond are semi-octagonal and probably
a later remodelling. The muddle in the N transept W wall, where
the aisle opens into it, has already been remarked on. In the
aisle is a blocked doorway which cannot be *in situ*. Also visible
from the transept are two arches, one above the other. The
upper windows of both transepts are shafted with shaft-rings.
The S transept W wall has windows with oddly rounded
trefoiled rere-arches. They indicate an early stage, and continue
by a bay in the nave.

The NAVE is fine and harmonious room despite its asymmetry. The C18 E partition wall is glazed with a big three-light
window under a basket arch, through which the ruined crossing can dimly be seen. The S side, there being no aisle, and
there being a cloister, has a high, completely bare wall, and
only above that four lancet windows and the clerestory with its
wall-passage. Of the main windows, to repeat it, the first has
the rere-arch we saw in the transept, the others have them no
longer. On the N side the arcade consists of an E arch separated
from the others by a piece of wall, corresponding with the masonry break noted outside. Stuart Harrison suggests that only
the easternmost bay of the aisle was originally intended.* The
rood screen stood here; the pulpitum was a bay further E,
under the crossing arch. Then three bays with standard
octagonal piers and triple-chamfered arches. The E respond has
stiff-leaf, the first we come across. The clerestory wall-passage
gives some indication of the details of building progress. On
the S side the first three bays from the E have no adornment,

---

* In H. Summerson and S. Harrison, *Lanercost Priory, Cumbria* (*CWAAS Research
Series* 10, 2000), as also the other authorities quoted here.

then dogtooth starts in the arch, then nailhead in the abacus, and finally dogtooth in the abacus as well. One capital and one only, the tenth of the sixteen (from the E), has stiff-leaf, and quite lively though not very thick stiff-leaf. On the N side there is no such hesitation. There are four bays without dogtooth, and then arch and abacus take them on together. In the clerestory a window every other bay. Another small alteration concerns these windows. They have single-chamfered reveals but turn to a hollow chamfer on N and S in the same place, one bay away from the E. The W wall has shafted windows. A much lower walkway crosses in front of the windows. The barrel ceiling is by *Ferguson*, 1872.

FURNISHINGS are mostly by *Ferguson*, or *Salvin* rearranged by Ferguson. – STAINED GLASS. The greenish grisaille windows are typical of the *York Glaziers Trust* in the 1740s. In the tiny window in the blocked E cloister doorway the quarries are medieval. Three C16 armorials in the E partition window come from Dacre Hall. *Morris & Co.* windows in the N aisle, all *Burne-Jones* designs but widely separated in time: NW, St Luke and St Peter at the beautiful gate, 1887; N, Moses and the angels, 1912; and, in the very tall lancet of the W wall, the First Noël, 1890, a beautiful design in the deepest colours. Also St Cecilia (N aisle E), a mucky window by *Evie Hone*, 1947, for Winifred Nicholson (who may have had a hand in it) in memory of her mother Cecilia Roberts (*see* Banks, p. 486). At the top of the scriptorium steps, a tiny heraldic window of 2006 by *Christine Boyce* commemorates Edward I's sojourn.

MONUMENTS in the E end. This was the burial place of the Dacres and Howards even long after it was unroofed. The tombs are described topographically N–S. Tomb-chest with five quatrefoiled circles and the arms of Vaux of Triermain, set into a four-centred recess, with fragments of an effigy on top. Phillip Lindley dates it to the later C14. – James Dacre, 'the last mail heir', †1716; table tomb on six volutes. – Sir Humphrey and Lady Mabel Dacre. She died in 1510, having founded a chantry in 1503. Large tomb-chest with two angels and damaged heraldic panels, and probably once effigies. – Lady Elizabeth Dacre Howard †1883; terracotta by *Sir Edgar Boehm* of the child apparently sleeping; the tomb-chest designed by *Philip Webb*. – The Hon. Charles Howard †1879; incised granite slab by *Webb*. – Thomas, 2nd Lord Dacre and his abducted wife Lady Elizabeth (†1516). The big tomb-chest must have been barbarically splendid when complete and fully coloured, with the Dacre salmon and griffin as shield-supporters. Thomas is thought to have commissioned both his and his parents' tombs (*see* above), leaving the date of his own death as MCCCCC–. In the event he was killed, harrying the Scots, in 1525. The segment-headed canopy with anachronistic dogtooth was added some time between 1794 and 1814. – Charles Howard, 10th Earl of Carlisle †1912, tablet by *Lorimer*. – John Crow †1708, the letters crudely cut into a medieval effigy lying on a late C14 tomb-chest bearing the Dacre scallops. – Also many C12 and C13 slabs with incised crosses.

Nave. Sir Thomas (Lord) Dacre, †C15– (N aisle vestry). Latten blackletter, from the tomb in the chancel. – Hubert George and Christopher George Howard, †1898 and 1896 serving their country abroad; portrait medallions by *Onslow Ford* set in green stone. – Oliver Howard, †1908 in Nigeria, in similar style. – The Hon. Charles Howard †1879 and his wife of only one year, Mary (†1843). Excellent bronze tablet of 1879–81 with two profile medallions and underneath the Nativity and the Entombment. The portraits are by *Boehm*; the scenes, in an Italian Renaissance relief style, were designed by *Burne-Jones*.

CROSS-SHAFT. The larger part of the shaft is in the blocked N doorway. Dogtooth decoration runs along its edges. Inscription in Roman lettering, translated: 'In the 1,214th year from the incarnation ... Otto being Emperor in Germany, Philip reigning in France, John in England, William in Scotland, this cross was made.' It was reused to record the death of a child in 1657. The BASE stands on the green N of the church.

THE MONASTIC PARTS. The foundations of the E RANGE and the cloister were exposed in the 1930s by the Office of Works, when it was discovered that the first small chapter house within the range had been replaced *c.* 1250 by a larger one further E and slightly S of axis (fragment of the jamb moulding of the chapter-house entrance). The S range was largely reconstructed at the same time, with a new rib-vaulted undercroft under the refectory (octagonal piers, single-hollow-chamfered ribs), and an elaborate lavatorium or washing place facing the cloister. The lavatorium must have been very beautiful: elaborately moulded corbels, and the springings of four arches, with dogtooth. The upper floor has gone. Three extra bays were added at the W end in the mid C14, extending under what is now the Dacre wing; probably a warming room. The W bays have thinner piers and two large windows to the W. From the W bay a small doorway with shouldered lintel led into a further two-bay rib-vaulted room under the W range.

The W RANGE, still in use, is the most complicated part. It retains some of the earliest masonry, but has been repeatedly altered to suit changing roles. It was refashioned as the Dacre residence in the mid C16, with new windows in runs of three, four or five, a stack jutting out into the W cloister walk, and a large kitchen/solar tower at the S end. The windows are straight-headed, with uncusped pointed lights. A link at the N end to the vicar's pele (*see* below) and its attendant buildings. The important rooms are all on the upper floor. The SCRIP-TORIUM, so called, is a small room over the slype, forming a retiring room behind the dais of Dacre Hall. It has a late C16 painted plaster frieze of Dacre shells, winged angels, and what look like corn cobs. Next comes the long DACRE HALL, partly divided up now for village purposes, with a very large fireplace dated CD 1586.* On the N end walls are traces of painted Antique work of *c.* 1560: black-and-white grotesques and shields, with a little red. Heavy kingpost roof (tree-ring date 1465) with raking queenposts and longitudinal braces to the ridge. The ruinous DACRE TOWER projects from the W end of the S range. This may incorporate the remains of the abbey kitchen, but appears to be mainly post-Dissolution, with numerous reused stones. The first floor was evidently a kitchen, with opposing fireplaces, one flanked by ovens. The upper chamber has large square-headed transomed windows.

The VICARAGE is on the site of the priory farm, beyond the W range. The prominent tower has been dated by the large dogtooth frieze under its parapet to the C13, but circumstances make a C14 date more likely. It was formerly joined to the cloister ranges by a low E extension. The building was much altered by the Dacres in the C16, by *Salvin* in 1850–1, and again by *Ferguson* from 1873. A spiral staircase to the first floor in the NW corner, from the first to the second in the NE corner. Some windows like those of the W range, but mostly with mullions and transoms. In the lower room of the tower is another frieze of Dacre shields held by angels, with corn cobs, as in the Scriptorium. In the angle between tower and lower range is fitted a good stair, with turned balusters.

GATEHOUSE. Mid-C13. Only the inner (E) arch survives: a wide segmental arch, twice chamfered, springing direct from the walls. It was evidently rib-vaulted, probably in two compartments. On the W side the springers of the vault are preserved. Hollow-chamfered ribs. A length of the PRECINCT WALL stands N along the road.

ABBEY FARM. The barn is C16, perhaps even monastic in origin. The farmhouse is by *Salvin*, 1859, and so is the state-of-the-art steading. Under redevelopment 2006.

OLD BRIDGE. Two soaring elliptical spans and a central cutwater. Medieval in appearance, but rebuilt in 1724.

BANKS, 1 m. NE, high up on the Wall, was much favoured by C20 artists. The Nicholsons, Ben and Winifred, grand-daughter of George Howard, 9th Earl of Carlisle, bought BANKSHEAD in 1924, putting in the picture windows which so often frame her paintings. Here Winifred lived for the rest of her life. In 1972 she helped the refugee artist Li Yuan-Chia set up a museum and gallery at BANKSIDE. He extended the three-bay cottage in a long line, Cumbrian vernacular in style if not in detail.

HADRIAN'S WALL. ¼ m. W of Banks at HARE HILL (Burtholme) is the tallest surviving fragment, seventeen courses high, the facing stones (including a centurial stone in the seventh course) replaced *c.* 1890. This is the Late Hadrianic narrow replacement for the Turf Wall, succeeded on the E by a medieval boundary wall marking the limit of the Lanercost lands.

---

*A fancy wooden overmantel of 1618 went to Kirklinton Park and then to the Bowes Museum, Co. Durham.

LANGDALES (W)

(Great Langdale, Elterwater, Little Langdale)

Everything the Lake District holidaymaker could want, from loitering by the limpid string-of-pearls of Elter Water to a strenuous hike on the Pikes, and consequently hugely popular. Much is owned by the National Trust, and tightly managed, though occasional lapses prevent it becoming too precious. Tough farming and industry – gunpowder, slate; the latter still in operation – keep it all in balance.

Industry came early to Upper Langdale; the crags and screes high on the s face of Pike o' Stickle and its neighbours were a centre for the manufacture of stone axes from *c.* 3800 B.C. until *c.* 2300 B.C. Thousands of worked Langdale stones have been found across the British Isles, with a particular concentration around the Humber, suggesting, perhaps, an export trade. A man-made CAVE near the 2,000-ft (615-metre) contour on the scree may be connected with these early operations.

HOLY TRINITY, Chapel Stile, Great Langdale. On a steep fellside, under a crag. Rebuilt in 1857–8 by *J. A. Cory* for Messrs Robinson and Wheatley-Balme, of green cut slate from the quarries that it overlooks. Short nave, extended w by a bay in 1878, short chancel, chubby s tower, windowless N aisle. Victorian Dec with unaltered and typical interior: pews and choir stalls, arch-braced roof. – STAINED GLASS. E, chancel s, and w windows by *Burlison & Grylls*, 1888, 1896. s, by the pulpit, dated 1910 and scratch-signed *A. L. Moore*. SS Peter and Paul and All Nations, including a Red Indian. Richly shaded purples. Mid s, St Francis with scenes from his life, designed and made in 1937 by Mr and Mrs *Dean Walmsley* of Great Langdale. – Millennium TAPESTRY, N wall, designed by *Shelagh Sutton, Meg Riley, Mary Quine*, under *Mary Hall*.

ELTERWATER, ⅓ m. sw of Great Langdale church. The village is a double row of white cottages. To its s, ELTERWATER YOUTH HOSTEL. Large bank barn adapted in 1939 by *Pattinsons* of Windermere: outshuts removed, new roof, large metal windows, i.e. without the present-day regard for integrity. Attached is the farmhouse of 1692, then an C18 cottage called ST MARTIN'S, once the base and weaving house for hand spun Langdale Linen.*

LANGDALE ESTATE, E of Elterwater village. Hotel, country club, timeshare. Architects *Unwin Jones*, from 1982. On the site of the gunpowder works and pinching some of its vocabulary. Four sizes of Scandinavian-style lodge; high-specification work in black wood, white roughcast and local green slate, interspersed with much water, trees and industrial remains. The hotel skulks low, with lots of roofs.

---

* Started in 1883 by Albert Fleming, a retired solicitor, and his housekeeper Marion Twelves, inspired and encouraged by Ruskin and Hardwicke Rawnsley.

MERZ BARN, not much more than a shed, across the road in Cylinders Wood. Here *Kurt Schwitters*, one of the most interesting artists to fetch up in the Lakes, created his third *Merzbau*, a Dada assemblage of found objects. At his death in 1948 he had completed only one wall, which was detached in 1965 and removed to the Hatton Gallery in Newcastle upon Tyne.

ELTERWATER HALL (now Eltermere Inn), ¼ m. S of the village. Built in 1756 for William Robinson. Three-bay front raised on a basement, with double steps to the front door, which is under a bay carried on Doric columns. KITTY HALL is tucked in below the slope in front. Minute, but not lowly. T-shaped, with swept valleys. Entry under a pent roof in the angle. Tiny upper windows under the eaves. A wooden-mullioned window discovered downstairs has shutters but no provision for glass. Two-room plan with the downhouse in the cross-piece T. C. Pattinson of Windermere, proprietor of the Langdale Green Slate Co. from the 1920s, kept Kitty Hall as a holiday house. The parlour extension at the S end, with plaster frieze with acorns and fleur-de-lys, and the new stair, must be Pattinson.

HIGH CLOSE (Youth Hostel), 1¼ m. E of Great Langdale church, on the fell road from Grasmere. C17 farmhouse, in 1857 turned into a mansion for Edward Balme Wheatley-Balme of Mirfield by *John Cory*, with further additions to designs of 1866 by *Cory & Ferguson*. Ranges S and W were added *en echelon*, creating a complex and rambling pile round a narrow courtyard. The garden front, towards the great Windermere view, advances in a series of angles bound together, and to the farmhouse, by a meandering veranda. The new parts are raised over a tunnel-vaulted basement. Back and N end are sheer and plain onto the narrow road. Double-height hall with baronial fireplace and bracketed-out stair. Main rooms of complex shapes, with decent fireplaces.

Now proceeding up Great Langdale W from Chapel Stile. ROBINSON PLACE is a three-bay gable-entry house on the r. T & AF (Thomas and Agnes Fearon) 1692 on a carved spice cupboard, 1693 on a plaster panel. Close by is ROBIN GHYLL. Firehouse with end entry by the fire, buttery and parlour opposite the fire, stair in the firehouse, i.e. all in the simple rectangle. Plenty of plank-and-muntin panelling, typical of the late C17 or early C18. Further on, RAW HEAD FARM has a fire-window and stack on the r., downhouse projecting forward on the l., with a couple of odd recesses in its end wall. Entry under a pent roof between the two. The big bank barn was converted for the Achille Ratti Climbing Club into BISHOP'S SCALE, with the R.C. CHAPEL of Our Lady of the Snows.

NEW DUNGEON GHYLL HOTEL and STICKLE BARN, further W, are the principal fleshpots of Langdale. The inn looks *c.* 1860s, symmetrical about a central gable, of green stone with invisible pointing and dripmould done in bits of slate standing proud: pretty harsh. The barn is a heavy-handed conversion.

STICKLE COTTAGE, between the two, has a wide porch with benches, and a cantilevered chimney on the r. gable. The lower window on this side is pushed in to accommodate the fire-hood and possible fire-window. Continuous slate drip over first floor. Whitewashed boulder foundation. Behind and across the stony beck to the NE is MILLBECK, standing bravely against the bracken-strewn fell – a classic Lake District picture. Long low range with a three-bay bank barn l., whitewashed house in the middle with porch and deep-set windows, and a small outhouse r., now domestic and whitewashed over the rough stones. The main stack at this end is indicated by the fire-window. A small lean-to at the back accommodates the stair.

The OLD DUNGEON GHYLL HOTEL is higher up the valley. The inn was bought in 1862 by *Miles Thompson* who no doubt added the tall three-storey section. The public bar was the cowhouse and retains its whitewashed slate and timber stalls or boskins.

At the head of Great Langdale is a low BARN by the road with three cruck-trusses. The blades, nearly straight, fail to meet at the top; instead the ridge is carried on a little collar and kingpost. Trenched purlins (there are no mortice joints) with thin curved wind-braces, indicating that the crucks were erected first and the galletted boulder wall built round them. Martin Higgins and Janet Martin have established that it belonged to a lost farmhouse across the road, and was built by Robert Satterthwaite between 1613 and 1616. WALL END, a little distance N, has a dog-leg stair at the back, next to the buttery also in the outshut, which means that the parlour can be full-width. Press cupboard in the partition dated 1725. Two bank barns to the N, attached to the house in L-plan.

LITTLE LANGDALE is S of Great Langdale. The two part company W of Skelwith Bridge. Several good villas here. (BRATHAY HOW, high up overlooking the road. Large Voysey-ish house of c. 1913. By *Mawson*? White, with some timber framing.)

HIGH BIRK HOW shelters in a hollow above Little Langdale Tarn. Two houses end-to-end, chimneys back-to-back, each with its wide-cheeked porch. The r. house has wooden mullioned windows deep-set; a four-lighter and tiny fire-window indicate the firehouse. It retains its timber-framed smoke-hood, suggesting an early date, possibly C16. Stone semicircular stair in an outshut at the back. The downhouse at the other end is unheated, whereas the l. house, late C17 or C18, has a fireplace at both ends.

SW over a beautifully satisfying three-part CLAPPER BRIDGE is LOW HALL GARTH (cupboard dated 1689), built at right angles to its barn, following the bend of the lane. From here we look across N to BUSK FARM, unusually of four bays. HIGH HALL GARTH, built end-on to the hill is basically a single C17–early C18 unit, with a small shippon now part of the house at the uphill end, and parlour and cruck barn at the back. It appears to have lost its uphill chimney.

Continuing w, BRIDGE END is a classic small Lake District farm. House and barn under one long roof, facing s. Small fire-window and big firehouse window, deep-set under wooden lintels, with continuous slate drips growing house-leeks. Tiny windows at the back light the stair and pantry. That was the whole extent of the c17 house; parlour, barn and broad-cheeked porch are additions.

Finally, FELL FOOT shines out with its big white chimneys at the head of the dale, where the road begins its hair-raising climb up Wrynose Pass. Substantial house of the early c17, owned in the c18 by Fletcher Fleming of Rydal (1707 arms), and in the c19 an inn. Distinguished by a windowless projection jettied out over the road. The door is underneath, but there is also the expected through passage in the wing, behind the stack. (Plaster overmantel moulded with grapes and leaves, with traces of a frieze. c16 cottage on its N side with crucks and a stone smoke-hood.)

LANGWATHBY (C)

Sizeable village surrounding a wide green and the Shepherds Inn. The houses, many with the characteristic double sashes, are generally parallel to the green, but some are end-on.

ST PETER. Partly rebuilt in 1718. Five-bay nave and two-bay chancel with tall narrow round-arched windows, coved cornice and alternating quoins. Large w porch added in 1836, E window probably later yet. But on the N an almost windowless aisle with its roof sweeping down low. The three-bay arcade has rough octagonal piers with E.E. capitals (one is round) too small for them, giving an odd waisted effect. Two-step chamfered arches, also E.E. The chancel arch, also twice chamfered, is whitewashed with plaster faces as springers.

WESLEYAN CHAPEL. 1860, extended to a T in 1900.

STATION. The Midland Railway, arriving in the 1870s, has a considerable presence. Stone station building of the middle

Langwathby, station, platform elevation.
Drawing, 1973

size, resplendent in blood-and-custard livery. Wooden shelter on the other side. Large GOODS SHED, with three loading arches. STATIONMASTER'S HOUSE, and a terrace of six COTTAGES with double porches.

At Little Salkeld, 1½ m. N, a WATER CORN MILL. Typical of the modest country mills of Cumberland. Built *c.* 1750, extended 1870. Less typically, it was carefully restored in 1975 and the original machinery is still working. Two-storey miller's house, barn, mill with two overshot wheels, kiln and stables straggle along the site, all built of the local red sandstone rubble. Altogether charming.

LAZONBY (C)

5040

ST NICHOLAS. Rebuilt by *Salvin*, 1864–6, at the expense of the Macleans of Lazonby Hall. Strong and unpretentious inside and out. The church is built of unusually small stones. W tower with higher stair-turret. Triple belfry windows, the side lights blank. Tracery partly in the style of 1300, partly with ogees. Three-bay N arcade, wide-stepping with circular piers. Notable WOODWORK by Canon *B. W. Wilson*, rector 1877–1920: S door, N vestry door, pulpit, and chancel, organ, tower and NW vestry screens. Passionflower, vine, wheat and rose luxuriate within disciplined frames, but his few ventures into the animal kingdom are inhibited. – Unornamented wheel CROSS, C10(?), at the highest point of the churchyard. Over 6 ft (1.8 metres) high. A fine view of the church below and, the other way, a surprise view of the STATION, a typical Settle and Carlisle job (1876).

WAR MEMORIAL of 1920. Another cross, by the path.

SCHOOL. 1863, enlarged 1907. Unusually decorative, with a tower and scrolly gables.

LAZONBY HALL, ⅔ m. NE. 1848. Large and complicated, with mansard roofs. In multiple occupation.

LEVENS (W)

4080

ST JOHN THE EVANGELIST. A plain nave and chancel of 1826–8 in the local limestone, with a W steeple and spire (added 1831) turning octagonal at the belfry stage. Lancet windows. Architect, inevitably, *George Webster*. The only drama is inside, where a W gallery runs behind the three arches of the tower and its flanking spaces. Surprisingly utilitarian roof, scissor-braced, of thin members with packing pieces and painted brown. – LECTERN, a fine wooden eagle. – Minimally Gothick PEWS. – STAINED GLASS. E window by *A. K. Nicholson*, 1922.

Chancel N and S by *Abbott & Co.* of Lancaster, 1952. – N of the church, three BELLS mounted in a wooden Scandinavian-looking shelter.

47 LEVENS HALL. The de Redman family held Levens from *c.* 1225 to 1578. Their house can be found in the basement level of the present house, with features in C14 style. The house we see is essentially Elizabethan, the largest and most complete in the Lake Counties. James Bellingham (†1641) built most of what makes it memorable. It is grey and informal, kitted with towers, gables, ornamentally leaded windows and wildly assorted chimneys including an enormous conical one for the hall fire. Intensely romantic within, rich in carved wood, embossed leather, armorial glass and geometric plasterwork. To Colonel James Grahme or Graham (of the Netherby family), who bought Levens in 1689, we owe the fantastic garden. Later by marriage the Howards, Earls of Suffolk, had the house; now the residence of the Bagot family.

The main block of the house faces N, across the C17 entry court. It approximates to the medieval H-shape but is unwontedly tall. It has in front of the Hall a big embattled tower, and to its r. one gabled bay, to its l. two. The windows are mullioned-and-transomed. The main doorway (with ears) of *c.* 1690 (dates on rainwater hoppers 1691, 1692) is inserted into one such window. Overhead the gable is carried over on a beam to make a dark recess. On the l. is the hall bay window with six lights to the front and two to the doorway. The E side towards the garden with its famous topiary is as asymmetrical. First one canted bay window, built out over a medieval shouldered-arched doorway in the basement, then one square projection. Then a recessed part continued as a long S wing aligned E–W, but interrupted at the angle by the four-storey Howard Tower, begun in 1807 by *Francis Webster* for Mary Howard. It has a higher stair-turret. The tower has an air of stage scenery, but succeeds as a visual link between house and garden. The S wing is documented as of 1692, for Col. James Grahme, by a Yorkshire mason, *Henry Cuthbertson* of Coxwold, and a Yorkshire joiner, *John Milburne* of Henderskelfe, to provide service rooms below and bedrooms above, and is in its present form regular. Mullion-and-transom cross-windows, and a 'cubaly' or clock tower in 1692. The rainwater heads now say 1788, the clock face of the turret 1773, but the bell inside 1707. The end block, at the SW corner, is the C16 brewhouse. However, the one-step four-light window in its gable is as a rule a sign of the late C17.

Entry on the N side is roughly central, up a flight of steps. How can we explain the level of the Hall, eleven steps up from the ground but four or five below any of the other principal rooms? And where was the medieval entry, which cannot have been central? To answer it is best to go first to the BASEMENT, and the SERVANTS' HALL (now teashop). Good stone fireplace with the Bellingham bugles and the date 1589; contemporary panelling. If the partitioning for serveries and kitchens is ignored, we can identify the medieval hall and its cross-wings. In the NW corner a wide doorway with a pointed arch, hollow-chamfered, leads to a spiral stair in the front tower. Next to it in the W wall a good medieval doorway, hollow-chamfered and pointed-arched again, and two more openings which may represent medieval doors, though missing their heads or jambs. At any rate it seems we have found the screens and entry. At the high, E end the doorways are shouldered-arched (1350s). The E cross-wing basement, under the drawing rooms, is tunnel-vaulted. Three doorways in different directions, all with shouldered lintels.

Now for the Elizabethan HALL. It is in the medieval position but raised up, although not as high as first-floor level, so still allowing it an impressive headroom. It is a magnificent room, with late C16 panelling, plaster ceiling with interlocked quatrefoils, and a plaster frieze divided into bays by short pilasters. In each bay is a Bellingham coat of arms, and over the fireplace a royal achievement of Queen Elizabeth. Painted glass with Bellingham alliances and heraldry. The bay window corresponds of course to the high-table end. Opening out of the Hall on the SW is the principal STAIR, obviously Grahme's, with three rather heavy balusters to the tread, early C18 panelling, and stamped leather. In the E wing, which must have been the solar over the vault, is the DRAWING ROOM, with a ceiling of eight-pointed stars formed of ribs of quite some depth of relief and with little pendants. Chimneypiece dated 1595. It is illuminating to consider that work at the neighbouring mansion of Sizergh was complete by *c.* 1575, whereas it seems to have started here after 1578. So the only ceiling at Sizergh similar to this one is the latest there. The chimneypiece is very grand, with short columns and pairs of short columns in two tiers in the overmantel, Ionic and Corinthian, but fluted pilasters l. and r. of the opening. The columns mostly frame coats of arms. The cartouches derive from a Vredeman de Vries design published *c.* 1560–3.

The adjoining SOUTH DRAWING ROOM has a simpler ceiling, but an exceptionally interesting chimneypiece of *c.* 1640 in the Newcastle style, inscribed:

THUS THE FIVE SENCES STAND PORTRAITTED HERE
THE ELEMENTS FOURE, AND SEASONS OF THE YEARE
SAMPSON SUPPORTS ONE SIDE, AS IN A RAGE
THE OTHER, HERCULES IN LIKE EQUIPAGE.

Samson and Hercules stand l. and r., figures of Touch, Smell, and Taste above, and Hearing and Sight recline on the open pediment above. Also carved panels of the Four Elements and the Four Seasons – a whole panoply of uncomplicated allegory. Wall panelling with lozenges, as at Sizergh.

The DINING ROOM W of the Hall has a chimneypiece dated 1586 and a stucco ceiling whose chief motifs are apsidally ended Greek crosses. More leather, adding warmth with its golden brown sheen. Nice triangular heads (not really

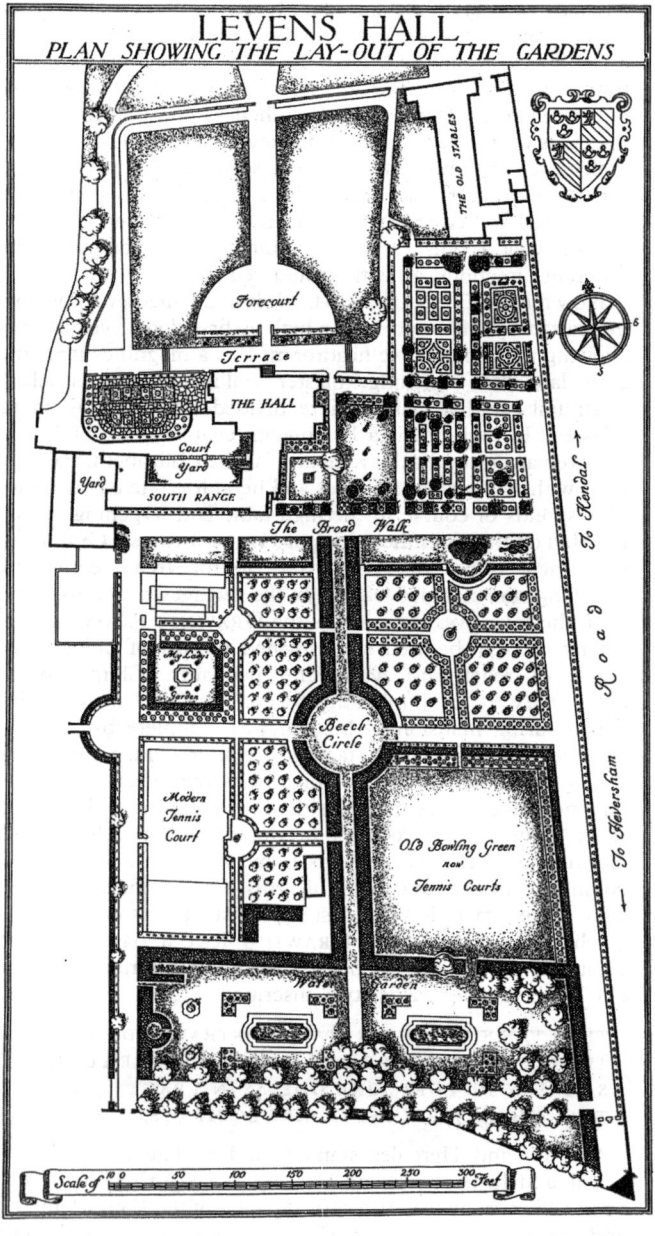

Levens Hall, gardens.
Plan, 1936

pediments) over the doors, with inlaid architecture. The
SMOKING ROOM behind the Dining Room has a
chimneypiece with C16 figures of Wisdom, Justice and Truth,
and panelling with Corinthian pilasters, obviously not
all Elizabethan, but equally obviously intended to look
Elizabethan. It was installed *c.* 1810 by *Francis Webster.* More
of the same panelling in the other rooms.

Now the N TOWER, which stands in front of the screens
position. Could this have been a porch-cum-stair on the North
Lancashire pattern? The turning stair changes direction part-
way. Lack of direct access from stair to Hall reinforces the
suggestion that the floor level is altered.

The BACK STAIR, with chunky turned balusters and
continuous string, was added in 1717. It leads to the BED-
ROOMS, with more stamped leather and C16–C19 panelling,
some imported. On the first floor above the Hall was originally
a Long Gallery.

The ROOFS provide a further surprise: over the principal
stair, a pair of medieval trusses, many-pegged. Canted collar
with trefoil shape above and mortices for massive braces below.
If *in situ* it suggests an earlier cross-wing, though it is very high
up to have been over an open room.

Family accommodation is now in the S WING: large
kitchen/living room below, bedrooms and smaller sitting rooms
above. One sports mock-Chinese painted wallpaper done in
the 1960s by *Harry Kellard.* Also a room with typical late C17
panelling and a staircase with equally typical twisted balusters.

GARDEN. Designed by Monsieur *Guillaume Beaumont,*
'Gardener to James II and Col. James Grahme'.* Work
started in 1692 with the boundaries. Walks and borders were
laid out in 1694, planting was done in 1697. A lead cistern has
the date 1704. On the E side is a long wall, which meant altering
the line of the road. On the W in contrast an outward-looking
HA-HA – a very early example – with a bastion. E of the house
is an intricate topiary garden, mad as a hatter. To the S the
brush is broader, with a long beech walk and *rond-point.* This
and the two cross-alleys are the only long vistas. There are no
diagonals. Nor are there any terminations to views, except a
niche on the S wall made in the 1920s, and the Second World
War PILLBOX in the park which is so prominent from the
Broad Walk. No fountains except a modern one. Yew, box and
beech. The PARK, across the road to the E, was also laid out by
M. Beaumont, mostly following a destructive storm of 1701.
Not large, but very beautiful with the steep banks of the River
Leven, big oaks and beeches and fallow deer.

NETHER LEVENS, or LOW LEVENS. Less than ½ m. W of Levens
Hall, but owned by Dallam (*see* Milnthorpe) and hidden by a
judicious clump of trees. Long and powerful building down by
the tidal River Kent, with a display of four huge round

---

*Grahme, as Privy Purse to James II, brought Beaumont from Hampton Court to
Levens after 1688.

chimneys and one smaller one. Hall and cross-wings originally (tree-ring date mid 1540s), but the S cross-wing shown by Machell has gone; its SE corner stands as an isolated ruin, and a little of its SW corner stands in line with the back of the hall. A blocked door in the hall evidently led to it, and a small raised door in the corner probably to a turning stair in the angle, as at Beetham (q.v.). The hall door and screens were at the N end where the stair is now. A garderobe and stair-tower at the back has the only doorway to retain its pointed and chamfered head. The date 1594 with T & AP for the Prestons probably refers to the hall's subdivision and the addition of a great stack with broad arched fireplace its W wall – and so probably also to the chimneys, and mullioned-and-transomed windows on the E side. The hall window, of four lights with four-centred heads, also fits that date, but the stair is typical of 1694 when the house came into the possession of the Dallam property. It resembles those at Beetham and Cowmire (Crosthwaite), with well-turned balusters, but if it had ball finials they have been sawn off. The small-scale panelling in the chamber above is late C17 too. The N wing remains in part, but is broken off where Machell shows an entrance arch. An upper fireplace can be seen here. The two wings reached out to a barmkin wall by the river, still partly standing with its wall-walk. Machell shows what could be a chapel (oratory licence 1452) at the N end. Here there is now a long kitchen wing with two more giant chimneys. It is astonishing how much internal space these stacks occupy, enough for a London flat.

Large and fine BANK BARN. The large DOVECOTE (C17: DCMS) has lost its roof in a fire, and the tops of the walls. The small DOVECOTE (C18: DCMS) is more ornamental, with a pyramid roof; two-storeyed within.

HEAVES HALL (hotel). A Grecian remodelling of c. 1818 by the *Websters* for James Gandy. Three widely spaced bays. The l. and r. ground-floor windows are tripartite. Porch of four unfluted Ionic columns. The mansard roof, not an improvement, was added by *Austin & Paley* in 1932. Octagonal entrance hall with rounded corners with niches, and a lightly canopied Soanian ceiling. Big square central space, presumably top-lit before the extra storey was added, in which climbs the delicate cantilever stair. Ionic screen upstairs. Sarcophagi over the doors, Greek key in the iron balustrade and the plaster cornices.

LINDAL-IN-FURNESS (L)

2070

ST PETER. For the 6th Duke of Buccleuch by *James Murchie* of Carlisle, 1885–6. Of red sandstone, rock-faced for the battered plinth, chisel-dressed above, ashlar dressings. The form is original and successful. Nave and lower chancel. Off the chancel a pair of transepts, cross-roofed. Off the E end of the nave a pair of one-bay aisles with lean-to roofs with the same reach, the N and S walls continuous. Near the E end of the nave a large wooden slate-clad bellcote and spire. Tracery is of the plate variety. Inside it turns out that the chancel transepts are screened off for vestry and organ. One of the nave aisles serves as choir vestry, the other houses a MODEL of the (haematite) pit top at Roan Head, made by *Thomas Quirk* (†1998). The chancel is ashlar-lined, the nave white. The cradle roof surprisingly shows no strengthening for the bellcote. Full pitch-pine FUR-NISHINGS of the period. – STAINED GLASS. E window by *Clayton & Bell*. NW, Magnificat and Nunc Dimittis window by *A. K. Nicholson*, 1962. The rest clear-glazed but leaded.

Attractive railed GREEN off the main road, ringed with trees and pleasant houses. CHURCH FARM is dated WAS 1635. Baffle-entry, still with the obtusely pointed lintel typical of the 1550s. Fire-window. Several Buccleuch estate buildings in limestone rubble with red non-ashlar dressings and hoodmoulds, e.g. High House Farm, 1879.

LINDALE (L)   4080

ST PAUL. 1828–9. A mean building in a lovely situation, high enough up to command wide views. *George Webster* probably provided the design, without fee; it anticipates closely the Carus Wilson model (*see* Casterton). Waisted tower with tightly pursed belfry lights and clumsy battlements. Plain lancets and a base mould complete the architectural dress. The chancel was added in 1864, in boringly correct Dec, and a flat-roofed N aisle in 1912 (when a bloomery was found), with paired lancets and buttresses. – By the S door the massive *Webster* MAU-SOLEUM, severely classical (Francis Webster †1827). On top an inscription slab surrounded by a cast-iron railing.

OBELISK to John 'Iron Mad' Wilkinson, ironmaster, †1808, in a tiny public garden in the centre of the village. Massive (40 ft (12 metres) high, 22 tons), black, of iron; an object of considerable power. Inscriptions in beautiful Trajanic lettering and the head of Wilkinson in profile in a medallion. 'His life was spent in ACTION for the benefit of MAN.' Prepared by *Wilkinson* himself at his Bradley Ironworks at Bilston in Staffordshire, and an important early example of the technique of box casting.* Removed in 1863 from the grounds of Castle Head (*see* below), where it had stood over his body buried in an iron coffin. Restored 1984.

*Wilkinson's father Isaac was a farmer and furnace-keeper at Clifton (C), then at Backbarrow (*see* Haverthwaite), where he developed furnaces and patented and manufactured box irons, for pressing linen. Financial success enabled him to apprentice his son in 1745 to a Liverpool ironmonger. In 1756 John followed his father to Denbighshire, where Isaac developed the famous Bersham Ironworks; in 1757 John was at Broseley (Shropshire) setting up the New Willey works; in 1766 John established the Bradley works. As a supplier of engine cylinders to Boulton & Watt, Wilkinson's skill and ingenuity underpinned much of the early development of reliable steam power.

Over the road, HADWIN'S GARAGE shows how the National Park's conservation policy has spread outside the Park itself. By *Bob Reynard* of *Unwin Jones Partnership*, Carlisle, completed 1998. Vaguely industrial or agricultural. The main entrance is brought forward in cheeks like that of a bank barn. Slate roof, limestone walls, timber trusses.

ELLER HOW, ⅓ m. NNW. The Websters' country retreat, a *cottage orné* backing against a steep wooded hillside, with tall chimneys (some cut down), hoodmoulds, bargeboards, finials and balconies. It grew in stages from *Francis Webster*'s L-shaped cottage of *c.* 1818 at the NE end, reaching SW to the larger rooms in a single storey over a basement which were added by *George Webster* after his father's death in 1827. The veranda at the extreme SW is of after 1847. This section cranks forward a little. An almost detached Italianate stone porch at the N end provides the balance. It demonstrates the firm's range of tooling of the local limestone. The interiors are quite modest, though an inventory of 1864 shows the house stuffed with paintings, 'articles of Vertu', and a sizeable library. Dining room made out of two smaller rooms, with a chimneypiece incorporating antique bits. Larger drawing room, L-shaped, originally giving onto a balcony by a sash window which disappears into a slot. The pentangular room in the cranked end section has a shallow plaster dome and grotesque figure corbels. Elaborate Reptonian GARDENS, too heavily wooded now, the artfully contrived clearings and sight lines growing out. A pool is crossed by an arched and railed bridge over a cascade. Paths and steps wind up to a (ruined) gazebo and other rendezvous.

CASTLE HEAD, ⅓ m. SE. A rocky island in the drained bog, like Meathop (q.v.). Built by John Wilkinson, ironmaster, in the late C18, and remodelled and extended in the late C19. Plain, white, blocky three-storey house with a veranda round three sides. STABLE with tower. Castellated farmyard, boathouse, boundary walls. LODGE to the SW, mid-C19, with its own little tower and veranda.

LINSTOCK (C) *see* HOUGHTON

LITTLE CORBY (C) *see* WARWICK

LITTLE SALKELD (C) *see* LANGWATHBY

LITTLE STRICKLAND (W)

Open-plan settlement loosely built around an indeterminate green. Small church islanded on the green. The old chapel of ease was on another site.

ST MARY. 1814. Colvin suggests, by *George Gibson* of Crosby Ravensworth. W narthex but no E chancel. Bellcote on the W gable, behind the narthex. Lancets with Y-tracery. Simplest whitewashed interior with a little W gallery on slender Doric columns. Altar table in a three-sided pen.

LOW HALL. T-shaped house hidden behind farm buildings and divided from the farmyard by a fence. The hall range was probably built *c.* 1540 by the Crackanthorpes of Newbiggin (W), whose arms are recorded in the blank panel in the S front. The hall is in the cross-piece, which has mullioned-and-transomed windows on both floors. A parlour at the N end on the first floor, with a plasterwork ceiling of *c.* 1600 after a well-known design in Serlio's Book IV. Close octagons, crosses, etc., and the panels filled in with roses, scrolls, etc. Entrance in the downstroke through a two-centred doorway. The plan shows a turning stair here.

HIGH HALL, over the road, was also built by the Crackanthorpes. The date 1600 over the fireplace, and the Crackanthorpe arms. Mullioned windows with labels. A fire-window by the front door suggests that a central stack has been replaced by stacks at the ends.

LONG MARTON (W)

ST MARGARET AND ST JAMES. Essentially C11 and C12, mixing in a suggestive manner Norman features with those we consider Saxon. Nave and W part of the chancel of *c.* 1100, with enormous quoin stones – the nave NE ones long-and-short. Tall and narrow S and W doorways both carrying forceful and barbaric tympana carved in shallow relief. The S one has a winged dragon with a knotted tail, a quadruped with wings on its neck and a tiny head, and a winged shield. The W doorway now leads into the W tower. This must have been added a little later, with (renewed) bell-openings of later C12 type, though in shape and form it is like that at Morland. It originally had a W doorway. The inner W doorway bears another two-legged dragon, and a figure with tiny head and upraised arms, identified by Malcolm Thurlby as Jonah and the Whale. The chip-carved saltire crosses below and the trellis of the lintel on the other hand are familiar Norman motifs. The blocked N doorway is definitely Norman, i.e. C12, but the small blocked windows must go with the original build. The lengthened chancel is Dec – see the E window, S doorway and windows, SEDILIA and PISCINA. The S transept, called the Knock Porch and set aside for the inhabitants of that village, was added in the C15. Most of the furnishings date from *John A. Cory's* restoration of 1880. – STAINED GLASS. In the blocked N doorway, 1930, St Margaret and St James. Next to that SS Cosmas and Damian, physicians and martyrs, by *Stanley M.*

Scott, 1967. S transept, 1925, in memory of George Dominic Stampa, architect.

WESLEYAN CHAPEL. 1818. On top of a cottage and reached by a flight of stone steps under a fine iron lantern arch. Trefoil-headed doorway, arch-topped windows, large carved name with vases of lilies. The cottage has ordinary sashes, not in line. Its front door is round the l. side, where the date is carved, with more symbols.

PARISH INSTITUTE, 1893–4. Designed by *George Stampa*. Born in Constantinople, he trained with Edward Walters in Manchester, and erected buildings in Constantinople and Egypt in 1859–78 before returning to Appleby. The Institute stands prominently in the village, looking like a Nonconformist chapel with a bellcote, but with large windows and a porch on the N side. The other newcomer is the former STATION of the Midland Railway, 1876, perfectly placed on one side of the cul-de-sac of the prettiest part of the village.

(BRAMPTON TOWER, SE of the village. Three-storeyed Victorian tower of red sandstone with lower wings, stepped gable, and corner turret.)

LONGSLEDDALE (W)

5000

CHURCH. Rebuilt 1712 and again 1863 by Lady Mary Howard of Levens. Her initials MEH and the date are carved on the chancel arch. Simple but ecclesiologically correct. AUMBRY door dated RLM 1662. The church, and its attendant school and parsonage, are all probably by *Miles Thompson*.

UBARROW or YEWBARROW HALL. Tucked under the wooded valley side with a big oak in front. Small C17 farmhouse with deep-set windows and a central porch, attached to a defensive tower with crowstepped gables and tiny plain windows. Tunnel-vaulted basement. BANK BARN.

Near the head of the valley, on the summit of Tarn Crag (2,176 ft, 670 metres), a SURVEY POST for the underground aqueduct taking water from Haweswater to Manchester (1925–31). ½ m. further, on the W side of the valley, the ruined miners' barracks and remains of a narrow-gauge tramway from WRENGILL QUARRY.

LONGTOWN (C)

3060

First mentioned in 1584. The town was laid out in the later C18 by Dr Robert Graham of Netherby (q.v.), two miles away, in rivalry with his Scottish neighbour the 3rd Duke of Buccleugh at Newcastleton. He also built a small harbour at Sarkfoot. The square of four streets, wide and lined with trees, is without accent except for the GRAHAM ARMS, a stately inn with two canted bays and a Doric porch. The houses are colourwashed, generally terraced and of three bays with a middle entrance. Mostly two-storey, but sometimes single-storey in the Scottish mode, and not too regimented. Often they have arches through to back parts, sometimes with a symmetrical arrangement of doors on each side. Many of the inhabitants in 1802 were home-weavers for Carlisle manufacturers. No parish church – that is at Arthuret (q.v.).

(St ANDREW (Church of Scotland), back of Bridge Street. 1834.)

(LOCHINVAR SCHOOL (comprehensive). By *Cumberland County Architects* under *D. W. Dickenson*, 1964. Mostly load-bearing brick, with pitched roofs.)

BRIDGE. A fine bridge of red sandstone ashlar carries the A7 over the River Esk on the northern edge of the town. Five segmental arches with solid parapets. Dated 1756 'for the Rev. Robert Graham', but widened in 1888 and sitting on C20 concrete rafts on the river bed.

GLOBE TAVERN, corner of Bank Street. Redesigned in 1916 by *Harry Redfern* for the State Management Scheme (*see* Carlisle, p. 223). Outside very plain, stone. This was a rough drinking-house catering for munitions workers – but carefully managed. The barn-like public bar, with an open roof and simple trusses, has a stage, and a good deal of the original furniture. Smaller bar at the back, leading to a garden formerly with a pergola. Upstairs a function room, again with open trussed roof, used by the Catholic Church among others. There was a restaurant and an off-licence.

M.o.D. LONGTOWN. The establishment in 1914–15 of the Army Cordite Factory affected the whole region, bringing in its train the State Management of drinking (*see* above). It covered 9,000 acres, partly in Scotland, and employed 19,772 people by 1917. The cost was £9,295,000. It was converted to a storage depot in the 1930s.

   HOUSING for the factory was the responsibility of *Raymond Unwin* of the Local Government Board, with *C. M. Crickmer* as resident architect, though the prime development was in Gretna (see *The Buildings of Scotland: Dumfries and Galloway*). Further housing at Moor Road by *J. S. Jones* of *Unwin Parker & Jones* with Border RDC and Carlisle City Council, 1976.

LORTON (C)

St CUTHBERT. Rebuilt *c.* 1807–9. It is faced in incised flat render, with an embraced W tower, lancet windows with wooden tracery, and a short chancel. Stone tracery was inserted in the E window in 1903, with vulgar STAINED GLASS by *Mayer* of Munich.

METHODIST CHAPEL. 1840. Cute building with two tall arched windows, a porch and a plaque on the long side.

LORTON HALL. Mostly of 1889–90, including the pele tower. The mid-section (now called Winder Hall) has a long even E front dated 1663 with triangular pediments above a continuous dripmould. Royal arms in plaster in an upstairs room.

Water-powered linen MILLS were established in the village in the C18 beside the Boon Beck Bridge. In 1828 John Jennings adapted one of them as a brewery (now in residential use), drawing supplies from a malthouse established by his father in the building that is now the VILLAGE HALL.

LOWESWATER (C)

ST BARTHOLOMEW. The gaunt grey church composes ill with the splendour of its setting. Four-bay box of 1827–9, unattractively Victorianized in 1884 by the addition of a polygonal chancel with Geometrical tracery, transept, porch, false buttresses and steep roof. The lancets were altered to take stone Y-tracery, but the round-arched W doorway of 1829 is still there.

A clockwise circuit round the lake of Loweswater, starting by the church, illustrates the development of domestic architecture. First the former SCHOOL, now Parish Hall, given in 1839 by John Marshall, Lord of the Manor. MILLENNIUM MONU-MENT, sculptor *B. Porter*, Pardshaw. Miniature bronze landscape labelling the fells with their respective heights. To the W, WATERGATE FARM under the fell edge looks prosperous, with small-paned double sashes and extensive outbuildings. HUDSON PLACE at the NW end of the lake is a confident, ample and handsome three-bay farmhouse, with shell-hood and ornamental datestone WW (Woodall) 1741. With LOWESWATER HALL on the N bank of 1868, like a Victorian vicarage, a new self-consciousness has arrived: unnaturally steep roofs, high-maintenance valleys and bargeboards, plate tracery for the stair window, gloomy evergreenery. Above it on the bridleway the ruins of SPOUT HOUSE, a failed settlement where the land was too marginal. Back on the N lakeside CRABTREEBECK, dated FB AB 1660, low and white, noses into the hillside. Deep-set windows under wonky wooden lintels, semicircular stair-turret by the beck at the back: pure vernacular. Contrast THRUSHBANK: house and barns dated 1697 but painfully smart with plastic windows and a uniform cover like yellow marzipan. HIGH CROSS, late C18 or early C19, approaches gentleman-farmer status. Five bays, arched farmyard entrance, sycamore avenue.

(LOW HOLLINS, Brackenthwaite, 1¼ m. NE. Dated 1687 RCS (Robert and Catherine Stubbs), with some mullioned windows and a continuous dripmould. Inside, plaster frieze of horses and doves.)

LOWICK (L)

St Luke. Red and green stone. Lancet style, with a w tower. It looks 1845 rather than 1885 as per the datestone. The style suggests *Grundy*. – stained glass. On the n side c17 bits assembled. e window by *Ward & Hughes*, *c.* 1885, pictorial. w, by *Gibbs & Howard*.

Lowick Hall. 200 yds w of the church. The three-storey s wing is c16; wooden mullions, a central Westmorland chimney and a non-projecting half-spiral stair of wood round a mast. The rest is c18, of five bays, its cramped proportions determined probably by a lost n wing. The porch was added by *J. W. Grundy* in 1880; his scheme for dressing up the whole front *à la* Graythwaite is preserved. Doorcase probably of 1746 (rainwater-head date; or later?) with fluted pilasters and a triglyph frieze. Good stair with moulded ends to the treads, to the upstairs drawing room and master bedroom (were they intended as a single room?), with eared and pedimented doorcases. Interesting waterworks in the garden, and a small Japanese garden presumably of *c.* 1910.

LOWTHER (W)

Lowther Castle. Seat of the Lowthers, Earls of Lonsdale, the dominant family of Westmorland. In architectural terms it has been an unlucky place, but the record of its failures is an absorbing one.

The first house we are aware of consisted of hall and towered cross-wings. John Lowther, later Sir John, rebuilt the centre and offices in 1628–30, buying the roof of the great hall of Kirkoswald Castle for lead and timber. His son, also Sir John (1st baronet), added a new w wing in 1640–1, a new n porch in 1642, and in 1655–6 a matching gallery wing. The porch was executed in white stone by *Alexander Pogmire*, and so probably were the wings. They had regular mullioned-and-transomed windows and a canted bay, open below. Pogmire's 'pilasters and other cuttwork' may have mixed classical and Gothic in the same curious way as his remaining gallery wing at Hutton-in-the-Forest (q.v.). In 1691–2 Sir John, later 1st Viscount Lonsdale (†1700), demolished the middle and built an up-to-date thirteen-bay house between Pogmire's wings. *Talman* supplied the design, but with the 'correction and approbation' of his friend, the mathematician and inventor *Sir Samuel Morland*, Lowther claimed the completed house as 'principallie my own thought'. The builder was *Edward Addison*. This was the house described at muddled length by Celia Fiennes in 1698, depicted by Kip in 1707, and painted by Mathias Read. The 2nd Viscount (†1713) commissioned the

Lowther Castle, garden front.
Engraving, 1825

unattributed scheme which appears in the second volume of *Vitruvius Britannicus*, and in 1717 the 3rd Viscount invited *Gibbs* to rebuild the C17 wings and update the house. However, in 1718, before anything could be done, the centre burnt out. For the rest of the century the family lived in the patched-up wings, meanwhile commissioning another design from *Gibbs* (*c.* 1728) and one from *Colen Campbell*.

In 1751 the estate passed to James, 1st Earl of Lonsdale, who in 1756 inherited the vast Whitehaven estates as well. Neoclassical designs were obtained from *Matthew Brettingham* (1759–63) and '*Capability' Brown* (1763), and around 1767–73 both *Robert* and *James Adam* supplied designs, some of the latter's being castellar Gothic and externally symmetrical. One was octagonal with a ring of towers round a central court; another had a huge central tower. Gilpin in 1772 said that materials were being collected for a grand structure, but still nothing was done. The last paper-only designs, by *Thomas Harrison c.* 1800, included one combining castle and ecclesiastical elements in a bold asymmetrical design.

Finally, in about 1799 *Francis Webster*, who may also have made 'Abbey or Convent-style designs', was set to work modernizing the W wing. Sir William Lowther inherited (as Viscount Lonsdale) in 1802, and in 1807 was elevated to first Earl of the new creation. *George Dance Jun.* made proposals in his Indian-flavoured Gothic in 1803–5 but, daunted by the distance, recommended instead *Robert Smirke*, just returned from Greece and the Near East.* Farington records in 1806 that Smirke 'in His Plan for the House to be built at Lowther has adopted principally the idea of

---

*Dance had been recommended by Lowther's close friend Sir George Beaumont, who employed him at Coleorton, Leics.

Dance, – which His Lordship is pleased with.' So it was Robert Smirke and the new 1st Earl of Lonsdale who finally built the present Lowther Castle.

Lowther was the young *Smirke*'s first job. He built the new castle clear and to the N of the old Lowther Hall, which meant moving the centre forward in relation to the wings. He began in 1806, remodelling Webster's offices on the E, and then starting on the new stables (executed by *Webster* and *B. Proctor*). By 1809 the family were able to move in to the E wing. Staircase and hall were complete in 1811, and in 1813 the W wing. Smirke submitted his account in 1814: £77,000, but building materials from the estate would have doubled the true cost, and as late as 1826 work was still needed on the billiard room. Plasterwork was by *Simpson* of Kendal but mainly by *Bernasconi* of London; painting by *Colvin* of Penrith and *Dixon* of London. Sculpture galleries and a conservatory were added in 1866 by *James Mawson*.

Here the Lowthers maintained great state until New Year's Day 1936, when the flamboyant 'Yellow Earl', Hugh, 5th Earl of Lonsdale was forced to close the castle. The largest-ever country house sale took place in 1947, realizing very little cash and robbing the castle of a viable future. In 1957 it was unroofed and thoroughly stripped, and is now a melancholy shell. Stabilization and structural repair are in progress, including in 2004 the insertion of a steel ring beam (engineer *Charles Blackett-Ord*).

THE HOUSE. Lowther is an extraordinary illustration of the northern pastime of castle building. Comparisons can be made with Porden's Eaton Hall near Chester (begun 1804), James Wyatt's Ashridge (1808) with similar massing and planning, with Nash's Ravensworth Castle, Co. Durham (begun 1808); and it was followed in the 1830s by Brougham Hall across the valley. As with many of these outsize houses Lowther may work better as a ruin than a habitation. The shell does a splendid job in holding together the grand landscape. A gravelled terrace 550 ft long and 100 ft wide (170 and 31 metres) on the park side (N) sets the scale. It is approached by ramps 30 ft (9 metres) wide from the massively battered and machicolated GATEHOUSE, which is set in a curtain wall punctuated by towers. The pinkish-grey ashlar N FAÇADE is 420 ft (129 metres) long. It rises in receding planes, its parts lined up and arrayed by size like a team photograph. The nine-bay centre is raised in the middle; behind that a yet higher, square, keep-like tower appears, and in front a porte cochère with octagonal turrets. The wings are book-ended in round turrets. Then there are low links and angle pavilions, higher than the links, but lower than the centre, with octagonal turrets again. The central keep or lantern has its own round turrets. The composition seems childish in full-frontal elevation, but works superbly as a piece of giant sculpture to be circumambulated, when the parts group and regroup in picturesque fashion.

The S or GARDEN FAÇADE has a contrasting ecclesiastical flavour, hence Wordsworth's lines, 'Cathedral pomp and grace, in apt accord/With thy baronial castle's sterner mien'. On this side are two round towers, crocketed pinnacles, buttresses, and a central Perp porch in front of a big traceried Perp window set in a steep gable. The gable top and statue niche have fallen. Matching galleries reach forward into the former gardens. These may have been added for the 2nd Earl's collections in the 1840s. One precariously retains its roof, plaster vault, and iron traceries. The ruined interiors cruelly reveal how skin-deep was the magnificence. All we are left with is rough stone and brick, with no stairs or vaulting and none of the shafting or modelling. The entrance hall is 60 ft by 30 ft (18 by 9 metres), the 'keep' 60 ft by 60 ft by 90 ft (28 metres) high. This originally contained the cantilever stair and was surrounded by arched corridors on each storey, now open to the elements. The state rooms were on the S front; drawing and billiard rooms E, breakfast room W. A great vaulted corridor 22 ft (7 metres) wide ran from E to W, flanked on the N by the oak-lined library and the family apartments. Now the outer ashlar skin is being slowly exploded away by the iron cramps buried within it. Areas of weakness created by the flues as they travel to the nearest turret, where they are carried up in brick, have had to be stitched.

The STABLE COURT forms an open U on the E side. Riding school behind the open-arched coach-house in the centre. This was the last section to be used – as a pig farm – and retains most of its roof. The remaining fittings date from the Kaiser's visit in 1893.

The GARDEN was vast, bounded on the W by the great C17 terrace and retaining wall nearly a mile long. Sir John recorded in 1653 how he fenced the new park 'with a great cast earthen hedge and brushed above and rail above that, so that never any Deer troubled it'. *Thomas Wilkinson* of Yanwath advised Lord Lonsdale on the walks and landscaping while the castle was being built in 1806–11. Garden doorway under a grotesque portico with columns part-fluted, part strapwork, and capitals with a ring of volutes, perhaps displaced from the house.* Of the Yellow Earl's phlox border, rose garden, Japanese garden, and Fountain Garden nothing can be seen; the 7th Earl, to whom the place was anathema, blotted it out with forestry conifers right up to the castle walls.

ST MICHAEL, N of the castle. Almost totally rebuilt in 1686 by Sir John Lowther, later 1st Viscount Lonsdale, after he had relocated the village. He may have consulted *Robert Hooke*. A strange, baffling exterior. Nave and aisles, a high central tower, a low S transept, and a chancel. The high tower has groups of three lancets as bell-openings and also for the stage below, and that is clearly Victorian. It dates in fact from 1856. But to the

---

*In 1731 Sir John Clerk of Penycuik described a portico 'of so bad proportions', the capitals 'monstrous'.

s the lower tier is replaced by a rectangular window with a moulded frame, unexpected in a church, and the aisles and clerestory have the same windows, making the church unusually transparent. Lowther's is the s transept as well with its steep pediment, and also allegedly the tall round-arched windows at the w and e ends. The n side of the tower shows that it is still c17 under the c19 skin. Lowther finished the tower with a dome and lantern, regrettably replaced by a more conventional top between 1814 and 1827. But the church is still an arresting building, magnificently sited and making an evocative group with the extraordinary mausoleum and the hearse/bell house behind.

The interior is much older than we have been led to expect. The massive N arcade must be of c. 1165–75. It has round piers with square abaci and single-stepped arches. One capital is multi-scalloped, the others have foliage, with little heads towards the nave, unfortunately totally re-tooled. The foliage capitals are of two types: those with the heads are earlier in style (though not in date); the others, e.g. the NW respond, look more Transitional. One pier and the E respond have base spurs. Square bases. The s arcade is a little later, say c. 1200, and less ambitious, with octagonal shafts but still round arches, with two slight chamfers. The arches from the aisles to the transepts look early c13. That is also the date of the central tower. The responds on all four sides are triple, with the big middle shaft keeled. That suggests the early c13. Steeply pointed arches. Only the intermediate columns inserted in the N and s arches are c19, presumably when the dome was rebuilt. These mid-piers have an unpleasant Siamese-twin section. The whole interior is lightly limewashed, disguising its texture – grey-white for the columns and shafts, pink for the arches and yellow for the walls.

FURNISHINGS. The chancel furniture goes with the walls, i.e. late c17 and very plain. REREDOS. Big square panel with bolection moulding; Lord's Prayer board above. – COMMUNION RAIL with twisted balusters. – Red and white diamond PAVEMENT. – PULPIT. c18. – FONT, a turned baluster. – SCULPTURE. In the w porch two-and-a-half c10 HOGBACKS, one with eight warriors in a ship, and a broken cross-shaft.★ – STAINED GLASS. Second World War memorial pair at the E end; artist *Herbert Hendrie*, maker *Charles Blakeman*. Two armorials, s, by *A. G. Moore*, 1938.

MONUMENTS. Nave s, four Neoclassical Lowthers dating from the 1870s–80s, highly coloured. – s transept. Sir Richard Lowther †1608. Alabaster effigy. – Sir John Lowther †1637 and Sir John †1675 share the same monument, made about the latter date. Between their busts a nonchalantly rolling skull on a black cushion. Black drapery behind, garlands and a cartouche below. Attributed to *Jasper Latham* (GF). –

71

★Parts of a very fine vine-scroll CROSS are in the Great Court of the British Museum. Part of another is in the Burrell Collection, Glasgow.

John, Viscount Lowther †1700. He reclines on a cushion, holding a coronet, wearing a curly wig and lace cravat. Reredos background with open segmental pediment. By *William Stanton*. – Gerard Augustus Lowther †1916, elegant cartouche. – Lord William Cavendish Frederick Bentinck †1828, urn and plinth. – The N transept centres on the huge white marble double sarcophagus of William and Augusta, 1st Earl and Countess Lonsdale, †1844 and 1838. – James, 1st Earl Lonsdale †1802. Made in 1805 by 'Messrs *Fishers* of York'. Tablet with sarcophagus. – Made by the same at about the same time, Richard, 3rd Viscount Lonsdale †1751. The sarcophagus here has a background of scythe, hourglass, caduceus, etc. – Also a couple of *Webster* tablets, and a clutch of brasses. The finest of these, by *Matthews & Sons* of London, shows Henry, 3rd Earl of Lonsdale, †1876 as Colonel of the Cumberland Militia, with handlebar moustache and silvered and gilt breastplate. – Chancel. Emily †1917, wife of the 3rd Earl. By *J. Froment-Meurice*, 1935. White marble, all in low and indistinct relief. On the plinth a greyhound, round the coffin angels and cherubs. Overhead, in mosaic, two more angels scatter flowers. Above the frame a portrait medallion. – Opposite (N), Lancelot Edward, 6th Earl †1953, a simple relief carved in wood, something that earlier Earls would never have countenanced. – Nave N wall, an elegant brass to Frances Mary Thompson who died in Rome in 1844.

80   MAUSOLEUM, above the River Lowther. By *Benjamin Baud* of London for the 2nd Earl in 1857, with carvings by *Thomas* and/or *James Nelson* of Carlisle. Perched on the lip of the valley on a grassy plinth, it is an architectural monsterpiece, all hideously crystalline forms, especially the solid side walls of three panels presumably for future epitaphs, with triangular heads and the jambs sloping forward as they go downward. Corner turrets. Inside, all white and all alone, the seated earl, a picture of loneliness. He is by *E. B. Stephens*, 1863.

BIER and BELL HOUSE, N of the church in the equivalent position to the mausoleum S. The bell is in the cupola.

VILLAGE. The village lining the road between the N front of the hall and the church was cleared away *c.* 1682 by Sir John, 1st Viscount, to enlarge his domain and better the prospect of his house. A very early example. The neat terraces of LOWTHER NEW TOWN, built in 1683–4, line the road facing the E wall of the park, punctuated a pair of Baroque gatepiers. The houses are mostly of five bays and two storeys, single or semi-detached, with plain window and door surrounds. The roofs are hipped. At the N end is the ESTATE OFFICE. Built as a manufactory for the new town *c.* 1680, plausibly by *William Thackeray*, mason, and *James Swingler*, carpenter. In 1697 it failed and, as Sir John Clerk of Penycuik put it when visiting his son in 1731, was turned into 'a manufactory for youth'. He described a large building with two great halls and twenty-two rooms for scholars. It closed in 1740.

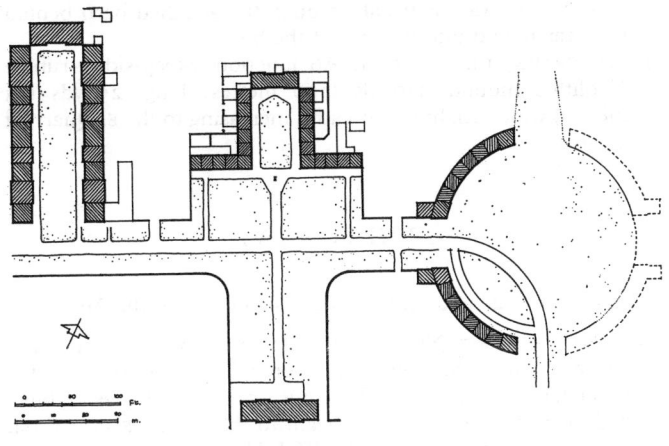

Lowther village.
Plan, 1967

LOWTHER VILLAGE, ½ m. SE. A second estate village, intended
to halt expansion of the first, which was still too near the house.
The plan was made by the *Adam Brothers* in 1765 or 1766 of a
circus and two Greek crosses. Building continued until 1773
but less than half was completed. Richard Warner in 1802
commented on 'the fantastic incongruity of its plan which
exhibits the grandest features of city architecture, the Circus,
the Crescent and the Square upon the mean scale of a
peasant's cottage'. It consists of two closes, both ending on the
N side with a seven-bay, two-storey house with a three-bay
centre and a hipped roof. The side ranges of the W close are
twenty-one bays long and articulated in height and roofs. The
second close has as its side pieces single-storey terraces with S
returns running E and W. Finally the E end of the composition
is a crescent open to the E and broken by the road in the
middle. Beginning and end of either half are marked by a
higher square pavilion with a pyramid roof. The original plan
provided for four, not two ranges, i.e. a complete circus.
Restored by *Johnston & Wright c.* 1973.

Earl Henry's Drive leads 2½ m. N to the PENRITH LODGE of
1877, by *James Mawson*, at Eamont Bridge. Castellated, with
an asymmetrical tower. Emperor's Drive, built in honour of
Kaiser Wilhelm's 1895 visit, runs 2½ m. S to the THRIMBY
LODGES, on the Shap road, though now cut by the M6
motorway. *B. J. Bardgett*, estate architect. Large; Tudor.

HACKTHORPE HALL, 1½ m. SE. Now Hackthorpe Business
Centre. The house, built by Sir Christopher Lowther in the
early C17, still looks quite hoary but the former farmstead is
spankingly restored, or new. The house has four-light
mullioned-and-transomed windows. Two-storey porch. The

earlier entry was, as usual, through the attached barn behind the hearth, and into the end of the house.

LONG CAIRN, 1 m. E, at the A6 junction. Steep-sided rubble Neolithic mound, 110 yds (100 metres) long, 25 yds (23 metres) wide; height and breadth increasing to the E. Quarried on the S.

LUPTON (W)

5080

Church, vicarage and school on an island site off the A65.

ALL SAINTS. 1867. Neo-Norman. Titchy – just three bays and an apse, with a bellcote and a porch. The S doorway on the other hand is enormous. Pleasing interior in shades of blue, with a cradle roof and rood beam to the apse. – FONT. From Kirkby Lonsdale church. The RCHME says that a date 1686 is assigned to it. However, it does not look that period.

Small BANK MILL on a site recorded in 1301. The breast-shot wheel ran in stone bearings, grinding corn until 1964.

GREENLANE END FARM. Datestone T & SW 1747 at the back, by a craftsman who delighted in foliage swags and flowers (also Badger Gate 1747, Boxtree Farmhouse, and others). Front garden with ball-topped gatepiers. The front has been sashed but the back retains its mullions and transoms. The stair is C18, with slender balusters, but there is at least one bolection-moulded fireplace.

FOWLSTON HALL. The two-storey porch looks like an C18 addition, though it bears the datestone E & AB 1655, probably moved. The inner front doorway is bolection-moulded. The house retains its fire-window to the r., and its side entry through the cottage porch behind the stack. (Stone stair rising through all three storeys.)

LUPTON TOWER. The tower is Victorian but it backs onto the C17 BOXTREE FARMHOUSE and its converted outbuildings, with nice datestones (see above) of 1720 and 1731.

MALLERSTANG (W)

7000

The beautiful and remote valley of the upper Eden is marked by a string of castles. The Settle and Carlisle railway climbs steadily up the valley side.

ST MARY, Outhwaite. 'Newe repayred by the Lady Anne Clifford' in 1663, according to a renewed inscription in Roman capitals over the S porch.* She tended to exaggerate the ruination, but the church does appear to be of 1663, with S windows of 1768, and C19 and C20 repair and updating. 1663 the S doorway, the N windows, and the E window (renewed)

---

* Of the LADY'S PILLAR erected 2¼ m. ESE by the Lady Anne in 1664 nothing of any shape remains.

with its two transoms. 1663 too the little octagonal PULPIT, and FONT. – STAINED GLASS by *Abbott & Co.*, 1920s.

Outhwaite is only a tiny hamlet, but it had a WESLEYAN CHAPEL too, of 1878.

PENDRAGON CASTLE, ¾ m. N. First mentioned in 1228, but apparently begun much earlier as an earth and timber RING-WORK, artificially scarped on the S and SE sides, and defended on the N by a deep crescentic ditch. Upcast dumped internally on the N and externally on the SE; causeway to the E. Within is an impressively massive ruin, shapeless but informative when examined. It was a free-standing Late Norman keep, apparently unsupported by other buildings. It measures *c.* 65 E–W by 59 ft N–S (20 by 18 metres), to Brough's *c.* 65 by 52 ft (20 by 16 metres), with a good plinth, and corner towers indicated by a slight bringing forward of the wall, as at Brougham. Twice-chamfered loops remain on the E. The diagonally placed garderobe tower, SE (cf. Dacre), complete with dig-out, is clearly an addition. The entrance is at ground level on the N, with a portcullis slot, and flanked by turning stairs. Unusually the walls are honeycombed with mural chambers even at the lowest level. The keep was not vaulted, but tunnel-vaulted chambers at two levels remain in the walls. Burnt accidentally in 1541, Pendragon was restored in 1660 by Lady Anne Clifford, to whom some of the internal openings are due (and perhaps also secondary causeway to the NW), but was dismantled by her grandson *c.* 1685. The interior is still piled high with grown-over rubble.

LAMMERSIDE CASTLE, 1⅜ m. NW, across the Eden. The square ruin of another defensive tower, but different from Pendragon in almost every way. Probably C14, it is the remnant of a bigger dwelling represented by nettle-grown foundations N and S. No ditch, but signs of enclosures. Its ground level is unusually complicated, with a cross-wall and large and small chambers vaulted in different directions. A passage went straight through the middle (cf. Burneside Hall, Wharton Hall, Preston Patrick Hall). Access to the upper floor was by a turning stair on the N from a presumed hall; a door-jamb here too. The S doorway actually belongs to that wing, not the tower; perhaps a kitchen. One large chamber above – now an alpine meadow over collapsing vaults – with a garderobe in the SW corner.

SCULPTURE, 2 m. S. Water Cut by *Mary Bourne*, 1996. The best of the Eden Benchmarks (*see* p. 75), set high up on the skyline at Hanging Lund Scar. Like a tombstone cloven in two. It is surprising how the serpentine cut tells from any distance and in any weather. A simple and powerful statement.

DALEFOOT, 1½ m. N by the cattle grid, incorporates a wide Norman arch presumably from Pendragon. On the barn end the top of a loop window.

BRIDGE across Fothergill Syke, Settle and Carlisle railway (N of Birkett Tunnel). A small but unusual double-decked bridge. A single slightly pointed arch supports a pair of segmental form. 1870s.

MANSERGH (W)

St Peter. 1879–80, replacing an earlier building. By *Paley & Austin* in their Late Perp style. Of dark limestone with thin sandstone bands. w tower with saddleback roof. The pretty wooden porch was added in 1903. Bare interior with a panelled barrel ceiling. The chancel is wainscoted with ashlar. – Large tub FONT. – STAINED GLASS. Re-set w window by *Lavers, Barraud & Westlake*, †1865. N, *Hardman*, †1878. – Fussy MONUMENT to Christopher Wilson †1845 in the tower; Gothic tablet, with a nodding ogee canopy. – SCHOOL. 1839.

RIGMADEN PARK. Wonderfully sited, severely Greek. By *Francis & George Webster*, 1825–8, for Christopher Wilson. Of finest buff ashlar, with corner pilasters, it has a grand porte cochère on the entrance side and a semicircular bow framed by tripartite and pedimented windows overlooking the valley. Wartime neglect led to the house being unroofed and gutted in 1948; then the line of the M6 was pegged out immediately below the ha-ha. In the event the M6 took a more westerly route, and in 1991–2 the family constructed a new house inside the shell and was able to move back. The architect was *Edward Mason*. Outside there is little change, save that the Websters' projected colonnade on the s front has been realized as a conservatory. The plan with its two cross-walls was largely reinstated, though the main staircase has been made smaller, allowing the morning room with its bow to be made larger. The extra part, marked off by an arch, forms a room-within-a-room. Three chimneypieces and three doors from the old house have been put back. The service wing on the N has gone, as has the conservatory (plans exist to rebuild). The billiard room of 1878 remains a ruin. Beyond that is the stable yard, now residential, and the walled garden. Down on the road is the HOME FARM, dated 1848.

Rigmaden was lit by hydro-electricity in 1882, just a year after the pioneering Cragside in Northumberland. The system still works.

MARDALE (W) *see* HAWESWATER

MARTINDALE (W)

St Peter. On the ridge, looking back down the wiggly road towards Ullswater, forward into the paradisical valley of Martindale. By *J. A. Cory*, 1880–2. Of local Hallin Fell stone contrasted with red dressings. A prim Victorian church sits uneasily here, but the interior shows originality. Narrow lancets throughout. They have emphatic rere-arches and wide splays, so wide that the two w ones fill the wall. Chancel with a bank of four N, but just one S, plus a recess for a massive parish chest. – STAINED GLASS. Apart from the grisaille E window, all by *Jane Gray*. Chancel N, three for the Jubilee, 1977. Chancel S, St Cecilia 1981, musical instruments only. Nave N, including HMS *Glorious*, 1975. Nave S, 1976 and 1979. They are without figure drawing, but often show a relevant church at the top. W, in the two tallest lancets, the Benedicite.

ST MARTIN, down in the valley, ¼ m. S. Rebuilt *c.* 1633. 'It differs little from a barne', said Machell, 'but a bell hanging at the west end of it'. Nave and chancel in one. Plain bellcote. Oblong windows. A remarkable survival. Interior of Quakerish simplicity. – PULPIT. 1634, with simple patterns on the panels. – Along the sides BENCHES, the ends of a plain, but unusual design, and PANELLING. – Plain COMMUNION TABLE dated EB 1674 without a rail. – The FONT could be a hollowed-out Roman altar.

FARMS scattered through the forked valley shelter each under a handy crag, or a clump of sycamores. Roofs, as simple as possible, run along the valley; the cross-ways orientation of St Martin is very noticeable. Many have a crowstepped gable at the windward end. Often the through passage or hallan between barn and house is retained, running behind the stack. Windows are set deep. The front door usually has a cheeked porch with lean-to roof. COTE HOW, poetically placed on the mountainside, was the Star Inn. THRANCRAG (modernized windows) makes a picturesque group under the great crag of that name. THE LODGE is on the bridle path to Sandwick. The end entry by the stack to the firehouse has been blocked, and a front door inserted instead. (Upper crucks.) DALEHEAD has a strong cheeked porch, the upwind cheek carried up to the upper floor. Hallan entry behind the stack, corridor behind the firehouse. A large room at the S end was added in the C18 for 'the yearly chace of red deer'. Many isolated BARNS, generally in good shape thanks to a DEFRA scheme, but ruined farms testify to the hardship of subsistence farming.

THE BUNGALOW, Dale Head. Built by the 'Yellow' Earl of Lonsdale in 1910 as a shooting lodge for the Kaiser. Of corrugated iron, painted green for the walls, red for the roof, with a veranda round three sides, lined inside with wood. Servants' accommodation is removed to a separate building below.

THE OLD VICARAGE, Boredale. The prettiest C18 white doll's house, with a triangular pediment over the door and low symmetrical wings.

MARYPORT (C) 0030

A valuable haven from Roman times. A settlement existed before the mid C18, but it became Maryport only when Humphrey Senhouse II, Lord of the Manor, named the village after his wife

and decided to develop it as a coal port. That was in 1748–9. By
1752 twenty-six 'colonists' had bought blocks of the grid. In 1754
an iron-smelting furnace by the river was blown in. *Sally*, the first
Maryport-built ship, was launched in 1765. By the late 1830s
almost 100,000 tons of coal were being shipped out per year.
Another Humphrey Senhouse promoted a railway to Carlisle in
1836, with *George Stephenson* as engineer. The line was complete
in 1845. But with its coal and iron worked out by the 1930s,
Maryport was the worst-hit of all West Cumbrian towns in the
Depression. It is still unnaturally quiet.

St Mary. The Senhouses' proprietary chapel of 1760, built
   outside the town grid near their mansion of Netherhall.
   Initially a two-storey box with an embraced w tower, like the
   first church at Whitehaven. Its datestone is set in the tower. Is
   the inner doorway *in situ*? It was lengthened and given
   transepts in 1837, and a new tower in 1847. This has high
   pinnacles, and its bell-openings as three stepped lancets. The
   nave was rebuilt with aisles in 1890–2 by *J. H. Martindale*. It is
   large and pretty plain, with a long blind storey. Red sandstone.
   – Font. A square baluster dated 1764. – Anachronistic royal
   arms of 1661, from St Michael, Appleby. – stained glass.
   Fine collection by *Heaton, Butler & Bayne*, 1891–1919. The e
   window of 1878 is by *Hardman*, and the two in the w walls are
   by *Atkinson Bros*.
Christchurch. Down by the harbour. 1872, by *Charles
   Eaglesfield*. Red sandstone, E.E., with a round apse, and a ne
   steeple with a band of portholes below the bell-louvres.
All Souls, Netherton. Big town church in the lancet style –
   even the circular window in the w gable is filled with lancets.
   Incomplete. The nave, by *C. J. Ferguson*, was 'yet to start' in
   1886. Chancel and s aisle (with *Harry Foxall*), 1899–1906.
   Little bellcote ne, where toothing and buttresses show a tower
   was intended. On the other side the yellow and red brick of
   the interior appears in the blanked-off arches of an unbuilt
   transept. Well-recessed nw entrance under a big arch and
   gable, hardly protruding.
St Mary and St Patrick (R.C.), Crosby Street. 1844. Nave
   with three tall w lancets, s aisle with stepped lancets in threes,
   both built right up to the pavement. Chancel hidden behind
   unfinished-looking accretions.
cemetery, on the Silloth Road. chapel, *c.* 1855 in the Norman
   style. By *Charles Eaglesfield*. The same design as his church at
   Ennerdale Bridge, except that a porte cochère has been
   incorporated by the ingenious expedient of leaving the w bay
   open under three arches.
Senhouse Roman Museum. On the cliff top immediately w
   of the fort. Built as a Naval Reserve training battery, 1885. Of
   red sandstone with generous white dressings from the
   Admiralty's Portland quarries. The semicircular tower in the
   centre is turned landwards rather than seawards, for effect
   rather than serious defence, with mock machicolations. The

Senhouses gave the land on condition that Lady Senhouse approved the design. The guns were in the low wings. The museum contains a quite exceptional collection of Roman altars, and architectural and religious sculpture and inscriptions, of local stone. The timber WATCH TOWER (*c.* 2001) – an evocation of the towers of the C2 defences here – is based loosely on examples depicted on contemporary reliefs.

ROMAN FORT. The square platform of the fort was much quarried for building stone in the C18 and C19 as the town expanded (*see also* Crosscanonby, St John Evangelist). Facing seaward, this Hadrianic fort (preceded by a timber fort and annexe, immediately SW) was the keystone of the coastal defences. It had a stone wall backed by a clay rampart, and three or four external ditches; angle bastions may have been added in the C4. The usual suite of internal buildings – central headquarters, commanding officer's house, and barracks – is known from antiquarian reports. An extensive civil settlement lies beneath the fields to the NE.

On the other side of the fort, at the very top of Camp Road, are CAMPHILL and PARKHILL, twin mansions built by *Charles Eaglesfield* for the Hine brothers who founded the Holme shipping line in 1873. They are an exact pair, each with an Osborne tower.

CASTLE, Castle Hill. Impressively sited small ringwork castle, above the mouth of the Ellen; internal rampart and external ditch, eroded on the SW. Probably overlying a tower in the Roman defensive scheme. C20 gun emplacement on the summit.

STATION. The principal station and headquarters of the Maryport & Carlisle Railway. All that is left is a signal box, and an archaic way of working the station with a single long platform to serve both up and down lines (cf. Cambridge).

HARBOUR. The tidal wharf along the river can be seen, and the wooden grid on which ships sat at low tide. Elizabeth Dock was made in 1857, Senhouse Dock in 1881–4. The iron LIGHTHOUSE was erected in 1846. The docks revived in the Second World War, but by the 1950s traffic had fallen to almost nothing. Final closure came in 1960. Efforts at regeneration include the AQUARIUM, 1997, a yacht basin in Senhouse dock, and housing along Elizabeth Dock started in 1989, called RITSON QUAY, by *Anthony Collier Associates*. On the pivot stone of a long-gone swing bridge is a nostalgic fisherman's SCULPTURE by *Colin Telfer*. DESTINATION MARYPORT, Irish Street, was under construction in 2008. A big public hall, for Allerdale Council. Project architect *Richard Dryell*, of *Capita DBS*. Wave roof, glass ends, portholes at the sides.

THE TOWN. The planned layout started with Senhouse Street, running down to the harbour, and Crosby Street and High Street crossing it at right angles towards the Roman fort. The Georgian grid developed from this, with a space left for

Fleming Square. The houses are individual and modest, conforming to a pleasant Cumbrian language of colourwashing with contrasting window surrounds. A bonded warehouse can be seen at the corner of John and Church streets; three bays, stone. In High Street No. 11 of 1832, with attached Greek Doric columns framing the doorway. No. 35 was the Athenaeum of 1855, of five bays with arched windows and an Ionic porch. At the corner of Senhouse Street is a former bank, four bays, in a cheerfully ignorant Italianate, with alternately blocked columns. Fleming Square is oblong, sloping, surfaced with cobbles.

With the coming of the railway the town extended towards the station, centred on Curzon Street, and the language changed. Now we see long, regular terraces in sombre red sandstone, usually rock-faced, fussy and mechanical at the same time, with the street names carved in the stone. The grid was maintained, however, with one obtuse angle introduced for Station Street. Senhouse Street links all three phases, from the pre-Georgian steep of Shipping Brow to the red sandstone Victorian terraces towards Curzon Street.

INDUSTRIAL REMAINS. Furnace Road leads s from the C18 town to the site of a major blast furnace, built under a lease of 1752 granted by Humphrey Senhouse to Whitehaven venturers who built a furnace of 200 cubic ft capacity, then the biggest in the country. In 1777 they equipped it with blowing cylinders, the latest technology, but chronic water shortage forced its closure in 1783. It stood complete until 1963, when the site was cleared in an act of extraordinary vandalism. The ruins remain of four of the seventeen coke ovens, high on the bank behind the Co-op supermarket.

NETHERHALL. The seat of the Senhouse family was abandoned in the 1960s. All that is left since demolition in 1979 is the ruinous pele tower. The ministry inspector found it 'a most unbelievable and ponderous heap, the result not of a complex history but of maniacal growth in the C19'. Their famous Roman collection, which seems to have been displayed under a long loggia, is now in the Senhouse Roman Museum (*see* p. 514). Ditto an achievement of arms carved by Mr *Smith* in 1726. (In the grounds, re-erected Ionic PORTICO from the first Wigton station of 1843.) The adjacent rugby club and Netherhall School have not added to its amenities.

EWANRIGG HALL, Ellenborough. Another sad remnant, in a patch of relict parkland. 'Mr Ewan Christian hath built a good house out of the shell of an old tower', recorded Denton in 1688; this was designed by *John Addison*. It was extended and fronted with ashlar in 1783 to make a fine house of seven bays and three storeys with three-bay wings, but in 1903 it was demolished to the level of its first-floor windows. The SW wing, with big blank super-arches, is still inhabited.

MATTERDALE (C)

CHURCH. Nave and chancel in one, domestic windows. On a tie-beam, 1573 in clumsily additive Roman numerals (no 'L'), and a set of initials including supposedly those of *Lancelot Pattinson*. 1573 is the date the church was licensed. Above the blocked priest's door a stone was found loose in 1848, inscribed IW churchwarden, CS mason and the date 1686. Absurdly small w tower of 1848 with a crowstepped roof set transversely. Very nice inside. Strong kingpost trusses, the ties markedly cambered, the slates back-pointed, not ceiled. Until 1848 it was thatched. Plain enclosure of seats to form the chancel. – ALTAR TABLE, C17. – COMMUNION RAIL also C17, a pen of stout balusters. – Two-decker PULPIT, C18. – BENCHES. Plain and pleasant, just with a knob on the corner of back and arm. – FONTS. A tiny baluster, and a stout octagonal one (re-tooled). – STAINED GLASS. E window with glass by *Kempe*, *c.* 1881.

LYULPH'S TOWER, 1¾ m. SE. One of the first Lakeland houses built for the view; a hunting lodge built, and probably designed, in 1780 by *Charles Howard*, future 11th Duke of Norfolk (*see* Greystoke). Castellated screen wall forming three sides of an octagon, like a fire-screen, with four polygonal (not all the same) towers, one at each angle. The shape makes the most of the fabulous views up, down, and across Ullswater. The windows are wide and round-arched, the glazing Gothick; 'Mere modern make-believe', wrote Eliza Linton (1860s), 'with glazed windows among the ivy and cucumber frames'. Construction is rough. Behind the screen a lean-to house runs round the three sides, comfortable and markedly informal. Narrow stairs at both ends climb up three sides. The sitting room is upstairs, with the best views. A Late Victorian extension, hip-roofed, is fitted in the centre, forced to partake of its steep angles. Both exterior and interior are confusing – it is easy to forget which facet of the octagon you are in, or which of the four towers this is.

The dramatic paths, steps and bridges of AIRA FORCE (to the NW) were initially laid out for Lyulph's Tower.

(COCKLEY MOOR, 1 m. WSW, above Dockray. A cottage with some Victorian and post-Victorian additions and further additions of 1938 by (*Sir*) *Leslie Martin* and *Sadie Speight*. An uncommonly sensitive blending of modern and old.)

MAULDS MEABURN (W)

Crosby Ravensworth

Handsome open-plan village, its houses and farms scattered over the greensward of a wide valley. A broad shallow BRIDGE is the centrepiece. No church. Islanded in the green, MEABURN LODGE. Small single-storey Gothic of *c.* 1850. ELIZABETH

COTTAGES, E side of the green. 1859. Treated as a formal row
with classical detail, e.g. central pedimented doorway.

MAULDS MEABURN HALL, at the N end of the village. The
house has known greatness, and fallen on hard times. It was
rebuilt in the C16 for the Vernons. As the seat of junior
Lowthers from 1602 or 1606 it saw improvement, but in 1750
Sir James ('wicked Jimmy') inherited Lowther itself. He pulled
down the S part of the centre, which was eventually rebuilt as
a temporary-looking single storey. This makes navigating and
understanding the house difficult. Tall wings projecting to the
E at both ends. The N wing is L-shaped, with three-light
mullioned-and-transomed windows upstairs, and a fine
dormer. A loop window surviving on the ground floor may
indicate its original defensive nature, and upstairs living. A
narrow stone stair climbs up beside the fireplace. The
inscription 1610 above the two segmental arches of the door
lintel probably gives us the date of the S wing. This has been
49   clumsily altered to 1676, which fits the stair, the house's great
feature (although accommodated in a poor lean-to to the W).
It climbs round a well, with bottle balusters, and ball finials
not round but slightly flattened and grooved, like bowls. The
newels are decorated with applied leaf garlands. The S front of
this wing is symmetrical l. and r. of a chimney-breast.

Walled GARDEN in front, with fine gatepiers and yews.
Bowling green S, with a raised perimeter walk and two
charming pavilions of c. 1700. One houses a multi-hole privy.
There was a formal garden at the back too. The high-walled
PARK rings the house on both sides of the road.

FLASS HOUSE. Picturesque mansion of 1851–3 in the Italianate
style by *G. J. J. Mair*, a pupil of Decimus Burton, for Lancelot
Dent (cf. Skirsgill at Penrith). The Dents, with Jardine
Matheson, controlled the opium trade. Of limestone and
render both limewashed white, giving it a ghostly appearance.
Emphatically off-centre, the essential Italianate tower. The
symmetrical garden front is set lower because of the river bank,
so the Doric porte cochère is halfway up the grand stair.
Pedimented wings with tripartite upper windows with an odd
extra semicircle above, suggesting a Venetian window.
Rectangular bays below, with the remains of an iron
conservatory. (Opulent interiors – scagliola, gilt, marble, cast
iron and fine plasterwork, done by *Gillows*. The scale is large –
a saloon 60 ft (18 metres) long and a hall 35 ft (11 metres)
high with a gallery. Chinese bedroom with C18 painted
wallpaper.) Well-watered Victorian garden with specimen trees,
shrubberies, ornamental bridges and tunnels.

MEALSGATE (C)

ALL HALLOWS, on the B5299 road. By *C. J. Ferguson*, 1896–9.
Low and solid W tower (like Ferguson's at Raughton Head and
Selside), out of which grows the S porch and a stair-turret

finishing with twin gables below the bell-stage. Long aisleless nave and chancel with single and grouped lancets. – BENCHES and FONT also by *Ferguson*, good and honest. – STAINED GLASS by *Powells*, 1913 (E), 1919 (N) and 1925 (W). – Spare FONT in the churchyard, dated 1833.

OLD ALL HALLOWS, 500 yds WSW of the A595/B5299 crossroads. A sad little remnant in a romantically overgrown churchyard overlooking Whitehall (*see* below). The chancel, with its plain arch less than 6 ft (1.8 metres) wide and tiny N lancet, is Norman. So by the looks of it was the demolished (1935) nave. SE chapel built by Lancelot Salkeld, 1587, but rebuilt in 1862 as a Moore mausoleum. Three excellent white marble MONUMENTS in the dust and dead leaves. George Moore, the original self-made man †1876, portrait bust by *John Adams-Acton* (as in Carlisle Cathedral). – Eliza, his first wife †1858, marvellously romantic rising-up figure in loose drapery. – Agnes, his second wife †1888, sensible profile medallion.

HARBY BROW, ⅞ m. SSE of the new church. Four-storey tower and attached farmhouse. The tower, said to have been built by Robert Highmore c. 1465, was restored c. 1861 for George Moore of Whitehall, and again in 1989. The tower is in an excellent state, lacking only its intermediate floors, roof and merlons. Vaulted basement through a renewed N doorway. SW doorway, pointed-headed – as they all are – to a left-handed spiral stair. First and second levels with fireplaces, garderobes and paired cusped lights on two sides. Stair and garderobes occupy equal cut-off corners, so that no projections are necessary; as at Hardrigg (Skelton), perhaps by the same mason. Original stone seats and hand basins. A blocked doorway by the first-floor fireplace goes through to a bedroom in the farmhouse, where there was probably a first-floor hall. The house is narrower and lower than its predecessors, which are indicated by roof-lines in the tower's N wall. Inside is preserved a little stone inscribed in inscrutable blackletter: 'Thys house was builded in the fourh yere of the ryne of Kyng Edwarde the sex [i.e. 1550/1] when a boushel of wete was at viiis a boushel of bere a nowbel malt iiiis st. more'. Another displaced stone says F.1594.H. The porch is inscribed THE BLESSING OF THE LORD IT MAKETH RICH G.A.M. [George Moore] THIS PORCH WAS BUILT AD 1876.

WHITEHALL, ¾ m. SE. A peculiar tower house probably C15, partly three-storey, partly two. A defaced stone inscribed 1589 with the Salkeld arms is on the lower section. George Moore, who was born close by, bought it in 1858, and had *Salvin* transform it into a mansion from 1862. Here he was at his best, 'frisking on my own soil'. The house, we are told, was nearly always full, one party succeeding another. Salvin's additions have been demolished again (1951), leaving the ground-floor walls as a garden feature. Salvin re-windowed the tower in typical fashion, leaving few original features. Whitehall does not seem to fall into the usual hall-plus-tower pattern. The higher and lower parts were clearly built as one, with equally thick walling. It may be that it was closer to a bastle, with first-

floor entry as shown in Bland's C19 drawing, and that the
N part was later raised to a tower. Moore's GARDENS were
by *Nesfield*. *Salvin*'s STABLE dated 1861 remains, now a
restaurant, and so does his LODGE. The gatepiers are
characteristically inscribed:

> MAY PLENTY AND GRACE
> ABIDE IN THIS PLACE
> LET TRUTH BE OUR GUIDE
> FAITH BE OUR STAFF.

STATION. Of *c.* 1866, showing the ambition of the Maryport &
Carlisle Railway. Disused, but well preserved. On the bridge
the GEORGE MOORE MEMORIAL HALL, 1879.
BLENNERHASSET. *See* Aspatria.

MEATHOP (W)

4080

An island in the marshes, now flat fields. By the causeway that
connects it with the mainland is MEATHOP HALL. Late C17.
Main house of four bays with three dormers and round
chimneys. The dormer windows are graded triplets, the middle
rising higher. Their gables have early C19 fancy bargeboards.
Windows mullioned on the first floor, mullioned-and-
transomed below. Doorcase with moulded lintel of the type
generally called 'Yorkshire'. Cottages added at both ends, both
with substantial porches, the r. one with fat round chimneys.

MELMERBY (C)

6030

ST JOHN BAPTIST. Restored 1848 and 1895. The lopsided
position of its E window shows that the nave and a N aisle have
been thrown into one under a high overall roof. Nave and
chancel, if the windows represent what was there before, are a
rarish example of Cumbrian Dec, with a continuous sill course
and diagonal buttresses. But there is also an odd blocked
window, small and set high on the S side. Two more of the
same, but glazed, on the N. Nothing is left of the N arcade but
a single compartment at the E end, with a steep twice-
chamfered arch to the chancel. An uncomfortably thin,
unmoulded chancel arch has been thrown across. The NW
tower, a poor effort of 1848 with a higher stair-turret, has a
high-level doorway into the nave. The high windows and upper
tower door may be relics of a defensive phase.
MELMERBY HALL. Austere C18 front of three storeys, five bays,
with an older wing with some mullioned-and-transomed
windows behind. Dates in the wing 1658 with Threlkeld arms,

1794 on rainwater hoppers of the added top floor, and 1660 in plaster within. The main block is T-shaped, the stair as usual being in a rear projection; three balusters per tread. Underneath apparently a pair of barrel-vaulted cellars.

The VILLAGE is grouped round a broad green, with stream and trees. The former Post Office, with segmental-hooded doorcase, and the Shepherds Inn with triangular pediment over the door form a typically Cumbrian group, well spaced and amply proportioned. The Village Bakery, founded in 1976, occupies a three-bay stuccoed house and its former barn, with a new bakery behind. The Clock House and Old School House have a clock tower between them.

MIDDLETON (W)   6080

HOLY GHOST. Datestones 1634 and 1772, but the present building is of 1878–9, by *C. J. Ferguson* for Margaret Elizabeth Moore of Grimeshill (which has been pulled down). Perp style, nave and chancel with a bellcote on the chancel arch. The curious E tracery was devised to incorporate *Wailes*'s STAINED GLASS, installed in the old church in 1862. The side lights and tracery added by *Lavers, Barraud & Westlake* in 1879 are not as good. All the other glass is by *Wailes* or *Wailes & Strang*. – Woodwork carved and plain by Mr *Martin* of Sedbergh, presumably including the PULPIT, READING DESK and LECTERN in Jacobean style.

MIDDLETON HALL, ⅞ m. NNE. The approach is forbidding. The house skulks behind a high curtain wall complete to the corbelled parapet, two guardroom windows peering out above the segmental gate arch. Through the arch can be glimpsed the otherwise undefended hall and cross-wings, probably late C14. The curtain originally enclosed a back courtyard as well, but is largely removed. The gatehouse itself is lost, but the scar can be seen as well as the two windows, trefoil-headed and cusped. The hall has lost most of its N service wing. The screens passage runs straight through in the way of the region, without doors, so more outside than in. Outer doorways pointed and moulded with headstopped dripmoulds and sunk quadrant mouldings. A run of three pointed and single-chamfered doorways on the N led to the lost buttery, kitchen corridor and pantry. Unlike the outer doorways these have all been fitted with doors. An elliptical-headed S doorway leads into the hall. The two-light hall windows are either transomed or have simple Perp tracery. Straight heads. Unusually, the hall has not acquired a second storey, though a few courses of smoother stone and the datestone 1647 indicate a flattening of the roof pitch. Fireplace and stack are inserted in front of the screens. Beamed ceiling (poor) of the hall C16 or C17. Bits of old stained glass in the tracery – sun, star, monogram MR, IHC. At the high (S) end of the hall a shouldered doorway leads to the stone solar stair, another to the parlour. This retains some panelling and a plain fireplace with the date 1670. Its windows are simply arched in threes. Lower and rougher C16 outer wings extend on the E into the rear courtyard, with trefoil-headed windows (perhaps *ex situ*) in their E ends. A former guest hall, now barn, fills the N corner of the front court. It has another trefoil-headed window (E) and a very large arched fireplace.

ROMAN MILESTONE, ¼ m. S, close to the Roman road down the Lune valley. Slender shaft inscribed MP LIII (53 miles, from Carlisle), unusually not naming an emperor; found nearby in 1836, as a contemporary inscription records.

MILBURN (W)

The village is clearly made – perhaps in the late C11 – and not grown, the houses and their barns lined up around a large rectangular green with a maypole. The little SCHOOL of 1851 encroaches at the top. The approach roads are managed to bring one in at each corner. They were walled up every winter for defence or livestock enclosure as recently as 1826. Houses in C18 and C19 dress stand behind low walls or railings.

ST CUTHBERT. The planning of the village did not include the church, which stands apart, its long narrow churchyard hemmed in by trees. Nave and chancel in one but with a break in the masonry. S aisle also in one, i.e. under the same roof. Traces of a W doorway and porch. Double bellcote dated 1894. The windows are of late C16 or C17 type, though those on the N side are new; perhaps there were originally none. The re-set S doorway is Late Norman, with a single order of colonnettes. In the W wall is a short re-set Norman piece with chip-carved saltire crosses (cf. Long Marton), and the chancel masonry is probably Norman too. But the S arcade of two bays is early C14, modelled on Appleby. Quatrefoil pier with fillets on the foils, double-chamfered arches. A third bay has been opened with just a flat joist. Small PISCINA, and another in the aisle. – PANELLING. Behind the altar; made from C18 pews. – ROYAL ARMS. Jolly sign-painter's art. – Tiny FONT on a baluster, turned in one piece. – STAINED GLASS. E and W windows by *Powells*, 1904. Three by the same interesting maker, *Marjorie Kemp*: a three-lighter, E end of the aisle, of 1934, and two in the S wall of 1930 and 1946. On the N a two-lighter by *Alex Haynes*, 2003. Nativity and Resurrection, with the WRNS insignia and a fell pony.

HOWGILL CASTLE. High up and remote on the Pennine shoulder. First impressions are of a three-storey mansion of the Wren era, H-shaped and symmetrical, but unusually dour and massive. This is because underneath the skin is a C14 fortified

mansion of brilliant planning and immense strength, fully
defensive in all its parts. The first stage in its transformation was
in the late C17, when it was made 'elligent and uniform'
for Edward Sandford by the Rev. *Thomas Machell* and *Edward
Addison*. A staircase extension was added at the back,
battlements and corner turrets were replaced with 'rails and
Ballisters', windows enlarged and given double transoms
curiously carved. In 1733 (rainwater hopper) it was altered
again. Now the windows were sashed, and the roof was
sprocketed out over the eaves, eliminating the parapets. Machell's
'Ionic Bellcony' was replaced by a demure segmental overdoor.

The ground-floor rooms are oppressed by the great
thickness of the walls. The tower basements, roughly tunnel-
vaulted, are particularly dungeon-like, though efforts have
been made to get light into the E tower kitchen. Machell's stair
rises broad and shallow, in three legs, with strongly modelled
dumb-bell balusters. The first-floor hall has a C17 fireplace of
grand size, with alternately blocked quoins at the angles and
fruit and foliage in relief. As you ascend and the wall thickness
steps back, from fully 11 ft (3.5 metres) at the base to 4 ft (1.2
metres) at the top, the house gets noticeably more cheerful, the
rooms more spacious.

The medieval circulation lurks, almost complete, behind
cupboard doors and flock wallpapers. The principal entry
was at the back, by-passing the ground floor, which was
presumably for storage, and ascending directly to the hall by
a long mural stair spectacularly arched over with ascending
trefoils. Its bottom end was severed by the C17 staircase, but
the top is complete, turning to enter the upper hall through a
wide C14 doorway. This must have been the low end therefore,
and the en suite W tower rooms buttery and pantry. Each has
a mural stair down to a vaulted cellar. From the solar in the E
tower another mural stair meanders down to the kitchen.
Upward progress, from the high end of the hall, is by another
long mural stair in the back wall parallel to the first but without
the stepped arches, to what was perhaps a great chamber on
the top floor. A spiral (the only one) climbs to the second floor
of the E tower and originally up to the leads. Fireplaces where
they survive are mid-C16, but the doorheads are earlier,
including at least one shouldered arch.

MILLOM (C)   *1080*

Medieval church and castle stand together on a low mountain
shoulder, looking down a couple of fields to the flatland where
the modern town is built.

HOLY TRINITY. A Late Norman foundation, see the N doorway
with one order of (C19) colonnettes and a manifoldly moulded
arch, one tiny chancel N window, and the plain re-set S

doorway. No tower, though the low arch in the w wall may have belonged to one. A s aisle was added in the early C13 – see the two round piers, octagonal abaci and scarcely pointed arches – and rebuilt in spectacular form about 1335. Flowing tracery in its s and w windows, the latter of an unusual vesica shape, reticulated tracery to the E (rebuilt 1955). Also C14 the E pier and w respond of the arcade. The church was subjected to a surprisingly drastic restoration in 1930, including rebuilding the chancel wider, by *Hicks & Charlewood* of Newcastle. Found then, and built into the NE corner of the chancel, is part of a CROSS-SHAFT with incised knotwork and a cable-edge, probably C10 or C11. Above it another fragment with a raised boss and central drilling, perhaps originally to take a 'jewel' of coloured stone, glass or paste. The aisle is very light thanks to the great windows whose sills are close to the floor. Both roofs are of rustic collar-beam type with wind-braces, some with rudimentary hammerbeams. Handsome WEST GALLERY of 1930. – COMMUNION RAILS. Partly of *c.* 1630. – BOX PEWS throughout. – (ROYAL ARMS. George I.) – STAINED GLASS. E window by *Clayton & Bell*. s aisle s by *Hugh Arnold*, given 1908, three archangels. More effective than the few other pieces is the entirely clear glazing of the renewed s aisle E window.

MONUMENTS. Sir John Hudleston †1484, sandstone tomb-chest with sculpted arms between buttresses on the sides. Worn top with a pattern of sinkings in the middle. – Richard Huddleston †1505 and his wife Elizabeth Dacre, alabaster tomb and effigies. The tomb-chest has the usual frontal angel weepers under ogee canopies, but on the long side at the feet of the angels kneel little daughters, on the one visible short side little sons. – Behind this and blocking one of the s windows Joseph Huddlestone †1700 and his wife †1714, with Ionic pilasters and a broken pediment. – Tablets in the chancel by *Fawcett* of Lancaster, *Franceys & Sons*, Liverpool and *Webster*, Kendal. – Also a beaten copper tablet to William Kewley †1907, perhaps by *Keswick School of Industrial Arts*.

MILLOM CASTLE. A peculiar complex, with a mighty tower house plonked in the courtyard of a much older fortified residence that was already oddly congested. The motte and ditch may go back to the granting of the manor in 1134. John de Hudleston, builder of the s aisle of the church, was in 1335 granted licence to crenellate; this is probably the date of most of the ruins, though the curtain may be older. The great tower filling the courtyard was built perhaps by Sir John Huddleston †1494. This is partly occupied as the farmhouse, with a modest kitchen extension to the w.

On the E is a fine pair of GATEPIERS, shown by Buck in 1739 as part of a formal garden. A flight of splayed steps leads up to the two-storey GATEHOUSE. This has lost its outer wall. To the N was the C14 HALL, identifiable by its large two-centred-arched windows with fragments of tracery and window seats. Two service doorways led to the KITCHEN on the NE corner. Fireplace and corner oven can be identified, and to the S a curious double row of small windows. S of the entry is what is interpreted as a detached GREAT CHAMBER. Entry doorway from the courtyard with a pretty ogee hoodmould into a lower storey with its own fireplace. This has its flue simply through the wall with a finial to the smoke-hole. The high upper room must have been a fine apartment, lit by big traceried windows N and E and warmed by a huge fireplace. The windows have round rere-arches. Wall passages link the upper chamber with the porch room and with the ruined section S of the pele. The GREAT TOWER is 50 ft (15 metres) square, with walls 7 ft (2 metres) thick. It has five storeys and is divided to its full height by a cross-wall running N–S. The ground level is vaulted in two parallel tunnel-vaults, reached from outside from the N. The original entrance was on the first floor from the E. There were here three, not two rooms. (The upper levels are interconnected by a spiral stair in the NE corner, and by an inserted C17 scale-and-plat stair, NW. The COURTROOM, probably the original Great Hall, is on the second floor, with a big fireplace with roll-moulded surround and Huddleston arms. The two rooms on this floor seem to have been connected originally by a passage in the S wall accessible through two small doors.) The parapets and corner turret shown by Buck in 1739 have gone, exposing paired hipped roofs. The surrounding park was dismantled in 1802.

The TOWN was officially inaugurated and named in 1866. The railway had arrived in 1850, and the first significant output of smelted iron from the rich haematite deposits of Hodbarrow was in 1862. Iron made Millom. Plans for a new town were hatched in 1865, though the best intentions were overtaken by its tumultuous growth. By 1876, from a standing start, the town's population was about 4,000, and in 1891 8,871.

ST GEORGE. The new town church, by *Paley & Austin*, 1874–7. A fine landmark with its crossing tower and recessed spire. Of red sandstone, markedly asymmetrical, with Geometrical tracery of varied patterns. A wide aisle and big transept for the organ on the N. The blank N transept wall has free tracery, including ogees. On the S only a low transept for the vestry, allowing (a typical Paley & Austin device) windows set low in the tower to light the crossing. Spacious ashlar-lined interior, visually stretched by the barrel ceiling and the lack of a S aisle. The tower arches frame the vista. The choir is under the tower. – FITTINGS. All *Paley & Austin* except the lectern. – STAINED GLASS. E window by *Heaton, Butler & Bayne*; also N, 1911. The equivalent on the S is by *Seward & Co.*, 1906. On the N a window commemorating Millom's unlikely poet Norman Nicholson (1914–87), of No. 14 St George's Terrace. It is by *Christine Boyce*, 2000. Deep blue and swirly, it includes a bee orchid, bloody cranesbill, Halley's Comet and the dazzle of the sea, as well as quotations.

BOER WAR MEMORIAL, 1905, outside the E end. Tall stone cross. Realistic running vine, E. Very fine dragon in a tremendous tangle but still eating its own tail, w. It is likely that, as Ruskin's cross at Coniston, it was carved by *H. T. Miles* to a design by *W. G. Collingwood*.

ST LUKE, Haverigg, 1¼ m. SW. In the lancet-and-buttress style typical of the 1840s, but the date is 1889–91, the architects *Settle & Farmer* of Ulverston. Of greenish-black sawn slate and red sandstone. No aisles, no tower, even the bellcote has been taken down. Five steeply graded lancets, w. Set-piece Victorian interior with pitch-pine benches and open scissor-braced roof. – STAINED GLASS. Highly successful w window by *Peter Strong*, 2002. Here is the life of the town that has fled. On the r. a heroic fisherman, hooking his great hands through the net, lively with fishes and rollicking billows. On the l. the sturdy miner, rope round his waist, lantern-flash behind. This side, all reddish haematite colours and claustrophobic vignettes, is especially effective.

OUR LADY AND ST JAMES (R.C.), Queen Street. By *H. V. Krolow* of Liverpool, 1888. Show front of red and green stone. The sides mix blue and yellow engineering brick with red, with lancets in pairs. Large plain interior with a small sanctuary under a semicircular arch.

STATION, Station Road. 1850. Of granite lump from Eskdale with red sandstone bands and dressings, as are all the stations between here and Seascale. On the triangle opposite, WAR MEMORIAL, 1925. Hexagonal steps, slim stone shaft. Round the base reliefs of soldier, sailor, airman. On top St Michael and the Devil. David Cross advises that the architect was *D. J. Brundrit* of Ulverston, the sculptor *Alec Miller* of Chipping Camden.

The TOWN PLAN was drawn up by *Wadham & Turner* of Barrow in 1865 or 1866. A plain grid, like Barrow. The streets are relatively wide, and there are no back-to-backs. Space for a market was left at the E end, between Market and Lonsdale streets, but the centripetal force of the station resulted in the laying out of MARKET SQUARE in about 1876 close to the new church. It has an air of the Wild West about it; grand façades, all in different materials, with nothing much behind them: MARKET HALL (1880), trying hard with its domed porch (cut down from the original tower and lantern) and Tudor symmetry, the former WEST COUNTY HOTEL on the N corner, three grand BANKS of the 1890s (the best one is now the Post Office), and round the corner the READING ROOM and LIBRARY (1882). MEMORIAL to the local industries by *Colin Telfer c.* 2000, of iron-ore dust and resin. A Hodbarrow miner pushes a real truck of ore; on the plinth a relief by *Will Todd* of a blast furnace, mine headgear and the lighthouse. Long regular terraces run straight out into slag banks, mostly now cleared away to leave lagoons and regenerating saltmarsh. In 1872–5 the Hodbarrow Iron Co. built houses of better standard at CONCRETE SQUARE at Haverigg (demolished), and in 1885–9 on Oxford and Surrey streets. Devonshire Road leads E to MILLOM PIER, just a piled edge facing the limitless sands. (On the shore at Haverigg a stone SCULPTURE, Escape to Light, by *Josefina de Vasconcellos*, 2003.)

INDUSTRIAL REMAINS. From Haverigg eastwards to Hodbarrow Point the curving sweep of a 2,290-yd (2,114-metre)-long SEA WALL by *James Mansergh* encloses a great lagoon, now given over to water sports and a nature reserve. The wall, constructed 1900–4, was the third attempt to keep the sea out of the Hodbarrow Iron Co.'s subsiding workings, which since 1873 had followed westwards a 60-ft (18-metre)-thick deposit of iron ore of remarkable purity. The second barrier, the last work of *Sir John Coode*, was a combination of concrete wall and puddle-clay embankment and lasted from 1888 to 1898. It can still be seen, rising above the waters of the lagoon, breached in the middle. The third wall is a broad composite of – from the landward side – a low bank of slag, a wide clay fill, a limestone rubble wall with a maximum height of 40 ft (12 metres), and a layer of tumbled 25-ton concrete blocks to break the force of the waves. It carries an iron LIGHTHOUSE, cast in the company's works and commissioned in 1905. The TOWER of the stone light of 1866 which it replaced stands near the E end of the inner barrier, close to the remains of the ENGINE HOUSES where two Cornish engines worked to pump the workings dry. The mine closed in 1968. The COMMODORE CLUB at Steel Green (N of the lagoon) was the Hodbarrow Mine office, now bar and restaurant. 1873. Probably by *Hornblower* of Liverpool.

(H.M. PRISON, HAVERIGG. Opened in 1967 in the Second World War hutment of R.A.F. Millom. New blocks 1996.)

GIANT'S GRAVE, a pair of slender STANDING STONES, ¼ m. NW of Kirksanton. 9 ft 10 in. and 7 ft 10 in. (3 and 2.4 metres) high; the NE one bears a cup-mark.

STONE CIRCLE, Swinside, 1¾ m. W of Duddon Bridge. An archetypal circle, 93 ft (28 metres) in diameter, of over fifty close-set stones; two additional 'portal' stones flank an entrance in the SE.

MILNTHORPE (W)
4080

A crossroads, an ill-defined market square, and a green encroached upon not least by the church. Until the Lancaster Canal came in 1819, Milnthorpe was the main port for Kendal and S Westmorland. The building of the viaduct to Arnside (q.v.) in the 1850s finally put paid to it. ST ANTHONY'S TOWER to the N, round and castellated, is Milnthorpe's landmark. It was built in 1832 by Henry Smithies of Bela Mill to celebrate the Reform Act.

ST THOMAS. 1835–7 by *George Webster*. Built of hard limestone with almost no detail. Windows and doors have an edge standing proud to facilitate limewashing, which would be an improvement. Lancets in tall narrow pairs. w tower, tall thin lancets in pairs, thin buttresses – i.e. of the Commissioners' type, though in fact for Mrs Thomasine Richardson (as was St Thomas, Kendal). The chancel is of 1883 by *Joseph Bintley*, in E.E. style with sandstone dress. Low church interior without a centre aisle, intended for 600 hearers. The w gallery has been removed, replaced in 1982 with a nasty subdividing wall the full height of the building. – STAINED GLASS. E window by *F. Burrow* of Milnthorpe, 1872. His workshop was at Sandside. He also did the nave s easternmost, 1885. Two in the sanctuary by *A. Burrow*, 1886 and 1890. Nave N by *Shrigley & Hunt*, 1898, and *Abbott & Co.*, 1928; nave s by *Heaton, Butler & Bayne*, 1879.

CHRIST THE KING (R.C.), Haverflatts Lane. By *Weightman & Bullen* of Liverpool, 1970 (job architect *Kevin Campbell*). A bunker! Blank rough limestone without windows, making an irregular seven-sided polygon. On top is an emphatic lid of green copper. Scoop-like entrance at the back with a descending roof, giving the feeling of going underground. Uncoordinated sacristies at the back, white-rendered. The interior is much better, though inadequately lit only by clerestory windows over the sacristies, by the *dalle-de-verre* Creation window by *Dom Charles Norris* of Buckfast Abbey, 1970, lighting the fluted concrete font, and by a glimmer of top light over the altar. White roughcast walls, boarded ceiling, dark slate floor. – SCULPTURE by *Adam Kossowski*: Christ the King at the entrance, Madonna and Child in the Lady Chapel. Stations of the Cross done by Kossowski as a continuous 29-ft (9-metre) frieze, the principals picked out in colour, the bystanders subfusc in green. The scenes rise and descend with the action.

The METHODIST CHURCH of 1904 on Beetham Road is by *J. F. Curwen*. Free Style, of rubble stone.

Two sets of ALMSHOUSES. TATTERSALL'S (St Anthony's) on the Kendal road, N, are by *J. Bintley* of Kendal, 1884. Six over-designed houses in an L, of grey limestone and yellow sandstone. Taller nurse's house in the angle with a Gothic oriel looking down the hill, and a raised inscription under an ogee canopy which grows out of the dripmould, cusped, crocketed, and with rosettes. BINDLOSS HOMES, off Main Street E of the centre, are of *c.* 1881. A single symmetrical block with a tall middle section. Arms over the top window, low verandas r. and l. Probably by *Eli Cox*, cf. Sleddall almshouses in Kendal.

BLUE ROW, the long terrace immediately N of the crossroads, was erected by the Milnthorpe Union Building Society in the 1840s. Of individual houses, HARMONY HALL, LABURNAM HOUSE and BELVEDERE form a nice group E of the church. Harmony was built *c.* 1795 by Joseph Fayrer, a sea captain. Ionic porch with a pediment, and fine sandstone ashlar. Three bays. Laburnam is lower, C19, with its roof hidden by a parapet. Of hammered limestone now painted, channelled on the ground floor. Belvedere was for a long time the vicarage.

Of hammered limestone with a side entry and a good deal of Webster detail. 400 yds from the bridge, BELA MILL. Three storeys and eight bays, built for twine and sacking but turned to comb manufacture in 1868. The 14-ft (4.5-metre) wheel survives. Converted to housing. The original little factory on the river brink was converted into a fishing house in 1951 by Percy Dobson. The mill-owner's house, BELA HOUSE of c. 1740, was kitted out at the same time with high-quality Georgian window and door surrounds, alcoves and fireplaces supplied by Crowther's of Syon Park. The house acquired a flat overdoor hood on console brackets and an iron-balustraded balcony. Up-to-the-minute for 1951 are the blue and green bathrooms, and the flat concrete-roofed extensions with *Crittall* windows.

The former WORKHOUSE by *Francis Webster*, 1815, is ⅓ m. E at Ackenthwaite. What is left is now called Ackenthwaite and Chelsea courts. Front range of four bays, a canted centre, and another four bays.

DALLAM TOWER, ⅞ m. WSW. A substantial, regular, gracious and symmetrical country house set in an undulating park with still waters, great trees and fallow deer – a typical English picture, but not a typical Westmorland one. The house rebuilt in 1720–5 by Daniel Wilson, as represented in a painting of 1812, is still recognizable: two storeys over a partly visible basement, seven even bays under a hipped roof with four dormers, single-storey wings. Typical of the date are the channelled pilaster-strips emphasizing the ends and the three centre bays, the tall sashed windows, and the door surrounds front and back with friezes pinched up in the centre. But in 1826 *George Webster* aggrandized the house, rendering the brick to imitate stonework, and adding a deep porch with four Doric columns and a pavilion in front of each wing – for a billiard room on one side and an ante-library and dining room on the other – and large outer pavilions with tall white cupolas. He also raised the grass bank to hide the basement completely, altering the proportions considerably. In the kitchen court, S, Webster inserted some of his Jacobean mullioned-and-transomed windows, but there are a couple of reused C17 ones in the basement at the other end. An old yew here shows the original ground level.

INTERIORS. The transverse corridors running between arched openings from the staircase are characteristic of the early C18, but many of the rooms were fitted out by *Webster*. The principal stair rising out of the entrance hall seems rather later than 1720; it is a wooden cantilever, with three slender mahogany balusters per tread. The treads and landing are surfaced with polished marquetry. The back stair too is quite fine, all four floors of it, of oak with two balusters per tread. (The drawing room of c. 1720–5 has pilasters and panelling, all very beautifully detailed; another room has enriched panelling of c. 1730–50. *Gillows* were employed. Also some *ex situ* C17 panelling.)

GARDENS. Along the garden front is a long terrace and an odd spur of raised ground, upon which is the curvaceous trefoil-plan ORANGERY backing onto to the stable yard. Of the Webster phase, it was supplied by *W. & D. Bailey* of Holborn, and looks amazingly modern. The extensive ROCK AND WATER GARDEN was laid out in the 1930s, probably by *Hayes* of Ambleside, but there are traces of a much older landscape represented, e.g. rows of old yews. The gateway to the WALLED GARDEN is dated 1683, still in the impure classical of the mid C17; perhaps the doorcase of an earlier house.

The beautiful rolling PARK lends the A6 road S of Milnthorpe unusual distinction, with the Tuscan-columned DEER SHELTER of *c.* 1851 above the river. – BRIDGE by *Francis Webster*, 1813. A single segmental arch takes the Arnside road over an artificially widened and still part of the River Bela. Not slender enough to be truly elegant. There is an older bridge too. – FARM OFFICES. Symmetrical group near the bridge, by *George Webster*.

SHORELINE BUSINESS PARK, Sandside, 1¼ m. E, commanding a wonderful prospect over the vast sands. By *Tom Mellor & Partners*, 2005. A striking building curved at the E end, buttressed over car parking below, with continuous windowing under the outflung roof. Wavy-line railings, a nice touch.

MORESBY (C)

In the messy coastal sprawl N of Whitehaven, the Baroque hall in its hollow, the blocky church above, and the bare promontory squared off for a Roman fort make a memorable picture.

ST BRIDGET. 1822–3; consecrated the same day as St John, Workington. By *George Crawford*. Embraced W tower with round bell-openings, nave of four bays. Two tiers of arched side windows. The tactful chancel with its Venetian E window and pediment was added in 1885–8 by *Joseph Bintley*; 'The present church is Italian, so I have grudgingly adopted this style.' (WEST GALLERY on cast-iron columns with Gothic spandrels. – ORGAN, LECTERN, PULPIT, COMMUNION TABLE all by *Bintley*; the pulpit made by *Arthur Simpson* of Kendal. – STAINED GLASS. *Heaton, Butler & Bayne* produced a plan for all twenty-seven windows, but only nine were executed, *c.* 1900–29. – MONUMENT. Mary Ann Benn †1843 by *Dunbar*. Grecian, with curtains, weeping willow and portrait medallion.) – In the churchyard the CHANCEL ARCH of the medieval church, with semicircular responds. – Former RECTORY also by *Bintley*.

Underlying the W half of the churchyard and extending to the W, overlooking the former inlet, the rectangular platform of the ROMAN FORT, part of the Hadrianic defences of the Cumbrian coast. Built between A.D. 128 and 138, occupied into the C4.

MORESBY HALL. The splendid façade, built for William Fletcher
c. 1670, is rusticated all over, as if it were in Bohemia. The
centre is emphasized but the ends run off into space, with the
rustication creating a ragged edge. Seven bays and three
storeys, faced in alternating bands of 'headers' and 'stretchers',
like English-bond brickwork. The fashion seems to have
emanated from Bishop Auckland, brought here by *William
Thackeray* and his partner and carpenter *James Swingler*. The
doorway has pilasters crossed by bands, fixed to them, as it
were, by lozenge-shaped nails (cf. Catterlen Hall at Newton
Reigny), and a broken segmental pediment. Nicholas Cooper
derives this from a design of 1631 by *Henryk de Keyser*, whose
grandson worked at Auckland. The windows have moulded
frames and are cross-mullioned, with double transoms for the
piano nobile, which has alternating triangular and segmental
pediments. The middle pediment is on brackets. The C17
rooms are ample and plain, with bolection-moulded fireplaces.
A plaster ceiling is retained in the E room, with a guilloche
pattern. The stair is in a rear wing. 6 ft (1.8 metres) wide, it
rises in gentle stages round an open well to the top of the
house. Balusters shaped like bottles upside-down. The
grandest room is in the centre of the *piano nobile*, lit by three
tall windows, with double doors into the end rooms.

Behind is an older house, U-shaped, with a massive stack at
the N end, mullioned-and-transomed windows, and the V-
arched door lintels characteristic of the 1550s. In its SW angle
a wide spiral stair. In the middle, between the two components,
is a tiny dark courtyard, almost filled by the 1670 stair-tower
and a glazed passage linking the C16 parts.

ROSE HILL, ¾ m. NE, is quite a distinguished late C18 house of
red stone. Bold convex front with fluted Doric porch *in antis*.
Circular vestibule, and a curved stair lit by a long window. Two
canted bay windows overlook the garden. – ROSEHILL
THEATRE, at a short distance. Clad in weatherboarding, it is
a C19 barn converted in 1959 for Sir Nicholas Sekers by *Gavin
Paterson & Son*. The theatre designed by *Oliver Messel* seats
200; a delightfully festive little space with pretend boxes. The
sign-painter's proscenium arch came from the Royal Standard
Hotel at Whitehaven.

MORLAND (W)　　5020

Large pink and grey village.

ST LAWRENCE. The only tower of Anglo-Saxon character in the
NW counties. Canon Gervase Markham attributes it to Siward,
Earl of Northumberland, between 1041 and his death in 1055,
though other authorities make it as late as 1120, when the

church was given to St Mary's Abbey, York. It is impressively sheer, with no buttresses or outer door and only tiny windows until we reach the belfry with its characteristically deep-set baluster mullions. A higher belfry was superimposed probably in 1588 (date of the bells), although there is little obvious break in the masonry. Yet later the pretty lead-covered spire. A blue clock face set very low on the w face completes the picture. Marks of a very steep roof upon its E face. Of the Norman church we have some lengths of zigzag, perhaps belonging to a chancel arch, above N transept and N aisle w windows. This church was extended by aisles in the late C12. The present building is cruciform, the transept ends E.E. of c. 1225, with deep-set double-chamfered lancets between strange stop-chamfered buttresses. Sitting uncomfortably above that a close-set pair of lancets similar to those of the s aisle. The s transept s windows at the lower level have dogtooth in the hoodmould. The s doorway with shafts and several rolls goes with the transepts. Nave and aisles are under one swooping roof. The N aisle was rebuilt in the C18. It has Georgian arched windows with keystones. The chancel was rebuilt in 1600, when the s chapel was removed, and has large four-light Perp windows, plain-arched under a square head and domestic in character. The church was restored in 1896 by *C. J. Ferguson* and, for the chancel, *W. D. Caröe.*

The s porch entrance of two continuous chamfers is *ex situ.* Four steps lead down to the interior, usually a sign of antiquity. Only the narrowest high doorway into the tower, another Anglo-Saxon feature, with no sign of a w door belonging to an earlier church, as are found at Long Marton and Ormside. The s arcade has round piers with octagonal abaci and double-chamfered pointed arches. The N arcade is the same but has one octagonal pier with a scalloped capital, and also the w respond with such a capital. So this probably came first. E responds of the characteristic lobed form with a fillet, *see also* e.g. Crosby Ravensworth. These were only provided c. 1225, when transepts were decided on. Elegant transept spaces; arches for E chapels, and an ogee – i.e. Dec – niche on the s transept. The chancel arch was rebuilt in E.E. style in 1896. The l. respond is waterleaf, the r. respond a plain moulded capital, both interfered with when the arch was widened. There is a one-bay N chapel whose standard details point to the C13. Such a chapel existed also E of the s transept. The chapel arch here is blocked.

FURNISHINGS. REREDOS by *Caröe,* 1926. – ALTAR RAIL. Late C17, with stout balusters. – Chapel SCREENS. Only the rails survive, with male heads and an angel bust. Late C14 or C15. – PULPIT. Cut down from a three-decker of 1721. – SCREEN to s transept chapel c. 1984, with a run of miniature balusters from a redundant pew, and springy ironwork. – POOR BOX, 1648, cut out of a log. – FONT and inscribed COVER 1662. Small; octagonal bowl. – (Tower LADDERS, 1660s.) – STAINED GLASS. Only one window, E, by *Powells,* 1926. – MONUMENTS.

(Brass to the Rev. John Blythe †1565, rediscovered 1896 and mounted on a hinged board because it is a palimpsest of an early C16 brass with an 11-in. (28-cm.) figure of a knight.) – Three C18 tablets in the chancel. – In the S transept a specially handsome late C13 coffin-lid with foliated cross.

In the churchyard, E, two fine cedars – sure sign of a gentleman parson.

MORLAND HOUSE, E of the church, on the Square. The vicarage was rebuilt by Thomas Warwick in the late C16, enlarged and gentrified at the end of the C18, and largely rebuilt into a gentleman's residence in 1871. After 1980 in addition the headquarters of the clothing company, Travelling Light. Every stage since 1828 has been in the hands of the Markham family; Gervase Markham (†2007) must have been one of the last squire parsons. The main rooms were kitted out in the 1880s with dark woodwork of many provenances and dates. The shop is in the Late Victorian stables, completely preserved. – GARDENS created by the Rev. John Jackson between 1773 and 1811, enlarged and elaborated in the 1870s. The W garden around the house is quite formal; a large artificial terrace with lawns and straight paths, old yews. Romantic steps lead down a riverside walk and, on the E side, the free-form quarry garden.

FORCE BRIDGE. 1680, widened 1878. It stands on a natural limestone cliff over which the river cascades as a force. Turbine.

HALL FARM faces the bridge on the E side. Large H-shaped, roughcast farmhouse, late C17 or early C18, with a mixture of mullioned and square sash windows. Rustic porch to the N. Converted to dwellings in 2005. (C18 stair with turned balusters, moulded strings and the handrail ramped up at the ends.)

At Byresteads, ¼ m. S, a set of double LIMEKILNS with low draw-holes.

NEWBY, ¾ m. SW, was new in the C12. It has shrunk since the Middle Ages. Single wide green with farmhouses and cottages on either side and the manor on high ground at the W.

NEWBY HALL. Set back behind a little formal walled garden with pollarded limes and C17 gatepiers. Over the side gate IEN (John and Elizabeth Nevinson) 1685. Over the door, sadly worn, the Nevinson arms. Mullioned windows in twos and threes with joined-up dripmoulds, i.e. characteristic of the late C16 rather than late C17. The house is U-shaped, i.e. with wings reaching forward but a flat back, apart from the outshut for a turning stair and a huge rough buttress against the W wing. The front is symmetrical, with a central entry, but there seems to be the outline of a doorway in the E angle, and the hall has a definite high end and low end. The great fireplace is at the high (W) end, with a family door to one side. Three unequal doors at the low end. One leads to a neat front parlour with bolection panelling, the centre and smallest via a narrow unheated room (called Jubilee) to a blocked outer doorway, the third to the stone stair at the back. Over the hall, which

has traces of painted imitation panelling, is the Great
Chamber. Over the E wing the solar. So the hall range and E
wing could function as one, and the W wing is either an
addition, perhaps when the house was made symmetrical, or
functioned as a separate dwelling. Over hall range and E wing
a high-quality roof with curved upper collars.

MOSSER (C)

1020

No village, but a series of large drive-through farms.

ST MICHAEL. Tiny fell chapel rebuilt in 1773. Nave and bellcote
with chancel. Plain oblong doorway, plain oblong windows,
given fancy glazing in tropical hardwood c. 2000. – (STAINED
GLASS. E window by *Joan Howson*.)

MUNCASTER (C)

1090

ST MICHAEL. Within the castle grounds. Low nave and lower
chancel. W bellcote, plus a Sanctus bellcote on the chancel
arch. The chancel windows look Late Perp, the nave windows
are plainly mullioned. Curious W window head with thin lines
of decoration in the spandrels. N side still roughcast, as the rest
evidently was. *Salvin* restored it in 1873, adding the Dec N
transept, and the battlements. He also made the handsome
Dec tracery partition between the annexe E of the transept and
the chancel. – STAINED GLASS. Mostly angelic. E window,
Passiontide, with cherubim in the tracery. W, a Doom, with an
avenging angel. Both by *Hardman*, 1870s. Chancel SE, the
Shepherds and the Heavenly Host, rather pale. Chancel N and
S, four more angels (1882) in hieratic pose with iridescent
wings. Nave S, two more (1887), still more gorgeous in colour.
All these by *Henry Holiday* for *Powells*. (In the vestry, a *Morris
& Co.* Virgin and Child by *Dearle*, c. 1928.) – MONUMENTS.
Numerous Pennington cartouches, the most splendid to Sir
Josslyn †1917. – The brass incriptions in a fake ancient script
were put up by John Pennington, 1st Lord Muncaster (†1813)
some time in the late C18. – Also bogus the inscribed slabs
stacked against the E wall outside, recollecting ancestors in the
imagined styles of the time.
    CROSS-SHAFT in the churchyard, C10–C11. Coarse, large-
scale interlace, including Dearham-style ring-chain on the W
side. Below, on all four sides, a Greek-key-like meander. A
broken wheel-head is in front.
    PARSONAGE, across the road. Now called The Chase. By
Salvin, 1872–4.

MUNCASTER CASTLE. In an excellent strategic position on a spur in the Esk estuary, and with beautifully landscaped gardens, including the famous Terrace Walk. Bulmer in 1901 called the castle a handsome modern structure. 'Modern' means *Salvin*, 1862–6 for the 4th and 1872–4 for the 5th lords Muncaster, followed in the 1880s by *C. J. Ferguson*. Salvin recast not the medieval pile but one already reconstructed in the late C18 by the 1st Lord. The medieval house consisted of a long range bordering the N terrace, and a thick-walled tower SE of it, of four storeys with a higher NW turret. It is not clear how or even if they were joined (cf. Isel, Irton). Thick spine walls at the back of the Hall and Drawing Room relate probably to a double piling of *c.* 1600, or to a probable 1670s phase involving *William Thackeray*. The 1st Lord Muncaster (†1813) Gothicked the house, covering it with smooth scored render embellished with sunk quatrefoils (as the stable wall still is), and perhaps with wooden traceries. Bits of quatrefoil decoration (not really tracery) in the top window heads of the tower may be a remnant. He built the double-height octagonal Library at the NE corner and a kitchen tower (now dated *c.* 1830) at the NW end, both of which survive, and an arched loggia or orangery facing S, which has gone. *Salvin* made the house altogether more serious. He gave the Library the semblance of a tower by squaring off the top and battlementing it, without altogether losing its octagonal shape. He added a service tower at the SW corner to answer the pele, and replaced the loggia with state rooms with mullioned-and-transomed windows. *Ferguson*'s external work is confined to the billiard room and part of the service court, but is extensive inside.

The castle is built of red granite, with red sandstone dressings. It is not easy to distinguish the phases, so thorough was the C19 work. Distinction can just be made between Salvin's crazy paving, intended to be seen, and the rougher coursing of the earlier masonry which was covered. On the other hand Salvin's punchy mouldings and diagonal tooling are easily told from the sensuous profiles and silky finish of Ferguson's work.

INTERIORS. Salvin's tiny ENTRANCE HALL shelters under a flying arch, turning away from the wind. Maximum impact in a small compass, claustrophobic after the great outdoor space. A boldly modelled fireplace, a two-bay rib-vault, armorial stained glass, black-and-white patterned tiles, leaving hardly enough space to turn round. The HALL is super-baronial, crammed with objects of virtu. The chimneypiece is dated 1864, with the 1917 arms of Ramsden over. It is lit principally by a large bay in the SW corner, with more armorial glass. Dark Continental panelling. Tantalizing glimpses of the stair through three little descending windows. Off to the S is the medieval TOWER. Its base storey has a segmental tunnel-vault, strengthened by chamfered cross-arches; these seem too weedy for Salvin. Could they be of the 1920s, when the Elizabethan stone chimneypiece, requiring extra height, was brought in by the

Ramsdens? Newel stair in the NW corner, and on the SE side the remains of another, starting higher up, which makes one suspect altered floor levels. Lord Muncaster's LIBRARY of 1780 was completely Salvinized in 1862. Even the wall surface is brought forward in front of the C18 plasterwork. Heightened as well perhaps, with a ribbed ceiling and a perfectly simple brass railing to the gallery. The DINING ROOM is a squarish C18 apartment with niches, mahogany doors and panelling. Salvin added the large bay, and may have raised the ceiling too, giving the room C19 rather than C18 proportions. Embossed leather wall covering. Passing the stair for now, Salvin's grand DRAWING ROOM has, as was customary, a more feminine ambience. Segmental plaster ceiling richly decorated. Superb late C18 white marble fireplace brought from Bulstrode (Bucks.), with figures of Diana and Apollo and a lintel with Apollo and the Nine Muses. Next a delightful little LOBBY, groin-vaulted with a mosaic floor, acts as a tobacco-resistant airlock to *Ferguson*'s BILLIARD ROOM, which replaced a jumble of small rooms in 1886. This is opulently fitted out in a rich Renaissance style, with different woods and tactile mouldings. Oblong skylight. A jib door in the N corner reveals the extensive SERVICE QUARTERS: bare, cream-painted, cool, with specialized rooms for everything and the strict segregation of the sexes advocated by Robert Kerr. The kitchen floor is dropped to give plenty of volume, well lit, with a battery of cooking alcoves. Sculleries, larders, and bakeries beyond with marble shelving supported on slate. A hidden spine corridor cuts back to the Hall, emerging through a Salvin entry cleverly altered by Ferguson to take a swing door.

Now for Salvin's PRINCIPAL STAIR, which is stony, with cross-arches, branching part-way up. The E branch rises further, above the state rooms, to a stone-flagged corridor resting on the thick wall between Hall and Dining Room. A hexagonal top-lit lobby gives access to the gallery of the Library, and to the private apartment in and around the Tower. The former solar of the Tower, with an oriel, is fitted with Arts and Crafts panelling with a dado of birds and animals. The other branch of the stair leads W to the RED CORRIDOR. This is an insertion, throwing the earlier bedroom fireplaces off-centre, except for the KING'S BEDROOM with its Jacobean panelling and chimneypiece. In the TAPESTRY ROOM an Elizabethan chimneypiece, said to be imported, with intricate strapwork and two tiers of caryatids and atlantes. Elizabethan and Jacobean fireplaces also in some other rooms. At the W end, around the kitchen tower, are more family apartments, fitted out by *Ferguson*, and partly opened up *c.* 1958. A neat stair lit by a shallow bow leads up to the top-floor nursery quarters. Beyond and still higher is a bewildering world of maids' rooms, ironing rooms and closets, and finally the leads, impressively renewed with English Heritage assistance in 1996.

SERVICE BUILDINGS, N. ICE HOUSE, by the back door, with a kennel on top. DAIRY, by the stableyard. Octagonal with a complicated spire roof. Slate shelving on sandstone. STABLE. C18 Gothick screen wall with blank circles, quatrefoils and cross-slits, preserving the style of the castle as it was before Salvin.

GARDEN. The site and subclimate are unsurpassed, maritime yet sheltered from the sea. A long rising TERRACE was made in the 1780s by the 1st Lord Muncaster, commanding the broad Esk valley and the receding heights beyond. A bridge leads to a second terrace, somewhat later but still before 1810. Two rustic SUMMERHOUSES, late C19. The Rhododendron collection was started in 1840; many have grown to great size. – Stone URN, more like a trophy cup, s of the house, in trees. Inscribed *Conjugi incomparabili* 1806, with a long poem, partly weathered away, in commemoration of the 1st Lord's wife Penelope.

The main GATE ARCH to the N, C18, is curiously two-faced. Fine buff sandstone ashlar within. Rusticated granite without, with *Coade*(?) stone medallions. The HOME FARM (NW) is C18 too. Symmetrical, of rusticated granite.

The three LODGES and SCHOOL are Victorian, by *Salvin* and then probably the local practice of *Banks*. The SCHOOL HOUSE (1876) is a charming piece of Victorian over-design, see the way the set-off jumps up and down, and the panelled chimney.

MONUMENT, ¾ m. NW. 1783. A dim tower in a forest green. It commemorates the meeting of Henry VI with the shepherd in 1461. Gothic, octagonal, of three stages both telescopic and slightly battered, and a blunt spire. Crudely built of rough stone, but structurally remarkable. Broad pointed doorway. The ground-floor chamber is niched in the angles and lit by a ring of oculi beneath a domed vault. The walls do not appear thick enough to resist its thrust; a ring of rust marks make one suspect hidden strengthening. The inaccessible second stage, with cross-slits, rests partly on the vault. The third stage pulls in again, with no direct support down to the ground. Over that, through the lancets and under the stone pile of the spire, can be glimpsed another dome.

MUNCASTER MILL, ⅛ m. NW, by the Ravenglass & Eskdale Railway. Rebuilt at least in part after a fire of 1801. A 13-ft (4-metre) diameter overshot wheel fed by a ¾ m. leat drove three pairs of stones until 2003. Now a house.

MUNGRISDALE (C)

3030

Right against the massy brown shoulder of the Blencathra/Skiddaw range, which opens out invitingly here and at Mosedale.

ST KENTIGERN. Of 1756 on a medieval site. Restored 1925. Whitewashed nave and chancel in one, with arched windows with keystones. Bellcote. Kingpost roof. – Low three-decker

PULPIT with graffiti of 1679 on one panel. Probably made up from pews when the church was rebuilt. – BOX PEWS, cut down.

At MOSEDALE, 1¼ m. NW, FRIENDS' MEETING HOUSE, 1702. Windowless to the lane. Two Doric columns support the roof where the wall was pushed out in the later C18. Interior fairly well preserved. Part used as tearoom. Walled BURIAL GROUND across the road.

THWAITE HALL, Mosedale. Small house of big rough stones, with a massive stack and tiny fire-window. End entry next to the stack. B & SM 95 (Benjamin and Sarah Mark, 1695) on a window of the side extension. Tiny byre in line at the other end. Next to it is MIDDLES FARM, quite a swagger five-bay house dated C & MM 1722 in the open segmental pediment over the door. Above that a round window with four keystones. Windows are cross-mullions, and the hall window on the l., as late as this, is bigger than the others. Space for a blocked fire-window at this end. Beyond that an extra half-bay and door indicates an end-entry plan, into the hall beside the stack. The traditional farm plan, in fact.

(SKIDDAW HOUSE (Youth Hostel), right in the middle of the massif at 1,550 ft (478 metres), 4 m. SW from Mosedale. Like a plain terrace of houses, grey roughcast, with three front doors. Built *c.* 1830 as a shooting lodge.)

MURTON (W)

ST JOHN, by the roadside on the way to Hilton. 1856, by *George Robinson*. Single cell with a porch. Flat-topped bellcote with four obelisk pinnacles. Narrow lancets, grouped into three E. Astonishingly, a triple-decker PULPIT near the middle of the N side. A niche in the wall to accommodate it shows that it belongs.

MURTON HALL, in the village. A gorgeous old house. The grandly scaled main section appears to be C17, with a commodious porch castellated with three shields on the lintel. To its r. the five-light transomed hall window. Three-light windows above, and a circular window in front of the stack. A low dairy wing, now demolished, came forward here. There is an upright oval window in the gable-end. However, the stack behind the round window sports a beautiful medieval chimney-top, octagonal with trefoil vents. The roof was apparently much steeper, suggesting that the upper floor is C17 but the range basically medieval. More medieval work in the lower link to the l. of the porch. First a lean-to stair projection and stack, then a magnificent Dec window head of three cusped ogee lights under a stepped hood with Musgrave arms and emblems. Thomas Bland in the 1840s drew this with long mullions, with a smaller trefoil-headed triplet above. When the

RCHME Investigator called in the 1930s it was a cowhouse door. Now it is filled with a wooden window. The Investigator reported an open kingpost roof over the upper floor of this section, with curved principal rafters and longitudinal braces to the ridge.

LYNDENE, a dull house at the village crossroads, shows with its massy C21 stone porch that inventive masoncraft is not yet dead, though its motifs are unwisely mixed.

(BRACKENBER HALL, 1½ m. S. Three-storey C17 house of five bays, each floor marked off by a drip course. Doorway with a Yorkshire lintel. Inside, a good stair with turned balusters and ball finials.)

INDUSTRIAL REMAINS. Records of lead mining in the Pennine escarpment above the village go back to the C14. From the 1820s Murton, like Dufton to the N, formed part of the London Lead Co. estates for fifty years. By 1930 all the mines had closed, and the mills were dismantled.

Upstream from Hilton Town head (E), the first substantial remains include foundations of an early C20 SMELTER on the l. bank of Hilton Beck, with associated leats and wheel pit and a collapsed 600-ft (185-metre) chimney. At the foot of Lowfield Hush is a complex of adits, ore bins, mill and ORE DRESSING AREAS, with wheel pit, leat, and a substantial limekiln. ¼ m. NE, under the crags of Amber Hill, is another stone-built wheel pit and the remains of what was probably a dressing mill and its settling ponds.

The principal mining and processing area was at the confluence of the Stow Gill and Great Augill with Scoredale Beck. Here are the remains of two MILLS each with its own wheel pit, the mine office, washing floors including round buddles, reservoirs and water courses, and half-a-dozen adits; also plentiful waste tips. From here a track or tramway formation contours back westwards on the r. side of the valley to at least two RESERVOIRS, which seem to be associated with early C19 hushing activities. Also a probable miners' lodging house, and a number of adits. This belvedere offers panoramic views of workings high in the crags on the S side of the valley.

MUSGRAVE (W)

ST THEOBALD. Prettily situated by the river and across a field. The church, not so pretty, was rebuilt in 1844–6 by *George Robinson* of Appleby. The old church appears to have been Norman. Thin W tower, nave and chancel in one, lancets and meagre buttresses. There is however a chancel arch inside, standing slightly E of the relevant buttress. – FONT. It looks *c.* 1662. – BRASS, inside the altar rail. Small (13½-in., 34-cm.) figure of Thomas Ouds †1502, priest, robed and albed, an inscription across his chasuble. – MONUMENT. Joseph

Collinson †1772 and his wife Agnes †1793 by *T. Joplin*. – Built into the E wall outside, a late C13 COFFIN-LID with foliated cross and sword. Sprigs emanate from one side of the cross stem.

BRIDGE. A fine flat two-archer.

NATLAND (W)

ST MARK. The continuing fertility of invention shown by late *Austin & Paley*, without departing from the canon of the English parish church, is astonishing. In 1908 they found *George Webster*'s church of 1825 seriously wanting: 'a very poor design'. The present church, of Lancaster sandstone, went up in 1909–10 – one of *Hubert Austin*'s last churches, and almost the last moment such a building was possible. It is Perp, with a sturdy W tower, nave and aisles, chancel and SE chapel. The tower is broadly buttressed below the belfry, but the taller stair-turret goes straight up from the ground – a piquant contrast. The S porch opens into the tower not the nave. On entering one is faced with an astoundingly fat and round pier, with arches dying into it. Its twin, the other tower pier, is built into the wall. There is an answering pair, not quite so fat, for the chancel arch, but the arcades between alternate round and octagonal. The idea may have come from the arcades of the mother church at Kendal. Their capitals have square flowers – a typical late Austin & Paley feature. Two-bay chancel arcades without capitals, taller on the N for the organ. The stonework inside and out is beautifully executed. Tie-beam nave and chancel roofs with kingposts and curved raking queenposts, under a semicircular ceiling. ALTAR RAIL, STALLS, PULPIT, PEWS and FONT all by the architects. – STAINED GLASS. E window, a Second World War memorial, by *E. R. Smith*, made by the *A. K. Nicholson* studio. Chapel E likewise, in memory of Adrian Sinker †1937, who is kneeling, with angels blowing trumpets on the Other Side. Millennium window, S, by *Sarah Sutton*, 2001: Adam lay y-bounden, with simplistic but emotional images. Keesey window by *Howard Martin* of *Celtic Studios*, Swansea, 1947, with battle scenes from both World Wars. – INSCRIPTION. Inset chancel N, dedication to William Dilworth Crewdson †1908.

HIGH HOUSE FARM, Helm Lane. L-shaped farmhouse with a sub-circular stair projection in the angle. Round-topped chimneys, deep-set mullioned windows. Firehouse and downhouse have their fireplaces back-to-back. TEW 1666 on the spice cupboard. Instead of a heck, a long corridor runs along the back of the house; perhaps a secondary arrangement. Half-turn stair of wood with a nice run of symmetrically turned balusters at the top. The upper corridor is lined with panelling, which also forms an internal porch and partition to the end bedroom. Another half-turn stair to the attic, which is lit at the end. Tie-beam trusses with raking queenposts. Close to the side door is a hennery-piggery: hens above, pigs below.

SPENCE HOUSE, Helm Lane. Trim little house by *Donald Haigh*, 1948, for Canon Edward Miller, builder of the church, on his retirement. White roughcast, green paintwork, metal windows with slate eyebrows, catslide roof.

SEDGWICK HOUSE, 1½ m. SSW. By *Paley & Austin*, 1868–9. Probably a Paley design. For W. H. Wakefield. Gothic, with a big square tower over the entrance and the spired clock tower on the stable block. It looks like a small lunatic asylum, especially at night when the huge illuminated face of the clock shines threateningly. Porte cochère, then a darkish lobby leading to a tremendous three-storey staircase hall at the heart of the house, lit by a clerestory and by dormers within the roof itself. The stair climbs in ponderous stages up one side, over the baronial fireplace in the centre (paired granite colonnettes and the inscription BE JUST AND FEAR NOT) and high up the other to gain an arcaded gallery over the entrance. Parkland with cast-iron rail in front. The elegant gateway belonging to the previous house (*Francis Webster* of 1810) is overgrown by the river bridge.

GUNPOWDER WORKS, S of the village. Opened in 1764 by John Wakefield, the Kendal banker, on the E bank of the River Kent, using the water race of an existing corn mill.* The New Sedgwick Works on the other side opened in 1858 and closed in the late 1920s. Much more survives here, now within a caravan park. The MANAGER'S HOUSE and WORKS OFFICE guarded the gates through which the finished gunpowder passed. The works stretched along the bank, each of the dozen or so stages taking water to power its machinery from the parallel leat (gunpowder works always cover a lot of ground, to keep materials and processes well separated to reduce the risk of explosion). Most of them can be traced in this now heavily wooded site. At the PREPARING HOUSE the ingredients (including charcoal from the surrounding coppice woods) were loosely mixed to produce a 'green charge'. The pairs of INCORPORATING MILLS combined this green charge under the pressure of great stone rollers; these are surrounded by substantial blast walls and banks. The PRESS HOUSES, with the even more dangerous job of pressing the 'ripe' charge into inch-thick cakes between copper plates, required more blast walls. Most dangerous of all was the CORNING HOUSE, where the cake was broken up into grains and sieved into the various grades of powder. At the GLAZE AND REEL HOUSE a 20-ft (6-metre) wheel drove wooden glazing drums which polished the grains with granite. Less specialized buildings were for

---

*Little remains of the Old Works, largely because of the Board of Trade's safety requirement that abandoned gunpowder establishments be dismantled and all the timbers burned.

cartridge making, packing and storage. Strong walls and flimsy roofs were the rule throughout, so that the force of any explosion would be directed upwards.

AQUEDUCT on the Lancaster Canal, 1¼ m. s at the village of Sedgwick. A substantial stone skew of 1819. John Rennie has been credited with the design, which resembles his now-replaced aqueduct which carried the canal over Bulk Road in Lancaster in 1796. But Rennie had in 1813 ceded his position to *Thomas Fletcher* for all works as construction moved northward, though it is plausible that his successor should have adopted much of his master's style. The curved retaining walls, the pilasters flanking the road arch and the arrangement of the two string courses and framed stone panel recall the portals Fletcher provided to the Hincaster Tunnel near Heversham. At the SE end of the aqueduct are four wheelwright's HOOPING STONES, used in fitting iron tyres to cart wheels. No doubt the canal water was handy for dousing the red-hot tyres when they were in place round the wooden rim.

OXENHOLME RAILWAY STATION, ¾ m. NW. The main Lancaster & Carlisle line opened in 1846, the Windermere branch a year later. Buildings in the mild Tudor style adopted for the L. & C. by *Sir W. Tite*, who at the time had the young *Thomas Worthington* working for him, completed in 1852 and extended in 1881. The branch-platform train shed was rebuilt in approximate replica, late C20.

Oxenholme VILLAGE is largely a railway creation. Five dwellings were attached to the station itself. Nearby are the twenty-five Helmside Cottages, brick, of 1885. Natland Terrace and Hill Place followed in 1897. The untidy bungalows were built as retirement homes, the railway houses being tied to the job.

CASTLESTEADS, ½ m. SE of Natland. Spectacularly sited small HILL-FORT on the s tip of a narrow ridge, The Helm. Two ramparts, a broad ditch and counterscarp bank on N; slighter s defences.

NAWORTH CASTLE (C)

Fortified seat of the Dacres, then Howards. 'A true specimen of ancient inconvenience', remarked Pennant, who saw Naworth in 1773 before it was burnt, 'with most frequent sudden ascents and descents into the bargain'. The castle lies low, but in a position of natural strength at the meeting of two narrow and deep ravines. It consists essentially of a massive quadrilateral curtain wall distorted by the geography, with the vulnerable SE wall across the isthmus strengthened by two ditches and two towers. Two detached buildings are on this side too, the Gatehouse and the so-called Bote House. Inside are buildings against three and originally all four sides.

The history of Naworth is marked by cycles of development and neglect. The Dacres had come to prominence in the Scottish wars when William Dacre of Dacre (†1269) was appointed Sherriff of Cumberland and Yorkshire. Naworth came to them in 1317 with the marriage of Margaret Multon to Ranulph, later Lord Dacre (†1339). He was granted licence to crenellate in 1335. Of this date probably the curtain and the lower part of the Dacre Tower projecting at the s corner. A blocked doorway with two-centred arch on the courtyard side of the SE range would also fit this date. The next development phase followed the dynastic marriage of Thomas Dacre (*see also* Askerton Castle) to Elizabeth of Greystoke in 1485, who brought with her Morpeth, Greystoke and the Yorkshire estate of the future Castle Howard. This phase is characterized by the grid-like Perp windows facing the courtyard. By 1588 all was in decay again, but in 1604 Lord William Howard came into possession; the third son of the Duke of Norfolk and 'a singular lover of venerable antiquitie, and learned withall', who had married the Dacre heiress. He refurbished the place with an antiquarian eye, bringing in materials from Kirkoswald Castle to the tower at the NE corner that bears his name. Naworth was deserted for Castle Howard in the C18 and early C19, and in 1844 fire swept through. *Salvin*, inevitably, was called in by the 6th Earl of Carlisle to make good. This he did in 1844–51, adding the Morpeth Tower (for bedrooms) to the outer side of the NE wing. In the late C19 the artist the Hon. George Howard, later 9th Earl of Carlisle, and his redoubtable wife Rosalind (née Stanley, of Alderley) decided to make Naworth their home. *Philip Webb* worked with them in 1874–9, as he did at their London house, at Lanercost and in Brampton, but a disagreement led to his handing over to *C. J. Ferguson*, who was in sympathy with both parties. Ferguson's major creation was the Stanley wing on the W side, but this has been removed. More neglect followed, but the Hon. Philip Howard has taken the castle in hand again. The family lives in the entrance wing, on the SE.

The GATEHOUSE s of the s front is tunnel-vaulted over a widely splayed carriageway. Dacre arms over. They and the whole building are much renewed. The early C16 BOTE HOUSE (bote = fuel) to the NE is a strange building, free-standing in front of the curtain and jutting into the former ditch. Square and crenellated, with the Dacre initials in the top frieze. Both buildings were probably once part of a walled forecourt. The Bote House was converted to a studio for George Howard by *Philip Webb* in the 1870s. The medieval fabric, following newly formulated SPAB principles, was not touched. Webb got extra light in by inserting a skylight and glazing an upper doorway, and heated it by a stove and external flue. Now it is a garage.

The ENTRANCE through the SE range is defended by the largest of Naworth's three iron yatts, i.e. a gate or door of iron bars, here retaining its wooden infilling. It leads through a tunnel-vaulted passage to the COURTYARD.

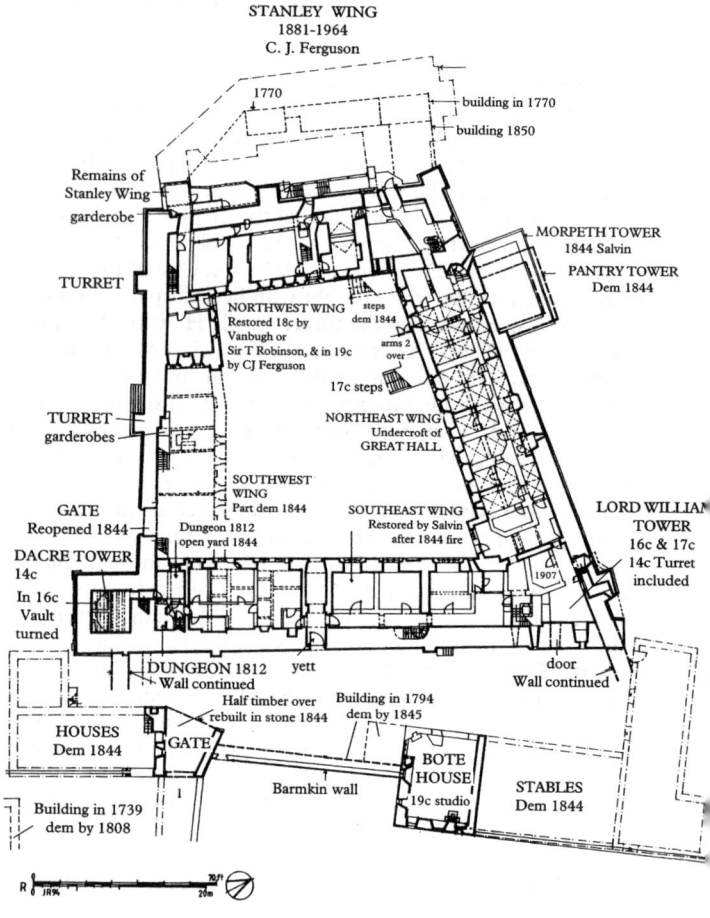

STANLEY WING
1881-1964
C. J. Ferguson

1770

building in 1770

building 1850

Remains of
Stanley Wing
garderobe

TURRET

NORTHWEST WING
Restored 18c by
Vanbugh or
Sir T Robinson, & in 19c
by CJ Ferguson

steps
dem 1844

arms 2
over

17c steps

TURRET
garderobes

NORTHEAST WING
Undercroft of
GREAT HALL

SOUTHWEST
WING
Part dem 1844

GATE
Reopened 1844

Dungeon 1812
open yard 1844

SOUTHEAST WING
Restored by Salvin
after 1844 fire

DACRE TOWER
14c

In 16c
Vault
turned

MORPETH TOWER
1844 Salvin

PANTRY TOWER
Dem 1844

LORD WILLIAM
TOWER
16c & 17c
14c Turret
included

1907

DUNGEON 1812
Wall continued

yett

door
Wall continued

Half timber over
rebuilt in stone 1844

Building in 1794
dem by 1845

HOUSES
Dem 1844

GATE

1

Barmkin wall

BOTE
HOUSE

19c studio

STABLES
Dem 1844

Building in 1739
dem by 1808

Naworth Castle.
Plan, 1998

The HALL RANGE is on the r. The high-table bay window of the
Great Hall – the largest window to the courtyard – has close
panel tracery of *c.* 1515–25. Great halls, in the sense of a
baronial apartment open to the roof, are not common survivals
in Cumbria. This at 78 ft by 24 ft (24 by 7.5 metres) is much
the largest, uncomfortably so in fact, and very empty without
its furnishings.★ Large fireplace with segmental head. The roof
is by *Salvin*, replacing one of Lord William's importations from
Kirkoswald, which was painted, like the Deanery ceiling at
Carlisle. Behind it, outside the curtain, is the MORPETH

★Three early C16 figures, the four heraldic Dacre Beasts of *c.* 1520 probably from
Kirkoswald, and the tapestries were sold in 1999 and 2000.

TOWER added by *Salvin*. Oak staircase by Salvin with a top section by *Webb*.

The NORTH-WEST RANGE, facing the entrance arch, may partly be the work of *Sir Thomas Robinson*.* The prominent clock was installed by *Webb* in the 1870s. It is uninhabited, stripped of plaster and much of the timber. Two or three staircases of different dates remain. A full-height KITCHEN adjoins the N end of the Hall. A doorway knocked through the ancient curtain by George Howard in 1879 to the proposed new Stanley wing without Webb's leave was the cause of their estrangement. The wing was built by *C. J. Ferguson*, but has been expunged again, leaving an extraordinary, little-seen elevation outside: a covered stairway rises over graded arches, next to an utterly incongruous bit of timber framing.

SOUTH-WEST RANGE. The Parapet Room, balanced on top of the mid-turret and garderobe projection of the curtain wall, is a *Webb* creation of 1877–8 for Rosalind Howard. A suicidal walkway continues across a section of plain wall, over an entrance arch opened in 1844. The walkway leads to the DACRE TOWER. This has a taller stair-turret in one corner, from early C16 heightening. A sculpted armed man threatens from its topmost point, an iron yatt (missing its woodwork) defends the bottom. The basement chamber has a vault strengthened by ribs square in section, as at Greystoke and, as we shall see, in the Lord William Howard Tower.

LORD WILLIAM HOWARD TOWER, at the NE angle, has to this side a strange mid-recess and corbelling-out inside it. There is also a garderobe higher up. The top masonry of the tower is different and may be a renewal of Lord William's. *Salvin* inserted a square stone stair rising around a dumb-waiter in a stone cage. The curtain wall is full of mural passages; a cupboard door in a window recess of the small kitchen on the first floor reveals one disappearing into the distance at waist height, showing that floor levels have been changed. The spectacular vault is strengthened by big, broad vault ribs, square in section and set diagonally across. The device is more logical than it appears, bridging the acute angle of the outer walls. This and an iron yatt, with its woodwork complete, saved the top storeys from the 1844 fire. A stone spiral stair leads up to the STUDY and CHAPEL, both very irregular in shape. The study is capped with a magnificent C14 camber-beam roof brought by Lord William from Kirkoswald Castle. It has richly moulded beams and bosses, and the panels are decorated with blank flowing tracery. In the chapel a PAINTING on boards, again fitting the wall, and representing the Flagellation, Crucifixion and Resurrection. It is dated 1514, the year after the Battle of Flodden. Possibly it was the high altarpiece at Lanercost; presumably a thank-offering for the victory. (Also parts of a very rich SCREEN probably from Lanercost, with crocketed ogee panels.)

---

*He took away a number of Roman altars to his seat at Rokeby, Yorkshire (North Riding).

FAMILY (SE) RANGE. In this range was the chapel (later library) and other rooms. The chapel windows to the courtyard are much larger than any of the others. Close panel tracery here, as in the bay window of the Great Hall. The apartments have been made pleasant and bright, though there is always a sense of redundant spaces walled off out of sight. The double-storey LIBRARY was re-fitted by *Ferguson* in 1881 following *Webb*'s sketches. A gallery along the shelves disappears behind the cove of the chimney-breast to reappear on the other side. The overmantel relief of the Battle of Flodden Field, 1880–6, was modelled in gesso by *Sir Edgar Boehm* to a design by *Burne-Jones*, who then modified it before final painting.* The large and low KITCHEN for C21 living on the ground floor was made out of the billiard room. On the top floor is the LONG GALLERY, more a broad corridor lined with pictures than an apartment.

NAWORTH PARK STONEHOUSE. A fine bastle house of superior type of *c.* 1590, but roofless and falling down. Walls about 4 ft (1.2 metres) thick. Lower floor with slit windows, one still barred, the door in the N wall. The joists may have been covered with flags rather than floorboards. Comfortable upper floor with a large fireplace corbelled out on the N and a smaller one on the other side. The upper entrance seems to have been on the S. A kingpost roof was still there in the 1970s.

Nearby is DENTON FOOT (*see* Denton), another bastle; they often clustered in groups.

NEAR SAWREY (L) *see* SAWREY

NENTHEAD (C)

Bleak Pennine settlement in mining country (lead, zinc, silver, fluorspar, coal), and still bearing the scars. Forfeited by the Jacobite Earl of Derwentwater in 1715, the manor was given by the Crown to Greenwich Hospital, which retained a controlling interest until the mid C20. From 1745 until 1882 its agents were the Quaker-owned London Lead Co., in charge not only of mining and smelting but also of miners' welfare – better here than in most places – and of the building of the town. From 1896 to 1949 a smaller-scale operation was carried out by the Vielle Montaigne Co. of Liège. Mining activity ceased in 1965. The remaining mine buildings are preserved as a museum.

ST JOHN. Of 1845 by *Ignatius Bonomi & J. A. Cory*, restored 1905–7 by *Hicks & Charlewood*. The polygonal bell-turret must

---

*George Howard commissioned a 21-ft (6.3-metre) painting by Burne-Jones, The Sleep of King Arthur in Avalon, for this room (now at the Luis Ferré Foundation, Puerto Rico).

belong to 1845, the fenestration and flowing Dec tracery to
1907. (ALTAR RAIL. From the pre-Victorian church at Alston.)
Big bare churchyard.

METHODIST CHAPEL (former), 1873. Two storeys, with a
pattern of round-arched windows and twin entrances.
Methodism was strong here; Methodists now use the lead
company's WORKMEN'S READING ROOM of 1855–9.

PUMP. Under a diminutive fancy cast-iron canopy, with four
crocodiles at the top of its legs. Presented in 1877 and made
by *Geo. Smith*, Glasgow. Near-identical designs at Askam-in-
Furness and Dalton-in-Furness.

SCHOOL, now village hall, very prominent from the S. 1864,
symmetrical about a polygonal bow.

BUS GARAGE (Wright Bros). Built by the Vielle Montaigne Co.
in 1909 as a dressing mill. Distinctive building of brick in an
exposed metal frame, with roof of Belgian mansard shape and
a V-shaped skylight.

RAMPGILL MINE (North Pennines Heritage Trust), at the S end
of the village. Opened as a heritage centre in 1996. The 200-
acre site extends ½ m. up the valley of the Nent, where
consolidated and restored buildings illustrate C19 mine
processes.

The reception buildings occupy the MINE OFFICES of
1850–5, on the NE side of the walled courtyard. Museum and
exhibition spaces in the ENGINEERING WORKSHOPS
opposite. From here the path takes the visitor past the timber
yard and joinery workshops and the site of the crushing floors,
now occupied by demonstration models of hydraulic power, to
the still-impressive SMELT MILL area. Here is the ASSAY
HOUSE of 1833 and 1855, for ore-testing. A domestic-looking
façade: two storeys and four big-windowed bays in coursed
rubble, hipped flagstone roof. Surprisingly tall central
chimney, to carry away the fumes of the testing furnaces. The
house is blind on the other sides, built into the steep valley side
with a single door to the upper floor. Opposite, the BARRACKS,
also built into the hillside, though there are signs on the gable-
end that the upper storey is added or rebuilt. Slit windows for
ventilation on the ground floor. Latterly used as a lodging
house, but said to have been in origin a peat store; it may be
a survivor of the early stages of the smelting works erected by
Col. *George Liddell* in 1737 (might it have been a stable for the
pack ponies?). Nearby above the river bank, a small store or
SMITHY. The greatest area is occupied by the remains of the
SMELT MILL and ORE BINS, the most impressive structure the
sloping spine wall which supported the great flue which took
away the smoke and fumes of the ore hearths standing against
it. By the time the mill closed in 1896 there were six such
hearths, as well as reverberatory and refining furnaces and a
de-silvering house where silver was removed from the lead by
the Pattinson process, invented locally in 1833.

BIG WHEEL PIT, on the hillside above. Striking evidence of
the powerful 50-ft (15-metre)-diameter water wheel of the

fume condenser, devised in 1840 by *Joseph Stagg*, manager of the mill, in order to draw the furnace gases through condensing chambers.

Also accessible from the Heritage Centre is the capped head of the BREWERY SHAFT, 328 ft deep and 12 ft in diameter (101 and 4 metres).* The shaft seems to have been sunk in the early 1840s to connect with the NENT FORCE LEVEL or Nenthead Level (*see* Alston, p. 97).

The moors around Nenthead are riddled with old MINE WORKINGS, including DOWGANG HUSH, ¾ m. SW of Nenthead on the road to Garrigill (for the hushing process *see* Caldbeck, p. 213).

NENT HALL (hotel), 1½ m. NW. Italianate, with a tower, the initial W, date 1858, and motto SEMPER VIGILANS.

LOVELADY SHIELD, another hotel close by. Late C18/early C19, with a pretty ornamental BRIDGE.

HIGH LOVELADY SHIELD. Ruin, romantic now in decay, but a tramway track passing the front door from a mine exit to a spoil tip tells a story of hard graft. Small square tower, extended uphill and down, with an outshut at the back. Dated 1691 with a set of initials on a window lintel, 1720 on the outshut doorway. The upper floor with its small square windows appears to post-date the very steep roof-line (presumably indicating heather thatch) that is visible at the downhill end.

NETHER DENTON (C) *see* DENTON

3070

NETHERBY HALL (C)

Border stronghold of the Grahams until *c.* 1986, with a medieval tower and probable hall. In 1757 Dr Robert Graham found 'waterlogged acres almost treeless and unenclosed, poverty stricken tenentry, a derelict and antiquated mansion'. He galvanized the estate, extended and refurbished the house, and laid out a planned settlement at Longtown (q.v.). From the 1830s Sir James Graham extended the mansion further and romanticized it in the spirit of Scott and Lochinvar, though with curiously scant regard for his genuinely ancient tower. His architect was *William Burn*, whose plans went through several stages during 1833 without fully resolving the circulation of what was already a sprawling mass of buildings.

The enormously long red E side is composed – if that is the right word – of wildly assorted parts. Far r., detached, a toy clock tower, part of *Burn*'s work, with a pyramid roof. Next a harmless three-bay house, colourwashed, also detached. The main E FRONT starts with a three-bay servants' hall (MOOT

---

*The Vielle Montagne Co. installed a hydraulic compressed-air system in 1903–5.

HALL), very low-set. Then another three-bay section (GUN ROOM ENTRANCE), still small, but tricked out with every sort of Scottish baronial twiddle; *Burn*, no doubt. A three-bay C18 section follows, taller and very plain. Then a three-storey tower which is the C15 pele, though you would hardly know it. It is not the highest part, and Burn's refacing with the addition of a comical knight in a niche, an over-sized oriel, and corner tourelles have robbed it of any impression of authenticity. Next comes the overtopping entrance tower, octagonal, top-heavy, flat-roofed. Now the house falls away again in grand but weakly composed stages, to finish abruptly in a blank wall, where a plain three-bay range matching the one already noted has been demolished. These two alone gave some balance and sense of structure to the whole farrago.

The PARK FRONT to the W is calmer; mid-C18 (i.e. Dr Graham again) though tricked out by *Burn* with pediments interrupted by shields, alternately blocked pilasters etc. Five-bay centre, with canted projections at each end. Further low three-bay sections on either side, each with a central super-arch. On the N there follows a former orangery, now the kitchen, and then fairly derelict service accommodation. Burn's plan shows that there was a matching conservatory and court on the S. The odd thing is that the E ranges appear over the top of all this, with the same turrets, pepperpots and battlements on their rear elevations as on their fronts. So the house looks like two parallel ranges with a gap between, as is indeed partly the case.

INTERIORS. Entrance is into *Burn*'s hallway in the tower, circular with a patterned floor. The inner hall houses the C18 cantilever main stair, with tulip balusters. If we turn r. we walk through the medieval tower almost without noticing, because in 1937 Sir Fergus Graham bashed a corridor straight through its thick walls, subdividing the vaulted basement. Architect *H. J. Harding*. Burn had already proposed this in 1833. Back-to-back with the tower is the DINING ROOM, which overlooks the park from the northern of the canted bays. This is lined with Continental woodwork, with an overmantel dated 1681. Its S door reveals a suite of white-and-gold mid-C18 rooms *en enfilade*, all the more delightful for being unexpected. They run along the park front. The ANTE-ROOM has pedimented doorcases with egg-and-dart, mahogany doors, fireplace between two big arched alcoves. The DRAWING ROOM has richer doorcases with plenty of gilt, and a swirling Rococo ceiling also gilt. The MUSIC ROOM fills the southern canted bay, but is round, with deep alcoves to fill the corners, and curved doors. Beyond that the LIBRARY, with a coved ceiling with urn-and-triglyph frieze. The walls are articulated by very fine Corinthian pilasters, but pilasters and ceiling are evidently of two periods and do not go together. Behind the round room is *Burn*'s PRINCIPAL STAIR, cold and grand. His first proposal was for a central E entry where the old one had been, but pushed forward – in which case the C18 stair would have been demoted to secondary status. With the introduction of the entry tower leading straight to the C18 stair this one has little obvious purpose. We regain the E entrance through Burn's huge empty SALOON or Great Hall, with more Continental woodwork and a geometrically coffered ceiling.

At both ends of the house there is open space between the front and back ranges. On the S open indeed, a narrow yard with kennels; on the N what is called the Crystal Palace, iron and glass for the roof, an expanse of flags for the floor.

GARDENS. Dr Graham took advice from Mr Howard of Corby, but his efforts were spoiled by a giant irruption of the bog in 1771. Aeration by large flat round stones with blowholes in the middle was the solution. WALLED GARDEN, to the SE. The garden front offers a grand prospect down a sweep of parkland to the River Esk and Kirkandrews Tower and church (q.v.). An additional incident is provided by the COOP HOUSE on the river bank. Built between 1772 and 1782 as part of Dr Graham's improvements, overlooking salmon coops and a fish ladder. Gothick; a central bay-windowed room flanked by a pair of towers. Restored by the Landmark Trust in the 1990s.

The ruins of a ROMAN FORT, an outpost of Hadrian's Wall, were levelled after 1757 for Graham's new house. From c. A.D. 130 this was *Castra Exploratorum* – the 'Fort of the Scouts'.

NEWBIGGIN (W)

near Temple Sowerby

ST EDMUND. In the shadow of the hall (*see* below). Nave and chancel in one, with a bellcote. The shallow W buttresses indicate Norman work; the N wall is probably Norman in its masonry, the E end C14. Dec-style windows, the E window reticulated. The N chapel is Tudor. James Crackanthorpe rebuilt much of the rest in 1853–4: a new and higher roof, the S wall rebuilt, windows regularized. – C12 PILLAR PISCINA in the N chapel; a tiny bowl on a square pedestal shaped into eight colonnettes. – PAINTING, Psalm 121, on metal, like an enormous cartouche; Probably C19. – STAINED GLASS. E, in the tracery, C14 armorials set against fragments of figurative glass. – MONUMENTS. Arched niche in the S wall. By it a C14 grave-slab with sunburst cross. N chapel, two Crackanthorpe urns of alabaster, 1896 and 1913. By *A. Mackmurdo* of London.

The over-sized former RECTORY over the road looks mid-1850s too.

METHODIST (WESLEYAN) CHAPEL. 1880. Small, very Victorian. The essential style is that of the 1830s but entrance is now, as has become customary, on the gable-end. The round-arched windows have acquired dripmoulds, gables have pierced bargeboards and finials, ridges have decorative crests.

NEWBIGGIN HALL. Fortified and castellated border house of rosy red sandstone. It has five component parts. The formidable East Tower jutting forward with its corbelled-out corner turrets commands the driveway. Armed men of stone from the battlements (cf. Raby and Hylton castles in Co. Durham) are preserved inside. The West Tower is a rebuild of 1844 by *Salvin*. Between is the unimpressive hall range, many times altered. Attached at the back of the E tower is the smaller Jerusalem Tower; and sticking out from that, along the river bank, a high-quality drawing-room wing of 1890–1 by *C. J. Ferguson*. Although there are plenty of datable features and several datestones the house is difficult to understand. Walls, roofs and floor levels have skipped about over time, and datestones are usually in the wrong place.

Newbiggin was granted to Robert, Steward of Appleby, in the C12. It passed by marriage to the Crackanthorpe family in the C14. Christopher Crackanthorpe rebuilt the hall in 1533 (inscription now on the E tower). Documentary sources suggest *c.* 1460 for the Jerusalem Tower, but the doorways at this end are all of the flattened pointed form characteristic of the mid C16. In 1677 *William Thackeray* was working on the roof 'to be uncovered . . . to amend the timber and imediatly againe covered' for Richard Crackenthorpe. This may give us a date for the rejigging of the floor levels of the East Tower. A putative basement was filled in, and the flat lead roof replaced by a pitched one which half-buries the corner turrets. The tower looks squatter than it should because of the building-up of the terraced lawn around it. Early sashes remain on its E side. The W ones, overlooking the courtyard, were made to look older in the early C20.

The medieval hall is represented only by its roof scars and doorways in the cross-wing walls. The masonry suggests that the both towers were built around it rather than *vice versa*. In 1759 the back wall was rebuilt further out, and in 1796–7 an elegant dining room with curved end walls was inserted, capsule-like, at first-floor level. The front wall was moved to accommodate the principal stair. The C16 kingpost roof with curved raking queen-struts is still there; a painted timber ceiling dated 1539 was recorded in 1796 and again in 1844 but nothing is visible now. Down in the basement are three service doors (one emerging from behind a later fireplace). They represent presumably a ground-level hall and service cross-wing, although their mid-C16 form seems anachronistic, and their position overlapping the Jerusalem and East towers is hard to explain. A turning stair rises from the screens between the two, again with C16 doorways.

Diminutive *Salvin* BELL TOWER between W tower and church. STABLES and COACHHOUSE, POULTRY HOUSE-cum-

PIGGERY (quite an architectural piece), and WALLED GARDEN, all 1794–6.

NEWBIGGIN HALL (C) *see* CARLETON

NEWBIGGIN-ON-LUNE (W) *see* RAVENSTONEDALE

NEWBY (C) *see* WARWICK

NEWBY (W) *see* MORLAND

NEWBY BRIDGE (L)

BRIDGE. Labelled as 'New Bridge' on Saxton's map of 1577. Five segmental arches with massive cutwaters and triangular refuges. The outflow from Windermere is sometimes alarmingly impressive. With the SWAN HOTEL (C18, with a columned doorway), including its attractive wing of *c.* 1965, it makes a satisfying picture. For the TOWER on the hill *see* Finsthwaite.

LAKESIDE STATION. The Furness Railway's Lakeside branch opened in 1869, making possible their enormously popular circular tours by rail and steamer. There was a raised restaurant with orchestra and potted palms, iron and glass canopies to the platforms, railway offices and a tall clock tower. When the railway closed much of this was lost, although since 1973 the line has been partly reopened for steam trains. Surviving are the long curving platforms, a Furness Railway signal box, some minor buildings of yellow brick with red and black brick and red stone trim, and the upper-level café on iron stanchions minus its pretty hipped glass roof. It is proposed to rebuild the canopy over the platforms. An incongruous newcomer is the AQUARIUM OF THE LAKES clad in matching polychrome brick, by *Alan Rhodes*.

LAKESIDE HOTEL. A typical late C19 *Pattinson* job, large and joyless in black and green stone.

FELLFOOT. *Mawson* garden, but no house. A large plain villa of *c.* 1780 for Jeremiah Dixon of Leeds was demolished in 1907 by Mrs Hedley, but her intended rebuilding got no further than the foundations. However the miniature DOCKYARD constructed by Col. G. J. M. Ridehalgh of Manchester remains. He bought the property in 1859, and was joint founder of the (Royal) Windermere Sailing Club. The boathouses are castellated. Giant lumps of limestone pavement like elephant's teeth are used for their lintels and other decorative bits. GJMR 1869 over a fireplace, which has a balcony-like overmantel on monster iron brackets.

NEW HUTTON (W)   *5090*

St Stephen. By *George Webster* in inglorious mode, 1828–9. Brown roughcast box, with bald lancets, a thin w tower embraced, and a bare alcove of a chancel. – PULPIT and READING DESK of 1885. – STAINED GLASS. E windows by *H. Gustave Miller, c.* 1902. – MONUMENT also by *Webster,* Ralph Fisher †1837. With a Grecian sarcophagus. – Two sets of GATEPIERS sculpted by the wind, with iron hounds on top.

Old Parsonage, w. 1805. With a veranda on trellis iron supports.

(Strawberry Bank, ⅜ m. SW. Late C16 or early C17, with C18 additions. In a room over the fireplace a very fine stucco panel of the early C17 with a close pattern of leaves and grapes, probably by the artist of the ceiling at Blease Hall, Old Hutton.)

(Hill Top, 1 m. w. Bought by Ralph Fisher of Liverpool and extended for him *c.* 1820, work attributed to *Francis & George Webster.* New dining-room and drawing-room wings with tripartite windows, and presumably the tetrastyle porch. Hexagonal entrance hall.)

NEWLANDS (C)   *2020*

New in the C12, when Husaker or Uzzicar Tarn was drained. The valley, and the farm of Littletown, feature in Beatrix Potter's *Mrs Tiggy Winkle.* Littletown is no more than a large farm and a cluster of cottages, now rather spoilt.

CHURCH. At the head of the valley. Plain whitewashed box of 1843 with round-arched windows, updated but not spoiled in 1885. – PULPIT and READING DESK from a cut-down three-decker. – FONT. Tiny octagonal bowl with the LECTERN demountable on top; the stone stalk is dated 1843. – BOX PEW-ENDS against the walls. – ROYAL ARMS. 1737. – STAINED GLASS. War memorial by *Shrigley & Hunt c.* 1920. – SCHOOL-ROOM of 1877, attached w.

INDUSTRIAL REMAINS. 1¼ m. SE on the slopes of Cat Bells, traces of the C19 Yewthwaite LEAD MINE, including the main adit and fine cobbled ore-dressing floor. 1 m. S towards Dale Head, the Goldscope COPPER AND LEAD MINE of 1564 scars the NE end of Hindscarth's ridge. An important example of the work of the German miners invited by the Company of Mines

Royal to England (the name is a corruption of *Gottesgab*, 'God's Gift'). The mine shows as a great fan of lead-mining scree falling towards the intake wall. Two dark gashes above mark the copper veins worked by the Germans, before explosives were used in mines. At the foot of the upper gash is a splendid hand-chipped 'COFFIN LEVEL', broadest at shoulder height. At the foot of the lower gash is a wider opening, the GRAND LEVEL, displaying a rougher, more vertical face to the r., where the C16 coffin profile was enlarged in 1850 for lead mining. From the Grand Level entrance, a dry LEAT leads 250 yds (231 metres) S down to a dressing floor. This is the last stage in an extraordinary feat of C16 hydraulic engineering; for *Daniel Hochstetter* contrived to draw water from a dam on the other side of the ridge, leading it 1 m. N before turning it into a tunnel through the mountain to a 40-ft (12-metre) water shaft, where it fell into a wooden cistern. From there it could be released to drive a 22-ft (7-metre) water wheel housed in a hand-cut pit at the Grand Level, to pump the lowest levels of the mine some 200 ft (62 metres) below. The water drained out along the Grand Level and was used again at the dressing floor.

Goldscope ore went to a SMELTER established by 1613 in Stonycroft Gill, off the main Newlands valley at Stair, to the NW. The likely site has been largely destroyed, but a 300-yd (280-metre) flue remains, rising eastwards from ruins and slag banks at a point where a track along the flank of Rowling End crosses from the r. bank of the beck. The whole middle section of the gill from the main road up to the 1,000-ft (308-metre) contour is rich in mining remains, complicated and difficult to interpret.

NEWTON ARLOSH (C)

1050

In 1301 Edward I granted to the abbot of Holm Cultram the privilege of a weekly market at Skinburness (Silloth), but following storm damage the charter was transferred in 1304 to the planned settlement of Newton Arlosh. Bishop Halton authorized the abbot to build 'one chapel or church afresh', entrusting its cure and upkeep to the Abbey. 'As a new town, Arlosh is a disappointment. One ought not to think of Montpazier or even New Winchelsea' (Pevsner). Maps show the shape of a wide central green, but it has been encroached out of existence.

32   ST JOHN. Building may have started in 1303, before the charter was ratified. The church, though small, is formidably tough-looking. It is built of cobbles and a minimum of cut stone. The tower is effectively a pele, tunnel-vaulted on the ground floor, with thick walls, no external door, slit windows including a

ground-level w slit, and functional battlements. A taller turret is corbelled out on the s. The first-floor room has a fireplace and garderobe. The short nave (no chancel) looks like an attached domestic hall. It is also strongly defensive, the walls thick, the windows tiny, originally barred, and set high, the only door narrow. The tower base is open to the nave by a wide twice-chamfered arch. A doorway is cut into the tower at first-floor level.

With the dissolution of Holm Cultram the church fell into decay. In 1589 sheep lay in it, and it is not mentioned in Bishop Nicholson's visitation of 1703. In 1843 a restoration and reconstruction was undertaken by *Sara Losh* of Wreay (q.v.). She added a parallel nave to the N which is larger than the old building, but by being wider than long avoids intruding on the medieval picture from the s. The extension is an interesting work in its own right. Superb w doorway with two rings of mighty voussoirs absolutely flush and unmoulded, like those in Palma de Mallorca. The altar was in the e apse, which has a scalloped stone roof, as at Wreay. In 1894 *George Dale Oliver* spoilt the extension by turning it to the N, making the old fortified church into a narthex, the 1843 apse into a vestry, and inserting triple lancets at the N end over the new altar. The interior, still facing N, is a bit bleak. Pair of rams' heads from the 1843 work at the e end of the old church (shown on a plan of 1873 as a vestry). – FITTINGS are few, since *Sara Losh*'s bog-oak lectern was stolen. – FONT. Octagonal, with crocketed gables; battered. Probably c14.

NEWTON REIGNY (C)

ST JOHN. The steep-roofed chancel is a rebuild by *Ewan Christian*, 1876. Small-scale nave, aisles, bellcote, with exterior details of 1882 and 1892. The interior is late c12 to c13. First the s arcade: round piers, round abaci, and pointed arches with only slight chamfers. Then the chancel arch, and then the N arcade with octagonal piers and fully double-chamfered arches. Small fluted PISCINA under the NE respond. The roof is dated 1585 and signed by the carpenters, *John Atkinson* and *Henry Bemert*. – STAINED GLASS. Medallion in chancel s window by *Shrigley & Hunt*, 1963.

CATTERLEN HALL, ¼ m. N. L-shaped house of three visible components and one largely invisible. A small defensive tower at the N end, vaulted on its ground floor and with a spiral stair in the sw corner by its entrance. It is a late example, attributed by Curwen to William Vaux *c.* 1460. Most of the windows are straight-headed with cusped arches. Also one larger and later window (uncusped arches). The third floor with its square-headed fireplace may be a heightening. The door at the back at this level was perhaps for a wooden garderobe, supported on the adjacent corbels (w side). Next the hall range s of the tower, signed and dated Rowlande Vaux 1577 over the door. The round-headed mullioned windows are consistent with this date, as is the ingle fireplace, but the mural stair in the E wall suggests something older. Anthony Emery reports chamfered timber ceilings 'which explode in the parlour in a sophisticated ribbed structure of three bays with curved cross members'. The third and spectacular component is the banqueting hall wing projecting to the E from the S end, which was remodelled in 1657 by Christopher Richmond of Highhead to celebrate his marriage to Mabel Vaux. Sixteen broad steps lead up to the wild and gorgeous first-floor central doorway, its jambs with alternating raised bands fastened, as it were, by lozenge pegs (cf. Moresby Hall). Big console as a keystone and a radiating pattern filling the space between the arch and the dripmould. Over that a heraldic achievement between Ionic pilasters and cherub supporters, and finally a flattened pediment. The large windows plainly mullioned-and-transomed to l. and r. and at the back are probably c16. (Inside, two rich stone chimneypieces, the bigger one with enormous scroll supports. The detail of the lintels is much the same as that of a chimneypiece in the adjoining S corner room of the older range, and this is dated 1657. It has funny caryatids.) The hardly noticeable component is at the E end of this range – the vaulted basement and newel stair of what may have been a second tower. Its presence suggests a defensive enclosure with towers at opposite corners. Now a by-road goes through the yard, crossed by a BRIDGE dated 1856 to farm buildings on the other side.

NICHOLFOREST (C)

Close to the Scottish border. Not marked on maps; the name applies to the church and civil parish.

ST NICHOLAS. By *Alexander Graham*, 1866–7. Fiddly Victorian church on the Netherby estate, with a wooden flèche and wooden porch, both painted white. Rock-faced, with a patterned slate roof. The chancel ends in an apse. Plate and bar tracery, e.g. a plate-tracery W rose. – (STAINED GLASS all by *J. Scott & Son*. – MONUMENT. John Ewart †1871, with a portrait medallion.)

(SCHOOL, at Warwickisland, ¾ m. SW. 1870, also by *A. Graham*.)

STONEGARTHSIDE HALL, 3 m. NE. Lonely, fierce-looking seat of the Forsters, restored in 1969–70 by David Lockhart Smith and now let by the Vivat Trust. It bears a date 1682 on a kneeler and is probably all of that date, though there are some anomalies inside. The rough walling of the house incorporates many reused carved stones. The rear windows have all had bars. The house is wholly Scottish in character, the three storeys rising sheer from the cropped grass to crowstepped gables and false chimneys. Alternating quoins each with a scallop step, like e.g. Heriot's Hospital in Edinburgh. Its U-shape is made into a double pile by enclosing the courtyard with a high curtain wall with a doorway and windows, as at another Scottish prototype, Methven Castle (1664). Gothick battlements, sunk quatrefoils and ball obelisks on the screen wall. The courtyard was apparently lead-roofed until 1804, and is now roofed again, but its lower windows to the front are blocked, upper ones mere holes, so it is still not sure whether it is inside or out. Inside, a wide stony dog-leg staircase rises between solid walls to the full three storeys, and a bit more. At the top is a redundant half-flight and landing, possibly once leading to a belvedere. Blanked out fourth-floor windows in the gables, probably dating from when the house was converted to tenements in the C19. The garth is enclosed by walls and a ditch, partly filled. Fine BARN on the roadside.

(MONUMENT, 2 m. NE, s of Green Rigg. In memory of William Forster, a gamekeeper shot by a poacher in 1891. Signed *G. Hope*, Smithfield. Tall tapering sandstone obelisk, polished Dalbeattie granite base. Surrounded by railings.)

OLD HUTTON (W)   5080

ST JOHN BAPTIST. Rebuilt in 1873 by *Daniel Brade* or *Brade & Smales*. Small. Round apse, spirelet growing naughtily out of the s porch. Plate tracery. Few buttresses. Old Perp window reused in organ chamber. Big uncomplicated interior. – ALMSBOX. Late C17; a strong, classical baluster and a small bowl and lid on top. – STAINED GLASS. E window, a Second World War memorial by *Abbott & Co.*

(BLEASE HALL, ¾ m. NW. The house, built *c.* 1600 for Roger Bateman, cloth manufacturer, has lost its s wing. The two-storey hall bay has large mullioned-and-transomed windows of three-plus-three lights and one each round the corners (cf. Levens Hall). Inside, a fragmentary plaster ceiling with a large spiral with grapes and leaves. Restored 1985.)

ORMSIDE (W)   7010

ST JAMES. This little church with its humpy silhouette and wildly assorted windows is not going to yield its story easily. It straddles the flat summit of a pronounced circular mount, overlooking the Eden and a series of old river courses. Defensive w tower of about 1200 with flat clasping buttresses,

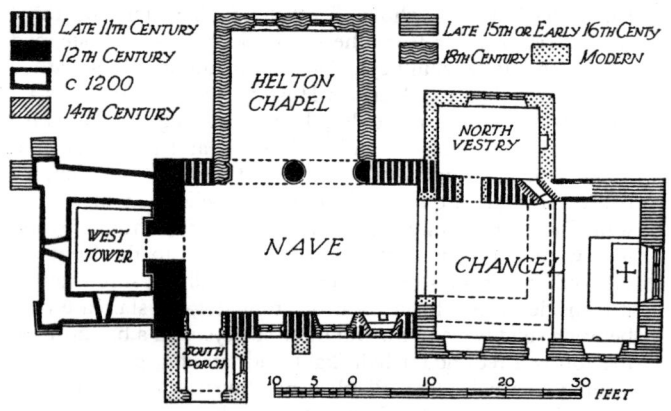

Ormside, St James.
Plan, 1936

windowless on the N but with three tiers of narrow lancets W and S; no external doorway. Its top has been shorn off and replaced by a pitched roof, but a few corbels of the parapet remain to E and W. It steps back halfway up. The nave and a small chancel were built in the late C11. Clearly of that date the blocked S doorway, tall and narrow, its round arch filled with a small blank tympanum on a big rough lintel carried on shouldered jambs. Its C19 replacement, in a rebuilt C16 or C17 porch, is immediately W. The W doorway to the tower is equally tall and narrow. From inside the tower the W wall can be seen to have been thickened on either side of it, presumably for a bellcote pre-dating the tower. There is an upper doorway into the tower as well, a defensive feature. The chancel was extended E and S in the early C16, making it wider than the nave. The window with ogee lights over the doorway must be re-set. On the N side are vestry and hearse house, and the Hilton Chapel of 1723 with silly C19 tracery inserted into round-headed windows. One of the S windows is of the same form, but with its sill dropped.

The two-bay N arcade of say *c*. 1140–50 shows that the Hilton Chapel replaced an aisle. The arches have one step only, the round pier and respond a square abacus. The capitals have scallops. Good C16 kingpost and raking queenpost roof to the chancel. Peter Ryder identifies the nave roof with its crown-posts and scissor-bracing as possibly medieval. C14 SQUINT, with trefoil head; PISCINA and AUMBRY in a double arch in the chancel. – FONT, a square bowl, Norman. – Hilton ARMS (chapel). 1723, coloured, with billowy feathers and a foolish face.

ORMSIDE HALL. Below and SE of the church. Gatepiers, cobbled yard with barns on either side, hall and SW cross-wing tower. The tower lost its parapet in 1811, but retains some fine

C14 features: two-light trefoil-headed windows for the first-floor solar, and for the second-floor bedchamber two-light cinquefoiled ones. A huge fireplace – unusual on the ground floor of a tower – backs onto the hall range, and great beams are carried on three-stage corbels; so no vault. If this was the kitchen it tells us that there was no matching service wing. The fireplace in the solar is on the opposite wall; this probably means that the ground-floor hearth is secondary, and there is a partly preserved acanthus frieze in plaster.

The BARN on the N side of the courtyard shows signs of domestic windows, but no obvious stack. If it was formerly a dwelling it can be compared with a similar set-up at Johnby Hall, Greystoke. The walled gardens are modern.

CROSS. Medieval. Just a square of steps falling away from a big sycamore tree.

VIADUCT, Settle and Carlisle railway. Prominent from the church, it seems unnecessarily high, with massive embankments. The railway is already making its great climb to get over the summit into Yorkshire. Former STATION and station-master's house, 1876. Solidly built to standard patterns, but in local stone.

ORTON (C)

3050

Also called Great Orton.

ST GILES. This gives a better idea of the small and primitive Norman churches of the Solway Plain than most. Nave with bellcote and chancel. The stout low walls of big rough stones are falling about under a long stone roof, and the way outer and inner skins are separating suggests a filling of not much more than loose stone in earth, as was recorded at the rebuilding of Aikton church. The excessive length is due to the addition of a school at the W end, possibly in the late C17. The change in the masonry is obvious, as are the blocked N and S doors. The faux-Norman N door and wooden porch go with a restoration of 1886. The E wall was rebuilt at the same time. Apart from the E lancets the windows are crudely arched and chamfered. Over the low-side window is a length of nailhead. The interior is charmingly informal and organic. Extremely wide splays to the furthest NE and SE lancets. Two massive and low trusses mark the chancel, with kingposts and raking queenposts. The position of the missing W wall is obvious. – PULPIT. Neo-Norman. Two sides only of stone arcading meeting at a little twisty support for a lectern. – FONT. Big and square, with a cute cover in the shape of a Romanesque tempietto with conical shingled roof. – STAINED GLASS. E window (†1857) by *Powell Bros* of Leeds. St Giles and the white deer, by *Millican, Baguley & Atkinson*, 1955.

The village is long, with bits of green. Several farms on the village street, gentrified or awaiting gentrification. At Baldwinholme, 1½ m. SW, was the cruck barn chosen for illustration by Pevsner. Now THE FARM is an awful lesson of the effect of C21 suburbanization. Only the farmhouse and a small wind-braced barn are left, daintily re-thatched with Home Counties eyebrow dormers. The farmhouse, which may have started as a genuine longhouse, is of clay construction and originally single-storey. Its cruck-trusses have yielded a dendro-date of c. 1575.

ORTON PARK, 2 m. SE. Unusual building of the 1830s for Sir Wastel Brisco. Garden side of five bays with giant pilasters throughout. On the entrance side the rhythm marked by giant pilasters is 2–3–2. Greek Doric porch of four columns. Cantilever stair with wrought-iron balusters. LODGE dated 1839.

TEMPEST TOWER at Little Orton, 1½ m. NE, makes quite a statement in this flat muddy country. Four-storey folly gatehouse of very mixed stone, attached to a harmless three-bay farmhouse of Carlisle Flemish-bond red and yellow brick. An inscription set between colonnettes dates the tower to 1875 and names its author, Ruth Sibson. Recessed columns flank the arch. Round-headed windows on each floor, trefoil-headed ones in the square turrets. Peculiar barely-projecting oriels on the farmhouse side. Two of the parapet corbels are carved as wolf-heads.

ORTON (W)

ALL SAINTS. Strong on horizontals. Blunt Perp w tower with diagonal buttresses with many set-offs, wide porch dated 1607, Late Perp windows, wide aisles and flat leads. *Paley & Austin*'s discordant steep-roofed chancel of 1878–9 overtops the nave; it replaced a much lower but still steep-roofed chancel. In 2005–6 the tower was lime-rendered white, a startling landmark. The church started cruciform in the early C13. Of that time is the arch to the former s transept (tripartite with the centre part keeled, as at Crosby Ravensworth and Greystoke, for instance), and the trefoiled PISCINA with a delicately fluted dish, re-set in the s aisle. The w arch of the crossing is represented only by the lowest part of the s jamb, with two nook-shafts. There is also a base in the same pier indicating that a s aisle existed. The N aisle belongs to the same period as the w tower; three wide steps with slim octagonal piers. The present s aisle is later Perp, and considerably wider than the N aisle.

FURNISHINGS. PULPIT. Victorian. Good simple octagonal pen on a low stone base. – Spirited ROYAL ARMS of 1695 over the s door. – FONT. Dated 1662, and very characteristic of those years. Octagonal, with the date, initials, some stylized flowers, and the blank head of a Perp window. – Round it some old BENCHES, BALUSTRADING and a CHEST. – STAINED GLASS. E window, *Clayton & Bell.* Chancel S, good strong colours, by *Abbott & Co.*, 1897. S aisle W, 1892, designed by *Beatrice Whistler* for *Campbell, Smith & Co.* Streaky sky, girlish angels (two appear to be pregnant), daisies and lilies. Conventional S side windows by the same firm and similar date, designed by *F. G. Christmas.** S aisle E by *Stanley Murray Scott*, 1959, for *Reed Millican*, SS Ninian and Martin with Dan Dare cheekbones. – MONUMENTS. Three good tablets in the chancel to members of the Burn family: †1785 (Dr Richard Burn, Chancellor of the diocese and antiquary, 'conspicuous for his Judgement, piety and candour, and the general complacency of his manners'), †1802, †1898. – Tablet by *Jones & Willis* to William Sharp †1914, of alabaster and tiles. – Free-standing war memorial, 1920.

METHODIST CHAPEL. 1833, with just a touch of Gothic.

Loose-plan VILLAGE with streams, bridges, and a couple of marshy fields in the middle. One or two upper-entry houses, like Alston bastles, e.g. Westmorland House. By the church the WAVERLEY TEMPERANCE HOTEL, plain and white. Close by, in the village, is SWAN VILLA (on gatepost; now called Stone Leigh), dated 1872. Yellow brick front with bits of Gothic stonework. Two-storey Gothic bay, arched window heads of two-light mullioned windows incorrectly pierced with a little glazed quatrefoil above the centre mullion. On the W side of the green is the former TEMPERANCE HALL of 1858, looking like a very plain chapel, of hammer-dressed limestone. RED-MAYNE HOUSE, 1872, is another curiosity with an elaborate porch of bits of carved work.

ORTON OLD HALL or PETTY HALL, at the S end of the village. Handsome cottage, house and big barn in line, the barn retaining pinkish limewash. Irregularly placed two- and three-light mullioned windows with dripmoulds which have fancy terminations. The hallan passage goes right through, as at Kentmere Hall (q.v.), with GB 1604 MB (Birkbeck) on three shields over the lintel. CMP 1689 (Christopher and Mary Petty) over cottage fireplace, with three castles and a pair of compasses. WG 1740 over the barn.

ORTON LIBERAL CLUB, almost in the hall garden. 1858. Little three-bay building like a small school. A frowning gentleman with wing collar and sideburns holds the name, as in a *Beano* cartoon.

ORTON HALL, S of the village towards Tebay. Late C18 house for Dr Richard Burn, the antiquary. Tripartite entrance with Venetian windows over and in the wings. Screen walls link the house with a pair of pavilions with Gothick ogee windows. Broken pediments to the pavilions and the centre. A little cupola on the roof is almost hidden from the front. In 1905

---

*The *Westminster Gazette* (1892) attributes these to *Heaton, Butler & Bayne.*

the front was refaced and extended, and perhaps the canted added bays added, by the Rev. Sidney Swann, who devised a stone-cutting machine for the local firm Parkin & Son. He also built a flying machine in 1910 and tested it at Maulds Meaburn Hall.

STONE CIRCLE, 1 m. E, at the foot of The Knott. A large sub-circle of about forty granite boulders, possibly set in a low bank.

OSMOTHERLEY (L)

The name pertains to the valley and the church. The nearest settlements are Netherhouses and Broughton Beck.

ST JOHN EVANGELIST. 1873–4 by *Paley & Austin.* Green slate and red sandstone. Lancet windows. Wooden bellcote and spirelet just big enough to have tiny broaches and lucarnes. Wooden porch, and a round apse.

OUSBY (C)

ST LUKE, ¾ m. SE of the village at Townhead, against a Pennine backdrop. Long narrow nave, long narrow chancel. Rebuilt in the late C16 and 1858, but the masonry is older and a couple of E.E. lancets are visible. Porch 1896. PISCINA, and stepped SEDILIA, mostly renewed. – MONUMENT. Excellent, elegant C14 oak effigy of a knight. He is dressed in mail with a surcoat, and has crossed legs.

RAYSON HALL, close to the church. Built for Hugh Rayson, rector. HR MR 1606 on a lintel. Doorway with carved label stops. Small square windows with dripmoulds but minus mullions. The l. extension is C18. Barn by the road with the initials IR, I & AR, and the date 1691.

HOLE FARM, at the SW end of the village. 'John Hall 1743' is inexpertly inscribed in the segmental pediment over the doorway, but it looks like an up-to-date house of a generation earlier. Five bays with sash windows, all small-scale. The doorcase still has a bolection moulding. Windows and cornice have the same mouldings as Nunnery, Armathwaite (1715).

LIMEKILN, 1 m. E of Townhead on the slopes of Cross Fell. A large commercial kiln 35 ft (11 metres) high, with a single oval pot but two tall pointed arches, each with three draw-eyes. This design indicates continuous burning, i.e. holding the burning zone in the middle while burnt lime was withdrawn at the bottom and fresh stone and coal loaded at the top.

OXENHOLME (W) *see* NATLAND

PARSONBY (C) *see* PLUMBLAND

PATTERDALE (W)

3010

St Patrick. The old church made way in 1852–3 for this dull building by *Anthony Salvin*, for William Marshall. Geometrical traceries, and a NE tower with a saddleback roof. More interesting extension, of 1995 by *BDP* Preston (*Ed Hill*, with *Paul Grout*). It forms a new entrance and foyer and a fine parish room. Roofs with scissor-braced trusses of pitch pine. – EMBROIDERIES. *Ann Macbeth* (1875–1948), embroideress, potter, teacher, settled here in 1921. The Good Shepherd (1935–6) is set in Patterdale and the faces are Patterdale portraits. The music is Parry's 'Jerusalem'. Its companion, The Nativity, is kept in Glasgow, where she trained, but returned here annually. – STAINED GLASS. Chancel windows and one nave s by *Henry Hughes*, 1876 etc. Others mostly *Ward & Hughes* or *Curtis, Ward & Hughes*, 1890s.

PATTERDALE HALL, overlooking Ullswater from the slope above the main road. The Mounseys were known as kings of Patterdale, and the house was known as the Palace. Of the house built by John and Dorothy Mounsey there remains a doorhead with their initials and the date 1677. Machell made a 'light touch or scratch' of the house in 1680, showing hall, buttery, pantry, and kitchen, probably with solar above, a terraced courtyard and a 'folly'. The present house has some C18 work but is mostly by *Salvin*, 1845–50, after John Mounsey sold the house to William Marshall of Leeds, owner of the Marshall Mills, in 1824. Asymmetry of the sort that looks incomplete rather than organic, with one broad square tower and one polygonal bay, formerly encircled by a veranda. Porte cochère at the back. Large U-shaped STABLE block, with a memorable Italianate clock tower. Ornamental DAIRY, its polygonal front echoing the house and its rustic veranda still in place. Elaborately terraced GARDENS, with exotic planting.

PATTON BRIDGE (W)

5090

Shaw End. 1796–1802 by *Francis Webster* and *William Holme* for Arthur Shepherd. Smart white house of seven bays and two storeys. Four-column porch with a pediment. The centre window above is enriched. Otherwise the house relies for its effect solely on proportion and position. Ha-has allow an august outlook. STABLE with an octagonal cupola. A BRIDGE takes the drive over a public footpath. House, stables, bridges, drive and garden walls cost Shepherd £3,735.

PENNINGTON (L)

ST MICHAEL. W tower and nave were built in 1826–7, originally with Y-tracery and a flat E end and flat ceiling. The blocky polygonal chancel, the porch and the straight-headed Dec two-light windows were added in the sweeping restoration of 1924–6 by *Austin & Paley*, i.e. *H. A. Paley*. New roof, new furnishings at the same time. However, it is an ancient and commanding site. Built in by the font is a Norman TYMPANUM with worn runes (transliterated) KML:SET:THESA:KIRK:HUBIRT:MESUN:VNM:MIA, i.e. Gamul was the founder, *Hubert* the mason. In the middle is the risen Christ, winged, with uplifted hands and the Cross behind his head. Other relics are a pair of semi-octagonal capitals with pairs of little faces, presumably from a chancel arch and now behind the organ. Some damaged Norman scallop capitals built into the porch. – Medieval FONT, a big tulip-shaped octagon. – STAINED GLASS. All by *Powells*, the side windows in their recognizable style, the E much more modern (1971) and spare.

RINGWORK CASTLE, Castle Hill, ½ m. NW. Strong defensive bank on E and N; steep slopes above the beck on W and S.

DEVIL'S BRIDGE, 2 m. N, above Pennington Reservoir. A fine unaltered packhorse bridge spanning Rathmoss Beck. C17 or C18.

PENRITH (C)

'So red that at my entrance into the town thought its buildings were all of brick', scribbled Celia Fiennes in 1698, 'but after found it to be the coullour of the stone which I saw in the quarrys . . . their slatt is the same.' Paving stones too. Not a large town (population 14,756 in 2001), but significant, standing at the cross-roads of Cumbria. The town is irregular and tight, all interconnected spaces rather than streets. It is arguable that this was defensive, certainly a way of managing and containing livestock. Augustinian Friars settled here in 1291, leaving no upstanding remains. The castle shows by its regularity that it is a relative latecomer on the edge of town. Border raids and incursions are recorded as late as 1601, followed by Civil War and then the C18 excitements of Bonnie Prince Charlie. Large hotels and inns are represented by the George, and formerly the Crown, and there are several fine town houses. No industry to speak of, but 'a good market for cloth that they spinn in the country' (Celia again).

Penrith is also the metropolis for a rich hinterland. Immediately s is the crossing of the River Eamont and the boundary with Westmorland, a crucial spot as the concentration of significant constructions of every age on both sides of the river shows. Beyond the crossing immediately s are Yanwath, Lowther and Brougham; to the E is the Eden valley and a rich crop of historic houses and villages; N and W are Hutton-in-the-Forest and Greystoke, and the road to Ullswater, passing Dalemain.

PLACES OF WORSHIP

ST ANDREW. Rebuilt in 1721–2. The immensely strong w tower remains from the medieval church. Its lower part, built on a grand scale, appears to be c13, unbuttressed, with thick walls, tiny windows, no external entry, and a high vault – i.e. defensive. However, its tower arch is open (*see* below; also Barton, Workington and others). The belfry stage was constructed (reconstructed?) in the c15 by Warwick the Kingmaker, i.e. *c.* 1460–70, with two pairs of straight-headed two-light openings with cusped arches for the lights, as at Appleby and Brough. The diagonal buttresses were probably added at the same time. The w doorway was broken through in the c18. It has a classical surround, with triangular pediment, trigyph frieze, and Doric columns.

The body of the church is the stateliest, and the earliest, of quite a crop of Georgian churches in Cumbria. The designer can be identified with confidence as *William Etty* of York, to whom a survey payment was made in 1719. The elevations match some of those at Castle Howard, Yorks., where Etty was working under Hawksmoor after 1721 (Terry Friedman). *Robert Harrison* and *Joseph Simpson* were paid for the masonry. It is built of the town's deep red sandstone. Eight bays of round-arched windows in two tiers, rather closely spaced between very broad pilasters. At the angles these are rusticated with bold grooving. Then what appears to be a two-bay chancel, and finally the shallowest of square apses, with a triplet of E windows under an enormous super-arch.

INTERIOR. The tower base is taken up by the c18 stairs to the galleries, two broad flights with three plain balusters to a tread. High c13 tower arch with two steps of chamfers, dying in to the imposts. It bears the marks of an iron grille. The walls are impressively thick. There is a square, domical vault, featureless except for the bell-hole, set high and thickly whitewashed. The first bay of the nave is taken up by a broad cross-passage to the side doors (cf. Ravenstonedale). The auditorium is a full nine bays; the apparent chancel is really just a narrowing of the outer walls, and the colonnades of the galleries march straight through. Tuscan columns below, tall thin quasi-Tuscan columns (of wood) above. The raised choir and large SE organ are C19 interventions (1887). The altar is still in the E alcove.

FURNISHINGS. PAINTINGS in the E alcove by *Jacob Thompson* of Penrith, 1845, replacing a scheme by *Mathias Read*. Angel and shepherds N, Agony in the Garden S, filling the side walls and running up into the vault. They are said to include recognizable Penrith portraits; to modern eyes they recall Sunday School prints. – COMMUNION TABLE. 1722, lengthened 1951. – CHANDELIERS. Of brass, in a usual Baroque shape. Paid for by the 2nd Duke of Portland in recognition of the town's defence against the Young Pretender, 1745. – PULPIT. The top of the Georgian three-decker, with fluted angle colonnettes, arched panels. – ROYAL ARMS, 1723, at the back of the gallery. By *Mathias Read*. – FONT. Plain octagonal bowl, dated 1661. – STAINED GLASS. E window by *Hardman*, 1870. N aisle E, *Burlison & Grylls*, 1889. N aisle N, E end, a jumble of medieval glass including a supposed image of Richard II, 1397. Also windows by *G. J. Baguley*, 1877; *Powells*, 1913; *Cox, Sons & Buckley*, 1893. S side, two medieval portrait heads identified as Richard Duke of York and Cicely Neville, married in 1438. Incorporated into a geometric window, all silver-stain and black, vines and flowers. Also Christ Church window, 1868, 'after *Heaton, Butler & Bayne*', commemorating the Rev. William Holme Milner, who is portrayed offering his church. To its W, Abraham and Isaac, by *Clayton & Bell*. – MONUMENTS. Two coffin-lids with foliated crosses in the tower; the larger C14, the smaller but more elaborate possibly late C12. On the gallery stairs, badly preserved stone effigies of Anthony and Elizabeth Hutton, commissioned by the widow in 1637 who then survived thirty-seven more years. Well be-ruffed, but with tiny heads.

CHURCHYARD MONUMENTS. N of the N wall of the church, GIANT'S GRAVE. Composite C10 monument consisting of a pair of crosses and four hogbacks between them set two and two. They have been arranged thus since at least 1664–5 when drawn by Dugdale, though the hogbacks are now mounted on sleeper walls. What do they signify? They are sadly worn and decayed, even since Calverley and Collingwood's photographs of 1899. There is in truth little surface decoration to describe. The crosses are of the tapered cylindrical type, turning square at the top. Pevsner noted the W cross over 11 ft (3.5 metres) high with much interlace and an unusually small cross-head, with free arms. The E cross is 10 ft 6 in. (3.2 metres) high and has interlace too, and on one side a bound figure and a woman next to him, with a serpent above his head. NW of the W tower, GIANT'S THUMB. Another C10 cross, re-erected in 1887. Shorter than the others, with a wheel head and interlace on its sides. Collingwood drew figures on both sides in 1919. Also identified recently, a cross base mounted upside-down to show its tenon. – Robert Vertue †1846, railway engineer. Gothic

tracery between two flat piers with pinnacles on top. – WAR
MEMORIAL, 1919. A Celtic cross with the characteristically flat
but soft-edged carving of the genre.

The other churches and chapels are grouped NW of the centre.

CHRIST CHURCH, Stricklandgate. By *Travis & Mangnall* of
Manchester (tender £2,500). Built in 1848–50, partly to
provide a new graveyard. Unexciting aisled building with a
blind storey and a thin W spirelet on a mid-buttress. Perp
tracery. Chancel remodelled by *J. H. Martindale*, 1905.
(STAINED GLASS. E, re-set figures from the window of 1850 by
J. G. Howe for *Powells*. Chancel s, *J. Scott & Son*, 1875. s aisle:
E by *W. Wailes*, 1850; s by *Clayton & Bell*. N aisle, †1904, *Shrigley
& Hunt*.)

ST CATHERINE (R.C.), Drovers Lane, its three-sided apse
overlooking Christ Church's graveyard. Nave, porch and
presbytery of 1849–50 by *Atkinson* of Carlisle, Pugin-like in its
early and earnest Gothic revival. Transepts and apse added in
1860 by *John Seed*. No tower. Tracery Geometrical to Dec.
Dinky interior sloping down towards the altar, with Puginian
slender open roof. The only stone exposed is in the two-bay
arcades for the transepts – i.e. there is no crossing. – STAINED
GLASS in the s transept by *John Scott & Son* of Carlisle, in the
Wailes manner. Apse glass signed *A. K. Nicholson*, 1926.

METHODIST CHAPEL, Fell Lane. 1815. Large, of three by three
bays with three-bay pediment, doorway with Doric columns
and broken pediment, and arched windows in two tiers – the
proper spacious Late Georgian preaching box.

WESLEYAN CHURCH, Drovers Lane, by Christ Church's N gate.
1873. Grand, dignified preaching box of red stone, pedimented
and handsomely proportioned, with Italianate detail. Usual
extensive social rooms behind, linked by a new entrance of
tubular steel and glass. The auditorium has kept its oval gallery
and coffered ceiling, but the ground-floor furnishings have
gone.

CONGREGATIONAL CHAPEL (former), Duke Street. 1865, by
George Watson of Penrith. All churchy, with an asymmetrically
placed steeple and Geometrical tracery.

UNITED REFORMED CHURCH, formerly Presbyterian, Lowther
Street. 1884. Red stone. Five graded windows at the end, porch
and turret at the side.

QUAKER MEETING HOUSE, Meeting House Lane. The Quakers
bought a C17 farmhouse in 1699, adding a loft and outside stair
in 1730. In 1803 a wing was built on the s side, making the
building T-shaped, with a new entrance. (Interior divided by
shutters.) Graveyard with typical Quaker stones, e.g. '5th
month' instead of May.

CEMETERY, Beacon Edge, N of the town. 1872. At the top of the
town on the E, commanding a tremendous prospect to Lowther
Castle and the central fells. Gothic keeper's house, and a pair
of chapels linked by an arch over which is placed a belfry and
spire, fat with four fat corner spirelets. The links are balanced

by a pair of outer porches, in fact the composition is precisely symmetrical. How pleasant such buildings can be when they are kept well.

PUBLIC BUILDINGS

PENRITH CASTLE. Sterile ruin opposite the station, which with its approach road has absorbed part of the defences. Although a tempting target for the Scots, and repeatedly despoiled, Penrith lacked a castle until 1396–7, when the competing ambitions of Walter Strickland, later Bishop of Carlisle and Archbishop of Canterbury, and Ralph Neville, 1st Earl of Westmorland, caused it to be built.*

Penrith Castle began as a square curtain-walled enclosure surrounded by a ditch, with a tower projecting in the middle of the E (actually NE) face, towards the town, guarding the gateway and drawbridge. The ditch is cut by the road on the W but impressive elsewhere. Only the base of the E tower is left, with its vault. In the early C15 the Nevilles added a second tower on the N side close to the E corner. Of this tower a high chunk of blank wall remains facing the station, and half of the barrel-vault. In the 1470s Richard Duke of Gloucester (the future King Richard III) made the castle into a major residence, with a new gateway and forebuildings against the N tower on its W side, and new first-floor apartments inside the curtain. Anthony Emery has interpreted the results as follows. The hall was on the E side N of the tower, with private apartments along the S wall. Buck's engraving of 1739 shows that three large windows lit the hall on the outer side. The inner wall of the former S range was raised to accommodate the apartments, which were warmed by inserted fireplaces. The S curtain is now the most impressive part, standing sheer to its corbelled-out parapet, with a mid-buttress. Only a few slits at ground-floor level outside. A two-storey chapel filled the SE corner, with large clerestory windows with four-centred heads. Diagonal SW angle buttress, formerly topped with a little turret. In the SE angle was a kiln, venting to a smoke-hole in the S wall. The kitchens were along the W side. The castle was excavated, conserved and tidied in the manner of the day, 1923.

CASTLE PARK. Opened 1923, along with the war memorial LYCHGATE. The SOUTH AFRICA WAR MEMORIAL, erected in 1906 in front of the Town Hall, was removed here in 1964. 'Peace crowning the heroes'. Bare-breasted but severe of face, she reaches forward on tiptoe with a wreath. By *T. W. Doyle Jones*, a copy of his Gateshead war memorial.

---

*Licences to crenellate were given to Strickland in 1397 and 1399, but Neville may have completed the work.

TOWN HALL, Stricklandgate. 1905–6 by *J. J. Knewstubb*, Surveyor and Engineer to the Council. The style is an out-of-date Italian or Dutch Renaissance, in pink and buff stone. Surprisingly, this is not a new building, but the conversion of a pair of superior Wyattish houses of 1792 – not something a more dynamic town would have countenanced. The polychromy was an original feature, but the round-arched windows in twos and threes were originally Venetian or single openings. Knewstubb retained the roofs and party wall, hence the bipartite composition. To the r., a richly multiple Corinthian porch and frontispiece. Centre l. a subordinate bay marking the Council Chamber upstairs. The cantilevered upper flights of the stair are C18 too, with shaped tread-ends, though with new cast-iron balustrades. Knewstubb, evidently unsure of them, provided a decorative girder underneath. Several C18 chimneypieces survive. In the Council Chamber a peculiar Corinthian temple front, with two pairs of columns. Are they from the C18 hallways?

GRAMMAR SCHOOL, Ullswater Road. Economical grey Neo-Georgian building, roughcast. E-shaped, with a central cupola and a doorway with curly pediment. By *Harrison & Ash* of Newcastle, 1913–15.

STATION. 1846, by *Sir William Tite* for the Lancaster & Carlisle Railway. Pretty Tudor Gothic building, asymmetrical, in red stone with pink dressings. The island platform was added in the 1860s for the Keswick and Workington line; it has a distinctive canopy built bridge-wise, supported on shallow arched girders.

PERAMBULATION

The irregular, interconnecting medieval spaces of the centre, as so often in England, present fairly uniform fronts of two and three storeys essentially Georgian in character and proportion. Older work behind is indicated by C17 and occasionally C16 datestones (not always noted hereafter) over yard entries and floating in later façades.

MARKET SQUARE is only roughly square, with a triangular road junction. The central CLOCK TOWER, a feeble Gothic edifice, was erected in 1861 to commemorate Philip Musgrave of Edenhall (†1850 in Madrid). The gates of the parish church stand slightly aloof to the E, through a gap between two early C20 banks. BARCLAYS, S (originally Bank of Liverpool), of 1912–13 by *J. F. Curwen*, is the jollier: red stone, Tudor, with playful oriels and turrets topped by four little copper spirelets. To the N NATWEST of 1928 (originally Barclays), smoothly classical, with paired giant pilasters, of alien Portland stone diagnostic of the date. The GEORGE HOTEL a little way N is the town's principal rendezvous, rather than the Town Hall which is relatively incidental in position and presence. It has three parts, stretching N into Devonshire Street. On the l. the early C18 George and Dragon, commandeered in 1745 by Bonnie Prince Charlie. Six bays and three storeys. Shops under, bedrooms above, broad entry with segmental pediment. The mid-C19 middle section, now the main entrance, has two-storey canted bays with tripartite windows over, and tripartite lunettes over them, i.e. four floors. Porch with Doric columns. On the r. a generously wide section built by the Duke of Devonshire c. 1807 over the entrance arch to his New Shambles. The pedimented tripartite window over the arch lights the assembly room. Good early C20 interiors, perhaps by *Gillows*, with plentiful woodwork, coloured glass and Lincrusta. The stair with its over-complicated balusters is perhaps of 1807. DEVONSHIRE ARCADE, 1807, leads through the arch to the GENERAL MARKET of c. 1855. Both were fettled up in 1991 by *Nichol Armstrong Lowe*, connecting through to their new LIBRARY on the first floor. Also in Devonshire Street, ARNISONS' (No. 18), a prominent old-fashioned draper's shopfront appearing in photographs of c. 1900 exactly as now (cf. the shopfront of Grahams' provisions, Nos. 6–7 Market Square). On the N side of the square in its wider part is HSBC, formerly the London, City and Midland Bank, by *T. B. Whinney*, 1912–13. Red brick and pale sandstone, Wrennish Baroque.

The Scottish Baronial turret in the SW corner of the square, an effective intrusion of c. 1986, signals the ANGEL SQUARE shopping centre. A series of small-scale pedestrian spaces and pastiche façades by *Nichol Armstrong Lowe* and the *Hives Partnership*. Self-effacing, perhaps even worthy of muted praise. Down ANGEL LANE, SW, the BLUE BELL BOOKSHOP has an engaging, crowded little façade. An illiterate inscription in the joint segmental pediment over the double doorway describes its acquisition in 1763. Doorcases with old-fashioned bolection mouldings and pulvinated friezes. Semi-double Venetian window, i.e. low, arched and high, arched and high, low, flanked by two ogee-headed Gothick ones, and on the top floor, but not central, another and smaller double Venetian.

Now we are in GREAT DOCKRAY, another open space of no determined shape. The GLOUCESTER ARMS was named for the future Richard III who had a house here in 1471, but the present building – formerly Dockray Hall – fits the date 1580 on the two-storey porch. One Elizabethan cross-mullioned window between bay and porch. The porch opens onto the side of a great fireplace with a passage on either side. The door lintels, cut away in a shallow Tudor arch, and the segmental arch of the fireplace typical of 1580. Current entry is through an inserted bay. The TWO LIONS INN on the S side, long closed, originated as the New Hall purchased by Gerard Lowther in 1584. His house, incorporating something of the New Hall, is still there behind the mess of C19 and C20 accretions. Hall and E cross-wing. Damaged C16 windows with

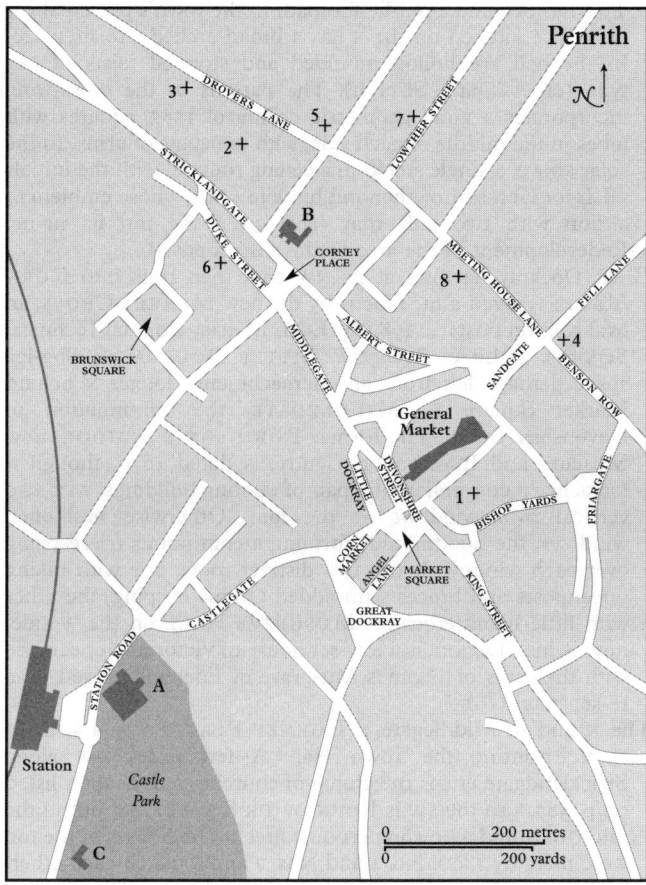

Penrith

1 St Andrew
2 Christ Church
3 St Catherine (R.C.)
4 Methodist Chapel
5 Wesleyan Church
6 Congregational Chapel

7 United Reformed Church
8 Quaker Meeting House

A Castle
B Town Hall
C Grammar School

hollow-moulded mullions and arched heads remain here and there, and a plain mullioned window in the kitchen. A stair-turret is known to have been removed from the E end. The main entry, retaining a fine studded door, opens into a cross-passage behind the hall fireplace in the Cumbrian manner.

This has become a public footpath to the town's principal car park. The kitchen on the E has a broad-arched C16 fireplace. In the hall are hollow-moulded and stopped joists of C15 type (cf. Askham, Sizergh). The parlour in the cross-wing incorporates a good geometric ceiling of 1585, squares with lobes in the middle of each side, with ten coats of arms. In the solar above, a single shield in a ceiling roundel with the initials GLL for Gerard Lowther and his wife Lucy, whose emblem of a lion with two tails may have given the inn its name. Redevelopment of the area to the S is proposed.

Great Dockray narrows at its NW end, then runs into CORN MARKET, given a nice focus by the new MARKET CROSS, an oval roof on posts; *c.* 1984 by Eden District Council Technical Services, architect *J. Caygill*. LITTLE DOCKRAY, a dog-leg space perhaps left from an encroachment, dodges N behind Market Square to MIDDLEGATE, the continuation of Devonshire Street. The former ROBINSON'S SCHOOL, now Museum and Information Centre, is dated 1670, though it looks like a conversion of a pair of existing buildings, with two vertical oval windows at the join. Otherwise mullioned windows, the hoodmoulds forming a continuous frieze rising over each window. It has two distinct roofs; one with raking queenposts and braces with added Gothic cusping, the other with little hammerbeams. MUSGRAVE HALL on the W side, now British Legion, is a low-set house of Victorian appearance with the arms of Thomas Musgrave of Edenhall carved on a re-set lintel (1615).

The N end of Middlegate is CORNEY PLACE, now a swirl of traffic fronting the Town Hall. A few paces NW along Stricklandgate etc. is the clutch of churches and chapels listed on p. 567.* To the SW is BRUNSWICK SQUARE, set out in the mid C19 round a bowling/croquet green. The houses at the top were there by 1860. No. 1 and Nos. 7 and 8 match each other, faced with Greystoke ashlar, with curved steps. The rest not until about 1900. The other way along Corney Place, SE, takes us to CORNEY HOUSE, now National Farmers' Union. 1777. Five-bay, three-storey house of red stone with emphatic string and sill courses. No central door, but identical entrances in little side wings. Immediately l. is a low folly front of reused stones: two arches over an octagonal pier and capital. Two crudely carved faces. Where are they from? From here Albert Street curves E. On its S side, ALTHAM'S IRON WORKS, early C19. The three-storey office and entrance building remains, symmetrical coursed sandstone rubble with generous windows and an arched cart entrance and taking-in door above on the top floor. The necessary water and power were taken from the Thaka Beck, passing below in a culvert.

---

* On Stricklandgate in the grounds of Shepherd's Hill, a fine square C18 stone MALTHOUSE with central louvred ventilator atop a pyramid roof. Interior complete with furnace, well, and pierced drying-floor.

Albert Street leads into SANDGATE, the largest open space so far. At its head on Fell Lane is CROZIER LODGE. 1826 for William Harrison, and named after his wife's family. Ashlar, of three bland bays and two low wings with a Venetian window each. Doorway with broken pediment. BENSON ROW runs SE between Sandgate and Fell Lane, part of an ancient by-pass: Drovers Lane, Meeting House Lane, Folly Lane, etc. (At the far end of Drovers Lane, COCKELL HOUSE. Partly c. 1660, partly mid-C18. Doorway with Doric columns. Staircase, etc., and also some windows C17.) On the r. side of Benson Row is the intriguing garden wall of Hutton Hall, with several blocked openings, and the best view of its tower (see below).

Turning r. into FRIARGATE we enter an undefined open space E of the parish church. Here is a group of significant houses. First HUTTON HALL (now Gregg's offices and bakery). Broad and even mid-C18 seven-bay front of red ashlar with a strong cornice and originally a balustraded parapet, evenly spaced chimneys, and a horizontally channelled plinth. Doorway with segmental pediment on brackets. A single pile with the stair wing at the back making a T, a typical Cumbrian plan of the time. On the r. is a lower C17 part, and behind and overlapping both is the defensive tower seen from Benson's Row. This is a late but well-preserved example, square not oblong, and unvaulted. Pyramid roof, replacing a presumed flat and parapet. Otherwise unaltered outside, with tiny windows (some cut out of a single stone) distributed apparently at random, and retaining its covering of roughcast. Larger windows on the S indicate the solar on the first floor, with a good fireplace with the initials WDH (William and Dorothy Hutton). The turning stair is unusually wide. The interiors of the main house are cut about for offices but retain a good deal of small-scale floor-to-ceiling panelling. Fine stair with two balusters per tread. Opposite is ABBOTS BANK of 1820, a handsome three-bay stuccoed house with a Doric porch. Good stable yard to one side. Then THE FRIARAGE of 1717, and NORTH FRIARAGE, on the site of the Austin Friars' house. MANSION HOUSE, now Eden Council Offices, adjoins the E end of the churchyard. Stately stuccoed house built in 1750 by the Rimingtons, of five bays and two-and-a-half storeys on a basement. Doorway with segmental pediment on brackets. The string course intersects the pediment. Subordinate wings standing forward, with Venetian windows at their ends. The arches of the windows have rustication of alternating sizes. Short Gothick links bridge the gaps. The front courtyard without cars would be an elegant space, with curved dwarf walls and rusticated gatepiers. One side wall has orientalizing cusped ogee niches.

Bishop Yards and St Andrew's churchyard encircle the church to its S and N. It can be seen how the graveyard has risen, half-burying some of the older houses. In BISHOP YARDS the PARISH ROOMS by G. Watson, 1893–4; a big, red, gabled front with tiers of pilasters and a Baroque doorway. Next an C18 house with moulded window frames and a doorway with a thin moulded surround, then a five-bay house with broken pediment over the doorway. TUDOR HOUSE in St Andrew's Place, w, is minor Tudor; RB 1563 on a two-storey bay, with uncusped round-headed lights. And back to the market place.

OUTLYING BUILDINGS

SCAWS HOUSING ESTATE, on the hillside above Hutton Hall and E of Fell Lane. 1949 *et seq*. Billed as Penrith's Garden Suburb – well behind the times – but the initial standard proved too expensive to maintain. The earliest houses, designed by *Frank Blanc*, are on Hutton Hill. Stone-faced semis arranged *en echelon*, with plenty of green space. They have catslide roofs of green, graded slate, homely porches, and dormers distinctively gabled like a Gothic arch (after Lorimer, e.g. at Brackenburgh, Plumpton, *c.* 1904).

BEACON TOWER, Beacon Hill, E of the cemetery and NE of the town centre. In its present form of 1719, repaired 1780. Red sandstone, square, with round-arched openings and a pyramid spire. Near the cemetery in Fell Lane, CAROLINE COTTAGE, built in 1818 by the 1st Earl of Lonsdale as a lodge to the Beacon estate. Gothick and castellated. Three bays, the centre of two storeys, the side parts of one.

57 TYNEFIELD HOUSE, Bridge Lane, SW. Dated M & ER (the letters are reversed) 1804 under the arch of the front door. The Rimingtons were prosperous Quakers, owners of Greenside Mine at Glenridding (q.v.). Cool, elegant and very restrained façade of Greystoke ashlar. Three widely spaced bays and two visible storeys under a shallow hipped roof. Tripartite ground-floor windows, brought almost down to the ground, and a tripartite doorway, each under a super-arch recessed just enough to create a pencil line of shadow (this was quite a Penrith fashion, but other examples have gone). Central eight-fold stack. Restrained interior too: stone stair, plain mahogany rail with square balusters.

CARLETON HALL (Cumbria Police headquarters), SE. Cut off by the new A66, it looks out to Brougham Castle across the flood meadows of the Eamont and Lowther confluence. Entrance front C19 and 1937, probably filling the original U. The six-bay centre of the garden front looks early C18. The two canted bays are a little taller and perhaps later, though both have the same coved cornice and window detail. Spacious staircase with three balusters to a tread. Pretty low-relief geometric ceilings in the Adam manner behind the garden front. The E room is especially handsome: octagonal with two niches.

CARLETON FARM, a little E on the Edenhall road. Three-bay house and byre in line, with their backs to the road. The house was given a smart new ashlar front in the early C18, with quoins, a full Gibbs surround and pediment to the doorway.

The trunk road intersection SE of Penrith has engendered the inevitable shedsville. CRANSTON'S FOOD HALL on Ullswater Road, 2003, has a slate roof and a bit of dry-stone wall to make it Cumbrian. Artfully cut away and folded at one end to catch the eye of the motorist. NORTH LAKES HOTEL, 1985, extended 2004. A design-and-build package by *Lesser Design* with *Richmond Design* for the interiors. Low, under slate roofs and blue-painted roughcast. Residential wing of three storeys, public parts mostly roof. Entrance lined in exaggeratedly rough stonework, with dramatic roofing of enormous reclaimed wooden trusses. The spaces flow freely through arches and down steps. GHYLL MOUNT (Environment Agency Office), Gillan Way, is by *Ross Erwin* of *Hills Erwin Partnership*, 1998. Bigger than it looks, being partly buried in the hillside. Two leaves of pink pressed blocks and grey metal, hinged about the stair atrium. The two colours are not particularly happy together. Interiors open, with much woodwork. The building ticks all the environmental boxes, e.g. reusing 'grey' water, solar heating, natural ventilation.

SKIRSGILL, I m. SSW, W of the motorway. Hemmed in first by the railway, then by the M6 and the A66. Plain but generously scaled three-storey house of 1795 for Hugh Parkin, with shallow bows looking S over the Eamont, a pediment N, and single-storey wings. It was remodelled in the 1840s by *G. J. J. Mair* of London for the Dents, opium traders instrumental in the founding of the Hong Kong and Shanghai Bank. Mair raised the wings to two storeys, ending in oddly emphatic stops on the river front. He added a porch on this side, a four-column Doric loggia on the N, and made a new 'railway' grand entrance at the E end, intended to be balanced by a conservatory, W. This was never completed. Interiors are generously gaunt in scale, with high ceilings and a broad spine corridor. Sparse plasterwork and frosted and coloured glass by *Mair*, as is the staircase. The private CHAPEL (R.C.) in the W wing was fitted out and decorated by *Gillow*. The STABLE BLOCK has been converted to business use.

RHEGED, off the A66 W of Skirsgill. By *Jak Jones* of *Unwin Jones Partnership*, Carlisle, 2000. A visitor attraction: petrol, refreshments, shops, cinemas and exhibition space.* It was built in a limestone quarry and bills itself as Europe's largest grass-covered building. Entrance apparently into the side of a hill, themed as a limekiln (there are four real ones on site), with a sliding glass door by *Colin Williams Design*. The interior, brightly lit by a wall of S-facing glass, offers an exciting progression of levels and spaces but does not bear close inspection. The great limestone outcrops are of theatrical fibreglass by *Terance Dickson & Associates* and *Dan Sharp*. Very large PAINTING, Scafell Crag, 2001 by *Julian Cooper*.

OLD PENRITH ROMAN FORT. *See* Plumpton.

---

*Rheged was the kingdom of the Carvetii.

PENRUDDOCK (C)

ALL SAINTS. 1902 by *C. J. Ferguson*. An economical church, roughcast with red sandstone dressings. Nave and chancel in one, with a NW porch facing w. Late Perp windows.

UNITED REFORMED CHURCH. Built by a Presbyterian congregation in 1789. Cute, with arched and keyed windows and a porch set in the long side. Victorian interior.

PIEL CASTLE (L)

Visible from as far away as Cockersand on the Lancashire mainland. The island was part of the original grant to the abbey of Furness in 1127 by King Stephen, on condition that the abbot 'make, sustain, repair and guard a fort' here. It guards the harbour and the seaward approach to the abbey itself. The present castle is constructed of beach cobbles with generous dressings of red sandstone.

The tower or keep was probably built in the early years of the C14. A licence to crenellate of 1327 would seem to have been retrospective, relating to a prompt strengthening after the Scottish raids of 1322 (porch or forebuilding, and the outer defences). The castle makes an impressive statement in this flat neither-sea-nor-land-scape, but its apparent completeness turns out to be fortuitous. The sea has taken away the whole of its s and E part, including the E wall and the E ends of the N and s walls of the keep; it just happens that the remainder has a turret on each corner, and one of the two cross-walls acts as a satisfactory stop.

Tall square TOWER with diagonal and mid-buttresses, corner turrets, and on the N side the deep full-height porch or forebuilding ending in two diagonal turrets. This led into a corridor with a room l. and a room r. There is a wide spiral stair just within the inner entrance arch. This entry bay is vaulted, and so is the small chamber above it. None of the main floors was vaulted. A smaller spiral stair climbs up the NW corner, and there are others at high level. At the SE corner is a narrow oblong projection containing one room on each floor, with slightly different floor levels. The characteristic shouldered 'Caernarvon' arches appear in every part. The W rooms have fireplaces on each floor. These and the large pointed-arched windows of two lights with evidence of quatrefoil tracery point to comfort more than serious defence, although the lower ones have been blocked. The keep was given extra protection by the ditched INNER BAILEY with its own gatehouse and remains of three towers, of which the NW tower is five-sided. In the SW tower are three doorways and the remains of a corbelled-out parapet. The gateway is on the W and has a room with a fireplace over. This bailey is in turn protected a rectangular OUTER BAILEY, also ditched and also surviving only to the N and W. It still has three recognizable two-storey towers. None of the gateways line up. A small building at the NE corner of the outer bailey (31 ft, 9.5 metres long) may have been a CHAPEL.

The use of polygonal and particularly of five-sided structures seems characteristic: polygonal buttresses to the porch, the pentagonal NW tower to the inner bailey, pentagonal turrets on top of the great buttresses of the keep.

The only other buildings on the island are the C18 SHIP INN, and a row of roughcast PILOTS' COTTAGES dated 1875. Of typical 'estate' design, by *Paley & Austin* for the 5th Duke of Buccleuch.

PLUMBLAND (C)   *1030*

Three townships: Plumbland, Arkleby and Parsonby.

ST CUTHBERT. At Parsonby, on a hilltop. Rebuilt by *J. A. Cory*, 1869–71. A masterly work, strong and personal. SW tower with four-way-gabled top, not tall enough to clear the nave. The clerestory on this side has three cross-gables, each with a trio of stepped lancets. The side windows are paired lancets. The N side has just single lancets with rere-arches inside, and quatrefoils in the clerestory. The E window is Dec. The plain Norman doorway re-set in the porch and the lancet re-set in the vestry E wall promise surprises, and indeed the best parts of the old church have been reused. While the arcade with its circular piers and red and yellow voussoirs is Victorian, the chancel arch is the Norman one of *c.* 1130, heightened and partly re-cut. Tripartite responds, capitals of only a few big scallops, and an arch with an early moulding. Two orders of zigzag. The C13 E window is rebuilt in the N transept. The vestry doorway is E.E. of the C13, and so is the PISCINA, whose mouldings are of a slightly earlier type. In the vestry an ogee-arched piscina, some chequer frieze over the fireplace, and a C17 inscription from the old roof.

SCULPTURE. In the porch, two bits of a C10 hogback, reused in the C13. The carving is still quite sharp: shingle roof, interlace on the end, beast on the side. The C13 half-capital which cannibalizes one of the bits is superb. – STAINED GLASS. E window, to a whole raft of Dykeses, by *Clayton & Bell*, after 1873. N transept by *Alexander Gibbs* 1878. N aisle, four by *Powells*, after 1879. S aisle, mostly *Cox & Sons*. W, war memorial, *c.* 1920 by *A. K. Nicholson*. – MONUMENTS. Rev. Peter and Sara Farish, early C18. A Doric aedicule with winged cherubs in the pediment, skull and crossbones underneath. – Tablets by *Nelson* of Carlisle, *J. Forsyth* of Hampstead (Gothic, to F. L. Ballantine Dykes †1866), *Wilson* of Whitehaven. – Outside s, against the chancel, Mary Hall †1832, very good headstone of the local type with books, hand and hammer/cross, eye in sunburst, urn and sarcophagus, vine. – By the gate Hannah Kennedy †1871, a monstrous piece like a Baroque gatepier. Over-sized leaves hang out like scrolly bosses.

VICAR'S DOVECOTE, s of the church. Perhaps C16. Square, with a pyramid roof.

SCHOOL. Also at Parsonby. 1799, with C19 additions. It looks like a Scottish kirk, a long T with a bell-tower forming the downstroke. Probably C19, this has four pinnacles angled out like ears (cf. Troutbeck church), pyramid roof, twin louvred belfry lights and, below that, a clock. The school has a bellcote on its w gable as well.

THREAPLAND HALL, 1 m. w of the church. Interesting three-storey house of C14 origins with small square windows irregularly distributed. Stack at each end, full-height spiral stair in the NE corner.

ARKLEBY HALL, ¼ m. N. Tall three-storey house of *c.* 1740 for Gustavus Thompson, though with an internal datestone of 1725.

4030

PLUMPTON (C)

ST JOHN EVANGELIST. By *Robert Lorimer*, 1907–8, for the Harrises of Brackenburgh. Small, but with a strong sense of rootedness conveyed by the battered walls of the low SE tower, porch front and w wall, and the markedly sprocketed roofs. Decorative elements strictly controlled. Bell-openings filled with reticulated tracery, the datestone, and the eagle of St John at the apex of the gable of the bare windowless E wall. The windows are more conventional, still Gothic Revival with tracery. In the interior, strongly lit by the broad clear-glazed w window, just a few carefully judged furnishings. The REREDOS, brought here in 1999, introduces a new note with its filigree Gothicism and gold leaf. It is however also by *Lorimer,* so the logic is impeccable. It comes from St Mary Mission Church, Bells Brae, Edinburgh, and was presented by Alexander Dunbar, who bought it in 1976. The paintings are probably by *William Hole.* – STAINED GLASS. Only one window, by *Morris & Co.*, 1907. – FONT (outside). An octagonal baluster, from the previous church of 1767.

BRACKENBURGH, 1½ m. NW. Very bleak on its flat hilltop. A late example of a defensive tower (datestone 1600; little remains of its internal dispositions) was incorporated into a crowstepped house of 1852 by *William Atkinson,* with extensive farm buildings. In 1902–3 *Lorimer* turned it into a mansion, his first, for Joseph Harris. The builder was *Hall* of Galashiels, the stone a pale buff sandstone from Lazonby Fell. It reached out in a giant L to join the tower and 1852 house with Atkinson's outbuildings at the SW end. However, outbuildings and a complete service court were demolished in 1960. The scar was healed in 2002 with a new kitchen porch. Lorimer's style is sternly Tudor, very sparing of detail. The house sprawls, eschewing regularity or rhythm, but any levity is firmly checked by the long horizontals of the parapets, with the roofs kept well back. On the entrance front much bare wall is contrasted with the occasional small detail, light-hearted in itself – paired dolphins hold the rainwater spouts, lions bite the corners of a bay – but there is nothing light about the totality. The warmer garden side is dominated by big mullioned-and-transomed windows, all different, with an enormous five-rise (i.e. four transoms) 'Kirby' window to the Great Hall.

The INTERIORS are baronial in scale, with the same spareness of detail. The GREAT HALL was designed around a large tapestry, and an organ which is no longer there: uncomfortably tall for its length, with a gallery set too high. Pink and white MUSIC ROOM, originally all white – the house had almost no colour. Lorimer and the Harrises intended it for dancing. High, with chamfered corners and a polygonal bay. Stylized lovebirds in the plasterwork. Long spine CORRI-DOR with a segmental ceiling and occasional arches and beams of cross-lighting. DINING ROOM at the W end, lower, more comfortable, with plaster vines over the beams. Stern STAIR, with occasional panels of carving in the balustrade. Small Signs of the Zodiac are dotted about in the otherwise plain coved ceiling. The upper corridor rises and falls over the different room heights below: the house's section is as complicated as its plan. Many of the ceilings rise into the roof space.

The GARDEN was designed by *Lorimer* and *Gertrude Jekyll*. Not a great deal is left. Now the L encloses an expanse of lawn, terraced with bastions. STABLES, LODGE, COTTAGES by *Lorimer*, some with his characteristic curved dormers.

(BROCKLEY MOOR HOUSE, formerly Ivy Dene, ½ m. w. IS 1677 over front entry, IS 1717 at the back. Mullioned windows with continuous label course. IS 1677 on a court cupboard inside.)

ROMAN FORT, Old Penrith, 1 m. N of Plumpton beside the Roman road to Carlisle. Site first occupied c. A.D. 90. The visible fort (garrisoned from the 160s to the late C4) is a playing-card-shaped platform, enclosing over 3 acres, oriented N–S. A single outer ditch (late C3) survives on the W and N. The site of the W gate marked by a narrow gap in the defences. The principal, E, gate (opening onto the road) was cleared in 1811 when the fort wall was quarried. Double portals, recessed between gate-towers, the inner forward angles of which were quarter-drums. The mortices for butterfly clamps clearly defined in the upper surface. Base surviving of the rear central pier of the gateway. A length of cornice, with dentils, lies adjacent to the gate. Other architectural fragments recorded

include a capital with human heads and acanthus leaves, a slab
decorated with vines, and five small sculptures of gods, each
in a niche, now at Abbotsford (Borders). None of their original
contexts is known.

PONSONBY (C) *see* CALDER BRIDGE

4020   POOLEY BRIDGE (W)

Lake-end resort on Ullswater.

St Paul. By *Cory & Ferguson*, 1867–8. Lancet windows. A heavy
bell-turret with spire sits apparently on top of the slates at the
w end. Inside, this is carried on a triple w arcade with
octagonal piers and arches back to the w wall, forming a
nice three-dimensional space accommodating porch and
baptistery. – REREDOS carved by Mr *Cumpston* of Barton
Hall. – Geometric STAINED GLASS by *Scott & Co.* of Carlisle.

Eusemere House, ¼ m. SW, opposite the wooded cone of
Dunmallard and looking s over camp site, lake and the far fells.
Built *c.* 1794 as a retreat for Thomas Clarkson, pioneer
campaigner against slavery, by *Thomas Wilkinson* of Yanwath,
who also did the landscaping. Double-fronted Regency villa
with tripartite windows, pink-rendered with quoins. Extended
at both ends, and with an added Jacobean porch with red stone
dressings.

Fish Cross, in the village. 2000 by *James Banks*. Stone pillar
and leaping trout weathervane, which sometimes appears to be
of glass but no, it is stainless steel.

Waterfoot House, ¾ m. w, in Cumberland. According to
John Martin Robinson, built *c.* 1820 by Major-General James
Salmond of Bengal, grandson of Edward Hasell of Dalemain.
Ashlar-faced front and back. Five bays, the middle one
bowed. The ground-floor windows are arched. Ionic porch of
rectangular form attached to the lower part of the bow. Lake
front of seven bays, the windows arch-headed on the ground
floor, with a super-arch for the Venetian middle window, which
has Ionic columns set in. The upper windows plain sashes, the
middle one tripartite. The entrance hall is circular. Quite a
superior design.

5080   PRESTON PATRICK (W)

St Gregory. Rebuilt in 1852–3 by *Sharpe & Paley*. Dominant
on its hill, but unexciting in itself. Rock-faced limestone. NW
tower with higher stair-turret incorporating a genuine Perp

window on the w. It has a curious Y-shape in the tracery, and
beast drip-ends. The chancel was rebuilt by the firm, now
Paley, Austin & Paley, in 1891–2 as a memorial to Mary
Keightley of Old Hall. It differs externally only in its dressings
of yellow sandstone. Sharpe & Paley's nave is whitewashed
inside with a dumpy N arcade on limestone monolith columns.
The chancel in contrast is lined with fine sandstone ashlar, and
very wide. Original Perp are the two canopied niches flanking
the E window, with grotesques under. – STAINED GLASS. E
window, a Te Deum by *Shrigley & Hunt*. Two war memorials
of *c.* 1920: W, with lots of white glass, by *Powells*; S nearest W,
by *Heaton, Butler & Bayne*, Christ crowns the dead man in
front of a lovely streaky sky. Next S, Herbert Barker memorial,
1963, in scratchy style by *Alfred Fisher* for *Powells*.

FRIENDS' MEETING HOUSE. 1691, but altered out of
recognition in 1869, and later hidden from the road behind an
attached cottage in place of the external stair. The large stable
and coachhouse by the lane was converted to offices 2004–5.
(The meeting house retains the traditional raised balustraded
dais and seating on four sides.)

PRESTON PATRICK HALL. Thomas de Wyrkington founded an
abbey here in 1191, but within ten years the community had
taken itself off to Shap (q.v.). It is possible that the occasional
red stone dressings, e.g. of the slit window commanding the
front from the l. wing, date from those years. The present well-
preserved hall-and-cross-wing house can be dated to the C14
by its doorways of shouldered 'Caernarvon' type and windows
with ogee-headed lights. In about 1500 the hall was divided
horizontally, and its roof raised. The straight-headed windows
and panel tracery of the hall and E wing go with this phase.
Unusual tracery details: elongated trefoils with prominent
stylized flowers at the cusp points. In about 1625 the Court
Room was made in the upper-floor of the E wing, with an
external stair and doorway broken through a window.
    The present central entry was broken through a C16
window – its tracery head remains – which was itself inserted
when the intermediate floor was put in. The medieval entrance
and screens passage were at the E end. Machell shows a tower
porch here; the jamb of its outer doorway can be seen, and the
possible line of a vaulting-rib. The screens passage has gone
but the row of service doors remains, all it seems originally
with shouldered heads. From the central one a tunnel-vaulted
cross-passage runs to an outer door between the tunnel-
vaulted buttery and pantry – the same plan as Burneside (q.v.).
The airy COURT ROOM above is reached by a mural stair from
the northernmost door. Excellent kingpost roof of four trusses
with curved tie-beams and curved braces up to the ridge; so
the wing never had a fighting top. There is not a great deal to
see in the partitioned hall range, but the full-height C14
window reveals, pointed and four-centred, can be glimpsed
upstairs. The lower hall is still taller than the rooms in the
wings, and is provided with a large ingle fireplace – so it was

not moved upstairs, as so often in Cumbria (Burneside, Coniston). Modest dog-leg stair of late C17 character at the back. The W or family wing, not vaulted, but with another good kingpost roof, has a good C14 fireplace upstairs in the former solar, with a massive flat lintel on corbels. There is a smaller version downstairs. Transomed N and S solar windows with ogee trefoil heads, well preserved even to the shutter hinges and bolt fittings. The small wooden stair turning round a mast probably replaces a stone one in the scooped recess of the NW corner. Anthony Emery interprets the NW attachment as an original inner chamber.

Large cobbled farmyard with good OUTBUILDINGS. Machell shows a detached gatehouse. In 1969 the M6, on a two-level embankment, cut the farmland in half.

MILTON MILL, ½ m. SW. A splendid mill on the lowder principle (cf. Heron Mill, Beetham), with complete machinery, conserved by an enthusiastic owner. The site slopes steeply. The leat enters a small, possibly early C18 building with irregular fenestration. Its door is placed to allow easy access to the penstock outside and the stone floor inside, while allowing the miller to observe the approach lane. Three pairs of upper crucks support the roof. Attached at the gable-end a small kiln, of a different build. On the tail-race side a three-storey extension dated EW ESQ 1863. Its rubble masonry is more regular, with big ashlar quoins. Farmhouse snugly alongside.

(CHALLON HALL, ¾ m. NE. Dated RD 1760 but with C17 dates within. Five bays. Windows with flat surrounds with a continuous stone band to the heads. Door lintel of Yorkshire type with two large broadly curved ogee shapes, and rosettes. C18 oak staircase with turned balusters, closed string, ramped handrail and segmental bottom step. Court cupboard initialled and dated W 1616. Panelling with enriched frieze dated W 1611 in bedrooms; decorative plasterwork to landing ceiling.)

(BIRKRIGG PARK, 2¼ m. N, dated RS 1742 though probably C17, has similar flat window frames.)

RAMPSIDE (L)

ST MICHAEL. All by itself on the road to Barrow. Furness Abbey had a grange chapel here, but there is nothing to be seen of it. A rough datestone 1621 presumably represents a rebuilding. The present church is dated 1840 on the W tower, with the names of three wallers and a joiner, but no architect. Lancet windows, no buttresses. Porch and vestry 1866. Chancel 1892. Very plain, inside and out. – TILE PICTURE of Simeon by *J. A. Gibbs* in the tower, and a mosaic floor. – STAINED GLASS. E window by *Lambert & Moore* of Lancaster, 1892.

RAMPSIDE HALL. An early double pile, with twelve diagonally set chimneys (the famous Twelve Apostles) exhibited along the ridge. Probably mid- or late C17. Five bays and three storeys of cross-mullioned windows make a crowded symmetrical façade. Central door with castellated lintel. Ball obelisks on the kneelers. The plan centres on a massive spine wall containing all the stacks. The fireplaces indicate that there were two chambers front and back on each floor. (Handsome full-height staircase centrally at the back. Turned balusters and broad rectangular newels.)

LEADING LIGHT, lonely on the weedy foreshore opposite the sparse settlement. Of 1875. The only survivor of a set of three lights to guide ships into Barrow. 65-ft (20-metre)-high slim square tower of red and yellow brick. Brick lantern stage under a pyramidal roof.

ROA ISLAND, 1 m. SW. The tear-drop-shaped islet has figured in plans for a Morecambe Bay crossing since the dawn of the railway age. For a few years in the 1840s passengers took the train to Fleetwood, steamer from Fleetwood to Roa, then train again. That explains the CAUSEWAY. The railway station was in line with it occupying the NW corner of the island. Next to it was the Piel Pier Hotel, today the ROA ISLAND HOTEL. Henry Schneider's MARINE RESIDENCE of 1861/5 is the surprisingly grand red brick building with an Osborne tower, surprisingly by *E. G. Paley*. On the N shore, looking to Barrow, is the WATCH TOWER of 1849, built of cobbles and weatherworn sandstone, its gateway dramatically framing the sea. Railway company terraced HOUSING. Assertive concrete LIFEBOAT STATION, 2000 by *Bond Design*, with a wave roof.

RAUGHTON HEAD (C)

3040

Across the River Eden from Rose Castle (q.v.).

ALL SAINTS. The present church, of greenish stone, is of 1761, of five bays with round-topped, keyed-in windows. Venetian E window. EDW CARLIOL ME CONSECRAVIT 1678 on a stone at the E end, formerly over the W door. The W tower, broad, squat and red, with a semicircular stair-turret, was heightened in 1881 by *C. J. Ferguson*. C18 quoins below, lancets higher up. Very simple interior. The tower arch is full-width, allowing the tower space to be part of the nave and fully pewed (cf. Selside). – STAINED GLASS all by *Clayton & Bell*. S window to the Rev. John Carter †1901, a painterly scene in a conventional architectural frame: Christ kneels, richly robed, with a golden cup; behind and dimly seen a sorrowful angel, all blues and purples. – MONUMENTS. Rev. Robert Monkhouse †1822 aged thirty, a tablet by *Musgrave Lewthwaite Watson*. Watson was the most talented Cumbrian sculptor of those years (cf. Sebergham), and Monkhouse had been his teacher. This was his first work in marble, and he seems to have done it in 1828.

Small, pensive seated scholar on top of a sarcophagus. – Some good standing slabs in the graveyard, including a fine pair of 1854 by the E wall. At the NE corner James Knox, huntsman, with a bronze plaque including fox mask, whip and horn.

(ROEWATH, 1 m. SE. Five-bay C18 house, cement-rendered, and a lower C17 part l. which is sandstone. This has lost its mullions but retained its two small fire-windows.)

THACKWOOD NOOK, 1¼ m. SSE. Home of the Romantic dialect poet Susanna Blamire (1747–94), who comes across as a most attractive figure, blithe and vivacious. Datestone 1681 JS ES, i.e. John and Elizabeth Simpson (née Fetherstonhaugh of Kirkoswald). Irregular front, but the upper-floor fenestration more or less symmetrical. The mullioned windows are renewals. On the dormer gable a diminutive figure of a Red Spearman (a feudal tenure of Inglewood Forest). Perriam notes a mural stair, suggesting that the house had a look-out tower. Back-to-back with the C17 house is a Georgian one, with a cantilever stair.

(THISTLEWOOD, ½ m. E of Thackwood. Solar tower and five-bay C17 hall range set in a very large farmstead, now all converted to residential use. The tower basement is tunnel-vaulted, but lacks access to the upper levels, which are reached by an upper door from the hall range. This first-floor entrance has a shouldered head, suggesting a C14 date. The tower is finished with a pitched roof, i.e. no parapet. It has mullioned windows, the hall range two-light windows.)

(THE ASHES, 2 m. SE. Probably C15 in origin, with fine moulded beams in the lower hall of the same pattern as at Scales Hall and Dacre Castle (qq.v.). Traces of WALL PAINTING were found in 1974; a hunting scene.)

0090

RAVENGLASS (C)

A Roman then a great Viking settlement on the three-pronged estuary of the Irt, Mite and Esk. Beached ships were unloaded direct, the last one in 1914. There is no quayside, just a single street, broadening out for the market (charter 1208) and running straight out onto the foreshore. The old coast road, tide-dependent, continued over the sands. The houses are low, of C17 and C18 aspect. The BAY HORSE, a former inn, has an Eskdale door hood (cf. Eskdale Green) dated 1764 on the inner doorway. PENNINGTON HOUSE, C17, is a little grander. Five-bay, two-storey front with a hood over the front door. The OLD READING ROOM was built as a chapel in 1863. In 1876 Sir Josslyn Pennington, 5th Baron Muncaster, purchased the estate and carried out a good deal of new building, including a Public Hall (1878). The style is eclectic: granite, brick, roughcast, tile-hanging, timber framing. The mixture appears also in two large houses further afield: WALLS, near the Roman bath house (*see* below), of 1885 and 1898, and NEWTOWN.

RAILWAY STATIONS. The Furness Railway buildings, by *Paley & Austin*, 1873, were converted to the RATTY ARMS pub in 1974 by the adjacent Ravenglass & Eskdale Railway (*see* Eskdale). The R&ER station has an awning on the E platform brought from Millom in 1971; that on the W platform (1980) uses parts salvaged from Whitehaven (Bransty).

WAR MEMORIAL, ½ m. NW, at the road junction. By *Lutyens*, 1920. Slim, attenuated granite cross, knife-edged, with very short arms. Decoration is confined to the wreath on the plinth. Names in bronze on plinth and side walls.

ROMAN BATH HOUSE, ⅓ m. SE. An extraordinary survival, with masonry standing up to 12 ft 9 in. (3.9 metres) high: the W end of a building originally nearly 90 ft (27 metres) long, extending WSW–ESE, away from the modern road. Two parallel rows of rooms, of coursed red sandstone rubble, with many putlog holes for scaffolding. The walls are rendered with white mortar and coated internally with the waterproof pink *opus signinum*, patches of which survive. Buttresses suggest a substantial roof. Five deeply splayed window openings, with high sills; some window glass was found during excavations in 1881. Five doorways, all except one having low flat lintels. The first room in the N range was probably the changing room; an arched semicircular niche, for a statue, in its W wall, and traces of another in the E wall. An eroded threshold, with rebates for (stone?) jambs, leads into the S range. A culvert – or a stoke-hole for a furnace – through the wall in the SW room has a tiled arch. This room, and apparently all those to the E, were heated with hypocausts.

To the S and SW, between the bath house and the modern house called Walls, the slight earthworks of the ROMAN FORT, occupied from the C2 to late C4, its W half destroyed by the estuary of the Esk and by the railway of 1850.

RAVENSTONEDALE (W)

7000

ST OSWALD. C18 rebuild, similar to Bampton, with quoins and the same closely spaced round-topped windows, but with a little chancel. We know from Thomas Machell's *History* of 1631 that the old church had a tower, and three substantial round pillars and four arches, which sounds Norman; two pieces of beakhead survive loose. The new tower was built in 1738 (faculty) 'of ruff stone but coins windows and five foot on the top to be of ashler work of the old stones'. The designer may have been the incumbent, *Robert Mounsey*. N and S belfry lights, not identical, with Late Perp details; no W belfry opening. Old stones were used for the tower arch as well. The rest is of 1744, incorporating notably the outer doorway of the old s porch. It looks *c.* 1200.

The interior is atmospheric. A long dark panelled cross-passage, too narrow to be called a narthex, runs under the w gallery. A corridor rather than an arch turns into the tower, which has a pair of gallery staircases. Chancel arch incorporating medieval work. The church is seated college-chapel-wise, its great unobstructed width emphasized by the relatively low ceiling inserted in 1751–2. Six raked ranks of BOX PEWS on each side, and a full three-decker PULPIT with sounding board in the middle of the N side. The E end has been reordered with a couple of chancel steps, choir stalls and an organ (1893), but the altar is still penned by a shallow curved COMMUNION RAIL of turned balustrading. – PAINTING. A painter was evidently active in the early C18. LORD'S PRAYER and CREED, with a beardless and youthful St John, older, balding and bearded St Peter (the corresponding board on the other side hidden by the organ); ROYAL ARMS, George II; CLOCK FACE dated 1719, which must be from the old tower. – FONT. Small, octagonal, probably C17. – STAINED GLASS. E windows by *Shrigley & Hunt*, 1889. Others including nave s easternmost, St Margaret of Scotland, designed by *J. E. Nuttgens* for *Powells*, 1925, and St Cecilia, NW, a moody lady with flowers in her hair and a rich gown, playing a portative organ, by *D. Cottier*, 1890. – MONUMENT. Henry and Elizabeth Fothergill (a great name hereabouts), †1753 and 1788.

GILBERTINE CELL. Ineloquent ruin exposed on the N side of the church. The cell was colonized from Warton in Yorkshire in the reign of Henry II (1154–89). Represents E range of cloister, rebuilt in the C13 or C14 and extending further E. Machell described a quadrangle N of the church with some vaulted chambers. Three C13 cross-slabs were found in excavations in 1927–8.

SCHOOL, by the churchyard gate. Rebuilt 1872 by *Joseph Bintley* for R. Gibson, and extended 1895. Two storeys, five bays, with arched windows but otherwise pretty plain.

HIGH CHAPEL (United Reformed). 1727. Pretty, with round-arched windows inserted *c.* 1868, pink render, and upper and lower entrances at the uphill end. When the render was renewed two tiers of square-headed windows were revealed. The interior has been turned to face E, with just a W gallery remaining, which can be closed off by shutters. Closed 2006.

LOW CHAPEL (Wesleyan). Formed when the minister of the High Chapel turned Methodist in 1838. The trim little chapel, not gable-fronted but side-entry, is dated 1839.

ST AIDAN (closed), Newbiggin-on-Lune, 1¼ m. WNW. Built in 1892 for John Fothergill.

ELM LODGE. In the village. Mansion of 1885–7 for T. A. Metcalfe-Gibson, probably by *Robert Walker* of Kendal. Red and silver stone, strong asymmetry and a plethora of motifs. In the 1920s Rupert Metcalfe-Gibson changed its ramped grass platform for hard landscaping with terraces and steps.

Panelling and doors in the house come from Hwith (*see* below) and Brougham Hall (q.v.).

Walker designed the BLACK SWAN HOTEL close by (drawings dated 1897). It had an open spinning gallery with lyre balusters, now closed in, perhaps echoing the SCAR GALLERY next door. This has a three-bay spinning gallery going into a curved stair outshut with tiny windows.

PARK. N of the village, roughly oval. Enclosed by the 1st Lord Wharton (cf. Kirkby Stephen) in 1560–1. The wall was 12 ft (3.5 metres) high.

HWITH, high in the limestone hills, was built by *Joseph Bintley* in 1869–75 for John Hewetson and demolished in 1927.* It was a spectacular mansion in Jacobean style, with shaped gables and over-large mullioned-and-transomed windows. The bones of the strongly architectural GARDEN remain, strictly symmetrical, with matched castellated bastions and water features. The toolhouse was converted (1948) and enlarged (1960) to the present house. Designs by *Quinlan Terry* among others for a new house on the old cellars have so far been refused planning permission.

LANE FARM or LANE FARM COTTAGE, Weasdale, 1¾ m. W. Crazy *ferme ornée* dated 1870, 1887 and 1892 and inscribed '*T. Hewetson* del., *W. Hodgson* sculp.' A lintel dated 1767 is also incorporated. Unnecessary corbelling, rounded intersecting tracery, quatrefoils, circles and blank arches, knotty volutes are the motifs. A two-storey porch and a semicircular end projection are additions to what could once have been a normal three-bay front. The curved end is battered below and corbelled out above. The porch has a semi-octagonal top. Luscious carved detail, all very naughty, with fat rolls contrasting with crisp shallow sinkings. Lower windows are battered, upper ones set very deep, in one case behind colonnettes. One can perhaps see an Arts and Crafts derivation, but really the whole thing is completely wild. There is colour contrast too – buff dressings with pink fill for the porch front, pink dressings with rough grey limestone for the next section r. (Rich woodwork inside.) All this is small-scale, unlike the mighty BANK BARN adjacent, dated 1902.

TARN HOUSE. By the lonely A683, 2 m. SE. Set low and facing away from the road across a cobbled yard. 1664 GF IF (George and Julia Fothergill) on lintels of house and barn. The house is not quite symmetrical: three pairs of close-set windows r., two spaced out l. Two-storey porch in the middle. All roughcast except for the porch front. Unusual window in the porch gable of a stone pierced with five squares linked to make a St Andrew's cross. Below that a recessed panel with five coats of arms. Continuous dripmoulds terminated with hefty scrolls, with smaller scrolls where they drop between the windows, as well as either side of the porch window. The barn has the scrolls

---

*The name is an acronym of Hewetson's brothers in order, with his own name contributing the 'i'.

as well. Two trefoil-headed windows, presumably reused medieval, are in the E end.

106   RAILWAY VIADUCTS. Smardale Viaduct on the Settle and Carlisle railway is of 1875, curved, over Scandal Beck (2½ m. N). Smardale Gill Viaduct, ½ m. or so to its S, is on the Tebay–Barnard Castle line opened in 1861; engineer the ill-fated *(Sir) Thomas Bouch*.

6040   RENWICK (C)

ALL SAINTS. Dated 1844–5. By *John Kidd*, in simple Norman style, with simplest Norman chancel arch and wide splays to the windows. Bellcote. – Two-decker PULPIT from the previous church, rebuilt in 1733. Only the minimum Norman frill of *c.* 1845.*

METHODIST CHURCH, opposite. 1905. Porch mock-fortified in a half-hearted way, with battlements and a clock on a backless tower behind it. Flèche, Perp windows.

(HUDDLESCEUGH HALL, ¾ m. S. Early or mid-C16, extended. Datestones 1601 and 1617, the latter on an ornamented lintel.)

RICKERBY (C) *see* CARLISLE

ROA ISLAND (L) *see* RAMPSIDE

3060   ROCKCLIFFE (C)

ST MARY. Rebuilt in 1848 by *James Stewart* of Carlisle. It stands on a steep knoll looking N over the tidal sweep of the River Eden, towards the big house (below) and the sea. Dec, with an inhabited cornice right round. The S porch tower with its broach spire, completed only in 1881, had to be rebuilt in 1901 after a lightning strike. The belfry louvres are only halfway up. The N transept is the family chapel of the Mounsey-Heyshams. Steep open roof. – FONT. A shell and dove of white translucent alabaster, mounted on an alabaster quatrefoiled stem with a stylized rock at each end. Perhaps Late Georgian. – STAINED GLASS. Grisaille designs of *c.* 1848 by *John Scott & Sons*. The W window was sent to Gilsland and replaced by a *Hardman* window. – MONUMENTS. Elegant C20 Mounsey-Heysham tablets in green and grey marble with mosaic work. – C10 CROSS in the churchyard, in its socket. Solid circular head with very short projecting arms, the usual armpit piercings

* The Victorian HARMONIUM Pevsner noted has gone.

represented instead by bosses. The stout stem has two raised collars, as though made of separate pieces. The panels are carved with alternating interlace and fanged beasts. – WAR MEMORIAL, 1920. Granite cross with bronze relief of a soldier in full kit, with the rock cliff and River Eden behind.

CASTLETOWN HOUSE, ¾ m. WNW, on the river. By *Peter Nicholson* with *William Reid*, 1809–11, for Robert Mounsey, a Carlisle lawyer, possibly after a sketch by *Thomas Telford*. The river front, the original entrance, is ashlar-faced, of five well-spaced bays and a pair of pedimented wings. These and the centre have broad and very shallow angle pilaster-strips, again without capitals or bases. The short links are canted back, which jars a little, but allows the apsidal ends of the main rooms to be lit. Tetrastyle portico of square columns without capitals or bases, with incised decoration. Shallow bow at the N end. In 1851–2 *James Stewart* turned the house round for George Mounsey, extending the land side by six feet or so and creating a new entrance recessed behind a pair of Doric columns *in antis*. The doorway behind the portico is tripartite and has a segmental fanlight.

Entrance from the river terrace is into a wide hallway ceiled with a radiating Greek key motif; Nicholson planned a shallow dome here, and a grand cupola room at the top of the stairs, but neither happened. Through a Doric screen is the stair, a shallow and slender cantilever, smooth underneath. On the turn an odd oval window brings borrowed light through Stewart's extension. The principal rooms both have columned screens in front of an apsed end, Ionic on the l., Doric r. The w end libraries have been knocked together to make a fine music room.

ROSE CASTLE (C)

3040

Residence of the bishops of Carlisle. At first sight essentially C19, but its history is long and complicated. The manor of Dalston was granted to Bishop Walter Mauclerc by Henry III in 1230. Edward I and his court stayed here in 1300, by which time it was probably a large manor house, unfortified save perhaps for a moat. It was sacked by the Scots in 1314 and 1322, in 1337 while Edward III's licence to crenellate of 1336 was being implemented, and again in 1355. Rose Castle was rebuilt into a roughly quadrangular, inward-looking castle of the same type as Naworth (licence to crenellate 1335); probably not, as has been assumed, in stages but essentially in one campaign by the warlike Bishop John Kirkby (1332–52).* The NE or Strickland Tower and the massive N and W curtains survive, together with the outer

---

*See Tim Tatton-Brown in *Carlisle and Cumbria: British Archaeological Association Conference Transactions 27* (2004).

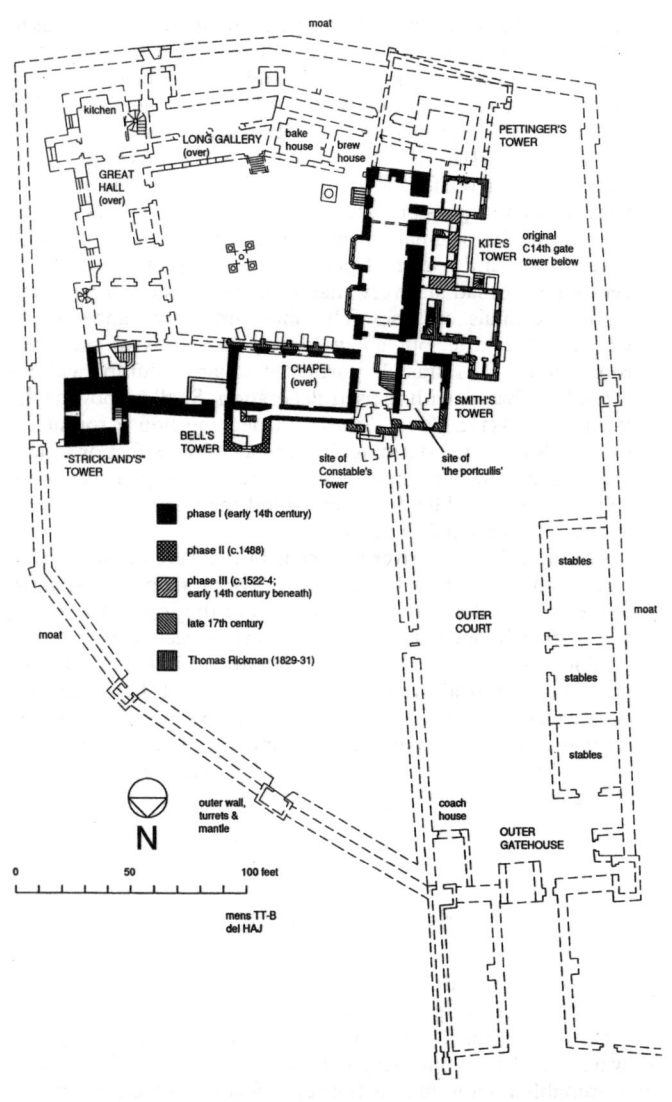

Rose Castle.
Plan, 2004

ward or mantle constructed at much the same time. The main gatehouse was in the middle of the W side, now part of the muddled agglomeration called Kite's Tower, opposite the hall formerly on the E side. Bishop Bell added a tower in the middle of the N side in 1487–9 to go with his rebuilt chapel.

Wasted in 1648 and lying roofless during the Commonwealth, the castle was patched up in 1660–4 by Bishop Sterne and

probably *Alexander Pogmire*. The ruined S and E sides of the
quadrangle were demolished, including the bishop's hall, one of
the finest apartments in the North, together with the Great
Chamber between the chapel and Strickland Tower on the N side.
In 1668–74 Bishop Rainbow and *William Thackeray* remodelled
the remaining W and N sides in a regular and classicizing
form, shown in Buck's engraving of 1739. In the 1760s Bishop
Lyttelton and his nephew *Thomas Pitt* undertook a whimsical
Gothicization, but as at the cathedral this was wiped out by more
serious Gothic work under Bishop Percy (1826–56). *Thomas
Rickman* refashioned the living quarters in 1828–30, building out
on the W side, and in 1851–2 *Anthony Salvin* restored the
Strickland Tower.

Rose Castle is approached from the N, reaching first the gate in
the outer mantle, which rises here to its corbelled parapet. A
turret appears in the NW corner, but otherwise the wall is cut
down to lawn level. Ahead is *Rickman*'s entrance, called the
Percy Tower; not the medieval entry, though there may have
been a postern here. To its l. appear the C14 curtain wall with
Bishop Bell's Tower projecting from it, and at the far end,
partly isolated by the removal of the chamber, the STRICK-
LAND TOWER. So we shall start there. The fighting top is
entirely *Salvin* – a drawing at Rose shows that Thackeray had
capped it with a pyramid roof. The same drawing proves that
the semicircular stair projection on the S is original, though it
looks all Salvin now. Entry is at first-floor level by shouldered-
arched doorways to the W (blocked) and S, once connecting
with first-floor apartments. A pointed-trefoiled piscina (heavily
restored) inside suggests that part was a chapel. The forms of
the doorways and piscina show that the tower was built in the
C14, probably after the first licence to crenellate (1336), rather
than in Strickland's time (1400–19). A straight mural stair goes
clammily down to the vaulted basement, its only access, lit
from two tiny windows reached by steps in the wall. Salvin's
spiral stair is carried up to a turret. Excavation in 1994
suggested that the demolished E curtain wall, fronting the hall
range, was bonded in to the tower.

The N CURTAIN WALL, also bonded in, was lowered by
Bishop Law (1769–87). The scar can be seen on Strickland's
Tower, and a short section still rises to full height by BISHOP
BELL'S TOWER, identified by Bs and bells in the string
course. This was built in front of the curtain in 1487–9 in
conjunction with Bell's Chapel behind. It has two-light
windows, the lights with two-centred uncusped arches. The E
bell-turret on top of the curtain must be *Rickman*'s in its
present form. More curtain wall, now full-height and retaining
its C14 corbel table, shelters the chapel (*see* below). At the
PERCY TOWER Rickman's smooth Gothic entrance disguises
Thackeray's interesting C17 rebuild, which had cross-mullioned
windows and pediments either triangular or curved, with flat
bits at the ends. Thackeray's proportions and openings are

29

unaltered, just Gothicized. His tower in turn replaced the medieval Constable's Tower. Round the corner on the w side is SMITH'S TOWER, also refronted by *Thackeray* and then *Rickman*. It was the site of the 'Portcullis' identified in a plan of *c.* 1671, which suggests a diagonal secondary entrance here. Medieval masonry appears on its lower w face, still containing a small blocked window. In the middle of the w side, now recessed to insignificance between Rickman's additions at the sw corner, is BISHOP KITE'S TOWER. As modified in 1522–4, it bears Kite's arms as Archbishop of Armagh on the upper string course. This was the principal C14 gatehouse, and still has a wide archway at its base, though the head has been altered. The paired Tudor windows of the lower three floors are evidently insertions into earlier masonry, only those of the fourth floor being entirely of Kite's time. The tower was repaired by *Alexander Pogmire* in 1653–5, to compensate for the loss of the e and s sides. The truncated s end carries the initials JB for Bishop Bloomer and the date 1955, where the Victorian kitchen was removed.

In the COURTYARD the fronts are almost entirely by *Rickman*; especially characteristic the two great bays of the superimposed State Dining Room and Drawing Room in the w range facing e, Late Gothic rather than Tudor. Again this is but window dressing: *Thackeray*'s double transoms, pediments and quoins were replaced, leaving proportions and openings untouched. The chapel windows on the n side are square and mullioned below, Perp above, with the thin buttresses and low-pitched roof of the 1830s.

STATE ROOMS. The front door in the Percy Tower is still locked by Lady Anne Clifford's key and lock, given according to her oddly possessive custom to Bishop Rainbow and carrying her initials AP and the date 1673. *Rickman*'s heavy Gothic STAIR with its cinquefoils, roses, and diocesan and Percy arms stands rather too close to the door for comfort. The splayed doorcases still have a feeling of Gothick. Beyond is the long STATE DINING ROOM with two Rickman chimneypieces. What is not immediately apparent is the great thickness of the C14 curtain wall behind the fireplaces, between the state rooms and the outer accretions. The further fireplace blocks the medieval entry through Kite's Tower. The principal rooms are as usual upstairs. First the DRAWING ROOM with its delicious C18 Chinese wallpaper (Bishop Lyttelton?) and a more elaborate pair of *Rickman* fireplaces. Rather sparse Gothic ceiling, as in the State Dining Room. In the n wing is the first-floor CHAPEL. Another multi-phase structure: early C14, then Bishop Bell's of 1487–9, repaired in 1673–5 by *Thackeray* and Bishop Rainbow. What we see now is *Rickman*'s, though it would be interesting to know if anything of Bishop Lyttelton's and *Thomas Pitt*'s work survives; the three tall w niches give it a whiff of Strawberry Hill. Panelling and pews with linenfold, some medieval, from Lambeth Palace.

SETTING. Further stretches of the C14 outer defence or mantle survive on the E and S, heavily buttressed to the E overlooking the Caldew valley, with bases of interval turrets. Successive bishops have gone in for gardening in a big way, including a rose garden and terracing by *Joseph Paxton* for Bishop Percy. A long line of Redwoods leads towards Carlisle, passing *Rickman*'s Home Farm and a small square DOVECOTE dated 1700 (Bishop Smith).

ROSLEY (C)

3040

HOLY TRINITY, 1½ m. N of the village. 1839–41 by *John Rook*, surveyor. Decidedly pre-archaeological. Thin W tower with steep pyramid roof. Wide lancets, low flat ceiling, tiny chancel. Dec E window inserted. Wooden tracery on the N; on the S it has been removed for STAINED GLASS, including a Millennium celebration of the village, by *Alex Haynes* of *Albion Glass*. E window by *Hardman*, 1909.

RUSLAND (L)

3080

ST PAUL. On a rocky knoll; not a habitation in sight. 1745, enlarged and given a new character in 1866–9 by *Ewan Christian* and *Miles Thompson*. Aisleless nave, W tower. The S wall of the new chancel had to be arched over the MONUMENT of James Twisaday †1844. – STAINED GLASS. E window by *Hardman*, the rest by *H. W. Lonsdale*, 1870s–80s.

(RUSLAND HALL. Early C18, with additions of *c.* 1850 attributed by Angus Taylor to *Thompson & Webster*. Of five bays and two-and-a-half storeys, with two-bay additions. Elegant doorway with Doric columns and a triglyph frieze.)

FRIENDS' MEETING HOUSE, Rookhow, ⅓ m. W. The date 1725 is cut in the iron latch. Built to accommodate the get-togethers of the Swarthmoor Monthly Meeting. Meeting house with gallery l., two-storey cottage r., wide, open porch between. Former coachhouse and stables on either side in front.

INDUSTRIAL REMAINS. ¼ m. W. on the l. bank of Force Beck, STONEY HAZEL FORGE. This was the last bloomery forge built in Furness, not long after the first blast furnaces in the area were established (*see* Haverthwaite). The site was leased in 1718 to a consortium led by *Edward Robinson*, and had been abandoned by 1743. A pond and leat, now dry; the roofless forge with its water-wheel pit; the remains of a charcoal store; and a house. In the woods above, charcoal pitsteads are clearly seen. The survival of such a complex is probably unique in the country.

½ m. s, a surprisingly complete CI8 TANNERY. A set of pits for soaking, stone hogbacks on which the skins were scraped, and – most remarkably – a bark mill, with a curved wall to accommodate a horse gin to crush the bark needed for the process.

3000

RYDAL (W)

A beautiful spot with many artistic and literary associations, indeed with some claim to be the place where Picturesque appreciation of landscape originated. The (le) Flemings acquired the estate in about 1468, taking up residence at the new hall in 1589. Since 1940 they have lived in Dorset, but still own the village. All the houses are permanently occupied, which is a rare thing in the Lakes.

ST MARY. Built by Lady le Fleming in 1823–4 (£1,500) to avoid her drunken brother-in-law, Richard, Rector of Grasmere. *George Webster*'s first church, and sadly hideous. Painfully starved w tower with cement corner-pieces and over-sized buttresses. Low bays l. and r. Battered base to nave and tower. The nave window surrounds stand proud, presumably for rendering, but instead the stone has been ribbon-pointed. Wooden tracery. Only the rainwater goods are fancy, initialled and dated 1824 with the Fleming arms. In 1884 a chancel was added, with free Perp stone tracery and a conventional plinth. The family gallery is reached by a porch and steps on the N. Bare interior, flat ceiling. – STAINED GLASS. E window by *Ward & Hughes*. s, Arnold memorial window by *Burlison & Grylls*, 1889; two by *Powells*, one of them designed by *Holiday*, 1891, with pretty child angels and banners. The commemorative brass tablet which goes with it is a good Arts and Crafts specimen.

RYDAL HALL. The house forms a T. The top-piece was added in the 1790s with its central bow looking proudly down the park towards Ambleside. Sir Michael Fleming was in 1783 sent 'a plan and particulars of alterations' by Joseph Senhouse of Calder. This does not survive, nor was it executed. Drawings apparently by *Carr* and an executant architect probably relate to the existing structure. Lower entrance wing behind. The E angle is filled in by a jumble of older buildings. At the back of the entrance wing a wooden cantilever stair of typical Carr type. In the top-piece large dining and drawing rooms, fitted out *c.* 1824 by *George Webster* with typical plasterwork and chimneypieces. Upstairs library over the entrance hall, with mahogany door and bookcases. More work in Edwardian times, e.g. in the entrance hall, disguising what may be the original hall with its inglenook and heck. The unbeautiful cement rendering and concrete balustrade were done then.

GARDENS and PARK were improved in the late C17 by Sir Daniel Fleming for the sake of the view, and in 1669 he built the little GROT or VIEWING HOUSE, with a big window to frame a perfectly composed view of the falls – an early, if not the very first, instance of such sensibility. 'Here nature has performed everything in little that she usually executes on the largest scale', wrote William Mason in 1775. *Thomas Mawson* remade the garden in 1909. Influenced no doubt by Reginald Blomfield's *The Formal Garden in England* (1892), and having visited Italy in 1905, he imposed Italianate straight lines and symmetry: a painful contrast with the wildness of the falls. The concrete balustrading, steps and urns disintegrated ungracefully, necessitating vastly expensive restoration in 2006. In 2007–8 a hydro-electric turbine was installed which will make the site carbon-neutral, but emasculate the falls. Truly there is no such thing as a free lunch. – SCULPTURE, Escape to Light by *Josefina de Vasconcellos*, 1996.

RYDAL MOUNT. Wordsworth's home from 1813 until his death in 1850. A multi-phase building. The oldest-looking part is the w wing, C17 with a spice cupboard dated EAK (Edward and Agnes Knott) 1710, bressumer, and fire-window. Dorothy Wordsworth's bedroom was above, the poet's study in the attic. The rest looks *c.* 1750, when it was turned to face the view, though it incorporates older parts. Five-bay, sash-windowed front. In the early C20 the house was opened up internally, with a broad bay window. The GARDEN is *Wordsworth*'s creation.* He used its given features. The mount in front was emphasized with steps, concentric paths and planting, the steepest bit at the side terraced into a series of not-too-formal walks.

UNDERMOUNT. Probably the Hare and Hounds Inn etched by Green in the early C19. Statesman's (i.e. yeoman's) house and bank barn forming an L. Gentrified in about the 1820s, with iron lattice windows and pretty interiors of *Webster* type. However, so steep is the hill that the old house, facing the other way, is largely complete underneath.

GLEN ROTHAY HOTEL. C17 inn extended at both ends and gentrified, 1817 and *c.* 1835. Gothick is the style. The old part is the bar and Oak Room; the latter retains the inglenook fireplace with its bressumer. IAF 1627 on the spice cupboard, AF 1627 on the overmantel – but this is *ex situ*, perhaps part of the court cupboard. The posh parts are lofty, with *Webster* ribbed ceilings and reeded door surrounds. Cantilever stair of wood, like that at Rydal Hall, with the same balusters.

COTE HOW, across the River Rothay, s. C16 or C17. Tucked in the uphill angle of the L, behind the pretty spinning gallery, is a rare survival in the region of exposed timber framing. The stout herringbone timbering, coloured red, is protected from the weather by the cantilevered gallery. Close studding within and a single wall-post suggest that the whole wing was timber-

---

*Wordsworth's disapproval of the exotic trees planted by the Flemings round Rydal Hall almost led to his eviction; *see* Foxe Howe, below.

framed. Cambered tie-beams, meant to be seen; cf. Coniston Hall, another Fleming house. A wall curves out at the back to meet the galleried wing, but inside is not a curved stair but a straight run of solid oak treads encased in C17 panelling.

3 NAB COTTAGE, ½ m. W. Home of de Quincey's wife Margaret Simpson, and later of Hartley Coleridge. Dated IAP (John and Anne Parke) 1702. Perfectly placed to cast its white reflection upon the stillness of Rydal Water.

PARK BARN, 1 m. S, near Rydal Farm and Crow How. Built in 1659 by Sir Daniel Fleming. One of the earliest ramp-entry or bank barns (but *see* Sizergh). Beautifully built and of a goodly size, with an extra gable in front for show.

FOX HOWE, Under Loughrigg, 1 m. W. Holiday home of Dr Thomas Arnold of Rugby, and then of his son Matthew, the poet. Arnold built the house in 1832 with advice from his friend, William Wordsworth, and from *George Webster*. Wordsworth had made a similar design for Dora's Field in 1825, when he feared eviction from Rydal Mount (*see* above). It is meant to be vernacular, with round chimneys and unplastered walls. The true date shows in the Gothick porch and Regency glazing bars. The mixture is surprisingly dour.

FOX GHYLL, next door, is prettier, with separately roofed sections of different dates. The overall character is Regency: tall sash windows with edge glazing, shallow pavilion roofs, cream-painted roughcast, Gothick porch. Heavily moulded plasterwork in *Webster* style. Taper-twirling balusters and boldly painted and etched glass on the stair.

ST BEES (C)

ST MARY AND ST BEGA. A Benedictine nunnery established *c.* 650 was destroyed by the Danes. The monastery, also Benedictine and dedicated to the legendary Irish princess St Bega, was founded from St Mary's Abbey in York by William de Meschines *c.* 1120. The W doorway was built not long after, and an E end of which we have fragmentary remains, but the parish may have had to make do with a pre-monastic building until the new nave could be built in the C13. The monastic parts have gone, but the PRIORY CHURCH is gratifyingly complete. After the Dissolution in 1539 the nave continued in parish use, with extensive repairs in 1611, according to a stone in the baptistery. In 1816 Bishop Law of Chester re-roofed the E end and established a theological college, the first outside Oxford and Cambridge. From 1855 into the 1880s *William Butterfield* restored and embellished the rest of the church, rebuilding the aisles and crossing tower and making a new chancel in the westernmost bay of the presbytery.

From the N the great length of the church can be appreciated. Strong crossing tower and transept, part-Norman and

St Bees Priory.
Engraving by Samuel and Nathaniel Buck, 1739, detail

part-*Butterfield* of 1855–8. Nave with Late Perp clerestory, aisle mostly Butterfield. The long and narrow E.E. chancel, presumably replacing a short Norman E end, is quite a spectacular piece (if one ignores the two separate roofs), with tall lancets originally shafted and still with waterleaf capitals, and shallow buttresses. The E termination had two tiers of shafted lancets, the upper tier cut down when the roof was flattened. Corbel table with faces and some nailhead. On the S side a blocked four-bay Dec arcade shows that a chancel chapel has been lost. Part of its outer S wall survives with a window jamb and part of a doorway, and a jamb of its large E window. All have complex hollow mouldings of the late C13 or early C14. The S transept front with its plain Norman-style windows is mostly *Butterfield*'s refacing; this of course is where the dormitory range abutted. Buck's print of 1739 shows the S aisle wall blind for the cloister, with small windows above the roof-line. A rough length of windowless wall at the W end shows where the western monastic range adjoined. The N transept front is also Butterfield's.

The W front faces a narrow yard at the side of the vicarage. It has three stepped lancets, and shallow buttresses later helped by bigger canted ones. The rich W doorway is of *c.* 1160. Three orders (the columns have gone, bar one) with scrolly capitals including figure-work, and much zigzag and also some sparse eroded beakhead in the arch. Also Late Norman the S aisle W wall. The fine DOOR with ironwork scrollwork is late C20.

The INTERIOR is dominated by *Butterfield*'s screen and E partition wall, and his cinquefoil openings separating the E end of the aisles from the transepts. Six-bay E.E. arcades; on the S octagonal piers alternate with round ones, but on the N the mid-pier has eight attached keeled shafts instead. Waterholding bases, on the S side at any rate. All the responds are keeled, and the E responds have leaf capitals. Capitals decorated with very small nailhead. The arches are simply moulded. Two labelstops have beasts' heads, one of them a Norman piece without doubt. The clerestory is as low as it can be, its windows fitting in the arcade spandrels, with their sills sometimes below the arch-heads. This looks like 1611 work, to go with the flat lead roofs shown by Buck. The present roof is characteristically Butterfield's, emphatically angular. The W piers of the crossing are clustered and keeled again, but the E ones are Norman, with just a fat half-colonnette with a crude Ionic-derived capital. The tall pointed arches do not sit comfortably on them. Chancel of a single bay with Victorian C13-style windows, but that on the N side has a round rere-arch with continuous moulding, i.e. it forms part of the Norman chancel. In the N transept E wall a small shouldered doorway, and a piscina.

FURNISHINGS. *Butterfield*'s partition wall acts as a REREDOS. Blank tracery, sunk circles, flat cinquefoils and bands in yellows, reds and black. *Minton* tiles. – ALTAR RAILS also by *Butterfield*. Iron, coloured gold, blue and red. – Butterfield's SCREEN is dated 1886, so right at the end of the job. It goes right up to the apex of the crossing arch. Metal, fully coloured in red, yellow, grey, light blue, and with a surprising mixture of correct and invented motifs. The top rail for instance has square gilded flowers like a medieval screen, but each merlon of the blue and yellow castellation has a little door and porthole windows, like a face. – N transept, SCULPTURE by *Josefina de Vasconcellos* 1955, the Vision of St Bega. – ORGAN, filling the S transept. An exceptionally large and fine instrument by 'Father' Willis of 1899. – FONT, 1858. Unmistakable *Butterfield* again; a great hexagonal block of pink-veined grey marble. – STAINED GLASS. All by *William Wailes*, to Butterfield's specifications. Strong primary colours and hieratic compositions. In the clerestory just one by *Shrigley & Hunt*, a bonny contrast.

MONUMENTS. Medieval monuments from the presbytery are gathered in the S aisle E. Prior Cotyngham †1379; tonsured portrait on an incised slab, smashed and reassembled. – Battered effigies of a knight in mail, perhaps Robert of Harington †1298, and another in plate armour holding a chalice, perhaps Anthony Lord Lucy of Cockermouth †1368. – D'Yrton stone, from Irton (q.v.). Linked to Adam de Yrton who travelled to the Holy Land *c.* 1100, though Peter Ryder dates it to the C13. Ringed cross on a stepped base, with sword and what may be a pilgrim's scrip. – Incised effigy of Joan de Lucy †1369. – Many other incised grave-slabs. – CROSS-SHAFT, on the window sill. C10, with spiral scroll decoration. – S aisle W, tablets. Capt. William Willcox †1798; weeper, sarcophagus, sword, musket and helmet, signed (*John*) *Bingley*. – William

Ainger D.D. †1840, with a portrait bust on top, signed *J. G. Lough*, London. – Capt. James Spedding †1857, signed *Nelsons*, Carlisle. – Chancel N, Maria Claudine Lumb †1865 aged four. White marble effigy in a sandstone Gothic altar recess. She lies on a rolled-up mat in a simple shift dress, with tiny hands and feet but rather an adult face.

OLD COLLEGE HALL, i.e. the E part of the CHANCEL. Used now by the school. A side door in the E partition wall gives access: a sudden shock of bright light and secular character. The wooden floor is inserted at sill level. Flat ceiling. Five very tall N lancets, wider at the E end, with continuous roll mouldings. Blocked S arcade of three bays (the fourth is W of the partition) with large plain-glazed windows inserted. Tall multiply-moulded arches, piers with quarter-hollows. The lower blocking is solidly done with a sloping sill for windows, showing that the chapel was lost before the Dissolution. Spectacular E wall. Three tall lancets, graded in width but not height, and separated by an elaborate system of tabernacles with colonnettes in two tiers. Sill walkway behind. Something has been chopped away from the middle tier; perhaps a continuous mid-level arcade across the windows. The ensemble can be dated to *c.* 1200, recalling the E wall of Kirkby Lonsdale (q.v.) which was also under St Mary's York. It is possible, standing here and looking back, mentally to reunite the whole great length of the church. In the storeroom underneath is the medieval floor, with altar step and more grave-slabs.

PRECINCTS. NEW COLLEGE HALL of 1863 is immediately S of the chancel. The personification of *Butterfield*: tough Gothic with no messing. Since the theological college closed in 1895 it has been used as a parish hall. Buck's view shows the monastic gatehouse W of the church, and what was presumably the refectory on the S. Nothing can be seen now, except perhaps the low wall retaining the vicar's front garden. Set in the vicarage wall W of the W end of the church is a carved LINTEL with a cambered top, found in the S aisle wall in 1868. It is in splendid condition. Viking in style, probably Norman in date, i.e. C12. Spirited dragon with wings and curly tail, warrior with sword, and several patches of interlace. In the niche below a wayside CROSS found on the Whitehaven road. – In the monastic graveyard, N, is another C10 CROSS-SHAFT, still in its socket stone. Interlace with animals. Beckermet group, Anglo-Scandinavian. – By the road a war memorial CROSS by *W. G. Collingwood*, 1919. The wall between the two sections of the graveyard consists of stacked grave-slabs.

ST BEES SCHOOL, opposite the E end of the church. Founded on his deathbed in 1583 by Edmund Grindal (*see also* below), Archbishop of Canterbury, who never forgot 'that little angle where I was born, the ignorantest part in religion, and most oppressed of covetous landlords, of any'. The centre of the school is the COURTYARD open towards the chancel of the church. Its N side is the original SCHOOL HOUSE of 1587, built of abbey stones, extended to the r. of the door *c.* 1697 to provide a house for the schoolmaster. The original schoolroom is scarcely altered, its wooden wainscot a mass of graffiti. The top storey was added in 1820 by Lord Lonsdale, who also contributed to the foundation of the theological college; conscience money perhaps, for he was extracting coal from under the school's lands. In 1842–4, after proper recompense had been agreed, the school expanded, with typical academic Tudor architecture of the time: the E side with a gate tower, and the larger S side with its own central entrance tower. Thin octagonal turrets. By *Thomas Nelson* (or was he only the contractor?). The CHAPEL and the LABORATORIES and LIBRARY to its N (1906–7), the HEADMASTER'S HOUSE (1886), and the GYM (1899) are all by the *Austin & Paley* practice, concurrently working at the schools at Rossall (Lancs.) and Sedbergh (then in Yorkshire, West Riding). The chapel is in a free Perp style, with a S tower with projecting top and saddleback roof. It slopes down markedly to the E, and has low passage aisles of unequal lengths below a clerestory. Stained glass by *J. H. Bonnor*, and by the other *William Morris*, i.e. of Westminster; sculpture, The Hand by *Josefina de Vasconcellos* (1955) in green slate. Also by the Austin & Paley firm SCHOOL HOUSE of 1885, some distance to the NE. To its E the MEMORIAL HALL, standard school fare of 1954. WHITELAW CENTRE of 1991, brick.

BRIDGE, over Pow Beck. Built by the will of Archbishop Grindal, 1585, with a stone to say so. Since widened. The original stone is in the school.

STATION (Furness Railway), 1870s. Of red sandstone, rock-faced. Small, slightly later SIGNAL BOX, with emphatically battered stone base and hipped roof.

W of the station, SCULPTURE, a flat-faced St Bega in her coracle by *Colin Telfer* of Maryport, 2000. Of powdered iron ore and resin. Also WAR MEMORIAL, by *J. D. Kenworthy*, c. 1920. Of St Bees sandstone; a Roman St George in toga and wreath, and a curled-up dragon.

MAIN STREET climbs up SE from the station. STONEHOUSE FARM, r., still a farm, has an entertaining exhibition of carved stones above its door including the date 1712. Over the door of the Georgian MANOR HOUSE HOTEL, l., a swan-necked pediment. The former CO-OP opposite sports a folksy shaped gable with giant scrolls, and a beehive. Much higher up is the little UNITED METHODIST CHAPEL of 1866. Sweet interior brightly lit by tall Gothick-glazed windows front and back, although there are none at the sides. A tunnel underneath leads to a pair of houses behind. This is followed by FAIRLADIES FARM (No. 102, r.): one-bay cottage, three-bay house, barn all in line, with arms of James Spedding and Elizabeth Harrington who married in 1779. On the other side FAIRLADIES BARN, of red stone, heavily converted.

FINKLE STREET runs E off Main Street at its lower end. MANOR STEAD on Cross Hill was Archbishop Grindal's birthplace, built between 1500 and 1520 by his father William, a tenant farmer to the priory. It has a round-headed doorway, and round arches to the lights of some of the windows. Other windows partly from remodelling in 1983–4. (Fragmentary wall paintings of *c.* 1580–1600.) Opposite is the long, even, rendered row of LONSDALE TERRACE of *c.* 1840, and, a little higher up, GRINDALL PLACE; both with Tudor dripmoulds.

NETHERTOWN, s of St Bees, towards Sellafield. A line of home-made SHACKS clings to the strand between the railway and the high-tide mark. Of beach cobbles, wood, felt shingles, and sometimes quite fanciful.

ST JOHN'S IN THE VALE (C)

ST JOHN. High above the vale, 2½ m. ESE of Keswick, on a gated unfit-for-motors road. A low single cell rebuilt in 1845, except surely for the tiny w tower/turret (cf. Threlkeld). The interior was reordered with pleasing simplicity in 1893. (The ALTAR comes from Crosthwaite church; by *G. G. Scott,* 1848. – STAINED GLASS. E window by *Shrigley & Hunt,* 1895.)

STONE CIRCLE (THE CARLES), Castlerigg (2 m. E of Keswick).   6 In an incomparable position, on the level summit of a low ridge amid the mountains. A circle, up to 110 ft (34 metres) in diameter, of thirty-eight close-set irregular boulders, all but five still standing. Tall 'portal' stones flank an entrance on the N. In the SE quadrant a rectangular setting of stones; its date and function both unknown.

SATTERTHWAITE (L)

CHURCH. Mostly by *Robert Walker* of Windermere, 1888: w gallery removed, new roof, windows etc. Dwarf w tower, diagonally turned SW porch. – (STAINED GLASS by *Shrigley & Hunt.*)

(BRIDGE, 1905. One of the first *Hennebique*-type reinforced concrete bridges in the country.)

GRIZEDALE HALL and FOREST PARK. The hall, 1 m. NW of the village, was a grim-looking affair of 1905 by *Walker, Carter & Walker* of Windermere for Harold Brocklebank of the Cunard shipping line. The estate was sold in 1937 to the Forestry Commission, and the fells planted with conifers. A prisoner-of-war camp during 1939–46, the hall was demolished in 1957 down to its base courses. Steps, outlines of bays and doorways remain, as do the balustraded terraces and ornamental planting, and lodges, kitchen yard and estate buildings. In 1968 the head forester, Bill Grant, returned from a travelling scholarship wanting to bring people back into the conifer desert. He established a gallery, craft studios, a theatre and, throughout the forest, environmental SCULPTURES. Ninety-two are listed in the 2003–5 brochure, scattered over many miles of forest trail. The best use found materials – wood, water, stone, wind, wilderness. Unannounced, unlabelled, hard to find, they sharpen one's perceptions. Change and decay are accepted, even celebrated.

The first artist in residence was *Richard Harris*. His Cliff Structure, Quarry Structure and Dry Stone Passage were all installed in 1977–8. Wooden Waterway is by *David Nash*, 1978. *Andy Goldsworthy* contributed Seven Spires (1984), Sidewinder (1984–5), and The Wall that went for a Walk (1990). The first works were abstract, but soon figurative pieces appeared. *David Kemp*'s Ancient Forester exists in two incarnations, 1987 and 1995, one overlooking the car park. Heart-stoppers in the deep forest are *Sally Matthews*'s Wild Boar Clearing (1987), Wolves (1993), and A Cry in the Wilderness (1990). C21 additions are brought in rather than the result of residencies; e.g. those by *Steve Blaylock* of Carlisle, 2005, in bright metal instead of forest materials, with modish *Lord of the Rings* overtones. His Mea Culpa of 2006 consists of two straining, linked figures of riveted metal strips.

INFORMATION CENTRE and SHOP by *Vis Williams Partnership*, *c.* 1986. In 2004–6 an education centre called THE YAN by *Sutherland Hussey Architects* was built around the ancillary buildings of the mansion. Of stone, Douglas fir and glass with a dramatically kicking-up roof.

SAWREY (L)
(Near Sawrey and Far Sawrey)

The W shore of Windermere is very different from the domesticated E shore. Forested, with clearings, all the way over to Coniston water, with no villas to speak of, few roads, no town. The forest is the preserve of large estates such as Graythwaite (q.v.) and the Forestry Commission. The settlement of Far Sawrey lies ⅔ m. E of Near Sawrey, and ¾ m. W of the ferry station.

ST PETER, Far Sawrey. 1866–72, by *Robert Brass* of London. Unattractively fussy and bunched up, with an undersized tower in the NE transept angle. Of black slate rubble with white sandstone dressings and a polychrome slate roof. Paired lancets, a triplet E and five W. Unexpectedly spacious and light interior. – STAINED GLASS. E window to Joseph Garnett †1869, by *Cox & Sons*. Transept ends by *R. B. Edmundson & Son*, 1870s. N transept W, 1886 by *Wailes & Strang* in hot orange colours. Nave, a musical window to Joseph Ridgway Bridson †1901 of Bryerswood.

FERRY HOUSE, Far Sawrey, by the lake shore. Large dispiriting former hotel of 1880–1 by *Joseph Pattinson* for his brother

G. H. Pattinson, builder, whose memoir conveys uncharacter-
istic regret for the destruction of the 'delightful' Ferry Inn. The
building is raised on a basement storey disguised by turfed
banking. To this the Freshwater Biological Association, who
took over in 1947, added the PEARSON LABORATORIES of
1967, by *Gill & Rhodes*. It was intended to be a storey higher,
hence the chopped-off stair-tower. Of reinforced concrete,
which shows in the upper floor with its continuous mullioned
windows but is hidden below by a frankly extraneous skin of
local stone.

CLAIFE STATION, high up behind Ferry House. The first of
Thomas West's viewing stations, as enumerated in his *Guide
to the Lakes* (1778). From the custodian's cottage and castellated gateway on the road a steep drive zigzags up to a rocky
platform. In 1799 William Braithwaite of Satterhow (demolished) built a two-storey octagonal summerhouse here,
designed by *John Carr* of York. A few treads of its cantilevered
stair remain in the curved rear bay, behind the chimney stack.
In 1802 ownership went to the Curwens of Belle Isle who
made it a Picturesque object itself, extending the sides and
adding the castellated screen wall linking it to the rock face
behind. The ground floor was a dining room, with a vaulted
cellar in the N wing. Upstairs was the viewing room, with
tinted glass to mimic the seasons. Clear of trees, whitewashed,
castellated, Claife Station was one of Windermere's landmarks, answering Belle Isle and Storrs temple on the lake (*see*
Bowness). Under National Trust ownership, it has fallen into
obscure ruin.

BRYERSWOOD, Far Sawrey, near the ferry. The plain square
structure of SOWLER'S TOWER on top of the hill was built by
Judge Sowler in 1865 so he could espy his villa, Sawrey Knotts,
when he stepped off the train at Windermere. The main estate
was developed in the C19 and C20. In *c.* 1886 Joseph Ridgway
Bridson had Bryerswood built, all decorative timber framing
and tile-hanging, by *R. Knill Freeman*; both of Bolton. It was
demolished in 1956/7, but much of *Thomas Mawson*'s first
GARDEN remains, including a large walled garden and specimen trees. Bridson's estate was sold to the Edmondsons of
Wigan, who built a sweet model farm in 1907, toy-sized
indeed, for their children; now called CLOCK HOUSE after the
mill clock installed on top. Two of the Whittaker family who
followed the Edmondsons are buried in Sowler's Tower. The
Naylors who came in 1936 planted the specimen *Cupressus ley-
landii* trees of different colourways. The present house is mainly
by *John Thompson* of Liverpool, 1964–6, with a terrace walk
over garages below.

HILL TOP, Near Sawrey. Beatrix Potter bought the farm in 1905
with the royalties of *Peter Rabbit* and *Squirrel Nutkin*. 'I never
saw such a place for hide-and-seek', she wrote, 'and funny cupboards and closets.' Even so small a house has a complex structural history, as suggested by the displacement of the l. window
of the doll's-house front, indicating the position of a blocked

fire-window.* On the other side of the fire was a wooden spiral stair. A blocked rear window shows that the rear outshut and c18 stair are additions. Beatrix's improvements are surprisingly eclectic: an elegant Adamish fireplace and c18 panelling with pilasters in the bower, fancy tops to the plain stone fireplaces upstairs. She added the FARMHOUSE on the W in 1906 for John Cannon, her farm manager, and extended it at the back.

4060

SCALEBY (C)

ALL SAINTS. Early c13 nave and chancel in one, with clasping buttresses at the E end, and W tower. The tower is clearly defensive, with no outside entrance and only extremely narrow and barred lancets, although not particularly thick-walled, nor vaulted. The top stage with its blunt pinnacles took its present form in 1828. No tower arch either, just a doorway with draw-bar slot. Further doors open into the church at two upper levels (what for?). The body of the church, described by Bishop Nicholson in 1703 as 'built chappel wise without a distinct chancel', has tall lancets with deep reveals. Round-headed S doorway, i.e. probably the earliest c13, with two continuous chamfers. In 1861–2, preparing for a proper chancel, *John A. Cory* rebuilt the E wall with a tall chancel arch, but instead an internal chancel was contrived between two little side chambers. A triple lancet fills the blocked arch.

FONT. Dated 1707, yet still a plain octagonal bowl. Very short, thick columnar stem. – SCULPTURE. Roman altar bearing an inscription to Jupiter, reused *c.* 1200 for a bishop or abbot in relief on one side, and another on the adjoining side round the corner. – STAINED GLASS. One with the white friar sign of *Powells*, 1928, and one by *Howard Martin* of *Celtic Studios*, 1954. – MONUMENTS. Mid-c19 tablets signed *J. Pickering*, Carlisle; *Nelson*'s Marble Works, Carlisle; *Fawcett*, Lancaster.

METHODIST CHAPEL. 1828. Low, with a hipped roof and slightly arched window surrounds, painted in a contrasting colour as is the local custom. Porch 1883.

SCALEBY CASTLE. The perfectly circular wet moat, large enough to enclose not just the castle but gardens and stableyard, is a striking feature on the map. In flat country, so close to Scotland and with no natural defences, Scaleby has suffered siege, lain waste, and changed hands more often than most, making the present building confusing to look at and to understand.

The de Tilliols were granted licence to crenellate in 1307. The five elements of the present castle are ranged around a tight and gloomy courtyard whose curtain walls rise to the full

---

*The farmhouse facing the National Trust car park has the same unbalanced symmetry.

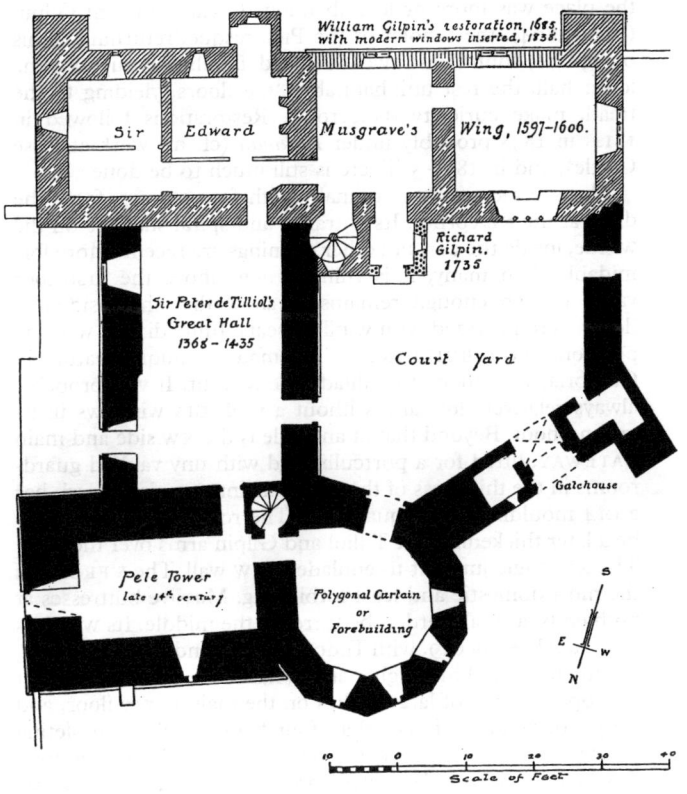

Scaleby Castle.
Plan, 1926

height of the house on the w and NW sides. Of the early C14
maybe the lower courses of the curtain and E range. The tower
at the NE corner may be early too, judging by its fine ashlar,
though Anthony Emery thought it cut across the hall to its s,
i.e. was built later. It was probably Sir Peter de Tilliol (†1435)
who raised the hall and s cross-wing. He may also have built
the unusual polygonal forebuilding that covers the tower's w
entrance. The s wing was rebuilt and extended w in 1597–1606
by Sir Edward Musgrave to make a second, outward-looking
front, facing s (cf. Hayton Castle). In 1644 and again in 1648
the castle was besieged by Parliamentarians, leaving it burnt
and uninhabitable. The Musgraves were forced to sell to
Richard Gilpin, ejected Presbyterian minister of Greystoke.
The Great Room over the hall vault was reconstructed by him
or by his son, William. Gilpin's grandson Richard rebuilt the

porch in the courtyard, signed RG 1737. From 1741 to 1772 the place was more or less abandoned again. William Gilpin (1724–1804), the scholar of the Picturesque, returning to his birthplace, found just two wretched families occupying the lower hall, the rest uninhabitable; 'the floors, yielding to the tread, make curiosity dangerous'. Restorations followed in 1814, in 1838 probably under *Rickman* (cf. his work at Rose Castle), and in 1853–5. There is still much to be done.

The SOLAR TOWER, originally with four storeys, faces the drive at the NE corner. Its entrance and spiral stair are on the W side, inside the curtain; other openings are recent. More formidable than many, it is ruinous now above the first-floor vault, though enough remains to show that the residential floors were provided with window seats. Immediately W is the polygonal FOREBUILDING or casemate, a unique feature in Cumbria, with loops to enfilade the N front. It was probably always relatively low and without a roof. C15 windows in its ground floor. Beyond that at an angle is the NW side and main GATEWAY, fitted for a portcullis and with tiny vaulted guard-rooms in the thickness of the wall. The inner, pointed arch has a C14 moulding (sunk quadrant). The round outer arch may be a later thickening. De Tilliol and Gilpin arms over the arch. The NW angle juts out to enfilade the W wall. The S FRONT is the most domestic and least forbidding. Massive buttresses at both ends, a small garderobe turret in the middle. Its W half is now largely early C19, with Tudor Gothic windows. The E half, slightly taller and of rougher stone, has three dormer gables at the top, a couple of large sashes on the main upper floor, and early C19 windows below that; four floors in all. Completing the circuit on the E side is the HALL RANGE, almost window-less below, with modern steps and entrance (1965), and big multi-pane sashes on the top floor, over the vault. Inside the courtyard it can be seen how the polygonal forebuilding has a secondary gate and portcullis to protect the entrance to the solar tower. The S wing shows its truer age here, with drip-moulds terminated with little fancies, which seem to have been a fashion in the 1590s (cf. Blencow Hall, Greystoke).

Inside, it may be noted how little access there is from the ground to the first floor; only the spiral in the pele, and the C16–C17 spiral in the S wing. Both hall and solar tower have tunnel-vaults set unusually high, enough for two storeys in the hall range, a feature more common in Northumberland and Scotland than the rest of England. The principal living accommodation however, here as in every other Cumbrian example (Johnby (Greystoke), Howgill), seems to have been on top of the vaults. High above the hall vault is the C17 Great Room, a splendid, nearly square apartment surveying the world from its tall windows, with a big door leading to the solar over the tower vault, and further accommodation at the top of the S wing including perhaps a garderobe on the turret noted outside.

Opposite the castle gate is HITCHENS ONSET, a clay-built farmhouse dendro-dated 1491 from the firehouse timbers. Single-storeyed as usual. Cross-passage behind the stack.

Heavily restored, with a stone roof in place of thatch. (HIGH
HILL FARM has the same plan. Another is BLOOMING
HEATHER at Scaleby Moss, 1½ m. WNW.)
(SCALEBY HALL, ¼ m. E. 1834 for Henry Farrer. Five-bay front
with a porch of unfluted Ionic columns and the gable-ends
treated as pediments. The comparative heaviness tells of the
late date.)

SCALES HALL (C)   5040

Very isolated, in flat country 3½ m. NW of Hutton-in-the-Forest.
Referred to in 1426, it came into the Brougham family *c.* 1520
when Peter Brougham married Anne Southwycke of Scales,
and was only finally sold in 1932, though in 1618 Henry
Brougham appears to have had to buy Scales again.
Pretty two-storey GATEHOUSE of *c.* 1580 to the NW, with roll-
moulded, segment-headed arch and fancy stone finials. BARN
on the r. side with domestic windows and doors on two levels.
The main house looks like a classic hall and cross-wings, with
a bay for the high table and entry at the low end – but it is too
long. Big mullioned or, upstairs, mullioned-and-transomed
windows of perhaps 1618, with a roll and flat hood which must
be early C18 floating above. Horizontal oval window in the
gable, set in a little aedicule, and another in the re-entrant of
the bay. The HALL RANGE, built of large, roughly squared
stones, is in fact a complete dwelling of two rooms and two
floors, with a stack at both ends and end entry (with drawbar),
in the Cumbrian fashion, beside the r. stack. This is perhaps
the Lodge referred to in 1426. The lower HALL has splendid
moulded beams, *c.* 1580s. Cross-beams, arched braces and
common joists all hollow-moulded and stopped. Fireplace with
a segmental arch with complex moulding, which has slipped –
hence the emergency buttress at the back. Fire-window under
the arch. Two pairs of Gothic windows at the back, slightly
pointed, uncusped. In the simpler ceiling of the adjoining
room, or PARLOUR, paintings of *c.* 1660 were found in 1992
but have been covered again. The KITCHEN WING on the r. is
planned like another dwelling, with fireplaces back-to-back,
the two rooms communicating by a flat-headed doorway
beside a large segmental-arched fireplace with single chamfer.
The spectacular LEFT WING and bay were added perhaps by
Henry Brougham in 1618 or soon after, and updated *c.* 1740.
The hall and kitchen doors, their mighty lintels tooled to look
like a rusticated flat arch, have the same frieze and floating drip
as the l. wing windows. The hall bay contains the STAIR, rising
round three sides of a well with spindle-shaped balusters and
square newels with fancy bits.* Excellent roof over the HALL

---

*Benjamin Furnival records the stair (1840s) at Brougham 'made from ancient oak
previously at Scales'; surely the Brougham staircase was far grander?

RANGE. Massive kingposts jowled at the top, with two pairs of raking braces plus straight longitudinal braces. The s window on the upper floor is of four lights, with a transom.

The BARN dated JB 1724 in the outer courtyard is the present farmhouse.

SCOTBY (C)

ALL SAINTS. By *Salvin* for George Head Head of Carlisle, 1854–5. Not small. Of rock-faced sandstone, with a SE tower. Cusped lancets, and plate tracery E. Interior unremarkable except for some good early C20 STAINED GLASS. By *William Morris* of Westminster, Jesus and the children including a black one, with good streaky sky. By *Heaton, Butler & Bayne*, Annunciation with a beautifully russet angel. By *Shrigley & Hunt*, a pair of war memorials.

(FRIENDS' MEETING HOUSE. 1718, closed 1913. Tiny, in a little graveyard with bollard-like headstones on the green. Converted.)

The village is typical of Cumberland, informally arranged round a long green. The new housing you would expect so near Carlisle has been sensitively done, especially SCOTBY GREEN STEADING, of dark brick and wood, mainly single storey, grouped round a former farmyard. OAK SQUARE is by *Johnston & Wright*, 1966–7.

ROSE HILL (Henry Lonsdale Trust), ¾ m. NNW on the A69 by M6 Junction 43. 1833–5, by *Christopher Hodgson*, for John Smith Bond. Three-bay centre flanked by unusual polygonal bays, canted diagonally outwards. Bowed-out porch on four Roman Doric columns, fluted in their upper halves. Wreaths in the frieze. Converted to an old people's home, 1980–1.

WHOOF HOUSE, ¾ m. E of Rose Hill, has the splendid C17 Gothic E window of Arthuret church (q.v.) mounted in the garden. It is quite a commanding object on the skyline. The composition is three plus three lights, each with a segmental arch and above intersecting tracery, and in the mid-spandrel an oval. Arthuret was rebuilt from 1609 onwards, but such an oval looks 1650–75 rather than 1610.

SEASCALE (C)

In 1879 *Edward Kemp* of Birkenhead planned a resort for James Ramsden of the Furness Railway: hotel, marine walks, promenades and villas. Little materialized, though there are some boarding houses N of the station, and few more on the low cliff top S including VICTORIA TERRACE, three houses dated 1886 with the name in highly glazed tiles. During the Second World War housing – as opposed to houses – appeared for munitions workers at Sellafield and Drigg (qq.v.), followed by more for Atomic Energy workers. Demolition of the station buildings, and of the Scawfell Hydro in 1997, has deprived Seascale of focus.

ST CUTHBERT. 1889–90, by *C. J. Ferguson*. Long, of red sandstone. Dec, with an almond-shaped SW window inspired by Millom church. Chancel, nave and bellcote, and S porch opening E, away from the sea. – Equal PULPIT and VICAR'S STALL, as Ferguson liked it. – Low SCREEN of 1912 by *J. H. Martindale*, carved by *J. Sharp* of Hensingham. – STAINED GLASS. All early C20, including the E window and one N by *Caroline Townshend*. The angels in the almond window are by *A. Seward & Co.*; also the nave NE.

METHODIST CHURCH, E of St Cuthbert. 1886, Gothic. Tripartite façade window and side porch neatly integrated with drip- and string courses and base mould.

WATER TOWER (Furness Railway). Seascale's most distinctive building. Of red stone, round, with a chimney and conical roof. Late C19. GOODS SHED of standard F.R. design, now Sports Centre, also of stone.

(SEASCALE HALL, 1 m. N. Probably of *c.* 1700, with a symmetrical five-bay façade, the doorway with a pulvinated frieze, but the windows still with crosses and hoodmoulds. At the back a datestone 1606. The cross-range r. is C19.)

GREY CROFT STONE CIRCLE, How Farm, 1½ m. N. Ten stones, with an outlier to the N. All but one buried in 1820, to aid the ploughing, but relocated and re-erected in 1949. Diameter 90 ft (28 metres).

SEATHWAITE (L)   2090

In the Duddon valley.

HOLY TRINITY, 2½ m. NE of Ulpha. The humble chapel of the Rev. Robert Walker ('Wonderful Walker'), celebrated by Wordsworth in his Duddon Sonnets and *The Excursion*. It was rebuilt in 1874 by *T. Bennett* of Barrow, largely at the expense of H. W. Schneider of Barrow. A dull effort in lancet style, of green cut slate with white pointing. Relics of Walker (†1802) include a small BRASS, and his clipping stone, outside. – STOUP, with a little trefoil arcade. – STAINED GLASS, †1897, by *Kempe*.

NEWFIELD INN, SW. C17 or C18, white, set in a corner between a large bank barn and a taller house. Notable for its stripy floors of Walna Crag slate.

0030

SEATON (C)

St Paul. 1881–3 by *George Watson* of Keswick (£2,213 13s. 4d.). Aisleless, with a small NE tower and pyramid spire rising out of the vestry next to a polygonal apse. Uncusped Geometrical tracery. – (STAINED GLASS. Apse, by *Abbott & Co.*, 1925, and (centre) *Wailes & Strang*, 1905.) Surrounded by brick terraces. Low Seaton is the old village.

SEATON HALL AND PRIORY (C) *see* BOOTLE

3040

SEBERGHAM (C)

Pronounced Sebberam.

St Mary. E.E. church of nave and chancel in one, the N side with just a single chancel lancet and another to light the pulpit. Three lancets (one blocked) to light the chancel S, but the E and assorted grouped nave S lancets are Victorian or later (restorations 1880, 1905). The chancel roof has been flattened, showing some timber framing where the higher nave roof starts. Short, thin W tower added in 1825, with external stair. Interior indeed a single space, with no chancel arch. Pretty oriel of 1905 looking down from the tower, with a carved vine. – BENCHES. Also 1905. Nice curvy ends, rather like North German Baroque. – Exceptionally good MONUMENTS. The centrepiece is a large white oval relief of the three Fates on a black setting, very flat, signed *Musgrave Lewthwaite Watson*, Rome, to his father Thomas Watson †1823. Sensational composition of three windswept women of Greek profile (Neoclassical attitudes indeed), three arms pointing forward, recalling Fuseli's Three Witches from Macbeth shown at the Royal Academy in 1783. Watson's most impressive work, up to the standard of the best that was done in these years in England. – Thomas Denton de Warnell †1616, stone, with four shields and crests. Latin inscription in distichs. – Benjamin Jefferson †1727, like an open book. – Series of Watsons, set up by Daniel Stalker in 1801. Large tablet with an urn and the large words *Virtus vivit*. Fan motif at the foot. – Rev. Josef Relph †1743, Adam style. – Ruth Ann Pasley Pain †1931 aged five. Brightly coloured mosaic and glazed tile in alabaster frame.

BRIDGE across the River Caldew, on the main road. A fine two-arched red sandstone structure of 1689. Its position between sharp bends at the foot of a steep hill means that its parapets bear the scars of many repairs. On the road E of the bridge is Brow Top. Five-bay C17 house retaining some two-light mullioned windows. Partially refronted in 1730 by R. Monkhouse with doorcase (still bolection-moulded), arched fanlight, and window over. BRIDGE END, dated 1737, also has two-light mullioned windows; late C20 alterations. Over the bridge on the NW GREENFOOT is dated JD 1715 though again incorporating an earlier house, dated 1687. Five-bay front with an open segmental pediment.

SEBERGHAM HALL, isolated ½ m. N of the church. Good late C17 façade of Tullie House (Carlisle) type, with alternating open-topped pediments over the ground-floor windows. Door and central window above emphasized with brackets.

CASTLE SOWERBY CHAPEL, ¾ m. SW, close to the Sour Nook Inn. Tin tabernacle with W porch and minute wooden bellcote.

SEBERGHAM CASTLE, 2⅜ m. NW. Impressive axial approach to this late C18 farmhouse folly front, all ogees and concave-sided gables. The centre is raised and castellated with an over-sized blank quatrefoil, then lower castellated screen walls, then ogee-gabled end pavilions. The symmetry is disturbed by a tower attached to the centre block. Windows in ogee-headed pairs with Y-tracery.

ST JAMES, Welton, 2½ m. NW. By *Cory & Ferguson*, 1874. Nave and chancel in one, Geometrical tracery. The bellcote is not on the apex of the W gable but by the NW corner.

SEDBERGH

See *The Buildings of England, Yorkshire West Riding: Leeds, Bradford and the North*

SEDGWICK (W) *see* NATLAND

SELLAFIELD (C)

Sellafield is Britain's most extensive nuclear landscape. Dominating South Cumberland's coastal strip, its great sheds and chimneys impose themselves unexpectedly on the views from many Lakeland summits. In essence a vast untidy chemical factory, its presence here derives partly from historical accident, partly from its need for the last natural resources the region still has in plenty – space and water.

The works began in 1939 as a Royal Ordnance explosives factory. Towards the end of the Second World War, Sellafield was increasingly drawn into the British support for the USA's nuclear weapons project. When the Americans unilaterally ended collaboration in 1946 the plant had an obvious role in the struggle to produce a British bomb, and by 1947 an atomic factory was rising.* Its main business was plutonium production, at first by the quick and potentially dirty process of burning uranium in air-cooled piles; hence the two 400-ft (123-metre) concrete CHIMNEYS topped by massive filters which for half a century were the characteristic silhouette of Sellafield. By the time the first significant plutonium was separated in 1952, the intrinsically safer Magnox process was already in development, and the next generation of plutonium factories was sold to an excited public as power stations which would deliver 'electricity too cheap to meter'. The world's first such POWER STATION opened at Calder Hall, across the river from Windscale, in 1956. In essence, the electricity the four Calder Hall reactors produced was a by-product of heat generated by the conversion of uranium oxide into plutonium. The *Chief Architect's Department, Ministry of Works* was involved with the design.

Britain's second generation of nuclear power was to be by ADVANCED GAS-COOLED REACTOR (AGR). A prototype was put to work alongside the Windscale piles in 1962, designed by the *Architects' Department, U.K. Atomic Energy Authority Engineering Group*. Its stainless-steel 'golf ball' pile was a notable contribution to the futuristic image of the site.

The original Windscale No. 1 pile has not worked since a disastrous fire in 1957, the blackest days in the country's nuclear history. It remains highly radioactive. No. 2, though undamaged, was also shut down for good.

Development of the planned third-generation Steam-generating Heavy Water Reactors took place mainly at Dounreay in Caithness, and at Sellafield the emphasis shifted to the problems of coping with radioactive wastes. In 1978, after lengthy public inquiry and Parliamentary debate, a Thermal Oxide Reprocessing Plant (THORP) was approved at Windscale. This opened only in 1994; by *British Nuclear Fuels Ltd Architects* with *Allott & Lomax*, engineers. Statistics illustrate its impressive size (114-ft, 35-metre) frame design, roof span of 130 ft (40 metres), 4,800 tonnes of steel), generous safety margin (able to resist a one-in-ten-thousand-years' wind), and vast cost (£2.7 billion). For reasons of security, secrecy and safety, the building can no longer give expression to the actual functions, and although the designers made valiant efforts to break up the bulk, nothing can make it exciting in the way of the pioneering structures. The 1991 VITRIFICATION PLANT, the 1997 MOX PLANT, and the NUCLEAR FUEL HANDLING PLANT of c. 2000 alongside Calder Hall power station thus became a succession of big bland boxes, with no opportunity for the bravura displays of pipework which enliven most conventional chemical plants.

Meanwhile concern has moved to the problem of decommissioning closed reactors and generators, the Achilles heel of the nuclear industry. Sellafield has become a laboratory for dismantling methods, experimenting on its own older buildings. The

---

*To avoid confusion with the Springfields uranium works near Preston the site was renamed Windscale, though locally it always remained Sellafield.

process started in 1980 with the chimney of Windscale's No. 2 pile, now taken down to the level of the reactor top. No. 1 chimney has also been shortened, but current expectations are that full decommissioning must wait until at least 2037, so the mutilated stump will stand for decades more. The famous 'golf ball' AGR closed in 1981 and is being dismantled, a job expected to take until at least 2030. In 1999 the Government declared that no more plutonium would be produced for military purposes, and in 2003 Calder Hall was switched off. Demolition began in 2007, the cooling towers whose 'noble shape' Pevsner admired in 1967 being the first buildings to fall. Although the conservation of nuclear industry buildings presents obvious problems, it may be wondered whether future generations will be pleased at the loss of so many pioneering pieces of technology.

The VISITOR CENTRE of 1986–8 (*Leslie Gooday & Associates*), placed a safe distance NE of the main site, attempts to rekindle some of the spark of earlier generations of building; but it is a muddle, joining glass pavilions distantly echoing the 1851 Crystal Palace with an overpowering windowless box by way of metallic tubes and a bizarre near-spherical structure looking like a deflating beach ball.

SELSIDE (W)   5090

ST THOMAS. Rebuilt in 1838 by a local amateur, *Richard Fothergill*; roughcast, with lancets typical of the period. Restored in 1894 by *C. J. Ferguson*, with a new tower distinctively and effectively broad, and entirely open to the nave, as at Raughton Head (q.v.). The battlements are later. Roof, E window, fittings all 1894. Opening into the side of the tower is the resited 1826 W porch. – (FONT. C18 marble bowl on a foot of 1894. – STAINED GLASS. E window by *Shrigley & Hunt*, 1912.)

SELSIDE HALL. H-shaped house, C14, though more like an L at the back, with a stair extension in the angle. Medieval two-light windows upstairs in both wings, but differing in detail. The r. one ogee-headed and cusped under a square head. The l. one transomed, with the spandrels of the tracery left solid. On the l. (s) wing a truncated octagonal chimney with what may have been a castellated top. Otherwise plain four-pane sashes and roughcast. The porch opens into a cross-passage behind the main fireplace, which is a full inglenook with heck on the front and opened-out fire-window at the back. It seems that the screens passage of the C14 open hall was at the other end, the door now opening into the stair outshut. The long s wing is tunnel-vaulted at basement level in two compartments.

A HENNERY-PIGGERY bounds the front garden on the l. Magnificent double BANK BARN in front, 150 paces long.

(LOWBRIDGE HOUSE, 1¼ m. N. 1837, also by *Richard Fothergill*. Large and asymmetrical, with bargeboarded gables.)

FOREST HALL, 1½ m. NW. Forbidding house of the C19 – or is it earlier? – looming over the A6 Shap road. Cross-shaped, with bleak mullions and transoms. Full cellar and attic floors. Knee-joints in the roof. The BARN fronting the road, now workshop above, doghouse below, was clearly a dwelling, and the principal accommodation was upstairs, i.e. a bastle. At one end remains of plasterwork with the initial B (probably Bellingham) and the date 16–. At the other a broken fireplace. The side walls have been rebuilt.

GRISEDALE FARM, immediately below Forest Hall though not readily accessible from it. Firehouse to r.; most of the windows have been made smaller, so the fire-window ends up much the same size. Bressumer of C15 type, deeply moulded and stopped (cf. Hartsop Hall). More bits reused under the stairs. Upstairs is quite intricately partitioned.

SETMURTHY (C)

1030

ST BARNABAS. Small and isolated. 1794, reconstructed 1870. Nave and chancel in one, with a polygonal NW turret and a polygonal SW vestry. – (FONT. Small, dated 1661 with initials and simple geometric decoration. – STAINED GLASS. E window, †1912, by *Wailes & Strang*.)

HIGHAM HALL (Adult Education Centre), ½ m. S. Naïve Gothick castellated house built in 1827–8 for Thomas Alison Hoskins. The design may have been his own, though it has Webster characteristics, especially the use of hammered limestone for the front. Symmetrical, with a pair of thin towers with angle-turrets making a rhythm 3:1:3:1:3. Large sash windows, pointed above, square-headed under dripmoulds below. The interiors are charmingly Gothick too, with castellated fireplaces, Gothick-panelled doors and plaster rib-vaults and bosses. Stained glass of 1996 by *William Davies* on the stairs.

SHAP (W)

5010

Famed for its granite, but this outcrops outside the village, which is built on and surrounded by limestone. Shap summit was notorious in earlier transport days, the village an emergency stopover in storm and blizzard. Now both railway and motorway pass by in cuttings, without stopping.

ST MICHAEL. Rebuilt by *George Dale Oliver* in 1897–8, leaving the unbuttressed W tower of 1828, the N wall with four-light

windows of Late Perp type, and inside a four-bay S arcade of
c. 1200. Round arches of two chamfered steps, round piers, the
simplest round capitals. Oliver's work is harsh in texture, his
style barely Gothic. Basket-arched windows, basket-arch-
section SE chapel ceiling. The builder was Mr *Grisenthwaite* of
Penrith. The Rev. J. Whiteside, evidently stung by criticism,
publicly regretted that so much of the old church was obliterated. – PULPIT (1899), SCREENS, ALTAR designed by the
architect and carved to a very high standard with lush foliage
and linenfold by *John Carlisle* and *J. M. Kilbride* of Barbon. –
FONTS. Small one of 1880 by the chancel arch. Big chalice-
shaped one of pink Shap granite, SW. Octagonal one turning
square loose in the tower. – ALTAR, SE chapel. Painted wood
front with chalice and two bowing angels; *c.* 1930s. – STAINED
GLASS. E window and two others by *Shrigley & Hunt,* SW by
Wailes & Strang, N aisle E (1904) designed by *J. F. Bentley.* Millennium window by *Adam Goodyear* of Huddersfield. Eagle,
cross, sheep; on the r. Shap Abbey ruins and the pink granite
quarry; on the l. Gogglesby stone, this church, Keld chapel,
and the railway.

MARKET HOUSE, in the village street, halfway down. The market
was granted in 1687, so the building will be of *c.* 1690. Three
by three bays, all rather miniature. Round arches, formerly
open, on short stubby columns. Small round-arched windows
above, now blocked.

WORKHOUSE, SSW. 1877 by *Perkin & Son* of Leeds, built by
G. H. Pattinson of Windermere. Long building with a central
tower with pyramid roof and a central projection for the
entrance.

THE HERMITAGE, Main Street. Pretty house in a plain village,
set back behind big trees. 1691 R & SE, I & SE over the door,
I & SE 1692 on spice cupboard, with *cottage orné* wings of
the 1840s coming forward, going with a general reconfigura-
tion. Parts of medieval windows have been found in the
fabric, including one with finely hollow-moulded jambs but a
crude replacement lintel. Inside is C17 panelling thought to be
from Newbiggin Hall (w), and stained glass from Lowther
Castle.

PLANE TREES (a recent name), towards the S end of the village,
end-ways to the road, which is unusual. Long-derelict house
of some quality, now restored, dated R & EI 1691. Four bays
plus blocked fire-window, then a byre with cross-passage entry
(now cottage), then another cottage – all with the same good
cornice. Mullions of two-light windows removed for sideways
sashes. Big stack at the road end; fire-window blocked. Tiny
spice cupboard *in situ.* Fireplace on the mid-floor at the opposite end with a profile head. Elegant roof with curved collars
and angle braces.

GREYHOUND HOTEL, at the S end. Render removed to expose
rubble. Stone inscribed AW WW 1703, with a greyhound. The
sculpted greyhound on the front canopy is by *Thomas Bland,*
i.e. C19. THE GREEN FARM, opposite. Handsome cottage,

house and byre/stable in line, fetchingly painted in shades of green. The same family and date as the Greyhound.

SHAP ABBEY, 1¼ m. w. The sudden sheltered valley of the River Lowther is almost miraculous in the bleak limestone plateau, the massive tower of the abbey even more so. Premonstratensian canons were brought from Blanchland (Northumberland) to Preston Patrick (q.v.) in 1191 by Thomas, son of Gospatrick, but by 1201 had settled here. The church was built across the valley, with the cloister and monastic buildings to the s.

Nothing stands more than 6 ft (1.8 metres) high apart from the shapeless corners of the E end, and the W TOWER, the last thing to be built before the Reformation. This was started *c.* 1500 by Richard Redman, Bishop of Ely, who retained the abbacy of Shap. It stands virtually complete, although cracked from top to bottom. It had a vast W window, like the late tower at Furness Abbey, and still has its three-light bell-openings. Tall tower arch, with just a single chamfer, but no side openings. What remains of the tracery is Perp uncusped. The Rev. J. Whiteside recorded a fireplace in the room below the belfry, presumably for a watchman. The CHURCH itself must have been rebuilt from the early to the later C13, and rebuilding as usual started from the E. The chancel is aisleless. Its straight-ended E half is a C15 lengthening to the brink of the river, but the W half is early C13. The difference in the base mouldings is striking. The base of the original E wall is now the first step of the two in the chancel. The crossing piers can still be guessed in their bases. They are so strong that in all probability they carried a tower. The transepts had two E chapels each. A patch of paving in the s transept is probably the foundation of the canons' night stair. A doorway leads into the cloister, a second from near the E end of the nave, a third from the nave further w. The long and narrow nave has only a N aisle. There must have been a break in building operations halfway down the nave. It is clearly visible in the masonry of the s wall, and also in the bases of the arcade piers. Those further w with their thin mouldings are C14 rather than C13. The piers were quatrefoil, with fillets and slim shafts in the diagonals as well. The E bay is blocked by a wall put up probably because the crossing tower gave trouble. That would also explain the encasing of the NW pier in simple canted masonry. The W bay is partly blocked by the E buttress of the tower, but the springer of the W arcade arch appears to the N of the buttress. The W side of the tower shows the original roof-line and a second Perp one of flatter pitch allowing for clerestory windows. This change must of course post-date the tower.

The MONASTIC PARTS take their accustomed places s of the church, their modest scale reflecting the relative poverty of the house and the tightness of the site. s of the s transept it is easy to recognize the corridor-like SACRISTY with its door into the chancel, and the CHAPTER HOUSE projecting further E and its vestibule with three early C13 columns no doubt carrying a rib-vault. There are also two wall-shafts halfway down. The

WARMING HOUSE further S was a vaulted room, characterized by its large fireplace and three octagonal piers. The dormitory above was continued E from its S end by the REREDORTER or lavatories, with several surviving drains. Along the S walk is a wide paved passage or slype, then, partly disappearing under the present farmyard, the REFECTORY undercroft, with a row of piers along the middle. Two inserted tunnel-vaults survive of the W range, built into the C13 walls in the C14. Also some steps, and a WELL tucked in the angle with the nave.

The slype leads to the INFIRMARY on the river bank S of the reredorter, of irregular plan and not on axis with the rest. Of the abbot's quarters nothing is left at all.

The FARMHOUSE S of the cloister may be C16. Built in over its front door a figured corbel of secular character, and another, more fanciful, on the gable-end.

KELD, ¾ m. SW, upstream of the abbey, via a high arid limestone wilderness of walls. Sequestered little settlement like a miniature Askham (q.v.). Plain oblong CHAPEL with a reused three-light Late Perp E window, otherwise nothing to mark it out. Partition wall with fireplace towards the W with a lobby behind it, like the standard Cumbrian cross-passage plan. Three-arch BUTTERMARKET to rival Shap's Market House, but with plain square piers. Gate and cattle grid, then straight on to the fells.

STANDING STONES. GOGGLEBY STONE is a massive monolith over 7 ft (2.2 metres) high, re-erected 1975: a survivor from an avenue of stones that extended from the Thunder Stone, a natural erratic ¾ m. WNW, to a STONE CIRCLE, 1¼ m. S. Of this only six large rounded boulders are visible, the E half having been overlain by the railway embankment.

STONE CIRCLE at Gunnerwell, 1½ m. NNE, beside the M6. Of the outer circle of boulders, about 100 ft (30 metres) across, only three are upright – two on the N forming a 'portal' and one on the S. The smaller stones of an inner circle 55 ft (17 metres) across surround a low mound, in the centre of which was a burial cist.

SHAP WELLS (W)

5010

Tucked away in a sheltered valley, like Shap Abbey. *The Beauties of England and Wales*, 1814, described it as much frequented by 'persons afflicted with Scorbutic complaints', and by lead workers from Alston (q.v.). The waters were analysed in 1828, the spa HOTEL built by the 1st Earl of Lonsdale in 1830–3. It was a popular stopping-off point in the long journey to Scotland. Large, quadrangular, and rather grim as such places often are. It was reconstructed with a mansard storey in 1914–16. The SPA WELL, a little up the river to the S, is a simple C19 font capped with a pump, under a hexagonal shelter.

QUEEN VICTORIA MONUMENT, 1842. Octagonal column designed by the Lowther estate architect, Mr *Mawson*. Too small for the landscape, and now half lost in the trees. The sculpture is by *Thomas Bland* of Reagill (Crosby Ravensworth). Britannia, on top, is rather apologetic, but the relief of the British Lion and globe, like a kitten playing with a ball of wool, is splendid. On the other side relief, the goddess Hygeia offers a libation to a seated god – or is he a patient? A third relief is of a laurel wreath.

SILLOTH (C)

Planted in 1855 by the Carlisle & Silloth Bay Railway & Dock Co. as a deep-water port to supplant Port Carlisle (*see* Bowness-on-Solway).* The railway opened in 1856. The dock scheme was promoted by *John Hartley*. A jetty to his design opened in 1856, a dock, engineered by *James Abernethy* with *Thomas Nelson* as contractor, in 1859. Following the collapse of the entrance in 1879, a new inner dock was added, designed by *Thomas Meik & Sons* of Edinburgh. Railway steamers sailed to Liverpool and Dublin, and Silloth was energetically promoted in Scotland as a resort. Despite this, the town was never more than moderately prosperous, and the closure of the railway in 1964 has taken the heart out of it.

CHRIST CHURCH. Won in competition by *C. J. Ferguson* and erected 1869–70 by *Cory & Ferguson*. The church is offered up, like an architectural model, on the flat green left for the purpose when the town was set out (*see* below). Round E apse. The prominent NW porch-tower and broach spire was completed in 1878. Local sandstone contrasts with granite brought by the North British Railway from Newry in Ireland, in regular chequers on the buttresses, crazy-paving infill and ashlar dressings elsewhere. Paired lancets for the aisles, foiled circles in big blank arches for the clerestory. The tower-porch is rib-vaulted with a bell-hole. The internal proportions, judged to a nicety, are very satisfying. The church is lined with yellow brick trimmed with red, and also bands of brick used in projection and recession. Stone is reserved for the capitals, corbels and feet of columns, all still in the rough and not carved. High but not too high cradle roofs. Ditto the chancel arch.

    Good FITTINGS, all presumably by the architects, including the very large square FONT with fern motif. – STAINED GLASS. Apse windows l. and r. by *James Holmes* of Lancaster, *c.* 1930, centre (†1875) by *Wailes*. W end by *Heaton, Butler & Bayne*, the lancets in memory of William Banks of Highmoor, Wigton, †1878.

*The company's unauthorized expenditure on the town was revealed when the enterprise was leased in 1862 by the North British Railway.

SOLWAY COAST DISCOVERY CENTRE, Liddell Street. Made, clumsily, out of the Gilbert Scott-ish parochial school of 1857.

The TOWN PLAN is by *W. & J. Hay* of Liverpool. By 1857 a grid of very wide streets was taking shape, paved with granite setts and lined with sycamore trees. CRIFFEL STREET is effectively the prom, built up only on one side, with three-storey Italianate boarding houses and hotels of colourwashed stucco looking out over acres of mown grass and bent pines to the distant sea. Elsewhere the houses are of two storeys, then one, then quite suddenly nothing. The best bit of street architecture is on EDEN STREET: the NatWest bank and No. 5, with a nice syncopation of window levels and boldly arched cornice.

FLOUR MILL, the key to Silloth's survival as a working port. Erected on the E side of the floating dock in 1887, originally under the same ownership as Carr's biscuit factory in Carlisle. Plain and dignified, brick, of eight five-storey bays, embedded in gimcrack accretions. An off-centre Dutch gable proclaims the name. Inside, a treasure: a 1904 horizontal cross-compound steam engine by *Carel* of Belgium, still in working order. Until the 1970s it drove the mill through twenty ropes from an 18-ft (5.5-metre) flywheel. The mill's taller metal silos compete with the church spire for Silloth's skyline.

GOLF CLUB. Laid out SW of the town in 1892 for the North British Railway by *Willie Park Jun.*, with *David Grant* and *Mungo Park*. The clubhouse, terminating the main drag, overlooks the dock and former station. It was built in 1903, extended 1908 and later. Timber-framed, with a veranda (now closed in) and large skylights and dormers to light the formerly open roof spaces.

CONVALESCENT HOME, beyond the golf clubhouse. 1862. Also promoted by the NBR, which ran trains to its private platform. Low symmetrical group, rendered, with hipped roofs.

AERODROME, 1 m. E. Opened 1939 as a Maintenance Command Station, closed 1960. Very large hangars remain dotted about.

SKINBURNESS, 1½ m. NE. A town and market were founded in the C13 by Holm Cultram Abbey, but the sea took most of it in 1301 (*see* Holme Low and Newton Arlosh). There are traces of the planned layout by the hotel, and the garden wall of Whiteways incorporates bits of medieval stone. HOTEL built in the 1880s as a hydro by Edwin Banks of Highmoor, Wigton, with a lookout tower at the back. The fancy, vaguely Jacobean front loses heart as it gets higher. CHICHESTER HOUSE of *c.* 1880, with another tower, was Banks's marine residence. Apricot stucco, cast-iron cresting, bracketed eaves.

SIZERGH CASTLE (W)
Helsington

4080

The home of the Stricklands, now Hornyold-Strickland, rewarded for their defence against the Scots but fined in penal times for recusancy. An intensely Catholic house, romantic and atmospheric despite half a century of National Trust ownership. Substantially the work of Walter Strickland (1516–69), who developed the house beyond the Great Hall and solar, moving the principal rooms upstairs. C14 hall and cross-wings form the centre; the hall is much modified and the SW wing takes the form of a formidable tower, dominating the whole. The tower as we shall see is the constant feature; the hall is surprisingly insubstantial in its history. Long and much lower C16 ranges stretch NW from either end, enclosing an entrance courtyard.

The great TOWER is exceptionally large (60 by 40 ft, 18.5 by 12 metres), with walls 9½ ft thick at the base, 5½ ft at the top (3 and 1.7 metres). Staircase turret on the hall side, and a spacious oblong attachment called the Deincourt Tower on the outer side, both rising above the roof. The importance of the main tower is asserted by the heraldic achievement in a recess over the C14 three-light second-floor courtyard window. The tower dates probably from the time of Sir Thomas Strickland (c. 1343–76), though the upper windows preserved belong to the C15–C16. As for the battlemented HALL, its front (courtyard) wall was pushed forward in 1773–4 for Cecilia Strickland by *John Hird*, and the over-sized porch and mullioned-and-transomed windows l. and r. are due to Sir Gerald Strickland and *J. F. Curwen*, who punched a carriageway right through the hall in 1897–1902. There was some logic to this since in the 1550s the hall itself had migrated upstairs, but Westmorland winds make the arrangement impractical. The large five-light mullioned-and-transomed window in the tower replaced a pair of sashes at the same time, but sash windows remain above in the hall range, with an ogee hood over the main first-floor window. The unobtrusive SE CROSS-WING or service wing forms a single bay, gabled to the courtyard as well as to the garden side. It has Elizabethan mullioned-and-transomed windows on the courtyard side.

The long COURTYARD RANGES attached in the C16, near-parallel to one another but not at right angles to the house, also have mullioned-and-transomed windows so far as they are original. Those of the S range are regularly placed, indicating the intended gallery within. A pair on the ground floor in the N range light the Elizabethan kitchen, and there are two further W on the upper floor. This northern range is crowned with five huge Westmorland chimneys, square in three stages. A number of the C16 carved bargeboards survive.

On the GARDEN FRONT external steps of the C18 rise to the former first-floor hall, as old pictures show was also the case on the courtyard side. Beneath the steps a doorway with a chamfered two-centred arch is the best evidence for the C14 ground-floor hall, telling us that the low end was here at the N end. The Gothic fenestration of the hall is *John Hird*'s and 1770s above, the National Trust's in Hird imitation below (1968). The two first-floor Venetian windows in the tower and service wing introduce another phase, of the 1740s. The four-

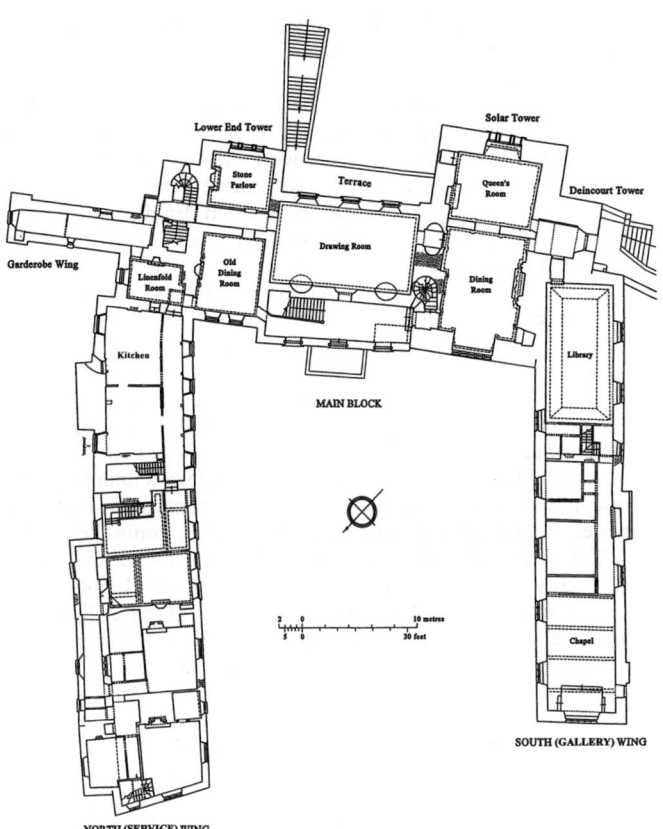

Sizergh Castle.
First-floor plan, 2005

light C15 window on the tower above is original (Buckler's drawing, 1822). The most remarkable feature to be seen on this side is a tall mid-C16 garderobe tower, or rather gallery, growing out of the service wing.

INTERIOR. Sir Gerald's carriageway runs slap through the HALL on wooden blocks. It is a double space, the outer part representing Hird's extension and the inner the C14 hall, though only the SE doorway and the window above are recognizably of that period. Between the two a wooden screen dated 1558, including parts probably taken from the C16 upper hall, introduces Sizergh's outstandingly rich woodwork. On the W side of the inner hall is the doorway to the tunnel-vaulted TOWER BASEMENT. Although the doorhead is altered, the massive hinges for an iron yatt suggest that the entrance is primary. A turning stair opens off the mural passage.

Returning to the hall, a flight of stone steps leads up to the *piano nobile*, as in a Roman palazzo. At the FIRST-FLOOR

VESTIBULE *Curwen*'s early C20 stair to the banqueting hall has been removed to the s wing, leaving its landing hanging at one end of the vestibule.

The famous PANELLED ROOMS are described in viewing order. No other house in England has such a wealth of high-quality Early Elizabethan woodwork. Moreover, it was one carver or one group of carvers who must have been at work over twenty years. They may have been English, but their source of inspiration was the Netherlands or France. Their chimneypieces are characterized by very lush acanthus and similar scrolls, swamping the coats of arms, by little children frolicking among them, by Early Renaissance baluster-type columns to flank the fireplaces and frame parts of the over-mantel, and by pediments, with or without a head in them. The carving has passages of outstanding quality. There is absolutely nothing here of that grossness and grotesqueness which mars so much Elizabethan woodwork (e.g. at Levens). The panelling also is excellent. The oldest here is linenfold, but much is of the most attractive type with lozenges set in oblong panels (Old Dining Room, i.e. 1563; Boynton Room, i.e. 1575).

The medieval tower solar was divided into two in the 1560s. The DINING ROOM, which was the C16 great chamber, has deeply framed panelling with Corinthian pilasters. Splendid armorial overmantel dated 1564 with bull and chained stag supporters. Pelicans and putti in the surround, bearded atlantes l. and r. of the fireplace with baskets of fruit on their heads. Also columns (rather than balusters). The ceiling, as in all of Walter Strickland's rooms, is geometrically patterned with thin wooden ribs: eight-pointed stars with small pendants. The smaller QUEEN'S ROOM beyond was a withdrawing room. A National Trust pastiche Tudor effort replaces Hird's fireplace. Overmantel with scaly dragon and skinny lion supporters to the royal arms, dated 1569 and inscribed VIVAT REGINA; green men and more lions as background. Pediment of the kind con-sisting of two shallow S-curves. Ceiling of octagons and Greek crosses, after Serlio. The DRAWING ROOM was the C16 upper hall, turned into a polite Saloon in 1773–4 by *John Hird*, but probably never completed. Three niches opposite the three windows, plain ceiling. It was heated by stoves in the outer niches. Moving now to the upper part of the service wing, we enter the small square STONE PARLOUR, a creation of the 1740s named for the black-and-white stone floor, and the vault that was inserted in the Muniment Room below to support it. Moulded ceiling perhaps by *Joseph Rose Sen.*, the only Geor-gian stucco ceiling in the house; Venetian window. The fire-place and the plain panelling date from a re-fitting of c. 1810 probably by the *Websters*. With the OLD DINING ROOM, over-looking the courtyard, we are back in Elizabethan times. Over-mantel dated 1563, with stag and ox supporters. Panelling with diamond inserts and Doric pilasters. Ceiling to a unique design of lozenges and elongated rectangles connected by short straight pieces. The LINENFOLD ROOM is a C16 closet to the

Old Dining Room. Bolection fireplace, no overmantel. Extra-complicated linenfold panelling of the early C16, somewhat juggled about. Beyond is the GARDEROBE GALLERY, from which an angled lobby added by *Curwen* gives access to the passage dividing Stone Parlour and Old Dining Room. A wide and straight stone STAIR (made necessary by moving the apartments upstairs) leads down to the kitchen in the N wing.

Up to the second floor by a turning stair. The BOYNTON ROOM is in the service range over the Old Dining Room. Overmantel dated 1575, with plant-men supporters and fluted pilasters. It is pierced work; a trace of deep blue shows through from the back panel. The BINDLOSS ROOM opposite has plainer C17 panelling (re-set), and an overmantel dated 1629 from Borwick Hall (Lancashire).

Up more steps to cross the hall range, with bedrooms and bathrooms on either side. The top two storeys of the N half of the tower were opened up in the C19 to create the BANQUETING HALL, which has an unconvincing themed air about it. A gallery created in 1948 gives access to the room above the Inlaid Chamber. The C14 and C15 windows in their deep reveals and fireplaces on two floors remain, as does the fine C15 camber-beam roof with its stop-moulded joists. So to the climax of the house, the INLAID CHAMBER. This fantastical room was created by Alice Strickland and her third husband, Thomas Boynton, shortly after 1575. The style is very different from the carved rooms below: plaster frieze and pendant ceiling with intricate rib patterns and floral etc. motifs in the interstices – the only ceiling in the house of the type which became current in the later Elizabethan houses – and colourfully inlaid panelling of delicate Renaissance character. The internal corner porch has its own little dome with a cherub on top. Ionic pilasters run round the room, with a smaller order for each panel. The inlays are of pale wood and black, floral above, geometric puzzles below. Armorial roundels of contemporary stained glass in the window. Out of place is the painted overmantel of 1805, showing a white-painted Sizergh in its setting. The Inlaid Chamber was dismantled and sold by Walter Charles Strickland to the Victoria and Albert Museum in 1891, but reinstated here on loan in 1999.

Now for the two long courtyard ranges of the mid C16. The S RANGE was intended for a row of lodgings on the ground floor, with a Long Gallery above, though there are doubts whether that was ever finished. In the mid C18 the end nearest the house was made into a chapel, with a coved ceiling. In 1897–1902 however this became the LIBRARY, and a new CHAPEL was made at the far end, reached by a corridor edging past the great gallery fireplace.

The N RANGE is more complicated. Nearest the house is the great KITCHEN, communicating with the Servants' Hall in the main house by a corridor and service hatch. The kitchen was originally open to the arch-braced roof, dendro-dated to *c.* 1557–8. It had three 12-ft (3.7 metre) fireplaces, one in the cross-wall and two at the back – awesome cooking power. Now it is divided horizontally, and a steep stair is inserted in one fireplace, the wood store in another; leaving just one open. An impressive room nevertheless. The enormous meal ark, though strictly furniture, cannot escape mention. The rest of the wing is a complication of family accommodation with features of every century from the 1560s on.

STABLE, SW of the house. Pretty late C18 building with a wooden cupola, probably by *John Hird*.

65   BARN. Ten bays long, with two ramps to the upper floor. If this is the 'new barne' recorded in 1569, with wheat, barley and oats above and livestock below, it is the earliest dated example of what is now called a bank barn. Thirty-eight paces long, which is not as big as later examples, with a simple tie-beam roof.

The ROCK GARDEN, all water-worn limestone, was made by *T. R. Hayes & Sons* of Ambleside in 1926–8 for Sir Gerald and his second wife Margaret. The designer is thought to have been *Charles Henry Wearing*.

5090   # SKELSMERGH (W)

ST JOHN BAPTIST. 1871. That most versatile architect *Joseph Bintley* is in muscular mode here. Tall narrow chancel, broader nave, powerful bellcote halfway to being a tower, supported on a double W wall. Geometrical tracery in the E window, but the rest are bald pairs of lancets. Plainly furnished, but three WALL PAINTINGS (St Peter, St John, and another), chancel N, look as though they were part of an overall scheme. – STAINED GLASS. E window by *Heaton, Butler & Bayne*, 1884, to the Morton family of the Hall. Nave s, Rabboni: Mary, of 1937 by *Joan Howson*.

SKELSMERGH HALL. C15 tower, tunnel-vaulted below, and C16 hall without a matching wing, though Machell indicates that there was one. Garderobe with slit window. C17 range with big mullioned-and-transomed windows at the back of the hall.

DODDING GREEN. H-shaped C17 house, roughcast. Left in 1723 by Robert Stephenson to the Roman Catholic Church, with an upper room converted to the chapel. Since 2005 it has been occupied by a religious community called Cenacolo. The datemark CB (Rev. Charles Brigham) 1840 on one end wall is about all that remains of an extensive *Webster* make-over; the decorative woodwork was all purged in 1968. Older bits inside, including a wooden turning stair round a mast at the back. Main stair early C18. CHAPEL. Ceiling partly raised to a cove. An overpowering white Italianate altarpiece is the only serious furnishing. Very fancy door in the corridor to the sacristy.

(GILTHWAITERIGG, ½ m. WSW. C15 hall and cross-wings. The hall now has a central entry. In the W wing two windows with cusped heads to the two lights.)

SUMMERHOW, ½ m. s. The coldly grand rooms at the front are said to be by *Webster & Thompson, c.* 1850. The one constantly inhabited room at the back (always a ready guide to the oldest bit) is the C17 firehouse. The fire-window is blocked by a cupboard, the bressumer smoothed, the heck turned into a corridor. Behind the hearth is a cross-passage to the C17 door and porch, which faces away from the road. The porch is perfectly preserved, with stone seats, pegs, and partial timber framing. The cross-passage was in the attached shippon, as is the usual regional pattern, with the main stair contrived within the rest of it.

SKELTON (C)

4030

ST MICHAEL. The tower looks C17 with its blunt pinnacles and squared belfry windows, but the tower arch is medieval and Christopher Brooke suggests the tower was defensive. Nave of 1794 with narrow round-arched windows and quoins. Short chancel also with quoins, but the vaguely Norman tripartite E window is of 1879. – (FONT. The former font is an octagonal baluster. – PULPIT. Mid-C18, with fluted angle colonnettes and arched panels. – COMMUNION RAIL. C18. – STAINED GLASS. E window and one s by *Wailes & Strang.* Another s, †1915, by *Kempe & Tower.*)

HARDRIGG HALL, 1 m. NW. The farmhouse is fronted by a ruined solar tower of the C14 or later. The half that is left reveals like an educational model its construction and organization. Thick walls of good stone. Basement showing the springing of a barrel-vault, and a stair-turret starting out in the corner. First floor, the solar, with a round-arched entry off the stair and a fireplace with mighty lintel. In the upper chamber a smaller fireplace and another stair door.

CRUCK BARN, a little apart from the farmyard, on a different orientation. Six bays, five cruck-trusses, oddly varied: two in the middle are much more slender and spring higher, like upper crucks. All emerge from the stone walls rather than resting on visible pads – though there is a massive pad at one end, where there is now no cruck. It seems likely that the stone walls are secondary.

SKINBURNESS (C) *see* SILLOTH

SKIRWITH (C)

6030

ST JOHN. 1856 by *Frederick & Horace Francis* for the rich and pious squire of The Abbey, William Parker. A set piece, all academically correct Geometrical Dec. Steep-roofed SW aisle. SW tower with a stone spire with two tiers of chunky lucarnes, Lincolnshire style. The tower is rather dwarfed by the high roof of the nave. Carlisle Diocese favours Evangelical simplicity, so a fully developed High Church building like this was, as Jill Kerr says, 'deeply shocking to the natives when new'. – FITTINGS. What a strange lot they are; the Parkers were evidently collectors as well. Rococo CHANDELIER from Brougham Hall (q.v.). – PANELLING C17, PUTTI C18, FURNITURE C17. – Hanging ROOD. – High-quality woodwork and stone carving of 1856, including the REREDOS and PULPIT. – The PAINTINGS on the panels of the altar were done in 1932. – LADY CHAPEL in the aisle, dedicated as a war memorial for Thomas Cooper Parker †1917. Riddel-post altar and modern screens. – STAINED GLASS. Twelve windows by *Wailes* commissioned by the church, gaining enormously by being a set. The E window however is by *Hardman*. Lady Chapel E window by *Percy Bacon*, c. 1919; artist *George Fellowes Prynne*.

Appropriately over-sized VICARAGE, S, also by the *Francis Bros*, 1856. Gothic of course, with its own stable block.

THE ABBEY. A four-square Palladian house standing proudly on level lawns. John Martin Robinson attributes it to John Yates in 1774, mason *Thomas Addison*; but a generation earlier would make more sense, relating to Dalemain and to Highhead (Ivegill). Square block of two storeys plus a full basement sunk in a broad railed area. A pair of lower wings are detached at a respectful distance either side of the lawn. Seven-bay front, the projecting middle three rather tight. Full-height canted bows at the sides. No pediment, but the frontispiece and bays emphasized with a balustraded parapet. Grooved masonry for the basement, end pilasters, and the rear centrepiece with its pedimented doorway. Hipped roofs, regularly spaced chimneys. Venetian windows to the detached wings. The plan is exceptionally interesting. Eight rooms form a peripheral parade, including a pair of octagonal rooms fitting the canted bays at the sides. The front hall and rear saloon also connect directly through the middle, as one would expect. Cross-arches in either side of the link reveal a pair of broad cantilever staircases ascending spirally, each in an octagonal top-lit well. They are equal in size, but the N one is slightly more fancy and rises only to the upper floor; the S one, plainer, rises from basement to attic. Hidden in the heavy spine of the house is a narrow stone newel-stair also going from top to bottom; a dumb-waiter balances it on the other side.

SMARDALE HALL (W)

2¼ m. W of Kirkby Stephen

Long narrow house, 86 ft by only 27 ft (26 by 8 metres), with big transomed windows on both floors, and a pair of fat round turrets flanking each end. It dates maybe from c. 1580, when

Smardale passed by marriage to the Dalstons. Of original details or even masonry surface, very little is preserved. The turrets are somewhat conical, i.e. battered, with conical slated roofs and a ball on top. Only one contains a stair. A wing attached at the NE end somewhat spoils the effect. Machell's plan of the 1680s tells us that this 'lofty spruce little room' was a first-floor hall, probably cut short at the through passage (cf. Sockbridge), and that beyond it were lodging rooms and 'the old tower', making a U with an enclosed garden to the N.

The Settle and Carlisle railway crossed the old North Eastern Railway line here; the NER's station (1861) is being restored. For the Smardale viaducts *see* Ravenstonedale.

SOCKBRIDGE (W)

SOCKBRIDGE HALL looks down across the fields to its greater cousin Yanwath Hall. A seat of the Lancasters, passing in 1638 by marriage to Sir Christopher Lowther, whose son Sir John did a good deal of updating. Two wings loosely attached at right angles, but once four ranges about a little court. The S wing, including a gatehouse, is probably late C16 and little altered. Stables below, offices above. Mullioned-and-transomed windows, and on the N side a window with uncusped arched-headed lights. The house, standing W of the court, is a mish-mash of different dates: C16 and mid-C17 on a probably medieval core. Stepped gable on the S end, pretty octagonal chimney in the middle. Windows mullioned, some with transoms and some with arched heads. Interior with an extraordinary diagonal corridor skirting the stair, indicating a good deal of juggling of spaces. Sir John Lowther re-roofed, re-floored and reglazed the house part.

Machell's tiny plan of the 1680s is the key to understanding the place. He shows the courtyard complete, with on the N side a hall and a 'little tower', and unspecified buildings on the E. The base of the little tower survives, now under a lean-to roof attached to the farmhouse. In its cut-off E wall is a run of three doors, now outside and half-buried in rubble and earth, with two-centred heads. This must therefore have been a C14 screens passage, directly opposite the gatehouse entrance, with a buttery and pantry in the little tower. The cross-passage itself, and the hall, have vanished.

STABLE, S of the hall. Built in 1687 for Sir John Lowther by *John Addison*. Stylish building of five bays, two storeys, the windows originally cross-mullioned; good enough for a house (except no chimneys). – BARN, to the w. 1699. Like that at Dalemain (q.v.), i.e. not originally a bank barn, though it later acquired two ramps. 123 ft long, 21 ft wide, 21 ft high (38, 6.5 and 6.5 metres), with two tiers of vent windows above and a ground-floor byre below. A lean-to cowshed was intended all along the back.

WORDSWORTH HOUSE, Quaker Lane. R & ED (Reginald and Elizabeth Dobson) 1699. It belonged to Wordsworth's father, then his brother. Smart little house of four bays, with bolection-moulded doorcase, quoins, cross-mullions, and a continuous drip or string over the first-floor windows. It looks to be a double pile.

SOULBY (W)

7010

ST LUKE. Nave and chancel in one. Built by Sir Philip Musgrave in 1662–3 (date 1663 over the door). The E ball finial and kneelers, the round-headed S doorway with its vaguely Perp moulding, and the W turret shaped like a tiny tower go with this date. The patently Victorian features are of 1873, but the E window with its flowing tracery is odd enough to be a copy of something of the time of Lady Anne Clifford. (STAINED GLASS. E window by *F. Burrow*, 1874. Two windows by *Henry Holiday* for *Powells*, 1890.)

SOUTH STAINMORE *see* BROUGH

SPADEADAM *see* GILSLAND SPA

STANWIX *see* CARLISLE

STAPLETON (C)

5070

ST MARY. All alone. Plain rebuild of 1829–31 by *James Hope*. W tower with obelisk pinnacles. Wide nave with lancets and a flat ceiling, short and narrow chancel with intersecting tracery in the three-light E window. – MONUMENTS. Arthur Forster †1680, Thomasine Hogerson †1752, both with achievements of arms. – Margaret Milbourn †1790, very large bowed tablet with Corinthian colonnettes.
(SHANK CASTLE, 2½ m. WSW. Slight remains of a tower house.)

STAVELEY (W)

4090

An industrial village – stone, slate, lead, diatomite, bobbin turning, wool, cotton.

OLD CHURCH (St Margaret). Chapel of ease to Kendal, built on land given in 1338. By the C19 it was a plain box with Gothick windows. Only the stout rustic TOWER of *c.* 1589 remains, horribly ribbon-pointed, with blunt obelisk pinnacles and a saddleback roof. Huge slate louvres run straight across the centre mullion of the belfry openings. Blocked tower arch off-centre, unmoulded. Three-light Perp w window with cusped heads and tiny niches on either side, both probably reused.

St James. On a new site at the top of the village. By *J. S. Crowther*. His initial design of 1861 shows a N aisle and a bell-cote perched on the chancel arch. As consecrated in 1865 it is a two-cell E.E. design with a double belfry and spirelet on an overpowering W buttress. The chancel with its tall and narrow triple E lancets is modelled on Wappenbury in Warwickshire, after Bowman and Crowther's *Churches of the Middle Ages* (1845), but in local materials. Steep roof, scissor-trussed at high level and with raking wall-posts and curved wind-braces. The chancel fittings and pulpit are later, by *A. W. Simpson.* – STAINED GLASS. Medieval fragments, chancel N. Lovely E triplet by *Morris & Co.*, 1881. Angel minstrels in three tiers in each side light, designed by *William Morris*. In the middle Crucifixion and an effortful Ascension with many angels, by *Burne-Jones*. The background is a midnight sky spangled with stars. 'A window of exceptional beauty', says Sewter, not an author given to hyperbole. Another *Morris & Co.* window, nave S: St Margaret and St James, to the Rev. William Chaplin †1904, who commissioned the church. Also glass by *W. Warrington & Son*, 1865 (nave S and further E, and nave N, at the W), *Heaton, Butler & Bayne*, 1881 (nave N middle) and *Powells* (nave N, at the E; 1931).

ABBEY HOUSE. Incongruously tall and grand, it was built as a hotel in 1844–5 anticipating the building of the railway. Doric porch and a pair of canted bays, rusticated quoins and a balustered parapet. Taller three-storey building with arched windows behind.

BOBBIN MILL, now effectively a small industrial estate. Coppice barn of fourteen bays. The open front, with its conical pillars of rough but skilfully laid stone, has been closed with waney-lap planking.

At the N end of the village a fine WEIR on the River Kent provided water to power a C17 corn mill on the E bank and the large Barley Bridge Mill on the W. The CORN MILL, now a house, used a 6-ft (1.8-metre) breast-shot wooden wheel until the 1950s. BARLEY BRIDGE MILL is a fine four-storey building, established as a cotton mill in the C18 and still in industrial use. It had added its own bobbin-turning shop by 1800. Clock and bell-turret on the front projection. Particularly impressive from the river side, showing signs of at least three enlargements.

Gas came to Staveley in 1865, after the Windermere railway provided a ready coal supply. The ROUNDHOUSE THEATRE, off Main Street to the W, is ingeniously built on the foundations of the gasholder.

CUMBRIA TOURISM HEADQUARTERS, Windermere Road. An older shed, adapted in 2006 (*Team Northern*, contractor). Roughcast; in front slate cladding added here and there, and some modelling, though the shed shape is still clear.

STAVELEY-IN-CARTMEL (L)

ST MARY. A church existed in 1618, and a window head on the N side carries the inscription EX DONO THO PRESTON 1678. (Another inscription on E gable.) The E window reflects these dates: three round-arched lights, then six, then intersecting tracery in the head. Other windows also with uncusped arched lights, one at least looking pre-C17. The dumpy W tower with flame-like pinnacles, and the S aisle with plain round-arched windows, may be 1793. Handsome C19 open timber roof with two tiers of wind-braces. There was a restoration in 1897 which included a new tower arch and a timber S arcade, replacing one of rubble.

STRANDS (C) *see* WASDALE

SWARTHMOOR (L)

SWARTHMOOR HALL. Plain grey house said to be of 1586. The Quaker George Fox came here in 1652, converted Margaret Fell and her daughters, and was tolerated and protected by her husband Judge Fell. Margaret and Swarthmoor provided the stable base the embryo movement needed. The house is L-shaped, three storeys, with a three-storey bay on the E side. The front doorway with its Yorkshire lintel is roughly central to the S, but there is no attempt at symmetry in the fenestration. Old pictures make it clear that the section l. of the door is considerably altered. On the r. side a doorway under a decorated lintel, under a first-floor opening with a tiny balcony (what for? Did Fox preach?). The house is built around a great stack in the angle, and the stair. This winds up to the top around a cage-newel with ten stages of sturdy, vertically symmetrical balusters. The best bedroom, at the back, shows that the C17 was not without comforts, with an internal porch, panelling, and an excellent chimneypiece, Ionic and Corinthian, with vines curling round the columns, as at the stalls at Cartmel Priory (q.v.). The fireplace itself has dentils. In 1912 the house was bought by *Emma Clarke Abraham* and restored as a Quaker 'shrine'. She panelled the ground-floor rooms, carved the strapwork decoration and made the winged lions. A four-poster bed, halved, makes the fire surround (1914) in the back room.

FRIENDS' MEETING HOUSE, Meeting House Lane, behind a door in a wall. Over the porch EX DONO GF 1688. George Fox bought a cottage in 1687, extended it and presented it to the Society in 1688, although it was not in regular use until 1690. The cottage to the r. with its mullioned windows serves as the smaller women's hall and gallery. The porch, which overlaps one of its windows, goes with the new meeting room. Its windows were sashed in 1829. Typical of the Friends are the ingenious dividers, both sliding and hinged, doubled up for soundproofing.

SWINDALE (W) *see* HAWESWATER

TALKIN (C)   5050

The tarn is a local pleasure dome, with a hotel and boathouses, boat hire, and café run by the Local Authority.

CHURCH. Still a proprietary chapel. Built, and very likely designed, by *Thomas Henry Graham* of Edmond Castle, Hayton, in 1842, in a jolly Norman style. A whiff of levity cheers the interior with pale pine benches, white walls, red ceiling, and plenty of daylight. Altar rail and pulpit have Norman arcading too. The PARSONAGE has both Norman and Gothick windows. Its STABLE has the Graham tower emblem in a quatrefoil.

TEBAY (W)   6000

Very remote, but a transport nexus, with old coaching inns, e.g. the Cross Keys. Here the Lancaster & Carlisle Railway, opened in 1846, girded its loins for the notorious climb to Shap. In 1857 the South Durham & Lancashire Union Railway arrived, bringing Durham coke through to the Barrow iron furnaces. Each company built its own HOUSING, in long terraces. The station (L&CR) has gone; it was by *Tite*, who at the time had the young *Thomas Worthington* working for him.

ST JAMES. By *C. J. Ferguson*, 1878–80; a 'mountain church' supported by the railway companies. An amusing building, constructed of Shap granite in squared lumps. The NW tower is round, with a corbelled-out bell-stage and fairytale-castle conical roof. Next to it and composing well is a semicircular western apse, for a baptistery. The ground falls away here, allowing a circular vestry or meeting room underneath in the battered basement storey. Porch immediately E of the baptistery. The interior is faced in yellow brick with red bands, with some notching, e.g. over the chancel arch. Closely single-framed roof with a fine ark-like effect in the W apse. The basement meeting room, slightly domed, has a central column. – ALTAR RAIL, CHOIR STALLS and ORGAN FRONT typical of *Ferguson*, with little turned spindles. – PULPIT (1930) of Shap granite. – FONT also of granite, part-polished, a powerful piece. The lid is spoked like a locomotive wheel. – STAINED GLASS. E window, 1911, and three-light war memorial, S, by *T. F. Curtis* of *Ward & Hughes*. Baptistery window by *Abbott & Co.*, 1916.

MOTORWAY. The M6 was completed in 1968. It would have contributed nothing to Tebay but for the enterprise of John and Barbara Dunning, whose farm was in the way. They created WESTMORLAND SERVICES. The northbound part was opened in 1972; *Gordon Stables*, architect. As Will Self remarks, it seems to pre-date the M6, rather than being a mere outgrowth of it. It turns away from the motorway and is deliberately low-key and domestic, in contrast to earlier such facilities. The buildings crouch low, under big pitched roofs, with plenty of wood. Water laps up to the walls. Extended in 1988 with very large industrial trusses resting on a stone pillar. The HOTEL by *Robert Gilchrist* opened in 1976, extended 1997. In 1986 came the Junction 38 truck stop off the A685, and in 1993 TEBAY EAST SERVICES, southbound. This is by *Unwin Jones Partnership*, Carlisle, and uses more reclaimed softwood king-post trusses, very large and set low. The trusses are mounted on themed stonework, with an imitation fireplace.

CASTLE HOWE, ⅓ m. NNW between Junction 38 (M6) and the River Lune. An impressive fragment of a Norman ringwork castle: a deep ditch and a high upcast bank on the S; the dished interior largely lost to the river. Possible bailey to the S.

TEMPLE SOWERBY (W)

An especially handsome open-plan settlement, with a maypole, though its spacious greens are turning into car parks. Mercifully, the A66 was diverted on to a by-pass in 2007.

ST JAMES. The churchyard is part of the green. The church was built in 1754, enlarged by an aisle in 1770, but the present two equal aisles with lancet windows look like 1877, corresponding to a datestone on the S aisle (*George Watson* supplied plans in 1868). Chancel attached to the N aisle, also with lancets. W tower 1807–8, still Georgian, with even quoins, round-arched W window and ogee belfry lights. The Victorian arcade takes the unexpected form of short cylindrical shafts on high square bases, with scalloped capitals and square abaci. – STAINED GLASS. E window by *Powells*, 1924.

Many gracious HOUSES round the Green: High Green House, Temple Sowerby House, and Mountain View, all fronted in dark early C18 brick; Sherriff House and Beech House, an identical late C18 pair, ashlar-fronted with paired sashes; an older house between. The Grange is dated 1817. Others, with late C18 or early C19 stone fronts on the A66, e.g. Edendale House, Woodbine House, Linden House.

ACORN BANK, ¾ m. NW.* A property of the Templars then the Hospitallers, taken over by the Crown at the Dissolution and bought by the Dalstons in 1543. Nearly everything we see is attributable to the Dalstons and their descendants, who had the house until c. 1930; much was formerly concealed by roughcast, hence the roughness of the earlier masonry. The house was resuscitated in the 1930s by the Yorkshire writer and folklorist Dorothy Una Ratcliffe (initials DP on rainwater heads for her married name, Phillips), and gifted to the National Trust in 1950. Today it remains under-used, although the attractive WALLED GARDENS are well known.

Long plain nine-bay S front of three storeys with lower wings, looking sedately over the park towards the village, but concealing a complex history. The earliest parts are early C17. The W WING retains mullioned windows (one with carved heads as label stops) and gabled closet towers on the W elevation, a series of first-floor fireplaces (for lodgings), and a stout wind-braced roof. For the MAIN RANGE, which was a single pile and just two storeys at first, one must look at the rear and W end for external signs of antiquity. It was shorter than now but probably had an E wing to balance the W (see the disrupted coursing on the S front). Inside, a service room divides a kitchen at the W end from the Hall. Both have large segmental-arched fireplaces and four-light windows to the rear (the Hall window renewed). A tight winder stair rises from the kitchen. Two first-floor rooms with C17 panelled wainscot. The date 1656 on a rear stair-turret (with initials I & LD, for John and Lucy Dalston) cannot refer to the C18 timber stair within, but must denote an earlier stair, in turn replacing a stone original. Generous winder treads from this stone stair are reused in the turret masonry and on the S front of the main range. So the S front must have been refronted at the same time, c. 1656. No long mullioned windows now, but tall mullion-and-transom openings (see the infilled transom sockets) whose proportions would later receive sashes gracefully. Probably in the 1670s John Dalston called in *William Thackeray* to extend the main range E – such is the implication of the channelled ashlar E end, with evidence of Thackeray's double transoms recognizable despite sashing. Dalston's neighbour Thomas Machell, writing c. 1690, commended the 'well wrought and polished' masonry. The mason's marks confirm that the rest of the main range was raised to three storeys at the same time. Some of the original roof trusses were re-set, but the E wing was probably lost.

*This entry was revised by Adam Menuge.

Another John Dalston (one of Westmorland's two M.P.s from 1747) transformed the house in the mid C18. His are the majority of the sashes, the segmental-pedimented entrance, the new E WING (unusually, a stable block over wine and beer cellars), the refacing of the W wing to match, and the Venetian windows on the ends of both. His too the two-storey screen wall to the stable yard, and the tall DOVECOTE adjoining, with a further Venetian window. (Did his death in 1759 cut short a matching outgrowth beyond the W wing?) Inside, a drawing-room chimneypiece with putto atlantes in profile, and a new cantilevered stone stair rising only to the first floor in a second rear turret. Its ceiling incorporates cherubs and a cornucopia in the central oval, and classical profile heads. Geoffrey Beard thought it perhaps by *Joseph Rose Sen.*

ACORN BANK MILL, in the grounds, on Crowdundle Beck. A charming and exceptionally interesting early C19 group. The upstream cell of the mill range is the two-storey KILN. The grates and baffle plates to spread the heat survive, but the tiled upper floor where the corn was spread out to dry awaits restoration. Downstream, the MILL has an inscription dated 1823, but may be twenty years older. It had three 12-ft (3.7-metre) wheels, one pitchback and two overshot; only the first complete at present. Most unusually, the final wheel was adapted to operate an endless wire rope to draw trucks out of a gypsum mine behind the big house. The machinery appears to have been made by *Stalker Bros'* foundry, Penrith. The mill looks across a narrow courtyard to the MILLER'S HOUSE and the usual PIGSTY, whose occupants enjoyed the husks and bran the mill produced.

ROMAN MILESTONE. Beside the old main road, ¾ m. SE, and 1 m. NW of the site of the Roman fort at Kirkby Thore. Still in position, but much eroded.

3010

THIRLMERE (C)

THIRLMERE RESERVOIR. A report by the Manchester Water-works Committee in 1874 warned that the city's Pennine reservoirs would within the decade be unable to meet demand, and boldly recommended looking at the Lakes a hundred miles to the N. The Act was passed in 1879, work started on the aqueduct in 1885. The works were ceremonially opened in 1894, and the following day a fountain of Thirlmere water spouted in front of Manchester Town Hall.

The DAM, 66 ft high and 857 ft long (20 and 264 metres), curves elegantly across the N end of the lake. Designed by the engineer *George Henry Hill*, built by *Morrison & Mason* of Glasgow (1890–4). It impounded 8,900 million gallons, uniting Leathes Water and Wythburn Water and drowning

Wythburn village and the picturesque triple packhorse bridge spanning the neck between the twin lakes. The dam is solid, with facings of Longridge (Lancs.) stone embracing concrete strengthened with rock 'plums'. The concrete aggregate includes local Threlkeld granite. In the middle, under the city arms, a proud granite plaque lists names and dates. Unusually for a solid dam, there is no visible spillway, a concealed swallow-hole at the W end taking the excess water. – VALVE TOWER. Castellated, in local stone with red sandstone dressings. – OVERFLOW. A two-arch footbridge crosses a chasm, which takes water under the road to a complex discharge chamber by the beck. – STRAINING WELL on the E shore, marking the head of the old lake. Castle-like rotunda with three wings. Another very large granite plaque outside, and an even more fulsome one within. The building, glass-roofed, covers a plunging circular well, out of whose depths rises a central iron tower. Wide Tudor arches lead to the side chambers. – The well feeds the 96-m. underground AQUEDUCT, with an average fall of 20 in. (51 cm.) per mile, avoiding the need for pumping.

Manchester rebuilt the roads on both sides of the lake, and planted the valley with conifers, rendering it gloomily magnificent.*

WYTHBURN CHURCH stands alone by the A591. Simple white-washed rectangle, domestic in style, with little to date it: recorded in 1554, rebuilt 1640 and again 1740. Small squarish side windows. Wordsworth called the church (unavoidably) a 'modest house of prayer'. In 1872 a churchy, taller chancel and rounded apse were added (*C. J. Ferguson*?), in greenish cut slate. – Arts and Crafts ALTAR, CHOIR STALLS and low SCREEN. – INSCRIPTIONS in beaten copper over the E window and at the back of the altar. – STAINED GLASS. Apse: centre light by *Henry Holiday* for *Powells*, 1892, side lights by *Hugh Arnold*, 1906. W window designed by *Temple Moore*, 1889.

DALEHEAD HALL (hotel), Thirlspot. Adam Laythes or Leathes brought his bride, Alice Blencow, here in 1577. The house was probably late C16, and was further modified in the 1620s and C18. In 1879 the family sold it and the lake to Manchester. Until 1980 it was owned by the city, and reserved for the mayor during August.

Plain Late Georgian lakeside front to a richly multi-phase building. The N wing was added after 1980 to balance the S wing, which although it looks Georgian contains a fine C17 open-well stair with twirly balusters. The spine corridor behind the Georgian rooms displays the rear wall of the C16 house, built of granite lump with a massive plinth. This house faces away from the lake, with a baffle entry against back-to-back inglenooks: not a common Cumbrian arrangement. A couple of wooden mullioned-and-transomed windows face the yard. Upstairs, now internal, are two little wooden mullioned windows towards the lake, still with their leaded glass. The

*The SAWMILL, now United Utilities offices, is at The Green, Legburthwaite.

tower-like NE wing in the yard, with massive plinth and tiny windows, incorporates a wooden half-spiral stair.

DUNMAIL RAISE. *See* Grasmere.

THORNTHWAITE (C)

ST MARY. Rebuilt in 1832–3 by *John Bowie*, enlarged in 1852–3 by *G. Watson* under the supervision of *Salvin*. Belonging to the later phase are the transepts, a W extension with its bellcote, and the roof. A possible survivor from an earlier building is the inner W doorway, with a shouldered lintel. – STAINED GLASS mostly by *Henry Hughes*, 1860s.

VICARAGE, now LADSTOCK, ⅝ m. S. By *Barry Parker & Raymond Unwin*, c. 1905, for the Rev. William Unwin. Shallow hipped roofs, shallow bows with slate-hung aprons, round chimneys. Scaled down for a C20 vicar.

(OLD MANOR, Little Braithwaite, 1½ m. SSW. Dated 1726 and already wholly classical, the windows with raised moulded frames and a doorway with Doric pilasters, a triglyph frieze and a pediment.)

THRELKELD (C)

ST MARY. The curious flat oblong tower with obelisk pinnacles, probably originally a W porch (cf. Embleton), remains from a C17 rebuild. Otherwise of 1776–7, a five-bay box with keyed-in round-headed windows and a Venetian E window with a flat surround. The S elevation is like a meeting house of the period, symmetrical about the porch with its broken pediment. The C18 church was probably seated around a pulpit in the middle of the N side. It was completely reorganized in 1911 by *J. H. Martindale*. A chancel was contrived by inserting little corner vestries and a canopy with hammerbeams and putti. The new work is in Renaissance style, with nothing Gothic about it. *W. Grisenthwaite* of Penrith was the contractor. Carving was by *George Fendley* of Carlisle; note the charming spandrel figures. The beaten copper inserts in the reredos are by *KSIA*. – Granite FONT made by *Samuel Knight*. – The coloured floors are *Harkewitz* TILES, made from granite dust (*see* below). – STAINED GLASS. E window by *Francis Skeat*, 1958. – MONU-MENT. Rev. Thomas Edmondson †1797 and his son, a merchant, who died at Baltimore in 1822. By *Webster* of Kendal, at the later date.

QUARRY, at the foot of Clough Head. Opened by *H. Harkewitz* in 1864 to provide granite railway ballast. In the 1890s Harke-witz developed a method of making pre-cast flagstones, and established a factory beside Threlkeld station. The quarry closed in 1982 and in *c*. 1990 *Countryside Consultants* converted the flag sheds into the BLENCATHRA BUSINESS CENTRE (job architect *John Widdaker*). The quarry is now a MUSEUM, including a reconstructed railway system and a demonstration mine adit. The original ENGINE SHED and WORKSHOP survive. (STONERAISE, 2 m. NE, near Scales. Mid-C17, with a two-storey porch.)

THURSBY (C)

3050

Pleasant houses, some in Dalston yellow and red sandstone, round a triangular green.

ST ANDREW. Quite a large church. Rebuilt in 1845–6. Plate tracery to the bell-openings. Chiselled buff sandstone and Dec windows (altered perhaps in 1878), which makes the broad and bald interior rather a surprise. Clumsy flat ceiling, alcove-like chancel. Three stepped lancets in the E wall. – PULPIT. Brought here from Carlisle Cathedral in 1878; it belongs to the 1765 restoration by Bishop Lyttelton and *Thomas Pitt*. Gothic, in oak. – STAINED GLASS. E window by *Clayton & Bell*, 1902. Window by the pulpit by *Tony Hollaway*, 1993. Dark, and not communicative in an obvious way, it represents a Lakeland landscape and commemorates his wife Joan and her parents. – S transept, a chapel for the Briscos of Crofton Hall, lined with good MONUMENTS, e.g. †1741, with an inscription worth reading, †1760, and †1805; the latter by *Kirkbride* of Carlisle.

CROFTON HALL, 1 m. SW. The Brisco family sold up in 1908, the mansion was demolished *c*. 1958. The grand Ionic GATE-WAY into the park from the A595 survives, with two pairs of fluted columns (but minus its huge stag on top), with paired pilastered LODGES behind, both in superb buff ashlar. By the mansion site a STABLE BLOCK dated 1826, also ashlar-faced, in a somewhat debased classical style. Seven bays, with the middle bay singled out by giant fluted Ionic pilasters, a pediment, and a cupola. Venetian window above the centre arch, and a more complex rhythm of rectangular and arched openings on either side. Lake, parkland, all rather melancholy. – GREENWAYS, an estate house NW of the stables. The front is three sides of an octagon. The windows are pointed, with Y-tracery. That also is probably of the 1820s. – Private RAILWAY STATION (former), built *c*. 1865 by the Maryport & Carlisle Railway for Sir Musgrave Brisco of Crofton Hall. Extraordinarily large for its purpose; indeed bigger than some of the railway's public stations. Tudoresque, H-plan with coupled chimneys. The M&CR indulged its local grandees to a remarkable extent (cf. Dovenby).

In 1935 Crofton was taken over for smallholdings by the Land Settlement Association, founded to alleviate unemployment in the worst years of the Depression. The whole estate is dotted with their white cubic houses. It was a Co-op, with a central buying policy and a marketing centre in the stables. The Cumbrian scheme was wound up in the 1970s. *See also* Cummersdale, Carlisle.

FIDDLEBACK, ¼ m. SW, on the A595. A curiosity. It has exactly the plan not of a fiddle but of the body of a guitar. The larger bulge is the house, the smaller the barn. The inscription EEH 1709 is over the side door, but the 1770s seem a more likely time, cf. other fancy farms at Greystoke and Workington Hall. The front doorcase, with a curly pediment, encloses a Gothick fanlight. The windows look Victorian; outlines of earlier round-topped windows can be seen.

CURTHWAITE STATION (former), ½ m. S. The stationmaster's house survives. Also a cast-iron WATER TANK inscribed *Hareshaw Ironworks*, Hexham, 1843, on a handsome ashlar base of three bays with plain semicircular arches and plain pilasters. There can be few other intact operational railway structures of this period.

MEADOW BANK FARM, West Curthwaite, 1 m. S. Excellent clay house, long, narrow, wobbly of wall, thatched, with crucks, offset chimneys, and minute windows to light a partial upper floor. Three props on the roadside, of great chunks of stone. 1666 IL DL over the cross-passage door, when the barn was added, still with the characteristic mid-C16 flat-arched lintel. The house at the uphill end may be older. INGLEDENE opposite is another dabbin, unsympathetically treated. The single-storey, long narrow shape and off-set chimneys tell.

THWAITES (C)

1080

ST ANNE. 1852–4 by *E. G. Paley*. The tender was £1,500. Of slaty rubble with streaky sandstone dressings, and great big slates for the roof. Nave, S aisle, and chancel, with a bellcote perched on the chancel arch. Three two-light windows in a row W, with a rose above – a favourite Paley motif. Lancets for the chancel, clerestory of quatrefoils, aisle with plate tracery. Good four-bay arcade with circular piers. – REREDOS. 1863, white stone arcading with marble colonnettes. – STAINED GLASS almost all by *Wailes*. Nave N, one by *Powells*, 1914.

On the W side of the main road a fine WATER MILL, built into the hill on the bank-barn principle. Two buildings, probably C17 and C18, with an overshot 14-ft (4.3-metre) wheel in a covered slot between them.

TIRRIL (W)

5020

FRIENDS' MEETING HOUSE (former). 1731, built by *Thomas Wilkinson* of Yanwath. Porch 1733, lengthened and re-windowed 1801 under the influence of his nephew, the poet, another Thomas Wilkinson. Now a dwelling, but little changed outside. Burial ground in front with but a single stone. The former WESLEYAN CHAPEL of 1879 is also now a dwelling but essentially unchanged. READING ROOM and LIBRARY, 1914.

TORPENHOW (C)　　　　2030

Pronounced Trepenna. Long village, still pungently agricultural and untidy.

ST MICHAEL. Bucolic Norman-and-later church, one of the best on the Solway Plain, with leaning-out walls. Nave and aisles under one big roof, and a N transept. Long chancel with three tiny Norman N windows and traces of three more E, broken into by a late C13 window with intersecting tracery. The N transept N wall must be C13; three stepped lancets. C17-looking W bellcote with miscellaneous stone spikes on top. The S aisle in its upper parts with windows and battlements seems C17. S doorway of c. 1150–70 with an outer order of bobbins with headstops, then an order of triple rope, then zigzag. Capitals of the colonnettes very crude, with little faces, a Torpenhow speciality. Two tiers of them l., ram's heads r. Odd jamb mouldings. The restoration of 1880–2 by *Cory* was benign on the whole, though we may regret the stripping of the walls. Porch, 1882.

Three-bay arcades of single-step arches on round columns with nice moulded bases and two-stage caps. The SW respond has scallops with another row of little figures including a dog on its head and a scroll. The NW respond has plain scallops. Piers and abaci are round. An arch at the W end of the nave is blocked with reused grave-slabs. Was a tower intended? The nave CEILING is splendid. Bishop Nicholson tells us that in 1689 Mr Thomas Addison 'offr'd to cover the middle aisle with a fair painted canopy of firr'. It is divided into square compartments and a central roundel, the powerful cornice breaking forward as though for pilasters. The delicious painting, almost monochrome, is quite accomplished. The subject matter is not very religious. In the centre dancing cherubs with a crown, in the panels fruity festoons, leafy faces, and more cherubs. The pilaster heads are gilded with acanthus and fruit basket, shell, eagle, lion etc. Magnificent Norman chancel arch of two zigzag orders. Octagonal capital on the N, suggesting an alteration, with a chain of little dancing figures interlocked by their knees and elbows. On the S, scallops with another row of animal and human heads. Scrolls and chequer on the abacus. Triple responds. The stylistic relations of this Norman work are with Carlisle Cathedral. The chancel N windows are widely splayed. Blocked ones can be seen on the S. Tomb-recess in the chancel S wall, with a double-chamfered arch. The N transept is oddly placed to overlap the chancel arch, and linked to the chancel by vaulted passage and internal porch. Barn-like tie-beam roof dated 1614, with raking queenposts. – PULPIT. Cut down from the Jacobean three-decker. – FONT. Round bowl with intersecting arches, and a sort of interlace, an interesting survival, under the bowl; probably Norman. – STAINED GLASS. E window (1882) by *Clayton & Bell*; some others also by them. – MONUMENT. Rev. Thomas Nicholson †1735. – In the porch the recumbent effigy of a lady, of worn sandstone, probably from the tomb-recess in the S wall.

ROMAN FORT at Caermote, 1¾ m. S. Occupied in the late C1. Defences of turf and timber, enclosing 3½ acres; inturned gateways; two ditches, each with a counterscarp mound. Overlying the NW quarter, a smaller simple FORTLET (1 acre): early C2, probably abandoned in the 140s.

TORVER (L)

2090

ST LUKE. By *Paley & Austin*, 1884. Chunky, robust, with a low central tower but no transepts, allowing a tall lancet to illuminate the under-tower space. The tower is carried on a pair of round arches buttressed by strong haunches. A variation on Finsthwaite (q.v.), but evidently with less money. The tower has a low pyramid roof instead of Finsthwaite's spire, with a fish weathervane. Again there are Norman references, including the inner doorway.

TROUTBECK (W)

4000

JESUS CHURCH, SW of the village. The simple tower with ears instead of pinnacles stands strong against the vastness of the fells. Datestone 1736, though its three-light W window still looks C17. Nave and chancel in one. The church was whitewashed until 1861, when the side windows were turned into lancets. Whitewashed interior with rustic C17 tie-beam roof. The textbook tracery in yellow sandstone of the E window introduced an alien note in 1872 – but its gorgeous *Morris & Co.* STAINED GLASS makes the church. Green is the overall tint, the Life of Christ the subject. All the principal artists were involved: *Burne-Jones* for the main lights, *Ford Madox Brown* the lower r. scenes. *Morris* himself did the angels, *Philip Webb* the trout and watery sunbeams. Another *Morris & Co.* window, of 1898, on the N, this time all red swirling seraphim above, greeny-gold angels below, a youthful Christ parting the clouds between. The design was by *Burne-Jones*. – Low SCREEN and CHOIR STALLS, of high-quality Jacobean panelling with blank arches and lozenges in them, from Calgarth Hall (*see* p. 642).

The VILLAGE ambles down braided tracks, following the spring line. To the N, near the top at HIGH GREEN is the Mortal Man Inn, named after its old sign (c. 1800) painted by Julius Caesar Ibbetson. LANE FOOT barn is cruck-framed; just one truss left, its feet embedded in the stone wall. BROW HEAD is signed on the outside render TBM (Thomas and Margaret Braithwaite) 1692. Gable entry via an end porch, under a balanced gable chimney. Blocked fire-window. Opposite the INSTITUTE of 1869 is LOW FOLD FARM (North Fold), C17, with an unusual five-light oriel on wooden brackets overhanging the road. In the yard is a gallery to the barn. Below the tarmac road on the l. is LOW HOUSE (datestones 1627 and 1811), startling in pink. The colour (haematite mixed with limewash) is traditional. THWAITE, in the same yard, provides a wonderful demonstration of Lake District vernacular. L-shaped, with wrestler slate ridges and swept valleys. The two-storey porch, hospitably wide, goes not into the house proper but into a cross-passage in the attached barn, behind the main hearth. Opposite the fire is the bower, raised a step and partitioned by plank-and-muntin panelling, with a small cellar underneath. A lobby paved with slates on edge in alternate squares leads to the downhouse in the other part of the L. Upstairs the partitions are arranged differently, allowing built-in cupboards and corridors. High-quality raked queenpost trusses to the roof, but buried in the E wall and unrelated is part of a cruck blade.

TOWN END (National Trust) is at the next road junction. The Brownes were semi-gentry and the house has developed somewhat beyond the vernacular, in the provision of a library for example. At the bottom end is the kitchen of c. 1620s, with its own porch, inglenook fireplace with two fire windows, and half-spiral stair. Its upper floor is partitioned into three small bedrooms. The late C16/early C17 centre range is called the firehouse, defined by a great round stack at the downhill end. Behind in a late C17 wing is the stair and George Browne's library. The upper rooms are partitioned with plank-and-muntin panelling, with the built-in cupboards so characteristic of the Lake District. The C18 uphill cross-wing has its own entrance under a corner pentice-roof, and its own great stack. It is not clear how the building worked; although interpreted as a single dwelling it could equally have accommodated three semi independent households. Opposite is the picturesque and much-photographed TOWN END BARN, dated GBE (George and Ellinor Browne) 1666 on a lintel. H-shaped, which is unusual, with a timber gallery between the wings, interrupted by the ramp of the cart entrance. TOWN FOOT, end-on to the road on the r., is a baffle-entry house, i.e the porch with its stone seat opens onto the side of the stack. GAB 1694 on the spice cupboard in the firehouse. Downhill is the bower with its panelling, uphill the downhouse, now the kitchen. 66

OUTLYING BUILDINGS are selected on a triangular itinerary: S to Troutbeck Bridge, NW along the lakeshore towards Ambleside, and back E up Holbeck Lane.

HOLEHIRD, Patterdale Road (E side). Long accumulative house in the Gothic style, built and altered for three successive Manchester men between 1854 and 1904, and characterized by a crescendo of gables and bays. The first two, J. R. Lingard and J. M. Dunlop, employed *J. S. Crowther*, the last, William Grimble Groves, *Dan Gibson* and *Thomas Mawson*.* Despite its additive history the house conforms to a favourite Crowther plan. The entrances are at the ends, offset from the long corridor so that it is lit from both ends. The middle of the corridor receives light from the stair through Gothic arches. Lingard's house was built in two instalments, conforming to a medieval H-plan but without the high-end wing. That was left to Dunlop to build; but it was made taller and more lavish, with tracery and iron cresting. Dunlop also built the large billiard room, complete with organ, the long service wing, and the porch initialled and dated 1869. Groves's indoor work is limited to the library of 1905 on the SW corner, replacing a splendid house conservatory. In 1961 the house became a Cheshire Home.

The GARDEN is now run by the Lake District Horticultural Society. Groves had a famous garden at Alderley Edge, bringing his head gardener Edward Robertshaw to Holehird in 1897. By *Gibson* the S LODGE (1897), HOLEHIRD COTTAGE by the N lodge (1905), and the former HORSE SHELTER in the stableyard, a cross-shaped windbreak with a roof.

HIGH CROSS YOUTH HOSTEL, Bridge Lane. A startling riposte to the vernacular on its hilltop: of poured and shuttered concrete painted white, with flat roofs. It was designed and made by Mr *Pickering c.* 1935 to replace his wooden house which had burnt down in 1915, of which the octagonal DOVECOTE is a reminder. Castle-like massing, but the YHA has removed its battlements and tower. Even the stairs and balustrade are concrete.

Manchester Corporation's THIRLMERE AQUEDUCT makes a brief appearance below the Youth Hostel, crossing the river in four great iron pipes on decorative iron arches and parapets with red stone abutments. By *Smith & Co.*, 1893.

At TROUTBECK BRIDGE, Short Bros built a factory and village in 1942 for the construction of flying boats. The site is now occupied by THE LAKES SCHOOL of 1965.

CALGARTH HALL, between school and lake. The principal seat of the Philipsons, but the object of a legendary curse and now scarcely habited. Hall and cross-wings, originally C15 or early C16. The N wing is disproportionately tall and tower-like, but square rather than oblong and not defensive – indeed there are no defensive towers in the central Lakes. It demonstrates its superiority with mullioned-and-transomed windows of imported sandstone and a massive round-topped stack and fireplace of late C16 type. Boldly moulded plaster overmantel

---

*Both Lingard and, curiously, Groves had Crowther houses at Alderley Edge in Cheshire.

with coats of arms of *c.* 1635, and an indistinct frieze of hunting scenes and mysterious letters. In the upper chamber a geometric ceiling of about 1638 with lions, cockerels, vines, pendants and bearded men. The panelling was removed by Dr Watson of Calgarth Park, some to Troutbeck church. An odd double porch gives independent access to both hall and wing, indicating multiple occupation. At the back of the hall range is another enormous stack, now with a puny chimney on top. The tiny upper window belongs to a powder room tucked in beside it. The S wing is now stabling, but a truncated stack corbelled out of its upper floor indicates domestic use.

CALGARTH PARK, ¼ m. NW of the former. 'I have bought a wild estate in this neighbourhood and am busy acquiring health and wealth by improving it', wrote Richard Watson, absentee Bishop of Llandaff, in 1788. His new house was built in 1789–90; a plain, but handsome and substantial mansion. Deep three-storey block, smooth-rendered, of just three well-spaced bays in front, four at the back, flanked by lower two-bay wings. The semicircular columned porch and Doric garden colonnade are probably early C19 additions. Hospital use *c.* 1915–70 explains the C20 extensions at both ends. The interior is planned round an arched longitudinal corridor, with a cantilever stair to one side balanced by the back stair on the other. Mahogany doors. The vaulted cellars have open arches on the garden side; evidently it was built four-storeyed then terraced up to the principal floor, as at Storrs (*see* p. 175).

CRAGWOOD (hotel), Ambleside Road. 1910, by *Frank Dunkerley*, a relation of the Gaddums of Brockhole (*see* below), for his cousin Albert Warburton. House and *Thomas Mawson* garden are more accomplished than Brockhole. Tightly composed front, symmetrical apart from an arched garden entrance. The stonework is exposed. Eyebrow dormer at the side, growing neatly out of the catslide and an upper inglenook chimney. Pale oak panelling and strappy cornices, nicely moulded ceilings, perhaps a bit spotty. – ROCKS OF NAMES, facing White Cross Bay. Laboriously carved in the intractible rock by *John Longmire* in the 1830s: Prof. Wilson, Dr Jenner and others in relief; political expostulations, more names, a potted biography of John Bolton of Storrs, deeply incised.

BROCKHOLE, Ambleside Road. By *Dan Gibson* and *Thomas Mawson*, 1897–1902 (during the short time they were in formal partnership), for W. H. Gaddum of Manchester and his wife Edith Potter, cousin to Beatrix. Photographs document the simultaneous creation of house and garden, from a virgin hillside (with badger sett). White and roughcast, the symmetrical lakeside front with its rhythm of bays and verandas invites comparison with the contemporary Broadleys (*see* p. 173), but Brockhole is frankly historicist in its shaped gables, dentilled cornices and Ionic gallery columns. In 1969 it became Britain's first National Park Visitor Centre, and the interior is largely lost. The surviving stair and backstair, of painted pine with slat balusters with heart cut-outs, suggest that it was never very lavish.

LANGDALE CHASE (hotel), Ambleside Road. In the late 1880s Mr Howarth of Manchester commissioned designs for a holiday villa, one Italianate, another Home Counties. When he died his widow went for something much more ambitious as a permanent home. It is credited to *J. L. Ball, J. T. Lee* and *Joseph Pattinson*, but the essence of the design is all there in *Pattinson*'s drawings of 1889. Mrs Howarth moved in in 1894. A rich Jacobean confection (£32,000), like a cream cake on the lakeshore, naughty but nice. It was built by *Grisenthwaite* of Penrith, of blue Brathay cut stone with generous sandstone dressings and carving. A wonderful sense of lift is given by the progression from the porch, to the big hall window with the rising stair behind it expressed as lights filled with carving instead of glass, onward and upward by a tiny corbelled turret and flying bridge to the bedroom eyrie in a domed corner tower.

INTERIORS. Outdoor clothing is shed in the apsed LOBBY built for that purpose, with its Italian mosaic floor. The inner HALL, almost suffocating in its welcome, occupies the centre of the house. Warm light filters in through the stained glass of the stair window and skylight; carved wood by *Arthur Jackson Smith* of Sale (Cheshire) twinkles darkly. Smaller stairs branch off the main stair and curtained balconies peep theatrically from the gallery. Mr and Mrs Willows of Scarborough, who bought the house in 1914, added the C17 chimneypiece and antique plates and paintings panelled-in. The DRAWING ROOM had an elaborate room-within-a-room round the fireplace, a paraphrase of the vernacular inglenook, now simplified. Dining room overmantel by the elusive '*Grasmere Hermit*', the small sitting-room fireplace made up from Continental carvings.

The GARDEN is one of *Thomas Mawson*'s best. Balustraded terraces, a cascade of steps, an ornamental bridge and a bastion. – BOATHOUSE. In the same style as the house, with a romantic bedroom over. For Mrs Howarth's steam launch. – LODGE. In the same style. A panel of the mullioned window is blanked out with armorial carving, like the stair window of the house.

BRIERY CLOSE, off Holbeck Lane. Embedded in the middle is the three-gable *cottage orné* in the *Webster* manner, 'newly finished' in 1839, where in 1850 Charlotte Brontë met Elizabeth Gaskell. The timber-framed and pargetted dining room and turret were added in the later C19. In 1910–12 *Francis Whitwell* of Ambleside turned it into a mansion for Oswald Hedley. The sprawling echelon of the house is validated by its magnificent position and virtuoso craftmanship, for instance the 1912 leadwork and aeroplane finial. It was divided in 1979 by *Robert Gilchrist*. *Thomas Mawson*, predictably, did the GARDEN from 1910. – COW BYRE and MOTOR HOUSE in the Voysey manner, by *Whitwell*. – Conical-roofed garden PAVILION, domed inside. – Out of sight at the top of the garden, a beautiful HORSE SHELTER with dry-stone piers supporting a big sprocketed roof.

TARN HOUSE, ¾ m. SE of Briery Close. A boathouse enlarged in 1939, and again in 1979 by *Robert Gilchrist*.

ULDALE (C)

ST JAMES, a long mile NW of the village. One of the few Lake District churches still kept whitewashed. Low and simple, just a nave with double bellcote (rebuilt 1914) and a chancel. Windows of 1730, arched with keystones and hinged for shutters, W doorway with moulded frame. But the E window is Dec; the chancel was rebuilt in 1837, but this may be the medieval one reused. The N wall has medieval masonry. Inside, the surprise is the wide low pointed chancel arch with two chamfers, springing straight from the walls. It is probably C16. The open timber roof goes with *J. H. Martindale*'s restoration of 1914.

(ST JOHN EVANGELIST, of 1869, was demolished in 1963.)

On Aughertree Fell, 1 m. NE, three well-preserved sub-circular LATE PREHISTORIC FARMSTEADS, each bounded by double banks. The E one the most complex: houses and stockyards are visible. Banks to S delimit a field system, probably contemporary.

ULPHA (C)

ST JOHN. Long, low, whitewashed, with domestic side windows, double bellcote and W porch. Perhaps C17 (E window), though not readily datable. Simple collar-beam roof. Bits of what must have been quite a spectacular scheme of WALL PAINTING found in 1934, in black and earth colours, including part of the arms of Queen Anne, and a couple of local names with C18 dates and putti.

ALMSHOUSES, N of St John. 1914, provided by John Gunson in memory of his parents. Three single-storey blocks curving across the valley, the middle one with a pediment. Recessed open porches at the end of each block. The gables have kneelers, the windows square dripmoulds.

(ULPHA OLD HALL, 1¼ m. SW. Ruin of a C16 or even C17 house with near-central entrance and opposed stair outshut.)

INDUSTRIAL REMAINS. Just upstream of the bridge over the River Duddon, on the Cumberland (r.) bank, impressive remains of the BLAST FURNACE established in 1736 by the Backbarrow and Cunsey companies, and excavated and conserved in the 1980s. From the road, the 40-ft (12-metre) high square block of the furnace stack dominates the view, a 15-ft (4.5-metre) arch defining the casting house, l., and the opening to the blowing shed on the adjacent face, r. The uppermost building (at the top of the site) is a large CHARCOAL STORE constructed across the slope in two campaigns (100 ft by 25 ft, 31 by 8 metres), with the original 50-ft by 13-ft (15- by 4-metre) store at the end, forming an L-shape. The square building between the arms of the L was the IRON ORE STORE, its walls still showing traces of red staining from haematite. Adequate storage was essential, since the furnace, once lit, would burn for six months, producing ten tons of molten iron every twelve hours.

Fuel and ore were wheelbarrowed gently downhill to the CHARGING HOUSE, level with the top of the furnace, of which little remains. Below and against the side of the furnace are storerooms, office, and other accommodation for the men, who were needed twenty-four hours a day. Now down to the CASTING FLOOR at the S side of the furnace. Through the arch can be seen the tapering, roughly circular form of the blast chamber with its lining of refractory brick, which would need rebuilding after each blow. On either side of the arch, holes through which slag was drawn off. The iron was tapped through the bottom of the chamber, to run into branching channels in the deep sand of the floor where it solidified into 'pigs'. Round the corner to the E face of the furnace are the footings of the walls of the BLOWING SHED, which housed a pair of bellows pushing air into the furnace to keep the temperature steady. It is possible that *Isaac Wilkinson* installed his prototype iron box bellows here in 1757; certainly, more efficient blowing cylinders were in place by 1785, along with a new 27-ft (8-metre) diameter water wheel, traces of whose mountings can be seen among the remains of the mill race immediately to the r. Its water was taken from ½ m. upriver, an unusually long channel for 1736. S of the furnace across a stream, a pair of COTTAGES and attached STABLES, recently restored as a single cottage. The furnace worked until 1867, always using charcoal (from the surrounding coppice woods) rather than coke.

DUDDON HALL, 1 m. NNW of the bridge. Early C19. Plain three-bay ashlar front with Doric porch, the rest roughcast. Converted to flats, with the loss of its interiors. Overlooking the bowling green and the river at the back is the exquisite Corinthian TEMPLE. Here is a puzzle: the most refined and highly wrought building in one of Cumbria's remotest valleys, built of an alien golden freestone, and dated 1843. Tetrastyle portico with monolithic columns and the crispest acanthus capitals. Pediment with wreath and swagged urns. The body of the building, which is tiny, is of ashlar with a honeysuckle frieze, fluted pilasters and pedimented windows. The cornice is the richest that a Roman building of this size would allow, as are the coffers of the portico. Windows with pulvinated friezes. The massive datestone sits on the pediment, with a stag on top.

In 2007 the temple was converted to a house by adding a 'floating' living space of glass and lead under the cedar tree to the r. A brave move in conservative Cumbria. The architect was *Alan Jackson* of *Ashworth Jackson & Walker*. Bedrooms, kitchen and bathroms have had to be contrived in the upper part of the temple and in a small extension behind.

ULVERSTON (L)   *2070*

Medium-sized market and industrial town (population 11,000), outside the Lake District National Park but, like Penrith and Kendal, emphatically not outside its orbit. Ulverston's dominant architectural accent is the BARROW MONUMENT on Hoad Hill, NE of the town. By *Andrew Trimen*, 1850–1. It commemorates Sir John Barrow, geographer and Secretary to the Admiralty. Visible for miles, it is an over-scale replica of Smeaton's Eddystone lighthouse of 1759, which was dismantled in 1882 and re-erected in truncated form on Plymouth Hoe.

ST MARY, Church Walk. Big, but low and unobtrusive amongst trees on the NE edge of town. *The Beauties of England and Wales* says it was almost wholly rebuilt in 1804. That does not go for the W tower, a very plain specimen rebuilt after 1540 when the old one was 'utterly destroyed' by a gale.* Nor for the Norman S doorway, with one arch moulding of incised zigzag, though its present position and outer surround make it certain that it is neither *in situ* nor complete. The aisle walls were rebuilt again by *Paley* in 1864–6, and the extended E bay of the chancel was added to the big basic rectangle by *Austin & Paley*, 1903–4. Spacious whitewashed interior. Arcades and clerestory look Perp but belong (says the VCH) to the 1804 rebuild. Wide low-pitched roof with alternate hammerbeams and ties, and two tiers of wind-braces. No chancel arch. Austin & Paley's sanctuary is ashlar-lined with typical sedilia and aumbry. The church was reordered in 2008. War memorial chapel made in the S aisle by *Paley & Austin*, 1923.

FURNISHINGS. SCULPTURE. Girl kneeling at a prie-dieu, her hair in a snood. White marble on a green marble pedestal; by *Pasquale Romanelli* of Florence (1812–87). – PAINTING. Entombment of Christ by *Ghirardi* after Van Dyck, presented by T. R. G. Braddyll for the pre-1866 reredos (cf. Egton-cum-Newland). – STAINED GLASS. E window by *Wailes*. The displaced early C19 E window has been re-set in the NW corner, but its painted glass has mostly fallen out of the iron armatures. Just one brown Reynoldsian figure left, eyes soppily cast up to heaven. Leslie Smith attributes the window to *Thomas Gray* of London, partly indeed after *Reynolds* (New College,

---

*A damaged INSCRIPTION recording a gift by William Dobson, Usher to Queen Elizabeth, refers not to Elizabeth I but Elizabeth of York (†1503), Henry VII's queen.

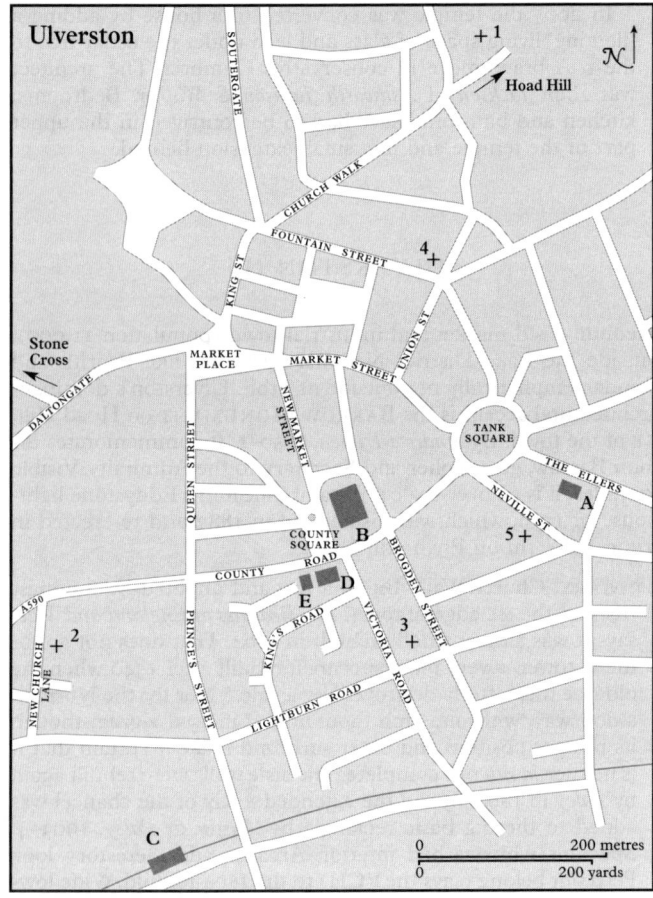

Ulverston

SOUTHGATE

+ 1

Hoad Hill

CHURCH WALK

FOUNTAIN STREET

4 +

KING ST

UNION ST

Stone
Cross

MARKET
PLACE

MARKET STREET

DALTONGATE

NEW MARKET STREET

TANK
SQUARE

THE ELLERS

NEVILLE ST

A

QUEEN STREET

COUNTY
SQUARE

B

5 +

COUNTY ROAD

D

A590

E

BROGDEN STREET

PRINCE'S STREET

KING'S ROAD

VICTORIA ROAD

3 +

NEW CHURCH LANE

+ 2

LIGHTBURN ROAD

C

| 0 | | 200 metres |
| 0 | | 200 yards |

1   St Mary
2   Holy Trinity (former)
3   St Mary of Furness (R.C.)
4   Catholic church (former)
5   Methodist church

A   Lanternhouse
B   Coronation Hall
C   Station
D   Library
E   Masonic Hall

Oxford). S aisle far W and SW by *Heaton, Butler & Bayne*, 1866.
N side by *L. C. Evetts, in memoriam* Joseph Rimmer, rector
1917–65. – MONUMENTS. William Sandys †1559, monument
erected 1588. Recumbent effigy in armour on a modern tomb-
chest. The carving of good quality. He was originally in the
centre of the SE chapel, and is to move back. – Myles and Margaret Dodding of Conishead, †1606. Two standing brasses in
a dark architectural surround of stone. A prosperous pair, he
in ruff, doublet, puffed breeches, trunk-hose, and fur-trimmed
cloak, she in coif, ruff, embroidered bodice and capacious

skirts. – Myles Dodding †1629. Tablet with miniature recumbent effigy in over-sized top-boots between Corinthian columns. Drums and armour in the background. – John Braddyll of Conishead †1727, signed *Christopher Mason*. C17-looking cartouche. – Thomas Braddyll †1776, with a small bust. – W. G. Braddyll †1818, by *R. Blore*; a putto weeps into a big drapery. – Plenty of other wall tablets.

HOLY TRINITY (former), New Church Lane. 1829–32 by *Anthony Salvin*. Severe rather than merely plain, with the stingy lancets, spare buttressing and mean clerestory of a Commissioners' church (cost £4,978). The NW tower only just clears the roof. Its fat spire goes some way to redeeming the rest. The short chancel was added in 1880 by *Paley & Austin*. (High octagonal piers inside.) Closed 1975, converted to a sports hall 1977, then to social housing in 1996.

ST MARY OF FURNESS (R.C.), Lightburn Road. By *James Sinnott*, 1893–5. Towerless church and presbytery joined in an L, enclosing a garden. All executed in chisel-dressed red sandstone with a minimum of buttressing and moulding. Pared-down Dec style, with Geometrical tracery reserved for the E and W ends. The interior is less successful. Arcades of polished granite, with unpleasant uncarved blocky capitals and over-sized chamferstops. – FURNISHINGS. Gothic spiry altarpieces with figure sculpture. – The PULPIT is an interesting piece. Populous scenes in low relief on the panels, saints in niches on the uprights, Latin inscriptions on their reveals. Angel supporters. Made by the parish priest, *Fr T.B. Allan*, 1898; also by him the paschal CANDLESTICK, and PAINTING, a copy of Leonardo's *Last Supper*. – STAINED GLASS. War memorial window in the baptistery perhaps by *Abbott*, who may have done the E window too. William Basil Weston V.C., †1945. Next to that a window by *Charles Lightfoot*, Manchester; sickly faces, sickly colours.

CATHOLIC CHURCH (former), later Oddfellows' Hall, Fountain Street. Ulverston's first R.C. church, built in 1821 on an irregular sliver of land, allowing windows on one side only. Gothick, with Y-tracery, iron pinnacles, and a little tower squeezed in the corner in 1832. The door at the altar end must be an insertion. The interior is well preserved in spite of some partitioning and enjoyable use as a junk shop. Plaster rib-vault with figure corbels. Gallery. Tiny sacristy behind the altar position, wall niche, door panelling. – Oddfellows' WAR MEMORIAL, a fine specimen of sign-painter's art including the occasional spelling mistake. – The former PRESBYTERY at the tower end is a Gothicized terraced house. Nearby is the former Catholic SCHOOL, another terraced cottage, with a castellated extension.

METHODIST CHAPEL, Neville Street. 1899–1901 by *John Wills* of Derby and London. Gothic, with plain sides and quite a fancy front. Tower and spire to one side, the spire interrupted by an octagon part-way up. Refurbished 1993, the windows reduced to holes by plain glazing.

115 LANTERNHOUSE, The Ellers. The headquarters of Welfare State
International, a spiritual centre based on the arts and community. Not a new building, but a resourceful conversion of
1987 by *Francis Roberts* of the National School of 1834. The
old building has been given a new character by knocking the
windows together vertically, framing them with lead, and filling
them with small-scale white glazing bars. The distant influence
of Mackintosh is evident. The wall-head has been altered to
insert a continuous clerestory under the eaves; its glazing
rhythm picks up that of the windows beneath. On the N a pair
of circular turrets have been added, painted a strong tomato-
soup red. On top of one is the lantern spire (designed by the
artist *Jamie McCullough*), a lattice of pale blue steel, its two-
stage silhouette making fun of the Methodist spire in the next
street. Detached on the N, but linked by a flying balcony, a
tower-like extension also tomato-soup-coloured picks up with
its vertical windowing the rhythm of the main building. The
ground floor is bare space, vaulted with jack arches on steel
columns. The lift is an entertainment in itself, apparently
worked by a little man of wire and fabric seen through a porthole. The top floor is open as the library. The 1834 kingpost
trusses rest in neat shoes in the steel posts.

Behind is the BARN, built in 1995 around three crucks of traditional type and extended in 1999 using wave trusses of laminated wood. They rest on the ridge-piece of the crucks, with
clerestory lighting interpolated. The walls are mostly glass, the
roof covering lead.

CORONATION HALL, County Square. 1914, but not opened
until 1920. Sub-classical. The auditorium with its passage
aisles, balcony and half-barrel ceiling is richly plastered, almost
the last time that such a thing would be possible for such a
building. Britannia over the proscenium, flanked by some of
the major colonies. Cherub musicians on the balcony front,
cherubs dancing round the roof vents, cherubs on the pilasters.
Fruit and flowers on all the structural elements.

POST OFFICE, next door. Of the same date, with grey terracotta.

STATION, Prince's Street, in a cutting S of the town. Built to *Paley
& Austin*'s design in 1878, after the Furness Railway had
absorbed the Ulverstone & Lancaster Railway. Surprisingly
grand for a small market town. Two Italianate storeys under a
Frenchy pavilion roof and a lofty clock tower, all in red sandstone with cream ashlar dressings with plenty of decorative
ironwork. Platforms for the main line and now-closed
branches, protected by glass and iron ridge-and-furrow
canopies on monogrammed brackets. On a neighbouring site
the Furness's handsome original terminus station of 1855, a
symmetrical composition of stone train shed fronted by a
glazed segmental arch flanked by hipped roofed offices. Now
a car showroom.

LIBRARY, King's Road. 1961, for Lancashire County Council. Pilotis, and interpenetrating volumes *à la* Mies, compromised by small size and requisite stone walling. The best thing is the proud Lancashire date-slate.

MASONIC HALL, next door. 1905–6, signed *W. Moss Settle*. Unusually good for the Masons. Neo-Georgian, in fine red ashlar, the classical language effortlessly used, even to an asymmetry, a circular window on the r. to make space for a beaten copper plaque perhaps by the *Keswick School of Industrial Arts*. An extension finished in 2004 corrects the asymmetry in an unimaginative way.

PERAMBULATION. The compact town mapped by John Wood in 1832 has been distorted by the development of Barrow and the necessity for an E–W through route (the 1960s County Road). The centre, N of the road, is pleasantly intricate and irregular, the houses smoothly rendered or roughcast, cheerfully colour-washed, only rarely exposing the rough limestone underneath.

In the NE corner of the MARKET PLACE a tall building dated 1736. It has quoins and an arcaded ground floor perhaps originally open. Overlording the square from the W the Manchester and Liverpool Bank of *c.* 1865 (now NatWest), attributed to *Miles Thompson*, with manager's house adjoining. WAR MEMORIAL, a slim Gothic pylon by *W. G. Collingwood c.* 1920. Pleasant houses in the square and adjoining streets, especially (to the S) QUEEN STREET. Over the through road in PRINCE'S STREET is Bellevue, early C19, with pilaster strips and a porch with Ionic columns. No. 20 is a *Webster*-style house of three handsomely proportioned bays in hammered limestone.

Back to the Market Place, from which KING STREET leads off N to the over-decorated Victorian front of the King's Arms. Bracketed doorcase, floral frieze, stained glass. On the corner of the adjacent mill four tiny sunk heads carved by *Edwin Woodburn*, 1896. SOUTERGATE continues N towards Broughton-in-Furness, lined with two- and three-storey colourwashed houses – the Lake Counties urban vernacular – attractive in sum but without accents, except No. 22, dated 1757. This is quite ambitious, with alternating quoins, window-sill brackets, and a pedimented doorcase with pulvinated frieze and ears. Returning again to the Market Place, NEW MARKET STREET runs S off the E end. New probably in the 1870s, with business premises bigger than had until then been the scale of Ulverston, and mostly in brick. Victoria Buildings 1878; Market Hall 1887, rebuilt 1935. Also the very fine Cumberland Union Bank (now HSBC), not advantageously sited, in buff ashlar with a big shell overdoor. To the S is COUNTY SQUARE, with a sculpture of Stan Laurel and Oliver Hardy (Arthur Stanley Jefferson – Laurel – was born in Ulverston in 1890) by *Graham Ibbeson*, unveiled 2009. They lean on a lamp-post. Opposite Coronation Hall (p. 650) is another excellent bank, Barclays (formerly Bank of Liverpool), 1901–2, almost certainly by *J. F. Curwen*. Red sandstone with a copper dome. Band of Renaissance foliage carving on top. Both doors have shell-hoods, one with grey granite colonnettes. Mullioned-and-transomed windows and ornamental leading to the lights.

MARKET STREET continues E and SE from the Market Place. The Co-operative Store of 1881 (N side) has very weird details: pilasters with bases that are no bases and capitals that are no capitals. A larger instalment stands opposite, dated 1892, in rock-faced limestone and buff ashlar. At the corner of UNION STREET is the former Trustee Savings Bank of 1836–8 by *George Webster*. Italianate, just three bays by one, but pedimented both sides. Limestone, rusticated below and ashlar above. On Union Street a heavy Grecian cast-iron balcony, to a two-light window with arched lights. The modestly Baroque clock tower and cupola (similar to the lost one on Webster's Kendal Town Hall) recessed behind the street corner was added in 1844. At the N end of Union Street in FOUNTAIN STREET, N side, two pairs of houses of 1832 with combined three-column doorways, built on a plot owned by *Webster* and attributable to him.

STONE CROSS. Gargantuan pile of 1874 on the NW edge of town, by *J. W. Grundy* of Ulverston for Myles Kennedy, ironmaster. It suffered a fire in 2004 and lies creeper-draped and fenced off at the time of writing. Of rock-faced silver limestone and yellow sandstone. Central tower, ponderously top-heavy with machicolations and French-style gargoyles, and at the top stone balconies bracketed out still further, each backed by an arc of sky through an open arch. The flanking wings are wildly asymmetrical, while aiming for the balance that Victorian architects liked. The r. wing is taller with a top-heavy chimneystack displayed in front, but the l. one reaches further, with dormers. John Martin Robinson gives a mouth-watering description of the interior, with its Wagnerian central hall arcaded all round on two levels and a truly Imperial stair, though its bottom flight was removed by an eccentric head teacher to facilitate indoor football. Dark dining room with another arcade, but the drawing room Adam style with Pompeian decoration. *Gillows* did the woodwork.

ULVERSTON CANAL. Built in 1793–6 (engineer *John Rennie*) and still in water, although formally abandoned in 1945. The canal runs arrow-straight for 1½ m. to the eastern outskirts of the town. It accommodated seagoing vessels, and ships were built and launched into the basin. The only lock was the SEA LOCK, a generous 27 ft (8 metres) wide. Near the mid-point, a steel ROLLING BRIDGE, designed by *Frank Stileman* for the Furness Railway's Bardsea branch and opened in 1882. A unique survival in England. Its ingenious mechanism enabled a section of the railway track, running at 45 degrees to the canal, to withdraw into the bank to allow ships to pass. Its tall brick hydraulic ACCUMULATOR TOWER still stands alongside.

LEVEN VIADUCT, 2 m. E. By *James Brunlees*, 1855–7; 737 yds (680 metres) long. An enterprise much admired at the time.

Forty-nine spans, until 1865 including a rolling section of 65 ft (20 metres) over the navigation channel. The main wrought-iron spans were replaced in steel in 1884–5, and in 1913 the original cast-iron columns were encased in brick and concrete. Further rebuilding from 2006 by Carillion Rail (job engineer *Matthew Wylde*), who renewed most of the deck in concrete. The history of rebuildings has been repeated on the similar Kent Viaduct (*see* Arnside).

CHAPEL ISLAND. *See* Conishead Priory.

UNDERBARROW (W)   4090

ALL SAINTS. The old church was condemned in 1867 by *Joseph Bintley* of Kendal as 'unsightly, unecclesiastical and utterly unfit'. New church built on the old foundations, plus part of the school, of 1869 by *Bintley* under the Rev. John Graves. Under the Rev. Thomas Snow (1876–93) the chancel was remodelled and the tower-porch built. The tower-porch is a clever piece of design, turning octagonal for the bell-stage and bearing a spire castellated at the base and with little lucarnes. Pretty doorway under a steep super-arch with dogtooth and red stone shafts. The side buttresses are an afterthought; perhaps the door arch showed signs of spreading. The window traceries were also improved, using buff sandstone; the N transept had to be cut away to accommodate the nave NE window. Cute vestry with bottle-shaped window and door. Long interior with single-framed nave roof, boarded chancel ceiling. – FONT. Constructed unusually of wood, with a lead bowl, and elaborated Dec in style. – LIBRARY CUPBOARD, 1793, probably from the school. – STAINED GLASS in apse only: E, 1870 by *Hardman*; S, 1907 by *Heaton, Butler & Bayne*; N, by *Shrigley & Hunt* in memory of the Rev. John McConnell, vicar 1893–1919; boy Jesus in the carpenter's shop.

UNDERLEY HALL (W) *see* KIRKBY LONSDALE

UPPER DENTON (C) *see* DENTON

URSWICK (L)   2070

The village has an uncharacteristically gentle setting, round a lowland tarn.

ST MARY AND ST MICHAEL. Nave and chancel in one, broad strong W tower of the local type, as wide as the nave. It gives the impression of belonging to the C13, except for the Perp upper stage. The W doorway is small and single-chamfered, with a segment-headed arch. In a niche (one of a pair) above the W window a C15 SCULPTURE, a Pietà of red sandstone, much decayed but still affecting. Long aiseless nave, long chancel. The chancel must be C13 too – see the one deep-set lancet by the chancel arch. But it was lengthened in the C14; hence the Dec windows. The E window is very peculiar and looks as if it were composed of two different portions (two lights of flowing tracery on three lights of late Perp). Yet it is said to be a facsimile of the original, made in 1908 at the restoration. Other windows of assorted shapes and styles. On the N side a C14 vestry. The chancel walls are new-lined with red ashlar, and a boarded ceiling of indeterminate profile inserted. Rubble exposed over the chancel arch. On each side is a tiny pinnacled niche – what for? On the S side a SQUINT. The nave walls are stripped down to the rubble. Steep king-post roof dated 1598. WEST GALLERY of 1828 on two pairs of Doric columns set in depth. In the gallery the stones of an arch can be seen, much wider than the existing upper doorway. Inside the tower it can be seen that there is indeed a tower arch, blocked by a relatively thin wall. The tower walls are immensely thick, enough to accommodate a stair on the N.

The church was restored in the early years of the C20, which resulted in the discovery of several ancient carved stones (*see* below) and a set of distinguished FITTINGS by *Alec Miller* of C. R. Ashbee's Guild of Handicraft at Chipping Camden, mostly given by Miss Petty of Ulverston in 1909–12. They are completely non-Gothic, not just in their language which is of the Renaissance, but in their forms, with a strong horizontal cornice rising to a semicircle for emphasis here and there. REREDOS incorporating a PAINTING by the local artist *James Cranke the Elder* (born 1707), flanked by carved figures of the Virgin and St Michael. – ALTAR RAILS, gently arched underneath, with turned balusters; scrollwork in the gates. – CHOIR STALLS with the arched cornice instead of poppyheads. Angel musicians play an unusual range of instruments including banjo, melodeon, pan pipes, conch, and barrel organ (with a monkey). – ORGAN with angel musicians and putti. – VESTRY DOOR with a carving of the Annunciation in low relief. – ROOD, supported by lively figures of St James of Compostela and John the Baptist. On the rood a bare cross, with angels holding the crown of thorns and cup. – GALE PEW, W of the chancel arch on the S side. Putti on either side of the door, swags of flowers on the panels. – Three-decker PULPIT, C18 of course, but the charming TESTER is of 1912, in the shape of a flat scallop held aloft by a pair of cherubs. – PEWS with roses and scallops. FONT, a massive stone egg-cup. Medieval. – FONT COVER, 1921, especially good, with disporting dolphins, angels, scallops; seaweed, conches and cockles around the rim. – S DOOR in memory of Thomas Shaw Petty, 1909.

SCULPTURE. Found in the walls in 1911 when the plaster was stripped, a CROSS-SHAFT (part), Viking rather than Anglian, probably C9, inscribed in runes 'Tunwini put up (this) cross in memory of his lord (son?) Torhtred'. It is signed '*Lyl* made this'. Collingwood remarks acidly, 'True it is that the worse the artist the bolder the signature.' Another fragment of a CROSS-SHAFT, found in 1909, with worn interlace; perhaps C10.

STAINED GLASS. In the SE lancet of the chancel, early C14 heraldic glass; in the SW a potpourri of fragments, some medieval, and the arms of Furness and Cîteaux. The 'Maiden's window', nave S, was made by *Guinevere & Margaret Kennedy* in 1912–13, so they tell us in the incised inscription below. The style is reminiscent of Tenniel. Leslie Smith attributes it to *Paul Woodroffe*, who perhaps assisted. Next to that, Doubting Thomas by *Powells*, 1931.

MONUMENTS. C13 coffin-lid with foliated cross, with an inscription referring to Amicitia filia Johannis Francissi. – A number of C18 and C19 tablets, one signed *Webster*, another *W. H. Burke*, London. – Outside are a number of monuments attached to the walls, including one erected by the Furness Cuirassiers to their drill sergeant Thomas Gardner, who fell from his horse in 1821.

LOW FURNESS PRIMARY SCHOOL, S of the church. 1992–6 by *Cumbria County Council Building and Design Dept.* An excellent building, square, spreading and low, with a shallow three-stage roof on top like a squashed pagoda. Each stage is a little steeper than the one below, with strips of glass between. Walls are clad in limestone to waist height, then wood. This clarity and simplicity is at odds with the complication of the interior spaces. The hall is in the middle, classrooms all round. But the hall is arranged diamond-wise, with double doors cutting off each corner, which means that the classrooms are basically triangular. However the deep eaves enabled the architects to push the walls out at the corners to give each classroom a semi-autonomous art area, and at the back are two small octagonal rooms. Porthole windows are a recurrent theme, and so is wood.

PREHISTORIC ENCLOSURE, on Skelmore Heads, ½ m. NNE. Not closely dated. The perimeter is marked by limestone outcrops, supplemented on the N side by a bank and external ditch, broken for a gate near the NW angle. Excavation suggested that a timber palisade enclosed an earlier phase. Immediately N, beside the field wall, a low and short Neolithic LONG CAIRN. Two upright stones within the mound, close to the E end, may have marked a burial; excavation established that two other stones stood further W, on the same alignment.

STONE CIRCLE, on Birkrigg Common, ¼ m. ENE of Sunbrick. Twelve irregular stones (enclosing Bronze Age cremation burials), tallest on the SW, lowest on the E; some evidence of an outer ring also.

WABERTHWAITE (C)

St John. Two farms, a mucky green, a spreading conker tree, and the primitive church on the brink of the tidal sands of the River Esk. Single cell, roughcast, low, with a bellcote (rebuilt 1796) and a curious cusped loop on the E gable. Perp two-light W window; windows otherwise of two or three arched uncusped lights, i.e. C16 or C17. The homely interior retains its flat ceiling and BOX PEWS (a little raised at the W end), both of 1806–7, small PULPIT (dated 1630), and CREED and COMMANDMENT BOARDS. – FONT. Cubic, with broaches in the corners, built into the wall. – ROYAL ARMS. 1778. – STAINED GLASS. E window by *James Holmes* of Lancaster, 1931. – Viking-age CROSS, outside. C10. Wide bands of interlace N, W and S. The E side is worn almost smooth. In its top two panels contorted and entangled animals may be discerned. The head is missing. Part of a second CROSS-SHAFT, of the C9, is too worn to decipher more than plant trails and interlace.

(STAINTON MILL, Bridge End, ½ m. N. A late C18 water mill with a small overshot wheel. There is a bobbin mill and a smithy downstream.)

WALTON (C)
with Birdoswald

The parish is very rich in remains from the Roman Wall.

St Mary. Rebuilt by *Paley & Austin*, 1869–70. A church of considerable personality. An early job, and the front still has something of the bluntness of early Bodley. Massive unbuttressed NW tower/porch with a flat but prominent staircase turret. The pyramid roof has tiny louvres, the belfry windows are E.E., with nook-shafts. The two sides of the church are completely different. The S side stands high and sheer, with tall lancets and just one pair with a quatrefoil over, not united under an arch. The N side is domestically cosy, with a cat-slide roof dropping in one from the nave ridge to the deep aisle eaves. The roof truss shows at its E end. Paired lancets and a rose W, three equal lancets and a quatrefoil E. Inside, as expected, is a N but no S aisle. Good single-framed roofs and shafted E triplet. – REREDOS. Mosaic framed in alabaster, 1899. – STAINED GLASS. E window by *William Wailes*, 1869. N aisle by *Heaton, Butler & Bayne*, including a tiny figure of St Leonard, *c.* 1912.

In the churchyard a HEARSE HOUSE, with a round-arched window probably from the 1813 church. – GRAVESTONE of Adam Jackson †1836. Draped urn, a pair of garlanded sheep's faces realistically portrayed, acanthus frieze, flaming urns and more acanthus.

CASTLESTEADS, 1 m. SW. A long house splendidly situated in a band of woodland overlooking a broad pastoral vale. Built between 1789 and 1794 for John Johnson of Whitehaven. A seven-bay double-pile block with a pedimented doorway, two-bay links, and wings reaching back. Judges' lodgings are provided in one of them. At the back, now the entrance front, the staircase projects apsidally. Victorian additions (1867 on downpipes) include a porch fronting the apse, a French pavilion roof over the apse, and raised dormers on the links. Inside, a broad cross-hall with two-column screen and arch, and a sweeping cantilever stair. The principal rooms are very understated in their decoration.

ROMAN FORT, Castlesteads. Levelled by Johnson in 1791, except for the SW angle of the fort platform, visible outside the SW corner of the walled garden. Separated from the Wall by the Cam Beck; the Vallum was diverted S to include it within the military zone. A rustic summerhouse contains a remarkable collection of ALTARS.

MILECASTLE 49, Hadrian's Wall. On the crest (Harrow's Scar) of the river-cliff above the W bank of the River Irthing. The E and W walls of the milecastle abut the S face of the Wall itself. The S gate – which had a tower, carried on the in-turned ends of the flanking walls – was narrowed in a later phase. The N gate, presumably similar, was destroyed by the track to Underheugh, which also took away much of the SE corner. Foundations in the SE quarter seem to mark the rear wall of a barrack block. The lower courses of a cottage (mentioned in 1603) occupy the SW quarter; ancillary buildings and its deeply tilled garden filled the rest of the W side. The Turf Wall began at this point (*see* p. 16; also below). The stone milecastle was built directly over its turf predecessor, the thick walls of which enclosed a smaller internal area.

ROMAN WALL. W to Birdoswald fort, the Narrow Wall replaced the Turf Wall. This stretch is notable for the frequent drains through it, and for several 'centurial' stones (marking lengths of Wall built by an army unit) and for carved phallic symbols (for luck). The easiest to find are a phallus, in the third course of masonry down, 26 yds (23 metres) from the W end at the modern road, and a stone of Cohort VIII, the century of Julius Primus, 167 yards (152 metres) from the road, in the top course. For the continuation W of Birdoswald *see* below.

BIRDOSWALD is a ROMAN FORT with a complex structural history, garrisoned in the C3 and C4 by Dacians, nominally 1,000 strong. In its principal phase the fort had four main gates, two minor ones, angle towers, and interval towers (in the N third only). In the original scheme the Turf Wall was constructed through this area, bounded on the S by the river-cliff above the Irthing.* In a rapid change of plan a small fort of turf and timber seems to have been thrown up, but this was occupied only briefly before a larger stone fort, covering

8

*TURRET 49A was also built, on the site of the later central headquarters building.

6 acres, was begun. This projected N of the Turf Wall, which met the fort defences immediately S of the main E and W gates. Probably before A.D. 140, and certainly by 160, the Turf Wall was demolished and replaced by Hadrian's Wall, which was now aligned with the N face of the stone fort.

Close to the NW corner, beside the road, is an interval tower, later extended as a BAKEHOUSE with a tiled roof; then the ANGLE TOWER, standing up to fourteen courses high. (This tower contains two ovens; several ovens were inserted into the rampart backing of the fort wall, throughout its circuit, and into the bases of the towers.) Further S on this W wall – its face robbed out here – an INTERVAL TOWER, and then the main W GATE. This had two arched portals, supported on six stone piers and flanked by towers, each probably three storeys high and linked by a room over the arches. Rebuilt in the C3. The W face of the S guard chamber is of ashlar of extraordinary quality, probably reused from an earlier monumental structure. S portal blocked in the C3 and used for iron-working. Stone-revetted CAUSEWAY across the external ditch, early C4. The gatehouse remained in use into medieval times.

The minor SW GATE was a single portal; one voussoir lies adjacent. When the stone fort no longer projected through the Wall, this gate, like its SE counterpart, was redundant and was blocked. The CURTAIN WALL of the fort is of coursed rubble, with much evidence of repairs and rebuilding; on the E this included blocks reused from the bridge at Willowford. The S GATE was a double portal; pivot-stones and part of the sill for the timber doors survive. The E portal was soon blocked, the W one later. On either side of the minor SE GATE the face of the curtain wall has fallen outwards. A dedication stone suggests that the main E GATE (with double portal) was rebuilt in 219. In the late C3 the W door of the N tower was blocked and a S door opened into a room formed within the gate passage. The N outer pier survives intact, with a simple bevelled impost block still supporting the lowest voussoir of the arch. The windows of the towers here had monolithic arched heads. At the N end of the E wall of the fort, a medieval corn-drying KILN.

Most of the INTERNAL BUILDINGS of the fort are underneath the pasture. An inscription of 296–305 records the restoration of the commanding officer's house, the headquarters building, and the baths. Barracks and workshops occupied most of the space. Inside the main W gate some buildings of special interest are displayed. On the N side of the principal E–W roadway – in front of the modern farmhouse, and behind a narrow frontage building – the S wall of a DRILL HALL: an aisled basilica in plan, and an exceptionally rare provision. To the S, two GRANARIES, known from an inscription to date from 205–8: formerly roofed with diamond-shaped sandstone slates, and possibly two storeys high, each needed heavy buttresses on its S wall; their floors were raised on dwarf internal walls and slots through the walls provided ventilation. Loading bays were provided in the gable-ends. In the mid C4 the S granary had another use; there were hearths at the W end, and it may have been used as a 'hall' in the late C4 or early C5. The N granary collapsed in the C4 and was quarried for its stone; after 395 a slightly larger timber building, supported by posts, was set up on the site. A second, even larger, timber HALL, 75 ft by 28 ft (23 by 8.5 metres), and of post-Roman date, was constructed (possibly in the late C5 and continuing into the C6) partly over the granary, encroaching on the street. The positions of its massive structural timbers, which were set on stone pads, are marked by modern posts. Two smaller SERVICE BUILDINGS, on timber sill beams, were constructed immediately to the W.

There is also evidence of a succession of much later buildings. Around the SW corner of the narrow frontage building, the footings of a TOWER HOUSE, possibly C14. To the E, the foundations of a BASTLE, probably late C16, are marked by pitched stones. The existing farmhouse is mid-C17, extended W in 1745 and then to the N; the castellated tower and the gabled porch were added in 1858.

WALL. For 1½ m. W of Birdoswald Hadrian's Wall was at first built of turf, soon replaced in stone. However, this rebuilding was on a separate, more northerly line, so here traces of the Turf Wall survive unencumbered. Walking from the W gate of the fort, on the National Trail, the secondary Stone Wall, with many drain culverts, is seen beside the road; its ditch, to the N, is well preserved for long stretches. TURRET 49B, butt-jointed to the Wall, was partly demolished in 1837; it was occupied into the C4 and refurbished several times. Unusually, its door was off-centre in the S wall rather than in the angle.

The DITCH of the Turf Wall becomes obvious in the slopes to the SW. To the E of the farm road to High House, where a line of trees follows the N side of its ditch, the steep bank of the TURF WALL itself is visible for about 275 yds (250 metres). The banks and the ditch of the VALLUM, here immediately to the S, confuse the eye.

Further W, back on the Stone Wall again, three turrets and a signal tower are displayed along the road to Banks. The former presence of the Turf Wall (much thicker than its successor) is shown by the way that TURRETS 51A and 51B, despite differing in size and proportions, each project forward of the N face of the Wall. Each contains a low platform internally against its N wall. On Pike Hill, ½ m. W, a fragment of a SIGNAL TOWER is all that survived roadworks in 1870. The tower preceded the Turf Wall, which zigzagged to meet it, and was set at an angle to its line; the later masonry butts up on the E. It probably provided a link between the fort at Nether Denton (*see* Denton) and a putative fort at Boothby, 2¼ m. SW. Just to the W, TURRET 52A stands eleven courses high. The plinth on the N face (and formerly on the S), and the poorly dressed flanks (originally hidden in the earthwork), are characteristic of turrets along the Turf Wall. Culverts drain through the Stone Wall.

WARCOP (W)

St Columba. The n wall of the nave is Norman, cf. a blocked doorway concealed by the boiler house. Otherwise E.E. and Perp is the general impression, if one counts the long C19 chancel as E.E. Apart from the chancel the n transept is E.E., but the two e lancets are again not physically ancient. The nave and s aisle windows are Perp. The chancel was rebuilt in 1854–5 by *J. S. Crowther* in E.E. style.* Three widely spaced e lancets, linked by a dripmould with tiny dogtooth. His buttresses are half-octagonal with square tops and bases, as at Crosby Ravensworth. Huge emergency buttress by the s door; all its stones tilted at right angles to the problem. A funny square bellcote turret on the w gable (cf. Bolton and Crosby Garrett). Machell in the 1680s noted an open triple bellcote 'delightful to look upon', so it must be later than that. Rebuilt more than once, most recently in 2006. The s porch appears to be vaulted. A very fine interior space. The chancel arch is C13, and the transept arches are C13 too, narrower than the transepts themselves. piscinas in both transepts; the different townships used different parts of the building. The two-bay s arcade, however, is Perp. Wide-stepping arches and octagonal columns. A buttress arch goes over to the emergency buttress noted outside; this pier has needed strengthening as well. The C15 nave roof is only tied by high collars, so it is not surprising that the arcade has been pushed out.

furnishings. Crowther rarely seems to have furnished his Westmorland buildings, and certainly not here. screen, stalls, altar perhaps by *Fowler*. The nave is full of C18 pews, one dated 1716. – stained glass. Chancel, largely by *Wailes*. s transept, two (†1875 and 1865–6), by *Heaton, Butler & Bayne*. Nave n, *Shrigley & Hunt*, 1893. s aisle, *J. N. Comper*, 1898. – monuments. Four coffin-lids bearing foliated crosses by the s door, three more built in round the n transept door, and an eighth by the s chapel altar. – Worn C14 effigy of sandstone, s transept. – Thomas Braithwaite, Gent., †1788. Elegant stele and cherubs in the nw corner. – James Wilkinson Breeks, †1872 at Ootacamund. Alabaster shrine in the n wall.

Outside, a re-erected medieval doorway with flattened ogee head from Burton Hall, dem. 1957.

Warcop Hall. Three parts in piquant contrast. On the l. an L-shaped Elizabethan kitchen wing, roughcast with mullioned windows. In the middle an ambitious Gibbs-style house of 1744 of six bays, faced with fine channelled ashlar. The doorway, with Ionic pilasters and a pediment, is not in the middle. And on the r. a mock pele tower of *c.* 1850 by *Matthew Charnley* of Kendal, which turns into a triple-gabled Gothic fantasy on the w elevation. At the back and inside is another phase of 1908–10, and we shall see work of 1835–8.

---

*Plans in Kendal Record Office. *The Ecclesiologist* however gives 1866 and *C. H. Fowler*.

The most valuable INTERIOR is the 1744 dining room, all 53
in beautifully faded colours. It gives the clearest idea of what
has been lost at Highhead (Ivegill, q.v.), the major Cumbrian
house of the period, and may indeed be directly related to it.
Swan-necked pediment and Corinthian pilasters to the
doorway. Corinthian columns, almost fully rounded, along the
rear wall (six of them) and flanking the fireplace. Rococo
ceiling with the same flying dragons recorded at Highhead. The
corresponding room on the l. was opened out in 1910, with an
arcade in dark wood. Of 1910 also the billiard room and library.
Good 1744 stair (date on keystone of Venetian window) up to
a cross-corridor and the upstairs drawing room. Of 1835 the
back bedrooms, showing that the house was not originally a
double pile.

WARCOP HOUSE. Deliciously faded Neoclassical house of the
early C19. Four-column Doric portico. Good central stair,
grand dining and drawing rooms with rich plasterwork r. and
l. Older parts behind.

WARCOP BRIDGE. C16. Three segmental arches, and cutwaters.
One of the finest in the county. It is very similar to the Eamont
Bridge (*see* p. 711).

WARWICK (C)   4050

Favoured satellite village E of Carlisle, with three worthwhile
churches and several major houses. The BRIDGE was built at the
behest of Peter Dixon, of Holme Eden Abbey and Shaddon Mill,
Carlisle; a fine job of 1833–5 by *Francis Giles* and *William Denton*.
It divides Warwick on the W from Warwick Bridge on the E.
Warwick Bridge runs into Little Corby, which is a short hop on
to Newby. All are included here.

ST LEONARD. Norman, and memorable for its semicircular apse 13
decorated by blank arcading – or if you prefer, bold square-
section pilasters joined by small arches at the top – and incorporating three tiny windows. Each of the deep recesses is quite
narrow, only about 18 in. (46 cm.) wide. The motif is exceptional in England, but occurs here and there in France (St
Loup, Bayeux, tower; Jazeneuil, Vienne; Thaon, chancel). It
was suggested by Neil Stratford (in *The Buildings of England:
Cumberland and Westmorland*, 1967) that it reflects the lost
Norman apse of Carlisle Cathedral – an attractive idea. The
apse is stopped by a pair of buttresses, one bearing the C16 tun
and thorn motif of Prior Thornton of Wetheral. The rest has
been rebuilt more than once. (It seems that the architectural
parts of these early Cumbrian churches, like the apse here,
were built in good masonry but the plain walling was rubble
bedded in clay.) The present nave is due to *R. J. Withers*, 1869,
correcting work of 1807 according to changed fashion, i.e

subsituting an open roof for a comfortable ceiling, and single and paired lancets for Georgian arched lights; also the bellcote on machicoulis-like brackets. Porch and narthex are by *J. H. Martindale*, 1908. Inside is another chunk of good Norman work: a western arch. Its arch mouldings and multi-scalloped capitals with single-incised decoration, with spurs at its feet, relate directly to Carlisle, so it can be dated not before the 1130s. Pevsner took this for the displaced chancel arch, so dating the apse as well; but Pennant in 1772 describes at the W end 'a good rounded arch, now filled up', and Bishop Nicholson wrote in 1703 that 'there has formerly been a square tower'. It looks to be *in situ*, and perhaps later than the apse, which is utterly simple inside and all the more impressive for it. Furnishings, monuments virtually nil. – STAINED GLASS. Three in the apse by *Daniel Bell*, 1870s, and a single light in the narthex by *Henry Holiday* for *Powells*.

SUNDAY SCHOOL, on the approach to St Leonard. Built by Thomas Parker of Warwick Hall before 1828, but used as a Methodist chapel by 1847. Stately front of ashlar with a big simple door surround and a pediment oculus but no other windows. It is flanked by short links and a pair of pavilions also pedimented. Corner pilasters smooth to the front, channelled at the sides. The sides, partly brick, have sash windows in two storeys. The auditorium was upstairs, and retains its dais. The pavilions were cottages. Now full of an inventor's oily machinery, with the living room in one wing, bedroom and bathroom in the other.

ST PAUL, Warwick Bridge. 1845–6 by *John Dobson* of Newcastle for Peter Dixon of Holme Eden Abbey. Neo-Norman, with a W tower whose bell-openings are correctly a little later in style than the church. Non-Cumbrian broach spire with lucarnes. Polygonal apse with a tripartite window in the E face, the others blank. (The apse has a plaster rib-vault. Contemporary STAINED GLASS; E window by *John Scott*.) – Contemporary too the PARSONAGE, S, presumably also by *Dobson*.

OUR LADY AND ST WILFRID (R.C.), Warwick Bridge. By *A. W. N. Pugin*, 1840–1. 'It is here and more or less precisely in 1841 that archaeological accuracy begins in English church design' (Pevsner). Built by Pugin's right-hand man *George Myers*, without Pugin's direct supervision (cost £2,586). Small but first-rate. Nave with bellcote and S porch, chancel, sacristy, and a linking section to the presbytery and stable also by Pugin. Triplets of graded E and W lancets. W doorway with naturalistic leaf capitals. In the S porch also one stiff-leaf capital. In the side walls narrow lancets alternate with large two-light Dec (elaborated Y-tracery) windows: presumably fictive rather than real history, as also at St Paul (*see* above). The interior is a Pugin jewel box, dark and claustrophobic, richly coloured and emotional. The chancel is tiny, yet finds room for three stepped SEDILIA and PISCINA in the S wall, AUMBRY, arcaded REREDOS, and in the N wall an Easter-sepulchre-like MEMORIAL in a recess to Henry Howard of Corby Castle, one of the donors, †1842. Every surface is painted and gilded. – ROOD SCREEN· and ROOD, of course. – Carved stone PULPIT, accessed from the sacristy. The nave is quieter. Stencilling in the lancet reveals but not those of the larger windows. Black-letter text round dado and cornice, more stencilling on the starved roof-tree. – CHRISM-CUPBOARD and STOUP by the font. – STAINED GLASS. E and W in a pattern of small quatre-foils with geometric filling, by *Warrington*, in the same rich reds and blues as the wall decoration. The larger windows by *Hardman*: dates commemorated 1860, 1865, 1867. Nave lancets signed LSL for *Lawrence Lee*, (19)62.

The PRESBYTERY is a good example of Pugin's stripped-down Gothic. Simple stone box with a hipped roof, welcoming porch and pointed windows of two and three lights as required.

Opposite the W end is HOWARD COTTAGE. It is built of clay, with five cruck-trusses (tree-ring date 1570/1). Howard Arms displayed on the gable-end. A long corridor has been built as an outshut on the back, and a brick wing added linking it with the stone BARN. This was used as a R.C. chapel until the church was built, hence the slabs of stone with cross-shaped holes inserted in the window openings.

WARWICK HALL. The house of 1828 was destroyed by fire in 1930. The classical STABLES and LODGE survive. The new hall was completed by 1934 for the Elwes family to the design of *Guy Elwes*. There is nothing else like this in the county. The sashes and rather bald cupola are Neo-Georgian, but the receding planes of the masonry, the five-sided bay overlooking the river and especially the pair of free-standing columns of the S front are unmistakably Deco. Elwes's proportions work well from a distance: the tight rhythm of his windows contrasts with the lazier rhythm of the service wing, speeding up still more round the central bay, and perfectly emphasized by the cupola above. The interior is planned about the swirling central stair, its cantilevered treads like high-heeled shoes, the gracefully backward-leaning balusters like Duchamp's 'Nude Descending'. Fat paired columns support a dome, and plain glazing allows the outside cupola to be seen as well. The thinness of the landing floor and non-alignment of supports demonstrates the structural freedom of reinforced concrete.

A beech-lined riverside walk to the large WALLED GARDEN gives splendid views of the house, and of Holme Eden.

HOLME EDEN ABBEY, Warwick Bridge. By *John Dobson*, 1833–7, for Peter Dixon, cotton manufacturer. *James Stewart* of Carlisle acted as site architect. The style is Tudor, elevations and plan asymmetrical, the stone red, the skyline with its bristling chimneys and turrets superb. Given to Benedictine nuns in 1921, whose graveyard still exists. The mansion was divided into twelve dwellings in 2004–6, by David Little. The house appears to have two storeys, but a third is hidden by the raised terrace. A vaulted tunnel gave access to the internal courtyard, whose elevations are indeed fully three-storeyed. This posed problems for the conversion, because so many rooms face inwards and not out. The internal decoration is of the coarse, gargantuan sort favoured at the time, with moulded plaster disguised as wood and stone. The principal rooms are allocated between flats, but the spectacular main stair with its monstrous brackets and hanging vaults remains communal.

Thirty-odd houses have been built in and around the polygonal walled garden; they are arranged formally, in an open square with their backs to the wall.

LITTLE CORBY HALL. Of 1702–8, for William Howard of Corby Castle. Handsome but slightly institutional-looking front of ashlar, seven bays with a three-bay pediment. Corner pilasters, grooved. A damaged inscription over the door appears to attribute the carved trophy of arms with the Howard lion to P. H. Howard and *J. Robinson* ('*scul.*'), 1842. The building was never finished internally and has stables in the r. half.

INDUSTRIAL SETTLEMENT, Warwick Bridge, tucked away s of the main road. Late C18 and early C19. A short street of two-storey red sandstone terraces leads to a nine-bay COTTON SPINNING MILL of three storeys plus attic, built 1790–3. For John Ferguson, Peter Dixon and William Waddell, whose initials are carved on datestones high up on the coursed rubble walls. A wooden bellcote with a weathervane at the w end, where an eleven-bay, four-storey extension was added in 1814. Cast-iron window frames throughout, and internally cast-iron columns. The leat and sluices are in place, and an arch shows the position of the original internal wheel. The mill is now split between office and light industrial uses. The HOUSES were all built for mill workers in 1814–16. The six to the N, with hipped ends to the terrace and more chimneys than should be expected, were originally twelve back-to-backs. The s terrace, with gable-ends, has an arched cart entrance separating four small houses from a three-bay house with a cellar, originally workrooms or a dyehouse.

On the main road, BROOKSIDE, an elegant sandstone house of three bays with a central gable. Built in 1853–4 as a miller's house for the nearby corn mill. The projecting chimneystack in the w wall bears the Howard arms and the initials PEHH, for Philip Howard of Corby Castle. The adjacent WATER MILL is a square bank mill of coursed rubble with an internal undershot wheel, made by *Blaylock* of Carlisle in the 1850s. It has a three-bay s extension and an internal loading platform to keep the corn dry. A weathervane on the ridge bears the Howard lion and the date 1839. Some of the machinery, which is complete, is of this date.

At NEWBY, overlooking the bridge, N, is a farmhouse done up as an eyecatcher for Edmond Castle at Hayton, *c.* 1840. Tower with outsized battlements and crowsteps, lower wing with a Scottish pepperpot angle turret, then a lower wing still. The garden wall looks over the river valley with a domed pepper-pot at each end. On the N side the large farmyard.

WHOOF HOUSE. *See* Scotby.

WARWICK BRIDGE (C) *see* WARWICK

WASDALE (C)

1000

Wastwater, England's deepest lake, is long and narrow, stern and desolate, with a waste of scree on its S side. At its head the valley widens to a characteristic arbour of fields and dry-stone walls hemmed in by the great mountain barrier of Lingmell, Kirk Fell and Yewbarrow.

ST OLAF, Wasdale Head. Date uncertain. In a grove of yews, and as minute and as humble as it should be in such august surroundings. Roughcast, with a stone roof and a tiny bellcote. Nave and chancel in one. The eaves on the N side are only nose height, the tie-beams inside not much higher. – Victorian IRON BRACKETS for oil lamps. – Outside, graves of young climbers.

CHURCH, Strands. The church of Nether Wasdale. Easily missed, so much smaller is it than the neighbouring dwellings. Whitewashed, domestic, C17; only the bellcote and gravestones identify it as a church. Nave and chancel in one. Some Georgian windows, including the arched E window. The interior is a joy. Coved plaster ceiling with exhortatory TEXTS. ROYAL ARMS (George III) at the W end. In 1837 Stansfield Rawson of Wasdale Hall added a N aisle behind an arcade of wooden posts and shallow arches, and brought in the late C17 PULPIT, LECTERN, and PANELLING said to have been rescued from York Minster after the incendiary fire of 1829. – STAINED GLASS. E window by *Shrigley & Hunt, c.* 1920.

WASDALE HALL (Youth Hostel), 1¼ m. E of Strands. Built as a holiday home by *Stansfield Rawson*, a Yorkshire banker, to his own designs in 1829 and 1839–40. He brought over as masons *John* and *William Aspinall* of Halifax. Of rough granite, with fine imported sandstone dressings. The earlier wing is timber-framed to a Yorkshire pattern. Dining room with Gothic fireplace with quatrefoils, cross-beamed ceiling with foliage bosses. Library with wild Jacobean chimneypiece with herms and lions. Stair with spiral balusters. From the recessed porch with its little vault one is face to face with the unfathomable lake and the plunging shivering scree, as often as not disappearing into the mist.

WASDALE HEAD INN. Legendary among climbers; the sport developed here from the 1860s. Enlarged from the original farm in the 1850s by the tall-story-telling landlord Will Ritson, and several times since. Good BANK BARN.

BURNTHWAITE FARM, Wasdale Head. Until 1928 two farms of the late C17/early C18, with the houses joined together.

WATENDLATH (C) *see* GRANGE-IN-BORROWDALE

WATERFOOT HOUSE (C) *see* POOLEY BRIDGE

WATERMILLOCK (C)

ALL SAINTS. Rebuilt in 1884 by *C. J. Ferguson*. Mauve slate and red sandstone. The W tower barely clears the nave roof but has the breadth and robustness to make its point. Square turret stopping short of the top, blunt pyramid roof. The windows are plain lancets in twos and threes, and a spread triplet at the E end under a vesica. The interior – this is not a small church – shows Ferguson as a Northern cousin of Paley & Austin. Polygonal waggon roof, closely raftered with just three ties; the chancel boarded. Low stone screen, just a dwarf wall. Geometric tiling in the chancel. – STALLS, ORGAN CASE, PULPIT, spare but good, by the architect. – FONT. A massive turned bowl of Shap granite, with some incised decoration; quite a feat in this stone. – STAINED GLASS. Good collection of a good period, 1884–*c*. 1908, by *Burlison & Grylls*, *Heaton, Butler & Bayne*, and *William Aikman* for *Powells* (NE).

(WATERMILLOCK HOUSE. Dated 1689. Three-light mullioned windows all under one label course. Oval windows in the gables. Late C18 addition behind.)

(LEEMING HOUSE (hotel). On Ullswater, 1 m. SE. Three-bay hip-roofed villa with an iron veranda. Bell in the clock tower dated 1831.)

WAVERTON (C)

CHRIST CHURCH, E of the village, at the crossroads. 1865. Nave with bellcote and chancel. Plate tracery.

(THE OLD MILL, Lessonhall. Dated WM 1834 over the mill-race arch. Two storeys, three bays. Rubble-faced red sandstone with flush quoins, with two channels over the mill race. Single-bay central gabled projection, single-storey l. lean-to. Under-shot water wheel inside.)

(HAWKRIGG HOUSE, 1 m. SE. J & SJ (John Jefferson) 1824 over the carriage arch. Nicely placed on an eminence and agreeable to look at. Rendered white. Three-bay centre with lower pedimented wings. The windows in the latter and l. and r. of the doorway in the centre are of the Venetian type, set in super-arches.)

WELTON (C) *see* SEBERGHAM

WESTNEWTON (C)   *1040*

ST MATTHEW. 1857 by *Hugall* of Cheltenham, who also did the SCHOOL dated 1858, and perhaps the estate cottages opposite. Thin w turret with clock and spire. Three-bay nave and little chancel; Geometrical tracery. – (STAINED GLASS. Chancel and w windows by *W. Wailes.*)

WEST CURTHWAITE (C) *see* THURSBY

WESTWARD (C)   *2040*

ST HILDA. Overlooking the little River Wiza. Of 1785–6, on older footings. A large bald church, rectangular, with lancets in equal threes. Thin w tower and square spire standing on a pointed arch forming the w porch, above which steps lead back to the tower. Pedimental E gable. The church was re-furnished in 1877–8. – (MONUMENT. Table tomb of Richard Barwis of Islekirk †1648, now set in the w wall, with two frames of dog-tooth, one framing his arms and epitaph on a brass, the other a brass of Francis Barwis's gifts.)

GREENHILL (hotel), on the A595. 1810–15. Seven bays, with a four-column Doric porch and tripartite window over. (The staircase is apsed inside. A corridor runs r. and l., and at its start are four pairs of tiny stucco caryatids and atlantes, two pairs r. and two l. They are reminiscent of Michelangelo and – though earlier – of Alfred Stevens.)

ROMAN FORT, at Old Carlisle, 1¼ m. NE. The prominent platform of a fort (*Maglona?*) on the Roman road from Carlisle to Papcastle. Probably Hadrianic in origin, and possibly occupied into the early medieval period. Defended by a double ditch and medial bank, enclosing 4 acres; the positions of the E and S gates are visible. A long history of quarrying of the stone buildings throughout the interior; the fort wall has been neatly filleted out. Broken ground between the fort and the modern road is part of the extensive civil settlement: long 'strip-buildings' (the lines of their walls marked by quarry-trenches), set gable-on, flanking the Roman road.

WETHERAL (C)

The village is given distinction by its triangular green ringed by the villas of Carlisle grandees, by the beautiful Eden gorge spanned by an exceptionally early and fine railway viaduct, and by the gardens and cascade of Corby Castle (q.v.) on the opposite bank.

HOLY TRINITY. Essentially early C16 in its outward parts, with most of the windows of two or three lights with uncusped round arches to the lights. A thin w tower added in 1790, with a round-arched w doorway. The tower was encased and given an octagonal top and half-octagon stair in R. J. Withers's restoration of 1882. The chancel was largely rebuilt by Withers in 1872. Blackletter *orate* inscriptions remain over a s chancel window for William Thornton, Prior of Wetheral in 1500, and over the door for Richard Wedderhall, who succeeded him in 1534. Less legible ones elsewhere, e.g. on a mullion on the N side. Attached on the NE is the fairy Gothick chapel of the Howards of Corby, added in 1791. This is as light a confection as iron tracery and a plaster vault can make it. Five bays of slim windows with slim buttresses and a large E window. The merlons have quatrefoil piercings as though to prove that they are not serious, but the teetering pinnacles have gone. The four-bay arcades are earlier than anything seen so far; C13, alternating round and octagonal piers with chunky caps and double-chamfered arches coming down to a neat little broach. The s aisle is much renewed. The C16 clerestory windows sit over the spandrels. The Howard Chapel is fenced off behind a wide arch. Bright and cold, it has a tight rib-vault of plaster on wall pilasters of trefoil section with delicate leafy capitals.

FURNISHINGS. FONT. Shallow C18 bowl on a Gothic base: a hollowed octagon with colonnettes and cusped arcading. – STAINED GLASS. In the tower, C15 coats of arms, a saint, Virgin and Child, donors. E window, 1886 by *Cox, Sons & Buckley*. s transept (†1886) and nave w windows by *Heaton, Butler & Bayne*. – MONUMENTS. The alabaster effigies of Sir Richard Salkeld of Corby †1500 and Jane Vaux, heiress of Triermain, much battered: not many arms, legs or noses between them. In the Howard Chapel, Adeliza Maria Howard †1833, by *R. Westmacott Jun.*; kneeling figure on a heavy plinth. – Lady Maria Howard, †1789 at the age of twenty-three, and infant girl. By *Nollekens* (it cost £1,500, and reportedly took ten years to make). White marble group, free-standing. Faith, generously draped, supports the dying mother and baby, 'dire ending of bright hope', and points to Heaven. It is one of Nollekens's major works. As Wordsworth wrote, we 'through this still medium, are consoled and cheered'. Fuseli called the monument superior to anything by Canova.

WETHERAL PRIORY, s of the church. Founded c. 1100 by Ranulph de Meschines as a cell of the Benedictine abbey of St Mary, York. Only the handsome GATEHOUSE is left, but that survives complete. It has been thought CI5, but the roof timbers are now tree-ring dated 1512–36. It stands three storeys high, with a crenellated top. The carriageway, porter's lodge, and basement of a removed building on the N are all tunnel-vaulted. The front wall projects a little over the outer arch, whose outer orders die into the imposts. Above, a two-light window, and above that another; cusped trefoil-headed lights, with dripmoulds. The turning stair is in a projection at the NE corner, with a small doorway inside. If the church was opposite the gatehouse then the cloister, represented by the quadrangular farmyard, was on the N. Some medieval walling remains with part of a two-light window. This may have been the E wall of the E range.

(CAVES, about ¼ m. S. Associated with St Constantine, and known to have been in use in the C14. Three cells, 20 by 9 by 9 ft (6 and 2.8 metres), cut out of the rock, with an entrance corridor enclosed by a wall, containing windows overlooking the river, and also a fireplace. For the statue opposite *see* Corby Castle.)

STATION. By *Benjamin Green* for the Newcastle & Carlisle Railway, 1835–8, later extended for the North Eastern Railway. Dramatically situated at the very end of the viaduct across the Eden gorge, the lines and platforms curving sharply into a cutting towards Carlisle. Original single-storey clerk's office in finely jointed red sandstone ashlar. Hipped roof. Iron and glass platform canopy added in 1861, tiny wooden-boarded ticket office in 1880. Standard NER iron FOOTBRIDGE, also 1880. STATION-MASTER'S HOUSE behind, two-storey in coursed limestone.

RAILWAY VIADUCT. Five very wide arches in beautiful red stone, with channelled rustication and radiating voussoirs. Inscriptions in Latin and English to Henry Howard who laid the foundation stone in 1830, and to *Francis Giles*, engineer, and *William Denton*, builder, 1831–4. Footpath over to Corby.

VILLAGE. On the green is KILLORAN (hotel), originally Oak Bank, a villa of 1869–71 for John Scott. Red Dumfries stone, Scottish dormer gables, tower at the back, rich internal detail. Directly opposite is EDEN MOUNT, 1872, similar but in Waterhouse-ish yellow brick and buff stone. Tenders to build were invited by both *John Hodgson* and *C. J. Ferguson*. At the other end of the scale are a few single-storey houses, of which HOLLY COTTAGE, to judge by its long narrow shape, steep and wobbly roof, and chimneys set off the ridge, is a clay dabbin. On Station Road, the CROWN HOTEL, originally *c.* 1800, with a top storey of *c.* 1930 by *Harry Redfern* for the Carlisle State Management Scheme (*see* p. 71). Seven irregular bays and a porch of Ionic columns, the capitals far better than the shafts. The OLD RECTORY is one of a handsome early C19 terrace of three double-fronted houses with Doric porches *in antis*.

EDEN BENCHMARK, 2000. Flight of Fancy, by *Tim Shutter*. Literally a bench, with stone cushions, Nollekens wings at the end, viaduct arches at the back.

(COTE HOUSE, 1½ m. SSE. Superior-quality bastle incorporated into a farmhouse. Late C16 or early C17.)

WHARTON HALL (W) *see* KIRKBY STEPHEN

WHICHAM (C)

1080

ST MARY. Wide single cell, roughcast, founded upon large boulders. The S doorway has a single-chamfered round arch said to be Norman. The E window is C17, the N transept with its wooden arcade is of 1858, when the other windows were 'improved'. – FONT. Heavy octagonal tub. – ROYAL ARMS. George III. – STAINED GLASS mostly by *Wailes*.

WHITBECK (C)

1080

ST MARY. The W front was rebuilt in 1883 by *Settle & Farmer* with rock-faced sandstone. The rest, a single cell roughcast without and plastered within, has early C19 twin lancets, perhaps in earlier masonry. – (MONUMENT. 6-ft (1.8-metre) effigy of a lady, early C14, rather rubbed off.)

WATER MILL, probably C18. Four-bay bank mill with 15-ft (4.5-metre) overshot wheel of composite wooden and iron construction.

WHITEHAVEN (C)

9010

Churches	672
Public Buildings	675
The Harbour	676
Industrial Remains	677
The Town	679
Outer Areas	683

A C17 and C18 planned town of great charm, breezily colourwashed and filled with the sound of seagulls. Favoured with coal deposits and a natural harbour, it was developed as a port by the Lowthers: first Sir Christopher, who built a quay in 1634 by the village which clustered round Pow Beck, where the Market Place is today, then Sir John, a Fellow of the Royal Society at the time of Wren, Hooke and Evelyn and the rebuilding of London after the Great Fire. His instructions from London to his steward

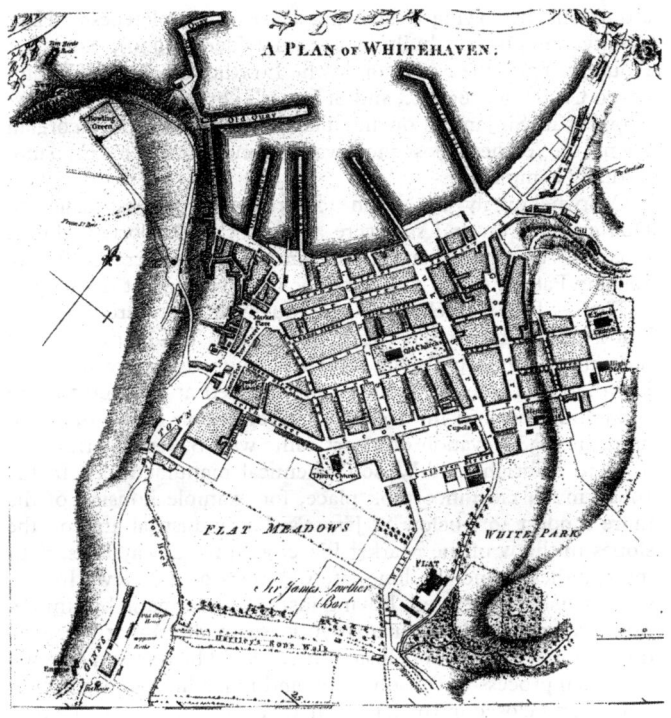

Whitehaven.
Map, 1774

begin in 1666. The town grid was laid out around the wide thoroughfares of Lowther Street and Duke Street, both leading up from the harbour, and the narrower Roper Street that comes down to the Market Place to the SW. A complete block was given to the church and churchyard of St Nicholas. Regulations determined that the houses stood right up to the street and butted up to their neighbours in a continuous row. Windows and doors were to be edged with hewn stone. Rules governing height seem to have been widely disregarded, although the houses are nearly always of three storeys. They are of differing widths, and were run up in ones and twos, presumably by small builders. This informality within the formal frame, and the wide licence of colourwashing (a recent phenomenon), are Whitehaven's particular charms.

Sir John died in 1706. James Lowther (later Sir James) was more pragmatic than his father, allowing for instance a shambles in Lowther Street. These were Whitehaven's most prosperous years, when it reached the natural limits imposed by the valley sides. Now, as Dorothy Wordsworth was to note, 'streets often terminated prettily; a hall, a church' – like the *allées* of the later sort of formal garden: another of Whitehaven's particular attractions, bestowing a satisfying sense of completeness.* Holy Trinity church was built in 1714–15 (dem. 1949), Somerset House in 1750, the extension to the Lowther mansion of White-haven Castle in 1766 etc., and St James's church in 1752–3; view-stoppers all. Sir James Lowther died in 1755, leaving the Georgian town, the earliest post-medieval planned town in England, virtually complete.

Overwhelmingly the main export was coal, especially to Dublin, but iron and salt were also shipped. Imports included tobacco, rum, grain, sugar and timber. Ships were built too, William Palmer (1702–78) being the most prominent shipwright.

The seeds of Whitehaven's subsequent decline were in its iso-lation and in the limited nature of its trade. Too many ships set out empty for Virginia, or returned empty from Ireland. The Lowthers lost interest. Coal exports peaked at 400,000 tons in 1928 and ceased in the 1980s. The Depression of the 1930s hit hard. In 1938 salvation of a sort came with Sekers Fabrics, and in 1940 Allbright and Wilson, chemical manufacturers. In the 1960s much clearance took place, for example housing of the more modest sort below St James's. The industrial area on the slopes to the w of the Market Place, with its railway lines, flour mills, pitheads and the long late c18 rows of the New Houses, was virtually obliterated, leaving just a few dramatic but myste-rious fragments. However in 1970 it was realized that if carried through to its logical conclusion there would be no town left, and a gradual process of consolidation and rehabilitation began. The last coal pit closed in 1986, though as late as 1992 phosphate rock was coming into the harbour to feed the chemical industry. A second lifeline has come with the help of BNFL Sellafield, and with the European Union. Whitehaven Development Company set up in 1992.**

CHURCHES

St Nicholas, Lowther Street. The proprietary chapel of 1693 was a big two-storey box with an embraced w tower and windows in two tiers along its sides. It was rebuilt in 1883 in red sandstone in a Dec-to-Perp style by *C. J. Ferguson*, his grandest church, for Margaret Gibson in memory of her parents. But all that is left after a fire in 1971 is the porch, w tower, and w transepts (the *parti* of Ely). The tower has detached buttress-shafts and pinnacles *à la* Somerset. It is sur-prising how successful the stump is, and how much has been fitted into it. Inside the w porch is the doorway of the c17 church, with Doric pilasters and pediment. The sw transept is fitted out as a chapel, the tower space and nw transept are

---

*Compare Millom, a c19 plan, where straight streets run out into nothing.
**For more on the planned town *see* Sylvia Collier, *Whitehaven 1660–1800* (RCHME), 1991.

divided horizontally as office and tearoom. Etched GLASS SCREENS by *David Peace* and *Sally Scott* fill the tower arch and the big buttress arch of the s aisle. – Mid-C20 STAINED GLASS by *Abbott & Co.*; also a window by *Heaton, Butler & Bayne*, 1880. – Splendid ROYAL ARMS of William and Mary in the office. By *Mathias Read*, 1693. The ruined fragments of the nave in the municipalized churchyard (Whitehaven's Central Park) work surprisingly well too, creating a sense of enclosure without dingy corners. – MOSAIC PAVEMENT, commemorating the miners and the pits of the area. – MEMORIAL near the Duke Street gate to children who lost their lives in the mines. Two boys, a girl and pit pony. By *Judith Bluck*, 2001.

ST JAMES, Queen Street. On the edge of the planned town and looking down on it from its hillside. Built in 1752–3, to a design 'produced by' Sir James Lowther's agent and mining engineer, *Carlisle Spedding*. No other building by Spedding is known, however, and Frederick O'Dwyer suggests as a likelier designer *Christopher Myers*, later active as an architect in Ireland (cf. Holy Trinity, Ballycastle in Co. Antrim, completed 1756 and convincingly attributed to him).[*] Myers was resident in Whitehaven in the 1750s, and is listed among the subscribers to the building. The type is that of the town's first St Nicholas, and of the lost Holy Trinity. The broad embraced w tower is provided with a larger pediment over the pedimented doorway. Arched bell-openings, obelisk pinnacles. The nave is a broad roughcast box with rectangular windows in two tiers. They look entirely domestic, without any adornment. Elliptical apse with blocked Venetian windows.

Serenely beautiful interior, entered through a SLIDING DOOR of etched glass (1997) – willow, poppies, falling water, water lilies – to a vestibule in the tower. Steps rise on each side to the gallery doorways; three thin turned balusters per tread (cf. Penrith parish church, 1720–2). Galleries on three sides, supported on Doric columns and with a full triglyph frieze, and carrying Ionic columns above. Flat ceiling with beautiful stucco roundels, Annunciation and Ascension, with angels and cherubs and Rococo bosses for chandeliers. *Robert West*, later a celebrated Rococo plasterer in Dublin, was paid £23 17s. 4½d. for these. In 1970 painted in Wedgwood colours. The shallow apse has four square Ionic pilasters and a PAINTING of the Transfiguration by *Giulio Cesare Procaccini* (1548–1628) in a pedimented aedicule. Said to have come from the Escorial; given by the 3rd Earl of Lonsdale in 1869. The apse was modified to suit in 1871, apparently by blocking the C18 Venetian windows (still visible externally) and introducing a glimmer of top lighting. In 1921 a baptistery and war memorial chapel were contrived under the E ends of the galleries, with Ionic screens composed of miniature Venetian motifs – classical veering towards the Baroque. In 1979 the altar was brought forward on an oval platform, the choir moved into the apse in

77

---

[*] See *Irish Architectural and Decorative Studies* 12, 2009.

Early Christian style, and the gallery balconies modified. Earlier alterations to the galleries by *C. J. Ferguson*, in a restoration of 1886.

PULPIT. C18, with fluted pilasters broken round the angles and arched panels with a little rocaille. The very tall columnar support and stairs have been parked in the gallery. – FONT of liverish marble, a shallow bowl and baluster. Given in 1876; reputedly Florentine and C17. – Early C18 PAINTINGS of Moses and Aaron from St Nicholas by *Mathias Read*. Also in the gallery. – STAINED GLASS. A fine collection, looking good in a church that was not designed for it. S aisle, several by *Abbott & Co.*, 1930s and later; also fourth and fifth from E by *Shrigley & Hunt*, 1917 and 1924. N aisle, second from W by the same, 1924, then one by *L. C. Evetts*, 1976 (minimal dove, wheat, houses), and two by *Wailes*, 1873. Bell-ringers' window, NW, with a hand and arm coming out of a cloud to grasp a stripy sally. Signed *Alex Haynes*, 1999. – MONUMENT. In the lobby a simply and beautifully carved tablet to the Rev. Thomas Spedding †1783.

ST BEGA (R.C.), Coach Road. Strangely isolated from the town. By *E. W. Pugin*, 1865–8, the first and best of his West Cumbrian trio. Typically swoonworthy in its exaggerated proportions. Long roof, high and even with patterns of green and blue slate, coming to a three-sided apse. Vertiginous W front, the tallness of its lancets emphasized by tiddly Dec tracery right at the top, the height of the gable emphasized by an overhanging angel. A heavy W bellcote and spirelet, unsupported by any buttressing, have been removed. Enormous aisle windows, so wide as to require inverted arches underneath. They have complex and varied six-light traceries. Entry is at first foiled by the glass capsule of the Crying Room (labelled as such). A pity, because it is designed for immediate and total impact, quite unlike the gradual mysteries of his father's churches. Flooded with light from the huge windows, almost unobstructed by the high and wide-stepping arcades, it is very tall, with a shiny sea of open benches. All focuses on the richness and colour of the E end. The arcades show a subdued alternation of red and yellow voussoirs, and an inset quatrefoil in each spandrel. Tricky scissor-braced roof. Small, rich chapels N and S, and the Miners' Chapel (NW) with a Pietà. The apse is elaborately arcaded right round, with four statue niches. Hanging over the arch in golden letters LUX LUCET IN TENEBRIS. The High Altar has been dismantled (though the lavishly carved reredos still runs round the apse), and the priest's chair now stands in the chord. The tall canopied tabernacle is now S of the chancel arch. The carved stone, done by *Boulton* of Cheltenham, is painted white, as are most of the fittings. Structural carving by Mr *Pickering* of Carlisle. – BENCHES. The ends are cast-iron. – STAINED GLASS. E windows by *Hardman*, *c.* 1868. – WAR MEMORIAL of tilework set in alabaster.

The older CHURCH of 1835 to the N is now a school canteen.

ST GREGORY AND ST PATRICK (R.C.), Quay Street. 1889. Dual-purpose church mission and school. Pink. Memorial to pit disasters on the polygonal apse outside.

KIRK MISSION HALL, High Street, E of St James. Scotch Presbyterian church, marked 'High Meeting' on a map of 1770; later Methodist. Two-storey ends, full-height centre indicated by a pair of tall arched windows. Later bellcote on the r. gable.

UNITED REFORMED CHURCH (formerly Presbyterian), James Street. 1904–5, a rebuild of the former Low Meeting. Gothic, stone, with a tactfully squat tower.

WESLEYAN METHODIST CHURCH (former), corner of Scotch Street and Lowther Street. 1877 by *T. L. Banks*. Crazy-paving granite and sandstone. Restlessly Gothic, without horizontals. The belfry lights of the NW tower run up into jabbing dormer gables, and so do the aisle windows.*

CHRISTIAN BRETHREN, Sandhills Lane, off Scotch Street. Built as a Quaker meeting house in 1724–5. White and simple, a double span with a central valley originally supported by 'great stone pillars', now apparently a steel joist. The interior was, as usual, divided into two unequal rooms by movable screens, but running the other way, i.e. across the line of the columns.

PUBLIC BUILDINGS

WHITEHAVEN CASTLE, originally Flatt Hall. At the E end of Lowther Street, not aligned with the town's grid. It was rebuilt by Sir John Lowther in 1676–84 as a square block with a small central light-well, in which state it is prominent in Jan Wyck's view of 1686. The architect was *William Thackeray*, the carpenter *James Swingler*. Then in 1766–75 for James, Earl of Lonsdale, *Robert Adam* turned it towards the town and the sea, adding castellations and the centre bow and tower-like wings that dominate the picture. Lowther, notorious for his meanness, reputedly never paid Adam's bill. *Daniel Benn* was the man on site. The N and W walls of Thackeray's house can still be seen, but his W front only appears between the bow and the N wing. Adam's urbane castle, anticipating his Scottish castles such as Mellerstain (Borders), stands against a beautifully wooded hillside, but the town fields it faced are now a supermarket car park. Of the C18 interiors, including some oval Adam rooms with niches in the diagonals, there seems to be nothing left.

WAR MEMORIAL, c. 1920. In the park next to the Castle. Sandstone stele with a tripping angel bearing a wreath in relief. Nearby on Lowther Street is *John McKenna*'s SCULPTURE, Man and Whippet, c. 2000, with an original 1859 drinking fountain.

---

*An equally eye-popping CONGREGATIONAL CHAPEL here, also by *Banks*, has gone.

CIVIC CENTRE, Lowther Street. Centre part 1953, dark blue brick blocky wings 1969. Architects *Graham, Roy & Nicholson*. The E wing joins up with the CARNEGIE LIBRARY of 1905–6 on Catherine Street, by *G. D. Macniven*. Built of deep red stone, it is in the Wren-verging-on-Baroque style favoured by Carnegie libraries everywhere: scrolls, swags, cherubs, keystones, all strongly modelled for light and shade and strictly symmetrical, with hipped roofs.

COPELAND CENTRE (Council headquarters), Catherine Street. 2003–5 by *Leach, Rhodes & Walker*. Red and cream. A tactful job, given its size, acknowledging the street rules on Irish Street but presenting a public front to the car parks at the back.

THE HARBOUR

Noble breakwaters of interlocking pinkish stones, worn by the fretful sea, protect the HARBOUR. The QUAYS within the enclosed area are helpfully named and dated by the Development Company. The OLD QUAY, built in 1634 by *Robert Storey* on the harbour's W side, was extended in 1665 and 1681 by *Richard Caton*. The BULWARK at the end of Duke Street followed in 1693 on the E side; the OLD TONGUE to its W (sometimes called the Sugar Tongue) in 1735; the confusingly named OLD NEW QUAY, N of the Old Quay, in 1742; the NEW TONGUE (or Lime Tongue, between the Bulwark and Old Tongue) in 1754. *John Smeaton* added the OLD NORTH WALL in 1785. *Sir John Rennie* designed the beautiful WEST PIER (1824–32).* His NORTH PIER completed the outer works in 1833. The enclosed QUEEN'S DOCK (1872–6, designer *Sir James Brunlees*) was the last major change until the development of the marinas in the 1990s (*see* below).

LIGHTHOUSES. The first was built on the Old Quay in 1710, a 42-ft (13-metre)-high tapering cylindrical structure. Moved as the quay was extended, it settled in its present position in 1767, and at some stage it lost the oriel on the sea-facing side. Its sundial is dated 1730. The harbour's most elegant lighthouse has shone from the end of the West Pier since 1832. It is a lovely tapering cylinder, rolling out at third-storey level to support a railed gallery with a slender lantern above, capped by an ogee roof with a ball finial. A shorter fatter light, dated 1841, answers from the North Pier opposite, and the Old New Quay carries a FLAG TOWER. The SWING BRIDGE for trains to cross a C19 slipway by the Lime Tongue is a relic of the shipbuilding industry. The lack of large dockside warehouses seems surprising, but Whitehaven's coal exports needed only secure yards, and the town's merchants preferred to store high-value, low-volume imports like rum and tobacco in their own houses where they could keep an eye on them.

---

*Though the builders deviated from his plan, and the seaward extremity had to be taken down and rebuilt on Rennie's alignment.

The architects *BDP* were charged by the Development Company with overseeing the REGENERATION of the harbour (project architect *Peter Shuttleworth*). A tidal lock was completed in 1998, new facilities for the fishing fleet in 1999. A posh marina occupies the N part of the harbour, a cheaper one the S. THE BEACON, like an over-sized lighthouse, was built in 1994–6 on the site of the 'hurries' (coal loading staithes) at the foot of the Howgill Incline. It is already being refurbished, after an unsatisfactory spell as a museum. Of the SCULPTURES, Wavy Line runs along the quay called Old or Sugar Tongue. It is what it says, illuminated at night. At the far end is Crow's Nest Mast, a shelter and a tall mast, placed as a view-stopper for Lowther Street and the distant Castle. Decorative surfaces and shelters abound. Benches supported on whale tails are inscribed with historical reminders in bronze, like bullet points or exam pass notes; by *Melanie Jackson* for *Stephen Broadbent* of Liverpool and *Oblique Partnership* of Glasgow. Figure sculptures include bronzes of sailors on the quayside, and Boy on Capstan on the pier, by *Judith Bluck* of Skipton. By The Beacon, John Paul Jones (bronze), and The End of an Era by *Colin Telfer*, 2005: a pillar of coal, miner, deputy, screen lass. Like most of his sculptures it is of resin coloured with the relevant mineral dust. Only John Paul Jones is a specific person, and an anti-hero at that. Where are Sir John or Sir James Lowther? Or Carlisle Spedding? The others are types, simply life-size, without pedestals or inscriptions, casually doing what they do. Together they give the impression of working to a budget rather than to a programme.

INDUSTRIAL REMAINS

The slopes S of the harbour bear many clues to the early history of the COAL INDUSTRY. Mathias Read's painting of *c.* 1738 shows the grooves of at least two gravity-worked WAGGONWAYS bringing coal to the harbour, novelties celebrated in J. E. Weeks's *Poetical Prospect of Workington and Whitehaven* of 1752 ('Down the descent, so vast the power of art/The waggonway retains the flying cart . . . Down planes inclined the self-moved engines fly/To load the ships which near the Hurries lie'). The straight track intercepting Rosemary Lane near Mount Pleasant is almost certainly the course of the Parker Waggonway, laid out in the 1730s. It passes behind fragmentary remains of the largest and earliest Guibal FANHOUSE to survive in Britain, once home to a 36-ft (11-metre)-diameter fan. Installed here in 1870, it ventilated the Duke Pit first sunk in 1765. Beyond, immediately behind The Beacon, the clear course of the first Howgill Incline (1813) crosses at a right angle, descending between stone walls from the hill brow. Here is the 'candlestick' of Wellington Pit, a tall ornamental CHIMNEY with a stepped square profile turning hexagonal.

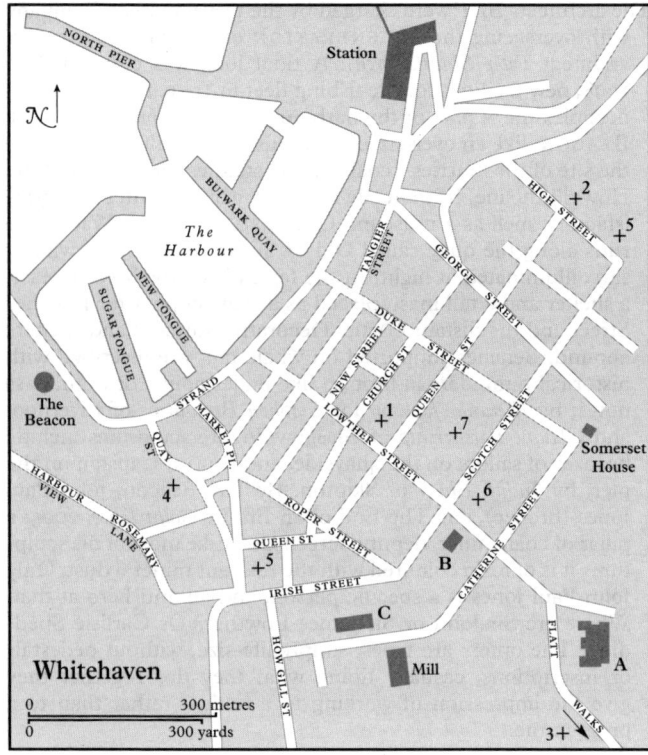

1   St Nicholas
2   St James
3   St Bega (R.C.)
4   St Gregory and St Patrick (R.C.)
5   Kirk Mission Hall
6   Wesleyan Methodist (former)
7   Christian Brethren

A   Castle
B   Civic Centre
C   Copeland Centre

Also some massive retaining walls, and WELLINGTON LODGE, an irregular polygonal tower with a crenellated top. The first shaft was sunk in 1840, and the 1st Earl of Lonsdale commissioned *Sydney Smirke* to design the pithead buildings in a style fitting for so prominent a site. The picturesque composition, completed in 1845, also incorporated a round tower and heavily battlemented walls. The pit closed in 1932 and the site was thoughtlessly cleared in 1969.

Harbour View Road offers a splendid view of harbour and town. From its end, a footpath continues to the top of the hill beside the upper course of the second HOWGILL BRAKE, 1925, the incline which lowered wagons from Whitehaven's southern mines down to the quays. At its head on the l. the capped shaft of KING PIT, once the deepest mine in the world. Sunk in 1750 by *Carlisle Spedding*, the Lowthers' energetic and ingenious agent, by 1793 it had reached 160 fathoms. A few hundred yards further, the cliff top on the r. affords a view of the ruins of SALTOM PIT, 1729–31. Of great importance in the history of coal mining: the first pit to extend under the sea, and the prototype of *Spedding*'s oval shaft, subdivided by wooden shuttering so that the drainage pump could work in one compartment and the winding operations in the other. It also allowed Spedding to ventilate the pit ('coursing the air') without the expense of sinking a separate upcast shaft. Spedding's sea wall survives, an engine house still stands, and the circular track of the horse gin is still visible, but the site, the best example anywhere of an integrated C18 coal mine, has suffered gravely from vandalism and erosion. It is a matter of great regret that local officialdom seems to prefer imaginary 'heritage' over effective consolidation and conservation of genuine items of serious historic interest.

The cliff-top path continues towards the HAIG PIT, Whitehaven's last coal mine, fortunately conserved by the Haig Colliery Museum Trust. Sunk 1914–18, closed 1986. Its workings extended more than 4 m. under the sea. The winding wheel stands over the square brick engine house, with five tall round-topped windows. Inside, a steam winding engine survives in a lofty room at the head of each of the two shafts, one of which keeps its full headgear. The engines themselves are horizontal cross compounds, supplied in 1914 by *Bever Dorling* of Bradford. The smaller of the two now operates on compressed air for demonstration purposes.

THE TOWN

Perambulations are never easy on a grid, as those who have tried it in New York or Baltimore will agree. The comparison is good; Whitehaven gives a flavour of what the North American ports may have been like in their C17 and C18 days.

The MARKET PLACE is broadly triangular, following the course of the culverted Pow Beck. It is mostly filled by the unexciting MARKET HALL of 1881 by *T. L. Banks*, replacing a much smaller building by *Robert Smirke*, and by a Gothick island block with an odd mezzanine of lancets. On the corner of Roper Street to the E is the GOLDEN LION; four storeys, with the moulded window surrounds typical of the early C18. To the S, James Street is terminated satisfyingly by the YMCA (Nos. 44–45 IRISH STREET), a U-shaped mansion with its own courtyard built between 1713 and 1734 by James Milham. Altered in the C19, and the wings heightened in the 1900s. Irish Street runs E, but shortly we turn S again into HOWGILL STREET for the ASSEMBLY ROOMS of 1736, set back, with a double stone stair up to the *piano nobile*. Four bays. First-floor doorway with Tuscan columns and pediment. Pedimented doorways are features of the C18 and early C19 in many streets of Whitehaven. At the s end of the street CATHERINE STREET runs E, with the former BARRACKS MILL end-on to the s side. An impressive former flax mill built in 1809 for the Quaker Joseph Bell. Four storeys, fifteen bays long including a central projecting pedimented bay, and two bays wide. Inside, fire-proof construction with cast-iron columns and beams carrying brick jack arches under an iron-framed pitched roof. A very early example of the type, with the further novelty of centrally placed engine house, thus reducing the length of the shafting needed to drive the machines. Sympathetically converted to housing.

Back in Irish Street, No. 7 (N side) has a good mid-C18 doorway. READ HOUSE on the corner of Cross Street was built by the artist Mathias Read in 1713; a single-cell dwelling of three floors with a turning stair in an outshut. The Copeland Centre (p. 676) occupies the s side, followed further E by an over-scaled palazzo by *Sydney Smirke*, c. 1845. Six bays and three storeys with a mighty cornice. Next on the s side, No. 18 has delightfully syncopated fenestration, No. 17 Mannerist stucco additions to the window surrounds.

At the site of Holy Trinity church, Irish Street turns NE into SCOTCH STREET. Here an unusually even row faces the side of the Civic Centre, but still there are variations of width between two and three bays, and the colour possibilities are well explored.

ROPER STREET, relatively narrow, runs NW from the angle of Irish Street and Scotch Street.* It is full of interest, beginning with the first three buildings. No. 30 (i.e. the corner with Scotch Street), c. 1745, has a swan-necked doorcase in the gable-end. Perhaps by *Christopher Myers*, who had connections with the family of the client, James Spedding (Frederick O'Dwyer; cf. St James's church, p. 673). No. 29 is much smaller, with a Victorian Italianate front with a shaped gable, and then comes Stout's warehouse (No. 28, now flats), late C18, of stone and six storeys tall, again with its gable to the street; a satisfying if untypical little group. Nos. 36 and 37 (sw side) share a fine hopper dated 1740, with Ionic volutes. No. 25, Captain Brocklebank's house, has tripartite windows. Nos. 23 and 24 are a fine tall pair, defined by a giant Ionic pilaster at each end, with open-pedimented doorcases framing urns. The block between Queen Street and Church Street is lost to Wilkinson's supermarket; boring but not harmful. Holt's Art shop, No. 45, is amusingly Gothick. No. 51 of c. 1715 has giant pilasters again, this time with a late C18 honeysuckle motif in the capitals. Fluted Doric doorway pilasters, moulded window surrounds. Nos. 57–58 fits in perfectly despite being unashamedly Victorian. It is a small Italian palazzo, blue and

*Demolished, the THEATRE of 1769, remodelled internally in 1909.

white, with alternating pediments with faces and brackets on the middle floor and an attic of horizontal round-ended openings. No. 60 has the rope motif seen here and there round its Victorian shop window.

A longer perambulation can be made from Market Place to Dockside, then SE up Lowther Street, with diversions.

DOCKSIDE and STRAND. The Old Custom House, l., and the George Inn (former), r., were built in 1686–7 by Sir John Lowther for Samuel Brownrigg. Single pile with back outshut for the stair, plus a rear outrigger. The inn has a porch with thin Tuscan columns. At No. 13 the ROYAL STANDARD HOTEL, Early Victorian. The interior fittings of the Music Hall at its back have been partly reused at Rose Hill, Moresby (*see* p. 531). Before heading up into town a diversion along the quay to the former BATHS of 1885 opposite Bulwark Quay, by *T. L. Banks*. Baroque, of red stone, with a tower and cupola and reliefs of a mermaid and Neptune. A little further on is TANGIER STREET and the WAVERLEY HOTEL of 1686–7, with wings *c.* 1700, heightened and altered. Set back in a courtyard, it has a five-bay front with C19 triangular pediments on all the ground-floor openings.

LOWTHER STREET is the main thoroughfare, and in consequence has lost much of its C18 character. Not so however the first short length from Quayside to Strand, which of all Whitehaven's streets, seems to look to the sea.* Nos. 37–41 are a homogeneous early C18 row. No. 42, with a little oriel overlooking the harbour, was rebuilt *c.* 1750. It preserves much of its panelled interiors, reeded window alcove, and open-well stair with three balusters per tread under a circular dome. The SAVINGS BANK on the corner of New Street is by *Rickman*, 1833; three bays, Greek Doric porch carrying a balcony with cast-iron railing, pilasters above, royal arms on the parapet.

We may pause a block up in the garden of St Nicholas to analyse in some detail the Whitehaven Georgian of CHURCH STREET on the N side. The houses vary in height, width and colour, all within the basic rules. No parapets, no valleys, so the roofs are prominent and the upper windows are immediately below the eaves. Front doors are raised up a few steps, but there are no areas, no railings; the building line is right on the pavement. The specified wrought stone surrounds to doors and windows have discouraged alteration, and are easily imitated in modern materials. Colour is the great thing; one colour for the walls, another for the door and window surrounds, although it is clear from Mathias Read's paintings, for instance, that this was not a feature of the Georgian town.

Back on Lowther Street, the WESTMINSTER CAFÉ (formerly Westminster Bank) is on the Queen Street corner of the churchyard. Three by four bays, restrained mid-C19 classical,

---

* No. 40 also has, on its top floor, a window ingeniously fitted with an angled pane and a sill behind it broad enough to rest an elbow supporting a telescope conning the harbour entrance.

with very tall windows, a stone balcony, and a balustrade on the cornice. Both this and the former CLYDESDALE BANK next door are in buff ashlar, the latter simply classical with an Ionic porch. Next comes a Late Victorian trio in red ashlar: the HSBC bank, the POST OFFICE (1898) in a compressed Wrennish style set back on the site of the Old Public Offices, and NatWest, built as the Bank of Whitehaven. The Methodist church and Civic Centre make major interventions at the Scotch Street cross-roads. No. 14 Scotch Street is worth noting here, built *c.* 1760 for Joseph Littledale. Stone, of five bays and two storeys. Centre emphasized by rustication and quoins of even length. Top balustrade. Doorway with attached Ionic columns, a pulvinated frieze, and a pediment.

At the top of Lowther Street No. 80 is another mid-C18 swagger house, with a Venetian doorway also incorporating a broken pediment. Rusticated centre and marked quoins, balustrade. No. 1 opposite, of the 1750s, likewise of two storeys instead of the usual three, plus basement and area. Five bays, with a triangular pediment for the central doorway.

Turning l. by No. 80 into CATHERINE STREET which is at the SE edge of the grid. The TELEPHONE EXCHANGE of 1962 damagingly ignores all the rules. Its front section retreats from the pavement and from its neighbours, overhangs, and is low and flat-roofed with a visible frame and chequered cladding. Behind looms a four-storey block with higher stair-tower. Compare the manners of the LABOUR EXCHANGE opposite, dated 1937 on the fanlight, of fine streaky buff ashlar, with large round-topped sash windows with stout glazing bars, and a hipped roof slightly sprocketed and graded. Five bays, only a single storey.

The far end of Catherine Street crosses DUKE STREET, with one of Whitehaven's most distinctive houses, SOMERSET HOUSE, as a splendid vista-stopper. Built in 1750 for Samuel Martin, it is cubic, stone-faced, with tripartite windows without surrounds. This unusual severity is set off by a charming porch with clustered Gothick shafts, tripartite again, with a perron. A long row of chimneys faces down Duke Street. (Gothick entrance hall.) Opposite is THE CUPOLA, a grand house of 1708–10 converted in 1851 into the Town Hall by *William Barnes* of London. He made two storeys in place of the original three, five bays in place of seven, and added the portico of four sturdy Doric columns and rear stair extension. Venetian windows on the ground floor to l. and r., probably of 1851; Mathias Read shows plain sashes. They have Ionic capitals, and bits of entablature. Typically Early Victorian upper windows crowned by pediments on very demonstrative brackets. Two early C18 wings have been demolished.

Further down on the same side more houses with nice pedimented doorways (e.g. Nos. 43–44, mid-C18). Further on, we turn NE up Queen Street. At the top is HIGH STREET, with some good post-1750 houses of two storeys not the usual three, and a railway tunnel ventilation shaft. QUEEN STREET is a perambulation in itself, running right through the grid from St

James to the Market Place. Dropping down, we note No. 43, a fine plain five-bayer of *c.* 1750 set back behind an area, with pedimented doorway over pulvinated frieze and eared surround, and No. 35, *c.* 1760, with an inset shell-hood. Cross Duke Street, hug St Nicholas's churchyard, cut Lowther Street. Opposite Wilkinson's, No. 140 is a four-storey warehouse of stone. SW of Roper Street is a particularly attractive section where the grid is kinked. No. 150 has an interesting window rhythm – five bays for the lower two storeys, three widely spaced ones above. No. 151, Gale House of *c.* 1733, is very nice, set back behind railings and two-storeyed. Five bays, with a pretty doorway with fluted Ionic pilasters. Entry through at one end. And so back to the Market Place.

OUTER AREAS

Whitehaven's suburbs do not share the cheerfulness or the informal formality of the centre.

St ANDREW, Mirehouse. 1956 by *H. B. Stout.* Brick. Utilitarian, with schooly rectangular windows and a thin oblong tower.

St BENEDICT (R.C.), Mirehouse. Sub-George Pace and even more distantly sub-Ronchamp design by the *Cassidy & Ashton Partnership* of Preston, 1973–6. Rectangular, with no obvious orientation, and the defensive look increasingly typical of post-war urban churches. Metal cage over the entrance, a few narrow windows of random size and shape. Principal lighting out of harm's way in the dormers of the roof. – (STATIONS OF THE CROSS by *Ray Schofield.*)

St PETER, Cliff Road, Kells. By *Hubert Worthington,* 1938–9. White Italianate basilica, with sloping buttresses to bridge the narrow passage aisles. Small round-topped windows. (Good modern style inside. Chancel and side chapel furnishings by *Thomas Worthington & Sons,* 1939, made by *Arthur Simpson.*)

St MARY (R.C.), Kells, near the empty offices and chemical works of Albright & Wilson. By *Wilfrid C. Mangan* of Preston, 1960–1. Of orange brick gone green in the sea air, with concrete-framed openings canted in at the top, and occasionally at the bottom too. Big W tower with clasping buttresses, but then cut back at the belfry stage to an irregular octagon. – (STAINED GLASS. Baptistery window by *John Hardman Studios,* 1961.)

INCLINE. Opposite St Mary's church, a disused railway track leads E towards the CORKICKLE BRAKE, which dropped precipitously to a junction with the main line S of Corkickle Station. Installed in 1881 to provide an easier connection for the cliff-top collieries, closed in 1931, but refurbished and reinstated in 1955 to serve the Marchon Chemical Works which opened in 1943 on the site of the Ladysmith Coke Works. It worked until October 1986, the last standard-gauge example of a cable-worked incline.

WIGTON (C)

The town is signalled by a quite elegant 325-ft (100-metre) metal chimney supported by a lattice PYLON. It was put up in 1966 by Sidex, makers of polypropylene film, now Innovia (*see also* p. 686). Approaching from the s, the crazy tower of Highmoor (p. 686) is the landmark.

ST MARY. There was a c12 church, which by 1375 had a defensive tower. The present handsome building is dated and signed at the bottom of the gallery stairs: *Pattinson & Holmes* joiners, *Nixons & Parkin* (i.e. *Nixon* father and son) masons, 1788. On the opposite pillar is inscribed: Restored 1881. The restoring architect was *C. J. Ferguson*. Two-storey elevation of red stone, the ends slightly emphasized with doorways in bays one and eight. They and the w doorway with rustication of alternating sizes. The tower is embraced by the rooms housing the two arms of the staircase. It has an open top with parapets and pinnacles, unlike that of St Cuthbert at Carlisle, a church which is otherwise very similar. Three galleries on Tuscan or Doric columns, and with upper Doric columns each carrying its own bit of entablature with a triglyph. Flat ceiling prettily decorated with stucco ornament in two roundels and an oval. Venetian E window with fluted Ionic columns in the short chancel. – PULPIT. Handsome, with swags. No doubt late c18. – RETABLE of the N aisle altar, made up of c16 and c17 North German woodwork (said to come from Cleves). The panels with religious scenes. – READING DESK of Continental work, with wondrous double tracery. – LECTERN. Given in the c19 by William Banks of Highmoor. – STAINED GLASS. E window by *Edmundson & Son*, 1865. s aisle, far w, to William Story †1906; the Light of the World, with a wide border of cherubs, signed with a crane, i.e. *Walter Crane*. N aisle E, †1921, by *Powells*. In the gallery a small blue window, the Annunciation, 1926, by *William Morris* of Westminster. (Three windows of 2009 designed by *Brian Campbell*, given by Melvin Bragg (Lord Bragg) and made by *Alex Haynes* of *Albion Glass*.) – MONUMENTS. Slab of Thomas Warcup †1653, prepared, as he tells us, by himself. In the churchyard a two-light cusped window with a sexfoiled circle over, perhaps late c13.

ST CUTHBERT (R.C.), Burnfoot. By *Ignatius Bonomi*, 1836–7. Red sandstone, with Y-tracery. Blank arches at the sides for transepts, never built. In 1857 it was extended E, with five stepped lancets, and w, with a façade of shafted lancets, for Elizabeth Ann Aglionby. She also founded a CONVENT for the Sisters of Mercy, with a chapel at right angles to the main altar. The church ceiling is mid-c20. – STAINED GLASS. E window by *Francis Barnett* of Leith, *c.* 1857. Convent, school and presbytery buildings are grouped round the E end of the church (ecclesiastical orientation used throughout). Their Gothic style was modelled on J. & C. Hansom's contemporary Carmelite convent at Darlington.

METHODIST CHAPEL, High Street. 1883. Grand Gothic front with plate tracery.

INDEPENDENT CHAPEL, now United Reformed Church, Water Street. 1834. Blocky building with arched windows above, flat-headed below; schoolroom in basement underneath.

FRIENDS' MEETING HOUSE, West Street. Dated 1830, and probably by *William Alderson* of London. 'Unusually stylish for Friends', says David Butler (*The Quaker Meeting Houses of Britain*, 1999). Of fine ashlar, with fashionable tapering window surrounds and broad rusticated angle pilasters.

CEMETERY, Aikhead Road. 1856. Beautifully kept. Twin chapels. Grandiose focal memorial to William Banks Jun. of Highmoor †1901. Red and grey granite stele signed *Macdonald Field & Co.*, Aberdeen; but who did the sculpture of Justice, with scales and sword?

FOUNTAIN, Market Place. The crux of the town. 1872–3, by *J. T. Knowles Sen.* of London for George Moore in memory of his first wife (†1858). It was dazzlingly re-gilded in 2004. In red granite, an eight-ton block and blunt pyramid spire with leaves in flat relief against a gold ground, and an elongated ball-and-cross finial. Reliefs by *Thomas Woolner* in aluminium bronze show Mrs Moore's bounty to the poor: Instructing the Ignorant, Clothing the Naked, Visiting the Afflicted, and Feeding the Hungry. Pevsner judged them very good, still with classical discipline, but also with genuine feeling. George Moore (1806–76), of Whitehall, Mealsgate (q.v.), textile millionaire and inexhaustible philanthropist, was held up by Samuel Smiles as the archetypal self-made man.

COTTAGE HOSPITAL, near the cemetery on Cross Lane. Built as the workhouse in 1838–42. Of brown stone, long and low with a five-bay centre.

NELSON THOMLINSON SCHOOL. In the grounds of Floshfield Hall, of *c.* 1860. *C. J. Ferguson*'s new hall of 1898–9 'in the scholastic style of the C17' is now the library. Later buildings include J BLOCK, *c.* 2000, on a gentle curve, two-tone brick, with a cupola, and the MATHS BLOCK, 2006 by *David Swarbrick*, with a ship-like prow. In the courtyard, SCULP-TURE, Messenger by *Stephen Hitchin*: two sharply carved stones with spiral forms.

WESTMORLAND HOUSE, High Street, was the girls' school and is now the Junior School. Late C18 house called The Flosh, altered and extended 1800–7 for John Westmorland. Five bays, with a deep Tuscan porch and a tripartite window over. Also a Gothick bit of 1815 and school additions of 1898 by *Oliver & Dodgshun*. – GATEPIERS, cylindrical with stylized rocks or icebergs on the sides.

LIBRARY, High Street. A poor building of 1975, long and mono-pitch-roofed, redeemed by the little concrete cloister in front enclosing a scrap of garden. Its arches take their cue from the C18 entry next door.

101

BATHS, in an oddly isolated position in fields behind the school. Built in 1902 by Edwin Banks of Highmoor. Brown stone, with half-hipped roofs and a square chimney.

STATION. Nothing much now. The first of 1843 was grandly classical, with an Ionic portico on the platform. It went to Netherhall, Maryport, for a summerhouse. The second, of *c.* 1880, was conventional, with an iron-and-glass canopy.

INNOVIA, West Street, right in the town. It was a jam factory, now cellulose-based packaging. WIGTON HALL, *c.* 1801, is now company offices. Eight bays. Ashlar facing, Neo-Tudor detail, i.e. Georgian windows under hoodmoulds, porch with pointed arch under a straight hoodmould and crowned by a pedimental gable with a parapet decorated with quatrefoils. RESEARCH AND DEVELOPMENT BUILDING, *c.* 2000. Kidney-bean-shaped, glass-faced, in the international style of UCB which was then the parent company.

THE TOWN. Wigton is pleasant enough. Once mainly clay-built, it is now a colourwashed Georgian and Victorian town of about 5,000 people, though much of its back-street intricacy has gone. The best houses are in the short narrow length of West Street, especially ARLOSH HOUSE of 1716, candy-floss pink, with a swan-necked pediment over a round arch with a sculpted keystone. The jambs are moulded to an elaborated bolection section.★ Pleasant doorways also in the streets running E from the Market Place, i.e. King Street–East End–Bankfoot. On Market Hill S of King Street is Dr Thomlinson's FREE GRAMMAR SCHOOL of 1730, with a similar pediment inexpertly executed. At the bottom of the hill is the interesting group of ST URSULA'S SCHOOL and BURNFOOT GRANGE. The school part is Greek stucco, the hall part of C17 brickwork with raised patterns.

Immediately N of the parish church is the plain MARKET HALL of 1882, and the COLLEGE OF MATRONS, almshouses founded by John and Robert Thomlinson in 1724 but remodelled in the C19 as three Tudor Gothic houses. Opposite, on High Street, is the KILDARE HOTEL, built by Edwin Banks of Highmoor in 1887 as a Conservative Club. Tall, of red ashlar, with an oddly canted bay. In South End, S of High Street, the OLD VICARAGE, *c.* 1800 and later. In its side wall is set a small Roman statue from Old Carlisle (*see* p. 667).

HIGHMOOR, off High Street. It started as a harmless enough house built in 1810 for Joseph Hodge, of five bays with a three-bay pediment. His business partner William Banks, exporter of factory-made clothing to Australia, enlarged it in 1870, adding an Osborne tower and enclosing the park with two miles of iron fencing. In the 1880s Banks's sons Henry and Edwin heightened the tower to a crazy 136 ft (42 metres) and installed a full Belgian carillon. On top is a gilded eagle on a green copper dome of ogee outline, then an octagonal drum for the carillon, with four gablets and four corner turrets at its base:

★ The former Mechanics' Institute of 1851 has gone.

Russian if anything, so far. Below that was the great bell called Big Joe; now just open arches of sky and the spindliest of spiral stairs. The lower part is thrown off-balance by a square stair-turret on the N, with its own little green dome and a balcony halfway up. Pevsner suggested *James Henderson* as architect, or as builder, and 'what the decades themselves called "Mixed Renaissance"' for the style. Traces of the planned landscape to the S, including a lake. A housing estate has been built around, not quite close enough to ruin it completely. – LODGES named Alpha and Omega, *c.* 1880, on Lowmoor Road. With applied timber-framing, tile-hanging, bamboo-like supports to the porches, dragon finials. – (Further up is LLAMA COTTAGE, for the estate bailiff, and the llama. – Off West Avenue, now lined on one side with 1930s houses, are the RACING STABLES and HOME FARM.)

WINDMILL. At the foot of Station Road, a 55-ft (17-metre) tower windmill of sandstone rubble, without sails since the mid 1840s. Late C18 in origin, it is unusual in its elliptical plan and in its asymmetrical batter, greatest to the E. Michael Davies-Shiel has suggested that it may have had a fixed cap with sails facing the prevailing wind to the W, the E side of the tower acting as a buttress to resist its pressure. No other example of such an arrangement is known in England.

(ISLEKIRK HALL, 2½ m. S. Mid-C16, with late C17 and C19 alterations. The house retains some mullioned windows with arched lights. DCMS)

WINDERMERE (W)

4090

'Young as the place is', wrote Harriet Martineau in 1855, 'it already has a public news-room and library, and a gallery of pictures. . . . The new buildings (and all are new) are of the dark grey stone of the region, and several of them are of a medieval style of architecture.' A railway had been announced in 1844, to run from the Lancaster & Carlisle at Oxenholme to Low Wood on the lakeshore. William Wordsworth, both the chief attraction and leader of the opposition, launched a counter-attack ('Is then no nook of English ground secure/From rash assault?'), ensuring that the line got no further than a rocky field at Birthwaite. The lake, visitors are dismayed to find, is a good two miles away. So the town of Windermere is purely a railway creation. In 1848 the railway brought 120,000 rash assaulters. 8,000 arrived on a single Whit Monday in 1883.

Windermere's architecture can be viewed as a search for a Lake District vernacular, without necessarily attending closely to the real thing. It takes several distinct forms, as will be seen.

ST MARY, Ambleside Road, Applethwaite A proprietory chapel was built by an offcomer from Liverpool, the Rev. *J. A. Addison*,

Windermere, St Mary.
Drawing, 1848

in 1847–8: nave, chancel and s porch, with a bellcote on the chancel arch. Modest enough, but up with the latest in Ecclesiology in the exaggerated steepness of the hexagonal-slated roofs and the articulation of each part. Of this hardly anything remains. In 1852 a s aisle was added by *Miles Thompson*, under its own roof, with a dumpy arcade of Webster-style hammered limestone. Round piers, far-projecting, deliberately primitive capitals, round arches. By now Addison was in financial difficulties. In 1855 the chapel was purchased for the town, and in 1856 consecrated. Next was a N aisle and porch by *J. S. Crowther* in 1857–8, with an arcade of pointed arches in fine streaky sandstone crisply moulded. Round piers, normal details. In 1861 the nave was extended w, but not the aisles, and in 1871 Crowther added a N transept and vestry. By now it was an untidy three-equal-vessel church, poorly lit at the centre despite dormers added in 1875. *Paley & Austin* rebuilt the E end in 1881–2 with a strong central tower, short chancel, and vestry. Their tower characteristically allows side-lighting at the crossing, by tall two-light windows. Below are two-bay arcades, with no capitals. Later still Paley & Austin extended the aisles to level up the w end, and rebuilt the s transept. The NE vestry of 1961 with its semicircular apse and flat roof is unmistakably by *George Pace*. In 1988 fire destroyed the nave roof, the last part *in situ* of Addison's proprietory chapel. Only his s porch, rebuilt outside the 1852 aisle, survives. Restoration after the fire was by *Michael Bottomley*, 1989–90. In 2005–6 the aisles were partitioned off behind glass; architect *Paul Grout*. – Remaining FITTINGS by *Paley & Austin*. – STAINED GLASS. E window by *Burlison & Grylls*, 1893. The w windows, figures floating in clear glass, date from the late 1950s; sides by *Francis H. Spear*, centre by *G. E. R. Smith*.

Addison had a passion for Gothic architecture, linked with his social aspirations for the new community. w of the church are the GATEPIERS of his own house, The Abbey (dem. 1962): started 1847, extended 1853 in a more refined style. It was thoroughgoing Gothic, with a high octagonal tower. The ENDOWED SCHOOL SE of the church is of 1850, enlarged 1857, 1872, 1877. Gothic, with hexagonal-slated roof. E of the church is ANNESDALE, now St Mary's Surgery, 1850, which served as the vicarage from 1859. L-shaped, with hexagonal slates and tall Tudor chimney pots. The N gable-end has crockets of yellow terracotta; the window traceries of these early houses seem also to be terracotta, now painted. The present VICARAGE, between the two, is of the early 1990s, nicely demonstrating the uses of local stone; by *Michael Bottomley* of Kendal. Further w along Ambleside Road is ST MARY'S COTTAGE, now Cedar Manor Hotel. Extended and Gothicized in the 1850s when Addison and his family moved from The Abbey. It has the hexagonal-slated roof of Annesdale, but the traceries are of wood. THE COLLEGE for young gentlemen and sons of the clergy opened in 1853, closed 1965. A large Gothic establishment with a collegiate tower. Parts remain s of the church on Phoenix Way, with a house called THE HIDE-AWAY (hotel). BIRTHWAITE LODGE, 1853–4, has a fine oriel which composes well from St Mary's Cottage. It is similar to J. S. Crowther's own house at Alderley Edge in Cheshire.

STATION, Church Street, to the E. Opened 1847, rebuilt 1853 with iron-and-glass canopies and a porte cochère. It was converted to Booth's supermarket *c.* 1984 by *Gill Dockray & Partners*. Behind is the single platform and pretty but apologetically small wooden building of the present station. Extension, quite nice but still small, 2006.

Looking out over the station towards the lake and fells, is THE TERRACE. Five Gothic double-fronted houses built by the railway company for its managers in 1853–4. Gothic interiors with details characteristic of *J. S. Crowther*, the architect busy on the church. On the old goods yard, LAKELAND LIMITED [119] store. By *Hanson Walford Marston* of Kendal, 2003–5. One of the best new buildings in Cumbria. Showy from the front but well hidden from above and behind, with grass-clad roofs. Four functional parts clearly expressed: flat recessed entry and circulation under a wave roof; big glazed rotunda, for shopping downstairs, café upstairs; a solid block clad in polished Italian stone for the call centre (adapted from an existing building); and, round the corner, large-windowed but not fully glazed offices. Interior materials and lighting are carefully controlled. The functional sections are not completely isolated: an open flying bridge crosses the foyer to the offices, and internal windows allow call-centre staff and shoppers to see each other. The WINDERMERE HOTEL N of Church Road shows the scale and confidence of the original venture. Built by Richard Rigg, coach proprietor, in time for the arrival of the railway, it was the only building in sight when the terminus opened in 1847. *Abraham Pattinson* was the builder, *Miles Thompson* the architect. It has an Italianate tower and cast-iron veranda and porch.

The VILLAGE lies to the SW. It took shape a little later than Addison's campus round the church; datestone average *c.* 1875. It is not a bit like a genuine Lakeland settlement, but exhibits a Lake District vernacular nevertheless, invented by local builders such as *Pattinsons* for boarding houses, banks and shops (but few pubs). The buildings are tall and solid. Bargeboards, finials, fancy dormers, timber framing and pargetting abound, set against the dark fissile local stone, unpointed. From the station, first HIGH STREET, with a bank, now NATWEST. This is outstandingly good; *c.* 1890, artfully asymmetrical, in a restrained Jacobean style, of sawn blue stone contrasted with buff sandstone dressings. Next, down VICTORIA ROAD, two 'vernacular' houses, now an Outdoor shop and a small hotel, built by *William Harrison* in 1854. Dark unpointed stone with limestone quoins and clumsy dripmoulds, leavened with decorative bargeboards and dormers, and both with a touch of Gothic. Further S, filling the island between Main Road and Crescent Road is ACME HOUSE, dated 1877, with an enterprising repertoire of timber framing, pargetting, and plate glass. Attached, the former Embassy Ballroom, equally enterprising with tripartite arcading and an Italianate wheel window in a teardrop-shaped setting. The gatepiers of FAIRHAVEN, *c.* 1850 by *Miles Thompson*, are in Crescent Road but the villa itself now stands on Main Road, so rapidly was open country swallowed up by building. Big and four-square, rendered, with limestone quoins. Tripartite entrance at the side. The cellar floor is banked up rather than excavated. To the W on College Road, APPLEGARTH (hotel). Square house on a tight site, insouciantly mixing Gothic and Norman Shaw Renaissance. The earlier parts bears the trademarks of *J. S. Crowther*, *c.* 1860, particularly the triplet of Gothic arches between inner hall and stair. The stair is peculiar to Crowther with its octagonal and castellated newel, two-tier rail, and stopped panelling. Phase two, dated 1891 on the porch, shows in the hall fireplace, the light oak wainscot, the dining-room fireplace, and the delicate stained glass. The STABLE has a gaping entrance arch and two oculi, like a face.

HUNTER HOUSE, off Birthwaite Road, W. By *David Matthews* for the Cooper Pattinson Trust, *c.* 1990. Eight sheltered flats, plus the warden's house at the end, arranged as half a polygon around an internal 'street', top-lit from ridge glazing.

GATESBIELD, New Road, S. Late but quintessential Arts and Crafts: another self-conscious 'vernacular'. Designed and built by *Stanley & Emily Davies*, 1926, as the initials over the door record. They harvested the stone on site, which was then turned into a garden. Much of the carving was done by Emily. They were Quakers, and everything is cunningly simple. Living room and kitchen interconnect by a large dresser, a paraphrase of the Lake District court cupboard, the drawers and cupboards of which open into both rooms. Framing Stanley's radio cupboard are Emily's carvings of men climbing the primitive scaffold to do the roof. By the road is CRAFT COTTAGE, their furniture workshop and showroom, designed by *Kenneth Cross* in 1923. 'The never-failing beauty of simple things' was the firm's credo. Since 1983 sheltered housing, with sensitive additions.

VILLAS. Generally for the comfortably off rather than the super-rich, who preferred nearby Bowness and Troutbeck. First the Elleray estate. ELLERAY was bought after 1807 by one of the first and most colourful, John Wilson, pugilist, prankster, professor and (as Christopher North) poet. He turned the barn into a drawing room, white and simple with a couple of tall inserted windows. Today this is CHRISTOPHER NORTH COTTAGE. Then, with advice from *Alexander Nasmyth*, he built a new house, low, unobtrusive, open to the landscape, and by the sound of it largely open-plan. In 1855 however its land was split up for villas by William Eastted, railway entrepreneur and land speculator.* Wilson's house was rebuilt in 1869 by *Thomas Pattinson* as a joyless mansion for A. H. Heywood, of the philanthropic Manchester banking family, now part of ST ANNE'S SCHOOL. CLEEVE HOWE and OAKLAND are by *J. S. Crowther*, 1853 and 1855. Gothic of course, of local stone contrasted with long ranges of mullioned and traceried windows in pale sandstone. Oakland has a full-height staircase hall lit by two large Dec windows. Both have later *Mawson* gardens (at Cleeve Howe of 1881) and glasshouses. ELLERAY BANK of 1856–61 is by *Alfred Waterhouse* for G. G. Cunningham, Italianate, and rather harsh. WYNLASS BECK, overlooking Cook's Corner, is a smaller *Crowther* house, of 1854, the least fussy (no traceries) and best planned of the three. The entry in the double-gabled end is pushed aside to allow light into a longitudinal corridor. Three Gothic arches, paraphrasing the service doors of a screens passage, allow additional side-lighting from the stair. Characteristic Gothic stair made with flat balusters and chamfered newels.

OUTLYING BUILDINGS

KELDWITH, to the NW, S of the Troutbeck Road and high up above Cook's Corner. Large multi-gabled holiday house of 1910–11 by *Herbert Luck North* for Alec Rea of Liverpool (nephew of J. H. Rea of Gatehouse, Eskdale (q.v.), who had met North at Llanfairfechan, Caernarvonshire). *Arthur Jackson* of Kendal built it. Sun-trap plan, with the dining and drawing rooms splayed to make a V. The effect of gables turning this

---

*Eastted did the same thing at Malvern, Worcs., and at Alderley Edge in Cheshire.

way and that to capitalize on the views and terrain is very marked. Porte cochère, Gothic-arched and battered, over which is Mrs Rea's boudoir, gabled in three directions. A chapter-house-like gazebo was added in 1913, now glazed in. The route from entrance to stair involved a circuit round the house, a Lutyens trick (North had trained with Lutyens). The interiors were conspicuous for the quality of materials and the unusual ways they are displayed. The principal rooms were not panelled but lined with almost Deco sheets of elm, filleted at the edges. The house was centrally heated and electrically lit from the start. All bedrooms had bathrooms en suite, and there was a lift.

FOOTPRINT, at St Catherine's (National Trust), Patterdale Road. Inspirational outdoor classroom built 2006–7, after a design by *Paul Crosby*. An exercise in sustainability, the building is boat-shaped, raised on stacked car tyres, with floors of beech and larch. A lovely fat wall of daubed and ochre-washed straw bales, randomly fenestrated, wraps around the N and W, but the S and E are largely open, and a veranda runs right round. Hump-backed shingle roof over a green oak frame and laminated crucks. A warm and welcoming sight through the trees.

From Cook's Corner S along Rayrigg Road

THE PRIORY, Rayrigg Road. 1869, by *Ernest Bates* of Manchester, built by *Pattinsons*, for William Carver of Manchester, carrier. Dec Gothic in imported golden sandstone, used as coursed rubble with ashlar dress. Prominent belvedere tower with oriel and Rapunzel turret. Windows with tracery with half-quatrefoils at the top, leaving a flat top. The STABLE, in dark local stone with sandstone dressings, looks down the road with a large wheel window.

MILLERGROUND. At first sight a picturesque C19 cottage. Only the door position in the gable end, and blank walling at the ends where fire-windows have been blocked, give it away as a C17 statesman's or yeoman's house: the true vernacular at last. End porch with stone benches leading into a rear corridor with plank-and-muntin partition. The main hearth has its bressumer and heck and a good array of spice cupboards, one utilizing the blocked fire-window. Facing the fire is the usual panelled partition, with the court cupboard inset between two doors. These lead to the snug or bower, with its own fire. At the back is the downhouse with its range, and the stair. It is possible that this was the earlier dwelling, with a half-spiral stair on the E side, and a shippon in line where the present firehouse is (cf. Low Millerground, below). Aga extension 1927. Upstairs is intricately partitioned, with extra rooms and storage spaces.

LOW MILLERGROUND. On the lakeshore. The unusual feature is a bellcote on the W gable to summon the ferry. C17 house and shippon in line, of two builds; the house as usual limewashed. Almost windowless on the N, with a half-turn stair jutting into the lane. Deep-set wooden windows on the S. The small fire-window and five-light firehouse window are readily identified. Entry is through the shippon, behind the hearth, and in at the far corner behind a heck – the standard regional arrangement.

RAYRIGG HALL. C17 and C18 lesser-gentry house in a delectable position by the lake. This is as grand as Lake District houses got before the influx of Manchester money. It was the seat of the Philipsons (arms over the door) who sold it to the Flemings in 1735. William Wilberforce took a seven-year lease in 1780 and did much of his best writing here. It was bought in 1913 by *G. H. Pattinson*, who built white sub-Arts and Crafts houses on the estate. The house was restored in 1946, with some misleading recycled materials, and again in the 1990s.

Low, two-storey front, U-shaped, facing the road, with deep-set windows mullioned-and-transomed in wood. The central entrance is somewhat unexpected. There is no sign of an earlier doorway, although the house is full of unexplained recesses and internal apertures. In the late C18 the S side was opened up to the lake view with sashed windows and a shallow curved bow at each end. This was done without gaining any extra height; its lowness and slight wonkiness are endearing.

The interior is a shock to those not used to old Lake District houses. It is so dark. The deep-set windows create islands of brightness rather than general illumination. Black Brathay flags, dark polished wood, low ceilings. The N wing, still the centre of daily life, is the nucleus around which the rest has grown. The position of its great bressumer and heck can be seen, and in the NE corner a neat wooden stair. This wing, which is three-storeyed, incorporates a good deal of structural timber. The C18 rooms belong to a different concept of living, bright, outward-looking, draughty. The main stair, now one broad and shallow flight, may have been built as a dog-leg. Upstairs an C18 panelled room with fluted pilasters, perhaps a private drawing room. Off the main bedroom in the SE corner is a perfectly preserved powder closet, panelled and pegged, with a tiny window and shutter.

Double BANK BARN, with two winnowing doors but only one ramp. Floor levels adjusted for cattle at one end, with boskins or stalls of big slates framed in wood, and horses (who need more headroom) at the other. They have C17 stalls, wooden-arched with pendants. Sympathetic conversion for small businesses, 2005–7 by *David Matthews*. – GAZEBO in the walled garden. Also by *David Matthews*; 2004. Of oak and slate, with striking use of small slates stacked. – BOATHOUSE. Probably late C18, a pretty picture.

On the inland side of the town

DAWSTONE, Lickbarrow Road, presently Heathwaite Manor. Major house of 1903 by *Dan Gibson* for Alexander Millington

Sing (later Synge), extended in 1912 by *W. L. Dolman* after Gibson died aged only forty-one in 1907. Irregular composition in white roughcast, with big round Westmorland chimneystacks and deep-set windows, sometimes in long bands. Full of excellent detail, from the rounded edges everywhere, to the artfully composed window seats with two little oak columns over a middle cupboard, to the tiny decorative ventilator lights set in each large window. Nice plasterwork here and there. The extension consists of a vast music room, with extra bedrooms over. The craftsmanship is the same but the design is more lavish, with a big inglenook to the music room and a coved ceiling with flowered plaster and canted fireplace recess to the master bedroom.

LODGES of 1912 for gardener and chauffeur, joined in a V, with swept valleys and Westmorland chimneys made terrific by the relatively small size of the building. The chauffeur's half neatly extended by *Roger Haigh* (*Haigh Architects*).

WATERBECK. Grey outside, white within. By *W. L. Dolman*, 1913, who had a reputation for ruining his clients. Mr Hislop of Manchester is supposed to have died when he got the bill, and one can see why. The style is like Gibson outside – the same roughcast, round chimneys, deep-set windows, though a little more formal in massing – but it is much more lavish inside, and moving away from the Arts and Crafts ideal. The plan is a big T, but large triangular bays are pushed out from the crosspiece to make a butterfly front to the garden and view. These are articulated inside with pairs of Doric or Ionic columns all in white. Elaborate plasterwork, fine tiled fireplaces. Only the stair is unpainted oak.

GARDEN by *Mawson*, eminently characteristic and well preserved. Three or four formal terraces drop away from the loggia with its unattractively made-up columns. Water is fed down the middle via Italianate pools to a round pond at the bottom, stone steps manoeuvre symmetrically from terrace to terrace.

THE CORBELS, Thornbarrow Road. By *Thomas Mawson* for himself, 1900. Quite a spectacular house. White roughcast. The upper floor is corbelled out over the sloping buttresses of the ground floor. Twiddly iron rainwater brackets designed by *Dan Gibson*. Chimneys with eye-catching raised lids of slate with stone balls on top. – BURROWFIELD across the road is one of a pair of Mawson semis, with mid-columns to the windows in Gibson imitation. SHRUBLANDS was designed by *Mawson* for his brother Robert opposite the nursery (now Windermere Social Club).

WINSTER (W)

4090

HOLY TRINITY. 1874–5, without attempt at architectural display. Of green stone. Nave and chancel in one, with a bellcote on a mid-buttress. Surprisingly, it has a chancel arch. Preserved from the old chapel, which Machell described in 1692, are five oval BOARDS with painted texts. One by the altar commemorates Henry Philipson 1796, with two psalm chants; another the Rev. Mr Elleray, curate, with a painted prayer book. The ORGAN was given in memory of Edward Holt of Blackwell, Bowness, †1928, and there is a bronze PLAQUE signed *Harold Stabler* to the Holts' son Joseph †1915. – STAINED GLASS. E window by *Henry Holiday*, in memory of Mrs Staniforth of Storrs. S, St Kentigern, signed *L. C. Evetts* 1941.

BIRKET HOUSES. By *Dan Gibson*, 1907–8. The last, finest and best-preserved work of his too-short life. Not a villa but a country house for a landed family, the Birkets. The house shone out white in its lush valley when it was built, but now, creeper-covered, mossy and shaded by enormous trees, looks as though it has been there for ever. It has neither the stripped-down modernity of Voysey nor the inventive three-dimensional planning of Baillie Scott, but excels in its evocation of the vernacular and in the quality and variety of its fitting out.

The family part, facing S, is planned like a medieval hall-and-cross-wings, but not slavishly. Mullioned-and-transomed windows in stone, moulded to a C17 profile. The service accommodation to the N has deep-set wooden-mullioned windows in the local manner. The three-storey porch leads to a cross-passage like a screens, with turned balusters allowing a look into the single-storey hall on the l. Beyond the hall are the drawing room and billiard room. The dining room is on the other side, where the buttery and pantry would be. The principal stair opens off the back of the hall, so no corridors. The staircase pauses part-way for an unnecessary, but delightful, little snug landing. The bedrooms are linked by the wide panelled passage beloved of the Edwardians. Some of the ceilings are raised into a cove. The NW bedroom over the billiard room is the only place where Gibson's has attempted the multi-functional complexity of Baillie Scott's hall at Blackwell: it is divided into sleeping and sitting areas by an ornamental truss, and has an extra raised annexe over the W bay.

The fitting-out everywhere is superb. Eclectic within limits – not a hint of Gothic. The dining room is fully classical, with Corinthian pilasters. The Hall is similar but without the pilaster order. The drawing room on the other hand is creamy and feminine, with more than a touch of Grinling Gibbons about the carved fruit of the fireplace. Chimneypieces are never repeated. No inglenooks. Brian Scowcroft added in 1997 a CONSERVATORY in the NW angle of the house. *Colin Rigg* of Kendal did the detail design. A huge KITCHEN of 2003 occupies the former scullery, larder and coals, with spectacular trusses modelled on that of the NW bedroom. *Jim Cooper* did the artistic ironwork.

The compartmented GARDEN is of course by *Mawson*. Local rough flags. Rhododendrons. Tightly planted group of giant pines against the hill at the back.

WITHERSLACK (W)

ST PAUL. The result of a bequest by John Barwick, Dean of
St Paul's, as an inscription in a cartouche over the subsidiary
S door explains: REVEREND JOHN BARWICK S.T.D. BORN IN
THIS HAMLET LATE DEAN OF ST PAUL'S BUILT THIS CHAP-
PELL A.D. 1664. His brother Peter, physician to Charles II, got
it built in 1668–9 and consecrated in 1671. An almost perfect
example of a plain Gothic church of that date, honest and
unpretentious. Chancel and wide nave in one, strongly battered W tower, all roughcast but not white. Tiny arch-topped
windows in the tower, three-light windows with arched heads
at the sides, E window of five stepped lights under a segmental arch. Porch and priest's doorways are round-headed with
cyma reversa mouldings. In 1768, as recorded on a board by
the organ, *John Hird* heightened the walls, adding a transom
and extra tier of lights to the side windows to match the E
window (Machell shows single-tier side windows but two-tier
E); a surprisingly tactful job, making a most harmonious and
peaceful interior. He added a screen of two Ionic columns to
separate the sanctuary, and a coved ceiling with a good cornice.
– REREDOS. By *Paley, Austin & Paley*, 1889. – PULPIT. Made
up in 1880 from the C17 three-decker, which stood a bay
further W under the square domestic-looking window. The
carving still looks Jacobean. Sounding board 1768, again surprisingly tactful. – ROYAL ARMS of goodly size, 1710. – Painted
HATCHMENTS, one of them Dean Barwick's. – FONT, a tiddly
baluster, 1666. – STAINED GLASS. E window, arms of the Stanleys and of Dean Barwick, characterful cherubs, and IHS.
Attributed to *Henry Gyles* of York, probably 1671. – MONU-
MENTS. Numerous tablets including Dean Barwick, founder,
†1664. – Geoffrey Stanley †1871 aged two: baby effigy in white
marble, very sweet and touching. Signed by *C. J. Miller*. The
pattern for this type of monument is Thomas Banks's Penelope Boothby of 1793 at Ashbourne (Derbys.) and Chantrey's
Robinson Children of 1817 at Lichfield. – The churchyard
GATEPIERS with their pine-cone finials and touch of Gothickry
are eminently typical of *Hird*.

By the gate is the large plain PARSONAGE provided by the
trustees in 1844, and the small SCHOOL, rebuilt 1874–6.

WITHERSLACK HALL. Hunting lodge for the 15th Earl of Derby,
now a special school. By *Paley & Austin*, 1874. Lintel dated
1874 in an inconsequential position at the back. It is mansion-
sized but relatively crude in the internal execution, as befits its
purpose. Big L of limestone and red sandstone, with a four-
storey tower at the hinge and a three-storey one terminating
the service wing. Big show of glass over the front door with
three tiers of arched lights coming out into an oriel in the
middle. Uncarved lumps of stone either side of the door.
Inside, a full-height stair hall, the stair climbing three sides to
a gallery on the fourth. Coved ceiling with cross-bracing. The

wood is pine. Extensive terraced GARDENS in front and at the side, lake behind. The OLD HALL is by the gate, a roughcast five-bay C18 house with kneelers and casement windows divided like sashes. Also the E-shaped KENNELS.

HALECAT HOUSE. Early C19 house of *Webster* type, remodelled in the 1950s by *Francis Johnson* for Michael Stanley. Tripartite entrance. Seven-bay garden front with the middle three making a bow. Charming octagonal SUMMERHOUSE by *Johnson*, Gothick with ogee windows and little plaster fan-vaults between them.

WOODLAND (L)

ST JOHN EVANGELIST. The third on the site: 1689, 1822, and now 1864–5, by *E. G. Paley* to a design of 1862. Small and remote. Flat-topped bellcote with four little obelisk spikes, nave and apse.

A series of other small nave-and-apse churches in the area can cause confusion. GOOD SHEPHERD at Grizebeck, of 1891 by *J. W. Grundy & Sons*, is probably the mission church noted by Pevsner. HOLY INNOCENTS at Broughton Mills, planned in 1896 and stylistically also by *Grundy*, was closed as unsafe in 2007. Its apse is smoothly integrated with nave roof, with lancets single for the apse, paired for the sides, triple for the W end. Wooden porch and louvred bellcote. Osmotherley (q.v.) is another.

2 m. NE of Broughton Mills, two fine POTASH KILNS in which bracken was burned to produce potash for washing woollen cloth. One is built into the wall of the road rising from the bridge over the River Lickle; the second is 100 yds along the path NE from Stephenson Ground farmhouse towards Walna Scar.

WORKINGTON (C)

J. Smith's paintings of 1791 show a small town straggling down from the hall on its steep bank to the church and harbour. It was already growing from a fishing village into a coal and iron town, under the energetic and competing patronage of John Christian Curwen and the Lowthers. Hutchinson's map of 1793 shows Portland Square and Elizabeth Street at the hall end, a ropewalk and a timber yard at the harbour, and Pow Street linking the two. The town's essential dichotomy is ritualized every Easter Tuesday in a 'football' contest between the Uppies and Downies, held at High Cloffocks. Up is the planned C18 town by Workington Hall, which was provided in the early C19 with St John's church. Down, a good ¾ m. w, is the port and the ancient church of St Michael. The gap between was only fully built up following the laying out of Oxford Street in 1906. The tidal cut of the River Derwent of 1763–9 was improved in 1798, to be supplanted by Lonsdale Dock in 1864–6, enlarged in 1927. Hope Pit was opened up by Curwen in 1789; he instituted social insurance and mutual benefit for his colliery workers. Jane Pit (*see* p. 702) was sunk by the Curwens in 1843–4. Closure of the modern Solway Pit in 1973 signalled the end of the coal industry. Iron-making started in 1763. The Moss Bay iron works of 1872 (later Workington Iron and Steel Co.) and the adjacent Derwent Iron Works produced Bessemer steel until 1975. Steel rails bearing the legend WORK-INGTON were made until 2006, though using steel from else-where in latter days.

ST MICHAEL. Overlooking the harbour. The Norman church had three cells. So the massive two-scalloped capital displayed in the partly surviving tower can only have been a respond, perhaps for the chancel arch. The church was rebuilt in 1770–2, but fire destroyed it in 1887. The next rebuild was by *W. Bassett-Smith* of London and *James Howes* of Workington, 1887–90. The outer walls were kept at least in part, so the church retained its short chancel and two-storey elevation embracing the short broad w tower, but with its windows made Perp, plus battlements and pinnacles. Aisles under their own gables. Fire struck again in 1994, and again it has been reconstructed inside the shell, this time by *John Bailey* of Kendal. The reopening was in 2000. The tower survived both fires, protected by its high barrel-vault and (partly rebuilt) Norman arch.

The bishop wanted the new church to be 'holy but not too holy'. While plentifully supplied with toilets, kitchens, and meeting rooms it has kept a good-sized worship space of some presence, and a smaller NE chapel. Bailey has reinstated the galleries as offices and a library, partitioned with wood and glass behind a narrow gallery walkway. The cylindrical piers of the superimposed colonnades are grooved and coloured like stone, but sound like drainpipes when tapped. They have only a suggestion of a capital, and where they get in the way some of the lower ones are simply omitted. The roof is ribbed in wood and incorporates small skylights.

FONT. Octagonal, with the same scalloping as the capital mentioned above (though Pevsner thought it Perp). – STAINED GLASS. The new scheme is by *Roy Comber* of *Pendle Stained Glass* (E) and *John Lawson* for *Goddard & Gibbs* of London. It is unusual in 2000 to see such unstinted large-scale design with plenty of figures and direct biblical story-telling. The Annun-ciation in the Lady Chapel is particularly effective. The etched glass in the galleries is by *Norman Blood* of Clifton, as are the sculpted images of Northern saints, and the very lively St Michael. – SCULPTURE. A number of pre-Conquest fragments were found in 1887 (though some have been lost again), and in 1994. The most interesting is a C10 cross-shaft bearing a plaited or 'fretty' pattern on its faces and attenuated animals on its edges, more typical of the Isle of Man than England. – MONUMENTS. Tomb-chest and effigies of Sir Christopher Curwen †1450 and Elizabeth de Hudleston, miraculously pieced together after the last fire by *Seamus Hannah* of York. Two angels by her pillow, two puppies biting her skirt. Against the tomb-chest shields under ogee gables with very flat, summary leaves. – C18 and early C19 tablets in the tower, enjoyable for their lettering and maritime flavour.

OLD RECTORY. Immediately E of the church, behind high walls. Neglected and thickly roughcast H-plan house, with screens passage (W) and high-end bay (E). Two-storey hall, big stack at each end, staircase extension at the back. Like Brigham parsonage it seems to have no defensive features except the perimeter wall – which has a crenellated section with wall-walk on the N – and an unexplained section of corbelling over the approach to the front door. This could imply an origin in the peaceful C13, but apart from the plan the only possible corroboration is a two-centred arch over the E end door.

ST JOHN, Washington Street. 1821–3 by *Thomas Hardwick*. The only representative in Cumbria of the first batch of Commissioners' churches, which were much more individually expensive than the second batch. The contractor was *Paul Nixson* of Carlisle. It is an enlarged version of Inigo Jones's 'Tuscan barn', St Paul Covent Garden, as it looked after Hardwick's restoration of 1795, plus a wooden tower. This was rebuilt in stone in 1847 by *Nelson*. It starts square, goes octagonal with diagonal pairs of pilasters, and finishes with a round stone cap. Mighty portico of two giant columns *in antis*. Shallow-pitched oversailing roof, tall arched side windows. The interior has galleries on thin iron columns. Flat ceiling with a thin rib pattern and leaf motifs. No chancel at all. The organ is in the tower, and the opening is flanked by fluted Corinthian pilasters.

Like its exemplar as originally built, the church is oriented the wrong way; tower and portico are at the E end. The solution was to ignore the compass and place the altar at the other end, in accordance with the architecture. In 1897–9 the order was reversed by *W. & C. A. Bassett-Smith*, with the altar under the tower; but in 1930–1 under *Ninian Comper* it reverted to the original arrangement. Comper's proposals were made in 1915; the executant architect was *Oldfield*. Comper's are the dazzling Italianate BALDACCHINO, gilded from top to toe, FONT COVER, and STAINED GLASS (E window). – ORGAN CASE. Ionic, also by *Comper*.

ST MARY, Westfield. Dark and rather drab church of 1889. (Interior redesigned by *Kevin Parker* in 1958, with parabolic (false) arcading, and reorientated N–S.)

OUR LADY STAR OF THE SEA (R.C.), Banklands. By *E. W. Pugin*, 1873–6. Big church of red and pink stone. Soaring front with plenty of sculpture (Our Lady by *Fr Laurence Benevot*) and a bellcote. Geometrical tracery. Pevsner called the interior 'terribly debased', so one longs to see it. It is true that E. W. Pugin was not one for purity or restraint, but the soaring proportions and sheer size compensate for any vulgarities. The model is that of the Counter-Reformation: good sight-lines, plenty of light, rich colours and much figurative sculpture. The space is dominated by three towering and richly sculpted altarpieces raised high at the E end. The composition of the arcades is worth enumerating. They stand on high red stone blocks of no recognized shape. Next come polished bases of raw-meat appearance. The piers themselves are of white Newry granite, the capitals of yellow Derbyshire stone, again after no known provenance, and the arches are plastered white. What a mixture! The semi-detached octagonal baptistery is painted all over inside with roses. – ALABASTER RELIEFS, C15, from Jervaulx. – STALLS. By *Robert Thompson*, 1926. Eight misericords, including lion and mouse, jackal and cadaver (after Carlisle), and a dog with a real bone. – STAINED GLASS. A full set, and good. By *Hardman*? (E. W. Hodge thought the E window was Continental work.) The latest date is 1917.

The Benedictine PRIORY of 1813 is at the back, with a large CHAPEL marked by a huge window with intersecting glazing.

TRINITY METHODIST CHURCH, South William Street. By *Charles W. Bell* of London, 1890. One of the few really grand Nonconformist churches in Cumbria. Renaissance style, with a red-and-white striped front with Venetian tracery and a domed tower prominent at the SW.

WORKINGTON HALL. Very sad. The chief Curwen mansion, not permanently inhabited after 1929, occupied by the army during the Second World War, was bequeathed to the town in 1946, then left for the populace to dismantle. Now a bare shell. Licence to crenellate was given in 1380. Of that time is the unusually massive tower in the SE corner with its vaulted basement and lots of mural passages and garderobes. The house probably started off (according to Anthony Emery) with a rectangular curtain, like Penrith Castle. The hall was N of the tower at first-floor level on the E side, overlooking the steep bank of the river, above a series of vaulted rooms. The kitchens adjoined the hall on the N side. The house developed continuously, with rebuilding of the hall and elimination of much of the curtain, in the C16 and C17, and now appears quadrangular. On the W side a C15 tunnel-vaulted gatehouse, i.e. opposite the hall. In 1783–95 *John Carr* made rich interiors and a courtyard corridor. The tower and hall have large arched windows. The N side is a long, even twelve-bay front with raised, flat window frames. The W side has, apart from the gatehouse, angle pavilions with round-arched windows with Y-tracery.

The PARK, designed by *Thomas White* in 1783, stretched both sides of the road, originally connected by a bridge. John Christian Curwen's experimental farm of *c.* 1800 is at SCHOOSE, in the High Park. It is polygonal and mock-castellated, like the Duke of Norfolk's model farms at Greystoke (q.v.); an elongated hexagon, with a gateway at each end. A pre-existing bank barn upsets the symmetry. Beyond the farmhouse at the NE corner is a handsome STABLE range, then a MILL running down to the stream. This is long and narrow, with three storeys, the lowest with lunette windows and groin-vaulted in five bays in brick; now a wonderful glory-hole of abandoned machinery and bikes. SE is a square DOVECOTE, now a house. All these buildings have the same detailing (*Carr*?). In 1809–10 the tall WINDMILL was added. It has Egyptianizing openings and was fitted with six sails. To the SW is a square enclosure, now full of static caravans, ringed on three sides by a long series of deep stone arches, like a low viaduct. What was it for?

WAR MEMORIAL, Vulcan Park. Low granite tower by *Sir Robert Lorimer*, 1928, with inset bronze reliefs by *Alex Carrick*. A soldier with helmet and rifle bids farewell to his wife and child. A greatcoated soldier carries a wounded comrade. Roundels on the other sides show the steel-workers and miners at home. Memorial sculpture at its best, tender without being mawkish, strong with no hint of belligerence.

STATION. At the bottom end of town, by St Michael. A proper main-line station of 1886, in LNWR style with two signal boxes and four tracks between the platforms. Yellow brick buildings, covered overbridge, platform canopies, all well preserved.

HARBOUR. Essentially a development of riverside quays, unlike that at Whitehaven. The original harbour lay on a creek, S of the Derwent. Its prime business was the export of coal from the Curwen estates. The first dock was not built until 1864 on the N bank, close to the Oldside Iron works which had opened under Lowther patronage in 1858 and 1860. Designed by *Alexander Meadows Rendel*, and named the LONSDALE DOCK, it proved inadequate within a decade. A satisfactory enlargement, the PRINCE OF WALES DOCK, was not constructed until 1927, with an opening direct to the sea and a 700-ft (215-metre) pier, to a scheme of *Rendel, Palmer & Tritton*. This is still working. On the quay along the S bank of the river is an odd little WATCHMAN'S HUT of random rubble, circular under a domed roof like a petrified bee skep.

WORKINGTON BRIDGE, ¾ m. upstream from the river mouth, for long the first crossing point, was destroyed by floods in 2009. It was dated 1841, and signed *Thomas Milton* Civil Engineer, *Thomas Nelson* Builder. Three segmental arches with rusticated voussoirs and a solid parapet. The town's other bridge, Calva Bridge, was deemed unsafe at the same time, leaving only the railway crossing the Derwent.

THE TOWN

Starting at the top end, the C18 town, small in scale, is a grid of streets centred on the sloping oblong of PORTLAND SQUARE. It was planned by John Christian Curwen and Thomas White in the 1780s. The square is long and narrow, with trees, and is laid with cobbles patterned in star shapes around the Peat Memorial OBELISK of 1881. The houses exhibit the West Cumbrian blend of Georgian, each a little different within strict limits, colourwashed with emphatic window and door surrounds in a contrasting colour. No basements or areas, parapets or valleys. The third floor, if present, is low. On Portland Street to the w is the entrance to the former covered market. Close by to the w is the tiny irregular MARKET PLACE. From here Jane Street leads w, then Washington Street s to St John's church. Across the road from the church in Ritson Street is a LOCK-UP of 1825. Two cells, two doors, two slit windows. Half-cylindrical stone roof – a naked tunnel-vault.

w of St John's the vocabulary changes. Now we have C19 and early C20 rock-facing with dormers and bargeboards. The chief area of interest is some way to the NW, above the river and around the Methodist church (p. 700), where Finkle Street becomes South William Street. The former CARNEGIE LIBRARY and THEATRE, 1903–4 by *W. A. Mellon & George Wittet* of York, is now a café and arts centre. The Baroque style is unmistakable and so is the Library plan, with the different sections around a rotunda for issues. Opposite, behind a little lodge, the TRADES HALL CLUB occupies a pretty villa, Victorian on this side but possessed of a pleasing Georgian front overlooking the river on Derwent Street. Set back opposite James Street is TUSCAN VILLA, said to be by the same builder as Grecian Villa in Cockermouth (p. 285). Despite the delicious name it is a gabled Tudor house in Goodwin's style, dated 1845.

HELENA THOMPSON MUSEUM, e of Portland Square on Park End Road. A grander late C18 house, detached, with its own garden and stable. Five bays and two storeys. Doorway with fluted Ionic pilasters and a pediment. Venetian window in the N gable. Good stair with three balusters per tread.

FOUNDRY, between Church Street and the river. Late C18 or early C19, a surprising survival. Coursed rubble with flush quoins, three storeys with Gothick windows and attached chimney, the uppermost four stages stepped brickwork.

BREWERY TOWER, Ladies Walk. An important visual incident against the steep hill rising behind it. An exuberant six-storey mid-C19 battlemented tower, with a tall chimney and projecting glazed lucams front and back. Windows with heavily quoined surrounds. Attached three-storey maltings. Closed 1989, converted to flats 2004.

JANE PIT, Mossbay Road, s of the town. Sunk for the Curwen family in 1843–4. Still a remarkable architectural statement, even though it stopped work in 1875. What remains is a three-storey oval PUMPING ENGINE HOUSE with an attached circular chimney, and a similar detached CHIMNEY alongside. The engine house is battlemented, and each chimney has a matching battlemented parapet, through which the flue continues for another 10 ft (3 metres). All in a fine pinkish sandstone ashlar. The engine house has a flywheel pit on the side away from the chimney, and there are traces of a circular horse gin in front of it. Built not long after Sydney Smirke's similarly medievalized Wellington Pit at Whitehaven for the Lowthers, the Curwens' great rivals, Jane Pit suggests a similar quasi-feudal expression of family pride.

WRAY (L)

3000

WRAY CASTLE. A modern castellated mansion of exactly the kind lampooned by Pugin in his *True Principles* (1841). It was created by Dr James Dawson, surgeon, of Liverpool, in 1840–7. The architect, a close friend of Rickman, was *J. J. Lightfoot*, who 'killed himself with drinking before the house was finished', according to Beatrix Potter who knew the house well. Wordsworth said it 'added a dignified feature to the interesting scenery in the midst of which it stands'; yet Lightfoot appears not to have glanced at a real Northern castle. A vast turreted porte cochère and a tall central lantern tower dominate the asymmetrical and top-heavy mass. The battlements are assertively machicolated, and punctuated by high-level turrets, daringly corbelled out. The window openings are inauthentically splayed on the outside. Arrowslits are sinkings of iron, dressings of hammered grey limestone, the rest of sawn slate.

The interior is astonishingly profligate of space. The broad central axis is articulated into three parts by triple Gothic colonnades without capitals. Each section looks up through a hole into the upper landing, the central section right up into the zooming verticals of the lantern, with its tall windows and niches and its turrets corbelled in at the corners (no sign of them outside). The upper landing offers not just the reciprocal views to the floor below, and the lantern above, but also – an extra *coup* – an extended vista into the billiard room over the porte cochère. The principal rooms are themed Gothic, though they have lost much of their richness. Mouldings, doors, skirtings are on a gargantuan scale, but the window traceries with their armorial glass are rather fiddly. Were the main lights always fitted with plate glass? All the openings are splayed at the sides and top; a recurring motif. The Music Room on the w, reached awkwardly across a service corridor, has a Jacobean theme, its ceiling threatening the beholder with gross pendants. The Morning Room (SE), incorporating a turret, has a bastard classical ceiling, linenfold panelling and curious alternations of windows and niches. The back stair is the most dramatic space of all, climbing up in vertiginous stages to the lantern tower.

FERNERY. A castellated glasshouse, no less. Its pyramid roof is ingeniously framed with chunks of limestone pavement. GARDENER'S HOUSE and BOATHOUSE in the same style, the latter with a complete miniature dock.

The LODGE is a little later than the mansion (1856?) and lacks some of its characteristic detail, but is still castellated and asymmetrical.

ST MARGARET OF ANTIOCH, by the Castle lodge. A very odd dedication for a C19 church. Kelly says: erected 1845, endowed (by J. Dawson) 1865. The sundial on the porch is dated 1856. The tower with its corbelled-out parapet chimes in with the castle. Otherwise it is very like the Rev. J. A. Addison's proprietary chapel at Windermere (q.v.) of 1848: a diminutive nave and chancel with exaggeratedly steep roofs and fancy late C13 to early C14 traceries. It retains on its porch the hexagonal slating favoured by Addison and the architect *Miles Thompson*. Simple interior with single-framed roofs. Only the low dying-in arch to the tower recalls the castle. – STAINED GLASS by the pulpit commemorating Dr Whittaker of Belmount, Hawkshead, †1854 and his wife †1871. – MONUMENTS. Marble tablet in Latin and English to James and Margaret Dawson †1862 and 1873. Their tomb is outside. – Brass plates to three MacIvers (*see* Ambleside), †1915, 1915 and 1916.

(LOW WRAY. Dr Dawson's home farm. Retaining the C18 farmhouse, he built a new stable and coachhouse and a new bank barn in the 1840s.)

PULLWOODS, ¾ m. NW. An amusing contrast to its castellated neighbour. The engineer Sir William Crossley of Manchester wanted something like Bramall Hall in Cheshire, i.e. picturesquely timber-framed. *G. Faulkner Armitage*'s many-gabled mansion of 1890–1 is more Home Counties than Cheshire, and thoroughly out of place. He used broken bricks or tiles in the infill between timbers, and brick chimneys, so it looks pink. No jettying, suggesting that the timbering is purely decorative. Big welcoming hall with a hooded fireplace and mosaic floor. Extended by the same architect in 1901–2, and now apartments. – BOATHOUSE, LODGE, and HOME FARM in the same style.

WREAY (C)

ST MARY. The remarkable creation of *Sara Losh*, in memory of her sister Katherine, who died in 1835. The church was consecrated in 1842. It cost £1,200. The Loshes were an old Cumberland family (Arlosh). John Losh, educated at Sedburgh and Trinity College Cambridge, had founded alkali works and iron works at Walker near Newcastle. The family had many intellectual connections, and were well travelled. Sara was calm, dignified and beautiful, a scholar of languages and mathematics. Katherine was lively and hearty.

A description first. The church is an aisleless basilica with a steep roof and a semicircular apse. The corner pilasters are adorned with very large and boldly carved brackets, not gar-

goyles: turtle, snake, crocodile, furry bat, dragon with wings
and big toenails. On the bellcote perches an eagle, as at
Newton Arlosh (q.v.). Blank arcading round the apse, with tiny
windows under the eaves. In the side walls, over each main
window, an extra triplet of tiny windows set in a sunk rectangle. On the w front more tiny windows climb up each gable
slope to a pair of figures in niches at the top. Number games
with threes and sevens can be played with the windows; the
total number is eighty-four. The reveals of the three w windows
and doorway are boldly and unconventionally carved; the
doorway with water lilies, the l. window with fossils such as
ammonites, crinoids and coral, the middle with poppies, lilies,
corn, caterpillar and butterflies, the r. with pine cones, birds,
a beetle and a bee. They are naturalistically but flatly carved,
a stylization which would be expected of 1900 but is unique in
the 1840s. The carver was *William Hindson*, working under
Sara's direction from nature in a way that anticipates Wood-
ward, Ruskin and the O'Shea brothers in the 1850s. The door's
interior arch is carved with a climbing gourd; a caterpillar
gnaws its stem. After the open narthex and baptistery, bounded
by a low stone wall, the floor drops three steps into the body
of the church, then up again with more steps at the E end, so
the nave reads like an arena (cf. St Wilfrid, Brougham). Round
the apse a close arcade of strong columns, a French and
Romanesque motif, its capitals carved with animals and plants. 82
The apse arch terminates in the only human faces, a man and
a woman, forthright, modern in the Neoclassical sense, iden-
tity-less. The glazing of the windows is uniquely effective. They
are filled with broken bits of STAINED GLASS (rescued by
William Losh from the Archbishop's palace at Sens), arranged
like grisaille in patterns so that each has a flower as centrepiece. Sara's accounts record *Wailes* for windows – £42 16s.
8d. In the 'clerestory' the middle light of each triplet is overlaid with a stencil. A single tiny clear window, deep-set, lights
each reading desk. The windows round the apse are very deep-
set too, so that only three or four can be seen at once. Alabaster
stencils of plant forms cover clear glass. Beneath, in the arcade,
are seven dim roundels of orange glass, like lamps. A floral
design painted around the continuous upper windows of the
apse gives an overall impression of marbling. Behind each seat
below are symbols, some surprising, of Christ and the apostles
in roundels, and texts from the Creed in banners.

Sara's choice and mixture of styles is highly original.
The climbing dwarf windows of the w gable are Italian
Romanesque, but the three principal English examples of the
style – Wilton church by Wyatt & Brandon, Christ Church
Streatham by Wild, and Christ Church Watney Street by John
Shaw – were all begun in 1840, i.e. just after the design of
Wreay. Edmund Sharpe's revival of Italo-Romanesque forms
in Lancashire in the 1830s, e.g. at St Mark Blackburn, may
have given her food for thought. She herself called the style
'early Saxon or modified Lombard'. The phrase echoes

Thomas Hope's *Historical Essay on Architecture*, published by Hope's son in 1831. In it the elder Hope warns that the Lombard or Italian Romanesque style became 'modified' as it spread to other countries. By 'Saxon' Sara probably meant English or Norman Romanesque.

FURNISHINGS. The ALTAR, set in the forward position so that the priest faces the people, is an uncanonical slab of green marble supported by a pair of bronze eagles. – PULPIT. A hollowed tree trunk of bog oak, out of which springs a new shoot. – LECTERNS. A pair, Early Christian style; one a pelican, the other an eagle, both carved in back glistening bog oak. On the E wall a pair of angels, more conventional than the rest. On the N wall a corbel carved with a watchful owl and cockerel. Above the chancel arch a beam carrying seven angels and eight palm trees. Was it meant to go across the arch, like a rood? – The FONT is a pretty conceit. Small, of alabaster, with ten panels of carving including pomegranate, a dragonfly and a dove. The motifs include Norman zigzag and Greek fluting. The lid is a sheet of mirror bearing lily pads and flowers reflecting in its surface. Carvers *William Hindson, John Scott*, and *Sara Losh* herself.

To understand the programme of carving, it is worth knowing that Sara's beloved Major Thain was killed on the North-West Frontier in 1842 by an arrow, and that shortly before his death he sent her a dry pine cone, from which she was able to germinate a seed. Arrows form the fence to the WELL-HEAD outside the W front, and the bars of the W door. A single arrow sticks out of the wall above the organ. Pine cones are everywhere. Christian symbolism can be seen, e.g. in the thirteen seats, as at the Last Supper, around the apse – but it is abstract, intellectual. Otherwise the images are from nature and from the fossil record. Life, death and resurrection. Buds, leaves, flowers and seeds. Larva, pupa and imago. Creation glorified in a detached, scientific, classifying sort of way as in the museums of the time, echoing the *Natural Theology* (1802) of William Paley, who had been a regular trencherman at the Losh table, and of Richard Payne Knight in his *Enquiry into the Symbolical Language of Ancient Art and Mythology* (1818, reissued 1836). Paley took the intricacy of Creation to prove the existence of a 'watchmaker' God, whereas for Payne Knight, essentially a pantheist, the themes of birth, life, death and immortality are common to all religions. Virtually all the symbols identified in his book appear at Wreay, where the lotus, pomegranate and ear of corn are identified as receptive and female, the pine cone as active and male. We see the same uneasy reconciliation of religion and science in the Oxford Museum, commissioned in 1854.

THE SETTING. The church stands upon a symmetry of mounds and ramps. This is the start of a grand vision, using the landscape in an C18 way but modelling its incidents on the earliest Christian and pre-Christian forms. Church, school and schoolmaster's house form a group. N of the church is the family grave enclosure, the cross and mausoleum. A fold of biblical sheep follows, and then the walled cemetery with its mortuary chapel and sexton's cottage.

CROSS, *c.* 1843, in memory of Sara's parents. A copy of the Bewcastle Cross as it was understood at the time, the first attempt at a scientific reproduction. The same size as the original, the same shape, the same elements even to the sundial, which looks as though it was not understood as such, but with Latin inscriptions instead of runes, Virgin and Child in place of St John the Baptist, and a conventional cross-head sitting awkwardly on the squared-off head. The figures imitate the Bewcastle poses but have an Early Victorian flavour. Sinkings are uniformly deep, edges rounded. – MAUSOLEUM. 1850. Cyclopean, roughly coursed masonry left quite accidental in shape and surface, flat roof. Sculpture, Catherina Isabella Losh, by *David Dunbar* after a sketch by Sara made near Naples in 1817.* She sits in plaintive mood, holding a pine cone and branch. Portrait medallions to Isabella, John, and George Losh, †1799, 1814 and 1846, also by *Dunbar.* – Family GRAVE ENCLOSURE. Rough and massy gravestones overlaid with pine cones and jointed fossil plant forms.

CEMETERY. Further N, across a field. Walled with cyclopean masonry like the mausoleum, with a single giant pine tree in the centre. CHAPEL, *c.* 1835. A copy (from reports in the *Gentleman's Magazine*) of the Early Christian oratory of St Piran at Perranzabuloe, Cornwall, which caused great excitement when excavated from the sand dunes in 1835. Sara Losh went for the Antique, every time. Only 29 ft by 16½ ft 6 in. (9 by 5 metres) in size. The two doors have her double roll moulding with idealized male and female heads at the springing and a lion at the head. The heads are Neoclassical in character, the arch is a basket not a semicircle. Inside, a rude altar and palm tree. – CEMETERY COTTAGE, now called Candlemas Cottage, for the sexton. Rows of tiny (blocked) windows in fives and a seven.

SCHOOL. 1830. Much altered, but retaining its Losh chimney.

POMPEIAN COTTAGE. For the schoolmaster, *c.* 1830, after a house excavated in Pompeii. Monopitch roof, with blanked-off recesses climbing up the slope, as in the church.

WOODSIDE, 1¼ m. NW. *Sara Losh* and her sister transformed the plain seven-bay Georgian front of the family home into a good C17 imitation, with an asymmetrical bay and mullioned-and-transomed windows with cusped heads. She did much inside too, but only the l. end remains after partial demolition in 1936.

KATHERINE WELL, ½ m. SE. In memory of Katherine Losh †1835, in a simplified version of Sara's style. Small arches all along the top, larger ones below. The design is exactly such as to be worked out with a child's wooden bricks.

SCALESCEUGH (residential home), on the A6. Substantial country house of 1913–14 for John R. Harrison by the Beaux-

*Katherine is sometimes Catharina, Sara is sometimes Sarah.

Arts-trained *Alexander N. Paterson* of Glasgow. H-shaped. The cross-bar is gently convex (a favourite motif of the time?), and the r. wing is half-hidden behind the original farmhouse, with its own cross-gable, dated 1746; both adding subtlety to the view from the drive. Lorimer's Brackenburgh (Plumpton, q.v.), of the same pale sandstone, seems to have been the exemplar, but this is more cheerful. Paterson insouciantly mixes his styles: Baroque for the gatepiers and curvaceaous garden perron, Jacobean the strapwork of the stairs and screens, Greek for the fireplaces, Rococo the swirling plasterwork of the drawing room. Even a touch of Gothic in the occasional carved accents. There are spatial subtleties too: the semicircular garden portico, forming with its recessed entry a complete circle, is echoed by a circular lobby upstairs. The stair has a curious rostrum on the landing from which Mr Harrison could address his assembled household. The cross-piece of the H holds not a great hall but a lobby and a broad, gently curved corridor. Its decoration in plaster and wood is sumptuous, but the concept recalls a pavilion-design hospital.

WYTHBURN (C) *see* THIRLMERE

1030

WYTHOP (C)

St Margaret. 1¾ m. ene of Embleton church, and, as so often, far from any village. 1865–6 by *Bruce* of Whitehaven. A Victorian set-piece, above a high retaining wall with paired lychgates and steps and a comfortable seat. Nave with fussy bellcote, chancel. In the porch, the lintel dated 1673 from its predecessor on a different site. – STAINED GLASS. Chancel side windows, †1908 and 1916, by *Burlison & Grylls*. w windows by *W. E. Tower* for *Kempe & Co.*, c. 1911.

HILL-FORT, Castle How, on a steep rock boss by the NW shore of Bassenthwaite Lake. Two rock-cut ditches, with counterscarp banks, on the E; three on the W, the innermost visible as a terrace on the N.

5020

YANWATH AND EAMONT BRIDGE (W)

31

Yanwath Hall. Arguably the best of all Cumbria's towered houses, providing generously for comfort and self-sufficiency as well as defence. It stands on the steep s bank of the River Eamont at that most strategic spot where all the N–S routes cross between Westmorland and Cumberland. Fine and complete tower, hall and kitchen in line, with E and N ranges behind

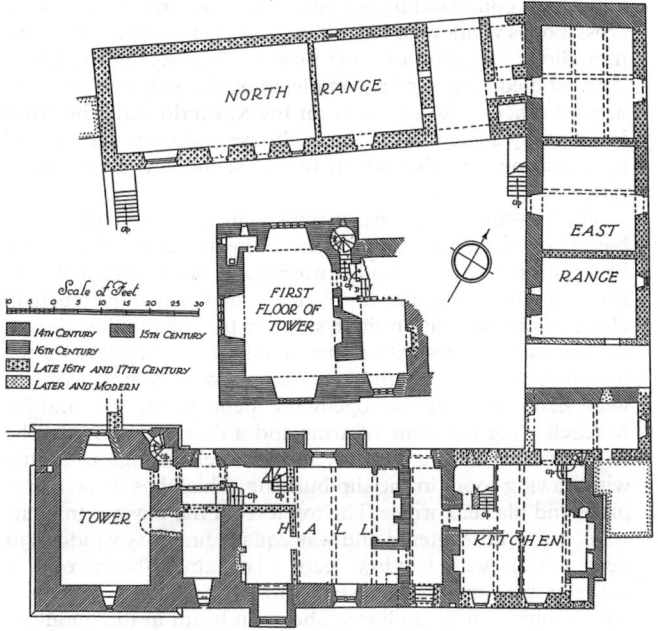

Yanwath Hall.
Plan, 1936

making a three-sided courtyard. The Lowthers bought Yanwath
in 1654, since when it has been tenanted and largely left alone.

The big solar W tower appears to be of two phases: late C14
and C15. Some of its small windows survive, notably a single
cusped window in the W wall, but the large five-light mullioned-and-transomed windows of the mid-floor are Elizabethan insertions. The tower does not abut directly onto the
hall. A narrow slip building or chamber block of two storeys is
interpolated, contemporary with the tower and like it uninhabited since the C18. The hall and kitchen are probably mid-
C15, though as we shall see modified internally. The hall sports
a bay window with a transom and rather coarse cusping of both
tiers of arches (cf. Chetham's Hospital, Manchester, with two
tier cusped windows, 1421). Small similar windows in the hall
front and back. Hall and kitchen do not butt directly up
directly either; between the two is a broad cross-passage, the
equivalent of the southern screens but more outside than in,
running behind the hall stack and not sharing its warmth or
light. The outer (S) screens door is unobtrusive under a rustic
porch, but the (N) courtyard entrance makes a magnificent
statement with a round multiply moulded arch and a massive
doorway made up with linenfold and a traceried opening. The
kitchen end, now the farmhouse, has fanciful detailing of the
C16(?) like that at the gatehouse range of Askham Hall (q.v.):

a gunloop commanding the roadway, a St Andrew's cross or cross-bones window, and another like a B on its back. The rope moulding and corbels on the massive chimneys go with this. The cobbled courtyard is completed on the E by a set of lodgings or offices, also C15, and on the N, overlooking the River Eamont, by a late C16 or C17 gatehouse and stables, protected by a playing-card-thin watch tower on the end of the office range.

The TOWER has its own turning stair and a tunnel-vaulted basement of fine size. Entry lobby to the first floor with its own little blocked window and a wash-hand basin. Machell calls this the Dining Room, a splendid chamber of Elizabethan character brightly lit on three sides by the big mullioned-and-transomed windows with a surviving mid-C16 fireplace on the fourth. Arms of Elizabeth I in plaster above it. Beams plastered with nailhead, with an openwork pendant in the middle. Machell recorded coats of arms and a date 1586. Garderobe in one corner, and a doorway in the other through to a little withdrawing room in the slip building, which has its own fireplace and plaster cornice. The top level of the tower is in a raw state, but is little altered and was equally fine. C15 windows in deep reveals with window seats. Flat camber-beam roof, a superior version of e.g. Dacre, Sizergh or Scales, decorated with nailhead in the hollows. The main beam in the middle is arched like that at Dacre. Wash-hand basin with drain at the top of the stair, another in the garderobe. Traces of painted 'Antique' work, in the Elizabethan fashion. The roofscape is magnificent. Nearly flat leads in the middle, broad flagged parapet walk over the thickness of the wall. Turrets in the corners each with a little room below and steps to a flagged platform above. The battlements step up to the turrets. One, and probably once two, decorative chimneys with a cap like a little conical-roofed house.

The HALL is still double-height, but considerably reduced; the remaining space is uncomfortably proportioned. It is ceiled, divided short of the bay-window section, and an enormous arched fireplace and integral door is inserted in front of the the cross-passage. The inserted W partition bears a painted clock face with a single hand. The stolen two-storey bit behind is divided horizontally into a snug below, clock room above, each with half of the bay window. The C15 hall roof, accessible from the tower stair, has massive collar-beams braced to form arches, kingposts, and cusped wind-braces.

The E range has a king- and raking queenpost roof with mortices for longitudinal bracing. Signs of partitioning, fireplace, and the regularly spaced doors suggest lodgings. At its N end the flat watch tower, with stepped access from the upper floor. The N range, of eleven bays, has steps to the upper floor at both ends.

Excellent C19 Lowther estate STEADING surrounding a second courtyard on the E, closed in by a massive stone retainer on top of which pass West Coast main line trains.

(Thomas Wilkinson (1751–1836), Quaker poet, farmer and land-scape gardener (cf. Pooley Bridge, Tirril, Lowther) had a house called THE GROTTO in Yanwath village. There he built an underground summerhouse, on which he inscribed 'Beneath this moss grown roof, this rustic cell/Truth, Liberty, Content, sequester'd dwell.' New houses there now.)

YANWATH WOODHOUSE, 1¼ m. SE, on the Lowther drive. 1697. Built for Sir John Lowther by *William Idle*. Front part originally with cross-mullioned windows, but refenestrated and rendered in the C19, when the added rear part converted it to a double pile, and a steading was added to what may have been a hunting lodge rather than a farm. Arms over the door, carved, according to Blake Tyson, by one *Dowthwait* in 1697.

EAMONT BRIDGE village runs along the A6 from the bridge at its N end to the Lowther bridge at the S. Within this short length there is plenty to see. Starting at the S end, the LODGE and GATE to Lowther Castle (*James Mawson*, 1877) and the road up to Brougham Hall, with a typical estate house, face one another; on the skyline the pele tower of Clifton Hall (qq.v.). On the l. as we enter the village the two ancient earthworks of King Arthur's Round Table and Mayburgh Henge (*see below*). South Africa War MEMORIAL, 1901; a Celtic cross in best Westmorland green stone. The two casualties are portrayed in bronze relief, in slouch hats. Signed *W. Grant Stevenson desig. et illust.*, *W. Grisenthwaite fecit*. CROWN INN, 1770. In the garden, remains of a Real Tennis court built in 1853 for William Brougham. Many of the houses carry C17 and C18 datestones; others, presumably estate houses, are single-storey and minimally Gothic. MANSION HOUSE, dated 1686 RLB (Rolland Barrow, rector of Brougham) and probably by *Thomas Machell*. An impressive up-to-date double pile. Five bays, three storeys. Porch with quoins and a balustrade. The centre window above has a broken curly pediment and bolection-moulded surround. Windows now mullioned, originally cross-mullioned, as they still are at the back. Oak stair with barley-twist balusters and heavy moulded handrail. (There is a stone turning stair as well.) The EAMONT BRIDGE, C16 but widened on the downstream side, has three segmental spans, ribbed underneath, with triangular cutwaters.

EDEN MILLENNIUM MONUMENT. A 50-tonne lump of unworked Shap granite near the Mayburgh henge. Upon it are carved the Greek letters alpha and omega, the Latin cross, and the Arabic numerals 2000. That is all. How little there is to say; cf. the South Africa memorial. The brainchild of Canon Gervase Markham of Morland; consultant engineer *Charles Blackett-Ord*, letter-carver *Lida Lopes Cardoso*.

HENGES. A Neolithic group, each differing in form. MAYBURGH, SW, is of unusual design: a massive circular bank of water-worn stones from the River Eamont. The usual internal quarry-ditch was not required. The S and E sides of the bank, including the single E entrance, were emphasized, being up to 150 ft (45 metres) wide and 24 ft (7.5 metres) high. Four stones stood in the interior until the early C18, reduced now to one, 9 ft (2.8 metres) high; two more formerly outside the entrance. KING ARTHUR'S ROUND TABLE, E, is a smaller sub-circular henge of more conventional design and proportions: internal ditch, external bank. Entrance causeway on the SSE, and (formerly) a second on the NNW, flanked by standing stones. A trench in the NE quadrant yielded cremated bone. The earthworks were enhanced in the late C18 or early C19, creating a tea garden for the inn. A third possible henge, now levelled, lay 140 yds (130 metres) S, beside the Lowther Lodge.

GLOSSARY

Numbers and letters refer to the illustrations (by John Sambrook) on pp. 722–729.

ABACUS: flat slab forming the top of a capital (3a).

ACANTHUS: classical formalized leaf ornament (4b).

ACCUMULATOR TOWER: *see* Hydraulic power.

ACHIEVEMENT: a complete display of armorial bearings.

ACROTERION: plinth for a statue or ornament on the apex or ends of a pediment; more usually, both the plinth and what stands on it (4a).

AEDICULE (*lit.* little building): architectural surround, consisting usually of two columns or pilasters supporting a pediment.

AGGREGATE: *see* Concrete.

AISLE: subsidiary space alongside the body of a building, separated from it by columns, piers, or posts.

ALMONRY: a building from which alms are dispensed to the poor.

AMBULATORY (*lit.* walkway): aisle around the sanctuary (q.v.).

ANGLE ROLL: roll moulding in the angle between two planes (1a).

ANSE DE PANIER: *see* Arch.

ANTAE: simplified pilasters (4a), usually applied to the ends of the enclosing walls of a portico *in antis* (q.v.).

ANTEFIXAE: ornaments projecting at regular intervals above a Greek cornice, originally to conceal the ends of roof tiles (4a).

ANTHEMION: classical ornament like a honeysuckle flower (4b).

APRON: raised panel below a window or wall monument or tablet.

APSE: semicircular or polygonal end of an apartment, especially of a chancel or chapel. In classical architecture sometimes called an *exedra*.

ARABESQUE: non-figurative surface decoration consisting of flowing lines, foliage scrolls etc., based on geometrical patterns. Cf. Grotesque.

ARCADE: series of arches supported by piers or columns. *Blind arcade* or *arcading*: the same applied to the wall surface. *Wall arcade*: in medieval churches, a blind arcade forming a dado below windows. Also a covered shopping street.

ARCH: Shapes *see* 5c. *Basket arch* or *anse de panier* (basket handle): three-centred and depressed, or with a flat centre. *Nodding*: ogee arch curving forward from the wall face. *Parabolic*: shaped like a chain suspended from two level points, but inverted. Special purposes. *Chancel*: dividing chancel from nave or crossing. *Crossing*: spanning piers at a crossing (q.v.). *Relieving or discharging*: incorporated in a wall to relieve superimposed weight (5c). *Skew*: spanning responds not diametrically opposed. *Strainer*: inserted in an opening to resist inward pressure. *Transverse*: spanning a main axis (e.g. of a vaulted space). *See also* Jack arch, Triumphal arch.

ARCHITRAVE: formalized lintel, the lowest member of the classical entablature (3a). Also the moulded frame of a door or window (often borrowing the profile of a classical architrave). For *lugged* and *shouldered* architraves *see* 4b.

ARCUATED: dependent structurally on the arch principle. Cf. Trabeated.

ARK: chest or cupboard housing the

tables of Jewish law in a synagogue.

ARRIS: sharp edge where two surfaces meet at an angle (3a).

ASHLAR: masonry of large blocks wrought to even faces and square edges (6d).

ASTRAGAL: classical moulding of semicircular section (3f).

ASTYLAR: with no columns or similar vertical features.

ATLANTES: see Caryatids.

ATRIUM (plural: atria): inner court of a Roman or C20 house; in a multi-storey building, a toplit covered court rising through all storeys. Also an open court in front of a church.

ATTACHED COLUMN: see Engaged column.

ATTIC: small top storey within a roof. Also the storey above the main entablature of a classical façade.

AUMBRY: recess or cupboard to hold sacred vessels for the Mass.

BAILEY: see Motte-and-bailey.

BALANCE BEAM: see Canals.

BALDACCHINO: free-standing canopy, originally fabric, over an altar. Cf. Ciborium.

BALLFLOWER: globular flower of three petals enclosing a ball (1a). Typical of the Decorated style.

BALUSTER: pillar or pedestal of bellied form. *Balusters*: vertical supports of this or any other form, for a handrail or coping, the whole being called a *balustrade* (6c). *Blind balustrade*: the same applied to the wall surface.

BARBICAN: outwork defending the entrance to a castle.

BARGEBOARDS (corruption of 'vergeboards'): boards, often carved or fretted, fixed beneath the eaves of a gable to cover and protect the rafters.

BAROQUE: style originating in Rome *c.*1600 and current in England *c.*1680–1720, characterized by dramatic massing and silhouette and the use of the giant order.

BARROW: burial mound.

BARTIZAN: corbelled turret, square or round, frequently at an angle.

BASCULE: hinged part of a lifting (or bascule) bridge.

BASE: moulded foot of a column or pilaster. For *Attic* base see 3b.

BASEMENT: lowest, subordinate storey; hence the lowest part of a classical elevation, below the *piano nobile* (q.v.).

BASILICA: a Roman public hall; hence an aisled building with a clerestory.

BASTION: one of a series of defensive semicircular or polygonal projections from the main wall of a fortress or city.

BATTER: intentional inward inclination of a wall face.

BATTLEMENT: defensive parapet, composed of *merlons* (solid) and *crenels* (embrasures) through which archers could shoot; sometimes called *crenellation*. Also used decoratively.

BAY: division of an elevation or interior space as defined by regular vertical features such as arches, columns, windows etc.

BAY LEAF: classical ornament of overlapping bay leaves (3f).

BAY WINDOW: window of one or more storeys projecting from the face of a building. *Canted*: with a straight front and angled sides. *Bow window*: curved. *Oriel*: rests on corbels or brackets and starts above ground level; also the bay window at the dais end of a medieval great hall.

BEAD-AND-REEL: see Enrichments.

BEAKHEAD: Norman ornament with a row of beaked bird or beast heads usually biting into a roll moulding (1a).

BELFRY: chamber or stage in a tower where bells are hung.

BELL CAPITAL: see 1b.

BELLCOTE: small gabled or roofed housing for the bell(s).

BERM: level area separating a ditch from a bank on a hill-fort or barrow.

BILLET: Norman ornament of small half-cylindrical or rectangular blocks (1a).

BLIND: see Arcade, Baluster, Portico.

BLOCK CAPITAL: see 1a.

BLOCKED: columns, etc. interrupted by regular projecting

blocks (*blocking*), as on a Gibbs surround (4b).

BLOCKING COURSE: course of stones, or equivalent, on top of a cornice and crowning the wall.

BOLECTION MOULDING: covering the joint between two different planes (6b).

BOND: the pattern of long sides (*stretchers*) and short ends (*headers*) produced on the face of a wall by laying bricks in a particular way (6e).

BOSS: knob or projection, e.g. at the intersection of ribs in a vault (2c).

BOWTELL: a term in use by the C15 for a form of roll moulding, usually three-quarters of a circle in section (also called *edge roll*).

BOW WINDOW: *see* Bay window.

BOX FRAME: timber-framed construction in which vertical and horizontal wall members support the roof (7). Also concrete construction where the loads are taken on cross walls; also called *cross-wall construction*.

BRACE: subsidiary member of a structural frame, curved or straight. *Bracing* is often arranged decoratively e.g. quatrefoil, herringbone (7). *See also* Roofs.

BRATTISHING: ornamental crest, usually formed of leaves, Tudor flowers or miniature battlements.

BRESSUMER (*lit.* breast-beam): big horizontal beam supporting the wall above, especially in a jettied building (7).

BRICK: *see* Bond, Cogging, Engineering, Gauged, Tumbling.

BRIDGE: *Bowstring*: with arches rising above the roadway which is suspended from them. *Clapper*: one long stone forms the roadway. *Roving*: *see* Canal. *Suspension*: roadway suspended from cables or chains slung between towers or pylons. *Stay-suspension* or *stay-cantilever*: supported by diagonal stays from towers or pylons. *See also* Bascule.

BRISES-SOLEIL: projecting fins or canopies which deflect direct sunlight from windows.

BROACH: *see* Spire and 1C.

BUCRANIUM: ox skull used decoratively in classical friezes.

BULL-NOSED SILL: sill displaying a pronounced convex upper moulding.

BULLSEYE WINDOW: small oval window, set horizontally (cf. Oculus). Also called *œil de bœuf*.

BUTTRESS: vertical member projecting from a wall to stabilize it or to resist the lateral thrust of an arch, roof, or vault (1C, 2C). A *flying buttress* transmits the thrust to a heavy abutment by means of an arch or half-arch (1C).

CABLE OR ROPE MOULDING: originally Norman, like twisted strands of a rope.

CAMES: *see* Quarries.

CAMPANILE: free-standing bell-tower.

CANALS: *Flash lock*: removable weir or similar device through which boats pass on a flush of water. Predecessor of the *pound lock*: chamber with gates at each end allowing boats to float from one level to another. *Tidal gates*: single pair of lock gates allowing vessels to pass when the tide makes a level. *Balance beam*: beam projecting horizontally for opening and closing lock gates. *Roving bridge*: carrying a towing path from one bank to the other.

CANTILEVER: horizontal projection (e.g. step, canopy) supported by a downward force behind the fulcrum.

CAPITAL: head or crowning feature of a column or pilaster; for classical types *see* 3; for medieval types *see* 1b.

CARREL: compartment designed for individual work or study.

CARTOUCHE: classical tablet with ornate frame (4b).

CARYATIDS: female figures supporting an entablature; their male counterparts are *Atlantes* (*lit.* Atlas figures).

CASEMATE: vaulted chamber, with embrasures for defence, within a castle wall or projecting from it.

CASEMENT: side-hinged window.

CASTELLATED: with battlements (q.v.).

CAST IRON: hard and brittle, cast in a mould to the required shape.

Wrought iron is ductile, strong in tension, forged into decorative patterns or forged and rolled into e.g. bars, joists, boiler plates; *mild steel* is its modern equivalent, similar but stronger.

CATSLIDE: *See* 8a.

CAVETTO: concave classical moulding of quarter-round section (3f).

CELURE OR CEILURE: enriched area of roof above rood or altar.

CEMENT: *see* Concrete.

CENOTAPH (*lit.* empty tomb): funerary monument which is not a burying place.

CENTRING: wooden support for the building of an arch or vault, removed after completion.

CHAMFER (*lit.* corner-break): surface formed by cutting off a square edge or corner. For types of chamfers and *chamfer stops see* 6a. *See also* Double chamfer.

CHANCEL: part of the E end of a church set apart for the use of the officiating clergy.

CHANTRY CHAPEL: often attached to or within a church, endowed for the celebration of Masses principally for the soul of the founder.

CHEVET (*lit.* head): French term for chancel with ambulatory and radiating chapels.

CHEVRON: V-shape used in series or double series (later) on a Norman moulding (1a). Also (especially when on a single plane) called *zigzag*.

CHOIR: the part of a cathedral, monastic or collegiate church where services are sung.

CIBORIUM: a fixed canopy over an altar, usually vaulted and supported on four columns; cf. Baldacchino. Also a canopied shrine for the reserved sacrament.

CINQUEFOIL: *see* Foil.

CIST: stone-lined or slab-built grave.

CLADDING: external covering or skin applied to a structure, especially a framed one.

CLERESTORY: uppermost storey of the nave of a church, pierced by windows. Also high-level windows in secular buildings.

CLOSER: a brick cut to complete a bond (6e).

CLUSTER BLOCK: *see* Multi-storey.

COADE STONE: ceramic artificial stone made in Lambeth 1769–*c.*1840 by Eleanor Coade (†1821) and her associates.

COB: walling material of clay mixed with straw. Also called *pisé*.

COFFERING: arrangement of sunken panels (coffers), square or polygonal, decorating a ceiling, vault, or arch.

COGGING: a decorative course of bricks laid diagonally (6e). Cf. Dentilation.

COLLAR: *see* Roofs and 7.

COLLEGIATE CHURCH: endowed for the support of a college of priests.

COLONNADE: range of columns supporting an entablature. Cf. Arcade.

COLONNETTE: small medieval column or shaft.

COLOSSAL ORDER: *see* Giant order.

COLUMBARIUM: shelved, niched structure to house multiple burials.

COLUMN: a classical, upright structural member of round section with a shaft, a capital, and usually a base (3a, 4a).

COLUMN FIGURE: carved figure attached to a medieval column or shaft, usually flanking a doorway.

COMMUNION TABLE: unconsecrated table used in Protestant churches for the celebration of Holy Communion.

COMPOSITE: *see* Orders.

COMPOUND PIER: grouped shafts (q.v.), or a solid core surrounded by shafts.

CONCRETE: composition of *cement* (calcined lime and clay), *aggregate* (small stones or rock chippings), sand and water. It can be poured into *formwork* or *shuttering* (temporary frame of timber or metal) on site (*in-situ* concrete), or *pre-cast* as components before construction. *Reinforced*: incorporating steel rods to take the tensile force. *Pre-stressed*: with tensioned steel rods. Finishes include the impression of boards left by formwork (*board-marked* or *shuttered*), and texturing with steel brushes (*brushed*) or hammers (*hammer-dressed*). *See also* Shell.

CONSOLE: bracket of curved outline (4b).

COPING: protective course of masonry or brickwork capping a wall (6d).

CORBEL: projecting block supporting something above. *Corbel course*: continuous course of projecting stones or bricks fulfilling the same function. *Corbel table*: series of corbels to carry a parapet or a wall-plate or wall-post (7). *Corbelling*: brick or masonry courses built out beyond one another to support a chimney-stack, window, etc.

CORINTHIAN: *see* Orders and 3d.

CORNICE: flat-topped ledge with moulded underside, projecting along the top of a building or feature, especially as the highest member of the classical entablature (3a). Also the decorative moulding in the angle between wall and ceiling.

CORPS-DE-LOGIS: the main building(s) as distinct from the wings or pavilions.

COTTAGE ORNÉ: an artfully rustic small house associated with the Picturesque movement.

COUNTERCHANGING: of joists on a ceiling divided by beams into compartments, when placed in opposite directions in alternate squares.

COUR D'HONNEUR: formal entrance court before a house in the French manner, usually with flanking wings and a screen wall or gates.

COURSE: continuous layer of stones, etc. in a wall (6e).

COVE: a broad concave moulding, e.g. to mask the eaves of a roof. *Coved ceiling*: with a pronounced cove joining the walls to a flat central panel smaller than the whole area of the ceiling.

CRADLE ROOF: *see* Wagon roof.

CREDENCE: a shelf within or beside a piscina (q.v.), or a table for the sacramental elements and vessels.

CRENELLATION: parapet with crenels (*see* Battlement).

CRINKLE-CRANKLE WALL: garden wall undulating in a series of serpentine curves.

CROCKETS: leafy hooks. *Crocketing* decorates the edges of Gothic features, such as pinnacles, canopies, etc. *Crocket capital*: *see* 1b.

CROSSING: central space at the junction of the nave, chancel, and transepts. *Crossing tower*: above a crossing.

CROSS-WINDOW: with one mullion and one transom (qq.v.).

CROWN-POST: *see* Roofs and 7.

CROWSTEPS: squared stones set like steps, e.g. on a gable (8a).

CRUCKS (*lit.* crooked): pairs of inclined timbers (*blades*), usually curved, set at bay-lengths; they support the roof timbers and, in timber buildings, also support the walls (8b). *Base*: blades rise from ground level to a tie- or collar-beam which supports the roof timbers. *Full*: blades rise from ground level to the apex of the roof, serving as the main members of a roof truss. *Jointed*: blades formed from more than one timber; the lower member may act as a wall-post; it is usually elbowed at wall-plate level and jointed just above. *Middle*: blades rise from half-way up the walls to a tie- or collar-beam. *Raised*: blades rise from half-way up the walls to the apex. *Upper*: blades supported on a tie-beam and rising to the apex.

CRYPT: underground or half-underground area, usually below the E end of a church. *Ring crypt*: corridor crypt surrounding the apse of an early medieval church, often associated with chambers for relics. Cf. Undercroft.

CUPOLA (*lit.* dome): especially a small dome on a circular or polygonal base crowning a larger dome, roof, or turret.

CURSUS: a long avenue defined by two parallel earthen banks with ditches outside.

CURTAIN WALL: a connecting wall between the towers of a castle. Also a non-load-bearing external wall applied to a C20 framed structure.

CUSP: *see* Tracery and 2b.

CYCLOPEAN MASONRY: large irregular polygonal stones, smooth and finely jointed.

CYMA RECTA and CYMA REVERSA: classical mouldings with double curves (3f). Cf. Ogee.

DADO: the finishing (often with panelling) of the lower part of a wall in a classical interior; in origin a formalized continuous pedestal. *Dado rail*: the moulding along the top of the dado.

DAGGER: *see* Tracery and 2b.

DALLE-DE-VERRE (*lit.* glass-slab): a late C20 stained-glass technique, setting large, thick pieces of cast glass into a frame of reinforced concrete or epoxy resin.

DEC (DECORATED): English Gothic architecture *c.* 1290 to *c.* 1350. The name is derived from the type of window tracery (q.v.) used during the period.

DEMI- or HALF-COLUMNS: engaged columns (q.v.) half of whose circumference projects from the wall.

DENTIL: small square block used in series in classical cornices (3c). *Dentilation* is produced by the projection of alternating headers along cornices or stringcourses.

DIAPER: repetitive surface decoration of lozenges or squares flat or in relief. Achieved in brickwork with bricks of two colours.

DIOCLETIAN OR THERMAL WINDOW: semicircular with two mullions, as used in the Baths of Diocletian, Rome (4b).

DISTYLE: having two columns (4a).

DOGTOOTH: E.E. ornament, consisting of a series of small pyramids formed by four stylized canine teeth meeting at a point (1a).

DORIC: *see* Orders and 3a, 3b.

DORMER: window projecting from the slope of a roof (8a).

DOUBLE CHAMFER: a chamfer applied to each of two recessed arches (1a).

DOUBLE PILE: *see* Pile.

DRAGON BEAM: *see* Jetty.

DRESSINGS: the stone or brickwork worked to a finished face about an angle, opening, or other feature.

DRIPSTONE: moulded stone projecting from a wall to protect the lower parts from water. Cf. Hoodmould, Weathering.

DRUM: circular or polygonal stage supporting a dome or cupola. Also one of the stones forming the shaft of a column (3a).

DUTCH or FLEMISH GABLE: *see* 8a.

EASTER SEPULCHRE: tomb-chest used for Easter ceremonial, within or against the N wall of a chancel.

EAVES: overhanging edge of a roof; hence *eaves cornice* in this position.

ECHINUS: ovolo moulding (q.v.) below the abacus of a Greek Doric capital (3a).

EDGE RAIL: *see* Railways.

E.E. (EARLY ENGLISH): English Gothic architecture *c.* 1190–1250.

EGG-AND-DART: *see* Enrichments and 3f.

ELEVATION: any face of a building or side of a room. In a drawing, the same or any part of it, represented in two dimensions.

EMBATTLED: with battlements.

EMBRASURE: small splayed opening in a wall or battlement (q.v.).

ENCAUSTIC TILES: earthenware tiles fired with a pattern and glaze.

EN DELIT: stone cut against the bed.

ENFILADE: reception rooms in a formal series, usually with all doorways on axis.

ENGAGED or ATTACHED COLUMN: one that partly merges into a wall or pier.

ENGINEERING BRICKS: dense bricks, originally used mostly for railway viaducts etc.

ENRICHMENTS: the carved decoration of certain classical mouldings, e.g. the ovolo (qq.v.) with *egg-and-dart*, the cyma reversa with *waterleaf*, the astragal with *bead-and-reel* (3f).

ENTABLATURE: in classical architecture, collective name for the three horizontal members (architrave, frieze, and cornice) carried by a wall or a column (3a).

ENTASIS: very slight convex deviation from a straight line, used to prevent an optical illusion of concavity.

EPITAPH: inscription on a tomb.

EXEDRA: *see* Apse.

EXTRADOS: outer curved face of an arch or vault.

EYECATCHER: decorative building terminating a vista.

FASCIA: plain horizontal band, e.g. in an architrave (3c, 3d) or on a shopfront.

FENESTRATION: the arrangement of windows in a façade.

FERETORY: site of the chief shrine of a church, behind the high altar.

FESTOON: ornamental garland, suspended from both ends. Cf. Swag.

FIBREGLASS, or glass-reinforced polyester (GRP): synthetic resin reinforced with glass fibre. GRC: glass-reinforced concrete.

FIELD: *see* Panelling and 6b.

FILLET: a narrow flat band running down a medieval shaft or along a roll moulding (1a). It separates larger curved mouldings in classical cornices, fluting or bases (3c).

FLAMBOYANT: the latest phase of French Gothic architecture, with flowing tracery.

FLASH LOCK: *see* Canals.

FLÈCHE or SPIRELET (*lit.* arrow): slender spire on the centre of a roof.

FLEURON: medieval carved flower or leaf, often rectilinear (1a).

FLUSHWORK: knapped flint used with dressed stone to form patterns.

FLUTING: series of concave grooves (flutes), their common edges sharp (arris) or blunt (fillet) (3).

FOIL (*lit.* leaf): lobe formed by the cusping of a circular or other shape in tracery (2b). *Trefoil* (three), *quatrefoil* (four), *cinquefoil* (five), and *multifoil* express the number of lobes in a shape.

FOLIATE: decorated with leaves.

FORMWORK: *see* Concrete.

FRAMED BUILDING: where the structure is carried by a framework – e.g. of steel, reinforced concrete, timber – instead of by load-bearing walls.

FREESTONE: stone that is cut, or can be cut, in all directions.

FRESCO: *al fresco*: painting on wet plaster. *Fresco secco*: painting on dry plaster.

FRIEZE: the middle member of the classical entablature, sometimes ornamented (3a). *Pulvinated frieze* (*lit.* cushioned): of bold convex profile (3c). Also a horizontal band of ornament.

FRONTISPIECE: in C16 and C17 buildings the central feature of doorway and windows above linked in one composition.

GABLE: For types *see* 8a. *Gablet*: small gable. *Pedimental gable*: treated like a pediment.

GADROONING: classical ribbed ornament like inverted fluting that flows into a lobed edge.

GALILEE: chapel or vestibule usually at the w end of a church enclosing the main portal(s).

GALLERY: a long room or passage; an upper storey above the aisle of a church, looking through arches to the nave; a balcony or mezzanine overlooking the main interior space of a building; or an external walkway.

GALLETING: small stones set in a mortar course.

GAMBREL ROOF: *see* 8a.

GARDEROBE: medieval privy.

GARGOYLE: projecting water spout often carved into human or animal shape.

GAUGED or RUBBED BRICKWORK: soft brick sawn roughly, then rubbed to a precise (gauged) surface. Mostly used for door or window openings (5c).

GAZEBO (jocular Latin, 'I shall gaze'): ornamental lookout tower or raised summer house.

GEOMETRIC: English Gothic architecture *c.* 1250–1310. *See also* Tracery. For another meaning, *see* Stairs.

GIANT or COLOSSAL ORDER: classical order (q.v.) whose height is that of two or more storeys of the building to which it is applied.

GIBBS SURROUND: C18 treatment of an opening (4b), seen particularly in the work of James Gibbs (1682–1754).

GIRDER: a large beam. *Box*: of hollow-box section. *Bowed*: with its top rising in a curve. *Plate*: of I-section, made from iron or steel plates. *Lattice*: with braced frame-work.

GLAZING BARS: wooden or some-times metal bars separating and supporting window panes.

GRAFFITI: *see* Sgraffito.

GRANGE: farm owned and run by a religious order.

GRC: *see* Fibreglass.

GRISAILLE: monochrome painting on walls or glass.

GROIN: sharp edge at the meeting of two cells of a cross-vault; *see* Vault and 2c.

GROTESQUE (*lit.* grotto-esque): wall decoration adopted from Roman examples in the Renaissance. Its foliage scrolls incorporate figur-ative elements. Cf. Arabesque.

GROTTO: artificial cavern.

GRP: *see* Fibreglass.

GUILLOCHE: classical ornament of interlaced bands (4b).

GUNLOOP: opening for a firearm.

GUTTAE: stylized drops (3b).

HALF-TIMBERING: archaic term for timber-framing (q.v.). Sometimes used for non-structural decorative timberwork.

HALL CHURCH: medieval church with nave and aisles of approxim-ately equal height.

HAMMERBEAM: *see* Roofs and 7.

HAMPER: in C20 architecture, a visu-ally distinct topmost storey or storeys.

HEADER: *see* Bond and 6e.

HEADSTOP: stop (q.v.) carved with a head (5b).

HELM ROOF: *see* IC.

HENGE: ritual earthwork.

HERM (*lit.* the god Hermes): male head or bust on a pedestal.

HERRINGBONE WORK: *see* 7ii. Cf. Pitched masonry.

HEXASTYLE: *see* Portico.

HILL-FORT: Iron Age earthwork en-closed by a ditch and bank system.

HIPPED ROOF: *see* 8a.

HOODMOULD: projecting moulding above an arch or lintel to throw off water (2b, 5b). When horizontal often called a *label*. For label stop *see* Stop.

HUSK GARLAND: festoon of stylized nutshells (4b).

HYDRAULIC POWER: use of water under high pressure to work machinery. *Accumulator tower*: houses a hydraulic accumulator which accommodates fluctuations in the flow through hydraulic mains.

HYPOCAUST (*lit.* underburning): Ro-man underfloor heating system.

IMPOST: horizontal moulding at the springing of an arch (5c).

IMPOST BLOCK: block between abacus and capital (1b).

IN ANTIS: *see* Antae, Portico and 4a.

INDENT: shape chiselled out of a stone to receive a brass.

INDUSTRIALIZED or SYSTEM BUILDING: system of manufac-tured units assembled on site.

INGLENOOK (*lit.* fire-corner): recess for a hearth with provision for seating.

INTERCOLUMNATION: interval be-tween columns.

INTERLACE: decoration in relief simulating woven or entwined stems or bands.

INTRADOS: *see* Soffit.

IONIC: *see* Orders and 3c.

JACK ARCH: shallow segmental vault springing from beams, used for fireproof floors, bridge decks, etc.

JAMB (*lit.* leg): one of the vertical sides of an opening.

JETTY: in a timber-framed building, the projection of an upper storey beyond the storey below, made by the beams and joists of the lower storey oversailing the wall; on their outer ends is placed the sill of the walling for the storey above (7). Buildings can be jettied on several sides, in which case a *dragon beam* is set diagonally at the corner to carry the joists to either side.

JOGGLE: the joining of two stones to prevent them slipping by a notch in one and a projection in the other.

KEEL MOULDING: moulding used from the late C12, in section like the keel of a ship (1a).

KEEP: principal tower of a castle.

KENTISH CUSP: *see* Tracery and 2b.

KEY PATTERN: see 4b.

KEYSTONE: central stone in an arch or vault (4b, 5c).

KINGPOST: see Roofs and 7.

KNEELER: horizontal projecting stone at the base of each side of a gable to support the inclined coping stones (8a).

LABEL: see Hoodmould and 5b.

LABEL STOP: see Stop and 5b.

LACED BRICKWORK: vertical strips of brickwork, often in a contrasting colour, linking openings on different floors.

LACING COURSE: horizontal reinforcement in timber or brick to walls of flint, cobble, etc.

LADY CHAPEL: dedicated to the Virgin Mary (Our Lady).

LANCET: slender single-light, pointed-arched window (2a).

LANTERN: circular or polygonal windowed turret crowning a roof or a dome. Also the windowed stage of a crossing tower lighting the church interior.

LANTERN CROSS: churchyard cross with lantern-shaped top.

LAVATORIUM: in a religious house, a washing place adjacent to the refectory.

LEAN-TO: see Roofs.

LESENE (lit. a mean thing): pilaster without base or capital. Also called pilaster strip.

LIERNE: see Vault and 2c.

LIGHT: compartment of a window defined by the mullions.

LINENFOLD: Tudor panelling carved with simulations of folded linen. See also Parchemin.

LINTEL: horizontal beam or stone bridging an opening.

LOGGIA: gallery, usually arcaded or colonnaded; sometimes free-standing.

LONG-AND-SHORT WORK: quoins consisting of stones placed with the long side alternately upright and horizontal, especially in Saxon building.

LONGHOUSE: house and byre in the same range with internal access between them.

LOUVRE: roof opening, often protected by a raised timber structure, to allow the smoke from a central hearth to escape.

LOWSIDE WINDOW: set lower than the others in a chancel side wall, usually towards its w end.

LUCAM: projecting housing for hoist pulley on upper storey of warehouses, mills, etc., for raising goods to loading doors.

LUCARNE (lit. dormer): small gabled opening in a roof or spire.

LUGGED ARCHITRAVE: see 4b.

LUNETTE: semicircular window or blind panel.

LYCHGATE (lit. corpse-gate): roofed gateway entrance to a churchyard for the reception of a coffin.

LYNCHET: long terraced strip of soil on the downward side of pre-historic and medieval fields, accumulated because of continual ploughing along the contours.

MACHICOLATIONS (lit. mashing devices): series of openings between the corbels that support a projecting parapet through which missiles can be dropped. Used decoratively in post-medieval buildings.

MANOMETER or STANDPIPE TOWER: containing a column of water to regulate pressure in water mains.

MANSARD: see 8a.

MATHEMATICAL TILES: facing tiles with the appearance of brick, most often applied to timber-framed walls.

MAUSOLEUM: monumental building or chamber usually intended for the burial of members of one family.

MEGALITHIC TOMB: massive stone-built Neolithic burial chamber covered by an earth or stone mound.

MERLON: see Battlement.

METOPES: spaces between the triglyphs in a Doric frieze (3b).

MEZZANINE: low storey between two higher ones.

MILD STEEL: see Cast iron.

MISERICORD (lit. mercy): shelf on a carved bracket placed on the underside of a hinged choir stall seat to support an occupant when standing.

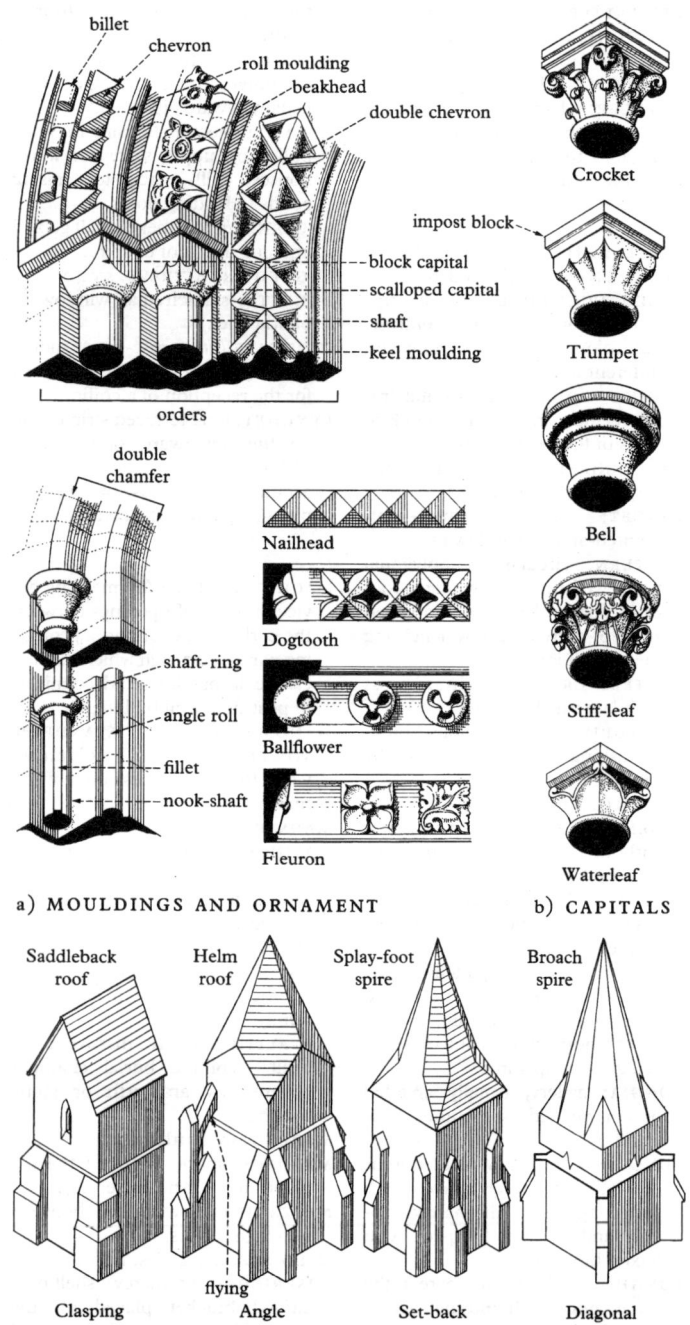

a) MOULDINGS AND ORNAMENT

b) CAPITALS

c) BUTTRESSES, ROOFS AND SPIRES

FIGURE I: MEDIEVAL

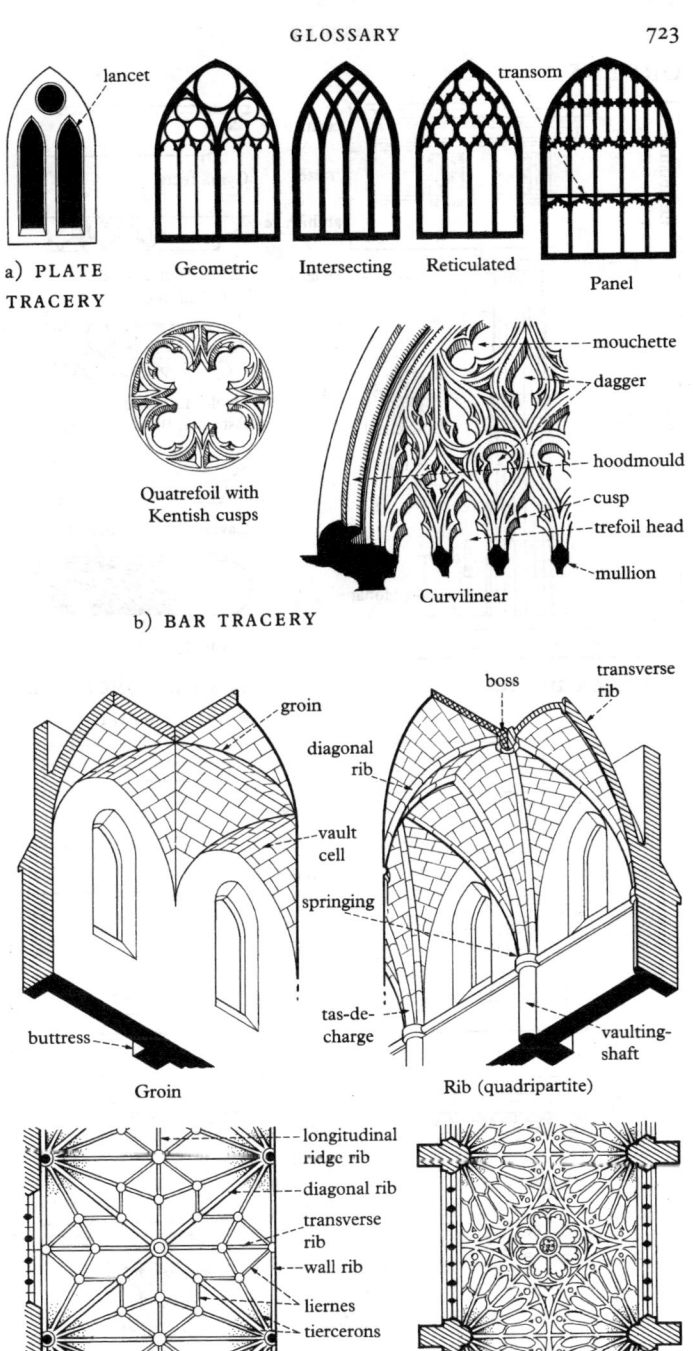

a) PLATE TRACERY

Geometric   Intersecting   Reticulated   Panel

Quatrefoil with Kentish cusps

Curvilinear

b) BAR TRACERY

Groin

Rib (quadripartite)

Lierne

Fan

c) VAULTS

FIGURE 2: MEDIEVAL

ORDERS

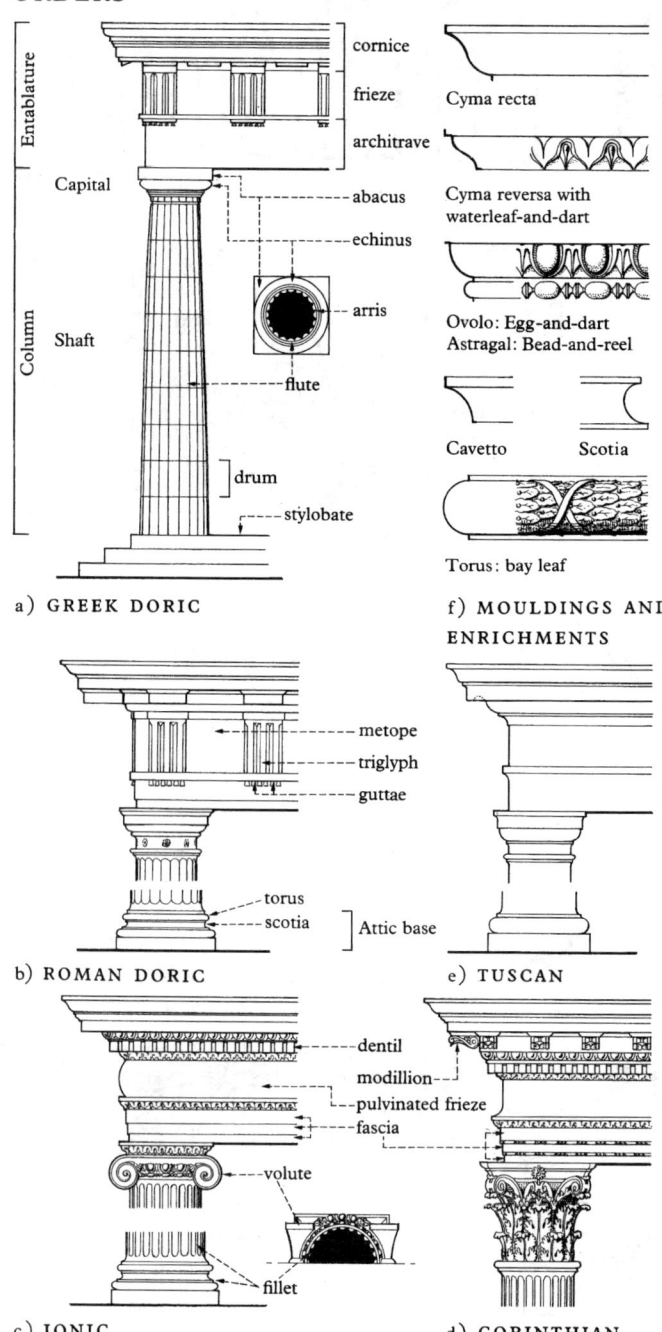

Cyma recta

Cyma reversa with
waterleaf-and-dart

Ovolo: Egg-and-dart
Astragal: Bead-and-reel

Cavetto   Scotia

Torus: bay leaf

a) GREEK DORIC

f) MOULDINGS AND
ENRICHMENTS

b) ROMAN DORIC

e) TUSCAN

c) IONIC

d) CORINTHIAN

FIGURE 3: CLASSICAL

a) PORTICO

Distyle in antis   Prostyle

Anthemion & Palmette   Guilloche   Key pattern

Rinceau   Husk garland   Vitruvian scroll

Console   Diocletian window   Acanthus

Broken pediment

Segmental pediment

Venetian window

Lugged architrave

Shouldered architrave

Open pediment   Swan-neck pediment   Gibbs surround

b) ORNAMENTS AND FEATURES

FIGURE 4: CLASSICAL

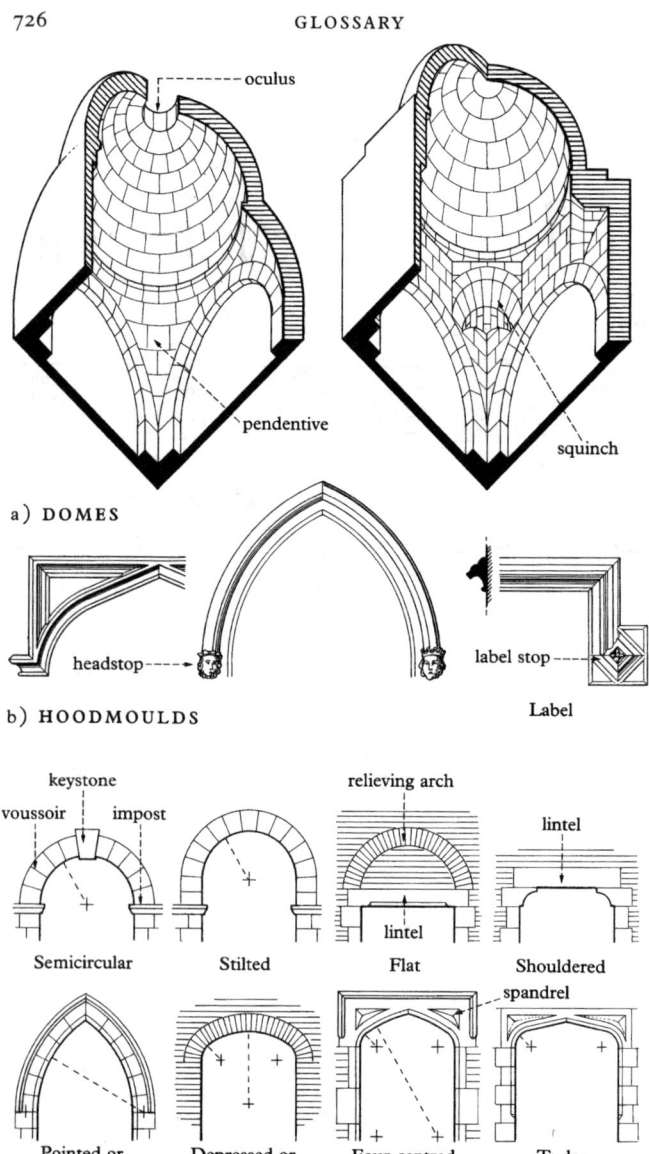

a) DOMES

b) HOODMOULDS

Label

c) ARCHES

FIGURE 5: CONSTRUCTION

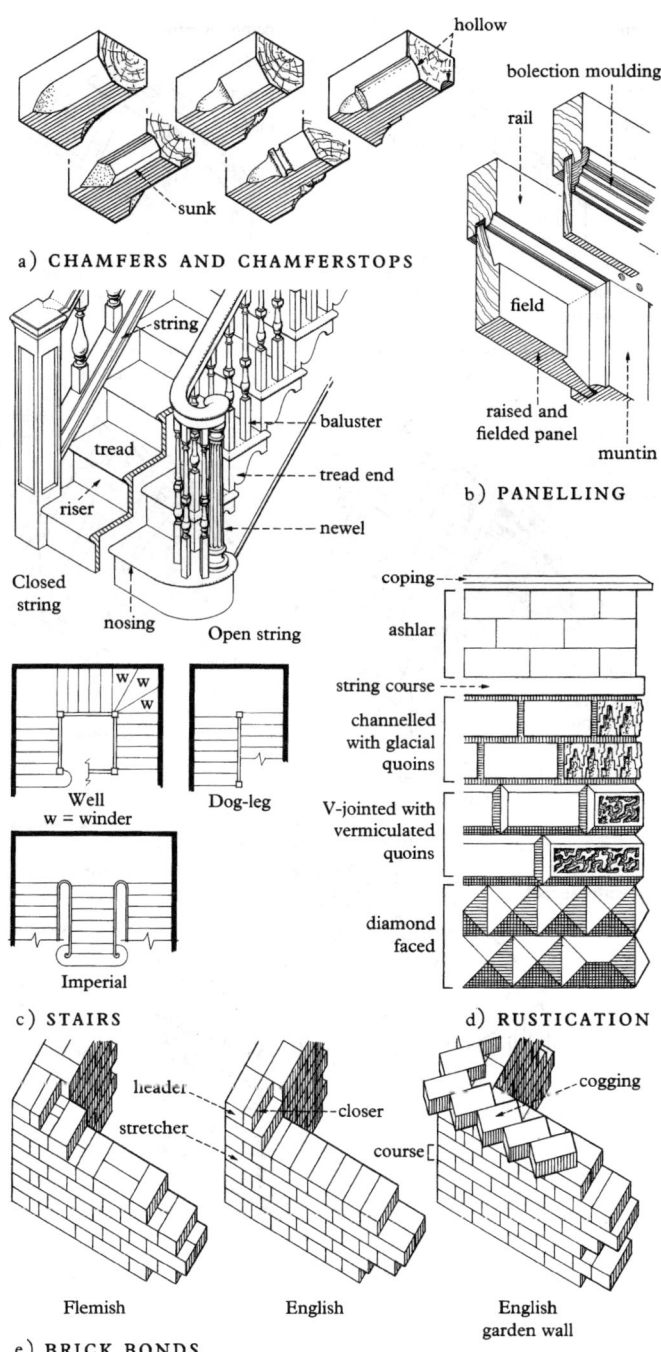

a) CHAMFERS AND CHAMFERSTOPS

hollow

bolection moulding

rail

field

raised and
fielded panel

muntin

b) PANELLING

string

baluster

tread

tread end

riser

newel

Closed
string

nosing   Open string

Well
w = winder

Dog-leg

Imperial

c) STAIRS

coping

ashlar

string course

channelled
with glacial
quoins

V-jointed with
vermiculated
quoins

diamond
faced

d) RUSTICATION

header

closer

stretcher

course

cogging

Flemish   English   English
garden wall

e) BRICK BONDS

FIGURE 6: CONSTRUCTION

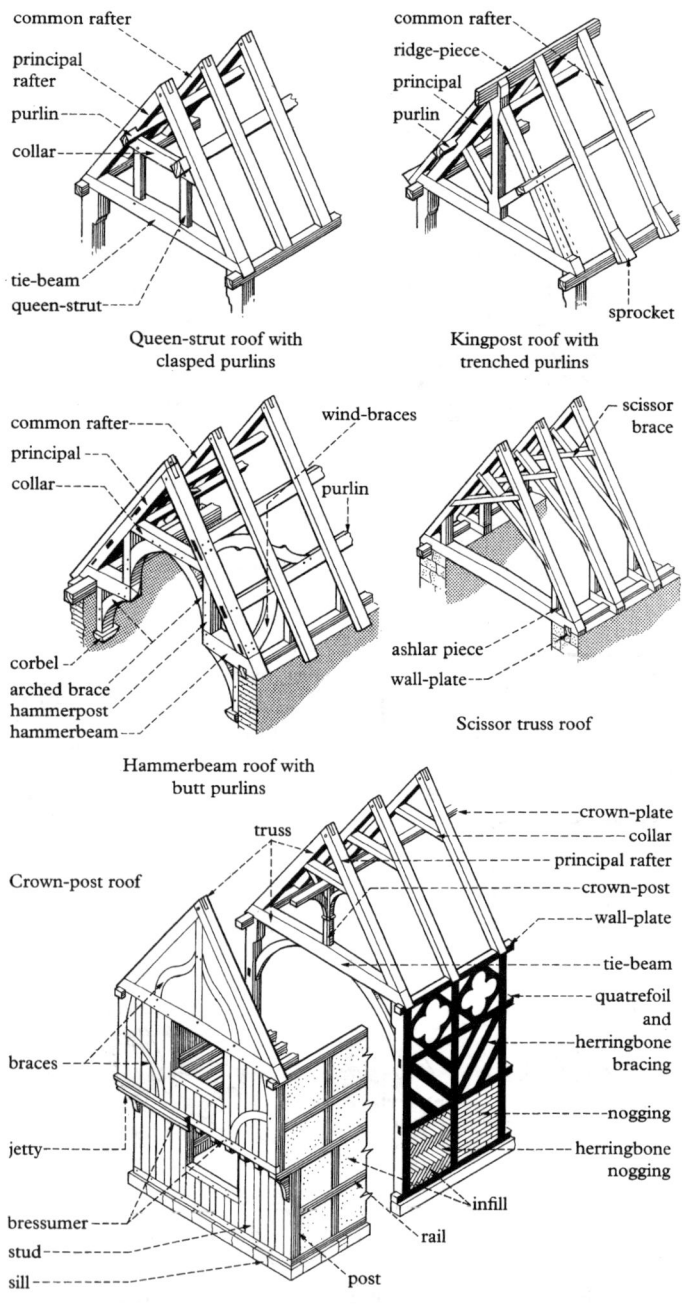

Queen-strut roof with
clasped purlins

- common rafter
- principal rafter
- purlin
- collar
- tie-beam
- queen-strut

Kingpost roof with
trenched purlins

- common rafter
- ridge-piece
- principal
- purlin
- sprocket

Hammerbeam roof with
butt purlins

- common rafter
- principal
- collar
- wind-braces
- purlin
- corbel
- arched brace
- hammerpost
- hammerbeam

Scissor truss roof

- scissor brace
- ashlar piece
- wall-plate

Crown-post roof

- truss
- crown-plate
- collar
- principal rafter
- crown-post
- wall-plate
- tie-beam
- quatrefoil and herringbone bracing
- nogging
- herringbone nogging
- braces
- jetty
- bressumer
- stud
- sill
- infill
- rail
- post

Box frame: i) Close studding   ii) Square panel

FIGURE 7: ROOFS AND TIMBER-FRAMING

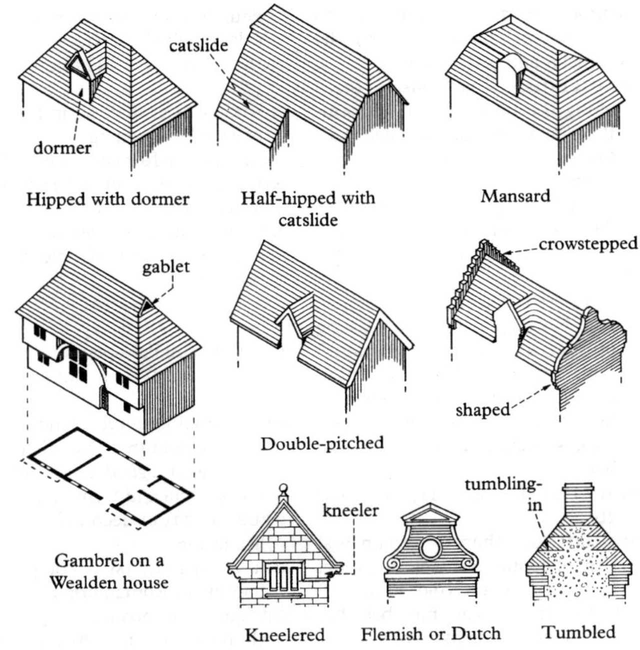

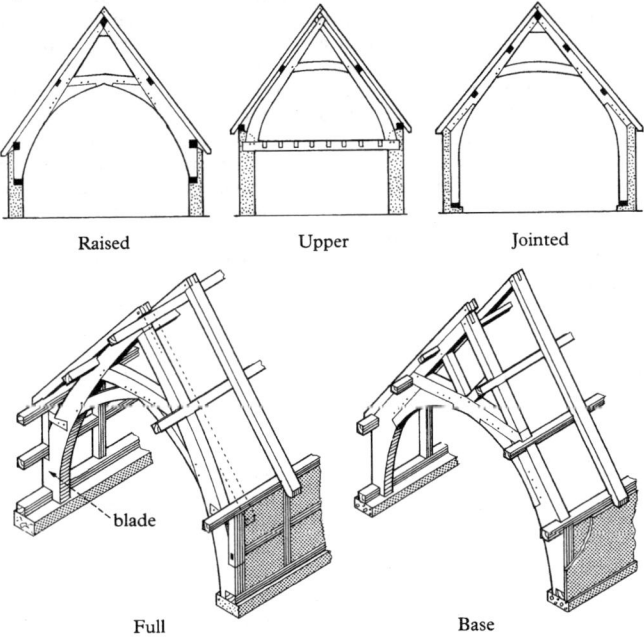

catslide
dormer
Hipped with dormer
Half-hipped with catslide
Mansard
gablet
crowstepped
shaped
Double-pitched
tumbling-in
kneeler
Gambrel on a Wealden house
Kneelered
Flemish or Dutch
Tumbled

a) ROOF FORMS AND GABLES

Raised
Upper
Jointed
blade
Full
Base

b) CRUCK FRAMES

FIGURE 8: ROOFS AND TIMBER-FRAMING

MIXER-COURTS: forecourts to groups of houses shared by vehicles and pedestrians.

MODILLIONS: small consoles (q.v.) along the underside of a Corinthian or Composite cornice (3d). Often used along an eaves cornice.

MODULE: a predetermined standard size for co-ordinating the dimensions of components of a building.

MOTTE-AND-BAILEY: post-Roman and Norman defence consisting of an earthen mound (motte) topped by a wooden tower within a bailey, an enclosure defended by a ditch and palisade, and also, sometimes, by an internal bank.

MOUCHETTE: see Tracery and 2b.

MOULDING: shaped ornamental strip of continuous section; see e.g. Cavetto, Cyma, Ovolo, Roll.

MULLION: vertical member between window lights (2b).

MULTI-STOREY: five or more storeys. Multi-storey flats may form a *cluster block*, with individual blocks of flats grouped round a service core; a *point block*, with flats fanning out from a service core; or a *slab block*, with flats approached by corridors or galleries from service cores at intervals or towers at the ends (plan also used for offices, hotels etc.). *Tower block* is a generic term for any very high multi-storey building.

MUNTIN: see Panelling and 6b.

NAILHEAD: E.E. ornament consisting of small pyramids regularly repeated (1a).

NARTHEX: enclosed vestibule or covered porch at the main entrance to a church.

NAVE: the body of a church w of the crossing or chancel often flanked by aisles (q.v.).

NEWEL: central or corner post of a staircase (6c). Newel stair: see Stairs.

NIGHT STAIR: stair by which religious entered the transept of their church from their dormitory to celebrate night services.

NOGGING: see Timber-framing (7).

NOOK-SHAFT: shaft set in the angle of a wall or opening (1a).

NORMAN: see Romanesque.

NOSING: projection of the tread of a step (6c).

NUTMEG: medieval ornament with a chain of tiny triangles placed obliquely.

OCULUS: circular opening.

ŒIL DE BŒUF: see Bullseye window.

OGEE: double curve, bending first one way and then the other, as in an *ogee* or *ogival arch* (5c). Cf. Cyma recta and Cyma reversa.

OPUS SECTILE: decorative mosaic-like facing.

OPUS SIGNINUM: composition flooring of Roman origin.

ORATORY: a private chapel in a church or a house. Also a church of the Oratorian Order.

ORDER: one of a series of recessed arches and jambs forming a splayed medieval opening, e.g. a doorway or arcade arch (1a).

ORDERS: the formalized versions of the post-and-lintel system in classical architecture. The main orders are *Doric*, *Ionic*, and *Corinthian*. They are Greek in origin but occur in Roman versions. Tuscan is a simple version of Roman Doric. Though each order has its own conventions (3), there are many minor variations. The *Composite* capital combines Ionic volutes with Corinthian foliage. *Superimposed orders*: orders on successive levels, usually in the upward sequence of Tuscan, Doric, Ionic, Corinthian, Composite.

ORIEL: see Bay window.

OVERDOOR: painting or relief above an internal door. Also called a *sopraporta*.

OVERTHROW: decorative fixed arch between two gatepiers or above a wrought-iron gate.

OVOLO: wide convex moulding (3f).

PALIMPSEST: of a brass: where a metal plate has been reused by turning over the engraving on the back; of a wall painting: where one overlaps and partly obscures an earlier one.

PALLADIAN: following the examples and principles of Andrea Palladio (1508–80).

PALMETTE: classical ornament like a palm shoot (4b).

PANELLING: wooden lining to interior walls, made up of vertical members (*muntins*) and horizontals (*rails*) framing panels: also called *wainscot*. *Raised and fielded*: with the central area of the panel (*field*) raised up (6b).

PANTILE: roof tile of S section.

PARAPET: wall for protection at any sudden drop, e.g. at the wall-head of a castle where it protects the *parapet walk* or wall-walk. Also used to conceal a roof.

PARCLOSE: *see* Screen.

PARGETTING (*lit.* plastering): exterior plaster decoration, either in relief or incised.

PARLOUR: in a religious house, a room where the religious could talk to visitors; in a medieval house, the semi-private living room below the solar (q.v.).

PARTERRE: level space in a garden laid out with low, formal beds.

PATERA (*lit.* plate): round or oval ornament in shallow relief.

PAVILION: ornamental building for occasional use; or projecting subdivision of a larger building, often at an angle or terminating a wing.

PEBBLEDASHING: *see* Rendering.

PEDESTAL: a tall block carrying a classical order, statue, vase, etc.

PEDIMENT: a formalized gable derived from that of a classical temple; also used over doors, windows, etc. For variations *see* 4b.

PENDENTIVE: spandrel between adjacent arches, supporting a drum, dome or vault and consequently formed as part of a hemisphere (5a).

PENTHOUSE: subsidiary structure with a lean-to roof. Also a

separately roofed structure on top of a C20 multi-storey block.

PERIPTERAL: *see* Peristyle.

PERISTYLE: a colonnade all round the exterior of a classical building, as in a temple which is then said to be *peripteral*.

PERP (PERPENDICULAR): English Gothic architecture *c.* 1335–50 to *c.* 1530. The name is derived from the upright tracery panels then used (*see* Tracery and 2a).

PERRON: external stair to a doorway, usually of double-curved plan.

PEW: loosely, seating for the laity outside the chancel; strictly, an enclosed seat. *Box pew*: with equal high sides and a door.

PIANO NOBILE: principal floor of a classical building above a ground floor or basement and with a lesser storey overhead.

PIAZZA: formal urban open space surrounded by buildings.

PIER: large masonry or brick support, often for an arch. *See also* Compound pier.

PILASTER: flat representation of a classical column in shallow relief. *Pilaster strip*: *see* Lesene.

PILE: row of rooms. *Double pile*: two rows thick.

PILLAR: free-standing upright member of any section, not conforming to one of the orders (q.v.).

PILLAR PISCINA: *see* Piscina.

PILOTIS: C20 French term for pillars or stilts that support a building above an open ground floor.

PISCINA: basin for washing Mass vessels, provided with a drain; set in or against the wall to the S of an altar or free-standing (*pillar piscina*).

PISÉ: *see* Cob.

PITCHED MASONRY: laid on the diagonal, often alternately with opposing courses (*pitched and counterpitched* or *herringbone*).

PLATBAND: flat horizontal moulding between storeys. Cf. stringcourse.

PLATE RAIL: *see* Railways.

PLATEWAY: *see* Railways.

PLINTH: projecting courses at the

foot of a wall or column, generally chamfered or moulded at the top.

PODIUM: a continuous raised platform supporting a building; or a large block of two or three storeys beneath a multi-storey block of smaller area.

POINT BLOCK: *see* Multi-storey.

POINTING: exposed mortar jointing of masonry or brickwork. Types include *flush*, *recessed* and *tuck* (with a narrow channel filled with finer, whiter mortar).

POPPYHEAD: carved ornament of leaves and flowers as a finial for a bench end or stall.

PORTAL FRAME: C20 frame comprising two uprights rigidly connected to a beam or pair of rafters.

PORTCULLIS: gate constructed to rise and fall in vertical grooves at the entry to a castle.

PORTICO: a porch with the roof and frequently a pediment supported by a row of columns (4a). A portico *in antis* has columns on the same plane as the front of the building. A *prostyle* porch has columns standing free. Porticoes are described by the number of front columns, e.g. tetrastyle (four), hexastyle (six). The space within the temple is the *naos*, that within the portico the *pronaos*. *Blind portico*: the front features of a portico applied to a wall.

PORTICUS (plural: *porticūs*): subsidiary cell opening from the main body of a pre-Conquest church.

POST: upright support in a structure (7).

POSTERN: small gateway at the back of a building or to the side of a larger entrance door or gate.

POUND LOCK: *see* Canals.

PRESBYTERY: the part of a church lying E of the choir where the main altar is placed; or a priest's residence.

PRINCIPAL: *see* Roofs and 7.

PRONAOS: *see* Portico and 4a.

PROSTYLE: *see* Portico and 4a.

PULPIT: raised and enclosed platform for the preaching of sermons. *Three-decker*: with reading desk below and clerk's desk below that. *Two-decker*: as above, minus the clerk's desk.

PULPITUM: stone screen in a major church dividing choir from nave.

PULVINATED: *see* Frieze and 3c.

PURLIN: *see* Roofs and 7.

PUTHOLES or PUTLOG HOLES: in the wall to receive putlogs, the horizontal timbers which support scaffolding boards; sometimes not filled after construction is complete.

PUTTO (plural: putti): small naked boy.

QUARRIES: square (or diamond) panes of glass supported by lead strips (*cames*); square floor slabs or tiles.

QUATREFOIL: *see* Foil and 2b.

QUEEN-STRUT: *see* Roofs and 7.

QUIRK: sharp groove to one side of a convex medieval moulding.

QUOINS: dressed stones at the angles of a building (6d).

RADBURN SYSTEM: vehicle and pedestrian segregation in residential developments, based on that used at Radburn, New Jersey, USA, by Wright and Stein, 1928–30.

RADIATING CHAPELS: projecting radially from an ambulatory or an apse (*see* Chevet).

RAFTER: *see* Roofs and 7.

RAGGLE: groove cut in masonry, especially to receive the edge of a roof-covering.

RAGULY: ragged (in heraldry). Also applied to funerary sculpture, e.g. *cross raguly*: with a notched outline.

RAIL: *see* Panelling and 6b; also 7.

RAILWAYS: *Edge rail*: on which flanged wheels can run. *Plate rail*: L-section rail for plain unflanged wheels. *Plateway*: early railway using plate rails.

RAISED AND FIELDED: *see* Panelling and 6b.

RAKE: slope or pitch.

RAMPART: defensive outer wall of stone or earth. *Rampart walk*: path along the inner face.

REBATE: rectangular section cut out of a masonry edge to receive a shutter, door, window, etc.

REBUS: a heraldic pun, e.g. a fiery cock for Cockburn.

REEDING: series of convex mouldings, the reverse of fluting (q.v.). Cf. Gadrooning.

RENDERING: the covering of outside walls with a uniform surface or skin for protection from the weather. *Limewashing*: thin layer of lime plaster. *Pebbledashing*: where aggregate is thrown at the wet plastered wall for a textured effect. *Roughcast*: plaster mixed with a coarse aggregate such as gravel. *Stucco*: fine lime plaster worked to a smooth surface. *Cement rendering*: a cheaper substitute for stucco, usually with a grainy texture.

REPOUSSÉ: relief designs in metalwork, formed by beating it from the back.

REREDORTER (*lit.* behind the dormitory): latrines in a medieval religious house.

REREDOS: painted and/or sculptured screen behind and above an altar. Cf. Retable.

RESPOND: half-pier or half-column bonded into a wall and carrying one end of an arch. It usually terminates an arcade.

RETABLE: painted or carved panel standing on or at the back of an altar, usually attached to it.

RETROCHOIR: in a major church, the area between the high altar and E chapel.

REVEAL: the plane of a jamb, between the wall and the frame of a door or window.

RIB-VAULT: *see* Vault and 2c.

RINCEAU: classical ornament of leafy scrolls (4b).

RISER: vertical face of a step (6c).

ROACH: a rough-textured form of Portland stone, with small cavities and fossil shells.

ROCK-FACED: masonry cleft to produce a rugged appearance.

ROCOCO: style current *c.* 1720 and *c.* 1760, characterized by a serpentine line and playful, scrolled decoration.

ROLL MOULDING: medieval moulding of part-circular section (1a).

ROMANESQUE: style current in the CII and CI2. In England often called Norman. *See also* Saxo-Norman.

ROOD: crucifix flanked by the Virgin and St John, usually over the entry into the chancel, on a beam (*rood beam*) or painted on the wall. The *rood screen* below often had a walkway (*rood loft*) along the top, reached by a *rood stair* in the side wall.

ROOFS: Shape. For the main external shapes (hipped, mansard, etc.) see 8a. *Helm* and *Saddleback*: *see* 1C. *Lean-to*: single sloping roof built against a vertical wall; lean-to is also applied to the part of the building beneath.
Construction. *See* 7.
Single-framed roof: with no main trusses. The rafters may be fixed to the wall-plate or ridge, or longitudinal timber may be absent altogether.
Double-framed roof: with longitudinal members, such as purlins, and usually divided into bays by principals and principal rafters. Other types are named after their main structural components, e.g. *hammerbeam*, *crown-post* (*see* Elements below and 7).
Elements. *See* 7.
Ashlar piece: a short vertical timber connecting inner wall-plate or timber pad to a rafter.
Braces: subsidiary timbers set diagonally to strengthen the frame. *Arched braces*: curved pair forming an arch, connecting wall or post below with tie- or collar-beam above. *Passing braces*: long straight braces passing across other members of the truss. *Scissor braces*: pair crossing diagonally between pairs of rafters or principals. *Wind-braces*: short, usually curved braces connecting side purlins with principals; sometimes decorated with cusping.
Collar or *collar-beam*: horizontal transverse timber connecting a pair of rafter or cruck blades (q.v.), set between apex and the wall-plate.
Crown-post: a vertical timber set centrally on a tie-beam and supporting a collar purlin braced to it longitudinally. In an open truss

lateral braces may rise to the collar-beam; in a closed truss they may descend to the tie-beam.

Hammerbeams: horizontal brackets projecting at wall-plate level like an interrupted tie-beam; the inner ends carry *hammerposts*, vertical timbers which support a purlin and are braced to a collar-beam above.

Kingpost: vertical timber set centrally on a tie- or collar-beam, rising to the apex of the roof to support a ridge-piece (cf. Strut).

Plate: longitudinal timber set square to the ground. *Wall-plate*: plate along the top of a wall which receives the ends of the rafters; cf. Purlin.

Principals: pair of inclined lateral timbers of a truss. Usually they support side purlins and mark the main bay divisions.

Purlin: horizontal longitudinal timber. *Collar purlin* or *crown plate*: central timber which carries collar-beams and is supported by crown-posts. *Side purlins*: pairs of timbers placed some way up the slope of the roof, which carry common rafters. *Butt* or *tenoned purlins* are tenoned into either side of the principals. *Through purlins* pass through or past the principal; they include *clasped purlins*, which rest on queenposts or are carried in the angle between principals and collar, and *trenched purlins* trenched into the backs of principals.

Queen-strut: paired vertical, or near-vertical, timbers placed symmetrically on a tie-beam to support side purlins.

Rafters: inclined lateral timbers supporting the roof covering. *Common rafters*: regularly spaced uniform rafters placed along the length of a roof or between principals. *Principal rafters*: rafters which also act as principals.

Ridge, ridge-piece: horizontal longitudinal timber at the apex supporting the ends of the rafters.

Sprocket: short timber placed on the back and at the foot of a rafter to form projecting eaves.

Strut: vertical or oblique timber between two members of a truss, not directly supporting longitudinal timbers.

Tie-beam: main horizontal transverse timber which carries the feet of the principals at wall level.

Truss: rigid framework of timbers at bay intervals, carrying the longitudinal roof timbers which support the common rafters.

Closed truss: with the spaces between the timbers filled, to form an internal partition.

See also Cruck, Wagon roof.

ROPE MOULDING: *see* Cable moulding.

ROSE WINDOW: circular window with tracery radiating from the centre. Cf. Wheel window.

ROTUNDA: building or room circular in plan.

ROUGHCAST: *see* Rendering.

ROVING BRIDGE: *see* Canals.

RUBBED BRICKWORK: *see* Gauged brickwork.

RUBBLE: masonry whose stones are wholly or partly in a rough state. *Coursed*: coursed stones with rough faces. *Random*: uncoursed stones in a random pattern. *Snecked*: with courses broken by smaller stones (snecks).

RUSTICATION: *see* 6d. Exaggerated treatment of masonry to give an effect of strength. The joints are usually recessed by V-section chamfering or square-section channelling (*channelled rustication*). *Banded rustication* has only the horizontal joints emphasized. The faces may be flat, but can be *diamond-faced*, like shallow pyramids, *vermiculated*, with a stylized texture like worm-casts, and *glacial* (frost-work), like icicles or stalactites.

SACRISTY: room in a church for sacred vessels and vestments.

SADDLEBACK ROOF: *see* 1C.

SALTIRE CROSS: with diagonal limbs.

SANCTUARY: area around the main altar of a church. Cf. Presbytery.

SANGHA: residence of Buddhist monks or nuns.

SARCOPHAGUS: coffin of stone or other durable material.

SAXO-NORMAN: transitional Romanesque style combining Anglo-Saxon and Norman features, current *c.* 1060–1100.

SCAGLIOLA: composition imitating marble.

SCALLOPED CAPITAL: *see* 1a.

SCOTIA: a hollow classical moulding, especially between tori (q.v.) on a column base (3b, 3f).

SCREEN: in a medieval church, usually at the entry to the chancel; *see* Rood (screen) and Pulpitum. A *parclose screen* separates a chapel from the rest of the church.

SCREENS or SCREENS PASSAGE: screened-off entrance passage between great hall and service rooms.

SECTION: two-dimensional representation of a building, moulding, etc., revealed by cutting across it.

SEDILIA (singular: sedile): seats for the priests (usually three) on the S side of the chancel.

SET-OFF: *see* Weathering.

SETTS: squared stones, usually of granite, used for paving or flooring.

SGRAFFITO: decoration scratched, often in plaster, to reveal a pattern in another colour beneath. *Graffiti*: scratched drawing or writing.

SHAFT: vertical member of round or polygonal section (1a, 3a). *Shaft-ring*: at the junction of shafts set *en delit* (q.v.) or attached to a pier or wall (1a).

SHEILA-NA-GIG: female fertility figure, usually with legs apart.

SHELL: thin, self-supporting roofing membrane of timber or concrete.

SHOULDERED ARCHITRAVE: *see* 4b.

SHUTTERING: *see* Concrete.

SILL: horizontal member at the bottom of a window or door frame; or at the base of a timber-framed wall into which posts and studs are tenoned (7).

SLAB BLOCK: *see* Multi-storey.

SLATE-HANGING: covering of overlapping slates on a wall. *Tile-hanging* is similar.

SLYPE: covered way or passage leading E from the cloisters between transept and chapter house.

SNECKED: *see* Rubble.

SOFFIT (*lit.* ceiling): underside of an arch (also called *intrados*), lintel, etc. *Soffit roll*: medieval roll moulding on a soffit.

SOLAR: private upper chamber in a medieval house, accessible from the high end of the great hall.

SOPRAPORTA: *see* Overdoor.

SOUNDING-BOARD: *see* Tester.

SPANDRELS: roughly triangular spaces between an arch and its containing rectangle, or between adjacent arches (5c). Also non-structural panels under the windows in a curtain-walled building.

SPERE: a fixed structure screening the lower end of the great hall from the screens passage. *Spere-truss*: roof truss incorporated in the spere.

SPIRE: tall pyramidal or conical feature crowning a tower or turret. *Broach*: starting from a square base, then carried into an octagonal section by means of triangular faces; and *splayed-foot*: variation of the broach form, found principally in the southeast, in which the four cardinal faces are splayed out near their base, to cover the corners, while oblique (or intermediate) faces taper away to a point (1c). *Needle spire*: thin spire rising from the centre of a tower roof, well inside the parapet: when of timber and lead often called a *spike*.

SPIRELET: *see* Flèche.

SPLAY: of an opening when it is wider on one face of a wall than the other.

SPRING or SPRINGING: level at which an arch or vault rises from its supports. *Springers*: the first stones of an arch or vaulting rib above the spring (2c).

SQUINCH: arch or series of arches thrown across an interior angle of a square or rectangular structure to support a circular or polygonal superstructure, especially a dome or spire (5a).

SQUINT: an aperture in a wall or through a pier usually to allow a view of an altar.

STAIRS: *see* 6c. *Dog-leg stair*: parallel flights rising alternately in opposite directions, without an open well. *Flying stair*: cantilevered from the walls of a stairwell, without newels; sometimes called a *Geometric* stair when the inner edge describes a curve. *Newel stair*: ascending round a central supporting newel (q.v.); called a *spiral stair* or *vice* when in a circular shaft, a *winder* when in a rectangular compartment. (Winder also applies to the steps on the turn.) *Well stair*: with flights round a square open well framed by newel posts. *See also* Perron.

STALL: fixed seat in the choir or chancel for the clergy or choir (cf. Pew). Usually with arm rests, and often framed together.

STANCHION: upright structural member, of iron, steel or reinforced concrete.

STANDPIPE TOWER: *see* Manometer.

STEAM ENGINES: *Atmospheric*: worked by the vacuum created when low-pressure steam is condensed in the cylinder, as developed by Thomas Newcomen. *Beam engine*: with a large pivoted beam moved in an oscillating fashion by the piston. It may drive a flywheel or be *non-rotative*. *Watt* and *Cornish*: single-cylinder; *compound*: two cylinders; *triple expansion*: three cylinders.

STEEPLE: tower together with a spire, lantern, or belfry.

STIFF-LEAF: type of E.E. foliage decoration. *Stiff-leaf capital see* 1b.

STOP: plain or decorated terminal to mouldings or chamfers, or at the end of hoodmoulds and labels (*label stop*), or stringcourses (5b, 6a); *see also* Headstop.

STOUP: vessel for holy water, usually near a door.

STRAINER: *see* Arch.

STRAPWORK: late C16 and C17 decoration, like interlaced leather straps.

STRETCHER: *see* Bond and 6e.

STRING: *see* 6c. Sloping member holding the ends of the treads and risers of a staircase. *Closed string*: a broad string covering the ends of the treads and risers. *Open string*: cut into the shape of the treads and risers.

STRINGCOURSE: horizontal course or moulding projecting from the surface of a wall (6d).

STUCCO: *see* Rendering.

STUDS: subsidiary vertical timbers of a timber-framed wall or partition (7).

STUPA: Buddhist shrine, circular in plan.

STYLOBATE: top of the solid platform on which a colonnade stands (3a).

SUSPENSION BRIDGE: *see* Bridge.

SWAG: like a festoon (q.v.), but representing cloth.

SYSTEM BUILDING: *see* Industrialized building.

TABERNACLE: canopied structure to contain the reserved sacrament or a relic; or architectural frame for an image or statue.

TABLE TOMB: memorial slab raised on free-standing legs.

TAS-DE-CHARGE: the lower courses of a vault or arch which are laid horizontally (2c).

TERM: pedestal or pilaster tapering downward, usually with the upper part of a human figure growing out of it.

TERRACOTTA: moulded and fired clay ornament or cladding.

TESSELLATED PAVEMENT: mosaic flooring, particularly Roman, made of *tesserae*, i.e. cubes of glass, stone, or brick.

TESTER: flat canopy over a tomb or pulpit, where it is also called a *sounding-board*.

TESTER TOMB: tomb-chest with effigies beneath a tester, either free-standing (tester with four or more columns), or attached to a wall (*half-tester*) with columns on one side only.

TETRASTYLE: *see* Portico.

THERMAL WINDOW: *see* Diocletian window.

THREE-DECKER PULPIT: *see* Pulpit.

TIDAL GATES: *see* Canals.

TIE-BEAM: *see* Roofs and 7.

TIERCERON: *see* Vault and 2c.

TILE-HANGING: *see* Slate-hanging.

TIMBER-FRAMING: *see* 7. Method of construction where the structural frame is built of interlocking timbers. The spaces are filled with non-structural material, e.g. *infill* of wattle and daub, lath and plaster, brickwork (known as *nogging*), etc. and may be covered by plaster, weatherboarding (q.v.), or tiles.

TOMB-CHEST: chest-shaped tomb, usually of stone. Cf. Table tomb, Tester tomb.

TORUS (plural: tori): large convex moulding usually used on a column base (3b, 3f).

TOUCH: soft black marble quarried near Tournai.

TOURELLE: turret corbelled out from the wall.

TOWER BLOCK: *see* Multi-storey.

TRABEATED: depends structurally on the use of the post and lintel. Cf. Arcuated.

TRACERY: openwork pattern of masonry or timber in the upper part of an opening. *Blind tracery* is tracery applied to a solid wall.
Plate tracery, introduced *c.* 1200, is the earliest form, in which shapes are cut through solid masonry (2a).
Bar tracery was introduced into England *c.* 1250. The pattern is formed by intersecting moulded ribwork continued from the mullions. It was especially elaborate during the Decorated period (q.v.). Tracery shapes can include circles, *daggers* (elongated ogee-ended lozenges), *mouchettes* (like daggers but with curved sides) and upright rectangular *panels*. They often have *cusps*, projecting points defining lobes or *foils* (q.v.) within the main shape: *Kentish* or *split-cusps* are forked (2b).
Types of bar tracery (*see* 2b) include *geometric*(*al*): *c.* 1250–1310, chiefly circles, often foiled; *Y-tracery*: *c.* 1300, with mullions branching into a Y-shape; *intersecting*: *c.* 1300, formed by interlocking mullions; *reticulated*: early C14, net-like pattern of ogee-ended lozenges; *curvilinear*: C14, with uninterrupted flowing curves; *panel*: Perp, with straight-sided panels, often cusped at the top and bottom.

TRANSEPT: transverse portion of a church.

TRANSITIONAL: generally used for the phase between Romanesque and Early English (*c.* 1175–*c.* 1200).

TRANSOM: horizontal member separating window lights (2b).

TREAD: horizontal part of a step. The *tread end* may be carved on a staircase (6c).

TREFOIL: *see* Foil.

TRIFORIUM: middle storey of a church treated as an arcaded wall passage or blind arcade, its height corresponding to that of the aisle roof.

TRIGLYPHS (*lit.* three-grooved tablets): stylized beam-ends in the Doric frieze, with metopes between (3b).

TRIUMPHAL ARCH: influential type of Imperial Roman monument.

TROPHY: sculptured or painted group of arms or armour.

TRUMEAU: central stone mullion supporting the tympanum of a wide doorway. *Trumeau figure*: carved figure attached to it (cf. Column figure).

TRUMPET CAPITAL: *see* 1b.

TRUSS: braced framework, spanning between supports. *See also* Roofs and 7.

TUMBLING or TUMBLING-IN: courses of brickwork laid at right-angles to a slope, e.g. of a gable, forming triangles by tapering into horizontal courses (8a).

TUSCAN: *see* Orders and 3e.

TWO-DECKER PULPIT: *see* Pulpit.

TYMPANUM: the surface between a lintel and the arch above it or within a pediment (4a).

UNDERCROFT: usually describes the vaulted room(s), beneath the main room(s) of a medieval house. Cf. Crypt.

VAULT: arched stone roof (sometimes imitated in timber or plaster). For types see 2c.
Tunnel or *barrel vault*: continuous semicircular or pointed arch, often of rubble masonry.

Groin-vault: tunnel vaults intersecting at right angles. *Groins* are the curved lines of the intersections.

Rib-vault: masonry framework of intersecting arches (ribs) supporting *vault cells*, used in Gothic architecture. *Wall rib* or *wall arch*: between wall and vault cell. *Transverse rib*: spans between two walls to divide a vault into bays. *Quadripartite* rib-vault: each bay has two pairs of diagonal ribs dividing the vault into four triangular cells. *Sexpartite* rib-vault: most often used over paired bays, has an extra pair of ribs springing from between the bays. More elaborate vaults may include *ridge ribs* along the crown of a vault or bisecting the bays; *tiercerons*: extra decorative ribs springing from the corners of a bay; and *liernes*: short decorative ribs in the crown of a vault, not linked to any springing point. A *stellar* or *star* vault has liernes in star formation.

Fan-vault: form of barrel vault used in the Perp period, made up of halved concave masonry cones decorated with blind tracery.

VAULTING SHAFT: shaft leading up to the spring or springing (q.v.) of a vault (2c).

VENETIAN or SERLIAN WINDOW: derived from Serlio (4b). The motif is used for other openings.

VERMICULATION: *see* Rustication and 6d.

VESICA: oval with pointed ends.

VICE: *see* Stair.

VILLA: originally a Roman country house or farm. The term was revived in England in the C18 under the influence of Palladio and used especially for smaller, compact country houses. In the later C19 it was debased to describe any suburban house.

VITRIFIED: bricks or tiles fired to a darkened glassy surface.

VITRUVIAN SCROLL: classical running ornament of curly waves (4b).

VOLUTES: spiral scrolls. They occur on Ionic capitals (3c). *Angle volute*: pair of volutes, turned outwards to meet at the corner of a capital.

VOUSSOIRS: wedge-shaped stones forming an arch (5c).

WAGON ROOF: with the appearance of the inside of a wagon tilt; often ceiled. Also called *cradle roof*.

WAINSCOT: *see* Panelling.

WALL MONUMENT: attached to the wall and often standing on the floor. *Wall tablets* are smaller with the inscription as the major element.

WALL-PLATE: *see* Roofs and 7.

WALL-WALK: *see* Parapet.

WARMING ROOM: room in a religious house where a fire burned for comfort.

WATERHOLDING BASE: early Gothic base with upper and lower mouldings separated by a deep hollow.

WATERLEAF: *see* Enrichments and 3f.

WATERLEAF CAPITAL: Late Romanesque and Transitional type of capital (1b).

WATER WHEELS: described by the way water is fed on to the wheel. *Breastshot*: mid-height, falling and passing beneath. *Overshot*: over the top. *Pitchback*: on the top but falling backwards. *Undershot*: turned by the momentum of the water passing beneath. In a *water turbine*, water is fed under pressure through a vaned wheel within a casing.

WEALDEN HOUSE: type of medieval timber-framed house with a central open hall flanked by bays of two storeys, roofed in line; the end bays are jettied to the front, but the eaves are continuous (8a).

WEATHERBOARDING: wall cladding of overlapping horizontal boards.

WEATHERING or SET-OFF: inclined, projecting surface to keep water away from the wall below.

WEEPERS: figures in niches along the sides of some medieval tombs. Also called mourners.

WHEEL WINDOW: circular, with radiating shafts like spokes. Cf. Rose window.

WROUGHT IRON: *see* Cast iron.

INDEX OF ARCHITECTS, ARTISTS, PATRONS AND RESIDENTS

Names of architects and artists working in the area covered by this volume are given in *italic*. Entries for partnerships and group practices are listed after entries for a single name.

Also indexed here are names/titles of families and individuals (not of bodies or commercial firms) recorded in this volume as having commissioned architectural work or owned or lived in properties in the area. The index includes monuments to members of such families and other individuals where they are of particular interest.

Abbott & Co. 64, 72, 92, 116, 135, 143, 278, 347, 362, 372, 420, 492, 511, 528, 557, 561, 610, 632, 649, 673, 674
Abernethy, James 618
Abraham, Emma Clarke 70, 630
Abraham, George 449
Acland, Cuthbert 102
Adam of Crookdale 187
Adam de Thweng 117
Adam, James 37, 504
Adam, Robert 37, 57, 109n., 504, 675
Adam Brothers 43, 509
Adams-Acton, John 65, 233, 235, 519
Addison, Edward 36, 37, 415, 473, 503, 523, Pl. 50
Addison, Rev. J. A. 60, 687–90, 704
Addison, James 35, 398
Addison, John 516, 627
Addison, Thomas 251, 626, 639
ad.hoc associates 77, 290
ADK Architects 161, 316
Aelicia *see* Pipard
Aglionby family 91, 115
Aglionby, Elizabeth Ann 684
Aglionby, Henry (c18) 115
Aglionby, Henry (c19) 219
Aglionby, John 115, 413
Aikman, William 666
Ainsworth, Thomas 279
Airey, William 444
Albion Glass 159, 331, 593, 684
Alderson, William 57, 94, 685
Allan, Fr T. B. 649
Allen, James 370
Allies & Morrison 171
Allott & Lomax 612
Alma-Tadema, Sir Lawrence 126n.
Almquist, Carl 128

AMEC 198
Andrews, G. T. 335
Andrews & Pepper 260
Antwerp Guild of Carvers 31, 234
Appleby, Edmund 474
Architects' Department, U.K. Atomic Energy Authority Engineering Group 612
Architects Plus 257
Argles, Thomas Atkinson 408
Armitage, George Faulkner 68, 70, 216–17, 704
Armstead, H. H. 65, 233
Armstrong family 26
Armstrong, William 412
Arnold, Hugh 456, 524, 635
Arnold, Matthew 596
Arnold, Dr Thomas 56, 596
Arup (Ove) & Partners 363
Ashworth Jackson & Walker 77, 647
Askew, Rev. Henry 366
Askew, Sir Hugh 160
Aspinall, John and *William* 665
Athelwold, Bishop 224
Atkinson, Conrad 279
Atkinson, Cuthbert 336
Atkinson, John 555
Atkinson, William (fl. 1795) 209
Atkinson, William (c19) 61, 475, 567, 578–9
Atkinson Bros 393, 514
Aumonier, William Jun. 306
Austin, H. J. 272
Austin, Hubert 62, 132, 407, 431, 540
Austin & Paley 58, 66, 116, 143, 151, 160, 200, 350–1, 372, 431, 462, 463, 496, 540, 564, 600, 647
  see also Paley & Austin, etc.
Ayris, H. E. 252, 325

Bacon, Percy 277, 320, 626
Bacon (Percy) Bros 422
Bagot family 492
Baguley, G. J. 367, 566
Bailey, John 75, 698
Bailey, W. & D. 530
Baillie Scott, M. H. 68–9, 171, 174, 695
Baines, Cuthbert 167n.
Baker, Sir Benjamin 143
Ball, J. L. 68, 644
Ballantine family 185
Ballantine Dykes family 185, 187, 578
Ballyedmond, Edward and Mary Haughey, Lord and Lady 301–2
Banks, E. H. 256
Banks, Edwin 256, 619, 686
Banks, Henry 686
Banks, James 580
Banks, John (C20, Kendal) 379
Banks, John (fl. 1903, Millbeck) 452
Banks, Thomas 234
Banks, Thomas Lewis 63, 218, 279, 339, 345, 394, 537, 675, 679, 681
Banks, William (d.1878) 618, 686
Banks, William, Jun. (d.1901) 685
Banks (T. L.) & C. H. Townsend 62, 287, 344, 478
Baracco, Alfredo 294
Barber, Samuel 377
Barbour, Robert 179
Bardgett, B. J. 509
Bardsley, Bishop John Wareing 65, 233
Barham, J. 146
Barker, Daye 396
Barker, John 387
Barn, John 337
Barnes, William 682
Barnett, Francis 279, 684
Barnett, H. M. 432
Barratt, John 299
Barrow, Sir John 66, 647
Barrow, Rolland 711
Barrowclough & Sanders 71, 117
Barry, E. M. 68, 127
Barry, T. D. 372
Barwick, Dean John 696
Barwick, Peter 696
Barwis family 667
Barwis, Thomas 187
Bassett-Lowke, W. J. 343
Bassett-Smith, W. 698
Bassett-Smith, W. & C. A. 699
Bateman, James 207
Bateman, Robert 420
Bateman, Roger 557
Bates, Ernest 372, 692
Baud, Benjamin 508, Pl. 80

Bayliff, William 464–5
BDP 76, 247, 677
    see also Building Design Partnership
BDP (Preston) 563
Beall (Newcastle) 247
Beattie (memorials) 66, 125
Beattie & Co. 90, 155
Beaulieu *see* Hugh of Beaulieu
Beaumont, Guillaume 44, 495
Beck, Thomas Alcock 399
Bective, Lord Kenlis, 4th Earl of 459, 466
Bell, Charles W. 63, 700
Bell, Daniel 163, 662
Bell, J. 259
Bell, James 451
Bell, John 276
Bell, Jonathan 400
Bell, Joseph (Grange-in-Borrowdale) 371
Bell, Joseph (Whitehaven) 680
Bell, Bishop Richard 32, 232, 233, 590–2
Bell, Spencer 451
Bell & Almond 166
Bell, Robert & James 223, 258
Bellas (or *Bellhouse*), *Henry* 54, 111, 191, Pl. 54
Bellhouse see Bellas
Bellingham family 381, 383, 407, 430, 445, 492–3, 614
Bellingham, James 492
Bemert, Henry 555
Benevot, Fr Laurence 699
Benn, Daniel 57, 109, 675
Bennett, Anthony 169
Bennett, Thomas 140, 609
Bennison, John & Thomas 128n.
Benson Harrison family 100, 102
Benson & Forsyth 76–7, 93, 376
Bentley, J. F. 455, 615
Benwell, John Wayland 326
Berkowitz, Maggie Angus 108
Bernasconi 505
Bever Dorling 679
Bewsey, J. C. N. 430
Billings, R. W. 61, 80, 263, 305, 325, Pl. 83
Bingley, John 598
Bintley, Joseph 62, 66, 148, 150, 317, 408, 420, 428, 440, 528, 530, 586, 587, 624, 653
Birch, Josiah 347
Bird, William 37, 285
Birkbeck family 318, 561
Birkbeck, Edward 198
Birkbeck, Thomas and Joan 198
Birket family 695
Birket, J. & L. 451
Birkett, Daniel 250, 254, 255, 256

Birkett, John 315
Black, Judith 673, 677
Black Tom see Curwen, Black Tom
Blackett-Ord, Charles 75, 390, 471, 505, 711
Blackmore, J. 125
Blakeman, Charles 507
Blamire, Susanna 584
Blanc, Frank 574
Bland, R. 308
Bland, Thomas 64, 67, 85, 310–11, 336, 538, 615, 618
Blaylock (C19) 664
Blaylock, Steve 602
Blencow, Henry 390
Blenkinsop, Thomas 188, Pl. 35
Blomfield, Sir Arthur 234
Blood, Norman 698
Bloomer, Bishop Thomas 592
Blore, R. 649
Bloxam, M. H. 422
Blücher von Wahlstadt, Countess 341
Bluck, Judith 251
Blyth & Cunningham 248
Bodley, G. F. 234
Boehm, Sir J. Edgar 484, 485, 546
Bolton, John 167, 169, 175–6
Bolton, William 398
Bond, John Smith 608
Bond Design 583
Bonner, Thomas 324
Bonnor, J. H. 600
Bonomi, Ignatius 61, 684
Bonomi (Ignatius) & J. A. Cory 546
Borough (Carlisle) 156
Bottomley, Michael 128, 338, 430, 431, 437, 443, 444, 688, 689
Bouch, Sir Thomas 51, 448, 588
Boulton (Cheltenham) 674
Bourne, Mary 75, 511
Bourne, Swaine 401
Bourne (Swaine) & Son 335
Bousfield, Major, M.P. 444
Bousfield, Samuel 254
Bowie, John 636
Boyce, Christine 75, 116, 339, 447, 484, 525
Boynton, Thomas 623
Braddyll, Col. Thomas Richmond Gale 292, 294, 341, 647
Brade, Daniel 146, 438, 557
Brade & Smales 127, 428, 557
Bradshaw Gass & Hope 439
Bragg, Lord (Melvin) 684
Braithwaite, Joseph 408
Braithwaite, Rev. Reginald 399, 400
Braithwaite, Thomas and Margaret 641
Braithwaite, William 603
Brammell, Chris 168

Brancker, James 102
Brass, Robert 602
Brassey & Field 130
Breeks family 191
Brettingham, Matthew 37, 504
Brettingham, Robert Furze 437
Bridgeman (Lichfield) 98
Bridson, Joseph Ridgway 170, 602, 603
Brierley & Rutherford 470
Brigham, Rev. Charles 624
Brisco family 637
Brisco, Sir Musgrave 638
Brisco, Sir Wastel 560
British Nuclear Fuels Ltd Architects 612
Broadbent, Stephen 677
Brock, T. 248
Brocklebank family 423
Brocklebank, Captain 680
Brocklebank, Harold 70, 601
Brocklebank, Sir Thomas 422
Brocklehurst, A. 252
Brogden, John and Alexander 374
Bromfield, Benjamin 150
Bromley (sculptors) 59, 315, 319
Bromley, J. W. 430
Bromley, John I 315
Bromley, W. (C20) 375
Bromley, William (C19) 59, 315
Brontë, Charlotte 644
Brooks, James 101
Brougham family 196, 197, 607
Brougham, Henry 607
Brougham, Henry Richmond 38, 425–6
Brougham, John 38, 426, Pl. 52
Brougham, Peter and Anne 607
Brougham, William 54, 197, 711
Brougham and Vaux, Henry Peter Brougham, 1st Baron 54, 196–7
Broughton family 200–1
Broughton, Sir Thomas 200
Brown, 'Capability' 37, 504
Brown, Edward 376
Brown, Ford Madox 640
Browne family 641
Browne, George and Elinor 641
Browne, William 185
Browne (Percy) & Son 254
Browning, Edward 361
Brownrigg family 316
Brownrigg, Samuel 681
Brownrigg, Dr William 316
Bruce (Whitehaven) 283, 708
Bruce, W. 352
Brundrit, D. J. 526
Brunlees, Sir James 116, 163, 652, 676
Brunsdon, Paul 108
Bryans, H. W. 208

Buccleuch, 3rd Duke of 500
Buccleuch, 5th Duke of 119, 132, 328, 361, 577
Buccleuch, 6th Duke of 496, 497
Buckeridge, Charles 283
Buckley, J. W. 174
Building Design Partnership 74, 76, 151, 251, 466
  see also BDP
Bullock, Thomas 176n.
Bunney, M. J. H. 434
Burgham, Odard de 196
Burke, W. H. 655
Burlison & Grylls 271, 487, 566, 594, 666, 688, 708
Burmantofts (terracotta) 137, 260
Burn, Dr Richard 58n., 561
Burn, William 54, 548–50
Burne-Jones, Sir Edward 114, 178, 200, 422, 455, 484, 485, 546, 629, 640
Burnet, Sir J. J. 265
Burns-Lindow, Jonas 423
Burrow, A. 64, 380, 528
Burrow, Frederick 64, 116, 150, 528, 628
Burrow, H. J. 217
Buss, A. E. 163
Butterfield, William 62, 64, 66, 185–6, 478, 596–9, Pl. 87
Buttress Fuller 170
Byrne, J. 134

Caine, Nathaniel 200
Caird, David 60, 141, 142
Caldebec, Thomas de 32, 384
Caldecotts (London) 410
Calverley, Rev. W. S. 65, 80, 125, 331
Camelford, Lord see Pitt, Thomas
Campbell, Brian 684
Campbell, Colen 37, 504
Campbell, Kevin 528
Campbell, Smith & Co. 561
Cannon, John 604
Cantwell, Robert 146
Capita DBS 515
Cardoso, Lida Lopes 711
Carel (Belgium) 619
Carleton, Thomas (C18) 112
Carleton, Thomas Junior (C16) 121
Carlisle, Frederick Howard, 5th Earl of 47, 51
Carlisle, George Howard, 6th Earl of 543
Carlisle, George William Frederick Howard, 7th Earl of 180, 346
Carlisle, George Howard, 9th Earl of, and Countess (Rosalind) 64, 177, 180–1, 479, 486, 543, 545, 546n.
Carlisle, John 127, 615

Carlton, John Metcalfe 191
Caröe, W. D. 63, 199, 282, 339, 532
Carpenter, R.C. 467–9
Carr family 220
Carr, John 54, 57, 170, 216n., 323, 399, 410, 434, 594, 603, 700–1
Carr, Jonathan Dodgson 261
Carrick, Alex 65, 701
Carruthers, Richard 55, 306
Carus, Roger 463
Carus Wilson *see* Wilson, Rev. William Carus
Carver, William 168, 692
Cash, David 76, 251
Cassidy, John 253
Cassidy & Ashton Partnership 683
Casson Conder 403
Catherall, Cyril 210
Caton, Richard 676
Cavendish family 135, 273, 354, 410, 457
Cavendish, Lady Evelyn 350
Cavendish, Lord Frederick and Lady 65, 132, 138, 140, 272, 350, 356
Cavendish, Lord George Augustus 58n., 410
Cavendish, Vincent, M.P. 350
Cavendish, William 458
Cavendish of Furness, Lord and Lady 411
Cawston (Arthur) and *Joseph Graham* 66, 247
Caygill, J. 572
Celtic Studios 540, 604
Chambers (or Chamber), Abbot Robert 30, 87–90
Chambers, Thomas 90
Chance Bros 362
Chantrey, Sir Francis 320
Chaplin, Rev. William 629
Chapman, Paul O. 92
Chapman & Son 98–9
Charles, J. A. 71, 137
Charles, John 138
Charlewood & Hicks 332
Charnley, Matthew 660
Cheere, Sir Henry 338
Chief Architect's Department, Ministry of Works 612
Chisholme, John 244
Christian, Ewan 103, 225–31, 238, 276, 419, 421, 456, 516, 555, 593
Christmas, F. G. 561
City Architects 247
Clahane, Danny 99
Clahane, Danny and *Lara* 407
Clark, James 132, 275
Clarke, James 470
Clarke, Joseph 61, 282
Clarke, R. 256

Clarke, Sarah Anne 372
Clarkson, Thomas 53, 580
Clayton & Bell 91, 146, 157, 163,
    185, 208, 233, 309, 313, 318, 320,
    325, 331, 346, 386, 407, 422, 469,
    478, 497, 524, 561, 566, 567, 577,
    583, 637, 640
Cleator & Sons 413
Cleburn, Richard de 280
Clerk of Penycuik, Sir John 506n.,
    508
Clifford family 106, 189
Clifford, Lady Anne (Countess of
    Pembroke) 34, 36, 104–8, 112,
    189–90, 192, 195–6, 198, 320,
    322, 380, 417, 437, 444, 510–11,
    592, 628
Clifford, Henry 198
Clifford, Robert 107, 189, 192
Clifford, Roger (father of Robert)
    192
Clifford, Roger (grandson of
    Robert) 189–90, 192
Clifford, Thomas 107
Close, Dean Francis 65, 233
Clough, Mollie 126n.
Coade (stone) 292, 300, 537
Coleman, Russell 247
Coleridge, Hartley 596
Coleridge, Samuel Taylor 182, 370,
    449
Collier (Anthony) Associates 515
Collingwood, Barbara 399
Collingwood, W. G. 65, 78, 79, 130,
    294, 297, 375, 399, 443, 450, 526,
    599, 651
Colt, Maximilian 36, 105, Pl. 72
Colvin (Penrith) 505
Comber, Roy 75, 698
Comper, Sir Ninian (J. N.) 275, 660,
    699
Coode, Sir John 527
Cooke, Elizabeth 399
Coombes, Chas W. 340, 438
Cooper, Alfred Heaton 101
Cooper, Jim 695
Cooper, Julian 575
Copley, Robert 369
Corby Hall & Sons 443
Corstorphine & Wright Hills Erwin
    441
Cory, John A. 62, 63, 68, 219, 398,
    475, 487, 488, 499, 512, 577, 604,
    639
*Cory (John A.) & Charles John
    Ferguson* 183, 253, 254, 318, 332,
    474, 488, 580, 611, 618, Pl. 84
Cottier, D. 586
Cottingham, L. N. 54, 196–7
Cotton, Thomas Dicey 412
Cotyngham, Prior 598

Coulthard, William 444
Countryside Consultants 637
Cowans, Sheldon & Co. 239
Coward, Elizabeth and William 349
Coward (John) Partnership 273
Cox, Eli 66, 428, 438, 443, 528
Cox & Sons 384, 577, 602
Cox, Sons & Buckley 282, 566, 668
Crackanthorpe family 499, 550–1
Crackanthorpe, Christopher 551
Crackanthorpe, James 550
Crackenthorpe, Richard 551
Craig & Green 137, 142
Crakeplace, Christopher 330
Crane, Walter 684
Cranke, James the Elder 654
Craven Dunnill (tiles) 66, 247
Crawford, George 530
Crewdson, William Dilworth (C19)
    444
Crewdson, William Dilworth
    (d.1908) 540
Crickmer, C. M. 501
Crittall 529
Crookdale family 187
Cropper family 205
Cropper, James 65, 205, 207, 433,
    434
Crosby, Paul 77, 692
Crosby & Hetherington 250
Crosley, William 409
Cross, David 315
Cross, Kenneth 691
Cross, Richard Assheton, M.P. (1st
    Viscount Cross of Broughton)
    200, 201, 235
Crossley, J. S. 115
Crossley, Sir William 704
Crosthwaite, J. 211
Crosthwaite, Peter 66, 79, 448, 450
Crowther, John Stretch 60, 61–2, 173,
    201, 308, 309, 310, 428–30, 444,
    629, 642, 660, 688, 689, 690, 691
Cruickshank & Seward 133
Crump, Mr 377
Culshaw (William) & Sons 200
Cumberland, Margaret, Countess of
    34, 36, 105, 195, Pl. 72
Cumberland County Architects 96,
    501
*Cumberland County Architect's
    Department* 74, 290
*Cumbria County Council Building
    and Design Dept* 76, 655
Cumpston, Mr 580
Cunningham, G. G. 691
Currer-Briggs, Henry 173
Curtis, T. F. 132, 632
Curtis (T.F.), Ward & Hughes 563
Curwen family 47, 54, 127, 170,
    218, 603, 697–9, 701, 703

Curwen, Sir Christopher (and Elizabeth de Hudleston) 32, 699
Curwen, Henry 393
Curwen, Isabella 170
Curwen, John Christian 43, 54, 170, 697–8, 700–1
Curwen, John Flavell 69, 78, 82, 155, 198, 273, 373, 393, 407, 408, 428, 430, 434, 435, 440, 441, 446, 463, 470, 528, 569, 620–3, 651
Curwen, Thomas ('Black Tom') 32, 219
Cuthbert, St 222
Cuthbertson, Henry 492

Dacre family 32, 54, 121, 177, 238, 272, 320–2, 386, 476–7, 479, 484–6, 542–4
Dacre, Thomas, 2nd Lord, and Lady Elizabeth 28, 32, 120, 164, 475, 477, 484, 543
Dacre, Sir Humphrey and Lady Mabel 32, 484
Dacre, Leonard 120
Dacre, Margaret 321
Dacre, Ranulph (fl. 1391) 120
Dacre, Ranulph, later Lord Dacre (d.1339) 543
Dacre, Sir Thomas *see* Sussex, 1st Earl of
Dacre, William (C13) 543
Dacre, William (C14) 321
Daighton see Deighton
Dalston family 318, 627, 633
Dalston, John and Elisabeth 325
Dalston, John and Lucy 633
Dalston, John, M.P. (fl. 1747) 634
Dalston, Thomas 198
Dalton, Sir George 325
Dalton, Sir John (fl. 1612) 325
Dalton, John (d.1844) 337
Dalton, Jonathan and Mary 337
Dalton, Percy 246
Dance, George Jun. 37, 504
Darbishire, H. A. 139
Darbyshire, Jane 244
d'Aumaret, Marion 404
David I, King of Scotland 21, 22, 87, 240, 244
Davies (Newcastle) 95
Davies, Rev. John Llewelyn 463
Davies, Lewis 240
Davies, William 614
Davies, Stanley & Emily 70–1, 690–1
Dawes family 144–5
Dawes, Lancelot 145
Dawes, Thomas 145
Daws, Thomas and Elizabeth 310
Dawson (Whitehaven) 370
Dawson, E. H. 372

Dawson, Dr James 703, 704
Dawson, Joe 465
Day Cummins 405
de Burgh, Thomas 186
de Quincey, Thomas and Margaret 79, 375, 596
Deakin, George William 373
Dearle, J. H. 114, 534
Deighton (or *Daighton*), Mr 393
Denman family 478
Dent family 309, 518, 575
Dent, George 34
Dent, James 469
Dent, Lancelot 518
Dent, Wilkinson 308, 309
Denton, William 661, 669
Derby, 1st Earl of 201
Derby, 15th Earl of 68, 696
Derwentwater, Earl of 546
Deuchars, Louis Reid 386
Devonshire, 7th Duke of 410
Devonshire, Dukes of 132
Dicconson family 93
Dickenson, Christopher 125
Dickenson, D. W. 74, 180, 186, 340, 501
Dickson (Terence) & Associates 575
Dixon (London) 505
Dixon, George 187
Dixon, Jeremiah 552
Dixon, John (architect) 276
Dixon, John, fl. 1824–45 414
Dixon, Peter 54, 661, 662, 663, 664
Dixon, Thomas 218
Dobson, John 54, 259, 414, 662, 663
Dobson, Percy 529
Dobson, Reginald 145
Dobson, Reginald and Elizabeth 628
Dockray, Brian 74, 428, 440, 462
Dockray & Moore 74, 100
Dodgson (or Dixon) family 208
Doggett, T. 317
Dolfin 21, 222, 234, 240
Dolman, W. L. 69, 166, 176, 694
Douglas, Clementina Sobiesky 349
Doulton & Co. 254, 255
Dower, John 73, 343
Dowthwait 711
Doyle, Harcourt M. 91
Drew family 408
Drury family 159
Dryell, Richard 515
Duckett, Thomas 431
Dudley, Edmund 122
Dunbar, Alexander 578
Dunbar, David 64, 235, 239, 303, 309, 530, 707
Dunkerley, Frank 643
Dunlop, J. M. 642
Dunn, Hansom & Dunn 257

Dunning, John and Barbara 632
Durand, Mr 174
Dyer, Jimmy 251
Dykes family 577
  see also Ballantine Dykes
Dykes Bower, S. E. 225, 226, 231–2,
  234, 238

Eaglesfield, Charles W. 63, 199, 283,
  285, 289, 342, 350, 514–15
Earley & Co. 72
Earley Studios 279, 432
Eastted, William 691
Eckroyd family 114
Eden District Council 108
Edmondson family 603, 636
Edmundson, R. B. 187, 346
Edmundson (R. B.) & Son 602, 684
Edward I, King 26, 155, 203, 222,
  225, 241, 242, 413, 479, 589
Egremont, Lady 283–4
Egremont, William FitzDuncan,
  Lord of 213
Elders Walker Millican Ltd 239
Elders Walker & Millican 335
Eleanor of Engayne 281
Elizabeth I, Queen 46, 222
Ellis, Rev. Robert William 408
Elwes family 663
Elwes, Guy 71, 663
English, Thomas 53, 169–70
Erridge, A. F. 131
Errington, J. E. 349
Erwin, Ross 77, 575
Etty, William 35, 565
Evans, S. 372
Evans (C.) & Son 403
Evetts, L. C. 317, 320, 648, 674, 695
Evill, Norman 266

Fairbairn, Sir William 262
Fairbairn & Hull 138
Fairer, William and Joseph 381
Farrell & Clark 464
Farrer, Henry 607
Faucet (Appleby) 337
Faulder, Joseph 393
Fawcett (Lancaster) 272, 524, 604
Fayrer, Joseph 528
Fayrish, Robert and Frances 89
Fearon, Thomas and Agnes 488
Fell, John Barraclough 329
Fell, Margaret 630
Fell, Robert 70, 420
Fendley, George 70, 218, 636
Ferdinand, A. 454
Ferguson, Charles John 62, 66, 68,
  70, 126, 127, 147, 156, 179, 180,
  183, 205, 211, 237, 245, 247, 250,
  253, 256, 263, 265, 277, 278, 312,
  314–15, 316, 319, 324–5, 326, 331,

333, 337, 339, 352, 361, 367, 384,
  385, 392, 413, 424, 475, 479, 484,
  486, 514, 518–19, 521, 532, 535–6,
  543, 545–6, 551, 576, 583, 609,
  613, 618, 631–2, 635, 666, 669,
  672, 674, 684, 685
  see also Cory & Ferguson
Ferguson, John 664
Ferguson, Joseph 262
Ferguson, Richard 414
Ferguson, Robert 252
'Fermer' workshop 386
Fetherstonhaugh family 476–7, 584
Fetherstonhaugh, Henry 476
Fetherstonhaugh, Timothy and
  Bridget 476
Fetherstonhaugh, Timothy, and
  Eliza Were 477
Fiennes, Celia 29, 37, 222, 247,
  503, 564–5
Fisher, Alfred 581
Fisher, John 438
Fisher, Ralph 553
Fisher, William 432, 438
Fishers (York) 150, 508
Fitchett, John 374
Fitzarthur, Henry 160
FitzDuncan, William 340
Fitzroy Picture Society 304
Flaxman, John 167
Fleming (le) family 375, 594–6, 693
Fleming, Albert 70, 487n.
Fleming, Sir Daniel 42, 43, 295,
  317, 375, 595, 596
Fleming, Fletcher 490
Fleming, Lady le 594
Fleming, Sir Michael 594
Fleming, Richard 594
Fleming, William (c16) 295
Fleming, William (c18) and
  Dorothy 446
Fletcher family 103, 418
Fletcher, Angus 375
Fletcher, Sir George 415
Fletcher, Sir Henry 415
Fletcher, Thomas 50, 409, 441, 542
Fletcher, Rev. Walter (Chancellor)
  118, 308n., 325
Fletcher, William 531
Foley, J. H. 180
Fontana, Petrus 59, 93
Forster, William 557
Forsyth, J. 577
Forwood, Sir William 165–6
Fothergill, George and Julia 587
Fothergill, John 586
Fothergill, Richard 613–14
Fothergill, Robert 109
Fowler, C. H. 660
Fowler, H. 444
Fowler, H. T. 134

Fox, George 35, 630–1
Fox, T. J. 250
Foxall, Harry 251, 514
Frampton, Edward 420
Franceys & Sons 524
Francis, Frederick & Horace 63, 318, 625, 626
Frearson 341
Freeman, R. Knill 68, 378–9, 603
Froment-Meurice, J. 508
Furuta, Hideo 248

Gaddum family 643
Gaddum, W. H. and Edith 643
Gaff, Mr 147
Gaffin & Co. 307
Gale family 129, 294
Galloway, W. & J. 116
Gamon & Humphry 72, 291
Gamul 24, 564
Gandy, James 408, 496
Gandy, Joseph Michael 175–6, 399
Gardner, Mark 41, 112, 123
Gardner & Ellis 205
Garforth, William 241
Garlick, Bill 366
Garnett, Annie 70, 169n.
Garnett, Anthony 442
Garnett, Thomas 463, 465
Garnett, Thomas, of Kendal 440
Garrett, Daniel 417
Gaskell, Mrs Elizabeth 644
Gathorne, Robert 463
Geddes, Wilhelmina 71, 128
Geldart, Rev. E. 182
Gell, William 53, 377
Ghirardi 647
Gibberd (Frederick) & Partners 74, 435n., 439–40
Gibbs/Gibbs & Co. (glass-stainers) 113, 342, 422
Gibbs, Alexander 186, 577
Gibbs, C. A. 333
Gibbs, James 37, 504
Gibbs, J. A. 582
Gibbs & Howard 401, 503
Gibson, Dan 68, 69, 103, 166, 378–9, 451, 642, 643, 693–4, 695
Gibson, George 57, 58, 64, 308, 470, 499, Pl. 81
Gibson, Ian 77, 295
Gibson, Margaret 672
Gibson, R. 586
Gibson, Rebecca 273
Gibson, S. 92
Gibson, T. G. 283
Gilbeck, W. & A. 340
Gilbert, John 97
Gilchrist, Robert 632, 644–5
Giles, Francis 302, 404, 661, 669

Gilkes, Gilbert 440
Gilkes & Co. 448
Gill family 319
Gill, John 168, 172, 428, 435, 438
Gill Dockray 77, 295, 428
Gill Dockray & Partners 101, 275, 373, 462, 689
Gill Dockray Rhodes & Moore 74, 168, 172, 428
Gill & Rhodes 74, 168, 603
Gillbank, Joseph and Mary 147
Gillows 373, 518, 529, 570, 575, 652
Gilpin family 605–6
    see also Sawrey Gilpin
Gilpin, Bernard 445
Gilpin, Richard (fl. 1644) and William 605
Gilpin, Richard (fl. 1737) 605–6
Gilpin, Rev. William (1724–1804) 52, 53, 79, 302, 450, 606
Gilpin, William (fl. 1375) 446
Goddard, D. 441
Goddard & Gibbs 75, 698
Goldsworthy, Andy 76, 84, 298, 602
Gondibour, Prior 31, 197, 225, 232–3, 236, 238, 239–40
Gooday (Leslie) & Associates 613
Goodwin, Francis 285, 291
Goodwin, Bishop Harvey 65, 233
Goodyear, Adam 615
Gordon, Alice M. 72, 411, 430
Gordon, Lord William 53, 452
Gospatrick, Thomas, son of 616
Gourdon, R. 448
Graham family 26, 118, 177, 403, 453–4, 548, 631
Graham, Alexander 556
Graham, Sir Fergus 549
Graham, James (Barrock Park) 409
Graham, Sir James (Netherby) 54, 233, 548
Graham, Joseph 247
Graham, Lady (Cynthia) 454
Graham, Richard (c16) 177
Graham, Richard and Jane (c18) 177
Graham, Richie 31, 244
Graham, Dr Robert 43, 453, 500–1, 548–50
Graham, Thomas Henry 403, 631
Graham, William 219
Graham, Roy & Nicholson 676
Grahme (or Graham), Col. James 44, 492–5
Grant, Bill 601
Grant, David 619
Grasmere Hermit 644
Graves, Henry 125
Graves, Rev. John 653

Gray, Charlotte 434
Gray, Jane 75, 513
Gray, Thomas 647
Grayme, William 115
Grayson, G. E. 67, 422–3
Green (sculptor) 95
Green, Benjamin 96, 669
Green, Clifford 142
Green Design Group 94, 405
Green, F. & W. 67, 316, 447
Greenall, Lt-Col. G. F. 451–2
Greenwell, William and Anne 156
Grey, John 180
Greystoke, William, 14th Baron 385, 386
Greystoke, Elizabeth of see Dacre, Thomas, 2nd Lord
Greystoke, Isabel de 475
Grindal, Edmund, Archbishop of Canterbury 599–600
Grindal, William 600
Grisenthwaite, Mr 67, 126, 615, 644
Grisenthwaite, W. 636, 711, Pl. 102
Grout, Paul 77, 133, 407, 563, 688
Grout (Paul) Associates 99
Groves, William Grimble 642
Grundy, James W. 67, 92, 341, 378, 503, 652, 697
Grundy (J. W.) & Sons 697
Gunson, John 645
Gunson, Joseph 405
Gyatso, Geshe Kelsang 293
Gyles, Henry 696

Habershon, Matthew 101
Habershon & Brock 63, 133, 257, 303, 406
Hadrian, Emperor 16
see also Places index, Hadrian's Wall
Haigh, E. Donald 338, 379, 434, 437, 541
Haigh, Roger 694
Haigh Architects 441, 694
Hall (Galashiels) 578
Hall, John 562
Hall, Mary 487
Hall, Philip 76, 471
Halton, Bishop John de 554
Halton, Miles and Dorothy 390
Hannah, Seamus 699
Hanson, Don 77
Hanson Walford Marston 77, 689
Harden, John 182
Harding, H. J. 549
Hardman 132, 144, 160, 233, 234, 235, 279, 282, 295, 315, 329, 386, 398, 462, 512, 514, 534, 566, 588, 593, 626, 653, 663, 674, 700
Hardman, Peter 417
Hardman & Co. 432

Hardman (John) Studios 264, 683
Hardwick, Thomas 58, 699, Pl. 79
Hareshaw Ironworks 638
Harkewitz, Herman 67, 447, 636
Harrington family 93, 600
Harrington, Lord John (d.1327) and Joan Dacre 32, 271–2, Pl. 25
Harrington, Lord John (d.1417) 269
Harrington, John de 366
Harris family 578–9
Harris, Alfred 463, 466
Harris, Joseph 578
Harris, Richard 602
Harris, Jonathan and William 290
Harrison, Daniel 439
Harrison, E. 315
Harrison, John 349
Harrison, John R. 707–8
Harrison, Robert 565
Harrison, Thomas 37, 441, 504
Harrison, Thomas (C19) 443
Harrison, Thomas and Dorothy (C17) 366
Harrison, William 60, 67, 690
Harrison, William (fl. 1826) 573
Harrison & Ash 569
Harrods 220
Hartcup, Capt. 242
Hartley, John 618
Hartley, John and Katherine (C17) 318
Hartley, Thomas, M.P. 147
Harvey, Harry 234
Harwood, Steve 161, 316
Haschenperg, Stefan von 29, 241, 242, 244, Pl. 94
Hasell family 43, 320, 321, 580
Hasell, Sir Edward (C17) 322
Hasell, Edward (C18) 38, 322–3
Hassam, Alfred 327
Haswell, F. R. N. 95
Haughan, J. H. 74, 96, 290
Haughey see Ballyedmond
Hay (Liverpool) 282
Hay, J. M. & J. 63, 263
Hay, W. & J. 60, 63, 380, 619
Hay & Henderson 63, 335
Hayes (Ambleside) 530
Hayes, R. 431
Hayes & Parkinson 443
Hayes (T. R.) & Sons 624
Haynes, Alex 75, 159, 163, 393, 522, 593, 674, 684
Haythwaite, Prior 232
Hayton, Lowthian & Lowrey 239
Head, Elizabeth 102
Head, George Head 253, 266, 404, 608
Healy, Michael 128
Heathcote, Margaret 370

Heaton, Butler & Bayne 105, 133, 142, 150, 202, 263, 278, 283, 306, 317, 327, 365, 386, 392, 404, 419, 425, 461, 514, 525, 528, 530, 561n., 566, 581, 608, 618, 624, 629, 648, 653, 656, 660, 666, 668, 673

Hedges, Nathaniel 323

Hedley, Mrs 552

Hedley, Oswald 644

Heelis family 105, 400

Heelis, Mrs *see* Potter, Beatrix

Heineman, I. N. 309n.

Hems, Harry 70, 335

Henderson, Gilbert 451

Henderson, James 687

Hendrie, Herbert 507

Hennebique 601

Henry I, King 21, 22, 222, 224, 234, 240

Henry II, King 21, 87, 241, 586

Henry, Earl 87

Hepworth, Joseph 261

Herbert, St 452

Hetherington, Rene 179

Hetherington & Oliver 250

Hewetson, John 587

Hewetson, T. 587

Heywood, A. H. 691

Hicks & Charlewood 91, 178, 361, 524, 546

Higginson, Henry 250, 251, 254, 257, 262

Higham, A. B. 66, 95

Highmore, Robert 519

Hill, Ann Nevell 380

Hill, Ed 395, 563

Hill, George Henry 634

Hill, Sandy & Norris 167

Hills, Judge Herbert Augustus 426

Hills, Tony 441

Hills Erwin Partnership 77, 575

Hilton family 558

Hindson, William 705, 706

Hine brothers 515

Hiorne, Francis 387, 388

Hird, John 53, 128, 201, 217, 323, 348, 395, 410, 434, 438, 620–4, 696

Hislop, Mr 694

Hitchin, Stephen 685

Hives Partnership 76, 570

Hochstetter, Daniel 212, 554

Hodder Associates 76, 373

Hodge, Joseph 686

Hodges, N. W. 449

Hodgson, Christopher 104, 245, 253, 266, 608

Hodgson, Gilbert 210

Hodgson, John 255, 262, 265, 669

Hodgson, Thomas 66, 448, 451

Hodgson, W. 587

Hodgson, William 414

Hodgson, Thomas & Isaac 67, 316, 447

Hodgson & Tritton 240

Hoggarth, Gawith 442

Holder Mathias Alcock 76, 198

Hole, William 578

Holiday, Henry 64, 69, 98, 126n., 132, 160, 185, 210, 217, 275, 303, 375, 400, 447, 461, 534, 594, 628, 635, 662, 695, Pl. 93

Hollaway, Tony 637

Holme, William 433, 441, 563

Holmes, James 618, 656

Holmes (J.) & Co. 191

Holt, Sir Edward 171, 695

Hone, Evie 484

Hooke, Robert 506

Hope, G. 557

Hope, James 628

Hornabrook, A. W. 252

Hornblower (Liverpool) 527

Hornby, Rev. J. T. 101n.

Horne, Willie 139

Hornyold-Strickland family 619

Hoskins, Thomas Alison 614

Hothfield, Barons 106

Hoton, Thomas de 415

Howard family 54, 55, 300–2, 387–8, 484–5, 492, 542–3, 664, 668

   see also Carlisle, Earls of

Howard, Mr (Corby) 550

Howard, Hon. Charles 178, 484, 485

Howard, Charles Jun. 387

Howard, Henry 300, 387, 662, 669

Howard, Henry Charles (C17) 387

Howard, Henry Charles (C19) 387, 388

Howard, Lady Maria 58, 668, Pl. 73

Howard, Mary 492

Howard, Lady Mary 500

Howard, P. H. 664

Howard, Philip (C18) 302

Howard, Philip (C19) 664

Howard, Hon. Philip 543

Howard, Thomas 44, 301–2

Howard, Sir William (C17) 300

Howard, William (fl. 1702) 664

Howard, Lord William (fl. 1604–12) 127, 543–5

Howard of Greystoke, Charles *see* Norfolk, 11th Duke of

Howard-Smith, W. 66, 247

Howarth, Mr and Mrs 644

Howe, J. G. 567

Howes, James 280, 698

Howie, J. W. 443

Howison, J. 304
Howson, Joan 71, 205, 234, 345, 534, 624
Hubert (mason) 24, 564
Huddart (father & son) 344
Huddart, Arthur 62, 67, 69, 344, 345
Huddart, Joseph 59, 93
Huddleston, Andrew and Dorathie 418–19
Huddleston, Sir John (d.1494) 524
Huddleston, John (fl. c. 1535) 160
Huddleston(e)/de Hudleston family 418, 524–5, 699
Huddlestone, F. 418
Hudleston family *see* Huddleston(e)
Hudleston, John de 524
Hudson, Thomas 431
Hugall (Cheltenham) 667
Hugh of Beaulieu, Bishop 25, 157, 224
Hughes, George J. 99
Hughes, Henry 166–7, 563, 636
Hughes, Rod 77, 290
Hulton, Rev. Arthur Emilius 425
Humphries, Jackson & Ambler 252
Hunt, G. H. 114
Hunter, T. C. and J. 140
Hurtzig, C. A. 143
Hussey, Richard Charles 197
Hutchinson, Christopher 253
Hutchinson, Nigel 100, 101
Hutton, Anthony and Elizabeth 566
Hutton, Cuthbert 418
Hutton, John 372, 431, 440, 444, 469
Hutton, Rev. William (Beetham) 151
Hutton, William and Dorothy (Penrith) 573

Ibbeson, Graham 651
Ibbetson, Julius Caesar 641
Idle, William 711
Image, Selwyn 304
Insall (Donald) Associates 390
Irwin, Thomas and Mary 215, 217
Ivo *see* Raghton; Taillebois

Jack, George 178, 250
Jackson (London) 248
Jackson, Alan 77, 647
Jackson, Arthur 691
Jackson, Rev. John 533
Jackson, Melanie 677
Jackson, W. 239
Jackson, William 449
Jacksons (Fleetwood) 92–3
James I, King of England (James VI of Scotland) 33, 118
James, Rev. Octavius 97
James, William 409

James (J. T.) & Partners 73, 142
Jekyll, Gertrude 579
Jefferson, Arthur Stanley (Stan Laurel) 651
Jefferson, Henry 339
Jefferson, John 666
Jenkinson, H. I. 448
Jennings, John (fl. 1829) 502
Jennings, John and Joseph 289
John, King 189, 192
John de Capella 228
Johnson, D. T. 263
Johnson, E. 307
Johnson, Francis 697
Johnson, James 151
Johnson, John 657
Johnson & Wright 252, 253
Johnston, David 265
Johnston & Wright 76, 247, 265, 509, 608
Johnstone Bros 96
Jones, Alan 253
Jones, F. W. Doyle 288, 568
Jones, J. S. 501
Jones, Jak 76, 575
Jones, John Paul 677
Jones, Owen 64, 231
Jones, T. Maldwin 313
Jones & Willis 561
Joplin, T. 540
Joy, Albert Bruce 65, 140

Kay-Shuttleworth, Sir James 127
Kayll & Co. 404, 455
Keightley, Mary 581
Kellard, Harry 495
Kelly, Chris 139, 203
Kemp, David 602
Kemp, Col. George *see* Rochdale, 1st Baron
Kemp, Marjorie 522
Kemp, Edward 60, 63, 68, 134, 317, 608
Kempe, C. E. 159, 200, 294, 339, 347, 386, 478, 517, 609
Kempe & Co. 144, 282, 315, 478, 708
Kempe & Tower 625
Kendal Milne 174
Kendall, Nick 244
Kendall, W. B. 356
Kenlis, Lord *see* Bective, 4th Earl of
Kennedy, David 306
Kennedy, Myles 652
Kennedy, Guinevere & Margaret 655
Kenworthy, J. D. 600
Kerr, Robert 536
Keswick School of Industrial Arts (KSIA) 70, 89, 132, 178, 182, 266, 315, 316, 320, 430, 445, 447, 448, 449, 524, 636, 651

Keyser, Henryk de 37, 531
Kidd, John 588
Kilbride, Joseph M. 70, 127, 174, 469, 615
King, Daniel Quall 293
King, James 348
Kinsman, Bunty 321
Kirkbride (Carlisle) 266, 404, 637
Kirkbride, J. M. 144
Kirkby family 457
Kirkby, Bishop John 589
Kirklinton-Saul family 474
Kite, Bishop John 590, 592
Knewstubb, J. J. 66, 569
Knight, Samuel 636
Knipe, Anthony 273
Knott, Edward and Agnes 595
Knott, Michael 296
Knowles (Manchester) 92
Knowles, J. A. 274
Knowles, J. T. Sen. 65, 685, Pl. 101
Kossowski, Adam 528
Krolow, H. V. 526
KSIA *see Keswick School of Industrial Arts*

Laing 250
Laing & Beattie 182
Lambert, Mary 92
Lambert & Moore 582
Lamont, David 265
Lamplugh, Richard 185
Lancaster family 310, 394, 627
Lane, Mr 134
Langstaff, Thomas 203
Latham, Jasper 36, 507, Pl. 71
Latham, John 182
Lavers, Barraud & Westlake 205, 208, 304, 319, 461, 512, 521
Law, Bishop Edmund 234, 591
Law, George 182
Law, George Henry, Bishop of Chester 66, 596
Lawson family 425
Lawson, John 75, 698
Lawson, Sir Wilfrid (c17) 405
Lawson, Sir Wilfrid (fl. c. 1800) 452
Lawson, Sir Wilfrid (C20) 124–5
Lawson, William 125
Laythes (or Leathes), Adam and Alice 635
le Brun *see* Richard le Brun
Leach, Rhodes & Walker 676
Lee, J. T. 68, 644
Lee, Lawrence 663
Legard, Sir John 175–6
Leigh, Sir John 424
Leigh, Thomas 215
Lennox-Boyd, Mark 411
Lesser Design 575

Lewyn, John 26, 241
Leyborne-Popham, Maud 389
Leyburn, Robert de 335
Li Yuan-Chia 486
Liddell, Col. George 547
Lightfoot, Charles 649
Lightfoot, J. J. 54, 703, Pls. 62, 63
Lindsay, Richard 339
Lingard, J. R. 642
Linton, Eliza 297, 517
Linton, William James 297
Little, David 663
Littledale, Joseph 682
Llewelyn-Davies 265
Locke, Joseph 51
Lockwood & Mawson 257
Longmire, John 643
Lonsdale, James, 1st Earl of (d.1802) 57, 109, 285, 504, 508, 518, 675
Lonsdale, William and Augusta, 1st Earl (2nd creation) and Countess of 65, 254, 504–6, 508, 574, 600, 617, 678
Lonsdale, William, 2nd Earl of 506, 508, Pl. 80
Lonsdale, Henry, 3rd Earl and Countess of 65, 508, 673
Lonsdale, Hugh, 5th Earl of ('Yellow Ear) 68, 505, 506, 513
Lonsdale, James, 7th Earl of 506
Lonsdale, Sir John Lowther, 1st Viscount of 503, 506–7, 508
Lonsdale, Richard, 2nd Viscount of 504–5
Lonsdale, Richard, 3rd Viscount of 504, 508
Lonsdale, Earls and Viscounts of 122, 503–5
Lonsdale, H. W. 398, 593
Lord, F. J. 142
Lorimer, Sir Robert 63, 65, 69, 182n., 263, 266, 325, 386, 484, 574, 578–9, 701, 708
Lorimer & Matthew 238
Losh family 704–7
Losh, James 413
Losh, John 704
Losh, Katherine 64, 704, 707
Losh, Sara 60, 64, 65, 555, 704–7, Pls. 32, 82
Losh, William 705
Lough, John Graham 315, 374, 599
Lowther family 36, 47, 111, 272, 354, 394, 410, 472, 503, 518, 670–2, 679, 697, 703, 709–10
see also Lonsdale, Earls of
Lowther, Sir John, 1st Viscount 34, 36–7, 44, 164–5, 503, 508, 627, 711

Lowther, Sir Christopher 43, 47, 509, 627, 670
Lowther, Gerard and Lucy 570, 572
Lowther, Sir James (d.1755, son of Sir John Lowther F.R.S.) 670–1, 673, 677
Lowther, Sir James (d.1802) *see* Lonsdale, 1st Earl of
Lowther, Sir John (d.1637) 36, 503, 507, Pl. 71
Lowther, Sir John (d.1675) 36, 507, Pl. 71
Lowther, Sir John, M.P. and F.R.S. (d.1706, Whitehaven) 43, 47, 670–1, 675, 677, 681
Lowther, Lady Mary 52
Lowther, Sir Richard 36, 507
Lowther, Maj.-Gen. W. H. 319
Lowthian (T.) & Sons 218
Lucas sisters 126n.
Lucchesi, Andrea Carlo 65, 233, 434, 450
Lucock, Joshua 285
Lucy (de) family 283, 598
Lucy, Thomas de 283
Lutyens, Sir Edwin 69, 70, 360, 451, 585, 692
Lyl 655
Lynn, W. H. 66, 135, Pl. 97
Lyttelton, Bishop Charles 58, 225, 591, 592, 637

Macbeth, Ann 395, 563
McCosh, Robert Hasell 324
McCullough, Jamie 650
Macdonald Field & Co. 685
Macfarlane (W.) & Co. 351
Machell family 157, 303
Machell, Hugh 37, 304
Machell, Rev. Thomas 37, 43, 57, 85, 108, 111, 188, 192, 251, 303–4, 394, 400, 433, 445, 446, 471, 473, 496, 513, 523, 563, 581, 582, 585, 586, 627, 633, 695, 696, 710, 711
McInnes, Miles 266
McIntosh, J. Y. 139, 140, 328
MacIver family 704
MacIver, David 101
McKay, John 404
McKenna, John 675
Mackereth, Thomas and Dorothy 101
Mackie, Chris 413
Mackmurdo, A. 550
Mackreth, William 398
Maclean family 491
McLean (J.R.) & F. C. Stileman 129
Macniven, G. D. 676
Maile (G.) & Son 163
Mair, G. J. J. 518, 575

Mangan, Wilfrid C. 74, 257, 264, 375, 683
Mann, Harrington 127
Mansergh, James 527
Mark, Benjamin and Sarah 538
Markham family 533
Markham, Col. 417
Markham, Canon Gervase 531, 533, 711
Marsh, A. E. 286
Marsh, R. S. 283
Marshal, William (C12) 267
Marshall family 67, 297
Marshall, John (d.1836) 447
Marshall, John (fl. 1839) 502
Marshall, William (fl. 1850–2) 450, 563
Marshall, William (fl. 1889) 276, 447
Marshall, William Cecil 296
Martin, Mr 521
Martin, Howard 540, 604
Martin, Sir Leslie (J. L.) 71, 181–2, 517
Martin, Samuel 682
Martindale, C. B. 104
Martindale, C. J. Fawcett 210–11, 264
Martindale, Isabel 389
Martindale, J. H. 63, 66, 70, 78, 88, 113, 114, 147, 218, 239, 277, 280, 304, 352, 426–7, 514, 567, 609, 636, 645, 662
Martineau, Harriet 56, 79, 102, 447, 687
Mary Queen of Scots 401
Mason, Christopher 649
Mason, Edward 512
Mason, W. 99
Mason-Hornby family 209
Matson, J. 294
Matthews, David 168, 690, 693
Matthews, Sally 602
Matthews & Hodgson 234
Matthews & Sons 65, 508
Mattison, J. 127
Mauclerc, Bishop Walter 589
Maude, Joseph 438
Mawson (architect, fl. 1842) 618
Mawson, C. L. 133
Mawson, James 505, 509, 711
Mawson, Joseph 121
Mawson, Robert 694
Mawson, Thomas 66, 68, 69, 138, 175, 345, 378–9, 411, 489, 552, 595, 603, 642, 643, 644, 691, 694, 695
Mayer (Munich) 315, 501
Mayer & Co. 118, 432
Mayo, 6th Earl of 285
MEB Partnership 448
Meik (Thomas) & Sons 618

Mellon (W. A.) & George Wittet 702
Mellor, Tom 305
Mellor (Tom) & Partners 530
Meschines see Ranulph; William
Messel, Oliver 74, 531
Metcalfe-Gibson, Rupert 586
Metcalfe-Gibson, T. A. 586
Milburne, John 492
Miles, H. T. 65, 137, 294, 526
Miles & Morgan 327
Milham, James 679
Miller, Alec 70, 526, 654
Miller, C. J. 696
Miller, Canon Edward 541
Miller, H. Gustave 553
Miller, James 264
Millican, Baguley & Atkinson 163,
    559
Millward, Edward 336
Milne family 173
Milner, Rev. William Holme 566
Milton, Thomas 701
Ministry of Public Buildings and
    Works 256
Ministry of Supply 335
Ministry of Works see Chief Architect's
    Department
Minton (tiles) 598
Minton, Hollins & Co. 261
Moffat & Bentley 339
Monkhouse, R. 610
Moore, A. G. 507
Moore, A. L. 487
Moore, George 65, 67–8, 235,
    519–20, 685
Moore, John 74, 168
Moore, Margaret Elizabeth 521
Moore, Temple 454, 635
Moore (A. L.) & Son 114
Morgan (de) (tiles) 172, 326
Morland, Geoffrey 208, 444
Morland, Sir Samuel 36, 503
Morris, William 422, 455, 629
Morris (William) & Co. 64, 92, 114,
    124, 178, 200, 217, 280, 347, 417,
    422, 423, 455, 484, 534, 578, 629,
    640, Pls. 90, 92
Morris (William) of Westminster 337,
    404, 600, 608, 684
Morrison & Mason 634
Morton, Alistair 126n., 181–2
Morton, Sir James 182n., 263
Morville, Sir Hugh de 477
Mounsey family 563
Mounsey, G. G. 363
Mounsey, George 589
Mounsey, John (C19) 563
Mounsey, John and Dorothy (C17)
    563
Mounsey, R. (C17) 123
Mounsey, Robert (C18) 585

Mounsey, Robert (C19) 55, 589
Mounsey-Heysham family 588
Mulcaster, J. S. 384
Multon of Egremont, Thomas de
    214
Muncaster, John Pennington, 1st
    Baron 534–7
Muncaster, Josslyn Pennington, 5th
    Baron 584
Muncaster, 4th and 5th Barons
    535
Murchie, James 63, 254, 496
Murray, J. 372
Murray, Ward & Partners 74, 439
Musgrave family 124, 157, 321, 338,
    401, 470, 471, 477, 605
Musgrave, Sir Edward (fl. 1609)
    401, 402
Musgrave, Sir Philip (C17) 628
Musgrave, Philip (C19) 569
Musgrave, Thomas (fl. 1615) 572
Musgrave, Thomas (fl. 1674) 384
Musgrave, William 389
Musgrave, Winifred and Grace
    389
Myers, Christopher 673, 680, Pl. 77
Myers, George 662

Napper Architects 76, 376
Napper Partnership 363
Nash, David 602
Nasmyth, Alexander 691
Naylor family 603
Nelson of Carlisle (C19 sculptors)
    391, 413, 577, 599, 604, 699
Nelson, George 59, 235, 325
Nelson, James 508
Nelson, Richard 248
Nelson, Thomas 58, 255, 508, 600,
    618, 701
Nelson, W. A. 444
Nesfield, W. Eden 68, 520
Neville family 568
Nevinson family 533
Nevinson, John and Elizabeth 533
Newby, C. L. 370
Newcastle upon Tyne University
    Projects Office 376
Newton, Chambers & Co. 397n.
Nichol, John 63, 240, Pl. 85
Nichol, Ray R.. 143, 163, 225, 239
Nichol Armstrong Lowe 76, 570
Nicholson, A. K. 72, 114, 167, 233,
    239, 256, 261, 337, 386, 407, 491,
    497, 540, 567, 577
Nicholson, Ben 180, 486
Nicholson, Sir Charles 225, 231–2
Nicholson, Christopher 180–1, 182
Nicholson, John 326
Nicholson, Norman 75, 79, 235,
    432, 525

Nicholson, Peter 55, 61, 244, 263,
    300–1, 306, 326, 414, 589
Nicholson, Ralph 261
Nicholson, Bishop William 35, 81,
    85, 87, 114, 118, 326, 384, 386,
    405, 421, 555, 604, 639, 662
Nicholson, Winifred 484, 486
Nixon (masons) 684
Nixon, William 387, 415–17
Nixons & Parkin 684
Nixson, Paul 64, 124, 146, 239, 245,
    252–3, 266, 414, 699
Noble family 126–7
Noble, John 125
Noble, Matthew 65, 138, Pl. 103
Nollekens, Joseph 58, 235, 668,
    Pl. 73
Norfolk, Thomas Mowbray, 1st
    Duke of 301
Norfolk, Charles Howard of Greystoke,
    11th Duke of (d.1815) 44, 53, 54,
    386–8, 517, 700
Norman, Graham 390
Norris, Dom Charles 133, 528
North, Christopher see Wilson,
    John
North, Herbert Luck 69, 451, 691
Northumberland, Henry Percy, 1st
    Earl of 283
Northumberland, Henry Percy, 9th
    Earl of 287
Northumberland, Siward, Earl of
    531
Nowell, Alexander 466
Nutter, William Henry 301–2, 370
Nuttgens, J. E. 586

Oakley, Major C. 138
Oblique Partnership 677
O'Byrne, James 295
O'Connor 95, 430
O'Connor, M. & A. 256, 425
Office of Works 254
Oldfield (fl. 1915) 699
Oldfield, Simpson & Saul 448
Oliver, Basil 223
Oliver, George Dale 67, 95, 251, 257,
    260, 262, 265, 286, 319, 475, 555,
    614–15
Oliver & Dodgshun 251, 339, 455,
    685
O'Neill, E. & C. 89
O'Neill & Pearse 134
Orridge, John 245
Osmotherley, Cuthbert and Mary
    187
Oxley, William 316

Pace, George 688
Paget-Tomlinson family 466
Paine, James 217

Paley (Manchester) 410
Paley, E. G. 62, 92, 119, 131, 132,
    135, 138, 141, 156, 160, 201, 209,
    268, 271, 275, 328, 341, 354, 359,
    373, 406, 457–8, 583, 638, 647,
    697, Pl. 104
Paley, H. A. 372, 564
Paley & Austin 59, 60, 62, 63, 64,
    68, 98, 131, 132, 134, 135, 138,
    141, 142, 165, 166, 200, 303, 313,
    317, 327, 342, 347, 359, 360, 361,
    395, 406–7, 410, 419, 456, 466,
    512, 525, 541, 560, 562, 577, 585,
    640, 647, 649, 650, 656, 688, 696,
    Pl. 98
Paley, Austin & Paley 70, 127, 316,
    347, 581, 696, Pl. 86
    see also Austin & Paley
Palmer, William 672
Park, Mungo 619
Park, Willie Jun. 619
Parke, John and Anne 596
Parker family 625–6
Parker, Kevin 699
Parker, Thomas 662
Parker, William 625
Parker (Barry) & Raymond Unwin
    636
Parkin, Hugh 575
Parkin, Robert Hogarth 309
Parry (Eric) Architects 405
Paterson, Alexander N. 708
Paterson (Gavin) & Son 74, 531
Patrickson, Hugh 474
Pattinson, Abraham 60, 67, 101n.,
    169, 690
Pattinson, G. H. 69, 101, 168, 169,
    174, 433, 603, 615, 693
Pattinson, Joseph 68, 69, 167, 169,
    174, 175–6, 602, 644
Pattinson, Lancelot 517
Pattinson, T. C. 488
Pattinson, Thomas 168, 169, 691
Pattinson & Holmes 684
Pattinsons 60, 67, 69, 73, 82, 101,
    173, 176, 448, 487, 552, 690,
    692
Paxton, Joseph 411n., 593
Payne, Edward 71, 116–17
Peace, David 673
Peacocke, Meg 76, 471
Pearce, W. 191
Pearson (Charles B.), Son & Partners
    2, 74, 246, 405
Pearson, John Bagot 191
Pease, Joseph 94
Peere, Heinrick van 241
Pembroke, Countess of see Clifford,
    Lady Anne
Pendle Stained Glass 75, 698
Pennington, T. F. 434

Percy family 287
  see also Northumberland, Earls of
Percy, Bishop Hugh 54, 325, 591, 593
Perkin & Son 615
Perritt, Thomas 417
Peter, Abbot of Furness Abbey 352
Petty, Miss 654
Petty, Christopher and Mary 561
Philipson family 446, 642, 693
Phillimore, Claud 128
Phillips, Norman 240
Pickering, Mr (Carlisle) 674
Pickering, Mr (High Cross) 642
Pickering, J. 604
Pickett (F.) & Co. 367
Pilkington (tiles) 246, 345
Pipard (or de Rumeli), Aelicia 314, 371
Pitt, Thomas (later Lord Camelford) 58, 225, 231, 232, 591–2, 637
Pitt, William (the younger) 207
Plaw, John 53, 169, Pl. 56
Plumer family 384
Pocklington, Joseph 53, 72, 79, 370–1, 450–1
Pogmire, Alexander 36, 415, 503, 591, 592
Pomeroy, F. W. 234
Ponsonby, Sir John (C17) 392
Ponsonby, Sir John (C20) 392–3
Ponsonby, Simon and Anne 392
Popplewell, John 117
Porter family 159
Porter, B. 502
Portland, 2nd Duke of 566
Potter, Beatrix (Mrs Heelis) 72, 298, 400, 553, 603–4, 643, 703
Powell, John Hardman 64, 233
Powell Bros (of Leeds) 113, 146, 335, 559
Powells 89, 95, 98, 124, 127, 163, 167, 182, 185, 199, 211, 217, 233, 266, 384, 392, 409, 425, 447, 469–70, 473, 519, 522, 532, 534, 564, 566, 567, 577, 581, 586, 594, 604, 628, 629, 632, 635, 655, 662, 666, 684
Preston family 359, 410, 496
Preston, George 33, 41, 268, 270–1, 272, 410
Preston, John 354
Preston, R. B. 328
Preston, Roger 105
Preston, Thomas 630
Prickett, Andy 161
Pritchard, Jonathan 93
Procaccini, Giulio Cesare 673
Proctor, B. 505
Proctor-Mitchell, R. 343

Prynne, George Fellowes 626
PSA Building Management 257
Pugin, A. W. N. 61, 235, 662–3, 703
Pugin, E. W. 61, 133, 278, 674, 699, Pl. 88
Pugin & Pugin 278
Purcell Miller Tritton 89
Puxley, Rev. H. B. L. 283

Quellin, A. 122
Quine, Mary 487
Quirk, Thomas 497

Race, Arthur 137
Radcliffe, Mrs Ann 161, 354
Raghton, Ivo de 231n.
Rainbow, Bishop Edward 37, 591, 592
Rainford, Christopher 363
Ram, K. 335
Ramsden family 535–6
Ramsden, Sir James 59, 60, 65, 130–1, 132, 137, 138, 354, 359, 608, Pl. 103
Ramshay, Thomas 180
Ranger, W. 432
Rank, Nicholas 429
Rankin, Sir Robert 201
Ransom, Gordon 98
Ranulph de Meschines 21, 23, 104, 110, 668
R.A.T. 174
Ratcliff, Sir John and Dame Alice 314, 315
Ratcliffe, Dorothy Una 633
Rathbone, William V or VI 147
Rawes, Richard 442
Rawlinson family 379
Rawlinson, Daniel 36, 399
Rawlinson, J. J. 380
Rawlinson, Sir Thomas 36, 399
Rawlinson, William and M. 380
Rawnsley, Edith 65, 70, 237, 315, 316
Rawnsley, Canon Hardwicke 65, 70, 72, 233, 237, 315, 316, 445, 450, 487n.
Rawson, John and Elizabeth 173
Rawson, Stansfield 665
Rayson, Hugh 562
Rea, James Henry Rea, 1st Lord 69, 344, 345, 691
Rea, Alec 69, 345n., 691
Rea, Hope 344
Read, Mathias 36, 123, 124, 187, 312, 390, 392, 423–4, 456, 503, 566, 673, 674, 677, 680, 681, 682
Redfern, Harry 71, 89, 223, 254, 255, 256, 257–9, 263, 265, 266, 501, 669
Redman (de) family 492

Redman, Richard, Bishop of Ely 616

Redmayne, George T. 182

Redmayne, Giles 182

Redness, Richard de 41, 245

Reed, Charles (later *Verelst*) 68, 316

Reed Millican 179, 254, 278, 335, 561

Reed Millican & Co. 185

Rees, John 239

Rees, Verner O. 71, 433

Regnart, C. 95, 126, 235

Reid, William 55, 306, 589

Reinforced Concrete Construction Co. 463

Remington, Rev. Thomas 374

Rendel, Alexander Meadows 701

Rendel, Palmer & Tritton 701

Rennie, John 50, 542, 652

Rennie, Sir John 676

Reynard, Bob 498

Reynolds, Sir Joshua 647–8

Rhind, William 335

Rhodes, Alan 552

Richard III, King 241, 568, 570

Richard of Bayeux, Abbot 352

Richard le Brun 164

Richardson family 97

Richardson, J. C. 437

Richardson, Thomas 94

Richardson, Mrs Thomasine 528

Richmond, Christopher 147, 556

Richmond, John and Margaret 426

Richmond, Susanna 38, 426

Richmond Design 575

Rickman, Thomas 54, 58, 75, 265, 591–3, 606, 681, 703, Pl. 29

Rickman (Thomas) & Henry Hutchinson 223, 413–14, Pl. 59

Ridehalgh, Col. G. J. M. 552

Rigby, Elaine 471

Rigg, Colin 695

Rigg, R. Morton 116

Rigg, Richard 689

Riggs, John 67

Rikard (sculptor) 24, 183, Pl. 16

Riley, Meg 487

Rimington family 573, 574

Ritson, Will 665

Roberts, Cecilia 484

Roberts, Charles 182

Roberts, Francis 76, 134, 650

Roberts (Francis) Architects 341

Robertshaw, Edward 642

Robertson, E. S. 166

Robinson family 186

Robinson, Mr 487

Robinson, Charles 349

Robinson, Edward 593

Robinson, George 538, 539

Robinson, J. (sculptor) 664

Robinson, John (County Architect) 246, 251

Robinson, John (Jack) 111

Robinson, John Martin 128, 652

Robinson, Sir Thomas 545

Robinson, W. 302

Robinson, William 488

Robley family 149

Rochdale, George Kemp, 1st Baron 451

Rofe & Raffety 397

Roger le Poitevin 21

Rogers, John 241

Romanelli, Pasquale 647

Rook, John 593

Rope, Ellen Mary 178, 450

Roper, Lanning 338

Roscoe, Norris 71, 117

Rose, Joseph Sen. 417, 622, 634

Roselieb, L. Fritz 125

Ross, John 67, 417, 448

Rotheram, Dr Caleb 432

Rothwell, Richard Rainshaw 400

Rowlinson, Michael 463

Rumeli, Aelicia de *see* Pipard, Aelicia

Ruskin, John 65, 68, 294–5, 297, 462n., 487n., 705

Ryder & Yates 403

Rymer, Thomas Harrison 216

Rysbrack, J. M. 411

Salkeld family 421, 519, 668

Salkeld, Prior Lancelot 232, 519

Salkeld, Richard de 300

Salkeld, Col. Thomas 326

Salmond, Major-General James 580

Salomons, Edward 437

Salviati 348

Salvin, Anthony 63, 67, 68, 120, 253, 280, 346, 385, 387–8, 415–17, 447, 450, 484, 486, 491, 519–20, 534–7, 543–5, 551, 563, 591, 608, 636, 649, Pl. 60

Sandes, Thomas 437

Sandford family 122

Sandford, Sir Edward 37, 523

Sandford, Mildred 122

Sandford, Thomas 122

Sandys family 400, 648

Sandys, Col. 400

Sandys, Edwin, Archbishop of York 398–9

Sandys, Thomas Myles, M.P. 378, 399

Sandys, William and Margaret 32, 398–9

Satterthwaite, Robert 489

Satterthwaite, William 400

Saul, George 306, 413

Saul, Jonathan 448

Saul, Silas 306
Savell (A.) & Co. 342
Sawrey Gilpin family 201
Sawrey Gilpin, William 43, 200, 233, 417
Sawrey, William 298
Schneider, Henry W. 65, 129, 131, 132, 135, 138, 139, 166, 171, 327, 583, 609
Schofield, Ray 683
Schomberg Scott, Walter 132
Schwitters, Kurt 100n., 488
Scott, Carl 312
Scott, Francis C. 182
Scott, George Gilbert 61, 77, 98, 314–15, 601
Scott, Sir James 176
Scott, John (carver) 706
Scott, John (glass-stainer) 662
Scott, John (Wetheral) 669
Scott, M. H. Baillie see Baillie Scott
Scott, N. Keith 74, 151
Scott, Paul 448
Scott, Peter 74, 174
Scott, Sir S. H. 366
Scott, Sally 167, 673
Scott, Stanley Murray 118, 335, 365, 499–500, 561
Scott, T. Taylor 250, 260, 403, 422
Scott, Walter 251
Scott & Co. 580
Scott & Drape 231
Scott (John) & Son 64, 98, 118, 124, 128, 148, 187, 189, 261, 312, 363, 422, 455, 476, 556, 567, 588, Pl. 91
Scott Wilson Kirkpatrick 450
Scowcroft, Brian 695
Scrope, Lord (C14) 241
Scrope, Lord (C16) 241, 242
Seddon, Joseph 71, 223, 258, 266
Sedgwick, George 34, 444
Seed, G. K. 125
Seed, John 567
Seely & Paget 71, 142, 264
Sekers, Sir Nicholas 74, 531
Sellers, J. H. 448, 475
Senhouse family 47, 66, 215, 291, 514–16
Senhouse, Sir Humphrey 370, 514
Senhouse, Humphrey II 43, 513, 516
Senhouse, John 66
Senhouse, Joseph 594
Senhouse, Prior Simon 33, 145, 235–6
Settle, W. Moss 143, 651
Settle & Farmer 63, 201, 291, 526, 670
Severn, Arthur and Joan 297
Seward (A.) & Co. 202, 525, 609

Sewell, Mrs 337
Shand Kydd 171
Sharp, Dan 575
Sharp, J. 609
Sharpe, Edmund 62, 91, 217, 705
Sharpe & Paley 143, 354, 580–1
Sharphouse, Mark 395
Shaw, Malcolm 428
Shaw, Stephen 63, 66, 116, 117, 305, 408, 428, 432, 433, 442, 443
Shearwen, John and Margrat 369
Shepherd, Arthur 563–4
Shepherd, Jonathan 352
Sheridon, John 74, 466
Shout, Robert 370
Shrigley & Hunt 64, 72, 91, 98, 116, 119, 127, 128, 132, 133, 135, 149, 150, 166, 172, 200, 205, 208, 271, 275, 309, 317, 328, 337, 348, 351, 372, 375, 377, 384, 407, 410, 419, 420, 430, 431, 454, 456, 461, 528, 553, 555, 567, 581, 585, 599, 601, 608, 613, 615, 653, 660, 665, 674
Shutter, Tim 669
Shuttleworth, Peter 677
Sibson, Ruth 560
Sievier, R. W. 167
Simpson (Kendal) 505
Simpson, Arthur W. 70, 166, 171, 173, 205, 274, 306, 379, 430, 443, 469, 530, 629, 683
Simpson, E. 372
Simpson, Hubert 443
Simpson, John and Elizabeth 584
Simpson, Joseph 565
Sing see Synge
Singer & Sons 99
Singleton, Trevor 99
Sinnott, James 649
Siward, Earl of Northumberland 531
Skeat, Francis 636
Skelton family 114
Skelton, Richard and Deborah 114
Slack, J. 404
Slack, Thomas 404
Slee, Prior Christopher 30, 225, 236
Smeaton, John 97, 676
Smirke, Sir Robert 54, 57, 58, 111, 121, 223, 236, 244, 248, 308, 319, 338, 403, 504–5, 679, Pls. 58, 94
Smirke, Sydney 403, 678, 680, 703
Smith, Mr 516
Smith, Arthur Jackson 644
Smith, David Lockhart 556
Smith, E. R. 540
Smith, Elizabeth 297, 399
Smith, G. E. R. 132, 239, 261, 689
Smith, Geo. (fl. 1877) 547
Smith, George (fl. 1815) 297

Smith, George H. (fl. 1825) 471
Smith, J. T. 361
Smith, John 339
Smith, Joss 110
Smith, P. W. 444
Smith, Ralph 323
Smith, Thomas, Bishop (previously Dean) of Carlisle 111, 238, 593
Smith, Thomas (London) 309
Smith, William 341
Smith & Co. 642
Smithies, Henry 527
Smithies, J. 345
Snow, Rev. Thomas 653
Somervell family 208
Southeran, Ann 126
Southey, Robert 315, 449
Sowler, Judge 603
Spear, Francis H. 689
Spedding, Carlisle 673, 677, 679
Spedding, H. A. 146
Spedding, James and Elizabeth (St Bees) 600
Spedding, James (Whitehaven) 680
Speight, Sadie 71, 181, 517
Stabler, Harold 70, 695
Stables, Gordon 73, 434, 632
Stables & Gilchrist 182
Stagg, Joseph 548
Stalker, Daniel 610
Stalker, John 440
Stalker Bros 634
Stammers, Harry 266, 317
Stampa, George Dominic 500
Stamper, Jonathan 427
Standish family 177
Stanley family 292, 343, 442, 696
Stanley, George Edward 217
Stanley, Michael 697
Stanley, Rosalind see Carlisle, 9th Earl of
Stanton, Thomas 36, 105
Stanton, William 36, 508
Stanton Williams 76, 247
Stapleton family 338
Stead, E. W. 326
Steel, John 290
Steell, John 235
Stephen, King 21, 576
Stephens, E. B. 272, 508
Stephenson, George 514
Stephenson, Robert 624
Stephenson Bell 439
Sternberg, Baroness de 55, 171
Stevenson, W. Grant 711
Stewart, I. 407
Stewart, James 67, 252, 363, 588, 589, 663
Stileman, Frank 652
Stordy, Thomas 204
Stordy, William and Tirzah 205

Storey, Robert 676
Story, Fred 203, 219, 265, 266, 403
Stout, H. B. 683
Streatfield, Ernest A. 258
Street, G. E. 225, 231, 236
Strickland family 619–20
Strickland, Alice 623
Strickland, Cecilia 620
Strickland, Sir Gerald 620–1, 624
Strickland, Sir Thomas 620
Strickland, Bishop Walter (C14) 26, 157, 225–6, 231–2, 568
Strickland, Walter (C16) 620–2
Strickland, Walter Charles 623
Strong, Peter 75, 211, 325, 526
Stubbs, Robert and Catherine 502
Sturgis, Tim 446
Sudwick, Sir John 145
Suffling, E. R. 276, 455
Suffolk, Earls of 492
Sumner, Heywood 304
Sussex, Sir Thomas Dacre, 1st Earl of 34, 321
Sutherland Hussey Architects 77, 602
Sutton, Sarah 540
Sutton, Shelagh 487
Swallow, J. 167
Swann, Rev. Sidney 256, 562
Swarbrick, David 685
Swingler, James 37, 282, 324, 508, 531, 675
Synge (Sing), Alexander Millington 693–4

Taillebois, Ivo de, Baron of Kendal 21, 458
Tait, Dean 225
Talbot & Co. 474
Talman, William 36, 415, 503
Tarbuck, Robert 100, 434
Tattersall, Richard 50, 57, 223, 261, 264, Pls. 70, 95
Taylor, Agnes 349
Taylor, Clement 348
Taylor, Edward 349
Taylor, Ferdinando 379
Taylor, G. E. 397
Taylor, George Ledwell 418
Taylor, Isabel 348
Taylor, T. 320
Taylor & Clifton 182
Taylor Young 444
Team Northern 630
Teasdale, John (father and son) and James 387n.
Telfer, Colin 75, 340, 515, 526, 600, 677
Telford, Thomas 57, 244, 589
Terry, Christopher 425
Terry, Quinlan 587

Thackeray, William 37, 219, 246, 326, 330, 393, 413, 508, 531, 535, 551, 591–2, 633, 675, Pl. 51
Thai 323
Thanet, Countess of 106
Thanet, Thomas, 6th Earl of 106, 108
Thanet, Earls of 106, 112
Theatre Futures 448
Thomlinson, John 686
Thomlinson, Dr Robert 93, 686
Thompson, Gustavus 578
Thompson, Jacob 566
Thompson, James 346
Thompson, John 603
Thompson, Miles 55, 57, 58, 60, 63, 67, 116, 206, 313, 335, 341, 376, 411, 422, 428, 430, 432, 437, 440, 441, 442, 463, 465, 489, 500, 593, 651, 688, 690, 704
Thompson, R. F. 437
Thompson, Robert 31n., 329, 700
Thompson, Alderman William 466
Thompson & Webster 207, 377, 439, 593
Thorneley, Thomas 400
Thornton, William, Prior of Wetheral 661, 668
Thornycroft, Sir W. Hamo 65, 233
Threlkeld family 370, 520
Threlkeld, Lancelot (d.1492) 308
Threlkeld, Sir Lancelot (d.1512) 309
Threlkeld, Thomas 370
Tilliol (de) family 604, 606
Tilliol, Sir Peter de 605
Tinkler, Richard 157
Tipping, H. Avray 176
Tirriol family 401
Tite, Sir William 59, 248, 542, 569, 631, Pl. 105
Todd, Will 526
Tole, Mark 293
Tonner, J. F. 403
Tower, W. E. 144, 708
Townsend, C. H. 345
  see also *T. L. Banks & C. H. Townsend*
Townshend, Caroline 71, 205, 234, 345, 609
Townson (or Tolson), Thomas 207
Travis, Henry 401
Travis & Mangnall 124, 567
Trimen, Andrew 647
Tufton family 106
  see also Thanet
Tunwini 655
Turner, George 128
Turner, Joseph 387
Twelves, Marion 70, 316, 487n.
Tyson, T. F. 272

U.K. Atomic Energy Authority 612
Umfraville, Gilbert de 283
Underwood, H. J. 159
Underwood, J. 92
Unwin, Mr 321
Unwin, Edward 409
Unwin, Raymond 501
Unwin, Rev. William 636
Unwin Jones 487
Unwin Jones Architects 262
Unwin Jones Partnership 73, 76, 498, 575, 632
Unwin Parker & Jones 501
Ushers (Coniston) 400

Vane family 418
Vane, Francis 415
Vasconcellos, Josefina de 75, 89, 98, 101, 236, 271, 386, 527, 595, 598, 600
Vaux family 484, 555–6, 668
Vaux, Robert de 363, 479
Vaux, Rowlande 556
Vaux, William 555
Verelst see Reed, Charles
Vernon family 518
Victoria, Queen 223, 248, 618
Vieuxpont (or Vipont), Robert de 189, 192
Vincent, Gabriel 34, 189
Vipont (Vieuxpont) family 105, 106, 189, 192
Vis Williams Partnership 602
Voysey, C. F. A. 68–9, 70, 173, 174, 223, 443, 695

Waddell, William 664
Wade (sculptor) 399
Wadham, Edward 361
Wadham & Turner 59, 526
Wadman, W. 374
Wailes, William 64, 91, 98, 105, 159, 185, 211, 233, 234, 293, 315, 325, 335, 339, 341, 350, 365, 401, 404, 420, 422, 455, 461, 521, 567, 598, 618, 626, 638, 647, 656, 660, 667, 670, 674, 705
Wailes & Strang 64, 89, 93, 105, 149, 187, 188, 211, 386, 392, 521, 602, 610, 614, 615, 625
Wainwright, Alfred 79, 210
Wakefield, John 541
Wakefield, W. H. 541
Waldegrave, Bishop Samuel 65, 233
Walford, Mike 437, 440
Walker, Charles 393
Walker, David 148, 170
Walker, George and Agnes 298
Walker, Leonard 71, 380
Walker, Richard 298

Walker, Robert 63, 168, 171, 586–7, 601

Walker, Rev. Robert 609

Walker, Carter & Walker 70, 601

Walker & Emley 283

Wall, A. R. 278, 372

Waller, John Green 469

Walmisley, A. T. 66, 248

Walmsley, B. D. 240

Walmsley, Mr and Mrs Dean 98, 487

Walter, Prior of Carlisle 413

Walton, George 223

Walton, J. W. 95

Warburton, Albert 643

Ward, Basil 74, 174, 439

Ward, Gilbert 279n.

Ward, W. H. 69, 146, 451

Ward, W. H. A. 403

Ward & Hughes 126, 132, 160, 167, 205, 239, 367, 430, 503, 563, 594, 632
  see also Curtis, Ward & Hughes

Waring & Gillow 174

Warre, Capt. Edmond L. 120–1

Warrington 98, 309, 407, 430, 663

Warrington (W.) & Son 629

Warwick, Thomas 533

Waterhouse, Alfred 68, 94, 102, 135, 182, 273, 451–2, 463, 691

Watson family 610

Watson, Dr 643

Watson, George 66, 91, 109, 111, 384, 567, 573, 610, 632, 636

Watson, H. E. 252n.

Watson, Musgrave Lewthwaite 59, 91, 235, 254, 257, 325, 583, 610, Pl. 74

Watson, Richard, Bishop of Llandaff 167, 643

Watson, S. 146

Watson, Thomas 610, Pl. 74

Wearing, Charles Henry 624

Webb, John 176, 275

Webb, Philip 62, 64, 68, 177–9, 180–1, 473, 484, 543–6, 640, Pl. 89

Webster family 55, 66, 72, 169, 272, 315, 328, 338, 348, 427, 430, 438, 442, 496, 497, 498, 508, 524, 596, 622, 624, 636, 655, 697

Webster, Mrs 309

Webster, Francis 37, 55, 57, 58, 101, 109, 151, 175, 272, 332, 380, 396, 399, 408, 428, 432, 433, 435, 438, 439, 441, 442–3, 459–61, 463, 492, 495, 497, 498, 504, 529, 530, 541, 563

Webster, George 55, 56, 57, 58, 66, 67, 92, 101–3, 128, 157, 171, 201, 205, 207, 272, 274, 277, 292, 327, 338, 349, 373, 374, 377–8, 380,

395, 408, 410–11, 411, 412, 415–17, 428, 431, 433, 435, 437–8, 442, 466, 491, 497, 498, 505, 527, 529–30, 540, 553, 594, 596, 644, 692, Pl. 61

Webster, Robert 272

Webster, Thomas 144

Webster, Francis & George 55, 66, 399, 433, 435, 444, 512, 553

Webster & Thompson 625

Wedderhall, Richard 668

Weightman & Bullen 75, 528

Weir, Alan 395

West, Robert 673

West, Father Thomas 52, 58n., 79, 327, 329, 603

Westlake (glass-stainer) 461

Westmacott, R. Jun. 668

Westmorland, Ralph Neville, 1st Earl of 568

Westmorland, John 685

Weston, Canon G. W. 309, 310

Weston, George F. 308–9, 310

Whall, Christopher 71, 205, 453

Whall, Veronica 72, 91, 234, 447

Wharton family 310

Wharton, Philip, 1st Duke of 470

Wharton, Thomas, 1st Lord 32, 470, 471–2, 587

Wheatley-Balme, Mr 487

Wheatley-Balme, Edward Balme 488

Whelpdale, John (de) 211, 386

Whewell, Dr William 428

Whinney, T. B. 570

Whistler, Beatrice 561

Whistler, Lawrence 320

White, K. C./White (K. C.) Partnership 131, 328, 431

White, Laura 471

White, Thomas 170, 700, 701

White, William (C19) 422–3

White, William (C20) 74, 466

Whitehead, Rev. Henry 177–9, 473

Whitehouse, J. H. 297

Whiteside, Rev. J. 615, 616

Whitfield, Nicholas 97

Whitridge, Joseph 160

Whittaker family 603

Whittaker, Dr J. W. 400, 704

Whitwell, Francis A. 69, 103, 379, 644

Whitwell, M. F. 400

Widdaker, John 637

Wilberforce, William 693

Wilkie, Kim 411

Wilkinson, Isaac 396, 497n., 646

Wilkinson, John ('Iron Mad') 396, 497, 498

Wilkinson, Joseph 452

Wilkinson, Thomas 53, 506, 580, 639, 711
Wilkinson, Thomas (uncle of the above) 638
Willement, Thomas 159, 293, 387
William I, King 21
William I (the Lion), King of Scotland 189, 454
William II (William Rufus), King 21–2, 25, 189, 222, 240
William de Fortibus 283
William de Meschines 21, 23, 339, 340, 596
William Rufus *see* William II
Williams, J. 254
Williams, J. R. & E. 309
Williams, William (fl. 1669) 421
Williams, William and Barbara (fl. 1675) 390
Williams, Arthur Y. & George 57, 254
Williams (Colin) Design 575
Williams & Watson 306
Williams-Ellis, Clough 74, 209–10
Willink & Thicknesse 68, 373
Willows, Mr and Mrs 644
Wills, John 649
Wills, W. & T. 285
Wilson family 150, 433, 434, 435
Wilson (Whitehaven) 578
Wilson, Canon B. W. 491
Wilson, Christopher (fl. 1785–8) 435
Wilson, Christopher (d.1845) 512
Wilson, Daniel 38, 434, 529
Wilson, George 434
Wilson, H. Warren 72, 291
Wilson, John (Christopher North) 53, 691
Wilson, Rev. John 437, 462
Wilson, Thomas 285, 289
Wilson, Thomas Newby 347
Wilson, W. 146

Wilson, Rev. William Carus 58, 274–5, 349, 377, 411, 497
Winder, Joseph 438
Wippell & Co. 131
Withers, Robert Jewell 63, 425, 661, 668
Withington, Rev. Thomas 432
Wood, Percy 65, 140
Woodburn, Edwin 651
Woodhouse & Willoughby 137
Woodington, W. F. 250
Woodroffe, Paul 655
Woodville, Thomas 297
Wooldridge (glass-stainer) 95
Wooldridge, H. E. 217
Woolner, Thomas 65, 98, 272, 375, 685, Pl. 101
Wordsworth family 375–7, 595, 628
Wordsworth, Dora 56
Wordsworth, Dorothy 285, 375, 595, 671
Wordsworth, John 285
Wordsworth, William 53, 55–7, 79, 98, 102, 169, 282, 285, 315, 375, 376–7, 398, 399, 420, 506, 595–6, 609, 668, 687, 703
Worthington, Hubert 683
Worthington, Percy 103
Worthington, Thomas 219, 542, 631
Worthington (Thomas) & Sons 683
Wrigley, Thomas 101
Wyatt, Sir Matthew Digby 54, 92
Wyatt, Philip 54, 55, 292–3
Wylde, Matthew 653
Wyrkington, Thomas de 581

Yates, John 626
Yeates, John 435
York Glaziers Trust 239, 484
Young, Francis Brett 399
Young, Gordon 247
Young, William 96
Yrton, Adam de 598

INDEX OF PLACES

Principal references are in **bold** type; demolished buildings are shown in *italic*.

Abbey Town (C) **87–90**
  Holm Cultram Abbey 23, 30, 32, 75, **87–9**, 164, 268, 385
  Raby Cote 30, **90**
Addingham (C) *see* Glassonby
Aikton (C) **90**
  St Andrew 24, **90**, 559
Ainstable (C) **91**, 239
Aldingham (L) **91–2**
  Aldingham Hall 54, **92**
  motte 21–2, **92**
  St Cuthbert 25, 72, **91–2**
Allithwaite (L) **92–3**
  Boarbank Hall 77, **92–3**
  St Mary 64, 72, **92**
  Wraysholme Tower 27, 42, **93**
Allonby (C) **93–4**
  baths and assembly room 57, **94**
  Christ Church 35, 59, **93–4**
  The Square 43, **94**
Alston (C) 10, 23n., **94–8**
  bastles 28, 95, **96–8**
  Clarghyll Hall 28, **97–8**
  Cross View Cottage **96**, Pl. 64
  Methodist Church 63, **95**
  mines 46–7, **97**, 548
  Nenthead Level **97**, 548
  Randalholme 28, **97**
  St Augustine **95**, 547
  Samuel King's School 74, **96**
  Town Hall 66, **95**
Ambleside (W) 2, 11, 14, 57, 67, **98–103**, 375
  The Knoll 57, **102–3**
  Low Wood Hotel 67, **102**
  NatWest Bank 74, **100**
  Roman fort 15, **102**, 343
  Rothay Holme 68, **102**
  St Mary and parish centre 61, 75, 77, **98–9**
  Waterhead 67, **101**
  White Craggs 69, **103**
Appleby (W) 10, 21, *23*, 29, **104–13**
  Appleby Castle 22, 26, 34, 41, **106–8**, 112
  churches **104–6**
    St Lawrence 34, 36, **104–5**, Pl. 72

    St Michael 25, 29, 30, 34, **105–6**, 188, 514, 522
  cloister 57, **111**, 470
  houses and streets 22, 104, **109–13**
    New Appleby 22, **110–13**
    Old Appleby **109–10**
    White House 54, **111**, 191, Pl. 54
  public buildings 57, **108–9**
    almshouses 34, **112**, 198, 437
    Grammar School 66, **109**
    Town Hall plans 57, 109n.
Arkleby (C) *see* Plumbland
Arlecdon (C) **113–14**
Armathwaite (C) **114–16**
  Armathwaite Hall *see* Bassenthwaite
  Chapel of Christ and St Mary 34, **114**
  Low House **114–15**, 276
  Nunnery and Nunnery Walks 23, 44, **115**
  viaducts **115–16**
Arnside (W) 67, **116–17**
  Arnside Tower 26, **117**
  Kent Viaduct **116**, 527, 653
  Methodist church 63, 71, **117**
  St James 63, 64, 71, **116–17**
Arthuret (C) 33, 64, **118**, 501, 608
Asby (W) *see* Great Asby
Askam-in-Furness (L) 60, 77, **119**
  Ireleth 11, **119**
  Marsh Grange 37, **119**
Askerton Castle (C) 27, 28, **120–1**, 164, 220, 363, Pl. 30
Askham (W) 3, **121–3**, 617
  Askham Hall 27, 41, **122–3**, 472, 572, 709
  Cockpit 13, **123**
  Cop Stone 13, **123**
  St Peter 58, **121–2**
  Widewath 39, **123**
Aspatria (C) 9, 20, **123–5**
  Blennerhasset 3, **125**
  St Kentigern 25, 59, 65, 89, **124–5**
    sculpture 19, 20, **124**, 163
Aughtertree Fell (C) *see* Uldale

Backbarrow (L) *see* Haverthwaite
Bampton (W) **126–7**
    limekiln 46, **126**
    St Patrick 35, **126**, 324, 392
    Thornthwaite Hall 42, **127**
Barbon (W) **127–8**
    Barbon Manor 68, **127–8**
    St Bartholomew 62, 70, **127**
    Whelprigg House 55, **128**, 466,
      Pl. 61
Bardsea (L) **128–9**
    Holy Trinity 71, **128**
Barrock Park (C) *see* High Hesket
Barrow Island (L) *see* Barrow-in-
    Furness
Barrow-in-Furness (L) 2, 45, 78,
  129–43
    churches etc. **131–4**, **142–3**, 313
      cemetery 63, **134**
      St James 59, 62, 130, **132**
      St John, Barrow Island 71,
        132, **142**
      St Mary of Furness (R.C.)
        61, **133–4**
      SS Matthew, Mark, *Luke* and
        John 62, **132–3**, *142*
    houses and streets 59, 62,
      129–30, **138–43**
      Michaelson Road **141**,
        Pl. 98
    industrial buildings 45, 48–9, 59,
      62, 129–31, **140–3**
      Devonshire Dock Hall 73,
        141, **142**
    outer districts **141–3**
      Barrow Island 60, 71, 131,
        141–2
      Biggar 129, **143**
      North Scale **143**
      Roose **142**
      Walney 129, 131, **143**
    public buildings **135–8**, 397n.
      Barrow Park 66, **138**
      Library 71, **137**
      statues 65, 75, **138–40**,
        Pl. 103
      Town Hall 62, 66, 131,
        135–7, 140, 359, Pl. 97
Barton (W) **144–5**
    St Michael 24, **144**, 565
Barwise Hall (W) 33, 41, 42,
  145–6
Bassenthwaite (C) 65, **146–8**
    Armathwaite Hall 52, 68, **147**
Beaumont (C) **148**
    St Mary 25, **148**, 211
Beckermet (C) 20, **148–9**
    St Bridget 19, **149**
    St John 59, 62, **148–9**, 599
Beckfoot milefortlet 17
Beckside (C) *see* Kirkby-in-Furness

Beetham (W) **149–52**
    Beetham Hall and Farmhouse
      27, 41, **151–2**, 496
    Blackberry Hill 74, **151**
    Heron Mill **151**, 582
    St Michael 21, 64, **149–50**
Belle Isle (W) *see* Bowness-on-
    Windermere
Bewcastle (C) 10, **152–6**
    Castle 18, 22, **155–6**
    Cross 18–19, 65, **153–5**, 222,
      313, 389, 406, 423, 707,
      Pls. 12, 13
    Presbyterian church 63, **155**
    Roman remains 15, 17, **155**
    St Cuthbert 24, **155**
Birdoswald (C) *see* Walton
Blackbeck (L) 49
Blackford (C) **156**
Blawith (L) **156**
Blencow Hall (C) *see* Greystoke
Blennerhasset (C) *see* Aspatria
Bolton (W) **156–8**
    All Saints 24, 75, **156–7**, 660
    Bewley Castle 27, **157–8**
Boltongate (C) **158–9**
    All Saints 28–9, **158–9**, Pl. 36
    Old Rectory 29, **159**
    Weary Hall 41, **159**
Boot (C) *see* Eskdale
Bootle (C) 10, **159–61**
    St Michael 31, **159–60**
    Seaton Hall and Priory 23, 25,
      160–1
Borrowdale (C) 38, 45, **161–2**
    Honister slate mines 45,
      161–2
Bowness-on-Solway (C) 1, **162–5**,
  314n.
    Anthorn Array 73, **165**
    Barrocks House 28, **165**
    Drumburgh Castle 17, 28, 120,
      164–5, Pl. 33
    Port Carlisle 50, **163**, 260
    Roman forts 17, 162, **164**
    St Michael 24, 30, 65, **162–3**
    Solway Viaduct 116, **163**
Bowness-on-Windermere (W) 11,
  165–76
    churches **165–8**
      Carver Memorial Church 63,
        168
      St John 132, 166, **167**
      St Martin and rectory 31, 34,
        40, 65, 70, **165–7**, Pl. 38
    town 60, **168–9**
      Elim Grove 60, **169**
      Old England Hotel 67,
        168–9
      Shepherds' boatyard 74, **168**
      Spinnery 70, **169**

villas **169–76**
  Belle Isle 53, 54, **169–71**, 176,
    Pl. 56
  Belsfield 55, 165, **171**
  Blackwell 68–9, 70, **171–2**,
    175, 176, 695, Pl. 112
  Broadleys 68–9, 70, **173**,
    174–5, 176, Pl. 109
  Gossel Ridding 69, 70, **174**
  Long Dales 74, **174**, Pl. 114
  Moor Crag 68–9, 173, **174–5**,
    176, Pl. 111
  Storrs Hall 53, **175–6**, 643
Brackenhill Tower (C) 26, **177**
Brampton (C) 9, 17, **177–82**
  Brackenfell 71, **181–2**
  Four Gables 68, **180–1**
  Green Lane House 68, **181**
  Moot Hall 57, **180**
  motte 21, **180**
  Old Brampton vicar's pele 29,
    179
  Old Church 24, **179**
  Roman fort 16, **179**
  St Martin and parish hall 62–3,
    64, **177–9**, Pl. 90
Branthwaite (C) *see* Dean
Brathay (L) **182**
  Brathay Hall 53, **182**, 400
Bridekirk (C) **183–5**
  Dovenby station **185**, 638
  St Bride 24, 32, 62, **183–5**, 278,
    362n., Pl. 84
    font 20, **183–5**, 320, Pl. 16
Brigham (C) **185–6**
  St Bridget 20, 25, 28, 62, 90,
    185–6
Bromfield (C) **187**
  St Mungo 19, 24, **187**
Brough (W) 14, 22, 47, **188–92**
  Augill Castle 54, **191**
  Brough Castle 18, 22, 26, 34,
    107–8, **189–90**, 198, 243, Pl. 28
  Helbeck Hall 54, 76, **191**
  St Michael 22, 30, 34, 104,
    188–9, Pl. 35
  South Stainmore **191**
Brougham (W) 14, **192–9**
  Brougham Castle 18, 22, 26, 34,
    108, **192–5**, 198, 574, 607n.
  Brougham Hall 27, 54, **197–8**,
    281, 505, 587, 626, 711
  Countess Pillar 34, **195–6**
  Hornby Hall 33, 40, **198**, 382
  Oasis, Whinfell Forest 76,
    198–9
  Roman fort **195**, 311
  St Ninian (Ninekirks) 34, 35,
    65, 192, **196**, 197
  St Wilfrid 31, 34, **196–7**, 234,
    705, Pl. 43

Broughton (C) **199–200**
  St Columba, Broughton Moor
    63, **199**
Broughton East (L) *see* Field
  Broughton
Broughton Lodge **347**, 400
Broughton-in-Furness (L) 43,
  200–1
  Broughton Tower 27, 29, 53,
    200–1
Broughton Moor (C) *see*
  Broughton
Burgh-by-Sands (C) 41, **201–5**
  Longburgh 41, **204**
  Moorhouse 41, **204**
  Roman fort 17, **201**
  St Michael 18, 28, 29, **201**
Burneside (W) **205–8**, 447
  Burneside Hall 27, 33, 40,
    206–7, 582
  Hollins 41, **208**
  St Oswald 70, **205**
  Tolson Hall 41, 54, **207**
Burton-in-Kendal (W) 42,
  208–10
  Dalton Hall 74, **209–10**
  St James 20, **208–9**
Buttermere (C) 34, **210**

Caldbeck (C) 3, **210–13**
  bobbin mill 50, **211–12**
  Caldbeck Fells workings 46,
    212–13
  Carrock Fell hill-fort 14, **213**
  St Kentigern 25, 29, 59, 64,
    210–11, 473
Calder Bridge (C) **213–18**
  Calder Abbey 23, 25, 45, 68,
    213–17, 340, 382, Pl. 23
  St Bridget 62, 215, **217**
Calgarth Hall (W) *see* Troutbeck
Calthwaite (C) **218**
  All Saints 63, 70, **218**
  Calthwaite Hall 54, **218**
Camerton (C) **218–19**
  St Peter 32, **218–19**
Cark (L) *see* Flookburgh
Carleton (C) **219–20**
  Newbiggin Hall 27, 120,
    219–20, 475
Carlisle (C) 2, 21, **220–67**
  Castle *see* public buildings
    below
  Cathedral 24, 25, 30, 58, 222,
    224–36, 241, 269, 389, 591,
    639, 661, 662, Pls. 17, 21, 24,
    26
    furnishings and monuments
      19, 30–2, 36, 58, 59, 64, 65,
      71, 105, 186, 197, **231–6**,
      519, 637, Pl. 44

monastic buildings 23, 225, **235–8,**, 265; Deanery and Prior's Tower 24, 29, 33, 145, **238**, 544, Pl. 40; Nos. 1–3, The Abbey 39, **236–7**, 247

churches etc. 75, **239–40, 256–7, 260–1,** 263
  cemetery 61, 63, **263**
  Christ Church 58, 223, 253
  Congregational church, Lowther Street 63, **240**, Pl. 85
  Dominican (Blackfriars') house 23, 222
  Franciscan (Greyfriars') house 23, 222
  Holy Trinity 58, 223, 253, 265
  Our Lady and St Joseph (R.C.) **257**
  St Aidan 72, **256**
  St Barnabas, Newtown 71, **264**
  St Bede 263, **264**
  St Cuthbert and Tithe Barn 35, 42, 91, 225, **239–40**, 684
  St George, Warwick Road **257**
  St John the Evangelist **256**
  St Mary 225, 239
  St Michael, Stanwix **265–6**, 412
  St Paul (former) **257**

districts:
  Belah 223, **265–6**
  Caldewgate **260–3**
  Currock 23, **263–4**
  Denton Holme **260–3**
  Etterby **265–6**
  Harraby 223, **263–4**
  Kingmoor **265–6**
  Morton 223, **264–5**
  Newtown **264–5**
  Raffles **264–5**
  Stanwix 17, **265–6**
  Upperby 223, **263–4**

houses, streets and commercial buildings 8, 9, 37, 41, 221–4, 239, **249–63**
  The Abbey *see* Cathedral *above*
  Apple Tree 71, **255**
  Botchergate 221, **257–9**
  County Hotel (Red Lion) 223, **254**
  The Crescent (pub) 71, **254**
  Crown and Mitre 223, **251**
  Cumberland (pub) 71, **257–8**
  Cummersdale **265**
  Earl Grey 71, **259**
  Horse and Farrier 71, **265**

  The Lanes precinct 76, 224, **251**
  Lowther Street 57, 223, **254–6**
  Redfern Inn 71, **266**
  Rickerby House **266**
  Rickergate 222, 246
  Rose and Crown 71, **263**
  Scotch Street 221, **251**
  Tullie House *see* public buildings *below*
  Warwick Road area 59, 223, **256–60**, Pl. 96

industrial history 45, 50, 51, 223–4, 250, 259, **260–3**
  Dixon's (Shaddon) Mill 50, **261–2**, Pl. 70

public buildings 57, 71, **240–54**, 257
  Athenaeum (Lloyds TSB) 57, **254**
  Bitts Park 66, 240, **248**
  Bochard Gate 29, 244
  Canal Basin 164, **261**
  Carlisle Castle 18, 21, 26, 31, 90, 190, 221–2, **240–4**, 306, Pls. 27, 41
  Citadel (and courts) 29, 57, 221, 223, **244–5**, 319, Pl. 94
  Citadel Railway Station and County Hotel 51, 59, 223, **248**, 249, **253**, 260, Pl. 105
  city walls 29, 57, 221, 222, 241, **244**, **253**
  Civic Centre 2, 74, **246**
  Covered Market 66, **247–8**
  Crown and Mitre Hotel 67, **251**
  Cumberland Infirmary 57, 223, **264–5**, Pl. 95
  Eden Bridge 57, 222–3, **248**
  Fish House, King Garth 57, **267**
  Guildhall 41–2, **245–6**
  Lakes Court Hotel *see* Citadel Railway Station *above*
  Old Town Hall 57, 223, **245**
  St Nicholas hospital 222
  Tullie House Museum 37, 66, 76, 219, 221, 224, **246–7**, 253, 300, 611

Roman remains (forts and Hadrian's Wall) 14–18, 220–2, 252n., 265, **266**

Carlisle Canal 50, 163, 165, 203, 222, 261

Carrock Fell (C) *see* Caldbeck

Cartmel (L) 1, 2, 21, 45, **267–73**
  Cartmel Priory 23, 24, 25, 30–1, 32, 33, 36, 41, 55, 64, 65, 75, 197, **267–73**, 630, Pls. 25, 42

Cartmel Fell (L) 273–4
  Hodge Hill 40, 274
  St Anthony 30, 31, 35, 273–4,
    Pl. 39
Casterton (W) 274–6
  Holy Trinity 58, 64, 274–5,
    Pl. 93
Castle Carrock (C) 276
Castle Crag (W) see Haweswater
Castlerigg (C) see St John's in the
  Vale
Castle Sowerby (C) 34, 276–7
Castlesteads (W) see Natland
Catterlen Hall (C) see Newton
  Reigny
Cautley 277
Claife Station (L) see Sawrey
Cleator and Cleator Moor (C) 48,
  60, 277–80
  Our Lady of the Sacred Heart
    (R.C.) 61, 72, 278–9
  St John Evangelist, Cleator
    Moor (1870–2) 63, 278
Cliburn (W) 280
  Cliburn Hall 75, 280
  St Cuthbert 24, 280
Clifton (C) 20, 280, 280–1
Clifton (W) 281–2
  Clifton Hall 42, 281
Cockermouth (C) 2, 9, 51, 282–91
  Castle and 'Mirk Kirk' 22, 24,
    283–4
  churches etc. 282–3
    All Saints 61, 282–3
    cemetery 63, 289–90
    Congregational chapel 63,
      283
  houses and streets 8, 22,
    285–91
    Grecian Villa (Manor House
      Hotel) 285, 291, 702
    Percy House 33, 287
    Wordsworth (William Bird's)
      House 37, 284–5
  public buildings 285–90
    Carnegie Library 66, 286
    Cockermouth School and
      Eco Centre 74, 77, 290
Cockermouth, Keswick & Penrith
  Railway 50, 448
Colby (W) 291
Colthouse (L) see Hawkshead
Colton (L) 72, 291–2
Conishead Priory (L) 23, 54, 55,
  67, 292–4, 411
  Buddhist Temple 76, 293–4,
    Pl. 116
Coniston (L) 2, 46, 294–300
  houses and farms 57, 295–8
    Brantwood 52, 68, 294, 297,
      Pl. 1

Coniston (Old) Hall and
  barn 40, 41, 42, 207, 295–6,
    446, 582, 596, Pl. 1
  Low Tilberthwaite Farm and
    sculpture 298, Pl. 118
  Low Yewdale 298, Pl. 67
  Monk Coniston Hall 53,
    296–7
  Tent Lodge 53, 297
  Yew Tree Farm (gallery) 40,
    298
  industrial remains 45, 48,
    298–300
    Hodge Close Quarry 46, 300
  Ruskin Museum 77, 295
  St Andrew 294–5
    Ruskin Cross 65, 294–5, 526
Corby Castle (C) 44, 55, 217,
  300–2
Corney (C) 303
Cotehill (C) 303
Cowgill 303
Cowmire Hall (W) see Crosthwaite
  (W)
Crackenthorpe Hall (W) 37, 291,
  303–4
Croglam Castle (W) see Kirkby
  Stephen
Croglin (C) 304–5
  St John Baptist and rectory 29,
    66, 304
  Townhead Bastle 27, 28, 304–5
Crook (W) 305
Crosby (C) see Crosscanonby
Crosby-on-Eden (C) 223, 305–7
  Crosby House 306–7
  Eden Grove 55, 306–7
  St John Evangelist 61, 305–6,
    Pl. 83
Crosby Garrett (W) 307
  Rayseat Pike long cairn 12, 13,
    307
  St Andrew 21, 23, 157, 307, 660
Crosby Ravensworth (W) 307–11
  Castlehowe Scar stone circle 13,
    311
  Crake Trees 42, 310
  Ewe Close 14, 311
  Image Garden, Reagill 64,
    310–11
  Reagill Grange 310
  St Lawrence 21, 25, 58, 62, 64,
    70, 75, 307–9, 470, 532, 560,
    660, Pl. 81
  Wickerslack Moor Roman
    farmstead 14
Crosscanonby (C) 311–13
  Crosby 3, 313
  St John Evangelist 18, 20, 21,
    23, 25, 89, 124, 311–13, 515
  Swarthy Hill mile fortlet 17, 313

Crosscrake (W) **313–14**
Crosthwaite (C) **314–17**, 449
　Cumberland Pencil Factory **316**
　St Kentigern 29, 30, 31, 32, 34,
　　59, 65, **314–15**, 601
　School of Industrial Arts (KSIA)
　　70, **316**
　Underscar 68, **316–17**
Crosthwaite (W) **317–18**
　Cowmire Hall 39, 41, **317–18**,
　　496
Culgaith (C) 35, **318**
Cumdivock (C) **318–19**
Cumrew (C) 29, **319**
Cumwhitton (C) 24, **319–20**
Curthwaite (C) see Thursby

Dacre (C) **320–2**
　Dacre Castle 27, 33, 34, 192,
　　320–2, 324, 584, 710
　St Andrew 19, 20, 34, 315, **320**
Dalemain (C) 9, 33, 34, 38, 42,
　43–4, **322–4**, 626, 627
Dallam Tower see Milnthorpe (W)
Dalston (C) 2, **324–6**
　Dalston Hall 29, 68, **325–6**
　Ratten Row 39, 41, **326**
Dalton-in-Furness (L) 11, 47, 58n.,
　327–9
　Castle 26, **328**
　drinking fountain 119, **328**
　St Mary 62, **327–8**
Dean (C) 3, **329–31**
　Branthwaite 37, **330**, 392
　Friends' Meeting House,
　　Pardshaw 35, **330**, Pl. 76
　St Oswald 59, 90, 158, **329**
Dearham (C) **331**
　St Mungo 24, 28, **331**, 473
　　sculpture 19, 20, 124–5, 146,
　　313, **331**, 534
Dendron (L) **332**
Dent 73, 332
Denton (C) **332–4**
　bastles 28, 29, **332**, 333, 546
　Hadrian's Wall:
　　Milecastle 48 (Poltross
　　　Burn) 16, **333–4**
　　Willowford 16, 17, **334**
　　Nether Denton 16, 17, **332–3**
　　　Roman fort **333**, 659
　　The Temon 28, **333**
　　Upper Denton church 21, **333**
Dillicar (W) **334**
Distington (C) 63, 70, **335**
Dovenby (C) see Bridekirk
Drigg (C) **335–6**, 609
Drumburgh (C) see Bowness-on-
　Solway
Duddon Bridge (C and L) see
　Ulpha

Dufton (W) 2–3, **336–7**, 539, Pl. 5
Dunmail Raise (W) see Grasmere

Eaglesfield (C) 35, **337**
Eamont Bridge (W) see Yanwath
Eden Benchmarks 75
　Appleby **110**
　Carlisle **248**
　Kirkby Stephen **471**
　Mallerstang 75, **511**
　Wetheral **669**
Eden Valley Railway 104
Edenhall (C) 28, 32, **337–8**, 471
Egremont (C) 22, 45, **339–41**
　Castle 21, 22, 215, **340**
　cemetery 63, **339–40**
　mining 47, 48, 339, **341**
　St John, Bigrigg 156, **339**
　St Mary 32, **339**
　Wyndham School and sculptures
　　74, 75, **340**
Egton-cum-Newland (L) **341**, 647
Elterwater (W) see Langdales
Embleton (C) **342**, 636
Ennerdale Bridge (C) 63, **342**,
　514
Eskdale (C) 48, **342–6**
　Boot **342–3**
　Brotherilkeld 30, **343**
　Dalegarth Hall 28, 40, **343**
　Eskdale Green 62, **344–5**, 584
　Eskdale Mill 50, **342–3**, Pl. 69
　Gatehouse 69, **345–6**
　Hardknott Roman Fort 14,
　　15–16, 45, **343–4**
　St Bega, Eskdale Green 62,
　　344
　Stanley Ghyll, Beckfoot Halt 67,
　　344
　Youth Hostel 73, **343**

Farlam (C) **346**
Far Sawrey (L) see Sawrey
Fawcett Forest (W) **346–7**
Field Broughton (L) 2, 62, **347**,
　Pl. 86
Finsthwaite (L) **347–9**
　St Peter 62, **347–8**, 640
　Stott Park Bobbin Mill 50, **349**,
　　Pl. 68
　Waterside 41, **349**
Firbank (W) **349–50**
Flimby (C) 17, **350**
Flookburgh (L) 1, 22, **350–1**
　Canon Winder Hall **351**, 411
　St John Baptist 62, 64, 347,
　　350–1
Frizington (C) **352**
Furness Abbey (L) 23, 25, 30, 47,
　48, 60, 88, 211, 216, 228, **352–61**,
　382, 616, Pls. 18, 19

Abbey House Hotel 70, **360**, Pl. 113

Abbotswood 137, 354, **359**

Furness Railway 46, 59, 60, 62, **116**, **119**, 129–31, 138, **140–1**, **160**, **329**, 354, **359**, **373**, **552**, **585**, **600**, 608, **609**, **650**, 652

Gamblesby (C) 3, **361**

Garrigill (C) 95, **361–2**
    bastle 28, **362**
    Redwing Chapel **361**, Pl. 75

Garsdale 362

Gatebeck 49

Gilcrux (C) 24, **362**

Gilsland Spa (C) 10, 21, **363–4**
    R.A.F. Spadeadam 73, 76, **363–4**
    St Mary **363**, 588
    Spa Hotel 67, **363**

Glasgow & South Western Railway 51, **264**

Glassonby (C) **365**
    Long Meg and Little Meg, Hunsonby 13, **365**
    St Michael, Addingham 19, 20, **365**
    White House Farm bastle 28, 39, **365**

Gleaston Castle (L) **366**

Glenridding (W) **366–7**
    Glencoyne Farm 40, **366–7**
    Greenside Mine 46, **366–7**, 574
    Inn on the Lake 67, **366**

Gosforth (C) **367–70**
    Gosforth Hall 218, **369**
    St Mary 24, 59, 187, **367–9**
        Cross and other sculpture 18, 19, 20–1, 32, 125, **367–9**, 423, Pl. 10

Grange-in-Borrowdale (C) **370–1**
    Barrow House 72, 77, **370–1**, 450
    Borrowdale Hotel 67, **371**
    Watendlath 3, 30, **371**

Grange-over-Sands (L) 1–2, 11, 12, 60, 67, **371–4**
    Netherwood Hotel 68, **373**
    Rockdene (Black Rock Villa) 55, **373**
    station **373**, Pl. 104
    swimming pool 76, **373**

Grasmere (W) 10, 314n., **374–7**
    Allan Bank 55, **377**
    Dove Cottage and Jerwood Centre 55, 57, 76–7, **375–6**
    Dunmail Raise 13, 23n., **377**
    Our Lady of the Wayside (R.C.) 74, **375**
    Prince of Wales Hotel 57, 67, **376**
    St Oswald 8, 30, 34, 35, **374–5**, Pl. 34
    Silverhowe 53, **377**
    war memorial 65, **375**

Grayrigg (W) **377–8**
    Roman fort, Low Borrowbridge 14, 311, **378**
    St John 58, **377–8**

Graythwaite (L) **378–80**, 602
    Graythwaite Hall 68, **378–9**, 503
    Lower Graythwaite (Graythwaite Old Hall) 41, **379**

Great Asby (W) 3, **380–3**
    Castle Folds, Great Asby Scar 14, **383**
    Gaythorne Hall 37, 38, **381–2**
    Grange Hall 30, **382–3**
    St Peter and rectory 27, 29, 34, 63, 71, **380–1**

Great Langdale (W) *see* Langdales

Great Musgrave (W) *see* Musgrave

Great Ormside (W) *see* Ormside

Great Orton (C) *see* Orton (C)

Great Salkeld (C) **383–4**
    St Cuthbert and rectory 24, 28, 29, 32, 304, **383–4**, Pl. 15

Great Strickland (W) **384**

Great Urswick (L) *see* Urswick

Greystoke (C) **385–90**
    Blencow Hall 27, 385, **390**, 472, 606
    folly farms (Spire House, Bunkers Hill and Fort Putnam) 54, **388**, 700
    Greenthwaite Hall **390–1**
    Greystoke Castle 24, 26, 54, 67, **386–8**, 545, 638, Pl. 60
    Johnby Hall 27, 28, 220, **388–90**, 559, 606
    St Andrew 30, 31, 32, 75, 320, **385–6**, 475, 560, Pl. 37
    Stafford House 54, **388**

Grinsdale (C) **391**

Grizedale Hall (L) *see* Satterthwaite

Hadrian's Wall 16–18, 162, 266, 363, **391–2**, *413*
    see also under place-names

Haile (C) **392–3**
    Haile Hall 330, **392–3**
    sculpture 20, 149, **392**

Hardknott (C) *see* Eskdale

Harc Hill (C) *see* Lanercost

Harrington (C) 47, **393–4**

Harrow's Scar (C) *see* Walton (Birdoswald)

Hartley Castle (W) *see* Kirkby Stephen

Hartsop (W) **394–5**
    Hartsop Hall 33, **394**, 614

How End 40, **394–5**
  spinning gallery 40, **394**
Haverigg (C) *see* Millom
Haverthwaite (L) **395–6**, 593
  Backbarrow 47–9, 77, **396**,
    497n.
  Low Wood Gunpowder Works
    49, **396**
  St Anne 58, **395**
Haweswater (W) 126, **396–8**
  Castle Crag, Mardale, fort 18,
    397–8
  Mardale 18, 21, 161, **397**
  Mullender 40, **397**
  water scheme 72, **396–7**
Hawkshead (L) 3, 11, 42, 314n.,
  398–401
  Betty Fold 64, 69, **400**
  Colthouse Meeting House 3, 35,
    400
  Esthwaite Lodge 55, 72,
    399–400
  Hawkshead Hall (Furness Abbey
    grange) 30, **399**
  Heelis office 379
  St Michael 30, 32, 34, 35, 36,
    65, **398–9**
  Town Hall 57, **399**
Hayton (C), near Aspatria 3, **401–3**
  Hayton Castle **401–3**, 605
Hayton (C), near Brampton **403–4**
  Edmond Castle **403**, 664
  Gelt Viaduct 51, **403–4**
Hazelstack Tower (W) *see* Arnside
Helsington (W) **404**
Hensingham (C) **404–5**
Hesket Newmarket (C) 3, 37,
  405–6
Hethersgill (C) 63, **406**
Heversham (W) **406–9**
  Hincaster Tunnel 50, **409**, 542
  Horncop 69, **408**
  St Peter 65, **406–7**
    cross-shaft 19, **406**, 430
Highhead Castle (C) *see* Ivegill
High Hesket (C) **409–10**
Holker (L) **410–11**
  Holker Hall 11, 54, 68, **410–11**,
    457, Pl. 107
Holm Cultram (C) *see* Abbey Town
Holme (W) **411–12**
  Farleton House 42, **412**
  Holy Trinity 58, 72, **411**
Holme Low (C) **412**
Holme St Cuthbert (C) **412**
Houghton (C) 223, **412–14**
  Brunstock 54, **413–14**, Pl. 59
  Drawdykes Castle 37, **413**
  Houghton House 55, **414**
  Linstock Castle 26, **413**
Howgill 414

Howgill Castle (W) *see* Milburn
Hugill (W) *see* Ings
Hunsonby (C) *see* Glassonby
Hutton-in-the-Forest (C) 36, 55,
  67, 300, **415–18**, 503, Pls. 48, 50
Hutton John (C) 40, **418–19**
Hutton Roof (W) **419**

Ings (W) 35, 62, 70, **419–20**
Ireby (C) 22, 25, 211, **420–1**, 421
Ireleth (L) *see* Askam-in-Furness
Irthington (C) 60, **421–2**
Irton (C) **422–3**
  Irton Hall 67, **423**, 424, 535
  St Paul 64, **422–3**, 598, Pl. 91
    Cross 18, 19, 65, 149, 294,
    423, Pl. 9
Isel (C) **423–5**
  Isel Hall 26, 27, 33, 39, **424–5**,
    535
  St Michael 20, 24, **423–4**
Ivegill (C) **425–7**
  Christ Church 63, **425**
  Highhead Castle 26, 38, 323,
    325, **425–7**, 626, 661, Pl. 52

Johnby Hall (C) *see* Greystoke

Kendal (W) 2, 11, 21, **427–45**
  churches **428–32**, **440**, 443
    All Hallows, Fellside 430,
      440
    Friends' Meeting House 58,
      432
    Holy Trinity 29, 30, 31, 32,
      34, 35, 36, 61, 65, 72, 104,
      269, **428–31**, 440; cross-
      shaft 19, **430**
    Holy Trinity and St George
      (R.C.) 58, **431–2**
    St George 58, 427, **431**
    St Thomas, Stricklandgate
      58, 72, **431**, 528
    Zion Chapel 63, **432**, 437
  houses, streets and commercial
    buildings 22, 40, 42, 427–9,
    435–45
    Angel Hotel (former) 37, **437**
    Aynam Lodge 55, **443**
    Bridge House 55, **443**
    Castle Dairy 39–40, **441–2**
    Collinfield 34, 41, **444**
    Cox's Organ Works and
      Sleddall Almshouses 66,
      443, 528
    Fellside **439–41**
    Helme Lodge near 55, **444**
    Helsington Lathes **445**
    HSBC (Westmorland Bank)
      57, **437**
    Little Holme 70, **443**

Low Fellside 74, **439–40**
  Parkside 173, **444**
  Provincial Insurance building
    74, 427–8, **439**
  Sand Aire House 55, **439**
  Skewbarrow Top 74, **440**
  Thorny Hills 55, **442**
  Vicarage 173
industrial history 45, 52, 427–8,
  435–45
  Gilkes of Kendal 50, 428,
    442
  K Shoes 65, 427, **443**
public buildings **432–43**
  Abbot Hall and Park 66,
    433, **434**
  Castle Howe motte 22, **433**
  Kendal Castle 22, **433**
  Library 66, 427, **434**
  Serpentine Walks 66, **440**
  Town Hall (and Assembly
    Room) 66, **432–3**, 652
  Westmorland County Hall
    71, **433**
Roman fort, Watercrook 14, **445**
Kentmere (W) **445–7**
  Kentmere Hall 42, **446**, 561
  longhouses 39, 41, **446**
Keswick (C) 2, 10, **447–52**
  churches **447–8**
    Our Lady (R.C.) 10, **448**
    St John Evangelist 63, 64,
      67, 72, **447–8**
  houses and streets 67, 447,
    448–52, Pl. 4
    Derwent Bay 53, 377, **452**,
      Pl. 55
    Derwent Island 53, 67, **450**
    Fawe Park 68, **451**
    Greta Hall 53, **449**
    High Moss 69, **451**
    Lingholm 68, **451–2**
    Millbeck **452**
  industrial history 45, 447, **450**,
    452
    Brigham Forge **450**
    Force Crag Mine 46
  public buildings **448–9**
    Crosthwaite's Museum 66,
      448
    Moot Hall 57, **449**
    Ruskin Memorial 65, **450**
    station and hotel 59, 67, **448**
Killington (W) **452–3**
  All Saints 71, **452–3**, 461
  Killington Lake Services 73, **453**
  Low Hall **453**, 467
Kirkandrews-on-Esk (C) **453–4**
  Kirkandrews Tower 26, **454**, 550
  Liddel Strength 22, **454**
  St Andrew **453–4**, Pl. 78

Kirkbampton (C) 24, 64, 210,
  454–5
Kirkbride (C) **455–6**
  Roman fort 16
  St Bride 21, **455**
Kirkby-in-Furness (L) **456–8**
  Burlington Slate Quarry 46, **458**
  Kirkby Hall 33, 40, 42, **457–8**,
    Pl. 46
  St Cuthbert 31, **456**
Kirkby Ireleth (L) *see* Kirkby-in-
  Furness
Kirkby Lonsdale (W) 11, **458–67**
  St Mary 23, 24, 29, 160, 211,
    458–62, 510, 599, Pl. 14
  Savings Bank 58, **463**
  Tearnside Hall **466–7**
  Underley Hall 55, 68, 74, 462n.,
    466
Kirkby Stephen (W) 11, 21, 51,
  467–72
  church 25, 30, 32, **467–70**, 472
  Cloisters 57, **470**
  Croglam Castle 14, **472**
  Hartley Castle **471**
  stations 109, **471**
  Stenkrith Park 75–6, **471**
  Temperance Hall **470**, Pl. 99
  Wharton Hall 27, 30, 197, **471–2**
Kirkby Thore (W) **472–3**
  Kirkby Thore Hall 27, 380, **473**
  St Michael 29, 210, **472–3**
Kirkcambeck (C) **473**
Kirkland (C) 344, **474**
Kirklinton (C) **474–5**
  Kirklinton Park 68, 220, **474–5**,
    486n
Kirkoswald (C) 9, **475–8**
  Castle 192, 321, 476, **477**, 503,
    543, 544, 545
  Ona Ash, High Windhill 39,
    477–8
  St Oswald (and College) 29, 30,
    32, 37, **475–7**

Lakeside branch railway 349, **395**
Lambrigg wind farm 77
Lammerside Castle (W) *see*
  Mallerstang
Lamplugh (C) **478**
  Kirkland Mission Church 62,
    478
  St Michael 62, **478**
Lancaster Canal 50, **409**, **411**,
  441–3, 527, **542**
Lancaster & Carlisle Railway 51,
  59, 409, **542**, **569**, 631, 687
Lanercost (C) 9, **479–86**
  Dacre Hall 484, **485–6**
  Hadrian's Wall, Hare Hill 479,
    486

Lanercost Priory 18, 21, 23, 25,
  30, 32, 33, 89, 217, 268, 333,
  458, **479–86**, 545, Pl. 20
  vicar's pele 29, 485, **486**
Langdales (W) 12, **487–90**
  Copt Howe 13
  Elterwater 73, 169n., **487–8**
  Holy Trinity, Chapel Stile 60,
    63, **487**
  Kitty Hall 38, **488**
  stone axe factories 12, 45, 487
  Youth Hostel 73, **487**
Langwathby (C) **490–1**
Lazonby (C) 9, **491**
Leven Viaduct (L) *see* Ulverston
Levens (W) **491–6**
  Levens Hall 32, 40, 44, 379,
    492–6, 557, 622, Pl. 47
  Nether Levens (Low Levens)
    40, 41, **495–6**
Liddel Strength (C) *see*
  Kirkandrews-on-Esk
Lindal-in-Furness (L) 63, **496–7**
Lindale (L) **497–8**
  Eller How 55, **498**
  St Paul 58, **497**
Linstock (C) *see* Houghton
Little Corby (C) *see* Warwick
Little Salkeld (C) *see* Langwathby
Little Strickland (W) 33, **498–9**
London & North Western Railway
  434, **701**
  Ingleton branch **349**
Longburgh (C) *see* Burgh-by-Sands
Long Marton (W) 21, 24, 472,
  499–500, 522, 532
Longsleddale (W) 63, **500**
Longtown (C) 9, 43, 223, **500–1**,
  548
Lorton (C) 36, **501–2**, 502
Low Borrowbridge (W) *see* Grayrigg
Loweswater (C) **502**
Lowick (L) **503**
Lowther (W) 64, **503–10**
  Hackthorpe Hall **509–10**
  long cairn 12, **510**
  Lowther Castle 36–7, 44, 54, 55,
    122, 191, 415, **503–8**, 567, 615,
    711, 712, Pl. 58
  St Michael and Mausoleum 20,
    23, 34, 36, 65, 369, 406,
    506–8, Pls. 71, 80
  village 43, **508–9**
Lupton (W) **510**

Mallerstang (W) **510–11**
  Eden Benchmark sculpture 75,
    511
  Lammerside Castle 27, **511**
  Pendragon Castle 21, 22, 34, **511**
  St Mary 34, **510–11**

Mansergh (W) **512**
  Rigmaden Park 55, 128, 444,
    465, **512**
Mardale (W) *see* Haweswater
Martindale (W) 38, **512–13**
  Bungalow 68, **513**
  St Martin 33, **513**
  St Peter 63, 75, **512–13**
Maryport (C) 2, 10, 47, 48, 51,
  513–16
  cemetery 63, **514**
  harbour 47, 51, 513–14, **515**
  houses and streets 9, 43, 59,
    515–16
  Netherhall 75, **516**, 686
  Roman fort 17, 18, 311, **515**
  St Mary 35, **514**
  sculpture 75, **515**
  Senhouse Roman Museum 66,
    514–15, 516
Maryport & Carlisle Railway 51,
  125, **185**, **259**, 514, **515**, 520, **638**
Matterdale (C) **517**
  Aira Force walks 44, **517**
  Cockley Moor 71, **517**
  Lyulph's Tower 44, 53, 54, 388,
    517
Maulds Meaburn (W) 3, 41,
  517–18, Pl. 49
Mealsgate (C) **518–20**
  Old All Hallows 24, 65, **519**
  Whitehall 67–8, **519–20**, 685
Meathop (W) 498, **520**
Melmerby (C) 24, **520–1**
Middleton (W) **521–2**
  Middleton Hall 27, **521–2**
  Roman milestone 15, **522**
Midland Railway **248**
  see also Settle and Carlisle Line
Milburn (W) 2–3, **522–3**
  Howgill Castle 27, 37, 322,
    522–3, 606
Millom (C) 10, 45, **523–7**, 585
  Holy Trinity 25, 186, **523–4**
  houses and streets 59–60, **525–7**,
    672n.
  industrial remains 48, 525, **527**
  Millom Castle 26, 114, **524–5**
  St George 65, 75, **525–6**, 609
  St Luke, Haverigg 63, 75, **526**,
    Pl. 117
  sculpture 75, **526**
  stone circle, Swinside 13, **527**
  wind farm 77
Milnthorpe (W) 49, 64, 116,
  527–30
  almshouses 66, **528**
  Christ the King (R.C.) 75, **528**
  Dallam Tower 38, 117, **529–30**
  St Thomas 58, **527–8**
Moorhouse (C) *see* Burgh-by-Sands

Moresby (C) **530–1**
  Moresby Hall 37, 41, 477, **531**, 556, Pl. 51
  Roman fort 17, **530**
  Rosehill Theatre 74, **531**, 681
  St Bridget 62, **530**
Morland (W) **531–4**
  Newby 3, **533–4**
  St Lawrence 21, 25, 30, 31, 308, **531–3**
Mosser (C) **534**
Muncaster (C) 344, **534–7**
  Muncaster Castle 26, 33, 67, 68, 424, **535–7**
  St Michael 19, 20, 64, **534**
Mungrisdale (C) **537–8**
  Great Mell Fell burial place 13
  St Kentigern **537–8**
Murton (W) 47, **538–9**
Musgrave (W) **539–40**

Natland (W) **540–2**
  aqueduct 50, **542**
  Castlesteads hill-fort 14, 17, **542**
  gunpowder works 49, **541–2**
  High House Farm 40, 41, **540–1**
  Oxenholme 59, **542**
  St Mark 58, 62, **540**
Naworth Castle (C) 24, 26, 29, 30, 67, 120, 164, 477, 479, **542–6**, 589
  Naworth Park Stonehouse 28, **546**
NBR *see* North British Railway
Near Sawrey (L) *see* Sawrey
Nenthead (C) 97, 119, **546–8**
  Rampgill Mine 47, **547–8**
NER *see* North Eastern Railway
Nether Denton (C) *see* Denton
Netherby Hall (C) 54, **548–50**
  Roman fort 17, **550**
New Hutton (W) 58, **553**
Newbiggin (W) **550–2**
  Newbiggin Hall 26, 40, 67, 68, **551–2**, 615
Newbiggin Hall (C) *see* Carleton
Newbiggin Hall (W) *see* Newbiggin
Newbiggin-on-Lune (W) *see* Ravenstonedale
Newby (C) *see* Warwick
Newby (W) *see* Morland
Newby Bridge (L) **552–3**
  Fellfoot 53, **552–3**
  Lakeside Station and Hotel 67, **552**
Newcastle & Carlisle Railway 51, **96**, 259, 302, 346, **403–4**, 669
Newlands (C) 46, **553–4**
Newton Arlosh (C) 22, 28, 60, **554–5**, 705, Pl. 32

Newton Reigny (C) **555–6**
  Catterlen Hall 27, 37, 322, 531, **555–6**
Nicholforest (C) **556–7**
North British Railway (NBR) 51, 60, 261n., 618, **619**
North Eastern Railway (NER) **259**, **627, 669**

Old Carlisle (C) *see* Westward
Old Hutton (W) **557**
  Blease Hall 41, **557**
Old Penrith (C) *see* Plumpton
Ormside (W) 3, 21, 28, 532, **557–9**
Orton (C; also called Great Orton) **559–60**
  St Giles 24, 25, 35, 308, **559–60**
Orton (W) **560–2**
Osmotherley (L) **562**, 697
Ousby (C) 32, 46, **562**
Oxenholme (W) *see* Natland

Parsonby (C) *see* Plumbland
Parton (C) 47
Patterdale (W) **563**
  Patterdale Hall 67, **563**
  St Patrick 60, 67, **563**
Patton Bridge (W) **563–4**
Pendragon (W) *see* Mallerstang
Pennington (L) **564**
  ringwork castle 21, **564**
  St Michael 24, 183, **564**
Penrith (C) 2, 3, 369n., **564–75**
  churches etc. **565–8**
    Austin Friars 23, 564, 573
    cemetery 63, **567–8**
    St Andrew 30, 35, 36, 65, 188, 392, **565–7**, 673;
    sculpture 19, 20, 369, **566**
    St Catherine (R.C.) 61, **567**
    Wesleyan church 63, **567**
  houses, streets and commercial buildings 9, 564, **569–78**
    Angel Square 76, **570**
    Hutton Hall 37, 476, 477, **573**
    Rheged 76, **575**
    Skirsgill 518, **575**
    Two Lions Inn 33, **570–2**
    Tynefield House **574**, Pl. 57
  public buildings **568–9**, **574–5**
    Environment Agency (Ghyll Mount) 77, **575**
    Penrith Castle and Castle Park 26, 66, 564, **568–9**, 700
    South Africa war memorial 288, **568**
    station 59, **569**
    Town Hall 66, **569**
    town walls 29

Roman fort, Old Penrith *see* Plumpton
Penruddock (C) **576**
Piel Castle (L) 26, 129, 137, **576–7**, Pl. 2
Plumbland (C) 20, **577–8**
Plumpton (C) 63, **578–80**
    Brackenburgh 69, 574, **578–9**, 708
    Roman fort, Old Penrith 14, 419, **579–80**
Poltross Burn (C) *see* Denton
Ponsonby (C) *see* Calder Bridge
Pooley Bridge (W) 144, **580**
    Eusemere House 52, **580**, 711
    Pooley Bridge Inn 197
Portinscale (C) *see* Keswick
Preston Patrick (W) 23, 27, 28, 40, 206, 304, **580–2**, 616

Rampside (L) 119, **582–3**
    Roa Island **583**, Pl. 2
Raughton Head (C) 35, 518, **583–4**, 613
Ravenglass (C) 1, 22, **584–5**
    Roman bath house and fort 14, 15, 343, **585**, Pl. 7
Ravenglass & Eskdale Railway 67, **343, 345**, 537, 585
Ravenstonedale (W) 11, **585–8**
    Gilbertine cell 23, **586**
    St Oswald 35–6, 126, 565, **585–6**
    Smardale viaduct **588**, Pl. 106
    spinning gallery 40, **587**
    Tarn House 111, **587–8**
Rayseat Pike (W) *see* Crosby Garrett
Renwick (C) **588**
Ribton Hall (C) 37, *393*
Rickerby (C) *see* Carlisle
Roa Island (L) *see* Rampside
Rockcliffe (C) **588–9**
    Castletown House 55, **589**
    St Mary 19, 20, 363, **588–9**
Rookhow (L) *see* Rusland
Roose (L) *see* Barrow-in-Furness
Rose Castle (C) 26, 28, 34, 37, 54, 234, **589–93**, Pl. 29
Rosley (C) 75, **593**
Rusland (L) 35, **593, 593–4**
Rydal (W) **594–6**, Pl. 3
    Cote How 40, 42, **595–6**
    Fox Howe, Under Loughrigg 56, **596**
    Nab Cottage **596**, Pl. 3
    Park Barn 42, **596**
    The Rash (projected) 56
    Rydal Hall and grot 43, 78, **594–5**
    Rydal Mount 55–6, 376, **595**

St Bees (C) 9, 10, **596–601**
    St Bees School 58, 66, **599–600**
    St Mary and St Bega (priory) 20, 23, 24, 30, 47, 62, 64, 75, 160, 384, **596–9**
    sculpture 75, **600**
St John's in the Vale (C) **601**
    stone circle, Castlerigg 13, **601**, Pl. 6
Satterthwaite (L) **601–2**
    Grizedale Hall and Forest Park 70, 76, 77, **601–2**
Sawrey (L) **602–4**
    Bryerswood 68, **603**
    Claife Station 52, 53, 54, 176, **603**
    Ferry House 67, **602–3**
    Pearson Laboratories 74, **603**
Scaleby (C) 28, **604–7**
    Scaleby Castle 26, 27, 28, 52, 54, 122, 220, 390, 401, **604–7**
Scales Hall (C) 28, 33, 197, 322, 584, **607–8**, 710
Scotby (C) 118, 413, **608**
Seascale (C) 60, 71, **608–9**
    Grey Croft stone circle 13, **609**
Seathwaite (L) **609**
Seaton (C) **610**
Seaton Hall and Priory (C) *see* Bootle
Sebergham (C) **610–11**
    St Mary 59, 583, **610**, Pl. 74
Sedbergh 73, 611
Sedgwick (W) *see* Natland
Sellafield (C) 45, 73, 340, 609, **611–13**, 672
Selside (W) **613–14**
    Forest Hall 28, 318, **614**
    Grisedale Farm **614**
    St Thomas 518, **613**
    Selside Hall 42, **613**
Setmurphy (C) **614**
Settle and Carlisle railway 51, 59, 104, **109**, **115–16**, 307, **318**, **471**, **490–1**, **491**, 500, **511**, 559, 588, 627
Shap (W) **614–17**
    Shap Abbey 23, 30, 356, 467, **616–17**, Pl. 22
    Shap Quarry 397n.
    stone circle, Gunnerwell 13, **617**
Shap Wells (W) 67, **617–18**
    Queen Victoria Monument 64, 67, **618**, Pl. 100
Shoulthwaite (C) 18, 21
Silloth (C) 2, 60, **618–19**
    Skinburness 22, 412, 554, **619**
Sizergh Castle (W) 27, 32, 33, 36, 40, 53, 58, 417, 429, 472, 493, 572, 596, **619–24**, 710, Pls. 45, 65

Skelsmergh (W) 624–5
    St John Baptist 71, 624
Skelton (C) 625
    Hardrigg Hall 27, 519, 625
Skinburness (C) see Silloth
Skirwith (C) 63, 64, 625–6
Smardale Hall (W) 33, 626–7
Smardale viaducts (W) see
    Ravenstonedale
Sockbridge (W) 627–8
    Sockbridge Hall and barn 26,
    42, 324, 617, 627
Solway Junction Railway 52, 163
Soulby (W) 34, 628
South Durham & Lancashire Union
    Railway 471, 631
South Stainmore (W) see Brough
Spadeadam (C) see Gilsland Spa
Stanegate 16, 17, 179, 333
Stanwix (C) see Carlisle
Stapleton (C) 35, 628
Staveley (W) 11, 628–30
    St James 64, 70, 629, Pl. 92
Staveley-in-Cartmel (L) 630
Stone Wall 16, 659
    see also Hadrian's Wall
Storrs Hall (W) see Bowness-on-
    Windermere
Strands (C) see Wasdale
Swarthmoor (L) 35, 630–1
    Swarthmoor Hall 35, 41, 70, 630
Swarthy Hill (C) see Crosscanonby
Swindale (W) see Haweswater

Talkin (C) 631
Tebay (W) 62, 73, 631–2
    ringwork, Castle Howe 21, 632
    Westmorland Services (M6) 73,
    632
Tebay–Barnard Castle railway 588
Temple Sowerby (W) 3, 304, 632–4
    Acorn Bank 37, 633–4
    St James 35, 632
Thirlmere (C) 52, 634–6
    Dalehead Hall 40, 635–6
    Legburthwaite village hall 397n.
    Thirlmere Reservoir 72, 634–5
Thornthwaite (C) 636
Thornthwaite (W) see Bampton
Threlkeld (C) 35, 59, 63, 70, 636,
    636–7
Thursby (C) 637–8
    Meadow Bank Farm, West
        Curthwaite 41, 638
    station and water tank 51, 638
Thwaites (C) 62, 638
Tirril (W) 638–9, 711
Torpenhow (C) 23, 24, 35, 417,
    639–40
Torver (L) 640
Troutbeck (W) 419, 640–5

Brockhole 69, 75, 643
Calgarth Hall 33, 640, 642–3
Calgarth Park 53, 643
Jesus Church 33, 34, 64, 294,
    640, 643
Langdale Chase 68, 644, Pl. 108
Thwaite 38, 41, 641
Town End 41, 167, 641
Town End Barn 40, 641, Pl. 66
Turf Wall 16, 17, 486, 657–9. see
    also Hadrian's Wall

Uldale (C) 645
    Aughtertree Fell farmsteads 14,
        645
    St James 34, 59, 645
    St John 420, 645
Ulpha (C) 645–7
    Duddon Bridge furnace 48,
        645–6
    Duddon Hall and temple 77,
        646–7
Ulverston (L) 2, 11, 45, 48, 77,
    647–53
    Barrow Monument 66, 647
    Catholic church (former) 58,
        649
    Coronation Hall 71, 650
    Lanternhouse 76, 650, Pl. 115
    Leven Viaduct 116, 652–3
    St Mary 32, 647–9
    station 129, 650
    Stone Cross 67, 652
    Trustee Savings Bank 57, 652
    war memorial 65, 651
Ulverston Canal 50, 652
Ulverston & Lancaster Railway 50,
    351, 650
Underbarrow (W) 60, 62, 653
Underley Hall (W) see Kirkby
    Lonsdale
Upper Denton (C) see Denton
Urswick (L) 653–5
    Low Furness Primary School
        76, 655
    St Mary and St Michael 19, 35,
        70, 653–5
    Skelmore Heads 12, 14, 655
    stone circle, Sunbrick 13, 655

Waberthwaite (C) 1, 20, 656
Walney (L) see Barrow-in-Furness
Walton (C) 656–9
    Birdoswald 657–9
        fort 17, 18, 334, 657, Pl. 8
        Hadrian's Wall (Turf Wall)
            16, 334, 657
        Milecastle 49 (Harrow's
            Scar) 333, 657
        Pike Hill signal tower 16, 659
    Castlesteads 17, 657

Warcop (W) **660–1**
  Burton Hall 660
  St Columba 21, 25, 29, 157,
    210, 307, 473, **660**
  Warcop Hall 38, **660–1**, Pl. 53
Warwick (C) **661–5**
  Holme Eden Abbey 54, 67,
    663–4
  Howard Cottage 41, **663**
  Our Lady and St Wilfrid (R.C.)
    61, **662–3**
  St Leonard 24, 224, 228, **661–2**,
    Pl. 13
  Warwick Hall 71, **663**
Warwick Bridge (C) *see* Warwick
Wasdale (C) **665–6**
Watendlath (C) *see* Grange-in-
  Borrowdale
Watercrook (W) *see* Kendal
Waterfoot House (C) *see* Pooley
  Bridge (W)
Watermillock (C) **666**
Waverton (C) **666–7**
Welton (C) *see* Sebergham
West Curthwaite (C) *see* Thursby
Westnewton (C) **667**
Westward (C) **667**
  Roman fort, Old Carlisle 18,
    667
Wetheral (C) **668–70**
  Holy Trinity 58, **668**, Pl. 73
  viaduct 51, **669**
  Wetheral Priory 23, 237, 301,
    302, **668–9**
Wharton Hall (W) *see* Kirkby
  Stephen
Whicham (C) **670**
Whitbeck (C) **670**
Whitehaven (C) 2, 10, 47, **670–83**
  Bransty 585
  churches **672–5**, 683
    Holy Trinity 35, *362*, 672, 673
    Quaker meeting house 35,
      330n., **675**
    St Bega (R.C.) 61, **674**
    St James 35, **673–4**, Pl. 77
    St Nicholas 35, 36, 62, 64,
      72, 75, *514*, **672–3**, 674
    Wesleyan Methodist church
      63, **675**
  houses, streets and commercial
    buildings 8, 43, 47, 60, 670–2,
    679–83
    The Beacon 76, **677**
    Queen Street 44, **682–3**
    Royal Standard Hotel 531,
      681
  industrial remains 47, 672,
    677–80, 683, 703
  public buildings **675–83**
    Carnegie Library 66, **676**

  harbour 47, 670, **676–7**, 701
  sculpture 75, **675**, 677
  Whitehaven Castle 672, **675**
Whitehaven, Cleator & Egremont
  Railway 279
Wigton (C) 9, 41, 47, **684–7**
  churches etc. **684–5**
    cemetery 63, **685**
    St Cuthbert (R.C.) 61, **684**
    St Mary 35, **684**
  fountain 65, **685**, Pl. 101
  Innovia 684, **686**
  Mechanics' Institute 75, 686n.
  station 516, **686**
  Westmorland House **685**
Willowford (C) *see* Denton
Windermere (W) 11, 52, 74,
  687–94
  houses, streets and commercial
    buildings 57, 60, 67, 69, 687,
    689–94
    Burrowfield 69, **694**
    The Corbels 69, **694**
    Dawstone 69, **693–4**
    Elleray 53, 377, **691**
    Gatesbield 70, **690–1**
    Keldwith 69, **691–2**
    Lakeland Limited store 77,
      689, Pl. 119
    Millerground 41, **692**
    Rayrigg Hall 40, 420, **693**
    Shrublands 69, **694**
    Waterbeck 69, **694**, Pl. 110
    Windermere Hotel 67,
      689–90
  public buildings 687, **689**
    Footprint centre 77, **692**
    station **689**
  St Mary 34, 60, 63, **687–9**, 704
Windscale (C) *see* Sellafield
Winster (W) 69, **694–5**
Witherslack (W) 34, 53n., 68,
  696–7
Woodland (L) **697**
Workington (C) 2, 77, **697–703**
  Burrow Walls fort 17
  churches **698–700**
    Our Lady Star of the Sea
      (R.C.) 31n., 61, **699–700**
    St John 58, **699**, Pl. 79
    St Michael and Rectory 24,
      29, 32, 35, 75, 565, **698–9**;
      cross-shaft 19, 149, **698–9**
    Trinity Methodist Church
      63, **700**
  houses, streets and commercial
    buildings 43, 59, 697–8,
    701–2
    Workington Hall and
      Schoose farm 54, 638, 697,
      700–1

industrial history 45, 47, 49, 51,
  697–8, **702–3**
  Jane Pit 698, **702–3**
public buildings **700–1**
  Carnegie Library 66, **702**
  harbour 47, **701**
  war memorial 65, **701**
Wray (L) **703–4**
  Pullwoods 68, **704**
  Wray Castle 54, 377, **703–4**, Pls.
  62, 63
Wraysholme (L) *see*
Allithwaite
Wreay (C) 60, **704–8**
  St Mary 60–1, 64, 65, 555,
  704–7, Pl. 82
Wythburn (C) *see* Thirlmere

Wythop (C) **708**
  Castle How hill-fort 14, **708**

Yanwath and Eamont Bridge (W)
708–12
  Eamont Bridge 661, **710**
    Mansion House 37, **711**
    South African War memorial
    65, **711**, 102
  Eden Millennium Monument
  710
  henges **710–11**
    King Arthur's Round Table
    12, **712**
    Mayburgh 12–13, **711–12**
  Yanwath Hall 26, 33, 322,
  708–10, Pl. 31